THE HABSBURG EMPIRE
1790–1918

THE HABSBURG EMPIRE
1790–1918

C. A. MACARTNEY

faber and faber

This edition first published in 2010
by Faber and Faber Ltd
Bloomsbury House, 74–77 Great Russell Street
London WC1B 3DA

Printed by CPI Antony Rowe, Eastbourne

All rights reserved
© C. A. Macartney, 1968

The right of C. A. Macartney to be identified as author of this work
has been asserted in accordance with Section 77 of the
Copyright, Designs and Patents Act 1988

This book is sold subject to the condition that it shall not, by way of
trade or otherwise, be lent, resold, hired out or otherwise circulated
without the publisher's prior consent in any form of binding or cover other than
that in which it is published and without a similar condition including this
condition being imposed on the subsequent purchaser

A CIP record for this book is available from the British Library

ISBN 978–0–571–25958–8

'What statesman inside or outside the Empire knows anything at all of the facts of Austria? It is a science in itself, nay, it is half a dozen sciences.'
MR GRANT DUFF IN THE HOUSE OF COMMONS, 1869

Contents

	Preface	xi
1	The Monarchy in 1780	1
	i *The Dominions*	
	ii *The Political Structure*	
	iii *Economic and Financial Conditions*	
	iv *The Social Structure*	
	v *Nationality*	
	vi *Cultural Conditions*	
	vii *The Monarchy in the World*	
2	Joseph II	119
3	Leopold II	134
4	Francis I (II): The Development of the System (1792–1815)	147
5	The System at its Zenith (1815–30)	199
6	The System on the Wane (1830–35)	232
7	The Vormärz	255
8	Before the Storm	306
9	1848	322
10	The Decade of Absolutism	426
11	Eight Years of Experiment	495
12	Intermezzo	569
13	The Foreign Relations of the Monarchy (1871–1903)	586

CONTENTS

14	Cis-Leithania under Dualism	603
	i *From Auersberg to Taaffe (1871–90)*	
	ii *From Taaffe to Koerber (1890–1903)*	
15	Hungary under Dualism	687
	i *Political Developments*	
	ii *The Face of Hungary*	
	iii *The Nationalities Problem*	
	iv *Croatia*	
16	Bosnia-Herzegovina 1875–1903	740
17	The Last Years of Peace	749
18	The End of the Monarchy	810
	Appendix 1: Titles	834
	Appendix 2: Currency, Weights and Measures	835
	Appendix 3: Place Names	836
	Bibliography	838
	Index	864

MAPS

1. The growth of the Habsburg Empire — 4–5
2. The administrative divisions of the Habsburg Empire, 1780 — 16–17
3. The Empire after the Treaty of Schönbrunn — 170–71
4. Hungary in the Absolutist period — 434–5
5. Austria-Hungary after 1867 — 572–3
6. Ethnic and Linguistic map of the Empire, 1910 — 826–7

Maps by Arthur Banks

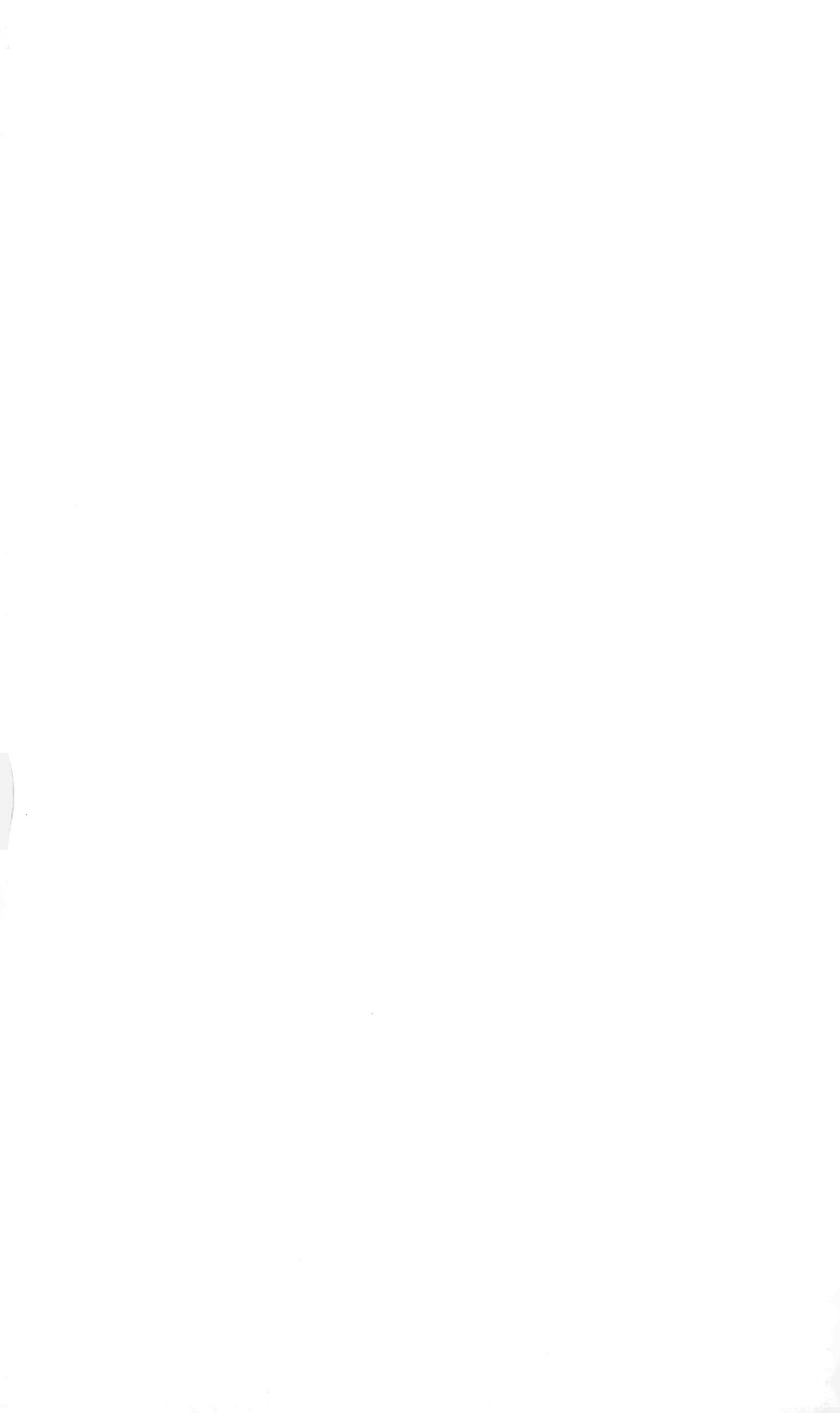

Preface

When I was a very young man, just after the First World War had ended, I spent several years in Vienna. I became keenly interested in the past of the great Monarchy among whose still-smoking ruins I had arrived, and read up everything about it that I could get hold of. I found general histories going up to the mid-nineteenth century, and for the later period, some personal reminiscences, studies of particular episodes, and also histories of different provinces and nationalities. I also found essays on the weaknesses of the Monarchy which had led to its break-up, but I looked in vain for any adequate general history of the Monarchy telling in narrative form just how and why that break-up had occurred. When I was in Vienna, only one man – Bibl – attempted the task, and I could not regard his book as definitive, or even comprehensive.

I conceived the ambition of writing the story myself.

In 1925 (I think) I talked to the distinguished Austrian historian, A. F. Pribram, and told him of my ambition. I still remember his answer. 'Yes, we all start with that ambition. I did myself, but gave it up because I did not know fourteen languages.'

I did not myself know anything like fourteen languages, and felt rebuked for my presumption. In any case, the enterprise would then have been premature, for as regards the latter part of the period in question, the flow of necessary material, primary works or secondary works on many special subjects, had hardly yet started. I put my ambition aside and waited for someone better qualified than myself to produce the book which I wanted to see.

But I have waited for forty years. So much material has appeared during those years that an attempt to write such a book as I had in mind would no longer be absurd. But the book of my vision has not yet appeared, and the prospect of its doing so in the foreseeable future seems actually to be receding, at least so far as the old Monarchy's own historians are concerned. Even in the old days, no Czech, Pole or Magyar even made the motions of writing a history of the Monarchy as a whole: he simply described the sufferings of his own people in the Babylonian captivity of the Habsburgs. The present-day historians of those peoples seem to be adopting the same attitude, only more so. While the Monarchy still existed, its German or Germanized historians were often still able to take a less parochial view of its problems, and such great figures as Springer still wrote *Gesammtmonarchisch* history. But a change came as early as 1867: Charmatz and Kolmer are already not historians of the Monarchy, but of Cis-Leithania. If we except Luschin-Ebengreuth, who writes of institutions, it is fair to say that the last important work of the type which I have in mind to appear before 1918 was Friedjung's unfinished *Austria from 1848 to 1860*. Since then, Pribram and others have investigated the Monarchy's foreign policy, Redlich and Walter have described its central institutions, and the modern German-Austrian historians have carried on their work with a brilliance and erudition with which I cannot hope to compete. But with the single exception of the venerable Kiszling (himself not an academic) they have, as soon as they have gone outside these central fields, adopted the particularist outlook of the other nationalities; what they write on domestic politics and social and economic developments relates simply to German Austria, with an occasional side-glance at Bohemia. The Hungarians are for them simply *lästige Ausländer*, and one could hardly gather from their books that the Monarchy had ever contained Poles, Ruthenes, Roumanians or Southern Slavs.

But the tribal histories which the local historians of today are now producing cannot be completely satisfactory even for their own tribes, for the political, social and economic development of each people was bound up with and largely conditioned by that of the others, without some knowledge of which it does not even make sense.

They certainly do not meet all the requirements of the non-Austrian reader, unless he is a diplomatic historian pure and simple. If his interests are wider than this, he will want to know something of what went on in all parts of the Monarchy, who its peoples were, what were the differences between them, by what means and how far they settled those differences, how far and why they failed to do so, what were the cohesive forces which enabled the Monarchy to survive until 1918, and what the forces of disruption under which it collapsed in that year. And this *Lebensfrage* of the Monarchy apart, something of how its peoples lived.

A man who by virtue of his birth and education stands at a distance from the countries which once composed the old Monarchy finds it perhaps easier than do their natives to take a wide-angled view of the subject, but it is, of course, far more difficult for him to acquire the necessary factual knowledge (which will certainly not have been imparted to him at school) and the no less essential psychological understanding. Thus very few non-Austrians have even attempted any major work on the problem, and of these, only Professor

PREFACE

A. J. May, in his *Hapsburg Monarchy, 1867–1914*, and his *Passing of the Hapsburg Monarchy* has thrown his net wide enough, and dredged deep enough, to meet the needs of those who seek for more than interpretations; and May's work, which is truly admirable as far as it goes, covers only a fraction of the period.

So a gap is, in my opinion, still there, and I have, after all, set myself, not to fill it, but to put something into it. No one knows better than myself, how inadequately. I still do not know fourteen languages, and the flood of recent publications has been so copious, especially in the Iron Curtain countries, which have been rewriting their histories on principle, that the proportion of works which I have read to those which I ought to have read is probably lower today than it was forty years ago. But man cannot wait for ever, either on his own perfection, or on others, so I have decided to face the world with my effort, imperfect as I know it to be.

This, then, is a history of the Monarchy, the Monarchy as a whole, and the whole Monarchy during what I regard, for the reasons which I give in my introduction, as the second great phase of its history, 1790–1918. It is primarily a history of domestic developments. These were, of course, constantly and strongly affected by the state and development of the Monarchy's international relations, but in dealing with these I have, out of considerations both of space and of my own lack of learning, omitted all details of diplomatic negotiations and military campaigns, confining myself to recording shortly the principal events and pointing out their influence on internal developments. The details omitted by me can in any case easily be found in many readily accessible works by specialist historians.

With more regret, but out of the same considerations, I have left out, except for the barest mention, all *Kulturgeschichte* proper, as distinct from literary, etc., activities which had their importance for the development of national movements. These sacrifices have left me more space, although still less than I should have wished, for the inner political, social, economic and national developments which I have taken as my main theme.

My introductory chapters are designed to show the origin and nature of the problems with the development of which my narrative history is concerned. I have tried to include in them all those facts, and no others, which are relevant to the narrative. Should this book ever fall into the hands of a native of the Monarchy, he will probably complain that much of this is elementary stuff, but my experience as a teacher of many generations of inquiring undergraduate minds has convinced me that most non-Austrians need something like this if the story with which they are then presented is to have any meaning to them at all.

Innumerable kind friends have helped me in various ways. It would be impossible for me to list them all, and I trust that those whom I do not now name will not think me ungrateful if I confine myself to expressing my especial gratitude to a few whom I have exploited with particular ruthlessness: Professor Hantsch, Director of the Historical Institute in Vienna, and his staff, especially Dr W. Bihl; Professor Hoffmann, of the Institute for Economic and Social History of the same University; Professors G. Otruba and Walter Knarr, also of Vienna, and Professor Fellner, now of Salzburg; the Director and staff of the Austrian Institute in London, and particularly its ever-helpful librarian, Frl. Erika Strobl; Dr L. Péter, now of the London School of Slavonic and East European Studies, a walking encyclopaedia of Hungary; Professor Skwarczynski, of the same School, for help regarding Poland. Last, but very far from least, the miraculous Mrs Pitt, the only person in the world who can read my handwriting and does not mind doing so, and no mere transcriber at that: a hawk-eyed detector to boot of mistakes in spelling and grammar, inconsistencies, repetitions, omissions and non-sequiturs.

Where any place has a name in common English usage, e.g., Vienna, Prague, Milan, I have used that form in writing of it. Otherwise I have used the name most likely to be familiar to the reader, i.e., the German form for places in the Western half of the Monarchy, the Hungarian form for the Eastern, except Croatia, where I have used the Croat form out of deference to the *Nagodba*. I give, however, at the end of the book a table showing the other names then or now current for the places which figure in my text. Exceptionally, I have referred to Treaties in the form in which they are familiar to readers of history books: the Peaces of Passarowitz, Carlowitz, Pressburg. For proper names, I have used the forms normally used by the bearers of them (except that I have not pandered to the Magyar habit of putting the surname first) except where a person is so familiar to English readers to have acquired a current English version of his name. This is certainly the case with the Monarchs with whom this book deals: Maria Theresa, Francis, Francis Joseph, Charles. I do not know why, but the Archdukes Charles, John and Francis Ferdinand seem to me to go better in English, and the rest in German. There would be a case for Anglicizing some more, such as Albert for Albrecht, but no one ever talks about Charles Louis, and one must draw a line somewhere.

I apologize for the inaccurate title of this book. I have adopted it, well aware that it is inexact and offensive to the susceptibilities of many former subjects of the Monarchy, in order to avoid confusion with other books.

I

The Monarchy in 1780

The history of the Austrian Monarchy falls into two phases. The earlier, and longer, is, from the point of view of the dynasties which styled and thought of themselves primarily as rulers of 'Austria', one of continued upward progress. The territories under their direct rule expand from a small, insecurely held marchland of forest and mountain to a vast agglomeration covering a large part of Central Europe, with outliers further afield; another area almost as great admits their titular supremacy. Their own title grows in dignity from Margrave, liege of the Duke of Bavaria, to Duke, Archduke, many times King, Emperor. This expansion outward goes hand in hand with an inner consolidation and an increase of their domestic power until it approaches the substance, if not everywhere the form, of absolute rule.

Then the tide turns. New rivals appear in Europe. The territorial advance gives way to a retreat in which one outpost after another is lost. At the same time, the forces of absolutism and centralism are driven back on the defensive, then into retreat, by the new forces of nationalism and democracy, until at last the peoples of the Monarchy, allied with its foreign enemies, repudiate not only the character of the Monarch's rule, but the rule itself. The end has come.

Obviously, neither the advance nor the retreat is quite unbroken. The earlier phase witnesses territorial setbacks enough, some of them enormous in scale, and a hard-pressed or personally feeble ruler sometimes exercises less effective authority than his luckier or more resolute predecessor. The latter period sees reassertions of the central power, and territorial additions – some of these achieved only a few years before the final dissolution. But it is unquestionably correct to speak of an advancing and a retreating tide, and it is not even over-straining the historian's licence to name a day as that on which the tide turned in Central Europe:[1] 28 January, 1790. On that day Joseph II, who had pushed absolutism and centralization further than any of his predecessors, admitted defeat at the hands of the Hungarian Estates and signed a Rescript revoking the bulk of the measures which he had imposed on Hungary since his mother's death. In this historic document Joseph admitted that the advance of centralism and absolutism had been

[1] The revolt and surrender in the Netherlands had, of course, come a little earlier still.

pushed beyond the line which it could hold, and with that admission the retreat, in fact, began.

The subject of this study is the history of the retreat; its narrative proper opens only with the year 1790. But the forces involved are so complex and so special to the Monarchy that the author has thought it well to prefix his narrative with a comparatively detailed description of the condition of the Monarchy before the retreat began. And it has seemed to him better not to take the conditions of January, 1790, for the situation in that year was a highly abnormal one: it was the climax of ten years of revolution (although revolution from above), and the practical problem which confronted Leopold II was what to keep and what rescind of the changes introduced in those ten years. Our picture will therefore be one of the Monarchy as Joseph found it when he succeeded to the sole rule on his mother's death in 1780. We shall follow this with a summary of Joseph's own reign, but only a very brief one, before turning to our narrative proper.

I THE DOMINIONS

The possessions bequeathed by Maria Theresa to her son were the following:

The so-called Hereditary Lands (Erbländer), consisting of the Archduchy of Austria, Below and Above the Enns; the Duchy of Styria; the Duchy of Carinthia; the Princely County of Tirol; the Duchy of Carniola, the Counties of Istria,[1] Vorarlberg and Gorizia-Gradisca and the City of Trieste.

The Lands of the Bohemian Crown, consisting in 1780 of the Kingdom of Bohemia, the Margravate of Moravia and the Duchy of Silesia (this only a fragment of the much larger Duchy inherited by the family in 1526).

The Lands of the Hungarian Crown, now divided into the Kingdom of Hungary, the Kingdom of Croatia, the Grand Principality of Transylvania, the Military Frontier and the *corpus separatum* of Fiume.

A number of smaller fiefs in Germany, collectively known as the Vorlande.

The United Austrian Netherlands.

The Duchies of Milan and Mantua.

Galicia and certain other areas formerly belonging to the Kingdom of Poland.

The (later Duchy of) Bukovina.

The Austrian Crown also exercised far-reaching rights over the episcopal sees of Brixen and Trent, which were, however, technically 'immediate'. The other enclave in the Hereditary Lands, the archiepiscopal see of Salzburg, was more genuinely independent.

These territories had come under Habsburg rule at dates extending over more than five hundred years, and as the result of very various transactions.

---

[1] To be distinguished from the larger Margravate of Istria, which remained Venetian until 1797.

THE MONARCHY IN 1780

The kernel's kernel of the Habsburg Hausmacht, as Austrian historians usually take it (and Francis I agreed with them when in 1804 he assumed the title of 'Emperor of Austria') was the Land of 'Austria', the Eastern March, founded in the tenth century (on the ruins of an earlier formation which had been unable to maintain itself) as a Margravate of Bavaria, on the eastern outliers of the Alps, to defend the Danubian frontier of the German Reich and of Christianity against the pagan Magyars. The capable dynasty first entrusted with this task, the Babenbergers, extended its frontiers eastward to the Leitha, northward to what then became the permanent frontier with Bohemia, and westward halfway to Salzburg (this westward extension becoming the quasi-separate Land of Austria Above the Enns[1]), in 1156 compassed the promotion of its status to that of an 'immediate' Duchy (the document confirming this promotion, the so-called *Privilegium Minus*, is a major landmark in Austrian history), and in 1192 secured the reversion, for the Duke of the day and his heirs, of the sister Duchy of Styria, its neighbour on the south and of similar origin. The male line of the Babenbergers died out in 1246, and their heritage then passed to Ottakar, Crown Prince and later King of Bohemia, who, however, in 1278 perished in battle against Rudolph, Count of Habsburg, and of certain other territories in Central Southern Germany, who had been elected German King five years earlier precisely because his Hausmacht was not dangerously large. In 1282 Rudolph enfeoffed his two sons, Albrecht I and Rudolph II, with the Babenberg heritage, as an escheated fief of the Reich. Rudolph (whose line in any case soon died out)[2] was forced to renounce his fief, but Albrecht's heirs showed a remarkable skill, which was also rewarded by singular good fortune, in augmenting their possessions, chiefly through inter-family compacts under which the survivor in the male line inherited the possessions of both contracting parties. By such or similar compacts they acquired a number of further Reich-fiefs, of similar origin to Austria and Styria: Carinthia and Carniola (then in the same hand) in 1335, the County of Tirol in 1363, the County of Istria in 1374, the districts afterwards consolidated under the name of Vorarlberg from 1375 onward, Gorizia in 1500. Trieste had submitted itself voluntarily in 1382, to escape annexation by Venice, from which a few further districts of Friule were conquered in 1511.

The main bloc of the Habsburg patrimony now composed the entire south-eastern corner of the German Reich, except the enclaves belonging to the immediate archiepiscopal sees of Salzburg, Brixen and Trent. Meanwhile, in 1453, the Emperor Frederick III, himself a Habsburg, had ratified the so-called *Privilegium Maius*, which, besides conferring various privileges on

---
[1] Austria Above the Enns was given a separate governor (Hauptman) in 1240 and its own Estates about 1400, but became a distinct Arch-Duchy only in the eighteenth century.

[2] He had only one son, the unfortunate so-called Johann Parricida (although the person whom he murdered was not his father, but his uncle), who died childless in 1313.

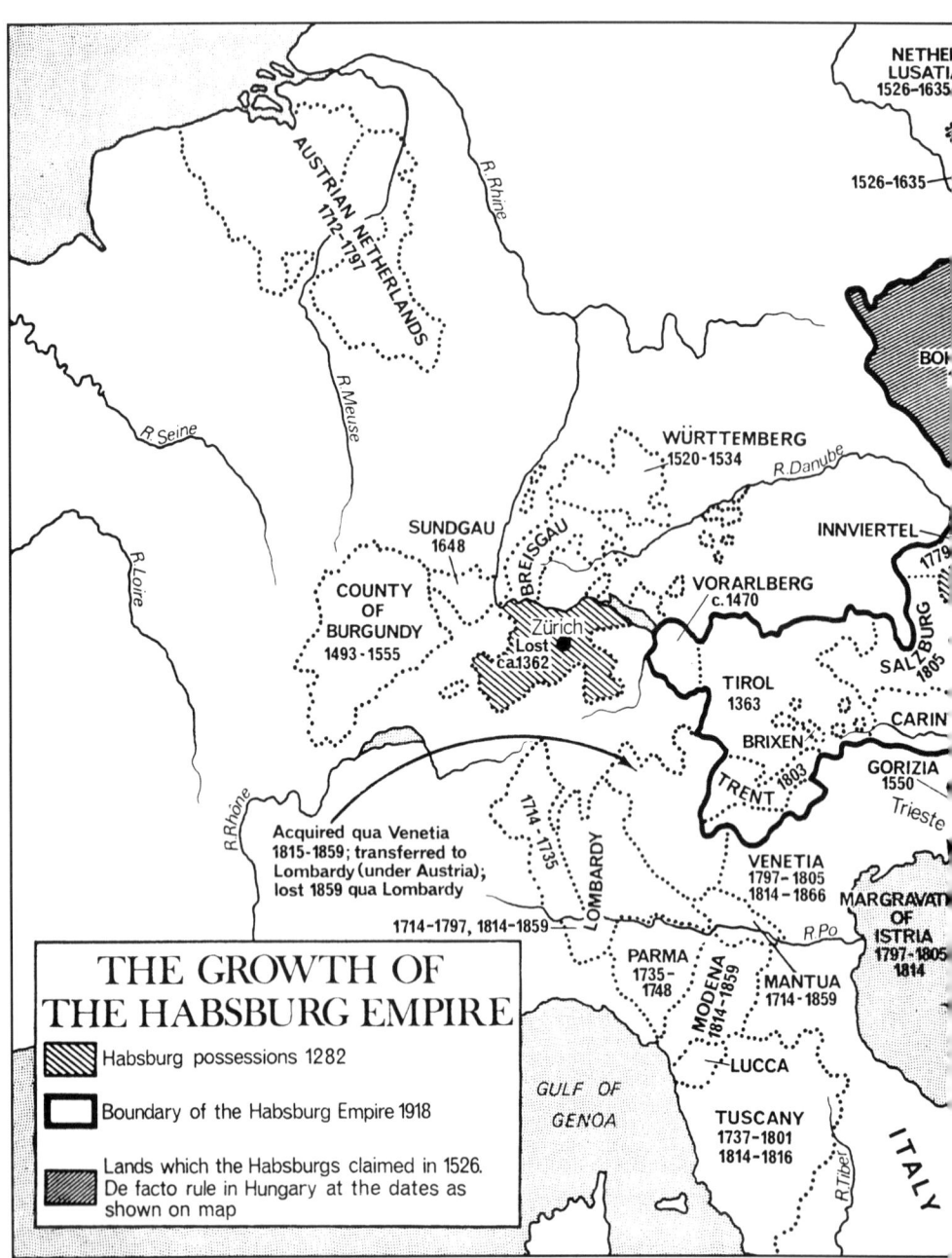

Map 1

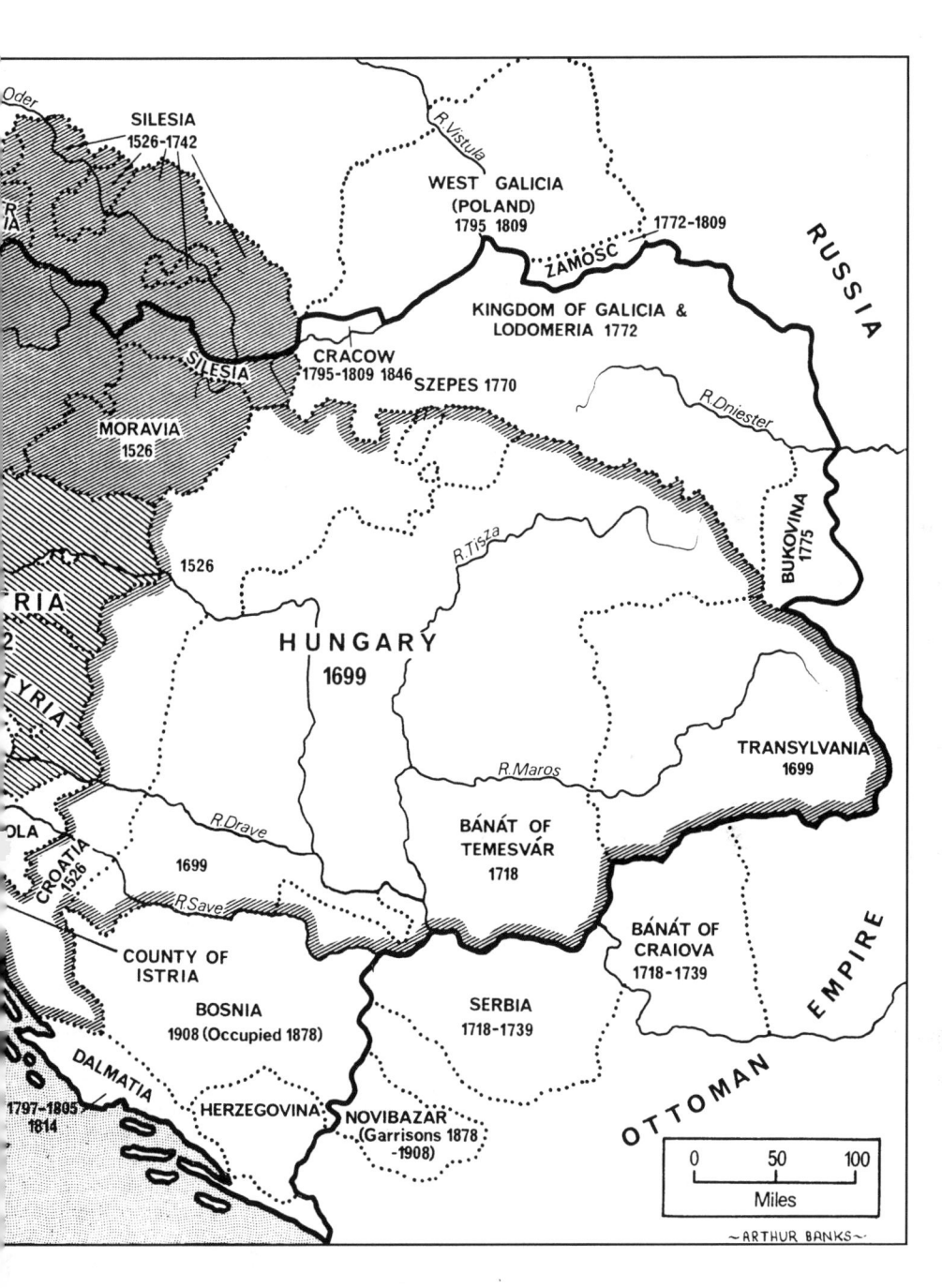

the rulers of Austria and the title of Archduke on all members of the Habsburg family, declared all Lands then held by the family to constitute an indivisible entail, hereditable in the male, or in default thereof, the female line of the House.[1] The bloc of Lands listed above were thereafter commonly styled the Erbländer, or Hereditary Lands, an appellation which it will be convenient to retain, although by 1780 it had long ceased to be exclusively, or even particularly, applicable to those Lands.[2]

The Habsburgs were, however, then still no more than a secondary dynasty, having greatly reduced their own power by their practice of dividing the family heritage between them, thus splitting it at times into two or even three blocs. One of its members, Albert v, had ruled also over Bohemia and Hungary, but he had died a couple of years after his accession, and his posthumous son, Ladislas, had died without issue, the two crowns then passing out of the family. Albert had, however, initiated the tradition that the dignities of Roman Emperor and German King were regularly held by the senior ruling Habsburg. The collateral lines having died out, Maximilian I succeeded in 1493 to the entire complex of the Habsburg Lands, and the fortunes of his family now took a sensational rise. Maximilian himself had married Maria, daughter and heiress of Charles the Bold of Burgundy, to whose possessions (the Franche Comté and the Netherlands) he had succeeded on Charles's death in 1478. His only son, Philip, married in 1496 Joanna of Spain, and their elder son, Charles, married Isabella of Portugal. When Maximilian died in 1519, Charles kept for himself the Spanish and Burgundian territories, with the Imperial title for his own lifetime, but ceded the Austrian possessions to his younger brother, Ferdinand I, who soon after became the beneficiary of yet another astounding marriage transaction. Maximilian had married him in infancy to Anne, daughter of Wladislaw Jagiellon, King of Bohemia and Hungary, while Wladislaw's son, Louis, married Charles's and Ferdinand's sister, Maria. It was agreed that if Louis died without male issue, his two crowns should pass to Anne and her husband. In 1526, Louis, who had succeeded to both thrones ten years previously, perished in the rout of the Hungarian arms by the Turks at Mohács, and Ferdinand thereupon claimed the two Crowns.

The Lands of the Bohemian Crown consisted at that time of the Kingdom

---

[1] The Privilegium had been devised by Duke Rudolph IV in 1358, but the then Emperor, Charles IV, had refused to ratify it on the ground that some of the documents on which it was based were not authentic. The effect of it was simply to take from the German King the right of disposing of the lordship of the Lands concerned. The Lands themselves, having (with few exceptions) begun their existences as fiefs of the Reich, had never had a voice in the question.

[2] In fact, it was always applied in official use to any Lands as soon as the dynasty's hereditary title to them became established, thus to the Bohemian group after the Vernewerte Landesordungen.

of Bohemia, the Margravate of Moravia, the Duchy of Silesia and the Counties of Upper and Lower Lusatia. Of these Bohemia ranked as the senior. It had, indeed, been a fief of the Empire since AD 895, when its princes, after throwing off the overlordship of Moravia, had done homage to the then Emperor, but a member of its capable native dynasty, the Premyslides, had achieved the royal dignity in 1086, and this had thereafter been recognized as hereditary in his line. When the dynasty became extinct (in 1306), the Emperor had claimed the right to fill the throne, which the Bohemian Estates, on the other hand, claimed to be elective, and after they had won, the second representative of the new dynasty, the Luxemburger, Charles IV, who was also himself Emperor, had, in his Golden Bull of 1356, assured the Estates of this right, should his own dynasty become extinct in both the male and the female lines. They had in fact exercised it, when the situation arose,[1] from 1439 onward.

Moravia had been associated with Bohemia since early times, having ranked, except for one brief interval,[2] as a fief of the King of Bohemia. Silesia had been acquired in 1335, the Lusatias in 1355 and 1368 respectively. The Golden Bull had pronounced all the dominions of the Bohemian Crown to constitute an indivisible whole, but how far this remained valid on the extinction of Charles's line was disputable, and when the point arose, the *Nebenländer* had usually claimed not to be bound by the decisions of Bohemia.[3]

The Lands of the Hungarian Crown consisted in 1526 of the Kingdom of Hungary proper (a kingdom since AD 1000) and the Kingdom of Croatia, Slavonia and Dalmatia (to which, however, Dalmatia no longer belonged, having been lost to Venice in the fourteenth century), which had become attached to the Hungarian Crown at the end of the eleventh century. The terms on which it had done so are totally obscure, the few texts relating to the event being capable of various interpretations, which are duly given to them by Hungarian and Croat historians respectively. It is certain that so long as the dynasty of the Arpáds, under which the union had taken place,

[1] It is important to remember, in connection with the 'elective' character of both the Bohemian and the Hungarian Crowns, that election was for a dynasty, not an individual; a king's undisputed heir succeeded him automatically, *jure hereditario*. Most disputes for the Crown in both countries were between rival candidates each of whom, while not his predecessor's heir apparent, could yet produce a hereditary claim of some kind. Genuine free election took place only when there was no such candidate in the field at all.

[2] Frederick Barbarossa made it an 'immediate' Margravate of the Reich in 1182, but it reverted to the status of a fief of the King of Bohemia in 1222.

[3] So in 1437, when Albert of Habsburg died, the Nebenländer recognized his widow and posthumous son as their lawful sovereigns; Bohemia 'elected' the boy only in 1457. After this Moravia and Silesia were for a time ruled by Matthias Corvinus of Hungary. In 1490 Wladislaw Jagiellon was first elected King of Bohemia; Moravia and Silesia followed suit later.

survived, the Croats recognized its right to rule over Croatia, by virtue of a single coronation. The King's rule in Croatia was exercised through a Viceroy (*Ban*), and each country conducted its internal affairs separately. Since the latter part of the sixteenth century, the Croats had sent delegates to the Hungarian Diet when matters of interest to both countries were being discussed.

In Hungary, too, the native dynasty died out at the beginning of the fourteenth century (in 1301), and the 'nation' claimed the right to elect its own king. Documentary evidence is lacking on what attitude Croatia took at such elections as took place, but it seems to have accepted the Hungarians' choice.[1]

On the death of King Louis, obscure situations arose in both groups of Lands. Moravia and Silesia recognized Maria, and Ferdinand as her consort, as their monarchs by hereditary right; and it should be noted that from this date onward the Estates of Moravia, whenever the question arose, consistently asserted their immediate relationship to the Crown, a thesis which was accepted by the Crown. The Bohemian Estates refused to recognize the Habsburg-Jagiello family pact as binding on themselves, but duly elected Ferdinand and accepted his successors after him, until 1619, when there occurred the famous rebellion which ushered in the Thirty Years War. After crushing the rebellion, Ferdinand II issued *Vernewerte Landesordungen* (for Bohemia in 1627 and for Moravia in 1628) which made the determination of the succession in both Lands a Monarchic prerogative, and thus vested it securely in his own family. Lusatia, however, was ceded to Saxony in 1635, and in 1740 Frederick II of Prussia seized all but a fraction of Silesia, so that the Lands of the Bohemian Crown to which Joseph would succeed on his mother's death were considerably less extensive than those over which Ferdinand I had ruled.

A Croat Diet also immediately recognized Ferdinand in 1526, but only a small minority of the nobles of Hungary proper 'elected' him, and that at a meeting which was constitutionally questionable. The majority elected a national king, John Zápolya; moreover, such effective rule as Ferdinand ever exerted over Hungary was confined to the north and west of the country; the remainder passed under Turkish rule, which was exercised directly over the centre of the country and in the form of a protectorate over Transylvania. Nearly two hundred years passed before Habsburg rule was established both *de facto* and *de jure* over the whole country, but Transylvania was reoccupied at the end of the seventeenth century, and under the Peace of Karlowitz (1699) Leopold I recovered all historic Hungary-Croatia except a small strip in the South which the Turks evacuated in 1718 under

---

[1] Both the two anti-Kings of the period, Charles of Durazzo and Ladislas of Naples, drew many of their followers from the South, but neither claimed the throne of Croatia apart from that of Hungary.

the Peace of Passarowitz.[1] Meanwhile, a Hungarian Diet had in 1683 accepted the Habsburg succession in the male line.

In Hungary, almost alone of their dominions, the Habsburgs departed from their rule of leaving untouched the political identities and frontiers of their dominions, as acquired. They had continued to recognize that all the Lands east of the Leitha recovered by them belonged in theory to the complex of the 'Lands of the Hungarian Crown', but Leopold I had kept Transylvania as a separate 'Principality',[2] with its own Constitution and Court Chancellery. He had also included within its boundaries certain areas, known in Hungarian terminology by the curious name of *Partium*, which, while not belonging to the recognized historic Transylvania, had been ruled by its princes in the Turkish era. Half of these had been restored to the Kingdom of Hungary by Charles III in 1738; the other half[3] were still with Transylvania in 1780.

The southern fringe of Hungary-Croatia was also under a separate dispensation. From the earliest emergence of the Turkish threat, the areas immediately behind the line of the Turkish advance had been organized as a defensive belt under direct military control. With time, this organization had been systematized and the areas concerned removed altogether from the control of the Croat and Hungarian Estates. When the Turks were driven behind the Danube in 1699, the frontier districts from which the danger had receded had been liquidated, but new ones formed behind the new frontier, as far as the Tisza, while when the area between the Tisza, the Maros and the Danube (the 'Bánát of Temesvár') was recovered under the Peace of Passarowitz, it was given a similar, but separate, organization, under a military Governor directly responsible to Vienna. In 1777, however, Maria Theresa had agreed to the liquidation of the Bánát, of which the northern portion was restored to civilian administration in 1778, while its southern and eastern portions were turned into Frontier 'Districts'. The Frontier now constituted a long, narrow strip, running the whole length of the frontier with Turkey, from the Adriatic to the boundary with Transylvania.[4] It was under the direct control of the Viennese Hofkriegsrat, and for fiscal purposes, the Hofkammer.[5]

---

[1] Under this Charles also acquired considerable territories in the Northern Balkans, but had to re-cede these under the Treaty of Belgrade (1739).

[2] It was promoted by Maria Theresa in 1765 to the rank of 'Grand Principality'. Kaunitz had then wanted the Queen to separate it from the Lands of the Hungarian Crown, but she had been dissuaded by the representations of the Hungarian Court Chancellery.

[3] The Counties of Közép-Szolnok, Kraszna and Zarand and the District of Kövár.

[4] It had not been thought necessary to extend the system to Transylvania, since the organization of the Szekel and, in part, the Saxon districts was already para-military. Joseph II afterwards formed two new 'Frontier Districts' in Transylvania, but the control of the Hofkriegsrat there was never so systematic as in Croatia or Inner Hungary.

[5] For these institutions, see below, p. 19.

Another area in South Hungary, the so-called Slavonian Counties, between the Lower Drave and Save, had in 1741 been placed under the Ban of Croatia for administrative purposes, but not legally incorporated in the Kingdom of Croatia.[1]

The manipulation had brought with it a change in nomenclature. The old 'Croatia' had lain chiefly in Bosnia, now still under Turkish rule. The area which now became known as Croatia had previously been called Slavonia, which name was now transferred to the area described, after a transitional period during which it was called 'Lower Slavonia'.

Finally, Fiume with its hinterland had undergone various vicissitudes, including incorporation in Croatia as recently as 1776, but in 1779 had been constituted a 'corpus separatum' under the Hungarian Crown.

It may be remarked that even the mutilations described above were much smaller than it had first been intended to inflict on Hungary, for on recovering the central and southern parts of the country, the Crown had claimed them as its own absolute property by right of conquest, and had for a time administered them as such through an organization known as the *Neo-acquistica Commissio*. The idea of turning this whole vast area into a new province had, however, been abandoned, and in 1722 the Crown, while retaining ownership of the land (large parts of which were then either settled with free peasants or sold or donated to individuals) had restored it to the civilian administration.

Of the remaining territories under Habsburg rule in 1780, the Vorlande, a set of enclaves in Western and Southern Germany, the most important of which was the Breisgau, were for the most part the fruits of purchases and sales, concessions and counter-concessions, too numerous to detail. Few of them had been very long in the family hands, since most of Rudolph of Habsburg's original patrimony had melted away quite early.[2] Milan, Mantua and the Austrian Netherlands, these former possessions of the Spanish branch of the family, represented salvage retained by Austria at the end of the War of the Spanish Succession.[3] The Kingdom of Galicia-

---

[1] The Counties in question were those of Szrem, Valkó (later amalgamated with Szrem), Pozsega and Verőcze. They comprised only the northern part of the area, for its southern half belonged to the Frontier, a salient of which cut them off from Croatia. The arrangement had been made in order to compensate Croatia for the non-recovery of the southern portion of its old territory, but the Hungarians had protested on the grounds that the area had never formed part of Croatia in historic times. They therefore stipulated that the three Counties should continue to send their delegates direct to the Hungarian Diet, and pay the full rate of taxation, which was twice as high in Hungary as in Croatia.

The population was, incidentally, almost entirely Serb.

[2] The bulk of it had been lost to the Swiss at the battles of Morgarten (1315) and Sempach (1384).

[3] The Treaties of Utrecht (1713) and Rastatt (1714) had also given Charles Sardinia, which was exchanged for Naples and Sicily in 1720. These were lost in 1735, when Charles received in compensation Parma and Piacenza, but these, again, were lost in 1748.

THE MONARCHY IN 1780

Lodomeria, with the Duchies of Zator and Oswiecim (Ausschwita) had been acquired by Maria Theresa herself under the First Partition of Poland; the Bukovina, previously the northern-most tip of the Danubian Principality of Moldavia, had been extracted from the Porte (its over-lord) in 1775 as 'compensation' for Austria's mediation of the Russo-Turkish Peace of that year.

Furthermore it had, as we have said, become habitual since the fifteenth century for the senior member of the House of Habsburg to hold the dignities of German-Roman King and Holy Roman Emperor. On the death of Charles VI, last of the true male line, a Wittelsbach, Charles VII, had been elected to them, but on his death, in 1745, they had reverted to Maria Theresa's consort, Francis Stephen of Lorraine, and then to their son, Joseph II.

All the Hereditary Lands and the Vorlande were, of course, like the Lands of the Bohemian Crown, parts of the Empire, but not those of the Hungarian Crown nor the Habsburgs' possessions in Italy.

We may mention here that after its attribution to Francis Stephen, the Grand Duchy of Tuscany was, in 1763, made into a secondo-geniture of the House of Habsburg-Lorraine. On Francis Stephen's death in 1765, it had passed to his second son, Leopold. His third son, Ferdinand, had married Beatrix, daughter and heiress of Ercole of Modena d'Este, after whose death in 1803 Modena became a family tertio-geniture.

As this outline will have shown, the Habsburg Monarchy of 1780 was essentially a dynastic creation. The diligence of Joseph's maternal ancestors had brought it together, and their single-minded pursuit of family aggrandizement had never been qualified by considerations of political, social, ethnical or geographical congruity; value and availability on the market had been their only criteria. If most of the Lands now composing the Monarchy formed a geographical continuum, this was simply due to the pragmatic fact that neighbouring estates are more easily and naturally acquired, and above all, more easily defended, than those which can be reached only across the territory of another, potentially hostile, ruler; not because any Habsburg had ever thought it improper or absurd that he should rule anywhere.

There was nothing peculiar about this mentality, or these methods. In the days when the Habsburgs built up their fortunes, every princely family, indeed, every baron, knight and squire in his own degree had been following exactly the same objective, by the same means, where he could. But in one respect, the Habsburgs had been unique. They had had their set-backs and their losses, but by and large, theirs had been a success story which no other European dynasty could rival. Again and again, a transaction which might have turned out either way according to the chance whether bridegroom outlived bride or vice-versa, whether this marriage or that proved barren, had ended favourably for them. The lines of Carinthia, of Meran and Gorizia, of Burgundy and Spain and Portugal, of Bohemia and Hungary, had died out; theirs had survived. It was true that it, too, had perished at last: Maria Theresa's father had been the last male Habsburg of the blood. Yet he had managed to salvage almost all the family inheritance for his daughter, whose son was succeeding to it now, under the old name.

But their very success had, inevitably, been achieved at the expense of homogeneity, of any sort. A little domain of a few villages may bear one face, geographical, social, ethnic: not so an empire so far-flung as the Habsburgs', sprawling clean across Central Europe, not to mention its outliers. And to the differences imposed by nature between its different parts and their inhabitants, there were added special ones due to the chance of the circumstances of its birth and growth. Fortune had set the cradle of Monarchy at the ethnic crossroads of Europe, where Teuton, Slav and Latin meet, and meet, moreover, precisely at that point which from time immemorial has constituted the last stage of their western journey for Europe's successive invaders from the Eastern steppes. If the original Marks of Austria and Styria had been German by definition, and in the main, also by population (since the foundation of them had been accompanied by colonization of their empty or sparsely inhabited spaces with German settlers), almost every single new acquisition made by the dynasty, except for the relatively few westward extensions, had brought at least one new element under its rule, and usually more. The first expansion southward had added a Slavonic fringe to the German core; the next, an Italian. The great *coup* of 1526 had added lands which were the national homes of the Czechs and the Magyars, and each of these had contained also many minorities: Hungary, amongst others, Croats, Serbs and Roumanians. The later expansion had brought in more Italians and Roumanians, also Poles and Ruthenes, Flemings and Walloons.

The variety of geographical environment had naturally brought about, and the ethnic heterogeneity had enhanced, wide variations in the economic conditions and social structures of the different parts of the Monarchy. And while political unity would clearly have facilitated a large measure of mutual assimilation in these respects, there was another feature of the Habsburg expansion which made such unity difficult to achieve. This was the comparatively late date of the family's rise to power, which had begun only in an age when the movements of the peoples in Central Europe were over, and the area had already achieved its basic political pattern of Kingdoms, Duchies, Margravates and Counties, each bounded by recognized political frontiers and each already possessed of its own political institutions. For centuries after this stage had been reached, almost all changes in the political map of Central Europe had been purely dynastic: they had consisted simply of the transference from one hand to another of this or that Kingdom or Duchy, within its historic frontiers and, at least nominally, without alteration of its political institutions; indeed, when the acquisition had been peaceful and justified by a claim of legitimacy, or by election – and almost all the Habsburgs' acquisitions had been of one or the other of these types[1] – it was customary for the new ruler to swear to keep those institutions intact.

A corollary of this method of Empire accumulation was that the links between the components, at least when first formed, were purely dynastic. Even where subsequent developments associated certain of them in larger groups – the Hereditary Lands, the Lands of the Bohemian and of the Hungarian Crowns – such association did not impair the mutual independence of each component within the group; still less did each group recognize any connection, except the dynastic, with any other. This individuality, constitutional and perhaps even more, sentimental, of the different Lands, was and remained a continual feature of the entire Monarchy, throughout its history.

It was their political relationship to their subjects which had chiefly interested the Habsburgs, and it is fitting that our survey of the Monarchy in 1780 should begin with a description of its political structure at that date. The picture was, indeed, one of extraordinary complexity, owing to the extremely various nature of the forces involved, and the great strength of some of them, and it may be added that the serious attempts at political unification outside the sphere of the *regia potestas* had begun only a generation or so before the date of our sketch.

II THE POLITICAL STRUCTURE

In 1780 the only recognized constitutional link between the components of the Monarchy was still the Dynasty, whose rule was acknowledged by all of them in the same, or nearly the same, terms under the Pragmatic Sanction issued by Charles VI (as King of Hungary and of Spain, Charles III) in 1713, and the Hungarian legislation (Laws I and II of 1723[2]) implementing it. These instruments declared all the Lands of the Monarchy to constitute an 'indivisible and inseparable whole' and bound all of them to accept as their future Monarch Charles's heirs in primogeniture in the male or female

[1] Almost the only exceptions had been the small sixteenth-century acquisitions made by Maximilian I at the expense of Venice, and the Bukovina. Maria Theresa's share of Poland was converted retro-actively into a 'historic-political unit' by identifying it with the mediaeval Kingdom of Halics-Vladimir, whereupon the annexation was justified by evocation of a claim derived from mediaeval Hungarian history. The Bukovina was made into a historico-political unit in 1849 (see below, p. 424).

[2] The Hungarian legislation was necessitated by the fact that Hungary, unlike all Charles's other dominions, had not previously been bound to accept the Habsburg succession in the female line, and her consent was legally necessary for any change in the law of succession. On this occasion, also, Croatia had spoken without waiting for Hungary: in 1712 a Croat Diet had declared itself ready to accept any Habsburg, male or female, who was also ruler of Inner Austria (Styria, Carinthia and Carniola) and could thus defend Croatia against the Turks.

line, or failing them, the heirs of his defunct brother, Joseph I, until the extinction of the line.[1]

The Pragmatic Sanction, as such, brought about no change in the mutual relationships of the components of the Monarchy. If some Austrian centralist historians have described it as turning the sum of these constituents into a 'State', this would have been vigorously denied in most of the Lands. No Hungarian could ever be found to acknowledge that Hungary formed part of any 'State' except Hungary itself. The Belgian and Bohemian Estates were on occasion equally emphatic in maintaining that the only 'States' to which they belonged were those of the United Netherlands and the Bohemian Crown respectively, and while none of the Hereditary Lands could claim either sovereignty or statehood, they would presumably have said that the State to which they belonged was the German Reich.[2] The usual term for the sum of the Habsburg dominions was, in fact, *Haus Oesterreich* in the sixteenth and seventeenth centuries, and in the eighteenth *Oesterreichische Monarchie* or *Gesammtmonarchie* (if the titles of some of the offices described below contain the word *Staat*, this was a mere matter of semantic usage). The conduct of the Monarch's government deferred to this thesis in so far that the Monarch conducted his transactions with each Land in his capacity of its *Landesherr*, as King of Hungary or Bohemia, Archduke of Austria, Count of Tirol, etc.[3]

The dynastic link nevertheless meant in practice something more than the bare fact that each Land acknowledged the same Prince, for in pre-Constitutional times the Prince of any land normally enjoyed, *jure majestatis*, certain important prerogatives in it. The main rights so enjoyed by the Habsburgs, in 1780, can be grouped under three heads:

(1) The right to declare war and conclude peace, to conclude treaties and alliances with foreign Powers, and in general, to conduct foreign policy. The Monarch's right in these respects was, in 1780, subject to no theoretical restriction whatever.[4]

[1] The Hungarian law further stipulated that the King of Hungary must be legitimate, an Archduke or Archduchess of Austria (i.e., of the Archduchy of Austria Above and Below the Enns), and a member of the Roman Catholic Church. As, however, Hungarian public law did not recognize the principle of *Ebenbürtigkeit*, any legitimate issue of an Archduke ranked under it as Archducal.

[2] So long as the Habsburgs were themselves subject to the German King, or Emperor, the supreme prerogatives in these fields were, of course, his and not theirs. We need not enter here into the complexities of this question.

[3] Moravia and Silesia were treated as 'immediate'. Croatia was addressed through Hungary. The Crown, while acknowledging that its title to Transylvania derived from the Hungarian Crown, yet corresponded with it directly. It was possible for Joseph to give orders to the Hereditary and Bohemian Lands *qua* Emperor.

[4] Under the rule of the weak Wladislas Jagiello both the Hungarian and the Bohemian Estates had forced the King to allow them a voice in foreign policy, but this right had lapsed under the Habsburgs. Some forced concessions made by the Archduke Matthias in 1609 had lasted only a few years.

(2) Connected with these rights were his prerogatives in the field of defence, where, again, he was usually supreme, subject to a fixed obligation, nearly always explicitly undertaken on his accession, to defend the frontiers of each Land, and in most cases limited by a provision that if he wished to undertake obligations which went beyond his own resources, he must apply to the Estates of his Lands for recruits or money, which they were entitled to refuse.

(3) His financial prerogatives in each Land included the determination of commercial policy and the levying of customs and excise, and, up to a point, internal indirect taxation.

Enjoying, as they did, these prerogatives in all the Lands subject to them, the Habsburgs naturally maintained certain central, pan-Monarchic, services for exercising them. These, in 1780, were as follows:

The Monarchy's foreign policy had since 1742[1] been conducted through the *Geheime Haus- Hof- und Staatskanzlei*, the head of which was in practice the Foreign Minister of the Monarchy. He was also, in general, the first servant of the State, and the holder of the office in 1780, Prince Kaunitz, bore the title of *Staatskanzler*. This, however, was a title conferred only occasionally, and *ad personam*;[2] heads of the Chancellery to whom it was not granted were usually called 'Foreign Minister'.

The head of the Chancellery was, it may be remarked, the only official in the Monarchy who took his decisions (subject to the Monarchic agreement) personally; in every other Ministry the system was that known as 'Collegiate', i.e., decisions were taken in Committee, by vote.

The military system of the Monarchy had passed through various stages of evolution. In mediaeval days the defence force of each Land had consisted of a local militia, the recruitment and conditions of service of which had been governed by local law and usage. These forces had increasingly been replaced by mercenary armies, which the Lands were required to finance by 'contributions' rendered by them in lieu of the personal service now no longer required of them. As this system had in its turn proved unsatisfactory, owing to the difficulty of recruiting and keeping together the mercenary troops, the defence system of the Central Monarchy[3] had, shortly before the date with which this sketch is concerned,[4] been placed on a new footing. A few relics of the older days still survived. All Hungarian nobles were still bound to obey the call when the *insurrectio* (*levée en masse*) was proclaimed.[5] The free peasants of the Tirol were under a similar obligation. In the

---

[1] Before that year they had been looked after by the Oesterreichische Hofkanzlei, from which the Geheime Kanzlei was then hived off.

[2] After Kaunitz, it was conferred only on Metternich.

[3] Milan-Mantua and the Netherlands had their separate services, which need not be described here.

[4] The system here described had been introduced in the Hereditary and Bohemian Lands in 1771 and extended to Galicia and the Bukovina when those territories were annexed.

[5] The order was issued by the Palatine, who commanded the force.

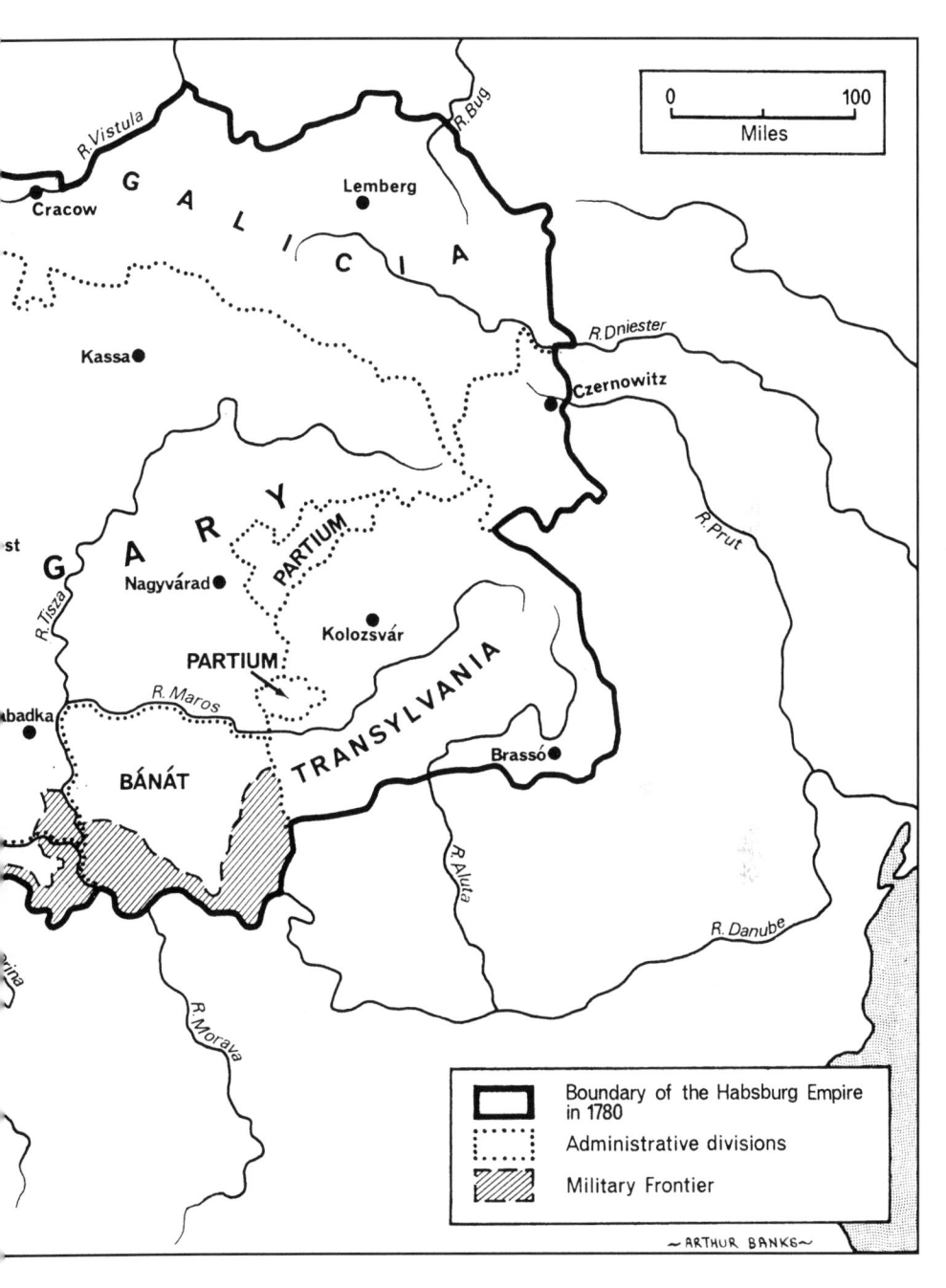

Military Frontier, outside certain 'Free Districts' which were exempt from this obligation, every able-bodied male was liable for military service, and those not serving with the colours did duty in rotation as pickets along the Turkish frontier. But the main defence force of the Central Monarchy now consisted of a standing army, the strength of which had been fixed in 1774 at 164,000.[1] Of these, 21,000 were recruited in Hungary by voluntary enlistment,[2] the rest by conscription, for which purpose all the Hereditary Lands, except the Tirol (which was exempt), the Bohemian Lands and Galicia-Bukovina, were divided into recruiting districts (thirty-seven in number), each of which was allotted a certain quota of recruits. All able-bodied males between the ages of seventeen and forty were liable to conscription, unless they belonged to an 'exempted' occupational category, and the quota was, in theory, made up by the drawing of lots. The exempted categories were, indeed, so numerous that in practice this device was seldom used.[3]

Austria also enjoyed, under Reich law, the right of recruiting in those Principalities of the Empire which did not maintain their own armed services (she made extensive use of this right especially to procure N.C.O.s, the non-Austrian Germans being regarded as constituting better material even than the Germans of Austria, let alone the non-Germans) and also accepted volunteers from other sources. Regular stations were kept up on the Silesian frontier for the reception of deserters from the Prussian army.

Subjects of the Monarchy could obtain commissions through entry from one of two cadet schools established by Maria Theresa, one for the sons of nobles from her dominions, the other for the sons of serving officers. A commission could, however, also be obtained through exchange from another service, or by simple purchase. In the 1770s a high proportion of the officers in the Austrian army came to it in one of these ways, and they were an extraordinarily varied body. Germans from the Empire furnished the largest contingent, but there were also Italians, Frenchmen, Spaniards, Irishmen and some of even more recondite origin.

[1] Raised from 108,000 after the annexation of Galicia.

[2] The famous Hungarian Diet of 1741 had agreed to contribute this number to the standing army, but had refused to accept conscription.

[3] The exempted categories included all nobles and priests, burghers and most skilled workers, including miners and chimney-sweeps and workers in 'privileged' (licensed) factories, and all peasants technically so ranking, and their heirs at law. It was thus in practice only the peasants' sons, other than his heirs, and the rural and urban proletariats, that were liable for conscription, and there were barely enough of these to make up the numbers. The quotas were largely made up by the method known as *Abstellung ex officio*, i.e., by the authorities seizing certain unwanted persons, including rogues and vagabonds, persons without papers, and renegades from Catholicism, and delivering them to the barracks (a court was not, however, allowed to condemn an offender to military service as part of a penal sentence). The remainder were selected by the lord of the manor, or his agent, to the number allotted to his manor. The 'volunteers' in Hungary were also largely produced by *Abstellung ex officio*, or by Shanghaiing.

THE MONARCHY IN 1780

The army was administered for the Crown by the Hofkriegsrat, a body established by Ferdinand I in 1560, originally as a small advisory Council, which, however, had since expanded into a permanent Ministry, employing a considerable staff, which was now divided into three departments: the *publico-politicum*, the *judiciale* and the *economicum*. All the regular forces of the Monarchy (including the Hungarian regiments[1]), came under the authority of the *Hofkriegsrat*, which also directly administered the Military Frontier and was thus the supreme authority, under the Crown, even for the civilian populations of that area.[2] All these forces were sworn to loyalty to the Monarch, and owed no allegiance to any other person or instance.

A third pan-Monarchic service, the Camera (*Hofkammer*) collected and administered the Crown's own financial assets – its revenues from the Crown lands, which were fairly extensive in most Lands, including the taxation paid by the Royal Free Boroughs, which were directly subject to the Crown, from mintage, from the revenues derived from the mining of gold, silver and salt,[3] the yield of customs and excise and of certain special taxes such as the 'toleration tax' paid by Jews, who ranked as '*Kammerknechte*'. This was naturally to some extent decentralized in its operations, and even in its organization: the Netherlands and Milan had their own Camerae which operated independently, subject to the obligation of paying over a quota of their profits to the central exchequer, and the Camerae of Hungary and Transylvania were also nominally independent, although in practice only sections of the Central Hofkammer, from the head of which they took their orders. But the Lands had no control over the operations of the Camera, over the apportionment of the revenues deriving from it, or over policy in the fields lying within the Monarch's financial-economic competence, although these included questions so important to them as those of foreign trade policy.

The central financial institutions included also a *Kreditdeputatio*, which administered the national debt, and a *Hofrechnungskammer*, or Supreme Court of Audit.

The field of operations of these bodies was in practice more extensive than the above words would suggest, for while, according to original theory, the Crown should have 'lived of its own', there had hardly been a time in the history of the Monarchy when it had succeeded in doing so. In times of war,

---

[1] When, in 1712–15, Hungary had agreed that the Pragmatic Sanction applied *et contra vim externam*, she had demanded her own Hofkriegsrat, but this had never come into being and the central Hofkriegsrat had even since exercised *de facto* control over the Hungarian regiments. Hungary had then asked that at least one Hungarian should always be a member of the Hofkriegsrat proper, i.e., the small 'Council' at the head of the organization. This, again, had never been granted.

[2] The economic affairs of the Frontier were administered through the Hofkammer.

[3] Its claim to this perquisite was, however, contested by the Hungarian Diet. Where the gold and silver mines were not directly owned by the Crown, it took a royalty on their production.

actual or threatened, it had always been obliged to call on the Estates of some or all Lands for special contributions, and once the defence system changed over from one of local militias to one of a paid standing army, it had, as we have said, become the practice to call on the Lands which were now relieved of the obligation of providing the service in kind (in the form of manpower) for a financial contribution in lieu thereof. The taxation system had been reorganized after the War of the Austrian Succession by Maria Theresa's great adviser, Count Friedrich Wilhelm von Haugwitz.

In principle, the Crown still financed its central non-military expenditure, viz., the upkeep of the Court, the Privy Purse, out of which special donations were made, and its own administrative services, out of its Cameral revenues; since 1763, also in part out of certain direct taxes levied by the exchequer without consultation with the Lands. The cost of the defence services was apportioned between the Lands on an assessment based on their populations and assessed wealth; this was made every ten years and then notified to the Estates of the Land (in Hungary, to a Committee of the Diet). In the Western Lands the central exchequer defrayed out of the *contributio*, as this was called, the cost of local expenditure for the housing, provisioning, etc., of the troops quartered in the Lands; it was in return for this concession that the nobles (who had previously been tax-free in most respects) had agreed to submit themselves (i.e., their demesne lands) to a land tax, out of which the bulk of the contributio was derived. In Hungary, the nobles had refused to submit to the land tax, and each Hungarian County still had to pay for the upkeep of the troops quartered in it. The sums paid by Hungary under the heading, known as *deperdita*, were appreciable. The direct contributio was, however, relatively small.

Central, in another field, and up to a point, was the Crown's advisory body. This, after changing its form and composition almost with every generation, had emerged by 1780[1] as a *Staatsrat*, consisting of three members of the higher nobility, three of the lower, and a bourgeois secretary. Each member of this body was sworn to give his true opinion on any question submitted to him, without fear or favour. Constitutional objections having been raised by Hungary, the competence of this body did not formally extend to the Hungarian Lands. Later a 'Hungarian Referent' was added to its members, but he reported independently on Hungarian questions; the other Councillors had no 'vote' on these.

All other questions were, in theory, dealt with on a Land by Land basis, being regulated either by the Crown in its capacity of *Landesherr*, and in virtue of its prerogative; by the Lands' own 'organs of self-government', in virtue of the autonomous rights possessed by them, or through negotiation between the two.

[1] The Staatsrat in this form had been established by Kaunitz in 1760, but its predecessor dated back to the reign of Maximilian I.

THE MONARCHY IN 1780

At this point we must interpose an outline of the political structure of the Lands, albeit an over-simplified sketch of a subject of unimaginable complexity and innumerable variants.

The structures of all the Hereditary and Bohemian Lands had by 1780 become almost identical, earlier differences between them having been ironed out in the course of time, chiefly through assimilation of the latter group to the former. The foundations on which all alike rested were the personal distinction which existed in all between their free and unfree populations, and the territorial distinction between the respective domains of the Landesherr in his official capacity[1] and the local nobles.

The personal distinction applied to both territorial groups, for the ordinary populations of most areas directly administered by the Camera were not free, but ranked as *Kammerknechte*. The burghers of the Royal Free Boroughs,[2] however, and certain communities of peasants, while not noble, ranked as free men; they owned no direct master except the Landesherr.

The rest of the area of each Land belonged to its nobles. It was divided into 'manors' (*Herrschaften*, or *Güter* – the former name was usually reserved for very large estates), a list of which, known as the *Landtafel*, was kept in each Land, and which, normally, could be owned only by a noble, although not necessarily an individual:[3] a corporation such as a Cathedral Chapter or a Monastery might, by a legal fiction, be granted 'noble' status entitling it to exercise manorial rights.

On such noble land, the direct link between the Landesherr and his subjects stopped at the manor; the unfree populations inhabiting each manor were, directly, the 'subjects' (the relationship was expressed by the term *nexus subditelae*) of the lords; for Maria Theresa herself, while introducing into the

[1] Where a Monarch owned land in his private capacity, his relationship to its population was that of any other landowner.

[2] It should be emphasized that by no means all towns possessing municipal charters were Royal Free Boroughs. Even of those belonging to the Crown, a considerable number were administered by the Hofkammer, and their inhabitants ranked as Kammerknechte: this category included even such important communities as the sixteen mining towns of the Szepes area in north Hungary. Half a dozen towns in Bohemia (the so-called Leibgeding towns) were the appanage of the Monarch's widow. Some towns were owned by archiepiscopal or episcopal sees, many of which enjoyed the right of granting municipal charters, as did certain individuals, especially in Galicia. The inhabitants of such places were the 'subjects' of their respective lords.

[3] While there were certain bizarre exceptions, the general rule was that a *landtäflich* estate could be acquired only by a person already possessing a title of nobility and *indigenat* in the Land (i.e., citizenship of it); a person buying such an estate had to prove his qualifications within a year or he lost it. In practice the indigenat was usually granted automatically to a 'foreign' noble of sufficient status, and in some Lands there was no legal ban to forbid an unqualified person from buying a landtäflich estate, but the acquisition was so difficult and expensive that most ambitious commoners found it easier to get their patent of nobility first. In some Lands the more considerable estates could be acquired only by members of the higher nobility.

relationship certain modifications (the resultant position is described elsewhere[1]) had, after certain waverings[2] resigned herself to leaving intact the political principle, which was that it was the lord of the manor only who was the direct subject of the Landesherr, the man of whom, alone, the latter took direct cognizance. Even where he had requirements which had in practice to be fulfilled by the unfree populations, such as the payment of taxes or service in the army, it was to their lord that he issued the orders, the lord then seeing to, and being responsible for, the execution of them by his subjects, apportioning and collecting the taxes, selecting and delivering the manorial quota of conscripts, etc. He also saw to the maintenance of public order and security among them, and of such services in connection with education, public health, etc., as the law required, and maintained a Court of Justice (usually known as the Patrimonial Court) which was the primary judiciary instance for his manor, himself dealing summarily with minor offenders and remitting others to a higher court, the dividing line varying, here again, with the size and dignity of the manor (the lords of some great Herrschaften were entitled to execute high justice and kept their own gallows, but smaller lords were as a rule competent to deal summarily only with comparatively light offences). When a manor was very small, several of them were often grouped together for the purposes of justice.

Every commune also possessed its own elected Council, which sometimes, by custom or local law, enjoyed a fair measure of autonomy, and could appeal to higher authority against abusive conduct on the part of the manorial lord. The Councils were, however, still their lord's subjects, not his partners in office.

The manorial lords were thus, looked at from the Landesherr's point of view, the last link in the chain of his direct authority; from that of the Lands, they were the basis of their political structures, which were simply the machinery through which the manorial lords settled their mutual differences, took joint decisions on matters of common interest where they could do so autonomously, arranged how to carry out orders issued by the Landesherr in virtue of his *potestas* (such orders naturally going to a single

---

[1] See below, p. 64 ff.

[2] In her earlier years, she had defended the institution on principle. 'It can never be practicable', she had written in 1742, 'to abolish the subjection altogether, for there is no country which does not make a distinction between lords and subjects; to free the peasant from his obligation towards the former would make the one party presumptuous and the other discontented, and would conflict with justice in every way.' Later in her life, when her inquiries had revealed to her the extreme misery in which the peasants were living outside the German-Austrian Lands, she had favoured cutting the Gordian knot at least in the Bohemian Lands by abolishing the nexus subditelae altogether in those Lands, but had been opposed so strongly, not only by the Estates concerned, but her own advisers (the entire Staatsrat had been against her, and so, to her extreme embitterment, had been her son) that she had given up the idea. Her hands had in any case been tied in Hungary by her Coronation oath, and she does not seem to have thought the measure necessary in the Hereditary Lands.

body representing the lords and not to each one of them individually) and also defended their collective interests against him. This was done through a 'Diet' (Landtag), for the composition of which practically all Lands had evolved a representational system of 'Estates' (*Landstände*, or simply *Stände*) which reflected the differences in real power and importance between the different classes of its lords. The pattern had, in this respect also, become practically identical in nearly all the Hereditary and Bohemian Lands (here, too, earlier differences had been ironed out[1]), although the relative numbers of representatives contributed by each Estate to the collective representational body varied considerably from Land to Land. Normally, the First and Second 'Benches' (these were sometimes counted together) were composed respectively of the great Prelates (the *Prälatenstand*) and the Princes, Counts and Barons (the *Herrenstand*), each of these being individually entitled to sit on his 'Bench'; the Rector of the local University (if any) and any important ecclesiastic not otherwise qualified also sat *ex officio* on this Bench (such representatives were known as 'Virilists'). The third Bench (the *Ritterstand*) was composed of representatives of the untitled nobility. The manorial lords were supposed to represent the interests of their respective 'subjects', who were therefore not represented on the Estates. Representatives of the Royal Free Boroughs (the *Bürgerstand*) constituted a fourth Bench, but usually possessed only a single collective vote among what might, theoretically, be a number running into three figures. In the Tirol, uniquely, the free peasants sent two representatives to the Diet. Silesia had only two Estates: the Dukes and Princes, and the smaller nobles.[2] The Littoral had none.

The Diets of these Lands were supposed to meet once a year, while Standing Committees, composed of representatives of each Estate, assisted by small permanent staffs,[3] were maintained to transact current business.

Even before the reforms described below, some of the larger Lands, notably Bohemia and Moravia, had found it convenient to divide their areas into sub-units – 'Circles' (*Kreise*) – and to keep in each an administrative representative and perhaps a judicial court of second instance. The Circle officials had, however, been only the local representatives and agents of the Estates; they had had no independent powers except in so far as the

---

[1] Earlier Bohemian Diets (before the arrival of the Habsburgs) had, for example, at one time excluded the Lords Spiritual, while allowing relatively generous representation to the towns. Ferdinand II had brought the Diet into line with those of the Hereditary Lands under the Vernewerte Landesordnung.

[2] Silesia was largely composed of tiny principalities, formerly the appanages of the very prolific ruling house of the Piasts. The Habsburgs had refused to recognize these rulers as immediate, but had left them quasi-sovereign status within their own dominions.

[3] The permanent staffs consisted of a few permanent clerks, etc., but most of them also contained a small number of doctors and surgeons, and many of the lists also show one or two more exotic figures: a dancing-master and a fencing-master, often a teacher of French and sometimes one of Italian.

Estates authorized them to deal on the spot with questions of secondary and local importance. They had had no deliberative assemblages of their own, and no representation in the Landtag.

We may pass over the constitutions of Lombardy and the Netherlands, only remarking that the latter, in particular, allowed considerable representation to urban and middle-class interests. The basic political structure of Hungary was the same as that of the Western Lands, in so far as it, too, rested on the distinction between free and unfree, and on the manorial system. But Hungary was too big to be managed on a two-tier basis. The founder of the Kingdom, St Stephen, had himself divided it into Counties (*Comitatus*, *Vármegyek*) setting in each of them a representative of his own authority, the *Comes* or *Ispán*. Gradually the Counties had changed their character and had developed into something halfway towards a Western Land. Each still had as its titular head a representative of the Crown, now known as the *Föispán*, but they had become autonomous entities, possessing a legal personality distinct from that of the Kingdom, exercising their corporate rights autonomously and technically acting in virtue of that autonomy even where they were in fact only giving effect to measures enacted by the government of the Kingdom. They could not refuse to carry out such measures if they were in accordance with the law of the land, nor could they themselves enact any unlawful measure. Subject, however, to this restriction, their authority was unlimited, and they possessed a recognized right to refuse to carry out an unlawful order – and in the situation which had developed in Hungary in the eighteenth century it was in fact possible to question the legality of a surprisingly high proportion of the orders which emanated from Vienna; while the sketchy condition of such laws as existed left the field in which they could exercise their discretion an exceedingly wide one. They had the right to submit their views to the Government on national affairs, as well as local, and to exchange views with each other. They had their own Diets (*Congregationes*) the franchise for which was enjoyed by all the local nobles, including the very large class of small nobles which was a feature of Hungarian society.[1] These electors periodically chose their own administrative staffs, the head of which was known as the *Alispán* (sub-*Ispán*).

Large Counties were divided into *járasok*, corresponding to the Austrian *Kreise*. The *járas* was not autonomous.

The composition of the Hungarian Diet reflected this development. It consisted of two 'Tables', the first of which was composed of the dignitaries of the realm, the higher Prelates, the male members of families of 'magnate' rank,[2] i.e., Barons and upward, the Föispáns of the Counties, and two repre-

[1] But see below, p. 57.
[2] At the end of the eighteenth century there were 108 Hungarian families bearing hereditary titles: 2 Princely, 82 of Counts, 24 Baronial.

sentatives from Croatia. The Lower Table was composed of Prelates not possessing their own Chapters, certain officials, two representatives from each County and from each of the four 'Privileged Districts,[1] one from the Royal Free Boroughs[2] and three from Croatia. Absentee magnates, or the widows of magnates, were allowed to send proxies to the Lower Table, but they could not address it.

The King was under a legal obligation to convoke the Hungarian Diet every three years.

Croatia had its own Diet, composed of local Lords spiritual and temporal, and lesser nobles, with a large number of *ex officio* members.

Transylvania had a peculiar constitution, dating from the Middle Ages, although since frequently modified. Its Diet had originally been composed of representatives of the 'Three Nations of Transylvania', viz., the nobles of the Hungarian Counties, the Saxons and the Szekels,[3] who met to deliberate together on matters of common interest, no decision being valid without the seals of all three bodies, so that in theory no measure affecting the right of any one of them could be passed without its consent. This provision was still in force, Leopold I having confirmed the Constitution in 1691, but the Diet's numbers had been stretched to include representatives of the Royal Free Boroughs and some other towns, local great landowners and other important persons invited by the Crown in the proportions of four Hungarian nobles and two Szekels to one Saxon, and officials appointed by the Crown. It met (or should have met) annually.

The Military Frontier had no self-governing institutions.

The Government, in 1780, was in process of constructing Estates on the normal pattern for Galicia. It had already organized first and second Estates, for the magnates and lesser nobility respectively, but had been unable to build directly on existing foundations, since at the time of the annexation there had been no legal differentiations between one noble and another. Families of 'Senatorial' status had been authorized to apply for the title of Count and those of somewhat lesser dignity, for that of Baron. Those who did so with success (not all applied, and not all applications were accepted) became members of the Bench of Magnates, while nobles paying a minimum land tax of fifteen florins a year (three hundred zloty) were entitled to membership of the Lower Bench (here, again, many nobles did not apply, while according to rumour, a considerable number of rich peasants and even Jews were allowed in, and given patents of nobility 'to make it so').

---

[1] These were certain districts originally settled by immigrants (Cumanians, Jazyges, etc.) who had received the privilege of freedom and self-government (under the Palatine or some other royal official).

[2] This number had been reached after a series of reductions. It had formerly been much higher.   [3] For these, see below, p. 78, n. 1.

Bukovinian families of boyar status were similarly being invited to apply for the higher Bench, and Mazil families[1] for the lower.

Provision had been made for a third Galician Estate, but the authorities had not yet decided what, if any, places in the province were important enough to be represented.

The Estates assembled in Diets constituted, then, the 'organs of self-government' of each Land. As opposite number to them, and representative of his own authority, the Landesherr, or Crown, maintained in each Land a representative known in the smaller Lands as the *Landeshauptmann*; in Bohemia, Galicia and Transylvania, as the Governor. In Hungary, the royal authority was represented by the Palatine (*Nádor*), who, however, was not exclusively the King's representative, but the official mediator between the Crown and the Hungarian nobles. As the powers which the Hungarian Constitution vested in the Palatine were too extensive for the Crown's taste (*inter alia*, he was the official commander of the armed forces in Hungary) the office was often (although illegally) left unfilled, a Viceroy being appointed in his place. This was the position in 1780. The Netherlands and Milan had Viceroys, usually junior members of the Imperial House.[2]

These officials had their own staffs, generally known as *Gubernia*,[3] while the link between them and the Crown was maintained through a series of 'Court Chancelleries', which were, in fact, the Monarchs' secretariats for handling their transactions with the different Lands, or groups of Lands (for the Monarchs had never found it necessary to maintain a separate Chancellery for each individual Land). When Maria Theresa ascended the throne there had been four such Chancelleries, the 'Austrian', for the Hereditary Lands, which, until 1742, had also carried out the work which was assigned to the Haus-Hof-und Staatskanzlei when it became a separate body in that year, the Bohemian for Bohemia, Moravia and Silesia, the Hungarian, for Inner Hungary and Croatia, and the Transylvanian.[4] Correspondence with Milan and the Netherlands was conducted through the Austrian Chancellery up to 1742; thereafter, through sections in the Haus-Hof-und Staatskanzlei.

All these bodies were now situated in Vienna, for whereas Ferdinand I

---

[1] See below, p. 94.

[2] The Viceroy of Milan at this time was Maria Theresa's third son, Ferdinand; her second surviving daughter, Maria Christina, was 'Governor-General' of the Netherlands, assisted by her husband, Albert of Saxony-Teschen.

[3] This was the generic term, and the official one in most Lands, but the office was known as Regierung in Lower Austria, and Landeshauptmannschaft in Upper Austria, Carinthia and Carniola. Hungary had a Consilium Locumtenentiale, which was, strictly, an advisory body to the Palatine, but maintained a permanent staff which corresponded to a *Gubernium*.

[4] Ferdinand I had established a single Court Chancellery for all the Lands of the Hungarian Crown, but his effective rule had, as we have seen, never extended into Transylvania. When Leopold II actually took possession of Transylvania, its Estates had themselves asked for a Chancellery of their own.

had established the Bohemian Chancellery in Prague, Ferdinand II had transferred it to Vienna, against the strong protests of the Estates, in 1623. The Hungarian Chancellery, after various earlier peripatetics, had been definitely established in Vienna in 1690.

The general pattern of the governmental machinery was thus, despite the variations in nomenclature, broadly uniform throughout the Monarchy. On the other hand, both the intimacy of the connection between central and local authority, and the degree of independence still enjoyed by the 'organs of self-government' varied very greatly indeed from one Land, or group of Lands, to another. The Viceroys of the Netherlands and Milan were almost completely independent – their correspondents in Vienna were in reality little more than post-boxes – and the local representative bodies enjoyed extensive autonomous powers. These will not be described here; it will only be remarked that the fact that these liberties existed, and that their beneficiaries were prepared to defend them tenaciously, was to prove of great importance for the history of the other parts of the Monarchy a few years later.

At the other extreme there now stood the Hereditary and Bohemian Lands, and Galicia. In these the regime was to a high degree autocratic, bureaucratic and centralized, the antique forms through which it was still in part exercised having become mere trappings devoid of reality.

The first of these attributes had, in a measure, always characterized the system of Government in the Hereditary Lands, where the Landesherren had from the first claimed the essential right *legis ferendae*, with the supreme headship of the administration and the judicature, while in Bohemia and Moravia, where the Crown's powers had been greatly trimmed under the weak Jagiellon kings, it had, under the Vernewerte Landesordnungen, assumed the same rights as it enjoyed in the Hereditary Lands.[1] Bureaucratization, on the other hand, was a relative novelty, for until the middle of the eighteenth century the lack of adequate staffs of trained administrators had forced the Crown to exercise its powers through the Estates' own apparatus; and the Counter-Reformation – the one really important political initiative taken by any of Maria Theresa's predecessors – once safely enforced, the Crown had left the new men to work through the old channels with little interference, not troubling greatly about methods so long as the required results were forthcoming – as they usually were up to the end of Charles VI's reign – nor about the Land's internal affairs. Up to the same date, centralization, too, had been carried only halfway.

Some of the Estates in both groups of Lands had, however, shown themselves conspicuously unreliable during the War of the Austrian Succession –

[1] These instruments also entitled the Crown to 'add to, alter and improve the Ordinances, and to take any other measures deriving from the Royal Prerogative'. The Estates were entitled 'to make suggestions and representations, but not to insist on them'.

the Estates of both Upper Austria and Bohemia had sworn fealty to the Elector of Bavaria in 1742 – and in general, the Estates had shown themselves so niggardly and obstructive over the contributio that Maria Theresa had had to break off or renounce more than one military operation for lack of money to pay the mercenary troops in her service. Besides excess of independence, there had also been too much provincial spirit: each of the Ministri and Capi, as the Empress complained bitterly, tried to protect his own Land (in which his own estates lay) to the disadvantage of the others 'as though they were foreign Lands and not subject to the same Monarch'.[1]

On the advice, therefore, of Haugwitz, she had carried through a series of drastic reforms. The problem which emerged after sundry transmogrifications (Haugwitz's original ideas having been modified later under the influence of Kaunitz) was that both groups of Lands, and also, subsequently, Galicia-Bukovina[2] were put under a single administrative Ministry entitled the 'k. und k. vereinigte böhmisch-oesterreichische Hofkanzlei' (the head of which was known as the *Oberste Kanzler*), and, justice having been separated from administration, also under a single *Oberste Justizstelle*, which combined the functions of Ministry of Justice and Supreme Court of Appeal.[3]

Simultaneously, the surviving powers of the Estates had been further reduced. Their most important surviving right had been that of querying or refusing the *contributio*. Under Haugwitz's reforms, the Crown's requirements in this field were now presented to them only at decennial intervals, but their consent to their assessment was still, in theory, necessary. In practice, however, this right now became purely illusory.[4] For the rest, they

[1] See her most outspoken comments on this point in her 'Political Testament', ed. Kallbrunner, Vienna, 1952, pp. 42 ff.

[2] Galicia had been given its own Hofkanzlei on its annexation, but the experiment had been abandoned a year or two later.

[3] Under the first reorganization the former body had also been given the financial business previously handled by the Austrian and Bohemian sections of the Camera. It had then been known as the Directorium in Publicis et Cameralibus. The Hofkammer had, however, recovered its functions in 1762, and the Directorium had then reverted to the title of Hofkanzlei. The Camera officials in each Land were, however, attached to its Gubernium.

[4] It is extraordinary, but true, that this all-important right gradually faded out of existence without any constitutional enactment abolishing it. The Tirol put up a fight to assert it in 1759–63, but ended by giving way almost completely. When the Styrian nobles tried to do the same, Maria Theresa called them to Vienna and threatened to place their private estates under sequester. Carinthia fared similarly. For a long time after this no Western Land ever even tried to appeal against its assessment. In 1847 the Bohemian Estates called their ancient right to mind and tried to assert it. The Hofkanzlei then argued that the Estates had never possessed a right to refuse the Contributio demanded of them – only supplementary demands – and appealed to the *usus* that since the days of Leopold II the Estates of all Austrian Lands had always accepted the State's assessment. The Bohemian Estates denied, indeed, that this long usage had caused their right to lapse, but the Chancellery retorted that the Crown could, if forced to do so, abolish the right (if such still existed) in virtue of its 'jus legis ferendae'. The point was still being argued when revolution broke out in March, 1848. How little the

apportioned locally and collected the taxation imposed by the Crown, administered certain local funds, considered applications for indigenat, and carried out a few other minor duties, mostly for the benefit of their own members. Quite often, the Crown did not even trouble to convoke them for their annual session. It would do so if they were docile, as a token of appreciation and good will; thus Styria, for example, never missed a year. If, as in Hungary, they showed a tendency to be recalcitrant, they were simply not called together. All the important administrative duties formerly performed by them corporately had passed to the Gubernia, over whose workings the Estates retained only so much influence that two members of them were attached to each Gubernium in an advisory capacity. The supremacy of the Gubernia over the Estates were further assured by the provision that the office of Landeshauptmann automatically carried with it the Presidency of the Estates.[1]

It was not only on Land level that the reforms had swept away the old local autonomy, for another, very important, change had made the Kreisämter (the number of which had been extended until they existed, under various names, in all the large Lands) into sub-branches of the Gubernia, and their staffs into employees thereof. Although, as we have said, the manorial system, as such, had been left in being, its scope had been greatly restricted by the transference of many duties formerly performed by the lords of the manor, to the Kreisämter, which had also been especially charged with the duty of seeing that the lords did not abuse their powers over their subjects. Similarly, the Oberste Justizstelle had taken over the entire judiciary above the Patrimonial Court level, and had substantially restricted the range of cases with which those Courts could deal summarily.

The urban and communal self-governing institutions had been left in being, but subjected to close official control.

In sum, the Monarch's powers in the Western Lands had now become so extensive as to enable serious writers[2] to describe them as 'unlimited'.

These developments had also brought with them a large amount of

---

will of the Estates counted may be seen from para. 17 of the Patent establishing the Galician Diet, which ran: 'As regards the proceedings of the Diet, the assembled Estates, on receiving intimation of Her Majesty's commands, will never have to dwell on the question 'whether', but only to debate the question 'how?'. They are, however, permitted to make representations and most humble suggestions, which, however, like everything else which the Estates wish to reach the ears of the Court, must always be sent to the Landestelle and forwarded by it, with opinion attached, to the Galician Court Chancellery' (this body, as has been mentioned, itself only survived a year or two, after which Galicia was put under the Vereinigte Hofkanzlei).

[1] There was one exception to this rule: the Estates of Bohemia had the right to elect their own President (known as the Oberstburggraf of Prague), and he automatically became the 'Gouverneur' of Bohemia.

[2] So Bisinger (*Staatsverfassung der oesterreichischen Monarchie*, Vienna, 1809, p. 17) and Rottinger (*Staatslexicon*, 1840, vol. X, pp. 331, 338).

centralization as between these Lands. Tribute was still paid to local particularism by the rule that the Landeshauptmann had to be a landowner possessing local indigenat, and the staffs of the Gubernia in the Hereditary and Bohemian Lands had also to be composed of local men.[1] But the Gubernia themselves were growing yearly less important. The real authority lay with the Hofkanzlei, which, it is true, sent out its orders separately to each Land, thus respecting their theoretical mutual independence, and the enactments sometimes contained considerable local variations,[2] but the general tendency of its operations, and of those of the Oberste Justizstelle, was to turn all these Lands increasingly into a *de facto* administrative and judicial unity.

Maria Theresa had not attempted to bring the Lands of the Hungarian Crown into this system, although the regime in Transylvania was in practice almost as autocratic. The Three Nations nominally possessed the right to elect the Gubernium (under the Governor himself, who was designated by the Crown), but this was a dead letter. The Crown simply filled the Gubernium by appointment. Moreover, it exercised its right to appoint ex-officio members ('Regalists') to the Diet so lavishly that its nominees always easily outnumbered the representatives of the Three Nations.[3] The Crown's 'postulata' were thus almost always accepted without argument, and if ever any objections were raised, a little pressure from the local military commander sufficed to silence them.

There was, however, a real, as well as a nominal difference in the position of Inner Hungary. The corpus of laws which made up the Hungarian mediaeval constitution did not limit the Monarch's powers much more than did the corresponding instruments in other Lands, except, indeed, in two important respects: that they made legislation dependent on agreement between the King and the 'nation',[4] and that they allowed the latter a formally enacted *jus resistendi* against illegal action by the King.[5] But Hungary

---

[1] Galicia formed, in 1780, an exception to this rule. Here, partly owing to Austria's mistrust of the Poles, partly to the Poles' own reluctance to enter Austrian service, the officials came from other parts of the Monarchy, in practice, nearly all from Lower Austria or Bohemia. In the Hereditary and Bohemian Lands an official served only in his own Land unless he was appointed to a central Ministry.

[2] Thus the *robot* Patents' described below (pp. 65 ff.) differed largely from Land to Land.

[3] Another effect of this was to increase further the weight of the Magyar element against the Saxons, whose representatives in 1791 numbered only 25 out of a total of 419.

[4] A legal stipulation to this effect was introduced only in the fourteenth century, but in practice many earlier Kings had been forced to accept the limitation. St Stephen and his successors had claimed the *jus legis ferendae*, but had in practice exercised it only in consultation with representatives of the 'nation'.

[5] The original clause in Andrew II's Golden Bull of 1222 entitled the 'bishops and dignitaries and nobles of the realm' to resist and refuse obedience to an order by any king violating the provisions of the Bull. This had been modified in 1231 to a declaration by the king that he and his successors would submit themselves to excommunication if they acted unconstitutionally, but this amendment had never been invoked, and had fallen into oblivion.

had maintained her rights where other lands had lost theirs. Leopold I had once annulled the constitution, but the national resistance had been so vigorous that he had been obliged to restore it soon after, with the sole exception that the *jus resistendi* was abolished, and the position as regards legislation was defined by the words 'as the King and the Estates assembled in Parliament (*dietaliter*) shall agree on the usage and interpretation thereof'.

After the great Rákóczi rebellion, Charles III had confirmed his promise, adding the assurance that he would never rule and administer Hungary except by its own laws, existing or to be enacted in Parliament, and customs, and not 'after the pattern of other provinces'. None of the bodies through which it was governed (in particular, the Hungarian Chancellery) was to be in any kind of dependence on any non-Hungarian body: the only authority recognized by Hungary was that of its own king.

These assurances were very far from giving Hungary complete self-rule. They did not give her any more voice than that possessed by any 'province' in the conduct of foreign policy, or defence, and the independence promised to her Camera was never more than nominal. The Consilium Locumtenentiale which was the top-level organ of administration, was in fact a Gubernium like any other, and although the Hungarian Court Chancellery, from which the Consilium took its orders, was in name subject only to the King of Hungary, it was often the hands of the Austrian Chancellery and *Staatsrat* which drafted those instructions which came to it through the mouth of the king. Finally, the Crown got round its obligation towards the Diet by not convoking that body at all, except to ask it (as it was still formally asking the Diets of Bohemia or Styria) for men and money (Charles, after he had got his way over the Succession Law, convoked the Diet only once again during his reign, and Maria Theresa, only on her accession and twice thereafter); and by treating any subject on which some ancient document did not give the nation an irrefutable right to speak, as one which the Crown was entitled to regulate at its own discretion, by Rescript. Education, 'colonisation', religious questions, industrial legislation, even the peasants' obligations to their lords, were so treated. When it was not a question of law, the minutest local and personal questions went up to the Chancellery, through the Consilium, and were decided by it.[1]

Nevertheless, Hungary's size, her strategic importance, her inaccessibility and the resolution of her noble class, had enabled her to maintain successfully the principle that she constituted an entirely separate body politic, linked to the Habsburgs' other dominions only through the Pragmatic Sanction, and quite unconnected, so far as her *interna* were concerned, with any of them, and in certain important respects she escaped the reality of central control. Her nobles retained intact the cardinal privileges of exemption from taxation, an extended right of *habeas corpus* and exclusive eligibility

[1] For examples, see B. Grünwald, op. cit., pp. 421 ff.

to public office. Her judiciary remained completely independent. The Counties, unlike the Austrian Kreisämter, were never etatized, and this provided a strong brake on the working of the central bureaucracy, since apart from their autonomy, they also provided the executive power through which the Crown gave effect to its decisions. Thus if they did choose to object to any demand, they put the Government in a position of real difficulty.

Finally, less because its law was different than because it could mobilize so large a *de facto* power of resistance, Hungary was really able to keep its consent to the contributio more than a formality. Here it was helped by the fact that when it was first assessed (in 1724) the country was exceedingly impoverished and depopulated after the Turkish Wars. Later Diets, in 1728, 1751 and 1765, did indeed vote increases to the contributio,[1] but only after debates the legality of which the Crown did not question, and not proportionately to the country's increase in wealth and population. It had also, as we have seen, maintained its exemption from conscription, so that it was able also to bargain over the number of 'volunteers' which it would allow to be enlisted, and to keep that figure, too, a relatively low one.

This real tenuity of the links between Hungary and the rest of the Monarchy and the real limitations of the Crown's authority in it were cardinal factors in the structure of the Monarchy, much of whose political history after 1780 consisted of the Crown's attempts to reduce Hungary to the status of 'other provinces', and the Hungarians' resistance to them.

The question of self-government versus autocratic control was, of course, only one aspect of the administrative problem of the Monarchy: the nature and quality of the resultant government was another. In this respect a very great difference indeed had developed since 1750 between the Western and Eastern halves of the Monarchy. The advantage in human comfort does not lie wholly with the West, for the ultimate objects of the changes carried through were only in a very minor degree the welfare of the subjecta, but far rather the military efficiency of the State, to which the predilections and the happiness of the subjecta were sacrificed ruthlessly enough. In her later years Maria Theresa came to think in more human terms, but by that time her son's influence was intruding itself into the picture. Many of the 'reforms' were thoroughly vexatious,[2] aimed solely at reducing the leisure, and the pleasure, of the people in order that they should have more work and money

[1] The figures were: 2,100,000 fl. in 1724; 2,500,000 in 1728; 3,200,000 in 1751; 3,900,000 in 1765, plus certain further sums from newly re-incorporated territories.

[2] One striking example of this was the abolition of a large number of holidays. Maria Theresa officially abolished twenty-two of these. It is true that it never proved possible to enforce the veto. Even the Viennese had revolted when ordered to work on Easter Monday. Others were the abolition of traditional folk-plays, games and amusements, restrictions on travel, etc., etc. A long list is given in Beidtel, op. cit., I. 46 ff.

to give the exchequer. Others were simply changes for change's sake, the spiritual offspring of bureaucrats who suddenly found the toy of power in their hands. But whatever the motives, the Vereinigte Hofkanzlei had developed within a few years into a vast body which combined in itself the functions of a dozen modern Ministries – Interior, Education, Church Affairs, Commerce, Public Works, Agriculture and Forestries, Social Welfare – almost everything, in fact, that human ingenuity could think up, short of Foreign Affairs, Defence and the financial business still transacted by the *Camera*. Every branch of it was engaged, not only in supervising what was already being done in those fields, but itself drafting for the Monarch's approval new 'laws, ordinances and enactments' which, since no one could say them nay, were at once put into effect if approved by the Monarch. By 1780 a generation of this bureaucratic rule had advanced the Hereditary and Bohemian Lands to a level of modernization far ahead of that reached by Hungary, not to speak of the newly acquired Galicia. The effects of these thirty years were plainly visible in the economic, social and cultural picture of the Monarchy; although they had, of course, only supervened on earlier conditions created by nature and by the past history of the different Lands.

The dignities of Roman Emperor and German King, both enjoyed in 1780 by Maria Theresa's son, Joseph, were very little more than titular. The Emperor could not intervene at all in the internal affairs of the German Princes, nor call on them to take any joint action without the consent of the Imperial Diet, and this was practically unobtainable. His revenues from the few dues and taxes which were his perquisite did not even cover the expenses of the surviving Imperial institutions, the Reichskammergericht in Wetzlau and the Reichshofrat in Vienna, both of which were, moreover, so hopelessly corrupt, inefficient and dilatory that even Joseph, after a futile attempt, had given up hope of reforming them.

III ECONOMIC AND FINANCIAL CONDITIONS

In 1780 the Austrian Netherlands and Milan stood no less far apart from the rest of the Habsburg dominions in respect of economic development and social structure, than they did in all other ways. With their dense populations (estimated in 1786 at 2,000,000 and 1,300,000 respectively), their busy cities, their flourishing trade and industries, their prosperous merchants and entrepreneurs, decent craftsmen and self-assured peasantries, they belonged in these respects where geography and history placed them, in Western Europe.

Very different was the state of the rest of the Monarchy. Most of the Hereditary Lands had never known wealth or ease. The Marches which formed the core of them were, except for the Danube valley, where agriculture was practicable on a modest scale, a mere tangle of forest-clad mountains, threaded by narrow and tortuous valleys which only rarely opened out into more spacious basins, and those usually occupied by lakes or marshes. The hill-slopes were fitted for little beyond cattle-raising, the forests inaccessible for exploitation except for local building or charcoal-burning. Of the other resources known before modern times, the iron of Styria and Eastern Carinthia, the gold and lead of the latter province, the silver and copper of the Tirol and the salt of Upper Austria were important, but the richest of the salt-mines lay outside Austrian territory, in the domains of the Prince-Archbishop of Salzburg, and difficulties of transportation limited the operations of the iron-mines to small-scale work: their chief products were scythes and nails.

It was, indeed, their inaccessibility that saved the Marches from succumbing to the barbarian attacks against which they had been founded, and under which their predecessors had perished; but the same inaccessibility denied them the possibility of accumulating wealth. They lay, moreover, on the very outskirts of civilized mediaeval Europe, far from its centres of wealth, or from the trade-routes linking them. Between the twelfth and the fifteenth centuries Vienna derived some prosperity as an entrepôt for the considerable traffic then passing by road or water between Central Europe and the Levant, but the Turkish conquest of the Balkans and Hungary put an end to this traffic and turned much of Austria into an outpost again. The only important trade-route now running across its territory was that which linked Italy with Germany via the Tirol. For the rest, the Hereditary Lands were thrown back on their own resources, which condemned their sparse population[1] to its old fate of a laborious uphill struggle against difficulties, natural or man-made. The latter were still far from inconsiderable. The peasant risings of the sixteenth century inflicted much damage precisely on the most prosperous Lands. While they escaped the full force of the Thirty Years War, the losses inflicted on them by the Counter-Reformation were not negligible.[2] In Upper Austria in 1663, 288 out of the 605 houses in Steyr were empty, 240 out of 426 in Wels, 133 out of 219 in Enns, 200 out of 288 in Freistadt. 120 out of 288 houses in Linz were uninhabitable. Lower Austria, Styria and Carniola were ravaged by Turkish armies (most notably, the great force which besieged Vienna in 1683[3]) or small raiding parties, or scarcely less destructive bands of Magyars, and their resources were further constantly and heavily taxed to maintain the defences against the invaders. Another recurrent and dreadful visitant was the

---

[1] This was estimated at two million in AD 1500.

[2] Hoffmann, op. cit., p. 243.

[3] According to contemporary sources, 14,933 'places' were burnt down in this campaign and 88,209 human beings carried off into slavery. Even if these figures are exaggerated, it is true that twenty years later nearly half the total population of many villages, etc., near Vienna was composed of new settlers (Zöllner, p. 275).

plague, which in some years and some places carried away half the total population.¹

Nature had dealt more generously with Bohemia and Moravia. The soil of their central plains was fertile and communications across them easy, while the mountains of the periphery had contained deposits of gold and silver which in the thirteenth century had produced the richest yields in Europe, and were also well adapted for the growth of certain industries, notably that of glass, which had early acquired a European reputation. In the early Middle Ages Bohemia had ranked among the wealthiest lands of Europe. It had conducted a flourishing trade with Germany and Poland, and thanks to the enlightened policies of several of its kings, had contained a far larger number of towns, relatively to its size, than any Alpine Land.² Silesia, while less naturally fertile, had early developed a textile industry which was very advanced for its age.

Here it was man that had been the destructive agent. All the Lands of the Bohemian Crown had suffered cruelly in the Hussite Wars of the fifteenth century. In spite of these, Bohemia is estimated to have contained some two million inhabitants in 1500, and Moravia and Silesia, another million each, and the population of Bohemia in 1620 is put at three million. Then, however, came the devastations of the Thirty Years War, which afflicted Bohemia more heavily than any other European land. Its towns were largely laid in ashes, its industry was ruined, its artisan class, with many of its nobles and even peasants, driven into exile, its very soil passed out of cultivation. Modern writers put its total population at the end of the war at only nine hundred thousand; some estimates are even lower. Moravia had suffered almost as severely.

Hungary, although never so densely populated or so highly developed economically as Bohemia, had also known considerable prosperity in the Middle Ages. When Louis the Great ruled over it in the fourteenth century, its population had been about three million, and it had boasted forty-nine Royal Boroughs, over five hundred 'market towns' and more than twenty-six

---

¹ Contemporary estimates put the losses by plague in Vienna and its suburbs in 1679 at 90,000. This is probably a big exaggeration, but the municipal records themselves listed about 8,000 victims (Zöllner, op. cit., p. 267).

² It is true that comparison of figures on this point might easily prove misleading. Because the Czechs, like all Slavs, were ill-adapted to urban life and pursuits, various Kings of Bohemia invited Germans into the country, and protected their settlements by granting them urban charters which *inter alia* allowed them to live under their own law. An Alpine settlement of the same size and performing the same social function would probably have grown out of the native soil and neither needed nor claimed urban status. The same remark applies to most of the German-inhabited 'Free Towns' of Hungary, many of which were smaller in population than many Magyar conurbations which ranked only as 'market centres', as much as to the Bohemian. Another area in which there were a large number of 'towns' was East Galicia, but few of these would have been recognized as such by a Western traveller (see below, pp. 46–7).

thousand villages. Its gold mines produced more than three thousand lb of gold annually, more than five times as much as any other European State. By 1500 the population had risen by another million.

But Hungary, too, had fallen from its high estate, later than Bohemia, but even more terribly. Here it was the Turkish conquest and a hundred and fifty years long occupation of the centre of the country, with its accompaniment of fighting and slave-raiding – both extending across the frontiers into the areas not actually under Turkish rule – that had spread over much of the country a desolation which the wars of liberation at the end of the seventeenth century had made almost total.[1] By the end of them the population of the Lands of the Hungarian Crown was down to about three millions (until recently, most estimates put it lower still), nearly all of it concentrated in North-West Hungary, or, to a lesser extent, Transylvania. In the centre of the country, most of the surviving population had huddled for safety into 'village towns', each of which harboured the survivors of twenty or more deserted villages. The population of the largest of these, Debrecen, was only eight thousand in 1720, and between each such agglomeration and its neighbour might stretch twenty-five or thirty miles, unmarked by human habitation save for a gypsy's or a herdsman's hut. South Hungary was in worse state still: in 1692 the three large Counties of Baranya, Tolna and Somogy had numbered between them a population of only 3,221 souls, 1,652 of them in the single city of Pécs.

It was, of course, not man alone that suffered under this devastation, but also his works. Cities fell into ruins, villages disappeared without a trace as the unfired bricks crumbled back into the clay of which they had been fashioned. The Bohemian industries almost died out. Prague in 1674 could muster only 355 artisans, as against 1200 when the Thirty Years War began. Iglau, where seven to eight thousand persons had been employed in the cloth industry, was left with only 300 burghers. 'Town' in Hungary had become simply a name for a large agglomeration of peasants. When Hódmezövásárhely, a community of seven thousand, wanted to rebuild its church in 1747, not a single carpenter, stone-mason or brickmaker could be found in the commune; it had to send away for all its craftsmen.

Even in the Hereditary Lands, it was the most skilled and enterprising elements of the population that the Counter-Reformation drove into exile.

The agriculture into which the economy had everywhere relapsed had itself returned to the primitive. The surviving inhabitants of Central Hungary had abandoned cereal farming for cattle-breeding, in which it was easier to evade the eye of the tax-collector. For the same reason, barns were no longer used to store such vegetable crops as were still raised; they were hidden out of sight in underground holes.

[1] It is true that the century before the invasion had already seen a big decline from the economic zenith of the fourteenth century.

It is true that the middle of the seventeenth century had marked the nadir of the economic fortunes of the Alpine Lands and Bohemia, and the beginning of the eighteenth, of those of Eastern Austria and Hungary. Since then all districts had made recoveries, some of them, in some respects, very large ones. With the end of the most destructive wars, and the abatement of disease (the last outbreak of plague in Vienna was in 1713) the population of Bohemia had recovered by 1750 to about one and a half million; after that it had been increasing very rapidly, and in 1780 was over two and a half million, and that of Moravia, about half as much. Rump Silesia had about three hundred thousand. The rate of increase in the Historic Lands had been slower,[1] but their population is estimated to have reached something over four millions (Lower Austria, 1,200,000; Upper Austria, 600,000; Styria, 750,000; Tirol, 550,000; Vorarlberg, 100,000; Carinthia, 270,000; Carniola, 400,000; the Littoral, 200,000) by the same date, while the increase in Hungary, where the natural growth had been supplemented by immigration from the Balkans and by the systematic operation of colonization known as the *impopulatio*, had been even spectacular. In some areas, where the previous devastation had been particularly severe and the immigration very intensive, the population had risen six, eight, or ten times and the total, for all the Hungarian Lands, was now some nine and a half millions (just under six and a half millions in Inner Hungary, nearly one and a half millions in Transylvania, 650,000 in civilian Croatia and 700,000 in the Military Frontier).

Economically, these increases spelled almost pure gain for the Monarchy, for the population was still almost everywhere well below the economic optimum. Most of the increase went at first into agriculture, which before then had been undermanned for its struggle with nature. Now swamps could be drained, brakes cleared, favoured areas put under intensive cultivation, practised by new methods which were gaining and sometimes applied to crops such as tobacco (later, maize and potatoes[2]) which had formerly been unfamiliar. Some of the masters of the land on which these processes were carried through accumulated big fortunes and lived very luxuriously, by their own standards.

The tastes of most of them were, however, not very diversified. They stood themselves large living accommodation, entertained their friends lavishly, and kept enormous armies of domestic servants (who came to constitute a considerable fraction of the population), but did not buy manufactured articles on anything like the scale of a modern family. Moreover, since

[1] Feigl, op. cit., p. 35, estimates that the population of Lower Austria probably remained approximately static from the fifteenth century to the middle of the eighteenth.

[2] The history of the introduction of the potato into the Monarchy would furnish material for an epic. In Galicia the peasants refused so obstinately to grow their own crops, or to eat the new-fangled thing, that Joseph had to have them cultivated by soldiers, who then 'carelessly' left them unguarded at night. The peasants stole them, and thus acquired the taste. Francis had similar difficulties in Dalmatia.

manpower meant wealth to them, they opposed any development of nature to draw it off their fields so long as it was in short supply – a condition which prevailed in large parts of the Monarchy until well into the nineteenth century, and was a factor of great importance in the economic history of the period which we are studying. Their wealth thus contributed relatively little to the diversification of the economy, and another factor with the same retarding influence was the policy of the guilds, which had developed the science of restrictive practices to a pitch from which any later age could have learned. Nevertheless, as one generation of internal peace followed another (most of Charles VI' wars were fought outside the Monarchy), the demand for diversification did inevitably grow, not least under the stimulus of the luxurious Courts kept by Charles and, in spite of her poverty, by his daughter.[1] The number of artisans and shopkeepers increased, and the towns expanded to receive them, and the old staple industries of the Monarchy – Bohemian glass, Silesian linen, Moravian woollens, Styrian iron – began to revive.

Meanwhile, moreover, the mercantilist doctrines of the age had found their adepts in Austria. As early as 1684 Johann Hörnigk had published a pamphlet entitled *Oesterreich über Alles, wenn es nur will*, in which he argued that if Austria developed her own resources, she could not only avoid the necessity of importing anything, but could herself become a big exporting country, besides enjoying greatly increased internal prosperity. His doctrines were taken up and elaborated by another writer, Johann Becher, and certain attempts were made to translate them into practice in the reigns of Leopold I, and still more, in that of Charles. What Charles effected for communications, in particular, was not insignificant, and the beginnings of some Austrian industries which later became important also date from his reign. Most of his attempts to introduce new industries came, however, to little, for various reasons, including the resistance of the landlords and the inexperience of the entrepreneurs; in any case, they did not very greatly affect the Austria with which we are concerned, since it was found easier to develop industries where they already existed, notably in the Netherlands and Silesia, than to found new ones elsewhere. The biggest development in his reign was in the luxury industries which grew up round the Court in Vienna.

But Maria Theresa, that remarkable woman, had a strong sense of the practical, and was keenly interested in economics from the day of her accession.[2] One of the first acts of her reign was to reactivate the semi-dormant planning offices set up under her father. Then the loss of Silesia,

---

[1] Maria Theresa's husband, however, was an excellent business man who, besides advising the Monarchy, accumulated a large personal fortune, on the later fate of which see below, p. 49.

[2] See on this G. Otruba, *Wirtschaftspolitik*, *passim*. It is, as Otruba says and shows, astounding how attentive the Empress was to the smallest detail, and usually, how sensible.

the most highly industrialized of her all provinces, increased this interest, under the dual stimulus of the need to make good the loss of the province (which had also disrupted the economy of Bohemia), and to revenge herself on 'the Prussian'. Industries were encouraged to move over from the lost province into the Monarchy (which they did on a considerable scale and with extraordinary rapidity), and entrepreneurs and skilled workers brought in, sometimes by morally questionable devices, from other countries, being then given facilities in the shape of exemption from taxation, subsidies, monopolies, etc., for the employers, and for the men (and also for workers inside the Monarchy) exemption from military service and from all restrictions on domiciliary rights in towns. Important was the classification, introduced in 1754, of industrial enterprises into *Kommerzialgewerbe* and *Polizeigewerbe*. The former, which were trades working on a large scale, and for a wide market (these included textile and metal works, glovemakers, opticians and jewellers, but also sculptors and painters) were as a rule freed from all guild restrictions, which continued to apply only to the second category, of establishments working for purely local markets (butchers, bakers, etc.).

As early as 1746 a central body, the *Universalkommerzdirektorium*, had been called into being to deal with the reform of tariffs,[1] the development of communications by land and water, the importation of industrial plant and the conclusion of trade agreements for the whole Monarchy. In 1753 tariffs were imposed against Prussia, with the avowed object of 'ruining Prussian Silesia economically'. In 1764 a tariff wall was erected round the whole Monarchy (except the Tirol, which was exempted owing to the importance to it of its transit trade) and in 1775 this wall, which was afterwards extended to take in Galicia,[2] was raised further, to an average of thirty per cent, the importation of many foreign articles being forbidden altogether. Now the internal tariffs between the Austrian and Bohemian Lands were abolished. Attempts were made to find new markets for the Monarchy's products in Russia and Turkey, and Trieste and Fiume (already declared free ports by Charles VI) were expanded to handle the trade.

Many of Maria Theresa's early experiments were no more successful than those of her father and grandfather, and both the governmental machinery and the methods used by it were changed repeatedly. The old difficulties had not yet been overcome, nor the basic economic structure of the Monarchy

---

[1] Until Charles's reign all Austrian tariffs had been low, and almost purely fiscal. Heavy duties had then been placed on a few specific articles, in the interests of his experiments, but there had still been no general rise in the level of tariffs.

[2] At first Galicia had been exempted, in order to allow its trade with the west to continue. When, however, Prussia (in order to damage Danzig) placed a tariff on exports from the province, the concession became valueless, and was withdrawn.

in any way transformed. The 'factories' themselves, where at all sizeable (when many of them were State enterprises, since few private entrepreneurs possessed the capital to start a big factory[1]) worked chiefly for the army; the smaller ones, largely for the Court and its hangers-on. Most luxury goods were still imported, in the face of numerous prohibitions made in the interest of the balance of payments, perhaps the chief effect of which had, indeed, been to give birth to a flourishing smuggling industry, which was often winked at by the authorities. The guild craftsmen still provided most of such more modest products for the wider market as could not be home-produced, but in most peasant families the womenfolk spun and wove the clothes and the men were their own masons and carpenters, and agriculture, much of it carried on by methods which differed little from those of the Middle Ages, with viticulture and forestry, was still the main occupation of by far the largest part of the population.

During the last years of Maria Theresa's reign an appreciable amount of industry was nevertheless growing up in the areas towards which the Government's mercantilist policy was mainly directed, these being chiefly the Bohemian Lands, Lower Austria, and the iron-fields of Styria. With it, trade was expanding. Agriculture, too, was growing more progressive, at least on the big estates, the advances here, too, owing much to government initiative and assistance. The economic picture was growing more diversified, and brighter.

It varied, indeed, widely from one part of the Monarchy to another. Vienna had been largely rebuilt and splendidly adorned since the retreat of the Turks had carried the frontier away from its vicinity. It was now the biggest city of Central Europe, with a population of over 200,000, and presented a magnificent picture. The spire of the grand old Stefansdom in the heart of the city looked down on fifty other churches, some of ancient construction, many of them new, but nearly all alike tricked out inside in the pompous baroque of the day. It looked down, too, on the splendid palaces of the Dynasty, the old Hofburg, newly rebuilt and enlarged, in the Innere Stadt and the great recent construction of Schönbrunn, three miles out, set in its vast formal gardens; both of them surrounded by great complexes of adjuncts, courtiers' quarters, Guards' barracks, and the sumptuous residences of the great aulic nobles, Prince Eugene of Savoy's enormous Schloss Belvedere and the magnificent palaces of the Schwarzenbergs, Liechtensteins, Starhembergs, Kinskys, Esterházys, Pálffys and a score more. There were museums, picture galleries, pleasure-grounds. The wider streets and squares were adorned with fountains and statuary. There were shops to supply the Court ladies with their finery, artisans' quarters in which some

[1] In an alarming number of cases the State advanced money to a private individual, and was then forced in the end to take over the enterprise from him.

of these articles were manufactured (although more were still imported). Further out, there were big new industrial suburbs, containing many factories, and beyond these, the adjacent hills were studded with the country houses of the rich, the more modest resorts where the tradesmen and artisans took their pleasure, and the homes of the farmers and vintners who prospered by supplying the needs of the capital.

But Vienna was a special case. It owed its splendour, less to the productivity of its own inhabitants, than to its position as capital and residence of the House which was ruler, not of Austria alone, but of Bohemia and Hungary, of the Low Countries and Lombardy, and not least, in its Imperial capacity, of the German Reich. Its growth did not even reflect a long accumulation of wealth in the Monarchy, for Charles's reign had been extravagant and unsystematic, and the first half of his daughter's, darkened by the Prussian wars, which had brought Austria to the verge of bankruptcy again; it had only been since the Peace of Hubertsburg that there had been a real recovery. Outside its immediate environment, the signs of prosperity soon died away. Upper Austria still made a good showing – far better than the Western half of Lower Austria itself.[1] Distinguished alike for the independent spirit of its peasants, which had secured for them the best social conditions in the Hereditary Lands, outside the Tirol, and for the progressive outlook of its larger landlords, who led even Bohemia in the introduction of modern methods, and favoured by nature, with stores of iron and salt in the hills and its plains open and fertile – lying, moreover, on the main highway from Vienna to the West – it could show comfortable farms and flourishing market centres, while Linz, its capital, contained a large cloth factory and Steyr, important iron works. Riesbeck found Linz so prosperous 'as to make the Bavarian cities appear like poorhouses in comparison'.[2] But in the Alpine Lands proper, there was little to tell of new times. Graz with twenty-five thousand inhabitants and Innsbruck with about twenty thousand were the only important centres until Trieste was reached, and both of them owed their dignity rather to the past, when they had been the residences of the Princes of considerable polities (Graz, not long before, had been the capital of an area larger than that directly controlled by Vienna itself). None of the other Alpine towns, except perhaps Laibach and Klagenfurt, and in the Tirol, the archiepiscopal sees of Brixen and Trent, which were only half inside the Monarchy, were more than small local centres; Marburg, the second town of Styria, had only five thousand inhabitants. Outside them, the pattern of life was still that of the scattered farm or hamlet, and such trappings of magnificence as these Lands could show were not in the villages but in the baronial castles which dominated them (and on which many of their owners bankrupted themselves, having overbuilt out of

[1] See Hoffman, op. cit., p. 283.
[2] Riesbeck, *Travels through Germany*, English tr., 3 vols, 1787, I, 207.

ostentation) and still more, in the great monasteries which held a considerable part of the more desirable ground. The Styrian iron works were, indeed, beginning to recover after a long depression, and there was some textile industry in Vorarlberg, but the big majority of the population lived from agriculture, pasturing herds in summer on the mountain alps and in the autumn, either driving them to market in Vienna or Italy, or slaughtering them and salting down their flesh. While the thrift and industry of the Alpine Germans still enabled them to maintain fair standards of comfort, under normal conditions, even they found the struggle against nature a hard one: devastating famines were not uncommon even in the richest of the Lands, such as Styria, while in the Tirol pressure of population was already forcing a considerable proportion of the menfolk to spend much of their time away from their homes, as itinerant journeymen or masons. The less advanced Slav populations of South Styria and Carinthia lived in poverty and squalor, their diets consisting of some form of pottage and their homes, of a single cabin, which was often shared with the poultry.

Bohemia and Moravia were economically more advanced than the Alpine Lands. Industrially, they had been able to build on more extensive ancient foundations. They had been the chief recipients of the immigrant industry from Silesia. The Bohemian landlords, too, had, for whatever reason, shown themselves far readier to engage in industry than their colleagues of the Alpine Lands, who, we are told, 'had, out of ancient caste spirit, shown themselves very unreceptive towards this new wish of the Crown's.'[1] Thus the two provinces were developing into the industrial workshop of the Monarchy. Bohemia now contained no less than 244 towns, of which Prague, with a population of 80,000, ranked after Vienna as the second largest city of the Monarchy. Ten years later (it is true that the intervening decade had seen a big spurt), 400,000 persons in Bohemia were employed in industry, and the value of their production exceeded that of the local agriculture – and that was the most progressive in the Monarchy after that of Upper Austria: the big landed proprietors who dominated it were among the first in the Central Monarchy to organize large-scale production for profit by modern methods, including modern rotation of crops, the introduction of fodder plants and the cultivation of such new products as potatoes.

But even here, the picture contained many shadows. The new industrialization had, after all, been a curative measure to make good the damage inflicted on the Monarchy by the rape of Silesia, and itself an operation of cold war, which had entailed many casualties. The new manufactures had arisen on the ruins of many of the older industries, and the enforced autarky had been extremely detrimental to what had once been a flourishing trade with Germany. When faced with demands for higher taxation, the Estates

[1] Otruba, op. cit., p. 46.

complained bitterly of their poverty, and if the landlord class was, nevertheless, prosperous on the whole, the same could not be said of their subjects. When Maria Theresa sent a Commission of Enquiry into the Bohemian Lands in 1769, its report revealed that the bulk of the peasants were living under really appalling conditions of squalor and near-starvation which in bad years became real starvation; in 1771 and 1772 there had been famines which had carried away fourteen per cent of the entire population. The sums earned by the spinners and weavers of the mountain districts, when they were able to work for money (much of their labour was performed gratis for their lords, as robot) were mere pittances, bare compensation for the infertility of their holdings and for the small size of them, for small plots were already frequent in these areas.

Across the Leitha, the economy was more primitive still. When the new industrial policy was inaugurated, it had been deliberately confined to the Western half of the Monarchy. This decision was destined later to have momentous political consequences, to which we shall have to return repeatedly, but it was not originally taken – at least not overtly – for political reasons, but out of simple economic calculation. Vienna was the seat of the Court and the headquarters of the army (and the Court and the army were easily Austria's chief consumers of manufactured goods), while in Bohemia and Moravia there already existed a considerable domestic industry, a relatively dense population accustomed to industrial work, and natural sources of power; moreover, to transplant thither the industries migrating from Silesia (and much of the new industrialization was effected by this method) involved only a short journey. In view of the contrast between these conditions and those in Hungary, with its sparse and rude population, its deplorable communications and its immense potential agricultural wealth, it had seemed only natural to divide the roles, allocating to Hungary that of producing the raw materials, and to Austria, that of turning them into manufactured goods. This division of roles was in any case meant at first to be only temporary, until Hungary should have reached a stage of development which made industrialization there practicable. Meanwhile, Government subsidies to Hungarian agriculture were to match those given to Austrian industry.

The Austrian industrialists, however, were not slow to argue that the Hungarian noble, paying as he did no taxation, could undercut his Austrian competitors under otherwise equal conditions, and Maria Theresa herself, although she always insisted that there must be no discrimination between her different dominions, admitted the force of this contention and agreed that Hungary should not be given facilities which enabled her to compete dangerously with Austria. As time went on, the Austrian and Bohemian magnates whose interests were bound up with the new establishments (and these were precisely the classes whose voices were heard on the Economic

Council) consolidated and systematized their advantage. In 1763 the Council got the principle established that the State should not found factories in Hungary.[1] Five years later, it tried to introduce a rule that even private individuals should never be given licences to establish factories there. This Maria Theresa rejected, but the Council, through whose hands applications for licences and other facilities passed, was usually able to reject those coming from Hungary. Further, when the internal tariffs between the Austrian Lands were abolished, that between Austria and Hungary was maintained, and so manipulated by discriminatory assessment of the commodities crossing it as to constitute another heavy handicap on Hungarian manufacturers.

Thus the remarkable situation was produced that industrialization was being deliberately held back by governmental policy in a part of the Monarchy which in area and population constituted nearly half of it; and not even industrialization alone, for the discrimination was often applied also against Hungarian agriculture. The Hungarians themselves were partly unwilling, partly unable, to counter this by self-help. All the weaknesses in their constitution to which Széchenyi later drew attention were in fact already operating against them. The nobles' privilege prevented the accumulation of public funds to mend their communications; the *aviticitas*[2] made it almost impossible for private individuals to obtain credit. To all this had to be added the potent congenital prejudices of the Hungarians themselves. The noble still could not be induced to think any career worthy of him, except that of landowner; nor the peasant, to do more work than he must, to escape the bailiff's whip.

Thus Hungary stood economically a step below Austria itself. One of its own writers testified in 1797 that its common nobles 'lived much worse than Austrian peasants'.[3] Ninety per cent of the entire population lived from agriculture, and nearly the same proportion, in villages or on scattered farms. There were in 1782 sixty-one Royal Free Boroughs, besides sixteen episcopal, mining or other 'towns', but their total population was only about 350,000. Not one town in the whole country had a population of thirty thousand, although Pozsony, the acting capital, came near it. Debrecen, Buda, Pest, Szeged and Szabadka were round the twenty-thousand mark, but of these Debrecen, Szeged and Szabadka were 'village towns', not truly urban at all. Many such smaller towns as there were lived primarily from their viticulture (Buda's own chief occupation) or from servicing the garrisons

[1] Maria Theresa had herself founded several such establishments, including the famous Herend pottery works, still today (1968) in production.

[2] Under this ancient Hungarian law, noble land was entailed in the family, and could be claimed on the owner's death by his nearest relative in the male line, however remote the degree of kinship. On the complete extinction of the line, it passed to the Crown. The system was open to endless evasions, and in practice, land was bought and sold extensively, but a transaction was always in danger of being upset by the intervention of some distant cousin.

[3] G. Berziviczy, *De Commercio et Industria Hungariae* (Löcse, 1797), p. 64.

quartered in them. 'Factory' industry was practically non-existent.[1] The non-agricultural needs of all but the wealthy, where not produced by their own womenfolk, were met by craftsmen, working entirely for the local market and protected against competition by the insuperable tariff of impenetrable roads. Of these, the Royal Free Boroughs between them contained in 1782 only 17,074 master craftsmen, 14,612 journeymen and 6,102 apprentices. Their products were bought in the town square on market day, or hawked round the villages by Jewish, Greek or Slovak itinerant pedlars. But even craftsmen were rare: most peasants were their own carpenters and wheelwrights, while their womenfolk spun and wove the family's clothes.

Naturally, in a country so vast as Hungary, conditions varied widely from one region to another. Those parts of the old Royal Hungary which had escaped the worst devastations of the Turkish wars had recovered a measure of prosperity. The great magnates of this area, the Habsburgs' favourites, drew enormous rent-rolls, and some of them had accumulated great wealth, the outward and visible signs of which were the sumptuous palaces which they took delight in building. The greatest of these, Prince Esterházy's at Esterháza, contained two hundred rooms and stabling for as many horses. It had cost sixteen million florins to erect. There were many other palaces which, if less magnificent than this, still answered every requirement of pride and luxury, and smaller manor-houses galore. The local towns, Pozsony, Sopron, Nagy-Szombat, wore an air of decent comeliness; even many of the villages were neat and clean, and housed a reasonably well-to-do peasantry.

But even in Royal Hungary there was much distress. The mines were no longer as productive as they had been, and the once very prosperous wine trade had been hard hit by the Prussian wars, military and tariff, for Silesia had been the biggest market for the North Hungarian wines. There was already frequent grim distress among the Slovak and Ruthene mountaineers. In the fat plains themselves, animal comfort when the harvest was good could easily be followed by famine when it failed; a rich harvest could not be taken to market for lack of communications and was sometimes even left ungathered, to rot on the ground. Ex-Turkish Hungary was much more backward still. Buda had been rebuilt and Pest was growing into a big commercial centre, but the village-towns of the Plain were much as they had been in Turkish days, only somewhat larger, while the same

[1] The latest investigation of the statistics had calculated that in 1783-4 Hungary contained only 125 'factories', 24 of them founded since 1781. Twelve of these were one-man enterprises (called 'factories' because they were exempt from guild restrictions); 62 employed less than 10 hands, 17, 10-29; 12, 20-49; 6, 50-99; and only 7, over 100. Far the largest was the spinnery of Sasvár, which employed 6,000 hands, nearly all of them outworkers (M. Futó, op. cit., p. 91).

unpopulated leagues stretched between them. This was still mainly a cattle area; the beasts were grazed in the open (where an unconscionable proportion of them perished) then driven on the hoof, as far afield as Germany and Italy. The cereal farming was on a low level. Only the vineyards were manured; otherwise, dung was used to build walls or patch roads. The German settlers, whose villages were islands of neatness, were the only people who practised the three-crop rotation, the Magyars contenting themselves with a two-year rotation of alternate crop and fallow, while the half-nomadic Serb and Vlach herdsmen of the South merely scratched a plot near their shacks and moved on to another when it was exhausted. Their own homes were pits sunk in the ground, with roofs of maize-straw and a hole at one end for door and chimney combined. The Bánát, settled largely with German colonists and organized under enlightened governors, was an outpost of progress, but the hinterland of Croatia (excluding, that is Fiume, which possessed shipyards and a large tobacco factory) and the Military Frontier were no more advanced than Central Hungary; the largest town in Croatia proper was Várasd, with 3,580 inhabitants. In Transylvania, the solid Saxon townlets and fortified villages had survived the troublous years reasonably well, but they were stagnating, for if the eighteenth century had brought Transylvania peace, it had also left it an economic backwater. Moreover, the birthrate of the Saxons – by far the most progressive element in the Principality – was declining, and the increase in the population was due to the growth of the Roumanian element, most of which lived in conditions of squalor hardly above those of the local gypsies.

In Galicia, the population of which, when it came to Austria, numbered about 2,300,000, conditions ranged in a descending scale, from West to East. In the Western half of the province, which had escaped serious devastation for several centuries, the population was relatively dense – in some districts too dense for comfort – and conditions comparatively orderly, the more so since no mean fraction of the population was descended from German colonists, long since Polonized but retaining testimonies to their ancestry and former freedom in the shape of soundly built cottages and well-tilled fields. Here there was even a little industry, mostly connected with the cultivation and preparation of flax, and some export of wheat still went on down the Vistula, although only a quarter of what had existed two hundred years before. But in the East, where Tatar slave-raids were still almost a living memory, the population, which was Ruthene, was sparse and primitive. Not only the forested Carpathians, in which only a few wild Huzuls lived by charcoal burning and game-poaching, but wide stretches of plain were almost uninhabited.[1] The large number of places ranking here as 'towns' simply meant that the population found it safer to live in company, while

[1] 'You can travel here for leagues', wrote Damian, 'without seeing a garden or a fruit tree.'

the landlords, too, derived some financial advantage from conferring urban status on a collection of houses. In fact, Lemberg was the only place which a traveller could recognize, and that with some repugnance, as a town. Of the others it was said that when a peasant stopped his cart at the Jew's shop (almost the whole urban population was Jewish), the nose of his horse protruded at one end of the town and the tail of his cart at the other. In 1802 a traveller in the parts was unable to get his horse shod in Stanislavov, the largest town after Lemberg, and in another, was unable to buy a candle. All Galicia in 1781 had only forty-three brick-burners, seventeen plasterers, 118 house-painters, two glovers, eight leatherworkers and similar numbers of other craftsmen.

The magnates' palaces, which were not numerous here, were sometimes imposing outside, but bare and comfortless inside; the houses of the *Szlachta* (small nobles) mere cottages.[1] Nine peasants out of ten lived in huts of wattle and daub, consisting of a single room which was shared by man and beast, windowless and chimneyless. An advantage of this for the peasant was that if he found his conditions burdensome, he simply did a moonlight flit. His home could easily be replaced; his portable possessions were as easily loaded on one cart.

The more advanced rotation of crops was one year's autumn-sown crop followed by two years' summer-sown, then one year fallow, but in some places a communal system was followed, several years' ploughing being followed by a long fallow. Ploughs were of wood; harrows consisted of boards studded with nails. Clover and fodder crops were almost unknown. The cereal crops were largely converted into rough brandy, of which the Galician peasants consumed fabulous quantities; but nearly half the area was pasture and ley.

In the Bukovina conditions resembled those of East Galicia but were, if possible, more primitive still.

When Maria Theresa ascended the throne, she had found the finances of her Empire in that dismal condition with which all her successors were to become so familiar. A long line of her paternal ancestors had regularly lived beyond their incomes, and an alarming proportion of the Crown's lands which had once formed the mainstay of its wealth had been sold. Many of the sources of indirect taxation had been farmed out, often on terms very disadvantageous to the Exchequer. The yield of the gold mines had long ceased to be appreciable, that of the silver mines was dwindling. The contributio had to be wrung painfully out of reluctant Estates, who were often themselves in difficulties and could not keep up with their payments (Carinthia, for example, owed the Treasury 2·8 million gulden in 1743).

---

[1] 'No better', wrote Damian, 'than an ordinary peasant's house in Austria, and sometimes worse.'

Charles's acquisitions in the Netherlands and Italy had been a welcome windfall, but most of the latter had been lost again in 1735–8. The State's revenues, which before the Turkish wars of 1736–9 had been estimated to bring in nearly forty million gulden, were in fact yielding barely half that amount in 1740. Meanwhile, Charles, like his predecessors, had kept an extremely extravagant Court.[1] Austria had already contracted the habit of borrowing from foreign bankers, who usually charged exorbitantly for the accommodation. When Charles died, his daughter had found only 87,000 gulden in her treasury, and the State debt was 101 m.g., sixty per cent of it owed abroad, much of this to the Bank of England. She herself was then at once embroiled in the War of the Austrian Succession. She clapped on a number of extraordinary taxes, in more or less arbitrary fashion,[2] but they were quite inadequate to cover the cost of the war, and it has been rightly said that the 'only prop' of Austrian finances during the following years was constituted by the English subsidies of £300,000 a year.[3]

Under Haugwitz's reforms, described on an earlier page, the yield from the contributio was stepped up considerably, and at the end of the Empress's reign the Crown was receiving about 32·5 m.g. from this source, of which 19 m.g. came from the Hereditary and Bohemian Lands and Galicia, 7 from the Netherlands, 3 from Lombardy and 3·5 from Hungary, while the Netherlands and Lombardy had already paid all their own military budgets and Hungary the deperdita, amounting to another half million or so. The yield of indirect taxation and of certain direct taxes now levied by the Crown, with the profits from the Crown lands and enterprises, had risen to about 27 m.g., approximately twice the figure of forty years earlier. Expenditure had, however, shown a tendency to rise *pari passu*, for although the Empress had made conscientious efforts to economize (and had, in fact, dispensed with many of her father's extravagances), and was a shrewd enough business woman, she was liable to costly lapses, especially when one of her favourites got out of his financial depth,[4] and had, of course, been faced with a second prolonged war only a few years after the conclusion of the first. Thus every year until 1775 had closed with a deficit, which had had to be met from 'extraordinary contributions' or by loans, which, since Maria Theresa was averse from borrowing abroad, were mainly raised inside Austria (lottery loans were a favourite way of raising the wind). Up to 1763 the State was

[1] Under Leopold I the Court spent 50,000 fl. a year on buying precious stones, and the Court operas, ballets and feasts cost enormous sums, as they did under Charles (*M.K.P.* II. 231).

[2] The list of these can be found conveniently in Arneth, op. cit., vol. III, c. 3.

[3] Otruba, op. cit., p. 21.

[4] She presented Count Chotek with 300,000 fl. for a house, and Prince Khevenhüller with 250,000. Frh. von Bartenstein got 100,000 fl.; Count Uhlfeld had debts amounting to over 100,000 fl. paid; etc.

paying 6% for its accommodation, and the service of its loans was becoming a heavy item in its expenditure. Her husband then took charge of the operation and managed to reduce the rate to 5%, and when he died, his widow and son devoted his entire public fortune[1] to amortization of the public debt, part of which was redeemed and the interest on the remainder brought down to 4%. In 1767, however, the debt still stood at 260 m.g., 38 m.g. of which was owed abroad, and the annual interest on it at 9·4 m.g.

In 1775 the budget was, for the first time for many years, if not the first in all Austrian history, balanced. The national balance of trade, long passive, had now also become heavily active. But barely had equilibrium been reached when there came the War of the Bavarian Succession, which cost another 30 m.g., which was again paid for out of borrowing, so that in 1780 the State debt stood again at 376 m.g.

Earlier in the century attempts had been made to establish a State Bank to help the Government in its financial operations, but they had broken down on the well-founded mistrust of the public. The conduct of the operations had then been transferred to the Wiener Stadtbank, a well-managed institution in which the public had more confidence, and which accordingly had succeeded in holding its own. Gradually this had slipped into the position of a Government bank, with the main function of floating government loans, to which was presently added that of a bank of issue, for in 1762 the Government had begun to issue, through the bank, non-interest-bearing notes of denominations ranging from five to one hundred gulden.[2] Later, as we shall see, these *Bankozettel* were to acquire a melancholy reputation, but at first they were issued only on a small scale (in 1780 only 6,798,000 of them were in circulation) and were taken readily at their face value, thus becoming an accepted part of the currency. They were, indeed, probably beneficial, as helping to relieve the stringency which must otherwise have resulted from the shortage of silver money.

IV THE SOCIAL STRUCTURE

Shielded as it had been by history against the impact of new economic forces, the social structure of the Monarchy had remained profoundly unmodern – a better word than 'mediaeval', for some of its features were less akin to those of a later age than were those of the mediaeval German Reich. In that, the Monarch had still been a human enough figure, whereas the Spanish Court ceremonial introduced by Ferdinand I and perpetuated under his successors (among whom Charles VI, who did much to revive it,

---

[1] This amounted to 22 million fl. in cash, besides estates in Bohemia, Hungary, Silesia, etc.
[2] Some notes of a different series had been issued earlier, but all these had been called in safely.

had passed his own youth in Spain) treated His Imperial Majesty not only as politically omnipotent, but socially, as a special class of man, almost halfway towards deity. A fabulously intricate system of etiquette separated him by a great gulf from the most exalted of his subjects.

Yet the Monarch's eye was not of the divine type, before which all men are equal. The central tenet of the Hungarian Constitution, which decreed that the *populus* of the Hungarian nobles constituted, with the Crown itself, the sole positive element in the polity, was not the Hungarian speciality as which it is often represented. With certain pragmatic exceptions (and these existed, although more rarely, also in Hungary) the constitutional position was as we have shown, no different from the rest of the Monarchy. The entire political structure of the Hereditary and Bohemian Lands, no less than the Hungarian, rested on the manorial system and its corollary, the nexus subditelae, and the manorial lords in each Land – in practice, its local landowning nobles – were the only category of its population of which the Crown took direct political cognisance; its relationship with the lords' subjects was only mediate.

Under the same system it was, practically speaking, only the nobles of each Land who had any voice in its public affairs (the self-government enjoyed by the boroughs and communes through their councils was, of course, limited to their own lives). Apart from the derisorily small representation accorded to the Royal Free Boroughs and the few other specially selected communities, the nobles alone were represented on the Estates of the Western Lands or in the Hungarian Diet and County *Congregationes*. The limits of the authority of the manorial lords and the Estates were, indeed, growing increasingly restricted as the Crown interested itself in a wider range of questions, but even this had hardly affected the nobles' near-monopoly. In the bureaucracy itself, the higher posts could be held only by nobles; only the lower grades were open to persons whose educational qualifications entitled them to the intermediate status of 'honoratior'.[1] If such a man's talents, or his expertize in law, finance, or some other technical field, demanded his advancement, he was given a patent of nobility corresponding to the post. This device was always open to the Crown, but Maria Theresa herself used it only rarely, while her predecessors had resorted to it only in the most exceptional cases. Far more often, a post was filled by the

[1] A 'honoratior' was officially defined in the censuses of the 1780s as 'any non-noble in the State services, regular employees of municipal councils, also all persons who, in virtue of the knowledge and learning acquired by them, exercise, under the public protection and toleration of the Landesfürst, callings serving the public (officia publica), such as doctors of medicine and law, procurators, notaries, etc.; also the superior employees of private persons (head bailiffs, head foresters, etc.).' The title was in practice generally conceded to any graduate in law, medicine or philosophy, and to any non-noble member of a profession. It carried with it personal freedom and exemption from military service, but none of the political rights or social prerogatives of nobility.

direct appointment to it of a person already holding the appropriate rank. Even where a noble youth entering the public service as a life career was required to start in a subordinate position, he climbed the ladder of advancement quickly and easily, while his ignoble colleague panted up it slowly and laboriously.[1]

The same system prevailed in the army, and even in the Church,[2] so that in all fields of public life the principle was maintained that the Crown exercised its direct authority only through nobles, and conversely, that the nobles by birth were the class from which the Crown took the great majority of its servants.

Any noble, landed or landless, enjoyed innumerable privileges. In Hungary he was exempt from all forms of taxation whatever, and in Austria, even after the eighteenth century reforms, his land was taxed at a lower rate than a peasant's and he was exempt from some minor taxes. Nobles were exempt from the obligation of military service, outside the Hungarian *insurrectio*. A noble, in all Lands, was tried before a Court of his peers. A Hungarian noble charged with any offence, even a criminal one, except high treason, or unless he had been caught *in flagrante* in the commission of highway robbery, arson, or one or two other crimes, could not be apprehended; he remained at liberty until his trial. No noble could be compelled to give evidence on oath; his word of honour sufficed. He was not above the ordinary law, civil or criminal, but it was extraordinarily difficult for a peasant to win a case against a landlord, or for a bourgeois creditor to recover a debt from a noble debtor desirous of evading his obligation (and the frequency of such evasions was one of the scandals of Austrian society). Special schools existed to which only pupils of noble families were admitted – the most famous of these, the Theresianum, had been founded by Maria Theresa herself. There were also specially endowed convents for the daughters, young or elderly but unmarried, of noble families, these being graded to match the rank of their inmates. A noble possessed of even a minor title would be extraordinarily unlucky if he fell into destitution, except through irremediable extravagance – and not always even then; Maria Theresa, as we have said, personally paid the debts of many of her favourites. A younger son for whom no place could be found in the service of the Government or the Estates could probably get a Court

---

[1] The scion of a well-to-do noble family often escaped the earlier stages of his service by the simple device of renouncing the salary, when he was not required to perform the duties. He was then quickly promoted as a 'supernumerary' until he reached a grade appropriate to his social standing, when he exchanged his supernumerary rank for a substantive one.

[2] In Hungary, admission to Holy Orders in the Catholic (Roman or Greek) Church carried with it the rank of common nobility.

[3] For the distinction, see below, p. 62. Strictly, all categories of land were taxed at the same rate, 18.45‰., but the noble was allowed to deduct expenses (labour, seed, etc.) while the peasant had to pay on his gross yield.

sinecure[1] or be received into one of the lay Orders which existed especially to provide for such cases.

The noble's other privileges included the right to wear special articles of clothing forbidden to lesser mortals, like Harrow bloods.

The nobility itself was far from being a homogeneous class. It fell into several categories, which in some respects were even legally differentiated, while the differences in their respective importance, and in the roles played by them in the State, were enormous. At the apex of this steep pyramid stood the *Hochadel* (itself tipped by the tiny elite blue-blooded enough even to marry into the Imperial family[2]) whose unblemished lineage procured them the privilege, denied to humbler mortals, of access to the Court and social intercourse with the Monarch and his family.

Generally speaking, possession of the title of Prince, Duke, Count or Baron (Freiherr) carried with it membership of this class, although even in the eighteenth century there were Counts and Barons who, although they could not be denied the legal privileges attaching to their rank, were not admitted by their colleagues as true members of the community.

It was a fact of great importance for the whole structure of the Monarchy that – whether of calculation, that they despaired of attaching to themselves more closely the wide, heterogeneous masses of their subjects, or whether it was that their eyes simply did not recognize the attributes of humanity in humbler guise – the Habsburgs (or at least, Ferdinand I and his descendants) had always sought the foundation and the instruments of their rule in a great aristocracy. Thus although in almost all their Lands the political supremacy which they now enjoyed had been achieved only after severe struggles in which the resistance to them was headed precisely by the local grandees, yet when the victory had been won, they had neither abolished the political prerogatives of the class as such, nor sought to weaken its economic basis. Only in the most exceptional cases had they kept the confiscated estates of rebels permanently in their own hands, for the benefit of other classes of the population.[3] Their general rule – applied by them alike in Bohemia, after the Battle of the White Mountain, and in Hungary after Wesselényi and

[1] Charles VI's Court numbered no less than 40,000 persons. This figure includes servants, but also a vast number of titular office-holders. Under Maria Theresa there were 1,500 Court Chamberlains. Many of these were, indeed, unsalaried and had even paid for the title. The sale of offices, ranks and titles was a considerable source of revenue to both Maria Theresa and Joseph II.

[2] Twenty-one families (15 of them bearing the title of Prince and 6 that of Count) might even marry into the Imperial family without the union's ranking as morganatic. These were families which had formerly been *reichsständisch*, although now mediatized.

[3] The colonization of South Hungary with free peasants was the chief apparent exception, and it was only apparent, for here the title-deeds had disappeared so completely that the land was really masterless. The considerations behind the settlement were in any case military.

Thököly and Rákóczi had shot their bolts – had been simply to replace the rebellious magnates by a new set of their own men, often even more richly endowed than their predecessors; for some of these favourites were given lands, not only of more than one great rebel, but of a dozen or a score of smaller nobles.

Perhaps one-third of the total area of the Monarchy was parcelled out among the few hundred great families of which this class was composed. In Bohemia, which was their stronghold, there were in 1792 only just over 950 manors, of an average size of 9,300 yokes (13,100 acres) each. Many of these were in the hands of one person. There were fifty-one princely families, whose property was valued at 465 million gulden, seventy-nine counts, worth between them 119 millions, and forty-four barons, worth 10·1 millions. In Hungary fifty-eight per cent of the cultivated land in Transdanubia, forty-one per cent of that in North Hungary, thirty-four per cent of the Great Plain consisted of *latifundia*. Some of the individual estates were enormous. The Prince of Liechtenstein held the Duchies of Troppau and Jägerndorf in Silesia, as well as great estates in Lower Austria, Silesia, Bohemia and Moravia – in that Land alone, forty-two square Austrian leagues – over 450 square miles – not to mention Liechtenstein itself. He, and some others, were feudal princes in their own right, entitled to mint coinage, to confer common nobility and to exercise other prerogatives of near-sovereignty. The Prince Esterházy owned something like ten million acres of Hungary, with over one hundred villages, forty towns or markets and thirty castles or palaces. His annual income was put at over 700,000 florins. That of Count Batthyány was estimated at 450,000 florins. Two other Hungarian magnates topped the 300,000 mark. The great Bohemian magnates, the Lobkowitz, Schwarzenbergs, Windischgrätz, etc., were probably richer still.

A great preservative of the wealth of these families was the institution of the *fidei commis*, introduced into Austria in the seventeenth century, but not used extensively before the eighteenth century. This was a form of entail, usually, although not necessarily, in primogeniture.[1] It could be instituted only with the Monarch's permission, which was given only in the case of the largest estates. The effects of this institution were very important. Vast estates had existed in almost all parts of the Monarchy at earlier periods in their history, but they had hardly ever been very long-lived; one writer has

---

[1] The entail could also be in *majorat*, when the estate was inherited by the eldest male among those of the same degree of kinship to the creator of the entail, or in *seniorat*, when it went to the eldest living male of the blood, regardless of the degree of kinship. The holder had only a life interest. He could borrow on the estate up to one-third of its value, but had to amortize the loan at five per cent annually. Creditors could not seize the land for debt. The holder could exchange land, lease the property, or even exchange into other forms of capital (which then remained entailed), but for this he had to have the permission of all known possible heirs, and of the Court.

calculated that up to the seventeenth century, the Hungarian latifundia had changed hands, on an average, every fifty years.[1] The glory of the families owning them had been equally transitory, especially before the introduction (which came only in the sixteenth century) of hereditary titles. It was the fidei commissa that created the great families whose names are bound up with the history of Austria from generation to generation.

The political function of the high aristocracy was to act as the Monarch's lieutenants in the government of his dominions. Their members constituted the second 'Bench' of the Estates of the Austrian and Bohemian Lands; in Hungary they, with the Lords Spiritual and chief dignitaries of the realm, formed the 'Table' of Magnates. The highest administrative offices, central and local, such as the Presidencies of the Hofstellen and the Gubernia, were reserved for them by law. In other services such absolute rules did not exist, but the practice was not very different; thus the highest commands in the Army were – greatly to the detriment of its efficiency – stocked almost entirely with members of the highest families, and the position in the Church was not very different.[2]

The Hochadel thus formed, under the Crown, a hereditary ruling class in the Monarchy. How far the magnates were actually more powerful than the Monarch himself, and how far they used their power in their own interests, rather than his, are questions on which much argument took place, at various times. The distinguished Austrian historian, Professor Josef Redlich, paints a very glowing picture of the relationship. According to him, the great nobles had developed by the end of the eighteenth century into a sort of 'pan-Austrian' class, with no 'national' attachment except that which expressed itself in complete subservience to the Monarch, absolutely devoted to him and possessed of 'a practical appreciation of the value of the firm and unitary association of all Lands' and of 'a very clear and fruitful conception of the "statehood" of the entirety of the Habsburgs' hereditary dominions.'

This is certainly going too far. It is probably true of the innermost ring of all, those in the immediate service of the Monarch and in daily contact with him, but of those who were chiefly based in their own Lands, the very fact that those bases were so broad, their interests deriving from them so large, tempered very noticeably their 'appreciation of the firm and unitary association of the Lands', at least if that 'association' was to express itself in the autocratic-bureaucratic government to which it naturally led.

---

[1] Agoston, *A magyar világi nagybirtok története* (Bp. 1913, p. 209), cit. E. Szabó, op. cit., p. 38.

[2] The Prince-Archbishop of Olmütz had to show his sixty-four quarterings. The Cardinal-Primates of Hungary were, at this time, almost always members of the very highest Hungarian families. It was practically unknown for a titled nobleman to be a parish priest; he passed straight to a bishopric or prelacy via some fashionable monastery.

Monarchs who over-bent the bow in this direction found the great aristocrats opposing a very vigorous resistance to them.

But Redlich's picture, exaggerated and over-generalized as it is, is by no means imaginary. Except for the disastrous year of 1742, Maria Theresa had found no reason to complain of disloyalty among her Austrian and Bohemian aristocrats, and little even of lack of subservience. Confident of her favour, they were fulfilling their side of the bargain honestly enough, and especially since the abolition of a distinct Bohemian nobility in 1752, they had grown very largely into a homogeneous class, 'pan-Austrian' within these Austro-Bohemian limits, and largely denationalized in any other sense, even the linguistic: not only Czech but even German was less fashionable among them than French or Italian. These were the fruits of seed which had been sown a hundred years before; in Hungary the growth was less advanced, for it was only Maria Theresa herself who had seriously undertaken the assimilation of the Hungarian magnates to pan-Austrianism. But she had been very remarkably successful, and already a substantial proportion of the Hungarian magnates were almost completely denationalized in the personal sense. They had forgotten their Magyar (or the younger generation had not learned it), taken to regarding Vienna as their spiritual home, learned to look down on the 'native savages' of their own country as loftily as any Anglicized Irishman on his bog-trotting cousins, and begun to intermarry with Bohemian or German families. Politically, where not actual centralists (for the special advantages attaching to Hungarian nobility were not lightly to be sacrificed) they were at any rate staunch upholders of the Gesammtmonarchie and often extremely hostile to any Hungarian particularism.

Constitutionally, the middle nobility – the *Ritterschaft* of the German Lands, the *Ryttersgwo* of Bohemia-Moravia, the *nobiles bene possessionati* of Hungary – stood one step below the Hochadel: their political forum was the third Bench of their Estates, or in Hungary, the Lower Table (in all these, however, they were represented only by delegates elected out of their own number), their field of service, the secondary offices.

But the step was a long one.

It was the middle nobles, rather than the bourgeoisie or the lower orders, against whom the Habsburgs' league with the magnates had chiefly been forged, and since the consummation of that alliance, their position had deteriorated steadily in every respect. Even their numbers were in decline in the West of the Monarchy: in all Bohemia there were only fifty-one families of knights. They were numerous only in Galicia and in the Lands of the Hungarian Crown, where the families reckoned as belonging to this class (for which no technical definition existed) may have numbered some 20–25,000. Their wealth, too, was modest. The total property of the fifty-one Bohemian knights was valued at only 7·5 million florins. A

Hungarian noble ranking as bene possessionatus usually owned 750–1,000 hold, and this, given the low return yielded by land, hardly did more than enable him to live comfortably on his own acres and visit or entertain his neighbours. An Austrian squire probably made even less out of his acres.

The restricted life of the middle nobles imposed on them a more provincial, or parochial, outlook than the magnates, but also brought them into closer touch with their own peoples. They were thus far less denationalized, and in so far as any national feeling at all existed in the eighteenth century among any of the Habsburgs' peoples,[1] it was in this class, rather than in the cosmopolitan magnates or the passive peasantry, that it was to be found. But their positive political importance, as a class, was small. Only in Hungary did they still represent an appreciable political force, for here the Lower 'Table' of the Diet had maintained its parity of status with the Upper;[2] the same principle of parity existed in all the main governmental offices (although this did not extend to the Presidencies of them); and most important of all, the middle nobles had succeeded in keeping in their own hands the machinery, and with it, a large part of the control, of the Counties, which, as we have said elsewhere, had been able to preserve a large measure of independence.

Even here, however, that independence had grown somewhat fictional in the eighteenth century: the Counties largely obeyed the dictate of the local magnate or of the Court Chancellery. In Galicia, where the equality of all nobles was, on paper, even more complete than in Hungary,[3] the *de facto* supremacy of the higher nobility was still greater, and in German Austria the middle nobility as a class played no political role whatever. Increasingly, its members were leasing their estates and moving into Vienna to take service under the Crown. As the successful *Briefadel*, for their part, had usually no more ardent ambition that to buy a country estate, the two classes

---

[1] Except the special cases, noted elsewhere, of the Greek Orthodox Serbs and Roumanians.

[2] The Hungarian freemen who in the thirteenth century had taken the appellation of 'nobles' had always jealously maintained the principle that every noble was equal in status to every other. In 1351 Louis the Great had confirmed that all the nobles of Hungary enjoyed *una atque eadem libertas*. The innovations (hereditary titles, division of the Diet into two 'tables', etc.) later introduced by the Habsburgs had conferred on the magnates a higher status than that enjoyed by the rest of the nobles, but left all those who were not magnates undifferentiated. Certain documents confined some privileges or duties to 'leading men', 'men of substance', etc., but without ever defining those terms; in any case the status conferred by them was not hereditary.

[3] In 1374 Louis, who at that time was doubling the Crowns of Hungary and Poland, issued the 'Privilege of Kassa', under which he conferred on the nobles of Poland the same rights as the Hungarians'. The Poles maintained their equality more completely even than the Hungarians, for Polish constitutional law did not legally recognize titles at all, and although here too the Sejm divided ultimately into an Upper and a Lower House, the former, the Senate, was exclusively composed technically of the holders of certain offices, for which any Polish noble was eligible.

of nobility were here becoming fused beyond distinction. The product played, indeed, a very important part in the public services, and although the plums and distinctions did not fall to them, it was probably on their shoulders that the Monarchy was really carried.

Every Land contained also its quota of small nobles. In the Vorlande there were 'manors', ownership of which entitled their holders to rank as *landsässiger Adel*, which consisted of a single house, or even half a house, and similar freaks were not uncommon in the Littoral, and even elsewhere.¹ Vienna and other Western 'towns' contained impoverished nobles in plenty, eking out miserable existences on pittances from Court sinecures, or surreptitiously, in employment from which their rank should have barred them. But the real haunts of the small nobles were Hungary and Galicia. In the former they constituted about 35–40,000 of the total of 65,000 noble families; in Galicia, there were about 30,000 families of them.² Even they, again, were no homogeneous class: there were some who were comfortable yeoman farmers; some who tilled no more than a single peasant holding;³ others who were entirely landless, and whose 'liberty' was only *quoad personam*. In Hungary, not all of the 'sandalled' or 'seven-plumtree' nobles even enjoyed to the full the most treasured of all the Hungarian noble's privileges of exemption from all forms of taxation: there were categories of them who had to pay their quota towards the *fundus domesticus*.

Their political privileges were more apparent than real. Any Hungarian noble, if he possessed any land at all, in theory enjoyed the franchise, both active and passive, for the County Congregatio, and was entitled to attend and speak at its business meetings. In practice, the passive franchise was confined to those whom public opinion recognized as *bene possessionati*, and while there were no fixed rules of procedure for the *Congregationes*, nor, for that matter, for the Diet, a generally accepted usage laid down that votes were 'weighed, not numbered': i.e., the President of a meeting announced its decision on any point in accordance with what the debate had shown to be the opinion of its 'senior pars.'. A small noble's opinion thus hardly counted, even if he had been allowed to express it. As a political factor, the 'sandalled' nobles came into their own only at the triennial electoral meetings, which ensured them a week's feasting at the expense of one or both candidates.⁴

¹ According to Feigl, op. cit., p. 10, there were in 1848 2,645 exercisers of manorial rights in Lower Austria.

² The total number of 'nobles' (men, women and children) counted in Galicia was 95,000, three-quarters of the number in all the Western Lands together.

³ In some areas small nobles were allowed to lease rustical holdings, against a rent.

⁴ Even then, the votes were seldom ascertained by counting of heads. One practice was for the supporters of each candidate to retire behind a screen and to shout his name, the loudest shout being judged the winner. For a highly entertaining description of a Hungarian election, see Eötvös's famous novel, *The Village Notary*.

The highest social grade among the non-nobles was that of the 'burghers', a burgher being a man entitled to practice a *burgerlich* trade in a town, to own real property in it, to exercise the active and enjoy the passive franchise for its council, share in its administration and grant or reject applications by others for the same status.[1]

The burgher's was a status which in some respects was not unenviable. Even where a town was not a Royal Free Borough, its obligatons towards its lord were usually light, and it enjoyed a good deal of self-government. In a Royal Free Borough this was almost complete. The City Fathers in such communities had their own dignities and ceremonies, to which were added those of the guilds and merchant corporations, with which citizenship of a town was usually closely connected, most master craftsmen and licensed tradesmen in a town (when not Jewish) being burghers of it, while conversely, the ranks of the burghers were mainly composed of these elements.

They had, also, their own rights and privileges, including that of being tried by their own Courts.

Its burghers, however, constituted only a very small proportion of the population of the Monarchy. The total urban population was small enough, and full burgher rights were enjoyed by only a small fraction even of this. In 1780 there were only 80,000 full burghers in all industrialized Bohemia, 4,450 in Styria, 2,013 in Carinthia. Hungary contained only fourteen towns with more than one thousand burghers. Highest came Debrecen, with 3,919 *civites*, a status enjoyed in virtue of ancient privileges. The proportion of the burghers to the total population of a town ranged from one in three in Sopron to one in ten, or in some cases, one in twenty or even thirty. The majorities were composed of domestic servants, apprentices, and humbly situated or casual workers.

With these small numbers, the burghers clearly could not constitute an important social, political or economic factor in the life of the Monarchy. We have seen how meagre was the representation even of the Royal Free Boroughs on the Estates, and even where allowed to attend those bodies, they were made to feel their inferiority. In Lower Austria, the most urbanised Land of the Monarchy, outside Bohemia, the burghers' representatives were allowed only to stand and listen in silence to the Government's *postulata*; then they withdrew, and signified their assent in writing. Boroughs which were not Royal were not represented on the Estates at all; it was taken that their lords spoke for them, as they did for their peasants. A craftsman or tradesman outside a town counted as a peasant, except for the personal advantage that he was usually exempted from military service.

It is, of course, true that the representation of the Royal Free Boroughs

---

[1] Their discretion in this respect was, however, not unlimited. The Landesfürst not infrequently ordered a Council to admit an applicant, or even, any person belonging to a certain occupational category.

on the Estates was anomalous in so far as those bodies were representing the interests of the Land *vis-à-vis* the Crown.

The political and social weight of the burghers in Bohemia and Hungary was, where they were Germans (as was often the case), further diminished by national antagonisms between them and the Czech and Magyar country nobles.[1]

It is probably safe to say that only one burgher in the Central Monarchy enjoyed, as such, real importance and dignity: the burgomaster of Vienna.

Where they held the money-bags the towns could, indeed, exercise a *de facto* influence which the law did not give them; more than one Prince in mediaeval Austria had discovered this to his cost. But the trend of the economic developments of the sixteenth to the eighteenth century had worked against the towns in this respect also, as had the Habsburgs' ineradicable partiality for the high aristocracy. Most of the big fortunes in the eighteenth century were made out of the land, in the form of rent-rolls or large-scale demesne farming; even the big industries, where not State-run, were more often than not founded by rich nobles, who worked them with their own unfree labour, sometimes supervised by foreign foremen and specialists.[2] Financial fortunes, where any, were made by 'privileged' Jews, chiefly by those who acted as Court moneylenders – a position which was, indeed, apt to end disastrously for all parties.

Writers on modern States tend naturally to include the members of the civil service and of the professions with the traders and industrialists as the 'middle classes'. So far as the State services were concerned, this classification was hardly applicable to the Monarchy of 1780, where those services were still mainly in the hands of nobles or their employees; the development of a special mentality of its own among this class was still to come. The modernizing State of the enlightened despots naturally needed more professional men than had sufficed for its simpler predecessors, and made them more important; above all, the rivalry described elsewhere[3] between State and Church for the ultimate spiritual allegiance of the people had put the teaching profession into something of a key position. Some individual members of it played roles of the highest importance in the councils of the Monarchy.

---

[1] The Hungarian Diet of 1687 petitioned Leopold I that 'since in consequence of the recovery of Hungary' (i.e., from the Turks) 'the number of Royal Free Boroughs, etc., had so increased that this Fourth Estate not only equalled but perhaps exceeded the others', he should not, unless in exceptional cases, grant any more charters.

[2] The native burghers had not as a rule the necessary capital to found considerable enterprises. Sometimes a foreign expert was invited into the country for the purpose, when, if successful, he was often ennobled. Another factor telling against the towns was the preference (on social grounds) of the authorities for siting factories in country districts, where the population was thought to be less liable to moral infection.

[3] See below, p. 110 ff.

This did not, however, bring the profession as a whole much increased prestige. Its two or three highest-ranking members enjoyed *ex officio* certain remarkable privileges,[1] but the rank and file were usually humble enough servants of the State, the lord of the manor, or the Church; the village schoolmaster usually doubled his post with that of sexton-verger, and was often made to act almost as the local priest's body-servant.[2]

The other professions, which, like that of teaching, were mainly staffed by honoratiores, enjoyed no more consideration. They were, incidentally, thin on the ground, especially in the more backward parts of the Monarchy,[3] which had little need of lawyers, except for complicated cases involving title to land, and tended to regard physicians as a superfluous luxury. The lists given by Damian of the occupations of the inhabitants of a number of towns in South Hungary hardly contains a single doctor. According to Damian, the almost universal remedy for any disease among the Croats was a draught of strong liquor laced with pepper (sometimes with other herbs) or, occasionally, a concoction of black hellebore. Thus even apothecaries were rare. The apothecary in Zirc, West Hungary, in 1938 exhibited a notice (and for all I know, may still do so) that it had been founded in 1784, on orders from Joseph II: before that date, the local wine had been considered the best remedy for any disease.

Surgeons (Wunderärzte) outnumbered doctors of medicine by two or even three to one in many country districts, but this was because they were also the official barbers; they were obliged by law to hang out a barber's pole and to shave customers on request (hairdressers were not allowed to perform this operation). It is one of the curiosities of the Austrian system that this obligation was imposed by law on men who were entitled to perform the operation of trepanning. Bleeding and the treatment of flesh wounds were also surgeon's work.

These conditions went on until long after the date of which we are

[1] Rectors of Universities always sat on the first Bench of the Estates of their Lands. The Rector Magnificus of Prague University and the heads of the two non-theological faculties were entitled to buy landtäflich estates. The Rector of Vienna University enjoyed the unique privilege of being entitled to demand audience of the Emperor whenever he wished; he was not even required to give advance notice of his visit.

[2] Endres, op. cit., p. 68 describes the life of a village teacher in the Vormärz, when it was certainly not more uncomfortable than fifty years before. He was teacher, verger and organist (ability to play the organ was actually one of the requirements for the post, and the organ was taught in the *Normalschule*). He also had to shave the priest on Sunday morning. The average stipend of a full elementary schoolmaster was 130 fl. a year; of an assistant, 70 fl. At this time a town magistrate was receiving 300 fl., his assistant, 150, and a servant, 50.

[3] The censuses of the 1770s give only about 20,000 'Beamte et honoratiores' for the entire Monarchy, a figure which leaves little enough for the professions when one deducts the public and private employees. 4,750 of the 20,000 were in Austria (Lower and Upper) and about 3,200 in Bohemia. Carniola could show only 427, Croatia only 438, Transylvania, with its total population of 1,500,000, only 771.

now writing. According to J. Springer, there were when he wrote (1845) still only 7 doctors and surgeons per 10,000 head of the population in Transylvania, 9 in the Military Frontier, and 10 in Galicia. The highest figure was for Lombardy (91), followed by Lower Austria (80). Styria had 46, Bohemia 34.

The term 'peasant', generically used for any non-noble cultivator of the land, actually covered as many variations of legal, social and economic status as the word 'noble'. One distinct category was formed by the free peasants, whose numbers were considerable in some parts of the Monarchy. In the Western Alpine Lands, the old Germanic tradition of the free community had maintained itself with some obstinacy; in the Tirol, almost all the peasants were free, as were a proportion of those in Upper Austria (and in the intervening Salzburg). At the other geographical extreme were the areas which had been settled with immigrant colonists who had had to be granted freedom as the inducement to venture into distant and often perilous lands. The Hungarian Lands, especially Transylvania and the newly-recovered south of the country, contained several such communities,[1] besides a number more, of slightly different origin, whose inhabitants could be described as free peasants with more or less exactitude.[2] Galicia contained some analogous classes,[3] and also some free peasants, as did the Bukovina. The class in both Hungary and Galicia would have been much more numerous if the political terminology of both Hungary and Poland had not equated the status of freedom with that of nobiliity. Many men who in the West would have counted as free peasants ranked in Hungary and Galicia as 'sandalled nobles'.

The free peasants' communities governed themselves on the lowest level; above that, they came under the authority of the State apparatus.[4] They paid the State taxation due from any citizen, and were subject to tithe to the Church, where this was exacted, as well as to contributions in cash or kind towards the necessary services of their commune: the upkeep of its roads and bridges, the maintenance of its Church and school, night-watchman, etc.

[1] The best known of these are the Transylvanian Saxons, who had been assured their freedom as early as 1224. Most of the eighteenth-century colonists on *neo-acquistica* land were free. In 1842 about 70,000 heads of peasant families in Inner Hungary, or one in eight, were free.

[2] These included the Szekels of Transylvania and the inhabitants of the Cuman-Jazyge Districts between the Danube and the Tisza, of the Hajdu towns, etc. Some of these had lost part of their freedom, but not all traces of it.

[3] These included the class of 'saltycze', who, although not noble, were exempted from taxation in return for military service.

[4] Some of the Hungarian communities were governed for the Crown by the Palatine or a special officer designated by him.

The big majority of the Monarchy's peasants were, however, still unfree men, the subjects of their manorial lords. The subject's position did not, indeed (except perhaps in Galicia, where the Polish legislation had not by 1780 been entirely superseded by the Austrian, although the supersession was on its way), involve bondage *ad personam*. He was not a chattel, could not be bought or sold, could own personal property, and was competent to bring an action at law in his own name. His personal freedom was, according to the writers of the day, complete in the German-Austrian Lands, and elsewhere incomplete only in the sense that he could not, even if he had fulfilled all his obligations, leave his holding, marry, or engage in, or put his sons to, a craft or profession without his lord's permission. These restrictions, if they still existed in law, had fallen into desuetude in the German-Austrian Lands, where the lord was entitled to demand a fee on such occasions (as he did elsewhere if he granted the permission), but could not refuse his consent. It was this distinction which Joseph II later invoked[1] to describe the condition of the peasants in the German-Austrian Lands as one of 'hereditary subjection' (Erbuntertänigkeit) and elsewhere in Austria, of 'serfdom' (Leibeigenschaft). Many writers have, indeed, objected to the latter term as an exaggeration.

The 'nexus' did, however, put the peasant in a position of legal inferiority and impose on him a number of material obligations. He was his lord's 'subject' in law, and legally bound to render him 'loyalty, obedience and deference' and to obey his orders and submit to the judgments of his Court; even when entitled to appeal against such orders or judgments, he had to obey them first, and appeal afterwards. The other side of this relationship was that the lord had to protect his subjects against unlawful exactions from any other quarter.

Of the unfree peasant's material obligations to his lord, some were due from all unfree inhabitants of a commune, whatever their economic category, being, in theory, his reward for protecting them and administering their affairs. The other payments depended on the legal quality of the land on which a peasant's home was situated, for all manorial land in the Monarchy was divided into two categories, known respectively in Austria as 'dominical' and 'rustical', in Hungary, as 'allodial' and 'urbarial'.[2] Dominical land was at the lord's free disposal: he could farm it directly through the labour of others (or his own), lease it, or leave it uncultivated or nearly so, perhaps simply preserving it for sporting purposes. Rustical land, while still owned by the lord in *dominium directum*, was divided into peasant holdings, the occupants of which enjoyed the usufruct (*dominium utile*) of them, in return for a rent paid in cash, kind or services, or a combination of the three.

[1] See below, p. 127.
[2] Common lands partook in some sense of the qualities of both categories, their benefits being enjoyed both by the lord and the peasants.

THE MONARCHY IN 1780

The rustical peasants were also the tax-payers in chief of the State, for under the system described above, the contributio, which was the largest direct tax, and most of the local expenditure by Kreise, Counties, etc., came out of the land tax, the whole of which in Hungary, and the greater part of it in Austria, was levied on rustical land. The occupant of a rustical holding also had to pay his quota of expenditure on communal services, and in places, tithe to the Church. He was therefore subject to taxation under five headings:

(a) to the State
(b) to the Church
(c) to the commune
(d) to his lord *qua* manorial lord
(e) to his lord *qua* landlord.

His payments under (b) and (c) need not detain us here. They were similar to those levied on the free communes, and not exorbitant by modern standards. The Church tithe was not even exacted everywhere, although sometimes, where the Church renounced it, it was added to the seigneural dues. On the other hand, the peasants' obligations under (d) and (e) had, up to the middle of the eighteenth century, been growing steadily more onerous, as their lords' tastes grew more luxurious, and in particular, as they found it possible to make a cash profit out of farming their demesne lands. For this purpose, and others,[1] they had taken to exacting more and more of the robot, as this service was currently known as most parts of the Monarchy[2] which was one of the traditional forms in which the peasants worked out their rent. Moreover, the robot, especially the field labour, was often exacted without any regard for the peasant's interest. Thus he might be required to spend his entire week at harvest time on his lord's land, with only his nights to get in his own crops. Where they did not exact the robot the landlords increased the peasants' dues in cash or kind, and they found means of increasing the yield from their other privileges. In many parts of the Monarchy they claimed the right to mill their peasants' corn (at a price), to distill strong liquors and to brew beer and to retail these beverages at the local tavern – this sometimes with dire results,[3] to retail their own wine throughout the

---

[1] The service did not have to be taken out in field labour: it could take the form of carting, etc., for building, or even of industrial work: the textile enterprises founded by many Bohemian landowners got most of their material from their peasants, who took out their service by spinning or weaving in their homes.

[2] From the Slavonic word *robota* = work.

[3] The *propinatio*, as this right was known in Galicia, was, owing to the Galician peasants' extreme addiction to strong liquor (see below, p. 96), actually the most lucrative of all the landlords' rights there. When an estate was to be sold, the first question asked by the prospective buyer was '*cos czyni arenda?*' (how much does the sale of liquor bring in?). Here the right of keeping the tavern was almost always leased to a Jew. In other Lands the right was less important, and in Lower Austria distilling was forbidden altogether.

year[1] and often, in practice, to force their peasants to buy practically all their requirements from them, and conversely, to sell them their produce, often making a large profit on both transactions.[2] They were entitled to call on their peasants' children for domestic service, usually for a limited period. They made their sporting rights extensive and exclusive, and often exercised them in a manner extremely detrimental to the peasants' interests.

A service often exacted in the most burdensome fashion was the 'long haulage', under which a peasant had to supply long-distance transport for a certain number of days in the year.

Another practice to which many lords resorted was to find some pretext to evict a peasant from his holding, and to convert this into allodial, and tax-free, land.

Meanwhile, the State, too, had been increasing its demands, sometimes in even larger measure than the lords;[3] and it should be remarked that these were not exhausted by the simple exaction of direct taxation; for when the standing army was instituted, the peasant was obliged in many districts to have soldiers quartered on him, to keep the local garrisons supplied, and to provide them with transport as required. He was paid for these services, but at a rate which seldom covered his expenditure.

It was a cumulative evil which to some extent had brought about its own partial remedy, or at least, alleviation. For eventually a point had been reached at which it was inescapably clear that the peasants could not fulfil the demands made on them from both sides, and exist. The attempts to make them do so were provoking unrest which was, indeed, regularly put down by force: but the inquiries instituted by her after some of these outbreaks convinced Maria Theresa that the degraded condition of the peasantry was humanly intolerable, and also a source of weakness to the body politic. Whether the stronger among her motives was the purely utilitarian, or the humanitarian, need not be discussed here: both considerations were certainly present in her mind, and it would be as misleading to ignore the former, as was done by most historians writing while her descendants were still on the throne, as unjust to deny the latter, as became the

---

[1] In wine-growing districts peasant vintners were also allowed to retail their own wine, but each family only for a certain number of weeks, during which a bush was put up over the door. One complaint made by the vintners of one Hungarian village was that the lord's wine was so good that their fellow-villagers preferred to drink it even when alternatives were available. More often, indeed, the complaint was that the landlord's wine was inferior.

[2] These rights, again, had fallen into desuetude in many of the German-Austrian Lands.

[3] In Bohemia, for example, the land tax had increased by twenty-nine per cent in the last years of the seventeenth century while the robot had remained unaltered (Kerner, p. 240). When Maria Theresa was arguing over her Robot Patent for Bohemia, the Estates repeatedly made the point that it was the State's exactions that were at the root of the trouble. The Hungarian Estates argued the same case.

fashion when dialectic materialism succeeded to the throne. At all events, she stepped in, and issued a series of Patents laying down maxima for the peasants' obligations to their lords, Land by Land.[1] At the same time, surveys (where such did not already exist) were carried out and registers drawn up showing what land in each Land was, at that date, dominical and what rustical,[2] and further conversion of rustical or common land to dominical forbidden except under special permit, for which cause had to be shown.[3]

When issuing her instructions for this work, Maria Theresa laid down the principle that whatever the lords' previous legal rights had been, the peasant must always be able 'to support himself and his family, and also to cover the general national expenditure in times of peace or war.' This would have seemed to foreshadow large changes in the legal position, but not only did the Estates, and also the Empress's advisers, oppose such changes obstinately, but the peasants themselves seem to have complained less against the law, than against the lords' disregard of it. At all events, the Patents, when they appeared (which, in the case of the Bohemian, was only after years of argument) were surprisingly unrevolutionary documents. They did away with a mass of illegalities and usurpations, including, in some Lands, many of the *banalités* and some other services for which no legal justification could be shown (written law or usage undisputed for thirty years being normally taken as constituting justification) and went into

[1] The series, nearly all of which constituted revisions of earlier enactments, began in the Hungarian Lands, where they were known as *urbaria*. The first of all, for the three Slavonian Counties, was issued in 1756, replacing an earlier enactment still, which had been issued in 1737, but had remained a dead letter. The urbarium for Inner Hungary was issued in 1767, by Rescript, the Diet having refused to collaborate in producing a Law. The Hungarians therefore regarded it as not possessing legal validity, but perforce obeyed its provisions. At that time Maria Theresa seems to have thought that it was only in Hungary that conditions were bad enough to call for her intervention, but in 1769 the peasants in Silesia struck against the robot. She set up a Commission of inquiry, and then instituted similar inquiries in Bohemia and Moravia. These revealed that conditions, at least in Bohemia, were no better than in Hungary. The Robot Patent for Silesia was issued in 1771, and Patents for Lower and Upper Austria in 1772. That for Bohemia followed in 1775 (extended to Moravia in the same year). Styria and Carinthia got their Patents in 1778, Croatia and the Bánát in 1780, Carniola in 1782. No urbarium was issued for Transylvania, where the authorities did not get down to making a survey, but regulations limiting the robot were issued in 1747 and 1768. No Patent was thought necessary for the Tirol or the Littoral, where robot was practically non-existent, nor for the Netherlands or Milan-Mantua. A provisional Patent was issued for Galicia in 1775, in advance of the survey, and confirmed in 1786, but this was left incomplete as regards its most important provisions, and the gaps were, in fact, never filled in.

[2] No surveys were carried out in Transylvania or Galicia, where the distinction continued to rest on local usage.

[3] The converse process was legal, and cases of it were not unknown, although a landlord not wishing to farm his demesne land directly more often preferred to lease it under one of the systems described below.

detail in regulating the legal length of a working robot day, the maximum number of days in any week when it could be required, etc., but except in relatively few cases, did not alter the existing law, confining themselves to codifying the local *status quo* and providing safeguards for its observance. In respect of the division of land, again, the *status quo* was registered; only proven recent usurpations were corrected. The main results of this, from our point of view, were two. Firstly although the Patents beyond doubt improved the situation of many of the peasants very greatly, especially in the Lands where abuses had been rife, they yet left the peasant position in the Monarchy incompletely solved, so that one of the first things Joseph did when his mother's eyes were closed was, as we shall see, to take up the question again. Secondly, since the situation *quo ante* had developed very differently in different Lands, according to the outcomes of earlier struggles in each between lords and peasants, so the obligations laid down in the Patents were almost equally various, both in their sums and in their distribution between the various forms of payment. Thus in Upper Austria an *Interim Relatio* issued in 1597, at the close of a peasant war in which the peasants had given almost as good as they had got, had laid down fourteen days in the year as the maximum haulage robot (performed with two yoke of oxen) to which a *Vollbauer* (viz., one occupying a full peasant holding, as legally defined[1]) was subject[2] and the Upper Austrian Patent of 1772 kept that figure. In the Bukovina, where the inhabitants were protected by a Patent issued by the Moldavian Prince Ghika, the initial figure was only twelve.[3] In Hungary, where fifty-two days had been laid down after the great peasant revolt of 1514, (again, as a penalty), this figure, again, was retained under the Urbarium, and it was also that legalized for Croatia, Slavonia and the Bánát. In Bohemia the figure had been fixed at 156 in the Robot Patent of 1738, which itself reproduced a figure laid down in 1570 by a particularly savage Diet, with which the then Emperor, Leopold I, had joined forces.[4] This, again, was

[1] A full holding was originally supposed to constitute the area on which a peasant could support himself and his family, while fulfilling his obligations. It varied slightly, in accordance with local custom, in each Land, and even locally inside a Land. In the West it was usually of the order of 22 yokes of arable plus 6 of ley (later, the criterion of size was replaced by that of the amount of land tax for which it was assessed). In Hungary it ranged from 16 hold (=yokes) arable plus 6 of ley for good land near the Austrian frontier to 38 plus 16–22 for poor land on the Tisza. Each holding also contained one yoke for house, outbuildings, garden, etc.

[2] The same figures were imposed at the time in the adjacent Salzburg and Passau. It is interesting for the development of the problem that when the *Interim Relatio* was issued, fourteen days constituted an aggravation of the peasants' obligations.

[3] This did not mean that the Bukovinian peasants were well situated. An inquiry undertaken into their conditions in 1804 showed that the landlords there found devices to reduce them to an exceptional state of servitude. See Meynert, *Kaiser Franz I*, pp. 321 ff.

[4] Leopold's language in publishing this Patent is extraordinarily similar to that used by the Hungarian Diet of 1514. It is remarkable how seldom attention is drawn to this correspondence.

retained and was made a sort of standard for the West, being adopted also for Moravia, Silesia, Styria, Carinthia, Carniola, Galicia (where, indeed, it constituted an improvement on the previous practice) and Transylvania. Lower Austria, however, got off with 102. For hand robot, performed without the use of draught animals, the figure was usually twice the above (so for Hungary, 104). A peasant holding a fractional holding did proportionately less, and a landless man less still, usually thirteen days, although sometimes as little as six to eight.[1] The landlord was entitled everywhere to call on his peasants for some additional robot, but the amount of this, the seasons at which it could be demanded, etc., were now carefully regulated, and such 'overtime work' had to be paid.

A landlord did not, of course, exact robot where he had no use for it, taking out his rent in other forms. Thus, apart from the Tirol, where the peasants were free, and the Italian districts, where they usually held their lands on a perpetual tenure payable in cash, little robot figured in the peasants' contracts in Upper Austria, Carinthia or the German parts of Styria. It, or its equivalent, was, however, regularly exacted in the Hungarian and Slavonic parts of the Monarchy, and also in Lower Austria.[2]

The payments in cash and kind which were, or might be, due from the peasant to his lord under headings (d) and (e)[3] constitute an almost endless list, many of them being rooted in antiquity, and some existing only on paper.[4] They, too, varied very greatly from Land to Land. Broadly, we may sum up the dues in kind as consisting first and foremost of the seigneural

[1] It is fair to point out that the robot attached to the land and not the person (beyond the cottager's due). Thus a Vollbauer with three sons (or farm-hands) and eight yokes of oxen would still have seventy-five per cent of his labour force available for himself even on his robot days.

[2] The figures for the Austrian Lands of the robot redeemed after 1848 are given in L.U.F., I. 70. The days of hand robot redeemed were (in round figures, thousands): Galicia-Bukovina, 16·5; Bohemia, 7; Lower Austria, 6·2; Moravia, 5·25; Silesia, Styria, Carniola, 1 each; Carinthia, 0·15; Upper Austria, 0·1; the remainder, insignificant. The figures for haulage robot show approximately the same proportions.

[3] These are treated together here, for while the distinction between them became important after 1848, when those falling under the former heading were remitted altogether, while those under the latter had, outside Hungary and Galicia, to be 'redeemed', before that date it was, for the peasant, one without a difference. They had, indeed, become so mutually entangled that it sometimes took the Commissioners months or years to sort them into their proper categories.

[4] Thus in Hungary a peasant was bound to pay a 'moderate and equitable' contribution towards his lord's ransom if he was taken in battle. This was a paper obligation, but one village in Bohemia still had to pay a levy for the maintenance of the seigneural wolfhounds, although wolves had long since been exterminated from the neighbourhood. It has been said that in Moravia, as late as 1848, 248 kinds of dues were being exacted (not all, of course, from the same holding), and in Carniola there were 71 possible dues in money and 52 in kind, including levies on fish, crayfish, martens, walnuts and chestnuts.

tithe, which usually amounted to about one-sixth of the peasant's produce,[1] plus, in most communes, extra dues on special days and occasions, such as a goose at Christmas, a 'present' when a wedding took place in the castle, etc. There were also taxes payable in cash: in most places a relatively small house or chimney tax, and other dues payable in connection with certain transactions, the heaviest of which were the *mortuarium*, levied on a change of tenancy following death, and the *laudemium*, levied on a transfer between living persons. Either of these could amount to as much as ten per cent of the value of the property transferred, although the former, in particular, was usually lower. The *Bergrecht*, an institution which was particularly resented, entitled the landlord to levy a special tax on all land suitable for use as vineyards, whether so used or not.

When the value of all these were added together, plus the indirect tribute paid by the peasant to his lord under the latter's economic monopolies, it is clear that the peasant's payments to his lord were still considerable, even under the Patents. In return, he received, indeed, certain counter-services from his lord, whose function in the mutual relationship was not by any means that of always receiving and never giving. Besides his duties in administering his commune and dealing out justice in it (which were not usually received by the peasants with gratitude, but involved him in considerable expense where, as nearly always, he exercised them through paid employees), the lord often bore the lion's share of the expenditure on the local schools and health services.[2] He was obliged to provide at least his *uneingekauft* peasants[3] with the material for keeping their houses, outbuildings and fences in repair, to provide them with firewood and to see them through harvest failures, if necessary advancing them seed for the next harvest. He sometimes enjoyed easements over their land, such as the right to graze his cattle on the village stubble after harvest, but they in return often enjoyed large easements over his land, particularly his forests.

In most Lands it was open to the subject, if his lord agreed, to commute (reluiren) his dues in labour, kind, or both, for a cash payment. The commutation of dues in kind seems to have been very general in the Vorlande

---

[1] To be distinguished from the Church tithe. It was not always exacted, and in some parts of Austria had become a marketable attachment to the land, and was sometimes bought by a working peasant on retirement to provide himself with a sort of pension. In Hungary it was called the 'none', the term 'tenth' having been appropriated by the Church. It had first been imposed there in 1351, when it had been supposed to constitute the peasant's entire obligations towards his lord, but had been retained when other dues were added. Crops grown on the peasant's 'home acre' were not subject to the tithe, and others could be exempted. Thus when the Government was trying to popularize the cultivation of maize in Austria, it declared it tithe-free (with very successful results).

[2] In some places he was under a specific obligation to provide treatment for his peasants if they were bitten by dogs, or contracted venereal disease.

[3] See below, p. 69.

and Lower Austria.[1] Commutation of robot was much rarer, except in Lower Austria, where it is common even now.[2] Elsewhere the peasant had not the cash, and the landlord could not be sure of finding hired labour. Since the robot was the obligation most hated by the peasants, and most easily abused by the lords, the Lands which were the strongholds of robot were also usually the chief foci of peasant unrest.

A rustical peasant's tenure, before the reforms, could be one of two main types.[3] In the Hereditary and Bohemian Lands, and also in Galicia, he had the right to 'buy in' (einkaufen) his holding.[4] If he did so, he could not be evicted from it except for negligent farming (liederliche Wirtschaft), and that only after inquiry by the Kreisamt, or if he was convicted of a criminal offence, or ran into heavy debt. He could borrow on it, up to two-thirds of its value, sell it (provided that his lord approved the purchaser) and bequeath it as he would on death or retirement,[5] subject again to his lord's approval of his successor.

The holder of an *uneingekauft* holding enjoyed no legal security whatever. His lord could, at his own pleasure, force him to exchange his holding for another, transfer part of it to another holding, or subdivide it, leaving him with only a fraction of it, or even reducing him to the position of a cottar.

The differences between the two categories were, however, smaller in practice than on paper, for while the *eingekauft* peasant's freedom was far from absolute, the man who had not 'bought in' was in practice seldom evicted except for grossly unsatisfactory conduct, and his heir (who by custom was his youngest son)[6] usually succeeded him without question. The possibility of reducing or dividing a holding, beyond certain limits, was limited by the fact – a most important one for the whole peasant question in the Monarchy – that it was the custom in most Lands, and the local law in many, that the farmhouse and sufficient land with it to form a viable farm had to be kept intact, failing special reason to the contrary. On the other hand, while buying in did not relieve a peasant of his obligations towards his lord, the latter usually maintained that it did relieve him of his counter-obligations. Consequently the transaction, besides itself costing the peasant money, was apt to leave him materially worse off.

Buying in was therefore fairly common among the thrifty Germans, but

---

[1] The 1848 redemption figures show no dues in kind at all for Lower Austria, the editors noting that they were nearly all commuted and were thus entered under the cash payments.

[2] See also below, p. 160, n. 2.

[3] Not counting, that is, the special form of tenure in the Italian-speaking areas, which was terminable only for repeated failures to pay the rent.

[4] This appears to have been a very old right: Grünberg (*Bauernbefreiung* I. 254) writes that it had 'always existed' in Bohemia. I cannot trace its beginnings.

[5] It was usual for a peasant to retire on reaching the limit of his working days. He then arranged with his successor for a sort of pension.

[6] If he was under age when his father died, the widow or a guardian appointed by the lord looked after the farm during his minority.

in the Bohemian Lands it was the lords who were in favour of it, as they said 'to be quit of the endless demands for seed and money'[1] and of the expense of doing-up cottages left in a state of dilapidation by unthrifty peasants; while the peasants refused to make the change. Maria Theresa favoured the buying-in system, but was unwilling to apply compulsion. She did abolish certain forms of tenure, widespread especially in Carinthia, which precluded it, but beyond this, confined herself to recommending it and urging the landlords to make the change. The results were, however, meagre.[2]

In the early 1770s one of the Empress's chief agricultural experts, Frh. von Raab, evolved a more radical plan. The landlord was to cede the *dominium utile* of his dominical lands to tenant farmers, who were then to pay cash rents for their holdings. In 1775 Maria Theresa introduced this system on a couple of estates confiscated from the Jesuits, and extended it afterwards to all such estates and to others over which she had direct control, including those belonging to the Royal Free and leibgeding boroughs. She was, however, again defeated (her son again leading the opposition) when, on 1 January 1776, she tried to get the system made compulsory in Bohemia. A few landlords, however, adopted it voluntarily, and these 'emphyteutic' tenants (as they were called even in common parlance) came to constitute an important category of the peasantry.

A landlord leasing a dominical holding to a 'contractualist' was not, on paper, allowed to impose on him harder terms than those in local usage for the rustical peasants. His landlord's rent was usually higher, since the peasant was not subject to some other obligations. The land tax, if any, was included in the rent and paid over by the landlord to the State. Here, again, the rent could be taken out in cash, kind or services. It was regularly paid in cash where the lessor was a municipality or other corporate body,[3] and cash rents were very common in the German-Austrian Lands, where many of the dominical estates were in the hands of Beamtenadel, who did not want to farm them themselves and were glad of the money rents. The monasteries also leased most of their lands, but took more of their rents out in services, partly out of conservatism, partly because they often owned big vineyards, for the cultivation of which this form was obviously appropriate.

[1] Grünberg I. 311.

[2] A patent for Bohemia was issued on 25 January 1770, and was followed by others, for Moravia, Silesia and Carniola. Only a few hundred peasants bought in their holdings in consequence of them, and these were nearly all men of German stock; the authorities in Silesia complained that the Poles refused to buy in, out of 'laziness'. F. Beidtel (I. 172) gives, indeed, a very different picture: he writes that during the next twenty years the peasants in the Bohemian Lands bought in their holdings so largely that by 1810 it was the exception to find one of the old type. I have been unable to find statistics on the point.

[3] In Hungary, in particular, the village towns leased for cash large areas of dominical land from neighbouring landlords, then sub-letting them in smallholdings, again for cash rents, to their civites. The technical status of these was 'free lease-holders'.

THE MONARCHY IN 1780

The landlord also made his own terms with his full-time labourers, and with rustical Innmänner who did more work for him than their obligatory stint. Such a man usually got a minute wage in cash, made up by an infinite variety of payments in cash or easements.

For a clear picture of the condition of the peasantry we should need to know many things more, such as the relationship between the areas of dominical and rustical land, and between the populations on them, the extent of the common lands, the average acreage actually held by a peasant cultivator, the proportion of cultivators to landless men, etc. Unfortunately, much of the information necessary for such a survey is lacking. No figures, for example, have survived of what counted respectively as dominical and rustical land in the Alpine Lands, and if they had survived, mere global percentages would be fairly meaningless, since those lands contained very much forest, much of which was unsuitable for peasant cultivation, and was, in fact, chiefly in the hands of the Crown or of big landlords.[1] They would, moreover, probably be misleading, owing to the large amount of concealment, especially of dominical land, practised by the lords in order to evade the land tax.[2] In this respect the censuses are only of partial help, since on the one hand they allow the title of 'peasant' to any person cultivating the required minimum of land, whether rustical or dominical;[3] on the other, they count as dwarf-holders or cottars not only all agriculturalists whose holdings fall below this minimum, again irrespective of the legal quality of their holdings, but also persons following a large number of occupations, not all of which are even rural.[4]

[1] Most Alpine communes, however, contained considerable tracts of communally owned forest land, and many of them extensive Alpine pastures for summer grazing, which were either communally owned, or, if belonging to the lord, subject only to an almost nominal fee.

[2] See below, p. 130.

[3] Technically speaking, only the cultivator of a quarter holding or upwards in Austria, or an eighth or upwards in Hungary (the eighth-holders in Hungary are said to have insisted on the rank out of reasons of pride) ranked as a 'peasant' (*Bauer, jobbágy*); those holding smaller parcels of land, or cottages only, or not even so much, were known by a variety of names: *Keuschler, Haüsler, Innmänner*, etc.; in Hungary, *házas* (housed) or *házatlan* (houseless) *zsellers*. The distinction was important from the recruiting sergeant's point of view, for a 'peasant' and his heir at law was exempt from military service, to which a dwarf-holder or landless man was subject.

[4] Under the instructions for Joseph II's census in Hungary (and these seem to have followed the normal rule) the term zseller was made to cover:
every married man, whatever his occupation, not entered as priest, noble, official, etc., burgher, peasant or heir at law of a burgher or peasant,
every widower with children,
all smaller employees of private persons,
regular workers in mines, salt-mines, shipping, road construction, felling and rafting of timber,
all males aged over forty or persons physically incapacitated for military service,
the sons of non-noble 'honoratiores' and of Protestant and Orthodox clergy.

In general it may be said that in the areas with dense populations and long records of uninterrupted cultivation, such as the Vorlande, the Italian-speaking areas and the Viennese Basin, a very high proportion, sometimes as much as ninety per cent, of the arable land and vineyards was rustical,[1] while most of the rest was leased, often for money rents. In other Lands the proportion was lower. In Bohemia fifty-eight per cent of the total area and nearly eighty per cent of the arable land was rustical; the area of arable dominical land in the province was about sixteen per cent of the total. About ten or twelve per cent of this was leased.[2] The figures for Moravia and Silesia were probably much the same. In Galicia as a whole 66·5% of the arable land was under 'rustical' cultivation (although the proportions varied considerably in different districts), but only a very small amount of the forests.[3] The great exception was that part of Hungary which had been recovered from the Turks round 1700, when large tracts of it had been almost uninhabited and there was practically no traditionally reserved urbarial land. Part of this, as we have seen, the Crown had reserved for itself, and settled with free peasants, but it had bestowed enormous tracts on great private beneficiaries. These landlords had to import labour from north and west Hungary, or abroad, and some of them established villages of urbarial peasants, but more usually, they kept most of their estates as sheep or cattle ranches, or alternatively, leased them to 'contractualists', sometimes via middle-men, such as municipalities. Thanks to these special conditions, Inner Hungary, the area of which was over 30 million hold, contained, according to Maria Theresa's urbarium, the abnormally low figure of only 153,528 whole *sessiones* (fractions being added together) totalling 5,639,029 *hold*.[4] This exceptionally high ratio of allodial to urbarial land, which did not alter greatly in subsequent decades,[5] proved a large factor in Hungary's later agrarian problem, since it meant that relatively little land was distributed under the 1848 reform. In the north and west of the country, however, where the population was denser, the relation between the arable and vineyards under the two types of tenure was probably not far from that prevailing in the Bohemian Lands and Galicia.

[1] So in the Viertel unter dem Wienerwald, east of Vienna, 86·4% of the arable land and 95·6% of the vineyards were rustical. The total proportion of rustical land was only 63·4%, but this was because 59·9% of the forests and 32·2% of the rough grazing were dominical.
In the two Austrias together, 79·8% of the arable land, 68·7% of the leys, 63·3% of the rough grazing and 20·4% of the forests were rustical.

[2] See Damian, op. cit., p. 75. Damian, working on 1792 figures, gives the total area of Bohemia at 7,769,601 yokes, of which 3,208,401 were dominical and 4,547,726 rustical. The figures for arable land alone were 3,608,205 total, 814,571 dominical and 2,793,633 rustical; for forests, 2,310,026 – 1,772,757 and 537,263.

[3] Brawer, op. cit., p. 59.

[4] Acsády, op. cit., pp. 389–90.

[5] According to I. Szabó, op. cit., p. 14, the arable land in peasant hands in Hungary in 1828 covered 5,020,675 hold and the allodial, 9,832,051. A figure for 1842 gives 69·5% of all cultivable land as allodial, but this included forests, etc.

THE MONARCHY IN 1780

In Croatia the figures were round sixty per cent rustical to forty per cent dominical. In Transylvania a high proportion of the total seems to have been dominical, but there again, the forests were very extensive.

The population was obviously denser on rustical land, since a lord cultiving his land for profit would employ as little labour as possible (and require little, on a forest or cattle-ranch). We must, of course, make allowance for the lease-holders,[1] but it is probable that three-quarters of the peasants in the Monarchy as a whole were rustical.

The average size of the holdings actually occupied again varied considerably, but in general, it is clear that by 1780 it was already the exception for either a rustical peasant or a leaseholder to hold a full sessio, still rarer, for him to hold more.[2] Here, again, it is possible to give figures for only a few Lands, but in Moravia, at the end of the century, there were 7,699 peasants holding whole sessiones, 4,375 with three-quarters each, 25,906 with half, and 25,616 with a quarter.[3] The figures for Bohemia and Silesia were probably similar. In Galicia the 'full' and 'half' peasants constituted only sixteen per cent of the total.[4] In Hungary (including Croatia and Slavonia), the statistician Schwartner found that in 1805 of the 1,426,579 non-noble holdings, dominical or urbarial, registered, 226,000 were whole or half, and 417,215 quarter.[5] The dwarf-holders and the even poorer classes of cottagers (*Keuschler, Gärtner, házas zsellerek*, etc.) who possessed their own cottages, normally with the conventional acre of allotment, and totally landless men (*Innmänner, házatlan zsellerek*) who had not even so much, formed the largest category of all: in 1781 they outnumbered the 'peasants' by three to one in the Hereditary and Bohemian Lands together,[6] the proportion being more favourable in the Tirol and the Littoral, where the figures were nearly equal, about two to one in Styria and Carinthia, and nearly four to one in Bohemia. In Hungary and Croatia the respective figures in 1784 were 509,823 'peasants' and 788,993 zsellers. Of these the poorest class of all, the totally landless men, may have numbered ten to twenty per cent according to the district.[7] For Galicia the figures were 89,824 'peasants' and 406,450 *Haüsler, Gärtner und beim Provinziale beschäftigte.*

---

[1] An inquiry held in Hungary in 1803 showed 762,593 non-noble 'houses' on rustical land and 494,402 on dominical.

[2] In Austria it was illegal for a peasant to hold more than one holding in villein tenure. He could, however, lease additional land. In Upper Austria it was not rare to find a peasant farming 200 yokes. In Hungary there was no legal bar, and there were cases in South Hungary of a peasant's holding up to six sessions.

[3] Grünberg, *Bauernbefreiung*, I. 52.

[4] Brawer, p. 23.

[5] Schwartner, *Statistik*, I. p. 204.

[6] The figures for heads of families were 555,000 and 1,596,810.

[7] The figures for Moravia gave 19,426 *Gärtner*, 71,086 *Haüsler* and 14,677 *Ausgedingshaüsler*, of whom only the last were entirely dependent on their labour.

This did not mean that more than half the peasant population of the Monarchy was living in a state of chronic destitution. As we have said, the terms Haüsler, zseller, etc., covered many persons not wholly or mainly employed in agriculture (the high figure in Bohemia, for example, is largely made up of home-workers in industry), and even the small agriculturalist might be a vintner or market-gardener (of the 783,344 zsellers found by Schwartner in Hungary in 1805, almost exactly 200,000 were vintners). Only urban 'intellectuals' unacquainted with the facts of rural life imagine that all members of rural society ought to be self-sufficient farmers. Even a peasant engaged exclusively in agriculture could often live comfortably enough, by the standards of the day, on as little as a quarter holding, especially if his commune was one owning much common land, or extensive grazing rights. Indeed, agronomes often complained that the size of the holding had been calculated too generously, and that smaller holdings, by compelling more intensive cultivation, would have resulted in bigger production.

At the date of which we are writing, the rural congestion which was later to become so alarming a feature of the Monarchy was only beginning to appear in certain districts of it, and there the peasant often had his remedy of decamping. The general economic problem of the Monarchy was still rather one of under- than over-population.[1]

The peasants' conditions were, however, greatly aggravated by their primitive methods of cultivation, and by the lack of storage facilities. If the harvest was bad, they were easily reduced to destitution. This had happened in Bohemia in 1771 and 1772, with the result that the population fell by fourteen per cent.[2] In 1782, when the harvest failed again, 32,000 persons in Bohemia were in receipt of public relief. In Hungary, in the same year, 24,995 *pauperes ostiatim mendicantes* were registered, and one person in every eighty in Pest, and one in every twenty-five in Pécs, was receiving relief.

The worst weakness of the peasant's position was his defencelessness *vis-à-vis* his lord and his lord's agents. In the Western Lands the Courts of the Gubernia took over from the Patrimonial at a fairly early stage, and the Kreisant officials supervised the work of the manorial officials fairly closely. But even there, and even as late as 1846, a writer, as we shall see, budgeted three per cent of a peasant's outgoings under the head of 'illegal exactions by manorial officials'.[3] In Hungary, where the local administration was even legally in the hands of the Counties, and still more, in Transylvania and Galicia, the supervision was hardly effective at all, and travellers in those

---

[1] I have found only one case (and that in the Vorlande) where Maria Theresa recommended the establishment of industries on the specific ground that the population was too dense to support itself by agriculture only. Far oftener it proved impossible to industrialize because man-power was short, even for agriculture.

[2] Kerner, p. 278.

[3] See below, p. 270, n. 1.

districts have horrifying things to tell of the tyranny exercised by bad landlords and abetted by Courts mainly composed of those same landlords.

At this date the Monarchy hardly possessed an industrial proletariat in the modern sense of the term. The craftsmen and journeymen of the guilds should be ranked rather as *petits bourgeois* (the apprentices were, indeed, sadly neglected and exploited). Many of the 'factories' were, as we have seen, minute enterprises, and the large ones, especially in Bohemia[1] operated largely with homework done in their cottages by small peasants or their families; sometimes the robot was taken out in this form. When Charles VI first tried to get factories going on a large scale, he tried to impress the sturdy beggars, mainly discharged soldiers, who were then roaming the countryside, to work them; but the sturdy beggars proved unsatisfactory workers, and the towns objected to their presence – this was one cause of the failure of his experiments. The newer factories, especially round Vienna, employed large numbers of foundling and other destitute children; some of them had been even set up by the State for the express purpose of providing for these unfortunates, who were very numerous. Women were also largely employed. The male adult wage-slaves were thus relatively few; they were still far from the day when they could rank as a factor in the State.

Austria would have been a white raven among States had it possessed much workers' protective legislation at so early a date, but it was not completely deficient in this respect. Apart from the guilds' own regulations, Maria Theresa issued a large number of enactments relating to working conditions.[2] Not a few of these were aimed at the difficult objective of compelling workers to honour their contracts, but a number were designed to prevent employers from exploiting them by imposing on them excessive hours of inadequate wages, and several laid down rules for the protection of young children.

V NATIONALITY

In the Hereditary Lands there had been no big shifts of population since the end of the great *Völkerwanderung* of the Dark Ages, and in 1780 the basic lines dividing the peoples were still approximately those on which they had halted nearly a thousand years before. All that the intervening centuries had brought had been some tidying-up through the natural assimilation of pockets of earlier populations which had survived the first arrival of the

---

[1] The great State woollens factory in Linz also operated exclusively with home-work.

[2] On these see Otruba, *Wirtschaftspolitik*, p. 182. His are almost the only pages on the subject known to me. Most writers tell us that Joseph II was the first ruler to introduce any protective legislation – even Brügel entirely ignores Maria Theresa's activities in this field. But while Joseph's enactments were far more extensive than his mother's, hers were by no means negligible.

newcomers; and in the opposite direction, the establishment of a few outposts of one people in what still remained basically the territory of another. Nearly all of these came from the foundation of German or Italian towns in predominately Slovene areas.

The tidying-up had been nearly complete in the main areas of German settlement, so that the Danube valley down to the Leitha, and the northern and central parts of the adjacent Alpine chain, comprising Austria Above and Below the Enns, northern and central Styria, northern Carinthia, the Tirol as far south as Solurn, and Vorarlberg (with the intervening Salzburg) were now as near as no matter solidly German.[1] In central and still more in southern Carinthia, where the early German colonization had been less intensive, enough Slovenes had survived to form, even so many centuries later, a perceptible minority, and in the southernmost third of Styria, all Carniola, Austrian Istria and the northern hinterland of Gorizia-Gradisca, the basic population was almost entirely Slovene, the German element being represented only in the towns.[2] Trieste, the South of Gorizia-Gradisca, and the Trentino up to Salurn, were Italian.

If we assume – and the assumption is fair enough for our purposes – that the proportions of the different nationalities were the same as half a century later, then the national composition of these Lands must in 1780 have been approximately as follows:

	Germans	Slovenes	Italians	Others
Lower Austria	1,200,000	—	—	—
Upper Austria	600,000	—	—	—
Styria	480,000	265,000	—	—
Carinthia	190,000	80,000	—	—
Carniola	20,000	370,000	—	10,000[3]
Gorizia-Gradisca, Istria, Trieste	10,000	130,000	55,000[4]	5,000[3]
Tirol	310,000	—	220,000[5]	20,000[6]
	2,810,000	845,000	275,000	35,000

[1] A few remnants of Romantsch or Ladin populations still survived in some valleys of the Tirol and Vorarlberg. The later Austrian censuses, which are based on language, count Ladin in with Italian, but the political historian should not follow this example, for most of the Ladins remained to the last *kaisertreu:* only a minority associated themselves politically with the Italians.

[2] South Styria also contained one island of German peasant population, in and around Göttschee, and Carniola, a few Croats, whose ancestors had taken refuge there from the Turks.

[3] Mainly Croats.

[4] Some German writers prefer to call the Italianate population of Gorizia-Gradisca 'Friulian' and there were indeed dialectal and other differences, still recognizable today, between the languages of these peoples and those of the Po valley. For all practical purposes, however, they may be counted as Italians.

[5] This figure includes the populations of the Sees of Trent and Brixen, which in 1780 did not, strictly speaking, belong to Austria.

[6] Ladins.

THE MONARCHY IN 1780

Czech and German historians dispute whether when the Czechs arrived – whenever that was – in Bohemia and Moravia, they found there remnants of an earlier German population. Whoever is right on this point, the general pattern which had emerged by the twelfth century was undoubtedly that of a Czech majority inhabiting the central plains of both Lands, partially surrounded by an incomplete ring of German settlements, some or all of which may have been autochthonous, and studded with German towns which had certainly been founded by German colonists invited in, chiefly in the twelfth and thirteenth centuries, by various Kings of Bohemia. This was still the ethnic pattern of the two Lands in 1780, although the proportions of the two nationalities had probably shifted since mediaeval times in favour of the Germans, for while both nationalities had suffered severe losses in the Thirty Years War, those of the Czechs had probably been the heavier, and after the wars, there had been some infiltration of Germans into devastated areas. The towns, which now probably contained a larger proportion of the total population than they had in the mediaeval Kingdom, were still almost entirely German, and the only gap in the German peripheral settlements was now on the Moravian-Hungarian frontier. Elsewhere they formed a thin but solid ring ranging in depth from five to ten to fifty to sixty miles, being deepest in North-West Bohemia and Northern Moravia. The same assumptions as before regarding the relative proportions of the two nationalities give a rough figure of 1,600,000 Czechs and 1,050,000 Germans in Bohemia, and 910,000 Czechs and 400,000 Germans in Moravia. Bohemia-Moravia also contained about fifty thousand Jews, some half of them concentrated in Prague.

Silesia, which had been attached to the Bohemian Crown only in the fourteenth century, contained, roughly, 150,000 Germans, 90,000 Poles and 60,000 Czechs, the Germans predominating in the West of the province, while the Poles and Czechs inhabited the areas adjacent to the frontiers of Galicia and Moravia respectively.

Ethnic conditions in the Lands of the Hungarian Crown were far more complex, for here a picture which had never been uniform had been further variegated by developments which in 1780 were still recent.

Arriving in the Middle Danube Basin as late as the end of the ninth century AD, the 'Hungarians' (who were themselves a mixed body, which included certain Turki and other elements besides the Magyars proper) had naturally found other peoples there before them: Moravian Slavs or proto-Slovaks[1] in the North-West, Slovenes in the West and South-West,

---

[1] This term glosses over another controversy on which the present writer does not feel himself competent to take sides. While most Czech writers maintain that the Slavonic inhabitants of Bohemia-Moravia and Northern Hungary originated as one people, which only later became differentiated into Czechs on the one hand and Slovaks on the other, the former

outposts of the Croats across the Drave, the mysterious people of the Szekels[1] in the central plains, and in Transylvania, a people described as Vlachs.[2] Furthermore, the pagan Magyars were a slave-owning people: they presumably brought non-Magyar slaves with them and certainly kept up the supply for nearly a century after by raiding their neighbours. These raids stopped with the national conversion to Christianity, but were replaced by a constant flow of immigration into the chronically under-populated country. More steppe peoples came in from the East, one body, that of the Cumans and Jazyges, who arrived in the thirteenth century, being a very large one. Germans were invited in, again in large numbers, to develop the country's economy as the burghers of the towns which now began to dot its surface, and to undertake special tasks; two of these latter groups were very large and important, the 'Transylvanian Saxons'[3] who were given extensive lands in Southern and North-Eastern Transylvania, as guardians of the passes, and another body of 'Saxons' imported to develop the mines of the Szepes area south-east of the Tatras. The Slavonic population of the north-west, now a distinguishably individual 'Slovak' people, was reinforced by further immigration from Moravia, Galicia and Silesia; Russians appeared in the north-east; more 'Vlachs' – these indubitably Roumanian-speaking – in Transylvania, and at least from the fifteenth century onward, Serbian refugees before the increasing Turkish pressure in the Balkans. By this time, moreover,

---

including most of the Slavs of Moravia, most Slovaks claim that the Czechs and Slovaks were always distinct, although kindred, peoples. The Slovaks had, indeed, formed part of the ninth-century 'Empire of Great Moravia', but the centre of gravity of that formation, in spite of its name, had lain east of the March (Morava).

[1] The ethnic origin of the Szekels is uncertain; they may have been of Turki stock. Within a century or so, however, their language was indubitably Magyar. Later they came to regard themselves, on the strength of a mistaken mediaeval Chronicle, as descendants of the Huns, and as the Magyars were at the time (again mistakenly) believed to be Huns, the Szekels looked on themselves as ethnically identical with the Magyars, but of older and purer lineage.

[2] When the documentary history of Transylvania begins (which is not until the thirteenth century), the only people mentioned in the documents, outside the Magyars themselves and others whose arrival there can be traced, is that of the 'Vlachs'. These 'Vlachs' are undoubtedly to be equated with the later Roumanians, but Hungarian and Roumanian scholars are not agreed whether they were descendants of the Roman settlers of the province of Dacia (or alternatively, of Romanized Dacians), who had survived the Dark Ages in their homes, or whether they were comparatively recent immigrants from the Balkans. In favour of the former view are the *a priori* probabilities, in favour of the latter, the fact that all the pre-Magyar place-names of Transylvania are Slav, except the names of four rivers, which are neither Dacian, nor Latin; and that the Roumanian language, while basically Latin, contains certain peculiarities which seem to indicate a formative period spent in the Western Balkans. If, however, the non-Magyar inhabitants of Transylvania in the Dark Ages were not Roumanian, they certainly Roumanized later, for no Slavs are recorded in Transylvania in historic times, except settlers whose provenance can be traced.

[3] In reality, most of these 'Saxons' came from the Rhineland or Luxemburg.

yet other elements had been introduced by the attachment to the Holy Crown of Croatia, with a population Italian on the sea-board and otherwise Croat.

It is true that by the sixteenth century much natural assimilation had taken place. All the peoples of steppe origin – the Magyars' original fellow-immigrants, the Szekels (who had been transferred to Eastern Transylvania, to guard its passes)[1] and the later arrivals alike – had Magyarized, as had nearly all the unfree populations of the central plains. These areas had become purely Magyar, and there were substantial pockets of Magyar settlement even in the periphery. Hungarian historians have calculated that around AD 1500 seventy-five to eighty per cent of the total population of Hungary (Croatia excluded) was Magyar-speaking. But the population of the north-west was still mainly Slovak; that of the north-east, such as it was (it was still very sparse), Russian, or, as these peoples were called, 'Ruthene'.[2] In Transylvania the Vlachs were now numerous, and the Saxons holding their own, and the Serbian immigration into South Hungary was growing extensive. And in Hungary, unlike any other of the Habsburg dominions, further very important ethnic changes had taken place between their acquisition of it, and Joseph II's accession. First the Turkish invasion and occupation, then the wars of liberation at the close of the seventeenth century, inflicted enormous damage on Hungary, and this was not evenly distributed. The brunt of it fell on the central plains, the strongholds of the Magyars. The population of the southern parts of these areas was practically wiped out – slaughtered or carried off into slavery – that of their central portions was grievously diminished, while the northern Carpathians – the national homes of the Slovaks and Ruthenes – and Transylvania escaped relatively lightly. Meanwhile, even under the Turkish occupation, a further immigration of Balkan elements had taken place, including a considerable movement of Croats north into that part of Hungary which was still under the Habsburgs. In the turbulent years round the turn of the seventeenth to eighteenth centuries there had been many fresh arrivals from the Balkans, including a large organized immigration of Serbs, perhaps two hundred thousand strong,[3] who arrived in South Hungary, led by their spiritual chief,

---

[1] Some Szekels were settled also on the Austrian frontier, but these soon lost their separate identity altogether.

[2] 'Ruthenus' was originally simply a Latin form of the word 'Russian'. Re-translated into other languages it then appeared as the special name for the persons of Russian descent living in Poland or Hungary. Meanwhile the centre of Russian national life had shifted north to Surdal and Moscow, whose peoples were recognizably distinct from the 'Ruthenes'. The ethnic and linguistic cousins, and geographical neighbours, of the Ruthenes were the peoples now called Ukrainians.

[3] This was for long the customary estimate. Later writers believe the figure to be an exaggeration, but many other, unrecorded, immigrations took place at about the same time, and the total of Orthodox immigrants was probably little, if at all, under 200,000.

the Patriarch of Ipek, in 1692, and many other, smaller contingents, including the Catholic Southern Slav peoples known as the Sokci and Bunyevci.[1]

These movements had slackened off (although they had not ceased altogether) by the time that more peaceful conditions returned; but the foreign element had been reinforced by the great process known as the impopulatio, or colonization of the empty spaces of Hungary with further settlers brought from abroad, these being chiefly Germans.[2]

Meanwhile, further changes in the distribution of the earlier populations had been going on. Many Magyars had returned to the plains from the mountains where they or their ancestors had taken refuge, while Slovaks, Ruthenes and Roumanians filled the empty spaces vacated by the Magyars and followed on their heels into the open areas adjacent to the mountains. A considerable number of Slovaks and a few Ruthenes were settled by landlords in the heart of the country.

By the end of the impopulatio, which coincided nearly enough with the end of Maria Theresa's reign, an ethnic map of Hungary which did not take account of the density of population would have looked very like one drawn in 1910, except that it would have been dotted more abundantly with small islets of local minorities. To begin with Hungary proper, the majority populations of the Northern Carpathians were Slovak in the west, Ruthene in the east, the line between these two running roughly southward from the Dukla Pass, although the Ruthene area of settlement extended west of this line in the higher mountains, and the Slovak, east of it further south. In these areas the Magyars were found chiefly in the towns and in a few of the more open basins. The 'Zipser Saxons' of the Szepes were dwindling, losing their identity to the Magyars or (more rarely) to the Slovaks.

The main dividing line between the Slavs of North Hungary and the Magyars followed, closely enough, the line where the foothills of the Carpathians melt into the plain, and from this line southward to one running roughly Pécs-Szabadka-Szeged-Arad the majority rural population was Magyar, but the fringe bordering the Austrian frontier was mainly German,[3] and there were many colonies of Germans (especially west of Buda), and some of Slovaks, and a chain of Croat settlements reaching right up to the Moravian frontier. The towns, except those between the Danube and the Tisza, were chiefly German, but many of them contained Serbian quarters.

---

[1] The Sokci came from Dalmatia, the Bunyevci from Bosnia. They were Serbs by origin, but had been converted to Catholicism by Franciscan friars, who then led them into Hungary. They seem to have arrived in 1682. See Macartney, *Hungary and her Successors*, p. 382 and n.

[2] These were generically known as 'Swabians', and Hungarian usage always distinguished rigidly between 'Swabians' and 'Saxons'. Only the older-established burghers of the towns were known as 'Germans'.

[3] Some of these populations, especially those of the extreme north-west, may have been pre-Magyar.

THE MONARCHY IN 1780

A surprising number of 'Greeks' (Hellenes, Serbs and Balkan Vlachs) were established throughout the country in one-man businesses.

The German fringe in the west ended below Szent Gotthard. Below it came a wedge of Slovenes, down to the Mur. The 'Muraköz' between the Mur and the Drave was now solidly Croat. There were other big German settlements north of Pécs and below the Pécs-Arad line the Magyars dwindled to a small minority. Here, in the great colonization area, were intermingled, Germans, Serbs and Catholic Slavs (Sokci round Mohács, Bunyevci round Szabadka). The colonists of the Bánát included Germans, Serbs, Bulgars, and even Frenchmen, Catalans and Cossacks. Its mountainous eastern end was chiefly Roumanian.

Civilian Croatia was solidly Croat outside the few towns, which were largely German, and the sea-board, where there were some Italians, but most of the Slavonian Counties were now Serb.

In Transylvania, the Roumanians were now indisputably the largest element: they had the higher land practically to themselves (except for the Hungarian landlords) and were even emerging into the plains. The Szekels, now completely Magyarized, formed a solid bloc of Magyar-speakers in the south-eastern corner of the Principality, and chains, not quite continuous, of Magyar settlement ran up the main valleys towards them. The biggest Magyar area, outside the Szekel Counties, was that encircling Kolozsvár. The Saxons were dwindling, not through assimilation, but because of their small families, but still strong in the south (round Nagyszeben), with small outposts at Brassó and Besztercze). Among the more interesting smaller ethnic fragments in the Principality may be mentioned the Armenians, descendants of a mass immigration which took place in 1672 to Transylvania and Galicia.

Finally, the gypsies of all Hungary were too numerous to be passed over in silence.

The approximate figures were as follows:

Inner Hungary: Magyars, 2,960,000; Germans, 775,000; Slovaks, 1,220,000; Ruthenes, 290,000; Roumanians, 635,000; Croats, 65,000; Serbs, 250,000; Sokci and Bunyevci, 40,000; Slovenes, 40,000; Jews, 85,000; gypsies, 75,000.

Civilian Croatia: Croats, 460,000; Serbs, 165,000; Italians, 15,000; Germans, 5,000.

Military Frontier: Croats, 360,000; Serbs, 240,000; Roumanians, 80,000; Germans, 30,000.

Transylvania: Roumanians, 850,000; Magyars, 400,000; Germans, 135,000; gypsies, 40,000; Jews, 5,000; others,[1] 10,000.

Total for the Lands of the Hungarian Crown: Magyars, 3,360,000; Germans, 945,000; Slovaks, 1,220,000; Ruthenes, 290,000; Roumanians, 1,565,000; Croats, 885,000; Serbs, 655,000; Jews, 90,000; gypsies, 135,000; others, 25,000.

[1] Including about 5,000 Armenians.

Statistics for Galicia are very uncertain, but broadly, the Western half, as far as the San, was predominantly Polish, the large German colonies settled there in earlier centuries having Polonized. The East was Ruthene by majority, but contained large Polish islets of population. Jews were very numerous in all Galicia, especially in the East. In the Bukovina, the northern half was Ukrainian, the southern, Roumanian. Here, too, there were many Jews. The total figures for Galicia-Bukovina were approximately 1,000,000 Poles, 1,500,000 Ruthenes-Ukrainians, 210,000 Jews, 50,000 Roumanians, and 10,000 Armenians.

If, then, we add in the 250,000 Germans of the Vorlande, the 1,500,000 Italians of the Milanese and the 2,000,000 Flemish and Walloons of the Netherlands, we get a grand total for the Monarchy of 5,650,000 Germans, 3,360,000 Magyars, 2,550,000 Czechs, 2,000,000 Flemish and Walloons, 1,800,000 Italians, 1,800,000 Ukrainians and Ruthenes, 1,600,000 Roumanians, 1,225,000 Slovaks, 1,000,000 Poles, 900,000 Croats, 700,000 Serbs, 350,000 Jews, 120,000 gypsies, with small numbers of Ladins, Armenians, Bulgars and other nationalities.

At later stages in this history, the population of the Netherlands will drop out, as will that of the Vorlande, but in place of the latter will come approximately the same number of Germans in Salzburg and the Innviertel of Upper Austria. The sees of Trent and Brixen will become integral parts of the Tirol. Venice, with 1·5–2 million Italians, comes in in 1797 and drops out finally in 1866. Dalmatia, when definitively acquired in 1815, had a population of a few thousand Italians and perhaps a quarter of a million Slavs, of whom about four-fifths were Croats (contemporary sources habitually describe them as 'Morlaks') and the remainder Serbs. The annexation of the Free City of Cracow in 1846 brought in another hundred thousand or so Poles, with the usual Galician leavening of Jews. Finally, the population of Bosnia-Herzegovina, when annexed by the Monarchy in 1908, consisted of about 1,600,000 persons, all of the same or kindred Southern Slav or Slavicized Morlak stocks, and speaking the same Slavonic language, with dialectical variants, but divided by religion into three elements, each with its own 'national' attachment: the members of the Orthodox Church, who regarded themselves as Serbs, the Catholics, who ranked as Croats, and the Moslems. The authorities never got down to taking a proper census, but authorities give the numbers as approximately 800,000 'Serbs', 600,000 Moslems and 400,000 'Croats'.[1]

---

[1] When, in the ninth century AD, the Slavs who had established themselves in the Balkans a couple of centuries earlier accepted Christianity, they did so roughly along the line already dividing the Eastern and Western Churches. This line ran through Bosnia, whose inhabitants west of the line accepted Roman Catholicism, and those east of it, the Orthodox Church.

A mere counting of heads would, however, give no adequate idea of the positions held by the different peoples in the political, social and economic life of the Monarchy of 1780. These differed very widely indeed. The crude picture so often drawn by publicists of 'ruling races' lording it over 'subject races' is, indeed, totally false so far as the Monarchy of the eighteenth century (and also that of the nineteenth and twentieth) is concerned. A certain master-subject relationship based on ethnic origin had indeed come into being in certain parts of the Monarchy, at certain earlier stages of their history; in the Alpine Lands when the Germans moved into them, on the Middle Danube when the Magyars first settled there. But even then the relationship had not been complete – not every German or Magyar had been a lord ranking above every Slav – and later centuries had blurred, where they had not entirely obliterated, the earlier ethnic dividing-lines between the privileged and the non-privileged. The social hierarchy which had developed since those early times took no account at all of ethnic origin in theory, and only accidentally, in practice. On the one hand, the vast majority of the eighteenth-century representatives of the old 'master races' now belonged to the non-privileged masses; on the other, the privileged classes now contained many men whose efforts, or their ancestors', had lifted them out of the servitude which had once been the general lot of their peoples.

It was, however, true that the start given to the national cultures of certain peoples by the military, political and (in some cases) cultural or economic superiority of their members over those of other peoples when contact between them first took place, had attracted to them those members of the weaker peoples who entered the ruling or propertied classes, or immigrants. There had thus really evolved hierarchies of national cultures, not, be it repeated, in the sense that any people lacked its unprivileged masses, but that some national cultures stopped short at the peasant-village priest level, while others continued upward through some or all of the higher grades of bourgeoisie, professional classes and lower or higher aristocracy.[1]

Bosnia seems at the time to have been chiefly Croat – the heart of the mediaeval Kingdom of Croatia lay, indeed, in Western Bosnia. These remote valleys, however, afterwards became a stronghold of Bogomilism, which was so persecuted by the Catholic Church that on the arrival of the Turks, most of the Bogomils, with some others, to a total of perhaps a quarter of the then population, accepted Islam. Later Turkish Governments established more Moslem colonists in Bosnia, and the proportion of Serbs to Croats was further changed, to the advantage of the former, by immigration of Croats into Hungarian Croatia, or even further, and by immigration from the South of Serbs, through which the so-called Lika district, far in the North-West of Bosnia, became almost purely Serb. The figures given above are those given by Südland (p. 585) and accepted by Hantsch (*Gesch.*, II. 568). R. W. Seton-Watson (*Southern Slav Question*) gives the Serbs and Moslems another 50,000 each.

[1] This brief sketch will not take account of the three peoples of the Monarchy whose position was quite peculiar: the Jews, the gypsies and the Armenians.

The special complexity of the pattern thus evoked in the Monarchy is due to the fact that the developments proceeded differently in the various Lands, or groups of Lands, before these came under Habsburg rule, while after that event, a new factor entered in the shape of *Gesammtmonarchisch* influences, these, again, being much stronger in some parts of the Monarchy than in others.

The national hierarchy in the Hereditary Lands very early assumed a shape which it was to retain into the nineteenth century. Here the Germans, of course, got off to a flying start. 'Austria' and Styria, on their foundation, were in every respect German principalities like any other in the Reich; the entire social hierarchies, from the princes through the nobility and educated classes, down to the peasantry, were nationally homogeneous. The extension of the Habsburg Hausmacht to its 1526 limits did not alter its political character, since practically all the additions had come into being as fiefs of the Reich, and most of the sub-fiefs had been distributed to German barons, knights or prelates, and in the Slovene areas, the social-national pattern soon adapted itself to the political. Where native nobles had been allowed to keep their estates, they or their descendants succumbed to the pull of the politically dominant and socially superior German element, and Germanized themselves. The same process took place also on the middle levels, for the Slovenes, then a very primitive people, had possessed neither towns deserving the name, nor a strong national Church. The local towns were founded or developed, the local Churches organized, by the Germans, and Slovenes entered them Germanized, like the nobles.[1] In these areas, therefore, the German national culture (although not the race, since many of the 'Germans' were of Slovene origin) did establish itself over the Slovene in a master-subject relationship, and the Slovenes remained a people of peasants and woodsmen, with no higher national culture of their own.

'Germandom' did not, it is true, acquire the same dominating position in the Italian-speaking Littoral and Trentino, for the Italians met the Germans, in most respects, on equal terms. Their language was one in which instruction could be, and was, given, and, not being averse to urban and middle-class occupations, they had their own national culture in their own strongholds,[2] and even imposed the same cultural and economic domination over the Slovenes of Gorizia and Istria (as they were doing under Venetian rule, over the Slavs and Morlaks of Dalmatia) as the Germans exercised further north.

[1] Cf. the circumstance, mentioned elsewhere (p. 111, n. 5), that as late as 1770 there were no Slovene schools at all in Styria, because the only purpose for which a Slovene ever sent his son to school was to learn German.

[2] Many of the 220,000 Italians listed above as inhabiting the South Tirol were politically only half in Austria up to the nineteenth century, being subjects of the medialized sees of Trent and Brixen. The independence of these sees from Habsburg rule was somewhat nominal, but sufficient to shield them against much interference from the lesser authorities. The administration of Trieste was purely Italian up to the eighteenth century.

Even politically, most of them had been governed by members of their own people, except on the very highest levels of all, until the great centralizing reforms of the eighteenth century.

The national evolution in the Lands of the Bohemian and Hungarian Crowns, up to their coming under Habsburg rule, was, of course, quite different. While due allowance must naturally be made for the differences between the mediaeval and modern outlooks on the question, yet it is fair to describe Bohemia-Moravia, at least up to the extinction of the national dynasty in 1311, as a Czech national state – Czech in its institutions, its spirit and its policy. The word 'national' could no longer be used of the policy of most of the foreign kings who ruled it from 1311 to 1458, but even under them, the Czech people had retained its near-monopoly of the nobility (whose non-Czech recruits Czechized) and thus constituted a genuine *Staatsvolk*, less solid than its German counterpart in the Historic Lands in the one respect that the towns and industries were mainly in the hands of the local Germans, but none the less, dominant; and if the Germans' charters and their economic and cultural standards, which were higher than those of the Czechs, preserved them from denationalization, except on the highest level, and even enabled them at times to play an important political role (especially in view of the political link between Bohemia and the Reich), they were still a minority.

The Czech national character of the Bohemian State had grown stronger again in the last half-century before the coming of the Habsburgs. From 1458 to 1471 the Czechs had been ruled by one of their own number, Georg Podiebrad; after him, until 1526, by the weak Jagiellon kings, under whom the native aristocracy completely dominated affairs. In that half-century the *officieux* compendium of Bohemian law, Victorin Cornelius Wscherd's *Nine Books on the Law of Bohemia*, laid down the principle that the Czechs were the only lawful inhabitants of the land; the Germans were 'foreigners'. In fact, all non-Czechs were so treated for many purposes, including the acquisition of noble estates and the holding of public office. Both German and Latin were almost completely banned from both administration and justice.

The political thought of mediaeval Hungary (excluding Croatia) simply equated the Hungarian 'political nation', the King's counterpart in the polity, notionally with the descendants of the original Magyar invaders, allowing no other element in the country a positive role or status in it. This theory, of course, no longer corresponded to the ethnic facts. The proposition that a Magyar was a free man had ceased to be true very soon after the Conquest with the growth of a Magyar or Magyarized unfree population, which by a very early date far outnumbered the freemen, and the converse proposition that a free man was a Magyar had also lost such anthropological truth as it had ever had with the large-scale ennoblement of non-Magyars, many of whom did not even speak Magyar. But the polity continued to regard itself as notionally Magyar in spirit and tradition, and its nobles as Magyars in the light of the higher truth, even if their names and their language itself might sometimes refute the claim.

Incidentally, the second or third generation of recruits to the upper strata of the nobility almost always Magyarized, even linguistically. Most of those 'nobles' who did not speak Magyar were really no more than free peasants who had been relieved of taxation in compensation for being required to bear arms.

Those inhabitants of mediaeval Hungary who remained non-Magyars in every sense of the term thus stood outside the community of the *Staatsvolk* in a relationship which was hardly the same in any two cases. Some of the Germans, notably the Transylvanian Saxons, maintained themselves as closely-knit national communities which on occasions even took up attitudes which were influenced by German national feeling, although they were usually content to live their own lives in a system which did not demand from them uniformity in non-essentials. The evolution of the Slovaks was more like that of the Austrian Slovenes, although the Magyar national culture being less penetrative than the German, they retained a fuller spiritual and intellectual life of their own than the Slovenes were able to do. Like them, however, they lost their most successful members, usually to Magyardom, and failed to develop any considerable nationally conscious aristocracy or bourgeoisie.

Assimilation to Magyardom was easy enough for either the local Germans or the Slovaks (or, once they had accepted Christianity, the immigrants from the steppes). It was more difficult for those peoples who were members of the Greek Orthodox Church, since while there was no linguistic test for the enjoyment of Hungarian nobility, there was a religious one: a noble had to be a Catholic, or, after their numbers had compelled the concession, a Protestant (Calvinist or Lutheran). The Serbs who entered Hungary in mediaeval times seem to have worn their religion very lightly, and to have accepted conversion and assimilation freely enough. Among the Roumanians of the day, the handicap of their Orthodox faith was reinforced by that of their vagrant habits, which made them look little better than gypsies to the lordly Magyars and smug Saxons. In their case too, conversion and assimilation skimmed off those members of the people who rose in the world, but such success stories were relatively few, and the position of most Roumanians could really be called that of a subject race. The mediaeval Constitution of Transylvania allowed them no separate representation *qua* Roumanians and little voice in practice in the affairs of the Grand Principality,[1] and the

[1] It should, however, be emphasized that the fashionable picture of a ruling Magyar 'race' dominating a subject Roumanian 'race' is incorrect. The three 'nations' of Transylvania were the Hungarian nobles, the Szekels and the Saxons. A substantial number of men of Roumanian stock enjoyed Hungarian nobility, and conversely, the great majority of the Magyars were non-nobles. But it is true that the Roumanian nobles were nearly all small men of the sandalled noble class, qualified to vote in elections but seldom or never standing as candidates unless they sloughed their Roumanianism.

Orthodox Church, to which at that time practically all of them belonged, did not rank as a 'received' religion.[1]

Croatia had its own nobility, which enjoyed the status and privileges of Hungarian nobility.

A new chapter opened with the unification of the three groups of Lands in 1526; although the changes which this initiated took place only gradually, and in a fashion which was far from simple.

The fashionable idea that the unification inaugurated an era of German domination is far from the mark. The Habsburgs of that day were not German-minded, nor even German. Ferdinand I came to Austria from Spain, and was himself unable, when he arrived, to speak German, bringing his courtiers and advisers with him, and his first violent clashes with his new subjects took place, not in Bohemia or Hungary, but in German Austria.[2] He insisted, indeed, from the first that the language of top-level administration must, in the interests of efficiency, be German, and employed some Germans even outside the capital in the offices through which he exercised his own functions (e.g. in the Camera), but did not attempt to restrict seriously the use of other languages outside those limits. Czech, for instance, was reaffirmed as the official language of all law-Courts in Bohemia as late as 1579.[3] Ferdinand's successors were born in Austria, and the usage which after the death of Charles V virtually vested the Imperial crown in the cadet branch of the family, restored the German element to the leading place among their subjects, direct or indirect, but the renewed division of the family property made the German lands ruled directly by the head of the House for many years less important than the non-German. The Emperor Rudolph made Prague his residence, and in the struggle between him and his brother Matthias at the beginning of the seventeenth century, the Moravian Estates extracted from Matthias recognition of Czech as the official language of Moravia, and in 1615 the Diet of Bohemia was able to secure inarticulation of a law that no one unacquainted with Czech might acquire noble *incolat* or burgher rights in Bohemia. Indeed, if any of the Habsburgs' subjects in the sixteenth century had to complain of denationalization, in any sense, it was the Germans of the Hereditary Lands. No one attempted to take away their German speech or *mores*, but their loyalty had now to be directed towards a supra-national dynasty.

But the Counter-Reformation was, in the main, carried through earliest in the German lands, and after that German nationalism was not identified

[1] See below, p. 107.
[2] It is true that from the day of his coronation Ferdinand was at war with that party of Hungarians who had elected Zápolya king, but he had no early 'national' difficulties with his own supporters.
[3] Under his reign German did, however, largely replace Czech as the official language in Silesia, the Lusatias, and some German areas of Bohemia.

with political resistance to Habsburg rule. Czech and Magyar nationalism were so identified, directly, or indirectly, through their continued association with Protestantism, and the consequence of the Czech rebellion of 1619 was that the Czech people fell from its position of a near-integrated *Staatsvolk*. Almost all the Czech nobility, higher and lower, perished or was driven into exile, their estates being confiscated and sold to or bestowed on a new set of Imperial servants (two-thirds of the land in Bohemia changed hands during the process). As the Czechs had possessed only a small urban middle-class, and even very few artisans, the effect was to reduce the nation, at one blow, to the peasant level, except in so far as any surviving aristocrats still acknowledged membership of it. They did not entirely fail to do so: they went on speaking Czech to their servants and their peasants (it was bad Czech, but their German was notoriously bad too) and their souls had room for a touch of Czech national consciousness, which was less an attachment to the Czech people than a romantic yearning for the ancient glories of the Kingdom of Bohemia, in which their ancestors had played such fine roles. A day was to come when, in a revived movement for the restoration of at least part of their old historic rights, a party among the Bohemian nobility found it worth while to protect and place themselves at the head of a wider Czech national revival, to which their patronage gave a weight not possessed by the parallel Slovene movement. But that day had not yet dawned when Joseph II ascended the throne. Meanwhile, the important families among whom a national tradition survived were only a handful.[1]

The downfall of the Czech aristocracy brought with it the first advance of the Germans to a leading position outside the Hereditary Lands. This still did not put the Germans of Bohemia quite into the position of those of the Slovene areas, for the new men on whom the lands confiscated from rebellious Czechs were bestowed were an extraordinarily miscellaneous set, drawn from all over Catholic Europe. They included Spaniards, Italians, Frenchmen and Irishmen. Some were 'Germans' by origin, but even they were not Germans by national feeling. At least in the seventeenth and eighteenth centuries the Bohemian aristocracy, as a class, constituted the most perfect representatives in the entire Monarchy of that special nationalism (there is no other word for it) which resided purely in attachment to the Monarch. Nevertheless, the real German element in Bohemia-Moravia took a step up. More colonists from the Alpine provinces or the Reich entered the country, and the new industrialisation brought the local Germandom further gains, since Czechs moving into towns or industrial centres usually Germanized. Meanwhile, the Vernewerte Landesordnung had already placed

[1] Only eight of the old great Czech families survived the change: the Czernins, Kinskys, Kolowrats, Lobkowitzes, Waldsteins, Schlicks, Sternbergs and Kaunitzes. That the names of three of the eight are German is due to the fact that the places from which they took their titles had German names.

the German language on an equality with the Czech in the Courts, while in the administration it was now the sole language, and a further important change was brought in the Western half of the Monarchy by the administrative reforms of Maria Theresa's 'first reform period'. Before their introduction, the language of top-level administration here had been partly Latin, partly German, while local administration and justice, which were largely conducted orally, were carried on, naturally and of necessity, in the language of the 'parties'. With the reforms, first the language of the Ministries became German, and then the change was extended right down to the lower levels, to satisfy the new and fussy insistence of the bureaucrats that everything possible must be in writing, so that it could be checked centrally. Thus the entire 'inner language' of the administration became German, and any person wishing to enter the State service had to be, or to make himself, a German-speaker.

The Germanization of the schools in Bohemia, described elsewhere,[1] was really only a logical and necessary consequence of the Germanization of the administration, but the two naturally worked together to produce a master-subject relationship of the two national cultures which was fairly complete, although time was to prove the impossibility of maintaining it in its entirety.

These changes had not reached Hungary[2] by 1780. Hardly any attempts had been made to Germanize that country before the series of conflicts between nation and Crown which opened with the 'Wesselényi conspiracy' of 1670. For a generation, then, strong efforts had been made to denationalize the administration[3] and aristocracy, but these had been abandoned under the Peace of Szatmár of 1711, having in the meantime met with only very partial success: the beneficiaries (unlike those in Bohemia, who had struck root and prospered there) had often found Hungarian conditions too outlandish for them and sold their estates, which had eventually found their way back into Magyar hands.

As has been said elsewhere,[4] Maria Theresa, using gentler methods, had, indeed, succeeded in largely denationalizing the magnates. But even less than their Bohemian counterparts did these men become German; in so far as they ceased to be Hungarian (and few of them were entirely exempt from occasional relapses) it was to become Habsburgists, pure and simple. And the Queen's blandishments hardly touched the great mass of medium and

---

[1] See below, p. 113.

[2] The following paragraphs do not apply to the Bánát or the Military Frontier, which, being under central administration, were being subjected to the same Germanization as the Western Lands.

[3] When the Constitution was suspended in 1673, Hungary was placed under a Directorate with a Council composed half of Germans. The official languages were proclaimed to be Latin and German, and officials were required to know German and 'Sclavonian', but not Magyar. But tthes measures had to be revoked in 1681.

[4] See above, p. 55.

small-medium nobles. If it was true that what interested them chiefly was the retention of their class privileges, political and economic, yet the national traditions and national culture were for them at once symbols and guarantees of their status, and they had not only maintained them themselves, but had been able to compel acceptance of the national tradition of the State even outside its frontiers.

It was true that the language of legislation and administration in Hungary, down to the County level, was Latin, as was that of practically all higher and secondary education, and of most of such literary products as the age could boast. Thanks to this, it was perfectly possible for an individual to rise to a high position in society, and even in the State apparatus, without knowing a word of Magyar; the Magyar character of the noble tradition was largely fictional. But this very quasi-fictional element in it made it the easier for the 'Magyar' national culture to maintain its priority in, and identification with, the State, and for the Catholic and Protestant non-Magyars to accept the position. They did not need their own national upper classes, because they could share in the Hungarian. Thus the Slovaks, in particular, were able to evolve a not inconsiderable intelligentsia which, if it found Slovak insufficient for self-expression, resorted happily enough to Magyar. If they rose a little higher still, they became trilingual (Slovak, Latin and Magyar). As nearly all of their neighbours who called themselves Magyars were trilingual also (they spoke Slovak, if only to make themselves understood locally, and most of them had picked up the language in infancy from their nursemaids, who, except in the snob families, were always Slovak peasant girls), it was really difficult for many of the inhabitants of North Hungary to say what they were 'nationally'.

In fact, the great majority of the Hungarian nobles were even now Magyar, by adoption if not by origin. The successful Slovaks, Ruthenes and even Swabians Magyarized in the second or third generation. Most of the non-Magyar speaking 'nobles' were sandalled nobles, whose 'nobility' amounted simply to exemption from taxation, and even they, although fairly numerous in certain outlying areas[1] constituted only a small proportion of the whole class,[2] and an infinitesimal one of its effective members. The reduction in the

---

[1] Prince Rákóczi, leader of the great Hungarian rebellion (or national war) at the beginning of the eighteenth century, who had started his campaigns in North-Eastern Hungary, had conferred common nobility very freely on his adherents, who included many Ruthenes, and also Slovaks and Roumanians. In 1787 the largely Roumanian County of Máramaros contained the highest proportion of nobles (16·6%) in all Hungary.

[2] Joseph II's censuses did not record language, but Fényes, in his statistical work published in 1842, states that when he wrote, there were in Hungary-Croatia (excluding, that is, Transylvania and the Frontier), 544,372 noble persons, of whom 464,705 were linguistic Magyars, about 58,000 Slavs and 21,000 Germans and Roumanians. Quite 35,000 of the 'Slavs' must have been Croats, leaving the Magyars a majority of something like ninety per cent in Inner Hungary.

proportion of Magyars to non-Magyars in the total population, fateful as it was to prove to Hungary in the nineteenth century, had thus had hardly any perceptible political effects in the eighteenth, since the only class that mattered was the effective fraction of the nobility.

Two of the peoples now inhabiting Lands of the Hungarian Crown remained, however, obstinately apart. The Roumanians (Vlachs) were one. When Leopold I confirmed the Transylvanian Constitution, he did so without amending it, so that the Roumanians, as such, remained unrepresented in the Diet and the Orthodox religion remained only 'tolerated'.

It is true that when the Uniate Church was introduced into Transylvania[1] the Roumanian representation in the 'Hungarian nation' was greatly increased, for all Greek Catholic priests, like all Roman Catholic, ranked as 'common nobles', and there were also an exceptionally large number of Roumanian sandalled nobles in Máramaros.[2] Thanks in part to this, a real Roumanian national renaissance had set in in the middle of the eighteenth century. Its inspirer was a certain Innocentius Klein-Micu,[3] who began to work as a Roumanian Uniate Bishop in 1732.[4] An exceptionally able and energetic man, Klein-Micu developed his see of Balázsfalva into a real centre of Roumanian national life, establishing there a primary and a secondary school, a seminary and a Basilite Monastery and further obtaining permission for some students to attend the College *De Propaganda Fidei* in Rome. He had strong ambitions for his nation, and besieged both the Transylvanian Gubernium and Vienna with petitions, not only for ecclesiastical facilities, but also for political concessions, asking that the Roumanian nobles should be admitted as a fourth political 'nation', with representation, in that capacity, in the Transylvanian Diet, a share in public office, etc. These requests were always justified by the theory of 'Daco-Roumanian continuity', which in his hands became a political weapon, never again to be laid aside by the Roumanians.

Eventually the Court got tired of him and when he went to Rome to ask the Holy See to intercede for him, persuaded the Pope to keep him there for the rest of his life. He had, however, left behind a considerable educated class, the product of his seminary, and an elite of men who had studied in Rome. Three of the latter, in particular, known as the 'Transylvanian Triade', carried on his work: his own nephew Samuel Klein-Micu (1745–1816) a grammarian and linguist; George Sinkay (1756–1816) author of a

---
[1] See below, p. 108.
[2] This was due to a lucky fluke. North-Eastern Hungary provided the bulk of Rákóczi's followers, whom he ennobled right and left. The Roumanians of Máramaros had accepted the Union just in time.
[3] Known alternatively by either of these names (both of which mean 'small') or by the two in combination.
[4] He had been consecrated Bishop in 1728, but was then still very young, and began officiating only in 1732.

'Chronicle of the Roumanians', a vast although ill-digested work strongly nationalist in tone; and Petru Maior, a slightly younger man who carried on Sinkay's work.[1]

Meanwhile the Orthodox Church, although not so well-endowed as the Uniate, was coming to represent another centre around which Roumanian national feeling could crystallize. At the same time, the social conditions of the Roumanians had become less tolerable than ever for them. In 1769 the Transylvanian Gubernium had issued an order, known as the *Gewisse Punkte*, the effect of which was to compel a large number of mountain shepherds to settle under landlords as peasant cultivators. This brought them within range of some more of the accepted trappings of civilization, but also forced them to work much harder, and the next decade was one of growing discontent.

This movement was genuinely national in a sense in which the word could not be used of any other in the Monarchy, except that of the Poles, because the Roumanians were, as has been said above, a semi-nomadic people, or at least, exceptionally lightly attached to the soil. Even in times of peace, the shepherds who formed a large part of the people were accustomed to drive their flocks to summer and winter pasturages which took little account of frontiers; when war harried them or social conditions became particularly onerous, either in Transylvania, or in the Principalities, whole communities would cheerfully transfer their habitats from one side of the Carpathians to the other. Consequently, an awareness of the identity of the whole Roumanian people always existed among them and any national movement among any part of them spoke for the people as a whole.

And in another respect, the Roumanian movement was more national even than that of the Poles, because the latter was identified with the noble class, and left the peasants untouched. The Roumanian people was socially almost homogeneous, for the few members of it who had climbed into the ranks of the higher Hungarian aristocracy had discarded their Roumanian feeling. No social gulf separated such Roumanian 'nobles' as there were – the Uniate priests and the inhabitants of various villages which had been enobled *en bloc* – from the rest of the people; at any rate, nothing to compare with that which separated any Roumanian from any Magyar or Saxon.

The Serbs were the other distinctive people. While the mediaeval Serbian immigrants into Hungary seem, as we have said, to have abandoned their faith and their language easily enough, it was otherwise with the large group led into Hungary by their Patriarch in 1692. Leopold I issued the newcomers with Privileges guaranteeing them the enjoyment of their customary rights, including the right of electing their own *Voivode*, or military leader. Meanwhile, they were to remain 'nothing other than an Austro-Politicum, and the nation itself a patrimony of the House of Austria and not of the Kingdom of

[1] Petru's history, which was in the main an extract from Sinkay's, was completed in 1815 but printed only (at Iasi) in 1851.

Hungary, under the sole jurisdiction of His Imperial-Royal Majesty'. It was in the Balkans, after their return thither, when the Austrian armies should have conquered the Northern Balkans, that the Serbs were to enjoy these privileges in perpetuity, but as the Austrian armies failed to accomplish this task, the Serbs perforce remained in Hungary. The Hungarians objected bitterly to the suggestion that the Serbs should receive a separate territory or 'national' organization, and in the end, they received neither: they lived, indeed, under a number of dispensations, some in Hungarian Counties, others in the Military Frontier, others in the Bánát, and they were never allowed to elect a Voivode, and only once a Vice-Voivode,[1] nor to extend their political organization to cover all the Serbs in Hungary. Nor were they given, as they had wished, their own Court Chancellery in Vienna, although they were allowed for a time a less imposing body (which gradually faded out and was abolished in 1777) called the *Hofdeputatio in Banaticis, Transylvanicis et Illyricis* to look after their cultural interests ('*quoad religiosa et spiritualia*'). Their religious liberties, however, were confirmed; a Serb Metropolitan See was established in Karlóca, and although the Orthodox Church was not 'received' in the constitutional sense, it yet enjoyed complete internal autonomy.

From the time of their establishment the Serbs of Southern Hungary[2] were, on religious and social grounds, bitterly hostile to the Hungarian State and to the Magyar people. These feelings were deliberately fostered by the Austrian authorities, who saw in the Serbs serviceable local tools to be used against Hungarian factiousness.[3] This role was assigned, in particular, to the Serbian Frontier Regiments,[4] which consequently became the apple of the Court's eye; its best soldiers for foreign wars, its most reliable agent for the preservation of the unity of the Monarchy at home.

We need not consider the position in Lombardy or the Netherlands. In Galicia history had brought about a position as between Poles and Ruthenes very similar to the German-Slovene relationship in the Hereditary Lands. The Poles of West Galicia formed a fully integrated nation, with a large class

[1] Once, however, in 1745, they were allowed to hold a 'National Congress'.

[2] The adjective is operative, for the Serbian trading communities further north (such existed in nearly all towns on the Danube, including Buda; the 'national centre' was in Szent Endre, a few miles north of Buda) lived in perfect amity with their Magyar and German neighbours.

[3] It is all too common to accuse Austrian monarchs of applying the principle of '*divide et impera*' when more often they were genuinely trying to unite incurably centrifugal peoples; but Kaunitz did write: 'the more obvious and disquieting the intention' (sc. of the Hungarians) 'becomes apparent of making a *vim unitam* out of Hungary, Transylvania, and the Illyrian nation, the more advisable and necessary does the principle of *divide et impera* become.'

[4] The officers in these regiments were Serb up to the rank of battalion commander inclusive: above that, they were drawn from the general professional pool, and thus were usually Germans.

of nobles, greater or smaller, weaker, indeed, than the Alpine Germans in that it had only a small native middle-class, trade and industry being mostly in the hands of the Jews, while the official classes had also been non-Polish since the Partition, and in that its peasantry was brutalized and oppressed, but still accustomed to regard itself as a Staatsvolk. In East Galicia the Poles had imposed their culture on the Ruthenes as the Germans had on the Slovenes. The entire Ruthene aristocracy had Polonized, and cultural life on its higher levels was dominated by the Polish Church, the Roman Catholic. The national church of the Ruthenes, the Greek Catholic, was ill-endowed and intellectually unpretentious, and outside its priests, the Ruthene people consisted almost entirely of peasants.

The Roumanians of the Bukovina had, during their Moldavian past, evolved their own land-owning aristocracy: the upper class of *Boyars*, and the humbler *Masils* and *Ruptaşi*, to whose ranks the Russians, during their occupation of the country from 1769 to 1774, had added a third category of '*Slactici*'. At least the big men were, however, thin on the ground in 1780, for a high proportion of them had emigrated, rather than submit to Austrian rule.[1] They had, indeed, been allowed to retain their lands, from which they drew rentals as absentee landlords, greatly to the detriment of the peasants, for the estates were sub-leased and sub-subleased, and every intermediary got a cut of some kind out of the unfortunate cultivator. The non-noble Roumanian people consisted of peasants, with a few village priests and monks of the Greek Orthodox Church, for here, as in Galicia, the secular 'middle-class' occupations were almost entirely in Jewish hands.

There was another national hierarchy in Dalmatia. The 'dominant culture' was Venetian, and the towns largely Italian or Italianized,[2] while the non-assimilated Morlak-Croat and Serb peasants lived, for the most part, under exceedingly backward conditions. In Bosnia, the landowning aristocracy was composed of the Moslem 'begs', and although the begs constituted only a small minority even among the Moslems, the humblest follower of Islam took precedence over any *giaour*.

The differences between the levels of cultural and material development achieved by the various peoples of the Monarchy did not, of course, reside solely in the fact that some of them possessed aristocracies and *hautes*

[1] Meynert, op. cit., pp. 321–2 writes that 'hardly a single landowner' in the Bukovina was not residing in Iaşi, where they had Court or administrative jobs. Prokopowitsch writes (op. cit., p. 36) that when the Bukovinian nobles were required, in 1779, to take the oath of loyalty to Austria, only twenty-one Boyars and 354 lesser nobles did so; all the rest preferred to emigrate.

[2] More the latter; surnames, both in Dalmatia and in Venice itself, reveal that a surprisingly large number of 'Venetian' nobles came from Croat families. The Dalmatian towns themselves were far more Croat, even in speech, than is often realized.

bourgeoisies of their own, while others stopped short on the peasant-village priest level. Travellers, both Austrian and foreign, who toured the Monarchy in these years, and set down their impressions of its peasantries (the classes above the peasant level are usually treated as broadly homogeneous, except for such special cases as the Polish or Hungarian small nobles, or the Galician and North Hungarian Jews), accepted this truth as candidly as though they were modern anthropologists investigating the lives of Central African or Polynesian natives. Thus the gypsies are invariably treated as practically sub-human, especially that sub-species of them which resided on the outskirts of every Transylvanian village, doing the jobs which no one else would touch, such as that of scavenger and public hangman.[1] These, writes Damian, lived in such degradation that the authorities did not attempt either to tax them or to press them into military service.[2] Bendant found them 'indolent and vicious', and 'the women, especially, very disgusting'.[3] The Transylvanian Vlachs (or rather, the male of the species: the women are usually described as hard-working and decent) come off little better. Damian writes of them that

... they are still some centuries behind the other inhabitants of the province in the development of their physical, moral and intellectual standards. One finds many of them who have hardly anything human about them except a human form, and even that is distorted and disfigured by goitres and other deformities. This physical barbarousness is coupled with an addiction to drunkenness and to sensual licence. Industry and diligence are no less foreign to them. Most of them laze about behind their sheep, others lounge round the country as carters.[4]

Bendant, writing rather later, is no kinder to the unfortunate Vlachs:

... of an aspect rather lively but of a brutal and perverse character ... filthy and ill-clothed ... immoderately addicted to drinking brandy.... Their national character is crafty, vindictive, pilfering and superstitious, with no fixed principles of morality or religion. To which, when we add that they are destitute of arts and civilisation, their condition must evidently be abject, and we need not wonder if the Hungarians, as well as other nations, treat them like slaves.[5]

The features of the life of the Polish and Ruthene peasant which strike observers most forcibly are the extreme squalor in which he and his wife live – a one-roomed clay and wattle hut, without windows or chimney,[6] shared by

---

[1] Gypsies were regularly used by the Turks as hangmen at least up to the 1870s.

[2] Op. cit. II. 44. According to Damian, Joseph II tried to extend these obligations to them, but the restoration of the Transylvanian Constitution in 1791 'gave them back their reluctantly renounced right to be degraded'.

[3] *Travels in Hungary*, p. 12.

[4] Id., p. 49. Damian has taken this from a little anonymous work entitled *Ueber den Nationalcharakter der in Siebenbürgen befindlichen Nationen* (Vienna, 1792).

[5] Op. cit., pp. 7–8.

[6] As late as the 1930s, the Ruthenes south of the Carpathians could not be induced to give their houses chimneys, because they took the noise of the wind howling in them for the voice of a malignant ghost.

the poultry all the year round and by the family horse and cow in winter – his invincible sloth, and his (and her) inordinate addiction to strong liquor, of which he (and she) consumed fabulous quantities. Damian writes:

> When a Galician peasant goes to market, he calles in on the way at various Jewish taverns and takes a drink on credit. On the way back he repeats the visit and drinks away half, sometimes all, of what he has made at the market. He drinks 20–30 glasses of schnapps at a sitting. His wife is not a hairs-breadth behind him. On Sundays after Mass they foregather in the tavern and drink schnapps all day, without a crumb of bread, until sundown, when they stagger home.[1]

'Altogether,' writes Damian, 'idleness and stupidity are still the chief characteristics of the Polish people.' And on this point, too, Damian's description, drastic as it is, is borne out by other testimony. An official in 1780 calculated the average annual consumption of spirits by a peasant family in Galicia at 122 quarts; 50 for the head of the family, 40 for its other members and 32 for 'feasts, solemnities, etc.' A quart cost 6 kreuzers, which was the calculated value of a day's haulage robot performed with two animals. One consequence of this was that the peasants were in permanent debt to the Jewish innkeepers, to whom, however, they seem to have borne no ill-will, regarding them rather as fellow-sufferers under the yoke of the landlord, the ultimate recipient of the money.[2]

The descriptions of the Southern Slavs of Hungary, Croatia and Dalmatia are usually kinder. The note of really venomous contempt which we find in almost all travellers' observations on the unfortunate 'Vlachs' does not recur in their accounts of the Serbs, Croats and Morlaks, who are usually credited with some attractive qualities: they are frank and hospitable, the men doughty fighters, the women pre-maritally chaste. But these peoples, too live under the most primitive material conditions imaginable; they, too, consume vast quantities of strong liquors and in their case, too, the need to satisfy this craving is the only inducement, other than compulsion, which can persuade their males to do a hand's-turn of work; practically all their other needs are taken care of by their women-folk, who spin, cook and even reap the fields (a sickle, with which the reaping was done, was regarded as an unmanly implement). The Magyar peasant is only a little better, especially in respect of industry: his own country-men, while claiming him to drink less than the Slovaks, and to be prouder, more intelligent and cleaner in his habits than they, admit him to be more indolent, less hard-working; all he asks of life is a weather-proof cottage, a sheepskin *bunda* and a sufficiency of bread and fat bacon, and if he has these, he will not stir for more. Risbeck robustly lumps together all the peoples of Hungary, except some of the

---

[1] Damian II. 27.

[2] Brawer, op. cit., p. 43. According to him, the records of the Lemberg Gubernium contain no complaints by peasants against the Jews, whom, on the contrary, they regarded as their allies and advisers against the landlords. For the propinatio, see above, p. 63, n. 3.

German colonists and the Court-polished aristocracy, as 'still in a barbarous state'.[1] Of the 'lesser' peoples of the Monarchy, only the Czechs come off better, and that largely *ex silentio*; travellers regard Bohemia as a German land, and only perhaps remark that some of its inhabitants speak 'Sclavonian', without finding any noteworthy distinction of *mores* or standards between them and the local Germans.

These testimonies agree too closely not to carry conviction, especially when we find them repeated almost exactly decade after decade. Bendant, writing in the 1820s, while favourably impressed by conditions in West Hungary, found the Magyar herdsmen of the Alföld 'as rude and savage as the animals among which they dwelt'.[2] The Englishman, Russell, notes of his journey through Silesia in 1824 that 'the nearer one approaches to the frontier of Poland, the further he recedes from the industry and diligence of the pure German portions of the province; instead of Saxon activity and liveliness, he encounters Polish misery and servility'.[3] Similarly, when passing southward through Styria, 'instead of the substantial dwellings in the other parts of the province, nothing can exceed the misery of the peasantry'.[4] The Slovene peasants seen by him lived in log cabins of one room, with one small window and no chimney. In Carniola they lived on 'black broth, thick with vegetables, still blacker bread, and sometimes a scanty platter of small, rank, watery potatoes'.[5]

Hain, at the end of the 1840s, has exactly the same hierarchy. He, too, concedes the Czechs' industry, and brackets them top with the Germans and Italians. The Magyars, Slovenes, Slovaks, Poles and Ruthenes come in a middle category, the Serbs, Croats and Roumanians last. The Southern Slavs are 'idle and negligent, and work only with the most miserable implements ... The Morlack, while brave and hospitable, dislikes work so passionately that only the threat of hunger can overcome his indolence'.[6] The East and South-East of the Monarchy has no conception of the diligence and unresting endeavours with which agriculture is carried on in the Alpine Lands and Lombardy.[7]

It is more striking still that Bruck makes exactly the same points in the memorandum submitted by him to the Emperor in 1860.[8] Of all the peoples of the Monarchy, he allows only the Germans, the Italians and the Czechs some willingness to work, whence the areas inhabited by them are relatively prosperous. But 'in nearly all Hungary and Croatia and Slavonia, in Galicia and the Bukovina', all development is held back for lack of satisfactory labour, 'because a few hours' work a day, or a few days' work a week, are often sufficient to satisfy the modest needs and claims of the family. The rest of the time is spent in brutish sloth, or in the tavern.'

[1] Risbeck, op. cit., II. 241.
[2] *Travels in Hungary*, p. 116.
[3] Russell, op. cit., II. 187.
[4] Id., p. 355.
[5] Id., p. 300.
[6] Hain, I. 189.
[7] Id., II. 16.
[8] See below, p. 497.

There is, indeed, no need to labour the point. The same gradations, if perhaps less steep, were perceptibly present in the inter-war years, and it would be surprising if they had vanished altogether even today.

There was one virtue which a member of such a 'backward people' might possess which made him a valuable 'subject', however unsatisfactory he was in other respects. He might be a good fighter. Such were, in particular, the Serbs and Croats, and we find them praised by travellers and esteemed by authority for that reason. Others of these peoples were not commonly credited even with this redeeming quality.

These observations obviously do not justify a God's eye classification of the peoples of the Monarchy into better and worse. None of the writers whom we have quoted had a true anthropologist's eye. All of them were, consciously or unconsciously, applying the criterion of social utility: how far were the objects of their observations profitable members of the community, in virtue either of military prowess, or of ability and willingness to benefit themselves, their masters, and the State by plus-values produced by their diligence, sobriety and thrift, stimulated by appreciation of the rewards of those qualities. And when that criterion was applied, the Germans and Italians unquestionably towered above the other peoples of the Monarchy. If not naturally more intelligent, certainly not more artistic, they had learnt to use their brains. They were, by comparison, industrious, methodical, dependable, sober and clean. They appreciated material comfort and did not mind working for it. They were unreluctant town-dwellers, skilful artisans, enlightened farmers, men capable of rising in the world.

These were the qualities (apart from that of usefulness as cannon fodder) which made a people valuable 'subjects' to a Monarch, and from the Habsburgs' point of view the Germans were, of course, far more important than the Italians. The latter were peripheral, and not numerous in the Central Monarchy, where the Germans, on the other hand, constituted the largest single nationality, which further enjoyed the unique advantage of being represented in practically every Land of the Monarchy, in most of them, in numbers sufficient to make them locally important: in the Central Monarchy, it was only in Galicia, the Bukovina, Croatia and Carniola that their numbers were insignificant in 1780.[1] They were even more easily the most numerous and important people of the Habsburgs' subjects if we take into account their indirect subjects in the German Empire; and this we must do. It was true that by this time the titles of German King and Emperor had, as we have seen, become mere shadows; nevertheless, they were still the loftiest of all those to which the Habsburgs could aspire and those most dearly cherished by them, and it was to the maintenance of their Imperial position that their world policy was nearly always primarily directed. While this did

[1] Joseph II afterwards greatly strengthened the German element in Galicia, the Bukovina and Hungary.

not in the least inhibit them from ruling over non-Germans, such rule was always in some sense a secondary objective, valued chiefly by the criterion of how far it contributed towards the real goal, and those peoples were essentially instruments or auxiliaries. There was still something of partnership in the relationship towards the Reich of the German King and his German subjects.

This apart, the prestige of the Austrian Court attracted to it a steady stream of ambitious young men from the smaller Principalities, desirous of taking service with it, so that if the Monarch ran short of native officers, civil servants or professional men and intellectuals, he could draw on a well-nigh inexhaustible reservoir of serviceable material from the Reich. The recruits so obtained were not few in numbers, and in quality probably superior, man for man, to the native products. We shall see in the ensuing pages how much Austria owed to them.

When all this is considered, it is not in the least surprising that when Maria Theresa and her advisers created their centralized administration in the Hereditary and Bohemian Lands, and also their centralized army, they should have made the language of the services German. If there were to be such central services, efficiency demanded that they should be conducted in one language, and as things stood, that language could be no other than the German. And when German (Austro-German and other) writers claim, as they are fond of doing, that Maria Theresa's measures, and even those of her son, did not constitute 'Germanization' in the later sense of the term, they are justified up to a point. Neither the Empress nor her son was a German nationalist in the sense that either would have derived any Treitschkeian satisfaction from a feeling of having advanced the ethnic frontiers or enhanced the glory of the German Volk as such. The German language and culture were for them simply vehicles for the consolidation of the Monarchy and the efficient conduct of its affairs, and they were quite uninterested in the ethnic origin of their servants, provided they did their work efficiently and loyally. For that matter, it was not even a hundred per cent Teutonic culture that their non-German subjects were being asked to accept, for their countless forebears who had acquired it in earlier times had brought to it their own contributions, which had made of it something which differed in many respects – often strongly to its advantage – from what the worthy and efficient, but stolid and unprepossessing Teutons could have evolved from their own stock, unlightened by this cross-fertilization.[1]

---

[1] In this connection we may draw attention to the fallacies and exaggerations in the claim made by some Germans that their ancestors had carried out a mission for which the world should thank them in civilizing the barbarous peoples round them, and had exhausted themselves in doing so. There is much truth in the first half of this claim: the work of the German missionaries (in the early days) and of German burghers and peasant colonists, down to the nineteenth century, bears witness to it. But it was rather the non-Germans who 'exhausted' themselves, in ceding to the upper stratum of the Monarchy their own more progressive and ambitious elements, who thereafter figured on the roll of honour of 'German' culture.

It is particularly easy to understand when we remember that when the reforms were first introduced, Austria had not yet acquired Galicia, and had only just lost, and still hoped to recover, Silesia; it was thus far more Germanic than it was destined to become a few years later. Silesia was, indeed, the place of origin of the chief author of the reforms, Count Haugwitz.

Nevertheless, the linguistic Germanization of the services, especially taken together with the Germanization of much of the educational system which was its necessary accompaniment, did amount to the imposition of a Germanic culture on the public and much of the social life of the Lands in which it was introduced, and once national feeling awoke among the other peoples of the Monarchy, none of them would gladly submit to having its affairs conducted in a language, and its general cultural life adapted to a pattern, which was not its own, least of all if the language and the pattern were those of a people living in political association with them. This would be galling even if the spirit of the State and of its servants was one of complete national neutrality; if either the Monarch or his servants departed from that neutrality, the relationship would become intolerable. And we may remark that it was putting a great strain on the Germans themselves to place their national culture in this favoured position, and to ask them to regard it as not their own.

Our narrative will be largely concerned with the awakening of the national spirit among the peoples of the Monarchy, and with its impact on the structure of the State. The problem at issue was really a two-fold one, although there was inevitably much overlapping of the two elements. One was the fundamental question whether the philosophic basis of the Monarchy was to be the national principle in any form, or whether the State was to be an a-national or supra-national one. One leit-motif of our story will be the slow and reluctant retreat from the latter position of its supporters, the Monarchs themselves and a band of their servants which, while never reduced to complete extinction, yet dwindled steadily from decade to decade. The second problem, which emerged increasingly into the foreground, was that of adjusting the rival claims of the different nationalities so as to form a multi-national State satisfactory to enough of them to be viable. This would hardly be possible if national aspirations were asserted to the limit, since the extreme claim of nineteenth and early twentieth-century nationalism was that all members of every nation ought to be united in a single sovereign national State; and it was the fatality of the Monarchy that in no single case was one of its political frontiers also an ethnic frontier. There were Germans inside the Monarchy, and Germans outside it; Italians inside it, and outside; and so too with the Poles, the Ukrainians (when the Ruthenes of the Monarchy came to feel themselves Ukrainians), Roumanians, Serbs and Croats, and in each case, except that of the Croats, the numbers outside the Monarchy exceeded those inside it. Only the Czechs, Magyars, Slovaks and Slovenes had no ethnic kinsmen outside the Monarchy, and if the Slovenes chose to regard themselves as Yugoslavs, they would drop off the list. If the Croats took the same view, they too would form part of a nation with its centre of gravity outside the Monarchy.

The history of the development of national feeling in the Monarchy is not, however, simply one of the growth of irredentism, even among those peoples who could be irredentist. Irredentism was hardly ever more than a last stage, and one which some of them, owing to their geographical situation, never reached at all; others, not until the clock had warned for the twelfth hour. Up to that moment, the centripetal forces in the Monarchy were still very strong, but the problem of producing general national satisfaction was extraordinarily difficult, partly owing to the history-produced stratification of national cultures which we have described. The peoples whom the developments of past centuries had left in positions of social, economic and cultural inferiority could not be satisfied until the leeway had been made up, and they had received political institutions which put them on an equality with those who had before led in the race. The latter, naturally, defended positions achieved by them in history and usually legitimized by historic rights. These, of course, were not only Germans, although the problem of the Germans affected the whole Monarchy in a way that no other did, but also, in their respective local spheres, the Magyars in Hungary, the Poles in Galicia, even the Croats and the Italians of Dalmatia.

These struggles came to turn largely round the eternal central problem of the Monarchy, the relationship between the whole and its parts. We have emphasized how very strong, both constitutionally and sentimentally, was the tradition of the separate entities of the different Lands. But these traditions conflicted with ethnic considerations. Hardly any Land in the Central Monarchy was ethnically homogeneous, and conversely, hardly any nationality was confined to a single Land. Of all the Lands with which this history will be concerned, other than incidentally,[1] only Austria (Lower[2] and Upper), Salzburg and Vorarlberg were uni-national, being in each case purely German. The Tirol contained a German majority and an Italian minority; Styria and Carinthia, German majorities and Slovene minorities; Carniola, a Slovene majority and a small, but important, German minority;

[1] That is, leaving out the Vorlande, the Netherlands and Lombardy-Venetia (which was also homogeneous), but including, for convenience' sake, Salzburg and Dalmatia.

[2] Vienna was always a great cosmopolitan city, and as it grew in the nineteenth century, it received many non-German immigrants from all parts of the Monarchy of which it was the capital, but these were generally irrelevant from the point of view of the national struggle. Only the Czechs were numerous enough to make their presence felt, and they could not constitute any genuine national problem. When Czechs tried to magnify, or Germans to minimize, the importance of this honest army of tailors, cobblers and maidservants, both were doing so with an eye on Bohemia, or on the Gesammtmonarchie.

the Littoral, Italians and Southern Slavs; Bohemia and Moravia, Czech majorities and German minorities; Silesia, Germans, Poles and Czechs; Galicia, Poles and Ruthenes; the Bukovina, Roumanians and Ruthenes. Inner Hungary contained eight sizeable peoples, besides Jews and gypsies; Transylvania, Roumanians, Magyars and Germans; Croatia, Croats and Serbs; the Military Frontier, these two, besides Germans and Roumanians.

Germans were found in every Land of the Monarchy, in perceptible numbers in thirteen of those considered here; Slovenes in five; Italians and Croats in four each; Czechs, Serbs and Ruthenes in three each and Magyars and Poles each in two. Only Slovaks were in one alone,[1] and if they identified themselves with the Czechs, the number of Lands in which Czecho-Slovaks were found would be four.

When the national struggle did develop, it turned largely round the Lands. Only a few very bold spirits ever advocated abolishing the Lands altogether, and the infinitely numerous arguments fall into two categories: those advocating, or resisting, adjustment of the boundaries of the Lands to agree with national distribution, these ranging from minor proposals for boundary revision to enormous schemes for dismembering Hungary or uniting all the Southern Slav areas of the Monarchy in one great unit; and those which concentrated rather on the relationship between the Lands and the central authority, these again taking innumerable forms of centralism, dualism, trialism and federalism. It should be added that it would be misleading to represent the struggles in the simple form of a battle between the new force of nationality and the antique forms of the historic-political individualities. In certain cases, as when the Slovaks demanded and the Hungarian Parliament refused an autonomous Slovak territory, this was true, but very often the new nationalism identified itself with the historic traditions, and tried to utilize them to its own advantage.

In 1780 there were still few signs that within a short term of years the Monarchy would fall victim to national convulsions which would not leave it until they had destroyed it. The administrative centralization thitherto carried through had gone off quite smoothly; whereas the earlier transference of the seat of the Bohemian Court Chancellery to Vienna had evoked the liveliest protests from Prague, no objections at all had been raised to the amalgamation of the Austrian and Bohemian Chancelleries; still less to the educational reforms described below.[2] These had, indeed, themselves sown the seeds of the later Czech and Slovene national revivals, for although the schooling which was now being administered to all pupils who got past the elementary stage was in German, it was nevertheless schooling, which did

[1] It is true that the south-eastern corner of Moravia contained some Slovaks. The family of President Masaryk was among these.
[2] See below, p. 113.

not preclude and might even stimulate interest in the national pasts. But the shoots which this seed was bearing had hardly yet begun to pierce the surface, and looked entirely innocent. Meanwhile, the Germanization of the schools had been rather welcomed than otherwise, as opening the doors of the public services to boys of Czech or Slovene mother-tongue.

As for the Austrian-Germans, they were quite content with the position of Austria in Germany, and of themselves in Austria. They did not feel this threatened, and there are no signs that they regarded it as conferring on themselves any 'national' mission in the Monarchy. Even in introducing non-Germans to the German language and way of life, their officials were not furthering their own national cause, but serving and helping to consolidate the State.

Thitherto, however, the application of these measures had been practically confined to those parts of the Monarchy which were controlled by the Vereinigte Hofkanzlei, where Germanic cultural domination was a long-established fact; no attempt had been made (outside the special case of the Military Frontier) to extend them to areas unused to that domination, and it was not intended ever to apply them to the Netherlands or the Milanese, which would remain, administratively, *corpora separata*. But it would hardly be possible so to leave Galicia, where the Polish nobles were already nationally awake in a high degree, smarting under the loss of their sovereign national State, entirely unreconciled to being under Austrian rule and certain to resent and resist any attempt to consolidate that rule. Up to 1780 Galicia had simply been ruled as a conquered country, but the problem of integrating it into the Monarchy would have to be faced one day.

Then there were the Lands of the Hungarian Crown. The Magyars' own historians count the years of Maria Theresa's reign as the most slumbrous, nationally, of all their history, and we can even understand Joseph's belief that they would not resist Germanization when we recall the recommendation of the Hungarian *Ratio Educationis* in favour of far-reaching Germanization of the schools, a measure which was, for that matter, urged also by the ardent young patriot, Kazinczy, the father of the later Magyar linguistic revival, himself. But Kazinczy's motive, and also that of the Hungarian co-authors of the *Ratio*, was not to further assimilation of Hungary into the Gesammtmonarchie, but to strengthen the Magyar people by making the works of Western civilization available to it and thus raising its cultural level.

It is true that Hungarian nationalism was still essentially political, a defence of noble privileges whose benefits to those enjoying them were mainly financial, and entirely unconnected with what language they spoke. The identification of them with Magyardom was still mainly presumptive. It would, however, require only a touch to turn the presumption into a conscious feeling.

And a national revival in the modern sense of the term was already setting in, this also owing something, indirectly, to Maria Theresa, for its first stirrings began among the young men who had studied at the academy founded by the Queen in Vienna for the sons of nobles (the famous Theresianum) or had served in the Noble Hungarian Bodyguard. It was young Guards officers who produced the first modern poems and dramas written in the vernacular. In 1776 the most famous of these, George Bessenyei, struck a genuinely modern note in his pamphlet '*Magyarsåg*', which was an impassioned plea for the Magyar spirit, free from all political and class considerations, and for the Magyar language; for, he wrote, 'never, anywhere on earth, did a nation acquire wisdom and depth until it had introduced the sciences into its own tongue. Any nation can become learned in its own language, but not in an alien one.' The pamphlet, incidentally, raised and faced Hungary's future problem by recommending the linguistic Magyarization of Hungary's non-Magyar peoples.

And many of these were not even so nationally passive as the Magyars. We have described the active nationalism still, or again, alive among the Serbs and Roumanians, and should not omit mention of the Transylvanian Saxons, who throughout all their history had ever found eternal vigilance the necessary price of their hard-earned religious freedom and advanced social and economic positions, and were in 1780 probably the most conscious German nationalists in the world.

VI CULTURAL CONDITIONS

The Dynasty's main prop *in spiritualibus*, and recipient in chief of its rewarding favours, was the Catholic Church. The connection had been a peculiarly intimate one in all the main groups of Lands in the Monarchy since their very foundation, Christianization and the establishment of kingship (in the German Lands, delegated Imperial authority) going hand in hand as two aspects of a single transaction. The association had, of course, known its troubles in later centuries. The great mediaeval contest between Empire and Papacy had not spared the Danubian lands; in the fifteenth century, the Hussite movement had split the Lands of the Bohemian Crown from top to bottom in a devastating struggle which had ended in the Utraquists' securing recognition of equality of their faith with the Catholic;[1] later, the doctrines, first of Luther, then of Calvin, had conquered the majority of the populations both of German Austria and of Hungary. Some of the Habsburgs themselves, notably Maximilian II, had inclined personally towards Protestantism. But Maximilian's successors had returned to the old alliance, enforcing the Counter-Reformation with their swords, so far as the range thereof reached. By the end of the religious wars, Catholicism had

[1] This was secured under the Treaty of Kutna Hora, 1485.

been re-established as 'the only ruling faith' in the Hereditary and Bohemian Lands. In them, Protestants were not even tolerated, except under licence, outside Silesia (where the intercession of the Protestant Powers at the Peace of Westphalia had obtained some protection for them) and, to a limited extent, Lower Austria.[1] Maria Theresa had not relaxed these general rules; as late as 1752 the profession of Protestantism had been declared a capital offence in Bohemia, equal to treason and rebellion,[2] and later still, unmasked crypto-Protestants in Upper Austria, Styria and Carinthia had been forced to migrate to Transylvania, or to leave the territory of the Monarchy altogether.[3]

In all these Lands, the Catholic Church occupied a position of great influence and dignity. The Prelates formed the first 'Bench' of the Estates,[4] and their princes ranked with the highest lay dignitaries. The Archbishop of Olmütz ranked as Prince and Duke: he possessed his own mint, Court and bodyguard, his estates covered twenty-six Austrian square leagues, and when he attended a meeting of the Moravian Estates, all other members of the Estates, including Princes and Dukes, walked on foot in procession before his carriage from his residence to the Landhaus. The state of several other dignitaries of the Austrian and Bohemian Church (five of whom, not counting Salzburg, ranked as princes) was only a little less magnificent, and in all these Lands the Chapters and monasteries, which were extremely numerous in most of them,[5] were among the biggest landowners. More than half Carniola and at least three-eighths of Moravia and Silesia (and that the most fertile parts) belonged to monastic Orders some of which were 'little

[1] The concession here applied to nobles and their peasants.

[2] It should be said that this draconic provision was partly prompted by political considerations, for Frederick of Prussia was trying to stir up Protestantism in Bohemia and use its adherents as his agents.

[3] In Salzburg, which was then not part of the Monarchy, twenty per cent of the population was driven out of the country. Most of the expellees went to Prussia, a few to Russia, whence their descendants moved later to Canada. Later in her life, Maria Theresa grew more tolerant and ordered 'little tolerance, but no spirit of persecution' when, in 1778, 10,000 Moravians in the *Kreis* of Hradcin reverted to Hussitism, although even then, she was prevented only by Joseph's opposition from having obstinate heretics pressed into the Army, if male, or sent to prison, if female, and finally transported to Transylvania. For all her devout Catholicism, she never boggled at employing Protestants, and even Jews, in special positions when she thought it conducive to the interests of the State. Protestant officers were admitted freely into the Army, numerous individual Protestants were licensed to practise trades or establish manufactures, and after 1778 Protestants were even promoted to Doctorates at the University of Vienna.

[4] This had been the rule in the Hereditary Lands since the inception of Estates in them. In Bohemia and Moravia the Prelates had been deposed from this position in the fifteenth century, but restored to it under Ferdinand's Vernewerte Landesordnung.

[5] According to *M.K.P.*, II. 320, the Monarchy in 1770 contained 2,163 monastic Houses (114 in Lower Austria alone) with 45,000 monks or nuns. Many of the Houses were extremely small.

principalities'. The Carthusians alone owned property worth more than 2,500,000 gulden. It is true that many of the Orders were heavily indebted.[1] The structure of the Church, like that of the temporal nobility, was, indeed, extremely hierarchical. The parish priests, most of whom were peasants' sons, lived poorly enough; their average annual stipend was usually around three hundred florins.

In Hungary the power and position of the Catholic Church were not quite so total. They had, indeed, once been even greater than in Austria. The Kingdom founded by St Stephen had been almost a theocracy, and while in it the wearer of the Holy Crown had enjoyed powers which made him the supreme head of the spiritual, as well as the temporal, arm of his nation, he had in return specifically exalted the former over the latter. The Crown itself was 'holy' and could not be born by any non-Catholic. The head of the Hungarian Church, the Cardinal-Primate of Esztergom, enjoyed extraordinary powers both *vis-à-vis* Rome (he usually ranked as a Legate of the Apostolic Church) and within Hungary itself. All bishops had from the first been *ex officio* members of the King's Council, and both St Stephen and several of his successors had endowed sees and monasteries with extraordinary generosity.

The Habsburgs had favoured the Catholic Church in Hungary as warmly as elsewhere, and here, too, it still enjoyed great power and wealth. The Cardinal-Primate was the highest dignitary in the land, after the Palatine. All bishops, including suffragans and bishops *in partibus*, of whom considerable numbers could be created if necessary,[2] and the prelates with independent Chapters, sat in the House of Magnates. The landed estates of the Church comprised nearly six million hold. The income of the Primate was estimated at 360,000 florins, that of the Archbishop of Egér at 80,000 and the Bishop of Nagyvárad at 70,000, the collective income of the other eight diocesan bishops at about 300,000.

In Hungary, however, the Turkish conquest had followed hard on the Reformation. The Turks, while on principle indifferent to the religion of their non-Islamic subjects, had tended to regard Protestantism as less dangerous than Catholicism, and had allowed it to exist unmolested in the territories under their direct rule, while in the vassal Principality of Transylvania, Catholics and Protestants had been so equally balanced that they had ended by agreeing on a regime of legal equality and mutual 'toleration' between themselves.[3] The Calvinist Princes had then repeatedly intervened

---

[1] Mitranov op. cit., p. 691.

[2] The Hungarian Church had throughout the ages prudently reserved its right to appoint titular bishops in sees in certain areas, such as Bosnia, which had been under its authority at one or another period in the Middle Ages.

[3] After certain preliminaries, this had been established between the Catholics, Lutherans, Calvinists and Unitarians in 1572.

to protect their co-religionists in Royal Hungary, forcing the Habsburgs to bind themselves by treaty to respect their rights;[1] and even apart from these obligations, the Habsburgs had not dared press the Hungarian Protestants too hard, for fear of driving them into the arms of the Turks. Thus Leopold I, on recovering Transylvania, had promised to respect its liberties, so that in 1780 the 350,000 or so Protestants of the Grand Principality[2] still enjoyed toleration, and were fairly well situated in most respects. The Protestants of Inner Hungary had been less fortunate, for their liberties had been steadily reduced as the Habsburgs' grip on the country tightened. The latest legal enactment on the subject, the *Carolina Resolutio* of 1731, had confined the public celebration of their services to a few specified places, and under Maria Theresa's regime (which became known to its victims as the 'Babylonian Captivity') many vexatious restrictions had been imposed on them. They had to observe Catholic feast-days, their clergy were subject to visitations by Catholic priests; a Catholic oath was required of all persons entering the public services, so that conscientious Protestants were debarred from such careers. In Croatia (where they numbered, indeed, only 3,500), they were explicitly debarred either from holding office or from owning land. Nevertheless, they were not forbidden to exist, and the census of 1782 recorded about 975,000 Calvinists and 600,000 Lutherans – a quarter of the total population – in Hungary-Croatia. It may be remarked that of these, the Calvinists were almost entirely Magyars. The Lutherans were either Slovaks from the North (where Lutheranism had succeeded Hussitism) or newly-arrived German colonists.

The Monarchy contained also a fair number of adherents of faiths outside these two main bodies of Roman Catholics and Protestants. Nearly all the 'Vlachs' or Roumanians found in, or immigrating into, Transylvania, had belonged to the Greek Orthodox Church, as, originally, had the Ruthenes who infiltrated into North-Eastern Hungary from East Galicia. These schismatics had been 'tolerated', i.e. allowed to live and to practise their religion unmolested, but the Orthodox Church had not been admitted to the status of a 'received' (established) one, nor included in the Transylvanian inter-confessional agreement of 1572. A bishopric had been established for the Orthodox Roumanians in the seventeenth century at Gyulafehérvár; it had been dependent on the Archbishopric of Târgoviste, in Wallachia. Meanwhile, numbers of Orthodox Serbs and Vlachs had been infiltrating into the

---

[1] The Treaties of Vienna (1606) and Nikolsburg (1621) had guaranteed equal rights to Catholics and Protestants but this had applied only to nobles, whose right to impose their own religion on their 'subjects' was assumed. The Treaty of Linz (1645) had extended freedom of religion to 'subjects'.

[2] There are no exact figures, since the census of the time did not count the religions of Transylvania, but the Saxons, who then numbered about 135,000, were all Lutherans (to be a Saxon was to be a Lutheran, and *vice-versa*), and of the 400,000 or so Magyars, probably some 350,000 were Calvinists and 50,000 Unitarians.

Military Frontier, where also they were tolerated (being needed as soldiers), and in 1692 the Orthodox Church received a powerful reinforcement when, as described elsewhere, the Patriarch of Ipek led his great body of followers into Hungary and was granted a Privilege guaranteeing his community their religious freedom and autonomy.

Meanwhile, various efforts had been set on foot to bring the Orthodox peoples of the Monarchy into the Catholic fold as 'Uniates'.[1] They were completely unsuccessful with the Serbs, but the Hungarian Ruthenes accepted the Union definitively in 1692, and in 1698 the Roumanian Bishop of Gyulafehérvár accepted it in the name of his people, so that for a time all the Transylvanian Roumanians counted as Uniates (Greek Catholics). Their attachment to the old faith was, however, very strong, and even the sincerity of the nominal converts doubtful. In 1761 Maria Theresa gave up the struggle, and while retaining the Uniate Bishopric, re-appointed a Roumanian Orthodox Bishop (this time, autonomous). His jurisdiction, however, extended only to Transylvania; all members of the Orthodox Church in the other Lands of the Hungarian Crown, whatever their ethnic origin, came under the Serb Metropolitan of Karlóca.

The membership of both the Uniate and the Orthodox Churches was reinforced when Austria acquired Galicia and the Bukovina, for the former Orthodox population of Eastern Galicia (in practice, to be equated with the Ruthene ethnic element) had accepted Greek Catholicism in 1596, under the Union of Brest Litovsk.[2] The Orthodox Roumanians of Bukovina were in 1780 still provisionally under their old ecclesiastical superiors in Moldavia.

Hungary contained a few more small Churches, including a Uniate Armenian community; the Armenians possessed another community, which even ran to a Bishop, in Galicia.

On her accession, Maria Theresa had very few Jews in her dominions. The thriving and important Jewish communities which had existed in mediaeval times in most of the Hereditary Lands had been liquidated in a series of expulsions.[3] In these Lands Jews were now to be found practically only in Vienna, where, although the community had been dissolved there also (although rather later than elsewhere)[4] some individuals had afterwards

---

[1] Union normally meant that the Uniates accepted the following four points of principle: the supreme authority of the Pope, the existence of purgatory, the use of unleavened bread for the Sacrament and the dogma that the Holy Ghost proceeds also from the Son. In return, they were allowed to retain their own ritual with certain other concessions (e.g. their lower priests might marry) and were admitted to the full civic and political rights enjoyed by members of the Roman Catholic Church.

[2] This is a very summary description of an exceedingly complex process, which had begun much before 1596 and was not finally completed until long after that date.

[3] From Styria in 1496; from Carinthia and Carniola in 1513; from the Tirol in 1518; from Upper Austria in 1596.

[4] In 1670.

been admitted under special permit. In 1776 there were about 300 of them. There were about 1,500 in the Vorlande, and a colony (of Sephardim Jews) in Trieste. In Bohemia-Moravia there were many more – about 40,000, most of them concentrated in Prague, where an old and famous community had contrived to maintain itself throughout the Middle Ages, and 20,000 odd in Moravia. In the Lands of the Hungarian Crown only twelve thousand had been counted at the end of the Turkish wars, but by 1775 the number had increased, chiefly by immigration from Bohemia-Moravia, or (illegally) from Galicia, to some 75–80,000, nearly all concentrated in the North-Western or North-Eastern Counties. The Jewish population of the Monarchy had then been more than doubled with the annexation of Galicia-Bukovina, where the Jews had constituted an appreciable proportion of the population, numbering, in the annexed areas, something like 200,000.[1]

Since the Counter-Reformation the Jews had had an unhappy time in the Austrian dominions. They were confined to ghettoes, made to wear a distinctive dress and subjected to a special Cameral tax, the Judensteuer,[2] on top of the usual taxation. They were, as a rule, forbidden to reside in towns (the Prague community was exceptional) and many occupations were forbidden to them. In Poland most of them earned their livings on the estates of the richer noblemen (almost all of whom kept a 'Hausjude') as estate managers, corn-brokers or licensees of the village inn. For the rest they were mostly small tradesmen, and most of them lived in extreme poverty.[3]

Maria Theresa was personally strongly prepossessed against the Jews, whom she described as 'an unparalleled plague, with their swindling, money-making and usury'. One of her earliest actions as Queen had actually been to expel them from Prague (as prelude to their total expulsion from the Lands of the Bohemian Crown) and it had taken strong representations from the Estates and the Hofkammer (and also from the tradesmen and artisans of Prague) to induce her to rescind the order; she extracted from them, however, a 'voluntary gift' of 150,000 fl., and later, a heavy annual tax.[4] She had maintained nearly all the restrictions on them throughout most of her reign; only towards the end of it was she allowing them to enter economic life in a larger way, for example as licensees of factories. It was, however, reserved for her son to confront the real problem presented by the huge sudden increase in the Monarchy's Jewish population entailed by the annexation of Galicia-Bukovina.

[1] The census of 1776 (for Galicia only) gave nearly 150,000; that of 1785, which included the Bukovina, over 210,000.

[2] This brought in substantial sums; in Hungary alone, 20,000 fl. in 1749, rising to 80,000 fl. in 1788.

[3] The Prague Jews had welcomed the invading armies of Bavaria and Prussia.

[4] 'The Jews of Cracow', wrote Russell in the 1820s, 'are sunk still lower than the peasants in uncleanliness and misery, and appear to be less sensible to it' (op. cit., I. 210).

In the partnership between the Crown and the Catholic Church both sides played their parts loyally, with the rarest deviations. If the Crown lavished wealth and honour on the Church, the latter both practised and preached the strictest loyalty to the Crown. It was no accident that the foci of rebellion, or at least, of contumelious self-assertion, had always lain among the Monarchy's Protestant subjects, and even in 1780, where such feelings (outside the special case of Galicia) were almost extinct, if they lingered on at all, it was among the Protestant middle nobles and yeomen farmers of Central Hungary.

Meanwhile, it is worth emphasizing that while nearly all the Habsburgs were themselves personally extremely pious, they guarded for themselves jealously the position of senior partner in the association.[1] Maximilian I had himself refused to allow the promulgation of a certain Papal Bull in his dominions, and his successors had repeatedly exercised the *placetum regium* in respect of Church appointments. Ferdinand II had confined the authority of the Church to *pura spiritualia* and had forbidden the spiritual arm, under pain of punishment, to intervene in the field of competence of the Landesfürst, for which he claimed, *inter alia*, jurisdiction between priests and laymen, and the right to supervise religious foundations. Church lands were treated as 'Kammergut' and taxed accordingly. Several of the Habsburgs intervened in what, under many definitions, would have been ecclesiastical questions, such as the determination of the feasts of the Church. And it is remarkable how few Churchmen figure in history as playing prominent parts in the political life of the Monarchy.

Maria Theresa, personally one of the most pious of her line, was as firm as any of them in this respect. She invoked her right as *suprema advocata ecclesiarum* to initiate pertinent inquiries into the management of Church properties and revenues; abolished Church punishments and restricted pilgrimages and Church feasts, and she advised her children not to make donations to the Church, 'which had enough' and misused its wealth. She hesitated at the last moment to allow Febronius' work, banned by the Vatican, to circulate freely in the Monarchy, but its doctrines permeated the educational system, which under her became strongly Erastian.

Up to a generation or so before 1780, all education had been in the hands of the Churches, who had conducted it through their own establishments, maintained out of their endowments, or out of subscriptions from their

[1] Another phase in this rivalry, now almost closed, had been the struggle between the temporal and spiritual power for actual authority. In the earliest days the German kings and emperors had granted 'immediate' status almost as freely to the great missionary sees, as to Dukes and Margraves. After themselves achieving immediacy, the Babenbergs and Habsburgs had gradually brought most of the local Church lands under their own jurisdiction, until in 1780, in the Alpine Lands, only the Prince-Archbishop of Salzburg and, in a more qualified sense, the Bishops of Trent and Brixen, were exempt from it.

THE MONARCHY IN 1780

congregations, which were not always generous.[1] The Crown had exercised its influence only indirectly, through its generosity or otherwise in conferring endowments, and its severity or otherwise in imposing restrictions. This influence had nevertheless been extensive, and it says much for the devotion and self-sacrifice of the Hungarian Calvinists and the Lutheran Saxons that in spite of their poverty[2] and of great administrative pressure they had succeeded in maintaining an efficient school system, both primary and secondary.[3] For the Catholics, all schooling was controlled by their Church and almost all instruction given by persons holding official positions in it; as a rule, only law and medicine were taught by laymen, and that within the framework of the Church-controlled Universities. This instruction was, incidentally, on a low level, and serious students often went abroad to complete their studies. Most higher and secondary education was mainly in the hands of the Jesuits (to a lesser extent, the Benedictines) whose secondary schools were nearly all gymnasia. Teaching in them was mainly in Latin, and was chiefly directed towards inculcating the true faith; the brighter pupils were trained on to become in their turn militant priests.[4] Primary education, where it had any pretensions at all, was to a large extent in the hands of the Piarists. Village schools were entrusted to the local parson, or not infrequently, the sexton-verger; they were thin on the ground, for one point on which the authorities and the adult peasants concurred was that it was useless, or actually harmful, to give a peasant-child book-learning.[5]

The first changes in this system had been inaugurated largely by Van Swieten, the Belgian doctor who came to Vienna in 1745, was appointed physician in chief to Maria Theresa and soon came to exercise an extraordinary influence over the entire educational system of the Monarchy. He was at first chiefly concerned to introduce the practical reforms which turned the medical faculty of Vienna into one of Europe's leading institutions in its field, but he was also a leading exponent of the Jansenist philosophy which now came to dominate educational thought in the Monarchy. The philosophical justification for reform was then furnished largely by that extraordinary figure, Josef Sonnenfels, who wrote a number of books expounding

[1] In 1723 the Jesuits had not enough money to maintain a Chair of history in Graz, let alone a medical or theological faculty.

[2] In 1865, when the Churches in Hungary had already parted with much land, the Catholic Church still owned 2½ million hold; the Protestants, only 28,900.

[3] For higher education Protestants had to go to foreign universities. For a time they were forbidden to do so.

[4] Most noble families who could afford to do so kept private tutors for their sons.

[5] In all the Slovene parts of Styria, there was not one single village school. A Commission reported in 1752 that the only reason why the parents of a Slovene child ever wanted him to receive schooling was that he should learn German, and in that case they sent him to a German school. Otherwise, 'no children were sent to school, so no schools were needed' (Pirchegger, *Steiermark*, II. 360). Even in the German parts many communes were without schools.

the doctrine that it was for the State to control closely the spiritual and intellectual lives of its subjects, the function of the Church being to assist it to do so.[1] But the changes were in any case rendered inevitable by the emergence of the autocratic-bureaucratic State, with its need for trained civil servants and its insistence on devotion to the Monarch as hardly less important than devotion to God. Education was now, as Maria Theresa told Cardinal Migazzi in 1770, when he objected to State supervision of confessional schools, a '*politicum*', i.e., a matter for State regulation. It had still to produce good Catholics, but it was even more important that it should produce good, loyal and civically useful 'subjects'.

Under the impact of these new ideas, the Jesuits were driven out of one stronghold after another, until in 1773 the Order was dissolved altogether by the Pope (incidentally, against Maria Theresa's deeper wishes). By this time a Commission was already considering the whole question of education in the Monarchy, and some of its members favoured complete laicization. After long hesitation, the Empress decided against this, partly owing to the difficulty of finding (and paying) enough lay teachers, so that the bulk of higher and secondary education was left in the hands of the Orders; but some further faculties at the Universities were entrusted to lay teachers, and in the gymnasia the curricula were broadened by the introduction of more practical subjects, and Latin largely replaced by modern languages as the medium of instruction. A considerable number of technical schools were also founded. The whole system was placed under State supervision.

At the same time, Maria Theresa took up the question of elementary education for the people, which, unlike some of her advisers, she thought useful and even necessary. She borrowed from Frederick of Prussia the famous educationalist, Felbiger, who worked out blue-prints for the establishment of a primary ('Trivial') school in every village, with grammar schools (*Hauptschulen*) in the larger centres and a sufficient number of training colleges (*Normalschulen*). An *Allgemeine Schulordnung* to this effect was issued in 1774 for the Hereditary and Bohemian Lands, where primary education now became (in theory) compulsory. As the Hungarian members of the Commission had objected that a scheme suitable for Austria would not fit Hungary, with its different conditions, a Hungarian counterpart, in the preparation of which several Hungarians had participated, and which took into

---

[1] Sonnenfels is one of the curiosities of Austrian, and indeed of all, history. The son of a Moravian Rabbi who adopted Christianity, he had an extraordinary early career which included some years of service as a private soldier in a regular regiment, then took up teaching and became Professor and Hofrat. He had a great influence over Maria Theresa, and was largely responsible for her Penal Code. Joseph II liked him less, and Francis ended by losing patience with him. His central ideas are contained in his *Grundsätze der Polizeiwissenschaft*, first issued in 1765, which was used as a textbook in Austria up to 1848. The most recent addition to the voluminous literature on this unpleasant but interesting character is an essay in A. Kann's *Study in Austrian Intellectual History* (1960).

account the entire educational system from the primary school to the University, was published in 1777 under the name of *Ratio Educationis*, although it did not receive official sanction until 1781.

It should be emphasized that these changes represented no victory for the principles of freedom of thought or instruction. Maria Theresa herself was no friend of abstract knowledge; in this, as in several other respects, the contrast between her and her grandson, Francis I, has usually been much overdrawn. It was on her hostility that the proposal to create an Academy of Sciences in Vienna foundered, to be realized only a century later on Metternich's motion. The goal of usefulness to the State was followed at least as rigidly as the Jesuits' objective of moral virtue. If some subjects, such as history and geography, were given a larger place in the latter system than in the former, this was simply because they appeared more useful for the new purposes, than for the old. Departures from the prescribed curricula, teaching methods, etc., were visited with heavier displeasure by the new civil authorities than they had been by the old ecclesiastical directors of studies.

It was in Maria Theresa's reign that the censorship, too, was for the first time institutionalized: characteristically, in a form which extended its supervision also to ecclesiastical works.[1]

It was utilitarianism, not German national feeling, that was responsible for one very important feature of the educational reorganization in Austria: its strong emphasis on the teaching of German. Maria Theresa and even Joseph II were not on principle hostile to non-German languages as such: early in her reign (in 1747) Maria Theresa had rebuked the Jesuits in Prague for giving too much instruction in Latin and too little in Czech. In 1763 officials in Bohemia had been enjoined to devote more time to learning Czech, and as late as 1774 a chair of Czech had been established in Vienna. But in the latter years of her reign, and especially, perhaps, under the growing influence of Joseph II, the idea of the centralized, bureaucratic State gained in strength and it was taken as axiomatic that this could only be run efficiently in German. Knowledge of the German language was thus one of the necessary accomplishments of a 'useful' *subjectum*, and the school curricula were adapted accordingly. The *Allgemeine Schulordnung* of 1774 made German an obligatory subject in all elementary schools in Bohemia, and in 1776 it became the language of instruction in the gymnasia; Czech was allowed to be used in only four of the sixteen Bohemian gymnasia, and that only for a grace-period of three years. Similarly, an Imperial resolution of 1774 ordered that 'children from the Illyrian districts should be taught German'; at first they were to be allowed to learn the catechism in their own tongue, but even

---

[1] There had previously been no State censorship in Austria, but as a Catholic State, Austria had admitted the control of the Holy See over the printed word. In 1753 Maria Theresa established a Committee of Censors, composed half of ecclesiastics and half of laymen, whose *imprimatur* was necessary before any work, religious or other, could appear.

this concession was to be withdrawn gradually 'as the German language made headway'. In 1775 and 1776 orders were issued that the elementary schools in the Slovene districts and even in the Military Frontier were to be Germanized.[1]

These measures did not apply to Hungary, where, as has been said, the proposals for the reorganization of education were still on paper when Maria Theresa died; and they did not go so far in the direction of Germanization as the orders enacted in the Western Lands. They provided that elementary education should be given in the pupil's mother-tongue – and most interestingly, they gave Magyar no preference over the six other languages (German, Slovak, Croat, Ruthene, 'Illyrian' and Wallachian) which they described as current in Hungary. But they still declared it especially important that every elementary school-child should be taught German. The basic language of instruction in the higher establishments was to be Latin, but the greatest weight was to be attached to the teaching of German in the gymnasia, and the Ratio actually expressed the hope that this would gradually lead to German developing 'as the Court had long wished' into the 'national language' of Hungary.[2]

These innovations had, of course, not got far beyond the blue-print stage by 1780. The German-Bohemian Lands possessed at that date, in all, fifteen training colleges, eighty-three grammar schools, forty-seven schools for girls, and 3,848 elementary schools. Bohemia was the most advanced of any Land after Lower and Upper Austria, but even in Bohemia, only about half the children of school age were attending the State schools. In Vienna itself the figure was only twenty-four out of one hundred (although here there were also many private schools); in Lower Austria, outside Vienna, only sixteen; in Silesia, only four.[3] In Inner Hungary only about forty-five per cent of all rural communes possessed schools at all – some 4,000 of them; 4,437 teachers were employed in them, giving an average of seven and a half teachers per ten thousand inhabitants.[4] These general figures cover very wide local variations; in West Hungary and in the area between the Danube and the Tisza, with its big, concentrated urbanizations, almost every commune had

[1] The instruction for the Military Frontier schools declared the measure necessary, to enable the boys to acquire the linguistic equipment to become officers and N.C.O.s 'without losing their time over the less necessary instructions in reading and writing in Illyrian'. To keep up 'Illyrian' schools as well as German was 'an unjustified burden, oppressive to the military communes'.

[2] Ratio Educationis, para. 102, *De Singulari linguae Germanicae utilitate.*

[3] Ficker, *Bericht über oe. Unterrichtswesen* (Vienna, 1873), I. 18.

[4] There were in Hungary in 1772 one University, with 42 teachers, 5 Roman Catholic seminaries, with 61 teachers, 58 Roman Catholic gymnasia, with 340 teachers, 51 grammar schools, with 329 teachers and 2,664 Roman Catholic elementary teachers. The Lutheran teachers numbered 629, the Calvinist, 1,600, the Greek Catholic, 40, the Greek Orthodox, 301.

its school, but they were much rarer in the Serb, Roumanian and Ruthene districts. In Transylvania the Saxons kept up, out of their own resources, the most complete system in the whole Monarchy, but that of the Roumanian Orthodox Church was still embryonic. In Galicia, when Austria took it over, conditions were worse still. In the whole District of Lemberg, with a Christian population of half a million, there had been only ten elementary schoolmasters, and the learning of eight of them had not got beyond the ability to read and write Polish. The Bukovina, we are told, had no educational establishments at all when Austria annexed it. The nobles kept private tutors (usually Greeks, who also acted as their secretaries) for their children. Otherwise, reading and writing were taught only in the monasteries, and few people except the monks and cantors were able to read or write.[1] When the Austrians took over Dalmatia they found conditions there, outside the Croatian coastal towns, equally backward.

In 1780 it was already a full half-century since Austrian 'culture' had reached what many regard as its apogee: that already slightly over-blown Hochbarock of Charles VI's reign which has been described as 'the outward and visible sign of the inward union between a high-aristocratic form of devotion and a Church no less hierarchic and very little less worldly' which

...had found at Charles's Court an expression surpassed nowhere in Europe either for splendour or for delicate and curious grace; for that Court was not only the seat of what was already the most august dynasty of Europe, but also a unique meeting-place where influences from Germany, Italy, Spain and the Netherlands met and mingled with those of the Danubian peoples to produce results which were not only magnificent, but also at once local and universal.

The Austria of 1780 had lost many things which the Austria of 1730 had possessed. It was not perhaps financially poorer, for against the losses of Silesia and some of Charles's Italian possessions must be set the general economic recovery in most of its remaining territories, but the rigid financial probity of that austere Silesian, Haugwitz, and perhaps also of that excellent business man, Francis Stephen, from whom Joseph II and Francis must surely have derived the strain of direct parsimony for which both were notorious, had curbed that sublime indifference to days of reckoning which had allowed the spending spree of the earlier day. It had lost a perceptible amount of the religious faith which had inspired the great ecclesiastical buildings of the High Baroque. The Italian influences which dominated the architecture, music and theatre of that age had grown perceptibly weaker.

None of these things, of course, had gone altogether. Maria Theresa, for all her conscientious efforts at economy, was too truly her father's daughter

---

[1] Ficker, II. 560. Joseph II wrote (with a touch of exasperation) that the Serbs and Dalmatians of the Monarchy had no schools at all, and that not one in thousands could read or write even in their own language.

not to be a good spender; the Church was still mighty and wealthy; if few of Austria's great buildings were now directly planned by Italian architects, very many of them were the work of pupils of Italian masters. And where the old forces were giving ground it was not only because of their own weakening vitality, but because they were being shouldered aside by new forces possessing their own vitality: a new spirit of nationalism, even new popular elements in drama and literature, as well as thought.

The Austria, especially the Vienna, of 1780 had its own special charm. If it was growing more German (signs of which were the popularity of popular farce in the Viennese dialect, as well as the adoption by the Empress herself of that dialect for habitual usage), it had not become repellantly Teutonic. The short-lived rococo into which the later baroque style had merged can show exquisite products, and the age was that in which that art of music which is Austria's special gift to the world was bringing forth its finest flowers, with Gluck, Haydn and Mozart still in their prime and Beethoven nearing his. But the music apart, the age cannot be conscientiously described as culturally great. The buildings (although may God bless Maria Theresa for her addiction to the shade of yellow which bears her name!) were nearly always smaller, plainer and cheaper than they would have been fifty years earlier. In thought and most of the arts, what was new had not yet filled the hollows left by the decay of the old. Neither had the beginnings of popular art been powerful enough to shake the tradition that the Monarch and the Court were the founts not only of political power, but also of cultural life. The Empress's long reign may even have strengthened, in this field also, the national Austrian repugnance towards true independence.

VII THE MONARCHY IN THE WORLD

The great treaties of partition between Maximilian's grandchildren had given the cadet branch two things: on the one hand, the Crowns of Bohemia and Hungary; on the other, not only the family Hausmacht in Germany, but also (to come to it on the death of Charles) the leadership of the Holy Roman Empire. It was undoubtedly the latter position which had taken pride of place in the eyes of Ferdinand and his successors. While not only the natural desire to make valid *de facto* their *de jure* claim to the territories of the Hungarian Crown, but also the requirements of self-defence, had forced them to devote a proportion of their attention to repelling the Turkish threat in the south-east of their dominions, they had always regarded the consolidation of their position there chiefly in the light of the necessary precondition for the expansion of their power in civilized Europe – Germany and – although here they had more often given way to the elder branch of the family – Italy. Consequently, their policy in the East had been mainly a defensive one, while they struggled in the West against their great rival,

France. It had been a struggle in which their position had, indeed, grown steadily weaker, not only in consequence of France's successes, but with the growth of the resistance of the German princes themselves to Austria's claim to dominate them. The Treaty of Westphalia had made their leadership little more than titular, but without diminishing its value in their eyes. Then had come the rise of Prussia, when Frederick had actually seized from Maria Theresa all except a fragment of the province of Silesia, 'the brightest jewel of her Crown'. It was this that had led to Kaunitz's famous *renversement des alliances*, the Treaty with France which was still in force in 1780.

The Seven Years War had failed to achieve its objective, the recovery of Silesia, and when she signed the Peace of Hubertsburg in 1763, Maria Theresa resigned herself to its loss, sweetened by the meagre compensation when first her husband, then her son, had been crowned Holy Roman Emperor. The renunciation was bitter to her, and when, in the last years of her life, she insisted on a peaceful settlement of the dispute over the Bavarian succession – whereas her son was prepared to face a full-scale war in order to add Bavaria to the family dominions – this was out of sheer abhorrence of war, especially war in a cause the justice of which was dubious. It did not mean that she, or still less her son, was willing to abdicate from Austria's leading role in the Empire.

Meanwhile, at the end of the seventeenth century, the decay of the Turkish power, and the brilliant advantage taken thereof by Prince Eugen, had changed the situation in the south-east. Hungary had been recovered. But these successes had not brought about any fundamental change in the Habsburgs' world outlook. True, Charles VI had twice carried his arms into the Balkans, but the first of these campaigns had aimed really at providing Hungary with a defensive *glacis*, while the second had been undertaken in fulfilment of an alliance with Russia, itself the price of Russia's recognition of the Pragmatic Sanction, and when the Turks proved unexpectedly difficult to beat on their own ground, Maria Theresa had willingly renounced any idea of adding to her dominions what she drastically described as 'a lot of barren mountains and feverish swamps, inhabited by unreliable Greeks'.[1] From 1768 onward Austria was actively supporting the territorial integrity of Turkey.

This was against the designs of Russia, whose rise to power the Empress saw without any pleasure whatever. 'The whole balance in the North,' she wrote to Starhemberg in Paris in 1762, when Russia's designs on East Prussia were revealed, 'would be upset, and the Russian power become too formidable for us and other Courts to enjoy seeing it in our neighbourhood.' And if, ten years later, she nevertheless expanded her territories on her northeastern frontier by participating in the First Partition of Poland, this was out

[1] I.e., members of the Greek Orthodox Church. The Empress was not speaking in ethnographic terms.

of no lust for conquest. The famous tears which she shed were not those of the crocodile. She took Galicia out of consideration of the Balance of Power, and to prevent Russia from reaching the Carpathians.

But the combined effect of these developments had been to leave the Monarchy in a paradoxical position. First the recovery of Hungary, second the acquisition of Galicia, had shifted the balance of her population strongly against the German element in its Hausmacht, and the hegemony in Germany which had doubled the strength of that element had already lost much of its real value. Yet it still retained so much of that value, and tradition was still so strong, that neither the Empress nor her son ever thought seriously of yielding the field to Prussia and moving out of the Empire.

Meanwhile, the immediate problem of Austria's rulers was to fortify their position in Germany, and in the East, to discover the best way to deal with Russia's expansionist ambitions. The latter problem was very acute in 1780, for Catherine of Russia was clearly a long way from being satisfied with the gains, large as they were, which the Treaty of Kutchuk Kainardji had brought her in 1774.

2

Joseph II

As we have said, a detailed description of the ten years of Joseph II's reign does not belong to the theme of this work. A brief account of them is, however, necessary, to show what it was that Leopold was summoned to alter, and, where he refused to do so, how the conditions which he left in being differed from those of 1780. The differences were very substantial, for outside the purely administrative patterns, Leopold could not have restored the *status quo ante* Joseph had he wished. For Joseph had a terrible genius. He touched not only the shape of things, but also the spirit within them; and even where the shape was restored, the spirit was found to have become different. The change was not always in the direction that Joseph himself had meant. In some cases the line which he laid down accorded with the spirit of the age and lived on after him; in others, it was in advance of, or contrary, to it, and evoked a counter-action, but even this was counter-action rather than reaction, for in resisting Joseph, it had changed its own shape.

Joseph II is perhaps the completest enlightened despot in European history, and the noun in the phrase is quite as fully operative as the adjective. His youthful reading had brought him certain doctrines of inherent natural rights of man, and had taught him that a ruler has duties towards his subjects: he even confessed the belief that he was there for their sake, not they for his. He certainly regarded his position as a charge, carrying with it a duty which he filled with scrupulous conscientiousness, and sparing himself as little as he spared others.

But he also believed that in all matters temporal, the ruler was absolute, responsible to no man. If he was bound to work for his subjects' welfare, it was for him alone to determine what conditions answered to the term, and what were the means by which they were to be achieved. And he was personally exceedingly dogmatic, self-opinionated and impatient of opposition, and, to boot, as unconciliatory in manner as he was in principle. He was capable of generosity, but not of tenderness or consideration; on the contrary, there was in him a streak of sadism which caused him to take real delight in humiliating and wounding those who, by their personalities or their positions, seemed to him to stand in the way of the realization of his objectives: especially the representatives of historic tradition, and the aristocracy as a class. Not only did he refuse to make concessions to opposition: he brushed it aside with a studied rudeness which doubled his victims' resentment. He could, indeed, probably have got far more of his reforms accepted, had he been more conciliatory in manner, but that was beyond him. His unpleasantness is sometimes excused as the effect of embitterment over the loss of his young first wife, whom he professed to have adored, and it probably does account in part for his really beastly treatment of her unfortunate successsor. But he was disagreeable even as a little boy; even his tutors complained of his manner. The fact is relevant to his history, and to that of his subjects.

In matters spiritual, Joseph professed himself a true Catholic, and even a champion of pure religion against its abuses, but he admitted the supremacy of the Church only in *pura spiritualia*, which he defined narrowly enough. In all other respects, he regarded his authority over the Church as no less absolute than over the lay arm. It may be remarked that this was the field in which the effects of his reign proved the most enduring of all. Leopold revoked a few of his measures, but not very many, and Austrian spiritual life at least up to 1847 remained dominated by a strong Erastianism which was rightly known as 'Josephinism'.

It is perhaps fitting to describe these measures first, since Joseph himself, logical as he was, considered control of the spirit to be the true condition precedent of all political control. It must, however, be remembered that the applicability of them to the entire Monarchy was made possible by the political enactments described later.

No complete list of them can be given here, for, as we said, he defined the phrase *pura spiritualia* in an extraordinarily restrictive sense; he even laid down, for example, the exact forms to be used in Church services, with the number of candles to be lit at each. But he also introduced some changes of the first importance in the relations of Church and State. He vetoed the publication of several Papal Bulls; abolished all foreign ordinariates and redelimited the Austrian episcopal sees to make them coincide geographically with the administrative units (these boundaries are still in force in Austria today), forbade direct correspondence between the bishops and the Holy See, and abolished the episcopal seminaries and monastic schools (which he described as 'nests of the fanatical hydra of ultra-montanism'), founding instead eight State-controlled 'General Seminaries' as the sole training-ground for intending priests.

An exceedingly important enactment, first issued as a Patent on 16 January 1783, and afterwards incorporated in the Code of Civil Law, made marriage a purely civil contract, the validity of which derived 'exclusively from the law of the land'. It was, indeed, contracted in front of a priest, who had to be the person in charge of keeping the State register, but he was not entitled to refuse to perform the ceremony on account of any circumstances regarded by Canon law, but not by State law, as constituting an obstacle to it.

One of the most far-reaching in its effects of all Joseph's measures was the 'Toleration Patent' of October 1781.[1] This did not introduce complete 'toleration', for it left Catholicism as the 'dominant' religion of State, and treated the smaller 'sects' with extreme harshness. But the Calvinist, Lutheran and Orthodox Churches were allowed to build their own places of worship and schools, where their numbers justified it, and their members became competent to own land, to become burghers of towns or masters of crafts, and to hold posts in the civil service, the armed forces or the educational system, without having to take an oath contrary to their consciences or to attend religious ceremonies contrary to their beliefs. The Jews were relieved of the obligation to wear distinctive dress and of certain other restrictions and taxes, and were allowed to attend Christian schools, as well as their own, to enter academic life and the free professions, and to practise trades, although they still could not become burghers or master-craftsmen and were left subject to many other restrictions.

Another famous set of enactments was directed against the monasteries. Here Joseph went far beyond his mother's tentative beginnings. First the mendicant Orders were dissolved, then the contemplative, and finally the teaching Orders, excepting only the Piarists, and their properties confiscated; in all, over six hundred Houses fell under the axe. The monasteries' lands were sold, leased or exploited by the State, and after provision, in the shape of pensions or gratuities, had been made for the dispossessed monks, the remaining proceeds were paid into a fund, part of which was devoted to founding new livings, on the principle that no village should be left more than an hour's journey from a church, while the rest was devoted to various welfare projects, notably hospitals and poor relief.

What Joseph set himself to create in the administrative field was a State entirely controlled by an efficient, smoothly-working machine which responded to and carried into effect his decisions in every field. The Monarchy, as he inherited it, obviously did not answer this description: even in the Austro-Bohemian Lands, absolutism was still only half in the saddle, and Hungary and the Netherlands still possessed constitutional organs entitled to a voice in the government of their countries. Had he accepted the usual conditions of a Monarch's accession, Joseph would have been obliged to swear to respect the rights of the Estates in those Lands, and he showed his hand at the very outset of his reign by refusing to submit to coronation in Hungary (or in Bohemia), replying to the embittered protests of the Hungarian Court Chancellery with the wounding words *pueri puerilia tractant*. The Bohemian Crown, the Ducal Hat of Lower Austria, the Styrian Sword of Office, were brought to Vienna to be kept in the Imperial Treasury; and finally, the

[1] This Patent was not promulgated in the Tirol or Vorarlberg.

Hungarian Holy Crown itself, the venerated and mystical symbol of Hungarian kingship, took the same road. This time Joseph's answer to the protest was: *risum teneatis, amici*.

In the Austro-Bohemian Lands the changes in the top-level administrative machine consisted only of adjustments. The financial Ministries (the Hofkammer and Banco-Deputatio) were united with the Böhmisch-oesterreichische Hofkanzlei under the name of Vereinigte Hofstelle; only the judiciary remained a separate instance. On the next level, the Gubernia were rationalized, Styria being amalgamated with Carinthia and Carniola under the name of Inner Austria, Silesia with Moravia, Gorizia and Gradisca with Trieste, Upper with Lower Austria, Vorarlberg and the Vorlande with the Tirol and the Bukovina with Galicia. These Gubernia now became all-competent (under the central Ministries); the *Capi* of the Estates were simply decorative figures, the posts being given to deserving officials past active work. Two 'assessors' representing the Estates sat in each Gubernium, but as State officials. The old 'Committees of the Estates' disappeared. The municipal Councillors were still elected, but their election had to be confirmed by the State, and they counted as State employees. The communal Councils were left with certain tasks, notably those of apportioning the prescribed taxation between the members of the commune, and collecting it, but with no freedom or discretion.

The only service newly extended to cover the whole Monarchy was the Hofrechnungskammer. Otherwise the Governments of Hungary, the Netherlands and Lombardy remained distinct, but their autonomy was reduced to the Austrian level.

Curiously, Joseph carried Austro-Hungarian dualism a long step further than Maria Theresa herself had done. Not only was the Hungarian Court Chancellery retained as a separate body directly responsible to the Crown, but its competence, now both political and financial (the Cameral agenda having now been transferred to it), was extended to all the Lands of the Hungarian Crown[1] (except the Military Frontier, which was left untouched), the Transylvanian Chancellery being abolished and its agenda transferred to the Hungarian Chancellery. But under this, the entire governmental system of Hungary was re-cast in 1785. The former Inner Hungary-Croatia was divided into ten Districts, the delimitation of which ignored the old historic division between Hungary and Croatia. Each District was placed under a Royal Commissioner. In the Counties, the office of Föispán disappeared; the Alispáns were now appointed by the Crown, and became Royal officials; the Congregations were allowed to meet only once a year, and then to no purpose, since they lost their autonomy. In Transylvania

[1] This important step, which the Hungarians themselves had not expected, and against which several of Joseph's councillors protested vigorously, meant that the dualist principle was now applied to the State finances.

the old Saxon and Szekel 'territories' disappeared. The entire area, including the Partium, was reorganized in ten Counties, under a single Gubernium, corresponding to the Hungarian Districts.

A similar absolutist regime was introduced in the Netherlands under two Decrees dated respectively 1 January and 12 March 1787; the Belgian Constitution, including the famous *Joyeuse Entrée*, which Joseph himself on his accession had promised to respect, was simply swept out of existence.

The offence to sentiment in the non-German Lands, except the Netherlands and Lombardy, was aggravated by the Germanization of the Government system. In Hungary the Consilium was informed, on 11 May 1784, that Latin, being a dead language, could not sensibly be used for official purposes. As Magyar was the language of only part of the population, the rest of which spoke 'German, Illyrian or Vlach', the only practicable language for official purposes was German, which was also the language of administration and the army in the Monarchy as a whole. German was therefore to become the official language, in the central offices as from that date, in the Counties after one year and in the lower instances after three. Officials unable to master the language within the prescribed periods were to be dismissed. Knowledge of German was to be a condition of admission to the Diet.

At the same time, German was made the sole language of instruction in all higher and secondary educational establishments, except that intending priests might study Latin in the High Schools. In the primary schools, religion might be taught in the pupil's mother tongue.

Similar orders were issued in respect of Bohemia, Galicia and Gorizia; in Galicia, it is true, it proved so difficult to find sufficient German speakers that Latin had to be re-instated provisionally (the question had not been officially settled by the time of Joseph's death).

In reply to remonstrances, Joseph denied that he was guided by any theoretical preference for German (which was not even his own favourite language). German had to be chosen because it was the language of the most important of his dominions (among which he included the Holy Roman Empire) and already the language of educated usage, including business and the professions. He did not, however, deny that his purpose was to Germanize, not all his subjects, but all his machinery of State, and in some parts of the Monarchy he pressed on Germanization by other means. More German colonists were settled as free peasants, 'privileged' merchants or artisans in Hungary, others in Galicia, and a number in the Bukovina.

As we shall see, these measures never became effective in the Netherlands, were rescinded by Joseph himself in Hungary and were even modified by his successor in the Austro-Bohemian Lands. But the tradition of them, too, lived on in Austria-Bohemia and even, in shadowy fashion, in Hungary. Under Joseph, the peoples of Austria learned beyond all un-teaching to regard bureaucratic rule, directed from a lofty and invisible centre, as the normal and indeed the right form of government; and if Hungary at the time rejected the application of the system to itself, it did so chiefly because the centre was then in Vienna. When, long after, it became free to establish its own system, it constructed a similar (although less elaborate) one centred on Budapest.

It was also under Joseph that the bureaucracy itself (outside Hungary, where his reforms had not time to take root – here the change came only later) emerged as a distinct class and social factor. As we have said elsewhere, most of the administrative work of the Monarchy had been carried on up to his day by local nobles, or their employees, either in their corporate capacities as Provincial Estates, or their individual ones as manorial lords. In either case, the administrator identified himself with his own local or class interests, or his employer's. Joseph's organized, centralized civil service was entirely different: it was a central service like the Army, owing its allegiance to the Crown and thus absolutely centralist in its political outlook, joining the Church, army and aulic aristocracy as a fourth great centripetal force in the Monarchy. Most of its members also developed strongly despotic mentalities.[1]

It was not only on the political grounds of centralism versus federalism that the bureaucracy came to represent an opposition to the provincial nobilities, but also on social. Even Joseph could not change the composition of his civil service entire, but he brought into it many more non-nobles, and facilitated their promotion by insisting on the criterion of merit. The bureaucrats thus came to feel themselves a distinct factor in the State, and as they found their feet, a strongly anti-aristocratic one. Even the nobles among them acquired a different mentality, that of servants of the State, not of their Lands or their class.

This new class had indeed, its own problems. Intensely parsimonious as he was, Joseph paid his servants badly,[2] worked them hard, and demanded of them high standards of integrity. He not only punished real corruption very heavily, but forbade many douceurs which had become so traditional as to be really harmless. They had very little independence, since Joseph decided everything himself, from issues of the highest policy to such problems as whether a zebra should be bought for Schönbrunn Zoo, or whether girls in State institutions should wear stays.

Moreover, the officials were under a constant galling, and even intimidating, supervision. Secret reports on their conduct were drawn up each

---

[1] The seeds of this change had, indeed, been sown by Maria Theresa when she founded the famous Theresianum, which was eventually a training college for bureaucracy. Its products were, however, only beginning to enter public life towards the end of her reign.

[2] A Kreishauptmann in Styria got only twelve hundred florins a year, out of which he had to pay three hundred to a secretary and a smaller sum to a clerk. A primary schoolmaster got one hundred florins.

year by their superiors, while spies reported on those in high offices. The secret police which was so notorious a feature of Francis I's reign was really of Joseph's creation. Before his day it had been a mere embryo; it was he who, in 1782, formed it into a separate service.[1] The new force, which reported directly to Joseph, enlisted a vast body of informers whose special duty it was at first to watch civil servants and officers; only later did foreigners and suspicious elements come under the same close supervision. With the most casual movement, contact and conversation liable to be reported, most civil servants lost the taste to exercise such initiative as would have been allowed them, and the bureaucracy became as notorious for its timidity as it was for its officiousness.

The secret police had also the duty of reporting on the state of public opinion, and in particular, on how it was receiving Joseph's various innovations. In this respect it must be said that Joseph personally showed great magnanimity, and the service, if not abused, could have been a useful substitute for the control by public opinion exercised in democracies by the people's representatives. The same purpose should have been served by the famous 'censorship edict' issued by Joseph as early as 11 June 1781. This did not abolish the censorship altogether, for immoral works or works calculated to bring religion into disrepute were still forbidden, but the preventive censorship was abolished and the limits of what could be printed extended fairly widely. Constructive criticism of all kinds was permitted, and might even be directed against the person of the Monarch himself. It is true that this licence was so inordinately abused by the vulgar scribblers of Vienna (and Viennese vulgarity can sink as low as Viennese refinement can climb high) that it was soon progressively restricted, and almost withdrawn a month before Joseph's death. But the years in which the importation of foreign works into Austria was relatively free undoubtedly brought new influences into the intellectual life of the Monarchy.

And these were, indeed, rather necessary, for while Joseph paid much attention to elementary schooling, which was already compulsory on paper and which he now extended in practice, by the foundation of many new schools, he had little use for higher education, except in specialist fields such as medicine, and in so far as it served to form efficient State officials. The number of gymnasia and humanist high schools was reduced, only Vienna, Pest and Liége being left with full University status. In particular, the axe descended mercilessly on all schools reserved for special social classes; even his mother's famous creation, the Theresianum, was abolished (to be revived, indeed, after his death). The survivors were placed under close State supervision, and the curricula severely rationalized, the humanist faculties suffering

[1] The head of the secret police, Count Pergen, was head also of the public '*Polizey*', and in 1789 the entire force was withdrawn from the control of the Hofkanzlei and made into an independent Hofstelle.

very heavily. Even the medical school of Vienna had difficulty in maintaining its four-year course. The number of pupils attending secondary schools in Hungary fell by fifty per cent, and in the Hereditary Lands, by a quarter.

The judicial system, the organization of which was now entirely independent, was completely re-cast. A new penal code was introduced, which abolished the death penalty, while, however, retaining many barbarous forms of corporal punishment.[1] The jurisdiction of the State Courts was extended to cover almost all cases above the Patrimonial Court level. The only separate jurisdiction to survive was that of the military; nobles and clergy became subject to the common law, although tried in separate courts.

Among the various changes in the civil law introduced in Joseph's *bürgerliches Gesetzbuch*, which was promulgated in 1786, two in particular may be mentioned: one, that the Einstandsrecht tying the ownership of landtäflich estates to certain birth, etc., qualifications was abolished; any purchaser might now legally acquire any such estate: the other that the value of an inheritance, real and personal, had to be divided equally between co-heirs, male and female.

Joseph's minor changes and reforms are too numerous to list, but it is fair to him to record that they included many of benefit to the helpless and unfortunate. Thus he was responsible for the establishment of Vienna's great 'General Hospital' (Allgemeines Krankenhaus) which became the foundation of the city's famous school of medicine; for a number of madhouses and institutions for the deaf and dumb; and for carrying on his mother's work in the field of what was for the day a considerable body of social legislation, including the prohibition of the employment in factories of children under nine years of age, and a system of poor law relief.[2]

In his industrial and commercial policy, Joseph, whose economic doctrines were a curious blend of the mercantilist and the physiocratic, built on the foundations laid by his mother. A new tariff introduced in 1781 prohibited altogether the importation of no less than two hundred articles, including cotton stuffs, linen cloths, stockings, buttons, needles, nearly all metal goods, watches, jewellery, butter, cheese and salt fish, except under licence, when they were subjected to an *ad valorem* duty of sixty per cent. More facilities were granted to persons prepared to start 'factories', and free competition was strongly encouraged; some of the guilds were abolished altogether, others had their privileges restricted, and they were placed under State control. Trade and industrial monopolies were abolished.

---

[1] Even the death penalty was abolished only because Joseph thought that 'it was never so effective a deterrent as a sentence of hard labour. The former was quickly over and forgotten, the latter remained longer in the public mind.'

[2] The obligation of every parish to provide relief for its own poor was laid down in 1783. A law of 1789 laid down that any person resident in a parish for ten years was entitled to relief in it; persons not so qualified were sent back to the parish of their birth.

According to Joseph's own statisticians, these measures had remarkable effects. The number of masters doubled in Bohemia between 1781 and 1788, and that of factory undertakings increased by 150%. The progress registered in Vienna was equally rapid. At the same time, it seems likely that some of this progress existed chiefly on paper; many of the new 'masters' were relatively unskilled men to whom the earlier restrictions had denied the name. The new competition certainly ruined many of the old craftsmen, and the growth of home industry was made at the expense of trade. One authority[1] has written that while Joseph hoped to speed up the economic evolution of his empire by a generation, he ended by setting it back by two. Nor was the planning always successful: for example, Joseph imported German stocking manufacturers into Galicia only to find that the peasants refused to wear anything but rags or straw inside their boots.

Perhaps the most economically beneficial of all Joseph's measures were those which had only indirect economic effects: the Toleration Patent and the freedom granted to the peasants – the purpose of this measure was, indeed, directly economic – to apprentice their sons to a trade.

There was one other respect in which Joseph carried his mother's economic policy further. The screw was tightened even more on Hungary, which was now practically unable to obtain from abroad any raw materials or manufactured goods except those which were produced in Austria. Further, in 1786, Joseph abolished altogether the duty on Austrian products entering Hungary, while retaining and even increasing that on Hungarian products entering Austria. Even Hungarian wheat and cattle entering Austria paid a higher duty than the same articles from other countries; and it was almost impossible for Hungary to export her products elsewhere.

This was part of Joseph's campaign to force the Hungarian nobles to pay taxation (*'cessante causa'*, he replied to their expostulations, *'cessabit etiam effectus'*). But the nobles proved obdurate, and Joseph's strength failed; thus his death left both cause and effect in being.

It would have been otherwise if he had lived to put through his reorganization of the land system, which was one of his most important fields of activity, but one in which he left his work uncompleted. A misleading impression of what he did in this respect, and even of what he meant to do, has, indeed, been created by the fact that one of his early Patents was entitled the 'Serfdom Patent' (*Leibeigenschaftspatent*), whence it has been concluded that Joseph transformed, or meant to transform, all the peasants of the Monarchy from serfs into free men. He actually never meant, any more than his mother, if as much, to abolish the *nexus subditelae*, but to establish throughout the Monarchy a condition of 'moderate hereditary subjection', such, as he himself wrote, already existed as in the Hereditary Lands. Most of the inhabitants of those Lands thus got no benefit at all under that particular Patent, and

[1] Kerner, op. cit., p. 225.

even those to whom it did apply[1] could hardly be said to have been serfs before. They did, however, get some very real improvements in their status under it, for it now universalized the peasant's right to marry, enter a trade or profession, or have his sons trained for one, without asking his lord's permission, and also to sell, exchange or mortgage his holding (up to two-thirds of its value) or leave it, again without permission. Further, all personal servitudes were abolished, except that the lord was still entitled to impress his peasants' orphan children for a term of paid domestic service.

Two other Patents, both dated 1 September 1781, improved the legal position of all peasants substantially. Under the 'Subjects' Patent' (*Untertanpatent*) any *Untertan* requiring redress against his lord, or feeling aggrieved at any demand made of him by his lord (or the lord's officials) and unable to obtain redress directly was given the right to appeal to the Kreisamt or equivalent State authority, when he could be given legal aid. The 'Penal Patent' (*Strafpatent*) limited further the penalties which a Patrimonial Court was entitled to inflict (it is true that these still included imprisonment on a diet of bread and water, forced labour in irons, and flogging, which, however, might not be inflicted by a professional) and laid down that only a legally qualified person might preside over a Patrimonial Court. If the lord of the manor was not so qualified, he had to provide a trained substitute at his own expense.

Some further alleviations of the peasants' position appeared later, mostly in 1788 or 1789. They included the abolition of the lords' remaining economic monopolies and other variants of the truck system[2] and limitation of their hunting rights and of oppressive game laws. Joseph also extended to most of his dominions, as a rule of law, the principle that a peasant holding might not be subdivided without official permission, and not at all into units smaller than a quarter holding (in Hungary one-eighth), the purpose of this ruling being to prevent the multiplication of purely agrarian holdings too small to support their occupants. One heir should maintain a viable holding, while the other children should go into other employment. He was, however, equally interested in avoiding the other extreme, and actually gave premiums to peasants prepared to subdivide holdings which were too large for them to

[1] It was first promulgated for Bohemia, Moravia and Silesia on 1 December 1781, then extended unaltered to Styria, Carinthia, Carniola and the Littoral, and Tirol, Vorarlberg and the Vorlande in 1782, and with modifications (usually in the direction of extension) to Transylvania in 1783, Hungary in 1785 and Galicia in 1786. It was held unnecessary to promulgate it in the Austrias, and in the other Western Lands it was promulgated only for safety's sake, and because it contained a provision, not already on all their statute books, that a peasant leaving his holding had to notify the military authorities.

[2] The Galician landlords, however, resisted the abolition of the propinatio so strongly that Joseph left it untouched, only forbidding the farming of the right to Jews. The right was not, in the event, abolished until 1882, when the Galician landlords were granted 1,000,000 fl. a year for twenty-two years as compensation.

cultivate fully, and allowed subdivision into very smallholdings in areas where the smallholders spent part of their time on industrial homework.[1]

Meanwhile, the rule of equal inheritance had made the *Bestiftungszwang* often extremely onerous in practice, since the heir taking over the farm might be crippled financially by payments to his brothers and sisters. Later legislation sought a remedy in arranging that the payments should be made on the basis of an artificially low valuation, but the problem thus raised was, as we shall see, still acute a century later.

Joseph, however, was not so much interested in alleviating the peasants' lot as in turning as many of them as possible into economically independent taxpayers and in reducing the area of thinly populated and lightly taxed demesne land. At the outset of his reign he tried to effect this in three ways; by extending the Raab and other emphyteutic systems, and by getting more peasants to buy in their holdings, and to commute their dues and robot for cash rents. He extended the Raab system to all estates under his direct control, and pressed private lords to follow his example; increased the inducements to peasants to buy in their holdings,[2] and allowed all peasants on Crown estates the option of paying their rents in cash or in kind. None of these endeavours, however, met with very much success. A few landlords in Bohemia put out some of their land on emphyteutic tenures, but not many; the peasants, at least outside the German districts, could not be persuaded to buy in their holdings, and commutation also remained a rarity outside those areas.

But meanwhile Joseph had been evolving a really radical plan. This was to raise the whole contributio exclusively from a single land tax, which was to be levied equally on all land in the Monarchy, at a rate of 12·22%[3] of its gross yield,[4] as calculated on the average return from it of the preceding ten years. The rustical peasant was, in addition, to pay his lord in cash (or if in kind, at its value at current market prices) a further 17·78% in lieu of all dues and servitudes, including the payments to the Church and the commune, which the lord was to take over. As at first announced, this measure was to come into force on 11 November 1789; the date was subsequently postponed to 1 November 1790.

---

[1] This provision, known as the Bestiftungszwang, was not introduced into the Tirol, Lombardy or the Netherlands.

[2] In 1789 Joseph allowed peasants who had not bought in their holdings practically the same testamentary, etc., rights over them as were enjoyed by the other class. This, however, was one of the concessions which vanished immediately after his death. In a memorandum submitted by him to Franz Joseph in 1849 (reproduced by Friedjung, *Historische Aufsätze*, pp. 58 ff.), Prince Windisch-Graetz wrote that 100,000 peasants in Bohemia were holding their land on Raab and other emphyteutic tenures, but most of these were probably Crown tenants, or had made the change later. In any case, many people find it difficult to distinguish between an emphyteutic tenure and one which had been bought in and its services commuted.

[3] In Galicia, 8·53%.

[4] That is, with no deductions for seed or working expenses.

This was a typical Joseph II plan. If it had had the effect of lightening the peasants' burdens at all – we have not the figures to be sure on this point – the alleviation would certainly have been small, nor was its purpose to confer benefits on the peasants, but simply to give the State a larger share of the fruits of their toil, which meant reducing the landlords' part. For the landlords, the increased burden would undoubtedly have been heavy, especially since Joseph was asking for increased taxation to finance his military adventures. But the plan was made even more objectionable to the landlords by a provision that the tax was to rest on all land really existing, not on land the existence of which had been disclosed to the revenue authorities. In 1784 surveys had been instituted in all Lands except the Tirol, and it had emerged that something like one-third of all land in most provinces had been concealed. This would now have become liable to taxation, or might possibly even be declared not to belong to its present occupant.

Many of Joseph's measures, enacted or proposed, naturally evoked acute discontent among the victims of them; the defenders of historic rights, above all in Hungary and Belgium, the representatives of the Roman Catholic Church, from the Pope (who in 1782 took the unprecedented step of visiting Joseph in Vienna) downward, the landlords, the conscious nationalists among the non-Germans, and all others on whose interests or susceptibilities he had trampled. He might, however, still have convinced a majority of his subjects that the blessings of his regime outweighed its burdens, but for his military and foreign policy.

From his early youth Joseph was by temperament an ardent and inveterate militarist. He was the first of his line to appear for preference in uniform, and he devoted particular attention to the army, improving the material conditions of all ranks and greatly enhancing the social status of the Corps of Officers, although he brought into it many men of non-noble origin. He also raised its strength to a target figure of 295,711 men,[1] which he tried at first to reach by putting pressure on the 'Conscription Lands' (most of which had, in the interest of their agricultural production, been boycotting the operations of the recruiting authorities by every device at their disposal, describing their labourers as skilled men or even concealing their existence) and by asking

---

[1] The orders to this effect were raised in April 1781. The force was now to be composed as follows:

57 infantry regiments of 3,061 men each	174,777
3 garrison regiments	6,995
17 Frontier regiments of 3,040 men each	51,680
Artillery	13,560
Sappers and miners	1,219
34 cavalry regiments of 1,252 men each	42,568
1 csaikist (river patrol) and 13 military cordon detachments	5,184
	295,711

Hungary to raise her quota of 'volunteers' to 52,000 (eleven infantry and eight hussar regiments). Since, even so, the figure could not be made up, conscription was extended to Hungary and the Tirol in 1785-6.

These proved to be among the most unpopular of Joseph's measures, and among those hardest to enforce. They evoked a torrent of complaints, chiefly from the Tirol and Hungary, but by no means confined to those Lands.[1] Many potential soldiers fled across the frontiers, or were hidden by their masters.

But worst of all was the fact that Joseph wasted this force in pursuit of a foreign policy which was over-ambitious and uniformly unfortunate. His heart's project, of exchanging the Austrian Netherlands for Bavaria, would have brought Austria a great accession of strength had it succeeded, but the end of it was simply to estrange France so deeply that the Austro-French alliance ceased in practice to exist, and to draw the German Princes into a Fürstenbund under Prussian patronage; he had already estranged the Netherlands. Not altogether of his own wish, Joseph found himself back on the old duelling-ground with Prussia, and it was largely for their mutual defence against Prussia that in May 1781 he concluded a treaty with Catherine of Russia.

But with this he was drawn into Catherine's schemes for expansion into the Balkans. In 1783, when a revolt, instigated by Russia herself, broke out in the Crimea, Joseph still preserved a measure of restraint. He mobilized to put pressure on the Porte, but rejected Catherine's grandiose project for a partition of Turkey, under which Constantinople, with Thrace, Macedonia and other parts of Turkey in Europe, were to be constituted a Russian secundo-geniture, while Austria was compensated with Serbia, Bosnia and the Herzegovina.[2] But in 1787, unwilling to see all the profits going to Russia (which had made large gains in 1784, while Austria got little), he forgot the circumspection which he had preserved on the earlier occasion. There was undoubtedly a *casus foederis*, for although all the real aggression was coming from Russia, it was the Porte that, skilfully egged on by Prussia, had declared war, and Joseph was only fulfilling his obligation when he in his turn declared war on the Porte on 9 February 1789. Even so, however, his treaty bound him only to provide an auxiliary corps of 30,000 men. Yet, although he spoke of the campaign with foreboding, a sort of madness seems to have seized him, and he sent an army of 200,000 men to the Turkish frontier.

[1] See Mitranov, I. 358 ff. Gorizia, for example, pleaded not only that its vineyards could not spare the labour, but that the Gorizian peasant was '*molle, timido, nullo meno que guerriero*', and would make a '*cattivo soldato*'.

[2] Among other provisions of this remarkable 'Greek Project', Austria was also to have received Dalmatia, then in possession of Venice, which was to be compensated with the Morea, Cyprus and Crete. Moldavia, Wallachia and Bessarabia were to be constituted an independent State of 'Dacia', and France, Britain and Spain to receive other fragments of Turkey in Asia.

The Austrian arms began by winning important successes, including the capture of Belgrade, but then everything went wrong. The other European Powers combined against Russia and Austria. Prussia, whose foreign policy was then directed by the ambitious and anti-Austrian Herzberg, negotiated with the Porte, with which it actually signed a treaty in January 1790. This was, indeed, afterwards disavowed, but Prussia also negotiated with the Poles for an understanding which was to include the restoration to Poland of part of Austrian Galicia, and mobilized on the Austrian frontier. There seemed every possibility that she would shortly actually attack the Monarchy. Prussia, England and Holland were allied, and Sweden attacked Russia in Finland. Thus threatened in her rear, Russia, which should have borne the brunt of the fighting against Turkey, was forced to leave this to Austria, whose troops, very incompetently led, were driven back into the marish plains of South Hungary. Here the army proved too large to be deployed effectively, and much too large to be supplied adequately, and was ravaged by the ague. Joseph himself went down to take command, but his own health was affected: he fell victim to a sickness which soon threatened to be fatal.

Meanwhile, he had chosen this precise juncture to threaten crass violence to the historic liberties of the Austrian Netherlands, where unrest had shown itself as early as May 1787 and had grown formidable in 1788. The situation was equally dangerous in Hungary, where the nobles were bitterly resentful of Joseph's ordinances, and now even the peasants were disaffected, for they were being forced to furnish the army with recruits and supplies, for which they were paid at half price, or in paper assignats. Discontent was rife in Vienna itself, where vulgar lampoons were hawked in the streets, almost within earshot of the dying Emperor.

In face of all this, Joseph showed incredible obstinacy, or courage. He brusquely refused any concessions whatever in the Netherlands until November 1789, when the Statthalter had already been forced to leave Brussels. Then he yielded there, revoked his ordinances and promised to agree with the Estates on their Constitution. It was too late: on 25 November the Estates of Flanders declared Joseph forfeit of the throne, and on 10 January 1790, Belgium – openly enough encouraged by Prussia – proclaimed its independence.

The turning-point in Hungary came in 1788 when, his own reorganization not having got beyond the blue-print stage, Joseph was forced himself to convoke the old County Congregationes and to appeal to them to produce for him the recruits and supplies which he needed. This gave the nobles their opportunity. They answered the request with protests and passive resistance. The Consilium and even the Chancellery supported them, advising Joseph that recruits and supplies could not lawfully be obtained without a vote of the Diet, and urging him to repeal his unlawful enactments, convoke the Diet, submit to coronation and swear to the Constitution.

This was the attitude of Joseph's most loyal Hungarian subjects. Others planned true rebellion, and emissaries of this group approached the King of Prussia (some directly, some through the Prussian Minister in Vienna, Baron Jacobi), asking him to propose a candidate for the throne of Hungary (Prince Karl August of Weimar was suggested for the post, although he hesitated to accept it), and to guarantee its Constitution.

Driven against the wall, Joseph yielded. On 28 January 1790, in a letter which emphasized how good his intentions had been, he revoked all his enactments relating to Hungary except the Toleration Patent, the Livings Patent, and the Peasant Patents. He acknowledged the right of the Diet to participate in legislation, but hoped that the Estates would not press for an early Diet, which would be difficult in view of the situation and of his own ill-health. In the same document he ordered the return of the Holy Crown to Hungary, whither it was escorted back amid scenes of indescribable jubilation. But he was not destined ever to be crowned King of Hungary. On 20 February he died.

3

Leopold II

When Joseph knew himself to be dying, he had sent for his brother and prospective successor, Leopold, whose previous portion had been the family secundo-geniture of Tuscany. The call was not welcome to Leopold. He was used to Tuscany, and attached to it, and he had been ruling it with a wise moderation, to his own satisfaction and that of his subjects. His somewhat timid and domestic nature could not but shrink from the prospect of being thrown into a maelstrom of huge conflicts, particularly as he thought that they had been misguidedly conjured up. Perhaps alone of all the Habsburgs who ever reigned, he was a genuine constitutionalist. He approved Montesquieux's doctrine of the division of powers, believed in the right of the people to fix taxation and to be protected against arbitrary rule, and even in a 'contract between sovereign and people', the latter no longer being bound to obey the former if he violated it, held it to be 'useless to try to impose even good on the people if they are not convinced of its utility' – force only 'estranged hearts and spirits without altering views' and even welcomed the first news of the French Revolution. 'The regeneration of France,' he had written to his sister Marie Christine on 14 June 1789, 'will be an example which all sovereigns and governments of Europe will be forced, willy-nilly, to copy. Infinite happiness will result from this everywhere, the end of injustice, wars, conflicts and unrests, and it will be one of the most useful fashions introduced by France into Europe.' He was absolutely unwilling to share the Government with his brother, as Joseph wished, for if he did so, both foreign Courts and the peoples of the Monarchy would believe that he endorsed Joseph's principles and systems, so that his credit would be irretrievably and uselessly compromised; besides which, he could 'get into conflicts with the Emperor every minute, and tie his hands for the future'.

He therefore delayed his coming, and was still in Tuscany when the news of Joseph's death reached him. Then, perforce, he started north. He reached Vienna on 12 March, and at once set himself to clearing up the mess which his brother had made.

The problems confronting him were both international and domestic, and he had, of course, to move simultaneously in both fields, particularly since the problems were to a large extent mutually inter-dependent, but it will make for simplicity if we describe first his handling of the international situation. The key to this lay, as he rightly saw, with Prussia, for although the only hostilities in which Austria was then formally engaged were those with the Porte, on the Danube, the operations there had reached something of a stalemate, with Austria holding a slight advantage through her possession of Belgrade, and she thus had no reason to fear the outcome of their continuance so long as Prussia did not intervene. But they still held down a part of her troops, leaving her with far too few to repel a Prussian invasion of Bohemia or Galicia. If, moreover, Prussia's privy negotiations (of which Leopold was fully informed) with the Hungarian malcontents prospered, there was an acute danger of a full-fledged Hungarian rebellion, supported by Prussia. This danger loomed so large in Leopold's eyes that historians have written that 'he looked at his relations with Prussia from the point of view of his Hungarian policy, not vice-versa'.[1] 'The King of Hungary concluded a Convention at Reichenberg with the King of Prussia, to enable him to remain King of Hungary at all, and to get that Kingdom secured to himself through coronation.'[2]

Only a fortnight after his arrival in Vienna, Leopold wrote his momentous letter – perhaps the most important of his reign – to Frederick William, protesting his own pacific intentions and his innocence of any wish to upset the *status quo*. Difficulties followed, bred of mutual suspicion and of frustrated ambitions in both camps, but on 26 June formal negotiations were opened in Reichenbach, and these led to the signature, on 27 July, of the Convention of that name. Under this, Leopold agreed to conclude an armistice with the Porte and to open negotiations for a definitive peace on the basis, subject to minor rectifications, of the *status quo ante bellum*. If the frontier was altered, Prussia was to receive equivalent compensation. Austria was not to help Russia if she tried to carry on the war; Prussia and her allies were to undertake the further mediation and guarantee the future peace. Leopold had already assured Prussia that he was not trying to upset the balance in Germany; now Prussia agreed that Austria's authority should be restored in Belgium, subject to an amnesty and the restoration of the former Constitution, which would be jointly guaranteed by Prussia and the Maritime Powers. Most important of all for Leopold was the King of Prussia's jettisoning of his Hungarian clients. He had suggested that he should be made a guarantor of the Hungarian Constitution, but when Leopold rejected this suggestion strongly, the Prussian dropped it, and therewith tacitly disinterested himself in Hungary.

[1] Silagi, *Mitarbeiter*, p. 30, quoted with approval by Wandruschka, II. 284.
[2] Wandruschka, l.c. Most European historians attach less weight to the part played by the Hungarian factor in determining Leopold's policy, and for that matter, few Hungarian historians suggest that the danger was as acute as Leopold believed; but what mattered was not how big it was, but how big Leopold thought it.

On 23 September Austria duly concluded an armistice with the Porte at Giurgevo, and the definitive peace, which brought Austria one or two small frontier rectifications, but lost her Belgrade, was signed at Sistovo on 4 August 1791. Peace between Russia and Turkey followed under the Treaty of Jassy (9 January 1792), which advanced Russia's frontier to the Dniester.

Kaunitz, and others, denounced the Convention for a diplomatic retreat by Leopold before Prussia's pressure (and he himself so represented it to Catherine of Russia), but it was rather a signal success for him. It marked, indeed, a retreat from forward positions which Joseph had tried to occupy, but most of those had been entirely untenable. If it entailed the end of Austria's alliance with Russia, it brought her far more elsewhere. It did not, of course, eliminate the old rivalry between her and Prussia, but it put it into cold storage. Prussia dropped her intrigues in Galicia and Hungary, and for the next two or three years accepted Austria's leadership in Germany (this, *inter alia*, making possible Leopold's coronation as Emperor, which took place, after an unopposed election, on 9 October 1790). It even made it possible, as an immediate result, for Austria to recover Belgium. When Leopold offered the Belgians the restoration of the constitutional *status quo ante* Joseph's innovations, they rejected it out of hand, but he in his turn rejected the proposals made (on 10 December) by the mediating Powers and sent troops into the country, which, now that Prussia was standing aside, they reoccupied without difficulty.

This success proved, indeed, short-lived, for it was only two years later that Dumouriez' victories ended for ever Austria's rule in the Netherlands. But in his other dominions, Leopold was able to turn to the work of internal pacification unhampered either by Prussian intrigues or by the expensive and exhausting war with the Porte – no small gain from the financial point of view alone, for Leopold had been at his wits' end to finance his armies, which were now quickly brought down to a more tolerable figure.

Even when in Tuscany, Leopold had kept himself well informed on events and conditions in the countries over which he might one day have to rule, and had probably reached fairly clear conclusions on the line he would follow. He might not have been abreast of every local problem, but he had been made acquainted with many of them before reaching Vienna, for in every Land through which he passed – the Tirol, Carinthia, Styria, Lower Austria, not to mention Mantua – deputations from the Estates, and in a few cases, also from local peasants, had waited on him, nominally to pay their respects, but in nearly all cases, also to present their grievances. He had returned non-committal answers to most of them, and on reaching Vienna, had made himself *incommunicado* for several weeks, studying documents and conferring with advisers. Then, on 1 May, invitations were sent out to the Estates to assemble at their several headquarters for discussion of their requests. The Hungarian Diet, which was to meet in Buda, was especially invited to consider the questions of Leopold's coronation, and of the election of a Palatine.

Hungary's was the only case in which any important negotiations behind the scenes had preceded the invitation, for even if only a minority of Hungarians had been privy to the intrigues with Prussia, a considerable number held the view that Joseph's unconstitutional rule had rendered invalid the contracts between the Crown and the nation concluded in 1687, 1715 and 1741, and were demanding a new election, accompanied by a re-statement of the relationship. Leopold had been adamant on the right of himself, and after him, his heirs-in-law to succeed to the throne, but he had been prepared to strengthen his supporters' hand by such concessions as he himself thought justifiable. The designation of Buda for the Diet's venue was one of these, the promise to fill the office of Palatine another, and he had already made one or two other popular moves, including the official reinstatement of Latin as the language of business of the Counties.

Thanks to these concessions, and even more to the news, which had soon filtered through, of Leopold's negotiations with Prussia, the extremists who had denied even his right to convoke a Diet had been overruled, so that it could be taken as certain that the Diet would meet. Nevertheless, its proceedings were bound to be turbulent. It would, indeed, be wrong to regard Joseph's reforms as having been universally unpopular in Hungary. By what he had done, and still more, by what he might do in the future, he had made himself the hope of the burghers and peasants, and the younger intellectuals were enthusiastic for him. As we have said, even the pioneers of the new Magyar linguistic movement, such as Kazinczy and, indeed, many others, took no exception to the Germanization of the schools, for they argued that this would bring enlightenment into the country, and enlightenment would bring reform. But precisely the County nobles, who would dominate the Diet, had had reason to object to practically everything that Joseph had done. For them the substitution of German for Latin meant that they would have to learn a new language, or if they were salaried, lose their incomes. The proposed new land tax would have swept away the most treasured of all their privileges (only recently reaffirmed 'for all time' by Maria Theresa) and the peasant legislation bore really hard on the Hungarian landlords, with their primitive, and largely still pre-monetary, economy. The discrimination against Hungary's trade and industry was another acute grievance.

Many of these measures, moreover, were not only wounding to the national pride, but constituted direct breaches of the national Constitution, and the natural consequence was that the resentment took the form, in the first instance, of a vociferous demand for the restoration of the Constitution and reparation for Joseph's violations of it. But many of the 'Congregationes' wanted more than mere restoration. By this time not only the doctrines of the Enlightenment, but also those of the French Revolution had reached Hungary. It was characteristic of the immutable national outlook that it still regarded the 'nation' as identical with the body of 'nobles' to whom Hungarian constitutional tradition still confined that term; there were very few suggestions for extending it to include the non-privileged classes. But many now interpreted the new doctrines as conferring greatly increased rights on the 'nation' vis-à-vis the King.

Thus when, in June, the Diet did meet, although Leopold's succession was no longer openly challenged, speeches were made on the *'independentia et majestas'* of the nation and on its rights vis-à-vis the Crown which would not have sounded outlandish in the Paris of the day. Speakers put forward the most far-reaching demands: for a separate Hungarian army and separate Hungarian representation at foreign Courts; for purely Hungarian central authorities in charge of the central services, including those concerned with the country's military and financial obligations. A 'treaty' was to be concluded with the Austrian and Bohemian Lands, respecting their shared obligations. The King was not to govern by Patents or Decrees; his proposals were to be submitted to a Council, which should be entitled to pronounce on their legality and suspend their operation if the decision were unfavourable (the *jus resistendi* was to be restored); all legislation was to be based on the joint deliberations of the King and the Diet, which was to meet annually. Provisions regarding the peasants were to be the concern of the Diet. The integrity of Hungary's old frontiers was to be restored, Transylvania, the Military Frontier and Galicia-Lodomeria being incorporated in them. In addition, the administration of the mines and the posts was to be restored to Hungarian hands; only Hungarians – as far as possible, nobles – to be employed in public office; the restrictions on Hungarian exports to Austria lifted. The King was to swear to all this in an Inaugural Diploma, which was to be regarded as a 'fundamental law'.

In addition, there was strong agitation for the repeal of Joseph's aggravations of the Austro-Hungarian economic relationship,[1] and finally, for the elimination of German from the administration and education; this last being accompanied by the new demand, which had quite suddenly caught the Diet's fancy, that the official language of the future should be, not Latin, but Magyar.[2]

Fortunately for Leopold, he had allies in Hungary itself. The Diet saw

[1] It is curious that not more was asked, but there seems to have been a fear that, in that case, the question of taxation would inevitably be reopened.

[2] For the sensational suddenness with which the Diet swung over from its previous demand for the restoration of Latin as the language of public life to the introduction of Magyar, see Silagi, *Jakobiner*, pp. 61 ff. To a large extent, the fashion had been set by the appearance of Dugonics' historical romance, *Etelka*, which caught the public fancy in an extraordinary degree. It should, however, be remarked that for many years thereafter some Hungarian Counties still, like the Croats, regarded Latin as the bulwark of their liberties.

the first emergence, in modern terms, of a problem which was to haunt Hungarian politics for the next century. The Croat Sabor which met before the Buda Diet had decided that the surest safeguard for Croat liberty against Habsburg absolutism lay in close co-operation with Hungary, and had instructed its delegates to work in harmony with the Hungarians and to submit themselves to the will of the majority in matters of common interest. But this attitude had made the assumption, which the leading Croat delegate, Skerlecz, expounded at Buda, that Hungary and Croatia were *regna socia*, whose union in AD 1106 had come about by mutual agreement, and that neither party was competent to enact laws binding on the other without its consent.

The Serbs, too, were astir, and in September Leopold allowed them to call a Congress, to which he himself allowed the name of a 'Diet'. At this assemblage, which met under the Presidency of the Serbian Archbishop, Stratimirovics, and of a bellicose General named Serujac, tumultuous speeches were made, speakers claiming to represent four million [*sic*] 'Illyrians' of Hungary against only two million [*sic*] Magyars, and describing the latter as 'orang-utans whom Vienna had turned into men'; the concrete demands were for a separate 'national' organization with a territory based on the Bánát,[1] with its own Government, lay and ecclesiastical, and its own representation in Vienna.

Finally, the Transylvanian Diet did not endorse the demand for union with Hungary, but asked for restoration of its own Constitution. And here, too, there was a cross-current. The two Roumanian Bishops[2] presented Leopold with a petition entitled the *Supplex Libellus Valachorum*. Much of this consisted of a historical exposé (Sinkay's work) setting out the thesis of Roumanian priority in Transylvania. Its positive demands were for recognition of the Roumanian nobles, as such, as a fourth 'nation' and of the Uniate and Orthodox Churches as 'received' religions. Roumanians should be represented proportionately in the Diet and public office, and in the Counties and Districts in which they formed a majority, Roumanian place-names should be 'restored'. A National Congress should meet to discuss details.

The sympathetic reception which Leopold gave to the Serbs, in particular, but also other devices employed by him,[3] cooled heads in Buda, and when the news of the Convention of Reichenbach reached the Diet, its members

---

[1] The liquidation of the Bánát, although enacted, had not yet been articulated in the Hungarian Corpus Juris.

[2] Bobb (Uniate) and Adamovitch (Orthodox).

[3] On these see Wandruschka, II. 281 ff. They included the establishment in the towns of 'burgher guards', which were mostly composed of Germans, the organization, through Leopold's secret agents, of petitions from the burghers and peasants, and the dissemination of a rumour that the King of Prussia had betrayed to Leopold the names of his Hungarian correspondents, who were going to be tried for high treason. Leopold had also replaced the garrison of Buda by Croat units.

finally realized that they could not hope for satisfaction of any very extreme demands. Leopold himself let it be known that many of the proposals which had been mooted were unacceptable, but that he was prepared to reach an honourable compromise. Accordingly, the coronation duly took place on 15 November, Leopold having, as he had stipulated, signed a diploma in the same terms as Maria Theresa's. The Diet then elected Leopold's fourth son, the young Archduke Alexander, Palatine, and then settled down in comparatively chastened mood to discuss the further re-statement of the legal and constitutional position.

The laws which emerged from these deliberations in fact secured the Diet most of the rights to which Hungary was historically entitled. The Diet expressly recognized Leopold's hereditary right, and that of his heirs, to the throne, and the King's right to 'govern' the country, but Leopold gave it a renewed and solemn pledge, which in substance did little more than repeat Charles III's declarations of 1715 and 1723 and Maria Theresa's of 1741, but was now embodied in a law, treated thereafter by the Hungarians as 'fundamental',[1] that although the succession united Hungary *inseparabiliter ac indivisibiliter* with the Habsburgs' other lands, yet Hungary, with its partes adnexae constituted a free realm, independent in all the forms of its Government, including the entire administration, not subject to any other land or people and possessed of its own forms of State and Constitution (*propriam habens consistentiam et constitutionem*). It could therefore be ruled and governed only by its own lawfully crowned hereditary King, and only in accordance with its own laws and customs, and not 'after the pattern of other provinces'.

Leopold agreed that the right to enact, interpret and repeal legislation resided jointly with the King and the Estates in session. Neither he nor his successors would rule by Patents or Rescripts, and the Courts were not obliged to recognize the validity of any such pronouncements. The Vice-Regal Council was entitled to query the validity of any executive act. Two loopholes by which Leopold's predecessors had evaded these obligations were stopped: the successor to the Crown was bound to submit himself to coronation within six months of accession, and the Diet had to be convoked triennially. The Palatine had to reside, and the Holy Crown had to be kept, in the country. The consent of the Diet was required for any demand for taxes or recruits and in a number of other fields. Foreign Affairs and Defence remained, however, Monarchic services, and no modification was made in the central structure of the Government, including the Staatsrat and Hofkriegsrat, and the Hungarian Court Chancellery.

For the rest, Joseph's retraction of the bulk of his work in Hungary had automatically restored the *status quo* of 1780 in a number of respects, which new legislation would be required to alter. Leopold refused to support the union of Transylvania, which was thus reinstated within its 1780 frontiers, as

[1] Law x of 1790.

were Croatia (the ambiguous position of the Slavonian Counties was not cleared up) and the Military Frontier. The Bánát, however, was duly 'provincialized', except for that part of it which remained assigned to the Military Frontier. Similarly, the administrative system recovered its old shape and competencies. The Serbs did not receive their separate territory, nor their 'national' organization, but in January 1791 Leopold did establish for them an independent 'Illyrian Court Chancellery'. Later, indeed, he was induced to state that this would be 'no different from the old Hofdeputatio', and thus not incompatible with the Hungarian Constitution.

The fact that Joseph had not retracted three of his Patents had not, in Hungarian eyes, left them legally valid, since they had not been enacted by agreement with the Diet, but Leopold insisted that the Diet should now enact legislation in the appropriate sense.

The Law passed in lieu of the Toleration Patent (which had in the end to be dictated by Leopold himself) gave Protestants freedom of worship both in Inner Hungary and Croatia, and in Inner Hungary, full equality with Catholics, but in Croatia their legal position remained that laid down by Law XLVI of 1741, under which they were unable to own land or hold public office, although allowed to settle in the country, lease land or practise a trade.[1] The Greek Orthodox Church became established and was admitted to full equality in Inner Hungary and the 'partes adnexae'. Jews received permission to settle in towns, except the 'privileged' mining districts of North Hungary, and to practise trades or industry in them.

The Diet, like the Estates of most of the Lands, was as obstructionist as it could manage on the peasant question, but eventually passed a law provisionally legalizing Maria Theresa's *urbarium*, instructing the County Courts to administer swift and impartial justice, and restoring the peasant's right to leave his land at will,[2] provided he had paid all his dues. The effect was, broadly, to legalize the substance, although not the wording, of Joseph's main Patents of 1781, but not that of his later enactments.

The nobles automatically recovered their exemption from taxation, and the proposed land survey was cancelled (in celebration whereof, even the completed surveys were ceremonially burned in all Counties except three). Otherwise, economic legislation reverted to the 1780 position, except that

[1] It will be noted that on this point the Hungarians gave way, in practice, to the Croats' demand that legislation with which they disagreed should not be imposed in Croatia. They were prepared to make the same concession on the linguistic question, but owing to Leopold's attitude, described below, the point did not arise. The difference of principle, however, remained unresolved, for although the Hungarians did not argue the point to a finish in the Diet (fortunately for the proceedings of that body) they did not commit themselves to acceptance of the Croat thesis, which a Hungarian publicist set himself to refute in a brochure published in 1791.

[2] Moving day was, however, only once a year (on St Gregory's day) and notice had to be given (at Michaelmas).

the price of salt was not to be raised without consultation with the Diet. On the important linguistic issue, Leopold consented to a law proscribing the use of a 'foreign language' (sc. German) as an official medium, but rejected a request (against which the Croats also protested) that Magyar should replace Latin in the public services. 'For the time being' Latin was to be used, but the Magyar language might be taught in the University and gymnasia with a view to the training up of a future supply of Magyar-speaking officials.

Many of these decisions were recognized by both sides as being provisional, and the Diet was to set up six Committees to work out proposals in a large number of fields. Leopold promised to consider their reports when the Diet met next.

In Transylvania, Leopold declared the Constitution restored and convoked the Diet, to which he submitted the *Supplex Libellus Valachorum* for its consideration. It is unlikely that the Diet would ever easily have admitted any request for equality from the Roumanians, and in 1791 it was in a particularly unyielding mood, for in 1784 the Roumanian peasants had risen under three leaders named Hora, Cloșka and Crișan, and had committed a frightful jacquerie in which many Hungarians, men and women, had been bestially slaughtered and their homes burned. The Diet rejected the petition out of hand and all that the Roumanians, as such, got out of it was the equality to which the Orthodox Church was promoted, here also. They were also allowed to elect their own Bishop, although he remained the subordinate of the Serb Metropolitan of Karlóca. The Roumanian (and other) peasants also received the benefit of Joseph II's Patent, which received legal validity here, as in Inner Hungary.

For the rest, the old Constitution was restored, and with it the independence of the Transylvanian Court Chancellery from the Hungarian, although in the economical form that the same body of men did the work of both offices, calling themselves the Hungarian or the Transylvanian Chancellery, according to their agenda. Transylvania, like Hungary, further received an assurance that it should not be governed after the pattern of other provinces.

The demands put forward by the Estates of most of the Hereditary and Bohemian Lands had not differed greatly in kind, *mutatis mutandis*, from the Hungarians'. Nearly all of them had asked for the restoration of historic rights, and the Bohemian extremists had been hardly less extravagant than the Hungarian. They wanted to revive the electoral character of the Bohemian Crown and to go back to the *status quo ante* the Vernewerte Landesordnung. There was to be a Constitution in the form of 'a contract between the Monarch and the nation', under which the legislative power should be divided between the King and the Diet, which was to meet annually. The King should swear to this instrument in an inaugural diploma. The Hereditary Lands of course asked for less, since they had never enjoyed so much in the past, but generally speaking, demanded restoration of the *status quo ante* Maria Theresa's administrative reforms, together with the restoration of such noble privileges as their monopoly of the higher posts in the State service. Nearly all the Estates asked for the revocation of Joseph's measures in favour of the peasants, particularly the new land tax. Most of the non-German Lands asked for concessions in favour of their 'national languages'.

Here, too, Leopold was willing to meet some demands, but not to compromise on the hereditary character of his throne, nor to set the clock back indefinitely. He accepted coronation in Prague (which took place on 12 August 1791), but ended by declaring 1764 the 'normal year' for the constitutional position, and treating as invalid only those changes which had been introduced after that date. As all Maria Theresa's essential administrative reforms had been completed by 1764, this meant that the regime of *de facto* centralization and absolutism was maintained, although the administrative and financial services were re-separated. The same datum year was taken for the other Lands, which meant, indeed, that Styria, Carinthia, Gorizia, etc. recovered their Gubernia, but the competence and composition of the Estates was extended only in minor respects: the burghers of Styria got more representation, the Tirol recovered some of its special privileges, especially in the field of taxation. All the Estates were, however, assured that their views would be heard before new general laws were introduced, or old ones amended; but they were not conceded the right to veto, or even delay application of, such measures.

Leopold refused to repeal Joseph's main Peasant Patents of 1781, in spite of the landlords' representations that they were seducing the peasants into idleness, drunkenness and contumacy, and in the Western Lands, unlike Hungary, he also left in force most of Joseph's later, minor concessions in favour of the peasants.[1] He did, however, duly withdraw the far-reaching Patent of 1789, with its proposed unified land tax, while reserving his right to reintroduce it after it had been reconsidered and subjected to any amendments which commended themselves. This meant that the system of direct taxation was back on its pre-1789 footing, and with it the rustical peasants' obligation to pay taxation, in its various forms, to their lords. It seems fairly certain that Leopold would have liked to see the Raab system, or something akin to it, generalized, or at least, cash rents substituted for the robot and dues in kind; but the Estates, who in 1789 had, at least in some Lands, not been entirely against this,[2] had now swung round completely and declared

[1] The uneingekauft peasants lost the concessions granted them in 1790, but the whole question of peasant inheritance was re-regulated in the direction of increasing the peasants' security of tenure and their powers to dispose of their property. These were now almost unrestricted, subject to the Bestiftungszwang.

[2] According to a report by the Hofkammer in 1792, cit. Blum, p. 56, the landlords of 1,600 estates in Lower Austria had agreed with their peasants to commute robot services against cash.

themselves strongly in favour of robot, so that Leopold contented himself with a Rescript affirming the legality of commutation in its various forms, if both parties agreed, and recommending it, but applying no compulsion.

Leopold allowed a Chair of Czech to be established in Prague, and when he died, was reported to be intending to restore instruction in Czech in the grammar schools and gymnasia of Bohemia. Knowledge of German ceased to be compulsory in the administrative services of Galicia and the Italian Lands.

He carried through, or at least began on (much of his work was left unfinished owing to his premature death) changes in many other fields, nearly all of them having the effect of rubbing the rough edges off Joseph's enactments, while keeping such core of good as they contained. He suspended the extremely harsh punishments in Joseph's penal code and set up a new Commission (to which no member of its predecessor was allowed to belong) to work out a new code. Another Commission was to establish a new educational system, leaving much more initiative and self-government to the teachers. This body had only half-completed its work when he died, but the State control had already been relaxed, and some gymnasia restored. Leopold refused to repeal the Toleration Patent or the dissolution of the monasteries (although some of these were reinstated),[1] or even to give the Bishops charge of the 'Religion Fund'. He liquidated the General Seminaries and dropped some of Joseph's interferences with ritual, but he maintained the *Placetum Regium* and the principle that the clergy were servants of the State and not entitled to speak except on purely religious questions.[2] He promised to consider changing Joseph's marriage law, but never had time for the consideration. The censorship was, indeed, made more stringent, all works being forbidden which 'criticized and blamed' the Government, and the reproduction forbidden of foreign writings, or parts of them, calculated 'to disturb public tranquillity by spreading dangerous doctrines'. This measure, however, had been impending when Joseph died.

The police were put back under the Hofkanzlei, and in connection with this change, Leopold liquidated a large part of Joseph's extensive apparatus of secret police, contenting himself with a much smaller number of confidants.[3]

Some import prohibitions were repealed, but Leopold had hardly touched the field of economic policy when he died.

---

[1] At the end of Leopold's reign the Monarchy (excluding Galicia) contained 416 religious Houses.

[2] His Decree of 3 March 1792 ran: 'Although the priest must be a shepherd of souls, as he should always be, yet he must be regarded not only as a priest, and as a citizen, but also as an official of the State in the Church, because the administration of the care of souls has unlimited influence on the sentiments of the people, and participates directly or indirectly in the most important political matters.'

[3] Silagi, *Jakobiner*, pp. 53 ff., points out that, contrary to the common belief, Leopold was no friend of secret police methods. He did organize his own service, but it was a small one, and he used it chiefly for purposes of information. This does not, indeed, apply to the

All in all, Leopold had carried through a singularly successful emergency operation of pacification, and how fine had been his judgment of what were the maxima that one set of parties could be manoeuvred into conceding, and the minima which others could be induced to accept without revolt, is shown by the fact that no revolts worthy of the name occurred against it. Even the peasants, who should have been thought to be the chief losers, soon calmed down: the considerable unrest which manifested itself in 1790 had almost died away by 1791.

But an emergency operation it was, and the position it created was certainly not that situation free from 'injustice, conflicts and unrest' which was Leopold's ideal and which he had come near to realising in Tuscany. Fairly certainly, he did not mean it to be permanent. He was a very reticent man, who took no one into his full confidence; moreover, many of the documents relating to his reign were destroyed by fire, as lately as 1945. Thus the exact nature of his future plans is not known. We have, however, glimpses of some of them, and the general shape of others can be deduced from his record in Tuscany, for, as Herr Wandruschka has rightly pointed out, his Tuscan experiences set precedents which largely guided his actions in Austria. It seems certain that while willing to allow some limitation of the Monarch's power through constitutional institutions, he was not prepared to let this be brought about by a simple abdication of the Crown's authority in favour of that of the Estates, as then composed. He wished to see the introduction of a genuine representative system, giving more rights to the burgher class, and more political weight to the peasants, with many more alleviations of their social and political conditions; the concessions which he made in these respects to the landlords were probably more reluctant than any others made by him.

Such changes would have meant reducing the powers of the Estates, and although Leopold had none of his brother's pathological hatred of the nobility, yet he was almost certainly prepared to pit his strength against the Estates as soon as he felt able to do so. How to manage this was a problem, in view of his rejection, on both pragmatic grounds and those of principle, of the methods of violent and undisguised revolution from above which Joseph had tried to apply, with such disastrous results. Yet soon after his

---

conspiratorial activities of a small band of agents described on the next page. It is also worth pointing out that the purposes of Leopold's 'secret police' (and, indeed, of his son's also) were not political only. When informing the Austrian public of the establishment of the institution, he emphasized the criminal side of its work, emphasizing the necessity of 'following criminals, who usually work in the dark, right into the most secret crannies where they seek to hide themselves'. He also declared that the police were 'expressly forbidden to use methods the application of which is then more dangerous to public and private security than the disorders which they seek to eliminate'. In particular, District Commissioners were strictly enjoined 'not to pry with inquisitive looks into the interiors of honest households, nor to disturb the quiet of respectable families by impertinent inquisitions'.

arrival in Vienna, he was engaged with certain secret agents in preliminary plans for what would have amounted to a real revolution from above in Hungary, the 'general purpose' being to introduce 'a sure equilibrium between moderate monarchy and democracy and an unshakable obedience of the people to the laws of the State and its ruler', while the 'more secret object' was 'to fight against the aristocratism, in all its forms, which everywhere thwarts the ruler and his intentions; systematic prevention of its despotic plans and endeavours; capture of popular opinion in the interest of the Government'.[1]

But although the conception of these plans was grandiose, the execution of them was amazingly unsystematic and even amateurish. So far as is known, Leopold got down to details only in respect of Hungary, and, oddly enough, Styria,[2] and he dropped his Hungarian plans in the autumn of 1790, taking them up again (after an interval in which he had been occupied with much other business, including a visit to Italy) only a long year later, with different agents. By that time it was too late to give them serious shape, for death carried him away, with tragic suddenness, after only a few days' illness. He died on 1 March 1792, and his eldest son, Francis, reigned in his stead.

[1] See Silagi, *Mitarbeiterkreis, passim.*
[2] He seems to have thought Styria a good subject for experiment, owing to its relatively small size and the sturdy character of its peasantry.

4

Francis I (II)

THE DEVELOPMENT OF THE SYSTEM

It is difficult to find words strong enough to convey the importance for Austria of the accident which set Francis II (or Francis I, as he was to become later)[1] in control of its destinies in his father's place at the unripe age of twenty-four. Francis does not altogether deserve the very harsh judgments which have been passed on him by many later Austrian historians, and adopted by their superficial foreign copyists. He was neither a bad man, nor a stupid one. The widespread popularity which he came to enjoy in his later years in Vienna (it was much smaller outside the capital) may have been somewhat fictitious: it was largely based on his affability and unpretentiousness – he received enormous numbers of his subjects in audience[2] and often took the air with his wife, unescorted, in the pleasure-gardens of Vienna – and perhaps even more, on his habit of expressing himself in a broad Viennese dialect. But his private life was virtuous; he was an affectionate husband and father, and must have possessed endearing personal qualities, for he inspired in at least one of his four wives a really passionate and romantic devotion, and the other members of his family circle seem both to have liked and respected him. He was an upright and conscientious ruler, strongly conscious of his duty towards his peoples and tireless in his endeavour to fulfil it; few of his servants spent such long hours as he did over the business of government. He took endless pains to establish a system of laws which ensured that justice should prevail among them and himself observed it towards them according to his lights, not squandering their substance on a luxurious Court – on the contrary, the modesty of his Court was proverbial, and the cause of much grumbling among the pleasure-loving aristocrats of the time – nor their lives on wars waged for the aggrandisement of himself or his House. Unlike his uncle, he was no militarist. It is true that nearly half his reign was spent mainly in wars, but these were always, at least in his

---

[1] When Francis was crowned Holy Roman Emperor, he became Francis II, his grandfather having previously borne that crown. When he renounced the Holy Roman Crown and adopted that of 'Austria', he became, in that capacity, Francis I.

[2] It is calculated that he gave twenty thousand audiences on his visit to Lombardy-Venetia in 1825. He used to give about eighty a week in Vienna.

own eyes, defensive, undertaken in the cause of preventing revolution from spreading to the dominions for which he was trustee – it must not be forgotten that these included the Empire, and that the Austrian Hausmacht itself included substantial areas as far west as the Rhine – or repelling actual attack on them, or under the compelling necessity of preserving the Balance of Power. He never favoured intervention in France itself, à la Pillnitz or à la Metternich.

He was shrewd above the average, with a disconcerting gift of drawing from any situation the conclusions which were correct by his own premises, and possessed, incidentally, of a sardonic sense of humour for which the shocked modern chroniclers of some of his apparently more outrageous sayings have made insufficient allowance.

But he had in him no trace of his father's genuine constitutional beliefs; he had rather absorbed from his uncle, under whose tutelage he had, as heir prospective to throne,[1] spent several unhappy years in Vienna, Joseph's unqualified faith in the doctrine of complete Monarchic absolutism – not merely, as Eisenmann writes, as a means, but as an end,[2] and his basic conception of the proper relationship between himself and his peoples was completely egocentric. He was entirely convinced that God had placed him where he was, over them, and if his duty was to rule them justly, theirs was to be 'good subjects' to him. The art of government, in his eyes, was to ensure that they should so conduct themselves, and his criterion of political institutions and of social conditions was their aptitude to produce this result. Withal, he had nothing of his uncle's social vision or imaginative power, or of his restless impatience with the imperfect. He was mentally near-sighted and unimaginative, incapable of appreciating large issues, or indeed, social issues of any kind. Actual distress – famine, pestilence, flood – shocked him, and he was willing that it should be relieved, but his mind simply did not reach to the consideration of underlying causes.[3] He could thus never have been a reformer for reform's sake, yet his absolutist tenets might have counselled him to attempt a revival of Josephinism, not as a means, but as an end in itself. But he was also quite lacking in Joseph's combative readiness to take on, even to provoke, opposition. On the contrary, he was mentally timid and suspicious, shrinking instinctively from the unfamiliar or the unknown, and strongly predisposed in favour of conditions, institutions and even persons to whom he had grown accustomed, over any form of novelty whatever. He also, as one of his tutors reported of him, shrank from unpleasantness in any shape, and was, moreover, quite shrewd enough to

---

[1] At that time he had been designated for his uncle's heir, since Leopold did not want to leave Tuscany.

[2] Op. cit., p. 54.

[3] An early essay of his is sometimes quoted as evidence to the contrary, but it is obvious enough that in this he was merely reproducing the views of one of his tutors.

appreciate the favourable contrast presented by Leopold's policy of moderate concessions to the Estates, to the fearful hornets' nest which Joseph's impetuosity had brought about the family ears. His instinctive reaction to the situation in which he found himself on his accession was therefore to freeze it, at least until the return of quieter times. The tragedy for Austria lay in the fact that those times did not return for over half a generation, and by that time the enforcement of the freeze had become a fixed system from which Francis had no longer any willingness to depart. Fortune then blessed him with another twenty years of life, and fortune again decreed that his dead hand should continue to hold the reins of government for thirteen years more, so that March 1848 found Austria in all respects in which governmental ingenuity could prevail – and these were considerable – in the condition in which Francis had found it in March 1792.

The international situation when Leopold died was really one which called for the utmost caution. In the last months of his life Leopold had patiently pursued the rapprochement with Prussia, and after painful negotiations in the course of which each side had made a token of goodwill, Frederick William by dropping Herzberg, Leopold by appointing Philipp Cobenzl to relieve Kaunitz (who was, indeed, eighty years of age) of part of his responsibilities, a preliminary treaty had been signed on 25 July 1791, and a definitive one, on 7 February 1792.

One motif in these negotiations had been the Polish question, on which, indeed, the two parties did not see eye to eye, Austria wanting from Prussia a guarantee of Poland's independence, to save it from annexation by Russia, while Prussia wanted a door left open through which she might increase her own Polish possessions. The final formula here was vague: the parties agreed only to work for the maintenance of a 'free' constitution in Poland. But they also mutually guaranteed the integrity of one another's territory and promised to help each other with twenty thousand men against any attack, or in the event of internal unrest.[1]

Meanwhile, Leopold had been pushed by his obligations as Emperor into a defence of the rights of certain West German rulers, lay and ecclesiastical, which various enactments by the Assemblée Nationale had violated. The French in their turn were annoyed at the protection afforded to the French émigrés by some West German Courts. Mutual irritation mounted, and Leopold's own originally favourable view of the French revolution became modified by its increasing radicalism, and by concern for his sister. On 6 July 1791, after the abortive Flight to Varennes, he had issued a proclamation to the sovereigns of Europe, inviting them to inform France that they regarded Louis' cause as their own, and demanded liberty and security for the King.

[1] This obligation did not apply to the Austrian Netherlands nor to Prussian Westphalia or East Frisia.

On 27 August, the preliminary treaty with Prussia having been concluded, he and Frederick William jointly issued the Declaration of Potsdam, which described conditions in France as a matter of common interest to all sovereigns, and expressed the hope that they would collaborate effectively to enable Louis freely to establish an order which took account both of the rights of sovereigns and of the welfare of the French people. The Declaration was cautiously worded: Austria and Prussia were prepared to mobilize the forces necessary to achieve the common end, but only if other States participated. This reservation, which Leopold described as constituting for him 'the law and the prophets', took most of the reality out of the threat, since it was already quite certain that England would not participate. But it played its part, not in averting the crisis but in precipitating it, in inflaming opinion in France against both the foreign interference and its own dynasty, which had seemed ready to profit by that interference. From this date onward war between France and Austria became an increasingly imminent certainty.[1]

The definitive Treaty with Prussia strengthened Austria's position, but further inflamed her relations with France, who regarded it as an open threat. Less than a month after his accession – on 27 March – Francis was confronted with an ultimatum calling on Austria to dissolve all alliances contracted without the foreknowledge of France, or directed against her, and at once to withdraw her troops from the frontier. The demand was rejected, and on 20 April Louis, with tears in his eyes, announced to the Assembly that France was at war with 'the King of Bohemia and Hungary'.

Under these conditions, it would have been extremely difficult for Francis, in common prudence, to provoke those classes among his subjects who traditionally constituted the strongest forces in each of his Lands, and on whose goodwill the integrity of his Monarchy, and even his own throne, might be supposed to depend. He must ally himself with them, if they were to be had as allies; and this they were, for the cardinal feature in the whole situation of the Monarchy – that which really determined all its subsequent development – was the deep anxiety of the Estates in every Land for a permanent peace with the Crown, which should definitively banish the threat of revolution: revolution from outside and below, infiltrating from France, and even more formidable, revolution from inside and above, should the unquiet ghost of Joseph II not prove to have been well and truly laid. As proof of the identity of their interests with those of the Crown, they could point to the course of the French Revolution, so demonstrably the work of men of the middle class and of intellectuals, and in its actions identifying the Crown and the aristocracy as its common enemy. Given reassurance of the Crown's conservative intentions, they were entirely willing, in effect, to

[1] It is true that after Louis had temporarily agreed with the Assemblée, Leopold thought that the French question was 'settled', and he was prepared to await future developments (see his circular note of 1 November 1791).

accept the reality of central political control which lay behind Leopold's recognition of their shadow-existence and to serve the Crown as junior partners in the common cause. Only the Hungarians were not ready to ratify the Leopoldinian compromise as it then stood; but even they wanted only amendments of detail, not destruction of the whole.

Unpretentious and almost kleinbürgerlich as he was in his personal tastes, Francis had none of his uncle's pathological hatred of the nobility. Nevertheless, easily guided as he was at this period of his life, he might yet have been led to question the wisdom of accepting this partnership if he had heard more arguments against it. But he was almost entirely surrounded by its advocates. There were, indeed, a considerable number of Josephinian-minded men in the middle ranks of the bureaucracy, and some men of this mental type had even given Francis lessons, at Joseph's orders, in certain subjects. It was characteristic of Francis's unwillingness to make any change that he never himself tried to replace a Josephinian civil servant, on grounds of principle, with the result that certain departments of the bureaucracy continued to work throughout his reign in a Josephinian spirit. But even Joseph had not altered the tradition under which the top positions in every Government department had been reserved for members of the leading aristocracy, nor the rigid Court etiquette which limited *Hoffähigkeit*, or social access to the Court, exclusively (with limited exceptions in the case of the military and the members of the Orders of Chivalry) to members of the higher nobility and persons bearing the rank of Geheimrat or Kämmerer. It was still rare for a non-noble to become a Geheimrat and by very definition he never became a Kämmerer (for which appointment sixteen quarterings were necessary; and failing possession of one or the other of these titles, he remained without access to the Court, however important his position in the administrative machine.

And Joseph himself, again, had shrunk from appointing anyone outside the charmed circle to be tutor in chief to the young Francis. Instead, he had chosen for that all-important position, Count Franz Colloredo. Honourable, unselfish and devoted to his pupil, to whom he also had the courage, even in later years, to tell home truths whenever he thought it necessary, Colloredo was yet a man of mediocre abilities and of a mental outlook as un-Josephinian as could well be imagined: strictly clerical and extremely Conservative. According to some writers, some of Francis's chief phobias, against the ideas of enlightenment and constitutionalism, against freedom of the Press and even against intellectuals in general, were directly inculcated into him by Colloredo. And his influence was most enduring, for in spite of his plain-speaking he inspired in Francis's unindependent mind a great devotion. Francis's very first official act as Monarch – done the day after his accession – was to appoint Colloredo head of his Kabinett or private secretariat, with the rank (previously unknown) of Kabinettsminister. In doing so, he told his old tutor, in touching language,¹ that he was to be always with him, advise him in every decision, and replace him in his absence.

Thus the road to the throne from every quarter except that of the Imperial family itself led through the office of Colloredo. From 1795 on he was also Head Court Chamberlain, in which capacity he controlled the giving of audiences. All important appointments were made on his advice, and he naturally nearly always recommended those of his own kidney.

In the first years of Francis's reign, when he was much occupied with his second wife, the Neapolitan Princess Maria Theresa, and with his rapidly growing family,² and less diligent than he afterwards became, he left practically the whole conduct of public affairs to Colloredo, who was thus probably the most important man in the Monarchy, the next most important being his assistant, Kabinettsrat Schoischnigg (another of Francis's old tutors).

The sum effect of this situation and these influences was that Francis accepted the aristocracy's thesis of the identity of their interests with those of the Crown – made acceptable as it was by their acquiescence in their subordinate role in the association – and the system which emerged was one which has well been called 'one of aristocratic bureaucracy, or if you will, bureaucratic aristocracy'.³ It was absolutist and centralist in its institutions but usually aristocratic and ultraconservative in the conduct of them; not, indeed, quite invariably so, for no purge was carried through in the existing bureaucracy, the middle ranks of which were staffed largely with Joseph's men, and now and then one of these would slip through some measure which was purely Josephinian.

The promotion of the Kabinett to Ministerial status, and the appointment of Colloredo to head it, were the only changes made by Francis immediately on his accession, either in the current machinery of Government, or in its personnel. He made one other change a year later, when he restored the police to the status enjoyed by it under Joseph II, of an independent Hofstelle

---

[1] 'I know well that the burden which has been laid on me is too heavy for me, since I am young and have so little experience. My only wish is to do good, and I hope that I may be so fortunate as to have my choice fall on righteous men to help me.'

[2] His first wife, Elizabeth Wilhelmina Louisa of Württemberg, who had been chosen for him by Joseph, had been married to him on 6 January 1789, but had died in childbirth on 19 February 1790, so that Francis had lost his bride and his uncle on consecutive days. The child, a daughter, lived only sixteen months. Francis's second wife, Princess Maria Theresa of Bourbon-Naples, had been chosen for him by his father; he married her on 19 September 1790. In their sixteen years of happy married life she bore him twelve children of whom, however, only four need recording: Maria Ludovica, or Marie Louise, b. 12 December 1791, Napoleon's bride; Ferdinand, b. 19 April 1793, the later Emperor; Franz Karl (Francis Charles), b. 7 December 1802, father of the Emperor Francis Joseph; and Leopoldine, b. 22 January 1797, who married the Emperor Pedro of Brazil.

[3] Beidtel, II. 45.

reporting directly to himself. Joseph's old Chief of Police, von Pergen, was put in charge of the office. Otherwise, the only changes of personnel in high places during Francis's first years as Monarch were a series connected with the conduct of foreign policy. Although Francis, like Leopold before him, left the aged Kaunitz in enjoyment of the title of Chancellor, and thus nominally in charge of foreign affairs, the actual conduct of these, after August 1792, was given to Count Philipp Cobenzl, and under him, Baron Anton von Spielmann. After Prussia and Russia had concluded the Second Partition of Poland behind Austria's back (January 1793), Cobenzl and Spielmann were dismissed, and in March Thugut was (on Colloredo's advice) appointed 'Director-General of the Haus-Hof-und Staatskanzlei'. When Kaunitz died in 1794, Thugut was given the additional title of Minister, although not that of Chancellor. He survived until 1801, but was inevitably retired after the Peace of Lunéville. Count Ludwig Cobenzl was now given the direct charge of foreign affairs, but placed under the tutelage of Colloredo, and these two men between them carried out such foreign policy as Francis did not keep in his own hands until their fall in 1805.[1]

In the event, Francis found it easy enough to reach an agreement with the Estates of all his dominions. The one problematic case had been that of Hungary, where final agreement between the Crown and the Diet was admittedly still to be reached, for the work of the Committees set up by the Leopoldinian Diet was still to be discussed and there was a possibility that some of the reports might contain far-reaching demands, political and even social. On the other side, there were influences in Vienna in favour of tightening up control over Hungary and even retracting the concessions made by Leopold.

Francis, however, was not of this party. He was at that time personally well-disposed towards the Hungarians, and held a high opinion (which he never lost) of the Hungarian Constitution as a guarantee of social stability.[2] As Crown Prince and co-Regent he had even played a part in mediating the settlement of 1791, and the Hungarians, knowing this, looked on him with confidence.[3] For their part, the radicals in the national field had been largely disarmed by Leopold's willingness to meet their chief demands, which the

[1] See below, p. 181.

[2] A famous expression of this conviction of his is his address to a deputation from Pest County in 1820:

'The whole world is crazy' (*totus mundus stultisat*) 'and leaving its ancient laws to go running after imaginary Constitutions. You have a Constitution which you have received intact from your ancestors. Love it: I, too, love it and will preserve it and hand it down to our heirs.'

[3] Wolfsgruber, II. 164 ff. According to Meynert (p. 15), Francis had also had a hand in persuading his uncle to restore the Hungarian Constitution and to send back the Holy Crown. Meynert does not, however, give his authority for this statement.

men then holding the highest offices – the Chancellor, Count Károly Pálffy, the Országbiró, Count Zichy, the Personalis József Örményi and Count József Haller of the Vice-Regal Council – all men who were able to combine attachment to their country with loyalty to the dynasty – held to constitute an acceptable settlement. In the social field, the conservative trend was growing rapidly stronger, as it was in Austria; the Committee dealing with the peasant question, in particular, was exclusively preoccupied with the preservation of the nobles' privileges and of their right to exact the maximum of services from their peasants. In any case, the Committees were not yet ready with their reports, which they were making extremely detailed.[1]

When Francis signified his intention of convoking a Coronation Diet, the Hungarians had not had time to prepare a detailed catalogue of wishes, and put forward only a short list, one of which was, indeed, of primary importance: the abolition of the Illyrian Court Chancellery. A second request was that Hungarian officers[2] should be given preference in appointments as commanders or establishment officers in the Hungarian and Military Frontier regiments, and a third that, as a step towards carrying into effect the language law (Law XVI) of 1791, instruction in Magyar should be made a compulsory subject in the gymnasia of Inner Hungary and an optional one in the partes adnexae. The young Palatine recommended his brother to accept all these, and Francis duly granted them on his coronation, which took place on 6 June. In return the Diet, while denying any legal obligation to do so, voted the war contribution asked of it, of five thousand recruits, one thousand horses and four million florins, and cheerfully postponed to a later date consideration of the reports set up by the Leopoldinian Diet.

Prague gave even less trouble: here no concessions of substance were required at all, and the coronation was effected on 8 August. That in Frankfurt had meanwhile taken place, again without difficulty, and without even any attempt by the Electors further to extend the Electoral Capitulations, on 14 July.

Francis was now able to devote his chief attention to the war with France; and while this work is primarily concerned with the internal conditions and developments in the Austrian Monarchy, it is, of course, necessary for the understanding of these to remember that for the next twenty-three years Austria was never really at peace. During nearly half of them she was actively at war; during almost all the remainder, either salving the wounds received in the last campaign, or preparing for the next. The wars further brought her repeated and important territorial changes, and also alterations in her status in relation to Germany. The essential facts of the first thirteen of these years are as follows:

[1] When completed, the reports filled 96 volumes.
[2] i.e., Hungarian subjects: the phrase thus covered Croats.

Austria's first war with France lasted, with varying fortunes, for almost exactly five years. Then, having been deserted by Russia and by the smaller German States, she was forced to sign the Preliminary Peace of Leoben (18 April 1797) and on 17-18 October, the even less favourable definitive Peace of Campo Formio. Her armies had early been driven out of Belgium; now she ceded that province definitively to France and secretly promised to support the cession to France of most German territory west of the Rhine. She also lost Lombardy, being obliged to recognize the formation of a Cis-Alpine Republic, extending eastward as far as the Etsch (Adige). On the other hand, she acquired Continental Venice, east of the Etsch, with the Margravate of Istria and Dalmatia. Meanwhile, in 1793, Prussia and Russia, taking advantage of Austria's preoccupation, had effected between them the second Partition of Poland, out of which Austria had come emptyhanded; but Thugut, who took over the Foreign Ministry from Cobenzl when Prussia's treachery was revealed, had shown his teeth to Prussia and when the total partition of Poland took place in 1795, after Thugut had concluded a secret agreement with Russia, Austria secured Lublin, Cholm, Cracow and Sandomir (then collectively known as 'West Galicia').

The peace established at Campo Formio lasted only eighteen months, for Thugut, the 'War Baron', unconcealedly regarded it only as an armistice and promptly opened negotiations for a new coalition against France. In March 1799, after agreement had been reached with Britain and Russia, as well as Naples and Portugal, Austria again declared war on France (having actually begun hostilities some weeks earlier). In this war, as in its predecessor, her armies won early successes, but the Russian Emperor, Paul, made his peace with Bonaparte, now in supreme charge in France, as First Consul, and in 1800 Bonaparte drove the Austrians out of Italy, following up this success with an advance which brought one of his armies down the Danube to within twenty leagues of Vienna, while another advanced on the capital from the South Tirol. On 2 February 1801, Francis had to conclude the Peace of Lunéville, the territorial provisions of which substantially repeated those of Campo Formio: only the Italian secondogenitures disappeared, the Grand Duke of Tuscany being promised compensation in Salzburg, and the Duke of Modena, whose territory was incorporated in the Cis-Alpine Republic, in the Breisgau (at Austria's expense). Austria even got the small gain that the episcopal territories of Brixen and Trent were assigned to her in the subsequent reorganization of Germany, but in other respects her influence in Germany was greatly diminished by the reduction of the power of the Catholic States, her traditional supporters, in favour of the Protestant.

This war had, moreover, been exhausting for her. The French armies had cruelly ravaged the territory through which they had passed, and some of the battles, notably that of Hohenlinden, had cost her a heavy toll in blood.

The population had been at best lukewarm for the war; the Hungarians, large numbers of whom had gone over to the enemy, less than that. In view of the exhaustion of his dominions, Francis now hoped to remain at peace. Thugut was retired in favour of the consortium Colloredo-Cobenzl, and in fact Austria remained neutral when war recommenced between France and England in May 1803; the only international event worth recording in Austrian history in 1804 was the assumption by Francis, on 10 August, of the title of hereditary Emperor of Austria, and this was an act of purely dynastic significance. It was forced on Francis on the one hand by Napoleon's assumption of the Imperial title, and on the other, by the obvious necessity of reckoning with the end of the Holy Roman Empire. If the Empire disappeared, Francis would find his own family inferior in dignity to the rulers of both France and Russia, unless he assured for it the Imperial style. But it had no further political significance: it did not signify any abandonment of Austria's claims to leadership in Germany, nor in general (as the history of the next decades amply proved) any alteration in her conception of her role in the world. Neither did it create any new bond, either *de jure* or *de facto*, between Francis's own dominions.[1] The Hungarian Chancellery demanded and, after argument, received, explicit assurances on the legal point.

This respite was again a short one. Francis changed his policy again: on 9 August 1805, Austria joined the Coalition with Britain and Russia. Hostilities broke out on the Danube in September, and this time the disaster was speedy and overwhelming. One of the main Austrian armies, thirty-three thousand strong, was lost when Mack capitulated at Ulm on 20 October; another was defeated at Caldiero ten days later. Napoleon advanced swiftly down the Danube, occupied Vienna and then, on 2 December, utterly defeated the chief remaining Austrian army, with a Russian army which had joined it, at Austerlitz, inflicting on the allies a loss of fifteen thousand killed and wounded and twenty thousand prisoners. On 26 December Francis was forced to sign the terrible Peace of Pressburg, which amply compensated for the relative leniency with which Austria had been treated at Campo Formio and Lunéville. She lost her recent acquisitions from Venice, these now going to the new Kingdom of Italy; Tirol and Vorarlberg to Bavaria, and her surviving possessions in West Germany to Baden and Württemberg. In addition, she had to pay an indemnity of forty million francs. Her only territorial compensation was Salzburg.[2] Other articles of the Treaty declared

---

[1] It is worth emphasizing that the title did not create any new 'Austria'; Francis took it only from the Archduchy of Austria Below and Above the Enns, as 'that one of my Dominions which has been longest in possession of my House, and most closely associated with it'. Proof of this may be found in the titles used by Francis's successors, of which one or two may be found in the appendix. No Monarch was ever crowned 'Emperor of Austria'.

[2] The ex-Grand Duke of Tuscany was transferred to Würzburg.

Bavaria, Württemberg and Baden sovereign States, and on 6 August 1806, when Napoleon had in addition created the Confederation of the Rhine, under his own protection, Francis, at his behest, renounced the title of Holy Roman Emperor and released all Estates from their obligations to the holder of it.

At this point we may return to pick up the threads of internal developments in the Monarchy.

The very fact that the war declared by France on Austria in 1792 was an ideological one, waged by Austria in defence of legitimate authority against revolution, would of itself have sufficed to prejudice Francis still further against innovations, even if his preoccupations had left him time to think them up. Nevertheless, he does not seem to have felt it necessary, during the first couple of years, to take any special measures against internal unrest: he was satisfied to let his agreements with the Estates take their effects.[1] But his mind and spirit were soon hardened by two severe shocks. One came from the increasing radicalism of the French Revolutionaries, culminating in the execution of Louis XVI in January 1793, and of the Queen (Francis's own aunt) in the following October. The second came when, in September 1794, the police reported the discovery of two 'Jacobin conspiracies', one in Vienna, the other in Hungary.[2] The Viennese 'conspiracy' reflected a real discontent with the war, and one or two of the participants (several of whom were well-known Viennese figures)[3] held genuinely treasonable views; but for the most part it was an almost ludicrously childish affair of a few men who had done nothing more than plant a 'tree of liberty' in a sequestered valley outside Vienna and dance round it, singing tipsy catches in praise of liberty. The Hungarian was a little more serious, and a good deal more mysterious. The chief figure in it, a certain Abbé Martinovics, had been one of Leopold's confidants in his plan for destroying the power of the aristocracy, and seems to have gone on conspiring after Leopold's death, ignoring the fact that the aristocracy was now allied with the Crown. The affair was fairly widespread, involving such various figures as the poet Kazinczy, afterwards one of the leaders of the Hungarian literary and linguistic renaissance, one member (a youthful one, it is true) of the aristocracy – a certain Count Sigray – several more 'intellectuals', and some officers. No two of them, however, seem to have had quite the same ideas. Martinovics had evolved a marvellous dream

---

[1] This seems to have been largely a (somewhat paradoxical) effect of Colloredo's influence; for that excellent but unperceptive man was firmly convinced that the French Revolution was the work of a few hot-heads and would soon burn itself out.

[2] There were some reports of similar stirrings in Prague, but they proved not to be serious.

[3] They included Josef Prandstätter, a Magisterial Councillor; Franz von Hebenstreit, a well-known author; Freiherr von Riedel, one of the Emperor's old tutors, the Imperial Councillor Franz Gotthardy, and the youthful Count Hohenwart, a kinsman of the Archbishop of Vienna.

of a republic run entirely by and for the benefit of the lesser nobility; the King and all his dynasty were to be deposed, the magnates swept aside, the property of the Church secularized, and although the peasants were to be personally free, they were to continue to supply the nobles with rents, dues in kind, and services. A second plan, revealed only to initiates, was more radical still. Others of the conspirators were pure national enthusiasts or idealistic reformers.

The conspirators were punished with extreme barbarity, several of them executed (after being pilloried publicly for three days) and others condemned to sentences of hard labour running up to sixty and even a hundred years, and after this Francis's dread of 'democracy' and allergy to change became pathological. The internal history of the next years is that of the elaboration and enforcement of a system designed to secure the most absolute stability which ingenuity could devise.

Political immobility was easily achieved in the western half of the Monarchy by the simple expedient of conducting all rule through the bureaucracy. The Estates were not abolished, for that would have been a revolutionary act, but their activities, where any (the Estates of Galicia were not convoked at all after 1782 until 1817), were purely formal, all their petitions for an extension of their powers being rejected. The meetings became a farce,[1] and few of those entitled to attend them troubled to do so. All Government was from above, which did not at all mean that during these years Austria suffered from lack of government. The *Vielregieren* of Francis's early years was proverbial; in respect of paper issued, they rivalled Joseph's. In the flood of enactments[2] there could not fail to be some that were beneficial, conspicuous among them an enlightened re-codification of the criminal law.[3] After he had been made President of the Hofkriegsrat in 1801,[4] Francis's brother, the Archduke Charles, introduced a number of reforms in the military services, including, besides technical reforms and many measures calculated to improve conditions for the troops and to raise their self-respect and their morale, the epoch-making change that the term of service was

[1] For a lively description of the meetings of the Moravian Estates, see Beidtel, II. 60.

[2] In 1808 Count Saurau, formerly President of the Gubernium of Lower Austria and later Governor of 'Inner Austria' and one of Francis's most outspoken and most intelligent critics, wrote to him:

'Your Majesty's Government has already issued twenty-four volumes of political (i.e. administrative) regulations alone. The most retentive memory cannot hold even the titles, let alone the contents of these orders, one of which often revokes another, nor combine the multifarious interpretations and modifications with the original orders.'

[3] This was promulgated by Patent on 3 September 1803. While reintroducing the death penalty, abolished under Joseph II, for certain very serious offences, it reduced the severity of sentences for minor offences and introduced a clear distinction between genuinely criminal acts and civil misdemeanours. It was, however, still more severe than the code which Leopold had planned to introduce.

[4] See below, p. 167.

reduced from life in all arms to ten years in the infantry, train, etc., twelve in the artillery and fourteen in the engineers. But against these, and a few other measures of real value, had to be set the near-complete fossilization of social, economic and intellectual life. On the land, Francis refused, indeed, to repeal (as the Estates of many Lands tried to make him do) his predecessors' reforms in favour of the peasants, but he also carried them no further, so that the peasants' obligations remained fixed, in general, at the levels laid down by Maria Theresa in her Patents.[1] On the principal question which Joseph's death had left undecided – how far the commutation of services and/or dues for cash rents should be imposed, or encouraged – an inquiry undertaken by the Hofkanzlei in 1794 in Bohemia showed that Leopold's appeal had met with small results.[2] Most of the landlords were now against commutation, and even the peasants were reported to be reluctant to bind themselves to cash payments, even where they could afford them. Opinions in the Hofkanzlei were divided: some experts still wanted the whole rural economy put on a cash basis, while others saw in the robot 'a good school of humility and obedience' and warned particularly against allowing the peasants to buy themselves out in perpetuity (Bareinkaüfe) as, other dangers apart, 'they would then in practice become free peasants, could dictate the price of cereals and would let the stocks of horses run down'.[3] In 1798 Francis issued a Patent reaffirming the legality of all forms of commutation, provided that both parties agreed, but commutations in perpetuity had to be approved by the Kreisamt, which was not to sanction them unless satisfied that the purchaser would pay. Then, in 1821, by a decision which, as has been justly remarked,[4] reversed what had been the whole general policy of the State since the days of Maria Theresa, he issued an order that commutation of robot on State properties was to stop, and Kreis officials were not to express 'a hint or wish' that it should be carried through on private estates, 'since it could be detrimental both to the yields of the properties, and to the "subjects"'.

The effect of this seems to have been practically to put an end to

[1] Some local abuses in the Bukovina were corrected, but the robot was also raised to the Galician figure of 156 days. A Robot Patent on the conventional lines was issued for West Galicia in 1799.

[2] The report covered fourteen of the sixteen Kreise in Bohemia. Up to that date there had been complete commutation on 351 estates and partial commutation on 108 more. 117 of the 351, however, had been Crown estates. Only sixty-four private estates had commuted for perpetuity, the rest for terms of years which were often quite short, and in many cases the experiment had not been renewed.

[3] A peasant whose holding made him liable to haulage robot was bound to maintain the horses or cattle necessary for the service, or else to hire them.

[4] Grünberg, *Bauernbefreiung*, II. 490–1. Neither Grünberg nor any other writer has any satisfactory explanation for Francis's decision to revert to the old fashioned pre-monetary economy, but it may well lie in the financial fluctuations of the time which, as noted elsewhere (p. 196), had involved many peasants in great difficulties.

commutation in perpetuity anywhere in Austria.[1] The more or less short-term commutation (Reluirung) inevitably went on in areas where it was convenient to both parties, which were, roughly, those in which money economy was now established and in which there was little demesne farming; so much so that travellers wrote that little robot, or none at all, was worked in the German-Austrian Lands,[2] and in Lower Austria payments in kind vanished almost completely.[3] Even this, however, remained rare in the less advanced Lands.

Francis also refused to introduce any general modification of the manorial judiciary system, although changes here would have been welcomed, not only by the subjects, but also by the manorial lords themselves, on account of the expense in which the system involved them. But precisely the same financial consideration, seen from the opposite angle, determined Francis against burdening the exchequer with the cost of a service which, as things stood, he was getting free. It is true that he did not introduce it in the territories acquired from Venice, and that on recovering the areas which had been under the rule of France and her allies from 1809 to 1814, and in which State judiciary systems had been introduced, he refrained from reintroducing the manorial system,[4] and after a general inquiry carried through in 1810, subsequently introduced minor modifications elsewhere.

Official policy towards industry wavered. One school among the bureaucrats was mercantilist-minded, and wanted the maximum development of industry, to increase taxable capacity and to obviate the necessity for

[1] Kübeck records (*Tagebücher*, I. 537) that in 1831 Count Kolowrat, the virtual Minister of the Interior and himself a large Bohemian landowner, was under the impression that commutation was not even legal. When corrected by Francis, he replied that the authorities made it so difficult that it might as well be illegal. Kübeck's wording (Ablösung) is ambiguous, but I think it fairly safe to assume that what was under discussion was commutation in perpetuity.

[2] So Turnbull, writing of his observations in 1837–8, says that '*robot* was practically unknown in Styria, Upper and Lower Austria, Tyrol, Carniola, Carinthia, etc. (with a few exceptions in Upper Austria, dues and services in those Lands having been either abolished or commuted against money payments' (Austria, p. 88)). Sealsfeld, too, writes that the German Austrians did no robot (Austria as it is, p. 92). The statistics showing the large amount of robot under the 1849 land reform (see above, p. 67 and n.) would seem to contradict this statement, but I am informed that the landlords, when making their contracts with their peasants, insisted that the word 'robot' should be used even when its value was being paid in cash, in order to be free to exact the service in labour should some circumstances such as another fall in the value of money make this advantageous to them. For the same reason, they concluded the contracts only for ten years at a time.

[3] So completely, that the statistics of the reform did not even list them separately. Considerable quantities of cereals were, however, being paid as rents in kind in Styria, Carinthia and Upper Austria, as in the Bohemian Lands and Galicia.

[4] The areas relieved of the manorial system (and also of the Bestiftungszwang) were thus Venetia, Dalmatia, the Littoral, the Villach Kreis of Carinthia, the Innviertel of Upper Austria, and the Trentino.

imports; others were physiocrats, and they reinforced their arguments that wealth lay in the land (for the exploitation of which labour was still generally short, especially during the campaigns), by appealing to moral considerations: urban life, they contended, was corrupting to morals, both private and political.[1] A middle course suggested by some was to develop industry in the rural districts, but not in the towns. The supporters of this view appealed also to the difficulty of supplying large towns in time of war.

Francis himself seems to have found it difficult to make up his mind on this question. On the point of economic principle, he agreed with the mercantilists, but he was very susceptible to the political arguments of the other school; he also shrank, on grounds of economy, from any expenditure which did not produce an immediate reward. In 1802, invoking the housing shortage, he forbade the establishment of any new factories in Vienna, although still allowing licences to be granted in rural districts. This device proved impracticable, since labour was available in the towns, but not outside them. Licences were now granted for the towns, but very sparingly, and even the import of machinery was forbidden until 1811. The shortage of manpower, not to speak of capital, was in any case very detrimental to economic development during the war years.

But Francis's pursuit of stability extended further than this. With his real gift for going to the heart of a problem and drawing the logical conclusion from what he saw there, he concluded that thought in general, except where directed towards purely technical subjects, was the enemy of stability. Rather interestingly, he did not share the view held by many of his advisers, and perhaps by the majority of landlords, that it was better for the poor to be unlettered. On the contrary, he wished that every child in his dominions should receive a sufficient elementary education, efficiently imparted by trained teachers, and that there should be a sufficient number of secondary and higher schools to produce the educated classes needed by the system. The number of schools of all kinds, especially secondary establishments, in the Monarchy increased largely during the first years of his reign, the Western Lands of which also saw the issue, in 1805, of a new '*Ratio*

[1] In 1806 Hofrat Ratschky pleaded strongly for limitation of the population of Vienna, and especially against the development of trade. 'The example of England', he wrote, 'which has made the world its tributary by the immense preponderance of its commerce, is not applicable to Austria, which is an agricultural State and not in a position ever to become a trading State of any importance, which, even if it were possible, would not even be desirable, because where the spirit of commerce which is followed by riches, luxury and moral corruption gains the upper hand there – as we have seen in Holland and will perhaps see also in England – the national character is ruined and the people, greedy only for profitable speculation, becomes emasculated by soft living and sedentary work and at last quite unserviceable for defence' (Wertheimer, *Geschichte*, II. 49). A year earlier, another bureaucrat, Della Torre, had wanted part of the factories in Lower Austria dismantled and their employees directed into agriculture. A compulsory costume, which women could weave at home, should be introduced (Meynert, *Kaiser Franz I*, p. 247).

Educationis' revising curricula and remodelling the organization of the educational system in many respects.

But like Joseph II and, for that matter, Maria Theresa, both of whose ideas on this point were more like his than is generally admitted, he believed the sole purpose of education to be the production of good, loyal and efficient citizens. The emphasis in the curricula was laid on practical subjects, with abundant instruction in religion, and in the higher schools, on those subjects knowledge of which was necessary for the State service, or *le cas échéant*, for entry into the Church.

Abstract thought was strongly discouraged, and teachers held to the strictest orthodoxy. To ensure this, they were placed under close supervision.[1]

The teachers, incidentally, were miserably paid (the annual salary of a village schoolmaster was 120 gulden, or less) and their quality correspondingly low. In 1811 Kübeck wrote, in a drastic memorandum, that they consisted almost exclusively of people unable to get any other job.

The chief anti-thought institution for the adult population was the censorship. This, as we have seen, was no invention of Francis's, but very early in his reign he gave the screw another turn – authors of books, or writers in the Press, were not only to abstain from any utterances calculated to disturb the public order but were not allowed to comment in advance on reports of planned legislation. Nothing could appear which represented the French revolution in a favourable light. Then reading-rooms were forbidden; then circulating libraries; and then literary reviews, on the ground that they published extracts from forbidden books. No Austrian might have a book printed abroad without permission from the censor.

In 1801 the power of censorship was transferred to the police, and became stricter than ever; also slower, since the police often referred a writing to

---

[1] A memorandum on this subject composed by Francis in 1796 has often been quoted. 'My especial heart's desire', he wrote in this, 'is the early institution of an educational authority with the duty of occupying itself not only with the supervision of the moral and decent behaviour of the young students at the high and lower schools, but also, and most especially, with the teachers, since their principles also determine the ideas of their pupils and thereby either result in furnishing the coming generation with a happy foundation for the formation of high-principled, religious and patriotic citizens, or, if the principles of the teachers are bad, they can spread them through their pupils, to the greatest detriment of the State in future generations.' The word here rendered by 'educational authority' (*Schulpolizei*) is often translated 'school police', which is misleading, for the word *Polizei* in Francis's day had a much wider connotation than our 'police'. In fact, he himself recommends that the supervision envisaged by him should be exercised by the Universities. The memorandum, however, shows both his conception of the purpose of education, and his mistrust of the teachers. But here again, Francis's work, the principles of which had been laid down by a Commission under the presidency of the ultra-Conservative Count von Rottenhahn, marked a retrograde step compared with Leopold's, in that it abolished the teachers' committees which had been a feature of the earlier scheme and placed the whole system under bureaucratic control.

one or more Hofstellen which might be affected for further opinions. The censorship was by now covering even mottoes on fans and snuff-boxes, monuments and toys. Next year an order appeared that when a man died, his books were to be passed on to his heirs only if the latter were suitable persons to receive them. In 1803 journalists were forbidden to print anything whatever on domestic affairs beyond what was contained in the *Wiener Diarium* (the official gazette) or Ministerial handouts; of foreign news also, only what the censorship passed. In the same year the famous 're-censoring commission' was set up to review all works permitted between 1780 and 1792. Within two years this body pronounced its ban on no less than two thousand five hundred works.

The result of all this was that the native production of literature, except the most strictly academic works on abstract subjects and fiction of the lightest kind, practically ceased. The habit of reading declined also. The books which were read were foreign products, smuggled in. Foreign newspapers could be imported but were subject to a heavy duty and often held up, or confiscated, if their contents were disagreeable to the Government.

It was very largely to the Church that Francis looked for help in the inculcation of proper sentiments. While the State retained the responsibility for the salaries of the teachers and the upkeep of the premises, the Church was responsible for seeing that the curricula were followed and that the conduct of the teacher (who was appointed by the Consistory on the proposal of the patron of the school) was satisfactory. The local parish priests exercised this supervision over the elementary schools and the Hauptschulen (outside Vienna), while the Archbishops and Bishops were responsible for the general supervision of the system, with the special function of 'seeing that the purity of Catholic doctrine was in no way endangered by the instruction'; ordinarily, they delegated this duty to one of their Canons. Higher teaching posts were given by preference to persons in Holy Orders.

The facilities for theological studies were increased and more gymnasia established in an attempt to attract more men to the priesthood, which had been losing much of its popularity as a career, partly owing to a growing apathy in religious questions. Yet, while personally pious enough, Francis held strictly to the Josephinian conception of the relationship between Church and State. The Church continued to be treated as a branch of the Civil Service, the function of which was the promotion of the useful virtues. Acceptance of this role led more quickly than piety to preferment, and the most influential prelates of the day, especially those connected with the teaching service or the supervision of it, were all pronounced Josephinians. Direct correspondence between the Bishops and Rome was still forbidden, and the Church properties were still administered by laymen.

The particular instrument perfected by Francis for the maintenance of the 'system' was the secret police. Here, too, he was only following his uncle and his father, but neither Joseph nor Leopold had taken into his service the enormous number of police spies recruited by Francis's ministers – from every walk of life, concierges, Legation servants, prostitutes (these in great numbers), as well as much more highly-placed persons, nor had kept so large a proportion of the population under observation. In Francis's day, not only the obvious objects of suspicion, foreigners and middle-class intellectuals, were constantly watched, their doings reported, their correspondence opened; but the surveillance was extended to the highest in the land, Ministers of State and even members of the Imperial family. Francis took a personal and lively interest in the spies' reports, many of which he had sent to him direct; he even had his own informers, who by-passed the police organization itself.

It is possible, indeed, to form an exaggerated opinion both of the omnipotence and the malevolence of this service; even probable that such exaggeration has been fostered by the circumstance that its operations were encountered at the Congress of Vienna by foreigners unaccustomed to the institution, and also by the fact that certain prominent and vocal figures fell victim to its workings in a famous case in Lombardy-Venetia, in 1821–2.[1] The Italian Provinces at the date in question were a special case, riddled with secret societies of subversive character, against which the authorities had no course but to employ secret counter-measures. The Congress of Vienna, in view of the importance of the business conducted at it, may also be fairly called a special case. It should also be remembered that the word 'secret police' covered criminal as well as political detection.[2] The whole purpose of the service was prophylactic rather than punitive. Even under Francis, Austria was never a police state in the sense in which Himmler and Beria have brought a later generation to understand the term. It knew no concentration camps. It was rare for persons to be arrested and kept in prison without trial on political grounds, and sentences for political offences, after the notable exception of those of 1794, were usually relatively mild, at least by modern standards. Francis himself, like his father and his uncle before him, used the police reports rather as a means of informing himself on current affairs, including public opinion, than for any more sinister purpose. Intercepted letters were never used against their authors or addressees. A man might have his doings and sayings reported for years, and yet live quite unmolested. Francis's first Chief of Police, although a thorough-going obscurantist, was no sadist, and Count Saurau, his deputy, an exceptionally enlightened man.

The service began largely as a defensive measure against the infiltration of revolutionary ideas from France and other foci of subversion which was thought to be threatening the Monarchy in the '90s. At that time, it was directed chiefly against the émigrés and their friends, and against the secret

[1] See below, p. 230.
[2] Cf. above, p. 144, n. 3.

societies, including freemasonry, which Francis and his advisers regarded, not without justification, as the main channels of those ideas.[1] It was really dangerous to be a mason, and in 1801 all State employees, at home and abroad, including the Archdukes themselves, were required to sign a declaration that they did not belong to any such society. To the last, membership of a secret society remained the most certain way of incurring disgrace or punishment.

This did not, however, nearly exhaust the field of the police's activities. While, strictly, it was only secret societies which lay under the ban, non-political and even religious associations were suspect also. The formation even of charitable associations required special permission, and learned societies were forbidden, except those devoted to the promotion of agriculture. The term 'association' was stretched so widely that permission had to be obtained even for a dance employing an orchestra of more than two instruments.

Especial and systematic attention was paid to the middle classes. Colloredo and others of Francis's early advisers had, from their careful and on the whole correct observation of the French scene, drawn the conclusion that the middle classes, and especially the professions, had provided the fermenting agency in the revolution, so that any 'intellectual' was an automatic suspect. Furthermore, since the security of the State depended on the loyalty of its civil servants and its officers (and the defeats suffered by Austria's Generals had been so constant and so conspicuous that Francis was not satisfied with the normal explanation of inefficiency, but smelt treason), it was thought necessary to keep these classes under the closest supervision. They worked under a twofold shadow: of confidential reports (which they did not see) regularly rendered on them by their superiors, and of secret reports by the police. Suspicious conduct might easily result in dismissal, or condemnation to a life of subordinate service in some remote corner of the Monarchy.

A notable weakness which made even the Vielregieren excessively difficult and inefficient was the cumbersome governmental machinery.

We have already mentioned[2] the institution of the Staatsrat, the duty of which was to advise the Monarch on any subject on which he chose to consult it. In practice the system had developed that the Ministers (so to call them; their titles varied with great frequency) of Foreign Affairs, Defence and (most often) Finance were regarded as exempt from the jurisdiction of the Staatsrat, and reported direct to the Monarch. Questions of home affairs, in the broadest sense, where they could not be decided departmentally, went on to the Staatsrat, which as the Austrian Dienstreglement prescribed, rendered an opinion on them in the shape of a written report

---

[1] The 'Jacobins' of 1794 had been freemasons.
[2] See above, p. 20.

by each member; these reports went up to the Monarch, via his Kabinett.

There were in this system, even as Francis inherited it, three major defects. One of these lay in the peculiarity of the Dienstreglement which had been built up during previous decades or centuries, and laid down which questions could be decided on a lower level and which had to go up to the top, both in an extraordinarily capricious manner, and one which more often allowed for too little devolution of responsibility, than too much. As one later critic wrote:

> Only the Emperor could exempt a single man from military service, whereas the determination of the size of the military forces lay in the unquestioned competence of the Hofkriegsrat. Crossing-sweepers and day-labourers employed on public works could receive a beggarly pittance only if the Emperor authorised it as an act of grace, while the Hofkammer carried out far-reaching financial operations independently. To deforest even a small piece of woodland required Imperial permission, while the Hofkanzlei issued decrees on important questions, which had the force of law, and no one cavilled.[1]

Given Francis's personal character, too mistrustful to delegate responsibility – he mistrusted the judgment, where not the loyalty, even of his senior officials – too conscientious to neglect it, and at the same time, constitutionally incapable of distinguishing between the important and the trivial, this meant that an enormous volume of business, some of it of the first importance, accumulated on his writing table, where a report might lie, literally, for years. By the summer of 1802 two thousand reports were awaiting his decision.

Incidentally, the arrears in the Law Courts became almost equally unmanageable, thanks to a sytem, the reflection of the administrative one, which not only allowed appeal from almost any decision taken in a lower Court, but made it almost mandatory.

The second great weakness lay in the absence of any machinery whatever for co-ordinating the policies of the Departments which came under the Staatsrat, with the others. It was only in the Monarch's hand that all threads ran together, and his Ministers had little idea of one anothers' operations and no recognized way of taking them into account.

Thirdly, the Staatsrat itself had developed, probably unintentionally and even unconsciously, into a sort of supervisory body controlling the work of the Departments reporting to it. The heads of those Departments frequently complained that the Staatsrat exceeded its competence by acting as an

[1] Hartig, *Genesis*, p. 25. These questions, it should be recalled, had first been considered by the Staatsrat, each of whose members had submitted a written report on them. Another writer quotes the following case: a certain cavalryman would have been entitled to a bonus of six florins if he had kept his horse for twelve years. The horse became a battle casualty after eleven years and ten months. The man asked for the bonus as an act of grace. The request had to go up to the Emperor, and passed through the hands of forty-eight officials, twenty-six on its way up and twenty-two on its way down.

executive, rather than an advisory, body; and where it did confine itself to advice, (a) its opinions were not necessarily any sounder than the Departments' own and (b) at the best, the procedure caused further irritating and unnecessary delays.

On his accession Francis had, as we have said, taken over this machinery (with the men staffing it) unaltered except for the few changes which we have recorded. He listened, chiefly to Colloredo or to subordinate members of his Kabinett such as Schoissnigg or Baldacci,[1] sometimes to his wife or his brothers, but without any attempt to co-ordinate their advice, or to let others do it for him.

Then, when, in 1801, the Archduke Charles was himself given an official post, as President of the Hofkriegsrat, he persuaded his brother to alter the system. Each of the chief Departments of State was to be placed under a 'Real Minister', genuinely in charge of and responsible for his Department. The Ministers, with the head of the Kabinett, were to meet weekly, or oftener if necessary, under the chairmanship of Francis himself. Questions touching on the work of more than one Ministry would be discussed at these meetings; otherwise, the Minister would report directly to the Emperor. The Staatsrat was abolished.

The Ministries were to be: Foreign Affairs, Defence, and Interior, the last-named to be a single gigantic Ministry dealing with all 'interna' (except the police, which would still report direct to Francis) throughout the Monarchy. The Ministers were the consortium Colloredo-Cobenzl for Foreign Affairs; Charles himself for 'War and Marine' (he received this appointment on 12 September) and the existing President of the Hofkanzlei, Count Kollowrat-Krakowski, for the Interior. Colloredo's assistant, Count Trautmannsdorf, sat in on the Conference, as did three 'Referendars' for special questions. There was also a secretary.

Francis promised himself great things from this reorganization, which was to produce an administration which ran like clockwork, and result in

... the advance of the general welfare, to be effected by the application of religion, morality and general peace, the execution of laws and ordinances, the prosperity of the population, of industry and trade, respect for every class and every individual subject, the due levying of all taxes and excises, the most exact business-like conduct of all branches of the State economy and the best administration of the public funds.

But in fact, no one except Charles really wanted the reform. He wanted it in order to influence foreign policy, and his opponents were against it precisely because they did not want him to gain that influence. The sessions

[1] Baldacci, who for some time reputedly exercised an extraordinary influence over Francis, was an enigmatic figure of uncertain origin: he was believed to be the natural son of a Hungarian nobleman, who had induced a Corsican named Baldacci to assume the putative parentage. Nearly all historians write ill of him, and he must have been a difficult colleague, but those of his memoranda which I have read have seemed to me full of good sense.

of the 'Staats und Konferenzministerium', as it was called, never frequent, grew rarer and rarer, and although Francis could not bring himself formally to abolish it, it soon ceased in practice to exist. The final blow to it was given when, in March 1805, the war party at the Court persuaded Francis to reinstate the Hofkriegsrat, under a new President, as an independent body subordinate only to the Emperor. Charles retained the title of Minister of War, but as he himself said, was now 'no longer an effective Minister, but only a rubber stamp'.[1]

The conduct of high policy in the Monarchy was back on its old basis of personal decision by Francis, taken after consultation with whatever person – it might be Charles, it might be Colloredo, it might be Baldacci – he thought best. Even Count Zichy, one of the least exacting critics of the system, complained that:

The most important questions, on which issues of war and peace depend, have not always been discussed with the Ministries of War and the Interior. The Ministry of War has taken its decisions, which affect most directly the political and financial administration, independently.

Meanwhile, after only a year, the Ministry of the Interior (whose aged designated head had himself protested his incompetence to direct so vast a body) had disintegrated into component parts. Finance had been erected into a 'Real Ministry', competent for the whole Monarchy.[2] For the rest, the Hungarian and Transylvanian Court Chancelleries had recovered their independence (against the loss of which they had protested) and the Vereinigte Hofkanzlei and Oberste Justizstelle[3] had been reinstated in their old functions of administrative and judicial Ministries for the German-Bohemian Lands and Galicia.

It is, incidentally, worth emphasizing that none of the complaints against Francis's rule during this period were on points of principle. In the inner ring, which was, necessarily, the arena of such argument as took place, no one questioned Francis's right to rule absolutely. The only man to raise that point at all was Charles, and he did so, to urge, not the relaxation of absolutism in Austria, but the extension of it to Hungary.[4] The other

---

[1] The excuse given was that Charles had been earmarked for command of an army in the coming war, and the Hofkriegsrat could not be left without a responsible head in his absence. The new President was Count Baillet-Latour. The real purpose was to make the new Q.M.G., Mack, who was Charles's rival, independent of him in order to eliminate his opposition to the war.

[2] The President of this was Count Zichy. His technical title was President of the Hofkammer, but he was also in charge of the other financial services of the Monarchy, including the Hofrechnungskammer.

[3] This was now divided into two Senates, one for the German-Bohemian Lands, the other for Galicia.

[4] Charles advocated this eloquently in a memorandum which he submitted to his brother in November 1802.

grumbles were all against the inefficiency of the system, and commonly reduced themselves to pleas that someone or other should be allowed less influence, and someone else (usually the writer), more. Charles, again, was the most vigorous advocate of administrative reform, but this was chiefly because he found himself unable to create an efficient army under an inefficient general system, although it is true that he condemned the general stagnation in agriculture and economic life generally, and would have favoured fairly radical reforms on Josephinian lines.

It should also be remarked that outside the special cases of Galicia, where the Poles were naturally unable to reconcile themselves to the loss of their independence and remained in a condition of sullen resentment which expressed itself in passive resistance to Austrian rule, and Venice, where the rising prices and mass unemployment which followed the annexation caused widespread discontent, the peoples to whom the system described above was applied, accepted it with perfect philosophy. The aristocracy did not greatly mind Francis's rule being dictatorial, so long as it was conservative. On 26 January 1793, the Estates of Lower Austria sent in a complaint against the 'Jacobin' tendencies of Francis's Government,[1] but they enclosed with it a substantial sum of money for the prosecution of the war against France. More real opposition came from the Josephinian elements in the bureaucracy, but even here, the reform party was in the minority: it was permanent officials who advised against abolishing the robot, or encouraging the development of trade and industry.[2]

As to the 'subjecta', the picture drawn by some pamphleteers of the Vormärz, and by some Liberal historians of a later age, of a freedom-loving people fretting against its chains, is, to say the least of it, misleading.

The class from which it would have been natural to expect the most discontent was that of the peasants, but in fact we hear hardly anything of peasant unrest during the first years of Francis's reign; a series of good harvests, coinciding with a time of high prices for agricultural produce, compensated them amply for the failure of the Government to carry through complete abolition of the robot and the Patrimonial jurisdiction. As for the 'intellectuals': while it is true that a small number of livelier spirits left the country altogether, the great majority wore their muzzles with most perfect grace. Such demonstrations of discontent as occurred during these early years were nearly all occasioned simply by anti-war feeling. The war of 1792-7 was clearly not popular, that of 1799-1801 even less so, but this was not

---

[1] Their chief grievance was Francis's refusal to reinstate the special Courts of Justice for persons of noble birth.

[2] It has been rightly remarked that fear of revolution, which was as strong among the bureaucrats as in other classes, had turned 'Josephinism' into little more than support of centralist autocracy against the alternative of government by the aristocrats through the aristocrats for the aristocrats.

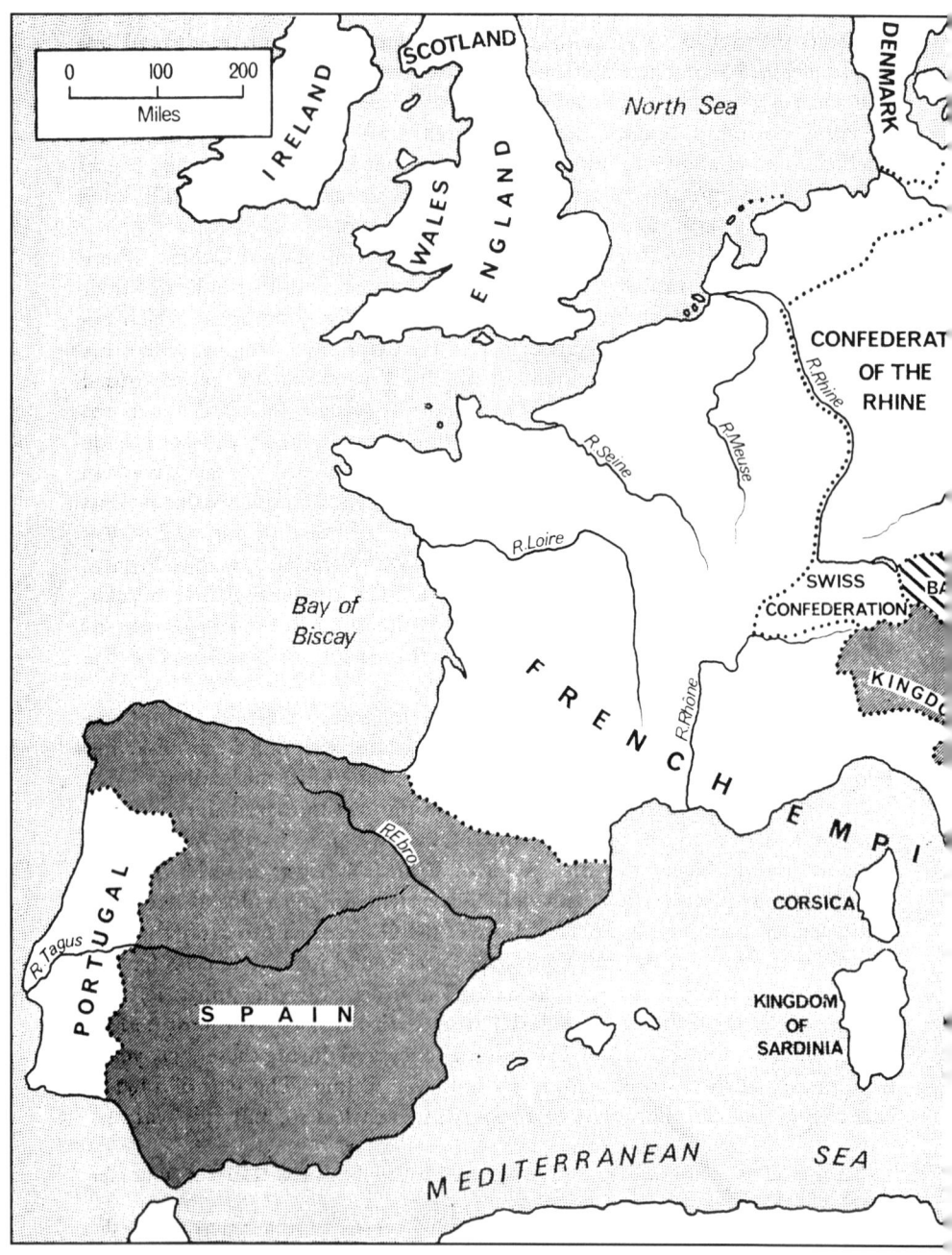

Map 3

because the peoples of Austria were ideologically opposed to fighting the champions of freedom. Neither, for that matter, were they interested in crusading against revolution; a people unschooled in the mysteries of the balance of power simply disliked seeing its sons dragged away to suffer and die on distant battlefields, and its own purses strained, in order that Cracow or Dalmatia should be added to the Emperor's territories. Himself cut to the quick by the terms of the Treaty of Campo Formio, relatively favourable to Austria as these were, Thugut wrote with deep bitterness of

> ... the scandalous degradation of our Viennese, who are drunk with joy at the mere word 'peace' – and nobody troubles to ask whether the conditions are good or bad. Nobody bothers about the *honour* of the Monarchy, or what will become of it in ten years' time, provided that now they can run to the ball and eat their roast chicken undisturbed.

Significant, too, is the reason which Francis gave Thugut for his dismissal on 1 January 1801: that 'all circles of the people are unanimously of the view that Your Excellency is holding up the conclusion of peace, and will always hold it up'.

There was thus, indubitably, popular feeling against the 'war party', but this was not directed against Francis's 'system', nor against himself, for the good reason that he was known to be a man of peace. Similarly, the great popularity enjoyed by the Archduke Charles was due less to the fact that (unlike most Austrian Generals), when he fought battles, he sometimes won them, than to the general knowledge that he was against fighting them at all, at any rate, with armies not properly equipped and supplied.

One consequence of this feeling was that Austria experienced extreme difficulty in getting soldiers to fight her campaigns at all. She started at a disadvantage, for Leopold, on grounds of economy, had not made up the wastage incurred in Joseph's Turkish wars, and at the beginning of 1792 only about 225,000 men had been under the colours. The Hungarian Diet had then denied the legality of introducing conscription into Hungary, and although, as we say elsewhere, they had agreed eventually to raise their quota to the standing army to 52,000, they had insisted that this must be done by voluntary enlistment, and the figure had seldom been reached. The Tiroleans were equally obstinate. In the 'conscription Lands' the numbers of exempted classes grew in such fashion that, according to the Archduke Charles's calculations, only 83,199 persons had then been liable for conscription, whereas in 1780 the figure had been 256,053 (out of a smaller total population), and 127,605 in 1788. The 83,000 were 20,000 short of the figure then required to bring the army up to strength.

In fact, the effective strength of the army, which in these years had ranged between 250,000 and 300,000 men, had been maintained largely by recruiting in the smaller German States. Nearly half the rank and file had been drawn from this source, and a still higher proportion of the N.C.O.s, since literacy was higher in the Reich than in Austria.[1]

The only one of Francis's dominions which was treated somewhat differently from the rest was Hungary; and here the differences were bigger on paper than in reality.

It is possible that Francis would have gone further than he did to meet the Hungarians, for he had after all taken part in the negotiations which had ended in the Leopoldinian Compromise, and only a year later had himself sworn to maintain the national rights, liberties and customs. The Martinovics conspiracy, however, awoke in him a mistrust of his Hungarian subjects even deeper than that which filled him towards his Germans and Czechs, and this was enhanced by an extraordinary memorandum sent in to him on 16 April 1795, by his brother, the young Archduke-Palatine Alexander.[2] The Archduke wrote that the Leopoldinian Diet had already been working for the ideas afterwards found to be behind the conspiracy, and he recommended the most stringent precautions. Germans troops should be stationed in the country, a censorship introduced, propaganda instituted in favour of the Dynasty, the higher officials 'taught obedience and be habituated to carrying out orders'. He further advised a policy of extreme social reaction. No reforms in the interests either of the towns or of the peasants were to be recommended. If any alleviations to peasants were found unavoidable, they should be confined to individual cases, not generalized; reforms in the interests of the peasants only unsettled them and disturbed 'the relationships and links between subjects and lord on which the well-being of both classes was founded'. To ensure the continuance of this harmony, the Archduke advocated the abolition of all instruction for peasants. The only end of instruction was to teach persons their official and vocational duties, and to that end a system of secondary and higher education might be organized. But 'more enlightenment and the multiplication of knowledge, especially for the common people, was altogether unprofitable'. The reading of newspapers only made the peasants neglect their work in the fields, education tempted their sons to desert that work for the easier existence of an *honoratior*. The clergy should instruct their flocks in morality, but in nothing else: all schools other than those for officials should be allowed to die away for lack of money.

On the other hand, the memorandum argued that the way to maintain the desired stability lay not through experiments, such as those in which Maria Theresa and Joseph II had indulged, but in working through the

[1] See E. von Glaise-Horstenau in K. Linnebach (ed.), *Deutsche Kriegsgeschichte* (1935, pp. 27 ff.); K. von Meynert (*Gesch. der k. u. k. Oe. Armée*), III. 47–9 and 147 ff., IV. 15 ff.

[2] The text of this is printed in Mályusz, op. cit., pp. 808 ff.

existing Constitution, for this safeguarded the rights of the Estates, and the Estates and the Crown had a common interest to exclude social instability. It should therefore not be abolished, but utilized as an instrument for achieving the desired effects.

The thesis that the Hungarian Constitution, if rightly utilized, was a guarantee of stability, was, as we have seen, already Francis's own – and it is tempting to suppose that he had imbibed it when visiting Hungary in 1790 from the same sources as those who had obviously inculcated the Archduke with it – those Hungarian magnates (among whom the young Palatine had in fact found his friends) whose arch-anxiety was to prevent a return of Josephinian 'revolution from above'. The question was whether the Hungarians would so behave as to justify these fair words about their national institutions. And it is not to be denied that their conduct during these years seemed to do so. The magnates and wealthy common nobles were as horrified as Francis himself at the developments in France, and the wider circle of lesser nobles had been frightened out of their wits by the Martinovics conspiracy, the wide-spread arrests which had followed it, the alarmingly general terms in which the indictment had been drawn up, and the glimpses afforded at the trial of sinister forces moving obscurely below the surface. Rumours ran round the country that the Court was planning a general extermination of the nobility and that the public hangman, escorted by the military, was making the round of nobles' houses in North Hungary.

The Diet which Francis then duly convoked in 1796 was in a thoroughly chastened mood. It voted a cash contributio towards the wars of 4,400,000 florins, with very large quantities of wheat, oats and oxen (in fact, what was needed to provision the entire army) and while still denying the existence of any legal obligation, agreed that the strength of the Hungarian standing army should be raised to 52,000 men (on the strength of which, three new Hungarian regiments were raised in 1798).[1] It consented without demur to the further postponement of consideration of the reports of the 1791 Committees and asked only for a few small immediate concessions: some facilities for the export of Hungarian wine to Galicia, and an assurance that the promises of 1792 regarding the national language, which the Court Chancellery had, to that date, succeeded in evading completely, should be honoured.

Meanwhile, one event had occurred, tragic in itself, which yet had most beneficent consequences for nearly half a century of relations between the Crown and Hungary. The unfortunate young Palatine perished in a dreadful accident (when experimenting with fireworks for a fête in Laxenburg) and his brother Joseph took his place. Joseph fell in love with Hungary. He left it as rarely as he could, adopting its traditional dress and moustachios

[1] The contribution of five thousand men voted in 1792, which had meant agreeing to one more regiment, was included in this figure.

(the language was too much for him)[1] and developed a great sympathy and understanding for its people and their just interests, earning for his reward a real affection such as no other member of his family, before or after, ever enjoyed. Withal, although nicknamed 'the new Rákóczi', he was impeccably loyal to his brother and always scrupulously safeguarded his interests.

During his very long tenure of office (he died only in 1847) Joseph did much to raise cultural and economic standards in Hungary, but his supreme value was that of mediator. Again and again he smoothed over difficulties and mediated understandings; that during all these years an open breach between the nation and its kings was always, somehow, averted was due in no small measure to this one man's devotion and honesty.

The Hungarians had much need of such a mediator, for the Palatine was the only man with direct access to Francis who was at all sympathetic to them. Baldacci hated them, and the Hungarian 'Referent' in the Staatsrat, Hofrath Izdenczy, whose function it was to report on all matters referred to the Council from the *Consilium* in Pest, was, although a Hungarian by birth, very hostile to his own country, and almost invariably reported unfavourably to its wishes, especially if he could smell Protestantism in the papers. All the representatives of the *Gesammtidee* at the Court saw in Hungary primarily a country which was contributing less than its share to the common burden, and setting a bad example to others by insisting on its right to speak. And these feelings grew stronger as the wars went on and Austria found herself increasingly pressed for money and manpower. Francis simply left the Diet unconvoked in 1799, thus violating, indeed, his oath but still avoiding the clash which increased demands on the country would inevitably have evoked; but the Peace of Lunéville produced conditions which made it impossible to leave the *status quo* undisturbed any longer. Count Kollowrat, in practice the Minister of the Interior, argued that the Lands of the Holy Crown were the only part of the Monarchy which was more prosperous than before the war, and suggested getting an increased contributio of two million florins out of them. While the rustical peasants could, admittedly, hardly shoulder this increased burden, it could be raised by taxing the peasants cultivating dominical land,[2] and the nobles themselves should be required to contribute to the fundus domesticus, or taxation for internal purposes.[3] The Archduke Charles, who had just completed his plans for reorganizing the army, said

[1] His one attempt to speak Magyar in Parliament provoked such merriment that he never tried again. When Magyar was made the language of the Diet in 1847 a special law was passed exempting the Palatine from the obligation.

[2] A recent investigation had shown that of the 1,256,995 non-noble houses in the country, only 762,593 were paying tax, the remainder escaping as being 'in noble service' (see above, p. 73, n. 1).

[3] The most important of these purposes was the upkeep of communications. The local officials were also paid out of the fundus.

that it was vital for them that the peace-time strength of the Hungarian contingent should be raised to sixty-four thousand[1] and conscription introduced into the country. He, too, pleaded for a higher contributio.

Some of Francis's advisers wanted him to send in troops and collect by force the men and money which he needed. He decided not to do this, and convoked the Diet in May 1802, but conducted its proceedings in a way which could obviously not satisfy the Hungarians. The traditional procedure was that a Diet opened with consideration by the nation of the royal *postulata*; when agreement had been reached on these, the Crown considered the nation's *gravamina*. In practice, what *qua* were to be given for what *quibus* was hammered out behind the scenes, usually before the Diet even opened. This time the Hungarians had got together a long list of wishes: for the attachment of Dalmatia to the Hungarian Crown, for 'wider use of the mother-tongue' in public life, and above all, for facilities to export Hungarian grain and cattle via Fiume, thus enabling those products to escape the stranglehold imposed on them by the ruling system, which as it stood, practically prohibited Hungary from exporting to them anywhere but Austria, and imposed a discriminatory tax on them on the frontier if harvests were good.

In the preliminary negotiations, Francis refused some of these demands flatly, and ignored the rest; and when the Diet opened, simply put his demands for men and money. The Hungarians dug their toes in. Instead of two million florins, they voted only 700,000, and they flatly refused to allow the war tax to be levied on any houses on dominical land, or to contribute to the fundus publicus. After long resistance, they agreed that the Hungarian contingent to the standing army might be raised to 63,264 for a trial period of three years, during which 6,043 men might be conscripted every year (if war threatened, twelve thousand men were to be conscripted 'once and for all'). But they refused obstinately to make the arrangement permanent, or to allow a war-time strength above sixty-three thousand. As soon as the agreement had been reached on these points, Francis dissolved the Diet, without allowing any formal consideration of the *gravamina* at all.[2]

Monarch and nation parted thoroughly out of temper with one another. The Crown had got much less, in terms of both manpower and money, than it had wanted, and less than it would have obtained if it had been able to apply to Hungary the methods which it was using in the Western Lands; moreover, the mere fact that the Monarch was obliged to ask, and might

[1] At this time Bohemia, with a much smaller population than Hungary, was contributing 56,000 men to the standing army, Galicia, 54,000 and Moravia, 30,000. The Hungarians' justification for their low figure was, of course, that Hungarian nobles were still subject to the 'noble levée'.

[2] This practice of his, which afterwards became habitual, had the pragmatic justification that the contributio and recruits were not legally due until the Diet rose, when the points agreed during it were articulated as laws.

suffer, a refusal, was offensive to the principles of Francis himself, and of his circle. The Hungarians had got nothing at all out of their own demands.

The Diet of 1805, held after the outbreak of the Third Coalition War, promised no better. The preliminary bargaining had begun in 1804, when the Coalition also was being negotiated, and Francis, ignoring the Palatine's advice, had insisted on asking only for 'sacrifices' in men and money, instead of taking the initiative in promising reforms. The Hungarians were at first inclined to regard the war as none of their business, and even to sympathize with Napoleon. Afterwards, when the French armies were nearing, and presently even crossed, the Hungarian frontier, they grew frightened and were prepared to offer not only the *insurrectio* but a large number of recruits towards the army, but the abrupt ending of the hostilities made the recruits unnecessary. The *insurrectio* had been proclaimed, but too late: it was obviously incapable of facing the disciplined French army, and Count József Pálffy, its commander (under the Palatine), was sent to the French commander, Davoust, to say that Hungary was not being defended. Francis's mistrust of the Hungarians, and even of the Palatine, was enhanced when Pálffy, misunderstanding his instructions, told Davoust that Hungary was declaring herself neutral.

Meanwhile the Hungarians had utilized the short period at their command (for the Diet itself was dissolved after only ten days, when the news of Mack's surrender arrived) to extract from Francis one linguistic concession: Hungarian was to be used, in parallel columns with Latin, in addresses to the Crown and might (not must) be used by local authorities in communications with the central authorities.[1] The economic grievances, however, remained unremedied, and so long as this was the case, and the Diet was treated so cavalierly, and clearly only regarded as a milch-cow, the nation could not be satisfied with its position.

If the Hungarians were not more restive than they were, this was chiefly because the period was a very prosperous one for the magnates and well-to-do nobles, whose voices were those which counted in the Diet and in the Counties. When the wars began, the demand for wheat and oats for the army rose sharply, while at the same time, the competition of 'Odessa wheat'[2] ceased. The price of wheat rose from a pre-war average of 30–40 groschen per Pozsony bushel to forty-five groschen in 1800, 143 in 1806, 152 in 1809. The Hungarian landlords who had successfully maintained their own exemption from taxation, while their fields and vineyards were untouched by the ravages of war, cashed in on this boom. Many of them accumulated substantial fortunes, and were able also to enlarge their estates by enclosure

[1] Law IV of 1805.
[2] Most of this came from the Danubian Provinces, which were normally able to under-sell the Hungarian producers owing to their even lower costs of production.

(which went on apace during the period) or by purchase, paying off their debts in the gradually depreciating currency.

In these conditions the question of industrialization became less acute. The landlords could employ all their own labour in the fields and were positively opposed to its being drawn off into the towns. The economic clashes with Austria were less over industrialization than over agricultural markets, Hungary wishing to exploit those of all Europe, while the Court wanted to keep Hungary's produce for Austria.

It was unfortunately true that in this respect the Palatine Leopold Alexander's thesis of the community of interests between Crown and Estates proved well-founded. There was one conflict – over manpower, which was still short in Hungary; and this shortage is one explanation for the tenacity with which the Hungarians resisted the Court's requests for more soldiers. But the Hungarian landowners heartily agreed with the Court on the desirability of keeping the peasants in their places, and they maintained social stagnation in Hungary as completely as Francis's officials enforced it in the Western Lands. Even the Robot law was often disregarded, since it was in the landlords' interest to extract the last ounce of labour from their subjects. It is with good reason that Hungarians count these years, with the decade that followed them, among those lost to their country in respect of reform.

There was, indeed, one other respect in which Hungary – that is to say, the Magyar element in it – contrasted strongly with the rest of Francis's dominions, in that there, and there alone, the interest and enthusiasm for the national language which had been so powerfully stimulated by Joseph II's attempted Germanization in many Lands had remained alive and active. As we have seen, the Diets of 1796, 1802 and 1805 had continued to press for more use of Magyar in administration and education, and in the country at large, a genuine linguistic and literary revival was beginning. In particular, young Kazinczy – the most important figure in the movement when Bessenyey grew older – when he emerged from the prison in which he had spent six years for his share in the Martinovics conspiracy, set himself the enormous task of 'renewing the language' purifying it from foreign corruptions, rationalizing its grammar, and enriching its vocabulary; and he and the little band of fellow-enthusiasts who had joined him in the task were achieving remarkable success in it.

Meanwhile, there was one thing which had resisted all efforts to keep it stable: the State finances.

These had been deteriorating since well before Francis's accession. Joseph II was, notoriously, parsimonious to excess, but although he underpaid his officials, his new administration was expensive, and the Turkish war sent things right over the edge. The cost of the army rose between 1787 and 1789 from 33 to 66 million gulden, the war cost in all 218 million, and the deficit in 1789 was 20 million, with a hangover of 27 million to be met in 1790. The national debt was up to 399 million. Moreover, Joseph had taken a step towards inflation. After making another public issue of Bankozettel in 1785, he had made a further, secret, one in 1788, bringing the real total in circulation to over twenty-eight million: still a relatively small sum, but growing nearer to the amount which it would not be easy to cash in case of a run. In addition, the provisioning of the army in Hungary had been paid largely in assignats.

Here again Leopold had effected some improvement: extraordinary military expenditure had been cut from 41·8 million gulden in 1790 to 16·4 million in 1792 and the circulation of Bankozettel slightly reduced. But the abandonment of the projected land tax had been an expensive luxury, and the national debt had risen a little further still during his reign, to 417 million.

The war with France involved fresh expenditure. The Minister of Finance reported himself unable to suggest either cuts in expenditure or new sources of revenue within the Monarchy: there was no help but to try the foreign bankers again, although they would probably make harder conditions than before. In fact, the foreign loans and subsidies received by Austria in the following decade never covered her needs, and became increasingly difficult to obtain when she fell into arrears with the interest and amortization of the first numbers of the series.[1] Little more was brought in by a few internal loans, some voluntary, some forced. Francis was always extremely reluctant to impose internal taxation,[2] more especially since he always persuaded himself that each war would be the last, and that after it he would be able to start a period of reconstruction; the remedy to which the Government regularly resorted was therefore the renewed issue of paper money.[3] By 1795 35·5 million fl. Bankozettel were in circulation; by 1796, 46·8 million.

Up to that year the public had accepted the Bankozettel without question, and it is likely that they had rather helped the economy by easing the monetary stringency. But now confidence in them began to waver. The Government issued a Patent ordering that they must be taken at their face value in payment of all State taxes and dues, and similarly, all employees and creditors of the State were obliged to take them at face value, and in

[1] A useful account of the British loans and subsidies is given in G. Otruba, *Englands Finanzhilfe für Oe. in den Koalitionskriegen*, etc. (Oe. in Gesch. und Literatur, Vienna, 1960, pp. 84 ff.). By the end of the First Coalition War, Austria's foreign indebtedness was about 116 m.g., one fifth of the total State debt. See also K. F. Helleiner, *The Imperial Loans* (Oxford, 1965).

[2] Some of his financial experts, on the other hand, thought 'low taxation harmful to the people, since it opens the door to idleness, and effort slackens off' (Beer, *Finanzen*, p. 9).

[3] Some money was also brought in by debasing the silver and copper currencies, the former by fifty per cent.

theory, they could still be exchanged for silver at any public counter (there were a dozen such in the Monarchy). In fact, however, during the panic when Napoleon was expected to march on Vienna in the spring of 1797, there was such a run on the counters that they had to be closed. After that silver vanished in practice from circulation, and Augsburg began to quote the Bankozettel at a discount.

Meanwhile, a series of exceptionally good harvests had kept the cost of living fairly stable from 1792 to 1794, but from 1795, prices began to rise, more or less *pari passu* with the increases in the currency.

After the Peace of Campo Formio (which itself was concluded largely on grounds of financial stringency) it was hoped that things would improve, but the deterioration recommenced when war broke out again in 1799. The Government resorted to an extraordinary number of expedients which it would take too long to describe here:[1] most of them were devices for persuading holders of State papers to exchange them into newer forms, and while sometimes bringing in small amounts of ready money, they increased the long-term State debt. Taxation, too, was raised by the introduction of a so-called *Classensteuer* (in reality, a graduated income-tax), but the deficit could never be met. More Bankozettel were issued, bringing the figure in circulation up to 200 million by 1800. They were now no longer convertible against silver, and the Government ordered that they must be taken at their face value in private transactions as well as public, but this could not be enforced in practice, and the Augsburg quotation rose to 115 in 1800, 117 in 1801 and 135 in 1804. The cost of living nearly trebled between 1801 and 1805.

Some classes of the population did very well out of a situation which left obligations to the State (even if these had been increased) payable at their old face value, while prices increased. Landowners and primary producers, big and small, prospered greatly; reports of the day were full of shocked comment on the luxurious living of the peasants, especially, of course, those who had commuted their services for cash (this was no doubt one contributory reason to the hostility of the landlords and the authorities to commutation). It was said also that many large fortunes were being made by Jewish speculators. On the other hand, State employees, pensioners living on State *rentes*, the clergy and other fixed-income classes were reduced to great distress.[1] Many of the lower-grade employees were carrying on second professions in the evening, some even, with the permission of their employers, in working hours. Some blamed the Jews, some the peasants, who were said to be sending up the cost of living by sabotaging the robot, but no one could devise a remedy.

[1] For an account of them see Beer, op. cit., pp. 9–11.
[2] The soldiers were comparatively little affected, since they received free quarters and rations and certain other allowances in kind.

After the disaster of Austerlitz, the Archduke Charles, who had warned his brother that 'the Monarchy was shaken to its foundations', renewed his representations, begging Francis to make a clean sweep of 'the obscure quacks gathered round the deathbed of the Monarchy', and to reorganize the conduct of affairs under younger and more energetic men. Up to a point, Francis listened to him. Colloredo and Cobenzl were dismissed[1] and Count Philipp Stadion placed in charge of Foreign Affairs, with full Ministerial rank. On 10 February 1806, Charles himself was made 'Generalissimus', a special title, rarely bestowed, which exempted him from any control by the Hofkriegsrat.

These changes were to the good. It was in every way profitable that Colloredo should have gone, especially as the post of *Kabinettminister* was abolished, so that one insulating layer between Francis and his executives disappeared. Charles's own promotion was also beneficial, as well as popular. Stadion, a Rhinelander and 'Imperial Knight', thus of the same class, and almost of the same local origin, as his famous contemporary Stein, who had, however, passed all his adult life in the Austrian diplomatic service, was a well-educated and intelligent man. And he had one idea which, for Austria, was revolutionary. He had been appointed, quite undisguisedly, in order to prepare a war of *revanche*, a task for which his strong personal hatred of Napoleon, who had confiscated his estates, his German national feeling and his connections, both in Germany and in the capitals where he had served which included London, Berlin and Petersburg, eminently qualified him; and he was convinced that to carry this through with success, more was needed than diplomatic alliances and army reform: it was necessary also to awaken national enthusiasm among the people, and for this, not only propaganda but also political and social reform were necessary. He favoured administrative decontrol, more power for the Estates (for the somewhat unexpected reason that this would form a counterweight to 'the influence of the Third Estate and the power of money, which is increasing in geometrical progression')[2] and liberation of the peasants.

It was beneficial, too, that Francis now began to draw the sensible and popular Archduke John into his councils, although not, for the moment, giving him any important official part. (Technically, he was employed at the time on supervising the fortification of the Alpine passes.) Yet another brother, Rainer, whom Francis also frequently called in, showed much common sense; the remarks credited to him in the records are always reasonable, and usually enlightened.

Yet to describe the period which now opened, as a recent Austrian historian has done, as one of 'great reforming activity, which reached its

[1] These dismissals had taken place before the conclusion of peace; Colloredo had gone on 28 November 1805, and Cobenzl on 26 December.
[2] Hormayr, Lebensbilder, cit. Rössler, *Oesterreichs Kampf*, I. 192.

climax in 1808',[1] is simply to divest words of their meaning. The one person who in 1806 and 1807 carried out any effective reforms at all was Charles himself, who dismissed twenty-five Generals, straightened out a number of administrative tangles, humanized the discipline and introduced the important change of keeping only part of the standing army permanently with the colours, the rest being organized as reservists, two reserve battalions being attached to each regiment. He also persuaded Francis to accept the idea[2] of a second reserve, or people's militia, for home defence service in case of invasion; the Archduke John was entrusted with the working out of the details.

But for the rest, the years were as stagnant as any which had preceded them. Stadion succeeded in getting the Emperor's signature to a proclamation promising the nation a freer intellectual life and Government support for 'all worthy and useful literary products', and rumours circulated that the censorship was to be abolished, but they proved unfounded. Francis refused to agree to a recommendation by Stadion – although both Charles and Rainer backed it – that the police should be demoted and placed under a man (Count Rotenhahn) 'whom the people believed incapable of resorting to the base methods of slandering, espionage and prying into family secrets in order to acquire in the Monarch's eyes a reputation for loyal vigilance, at the price of his integrity'. The police remained an independent service, and precisely in these years its activity increased rather than decreased. No move was made to enlarge the self-government of any representative body – on the contrary, it was precisely on 1 April 1808 that towns and marketplaces in Austria were deprived of their right to elect their own burgomasters and aldermen; these were now to be appointed by the authorities. The central administration was actually altered again for the worse, for on 4 January 1807, the remarkable decision was taken (on Baldacci's advice) secretly to limit the competence of the Staats-und Konferenzministerium to internal affairs. Thus all machinery for the wider co-ordination of policy disappeared, while the new organ for co-ordinating internal policy was even less efficient than the old Staatsrat had been. No important changes of personnel were made beyond those mentioned above; Francis insisted on retaining Zichy (who cheerfully admitted his own incompetence in the field) at the head of finances, in preference to Charles's candidate, Chotek; Baldacci remained his chief confidant in internal questions.

No social reform of any sort was introduced. It is true that the year 1806

[1] Hantsch, Geschichte, II. 279.
[2] The plan had been broached in 1796, but rejected by Francis on the advice of Colleredo who had thought it calculated 'literally to overthrow the throne'. In 1797 it had, after all, been introduced, but too late to develop beyond rudiments. There appear to have been two special considerations which now altered the Emperor's mind. One was that of economy: the *Landwehr* would cost much less than the equivalent number of regular troops. The other was the shock produced on his mind by Napoleon's dethroning of the King of Spain.

saw the establishment of a polytechnic and a Realschule in Prague, and the promulgation of the revised Hungarian *Ratio Educationis*, but the latter instrument had been years in preparation,[1] and apart from the fact that Francis, more progressive on this point than his advisers (for the Palatine Joseph shared the view of his predecessor on the detrimental character of education for the poor), had laid down that every child must receive elementary education; if the parish was too poor to maintain a school, the landlord must do it[2] – it could hardly be called a progressive document: the object of education was still to make a boy '*bonus homo, fidelis subditus et pius Christianus.*' For the rest, the new Ratio, yielding to insistent pressure from the Consilium, at last honoured Francis's promises (which the Court Chancellery had thitherto found ingenious ways of evading) to make the Magyar language a subject of instruction in the grammar schools *intra limites regni*, but all instruction was to be given in Latin from the eighth year upward.

Meanwhile, the financial situation went from bad to worse. English subsidies had covered a fraction of the cost of the war, but for the remainder, the printing-press had again been called in. By 1806 the circulation of Bankozettel had stood at nearly 450 million and the discount rate at 175, and the cost of living was still soaring. No one wanted to save a depreciating currency, so those who earned money indulged in a spending spree, but the situation of the fixed-income classes was growing desperate.

The problem was repeatedly discussed on the highest level, by a Finance Commission, which Francis himself often attended. Charles and Chotek favoured drastic deflation by the simple method of withdrawing a large proportion of the Bankozettel. But Zichy believed that this would cause too much hardship, and would be inequitable, as not hitting all classes of the population equally, and Francis supported him. A forced loan and a surcharge on indirect taxation brought in small sums which were at once swallowed up by the cost of rearmament, and the inflation went on.[3]

The financial situation was intimately connected with the Hungarian question, for the one point on which everyone at the Court agreed was that it was hopeless to expect any improvement in the finances of the Monarchy unless Hungary – now a considerably larger and more important proportion of the whole than it had been before the Treaty – could be induced to shoulder a larger share of the burden. In Hungary lay also the most obvious

[1] Francis had originally wanted to promulgate an uniform Ratio for all his dominions, but Joseph had persuaded him that Hungary must be treated separately. Francis had then insisted that the Austrian reorganization must be taken first, and had turned to the Hungarian only after the Austrian had been completed.

[2] His motive, however, seems to have been chiefly to ensure a supply of literate N.C.O.s for the Army.

[3] See Beer, op. cit., pp. 14 ff.

untapped resources of manpower,[1] and the Archduke Charles held it absolutely vital that conscription should be introduced there.

Most of Francis's inner ring of advisers wanted compulsion applied to Hungary. The Palatine, on the other hand, pleaded that the Hungarians should be presented with a clear and honest statement of the position, and also that consideration should at last be given to their wishes in other fields. Francis chose the middle way, which got the worst of both worlds. After unilaterally raising a number of indirect taxes[2] in 1806, he convoked the Diet in April 1807, and asked it for an increased regular contributio, to take into account the rise in prices, a single extraordinary contribution towards the cost of rearmament, and the introduction of conscription so far as was necessary to keep the Hungarian regiments up to strength. All he offered in return was a revision of the judicial procedure and of the law relating to bills of exchange.

The Diet in return displayed an obstinacy which earned it the historic soubriquet of 'the Accursed'. It began by demanding assurances (which amounted to something like budgetary control) that anything which it gave would really be used for stopping the inflation and restoring the credit of the State; further pressing for remedy for Hungary's economic grievances, and throwing in another request for the introduction of Magyar as official language and for more Magyar instruction in schools[3] (it was not satisfied with the 1806 Ratio, and moreover, denied education to be the exclusive prerogative of the Monarch). It was obstinate on the conscription issue.

After very long and acrimonious debates, interrupted and aggravated by a personal issue which aroused intense feeling, the Diet at last agreed to offer a contribution by every noble of one-sixth of his income from his real estate, and one per cent of his other income – this to be a 'voluntary gift', not on the basis of official assessment, for as one speaker said,

It is not advisable to disclose all our assets; the provident wisdom of our ancestors resided in never disclosing to the world how much they really possessed.

It also authorized the conscription of 12,000 men, but the old system of voluntary recruiting was to be retained for any reinforcement of the army above that figure. This was to be in return for consideration of their *gravamina*, which Francis promised to give. Instead, he closed the Diet on

[1] It was calculated that only one man in 130 was serving with the colours in Hungary, compared with one in 70 in the 'conscribed Hereditary Lands'. The number of Hungarians serving with the colours had been reduced again after the war of 1805 to 35,000 'in order not to withdraw too many hands from agriculture'.

[2] The excise duty on salt, the 'Jew tax', postal charges and certain customs dues.

[3] The requests were that Magyar should be taught, with the help of the pupil's mother tongue, in all elementary schools, and after ten years no pupil ignorant of Magyar should be admitted to a gymnasium, and that all teaching in gymnasia (except in philosophy and theology) should be only in Magyar. Magyar was to be taught as a subject also in Greek Catholic and Greek Orthodox schools.

16 December, not having considered one of the *gravamina*.¹ The disappointment and indignation were so great that observers described the country as on the verge of revolution.

All this might have been enough to counsel at least postponement of any thought of *revanche*, particularly since the international situation had taken another turn for the worse with Prussia crushed at Jena and France and Russia come to terms at Tilsit, so that only England, and her small allies, Portugal and Sweden, were left facing Napoleon. But the party of action in Austria now received a powerful reinforcement in the attractive person of Francis's third wife, the charming and vivacious Maria Ludovica of Este, whom he had married on 6 January 1808, after another conspicuously short period of bereavement.² Although Italian by birth (but brought up in Austria) the young lady adopted enthusiastically Stadion's idea of awakening Germanic national feeling. For her wedding no one bought anything new; the guests wore family heirlooms, and the Empress then set about popularizing a 'Teutonic fashion' which suited her better than it did some others who adopted it.

In 1808 things really began to move. The Archduke John had completed his plans for a *Landwehr*, or Home Guard, and a Patent establishing this force was issued on 9 June. Service in it was made compulsory for every male between the ages of eighteen and forty-five in the Hereditary and Bohemian Lands,³ unless he was already serving with the colours or in the reserve, or belonged to an exempted category. These were fairly numerous, but persons belonging to them were allowed to volunteer. Meanwhile, Francis had been collecting opinions on the central administration, and a Patent issued on 6 June had introduced another rearrangement. The Staats- und Konferenzministerium was abolished, and the Staatsrat reinstated. There was now no formal machinery for the co-ordination of policy on the top level, but Francis agreed that the Staatsrat should hold regular and frequent conferences under his own Presidency or that of a person delegated by himself, and that these might be attended by the heads of the Departments of Foreign Affairs and Defence. In practice, Francis seldom attended these meetings but the man whom he made his regular deputy, the Archduke Rainer, proved an efficient substitute. The new head of the Staatsrat, Count Zinzendorf, was not much younger than his aged predecessor, but far his superior in energy and freshness of mind. Finally, in August Zichy was replaced at the head of the Finance Commission by the far more competent O'Donnell, a Galician nobleman of Irish descent.

¹ In Hungary the insurrectio was to be the counterpart of the Landwehr. It was thought unsafe to introduce the system into Galicia; there a larger number of men were enrolled as reservists.
² The request for the introduction of Magyar had been flatly rejected.
³ Maria Theresa had died on 13 April 1807, of the effects of a premature confinement.

Then, on 31 August, Francis convoked another Hungarian Diet, on the pretext of having his new consort crowned. The lessons of the 'Accursed Diet' had been taken to heart. The Personalis, István Aczél, went to great pains to ensure that the Counties sent pliable representatives to Pozsony, and these, when they arrived, were mollified by lavish entertainment, a regular Danae's shower of orders and decorations, and in some cases, more tangible satisfactions. His efforts were successful: the Diet earned itself the name of 'the Handsome' by consenting that the strength of the standing army should be raised, if necessary, by a further 20,000 men and by giving the King authority in advance for three years to call out the insurrectio.

It was true that – as events were to prove only too quickly – the heart of the differences between the Crown and the nation had not been touched. But the immediate point had been gained. Meanwhile the spirits of the war party had been inordinately raised by Napoleon's difficulties in the Peninsula, and in particular, by the Capitulation of Baylen. Surely the spirit, and the efficiency, of Germans would not lag behind those of the Spanish guerillas! So the green light was given. The Imperial couple toured the Western Lands, enthusiastically received. A horde of publicists, some native, like von Collin and the Tirolean Hormayr, others, such as the famous Gentz[1] and the brothers Friedrich and August Wilhelm Schlegel, imported, were set to whipping up national enthusiasm in Austria, and still more, in the German States. Articles and pamphlets were poured out extolling conditions in Austria, on a basis which, ordinarily, would have made Francis faint. The appeals were directed not only to national, but to democratic feeling; even intellectual freedom was described as 'the first condition of all culture', and Austria was hailed as its champion.

A special feature was the agitation in the Tirol, where the Archduke John and Hormayr (acting, it seems, without the knowledge of the Emperor, and perhaps also of Stadion) got in touch with local leaders, whom they encouraged to organize a popular revolt, which was to begin simultaneously with the outbreak of war between Austria and France. Proclamations and patriotic literature were smuggled into the country, and military and financial help promised.

It throws a curious light on the mental outlook of the group then controlling the policy of what was already the 'Austrian Empire' (and for that matter, of the later German historians of the events) that they were able to ignore almost entirely the mainly non-Germanic ethnic composition of the Monarchy. Some of the patriotic literature was translated into Czech and Slovene, these peoples being, broadly, regarded as subjects of the Empire who happened not yet to speak German; but Hungary and Galicia were simply left

[1] Gentz had been in Austrian service since July 1802 but it was only now that he was given a free rein as publicist.

out of the reckoning. In fact, feeling in both countries was far from satisfactory. In spite of the success of the Handsome Diet, the Hungarians showed no enthusiasm whatever for a war which, if successful, would only increase the preponderance of the Germanic element in the Monarchy, while the Poles of Galicia made no concealment of their sympathies for Napoleon, to whom they were looking to restore the Kingdom of Poland. But the appeals went down well enough among the Germans of Austria. The Viennese burghers found vast pleasure in dancing at *redoutes*, Teutonically garbed, in listening to their favourite actors declaiming patriotic speeches, and in being rude to the Frenchmen in the city. The calling-up notices for the Landwehr were obeyed cheerfully enough, and many persons belonging to the exempted classes volunteered for service. By the beginning of 1809 the force numbered over 150,000. Vienna raised six volunteer battalions. Especially students and young people in general came forward in such numbers that the authorities had to restrain the students in the interest of the future intellectual life of the country.

Meanwhile, the international situation had not really improved at all. No foreign government had guaranteed any substantial help: only England had promised a subsidy and a diversionary attack in the Netherlands. The army was still exhausted and, to boot, in the middle of a great reorganization of its entire tactical methods – the old discarded, the new not yet fully learned. On this and other grounds, the Archduke Charles pleaded strongly with his brother at least to postpone the adventure and if possible, to reach a composition with Napoleon. But the war party, headed by Stadion and the Empress, with Baldacci in the background, was deaf to warnings. They believed implicitly in Germany's will to throw off the French yoke; further, some completely misleading reports from Metternich, then Austrian ambassador in Paris, had contained assurances of strong opposition to Napoleon in France itself; and the Government allowed itself to entertain equally crass illusions about the secret intentions of the Czar. As to finance, Stadion admitted that Austria could not afford a war; but she would be even less able to afford one later.

Seeing that the war was going to be waged, with him or without him, Charles gave up his resistance. In February 1809 active preparations were set on foot. On 6 April a fiery proclamation to his troops, signed by Charles (Friedrich Schlegel had composed it), assured them that:

> Europe seeks freedom beneath your standards. Your victories will loose her bonds.

On the 9th, Austria declared war on France. On the 10th, Charles led his armies across the Inn. Another army, under the Archduke John, entered Italy, while a third force, led by Field-Marshal L. Chasteler, penetrated the Tirol, where the local militia, headed by the famous '*Sandwirt*', Andreas Hofer, rose to help them.

Immediate disaster followed. All Stadion's calculations proved mistaken.

France remained perfectly united, the Czar made no motions to betray him. In Germany poets *schwärmed* for the cause and in one or two of the minor States there were small outbreaks of unrest, easily suppressed. But the people who mattered, the German Princes, refused flatly and even contumeliously to range themselves behind Austria; on the contrary, Bavaria and Württemberg sent large contingents to reinforce Napoleon's armies. Outside Austria's existing frontiers, only the Tiroleans fought for her, with obstinate courage. Inside them, the Landwehr often fought bravely, but could not constitute a serious force. Thus the story of 1805 repeated itself, with even more sensational celerity. Napoleon cut the Austrian armies of the Danube into two, and by 10 May had reached Vienna itself. The Queen's brother, the Archduke Maximilian, had been left in charge of the capital while the Court retreated to Hungary, and had vowed to defend it to the last, but a few hours' bombardment broke the will of the Viennese (who had earlier petitioned that the city should not be defended), and the city surrendered in the small hours of the 13th; its entire garrison was made prisoners of war.

Charles gave battle at Aspern on the 21st, at first with success, but inexplicably, to those who had watched the battle, failed to follow up his victory. The question was now whether Napoleon's Army of Italy, under Beauharnais, could reach him before the Archduke John, whom Charles's retreat had forced to retreat similarly, could join his brother; it was planned that he should make his way back through Carinthia and Styria into Hungary, where he was to join up with the insurrectio, under the Palatine. Meanwhile the Tirol had perforce been left to its fate: the Bavarians, who had been driven out of the province in April, re-entered Innsbruck on 19 May.

But John's armies moved slowly, and a disappointment awaited them when they reached Hungary. At the remarkable date of 2 April the Hofkriegsrat had informed the Palatine that it would be unable to supply the *insurrectio* with arms, or even uniforms, Nevertheless. the call-up was obeyed well enough, and a proclamation by Napoleon, dated 15 May, inviting Hungary to rise against Austria, fell almost flat. But when the junction was at last effected, the combined forces were heavily defeated at Györ, on 14 June. Beauharnais was able to join forces with Napoleon. Charles, after sending urgent messages to John to join him, gave battle again at Wagram on 6 July; but John's army did not come up in time, and Charles was defeated with heavy losses.[1] On the 11th/12th he signed an armistice with Napoleon.

Now there was hardly anyone left (except the Empress) who wanted to continue the war, and what enthusiasm had been left disappeared when the promised British diversion, in any case belated, proved a humiliating failure.

[1] On this occasion his Chief of General Staff, Count Wimpffen, was commanding the Austrian armies. It is thought that Charles may have been suffering from one of the epileptic fits to which he was subject. This may be the explanation also for his failure to follow up his victory at Aspern.

It remained to negotiate the peace, which was signed at Vienna on 14 October. It was even harder than its predecessor of Pressburg. Austria lost the entire Littoral (Trieste, Gorizia, Carniola, part of Carinthia, Istria, the Hungarian Littoral and Croatia south of the Save), all which areas, with Dalmatia, were formed into a new 'Kingdom of Illyria' under French rule; her Polish acquisitions under the Second and Third Partitions, all of which, except a small part taken by Russia, went to the 'Grand Duchy of Warsaw', and Salzburg, Berchtesgaden and part of Upper Austria to Bavaria. She had to pay an indemnity of 85 million francs, to reduce her army to 150,000 men, and to join the Continental Blockade.

The part of all this story which had, humanly speaking, the saddest ending, as it had been the most inspiring while it lasted, was the rising in the Tirol. This had been prearranged in January 1809, when Hofer had come to Vienna and negotiated with the Archduke John and Stadion, both of whom promised the Tiroleans money and arms if they rose, and the restoration of their ancient liberties, which had been largely disregarded under the Bavarian regime (it is interesting that Francis had at first opposed the plan, on the grounds that it constituted a violation of the principle of legitimacy, which was on the Bavarians' side, but Hormayr, who acted as intermediary in the negotiations, found a way of satisfying his scruples[1]). Hofer's militia and Chasteler's regulars were at first completely successful; they cleared the Tirol, and on 29 May, Francis assured the Tirolean Estates that he would not sign any peace which did not reunite the Tirol irrevocably with the Monarchy. He broke his promise – perforce – when he signed the Peace of Vienna, but the Tirolean peasants went on fighting alone, and it cost the French troops sent against them no little trouble to overcome their resistance. In the end, however, the big battalions inevitably prevailed. The fighting petered out. Hofer's hiding-place was betrayed. He was taken in fetters to Mantua and Napoleon had him shot there, although both Metternich (for Francis) and Beauharnais interceded for him. His lieutenant, Mayr, was offered his life if he would plead that he had not known of the armistice and the peace. He refused 'to buy his life with a lie', and he, too, was shot.

The reception by the Viennese of the news of the humiliating peace was less edifying. 'What a crush on the streets', wrote a contemporary; 'What joy! What delight! People embraced and kissed one another. Everything proved with what longing the day of deliverance had been awaited.'[2]

When these renewed disasters overtook the Monarchy, Francis changed his advisers once again. Stadion had renounced the conduct of his department when the armistice was signed, and resigned on 8 October, a week before the signature of the Treaty. Charles had been dismissed, in abrupt and ungracious fashion, after Wagram, and thereafter Francis pursued him with

[1] On this see *M.K.P.* III. 26 ff.   [2] Id. p. 35.

dislike and distrust, which seem to have been enhanced by the knowledge that Napoleon had suggested that Charles should take his brother's place on the throne. There is no evidence that Charles had behaved in the least disloyally, but he was now banished from public affairs, in which he never again played an important part.[1] For less apparent reasons, Rainer, too, fell into disfavour and lost his post of consultant on internal affairs. The Archduke John's positive disgrace came only three years later,[2] but meanwhile his influence at Court, too, diminished. Of Francis's 'cabinet of brothers', only Joseph, whose position in Hungary made him indispensable, survived, and he with some difficulty.[3]

Since the dismissal of Colloredo, Francis had devoted himself far more closely than before to the conduct of affairs, and had taken far more decisions personally. From 1809 on his rule became a personal one, in the fullest sense.

In so far as anyone now possessed his ear, this was Metternich, who took Stadion's place at the Chancellery, and it was only in an indirect sense that even Metternich influenced him, outside his own field of foreign affairs. In later days, when accused of responsibility for the hated 'system', Metternich repudiated it. 'He had often', he said, 'governed Europe but never Austria.' He had not been concerned at all with Austria's internal affairs. He had not invented the 'system', which he had found complete in every detail when he arrived. He had even disapproved of some aspects of it.

It is certainly true that Metternich was not the author of the system; and true in a sense which is highly unflattering to him. If we examine his so-called philosophy, we find in it certain notions, connected with his own special branch of foreign affairs, which can be traced back to his more general experiences: such, outside the all-dominant dread of the unsleeping menace of revolution, against which eternal vigilance was necessary (although this

[1] This was, indeed, largely owing to his own attitude. He was invited to command the Austrian army supporting Napoleon in 1812, but refused. After this he was put again under strict surveillance. He was made Governor of Mainz in 1815, but not offered any important post until 1830, when he was invited to lead the crusade against revolution, but declined. His name was mentioned in other connections also in that year, but nothing came of plans to instal him on the throne of Belgium, or of Poland. After Francis's death he offered to take over the army again, but the Staatskonferenz found a pretext to refuse the offer.

[2] This was in the spring of 1813, when a little group of Tiroleans concocted an odd plan for raising the men of the Alps, from Switzerland to Istria, in a people's war against Napoleon. Britain gave some money, and was to have sent naval units to help. One of the principals betrayed the plan to Metternich, alleging that John (who had been privy to the plan) was to marry a Russian Grand Duchess and have himself proclaimed King of 'Rhaetia'. This was probably entirely untrue, but John was banished from the Tirol and from the Court. He was, indeed, entrusted with various relatively unimportant duties, but played no further major part in national affairs until after Francis's death. The other leading conspirators were arrested, but released after Napoleon's fall.

[3] He was suspected of aspiring to the throne of Hungary, and of a liaison with the Empress. Metternich himself intercepted letters from Joseph to Maria Ludovica, and read them out to Francis, but this time Francis seems to have dug his heels in.

was then a commonplace of all except the revolutionaries), are perhaps his doctrines of the essential unity of Europe, of the salubrity of diversity within unity, of the virtue of balance. These ideas were at least sensible, if not particularly original; but we may at any rate be grateful to Metternich for their moderation. If he claimed for Austria the hegemony of Europe, at least he did not try to make it into a super-Europe directly ruled by her. But scrutiny of the rest of his 'political philosophy', pretentiously represented by himself and reverently expounded by his admirers as a coherent deductive system applying eternal verities to specific conditions, shows it to be nothing of the sort: it is an inductive justification of the Austrian Monarchy, and of the principles on which Francis's own instincts and his experience had led him to govern it. That the only sure foundation of order lies in the monarchic principle; that the Monarch should normally derive his title from the principle of legitimacy, but that that principle might be over-ridden if other considerations, notably that of balance, made this necessary; that the monarchy must be 'pure', bound, indeed, by the higher laws of justice and humanity but politically absolute, since between absolute monarchy and the sovereignty of the people, which is the child of revolution and the mother of anarchy, there is no intermediate stage, a constitutional monarchy being a contradiction in terms and a mask for popular sovereignty; that pseudo-constitutional institutions are nevertheless permissible so long as their functions are confined to discussion and tendering advice, and they are allowed no real power; that a Constitution may be permissible if it is hallowed by antiquity, represents conservative forces and does not embody the idea of popular sovereignty, and that the Hungarian Constitution conformed to these conditions; that there is nothing unnatural in a multi-national State, since common national feeling does not, any more than any other group feeling, give a body of subjects the right to choose their state – phrases such as 'rights of nationality' being mere shibboleths and the word 'nationalism' a mask for revolution; that a people deserved the name of nation and was entitled to the preservation of its political cohesion if in the past it had shown itself determined and able to preserve it; that this was not the case with the German and Italian peoples; that most 'subjects' are in any case uninterested in national questions and only want material prosperity and the efficient application of just laws – it is hard to see how Metternich could have phrased all these pompous dogmas differently by one iota had he deliberately and cynically set himself out to compose a justification of Francis's Austria and his own Europe.

Far from putting ideas into Francis's head, Metternich had in fact simply thought himself into the position to which Francis's temperament, his early tuition and his experiences had brought him as early as 1794. If, however, he was innocent of authorship of the 'system', he was not so guiltless of its extension and perpetuation. It is true that his direct influence on the conduct of Austria's internal affairs was limited – his enemies, who were numerous and embittered, saw to that. But he determined many issues by his insistence on the priority of considerations of foreign policy over internal, and his indirect influence over the entire conduct of Austrian policy was enormous. His 'Liberalism' was a farce. He thought the machinery of government imperfect, but so did everyone else, not least Francis himself. He was educated and personally civilized enough to realize that the system was narrow and obscurantist, and chafed against it when it was applied against himself, but he had no scruples whatever about applying its methods to others. He maintained a special spy service, paid for out of his own secret funds, for watching over developments in Germany, and as we have said, actually had intercepted, and himself read to the Emperor, correspondence between Francis's own wife and his brother, the Palatine.

He saw nothing whatever wrong with Austrian conditions[1] and details apart, entirely approved of the principle of keeping them just as they were. Thus he made himself the second father of the 'system' by his constant approval and endorsement of it. His responsibility is heavy indeed, for during many years he was spending an hour a day, sometimes two, in Francis's company; and impressionable as Francis still was, could assuredly, with his fluency, wit and polish, so much superior to the Emperor's, have influenced him in the direction of reform. Instead, he consistently assured him, at least by implication, that no reform, other than one of Governmental machinery, was needed; and Francis did not doubt him.

In his own field of foreign policy, Metternich undoubtedly called the tune, if only, as he himself put it, by the method of planting his own ideas in Francis's mind.[2] The immediate line was in any case marked out beyond much possibility of dispute. Whether, as he afterwards pretended, Metternich foresaw the speedy downfall of Napoleon and was concerned only to gain a breathing-space, or whether, as many believe, he held France's hegemony on the Continent to be a firmly established fact to which Austria must at last

[1] See his letter to the Countess of Lieven, written in 1819 (*Lettres du Prince de Metternich à la Comtesse de Lieven*, pp. 180–1).

'Tout ici', runs this devastating document, 'est bon; je ne connais pas un fait basé sur un principe ou faux en lui-même ou condemnable. C'est le régime qui, au monde, respecte le plus tous les droits et guarantie le plus toutes les libertés . . . Notre pays, ou plutôt nos pays, sont les plus tranquils, parceque ils jouissent sans révolutions antérieures de la plupart des bienfaits qui incontestablement ressortent de la cendre des empires bouleversés par les tourmentes politiques. Notre peuple ne conçoit pas pourquoi il aurait besoin se livrer à des mouvements, quand, dans le repos, il jouit de ce que le mouvement a procuré aux autres. La liberté individuelle est complète, l'égalité de toutes les classes de la société devant la loi est parfaite, toutes portent les mêmes charges; il existe de titres, mais point de privilèges.'

[2] 'What I want', Metternich's confidence to his mistress goes on, 'is always what he wants to do. He is convinced of this.' Even here, however, he confessed to a Russian General in 1829: 'If he' (sc., Francis) 'heaps favours on me, it is because I go the way which he prescribes to me, and if I were so unlucky as to stray from it, Prince Metternich would not remain Foreign Minister for twenty-four hours.'

seriously adapt herself, the situation to which the Treaty of Schönbrunn had reduced her was compulsive: for immediate policy, she had, as he told Francis immediately on his appointment, no choice but to seek France's, or rather, Napoleon's, favour, at whatever price it could be bought. Then she must temporize and flatter 'until perhaps the day of general liberation arrives'. The price, the hand of Francis's eldest daughter and favourite child, Marie Louise, was Metternich's own suggestion.[1] It was one which her father certainly did not find it easy to pay, still less, the victim herself, but Francis yielded. The marriage was celebrated on 2 April 1810.

For the rest, very various judgments have been passed on the value of the foreign policy followed by Metternich between 1809 and 1813. He had hoped to persuade Napoleon to pay for his bride with a number of concessions, including the restoration of the Illyrian provinces. In the less important fields he harvested little or nothing; Napoleon offered him Illyria only in exchange for Galicia, to be incorporated in a new Kingdom of Poland, and an alliance against Russia. It may have been an advantage for Austria that Metternich refused to commit her against Russia, and at the same time frustrated a plan sponsored by his own father for a defensive alliance with Russia against France. The immediate outcome was that Russia gained important territorial advantages at the expense of the Porte, while Austria came out empty handed. Then in 1812 Austria after all allied herself with France against Russia. Her obligations were not heavy: she had only to send an auxiliary corps of 30,000 men, and her promised reward great: she was to have Silesia. Only the war turned out badly, and Silesia remained Prussian.

Meanwhile, the Francophile line would itself have imposed the cessation of the appeals to national sentiment; but Francis needed no considerations of foreign political expediency to turn him against what had always been repugnant to his innermost convictions. The policy had proved, not only a failure, but a humiliating one. It had not been the German Princes alone who had shown themselves indifferent to it: Francis's own favourite Viennese had not behaved very differently. At first, it was true, they had received the conquerors sullenly, but they had consoled themselves quickly when the French not only took efficient measures to secure the capital's food supplies, but also relaxed the censorship. The patriotic songs and pamphlets had been hurriedly scrapped in favour of effusions of a very different tone. A gay social life had reigned, and when the news arrived of the shameful peace which cost Francis one-third of his dominions, the Viennese had embraced and kissed one another in the streets. It was not surprising that the policy of popular appeal should have been put sharply into reverse. Fortunate were those among the minor figures of the short-lived popular renaissance who scented the changing of the wind in time, for continued profession of the sentiments

[1] Napoleon had, indeed, hinted at his wishes before Metternich actually made the proposal.

so popular only a few months earlier now brought with it displeasure and, in some cases, heavy punishment.

Thus the political and social freeze was re-established, although not, altogether, the economic, for the European situation, in particular, the Continental Blockade, forced the authorities' hand, and with that and the advent, short-lived as it proved to be, of peace (among the consequences of which was the return to civilian life of a large number of soldiers) some economic life began to stir in Austria, especially in respect of her industries. Not all of these prospered: for the glass-makers, leather-workers and others who had depended largely on the export market, it was a hard time. But there was a big demand for articles required by the army, and for those products, notably woollen and cotton goods, in which England had formerly dominated the market. Many new factories producing these articles (sometimes out of local substitutes for cotton) were established in Bohemia and Moravia, where these years also saw the beginning of the sugar-beet industry, to replace the cane-sugar which was no longer available. Under the pressure of the circles interested, the Hofkammer changed its policy, and decided that in the future, 'liberalism' was to be the guiding principle. The distinction between *Kommerzialbetriebe*, which worked for export, and *Polizeibetriebe* (working for the local market) was, indeed, maintained, and the old guild restrictions kept in force for enterprises of the latter category; but for those of the former, all restrictions were lifted in 1809–10, and local authorities strictly enjoined 'in no case to lend an ear to the dangerous effusions of the spirit of monopolies and guilds, but steadfastly to maintain the spirit of free competition, dismissing all secondary considerations'.[1] The ban on the importation of machinery was lifted in 1811, as was that on the establishment of new factories in Vienna; it is true that, at the Emperor's wish, the countryside was still preferred.

The financial situation, however, was worse than ever. By 1808, when O'Donnell took over, the note circulation was 650 million and the rate 315. An attempt to raise a loan on the security of the Crown property brought in only small sums. The initial costs of the war had to be met again out of the printing press, the circulation rising to 729 million. Napoleon, in this respect as in others ahead of his time, was preparing to make things worse by printing forged Bankozettel for circulation in the occupied territories. Then had come the disastrous Treaty, with the indemnity, and the territorial losses, which brought a further aggravation of the currency situation; for the new masters of the ceded areas fixed dates after which the Bankozettel would cease to be legal currency in them, and the owners of the paper sent it to Vienna for exchange into commodities or small coins. On 19 December 1809, a new Finance Patent called in all silver (except spoons, watches, seals, surgical instruments and antiques) from the extra-Hungarian Lands, paying for it with Bankozettel at the rate of 300, or with tickets in a new State lottery. The

[1] Beer, op. cit., p. 45.

proceeds of this collection (which were far less than they should have been, since large quantities were smuggled into Hungary) yielded enough for the indemnity, but little more. A new plan for replacing the Bankozettel by bonds secured on the Church lands had no perceptible effect except to increase the public mistrust of the Bankozettel. The circulation rose to 846 million, the course sank to 469.

Then O'Donnell died, and in July 1810 Francis appointed in his stead Count Joseph Wallis, Oberstburggraf of Prague, an eccentric of brutal energy but with no recorded expertise in finance. The course of the Bankozettel promptly fell to 800, and at one moment at the beginning of 1811, even reached 1,240, although it then recovered slightly. The circulation was now 1,060 millions.

On 20 February 1811,[1] Wallis produced his remedy in the shape of a *Finanzpatent*, a measure of the most drastic deflation. All Bankozettel and also all small metal coins, were called in and exchanged for new paper, called 'redemption bonds' (Einlösungsscheine) at the rate of one new for five old, of the same face value. The Einlösungsscheine were thereafter to constitute the sole legal tender. All taxation, direct and indirect, was to be paid in the new currency, in which the Government was also to pay its own salaries, pensions, etc. Both taxes and salaries were thus multiplied by five. The rate of interest on State loans was, however, to be cut by half, so that the multiplication here was only by $2\frac{1}{2}$. The Government promised never again to allow the issue of paper money to exceed the new figure of 212 million Einlösungsscheine. The new paper was itself to be gradually amortized as funds became available.

For private debts contracted in the past since the currency began to fall, a scale (the *Wiener Scala*) was laid down, converting all such debts, if still outstanding,[2] into the new currency at a rate calculated on the average quotation of the Bankozettel in Augsburg in the month in which they had been contracted.

The necessity of stopping the inflation had been generally admitted, and there were some classes, notably the State employees and pensioners, to whom the Patent brought belated justice; what they retained of their incomes, after paying their taxes, was, provided nominal prices fell by 80% (as most of them did at first), multiplied by five. Some creditors also found their positions improved substantially. But the increased taxation was a very heavy blow to all taxpayers, many of whom were genuinely unable to meet

---

[1] It was published at 5 a.m. on 15 March. It was not the *ipse dixit* of Wallis as which it is represented by Springer and other older historians. It had been preceded by prolonged discussion in high places, and constituted only a variant of many similar proposals. See Beer, op. cit., pp. 70 ff. Beer's opinion of Wallis is higher, and perhaps juster, than that of the older writers.

[2] The measure did not apply to debts already settled.

the new demands. A large number of landed properties, big and small (including many *eingekauft* peasant holdings), were sold up, and the abrupt deflation even did much to nullify the embryonic industrial boom.[1] At best, the operation produced extraordinary confusion, and it remained a terrible memory to the people, who persisted (rightly or wrongly) in regarding it as a State bankruptcy for four shillings in the pound.[2]

Moreover, the Patent brought the sharpest crisis to date in the Crown's relations with Hungary.

The constitutional position in Hungary was that the right of mintage was the King's unquestioned prerogative, but indirect taxation should have been agreed with the Estates, and Hungary, although she had, of necessity, been using Bankozettel for a decade past, did not recognize any community between her currency and that of the rest of the Monarchy. Francis had at first intended simply to promulgate the Patent in Hungary, as in his other dominions, but on the strong representations of the Palatine he convoked the Diet for August. He still, however, announced in his 'propositions' that the Patent was applicable to Hungary; the Diet was to be asked only to consider the means of applying it. It was further to take over the amortization of one hundred million of the Einlösungsscheine and in addition, was asked to raise the contributio by 100%.

The Diet, when it met, resisted stubbornly. It argued that the issue of uncovered paper money was an abuse of the right of mintage and simply a disguised method of milking the taxpayer. It refused to admit the legality of extending the Patent to Hungary, or to take over the amortization. There were also bitter complaints against the *Wiener Scala*.[3] The argumentation was so long and bitter that the centralist party at the Court again strongly pressed Francis to suspend the Hungarian Constitution. Both Metternich and Wallis, however, warned him against the step, while the Palatine told him that it would provoke revolution, and even Napoleon, when consulted, was discouraging. Again Francis shrank from the irrevocable, but on 30 May 1812, he dissolved the Diet, and on 1 September introduced the Patent 'provisionally' into Hungary, pending the convocation of the next Diet. As in

---

[1] Whereas at the end of 1810, 63,218 persons had been employed in the factories and artisans' workshops of Lower Austria, the figure two years later was only 42,247. In Bohemia the fall in the number of employed persons was 69,144.

[2] So the historian Springer wrote, in a work published in 1863:

'To this day the memory of the Finance Patent of 1811 remains more rooted in the memory of the people than that of any other historic event, and constitutes for it the most important event in the modern history of Austria... Its consequences are still visible, its connection with later facts and conditions undeniable' (*Geschichte*, I. 143).

As we shall see, it was the fear of a renewal of inflation that triggered off the revolutions in Vienna and Hungary in 1848.

[3] A considerable proportion of the members of the Diet were landowners who had been borrowing extensively and now found the weight of their indebtedness suddenly increased.

fact he did not convoke a Diet for the next thirteen years, this meant that Hungary was ruled, during that period, almost as absolutely as the Austrian Lands. The Counties were, indeed, left unmolested, but where they proved recalcitrant, the Crown enforced its will by putting in Royal Commissioners.

And after all, the Patent did not achieve its purpose. The course of 1:5 had been chosen because the last time at which the Bankozettel had still stood at par had been when the circulation was at that figure; but in 1811 the rate had been not 500, but 900. The Einlösungsscheine were at once quoted at 180, and as they had no backing, their course fluctuated widely. Prices, after generally remaining for a short time at one-fifth (nominal) of the pre-Patent figure, rose sharply in the autumn of 1811. In 1812 they fell again and the course went down to 139. But even the relatively small military operation which was all that Austria was required to undertake in that year – the despatch of an auxiliary force against Russia – strained her resources (it had been paid for out of taxation) and in 1813 the foundations of the recovery were again sapped by the demands of foreign policy, which now took a new turn. The failure of his attempt to invade Russia, and Wellington's victories in the Peninsula, had weakened Napoleon's position. The war party at the Viennese Court took courage again and Austria began to rearm in preparation for intervention on the side of Napoleon's enemies. The armistice concluded on 4 June between France on the one hand and Russia and Prussia on the other placed Austria in a favourable position, for both sides were prepared to pay for her assistance. The alliance with France was discarded, in none too honourable fashion. By the Convention of Reichenbach (27 June) Austria promised to declare war on France if the terms, which she would offer, were rejected. Napoleon in fact rejected them; and fortified by a promise of subsidies from Britain (which came in on a fairly generous scale), Austria declared war on 11 August. Again she was involved in war, again without being able to afford it. As early as April 1813, when she had begun to rearm on a larger scale, the Government had been obliged to break its word, so recently pledged, and to announce the issue of another 45 million gulden of paper money, beautified with the name of *Anticipationsscheine*,[1] for equipping the army. When actual war broke out, this figure proved hopelessly inadequate, and that although the Austrian army was conspicuously and piteously the worst equipped in the field: official reports admitted that many of the soldiers called up could not be supplied with overcoats, some not even with boots. The army fought courageously, playing its full part in the Battle of Leipzig, and in general, in the campaign which ended in Napoleon's fall. But this was at a heavy cost, not only in blood to itself but in the tax which it imposed on the resources of the State. Conventional expedients all proved hopelessly inadequate: a loan floated for the 1815

[1] Because they represented the 'anticipated' revenue from the land tax for the next twelve years.

campaign was under-subscribed, although bearing interest at $8\frac{1}{4}\%$; a 50% surcharge on taxes other than the land tax (i.e., the *Gewerbesteuer*, *Einkommensteuer* and *Personalsteuer*) brought in only a few drops into the bucket. More paper had to be issued.[1] The fact was not admitted, and the '*Oberster Kanzler*', Count Ugarte, who was then in charge of finances,[2] hoped that the public would not realize what was happening, so that there would be no consequences.[3] But the public smelled a rat, and the old story set in again of rising prices and a falling quotation; in October 1913, the new money stood at 169, in April 1814, at 238, in April 1815, after Napoleon's return from Elba, at 408. Thereafter it was rarely below 300, often as high as 360. The circulation of the paper, new and old, was now, in reality, over 635 million '*Wiener Währung*', as the Einlösungsscheine and Anticipationsscheine were collectively called.

[1] There were seven secret issues.
[2] Wallis had resigned when the Government began issuing Anticipationsscheine.
[3] Beer, op. cit., p. 85.

5

The System at its Zenith (1815-30)

But Austria's fortunes were on the upgrade at last. When peace returned to her in 1815, it was with a different countenance from that which she had shown on her fleeting visits of earlier years. At the famous Conference, which was held in Vienna, the Emperor Francis acting as host, Metternich, on his home ground, largely dominated the play. Under the final Treaty of Paris, signed on 20 November 1815, Austria emerged with all the territory which she had lost since 1792 except the Netherlands and the Vorlande, and almost all the acquisitions made by her at any time since that date, except some of her more transitory gains under the Third Partition of Poland; and even here she had retained a right of co-supervision over Cracow, now a Free City. She dominated Italy through her own possessions of Lombardy and Venetia, through family connections (the secundo and tertio-genitures in Tuscany and Modena had been restored, and Marie Louise given Parma, Piacenza and Guastalla for life) and through her influence over the remaining Courts. The latest solution of the German problem – the constitution of the German Bund as a federation of thirty-five 'sovereign princes' and four Free Cities, under Austrian Presidency – probably gave the Emperor of Austria more influence in Germany than the Holy Roman Emperor had enjoyed for many generations. Austria, Britain, Russia and Prussia were jointly pledged to maintain the peace settlement, while every King in Europe (except our poor George, who was under tutelage) had signed a solemn declaration pledging himself to a Christian union of charity, peace and love. The three first signatories to this document had been its spiritual father, Alexander I of Russia, Francis, and Frederick William III of Prussia, and Metternich (who held, indeed, a realistic enough view of the declaration as such) believed that he had his Monarch's two partners well in hand. In short, he flattered himself that the Concert of Europe was firmly established and playing well in tune, with himself as its conductor, or leader.

Finally, Austria was booked to receive an indemnity (of 150 million francs), an agreeable change from the obligation of paying one with which she had grown accustomed to ending her wars; and instead of having to support a foreign army on her soil, she was keeping 30,000 men on the soil of France.

Many Austrian writers of later decades have thought that Metternich did not choose his prizes wisely; that instead of spending so much effort on securing territory and spheres of influence in Italy, which in the event cost her blood and money and had to be relinquished, ignominiously enough, after only a few decades,[1] he would have done better to recover for Austria the titular leadership of Germany – Francis could have had the revived Imperial Crown for the taking if he had been willing to reassume the responsibility – and to recover and extend the Vorlande, thus securing for the Dynasty a solid German Hausmacht. The Archduke John, while also doubting the wisdom of Austria's acquisitions in Italy, thought that she ought to have expanded into the Balkans and the Danubian Principalities. Either of these alternative courses might perhaps have served Austria better than that which she chose, although it must be remarked that either would have brought with it its own problems, which might have been, each in its different way, as intractable as those which actually occupied her during the next decades. But at least, on Metternich's own premises, he could (as he did) flatter himself that he had been highly successful. So much was sure, that the outward glory of Austria was shining more brilliantly than it had done for many a long year.

Against this there had, indeed, to be set the extreme financial chaos and economic distress to which the preceding twenty-five years had reduced the Monarchy. The situation of the currency has been described; further, the last campaign (for which Austria had undertaken to provision a large part of the armies of her allies, as well as her own) had almost exhausted her stocks, and then 1815 was a year of rain and floods, followed by a bad harvest; while the Congress of Vienna had 'danced',[2] at the expense of the city, prices had risen fantastically. The harvest of 1816 was a complete failure, and in many parts of the Monarchy there was literal famine. People were eating grass, clover and maize-stalks, and perishing in their hordes of starvation and its attendant diseases. In fat Hungary itself, 18,000 persons perished of starvation in 1816–17 in Arad, and 26,000 in Szatmár, Krassó Bihár and Bereg.[3] Conditions were as bad in Silesia and Friule. It could, however, be hoped that if the peace proved enduring, this last heritage of the unhappy past would itself become a memory.

[1] Here again, the Emperor's personal wishes may have operated more strongly than is often recognized, for Francis always had a *faiblesse* for his Italian titles.
[2] Too much importance has, indeed, been attached to this phrase, originally simply a *bon mot* coined by the *spirituel* Prince de Ligne. The Congress, of course, did much solid work.
[3] A. Mód. *400 év kuzdelem az önálló Magyárországert* (Bp. 1945), p. 88.

THE SYSTEM AT ITS ZENITH (1815–1830)

In fact, the next decade saw a recovery even in these fields, but it was slow, painful and incomplete. The one evil which was really remedied was the inflation. In 1814 Stadion had been put in charge of the national finances,[1] and in 1817, after an earlier, more ambitious, plan had foundered on the rocks of public mistrust,[2] he succeeded in bringing into definitive being a 'Privileged National Bank', which was established with the help of private capital and remained a non-Governmental body (a Government Commissioner sat on its board, but had only an advisory voice). The main long-term function of this institution was to act as banker to the State, but it was empowered to issue its own notes, for which, on foundation, it exchanged the Anticipations- and Einlösungsscheine at the rate of 250, i.e., somewhat higher than that which had prevailed in the previous year. The Government succeeded in holding the exchange at that rate; the Bank's notes gradually replaced the old paper money, and the Government was able to use them, and metal, which now began to reappear, interchangeably, and even, in 1820, to resume the full nominal payment on its own debt – a measure which raised its credit, although it met with a mixed reception from the public, since it was argued that most of the original buyers of the papers had sold them, so that the profits were going to speculators.

Stadion's operation, however, meant in effect the repudiation by the State of another twelve shillings in the pound of its obligations, for the owner of 250 gulden Wiener Währung could exchange them only against one hundred gulden Conventionsmünzen, although they had been issued with a solemn promise that their full value would be maintained. Moreover, the inauguration of this severely deflationary monetary policy, which created a catastrophic shortage of money (and private credit, at that stage, hardly existed), coincided with the opening of a prolonged and severe economic crisis of markets. A series of good harvests following the appalling ones of 1815 and 1816 brought about a local abundance of commodities of prime necessity. On the other hand, the conclusion of peace and the ending of the Continental blockade were followed by the reappearance of Odessa wheat

---

[1] Stadion's commission in 1814 was a special one, but in 1816 he was given an independent Ministry, the Hofkammer reverting to its original function of collecting and administering the revenues from the Crown properties, etc. Subsequently Stadion succeeded in making himself 'overlord' of all departments dealing with finance, although the 'Kommerzhofdirektorium' mentioned below remained *de facto* largely independent in its policy.

[2] This plan, which was promulgated by Patent on 1 June 1816, allowed holders of paper money to exchange part of it against a new metal currency (Conventionsmünze) to the same nominal value, part into notes, again to the same nominal value, issued by a new National Bank, these notes again being exchangeable for metal, provided the holders also bought State bonds in the proportion of five bonds to two notes, and paid for these in metal; or alternatively, to buy shares in the bank, paying for them in the proportion of ten in paper to one in metal. The Government placed its stocks of metal currency and its payments from foreign Powers at the disposal of the Bank. There was, however, such a run on the metal currency that the Bank quickly exhausted its stocks and had to close its doors.

on the agricultural market,[1] and of English manufactures on the industrial. The price of Hungarian wheat, which had risen to 143 groschen per Pozsony bushel in 1806, 152 in 1809, 158 in 1814, 513 in 1816, 413 in 1817, fell to 149 in 1818 and to 75 and even 60 in the 1820s; even in the 1830s it rarely rose above 100. The same fate overtook the Galician wheatgrowers, who complained in 1817 that the price of their produce had fallen by two-thirds and that their export trade had dried up altogether. The smaller owners in the Western Lands, many of whom were heavily indebted, found it impossible to meet their obligations. According to one writer:

> In many villages hardly one owner in ten could keep his head above water. Peasant holdings which had cost 4,000 gulden Wiener Währung three years earlier could now often be had for 200 gulden Conventionsmünzen. Perhaps half the smaller landowners and one in ten of the bigger were ruined.[2]

Manufacture suffered as heavily when Britain began throwing her accumulated stocks on the Continental market, often at dumping prices. The industries which had been built up in answer to the Continental blockade – in particular, textiles, small metal objects such as buttons, buckles, etc., and sugar – were the worst sufferers. In 1818 the production of cloth in Reichenberg was barely half what it had been five years earlier; in some other centres, only one-third. Conditions in the Moravian wool industry were similar; out of twenty-three enterprises in Brünn, only seven survived the crisis. There were also many bankruptcies in Lower Austria. Broadly speaking, it was only the larger enterprises, which were able to import the new machines, and now began to do so,[3] which escaped disaster. Many workers were thrown on the streets.

Things would have been worse still but for the inclusion of Lombardy-Venetia in the Austrian customs unit ordered by Francis in 1817. The population of these Lands, in which silver currency still circulated officially, provided a certain market for the Austrian industries, but the effect of this became really perceptible only after some years.[4]

A semi-autonomous *Kommerzdirektorium*, established, on Metternich's initiative, in 1816, to act as a sort of economic planning centre, with executive powers, did some useful work, particularly in securing the abolition of the remaining internal tariffs, and it laid the foundations for the later reforms in Austria's industrial legislation, but its director, the Prussian Freiherr von Stahl, could not get on with his Austrian colleagues, and the office was

---

[1] Even Dalmatia now imported its wheat from this source and so – so bad were communications in Hungary – did even some areas in Inner Hungary itself.

[2] I Beidtel, II. 303-4.

[3] See below, p. 265 f.

[4] For some years the provinces were, indeed, heavily passive owing to the cost of winding up the French administration and installing a new one and to a series of disastrous harvests, in consequence of which much taxation was remitted and expensive public works undertaken.

wound up in 1824. In any case, most of his proposals had foundered on Francis's antipathy to innovations. Official policy on industrial questions was practically confined to taking decisions for or against encouraging, or allowing, 'factories' to compete against the guilds,[1] and on this point, it changed repeatedly: the ban on granting new licences was reimposed in 1822, lifted again in 1827, imposed again in 1831. The effects of the continued protection enjoyed by the guilds was, incidentally, far from healthy for themselves; their fossilization grew even more pronounced.

Meanwhile, Austria's finances had not really been restored. In principle, the State had resolved to renounce the habit of letting its expenditure exceed its revenue, bridging the gap by issuing uncovered paper money; but it had found no substitute for that device. Under Stadion's regime, receipts really rose considerably; ordinary revenue, only 50·7 million gulden in 1814, had risen to a decimal point under 94 in 1817, and this was followed by further increases – another nine millions in the five years 1820–5 and 7·5 millions more by 1830.[2] The sensational increase of the first four years was, indeed, due largely to the increased number of tax-payers, the Monarchy having in these years recovered the territories lost in 1809; but the load of taxation had also been increased, notably by the raising of the tax on earnings by 50% in 1817. Francis was, however, still very reluctant to increase taxation, especially direct taxation, and his subjects equally reluctant to pay it. Thus it was decided in 1817 to introduce a new land tax imposing equal taxation on all land, rustical or dominical, everywhere outside Hungary, but the prerequisite for this was a new land survey. This proved such a formidable undertaking that as late as 1843, when the Government began arguing with the Estates on what were their commitments under it, it had still been completed only in Lower and Upper Austria, Styria, Carinthia, Carniola, the Littoral and Lombardy-Venetia, and only in those Lands were the dominical Estates coming under the higher assessment.[3] Meanwhile, the Government had been so extensively cheated over the valuations, especially by the big landowners, that the yield of this tax was actually lower at the end of the Vormärz than it had been in 1817.[4]

The biggest item on the other side of the balance-sheet was the cost of the armed forces. Francis laid down a ruling that ordinary expenditure on the army was never to exceed 40 million gulden yearly,[5] and although this figure was afterwards raised to 44, and the army was never held quite rigidly to it,

[1] Francis must, indeed, be credited also with founding a number of technical schools and colleges.
[2] Beer, pp. 170 ff.
[3] It was first put into force in Lower Austria, in 1834, with the result that taxation there was heavier than anywhere else in the Monarchy.
[4] Thus Prince Liechtenstein, who had 720,000 'subjects', paid only 150,000 gulden a year in land tax.
[5] Beer, p. 135.

very real economies were effected in this field. The strength of the army was substantially reduced, chiefly by the simple device of suspending recruiting, so that the fall-out due to men leaving the colours under the new age-limits was not made good. In this way, while the nominal peace strength of the army at this period was 400,000, its actual peace strength ranged between 200–230,000 men. Further, the army reserve was abolished and the Landwehr used in its place, the first Landwehr battalion of each regiment counting as the fourth battalion of each regular regiment. Finally, both training and equipment were neglected; it was only in 1830 that percussion muskets were introduced (and they were still muzzle loaders, with a range of three hundred yards). The allowance of ammunition was only ninety rounds per annum. By these devices the military budget was brought down to an annual average of 45–50 million gulden, but only against the embittered opposition of Metternich, whose thesis that foreign policy, under which he included the preservation by Austria of European order, must take precedence of internal, was obviously incompatible with large-scale military retrenchment. And it was really difficult to economize very extensively in this field. It is to be remembered that while, looking back, we see that in 1815 in fact opened a period of nearly thirty-five years during which Austria was never once at war in the technical sense, yet when that period opened it did not look like lasting nearly so long, and during its first years it looked less like peace than an armed and precarious truce. There was revolution, or the threat of it, in Germany, Italy, Spain, Portugal, the Balkans, even France. At each crisis Metternich renewed his Cassandra-like wails of impending disaster and his persistent warnings that the price of order was eternal vigilance; the smallest relaxation might undo all that had been so painfully achieved. He was blissfully indifferent to financial objections: one could always borrow, could one not? In 1820–1 it was only technically that Austria was at peace at all; in those years her armies occupied Piedmont and Naples. The cost of the expeditions was relatively small, and Austria succeeded in getting them paid for to the tune of 28 million franks; even so, it was enough to upset the budgetary equilibrium which Stadion had painfully achieved and to keep it upset for ten years, when it was overthrown again, in the very year of its recovery, by the same cause.[1]

In 1828, when there seemed a possibility that war might break out with Russia over the Eastern Question, the Hofkriegsrat reported that the army was quite unfit for a campaign; neither its numbers, its equipment or its morale were adequate.

The economies on the army, besides their effects in reducing the Monarchy's weight in international affairs, had the particularly embarrassing consequence (on which, as we shall see, the attempt to impose absolutism throughout the Monarchy ultimately foundered) that when troops and

[1] See below, p. 236.

THE SYSTEM AT ITS ZENITH (1815–1830)

subsidies were required for some foreign enterprise, there was no course but to apply for them to Hungary, thus presenting the Hungarian Diet with its opportunity to assert its rights.

The army was not, of course, the only big source of expenditure; the reincorporation of the recovered provinces entailed expenditure as well as bringing in revenues. Thus all economies and windfalls notwithstanding, there was still a regular and formidable annual deficit, ranging from 50 million gulden downward. The Government covered a fraction of this by auctioning (usually for very inadequate sums) State properties, including the last of the Church properties which Joseph II had confiscated. For the rest, it perforce resorted to internal loans, lottery or ordinary subscription, or borrowed abroad. Both types of loan were chiefly raised for it by Viennese bankers, or the Viennese representatives of international banking-houses, a small ring, composed for the most part of 'privileged' Jews, who now ousted the older firms (mostly Swiss) which had served Francis during his earlier years. Easily the most important of these new houses was that of Rothschild, whose representative, Salamon, founded a branch of the family house in Vienna in 1819. Within a very few years Salamon, who was given a barony in 1822, made his family not only far the richest but, after that of Habsburg, probably the most really powerful in the Monarchy. Hardly a decision on high policy could be taken without Salamon's approval, and an extraordinary number of them were taken on his direct advice. Metternich's relationship to him is one of the most curious in history. Rothschild's relationship to Metternich's publicist, Gentz, was, indeed, simple enough: he bribed him heavily to look after his interests.

The benefits of the connections (many of them running through the National Bank) between the Austrian Government and these circles were not altogether one-sided. The Rothschilds, in particular, rendered Austria extraordinary service in 1823, when they got her chief foreign debt – that to Britain – settled by persuading the British Government to renounce all but £2,500,000 of the £23,500,000 at which the debt then stood, and undertaking the transference of this sum, for which they then became the creditors of the Austrian Government.[1] And the bankers nearly always arranged that the Government should get a loan when it wanted one. But it paid through the nose for the accommodation. Up to 1820 it was seldom able to float a loan at over 70,[2] often only at 60–5, so that it actually paid 8–9% on what it borrowed.[3] Later the terms became somewhat easier, but during the whole

[1] For details, see Helleiner, op. cit., pp. 147 ff.

[2] Floating a loan at under par was actually a device invented by Austria's creditors, on the pretext that they had to recoup themselves against the risk of default, but wished to avoid the odium of charging a very high percentage.

[3] In fact, Austria paid back 38 m.g. for the 20 which she received as the first half of her 1820 loan, which was a lottery loan (at 6%) floated by the Rothschilds. Her loss on the second half was heavier still.

of Francis's reign no loan was ever floated as high as 90.¹ Thus, as time went on, the State debt became an enormous millstone around Austria's neck. Between 1816 and 1823 alone it rose from 739 to 905 million gulden, the interest on it from 8·9 to 23·5 and the gross annual expenditure from 12 to 36.

Meanwhile, the outcome of the Congress of Vienna had, not unnaturally, confirmed Francis in the conviction that he had been right all along, after all. In the preceding twenty-five years he had listened time and again to advisers who had wheedled him into trying this or that innovation; every time he had done so, he had lost a war, and usually a province. Since 1810 he had gone his own way, and now had emerged triumphant, all the lost ground recovered and twenty-three years weathered, twenty-one of them since the last serious hint of internal trouble.

In any case, he was genuinely unable to see what more remained for him to do in the political field. In his view, which Metternich reflected faithfully, all that the 'subjects' needed was material well-being and good laws. The well-being would come in time – in any case, he was quite blind to the problem of poverty except when it manifested itself beyond concealment in some natural catastrophe, a famine or a flood, when he was ready enough that relief should be organized; the laws were there, for following the new Penal Code, the new 'General Civil Code' – another very excellent piece of work – had been completed and issued by Patent in 1811.² It was now extended to the new or re-acquired Lands, and therewith Francis really felt that nothing more remained for him to do.

Finally, as Sedlnitzky of the police once said (probably with reference to himself and Metternich), 'although His Majesty had always had the system, it was only now that he had been fortunate enough to find the organs which reflected it without distortion.³

Among the 'distortions' which now vanished was a large part of the background influence which the great feudal aristocracy had, thanks largely to Colloredo's influence, succeeded in salvaging when Francis first ascended the throne. It is hardly possible to define exactly the stages by which the fall of the aristocracy took place. According to Sealsfield[4] it was after 1811 that they 'fell into disgrace'. Beidtel[5] puts the decisive change after 1815. Then, he writes, the aristocracy felt that many considerations which the Court had been forced to pay to the revolutionary situation no longer applied, and they would be able to recover their old near-monopoly of the leading positions

---
[1] Beidtel, II. 310.

[2] It was promulgated by Patent on 1 June 1811 to enter into force on 1 January 1812. This compilation, unlike the Penal Code, carried forward with little modification the principles initiated by Francis's predecessors.

[3] Bibl, *Zerfall Oesterreichs*, I. 44.

[4] Sealsfield, op. cit., pp. 161 ff.

[5] Beidtel, op. cit., II. 234 f.

THE SYSTEM AT ITS ZENITH (1815–1830)

in the Church, the administration and the army. Unfortunately for themselves, they voiced their views too openly, especially over certain Episcopal appointments, and the Emperor, offended, took the opposite line. It is certain in any case that during these years of its hey-day Francis's system underwent a perceptible reversion to Josephinism, in respect both of its composition and its spirit.

There was naturally no place in it for any kind of representative institutions. When Austria entered into possession of her new or newly-acquired territories, she found herself, indeed, under an obligation to introduce 'Constitutions' in some of them, in virtue of certain international instruments signed by her at Vienna.[1] Estates were accordingly set up in Tirol-Vorarlberg, Carniola and (in 1826, after its constitution as a separate Land) Salzburg. None of these 'Constitutions', however, provided for any genuine self-government. Even that of the Tirol, the least restricted of them, still gave its Estates less power than they had enjoyed under Leopold.[2] A law establishing Estates for Gorizia-Gradisca, although drafted, was never put into force, and no representative institutions were ever provided for Istria or (while Francis ruled) Dalmatia.

The provinces belonging to the old Hereditary and Bohemian Lands, with Istria and Dalmatia, were then simply put back under the old Vereinigte Hofkanzlei, or, as it was called after 1817, the Ministerium des Innern[3] (the head of which was now entitled 'Oberster Kanzler und Minister des Innern', and were governed as autocratically as ever,[4] and on highly centralized lines; even the spheres within which the Gubernia could act without reference to Vienna were extremely limited. The only changes in the administrative or

[1] Art. 13 of the German Bundesakte had laid down that 'in allen Bundesstaaten wird eine landständische Verfassung stattfinden'. Art. 1 of the Final Act of the Congress had declared that 'les Polonais, sujets respectifs des Hautes Parties Contractantes, obtiendront la conservation de leur nationalité, d'après les formes d'existence politique que chacun des gouvernements aux quels ils appartiennent jugera convenable de leur accorder'.

[2] It is true that these Estates were now more democratic in form. There were four Benches, the Prelates, the nobles (higher and lower), burghers and peasants, each having thirteen voices. The representatives of the three lay Estates were all elected by their peers.

[3] This body was now divided into three geographical sections, the Bohemian, the Austrian and the Illyrian. The Gubernia were: in the Bohemian section, Bohemia and Moravia-Silesia; in the Austrian, Lower Austria, Upper Austria with Salzburg (these were treated as one Land until 1826, when Salzburg was separated off), Tirol-Vorarlberg, and Styria; in the Illyrian, Carinthia (to which the Klagenfurt *Kreis* was re-attached in 1825), Carniola (the 'Illyrian Government'), the Littoral (Gorizia-Gradisca, Trieste, Istria, the northernmost Dalmatian islands, and until 1822, when they were returned to the Hungarian Crown, those portions of civilian Croatia and of the Hungarian Littoral which had belonged to Napoleon's Kingdom of Illyria – the military portions had been immediately re-incorporated in the Military Frontier) and Dalmatia (the historic province minus its northernmost islands).

[4] In 1816 the Estates of Carniola complained against certain administrative abuses. The document was simply sent back to them, and an investigation against its authors set on foot.

judicial systems on the lower levels were the small reforms of the Patrimonial Courts mentioned above.[1]

Hungary and Transylvania retained their own Chancelleries, or Chancellery, which remained in name directly under the Crown alone. It was, however, as truly an instrument of the Monarch's will as any of its sister bodies. The Diets were left unconvoked.[2]

The Government had decided in 1817 that it would be good policy to placate the Poles, lest they should gravitate towards Russian Poland. The severity of the regime in Galicia was consequently somewhat relaxed. The Province was given the style of a Kingdom, with a Viceroy, and its own Court Chancellery in Vienna. The Estates were remodelled, the Bench of Magnates being reinforced through the creation of new titles, and were allowed to meet again after thirty-five years. The real authority, however, remained entirely with the Gubernium and its officials, who continued to be drawn, with few exceptions, from the Hereditary and Bohemian Lands.

Only Lombardy-Venetia was treated somewhat differently. Francis had, indeed, rejected a request brought to him in 1814 by a deputation from Milan that Lombardy should constitute an independent Kingdom under the Austrian Crown, with its own institutions. His reply had been that Lombardy was his by right of conquest, and that he would inform the Milanese of the dispositions which he proposed to make concerning them. On 23 May Field-Marshal Bellegarde had then formally taken possession of Lombardy on the Emperor's behalf.

Nevertheless it was felt advisable to conciliate the Italians, and unwise even to attempt the impossible task of Germanizing them. Accordingly, Lombardy-Venetia was constituted a Kingdom, and after Francis had had himself crowned, an Archduke (this time an important one)[3] was sent down to represent him.

It was provided with a 'Congregations General', composed of representatives of the noble and non-noble landowners, and the larger towns, whose duty it was to see the local execution of Government legislation and its right, to bring the wishes and needs of the population to the attention of the authorities. Below this level, the Kingdom was divided into two Gubernia (the frontier being moved westward to the Mincio in order roughly to equalize the populations), each of which was provided with a 'Provincial Congrega-

[1] See above, p. 160.

[2] The last Hungarian Diet had been the disastrous one of 1811/12. The Transylvanian had not been convoked since 1810.

[3] The appointment was first offered to the Archduke Anton, but after he had refused to take up a post which carried no authority with it, Rainer was sent down instead. The Viceroy was, indeed, a purely decorative figure: the Gubernia corresponded directly with Vienna, without showing him their reports. Rainer occupied himself chiefly with holding modest Courts in the two capitals, organizing certain charitable institutions, and with laying out the truly beautiful ornamental gardens of Monza outside Milan.

tion' on the same representational pattern as the Congregation General. The Viceroy was to reside half the year in each Gubernium. Below this again, Lombardy was divided into nine, and Venetia into eight, Provinces, corresponding to the Austrian Kreise. There was an excellent system of local autonomy. At first each Gubernium was also given its own military command, but the command was afterwards centralized in Verona, with sub-commands in the two capitals, Milan and Venice.

The Kingdom had its own Court Chancellery in Vienna, and the language of the administration, education and the Courts was Italian. (German was taught as a subject in the higher establishments.) There was an abundance of educational establishments of all grades, from the famous Universities of Padua and Pavia downward, and a relatively modern judical system, all of it State,[1] with a separate High Court in Verona, officially regarded as a branch of the Supreme Court in Vienna. At the beginning all existing Italian civil servants, except those very closely associated with the previous regimes or found to belong to secret societies, were allowed to keep their posts; only a few civil servants and judges, and those picked ones,[2] were sent down from Vienna to initiate the Italians into the Austrian system and to exercise a measure of control over them. Another important concession to the Kingdom was that the debased Austrian paper currency was not made legal tender in it, the silver currency continuing to circulate.[3]

The top-level machinery of Government underwent various changes of form, none of which modified at all substantially its essential nature. The regular conferences, based on the Staatsrat, had ceased with the fall from favour of the Archduke Rainer, and no attempt was made to replace them until 1814, when another reorganization was carried through. The Staatsrat was again remodelled as a general supervisory body, to control the work of all Government departments outside Hungary except that of Foreign Affairs. It was divided into four sections, dealing respectively with legal affairs, 'politica' (internal administration; the head of this section was responsible not only for the Ministry of the Interior, but also for the Italian and Galician Court Chancelleries), finance, and defence. The heads of sections were to meet regularly in conference, under the presidency of Count Wallis.

'Beside and above' the Staatsrat – the relationship between the two bodies was expressed only in this vague phrase – there was to be a Konferenzrat, for the discussion of general policy on the highest level. All 'Real Ministers', i.e.

---

[1] I.e., there were no Patrimonial Courts in the Kingdom. The law, both civil and criminal, was Austrian.

[2] Many of them were chosen from among men who had proved their capacity in the 'difficult' province of Galicia (H. Benedikt, *Kaiseradler*, p. 114).

[3] An attempt to introduce the Austrian paper currency had evoked such strong protest that the order had been withdrawn. The same concession was made to the Tirol.

heads, past and present, of departments with Ministerial rank, were 'perpetual members' of this body, with the title of Staats- und Konferenzminister. Other members were nominated by Francis, either for life, or for shorter periods. The first President was Count Károly Zichy;[1] when he died in 1826, Prince (as he had been created in 1813) Metternich succeeded to the Presidency.

Metternich, who in 1821 had been made formal head of the Haus-Hof-und Staatskanzlei,[2] had also, in 1824, been given the title (vacant since the death of Kaunitz) of State Chancellor, with the emoluments of the office; but this, as he soon discovered, had given him no authority to control the work of other departments, or even to know what they were doing. And as the Konferenzrat met, in the event, no more often than its predecessors, there was still no one beside Francis himself even in a position to survey the whole field of the Monarchy's affairs, much less take a decision in the light of it. Nor was there any improvement in the cumbersome character of the machine, and its inability to distinguish between the important and the trivial.[3]

Under this system, the maintenance of stability was developed into a fine art as never before. In 1810 the censorship had, in theory, been slightly relaxed, owing to the representations of the then Chief of Police, Baron von Hagen, who was a relatively liberal-minded man, and had warned Francis that it was dangerous to overstrain the bow; and in October of that year Francis had issued new instructions for the censors, to the effect that serious works of learning containing new discoveries or points of view, and written for savants and specialists, were not to be forbidden without real cause; even serious and constructive criticism of the administration was to be allowed, so long as it contained nothing which was contrary to religion or morality, or subversive – although even so 'a careful hand should safeguard the hearts and heads of the immature from the deleterious products of an abominable fantasy, the poisonous breath of self-seeking seducers and the dangerous chimeras of perverse brains'.[4]

But Hagen grew old, and in 1815 the charge of the police and censorship was put in the hands of Count Sedlnitzky,[5] who appears, indeed, to have been

---

[1] Other members were Kolowrat-Liebsteinsky, Metternich, Wallis, von Dube, von Lederer, von Hamer and von Pfleger.

[2] Until that date he had used the Kanzlei for his secretariat, but his title had been only 'Minister of Foreign Affairs'.

[3] Charmatz, *Das Politische Denken in Oesterreich*, p. 10, records one case: the lower age limit for admission to a gymnasium was ten. The parents of one exceptionally precocious boy wanted him to enter a school earlier. They had to put in a *Majestätsgesuch*, which went right up to the Staatsrat, which referred it back to the relevant Hofstelle for a considered report.

[4] These words were the work of Gentz.

[5] Sedlnitzky became *wirklicher Präsident* only on 17 May 1817, but had been in effective charge since 16 August 1815.

by no means the terrorist as which he figures in the literature of 1848. According to sober observers, he was strict, not out of sadism but out of an excess of timidity. The effect, however, was that under his regime that criteria of what could safely be published became narrower than ever. A second police service, numerically smaller but still extensive enough, was under the direct control of Metternich. The agents of this service operated also outside the Monarchy.

Metternich, although he complained of the stupidity of the censorship and was annoyed when his own movements were spied upon, was second to no man in the Monarchy in his readiness to use espionage against others or in his fundamental obscurantism; and it was probably the reports of his spies from abroad, and his own glosses on them, that were chiefly responsible for the intensification of the anti-intellectual drive which set in after 1815. Not without reason, Francis regarded most of his own peoples (Hungarians, Poles and Italians excepted) as fundamentally innocent, provided they were not corrupted through infection from abroad. But the world abroad, and especially Germany, was full of dangers. If the *camisards* of the French Revolution were a bogey of the past, Liberalism was not, in Metternich's eyes, essentially any better than Jacobinism, and more dangerous when it was German; for, as he said, 'the French play with liberty. It is a more serious matter when the Germans couple perseverance with enthusiasm.' So students attending German Universities were particularly suspect in the years immediately after the Congress of Vienna, when some of those institutions, especially those of Jena and Weimar, in fact became foci of national and social unrest, and the *Wartburg Fest* of 17 October 1817 produced something of a crisis, for the Austrian authorities discovered to their consternation that student movements and organizations parallel to those in Berlin and Jena had come into existence in Vienna and Prague, Innsbruck and Graz. Duels were being fought, long pipes smoked, country walks undertaken, suspiciously hearty choruses sung. A swoop followed. The peccant students, except for a few ringleaders, got off relatively lightly, but not so their teachers, for as Sedlnitzky rightly pointed out, things would never have reached this pitch if the professors had been doing their duty.[1]

A grand inquisition accordingly set in against this professional class as a whole. A number of them, the best-known the famous Bolzano (who had particularly offended the Court Chaplain, Frint, by refusing to use his works as textbooks) lost their chairs; some of them emigrated. An order was issued enjoining that the strictest watch should be kept on the behaviour and utterances of professors and anything at all objectionable reported immediately. Lists of the books taken out by them from the libraries were sent to the authorities. Among other rules laid down were that foreigners might

[1] An unexpected by-product of this was the foundation of a Protestant theological faculty in Vienna, to obviate the need for Protestant students to go abroad.

not be employed as teachers, even as tutors in private families; that in selecting teachers for State schools as much attention must be paid to their political views as to the ability in their subjects; that teachers must do three years probation before their appointments were made definitive.

It was soon after this (1821) that, if the reports are true,[1] Francis made his famous remark to the teachers of the Laibach Lyceum: 'I do not need savants, but good, honest citizens. Your task is to bring young men up to be this. He who serves me must teach what I order him. If anyone can't do this, or comes with new ideas, he can go, or I will remove him.'

With this, the last traces of liberalism vanished from the Austrian educational system, as they vanished also from the conduct of the censorship. Here the regulations themselves were not altered (they remained, indeed, unchanged until 1848), and purely scientific or purely artistic work was still permissible. But the accepted criteria of what was purely scientific, or purely artistic, were devastatingly narrow. One serious medical work was forbidden because it contained a passing reference which criticized the state of the roads in Carinthia. Grillparzer narrowly escaped dismissal from the Civil Service for a romantic poem bewailing the fate of ancient Rome. His *König Ottokars Glück und Ende* only just reached the stage.[2] Schiller's *Piccolomini* could not be played, and his *Wilhelm Tell* only after it had been heavily cut.

Meanwhile the army of police spies multiplied enormously (at great public expense), the police pryed ever more closely into the details of the 'subjects'' lives and the list of activities in which a 'subject' might engage without police permission dwindled almost month by month.

If the 'system' changed at all in these years, it was in one direction only, that the Roman Catholic Church regained part of the political influence which it had lost since Maria Theresa's death. Francis became a widower for the third time in April 1816, and on 29 October of the same year took a fourth wife, the Bavarian Princess, Caroline Augusta. A pupil of the Jesuits[3] and herself extremely devout, the new Queen became the nucleus of a 'pious party' at the Court, and Metternich associated himself with this, partly for political reasons, to secure for Austria the sympathies of Catholic Southern Germany against Protestant Prussia,[4] and partly, it seems, under the influence of the romantic attachment which he conceived for Dorothea Schlegel's friend, Countess Julie Zichy, née Festetics, a fountain of piety.

Under the Empress's influence, and that of Bishop Wagner, the Court Chaplain, a devotional air began to pervade the Court, and various concessions were made to the pious. When, for example, the reconstituted

[1] The only authority for this famous speech is a newspaper.
[2] Here the objection was that the national susceptibilities of the Czechs might be hurt.
[3] Pope Pius VII had allowed the Order to reconstitute itself in 1814.
[4] See Bibl, *Tragödie*, p. 129 and the literature quoted by him in his n. 40.

THE SYSTEM AT ITS ZENITH (1815–1830)

Jesuits were expelled from Russia, they were given asylum in Galicia. There were, however, few changes of substance even in this field. In 1816 the Secretary of State to the Holy See gave the Austrian Minister a list of points on which the Vatican wanted Austrian law and practice changed; if this were done, a Concordat might be concluded. Francis appointed a Committee to consider the question, and it reported unanimously against a Concordat. When Francis visited Rome with his bride in 1818 the list was re-submitted to him, but again, under the influence of his Josephinian advisers, Francis made no concession, except that mentioned below,[1] to his Italian Bishops.

These were not propitious conditions for vigorous intellectual or artistic life, although modern Austrian writers are justified in repudiating the exaggerations of their predecessors who represented the era as completely barren of any cultural achievement whatever. Beethoven had, after all, not yet ceased to write, and Schubert was in his short-lived prime. Some of the Benedictine Monasteries were producing serious historical and other works, and Klemens Maria Hofbauer stirring consciences with his preaching. Fortune placed the charge of the Burgtheater in the hands of an exceptionally talented director, Joseph Schreyvogel, under whose auspices Grillparzer, a great literary figure by the standards of any age and any country, was able to get his plays produced. On a more popular level, the Hanswurst satirical farces, of which Ferdinand Raimund's comedies are a sort of sublimation, flourished greatly. But all cultural life was heavily overshadowed by the official control. Even the medical school of Vienna grew torpid under the restraints imposed by Francis's physician, von Stift. And the author who writes that Hofbauer 'raised Vienna to the position of the cultural centre of Catholic Germany'[2] might have mentioned that Hofbauer began his career in Vienna by being put in prison, and only just escaped ending it by being expelled.

Another restrictive influence was that of the financial stringency, or perhaps it should be said, the new attitude towards it. Shortage of money was, of course, a condition familiar to Austria, but it had been gloriously disregarded in the rollicking days of High Baroque. In Francis's day, the convention ruled that bills had to be paid, and the very buildings of the age reflected his staid and upright personality in a style which was economical, domestic and unpretentious, the style of an imposed discipline which was not even resented.

Curiously, however, the period was one of vigorous springtime for the national cultures of some of the non-Germanic peoples of Austria, particularly the Czechs of Bohemia. Deprived of other outlets for their energies, some of

[1] See below, p. 230.
[1] *M.K.P.*, III. 88.

the great families who dominated Bohemian society adopted the role of patrons of the local culture. Prince Schwarzenberg founded a national museum in Prague in 1818. Particularly important was the foundation, in 1822, by Count Kaspar Sternberg, of a 'museum of the homeland' (*Vaterländisches Museum*) and a 'Society of Friends of the Museum' to reinforce the already existing Royal Bohemian Society of Sciences.[1] Sternberg, and most of his colleagues in this field, were not playing at Czech nationalism: they were Bohemians, not Czechs or Germans, and interested in raising the cultural and economic standards of the poor people round them, not concerning themselves with 'national' questions.[2] But they were not anti-Czech, and it was largely as employees of Sternberg's or similar institutions, or as tutors in the houses of great families, that the scholars and writers found a living who came to form the advance-guard of the Czech national-cultural revival. The doyen of them all, Josef Dobrowský (1753-1829), who was, indeed, born in Hungary, but passed most of his life in Bohemia, had produced a History of the Czech language as early as 1792; a revised edition of this came in 1818, and a detailed Czech grammar. In 1820 he founded the first Czech scientific periodical, the *Casopis Musée*. Josef Jungmann (1773-1847) produced a History of Czech Literature (1825) and a great dictionary, besides translations into Czech from English and French. This severe, painstaking and rationalist work, which drew its inspiration from Voltaire and Lessing,[3] had as its chief object to make it possible for the Czechs to think, read and write in their own language, and in this it was notably successful; when Dobrowský and Jungmann handed on the torch, the form of the Czech language had been standardized, its grammar regularized, its vocabulary enriched. It was now fit to serve as a language of instruction at all levels, and as a medium of administration. The harvest of this work was reaped by a generation of 'romantics', the leading figures of which were two Slovaks who wrote in Czech: Jan Kollar, author of an extraordinary heroic epic, *Slavy Dčera* (The Daughter of Slava), the first part of which appeared in 1824 and its conclusion in 1832, and Paul Josef Safarik,[4] author of a *History of Slav*

[1] The Society itself had been founded as early as 1784 – under Joseph II – by a group of aristocrats.

[2] It is interesting that Kübeck, who at this time was serving as a minor official in a Moravian Kreisamt and kept a fairly voluminous diary, never once mentions the national question in it.

[3] In making these distinctions, I follow Denis, op. cit., II. 52. This work contains a far more detailed account than it is possible to give here of the Czech revival. For a shorter account, see R. W. Seton Watson, *History of the Czechs and Slovaks*, pp. 170 ff.

[4] Safarik was in fact a convert, and rather an unwilling one, to Czechdom. He was born in Hungary of a Protestant Slovak family which wrote its name as Šafáry and spent many years teaching in the Serb lycée in Ujvidék, which he had to leave because the Orthodox clergy objected to a Protestant's teaching there. He was then in difficult circumstances, from which Palacký rescued him, but insisted that he should in return write his name Czech fashion, and his books in the Czech language. He was always a good Slovak at heart.

THE SYSTEM AT ITS ZENITH (1815–1830)

Languages, published in Buda in 1826; although both of these men were far more Pan-Slav than Czech in inspiration. But by 1830 a third generation, embodying the more methodical and practical spirit characteristic of the true Czech, was beginning to emerge. Its leader was the man destined to be the most famous of all, František Palacký, a Moravian by birth, who had received his education in Hungary and come to Prague only in 1823. In 1827 he was appointed editor of the two periodicals which commenced publication in that year under the auspices of the Museum, and now began to work on his great *History of Bohemia*, the first volume of which was published in 1826.

At first, these men had appeared to be swimming against the tide: the evidence of contemporaries is that – contrary to the usual belief – German had been gaining steadily on Czech since the beginning of the century, and had not yet ceased to do so.[1] But the tide was turning, and that – again contrary to common belief – with explicit and effective official encouragement. A decree was issued in August 1816 introducing lessons in Czech (for Czech speaking students) in the gymnasia in Czech or mixed districts. The headmasters and teachers of the humanities in these schools had to be acquainted with the language. Further, students were to be informed at the beginning of each academic year that in appointments to the administrative services 'of the Bohemian Lands' preference would be given, *ceteris paribus*, to candidates who knew Czech.[2]

In all this, as it is necessary to emphasize, as a point relevant to the developments both of this period and its successors, even down to 1918 (and very strongly in 1848), the word 'Bohemia' used on a previous page was operative. With the southward economic orientation given it by geography (unlike that of Bohemia, whose waters, proverbially, flow north), Moravia had always felt closer to Vienna than had Bohemia, and its Estates were actually decidedly hostile to the Bohemian political movement, regarding Prague as a potential oppressor quite as dangerous as Vienna. National feeling among the Moravian Czechs was still little developed and even uncertain, so much so that many Moravians held their nationality to be a distinct one. In any case, national antagonisms were far less acute in Moravia, than in Bohemia. The two peoples lived, not in separate territorial blocs, but closely intermingled, spoke each other's language, and had grown accustomed to peaceful co-existence.

The Czechs of Silesia were only a minority of peasants, among whom national feeling was still quite primitive.

The local magnates among the Slovenes were less enterprising than the Bohemian, partly because they were less wealthy, but some of them played a

[1] See the remarkable testimonies quoted by Denis, op. cit., pp. 176–7.
[2] The text of this Decree is given by Fischel, *Sprachenrecht*, p. 54. Denis, p. 96, writes that its opponents 'got it repealed', but I can find no authority for this statement.

similar role of patrons (characteristically, one of the men who did most for Slovene culture was the Archduke John, the 'German Archduke', whose 'Johanneum' in Graz is a worthy counterpart to Sternberg's foundation in Prague).[1] But the Slovene national culture had been given a strong stimulus by the French administrators of the 'Kingdom of Illyria', which they had deliberately designed to make into a Slovene national State. They had drawn up blue-prints for an advanced system of general education, with an elementary school for boys in every commune and one for girls in every Canton, twenty-five gymnasia and a lycée, and a High School of University standing in Laibach. Instruction was to be in the 'local language' in the elementary schools; in the secondary and higher schools, partly in that language, partly in French and Italian. A weekly newspaper was published in the same language.

They had not got very far, for they had had to plough an almost virgin field; before they came there had been, as we said before,[2] no instruction at all in Slovene, and very little in any other language (when they took over Carniola and Istria, they found that only 3,000 of the 419,000 inhabitants of the two Lands had attended, or were attending, school)[3] and hardly any printed literature in Slovene except one or two devotional books including a Bible, which had been printed in Germany in the sixteenth century.[4] And they were only there for five years, after which the Austrians returned and in 1817 restored the *status quo* in almost every respect, including instruction in German in the schools.[5] But they had left behind them a new interest and pride in their nationality among the younger Slovenes, and, incidentally, had settled what had until then been an undecided question, what the Slovene language was to be. They had at first thought of making the language of instruction and public life the Što dialect of Southern Slav, spoken in Ragusa, the dialect which, as described below,[6] was afterwards adopted by both the Croat and the Serb linguistic reformers, and thus became the ancestor of the present Serbo-Croat literary language. But a Slovene philologist named Kopitar, the Keeper of Slavonic Books at the Court Library in Vienna, who was generally regarded as the leading authority on the subject,

---

[1] The Archduke retired to Styria after his disgrace, when Tirol was forbidden him. He settled down, made a morganatic marriage with the daughter of a Styrian postmaster, and devoted himself to raising the cultural and economic standards of the province. Before him a certain Baron Cojz had played the Maecenas in a small way, to the local culture (German as well as Slovene). The earliest at all memorable figure of the Slovene renaissance, a priest named Vodnik, owed much to his encouragement.

[2] See above, p. 111, n. 5.

[3] Wendel, *Kampf der Südslawen um Freiheit und Einheit*, p. 128.

[4] To make things worse, many copies of these products had been burnt as heretical.

[5] Theology was, however, taught in Slovene at the Laibach Lyceum and students of theology there were compelled to learn Slovene.

[6] See below, p. 252.

THE SYSTEM AT ITS ZENITH (1815–1830)

persuaded them to adopt the 'local language', of which he had himself just published a grammar.[1] Later intellectuals thought of reversing the decision, but were never able to do so,[2] and Slovene remained thereafter a separate language; it may even be true to say that the decision settled the question whether the Slovenes were to remain a distinct people.

There were even shy stirrings of a cultural movement among the Ruthenes. Joseph II, whom nothing in his Monarchy escaped, had not overlooked this people. He had ordered that Ruthene should be taught as a subject in the elementary schools of East Galicia, and at least religious instruction given in the language, had founded a seminary for Ruthene clergy in Lemberg, the counterpart of that established by his mother in Munkács, and had instituted courses in theology and the humanities at Lemberg High School. The seminaries developed into the foci of a modest national movement, the leaders of which belonged to a little group which had caught the infection of the Ukrainian national stirrings then perceptible in Kiev, shared some even of its political emotions[3] and emphasized the identity of the language then spoken on both sides of the Austro-Russian frontier.

The Ruthenes did not, however, get far in this period, for they encountered opposition from every quarter. The Poles insisted that the language spoken in East Galicia was a mere dialect of Polish, while the Russians denied the existence of Ukrainian language or nationality. They feared that the development of a Ukrainian movement in Galicia would strengthen separatism in the Ukraine, and even accused the Austrian Government of fostering the movement to that end. The Austrians, on the other hand, became frightened of the attraction of Russia on their own subjects. They therefore inclined to support the Polish view, and in 1816 allowed the reintroduction of Polish into all the primary schools of Galicia:[4] a concession prompted not entirely by political considerations, but partly also by the primitive condition of the local language and the lack of primers in it. The courses in Lemberg had already collapsed in 1808 for lack of interest.

The Roumanian national feeling already stirring in Transylvania had not yet spread across the Carpathians into the Bukovina. A Roumanian historian

---

[1] *Grammatik der Slawischen Sprache in Krain, Kärnten und Steiermark* (1808). Like all Kopitar's work, this was written in German, as was Palacký's history.

[2] See below, p. 299.

[3] When Poniatowski's Polish Legions entered Galicia from the Grand Duchy of Warsaw in 1809, the Ruthene Bishop, Mgr Angelovitch, called on the Ruthenes to rise against the Poles.

[4] This does not mean that the entire educational system was Polonized. Instruction in religion had always to be given in Ruthene where the children belonged to the Greek Catholic Church, and all instruction in schools where all the children were Greek Catholics was also to be given in Ruthene, but here Polish was to be taught as a subject. In mixed schools all instruction, except in religion, was to be given in Polish, but Ruthene children were 'as far as possible' to be taught to read and write in their own language.

has described intellectual conditions in the province at that time as 'a desert in which any spring of spiritual inspiration must dry up'. Two Roumanian journals founded in Transylvania failed to find a single subscriber in the Bukovina.

It may be remarked that the Roumanians were under at least as heavy a cultural yoke as the Ruthenes. In 1815 the Roman Catholic Consistorium in Lemberg had been put in charge of the entire educational system of the Bukovina. Thereafter all Greek Orthodox teachers were gradually replaced by Roman Catholics, almost all of whom were Poles (a few were Germans), and few of them even acquainted with Roumanian. It was not until 1844 that the *Studienhofkommission* proposed that this abuse should be remedied, and not until 1851 that the Orthodox schools were actually transferred to the Orthodox Consistory in Czernowitz.[1]

The strong encouragement which was undoubtedly given by the Austrian authorities to the Czech and Slovene national cultures[2] had been prompted, partly by their belief that purely cultural or practical studies would take men's minds off politics, partly because local Slav cultural movements seemed to them less dangerous than the more spacious visions of inter-Slav solidarity (not confined to the Monarchy) which appeared to be their strongest rivals; also less dangerous than the liberalism to which the German-Austrians were susceptible. But they were, of course, entirely wrong in supposing that any cultural development could fail to give birth, ultimately, to political aspirations – in this respect such men as the Palatine-Archduke Alexander and his advisers in Hungary showed a much juster appreciation of the facts of life, or at any rate, of Central European life. These Czech and Slovene 'cultural revivals' thus marked a further very important stage in the gradual transformation of the Monarchy from something which could be ruled as a non-national State to something the multi-national nature of which had to be admitted.

It was, moreover, not even true that most of the products of the age were non-political. Among the Czechs, in particular, there were few – possibly, among the better-known figures, only Dobrowský – whose nationalism was not already intensely and belligerently political. The *Slavy Dčera* is an allegory representing the sufferings of the Slav nation under its German and Magyar oppressors; it is full of the most megalomaniac glorifications of the greatness and virtue of the Slavs, and its last cantos depict a Paradise in which true Slavs and their friends enjoy their glorious reward, while their enemies and, in particular, renegades from Slavdom, are submitted to dis-

---

[1] Prokopowitch, pp. 65 ff. One consequence of this policy was that a large number of Roumanian priests and monks had emigrated to Moldavia (id. p 36).

[2] The Scotsman, Turnbull, travelling in Bohemia in 1839, notes (II. 112) that 'the Crown, after attempts to Germanize, seemed to throw itself into the opposite extreme. An official patronage was extended to the popular dialect which it had not enjoyed before.'

gusting tortures. Another 'literary' production of purely political intent (and great political significance, since it enormously enhanced the Czechs' national self-esteem) was a collection of poems, known from the sites at which they were 'discovered' as the Königinhof and Grünberg MSS., which depicted a glorious Czech civilization allegedly existing in the Dark Ages. In fact, the 'discoverer' of them, a certain Hanka, had forged them.[1] One of the warmest admirers of Palacký (who, incidentally, was deceived by these fabrications) has written of him that 'his essential merit was to have understood very early that political liberty was the necessary condition of national independence.[2] In his history, as another admirer has written, there are two closely-interwoven guiding threads, which run all through it: 'the racial conflict between Czech and German, the spiritual conflict between Rome and the Reformation',[3] Czech nationalism appearing as 'enriched and hallowed by the ideals of humanity, justice and rectitude,'[4] while the Germans are shown as interlopers and tyrants. The Magyars are condemned, not only for oppressing the Slavs, but for their very existence, since they are reproached with the historic sin of having cut off the southern from the northern branch of the West Slavs (in point of fact, the accusation is misplaced; the separation of the two branches of Slavs may or may not have been historically unfortunate, but it was not the work of the Magyars but of their predecessors, the Avars). So blatant was the political purpose behind much of this work that it is difficult to believe that it really escaped the eye of the authorities. We shall see in the next chapter that one man at least who after 1830 sat at the very heart of things made no bones whatever about encouraging Czech nationalism for political purposes. During most of the period which we are now describing, that man, Count Anton Kolowrat, was not a member of the central government, but since 1809 he had already occupied a key post in Bohemia as Oberstburggraf of Prague, and it is more than likely that already in that capacity he was actively furthering the cause for which he afterwards did so much. The decree reintroducing instruction in Czech into the gymnasia could not have been issued without his recommendation. And it is hard to think that Sedlnitzky, who was also a Czech, did not look the other way when the Czech cultural pioneers went so happily picnicking in political fields.[5] Palacký, for example, never received more than a 'hint' that

[1] The Königinhof MS. was 'discovered' in 1817; the Grünberg, a year later.
[2] Denis, op. cit., p. 193.
[3] R. W. Seton-Watson, op. cit., p. 151.
[4] Quoted by Seton-Watson, l.c., from Werstadt.
[5] Another reason for the relative indulgence of the authorities towards the Czech and other Slavonic movements was simply the imperfect linguistic equipment of the censors. Cases were recorded of literature which appeared in German and Czech; the Czech version purported to be a translation of the German but in fact contained subversive passages which were absent from the German text. The censors read only the German version, and passed both. Other cases are recorded in which mss in Russian, or even in Czech, written in Cyrillic

he should modify his anti-German effusions. He never got into any sort of trouble for them.

None of this activity, however, reached the surface of political life. The narrow basis of the composition of the Bohemian and Carniolan Estates would have excluded the young nationalists from membership of them; and in any case, the Estates never met except to give a purely ritual assent to the Government's 'proposals'. And once the small intellectual ferment among the Germans had been neutralized, the picture throughout the German-Bohemian Lands, from 1815 to 1830, was one of unbroken calm. Not a single political trial of an Austrian subject took place in the Hereditary or Bohemian Lands during the last twenty years of Francis's reign.[1]

More activity might have been expected from the Poles, who had certain real causes for complaint, apart from the loss of their independence. Viennese writers stress the benefits conferred on Galicia by Austrian rule, especially on the peasants, and it is probably true that those unfortunate beings were brought a long way nearer to humanity by the protection afforded them by the Kreis officials; later events were to prove that the peasants generally in fact regarded the local officials as their friends and protectors. Some local economic resources were developed: the yield of the salt-mines, for example, rose by 400%.

But against this, as Polish writers point out, taxation, both direct and indirect, rose enormously (by over 400% between 1773 and 1817), and against such active items as the considerable development of the linen industry, which was largely in the hands of immigrant Germans, had to be set such debit items as the increased cost of living and the almost total disappearance of Galicia's old export trade in wheat.[2]

The same writers accuse Austria of hostility to Polish culture and of 'Germanization', and the latter accusation has this much of substance that, besides the fact that administration and justice were conducted in Latin or German, which was also the language of all secondary education, both Joseph II and his successors had brought in numerous German artisans, etc. into Galicia; Lemberg had become almost a German town, and remained so up to 1848.

Nevertheless, the Polish nobles did not revolt during these years. They

---

script were passed because the censors could not read them. Many of the leading Czech and Slovene literary figures were themselves censors, and happily let through writings with which they sympathized.

[1] In 1815 and 1816 there were some riots against the high prices, the shortages and the increased taxation, but they were not repeated after conditions improved.

[2] The decline of the wheat trade was less Austria's fault than Prussia's. After the annexation Austria had exempted Galicia from the operation of her tariff, in order to allow the trade to continue, but when Prussia introduced a duty on wheat (in order to damage Danzig), the exemption was useless, and was cancelled. Some exportation of wheat still went on, but on a greatly reduced scale.

simply maintained their passive resistance to the regime, boycotting the Austrian officials and avoiding their own civil obligations as far as they dared,[1] but not attempting more.

Their hostility was even beginning gradually to weaken. In 1826 the Austrian Government sent up a new Governor, Prince Lobkowitz, with the avowed object of conciliating the Poles, and he was meeting with some success. The Roman Catholic Church, a very powerful local factor, was in any case more favourable to Catholic Austria than to Protestant Prussia, or Orthodox Russia.

Politically all was quiet among the Ruthenes. The Roumanians of the Bukovina resented its attachment to Galicia, the influx of foreign administrators, the Polonization of the schools and the control imposed on the Orthodox Church, but they submitted to their fate with sufficient philosophy.

In Hungary, as always in this half-century, things were much livelier. The Magyar national and cultural revival was by now in full spate. The work of Kazinczy and his circle of correspondents was already transforming the Magyar language into a vehicle capable of expressing deep poetry, high abstract thought and all practical requirements of public and private everyday life. An abundant literature in the 'renewed language' was coming into being, much of it still crude and imitative, but some of it fit to challenge comparison with all except the most advanced national literatures of the day. This pioneer generation included one man of real genius, Mihály Vörösmarty, whose grandiose epic *Zalán Futása* (The Flight of Zalán), which appeared in 1825, was at once hailed as a national achievement of the highest order. In fact, the linguistic and literary renaissance among the Magyars already possessed an immediate political significance which the corresponding Czech and Slovene movements had yet to achieve; for since the eventual replacement of Latin and German by Magyar in public life was already one of the nation's political demands, every new epic or drama in the native language whetted the national appetite for further concessions and was hailed as further justification of them. Thus the cultural movement itself helped stiffen the national resistance to Francis's absolutism.

But the Hungarians had also another weapon in their armoury, in the shape of their constitutional rights and *de facto* nuisance power in respect to their contribution to the common services of the Monarchy, and it was over this point that Francis's attempt to rule the country absolutely ended by breaking down.

[1] According to a traveller, it was a frequent habit of the nobles to leave their taxes unpaid until the officials distrained on so much corn as they calculated corresponded in value to the amount due. When it was put up for auction, the owner would buy it in himself. This often cost more than punctual payment would have entailed, but the spiritual satisfaction was counted as worth more than the money.

In 1813, when the Government needed recruits, to the considerable number of 60,000, for its new wars, it simply announced that in view of the urgency there was no time to convoke a Diet, and sent the demands straight to the Counties, sending down Royal Commissioners when these proved recalcitrant. This did not even prove necessary except in one or two Counties; most of them accepted the Government's case. When the Government tried to repeat the procedure in 1815, asking now for 30,000 men, there were more objectors, since another Diet was by then overdue, and by 1816 28,420 of the total 90,000 had still not been supplied. But after the unexpectedly quick close of hostilities, the recruiting campaign was called off and no recruits were asked in 1816, 1817, 1818 or 1819. Meanwhile, Hungary had accepted the inevitable and had paid her contributio in Einlösungsscheine.

Thus a certain breathing-space had ensued which, incidentally, the Court had used to strengthen its hand by the issue (in February 1819) of a ruling which formally conferred on the sandalled nobles, whom it could hope to find more amenable to influence than the economically independent *bene possessionati*, the right, which usage, rather than any written rule had previously denied them[1] of voting at the meetings of the County Congregationes.[2]

But in 1820, when Metternich felt the call to intervene in Naples and Piedmont, the Court announced that the Hungarian regiments must again be brought up to war strength, and told the Hungarian Court Chancellery to instruct the Counties to produce another 30,000 men. This elicited strong protests, whereupon the Court ingeniously said that it would content itself with the number in arrears from 1815 (a figure, in fact, only 1,580 smaller than its original demand but one which, it could maintain, had already been accepted). But on 13 August 1822, it further demanded payment of the contributio in silver, or, if made in Einlösungsscheine, at the new rate: $13\frac{1}{2}$ million instead of $5\frac{1}{4}$.[3] This time there was tumult indeed. Many of the Counties flatly refused to obey either order, and the Royal Commissioners found the task of getting in the men and money by force to be beyond their powers. Representations went to and fro for three long years until at last, constrained to realize that a single national body, one of whose two 'Tables' was safe to be on his side, was after all a more manageable proposition than fifty-two County Congregationes, some of them situated in almost inaccessible townlets, Francis yielded and convoked the Diet for 11 September 1825. Here he met with criticism so acrimonious and so prolonged – the Diet held 271 sessions, spread over very nearly two years – that he was obliged to make

[1] See above, p. 57.
[2] Another proposal, that the County salaried officials should remain in permanence at the County centres and transact all public business without calling on the Congregationes at all, only reporting to them retrospectively every three years, had had to be dropped owing to the opposition of the Counties.
[3] This figure was afterwards slightly reduced.

something of an apology for his recent behaviour and to swear all over again the respect for the Constitution to which he had pledged himself in 1792. The Diet further resolved to appoint a new set of Committees to prepare for its successor a re-edition of the national gravamina, bringing up to date, for the purpose, the reports of the 1792 Committees.

This Diet, by its successful defence of its own rights and of the Counties', had thus imposed the first check ever inflicted in the Monarchy on the steady advance of absolutism which had been proceeding since 1792. In this respect it deserves the place assigned to it by most Hungarian historians as the first Diet of the 'Reform Era'. It reflected the new spirit also in one other respect: in the increased extent of the linguistic demands which were put forward, as well as the vehemence with which they (and indeed, all the Diet's wishes) were pressed. This time, the Crown was asked to make Magyar not only the language of administration throughout Inner Hungary (in some branches, after a period of grace), but also that of instruction, even in elementary schools. It is true that the demands met with the accustomed refusal, and the only notable result of the Diet's work in this field was a non-contentious one: after one speaker had been enlarging on the need for a National Academy, and the difficulty of raising funds for it, a young man of whom much was to be heard in the near future, Count István Széchenyi, electrified the House by rising to his feet and offering a year's income from his estates for the foundation of the institution.

In other respects, however, the Diet hardly deserved the name of 'reform'. Ninety per cent of its energies were spent simply on defending the national Constitution against infringement or innovation – i.e., in practice, against the Crown's attempt to get money or recruits from the country without the Diet's consent. In all the instructions given by the fifty-two Counties to their representatives, not one contained any mention of social reform. On this issue, the Diet was fully as reactionary as Francis himself, or Metternich.

Nor was there any difference here between the 'Court party' and the 'national opposition'; the division between them was exclusively on the question of greater or less centralist control. If anything, the so-called 'Opposition' was the more reactionary of the two.

The literary and cultural revival was itself anything but reformist on social issues. Bessenyei himself had argued:

> Thanks be to Providence that we Magyars have always remained to this day a nation of landlords! Knowest thou why the multitude of peasants may not appear to speak for themselves at my nation's Diets? Because they are not landowners or landlords, but the nation's hereditary tenants living within the noble system. The noble cannot take the peasant's land from him, but neither can the peasant do ought but serve and support his lord.

A few of the young literati looked to the uncorrupted peasantry as the reservoir of the nation's strength, and even to their language as the pure well-spring from which a linguistic revival must derive; but not one of them (since their prison sentences had cured Kazinczy and his young friends of their revolutionary ardour) interested himself publicly, or even in private, in social reform. This was, indeed, the natural result of the social structure of the country, for the Hungarian noble class was so broad that most educated men belonged to it by birth, and the pride in membership of it so great that the honoratiores who won a half place in it (the number of those who did so had, indeed, been growing rapidly since Joseph II's reforms) almost always at once adopted its outlook, often in exaggerated form. And Hungarian history being what it was, it was inevitable that, especially when the waves of romanticism reached Hungary, the young poets and playwrights should, even more than in most countries, seek their inspiration in the national past, and sing the glories of a day when the Magyars were indeed a nation of warrior-conquerors, holding their land by the sword, and by constant vigilance against the foreigner; *Zalán Futása* itself is an outstanding example of this.[1] Thus the cultural renaissance, in this stage of its development, tended actually to reinforce the conservatism of the purely political movement.

During these decades Hungarian nationalism had occupied itself no more with the non-Magyars than with the peasants; each had been regarded as irrelevant to the problem of the day, which was the struggle against Vienna. And in fact, none of the nationalities of Inner Hungary made any impact on its political life during the period. This was, perhaps, remarkable in the case of the Serbs, who had demonstrated so vigorously against the Hungarian State in 1790, and were still under the leadership of the extremely bellicose Archbishop, Stepan Stratimirovics, who had presided over the 'Illyrian Congress'. Nor did Stratimirovics alter his political views with advancing years; when the Serb revolution broke out under Kara George in 1804 he wrote secretly to the Czar, asking him to establish a Protectorate, if possible under a Russian Grand Duke, to include not only Serbia and Bosnia, but also the Serb districts of Hungary.

Moreover, this was the age of the first real Serbian cultural rebirth, and since the terrain for this was extremely unfavourable in Serbia, where Miloš Obrenović could not write his own name, and mistrusted all education, and most of the Bishops, until 1830, were Phanariote Greeks, who were strongly hostile to Serbian culture, it was chiefly outside the Principality that the new movement developed, and not least, in Hungary. Hungarian Serbs founded a gymnasium in Ujvidék in 1816, and in 1826 a literary society, the Matica Srbska, which soon moved to the same town, which became known as the 'Serbian Athens', and was perhaps the chief centre of Serb culture of the day.

But the younger generation failed to fuse with the older. Stratimirovics was

[1] Zalán was the legendary Bulgarian king who, according to the romantic Hungarian chronicler 'Anonymus', was put to flight by Árpád and his paladins when they entered and conquered Hungary.

THE SYSTEM AT ITS ZENITH (1815-1830)

so intensely conservative that he opposed any new development whatever. He refused to allow a modern Serb liturgy to be used in place of the Old Slavonic, and petitioned the censor to forbid publication of a new grammar by Vuk Karadžić in his new orthography; throughout his long life (he died only in 1836) he imposed on his people, as far as he could compass it, a spiritual standstill as complete as that which Francis was enforcing on the Monarchy as a whole.[1] Thus the seed scattered from Ujvidék fell not in its own neighbourhood, but in the Principality. Meanwhile, in the new situation, with the canny Miloš installed in Belgrade, Austria supporting the integrity of the Porte and Russia turned discreet, Stratimirovics had no chance to go on playing at international politics.

It may be added that the decay of the Serb element in Hungary outside its strongholds in the South was already setting in. A writer who occupied himself with these questions noted in 1847 that 'for the past twenty-five years the Serb Orthodox communities in Transdanubia and west of the Tisza have been dwindling steadily, because many Serbs are migrating to Serbia'. Many parishes, including Székesfehérvár, Györ, Komárom, Miskolc, Tokay, etc. were closing down, for lack of funds to pay the stipends of the priest, and the Serbian shopkeepers in the villages 'had vanished completely, and now one hardly finds any shopkeepers except Jews'.[2]

Among the Slovaks[3] these were years of doubtful stirrings; years when the question – not to be answered finally for a full century, if then – what they were, or what they wanted to be, first became a subject of serious debate among them, as the similar question was becoming among the Ruthenes. We have already mentioned Kolar, Dobrowský and Safařik, who ended by writing works of Pan-Slav tendency in the Czech language, but they were individuals, who really outstepped the bounds of their nation. Round the end of the eighteenth century, however, the cause of Czecho-Slovak linguistic unity was also taken up by a group of Slovak Protestants (to whom the end of Maria Theresa's ultra-Catholic regime and her son's Toleration Patent had given fresh courage), to whom the idea came naturally, since the Bible used by them was a Czech one, introduced into Hungary by the Hussites. The leader of this group, a certain Juray Ribay, was a friend and correspondent of Dobrowský's.

The growth of this movement inspired a Roman Catholic priest named Bernolak (who then received much help and support from the Cardinal-Primate of Hungary, Rudnay, himself a Slovak who always insisted on his

---

[1] The Orthodox Popes described Karadžić's alphabet as 'the Devil's claws'. It was largely their hostility which drove Safařik, who had been a teacher in the gymnasium in Novi-Sad, to throw up his job there in 1832 and migrate to the kindlier atmosphere of Prague. Yet Karadžić himself was a strong Serb nationalist, and in particular, no friend of the Croats.
[2] Bárándy, *Ueber Ungarns Zustände* (Pressburg, 1847), p. 8.
[3] The following paragraphs are based chiefly on Gogolak, op. cit.

Slavonic origin and sympathies),[1] to start a counter-movement[2] for stabilizing the existing Slovak, of which they took the Western dialect as representing the 'national language', as an independent language and developing it from that basis, precisely in order to save the Slovaks from the 'Hussite tongue' of Czech ecclesiastical literature. Bernolak and his friends founded a number of literary circles and associations, and this in its turn stimulated the opposition to found their own institutions. One of these, a 'chair' of Czecho-Slovak linguistics at the Lutheran Lyceum in Pozsony, established in 1803, was important, for Georg Palkovic, who occupied it for many years, expounded the thesis of Czecho-Slovak linguistic unity to a whole generation of students, among them the young Palacký.

Both these movements, by the very fact that they interested themselves in the Slovak national culture, contributed their mite towards creating something which was bound one day to come into collision with Magyar neo-nationalism. In the early decades of the nineteenth century, however, neither was yet politically dangerous to the Hungarian State. Bernolak's and Rudnay's was specifically 'Hungarian', and even the Slovak Protestants at that time contrasted conditions in Hungary favourably with those in Bohemia, where the Protestants enjoyed far less freedom.

As for the Roumanians of Inner Hungary, those in the south, who were Orthodox, had some national feeling, but saw their chief enemy in Stratimirovics, who treated his whole Church as a purely Serbian institution and refused to allow any liturgy in it except the Old Slavonic. The Uniate priests, further north, were so far Magyarized that, according to one authority, many of them spoke Magyar in their homes and voluntarily conducted service in Magyar.[3]

None of these peoples had, indeed, any constitutional channel through which to voice their wishes or their grievances. The Croats had a whole hierarchy of them: their County Congregationes, the Zagreb Sabor, and the Hungarian Diet itself, in which they were represented. And in a sense, the Croat political case had been at odds with the Hungarian ever since 1790, for the Croat delegates to Pozsony never abandoned the Skerlecz thesis that laws passed there were not binding on Croatia unless the Croats had voted for them, when they were binding in virtue of that vote – a thesis which amounted in practice to a claim to exercise a *liberum veto* on any change in the existing order; whereas the Hungarians, as we have said, while not arguing the point out in

---

[1] Rudnay is, however, a typical example of the ambiguous state of 'nationality' in North Hungary, for his remote origin was in fact Magyar.

[2] The word 'start' is not strictly accurate, for Bernolak had had fore-runners, notably another Catholic priest named Josef Ignatius Bajza. Bernolak, however, thought Bajza still too 'Czecho-Slovak'.

[3] Gáldi and Makkai, op. cit., p. 322.

full Diet, had yet never committed themselves to acceptance of the Croat thesis.

In 1790, however, it had been possible to evade the point of principle by confining the application of the legislation to which the Croats objected *intra limites regni*, and for a whole generation thereafter the point had hardly arisen; for the questions on which Francis did consult the Diet reduced themselves in practice to the supply vote, on which the Croats continued to follow the principle which they had adopted in 1790 of submitting themselves to the will of the majority in matters of common interest; while Francis's refusal to consider changes in the fields in which a clash might have occurred, notably the language of the Diet and the central services, stifled discussion of them in the womb, although whenever such a question did arise, or showed signs of arising, the Croats always duly put in their caveat, so that the unsolved political issue did subsist. It was not, however, a national struggle between the Magyar and the Croat peoples. If it was true that the Hungarian delegates to the Diet were interested almost exclusively in maintaining the privileges of the class which they represented, the qualification can be omitted in the case of the Croats. They were totally uninterested in the Croat people, of which they formed an even smaller proportion than did the Hungarian nobles of the people of Inner Hungary,[1] as such. They were fully as conservative as the Hungarians on social policy in general; the condition of the Croat peasantry was even worse than that of the Hungarian, and as late as 1825 the Croat delegates to Pozsony objected to a proposal to allow peasants easier access to settle in the towns, because this would promote the growth of industry, and they did not want industry to grow. While the Hungarians were from the first always entirely willing that the Croat language should enjoy the same position in Croatia's *interna* as they were asking for Magyar in the *interna* of Inner Hungary, the Croats did not want even that. In 1805 the Congregatio of Várasd resolved that no other language than Latin should be used 'in these kingdoms', since if its use was abolished, 'the culture and the nation must decay and in the end the nation would not understand its own laws'. The language against the introduction of which the Congregatio was protesting was not Magyar, but Croat.[2]

In 1810 an aspiring journalist got permission to publish a paper in Croat, but had to give up the plan because he could find no subscribers.

Finally, one must concede that the introduction of Magyar in place of Latin in the Diet and the central services would in fact have placed the

[1] In 1789 the nobles of Croatia-Slavonia formed only 2·9% of the total population, while the figure for Inner Hungary was 4·8%. This, it is true, was due mainly to the conditions in the Slavonian Counties, where the figure was only 0·45, owing to the complete absence there of sandalled nobility. In at least two of the three Counties of Croatia proper (Zagreb and Körös) the figure was much higher.

[2] It is fair to point out that some Hungarian Counties expressed themselves in the same sense, at even later dates.

Croats at a disadvantage in those bodies, compared with the Magyars; the Croats would now have had to use a second language, while the Magyars would have been relieved of the necessity. But while sympathy must always go out to a minority defending itself against the tyranny of a majority, it should in fairness be pointed out that the official representatives of Croatia among the Magnates numbered only five (the Ban, the Bishop of Zagreb and the Föispáns of the three Croat Counties proper, or eight if the Slavonians were counted),[1] while the official representatives of Inner Hungary in that body numbered some 150.[2] On the Lower Table, there were only three representatives of Croatia (the two delegates from the Sabor and the 'Count of Turopolje',[3] plus the six from Slavonia. What their claim amounted to was that something like ten or fifteen times their own number should be debarred from conducting their national business in their own tongue, and should instead use a second language, to save this tiny minority from having to use a different second language.

For the central services the position was similar: the proportions were again about 1:15.[4] Since a high proportion of the Croat 'nobles' were 'sandalled', or, as they were called locally, 'seven plum-tree' nobles, and another considerable fraction were already Magyar-speaking, the number of Croat candidates who would really have been affected by the Magyarization of the central services would have been minute.

Between 1809 and 1822 the disproportions were even larger because during those years a substantial proportion of Croatia was under foreign rule, first French, then Austrian.

Thus if the Hungarians' wishes would have imposed a real inequality on the Croats, they could hardly be called unreasonable. The only real cure for the inequality would have been the drastic one of complete separation; and for that the Croats themselves was not yet asking.

In Transylvania there was little political or national life. Not only did the Crown convoke no Diet after 1810, but it also ignored those clauses in the Transylvanian Constitution which entitled the 'Three Nations' to repre-

[1] The Slavonian Counties, it will be remembered, sent their representatives direct to Pozsony.

[2] Croat magnates could also sit among the Magnates, but the Croat magnate class was so intermarried with the Hungarian that most great families could sit there as either Croats or Hungarians.

[3] Turopolje (in Hungarian, Turmezö) was a community consisting of fifteen communes of sandalled nobles (according to Damian, about five hundred families) in the vicinity of Zagreb. They enjoyed self-government under their own 'Count', who sat in Pozsony *ex officio*. As we shall see later, this tiny community became in the 1840s one of the storm-centres of the Hungaro-Croat relationship. Another community, in the Kalnoki mountains of Körös (this of 600 families), gave, oddly enough, no trouble.

[4] In 1787 there had been 9,782 male nobles in Croatia-Slavonia against 155,519 in Inner Hungary.

THE SYSTEM AT ITS ZENITH (1815–1830)

sentation in the administration; vacancies were simply filled with the Governor's own nominees. The autonomy both of the Saxon University and of the Lutheran Church was further curtailed.

The peoples took this quietly. The Saxon 'patricians', after at first resisting the new regime, found in it features which made it tolerable and even enjoyable. The Magyar or Magyarized landlords, whom the haphazard developments of the Monarchic legislation had left in an exceptionally strong position,[1] were ready to support any regime prepared, as the Gubernium seemed to be, to keep the Vlachs in their places. In any case, they were too few and too widely scattered over a number of small and remote Counties to combine against authority. Many Counties did not even trouble to hold their Congregationes.

Among the Roumanians, the 'Transylvanian Triad'[2] had produced their chief works by the early years of the century. Then they grew old, and found no successors of their own calibre. The Uniate Bishop, Bobb, managed the estates of his church well, and under his regime the number of Uniate priests, the leaders of the future, grew considerably, but Bobb himself was no crusader, and grew even more passive with advancing years (he died only in 1830, at the ripe age of ninety-one). The Orthodox Bishopric was vacant from Adamović's death in 1796 until 1811, when Vasile Moga was appointed to it. His regime, again, was destined to be prolonged, for he died only in 1845. He was another such as Bobb, a good administrator, under whose hand both the number and the quality of the Orthodox schools increased, but a non-combative personality, who cultivated friendly relations with the authorities and the Uniate Church and discouraged political agitation.

Under these conditions the more active and enterprising Roumanians of the Grand Principality tended to seek their fortunes in the Danubian Principalities, where they came to enjoy a near-monopoly of the teaching profession and were among the chief inspirers of the Roumanian national renaissance when it reached the Principalities. This, however, was hardly before 1830, and during its first phase, the attentions of its leaders were entirely preoccupied with the problems of the Principalities themselves.

In Lombardy-Venetia the population of the former 'Kingdom' had received the Austrians quietly enough in 1815, but there had been certain grievances from the first. The nobles of Milan, although they appreciated the Scala,[3]

---

[1] As has been said (above, p. 65, n. 1), the urbaria of Maria Theresa's reign had not extended to Transylvania. A rough survey was carried out in 1819, but the landlords succeeded in getting nearly half the land cultivated by peasants entered as dominical. The robot was not legally limited, and the customary stint was four days a week.

[2] See above, p. 91.

[3] Massimo d'Azeglio wrote: 'The Austrian government has for many years ruled Lombardy through the Scala, and it must be said, with a certain success.' (Cf. Benedikt, *Kaiseradler*, p. 114.)

found the Archducal Court insufficient compensation for the degradation of their city from its previous position of capital of the Kingdom of Italy; the Patricians of Venice were offended when a Heraldic Commission equated their rank only with that of the untitled nobility of Austria. The Italian clergy, although the Bishops were allowed the privilege of corresponding freely with Rome, were estranged by the Erastianism of the Austrian ecclesiastical system, which they described as 'half-Lutheran'. The entire population disliked the Austrian conscription system, which was enforced more generally than north of the Alps; several categories exempted there, including nobles, were made liable for service in Italy. Then, in 1820–1, the Kingdom became the scene of that incident which, probably more than any other, brought the Austria of the day into international disrepute. A group of men, some of them belonging to the highest Italian aristocracy and conspicuous figures in the local society, became involved in a plot as the result of which they were arrested, tried before special Courts, and, after the sentence of death passed on them had been commuted by the Emperor, sent to pass long and, for those days, particularly barbarous sentences of imprisonment in the dreaded fortress of the Spielberg, in Moravia.

This had not been a revolt of Francis's subjects against Austrian rule. Most of the persons arrested belonged to one or another secret society (of which that of the Carbonari was the most important) whose ramifications extended throughout Italy, and their main effort was directed against the regimes in Naples, Piedmont and the Romagna. It is true that the most prominent of the conspirators, Count Confalonieri, had worked out plans for risings in the chief cities of Lombardy, to break out when the revolt in Piedmont should have succeeded, but his plans seem not to have got much beyond the blueprint stage. In spite of the extreme efforts organized by Francis and Metternich, against the strong advice of wiser subordinates, to smell out every person tainted, however faintly, with the malodour of revolution, relatively few conspirators could be found in the Austrian Kingdom;[1] certainly no part of it was the scene of unrest comparable to that which in those years ravaged Sicily and Piedmont. But a vicious circle had been started. The General and Provincial Congregations sank into the same impotence as the Austrian Estates. The Government became purely bureaucratic, and highly centralized: the Archduke, who was neither stupid nor unenlightened, was limited to representational duties; the executive power lay wholly with the Gubernia, and even more, with the Court Chancellery in Vienna. More and more non-local officials were sent down,[2] and now the Italians themselves began to avoid the public service, complaining that the

[1] Only twenty-four death sentences were pronounced in Lombardy, and not so many in Venetia.

[2] A large number of these were, indeed, Italians from the Trentino. It is true that they generally returned to their homes Italian nationalists.

THE SYSTEM AT ITS ZENITH (1815-1830)

influential, lucrative and interesting jobs were reserved for outsiders. Large garrisons were quartered in the Kingdom and the network of police spies was spun ever finer – partly, indeed, in deference to the habits of the local population, among whom espionage was a national profession. Only the position of the Italian language was left untouched (and that not altogether, for correspondence with the Hofkanzlei had to be conducted in German). Otherwise, the Kingdom came to assume the aspect of a conquered land, ruled by its conquerors, and in it freedom slept as deeply as in Bohemia or Styria.

Administration and justice continued, indeed, to be efficient and uncorrupt, by local standards, taxation relatively low, and much was done for the material welfare of the population: roads were built, canals constructed, factories founded and trade with the interior of the Monarchy fostered. All this blunted the edge of the discontent, but it could not engender a genuine attachment for Austria in the bulk of the population. This remained passive, a fallow-land on which, when the spring winds came, the crop which would flourish would be that of Italian nationalism.

5

The System on the Wane (1830-1835)

Austrian historians count the Vormärz – the years in which the revolution of March 1848 was being gestated, and the Franciscan-Metternich system in obvious decay – as opening with the death of Francis in 1835; but in fact, the first challenge of the new age came earlier than that. Even by the late 1820s, the great economic depression whose weight on the Monarchy had paralysed resistance to the political stranglehold was lifting, allowing new economic and social forces to emerge which fretted against the *vis inertiae* of the 'system'.

Moreover, by Metternich's own philosophy, stability within the Monarchy could be assured only if 'order' reigned everywhere in Europe, and by the same date the European 'order', too, was cracking dismally. Britain had very soon repudiated Metternich's tutelage, insisting on a strictly limited interpretation of the Quadruple Alliance, as also of the Quintuple Alliance (set up beside it with the inclusion of France) in 1818. When Alexander tried to replace the Holy Alliance (which had never been more than a pious scrap of paper) with an effective instrument for maintaining the European 'order', neither Britain nor France would give its signature. The 'Protocol of Troppau' reduced itself to an alliance between the three despotic Powers of Eastern Europe, with an authority which never extended west of the territories under the effective control of one of them, and it had very quickly become plain that Alexander did not interpret the maintenance of order as excluding changes to Russia's advantage in the South-East European *status quo*. Metternich had persuaded the Czar to draw back in 1820, but he had not been able to prevent Russia from agreeing with Britain in 1826, and it was even more humiliating for him when, in 1829, the Peace of Adrianople had brought freedom to the rebellious Greeks and further foretastes of it to the other Balkan peoples, further enfeebling the Porte and dangerously strengthening Russia's power-position in the Balkans.

But the real turning-point had come in 1830, with the July revolution in Paris and its sequels in Belgium, Italy and Poland. Metternich had collapsed

THE SYSTEM ON THE WANE (1830-1835)

at his desk when he received the news from Paris, moaning 'my whole life's work is destroyed!' He had recovered his poise, and afterwards had shown all his old diplomatic expertise in retrieving from the wreckage far more than any lesser man could have salvaged. He sent Austrian troops into the Papal States, Parma and Modena, and after some dangerous moments when a clash with France seemed possible, 'restored order' also in Italy, an order which left Austria again the ruler, direct or indirect, of most of the peninsula. He re-established solidarity with both Prussia and Russia, agreeing with both at Münchengrätz, in September 1833, on the principle of mutual support against revolutionary agitation, smoothing over the differences which had arisen between Austria and Russia over both Poland and Turkey (which both Powers agreed to support, or to concert over the reversion if maintenance of it proved impossible) and most important of all, extracting from the Czar, Nicholas I, a promise to stand by Francis's son, Ferdinand, when he should succeed to the throne.

Nevertheless, Metternich himself could no longer see Europe as a system of ordered States obeying his direction. The Emperor's own advisers had been obliged to oppose his first wish to 'restore order' in France by a military expedition on the grounds that Austria's financial and military resources were simply not adequate for the task: in any case, the Archduke Charles had said, sensibly, foreign bayonets could not conquer ideas. So France had followed Britain in slipping right out of his grasp, and even in Germany Austria was steadily losing ground to Prussia as that State's real power increased with the extension of the Zollverein. That Austria missed her chance of adhering to the Zollverein in 1834 was not Metternich's fault; her refusal to moderate her tariffs was taken against his advice, in the interests of Bohemian industrialists, but it was one which enormously weakened her influence in Germany, where Bavaria, Württemberg, Saxony and half a dozen other smaller States all joined the Zollverein in 1833-5.[1] Only the Czar had reappeared as a real friend; and Russia's friendship, if better than her hostility, was by no means an unmixed blessing.

At home, the danger-year had, on a superficial view, passed over very satisfactorily for Austria. Of all the Kingdoms and Principalities of Italy, Lombardy-Venetia had been the most tranquil; there had hardly been a whisper of sympathy for the revolutionaries beyond its frontiers. The organizers of the Polish revolt in Russia, encouraged by Lobkowitz' arrival and his avowed programme, and seeing visions of getting Austrian support

[1] The question of freer trade between the Monarchy and certain German States had come up on many previous occasions, and Metternich, to do him justice, had regularly been in favour of the more liberal policy, especially with regard to food-stuffs. A strong consideration behind the rejection of all these opportunities had been the political one, viz., the fear that foreign ideas would slip in with the foreign commodities. The obstructionist in chief in this respect was probably Francis himself.

against Russia, had not included Galicia in their plans, nor even attempted to make trouble there. The province had in fact remained quiet, although a Committee had formed itself in Lemberg to organize the dispatch of arms, ammunition and medical supplies to the Polish forces in Russia, and a few volunteers, but only a few,[1] had crossed the frontier to join the fighting. After the failure of the rising the refugees, several thousand in number, who took shelter in Galicia, caused some trouble to the authorities, whose desire it was to combine a sympathetic attitude towards the Poles with a correct one towards Russia. They disarmed the refugees and returned their arms to Russia, but gave the men asylum. The consequent emotional outbursts made it seem advisable to replace Lobkowitz, who was superseded by the more imposing figure of the Archduke Ferdinand d'Este, brother of the late Empress Maria Ludovica, with a vigorous second in command (the Archduke himself was a very easy-going man) in the person of one Baron Krieg, who introduced a severer regime. It was to become apparent later that this had only driven Polish disaffection underground, not extinguished it; but at the time, the position in Galicia looked as satisfactory as that in Lombardy-Venetia.

Nevertheless, the events outside the Monarchy had produced among the people inside it a very widespread feeling that the 'system' was the enemy of their happiness, and moreover, that it was a weak and moribund enemy, which a determined effort could overthrow. A ripple of impatience swept over them, like the sudden gust which precedes the storm. The men at the top could no longer pretend that everyone was contented with things as they were: they had to decide whether to resist the demand for change, or to make concessions to it.

For Francis, the choice presented no problem. His abhorrence of change had by now become pathological indeed. Only in the religious field was it not absolute; in 1833 negotiations for a Concordat were opened with the Holy See, but even they broke down on Francis's refusal to surrender the prerogatives enjoyed by the lay arm over the ecclesiastical. For the rest: 'I want no change', he said to the Hofkanzler, von Pillersdorf, in 1831. 'Let the laws be applied justly. Our laws are good and just. Justice is all in all.' Pillersdorf suggested that change was sometimes necessary, but Francis replied: 'This is no time for reforms. The people are like men who have been badly wounded. One must not keep touching and irritating their wounds.'[2]

On another occasion, Count Chotek, Oberstburggraf of Bohemia, suggested reviving the commutation of the peasants' services. Francis said to Kolowrat, now his adviser in chief on internal affairs: 'Count Chotek, too, seems to me to have got infected with liberal ideas. What has happened to him?' Kolowrat ventured to remark that the Bohemian landlords, on the whole, favoured the

[1] One authority puts the number at five hundred, twenty-six of them Counts.
[2] Kübeck, *Tagebücher*, I. ii p. 438.

THE SYSTEM ON THE WANE (1830–1835)

change, but Francis broke off the conversation, saying: 'No! No! Leave well alone!'[1] And Metternich sang his old song of not being really an obscurantist, seeing that advances were necessary, but they must always be gradual; the present was 'no time for innovations'.[2]

Nevertheless, Francis himself was not the man he had been. He had been severely ill in 1826, and when he recovered, much of his old industry and determination were gone. As it happened, moreover, the change in public opinion coincided (there was more coincidence in it than sequence of cause and effect) with the appearance in the innermost councils of the Court of a man professing Liberal sentiments; a single individual, but one who from his position at the heart of things was able to influence the destinies of millions.

This was Count Francis Anton Kolowrat-Liebsteinsky, a Bohemian magnate of famous family and great estates, who, after serving as Burgomaster of Prague and Oberstburggraf of Bohemia, had been called to Vienna by Francis in 1826 and made head of the Political Section of the Staatsrat, with the rank of Staats- und Konferenzrat, to fill the place of Zichy, who had died; as such, he controlled appointments and promotions in the administrative services. The next year he was made, in addition, head of the Financial Section, which gave him supreme control over finances, for when Stadion died in 1824, although Count Nádasdy, President of the Hofkammer, succeeded to his title of Finance Minister, finances came under the Staatsrat, ceasing to be an independent Ministry.

In 1829 Kolowrat was appointed head of a special Committee to investigate the falling-off in State revenues, and in April of the same year Francis signed a document reserving to himself only a limited sphere of activities: the formal functions of Head of the State, including Acts of Grace, appointments to the highest offices, changes in existing legislature, and decisions on questions of the highest importance, or questions on which the Hofstellen had failed to agree. To help him perform these last duties, he appointed in 1830 a 'Permanent Inner Conference', consisting of Metternich, Kolowrat and Nádasdy with himself as President. His decision of the previous year had already meant that nearly all the business of State except that falling within Metternich's field, or that of the Hofkriegsrat, was now dealt with by Kolowrat, and furthermore, as the committee of investigation was found to be performing in effect the functions of a Ministry of Finance, Francis in 1830 made it permanent, Nádasdy becoming *de facto* only Kolowrat's subordinate.

Again in 1829, Francis made Kolowrat head of another Committee, nominally under the Presidency of the Archduke Ferdinand, for clearing up

[1] Id., p. 508. It is not clear from Kübeck's wording exactly how far Chotek's proposals went.
[2] Id., p. 439.

the arrears of business which had accumulated on his own desk. As these promptly accumulated again, yet another Committee, again under Kolowrat, was appointed in 1832 to deal with the fresh arrears.

Kolowrat left no memoirs. What we know about him comes chiefly from his enemies, above all, the garrulous Metternich (and his equally verbose biographers) and Kübeck. These sources are obviously biased, and against them must be set the high opinion of him which was held by Francis and by the sensible Archduke John. Yet he cannot at best have been an easy character. He was ruthless in shouldering aside those who stood in the way of his ambitions, but fractious and nervous in the face of real opposition. Thus he excused himself from that important part of his duties which involved Hungarian affairs because he could not bear arguing points with the temperamental Hungarian Chancellor, Count Reviczky. When he failed to get his way, it was his habit to tender his resignation, or pleading ill-health, which may have been been real,[1] to retire to his Bohemian estates. Somehow or other, these expedients always worked, for he held his position up to the outbreak of revolution and through the first days of the revolution itself.

Whether he was really a financial genius, may be doubted. His fame in this respect derived from his (or (Nádasdy's) achievement – if it was really due to either of them[2] – in having produced Budget estimates for 1830 which allowed for the smallest deficit within living memory, one of something under 10 million gulden.[3] This had been achieved partly by a further pruning of the army estimates (to 38 million gulden, ordinary expenditure,[4] partly to the introduction of a new consolidated tax on consumption in the form of a general excise, collected by levying an octroi on meat, wine, beer, and various other commodities. Although highly unpopular,[5] this tax had brought in 11 million gulden, or 7 million gulden nett, since certain other taxes had been remitted when it was introduced.[6] The estimates for 1831 had actually provided for a surplus, although a minute one.[7]

That these calculations were promptly upset by the outbreak of the July Revolution, so that the deficits recommenced,[8] was, of course, not Kolowrat's fault. The deficits were occasioned almost entirely by the increased military

---

[1] Metternich said that he had piles, which rose to his head.

[2] Kübeck claimed the credit for himself (*Tagebücher*, p. 479).

[3] Beer, p. 141.

[4] The Emperor had issued another ruling that 40 m.g. was to be the absolute limit for ordinary expenditure on the Army.

[5] Its introduction gave rise to riots in Vienna and Prague. The 'revolution' of 1848 in many country towns took almost the sole form of committal of mayhem on unfortunate excise-men.

[6] Beer, p. 172.

[7] The estimates had provided for 149·323 m.g. revenue and 148·195 m.g. expenditure.

[8] They were 40·3 in 1831, 28·5 in 1832, 25·0 in 1833, 26·5 in 1834, 31·5 in 1835. In these years the State debt rose by another 250 m.g., with a further annual charge of nearly 12 m.g.

THE SYSTEM ON THE WANE (1830–1835)

expenditure, and Kolowrat always maintained that this was due to Metternich's extravagant policy of keeping order in Europe by bayonet. But neither he, nor, for that matter, his critic and rival expert, Kübeck, had any real nostrum for Austria's financial condition. Both ruled out equally any substantial increase in direct taxation, and both rejected the drastic remedy of another 'State bankruptcy'. The only real difference between them was that Kübeck was content to go on raising loans *ad infinitum*, regarding the most important duty of policy to be that of keeping the State credit good, so that the loans could be floated cheaply, while Kolowrat – and on this point he was surely right – saw that the loans only increased Austria's ultimate expenditure.[1] He would have risked issuing more paper money, which in fact had to be done in 1831, when the paper currency doubled and its cover in silver sank from 1:5 at the beginning of 1830 to 1:10 at the end of 1831.

Kolowrat's own liberalism did not really go very deep. As a great Bohemian aristocrat he sympathized with his fellow-nobles' objections to the dictates of the bureaucracy, but he once told Metternich that the latter was mistaken in supposing that the two men's principles differed. He (Kolowrat) was himself 'an aristocrat by birth and conviction', and entirely agreed with Metternich 'that one must have conservative aims and must work systematically towards them'. But he disagreed with Metternich's methods of 'a forest of bayonets and rigid adherence to the *status quo*'. This only exhausted the Government's resources, made the masses wretched and discontented and provoked the middle classes to hatred of the aristocracy, which they would end by destroying, in alliance with the masses. The way to avert the otherwise certain revolution was to make concessions to promote the material well-being of the people, bringing them well-being as reward for their industry.[2] But he did, at least, succeed, if only once, in producing a balanced budget. That, after all, was something; the fact that he detested Metternich personally, and took every occasion to thwart him out of personal spite, if not principle, was even more. This, combined with the fact that he had Francis's ear, made him the hope of all liberals, even of anyone who on any ground was against Metternich, and this mere fact probably often led him into

[1] Very interesting in this connection is a note by Kübeck of a conversation between himself and Kolowrat in January 1831 (op. cit., p. 315). Kübeck said:

'To get money, there are only the ways of taxation, force' (by this he appears to mean a repudiation of obligations: cf. id., p. 316) 'or credit. The first two ways can hardly be chosen because they would be neither undangerous, nor productive of big results. Credit, on the other hand, is always there, only one must fulfil its conditions.' Kolowrat preferred the issue of paper, as did the Emperor (id., p. 470), but Kübeck was adamant for keeping the credit of the State good, and borrowing on favourable terms. On another occasion, in November 1832, the Emperor, according to Kolowrat, when warned that the excessive army expenditure and the repeated loans would lead to State bankruptcy, answered indifferently: 'What of it? Bankruptcy is a tax like any other. Only one must arrange it so that everyone loses in equal proportion, as when an honest tradesman goes into liquidation' (id., p. 593).

[2] Id., p. 626. The date is 1833.

supporting policies more liberal than he would otherwise have approved. And he must have been a competent administrator in his way. The confidence reposed in him by Francis would alone give proof of this, for Francis was an excellent judge of men. His supporters also included at least two members of the Imperial family, the Archdukes Charles and John, both of whom both agreed with his principles and regarded him as more capable than Metternich of creating internal order in the Monarchy. It was the combination Charles-Kolowrat (effectively backed, on this occasion, by Salamon Rothschild) that quashed Metternich's plan of intervening in France and Germany in 1830, and it was John, who had a high opinion of his abilities, who secured him his place as dictator of Austria's internal affairs after 1835 and worked with him in 1848 to bring about the dismissal of Metternich.

Apart from their difference of views on the prime question of priorities (international order or internal consolidation), Metternich and Kolowrat disagreed on a number of other points. Kolowrat was a pronounced Josephinian in his views on Church questions, whereas Metternich inclined even further to the 'Party of Piety' after he had, on 30 January 1831, taken as his third wife the young Countess Melanie Zichy-Ferraris, who shared much of the piety of her step-aunt-in-law, Metternich's earlier Egeria.

The Zichys were also one of the great Hungarian families, and his affection for his young wife, combined with his memories of the elder lady, may well have contributed towards strengthening his predilection for Hungary's aristocracy and confirming the view of the virtues of its Constitution which he had adopted from Francis.[1] On these points there was a profound and most important difference between him and Kolowrat, who would in any case have regarded the Hungarian Constitution with disfavour as an obstacle to the efficient government and financial equilibrium of the Monarchy and a shield for disloyalty. But in addition, he was an enthusiastic Czechophile, and beyond that, a warm Slavophile. In his days in Bohemia he had been an active patron of the Czech cultural revival, and when he became head of personnel affairs in Vienna, it was said of him that an applicant had only to say 'My name is Wenzel and I'm a Czech' to get his appointment.

Sentiment and reason worked together to make him further in every way at his disposal (and they were innumerable) the cause of the Slavs in both halves of the Monarchy: of the Czechs in the West and far more actively, since the opportunities were greater, of the Croats in the Lands of the Hungarian Crown. The following pages will give examples of this.

The two men differed also on other points. Kolowrat, essentially a bureaucrat, found Francis's system of direct rule through civil servants eminently suited to his genius. He was also, even apart from Hungary, a centralist. Metternich was impatient of *ronds de cuir*, and also held that, even

[1] He had also been granted Hungarian Indigenat in 1826, and had become a titular Hungarian magnate, a distinction of which he was vain.

THE SYSTEM ON THE WANE (1830-1835)

apart from Hungary, a highly centralized system was incompatible with the special nature of the Monarchy. Finally, while entirely accepting the principle that the Monarch's will was absolute, he thought it wise that a machinery should exist which might restrain the Monarch from hasty and ill-considered moves. His prescription was an advisory Reichsrat, which should include, besides Archdukes and elder statesmen, also assessors, nominated by the Crown, from the Estates of each Land. Soon after being appointed Chancellor, he expounded these proposals in a reasoned memorandum to Francis, who promptly put it into a drawer unread. He revived them unsuccessfully in the struggle for power which followed Francis's death, and once again on 12 March 1848, when they were again swept aside. It was reserved for the experimenters of 1860 to call into being an institution which in its functions and its composition recalled strongly Metternich's proposals of forty years earlier. It is true that the result was speedy failure.

Apart from Metternich and Kolowrat, Francis, in his last years, tended to lean chiefly on his youngest brother, Ludwig. Ludwig was, by all reports, the least talented of the whole family (most of whose other members disliked him), and Metternich's enemies accused him of having pushed Ludwig forward because he could dominate him, as he could not his more experienced and self-confident brothers. It is, however, true that, given Francis's predilection for employing members of his own family, he had little other choice, since the other brothers were either in disgrace, or embedded in other occupations. That later developments were to place Ludwig in a position of key importance for the destinies of the whole Monarchy was, in part, unintentional.

Ludwig's promotion arose, ultimately, as a result of a definitive decision taken by Francis, again in 1830, in respect of another family problem, that of the succession to his thrones. Francis's second wife, the mother of all his surviving children, was not only his first cousin twice over,[1] but also came of infected stock. One or both of these facts had rebounded on Francis's eldest son, Ferdinand, who was clearly incapable of becoming an effective ruler. Physically, he was subject to epileptic fits, and in general, extremely frail, while mentally, if not idiotic, he was on the verge of idiocy. This simplicity went hand in hand with an extreme goodness of heart, which earned him the deserved soubriquet of 'Ferdinand the Goodhearted'[2] and the effect of the combination was that he could never be got to see that the way to remedy any grievance was not promptly to grant the petitioner whatever he asked – a formula in any case genuinely inappropriate for dealing with the complex

[1] Her father was Ferdinand IV of Naples-Sicily, brother of Francis's mother, while her mother was Leopold's sister, Marie Caroline.

[2] *Ferdinand der Gütige.* This was the more official version: the more popular one was *Nanderl-Trotterl* (Ferdy the Simp).

affairs of the Monarchy, and nothing short of terrifying to his entourage, whose general prescription for ruling was, it is hardly unfair to say, the precise contrary.

Ferdinand's younger brother, Franz Karl, the only other of Francis's sons to survive infancy, was no genius and took little interest in politics, but he was a man of average capacities. In him, moreover, there rested what seemed to be the only hopes of the Crown's remaining with Francis's heirs, for Ferdinand, up to 1830, had been judged unfit to marry. Franz Karl, on the other hand, had taken a wife, Princess Sophie Wittelsbach, a younger daughter of King Maximilian of Bavaria,[1] and although by 1830 Sophie, in spite of several *fausses couches*, had not yet become a mother, she might clearly still become one: things were pointing that way again in the spring. There was obviously something to be said for passing Ferdinand over altogether, but Francis was reluctant to do this, partly out of affection for the poor young man, partly out of respect for the principle of legitimacy, and on this point he was supported by Metternich, nominally at least on the same ground of legitimacy, although his enemies maintained that his stronger motive was the calculation that if Ferdinand came to the throne, Metternich himself, as the hapless youth's mentor, would be the real ruler of the Monarchy. At any rate, the decision was taken in Ferdinand's favour, and Metternich arranged to have it made irrevocable by having Ferdinand crowned King of Hungary at the next Hungarian Diet.[2]

This still left the further succession with the younger branch of the family. In 1831 Ferdinand was, after all, given a bride, Princess Marie Anne Caroline of Savoy, a lady who bore her truly unenviable lot with Christian fortitude, but with so little interest in public affairs that she never even learnt to understand German. It was, however, soon known that the poor epileptic was never to be a father. Sophie, on the other hand, had, on 18 August 1830, given birth to a son, Francis Joseph, to whom she afterwards bore two brothers, Ferdinand Maximilian (b. 6 July 1832) and Karl Ludwig (b. 30 July 1833).[3]

This is the place to kill a couple of widespread and persistent legends.[4] Sophie was a very ambitious and very bossy woman – a famous description

---

[1] Thus, incidentally, becoming his father's step-brother-in-law, since Francis's own fourth wife was the King's elder daughter by another wife.

[2] Hungarian history contained several precedents, the first of them as early as the eleventh century, for the coronation of the king's designated successor in his predecessor's own lifetime. It was a convenient way for a dutiful father to secure his son's succession in times when the succession law was not yet fixed.

[3] There was also a daughter, Anna, born on 27 October 1835, who, however, died in infancy.

[4] The following lines are based chiefly on Corti's *Von Kind bis Kaiser* (Graz, 1950), a work for which the author went through the Archduchess's diary and letters with a magnifying glass. It is by far the most detailed and most authentic account of these family relationships.

of her, in 1848, called her the only man in the Imperial family – and she certainly fretted against the position of inferiority to which the principle of legitimacy relegated her menfolk, but it is quite untrue that either she or her husband (who is usually held, probably with some exaggeration, to have been mere wax in her hands) in any way resented the decision that Ferdinand should succeed his father: their own respect for the principle of legitimacy forbade this. Sophie was, indeed, aghast when Ferdinand married, but calmed down when assured that there was no prospect of her sons' being supplanted in the succession. Still less did either she or her husband bear Metternich any shadow of resentment for his part in the decision, or side with Kolowrat against him. Franz Karl was, on the contrary, the staunchest supporter whom Metternich had in the Imperial family during the next fifteen years, taking his side more consistently even than Ludwig, while Sophie had for him the deepest personal devotion. The Chancellor and his family were practically members of the Archducal family circle, and her distress when he fell sick was almost passionate.[1] Corti's book contains, on the other hand, not a single passage showing that she was aware of Kolowrat's existence.

Metternich was also the Archduchess' political Bible. She was in fact a silly woman who had no political ideas, in the true sense of the word, whatever, and the emotions which served her in place of ideas were entirely primitive. If the thrones of her menfolk and her in-laws were undisturbed, that was good; if they were threatened, it was bad. She swallowed whole Metternich's pontifications on 'order', entirely agreed with his recipe for preserving it (by bayonets) and accepted everything he laid down about the sinfulness of democracy, nationalism, etc. As Corti points out,[2] the best proof of her faith in his wisdom is that when the time came for Francis Joseph to be taught statecraft, it was to Metternich that she sent him to learn it.[3]

The stirrings of new life were not, in fact, very vigorous in the Hereditary and Bohemian Lands. In 1831 'Anastasius Grün' published his mildly political *Spaziergänge eines Wiener Poeten*, often hailed as the first blossom of the Vormärz; as a great aristocrat (the pseudonym covered the identity of Count Anton von Auersperg), he could afford the risk, and in any case, the book was published in Hamburg. The *Rheinische Merkur* reported during March that ideas of reform and of a Constitution had found their way into Austria and were widespread among the middle-classes; and private diaries show intellectuals envying the French their courage. But history does not record them as imitating it. Some riots which took place in Vienna had (as usual) material origins; they were against the new consumption tax.

[1] Corti, op. cit., p. 166.
[2] Id., p. 244.
[3] For the legend of her alleged lapse in 1848, see below, p. 325.

Sedlnitzky reported reassuringly that only the worshippers of novelty were interested in the new-fangled ideas; most people were quite content with things as they were.¹

The danger-year had passed over equally quietly in Prague, except for some sentimental outbreaks of sympathy for the Poles. Neither did the following years see any political developments worth recording in these Lands. In the Lands of the Hungarian Crown, on the other hand, 1830 ushered in a really eventful lustrum.

In the summer Francis re-convoked the Hungarian Diet, partly to crown Ferdinand and partly to receive the Crown's demands for the recruits and money which Metternich wanted for his actions against European revolution, and already this Diet was only half complaisant. It crowned Ferdinand, on 28 September, although not without some grumblings, and the magnates, who were as anxious as Metternich himself that revolution should not spread to the Monarchy, were prepared to grant the Crown's full demand for recruits, viz., 30,000 immediately, to bring the Hungarian regiments in the standing army up to strength, and 20,000 more if the defence of the State required them before the next Diet opened. But the Lower Table haggled. They ended by voting the immediate requirements, but only 28,000 (to show their independence), and made the supply of the other 20,000 dependent on various conditions (which Francis did not, indeed, accept), including that they should not be used for intervention abroad 'against popular liberties'. As the price for this they extracted, at last, one really substantial linguistic concession. No person not conversant with the Magyar language was in future to be admitted to the public services in Inner Hungary, and after four years, the same condition was to apply for admission to the Bar. The Chancellery and the Curia were to be bound to answer in Magyar communications addressed to them in that language by the Counties, and Magyar might also be used in the Courts.²

They had a great number of other requests as well, and when Francis, employing his customary device, sent them home as soon as he had gained his own points, they received the intimation with strong protests of their 'consternation'.

Up to a point, this Diet should still be regarded as the successor of that of 1825, rather than the inaugurator of the very different series which followed. Almost all its demands were directed towards maintaining Hungary's constitutional independence *vis-à-vis* Vienna; even the caveat regarding popular liberties abroad was made because speakers thought that the existence of other constitutional regimes would make it easier for Hungary to defend her own. But two years passed before the next Diet met, which was longer than

¹ Charmatz, op. cit., p. 12.
² Francis's pliability on this point is said to have been due to the eloquence of Reviczky, who persuaded him that a concession here would produce the recruits.

THE SYSTEM ON THE WANE (1830–1835)

it should have been; for on closing the Diet of 1830, Francis had promised faithfully to convoke its successor the following year, and give a proper hearing to the nation's wishes. But in 1831 a devastating outbreak of cholera, spreading from Russia via Galicia, ravaged Hungary with such dreadful effect that in the single year 536,517 persons sickened of it, 237,641 of the cases – one in twenty-five of the entire population – proving fatal.[1] Francis made the outbreak a pretext for leaving the Diet unconvoked, although it was freely said that his real reason had been fear of indiscreet demonstrations of sympathy for the Poles, if not something worse (reports had been reaching the secret police of Polish emissaries spreading revolution, and of Hungarian conventicles plotting it)[2] and when it did assemble, on 16 December 1832, its mood was not only more combative still than that of its predecessor, but different in kind. The change was due (apart from the general spirit of the age) to two influences.

One was the effect of the epidemic itself, and its concomitants. The authorities had sent round commissioners to pour chlorine into the wells, and had also made issues of bismuth. By ill-fortune, some persons using the disinfected wells, and some taking bismuth, had died, while others who had taken no medicaments had survived. The epidemic had been worst in the northern Counties, where the peasantry was most backward, and also most oppressed. A belief had spread that the authorities, the landlords and the Jews were in conspiracy to reduce the population by poisoning it off. Many landlords' houses were sacked and burnt, and a number of nobles and their bailiffs, priests and Jews were murdered, some of them in indescribably brutal fashion.

These dreadful excesses shattered the complacent belief of the Hungarian landowners that the peasant situation could be left to look after itself. A wave of near-panic swept over them. One party, indeed, called for severe repressive measures (such as were in fact applied in the affected areas), but another, not inconsiderable, group felt that the remedy should lie in reforming the peasants' conditions. Whichever the standpoint, the peasant question appeared to call for urgent action.

The second factor to alter the mood of the Diet was the personal influence of a single man, Count István Széchenyi, the man who had intervened so sensationally in the linguistic debates of 1825.

Széchenyi is one of the most important figures in the modern history of the Monarchy, one of the most admirable and of the most tragic, because the waters which he released, out of the deepest conviction and with the purest

---

[1] In Galicia there were 325,029 deaths (from all causes) in 1831, against only 157,855 births. The cholera reached Vienna, but there it was stamped out fairly quickly. Its effects in the other Lands were not serious, although it reached Moravia and Bohemia.

[2] In fact a considerable number of refugees from Congress Poland had sought shelter in Hungary and there had been a good deal of enthusiastic talk.

intention, turned within a very few years into a raging torrent which menaced the very foundations of what he still held to be essential to their useful operation.

István Széchenyi was a member of one of Hungary's greatest families, one which had, indeed, a tradition of national service: his father, Count Ferencz Széchenyi, was the founder of the great national library which still bears his name. But the family, whose estates lay hard on the Austrian frontier, was also one of those whose loyalty to the dynasty had always been total. Széchenyi himself had begun his career by serving his Monarch, with some distinction, as an officer of hussars, and even the tongue in which he thought and expressed himself most freely was German.

Loyalty to the dynasty was always axiomatic to him, and he never even saw Hungary except in terms of the Gesammtmonarchie.[1] He also had a realistic appreciation of Hungary's weaknesses, political, national and financial, and was convinced that the help, protection and financial resources of Vienna were essential to her. But his was a brooding and mystical spirit, which became possessed by a passion in which devotion to God was so mingled with an intense and compassionate love of Hungary and of the Magyar people that the elements defy separation. When peace came he had sent in his papers and thereafter travelled widely in Western Europe, especially England. He was shocked by the contrast between the progress, wealth and civic liberty which he found there and the backwardness, poverty and degradation of the 'great fallow-land', as he termed his own country, and had immediately set himself to diagnosing the ills which he found there, and to seeking remedy for them.

It is a curious feature of Széchenyi's activity that while his whole inspiration was essentially moral, even religious, his approach to problems and his arguments were always severely practical.[2] His first enterprises (apart from the offer to finance the Academy) sounded almost trivial: the foundation of an aristocrats' club, the introduction of horse-racing. But they had a practical purpose: the club was to enable its members to read Western literature and to exchange ideas, the races, to improve the breed of Hungarian horses.

After another visit to England he became interested in the navigation of the Danube, took shares in the recently-established *Donaudampschiffgesellschaft*,

---

[1] This was partly also a calculation: just before his suicide he said to an Austrian (Crenneville): 'Hungary can exist only in Austria. In German arms she may feel herself squeezed, but in Slav arms, she would certainly be crushed' (Corti, *Mensch und Herscher*, p. 253).
Interesting also is a letter which he wrote to Rechberg shortly before his death, that his programme was:
(1) Loyalty and devotion to the Dynasty and the person of the Emperor.
(2) Loyalty and devotion to Hungary in association with the Hereditary Provinces.
(3) Reasoned approval of Constitutional institutions.

[2] It is no less curious that he should have been unique in this respect, but he was in fact the only Hungarian of his age to occupy himself seriously with questions of the national economy.

which had begun plying between Vienna and Pest in 1830, and launched a plan for an independent Hungarian company, which was also to work the lower stretches of the river. At the same time, Széchenyi was launching propaganda for the most famous of all the children of his brain, the construction of a suspension bridge between Buda and Pest. Revolutionary in its grandeur, this project contained a proposal which was more revolutionary still, for Széchenyi proposed to exact a toll from all users of the bridge, noble or non-noble; if accepted, this would have constituted the first breach in the nobles' cherished exemption from taxation.

By this time all Hungary was humming with the activities of 'the Count'. Some laughed at him, others admired him, but he was the talk of the country. Then, in 1830, came his first full-scale book, *Hitel* (Credit).

Hitel is an astonishing book. The inspiration of it, apparent in every line, is a pure and intense love and pity for his country and its people, deserving, he thinks, of so much and capable of achieving it, but now in possession of so little. Yet he barely invokes the moral considerations which move him so deeply; his references to the incompatibility of Hungary's social system, above all, the unfree condition of the peasants, with the claims of human dignity are almost parenthetical. If he seeks souls, he does so through an appeal to pockets, by arguing that the Hungarian Constitution is materially disadvantageous to its supposed beneficiaries, the nobles, themselves. The inalienability of their estates imposed by the aviticitas makes it impossible for them to give them as security for the loans without which they cannot carry through essential improvements. Their exemption from taxation prevents the accumulation of funds to construct the communications without which their produce remains unsaleable. The landlord-peasant nexus and the robot system are unprofitable to the landlords themselves, because, as he calculates, a day's robot is only one-third as productive as the hired labour of a freeman.

Széchenyi suggested no far-reaching political remedies; certainly nothing like the introduction of Western democracy, which to the end of his days he thought dangerous for Hungary; his programme was always a paternal one, of reform from above. And yet his theses, severely practical as they were, were revolutionary in the fullest sense of the term. The proposition that the sacrosanct Hungarian Constitution was no fortress of liberty, but a prison, stood all Hungarian political thought on its head. Moreover, Széchenyi argued his case with a brutal frankness which did not spare his readers. He told his fellow-nobles, with great candour, that the ultimate cause of their country's backwardness lay, not in foreign oppression, but in their own sloth, selfishness and complacency, and that the remedy lay in their own hands.

Not unnaturally, *Hitel* met with a mixed reception. The rich magnates, on whom the weight of noble taxation would fall, regarded his proposals as simply highway robbery; the backwoods squires could not believe that any better existence than theirs was led by any class on earth; and for proof that they owed their blessings to their Constitution, pointed to the repeated complaints by Vienna precisely against that Constitution. Széchenyi was denounced as an unpractical dilettante, a bird fouling his own nest, a red revolutionary, a traitor.

But Széchenyi stood his ground. In 1831 he answered his critics and developed his arguments, especially his case for social and political reform, in the still more impressive *Világ* (Light).[1] And the very storm which his books aroused helped to increase their effect. The questions which they raised became the subject of hot controversy. The virtues and blessings of the Constitution were no longer assumed as automatic. They were still most generally maintained, but not a few people were found to agree on the weakness of the spots on which Széchenyi had put his finger. When the 1832 Diet met, Széchenyi had still very few supporters among the magnates, but the Lower House contained a considerable group of 'Liberal' advocates of at least some of his ideas. Among these, Ferencz Kölcsey was the man whose ideas were the most closely akin to Széchenyi's own, but the man destined to appear as the most important of all was Ferencz Deák, a sober, high-principled and respected medium landowner from Zala, who, quietly turning things over in his own mind, had come to the conclusion that far-reaching reforms, including the complete emancipation of the peasants and the extension of taxation to the nobles, were necessary on moral, political and economic grounds.

So battle was joined between the conservatives and the reformers, and if the latter were few, they were vocal, and since the Diet was now technically submitting to the Crown the revised reports of the Committees originally set up in 1791, they had a chance to talk on almost any subject they fancied. Progressives from all over the country had taken the opportunity to get their ideas into the reports, which accordingly contained a long series of proposals, some of them genuinely radical for that day: for far-reaching improvements in the condition of the peasants, for the removal of unequal restrictions on Protestants, for reform of the tariff system (to consider which it was suggested that discussions might be held between representatives of the Hungarian and Austrian Estates), for the abolition of the *aviticitas*, and a host more; besides such purely national demands as the re-integration of the Partium and more facilities still for the use of Magyar in public life; and to sweeten the mixture, a motion of sympathy for the Polish nation.

Against most of these proposals, the Hungarian magnates put up a stubborn resistance, and they were nearly always backed by the Crown, partly out of its innate conservatism, partly on the *a priori* reasoning that anything which Hungarians wanted must be undesirable. Heavy personal responsibility rests here on Metternich, who had snubbed Széchenyi in 1825,

[1] A third, more repetitive, work, *Stadium*, appeared in 1834.

THE SYSTEM ON THE WANE (1830–1835)

when the young Count had pleaded with him for reform from above, in collaboration with Vienna. 'No, no!' the old wise-acre had replied: 'Take one stone out of the vaulting and the whole thing collapses'– thus really damning in advance all Széchenyi's hopes. The result was that by the end of 1835, when the 'Long Diet', as it was baptized, had sat for three full years, it had very small results to show for so much talking. Perhaps the most conspicuous of them was that it had accepted, after bitter opposition from the die-hards (one of whom shed tears over the deflowering of the nobles' fiscal virginity), Széchenyi's toll-bridge. Besides this, the Magyar text of laws was to be the authentic one, lawsuits *could* be conducted in Magyar, registers were to be kept in Magyar in parishes in which the sermon was preached in that language. The peasants received a few concessions which brought their legal position up to that of their opposite numbers in the West: they were entitled to commute their dues and services for a money rent (although not to buy their holdings) and the competence of the Patrimonial Courts was somewhat restricted. The reintegration of the Partium was accepted on paper. But the Crown had made no concession at all on the tariff question, flatly rejecting the suggestion of Austro-Hungarian discussions, on the ground that the determination of tariffs was a prerogative of the Crown, in which the Estates had no voice, and practically none in the religious.

Yet it was only in appearance that the victory lay with the Crown and its allies. Széchenyi's criticisms of the Constitution had by now found very widespread agreement; and Széchenyi himself was already becoming a back number. If the reformers were still too advanced for most regular members of the Diet, they had become too slow-minded for the gallery. It was the custom of each Deputy to bring with him one or more *juratus*, or recent graduate in law, to act as his secretary or simply to gain experience by listening to the debates, and at the Long Diet no less than fifteen hundred of these youths had appeared, including many of the figures to become prominent in 1848.[1] Technically nobles, many of them were from landless families, or else younger sons for whom the paternal acres provided no fortune, so that they had no vested interest in the *status quo*, and they belonged, of course, to a younger age-group than the Deputies and were open to more modern ideas. Most of them were under the influence of the French Liberals of the day, Thiers, Lammenais, Victor Hugo, etc., whose writings easily slipped into Hungary past the slip-shod censorship of the day. A programme drawn up by a group of them in 1835 included, besides Széchenyi's demands, popular representation, Ministerial responsibility and Parliamentary control over the Budget.

The jurati could not, of course, intervene officially in the debates of the

---

[1] Berthalan Szemere, Kálmán Ghyczy, the brothers Madarász, Menyhért Lónyay, László Szalay, and many other figures prominent in later Hungarian politics, were among them.

Diet, but tradition and the national character permitted them to accompany its proceedings with applause, catcalls and interruptions, so that the Diet (and the Crown) were soon aware on which side the sympathies of Hungary's angry young men lay. And before the Diet had risen, the young radicals had found a leader, and still more, a mouthpiece, in the person of the man who was soon to drive Széchenyi out of the field, Lajos Kossuth.

Kossuth was a somewhat older man than the jurati, having been born in 1802. He came from the mixed Magyar-Slovak district of North-Eastern Hungary, and his family (which was Lutheran) was of originally Slovak stock on the paternal side,[1] although those who call him 'a renegade Slovak', 'a Slovak trying to be a Magyar', etc. only show that they do not understand the atmosphere of the place and time. His family had been Hungarian nobles for centuries, and for as long, spiritually Hungarians; if some of them still spoke Slovak, as well as Magyar, this was common in mixed districts up to at least 1918. But although noble, the Kossuths were also impoverished, and after various adventures (including an unsuccessful attempt to obtain a post in the Consilium), Lajos had found employment as estate agent to a rich widowed Countess in his native County. She fell in love with him and he spent seven years in her company, taking only a small part in local affairs. In 1832 they parted, but still, it appears, feeling affection for him, she found him a mandate to represent a distant relative of hers in the Diet, a post which, under the peculiar procedure of that body, allowed him to sit, not among the magnates but with the lesser men, but not to speak. Here, for the first time, he was drawn into national politics.

Although Kossuth soon had more political followers than any other man in Hungary, it is easier to draw out Leviathan with a hook than to reduce his political philosophy to a system; so much do his utterances abound in digressions and irrelevances, even in flat mutual contradictions. Their coherence is emotional, for all of them are instinct with a burning love of his country and his fellow-countrymen and a passionate wish to see them in enjoyment of every blessing which thought had anywhere devised for any people. In this he did not differ from Széchenyi, nor greatly in his view of Hungary's condition; but his remedy was very different. A true child of his age, Kossuth accepted its almost automatic identification of the good with liberty; on which ground alone, he wanted to see every Hungarian enjoying personal liberty (including equality before the law), liberty of religion, of thought, speech and the written word, and the rest. But again like most Central European reformers of his day, he put national liberty highest of all, not merely as the *summum bonum* to which all else would have to be sacrificed if necessary, but as the true pre-condition for any real social, economic or cultural advance. Blind, owing to his narrower horizon, to the material advantages which Széchenyi saw in the connection with 'Vienna', he saw

[1] His mother's family were Germans from the Szepes.

THE SYSTEM ON THE WANE (1830–1835)

the source of everything that was wrong in Hungary in the illegitimate[1] domination exercised over her by 'Vienna' and its servants. The first step must be to get rid of that domination; the political battle came first. He saw, and presented, every question in that light, thus repudiating (and quickly defeating, in the popular mind) Széchenyi's programme of reform through collaboration with 'Vienna'.

But if in one sense this attitude was simply that of the traditionalist *kuruc* squires, in another it was the opposite of theirs, for Kossuth wanted national liberty in the cause of reform, not of stability, and while believing that full social and political liberty must wait on national liberty, yet he also believed that internal reform, besides being desirable in itself, would bring national liberty nearer. Thus the emancipation of the peasants, itself a postulate of liberty, was also in the national interest because it would multiply twenty-fold the forces fighting for the national cause. The fiscal prerogatives of the nobles must go, not only because they constituted a negation of equality, but also because their chief beneficiaries, the magnates, were the allies of Vienna, and no true Hungarians.

Thus Kossuth made radical social and political reform a national postulate; and the greatest service which he rendered to his country (and he rendered it much service, as well as much disservice) was that he won over for the cause of internal reform many who would have rejected it had he not convinced them that it was desirable in the national interest. 'Vienna' argued that a thing must be bad because Hungary wanted it. Kossuth persuaded his fellow-countrymen that it must be good because 'Vienna' opposed it.

He was able to do this because if his thought was neither profound nor original, his facility in expressing it in convincing terms was unique. He was one of the most persuasive men ever to be born. He was of notably handsome appearance, with brilliant blue eyes under a magnificent forehead, a most winning manner and a beautifully modulated voice. As a speaker he possessed an unfailing readiness and gift of impromptu and an inexhaustible fluency which seldom failed to carry his audiences with him, at any rate if they were large. He was no less gifted with his pen, having an extraordinary gift of enlisting his readers' sympathy for whatever cause he was pleading, by emotional appeal rather than intellectual, but not the less strongly for that. He was a superb player on the heart-strings of the Hungarian people, because they were also his own.

With such gifts he was bound, given equal opportunities, to outdistance Széchenyi in popular appeal, for 'the Count's' literary style was involved, his oratory halting and even his command of the Magyar language imperfect. But the opportunities were at first not equal. Kossuth had no money to publish works of his own, and when he came to Pozsony in 1832 was gagged

[1] The word must be emphasized, for up to 1849 Kossuth was completely loyal to the dynasty.

by the terms of his mandate. Soon, however, he was offered, and seized with both hands, an unexpected chance. The Opposition had for some time been urging, and the Government refusing, the issue of a printed record of the proceedings of the Diet. Someone hit on the idea of having a handwritten record made. Jurati took down the speeches and Kossuth was given the job of editing them.

What emerged under his hand was no verbatim transcript. The speeches of the reformers were given at length, and in eloquent periods which sometimes owed more to the genius of the editor than to that of the speakers; those of the other side were dismissed in a few colourless or sarcastic lines. But – or rather, consequently – the 'Gazette' quickly achieved an enormous popularity. It circulated from hand to hand over Hungary, spreading everywhere the ideas of reform and the arguments in favour of them, and marking out Kossuth as the leading hope of Young Hungary. Naturally, too, it inculcated, by suggestion but most deeply, Kossuth's point of view of the priority of the political struggle.

And this had been underlined by the meagre results of the Diet itself. Even reformers whose positive programme did not go nearly so far as Kossuth's were bound to agree with him that 'Vienna' was the obstacle in chief to even moderate progress. Thus the close of 1835 found the cause of progress little advanced in Hungary, but the forces determined to achieve it strengthened immeasurably.

Simultaneously with the developments in Inner Hungary, Transylvania suddenly burst into political life. Even more than in Inner Hungary, this change was the work of a single man, Baron Miklós Wesselényi. Wesselényi had accompanied Széchenyi on some of his travels and had gathered much the same impressions as the other man, but he had none of Széchenyi's philosophical restraint or of his attachment to the Crown. He was a passionate character, big in every way: tall, with a great voice, tempestuous of soul, a vehement nationalist, very conscious of the need to defend the Magyars, both against the local Germans and Roumanians and also against the danger, of which he was acutely conscious, of Pan-Slavism, and a born rebel, of the type to see the root of all evil in 'Vienna'. His opportunity came in 1831, when the Gubernium began impressing recruits without having obtained from the Diet the vote which the Constitution required. Under his influence several Counties refused to supply recruits and announced that they would not obey the Gubernium until a Diet had been convoked and the administration reconstituted as the Constitution demanded.

The Crown sent down General Wlassics, the Ban of Croatia, as Royal Commissioner, but Wlassics himself reported in favour of remedying the grievances of the province. The Crown yielded, and convoked the Diet for June 1834, but took the precaution of packing it with no less than 231 official

THE SYSTEM ON THE WANE (1830-1835)

members, as against only ninety-two elected, and of replacing Wlassics by Archduke Ferdinand d'Este, sent down for the purpose from Galicia. Weeks of barren recrimination followed, the Opposition denying the legality of the Government majority; then on 6 February 1835, the Crown dissolved the Diet, suspended the Constitution, forbade the Congregations to meet and left the Archduke in charge with unrestricted plenipotentiary powers.[1]

The waves of this disturbance spread to Inner Hungary, for Wesselényi had been given an estate there and was thus entitled to attend the Diet as a Hungarian magnate.[2] In December 1834 he had made a typically forceful speech in a Hungarian town, denouncing the Crown's reactionary attitude over the peasant question. The Crown issued writs against him, both in Hungary and Transylvania, for subversive agitation. As he could not be arrested while the Diet was in session, he remained at large, a popular idol, while the Hungarian nobles fumed at what they described as an unprecedented and illegal infringement of their right of free speech.

Simultaneously with this again, the political atmosphere in Croatia was undergoing a transformation as sudden and as spectacular as that in Hungary itself.

If we seek any special cause for the extraordinary developments in these years in what had previously been perhaps the most rigidly backward-looking corner of the whole Monarchy, we may perhaps find it in the reincorporation in Civilian Croatia, in 1824, of areas (no small part of the country) which had passed fifteen years first under French, then Austrian, rule, so that men now walked the streets of Zagreb and Karlovac who had been instructed in revolutionary principles by French masters, and rubbed shoulders at German high-schools with romantic Slavomanes. Here was, as it were, a tinder impregnated with the spirit of the age; but as in Hungary and Transylvania, the spark to set it ablaze was struck by a single man, who was actually of a younger generation still.

This man was a certain Ljudevit Gaj, who had been born as recently as 1809, in Krapina, in the Zagorje, son of a village apothecary (who, incidentally, like his wife, whose name was Schmidt, was of German stock). The young Gaj's parentage was thus humble, but not so humble as to deny him education, and after leaving gymnasium in 1826, he attended University courses in Vienna, Graz and Pest. His months in Pest were crucial, for here he came under the influence of Kollar, who encouraged his political, literary and philological ambitions and largely shaped his ideas.

---

[1] It should be mentioned that in this year the two Roumanian Bishops, Leményi and Moga, sent in a petition on roughly the same terms as the 'Supplex Libellus Valachorum' of 1791. This was, however, refused.

[2] A friend, Count György Károlyi, had presented him with a small estate in County Szathmár for that purpose to qualify him.

The nationalism which Gaj brought back to Zagreb, when he returned there in 1831, was totally different from that rigid defence of noble privileges which thitherto had constituted the sum of Croat politics. This is not to say that it was revolutionary in the social or inner-political sense: Gaj and his friends were almost all students or honoratiores, whose minds were too full of higher things to trouble about the grievances of the Croat peasants. But they were also without positive interest in the maintenance of noble prerogatives: the object of their enthusiasm was their people as a whole, without distinction of class, and their goal the cultivation and satisfaction of everything which was 'national' – language, customs, tradition and the political ambitions devolving from them. In this sense their nationalism was modern, and total.

It was total also in its disregard of political boundaries: what mattered to it was the nation to which a man belonged, not whether he lived in Civilian Croatia, in the Frontier, in Dalmatia or even in Bosnia. But it was a curious fact, and one of considerable importance for the history of the next five years, that Gaj, the catalytic agent who released the modern Croat national movement, was not a Croat nationalist at all in the narrower sense of the term. He had learned, especially from Kollar, to hold that all Slavs were members of one family, but within this he discerned a closer relationship between the members of its Southern Slav branch – Croats, Serbs, Slovenes and Bulgars. These he regarded as forming a single 'Illyrian' nation *in posse*, and his first activities were largely devoted to trying to bring these peoples to adopt the common language which was the pre-condition of their becoming a nation *in esse*. This, in the end, had highly peculiar results. Gaj succeeded in swinging the entire literary language of his own Croat people from the *kay* dialect of Southern Slav native to them to the *Što* dialect spoken in Herzegovina and Southern Dalmatia, and already adopted by the Serb linguistic *maestro* of the day, Vuk Karadžić, for his own people,[1] written in an orthography modelled on the Czech; but he was unable to persuade the Serbs to adopt the Latin alphabet (which the priests denounced as a devilish machination of Rome's to seduce them from the true faith), nor the Slovenes to abandon their own spoken forms.[2] The net result was thus the survival of two[3] distinct although related spoken languages, Slovene and Serbo-Croat, and of two alphabets, the Latin, used by Slovenes and Croats, and the Cyrillic. used by Serbs; literary (and ultimately, spoken) Croat becoming the same language, in its forms, as Serb, but being written in the same orthography as Slovene.

But Gaj's linguistic manipulations were unimportant compared with the

[1] *Što* and *kao* are the dialectical forms of the word meaning 'what' used in various Southern Slav districts. A third form, the *ča*, was used in Istria, on the Croat littoral, in Northern Dalmatia and on the Dalmatian islands.
[2] See above, p. 225.
[3] Three if Bulgarian is included.

extraordinary stimulus which he – a totally unoriginal thinker, a poor writer, a man without birth or connections, and to boot, only in his early twenties – succeeded in giving to national feeling in his country. This was, indeed, awakening all round him, without his intervention: in 1832 one of Croatia's own magnates, Baron Rukavina, had addressed the Sabor in Croat, and in the same year a fiery pamphlet had appeared (in German) under the title *Sollen wir Magyaren werden?*.[1] But Gaj possessed an almost magical gift for making disciples and also securing patrons, and in 1833 he brought off two extraordinary *coups* in the latter respect.

He had decided to ask permission to publish a periodical. On this quest he travelled to Vienna, passing through Pozsony, where he called on the Croat delegates to the Long Diet, and one of these, Count Janko Drašković, he converted completely to his ideas. This was an event of extraordinary importance, for Drašković was no obscure young honoratior; he was a Count, a member of one of Croatia's most illustrious families, a member of the Hungarian (or Hungaro-Croat) House of Magnates, an Imperial and Royal Chamberlain and an Army Colonel. If he pointed to a road, a large proportion of those Croats who counted would follow it.

Gaj's second success was in Vienna. He saw Kolowrat, whom he told that his purpose was:

> Primarily, to influence opinion among the Croats and Slovenes against Hungary's purpose of achieving independence through the Magyar language, and to strengthen their (the Slavs) attachment to the throne; further, to influence in favour of attachment to Austria the Slav peoples bordering on the Austrian Monarchy, the Serbs, Bosnyaks, Herzegovinians, Montenegrins and Turkish Croats, who appear to be chained to Russia through the influence which it exercises in their favour.

These purposes seemed to Kolowrat admirable. Gaj got his licence, and in January 1835 his daily paper, the *Novine Hrvatska* (Croat News) began to appear, with a weekly literary supplement, the *Danica* (Morning Star).

The new militant Croat nationalism was now fairly launched, and it was, as we have said, something totally different from what had previously passed under that name. It was an orgy of ultra-chauvinistic self-glorification, which claimed for the Croats every virtue, and every reward of virtue, which fantasy could think up. And first and foremost, it was almost hysterically anti-Magyar. As Kossuth attributed every evil in Hungary to the domination of 'Vienna', so Gaj, even more vehemently, ascribed all Croatia's troubles

---

[1] According to R. W. Seton-Watson, *The Southern Slav Question*, p. 27, the author of this pamphlet, which was long attributed to Kollar, was A. Vakanović, at one time Vice-Ban of Croatia; but Wendel, *Aus dem Südslavischen Risorgimento*, p. 53, writing much later, still attributes it to Kollar, and says that it was 'originally only intended for Slovaks', which makes sense, because its whole argument was directed against linguistic enactments which the Hungarians themselves were not trying to introduce into Croatia.

to her association with Hungary. The following effusion, from Gaj's own pen, is an example of the pabulum dished out to the Croat public by its new leaders:

The hour of triumph strikes for us! Only unity! Hold together, be one! All is morning, all is astir, from the Adriatic to the Balkans. Slavs, born heroes, unfurl your banners, gird you with your swords, mount your steeds! Forward, brothers, God is with us, against us the Devil. See how the wild Tatar race, the Magyar, tramples on our tongue, our nation: but before he crushes us, let us cast him into the pit of Hell. Forward, brothers, God is with us, against us the Devil. The heroic Slav of the North clasps the hand of the Illyrian of the South in the heroic dance; the trumpet sounds, the swords clash, the cannon roar. Let us wash our honour clean in the blood of the enemy; let each cleave one skull and our suffering will be at an end. Forward, brothers, etc.

7

The Vormärz

On 24 February 1835, Francis was seized by a sharp fever, and in the small hours of 2 March he died. His peoples had grown so accustomed to his hand that when it was removed, leaving poor Ferdinand nominal ruler of the Monarchy, not only grief was felt, but deep anxiety over what the future would bring. A year before, Kübeck had prophesied that the Emperor's death would be followed by anarchy.

But the first sequel was merely an unseemly scramble for power. As Francis lay dying, Bishop Wagner had extracted his signature to two documents, both addressed to his heir. In the first he enjoined Ferdinand 'not to displace the bases of the structure of the State, to rule[1] and not alter', to hold fast to the principles by which Francis had guided the Monarchy through the storms of hard times. He was to preserve unity in the Imperial family and 'in important internal (innere) affairs'[2] to take counsel of the Archduke Ludwig. 'Bestow on Prince Metternich, my most faithful servant and friend,' the document concluded, 'the trust which I have reposed in him during so many years. Take no decision on public affairs, or respecting persons, without hearing him. I enjoin him, for his part, to show you the same sincerity and faithful devotion as he has always displayed towards me.'

The second document enjoined Ferdinand to continue the task, still incomplete, of correcting and modifying those parts of the Josephinian Law which impeded the free activity and other rights of the Church, and conflicted with the doctrines, constitution or discipline of the Church, and in particular with the decisions of the Council of Trent. Here, too, he was to listen to the advice of Metternich, and of Bishop Wagner.

The second of these documents had been literally composed by Wagner; the first had, except for the sentence relating to the Archduke Ludwig, not been actually dictated word for word by Metternich,[3] but very nearly so.

[1] i.e., to confine himself to high policy, not to meddle with details of administration.

[2] It will be remembered (see above, p. 239) that Ludwig had for several years been the only one of his brothers whom Francis still consulted. The designation of him as adviser in chief to Ferdinand was therefore, although unfortunate, logical enough, and should not be regarded as a piece of Macchiavellian intrigue by Metternich to increase his own influence. It was, in fact, the one part of the document which was Francis's own work.

[3] It reproduced practically verbatim a draft which had been composed by Metternich as early as 1832 (Bibl, *Kaiser Franz*, pp. 387–8).

Metternich's opponents naturally could not accept such a shameless jumping of claims, so transparently designed, not only to put Metternich in, but also to keep Kolowrat out. An embittered struggle set in, the details of which have little historic importance;[1] it ended on 12 December 1836, with the establishment of what amounted to a Council of Regency. A Staatskonferenz[2] was set up under the nominal presidency of Ferdinand; but in his absence (which, it was assumed, would be the rule), the Archduke Ludwig was to preside. Its other permanent members (it called in consultants *ad hoc* at will) were the Archduke Franz Karl, Metternich and Kolowrat. Metternich was to preside in Ludwig's absence, but his sphere of action and Kolowrat's were exactly defined: Metternich was in charge of foreign policy and Kolowrat, of domestic.[3] Only Ludwig could override either of them (Franz Karl was there simply to keep the place warm for his young son, and was not expected to play a much more active role than Ferdinand himself).[4]

The Staatskonferenz was advised, in certain of its functions, by a Staats- und Konferenzrat (the latest avatar of the old *Staatsrat*), now composed of the three heads of the Departments of the Interior, Defence and Finance, seven Privy Councillors and seven *rapporteurs* (Referenten) on special subjects. Metternich's proposal to create a Reichsrat had, however, been defeated, so that the whole Government machinery remained essentially bureaucratic and, except as regards Hungary, strongly centralist.

Thus anarchy was averted, and a regime restored the avowed purpose of which was to perpetuate the stability which Francis had regarded as the end of government; but it was an incomparably less effective instrument for achieving this than Francis's personal will had been. The only two members of the Conference who performed their duties quite adequately were Ferdinand himself, and Franz Karl; they had nothing to do, and that was what they did. Ludwig was not such a fool as he is often described, possessed of considerable experience, and not a null, and there was nothing obscure about his intentions; he was as conservative by temperament as Francis himself, and in any case regarded it as an injunction of piety to fulfil his brother's dying command and 'not to alter' (according to some writers, he had

---

[1] The most interesting feature of the prolonged intrigues is the warm support which Kolowrat received from the Archduke John.

[2] Sometimes called by contemporary writers the Staats-und Konferenzministerium.

[3] He gave up his direct official position, but all reports from the Staatsrat came to him for comment and report. He was in direct charge of high finance, including secret credit operations, with power to call on the advice of the financial sections of the Staatsrat and the President of the Hofkammer. He also was given charge of the police, subject only to the obligation of reporting to Metternich police business which touched on foreign affairs.

[4] His wife, the Archduchess Sophie (not, of course, an unbiased witness), represents his role as having been rather less passive than is usually supposed. 'Uncle Ludwig's modesty and timidity', she writes, 'need my husband's support whenever a decision has to be taken' (Corti, *Von Kind bis Kaiser*, p. 165).

actually sworn to do so); but he did not possess Francis's personal authority. He remained a weak ass couching between two burdens. If the effect of the labours of the two really important members of the Conference, Metternich and Kolowrat, was indeed to produce a high measure of immobility, it was not the purposeful immobility imposed by a single will, but the stalemate which results from equal and opposite forces. If one of the two tried to move in any direction, the other painstakingly thwarted him if he saw a chance; and the opportunities arose often enough, for no ingenuity could assign the questions of highest policy exclusively to the competence of one man or the other.

This however was only an immobility of the institutions and machinery for dealing with affairs; not of the affairs themselves. The old freezing apparatus – if the metaphor is permissible – was still there, but the radius of its effectiveness diminished year by year. The Vormärz was in fact a period big with change. While – to change the metaphor again – the structure stood unaltered, only growing visibly shabbier and losing a brick or a tile here and there, new forces, national, economic, social and political, were accumulating and surging round its foundations, threatening alike its internal stability, and its defences against the outer world.

Chief among the subjects on which Metternich and Kolowrat pulled in opposite directions was the old question whether Austria should follow an ambitious foreign policy such as the one desired, or should, as the other maintained, cut her coat according to her cloth. The issue was really a financial one, and in general, the state of the national finances affected so powerfully almost every development of the period that we shall only be paying the subject its due if we devote to it the first of the pages which follow.

In this field, stability had really been achieved in one respect. The National Bank had succeeded in withdrawing from circulation the great mass of State paper money, of various issues, leaving in circulation (besides the metallic *Konventionsmünzen*) only its own notes, which up to the very eve of the revolution were convertible against silver and accepted at their face value, both at home and abroad. Nevertheless, the Achilles' heel remained. Rigid economy in expenditure had kept the normal annual budgetary deficits to a relatively low figure,[1] but revenue, too, had remained low. Largely owing to the delays in introducing the new land tax, the yield of direct taxation in Austria had risen only fractionally;[2] while in Hungary, where noble land remained tax-free, it hardly rose at all.[3] That of indirect taxation, the

[1] In 1836 it had been 13·5 m.g.; in 1837, 8·5; in 1838, 15·5. The figures for the next decade were similar.

[2] Beer, op. cit., p. 172, gives the figures of 43·8 m.g. in 1831 and 47·9 m.g. in 1847. For the delay in introducing the land tax, see above, p. 203.

[3] In 1846 Hungary, with seven-eighteenths of the population of the Monarchy, was only yielding less than one-seventh of its total direct and indirect taxation (23,227,333 g. out of a total of 164,236,758).

most productive item of which was the unpopular 'consumption tax' (octroi), had risen faster, but still hardly more than the growth of the population,[1] so that revenue never matched even ordinary expenditure, and almost every year the State borrowed afresh, sometimes in the form of lottery loans, which had become a very favourite device, sometimes by borrowing directly from the small ring of private banking houses (Rothschild, Sina and a few more) which specialized in the operation.[2] Alternatively, the State borrowed from the National Bank, which, given the composition of the shareholders of that body, came to the same thing.

The two men who were in charge of Austria's finances during the period – Peter Eichhoff, who succeeded Klebelsberg as President of the Hofkammer in 1835, and in whose favour Kolowrat, whose protégé he was, then renounced the charge of 'high finance', and Kübeck, who took over in 1840[3] – devoted their chief efforts to keeping Austria's credit good, so that the loans could be floated on reasonable terms, and were not unsuccessful. These loans, however, were hardly ever devoted to developing the national resources and increasing taxable capacity; nearly always, they were simply used to cover deficits in ordinary current expenditure, so that the chief result of them was simply that the indebtedness of the State went on rising, and an increasing proportion of its revenues had to be devoted to payments (interest and amortization) on the debt. It was calculated in the 1840s that the State debt had more than trebled in twenty-five years (by 1847 it had reached the figure of 1,131 million gulden)[4] and the service of it multiplied tenfold, not counting payments on lottery loans; by 1847 the interest was 45 million gulden, plus 6 million gulden for amortization – almost as much as the total yield of direct taxation. It may be added that the political effects of this development were not inconsiderable, for to the oversimplifying popular eye, the State was becoming simply a gigantic machine which milked the many for the benefit of the few.

Meanwhile, even the convertibility of the bank notes was precarious. The public had not forgotten the experiences of its fathers. The scare of 1840, when the development of the Eastern crisis made war with France an apparent possibility, brought a run on the National Bank which reduced its metal coverage to 1:11.

In 1841 the State burdened itself with a new item of expenditure. Among the things to which the logically-minded Francis had objected had been

---

[1] Here Beer's figures are 62·92 m.g. in 1830 and 79·03 m.g. in 1847. These include the yield of customs and excise.

[2] For a list of these loans see Beer, pp. 159 ff.

[3] Eichhoff had resigned under suspicion of irregularities, which may have been unfounded; see Beer, pp. 149 ff.

[4] A. Gratz, op. cit., p. 250 gives a slightly lower figure: 984 m.g. at the beginning of 1848.

railways, which, he said, 'would only bring revolution into the country'. If, nevertheless, Austria had boasted the first railway on the Continent, a line between Budweis and Linz opened in 1832, neither the freight nor the motive-power of this had been alarmingly newfangled: salt the former, the latter, horses. But meanwhile an imaginative engineer named Riepl had worked out, single-handed, plans for a complete network of railways to link Vienna with Galicia. He had succeeded in interesting Salamon Rothschild, and hardly were Francis's eyes closed when Rothschild persuaded his patron (or client) Metternich to give him a concession to build a line from Bochnia, in Galicia, to Vienna. After prolonged initial difficulties, the stretch between Vienna and Brünn was opened in 1839. After this the network extended rapidly, the lines in the north being constructed chiefly under the auspices of the Rothschilds, while their rival, Baron Sina, secured the concession for a line to connect Vienna with Budapest and for the Südbahn which was to link Vienna with Trieste; the line from Vienna to Gloggnitz was opened in 1841, by which time 473 kilometres of line in all had been constructed.

For various reasons, among which the clever propaganda carried on by the Rothschilds was not the least, the public had not extended to the railways, in spite of the low yields on their shares,[1] its aversion to investing in private enterprise, but unfortunately for it, there were many irregularities and much money was lost. The State then decided to expand the railway network itself, as a matter of public interest. It carried on the work with some vigour, so that by the end of 1847 the length of the line had reached 1,401 kilometres,[2] 478 of which was State property. It was indeed obviously a necessity for the Monarchy that it should possess a railway system, but meanwhile, the construction cost the State considerable sums which, again, were largely raised by borrowing. Economies were partly achieved by underpaying the civil servants, whose position became steadily more difficult as prices rose (to the detriment of both their efficiency and their integrity) and partly, at the expense of the army, which, after the untimely death in 1837 of its competent Adjutant-General, Count Clam-Martinitz, had no influential champion to speak for it in high circles. On this point Kolowrat defeated Metternich. The annual army budget was kept down to some fifty to sixty million gulden annually. To achieve this, in spite of the rapidly increasing population of the Monarchy, the nominal peace strength of the army at the beginning of 1847 was still only a little over 400,000 (war strength about 630,000) and the number of men actually with the colours ranged between 210,000–230,000; it was, moreover, still composed largely, perhaps mainly, of elements whom local authorities found undesirable

---

[1] The Nordbahn shares paid only $2\frac{1}{2}$%. Nevertheless speculation in them drove them up to great heights.

[2] 1,048 in Austria, 161 in Hungary and 182 in Lombardy-Venetia.

and rid themselves of by the simple expedient of handing them over to the recruiting sergeant. Both the moral and the physical condition of the men were low. Its equipment had been little modernized for thirty years.

In spite of this essential weakness in his position, if it should ever be challenged, Metternich retained unmodified his old vision of Austria (and himself) as guardian of order in Europe, and it must be said that he exercised this with all his old diplomatic expertise. He was further supremely fortunate in having as his immediate negotiating partners men who sympathized with his ideas of order, and in many cases, were ready to accept his leadership. Nicholas of Russia remained loyal to the pledge given by him at Münchengrätz, and if there were considerable differences between Russia and Austria during the Eastern crisis of 1839–40, they were bridged over and the former friendship restored without Austria's interests on the Lower Danube, or in the Balkans, having been seriously impaired. Frederick William III of Prussia continued until his death in 1840 to obey faithfully his motto to work, not indeed under Austria, but always with her; and his romantic son and successor, Frederick William IV, readily acknowledged the supremacy of the 'Archhouse' of Habsburg. Up to almost the last days of the Vormärz the great majority of the Princes of Italy gratefully accepted that Austrian support to which, as they were well aware, they owed their thrones; even Charles Albert of Piedmont hid his true ambitions so well that when, in 1842, he married his son to a Habsburg Princess, Radetzky, commanding the Austrian army in Lombardy-Venetia, referred to the Piedmontese army as 'the advance guard of the Imperial forces'.

But this was pre-eminently a pool on which the ice was growing thinner year by year. In Germany and Italy both liberal and national feeling were growing apace, and to the votaries of both goddesses, Metternich's Austria now appeared as the arch-obstacle to the realization of their dreams. His 'system' was now resting solely on the goodwill of the Monarchs, and would find it difficult to survive, either if the peoples as a whole combined to overthrow his allies, or if one of them changed sides and put himself at the head of a national movement. And in both Germany and Italy the possibilities of either development increased in the 1840s. Although Frederick William IV's loyalty, and also his own exceedingly mediaevalist mentality, kept him aloof from the German movement towards unification, yet the continued extension and consolidation of the Zollverein was inexorably turning Prussia into the *de facto* leader of Germany. In 1841 Austria was given one more chance to reverse this process. Quarters in South Germany, to which the growth of Prussian influence was unwelcome on both economic and political grounds, invited Austria to join the Zollverein, or perhaps to place herself

THE VORMÄRZ

at the head of a rival grouping, but the Staatskonferenz, after long discussion and against the wishes of both Metternich and Kübeck, rejected the offer, partly owing to very strong objections from the Austrian industrialists, and partly because the mouthpieces of the Austrian producers were not prepared to renounce the protection which they still enjoyed against Hungary, as would be necessary if the Monarchy as a whole came into a German customs unit, while to leave Hungary outside would have weakened still further the links between her and the rest of the Monarchy, and been a blow to Vienna's own allies in Hungary. A year later, as is described elsewhere, the Staatskonferenz decided that Austrian production could face Hungarian competition, and tried to introduce inter-Monarchic free trade, but now the offer was rejected by the nationalists in the Hungarian Diet,[1] and Prussia, too, objected very strongly. When, eight years later again, Schwarzenberg, having crushed Hungary's resistance, tried to import the entire Monarchy into the Zollverein, it was too late.[2]

At the same time, Metternich's attempts (in which, again, he was supported by Kübeck) to counter the growth of Prussian influence by establishing a closer economic connection between Austria and Italy, especially through the development of railways from Central Germany to the Austrian ports, was one of the factors which stimulated Piedmont to greater activity and marked out its ruler as the future leader of united Italy.[3]

The end of all the talks was a decision to maintain the existing system of prohibitions and high tariffs, although modifications might be introduced in individual cases.[4]

There remained Russia; and not everybody was glad of it. The popular view that Metternich's Austria had sunk into the position of the Czar's European outpost and police-agent was certainly exaggerated; but it was true that the leading role in the partnership was passing, inevitably, to the partner which was in fact the stronger, and its perception, and resentment, of the fact was one of the causes of the suspicion with which Liberal opinion in the Monarchy regarded Metternich and his 'system'.

And the relationship with Russia itself became heavily overclouded at the end of the period.[5] The Czar conceived the idea of cementing it by marrying his beautiful daughter, Olga, to an Austrian Archduke, but when the Archduke Albrecht was sent to Petersburg in 1839, the young Grand Duchess would have none of him. In 1845, then, her father thought of marrying her to the more attractive Stephen, son of the Palatine of Hungary and his

[1] See below, p. 261.
[2] See below, p. 433 f.
[3] It is, however, noteworthy that in Lombardy, unlike Hungary, there was no national feeling against the Zollverein.
[4] The Emperor's decision to this effect was delivered on 9 May 1844.
[5] On this see Srbik, II. 138–9; also Corti, pp. 164, 218 ff.

father's successor-designate in that role, and to this she consented, but the Catholic party at the Court of Vienna insisted that the prospective bride must be received into the Catholic Church. Metternich, fearing that the marriage would have unfavourable repercussions in Hungary, fomented the opposition, and the Czar had to call the plan off. He was deeply wounded, and carried away from the visit to Vienna at which the snub was admistered the most unfavourable view imaginable of the Monarchy and its rulers; a tottering, ramshackle edifice, which was 'sick, very sick', and must soon perish, while the existing rulers were either born incompetents, or senile.

At home, the Staatskonferenz obeyed the injunctions contained in Francis's political testament with scrupulous loyalty. At the outset of the new regime certain gestures were made to popularize it, among them, an extensive amnesty for political prisoners, under which a large number of Italians, in particular, benefited. These, however, were not followed by any modification of the nature of the regime, which, so far as the western half of the Monarchy was concerned, remained one of bureaucratic rule, censorship and police supervision. In some few aspects, the rules were even more severe than before; thus it was made more difficult than ever for Austrian students to attend foreign universities, or vice versa. The only question relating to the nature of the regime on which there was any serious debate for or against the *status quo* was how far Francis's second set of injunctions were to be carried out. The 'Pious Party' had become very strong at Court, especially since the arrival of the Archduchess Sophie. Metternich had attached himself to it unreservedly. Other leading members of it were Metternich's secretary, Jarcke, and most important of all, the young and highly intelligent Joseph Othmar von Rauscher, who provided the movement with its theory. This was that while the authority of the Crown should be made unshakeable by any revolutionary force, the Josephinian system was not conducive to that end. The Church was the natural ally of the Crown against their common enemy, the subversive forces of enlightenment and godlessness, but it could not play its part in a condition of semi-servitude to a Government itself tainted with enlightenment. It must enjoy complete freedom, which should be ratified by a Concordat.

Rauscher is one of the most important figures in the history of the Monarchy, for in 1844 the Dowager-Empress got him appointed tutor in philosophy to the Archduchess Sophie's three sons, and the influence which he thus acquired over the mind of Francis Joseph largely determined the latter's policy in the field of Church-State relations when he came to the throne. In the 1840s the forces were still evenly matched, and the struggle ended in a characteristic draw. The Pious Party registered certain successes. The Society of Jesus was re-admitted to all parts of the Monarchy, and the Ligurians allowed to establish themselves there. In 1837 a small group of Protestants which had managed to survive in the Tirol were forced to emigrate.¹ But continued negotiations with the Holy See for a Concordat foundered on the opposition of the Josephinian Party, with which Kolowrat associated himself. In 1841 the Vatican made one concession, on mixed marriages – a question which events in Germany had made *actuel*: it recognized as *illicita sed valida* marriages contracted in Hungary before a non-Catholic Minister, but in Lands belonging to the German Bund such marriages were valid only if a Catholic Minister had attended the ceremony, and only if safeguards were given that the children of the marriage would be brought up in the Catholic faith. The concession did not apply at all to Galicia, Lombardy-Venetia, or Dalmatia.² The Vatican refused to go further, and put forward, on its side, wishes³ which the Government declined to accept; a Commission established to consider them had not completed its work by 1848.

A less easily perceptible, but not unimportant feature of the period was the recovery made during it by the great feudal aristocracy of much of the political and other influence lost by that class in the years when Francis's absolutism was at its height. The tide had already begun to turn again when Francis grew old and left the conduct of internal affairs to Kolowrat, for Kolowrat was a strong and systematic supporter of the class to which he himself belonged.⁴ It came in with a rush when Kolowrat got an entirely free hand during the 'despotism without a despot', as poor Ferdinand's 'reign' has been called.

This does not mean that the State bureaucracy re-ceded any of the functions which it was now carrying out to the 'self-governing institutions'. That would have meant changing the political structure of the State, which was a *noli me tangere* like all its institutions; for that matter, it was only when the High Vormärz was nearly out that the Estates themselves began asking for any such concessions. Nor does it mean that there was any reduction in the numbers of the bureaucracy, the size and expensiveness of which continued to elicit endless complaints from the malcontents of the day (Andrian's famous pamphlet, *Oesterreich und dessen Zukunft*, is full of them),⁵ but in vain, nor even

---

[1] This was a little group inhabiting the Zillertal, which had been transferred in 1816 from Salzburg, where the practice of Protestantism had been allowed, to the Tirol, where it was forbidden. They were given the customary choice between renunciation of the faith and emigration. Most of them chose the latter. The King of Prussia gave them asylum.

[2] It was, however, extended to Galicia in 1842.

[3] These were, roughly, those for which it asked after 1848; see below, p. 458.

[4] Not, however, of the lesser nobility, which, according to Beidtel (II. 228), he thought too numerous. But by now the lesser nobility had in any case lost its footing on the land almost everywhere, and most of such of its members as had escaped ruin had merged in the *Beamtenadel*.

[5] To us, indeed, the figures appear modest enough. Springer (*Statistik* II. 9) gives for the whole Monarchy when he wrote (1842) a total of 34,350 Grade A civil servants, of whom 27,430 were established, 5,190 '*Praktikanten*', or probationers, and 1,630 *Diurnisten* (extra hands, often ex-officers, who were taken on when there was a rush of work) and 91,880

that its composition as a whole became more aristocratic. Indeed, the proportion of non-nobles in it rose steadily during Ferdinand's reign, as it had during that of Francis. But the influx of non-nobles was almost all at the bottom end, into the obscurer and less well-paid posts, and the difference in salary levels between these and the higher grades was very large indeed.[1] These men were, moreover, kept for years, sometimes for a lifetime, before they even became established, against which the device of 'supernumerary service', which had been relatively rare in earlier times, now became almost the rule for the fortunate. It was even rarer than a generation before for a man of humble origin to reach an important post.[2] Thus the aristocrats dominated the Civil Service itself, and if they could not get the centralist system altered, they ruled the Western half of the Monarchy from inside it probably more completely than they had since the days of Charles VI.

So far as this recovered power of the aristocracy went, it was another factor operating against change, for the aristocracy lived in an even more remote past than the bureaucracy.

Meanwhile, however, life had not, after all, left the Monarchy untouched since 1792. The population, the growth of which had been slow in most Lands during the wars – in some, it had actually declined – had increased very rapidly after the return of peace. Still relatively modest in certain of the Alpine Lands, such as Upper Austria and Carinthia, and in North-Western and Northern Hungary, the growth had been almost precipitate in the Bohemian Lands and Galicia, and in those parts of the Monarchy such as

---

Grade B. 16,000 of the Grade A and 84,000 Grade B were employed in the financial services; in other words, most of them were douaniers or excisemen. The strength of the central administration was 100 *Hofräte*, 95 *Hofsekretäre* and 105 *Hofkonzipisten*. The staff of a Kreisamt in the 1840s still consisted only of one *Kreishauptmann*, two to four *Kreiskommissäre*, and a handful of copyists, messengers, etc. In the Monarchy as a whole, one person in every 1,030 of the population was an official. The proportion was naturally highest (1:298) in Lower Austria, where the central Ministries had their headquarters; in Styria it was 1:950, in Bohemia 1:647, in Transylvania 1:2,361 and in Hungary only 1:2,730. The total salaries paid amounted to 38,249,879 fl., while pensions, etc., cost another 6,758,250 fl. This, as will be seen, was substantially less than the cost of the armed forces, and less than that of the service of the public debt. The figures given by Turnbull (I. 371) are practically identical; those of the *Statistische Tabellen* for 1828 somewhat smaller (32,157 and 78,614), but the proportion to the total population is practically the same.

[1] The President of the Superior Court in Verona, for example, received 20,000 fl. a year, the Hungarian Országbiró, 14,000, etc., while a minor official might be getting only 3–400. For an interesting picture of the financial vicissitudes of an official family (which fared, indeed, far better than the average) see the biographical introduction to Beidtel, op. cit.

[2] The case of Kübeck, the provincial tailor's son who rose to be President of the Hofkammer, is often quoted as proof that promotion was not impossible for a man of lowly birth. But Kübeck's case was conspicuous precisely because it was so exceptional. Incidentally, it was Francis who first raised him out of the ruck, and according to Beidtel (pp. 224–5), he owed his further advance largely to his connections with the financial world.

Central and Southern Hungary into which internal immigration was going on. By 1843 the total population of the Monarchy was some 37·5 millions – 17·1 in the Western Lands, 15·6 in the Hungarian and 4·8 in Lombardy-Venetia, an average over-all increase on 1792 of some forty per cent.

Most of the absolute increase had still been on the land, but relatively, the growth had been much faster in the towns. Vienna had now a population of nearly 400,000, Milan, nearly 150,000, Prague, over 100,000 and Venice little short of it, Pest, 80,000 (with Buda, across the river, another 40,000), Lemberg and Trieste each over 50,000, Graz 44,000, etc.

While agriculture was still the largest single industry in the Monarchy as a whole, and in nearly all parts of it, other occupations were creeping up on it. Even during the last years of Francis's lifetime, the advocates of economic liberalism and of industrialization had been gaining ground, and after his death, practically all restrictions on the foundation of new enterprises, at least those falling within the category of *Kommerzialgewerke*, had been removed. The Government had still little positive economic policy except that represented by the maintenance of import restrictions and high tariffs (which, as always, were largely evaded by smuggling, which had developed into a major national industry) and measures which cost it nothing, such as the ennoblement of successful entrepreneurs, and especially under Kübeck's regime it had largely counteracted even these by its rigid restriction of the note circulation, its own repeated applications to the money market, resulting in the issue of an unending stream of State obligations, and its insistence that its own demands for any available credit must have priority.[1] The little ring of professional bankers found that it earned them both better marks, and more profit, to take their rake-off from Government loans, than to invest in agriculture or industry: this was so much the case that although the National Bank's original statutes had empowered it to make advances on real property, it had never made use of this power, which was actually omitted when the statutes were revised in 1846. The unofficial sources of non-exorbitant credit were the various foundations, and they, too, tended to put their profits into State papers, as did the big majority of small savers.

The investing public tended to follow the bankers' lead, with the single exception which, as mentioned above, it made in favour of railway shares when the first private railway companies were floated. After its unfortunate experiences in this field, it returned to its old habits, while the nationalization of the railways turned the cost of their construction again into a responsibility of the exchequer.

In spite of all these handicaps, the passing of the great post-war depression had after all been accompanied by a considerable amount of industrialization.

[1] In 1840 117·8 of the 170·8 m.g. transactions carried through by the National Bank were with the Government (Beer, p. 157).

The old-established industries of silk-weaving, leather goods, furniture, brewing, etc., which were chiefly centred round Vienna, expanded largely, as did the woollens industry of Moravia and Upper Bohemia. In the late 1830s the cotton industry of Lower Austria and, in particular, Bohemia, made a phenomenal spurt which was accompanied by a sudden change-over from relatively old-fashioned methods to highly mechanized modern ones, involving the use of labour-saving machinery operated under factory conditions.[1] The number of enterprises in the cotton-spinning industry (exclusive of Lombardy-Venetia) rose from 110 in 1829 to 135 in 1841 and 149 in 1843, some of these being really large: the Pottendorf works outside Vienna, which had been founded in 1803 by two foreign entrepreneurs, one of them an Englishman, had nearly 47,000 spindles. By 1847 the total had risen to 204 mills, with 1,356,000 spindles. The import of cotton yarn into the Monarchy multiplied eight-fold between 1835 and 1842 and that of raw cotton, three-fold. Where the cotton-spinning had led, other industries followed. The first steam-driven machine in the entire Monarchy (for a cloth factory in Brünn) had begun work in 1816, the first in Lower Austria, ten years later. The figure in 1841 was 219 (79 in Bohemia, 77 in Moravia-Silesia, 56 in Lower Austria, three in the Littoral, one each in Styria and Tirol) with 2,939 H.P.

These were also the years in which the first railways began operating, an event which laid the foundations for the true development of Austrian industry in a modern sense, especially of its heavy industries, the establishment of which on a large scale had previously been prevented by the impossibility of bringing fuel to them, or carrying their produce away from them. A considerable number of such industries sprang up (or old ones expanded) in connection with the railway programme itself, for which it was decided to use home-made products. In particular, a great stimulus was given to the production of iron and coal. The production of coal rose from 2 million Zentner in 1820 to nearly 10 million in 1848,[2] that of iron in the Bohemian Lands

---

[1] This was largely due to a freak of natural conditions. Up to the late 1830s the cotton-spinners of Bohemia, among whom the process began, had depended largely on small machines driven by water-power. Two abnormally dry years put many of these water-wheels out of action, and the cotton-masters went over in a hand's turn to steam-driven machines. (See G. Otruba in *Bohemia*, II. pp. 153 ff.) Whence they suddenly acquired the cash or the credit for this operation is a question to which I have vainly sought the answer. Zenker, however, quotes the following figures for imported machinery and parts (in m.g.):

	machines	parts
1836	93	40
1837	298	54
1838	345	46
1839	350	50

The figures remained on approximately this level for the next ten years.

[2] This was partly because coal was replacing charcoal. The first trains used wood, but they soon went over to coal.

alone rose from 300,000 to 900,000 Zentner, and that in Styria was almost as high.

Counting factory labour and the old handicraftsmen together, it was estimated that in 1846, 16·73% of the population of the Monarchy was deriving its living from industry and mining, against 73–74% from agriculture, a small figure compared with that of the England of the day, especially when it is remembered that in the less advanced Lands most of the 'industrialists' were still simply village smiths, cartwrights or cobblers, but still an appreciable change compared with half a century earlier. The stage of development varied, indeed, largely from Land to Land. The most highly industrialized part of the Monarchy was the Lombardy-Venetian kingdom. Then came Lower Austria and the Bohemian Lands, whose heavy industry was still in the womb, but which now led in respect both of woollens and of cotton, the latter, in particular, employing a very large number of home-workers; it was calculated that one-quarter of the population of German Bohemia did spinning, this being the sole occupation of half of them. Hungary was further behind, since, other difficulties such as bad communications and primitive credit facilities apart, the old customs line between the two halves of the Monarchy was still standing. There were only eight steam-driven machines with 80 H.P. in Hungary and Transylvania in 1841. Nemes gives, for 1848, only 23,000 factory hands, 35,000 miners and 78,000 handworkers.[1] The figures for Galicia-Bukovina, were they available, would probably be lower still.

Meanwhile, the pattern of agriculture itself was beginning to change. As markets for their products increased, and as improved communications made them more accessible, more producers, large and small, but especially the former, were going over to production for profit. Besides the old staple crops of cereals, vegetable, wine and cattle, sheep-farming for wool had become an important industry, especially in Hungary, and industrial crops such as sugar beet and flax were being produced in the Bohemian Lands and Galicia.[2]

These developments brought with them a big increase in the propertied (outside the landed) and bourgeois classes of the Monarchy, especially in its larger centres, and above all, of course, in Vienna. Besides the landlords and State employees who had previously dominated these classes, there was now a whole society of persons connected with the production of the new manufactures, or as traders, with the exchange of them, and in their train a growing multitude of lawyers, doctors, teachers, architects, artists. A few members of this society, the financiers above all and some of the manufacturers, who made vast profits in good years, had accumulated great wealth; many more

[1] *Forradalom és Szabadságharc* 1848–9, p. 273.
[2] The first sugar-beet factory was established in 1830; Francis gave it a ten years' exemption from the *Erwerbssteuer*.

enjoyed competencies which the exceedingly low cost of living made reasonable.[1] It is on the agreeable and, so far as its elite was concerned, praiseworthy existence led by these classes that the panegyrists of Austria's good old days love to dwell, and Viennese 'culture' in these days in fact experienced a revival which was not profound, but nevertheless brought with it much that was attractive. As both the extreme financial stringency and the extreme political repression relaxed, something of the old, irrepressible light-heartedness crept back into Viennese life. In furniture and decoration, a breath of rococo, another of the indefinable local genius, softened the austere Franciscan pseudo-Empire into the intimate and graceful Biedermeier style. Caroline Pichler held a *salon* which did not attempt to imitate the extravagances of the Congress, but had its own elegance. It was no age of giants: the best painter of the day, Schwind, emigrated, and Waldmüller went unrecognized. The popular musicians, Lanner and Johann Strauss, were turners of valse tunes, not to compare in genius with the generation which had perished with Schubert, and most of the best-known writers of the day, Raimund, Nestroy, Bauernfeld, were the authors of comedies (the greatest figure of them all, Grillparzer, was, of course, more than that). But the comedies were very witty, and the valse-tunes more than catching. It was not even the case that, as later romanticists would have us believe, the life of the day exhausted itself altogether in light music, wine and society gossip. There was plenty of all of these, and it is probably true that there are few societies which have obeyed so generally, and with so little reluctance, the order of authority to 'run away and play, and don't meddle with what is not your business' as the Viennese bourgeoisie of the Vormärz. But it is only fair to record that a minority of its members performed distinguished work in many fields. The medical faculty of Vienna University regained its old standards when von Stift ceased to direct it; it now produced two figures of European calibre in Rokitansky and Skoda. Three Austrians, Prokesch-Osten, Hammer-Purgstall and Fallmerarer, were among the leading travellers and orientalists of their day. 1846 even saw, at long last, the foundation of an Academy of Sciences in Vienna which was destined to become one of the leading institutions of its kind in the world.[2]

---

[1] Turnbull met 'a gentleman attached to the University in Graz' who told him that he lived on 400 fl. a year, out of which he was able to buy books. Many bourgeois families 'lived well on 1,000–1,200 fl. a year' (op. cit., p. I. 265). Graz was, it is true, an exceptionally cheap town. Wilde met an enterprising Jew who ran a kindergarten in Vienna, and was able to give his charges a solid midday meal for a kreuzer apiece.

[2] We remarked above that the Academy was founded on Metternich's motion, and in fact, after opposing it before, he himself proposed its foundation in 1846. It is a curiosity of history that Ferdinand signed the order exempting the proceedings of the Academy's proceedings and publications from the normal censorship on 13 March 1848, the day of the outbreak of the revolution.

THE VORMÄRZ

Yet wishful memory, and the ecstasies of tourists so dazzled by the slick charms of Viennese life as to be unable to appreciate how much in them was bogus, should not blind us to the truth that for a substantial and growing proportion of the population of the Monarchy the Vormärz was a period of material hardship, and for considerable numbers, of naked destitution.

It is, indeed, not easy to form a judgment on the material conditions of the villein peasants, and unsafe to adopt as universally true the Jeremiads which may be found in the works of some Left-wing writers. It is true that while the Bestiftungszwang was, according to the best authority on the subject,[1] fairly well observed where it was the law[2] (outside Galicia, where it was admittedly disregarded) so far as genuine farming land was concerned (permission to subdivide was freely granted, and even encouraged, where a family had other means of subsistence, such as home-spinning or weaving), this rule seems generally to have been understood only as forbidding the subdivision of a holding below the limit on which a family could live off the land, and this was now generally taken at much less than when the size of a *Bauerngut* was first laid down (on the basis, of course, of different standards of cultivation, as well as different population conditions). Thus whole Bauerngüter were by now a rarity almost anywhere, and even half-holdings not very common: the most usual size for a peasant holding was a quarter Gut or even smaller. So 'Tebeldi'[3] tells us that in Lower Austria, in the mid-1840s, there were 133,048 rustical holdings, of which 20,442 were whole, 27,119 half, 23,556 quarter and 62,131 smaller than a quarter. In Styria there were 11,302 full holdings, 21,080 half, 25,725 quarter and 91,273 smaller.[4] In Moravia-Silesia there were 6,766 full holdings, 3,242 three-quarters, 26,935 half, 38,425 quarter and 132,493 smaller.[5] For Hungary no two sets of figures agree, but what appears to be the most reliable list shows that about 1848 there were then in Hungary, exclusive of Transylvania and the Military Frontier, 624,134 sessionati peasants, with holdings divided as follows: whole, 40,380; three-quarters, 6,458; half, 281,264; quarter, 254,160; eighth, 41,872.[6] In Transylvania there were 63,940 sessionati peasants, with an

---

[1] Grünberg in *L. u. F.*, I. 24. Grünberg records, however, that in the 1840s there were complaints that the authorities were applying the rule laxly.

[2] For the exceptions see above, p. 160, n. 4.

[3] 'Tebeldi', p. 200. Extraordinary as it may seem, no one in Austria had been able to tell me where 'Tebeldi' got his figures from.

[4] Cit. Blum, op. cit., p. 172.

[5] Blum, p. 202.

[6] This list (which is quoted by Ember, *Forradalom*, p. 198) was drawn up in 1849 by the statistician, Fényes, for the then Hungarian Government, in preparation for the planned land reform. Fényes published the first edition of his *Statistics* in 1843, brought up to date in 1847; his figures are probably from the latter year. Merei, op. cit., p. 173, quotes a nearly identical global figure for 'just before 1848'—619,725 sessionati peasants, holding between them 234,629 sessions. Tebeldi gives nearly the same global figure, 643,215 holdings, of which, however, he reckons 226,000 as full or half, and 417,215 as quarter, etc. Finally, Merei quotes Austrian

average holding of 10 Magyar hold. In Galicia in 1842 only 8·4% of the peasants were occupying holdings of 20 yokes or more; 23·4% of the holdings were of 10–20 yokes, 29·3% of 5–10, 16·7% of 2–5 and 26·2% of under two.

It is also true that the villein peasant was still taxpayer in chief to the Monarchy, as well as income-provider in chief to his landlord, and that while the level of State taxation, and of the landlords' dues, had remained stationary for half a century, payments in local and communal services had risen substantially. Family budgets reproduced by various writers generally agree that a peasant's total payments under these headings amounted to anything between 50–70% of the assessed value of his land.[1]

The assessed value, however, like the English rental value, was not much more than one-third of the land's actual yield, so that if the peasant paid no more than what could legally be required of him, this was no very crushing burden by twentieth-century standards. And in calculating the value of his acres to a holder, we must not leave out of account the value of the counter-services which he received from his lord, nor, above all, the benefits which he enjoyed from common rights where, as was the case in most parts of the Monarchy, his commune possessed extensive common lands.[2] Many writers

---

figures from the early 1850s, not covering quite the entire country. Of 552,252 peasants who by then had benefited from the reform in the areas covered by him, 17,262 had received holdings larger than one session; 28,599, one session each; 43,865 between a half and one; 173,119 a half each; 239,692 between a quarter and a half; and 22,715 less than a quarter.

One difficulty with Hungary is that no two sets of figures cover exactly the same area; Tebeldi's, for example, presumably exclude the Partium, which Fényes' include. The figures for the 1850s probably include former dominical land held by peasants on lease.

[1] 'Tebeldi', pp. 204, 217, calculates that a peasant in the Western Lands paid 13·2% of the assessed value of his yield to the State in direct taxation, and 4·25% in dues in kind and services, 24% to his lord plus 3% to the manorial officials for illegal exactions, 6% to the Church and 5·25% to the commune (includng school fees and insurance). A Lower Austrian smallholder's budget reproduced by Bach, op. cit., pp. 368–9 gives the assessed value of the holding (of 17·2 yokes) at 83 fl., out of which he paid 12·24 in State and Kreis taxation, 1·18 for billeting soldiers, 24·04 to the landlord and 17·15 in various dues and services. The list however, includes 5·43 on a laudemium and 2·51 on a mortuary. Zenker, op. cit., p. 54 quotes a Silesian peasant whose holding, of thirty yokes, was assessed at 120 fl. a year, on which he paid 23·24 in State taxation, 1·44 in ground rent, 0·7 in 'spinning money' and services and dues to his landlord of a cash value of 61·40.

On the other hand, Le Play (II. 272 ff.), taking the budget of a Hungarian peasant family selected by him as typical, holding a quarter session, and calculating his real income and outgoings, converted in each case into cash values, puts the former at 1,179 fl. 60 kr. and the latter at 66·72 in dues in kind to the landlord and priest (these presumably include the tenth and the ninth), 35·24 in value of robot (thirteen days by the head of the family and two by the eldest son), 2·60 in house tax, 4·16 in payments to the Church and 2·34 in school fees for his children.

[2] In Le Play's commune the area of common land was nearly five times that of the rustical arable land, and he notes this figure as typical.

found little wrong in the condition of the peasants in the Western half of the Monarchy. Bisinger wrote that 'the fleshy faces of the Austrian peasants, their houses, which are usually built of stone, their clean clothes, their rising consumption of coffee, testify to a prosperity of which most European States cannot conceive'.[1] Sealsfeld, uniformly hostile critic as he was, yet found the villages of Upper and Lower Austria to enjoy a prosperity 'without equal elsewhere on the Continent'.[2] He thought the German-Austrians better off than the Czechs, which is the usual view. But Demian had found Bohemia (including its peasantry) the most advanced Land of the Monarchy.[3] Turnbull, who travelled extensively in the Western half of the Monarchy in the late 1830s, had an eye for social conditions, and made careful notes of what he saw, not only reports favourably of conditions in the Alpine Lands, but notes also the 'stout and healthy' look of the Bohemian peasants, who lived chiefly on 'rye and various forms of swine-flesh, with beer' while their clothing was 'warm and substantial'. He warns travellers against 'an ill-required compassion' for a people 'whose material conditions are probably better than those of the corresponding class in the observer's own country'.[4] Wilde thought them 'some of the happiest and most contented peasantry in Europe'.[5]

It was in those days – and for that matter still is today – a fixed article of faith among all German-Austrians that conditions in Hungary were always far inferior to those in their own homes in every respect, and especially the social, and that in consequence all Hungarian peasants were half-starved and pitilessly exploited wretches.[6] But even this is not altogether borne out as a generalization by those foreign travellers who braved the plunge into the land of terror and looked at it with their own eyes. Bendant found the condition of the Hungarian peasants 'not inferior to that of many farmers in France'.[7] Paget, who had been fed full with horror-stories by Austrian friends when he told them that he was going to Hungary[8] and 'expected to find among the peasants nothing but misery, attended by the most abject submission or stifled hate,[9] was agreeably surprised to be shown by one of his hosts, a nobleman owning an estate near Pest, a village whose inhabitants were indubitably both prosperous and contented and their relations with their landlord excellent.[10] Most striking of all is Le Play's analysis of the budget of a family which, be it repeated, he chose as typical. Many a middle-class family in the Western Europe of today might envy this 'typical'

---

[1] Op. cit., p. 208.   [2] Sealsfeld, pp. 91 f.   [3] Op. cit., p. 44.
[4] Op. cit., I. 89.   [5] Op. cit., p. 9.
[6] When the Prussian, von Stein, wrote in 1809 that 'the condition of the peasants in (the Austrian) Monarchy, except in Hungary, is much happier than in Prussia', it is fair to note that his travels did not take him into Hungary.
[7] Op. cit., p. 27.
[8] Op. cit., I. 2.   [9] Id., p. 285.   [10] Ibid.

Hungarian peasant's material standards of living, and for that matter, the lightness of his payments to assorted bloodsuckers.[1]

It is not, however, to be pretended that such happy conditions were universal, or even general. Other travellers,[2] and also many progressive Hungarians themselves, found the situation of the Hungarian peasants profoundly unsatisfactory (on this point, Széchenyi, Kossuth, Deák and Eötvös were completely at one).

Paget himself visited another village which lay in a remote and infertile part of North Hungary, and belonged to an absentee landlord who lived in Vienna and let his estate 'to a greedy Jew who ground out of the people every possible profit, no matter how injurious such conduct might prove to them or their master'. The peasants 'loved the brandy-bottle and hated their master', and lived in such filth and squalor that Paget could not bring himself to enter any of the rude timber shacks which served them for homes, such was the stink of the accumulated filth in front of them.[3]

Exacting and tyrannical landlords and corrupt and unscrupulous bailiffs on the one hand, and drink-sodden, slothful and brutalised peasants on the other, were undoubtedly no rarity in the Monarchy. In some parts of it, especially Galicia, they were perhaps rather the rule than the exception – although, as Tebeldi's calculations show, everything was not perfect even in the West – and where these existed, they produced grinding poverty. Yet gross as these evils sometimes were, they could be expected to diminish with time as the rule of law spread, the landlords grew more enlightened and other interests began to compete with the brandy-bottle in the peasants' minds. In these respects conditions were probably improving during the Vormärz, although very slowly in the backward areas. On the other hand, it was during these years that the less tractable curse was emerging which was to plague the economic life of the Monarchy for the next two generations and more, the pressure of a fast-growing population on means of subsistence which were expanding less rapidly.

The productive area of the Monarchy was, indeed, somewhat larger than it had been half a century earlier. The great vacant spaces of South Hungary and Eastern Galicia had been organized for cultivation, and in many communes elsewhere more marginal land had been made productive. These areas, however, did not even take up their proportionate share of population,

---

[1] For the payments, see above, p. 270, n. 1. The family consisted of husband and wife, three children (one adult) and a grandfather. It spent 44·35 fl. on 'amusements', including drink in the village inn. Its consumption included 1,096 lb. of rye, 57 lb. of fat bacon, 57 of beef and mutton, 213 of pork, 100 of poultry, 23 of fish, 684 of vegetables, 505 litres of wine and 12 litres of brandy. The amount spent by the family on 'amusements' and on alcohol consumed in the house equalled almost exactly the entire expenditure on taxes and dues of all kinds.

[2] So, for example, R. Bright, op. cit., pp. 111 ff. It should, however, be noted that Bright, like many others, finds the root of the trouble in the 'system', which, oppressive to the peasants, is also unremunerative for the landlords.

[3] Paget, l.c.

for the larger spaces reclaimed were chiefly owned by great landlords, and while it was not uncommon for them to turn parts into leaseholds, and not unknown for them to dedicate parts as rustical land, more often they farmed them directly, keeping on them only as many hands as were needed for the purpose.[1] The great majority of the enlarged population had to find its living on, or away from, an only slightly enlarged area.

In this the villein peasants, sheltered as they were by the Bestiftungszwang, formed, after all, something of a privileged class, and the very existence of the measure meant that in most parts of the Monarchy this class was already outnumbered by the small and dwarf-holders, by the cottagers who owned only a cottage with an acre or so of allotment, or by the *Innmänner, házatlan zsellerek*, etc., who did not even own a roof of their own. Thus in Lower Austria, as we saw, the holdings of less than a quarter Gut were already as numerous as those of a quarter or larger, and if we equate the rural population with that living outside conurbations of 5,000 plus and take the usual calculation of five members to a family, we find about 65,000 families – over one-third of the total – who were entirely landless, or practically so. In Styria the same calculation gives us 40,000 landless families, besides the 91,000 smallholders; in Moravia-Silesia, besides the 130,000 smallholders (themselves nearly twice as numerous as the holders of quarter-Guts or more), twice as many again landless families. In Hungary, Tebeldi gave 783,000 zseller families; the land reform calculation, 913,962 zsellers (heads of families), of whom 32,120 held some land and 773,528 their houses only, while 108,314 were 'houseless'. 193,421 families of 'servants' were counted separately. In Transylvania there were 137,421 families of zsellers, i.e., there were twice as many zsellers as villein peasants.

These figures include, at least in Hungary, the lease-holding farmers, a number, large in some areas, of small vintners and market-gardeners, and also the fairly substantial class who lived from rural occupations other than the tilling of the soil (carriers, lumberjacks, quarrymen, etc.); also the regular estate employees, farm-hands and domestic servants.[2] Above all, they

[1] Where rustical peasants reclaimed land previously uncultivated in an old-established commune, the lord usually claimed it as his own and charged them rental for it, but sometimes they succeeded in getting it classified as rustical. Law-suits over this point, and also over enclosures of common lands, were very frequent.

[2] It will be of interest to quote Le Play's analysis of the social structure of his 'typical' commune (in the Hungarian plain). It consisted of 355 *jobbágy* families, of whom 5 held two sessions each, 35 one each, 70 halves and 245 quarters; 160 'masters' (17 smiths, 27 joiners, wheelwrights and other workers in wood, 30 masons and other workers in stone, 40 weavers or tailors, 6 millers, 18 merchants, 15 Jewish pedlars, 17 various); 80 cottagers, some of whom lived by hiring out horses for the post, others by working for the villein peasants; 40 houseless men (how they lived is not stated); and 5 manorial employees.

In Hungary, at this time, Le Play found that where there were several sons, the eldest usually went into the army, the second inherited the farm, and the others either established new farms on land previously uncultivated, or became artisans.

include those families which, while ranking in the statistics as *Innleute*, etc., supported themselves mainly or entirely by industrial homework. But when all these are deducted, the number of agrarian families without regular means of subsistence was growing terrifyingly large. Many of them were now living chiefly from seasonal labour on the big estates, whence they took home a share in kind of the crops harvested by them. Of others, it is hard to say how they existed at all, where they could be said to exist – death from diseases of under-nourishment, or from sheer starvation, were common enough. The regional incidence of the distress varied widely: it was worst in German Bohemia, North Hungary, parts of Silesia and Galicia, and the Szekel areas of Transylvania. In these it was endemic, and acute.

In the Alpine districts, and perhaps in some others, and in the old-established industries, wages and conditions of industrial labour seem to have been tolerable, and the system easy-going and patriarchal, even in the 1830s. Turnbull found wages in Styria and Upper Austria to range from twenty to thirty kreuzer up to forty to fifty or more for a male adult worker. On this, he was able 'to eat, drink and smoke to his heart's content',[1] especially as he usually got his cottage with attached vegetable plot thrown in. These wages compared, in fact, not unfavourably with the earnings of the lower-grade civil servants and professional men[2] and Turnbull tells us that even the agricultural labourers, who got only ten kreuzer a day plus food or twenty kreuzer without it, ate meat three times a week.

He also tells us that the Austrian workers 'were never made to feel the immense value of time'. The industrial revolution had not yet reached Austria. When it did, 'it would increase the national wealth, but introduce unemployment and pauperization'.

But the conditions which Turnbull described were already passing – in some parts of the Monarchy they had perhaps never existed. By the mid-1830s the homeworkers for the Bohemian cotton-mills were earning no more than five, sometimes only two to three kreuzer a day. Up to that date homework was the rule in all branches of the textile industry. Then, in the late 1830s, came the sudden change-over to the factory system, and the

---

[1] Op. cit., I. 186.

[2] A primary schoolmaster in a country district got 130–150 fl. a year, his assistant, usually 70; in Vienna, about twice as much. An excise-man got 200 fl., a State official of medium grade, 400. A disgruntled man employed on public works in Vienna in June 1848, at 24 kr. a day, which was the top rate for unskilled labour, complained that he ought to be getting 36, which was what he had been earning in his factory. On that 'he had been able to afford three good meals a day, with coffee, wine and beer, and a decent lodging' (Violand, *Soziale Geschichte*, p. 131). Dr Fischof, President of the Committee of Public Security, before whom the complaint came, was not very sympathetic; he himself was getting only 40 kr. a day as consultant in a Viennese hospital, a post which allowed him hardly any time for private practice.

increase in the number of enterprises. This did indeed increase the national wealth, and brought some monetary benefit also to the workers who found employment in the factories, for in them they could earn perhaps three times as much as by homework. Adult male workers in employment earned a living wage (as the case quoted above shows), while even the much smaller amounts earned by women and children were at least large enough to tempt the women into the factories.[1]

But the machine age brought with it all the social evils which attend most industrial revolutions. Women and children were employed very extensively,[2] the latter no longer for philanthropic reasons, but out of the less worthy motive that their work cost less than a man's. The lower age limit of nine years set by Joseph II was raised to twelve in Hungary in 1840 and in Austria in 1842, but was often evaded. A child's working day was usually about 12½ hours, with a 1½ hour's break at midday, but Marx quotes a case where children in a factory were working 13–13½ hours a day for a weekly wage of one and a half florin Wiener Währung (52 kreuzer C.M.). Children over twelve counted as adults. Hours and conditions for adults were entirely unregulated. The average working day for adults in either half of the Monarchy was 13–16 hours in factories or 12 in mines, with only the shortest of breaks. There was no legal Sunday rest.[3] The Hofkanzlei three times (1843, 1844, 1846) suggested introducing some social legislation for the factory workers, but was forced each time to retreat before the objections of the employers.

Housing conditions were particularly bad, worst of all in the big towns, into which, especially Vienna, workers were now flocking in great numbers,[4]

[1] Wages varied so widely from trade to trade that there seems little purpose in giving figures, especially in the absence of figures on the cost of living. Some figures are given by Bach, pp. 217 ff., *M.K.P.* III. 85, Zenker, pp. 66 ff. and Marx, *passim*. *M.K.P.* gives for a skilled machinist in Vienna, up to 80 kr. a day, for a silk weaver, 40–50 kr., for a textile weaver, 30–40 kr.; about thirty per cent lower in the provinces. Women earned 20–30 kr., juveniles, 7–8. Bach's figures are for Bohemia. The highest (excluding compositors, who earned really good money) is 50 kr. plus food and lodging; the lowest, 2–8. Zenker gives an average of 5·22 fl. weekly for a man, 2·58 for a woman. For wages in country districts (especially Upper Austria and Styria) see Turnbull, vol. I, *passim*.

[2] Zenker, p. 61, writes that in 1845 in the cotton and paper industries of the Western half of the Monarchy, 433 of every 1,000 workers were men, 420 women and 147 children.

[3] There were, however, a large number of public holidays, and the peculiar Austrian institution of the 'Blue Monday', when a worker slept off his Sunday night hangover on Monday, was widely observed. One left-wing historian of the 1848 revolution in Vienna, which broke out on a Monday, explains the large number of workers who flocked into the city that morning with the simple words: 'since it was not usual to work on a Monday.' A worker in regular employment usually worked about 300 days in the year. Brügel, *Sozialdemokratie* I. 44, says that the absence of the Sunday rest was not one of the grievances resented by the workers, and Nemes, p. 255, says the same of Hungary.

[4] In 1846, 131,116 persons living in Vienna had been born outside it. In 1820 the figure had been only 13,552.

and in which the growth of accommodation lagged far behind that of the population.[1] The workers huddled together in dank cellars or stifling attics, for which the landlords exacted exorbitant rents, often one-third of a family's earnings, for the most miserable accommodation. Often two or three families shared a room, and the institution of the 'Bettgeher', where a person simply hired the use of a bed for a few hours out of the twenty-four, was not uncommon. In many factories the workers slept by their machines; the lot of those who did so, thus saving rent, was often envied. Immorality was naturally rife, and the lives of most workers were entirely devoid of any spiritual or intellectual interest.

But the greatest of all the evils brought with it by Austria's industrial revolution was that of technological unemployment. The new machines required much less labour than the old, so that the introduction of them made many of the old handworkers redundant; they were able also to undercut the craftsmen in the trades which they invaded, ruining large numbers of the old practitioners. In so far as they created a new demand they were, of course, able to give new employment to some of these (although at the cost of transforming them from independent men into wage-slaves), but as it happened, the years of precipitate mechanization were also difficult ones for Austrian industry. First the Eastern Crisis of 1839–40, then the development of the Zollverein, put not the textile industry alone into great difficulties. Even Kossuth's 'buy Hungarian' campaign, small as was its success in Hungary, caused a lot of damage to the Austrian producers. British competition was a permanent threat. The factories were therefore not so much creating new markets, as struggling to maintain themselves in existing ones. Many of them were under-capitalized, and therefore exceptionally vulnerable to even minor changes in trading conditions; not a few, actually fraudulent. But even the more solidly established enterprises found their capacity to employ labour at a profit fluctuating wildly. The average factory worker was out of work for at least three months in the year. The older, semi-patriarchal businesses usually tried to see their workers through bad times, but others simply dismissed them out of hand when sales fell off. Jewish employers, who were particularly numerous in the cotton industry, had an especially bad name in this respect; this was one of the causes of the widespread anti-Semitism of 1848. And to add to the difficulties, the shrinkage of the number of jobs coincided with something of a population explosion which, as we have said, was particularly violent in the Bohemian Lands, already densely populated. In bad years Bohemia, in particular, was filled with a great army of destitute men.

It is not surprising that the mechanization soon produced its obvious reaction in the form of machine-wrecking. This occurred sporadically in 1842 and 1843, and in 1844, when some of the mills introduced more machines

[1] In Vienna, including the outer suburbs, the population increased by 45% between 1827 and 1847, while the increase in housing was only 11·4%.

which threw many thousands of workers out of employment, the wrecking was on a major scale. A mass of the unfortunate men then flocked to Prague to beg for help, only to be met with fire from the muskets of the police and the military, whom the panic-stricken authorities had called in to their help.

The labour problem in this latest form was still almost confined to a few areas in Lower Austria and Bohemia, but this does not mean that labour conditions elsewhere were much better. The homeworkers in other parts of the Monarchy were still toiling for pittances which it is almost shameful to record, and the apprentices and journeymen in the remotest villages were labouring all day and far into the night for the barest subsistence.

Finally, prices rose steadily from the late 1830s onward, although the rise up to 1844 was still relatively slight.

The problem of real poverty in Austria made, at the time, little impact except on its immediate victims. Andrian drew attention to it in moving words,[1] but generally, it passed so unnoticed that a modern writer has been able almost to deny its very existence.[2] When a harvest failed badly in some area, there might be some distribution of relief, possibly a remission of taxation, but the idea that rural congestion was a condition which needed, and might be given, remedy occurred to no one. Official theorists still regarded the population as below the optimum. For industrial unemployment the only remedy was, again, relief or the organization of public works. This was left to Land and Kreis officials, whose plans were usually quite futile and were often wound up precisely when the need was greatest, because funds ran out, or to private charity. The authorities also intervened from time to time with various devices to counteract sudden sharp rises in the prices of articles of prime necessity. For the rest, the Austrian authorities, like those of most European countries of the day, regarded the proletariat chiefly as potential revolutionaries, forbade them any kind of association or organization,[3] and had the police keep a close watch on them. Society as a whole regarded the problem in the same light.[4]

Otherwise, a destitute man had no resource at all outside the meagre parish relief which Joseph II had instituted, and the parishes in which unemployment was highest were, of course, precisely those least able to provide relief.

---

[1] *Oesterreich und dessen Zukunft*, p. 24.

[2] Marcel Brion, *Daily Life in the Vienna of Mozart and Schubert* (English tr., London, 1959, p. 14), writes that 'entire poverty was practically non-existent in Vienna'.

[3] The guilds were, of course, trade associations, and 'brotherhoods' existed among the miners and in some other trades. When the crisis in Bohemia grew acute in the 1840s, a number of 'factory funds' (Fabrikscassen), which acted as strike funds, were founded, but new foundations were forbidden in 1845.

[4] The chief exception was the circle round Clemens Maria Hofbauer, who preached social reform through the Church; but his doctrines seem to have had no effect whatever on official policy, and his own approach was religious rather than social.

No one else was under any obligation to provide for the destitute, and the usual remedy of any local authority, if a factory falling within its jurisdiction dismissed its hands, was to order any unemployed workers from outside it to return to their native communes – a measure which was usually quite ineffective, for the deportee was told to make his journey on foot,[1] was unescorted, and was often back where he had started from a couple of days later.

When revolution broke out in 1848, fear of the workers played, as we shall see, a considerable part in its developments, at least in Vienna. But the precautions taken against them in the Vormärz were hardly necessary. The proletariat did not even regard itself as a distinct social class, and no socialist or communist leaders appeared among it. Employment, a living wage and relief if factory work was unavailable, were the most for which they asked, and they asked for that only as individuals.[2]

One social class, however, was succeeding in drawing attention to its grievances *qua* class. These were the villein peasants. Towards them, as in general, the Staatskonferenz was trying conscientiously to maintain the position as Francis had left it, which, as we have seen, was, with small modifications, that which he had found on his accession. But it had been unable to enforce unchanging acceptance of an unchanged law. While Austria stood still, other countries had advanced, and from being in the vanguard in her treatment of this problem, where Maria Theresa and Joseph II had placed her, she was now among the laggards, and the fact could not be concealed. For all the censorship and carefully supervised schooling, the peasants had become aware that subjection was not everywhere the inevitable and immutable lot of the tiller of the soil. Writers recorded mournfully that the peasants had lost belief in the justice and reason of the nexus subditelae and did not even believe that they were occupying their lands by grace of the rightful owners of them, and that their dues and services were a legitimate return for that grace. And by the 1830s the peasants were giving practical expression to their scepticism. Wherever the law allowed appeal from a decision of a Patrimonial Court, the appeal was made. Dues in kind arrived late, and then the quality of them was inferior: chickens stringy, eggs aged, honey mouldy. In their performance of the robot, the peasants had developed the arts of slow motion and passive resistance to a pitch of high virtuosity, against which the bailiff was powerless

[1] Local authorities on the roads were obliged to provide a night's shelter and a meal for those making the journey.

[2] All writers are agreed on this point. It is interesting to note the opinion of Wilde, the Irish doctor who visited Austria in 1840. Wilde not only found the Viennese artisans (as also the bourgeoisie) better off than their opposite numbers in England, but expressly praised the absence of discontent or agitation among the workers, contrasting it most favourably with the attitude of the English workers. He greatly praised the prudence of the Austrian authorities for insulating the workers against subversive doctrines (op. cit., pp. 8 f.).

when his unrestricted use of the whip was gone.[1] Széchenyi's calculation that a free man's hired labour was worth three times that of the *robot* has been quoted: other writers put the ratio at one to four, or more; one, as high as one to thirteen.

In respect of the manorial authority the peasants had long had a considerable proportion of the landlords themselves on their side, for they were finding the Patrimonial Courts and their manorial duties in general much more of a burden than an advantage. The salaries of the men whom they now had to employ to conduct the Courts, meagre as they were, yet added up to perceptible sums, when the incidental expenses of them were added in,[2] and the advantage which they derived from the tilting of the scales in their favour when a case was first heard was largely nullified by the cost and time-wasting of the inevitable appeal, which might well go against them. Their general administrative duties, too, were becoming increasingly burdensome and expensive. Consequently, they, too, would have been glad to see the manorial system replaced by a State-paid administration and judicature. As early as 1833 the Estates of Lower Austria petitioned to have this change introduced.

Opinion among the landlords in respect of the robot had not changed so generally. The landlord in a remote district into which money had hardly penetrated, even into his own household, let alone his peasants', where the population was so sparse that he could not have found free labour to hire if he could have afforded to hire it, where if his lands did yield an abundant harvest he could not take it to market for lack of roads – such a man simply clung to the sheet-anchor of his robot and took advantage of the absence or complaisance of authority to disregard the legal limitations on it. But the most conservative among them were impressed by the consideration of sheer fear. The nobles of Transylvania still quaked at the memory of the Hora rising, which had been followed by several others on a smaller scale.[3] Those of Inner Hungary had been uneasy since the beginning of the century,[4] and particularly since the outbreaks of 1831. Many landlords believed that even if the peasants did not use violence against them, they would one day occupy their

---

[1] The famous peasant tribune Kudlich, whose parents were villein peasants on a big estate in Silesia, has recorded that the local peasants used to keep a specially weak horse and even a specially small cart expressly for their robot services (op. cit., I. 50). It was a common landlords' complaint that the peasants sent their youngest son, a child, to do the service.

[2] *Inter alia*, the landlords had to pay for the upkeep of the village jail and for the maintenance of the prisoners in it. This may partly explain the predilection of the Courts for passing sentences of corporal punishment, rather than imprisonment.

[3] One of these occurred as late as 1845. For a description of this curious incident, in which the chief figure was a woman (incidentally, a Magyar of Inner Hungarian origin), see Helfert, *Geschichte*, I. pp. 68–9.

[4] When the insurrectio was called out in 1809, the women of many noble families had moved into the towns, because they dared not stay on the land unprotected by their men-folk.

lands in a movement so general that there would be no recourse but to accept the *fait accompli*. We hear of similar opinions expressed in Bohemia and Galicia.

The landlords who were producing for the market, especially in those districts in which hired labour, regular or seasonal, was easily available, were turning against the robot system for its economic inefficiency, as practised by the peasants – an inefficiency which every improvement in methods of cultivation made increasingly flagrant. They wanted the whole system of services and dues in kind replaced by money payments which they could invest in better implements and improved breeds of animals, used and tended by workers whose services were always available. Their problem was how to get the cash replacement for the robot. Where the peasant could raise the cash to commute, this could be done, despite the official discouragement, but he often had practically no cash at all, and where he had, he was seldom willing to pay what the landlord considered a fair price. The solution of letting him buy himself out by ceding part of his land was often considered and indeed strongly favoured by many landlords, but generally dismissed in view of the peasants' opposition, besides the formidable difficulty of deciding what piece of land would constitute a fair price for the rest. It would, moreover, have necessitated altering the law which forbade the conversion of rustical land to dominical, and this, like any other change, was opposed by the Government. The solution which the reformers came generally to favour was that of letting the rustical land go altogether in return for a monetary compensation in which the State should act as intermediary, the peasants buying themselves out through payments to the State, which would then pass the compensation on to the landlords in the form of bonds.

The movement among the landlords for peasant liberation first took shape (in the fashion described above[1]) in Hungary, which was, in the 1830s, the only part of the Monarchy affected by the problem where such a question could be raised publicly, and where the reform party was also interested in it for national reasons. It made, as will be seen, small progress: the Government was willing to allow the conditions of the Hungarian peasants to be brought up to the level of the Austrian (this was roughly what the reforms of the Diets of 1832–45 amounted to), but not beyond, as that would have set a precedent for the Austrian Lands. In none of the latter could the question be raised officially (although a considerable pamphlet literature was appearing) until the Lower Austrian Diet got its chance in 1843, over a question of taxation. The reform party in that body then persuaded it to adopt a petition to the Government asking it to carry through redemption, facultative for five years and compulsory thereafter. In 1845 the same Estates further petitioned to be relieved of a number of their manorial duties, on the ground that these involved them in much unpaid work and heavy actual outgoings.

[1] See above, p. 246.

The Estates of Styria, Moravia and even Galicia sent in petitions to similar effect in the same year.

The movement was held up by the Government, for various reasons. One was the old, ineradicable conservatism of the men at the top, for while the younger officials, who were in touch with conditions on the land, mostly agreed with the reformers, their superiors regarded this change, too, as smacking of revolution. Constitutionally, they objected to the Estates extending their interests beyond the narrow limits prescribed for them. Finally, their financial advisers held that the operation of financing the reform would overstrain the Government's credit. They therefore returned the Estates a series of snubs, telling them, none too gently, to mind their own business. Permission was even refused, except in the single instance of Galicia, for the foundation of agricultural credit banks, on the ground that these would compete with the State's demands for credit. The movement was, however, gaining ground rapidly in many of the Lands of the Monarchy in the years following Francis's death. Meanwhile, it is relevant to note that, whichever side was right in the social argument – whether the servile condition in which they were kept was the reason why the peasants produced so little, or whether to keep them in it was the only way to make them work at all – in any case, between their reluctance to work the demesne land and the primitive methods used by them in working their own, agricultural production in the Monarchy as a whole was in a most unsatisfactory condition. With nearly three-quarters of their populations still gaining their livelihoods from agriculture, the Western Lands still had to import foodstuffs, while Hungary's surpluses too often simply went to waste.

The peasant problem, however, was *sui generis*. It affected almost every part of the Monarchy, and in much the same way, but everywhere its solution would have required nothing more than an adjustment of class relationships which need not have entailed any modification of the structure of the Monarchy (a question to which no peasant devoted a thought). It was otherwise with the movements to which we now turn. These were mainly middle class in the sense that their chief inspirers came from the representatives of the new bourgeois interests, or from the new intellectual proletariats (with whom, indeed, some progressive aristocrats and civil servants associated themselves), but none of them was a class movement in the most exact sense of the term. They sometimes included in their programmes desiderata special to their own class or deriving from its interests – sometimes also measures of wider social reform – but primarily they were national, and subordinated all class interests to national considerations. It was these national movements that in the Vormärz dominated the political life of all parts of the Monarchy, with the single and qualified exception of its German-Austrian provinces.

As in the 'pre-Vormärz', so in the Vormärz proper, the parts of the

Monarchy in which national feeling was least apparent were those from which the most danger might, *a priori*, have been expected. Lombardy was still the most nationally passive of all parts of Italy except one, and Venetia, the most passive of all. Even those of Austria's Italian subjects who fretted against the rule of Vienna were by no means all enchanted with the possible alternatives to it, and particularly not by that of rule from Turin, where d'Azeglio himself described the atmosphere as less free than that of Milan. The historian of Austrian affairs, as distinct from Italian, may pass over developments in the Kingdom up to 1846 with no more words than these.

Galicia, too, presented a picture of almost complete surface calm, but here the appearance was deceptive, for the Polish Committee in Paris was now engaged in feverish plans to retrieve the reverse of 1830, and in these new designs, Galicia was assigned a part. Every second Polish noble was more or less initiated into the plans, and the province was honeycombed with secret societies (the conspirators were even thicker on the ground in Cracow, which Austrian troops occupied in 1836, when they found over 2,000 *émigrés* living there under false names; they abated the nuisance, but as soon as they left, it began again). A man well qualified to judge[1] has described the years as 'the quarter-century of conspiracy' and the Polish nobles as 'one vast band of conspirators'. The authorities, however, were never able to come on more than individuals or small groups, and most of the officials, exceedingly handicapped by their ignorance of the local languages, entirely failed to perceive that anything very serious was wrong. The Archduke-Viceroy, in particular, a kindly but not over-intelligent old gentleman, who had surrounded himself with plausible Polish nobles in order to form the nearest approach to a Court which he could compass, reported complacently to Vienna that all was well, and was not to be convinced to the contrary.

The plotting was in fact directed rather towards preparing the ground for future operations than organizing the operations themselves – the plans of campaign were worked out by the *émigré* headquarters in Paris, and it was thence that the signal for action would come. This preparatory activity was, however, considerable in one direction. In 1830 a number of the younger and more democratic Poles had wanted the call to arms to be accompanied by a proclamation emancipating the peasants, and they attributed the quick collapse of the rising largely to the refusal of the aristocratic party to accept this advice, with the consequence that the peasants had given little or no help to the Polish arms. A large number of the refugees in Galicia belonged to this party, the *Towarzystie Domocratyazne*, which also had its adherents among the born Galicians, and they initiated a social propaganda which was so active that for once it reached the ears of the authorities, who

[1] Anon., *Polnische Revolutionen*, p. 24.

arrested a number of them. The Polish landlords complained also, and the democrats agreed to drop the agitation, but it went on in secret, and meanwhile the peasants' disaffection towards their lords had become so obvious that in 1843 a party in the Galician Diet itself asked the Gubernium to sanction the appointment of a Committee of the Estates (who would thus be seen to be taking the lead) to take steps towards abolishing the peasants' servitudes, against compensation for the landlords. The Government raised difficulties – the same as it was advancing in other Lands, but was frightened to put the Estates into the position of being able to claim that they had wanted the reform, and the Government had refused it. The Committee was duly appointed in 1845, but by the next year, when the events described on another page took place, had not got beyond preliminaries.

Another important development in Galicia was the tentative re-emergence of a national movement among the Ruthenes, who, however, were handicapped by the difficulty which haunted them down to the end of the Monarchy, and, indeed, after it, of deciding what they really were – Russians, Ukrainians, or something different from either. In the 1840s the most influential figures in the movement were a group of Uniate priests attached to the Metropolitan Church of St George in Lemberg, and consequently known as the 'St Georgites'.[1] This group held that the Ruthenes were indeed a distinct nationality, which was the thesis most pleasing to the Austrian authorities, who therefore gave them such patronage as they could spare for any Ruthenes; in 1844 they gave the group permission to introduce instruction in Ruthene in the schools. The St Georgites, however, hampered their own cause by trying to impose as the national language the so-called *Jasisze*, a dialect which they had evolved in their own circle, consisting of an Old Slavonic basis, helped out with local, Russian, and Polish words. It was incomprehensible to the people, with whom the St Georgites had, in general, little contact.

Another group, composed generally of younger men, had begun to interest themselves in the language actually spoken by the local peasants, which was unmistakably a dialect of Ukrainian, and in their native culture. They were collecting folk-songs[2] and doing all the other usual work of national pioneers. They had, however, no friends in high places except only the Suffragan Bishop of Premysl, Mgr Joachimowycz, and the Austrian Government and the Poles combined against them, as they had against the earlier apostles of the same creed.

Yet a third group, which was supported by the Poles, but included a number of Ruthene country priests and also the Ruthenes' single local

[1] The name 'St Jurists', applied in some books to this party, is an attempt to reproduce for Western ears the Ruthene form of the name George.

[2] Interestingly, the first collection of Ruthene folk songs was published (in 1833) by a Pole, Zaleski, the later Statthalter of Galicia.

monastic Order, the Basilians, favoured bringing Ruthene into a closer relationship with Polish by various devices, including the substitution of the Latin alphabet for the Cyrillic.

Finally, the Ruthenes' national nest contained a cuckoo's egg. The famous Russian Pan-Slavist, Pogodin, had visited Galicia to spy out the land in 1835, and returned several times later, and had interested Government circles in Petersburg for the thesis that the Ruthenes were Russians *manqués*, who could one day be converted into real Russians. The egg, was, however still in process of incubation.

In striking contrast to the surface (and in the former case largely real) calm in Lombardy-Venetia and Galicia were the complex and tumultuous developments in the Lands of the Hungarian Crown.

The Staatskonferenz, in which Kolowrat seems to have directed policy towards Hungary in the first years after Francis's death, began by showing the iron fist. Thanks to Francis's forethought in getting Ferdinand crowned during his own lifetime, there had been no need for a special Coronation Diet, and the Long Diet ended quietly. But as soon as it rose, which was on 2 May 1836, Reviczky was replaced as Chancellor by Count Fidél Pálffy, an extreme exponent of aulic politics who did not even speak Magyar (incidentally, Kolowrat's son-in-law). The other key offices were filled with men of the same kidney. Several young jurati were arrested. In May 1837 Kossuth's turn came; he was arrested for a Press offence (he no longer enjoyed Parliamentary immunity) and sentenced to four years' imprisonment. Wesselényi's status entitled him to remain at liberty until convicted of an offence, but charges against him were prepared, and in 1839 he was sentenced to three years in prison; he was, indeed, allowed to remain at liberty, although under surveillance, in an Austrian spa.

There was great popular indignation at these sentences, especially at that on Wesselényi, who had made himself a national hero by daring work in saving life during great floods which devastated Pest in 1838, and the Staatskonferenz was in a difficult position when the Eastern crisis grew acute in the spring of 1839 and another Diet had to be convoked in April to receive demands for recruits and subsidies. The elections took place in a heated atmosphere, and a considerably increased number of reformers were returned to the Lower House. In the House of Magnates a group of some thirty-five aristocrats, including Counts Lajos and Kázmer Batthyáni, Baron J. Eötvös, Count L. Teleki, and Z. Perényi, constituted themselves a 'Liberal group', and another group, headed by the gifted Aurel Dessewffy, formed themselves into a part of 'considered reform', which admitted the desirability of change in many fields, but wished it carried through in concert with the Government, expressly disclaiming the name of opposition.

The Staatskonferenz, in which Metternich now seems to have taken charge of Hungarian affairs,[1] had come prepared to pay a price for its requirements. Pálffy was dismissed – only, it is true, in favour of the only slightly less unpopular Antal Majláth, and similar changes made in the other top offices. During the Diet itself, the Government yielded considerable ground in several minor fields,[2] and retreated a long step on the linguistic question. Magyar now became obligatory for communications from the Consilium and Camera to Hungarian authorities in Inner Hungary, and for the internal service in the country, and a knowledge of Magyar was required of all parish priests, of whatever confession. Finally, at the end of the Diet, Wesselényi (who meanwhile had lost his sight) and Kossuth were amnestied.

For their part the reformers in the Lower House, among whom Deák had by general consent taken the lead, were anxious to avoid a clash, and the Diet, its conditions having been met, duly voted the 30,000 recruits asked of it, also consenting that they should be enlisted by the Austrian method of conscription through the drawing of lots.

So the results of the Diet could thus be called another victory for the policy of grudging concession; but one that was unlikely to prove permanent. The reformers were far from satisfied, particularly since they had made no progress over several questions on which they felt deeply, including the position of the Protestant Churches. Thus the closing of the Diet was not even followed by the breathing-space usual in more tranquil times, when the legislators had been accustomed to return home to see what their wives and their bailiffs had been doing in their absence. The Counties remained in permanent session, and declaring, with some truth, that it was impossible to get legislation through the Diet, proceeded to pass enactments, often very radical, of national scope,[3] but with local application. The Crown regularly annulled these, but could not check the rising temper of public opinion, which its own

[1] I can find no authority for this statement (nor, for that matter, for saying that Kolowrat had handled Hungarian affairs from 1836-8), either in Metternich's own papers, in the biographies of him, or any other source. But it is a fact that from 1839 we find the threads of Vienna's Hungarian policy running together in Metternich's hands. In 1841 a mixed Austro-Hungarian Committee (the Hungarian members of which were all reliable centralists) was set up to devise means of coping with the Hungarian Opposition (see Hock-Biedermann, op. cit., p. 680).

In 1837, however, Metternich had been entirely in favour of the policy of the strong hand; see his letters to the Czar of April and May of that year, published by E. Andics (op. cit., annex, pp. 187-96). The documents do not reveal just why he became less rigid from 1839 onward; probably simply his urgent desire for recruits and the knowledge born of experience that he would be unable to get them out of fifty-two recalcitrant Counties. He was also sick in the latter half of 1839.

[2] These included laws permitting the peasant to commute his obligations in perpetuity (although not to buy his freehold), limiting the hours of child labour in factories, improving the procedure on bills of exchange, and allowing Jews to settle anywhere in the country (outside the districts under Cameral control), lease (although not own) real property, and practise a trade or profession.

[3] One County introduced taxation for its nobles in 1842.

best intentions promoted. Metternich had decided that the national passion for freedom of expression was something to which it would be wise to make concessions.[1] Papers and periodicals were now appearing in some numbers, and when Kossuth came out of prison in 1841, he was, under circumstances which are still obscure, allowed to become editor of one of them, the *Pesti Hirlap*, with a practically free hand, subject only to his undertaking not to attack the dynasty, or to write on conditions in Germany. Kossuth used his opportunity to extraordinary effect. The aura of martyrdom with which his imprisonment had invested him lent his words an almost oracular authority. They were read throughout the country – before long the circulation of the *Pesti Hirlap* had reached the figure, prodigious for the day, of 10,000 – and his readers became his converts. There was hardly any aspect of Hungarian affairs on which he did not comment, and always with the implicit assumption that true reform was impossible without political liberty. The three years of his editorship may be said to have established definitively in the Magyar popular mind the identification of reform with opposition to Vienna, and thus the priority of the political struggle.

He was, however, far from being the unquestioned leader of the Hungarian opposition.[2] Széchenyi, perhaps, could hardly be counted as any longer belonging to the opposition at all, for on the central political question he was nearer the party of 'considered reform'. He and Kossuth attacked each other in barbed pamphlets which did little to enhance the reputation of either man. But Deák distrusted Kossuth's wisdom and disliked his provocative tone, and another group – small but important – was emerging which also differed from him. This was a handful of men, the best known of whom today is Baron József Eötvös, known in derision as the 'Centralists' or 'Doctrinaires'. Without sharing Kossuth's nebulous allergy to all things Austrian, and genuinely concerned to preserve the integrity of the Monarchy, they went as far as he on the central political issue, in demanding a Government responsible to the electorate; and in another respect, further. While Kossuth regarded the Hungarian Counties with mystical devotion and still saw them as bulwarks against Viennese oppression, the Centralists held them to be strongholds of reaction and obscurantism, and argued for a strong central Hungarian Government, administering the country with modern efficiency, and equally efficient local government. On social issues they were more radical than Széchenyi and more logical than Kossuth. They were heavily outshadowed at the time by the more popular and spectacular Kossuth, but played a large

[1] The whole 1839–40 Diet had been overshadowed by a bitter conflict over this question.

[2] It must be remembered that no Party system yet existed in Hungary, and that the deputies of each County were rigidly bound by instructions given them by their Congregationes: if they wanted to depart from these, they had to go back to the Congregatio and persuade it to change its instructions. No Congregatio was in any way bound by any other. In so far as the leaders co-ordinated their ideas, this was by correspondence, or meeting if business took several of them to town at the same time.

part in the inner councils of the reformers, especially after 1844, when Kossuth quarrelled with the proprietor of the *Pesti Hirlap* and left the paper, which the Centralists then took over as their organ.

But if the Hungarian opposition was thus growing with headlong rapidity, so was the opposition to the opposition. In Croatia the movement had failed to follow the line which Gaj had marked out for it. He himself had begun by preaching pure 'Illyrianism'; he had initiated the 'Croat News' with an appeal to 'the famed Slav people in the Southern Regions, such as Croats, Slovenians, Dalmatians, Ragusans, Serbs, Carniolans, Styrians, Istrians and Bosnyaks', and the Danica had depicted the triangle between Scutari, Varna and Villach as 'the Illyrian lyre', the harmonizing of whose now discordant strings, Carinthia, Gorizia, Istria, Carniola, Styria, Croatia, Slavonia, Dalmatia, Ragusa, Bosnia, Montenegro, Serbia, Bulgaria and Lower Hungary, was the task of the future. In 1836 he changed his paper's name to *Illirske Narodne Novine* (Illyrian national news).

For a time Vienna continued to load him with favours; in 1839 Kolowrat got Ferdinand to present him with a gold ring for his 'services to literature', on the grounds that 'in view of the way in which the Magyars treat the Slavs living in their country, the latter need protection', adding, in words which show how little new there was in the ideas with which Francis Ferdinand was toying eighty years later, that 'a closer connection between the 3,000,000 (Southern) Slavs living in the German and Hungarian Lands could only be of advantage, especially in regard to Hungary'.

But in 1840, when the Eastern crisis grew acute, the Pasha of Bosnia complained that Gaj was fomenting agitation among the Slavs in his province, and this was embarrassing to Metternich, who was working to strengthen the Sultan's authority. Moreover, the other prospect held out by Gaj, that he would influence in Austria's favour the Slav peoples 'chained to Russia', did not materialize. The Serbs rejected 'Illyrianism', with its Western connotations, almost unanimously; as they grew more nationally conscious, they became, not more Austrophile, but more Russophile. Gaj himself visited Russia and took money from Russian agents. The pull appeared to be in the wrong direction. In 1842 Metternich complained to the Czar, who repudiated responsibility, sincerely enough – he was antagonistic towards all popular movements. But the fact remained that Illyrianism had become an international embarrassment, and was not helping Austria; that the Hungarian authorities were flooding Vienna with complaints needs no mention. So the word 'Illyrian' was forbidden, and Gaj had to change the name of his paper back to 'Croat'.

But the rescript communicating the prohibition contained the assurance that 'His Majesty wishes no obstacles to be placed in the way of the cultivation of the national language, and will most graciously defend the public rights of Croatia and its nationality, as built up under the shield of those rights, against any attack'. This was perfectly agreeable to nine out of ten Croat nationalists, on whom 'Illyrianism' had made as little impact as it had on the Serbs (or, be it remarked here, the Slovenes). It was not an 'Illyria' that they wanted, but a Great Croatia, to include at least the Slavonian Counties, Fiume and Dalmatia, and ultimately, Bosnia. It was to continue to be a part of the Habsburg Monarchy; but the really important postulate (which emerged, indeed, only gradually, for up to 1848 there was no fixed programme) was that it was not to be mediatized through Budapest, but to stand directly under Vienna.

These aspirations were now entertained by the majority of the politically active classes of Croatia; although still not by all. A second party, known, through a corruption of the word 'Magyaromane', as the 'Magyarones' – an unfair description, for they were not real Magyaromanes, but nor were the extreme nationalists 'Illyrians', as the Hungarians called them – preferred the traditional connection with Hungary. The Magyarones were strongest among the half-Magyar magnates, but included also the Croat sandalled nobles, and especially those of Turopolje, who, as we have said elsewhere,[1] had their own representative in the Diet at Pozsony. This was paradoxical, for in Inner Hungary, as we saw, the corresponding class had been enlisted on its side by Vienna in 1819;[2] but the Croat nobles of the Illyrian party chose to regard the extension of the decree to that effect to Croatia as another infringement of Croatia's historic rights; whereupon the Magyarones gratefully added the Turopolyans to their own voting strength.

By 1843 things were working up to a crisis. The Hungarians, while not admitting the Croat nationalists' thesis on the relationship between the two countries, had yet been trying to avoid a clash, and the language laws of both 1836 and 1840 had been made applicable only *intra limites regni*, i.e., not to Croatia. But the Croats' claim that they were entitled to leave the body corporate of the Hungarian Crown altogether, taking with them the Slavonian Counties and Fiume, was too much even for the Hungarian moderates. Deák himself rejected it flatly.

In the 1840s a new and unhappy chapter had also opened in the relations between the Magyars and the non-Magyar 'nationalities' of Inner Hungary.[3] This does not, of course, mean that a relationship which had previously been

[1] See above, p. 228, n. 3.
[2] See above, p. 222.
[3] The question of nomenclature is an awkward one, but important. The 'Hungarian nation' (magyar nemzet), in spite of the adjective (Hungary's enemies often objected to it as unfairly identifying a part with the whole, but exactly the same usage was, and is, current in many other countries) had no ethnic significance, but a political one: up to 1848 it denoted the politically recognized class, i.e., the nobles (in Latin, the *natio* or *populus*). The ethnic groups composing the population of Hungary were known as 'nationalities' (*nemzetiségek*); when all of them were listed the Magyars also figure as a *nemzetiség*, but more generally, the

THE VORMÄRZ

universally untroubled now became universally bad, for as we have seen, the Serbs of the South had since their arrival in Hungary been fundamentally hostile to the Hungarian State, while conversely, when the new phase opened, most of the Germans of Inner Hungary, many of the Slovaks and practically all the educated Ruthenes found no objection to it. Yet a new and disturbing element had entered into the general relationship between Magyars and non-Magyars, the unhappy but inevitable result precisely of the spread among both parties of modern, and to some extent, democratic, ideas. Before these entered the picture, the Hungarian political 'nation' had been, by definition, exclusively its 'noble' class, and it was a fact that, except for the denationalized magnates at the top, the overwhelming majority of its effective members,[1] who alone composed the Diet and the Congregationes and staffed the public services, whatever their ancestry, spoke Magyar and felt themselves Magyars. Up to the 1830s, the Hungarian nobles, in their demand for a wider use of their language, had had their eyes fixed almost exclusively on Vienna, and the point as they saw it had been the reasonable one that it was absurd and unnatural to forbid them to conduct their own affairs in their own language, for the convenience of a regime which in any case they regarded as a trespasser in most of the fields occupied by it. The fact that more than half the non-nobles of Hungary were non-Magyars was simply irrelevant, since they were not concerned with public life; and it was also a fact that up to that date the vast majority of the non-nobles whose mother-tongue was not Magyar, still accepted this point of view, and cheerfully learned Magyar as the price of advancement.

The new element came in, tragically, when Hungarian political thought became broader and more democratic in the sense that it came to take other classes besides the nobility into consideration. The Magyar-feeling nobles simply assumed that the new, broader State would have the same character as the old, narrower one, and the demand for more schooling in Magyar for non-Magyars (which in practice applied only to secondary and higher education)[2] was made, at first, in the honest faith that it was conferring a benefit on non-Magyars to enable them to acquire the necessary linguistic equipment for taking their place in the national political community. Many majorities in history have, of course, adopted this attitude, and many

---

word, in the plural, is used to denote the non-Magyar peoples of Inner Hungary. The Croats (of Croatia) were not a 'nationality'; their nobles constituted the 'Croat nation'.

The word 'nation' was, however, sometimes used also of any body corporate enjoying extensive rights of self-government. The Serbs of Hungary constituted a 'nation' in this sense, as did the three privileged communities of Transylvania: the Hungarian nobles, the Szekels and the Saxons. This, again, was not an ethnic term, for a Roumanian acquiring Hungarian nobility became a member of the Hungarian nation, and a Saxon domiciled outside the Sachsenboden did not belong to the Saxon nation.

[1] See above, p. 56 f.
[2] The more extensive demand made in 1825 was an aberration, and not seriously pressed.

minorities have welcomed it, as, even now, did many non-Magyars in Hungary.

But national feeling was awakening also among the non-Magyars, and the men touched by it felt that they had the same natural right as the Magyars themselves to use their own languages, cultivate their own national attributes, take pride in their own national pasts. And if the idea of inter-national equality was pushed to its logical conclusion, this would mean that Hungary must cease to be a Magyar State, and become a multi-national one. If few of them went so far as this in the Vormärz, more and more were beginning to want political institutions of their own on a lower level, with the appropriate languages of administration and education. It was a conflict of principle which in practice was made acute by the conviction of the Magyars that their State could not continue to exist at all, except on its old basis. For this they undoubtedly had reason. There was the irredentism being preached from Serbia and Roumania; the Pan-Slav effusions of certain Slovaks, which enormously affected Hungarian public opinion (if the dangers from this quarter were not so great as the Hungarians believed, this was not the fault of Kollar or Stratimirovics). Above all, there was Vienna, with its age-long hostility to Hungarian nationalism, and its traditional policy of allying itself with the non-Magyars. Many Hungarians felt that the only real safety for their country would have lain in turning the entire Magyar population – or at least, its whole educated class – into Magyars, an operation which, the ardent spirits added, would have strengthened the army of those championing and enjoying the blessings of freedom and progress which they proposed to bestow on Hungary, against Viennese (and Czarist) reaction and obscurantism.

So a dismal vicious circle took shape. The Magyar chauvinists, with some genuine cause for alarm, pressed their remedy to ridiculous excess, and began to see treachery in the mildest assertion of nationality by a non-Magyar; thereby in fact turning against Hungary many who would have been perfectly happy to admit even its traditional Magyar character, had this been combined with respect for the national susceptibilities of its non-Magyar citizens.

In this field also Magyar chauvinism reached a new high level in the excited years 1840–3. In this respect, too, Kossuth led the extremists, while Széchenyi sacrificed the last remnants of his popularity by publicly condemning the Magyarization campaign as both un-Christian and ineffectual.[1]

With all these passions in the air, Hungary in 1843 was like Aeolus's cave, and the elections to the Diet were turbulent to a degree. The Opposition, however, made an error in tactics: it announced that noble taxation was the key to all reform, and while not yet daring to attack the contributio, proposed

---

[1] The occasion was the Presidential Address delivered by him in 1842 to the Academy of Sciences which he had promised in 1825 to finance.

that the *cassa domestica* should be extended to all noble land; conversely, those not paying it should be excluded from representation. Either change would have inflicted a crippling blow on the sandalled nobles, whom the Government, in reply, mobilized as its allies. Thanks to their vehement interventions, many Counties returned Conservatives, and the Opposition increased its representation only slightly, while losing also much of its coherence and moral strength through the absence of Deák.[1]

The scales being thus fairly evenly balanced, the Opposition made only small advances in most fields. The Protestants got a concession over the long-debated question of mixed marriages, which could now be celebrated by a minister of either confession, while male issue followed the religion of the father, and female, that of the mother. Non-nobles received the right to hold public office and to buy noble land, and their obligations in respect of public works were limited. But a new codification of the criminal law which would have abolished the competence in it of the Patrimonial Courts and introduced universal equality before the law was rejected, as were a motion to introduce trial by jury, another to reform the statutes of the Royal Free Boroughs, and a third calling for the unification of Transylvania with Hungary.

The Opposition did, however, force through two important decisions. Shortly before it met, the Staatskonferenz had taken the decision mentioned above[2] against Austria's joining the Zollverein or a rival South German grouping. But soon after, Kübeck and Pillersdorf had reached the conclusion that Austrian production could stand up to Hungarian competition, and that if the Monarchy was to stand apart from Germany economically, it must form itself into an economic unit. This would have meant abolishing the internal tariff against which Hungarian Diets had protested so often; it would, indeed, obviously have necessitated also the abolition of the Hungarian nobles' exemption from taxation and the introduction into Hungary of the Austrian indirect taxation, including the excise on tobacco, the cultivation and consumption of which had hitherto been completely unrestricted there.

The big Hungarian agrarians thought that the advantages which would accrue to their exports would outweigh the new burdens; it is from this time on that they accepted the idea of noble taxation. But the economic unification would clearly also have strengthened the political unity of the Monarchy; also, as things stood, of the German element in Hungary itself, which then constituted Hungary's chief trading and industrial classes. Kossuth, moreover, had been reading List's *Nationales System der Politischen Oekonomie* and had been fired with the ideal of economic autarky, or at least of so much

---

[1] The scenes in Zala had been so scandalous (*inter alia*, a mob of sandalled nobles discharged pistols into Deák's house) that Deák announced that he would not accept a mandate if it could be got for him only through equal violence.

[1] See above, p. 261.

industrialization as would diminish the then excessive span of the 'agrarian scissors'. Inspired by him, the Diet demanded that the Crown recognize Hungary's right to decide her own tariffs. When the Crown returned an evasive answer, a group of reformers, again inspired by Kossuth, set up a 'National Association for the protection of Industry',[1] announcing that 'if it proved impossible to set up a protective tariff on the national frontiers, it was possible, and necessary, to set one up on the threshold of every citizen's home'.

The Opposition's second victory was one which, although hailed with immense jubilation, ended by bringing it little profit. At the elections in Zagreb which determined which delegates should be sent to Pozsony, the President, who was an 'Illyrian', had queried the right of the Turopolyans to vote, saying that he must ask Vienna for a ruling whether the Order of 1819[2] applied to Croatia. Meanwhile, he succeeded by an ingenious trick in getting the vote taken when the Turopolyans were absent. At Pozsony the Turopolyan Count, who sat there *ex officio*, queried the legality of the President's action, and consequently, the validity of the mandates of his elected colleagues. The question became entangled at the Lower Table with that of the language of debate there, and that again, with the linguistic question generally, and the heated nationalists produced a Bill to make Magyar the sole language of the legislature, administration and education in the central instances and in Inner Hungary, and of all communications between Hungarian and Croat authorities. The Croat delegates to the Diet had to use Magyar there. Only the three Counties of Zagreb, Várasd and Körös were allowed to rank as Croatia; the Slavonian Counties and Fiume were reckoned as Inner Hungarian. After violent scenes in the Lower House and unsuccessful attempts by the Magnates to mediate, the Crown eventually produced a compromise[3] which in fact gave the Hungarians almost all they asked, with the sole reservation, as regards Croatia, that the Croat delegates, if they did not know Magyar, might continue to use Latin in the Diet for another six years, and the Slavonian Counties and Fiume, which the measure counted as part of Hungary, were allowed the same grace before Magyarizing their administration. Croat authorities were to continue to use Latin among themselves, but Magyar when corresponding with the central or Inner Hungarian officials.[4] The Crown promised that all instruction in Inner Hungary above the elementary level should be in Magyar; elementary

[1] *Országos Ipárvédegylet*, usually known for short as the *Védegylet*. The date of the foundation was 6 October 1844. Kossuth's enthusiasm seems to have been due partly to the fact that, having lost the editorship of the *Pesti Hirlap*, he was without a regular outlet for his activities, or, indeed, a source of income.

[2] See above, p. 222.

[3] According to Srbik (II. 195 ff.), this compromise was largely Metternich's personal production.

[4] Latin where they were corresponding 'officially but in their own names'.

education would be the subject of a further enactment. In Croatia Magyar was to be taught as a subject in upper and secondary schools.

After this, Metternich changed his Hungarian policy once again. The turbulent course of the Diet had convinced him that Hungary was standing 'a pace from the Hell of revolution', yet true spiritual pupil of Francis as he was, he rejected as both wrong in principle and impracticable the Josephinian nostrum of suspending the Constitution. On the other hand, even he had come to see that the policy of pure negation was no longer possible. Instead of following it, he allied himself with the 'Party of Considered Reform', or, as they now called themselves, the 'Progressive Conservatives', on a plan which amounted to carrying out through them, and through a 'reformed' Parliament, a programme of political authority and economic reform.[1] The Föispáns were to reside in their Counties and themselves to take direct charge of the administration; if unable or unwilling to do so, they were to be replaced, as in the 1820s, by 'administrators'. The Föispáns or administrators were to see to it that the Counties sent right-minded Deputies to the Diet, and these were no longer to be tied by binding instructions from their constituents. The 'reign of terror of the jurati' was to be abolished, a proper procedure instituted for the tabling of Bills, and the Government was to submit its own proposals in the form of draft Bills. Other suggestions for strengthening the hands of the central authorities (it is not clear from which side these emanated) included increasing the constitutional weight of the German element by giving more power to the towns and strengthening the garrisons and police.[2] On the economic side, the programme, reflecting the interests of the big Hungarian landowners, scornfully denied the need for factories in Hungary or the utility of them, but stressed the importance of a flourishing agriculture and efficient communications. It accordingly accepted the customs union with Austria, with its consequences, including the introduction of the tobacco monopoly. There was to be a big programme of public works, carried through with the help of Austrian financial houses.

This programme seems to have been worked out while the Diet was still in session, and as soon as it rose (on 13 November 1844) the leader of the Progressive Conservatives, the young and energetic Count György Apponyi (Dessewffy had died suddenly in 1842), was appointed Vice-Chancellor (under Mailáth), to put it into effect. It was not an easy commission, for neither Mailáth nor the Palatine approved of the new policy, but Apponyi went ahead boldly. Administrators were put in in eighteen Counties (in most

[1] The authorship of the programme is not entirely clear. Most of it is contained in two memoranda by Metternich to the Staatskonferenz, and Srbik (II. 198) gives as Metternich's sources for these proposals Jarcke, Baron L. Ambrózy, L. von Wirkner and György Mailáth. But some of them must have come, if only indirectly, from Apponyi's own circle: they were not the men to have a programme simply dictated to them.

[2] The programme frankly recommends the use of military force and corruption if Counties are recalcitrant.

of the rest the Főispáns were already safe Government men). A special section for communications was created in the Consilium and put under the charge of Széchenyi (about whom Metternich had changed his mind, and Széchenyi was magnanimous enough to forgive him), who succeeded in interesting Viennese banks in a number of his pet projects, including the regulation of the Tisza and the development of the railway system along rational lines.

The bright prospects of economic development along the Government's lines were in striking contrast with the failure which was attending Kossuth's endeavours to make Hungary economically autarkic. A 'buy Hungarian' campaign launched by the Védegylet and its sister 'Hungarian Commercial Association' had enjoyed some popularity for a little while, especially among the ladies, but had soon broken down. A few really sound enterprises had been started in connection with it, but most of the Hungarian products had proved shoddy and expensive. The biggest material gains had gone to unscrupulous traders who smuggled in Austrian products, labelled them 'made in Hungary' and sold them at a profit.[1] The Government's economic policy seemed to many more practical, and was not ill-received. Deák wrote bitterly to Kossuth that: 'Hardly had the Government begun to come forward with practical proposals, and to tempt our fellow-citizens with well-paid jobs... and our former adherents are swarming over to range themselves under the Government's banner.'

Nor, it must be said, did the 'swarms' consist solely of place-hunters. Many honest Hungarians felt that it was better in their country's own interest to accept the half-loaf offered by Vienna than to continue an exhausting and quite possibly barren struggle for the whole quartern.

On the other side, however, stood the authoritarian character of the regime and the increased closeness of its connection with, and, it was felt, dependence on, Vienna. These were completely intolerable to the general body of Liberal and nationalist opinion, and it would have required courage to prophesy lasting success for Metternich's latest experiment.

Meanwhile, in Croatia, the 'Illyrians' had driven their opponents out of the field, for in September 1845, the Ban, General Haller, had formally excluded the 'sandalled nobles' from the meeting of the Congregation General in Zagreb, thereby at a stroke reducing the Magyarone voters in Croatia to a handful of landlords and high officials; when challenged to justify the legality of his action, he had produced a Rescript from Vienna authorizing it.[2] And by now the anti-Magyar front in the Lands of the Hungarian Crown could number other national components. The end of Stratimirovics' long reign over the Hungarian Serbs had brought no great

[1] The death-blow to the Commercial Association came when its cashier absconded abroad with its funds. This, however, was not until 1846.

[2] This coup had been approved by Apponyi, who regarded the Turopolyans as radicals and potential allies of the Hungarian Opposition.

immediate changes, for his successor was a somewhat passive and easy-going figure. But his successor again, Rajačić, who was enthroned in 1842, was another politician, 'Illyrian' in the sense of being prepared to combine with the Croats against Hungary, and also a stout champion of the particular Serb cause. A sign of the new activity to be expected from this quarter was that the Synod which elected Rajačić asked for the convocation of a General Assembly of the Serb 'nation' to consider the problems which had been adjourned in 1792.[1]

Other developments important for the later course of events had taken place in the Balkans. Old Miloš Obrenović had at last been deposed in 1839. His elder son, Milan, died only a few weeks later; his brother, Michael, was deposed in his turn in 1842 in favour of Alexander Karageorgević, grandson of the old hero, Black George. Alexander brought with him into Serbian public life a new set of men, the most important of them his Minister of the Interior, Ilja Garašanin. In 1844 Garašanin worked out a plan (which was based on a draft composed by the Polish *émigré*, Prince Adam Czartoryski) for the realization, when opportunity offered, of a Great Yugoslav State, which was to include all territories inhabited by Serbs, Croats and Bulgars, including Croatia and South Hungary. In certain respects this represented another version of the Illyrian idea, but Garašanin's variant definitely envisaged detaching the Serb and Croat territories from Austria and Hungary and placing them under the rule of Belgrade. Agents of the Serbian Principality were beginning to make cautious propaganda in favour of this idea in 1846 and 1847 among the people of Hungary.

Finally, the Slovaks were stirring, partly in response to the effusions of Kollar and his friends and disciples, partly in reaction to the unwise zeal of the Magyarizers, which, owing among other causes to the bogey of Pan-Slavism which the Slovak extremists had conjured up, was directed particularly against this people. The lead was taken here by a local magnate, Count Károly Zay, who in 1840 was elected Superintendent of the Hungarian Lutheran Church. Zay has secured himself a place in the history-books as one of the most fanatical Magyarizers on record. Magyarization, he announced in his inaugural address, was the 'sacred duty' of 'everyone who fights for freedom and common sense, every loyal subject of the House of Austria', and to hinder it, or to foster the spread of any other language 'would be tantamount to severing the vital artery of intelligence, of constitutional principles, of Protestantism itself'. The triumph of Magyarization was 'the victory of reason, liberty and intelligence'.[2] A particular project of his was to bring about the administrative unification of the Calvinist and

---

[1] The Government succeeded in pigeon-holing this request by referring it to a Committee which in the event never met.

[2] Extensive quotations from this address are given in R. W. Seton-Watson, *Racial Problems in Hungary*, pp. 65-7.

Lutheran Churches, which would have been nationally disastrous for the Slovaks, for while the Lutheran Church in North Hungary was largely Slovak, the much stronger Calvinist Church was purely Magyar. Some two hundred Slovak Lutheran pastors, headed by their Superintendent, petitioned the Crown, furthermore complaining bitterly of the intolerant Magyarization of their schools and of public life in their homes. Zay's plan was dropped, but Slovak nationalism was now awake, and was further promoted by another of Zay's activities. In 1843 he succeeded in getting the Pozsony chair abolished, on the ground that the assistant lecturer there, Ljudevit Štur, a pupil of Kollar's, was spreading Pan-Slav doctrines.[1]

This had the rather unexpected effect of promoting the development of an independent Slovak language, because Štur became convinced that it was impossible to maintain Czech as the language of Slovak culture, and after considerable debates, the Slovak intellectual leaders, Protestant and Catholic, agreed to adopt for the national language the purest of the Slovak dialects, that spoken round Turócsszentmartón. But even this was another step forward for the Slovak national movement. Štur and his collaborators, the chief of whom, Josef Hurban and Michael Hodža, were both Lutheran pastors, founded a newspaper in the agreed language, the *Slovenský Národný Novine*,[2] and in it developed a vigorous activity which, although primarily literary, contained many political undertones. On religious grounds, the group did not aim at separation from Hungary, where their faith enjoyed much more freedom than in Austria, but they now constituted, within Hungary, a vigorous national opposition to the Magyars' ambitions of creating a unitary Magyar State.

The situation in Transylvania was meanwhile developing on lines parallel to the Hungarian. The Diet which the Crown perforce convoked in 1837, for its members to swear loyalty to their new Monarch, showed in various ways that it had not forgotten recent events: it refused to submit the Archduke's name for Governor and wrangled hard over most of the other appointments. At the same time, many of its members were inclined to think that Wesselényi had gone too far, nor did they want to see extended to Transylvania the legislation in favour of the peasants enacted in Hungary. Accordingly, a quiet three or four years followed, but then feeling among the Magyar nobles began

[1] This was probably true enough. Štur was an unstable and inconsistent creature who held many doctrines successively and even simultaneously. Before 1848 he was Austro-Slav, sometimes even Hungaro-Slav *à la* Bernolak; then after 1848 he became a fanatical Russophile and Pan-Slav. See the study on him, *Ljudevit Štur, his place in the Slavic World*, by J. M. Kirschbaum, Winnipeg and Cleveland, 1958.

[2] This began publication in 1845. The Hungarians had tried to prevent it, but Sedlnitzky intervened. This was one of the few occasions on which he was able to get his will over a Hungarian question, for his direct authority did not extend across the Leitha. He used to make representations to the Hungarian Chancellery, but, as he used to complain, they were often ignored.

to change: the demand for union with Hungary grew stronger again, outweighing calculation, so that a small Liberal party appeared, and simultaneously, a strong demand emerged for the extension of the official use of the Magyar language. This had been raised in 1837, but rather half-heartedly; however, in 1841 the majority wanted Magyar made the sole language of all official transactions, and of all education, except that the Saxons might for ten years continue to correspond with the authorities in Latin, if they preferred, and might use German in their own schools and internal affairs

The Saxons protested vigorously against this proposal, which the Crown, on this occasion, refused to sanction, and the new Vice-Chancellor appointed in 1844, Baron Samuel Josika, who was a member of Apponyi's group and a man at once of determination and of strong aulic sympathies, was able to restore surface calm. But by this time Transylvania had reached the stage already achieved by Inner Hungary, of cold war between the component nationalities. The Saxons had found a leader, a village pastor named Stefan Ludwig Roth,[1] to rally them to a vigorous resistance to the Magyar unitary State; their natural remedy was the continuance of Transylvania's separate status, in the closest possible connection with Vienna. The Roumanians could be relatively indifferent to the language of an administration in which they did not participate, and an education which they did not receive. Moreover, Bobb's successor, Leményi, was another like him, practical, non-combative, an administrator rather than a politician. On the other hand, Roumanian nationalism in Transylvania was now in its turn being fed from the Danubian Principalities, become virtually independent of the Porte in 1829 and genuinely left to their own devices when the Russian troops evacuated them three years later. The *Règlement Organique* bestowed on them was exceedingly conservative, but it did provide them with national institutions of a sort, and within their framework the national consciousness of the Roumanian people developed mightily. The very fact that a large number of the teachers and civil servants in the Principalities were of Transylvanian origin ensured that that consciousness would always include an awareness of the unity of the Roumanian people,[2] and now, as the pupils began to emerge from the schools, the emotional and intellectual current reversed itself, or at least, became two-way. Roumanian books and literature from the Principalities entered Transylvania and stimulated the consciousness of the Roumanians there. By 1840 the younger generation was already in revolt against the 'Magyarone' tendencies of its elders.

[1] On Roth, see the detailed study by Otto Folberth, *Der Prozess Stephan Ludwig Roth* (Graz, etc., 1958).

[2] Characteristic are the words used by M. Kogalniceanu at the opening of the Iași Academy in 1847:

'I regard as my home the whole territory in which Roumanian is spoken and as my national history, the history of Moldavia as it was before they broke our brothers of Transylvania and Wallachia off from us.'

It was, of course, impossible to express irredentism openly; a Roumanian political programme had to be set within the framework of the Monarchy, and it went for the time no further than the old demands of 1791, for recognition of a Roumanian 'nation' and of the Orthodox Church. But it also included, or implied, strong hostility to the union with Hungary.

In Bohemia – as before, the movements now to be described did not extend to Moravia – opposition to the existing state of things was developing along two distinct lines which seldom coincided, but each to some extent cleared the way for the other; so long as both were against the Government, each found the other a useful ally.

The work of the linguistic pioneers, which had been carried on with great vigour and in complete freedom since 1835, was now complete; Czech had become a mature language, capable of use in any field, and thanks to the density of the schools in Bohemia, and to the important edict of 1815, now widely spoken well above the peasant level. Palacký, Hanka and others had created the national mythos.

A new stage opened about 1840, when a young generation, calling themselves the 'patriots' (Vlastenci), hurled themselves into the task of carrying further their elders' work. As the philologists' task was complete, the 'patriots' saw their task in securing for their language, and for the speakers of it, the place in education and public life to which they felt it, and them, to be entitled. At that time they asked, indeed, no more than equality with the Germans, but many of them were certainly dreaming of superiority, or complete predominance, and as even equality could obviously not be achieved without a struggle, a note of Germanophobia began to creep into their utterances.

It should be added that this younger generation had shed a good deal of the mystic Pan-Slavism of its elders. Few of them felt for Russia more than a certain sentimental veneration and that was weakened by the memories of 1830. There was still some general Austro-Slavism, but most of the young men were primarily interested in the Czech people, and in Bohemia. Even their interest in the Slovaks was relatively lukewarm.

The second movement was that of the Bohemian Estates. Here the Czech national *motif* was, indeed, much less strong, for a high proportion of the aristocrats who dominated the Estates did not even speak Czech. The movement was one for provincial rights; its participants wished to secure for themselves and their Land the same amount of independence from Viennese centralism and bureaucratic control as was enjoyed by their Hungarian counterparts, and although a relatively small Liberal party, led by Count Albert Dehm, evolved within it in the 1840s, the majority were arch-Conservatives; their constitutionalism looked back to the days before the Vernewerte Landesordnung and was more retrogressive than progressive.

The Bohemian Estates, after long years of almost total quiescence, began to stir in the late 1830s, when they caught the Oberstburggraf, Count Chotek, out in a technical irregularity,[1] and persecuted him until he resigned in July 1842. The Staatskonferenz replaced him by the young and agreeable Archduke Stephen, to whom they attached as assistant, Robert Altgraf in Salm, but the Estates discovered that Salm, whose lands lay in Moravia, did not possess Bohemian Incolat and was therefore ineligible for the office. A relative lifted Salm over this hurdle by giving him an estate, but the Estates had now got the bit between their teeth, the more firmly because the hand on the reins had slackened: the old Oberster Kanzler, Count Mittrowsky, who had been a strong man who stood no nonsense from provincials, had just died, and the new Chancellor, Count Inzaghi, was an amiable nonentity, easily over-awed by truculent opponents.[2] The Estates now utilized certain complicated and in themselves trivial incidents to assert a claim of principle, their right to approve the Government's budgetary estimates, and then, in May 1845, sent a deputation to Vienna, commissioned both to put forward certain specific requests, many of which were non-controversial, and also to establish the principle that the Vernewerte Landesordnung of 31 July 1627 was still the public law of the land, so that all diminutions of their rights and privileges suffered by the Estates since that date were legally null and void, and must be rescinded.

All this was extremely embarrassing to the Government, which could appeal to nothing except long-standing 'usus' in support of its claim that the Estates were not entitled to query its estimates. On the second question, it replied that both Ferdinand II and his successors had always reserved themselves the right 'to enlarge, alter, improve and treat in accordance with the *jus legis ferendae*' the Landesordnung. As this answer amounted to a claim by the Crown of a free hand, it left the Estates angry and disappointed, and they and the Hofkanzlei embarked on an acrid feud, thwarting each other in every way that their respective imaginations could devise.

The Slovenes, as before, were still lagging far behind the Czechs. Even the linguistic question had been thrown back into the melting point in the 1830s by Gaj's 'Illyrian' propaganda. After a good deal of controversy, the literary leader of the day, Dr Johann Bleiweiss (in spite of his name,[3] an enthusiastic Slovene and later revered as the 'father of the nation'), ended by adopting Gaj's orthography for the language in which he issued his little paper, a weekly appearing in Laibach, but insisted on the independence of the Slovene language.

[1] He had been spending, on public objects but not always wisely, and without getting the Estates' authorization, moneys from their domestic budget.

[2] Beidtel, II. 402–3, regards this change in the Chancellorship as having been a big factor in the rapid development of the Estates' oppositional movements, not in Bohemia alone, but in all the Lands administered by the Vereingte Hofkanzlei.

According to Beidtel, the real power in the Chancellery was now Inzaghi's second in command, Pillersdorf (the later Minister President). But Pillersdorf himself, although a centralist, was no man of iron.

[3] It was, however, a corruption of the Slovene Blavec.

In the 1840s the name 'Slovenija' began to appear (first in Bleiweiss's paper). Once the Slovenes had got the bit between their teeth, they were as chauvinistic as anyone else. 'From now on', wrote one of Bleiweiss's circle, 'let no Slav maiden give her hand to a German husband, unless to draw him over to her nationality'.[1] But lacking as they did any 'historic rights' to which to appeal, divided between four or five different Lands and possessing no aristocracy and only a minute bourgeoisie, they could do no more than chafe for more cultural freedom and more representation in local government; looking for both nowhere but to the Emperor.

It would be false to deny the German-Austrians of the Vormärz a national feeling, in the modern sense of the term. In particular, the younger 'intellectuals', headed by the High School students, among whom no less than nine more or less ostentatiously Germanic associations now existed, were by no means unaffected by the romantic nationalism of the day. They read the poetry of Schiller and Heine, the prose of Herder and Fichte, and thrilled to the thought that they belonged to a great, unspent people with its future in front of it. But to translate these enthusiasms into a political programme was a different matter. Even those few of them who felt a desire for unification with the other German States, an aspiration which in most of the smaller of those States synthetized so easily with Liberal aspirations, usually did so on grounds which were political rather than strictly national: they felt that in an united Germany they would obtain those Liberal institutions for which they could not hope in Austria as it stood. And those who wanted an united Germany achieved at the price of the disintegration of Austria were few indeed. The feeling of the vast majority was, as it has been well said,[2] that 'Austria and Germany needed one another': the 'Austria' of that phrase being, if not necessarily the Gesammtmonarchie, then at any rate those parts of it of which they were accustomed to think as truly 'Austria', viz., the Hereditary and Bohemian Lands. But for these they had no 'national' programme, cultivated no 'national' movement, because they saw no need for one, since it was axiomatic for them that in the Monarchy (at least, this part of it), the German element was not only entitled to play the leading part, as the only one qualified to do so, through its possession of a cultivated bourgeoisie, but would automatically do so.[3] Those of them who truly deserved the name of Liberal which has often been given, rather indiscriminately, to the whole class, accepted national liberty as one of the faces of the goddess of liberty at whose shrine they worshipped, but in their own way. They were able to approve of the separatist movements in Lombardy-Venetia and Galicia, and to sympathize with Hungarian Liberalism; they were even able to bestow patronizing encouragement on the cultural aspirations

---

[1] Cit. Helfert, op. cit., I. 17.   [2] Molisch, op. cit., I. 24.
[3] There are some excellent remarks on this point in P. Burian, *Die Nationalitäten in Cis-Leithanien und das Wahlrecht der Märzrevolution 1848/9* (Graz-Köln, 1962), pp. 15 ff.

of the Czechs and Slovenes,[1] but their benevolence was due to the fact that they simply attached no political importance to those movements, and therefore had not troubled to work out the political consequences for themselves if they did become political. The very few among them who even conjured up the picture of Austria as a multi-national State did so only to dismiss with ridicule the picture of a polity 'in which the sovereign people of the Slovak besom-binders and the Galician schnapps-peasants had a role to play'.[2] But the great majority never even played with such visions. They simply assumed that the political changes which they desired would come about without any alteration in the structure of the State, in the same way that they had come about, or might do so, in France or England. It has been well said of them that the European ideas of reform reached Austria, but were not given there 'a specifically Austrian stamp'.[3]

The Viennese Liberals' criticisms of the Monarchy as it then stood were thus not nationalist, but political, social and economic.

On the other hand, Vienna contained by far the largest and most powerful bourgeoisie, with its own class interests and consciousness, in the entire Monarchy.

Consequently, the Vienna of the Vormärz had its reform movement, as Pest, Prague and Milan had theirs; but its programme was not national, but political, social and economic.

This movement is generally described as a 'middle-class' and 'Liberal' one, but neither of those adjectives is entirely accurate. The greater part of the reformers were indeed middle class by origin and in outlook, but there were also aristocrats among them. It is, however, true that the 'feudal' character of the existing regime was, in the eyes of nearly all of them, one of its worst defects, and their attacks on it are often accompanied by vicious diatribes against the general personal qualities of the class.[4]

---

[1] It is remarkable how many German-Austrian romantic writers of this period drew their inspiration from episodes of Czech history; Grillparzer's *Libussa* and Lenau's *Ziskra* are familiar examples. It is hardly necessary to refer here to the role played by Herder and other German writers in stimulating the Slav national renaissances.

[2] From *Grenzboten*, 1847, cit. Burian, p. 17.

[3] Charmatz, op. cit., p. 16.

[4] The case against the aristocracy is put with great vigour in many works, among which may be mentioned those of Andrian (himself a titled man), 'Tebeldi', Beidtel himself and Violand. Violand was an extremist, but the others say much the same thing in more temperate words. It may perhaps be remarked that if one-tenth of what Austrian writers of the old days used to say about their own society was true, it is inexplicable that fire and brimstone did not descend to destroy the whole contraption. If, on the other hand, the picture presented by many modern Austrian historians has anything in it, one cannot understand why angels did not waft the place up into heaven.

But the Englishman, Russell, himself wrote that the Austrian aristocracy was 'the least manly in sentiment and the least enlightened in mind of the German nobility' (op. cit., II. 234–5.)

'Liberal' is a more doubtful description. All the would-be reformers were agreed in their dislike of the antiquated, obscurantist and inefficient regime, but when we come to suggested remedies, we can distinguish two trains of thought among them. The one, with which many men then actually serving the Government sympathized, really represented the old Josephinian tradition. What its adherents chiefly disliked in the regime was its inefficiency, and their true hearts' desire was to see a modernized, efficient bureaucratic State, run by themselves. This demand entailed, in their eyes, a number of reforms which in a later age would have earned them the name (only it had not yet been invented) of Right Radicals; and it did not exclude among many of them, a complete readiness to see the structure of the Monarchy as centralist as Joseph II himself could have wished.

The representatives of the new business and intellectual classes (but this group, too, contained many civil servants) were 'Liberals' of a more conventional type. They wanted all the popular freedoms generally desired by European Liberals of their day: intellectual freedom, including freedom of the Press and the abolition of the censorship (these were very strong demands) and freedom of conscience, although since the Jewish element among them was then still small, the anti-clericalism which later obsessed Austrian Liberalism was still embryonic; most of them were Catholics, and in the religious field, went no further than Josephinian Erastianism. They wanted the relaxation of bureaucratic control over business life, a small and cheaper Civil Service, and above all, control by the tax-payer over the public purse. All these things were to be achieved through effective constitutional institutions, in which their own class should be fully represented.

So long as the State was neither free nor efficient, no one needed ask to which of these two groups – which had, indeed, much in common – he belonged, and they combined happily enough. It was not long after Francis's death that they began to acquire mouthpieces and a certain measure of organization.[1] 1839 saw the foundation of the *Niederösterreichischer Gewerbeverein*, a body in which both the aristocracy and the leading figures of the new industrial and commercial world were represented; 1840, that of the 'Concordia', a society of artists, writers and actors whose members included Nestroy, Grillparzer, Endlicher, Baumgartner and others, and in 1842 followed the most important of all, the *Juridisch-Politischer Leseverein*, an exceedingly heterogeneous body, the members of which were mostly higher officials or army officers, but included also, on the one hand, such men as Count Leo Thun, the Bohemian aristocrat, afterwards the most uncompromisingly clerical Minister of Education ever possessed by Austria, and on the other, business men, writers, lawyers, University Professors and doctors. The future Ministers Bach, Schmerling, Doblhoff, Hornbostl and several others all belonged to this association, which became the meeting-place

[1] A good account of these developments is given by Georg Franz, op. cit., pp. 17–41.

for all leading representatives of the 'bourgeois opposition', and, as one writer has called it,[1] the 'General Staff' of the movement.

Although frowned upon by Metternich and Sedlnitzky, the Leseverein was, no doubt largely for that very reason, patronized and protected by Kolowrat, and was consequently able to allow itself a good deal of freedom. It even listened to lectures by J. N. Berger on constitutional history, in which the desirability of constitutional institutions for Austria was openly argued. Moreover, although it had itself no official standing, its membership partly overlapped with that of a body which had such a standing, the Lower Austrian Estates.[2] In the meetings of that body Schmerling, Doblhoff and others developed a reform programme which included in its political demands, besides the abolition of the *robot* and the tithe, such reforms as the broadening of the composition of the Estates by adding to them equal representation for the burghers and peasants, extension of their competences, and the institution of a sort of general Parliament (Allgemeine Reichstände) composed of representatives of the Estates of all Lands, to meet annually in Vienna, vote the budget, audit the State accounts and consider and advise on draft legislation. Other suggestions included the reduction of the length of military service, reformed taxation (including a general income-tax) and reform of the manorial system of communal government.

Some of the same requests were sent in by the Estates of other Lands – Bohemia, Moravia and Styria – and local associations similar to the *Leseverein* were founded in Graz and Prague (which at that time was a German town, so far as its propertied classes were concerned).

We should be flattering the honest Viennese bourgeois if we represented them as in any way seething with unrest during these years. The vast majority of them remained as insouciantly a-political as ever. For that matter, the 'Opposition', such as it was, was entirely loyal to the Crown; if its members wanted the 'system' overthrown, it was because they believed that it was undermining the solidarity of the Monarchy. But few and moderate as they were, their position at the heart of the Monarchy's economic and social life gave them an importance disproportionate to their numbers, and they were destined, as we shall see, to play a large, if somewhat reluctant, part in the revolution of March 1848.

As the Viennese bourgeoisie occupied a special position, so did the High School students studying in Vienna, who constituted a not inconsiderable body – in 1846 Vienna University had 3,719 students on its books. Some of

---

[1] Bibl, *Zerfall Oesterreichs*, II. 67.

[2] The Lower Austrian Estates had come to differ largely in character from those of most Lands, because although even there the towns, including Vienna itself, enjoyed only very meagre representation as such, many of the landed estates were owned by bourgeois or by members of the Beamtenadel whose sympathies and interests were rather with the bourgeoisie than with the 'feudal' aristocracy.

these were, of course, proto-bourgeois, coming from staid and respectable homes and destined to graduate into props of the regime. But they were a minority, and the sons of nobles a still smaller one, for both the nobles and the richer bourgeois preferred to have their sons educated at home, by private tutors. The majority of the students were sons of peasants, artisans or struggling Jewish professional men, whose best hope was one of the meagre careers open to a honoratior. Many of them were desperately poor. According to a contemporary writer,[1] they often subsisted for weeks together on a diet of bread and water, huddling by night in cellars, if they could afford so much; the writer knew of one who slept in the winter in barns and stables, and in the summer, in the open air. The poorest of all were the Jewish students, who had less easy access to the resource by which many of their Christian colleagues kept body and soul together, of giving private lessons.

The students were usually the most fervent nationalists of their peoples: in Vienna and Graz they were the strongest German nationalists, and their opposite numbers were equally fanatic Magyars and Czechs. Further, the material circumstances of many of them and the generous enthusiasms of more, predisposed them to social radicalism. As we shall see, they were largely responsible in 1848 both for touching off the spark of revolution, and afterwards for keeping its flame burning. In particular, they filled the indispensable role of liaison officers with the workers. Their chief demands for themselves were in the intellectual field: for freedom of teaching and learning, abolition of the censorship, etc.

As time went on, the resistance of the Konferenzrat and its servants to all these challenges to its authority grew increasingly ineffectual, even increasingly half-hearted. The Archduke Ludwig's conservatism was rooted in piety, but he was not intelligent enough to make it systematic. Metternich was himself too cultivated a man not to have a certain indulgence towards the things of the spirit, and in any case, too non-combative to impose his will against stiff opposition. Kolowrat, as we saw, posed as a Liberal and in fact undermined much of the work of his colleagues. An interesting tribute to the relative mildness of the Vormärz regime was paid by no less a person than Grillparzer, who wrote in his *Erinnerungen aus dem Jahre* 1848:

All these statesmen, however vigorously they carried on the old system, of free will or under compulsion, were yet at the same time much too good-natured and too humane to want also to carry on the old police pressure. And that was their ruin. Their feeling of decency, thinly as it flowed, yet brought down the March Government in Austria. The Emperor Francis's system of government could only be carried on if accompanied by his police system. As the pressure relaxed, the springs shot up automatically.[2]

---

[1] A. Füster, op. cit., p. 71. Füster, who acted as 'Chaplain in the field to the Academic Legion', was an extreme radical, but he knew how the students lived.

[2] *Erinnerungen, Werke*, vol. VIII, pp. 208–9.

THE VORMÄRZ

The censorship, in particular. while still applied fairly strictly to works printed inside the Monarchy – in 1845 Metternich personally rejected a petition from a group of writers, headed by Grillparzer, to relax it, saying that 'to do so would frustrate the good intentions of the Government' – had become almost nominal in relation to works printed abroad, which easily entered the Monarchy and were widely read. Persons in society read them openly and without fear, and even the students, for whom the nominal penalty for such an offence was perpetual exclusion from any academic institution in the Monarchy, clubbed together to buy them and passed them from hand to hand. Austria thus got the worst of both worlds, for attacks on her system and institutions were published abroad, chiefly in the Protestant States of North Germany, and these writings, many of which were the work of political refugees and correspondingly malevolent,[2] achieved a twofold circulation, wide in each case: in the place of their origin, and in Austria.

How lax the pressure had really become may be judged from Turnbull's experiences. It is hard not to think that Turnbull's spectacles were somewhat roseate, and that he did go rather far in describing conditions in the Monarchy as 'combining unrestricted individual liberty with the most perfect public order.' But he was no fool; he was a Fellow of the Royal Society, and took the trouble, not only to study statistics, but to see for himself how peasants were fed and what wages were earned by industrial workers. And his own experiences entirely bear out his description of the regime. He passed the frontier without having his baggage opened. He seems hardly to have encountered a policeman in the whole course of his travels, and he found ample provision of English, French, German and Italian newspapers in the reading-rooms of Carlsbad, Graz and Trieste. His description of 'the real indulgence of the Austrian Government which often tempers its nominal severity' is, after all, a fair enough anticipation of the definition of the same system given three-quarters of a century later by the Socialist leader, Viktor Adler: 'absolutism tempered by slovenliness'.

[1] Schuselka's various writings are good examples of such hostile products by malcontent émigrés; but Andrian's famous *Oesterreich und dessen Zukunft*, which enormously affected opinion in both Germany and Austria, was also published abroad, although its author was working as a civil servant in Austria, as was Möhrings *Sybillinische Bücher aus Oesterreich*, by the tutor to an Archduke's sons.

8

Before the Storm

In spite of the considerable stresses which accumulated in most parts of the Monarchy during the decade which followed Francis's death, the general atmosphere of the 'high Vormärz' (to coin a phrase) was curiously un-urgent. The spirit of Francis had reigned so long that it was difficult to imagine it as ever abdicating, and most men and women of the period did not nerve themselves to the imaginative effort. When their petitions were rejected, they shrugged their shoulders and left it at that. The proverbial Austrian who began his discourse on public affairs with the indignant exordium *da muss etwas geschehen* – and there were many who did – really ended it more often than not with the equally proverbial conclusion, *da kann man nix machen*. And the student of the period cannot escape the conclusion that he did so with a certain satisfaction. The devils he had learnt to know had ended by endearing themselves to him. Turnbull notes that the Viennese 'dread any change, as fraught with evil',[1] and here again he is only confirming the judgment of Russell, who found the Viennese 'more bitter enemies of everything like care or thinking ... than any other (people) of Germany, or perhaps of Europe',[2] and the Austrian people 'the most anti-revolutionary of Europe'.[3] It would be easy to compile a whole anthology of quotations to the same effect from Austrian writers; Schuselka, for example, wrote that 'the population of Vienna seemed to a serious observer to be revelling in a continuous state of intoxication. For them it was always Sunday, always Carnival.' The more turbulent spirits themselves did no more than toy with the idea of revolution.

Even economic conditions were not wholly unsatisfactory. Turnbull, as we have said, noted no signs of distress among any classes. Prices were rising, enough to cause some discomfort to the wage-earners and still more, to the fixed income classes, but the rise was still only slight. The most careful student of Austrian economic conditions of the day is still able to describe the years 1840–5 as 'the last good period'.[4]

But just as (we have suggested) the five years 1830–5 ought to be added

---

[1] Russell, op. cit., II. 217–18.   [2] Turnbull, op. cit., II. 226.   [3] Id., p. 323.
[4] So G. Marx heads the second section of his book. The heading is surprising, for the contents of the section read to the unsophisticated reader like a fairly unrelieved category of tribulations, but Marx gives it, and stands by it (see his p. 143).

to the beginning of the Vormärz, in its true spiritual sense, so the years 1846–7 should be lopped off it, as constituting a distinct historic period of their own. In them the atmosphere is quite unlike that of their easy predecessors. The complacent sense of security on the one hand and the only half-resentful acceptance on the other are both gone. In their place comes an anticipation of imminent change which is regarded with hopeful impatience by some, with anxious forebodings by others, but of which all are conscious.

The transformation was largely wrought by a single event – an extremely curious one, and one where, as so often in Austrian history, the flint on which the spark was struck, and in part, the tinder on which it fell, lay outside the frontiers of the Monarchy. In 1840 the Liberals in the Polish emigration had reached agreement with the Conservative party, and the 'national Government' had included peasant emancipation in its programme. The Polish Left in Galicia (as in Prussian and Russian Poland) had thereupon developed a vigorous social agitation: emissaries toured the country, leaflets promising the peasants land and liberty passed from hand to hand, secret societies and conventicles sprang up. The Resolution of the Galician Estates,[1] which itself owed something to the decision in Paris, lent colour to the propaganda.

Absurdly optimistic reports reached Paris that the peasants had been won over to the national cause. They were so plausible that in the autumn of 1845 the Paris Committee decided that the time was ripe to strike again. This time the peasants were to be invited to join in, being promised land and liberty for their reward. The revolution was to embrace the territories of all three Partitioning Powers and Cracow, but it was to begin in Posen, Cracow and West Galicia,[2] where the first objective was to be the *Kreis* capital of Tarnow. Zero day was fixed for 21 February 1846.

It need hardly be said that the secret was ill-kept. Russia and Prussia got wind of it and nipped the preparations in the bud. The Austrians, too, received warnings, but the Archduke was incurably optimistic and Metternich, too, underestimated the danger.[3] The Austrians therefore took next to no precautions. The garrisons were, indeed, brought up to strength, but left almost without ammunition.

Meanwhile, their failures elsewhere did not deter the Poles of Cracow and

---

[1] See above, p. 283.

[2] According to Sacher-Masoch, op. cit., the landlords in East Galicia, with one or two exceptions, had held aloof from the movement. There was to have been a rising in Lemberg. The local officers were to be invited to a grand ball and asked to stand up with the Polish ladies in a dance for which they would have to remove their daggers. They were then to be massacred on a given signal. The plan, however, was betrayed and the ball called off. Similar balls were to have been given in other centres, but it does not appear that any of them were held.

[2] Sacher-Masoch writes that the Poles employed double agents to feed the Austrians with misleading reports.

Galicia. On 17 February the Kreishauptmann of Tarnow, Frh. von Breinl, received a message from Cracow that the revolt was about to break out (the date having been advanced) there and in Tarnow. Breinl was a man well-liked and trusted by the local peasants, and the next day a stream of peasants from the neighbouring villages arrived at his office, all with the same story: at 11 p.m. that night they were to assemble, armed with scythes and flails, then to march on Tarnow and 'massacre the Germans there'. As reward they were to be allowed to loot the Jews' shops and afterwards to receive their land and liberty.

Breinl afterwards swore that all that he had told the peasants was that they were to obey only their lawful masters, i.e. the Austrian authorities. The Polish version, stubbornly maintained, was that he and other Austrian authorities had told them to attack their lords, and had even set a price on the heads of the Polish rebels.[1] One inclines to believe Breinl, for it is certain that he afterwards saved many nobles from the peasants' hands, but almost anything said in such a situation could easily be misinterpreted. In any case, it was on their lords that the peasants turned, and during the next three days a procession of peasant carts arrived in Tarnow laden with Polish nobles, some living, but others dreadfully mutilated corpses. They had done this, they said, 'because the lords were against the Emperor'.

Similar scenes, on a small scale, had taken place elsewhere in Galicia. Practically everywhere, where the peasants had moved at all, it had been to attack their lords, of whom 1,458 were counted afterwards to have been killed or wounded. With this the 'rising' was over in Galicia, before it had begun. In Cracow it lasted a few days longer. The Austrian General Collin had (at the request of the city Senate itself) occupied the Free City on 18 February with a little force of 750 men, but had withdrawn it on the 22nd, alleging a shortage of ammunition and supplies. The Poles then formed a 'Government', which sent detachments into the neighbouring country-side. Collin, assisted by an energetic young officer who won his spurs in this field, Lieut.-Colonel, as he then was, Benedek, drove them back with the help of primitively armed peasant auxiliaries. On 3 March, while

[1] This version was propagated at the time from Paris, and was widely credited. Some Polish writers go so far as to suggest that the whole incident was instigated by the Austrians (this is the plain sense even of the account in the *Cambridge History of Poland*, II. 353, written nearly a century later). This is certainly ridiculous. The lesser charge may have been justified in certain individual cases: Namier, *The Revolution of the Intellectuals*, p. 16, quotes (from Polish sources) an alleged instruction from a high official in Lemberg which, if authentic, would prove him personally guilty of it. Even so, it is hard to see the Poles' grievance, since on their own admission they had been preparing to do exactly what they found so scandalous in the case of the Austrians: set peasants to attack unsuspecting men. The text of one of their instructions for the rising, quoted by Sacher-Masoch, op. cit., p. 46, contains the words: 'On a certain day, and at a certain hour, the whole realm will rise in the following way: the associates will massacre the oppressors...'

these operations were still in progress, Russian troops marched into Cracow, followed on the 5th by a detachment of Prussians. Now the Poles outside the city agreed to call off any further moves in order to avoid waste of blood. They should rather complete their armaments and try again later. The ill-conceived and ill-starred enterprise was over.

This extraordinary episode had profound effects, direct or indirect, in almost every field of the Monarchy's public life. One consequence was, on the surface, a gain for her, for on 6 November, after concluding the necessary negotiations with the two other Partitioning Powers,[1] she announced the annexation of the Free City, consequently actually ending the Vormärz with wider frontiers than had been hers when the period opened. But this brought her perhaps the reverse of profit, even internationally. While the Czar had approved the annexation, it did not cause him to revise the feelings of dislike and contempt with which he was now regarding Austria's rulers. Prussia had given way only very reluctantly, and the annexation enhanced the jealousy with which she and the other German States viewed Austria. Britain disapproved deeply, particularly since Metternich had informed the Foreign Office of the impending annexation only ten days before announcing it. Palmerston denounced the step publicly, with the significant comment that the Acts of the Congress of Vienna 'constituted a single whole which, if not valid on the Vistula, can be declared invalid on the Rhine or the Po'. He was to give practical expression to this view in 1848, in a fashion which caused Austria great difficulties, when the settlement on the Po was really called in question. France swallowed the affront more easily, and in the autumn of 1847 Metternich reached an unwritten 'entente' with Guizot, but the event proved this worthless. In general, Austria's moral credit was weakened everywhere by the odium which the Polish Committee in Paris succeeded in casting on her for her alleged commission of the social crime of instigating peasants to massacre nobles.[2] How small her international influence had become was made dismally apparent in 1847, when Metternich's support was unable to save the Swiss Sonderbund from defeat at the hands of the Federation.[3]

[1] The details are given conveniently by Srbik, *Metternich*, II. 149–66.

[2] It is interesting that in April 1848, when the Cracow Poles were giving the Austrian Government so much trouble, Pillersdorf said that the acquisition of the Free City had been 'the root of all the trouble' and 'its separation from the Monarchy would be desirable'. Ficquelmont, indeed, objected that Cracow would then immediately be occupied by the Russians, and although this would indeed put a stop to the revolutionary agitation, it would put Russia militarily in a position from which 'it could operate in the heart of the Monarchy easily and almost unimpeded' (Walter, *Zentralverwaltung*, III. I. p. 67).

[3] This was, in essentials, another of the innumerable cases in which the financial considerations championed by Kolowrat proved decisive. Metternich wanted to send troops into Switzerland, or at least to grant the Sonderbund an armaments credit. He succeeded with

In Galicia itself the massacres left the Polish nobles, almost to a man, bitterly resentful towards the Austrian authorities, while the annexation increased the complexity of her internal Polish problem by adding to the numbers of her Polish subjects a contingent which was not insignificant numerically, and qualitatively very important, since it contained a large intelligentsia, and one steeped in nationalist tradition. The Government had to take strong measures. A big garrison was stationed in Cracow, and the troops in Galicia reinforced. The unsuspicious old Archduke was induced to resign, and the able and energetic Count Rudolph Stadion, President of the *Gubernium* of Moravia-Silesia, sent to Lemberg as 'Commissioner Extraordinary'. But the thorniest problem of all was that raised by the peasants, among whom the belief, right or wrong, had taken firm root that the Government had promised to reward them for their loyalty with their liberty, which they demanded vociferously; thereby placing the Government in a quandary. It feared that if it did nothing, the peasants would join hands with the Polish nobles (who, they claimed, had made them the same promise). On the other hand, it was anxious not to give the impression that it was rewarding massacre, nor to make a concession which would lead to further demands in Galicia itself (if the peasants stopped paying dues to their lords, the Staatskonferenz argued, they would go on by refusing payments to the State) and also set a precedent which would have to be followed elsewhere. Metternich was further afraid of incurring the displeasure of the Czar.[1] The sole early fruit of these conflicting considerations was an Imperial Patent, dated 13 April, which abolished a few special abuses, most of them already illegal, and extended the peasants' rights of complaint and appeal, but left the basic situation broadly unchanged.

This naturally did not satisfy the peasants, especially as the year was one of extreme distress for them. In the previous autumn there had been disastrous floods in the basin of the Vistula, the seventh in ten years, and the worst of any; these had destroyed the homes of no less than 60,000 peasants, besides ruining their fields and drowning many of their cattle. Much of the country was on the verge of starvation. Hunger typhus broke out and thousands of men, women and children perished. In many places, especially in West Galicia, the peasants refused to perform the *robot* and some villages more or less repudiated all authority.

In November[2] the Government ventured another Patent, which placed all rustical land in Galicia on the 'bought-in' basis and reduced the *robot* to the

---

difficulty (both Kolowrat and Kübeck objecting) in persuading the Staatskonferenz to grant the Seven Cantons a non-interest-bearing loan of 100,000 g., but his other proposals were rejected as financially impracticable. Lacking as it did any financial sinews, the 'moral support' which the Chancellor gave the Seven Cantons proved to be worth exactly nothing.

[1] Schlitter, pp. 39 ff.
[2] The Patent was dated 12 November and promulgated in Galicia on 25 November.

Bohemian level, but did little more, leaving, in particular, the peasants' dues in money and kind unaltered, and bringing the cottars and landless men no alleviations whatever. This naturally only increased the peasants' impatience, while the landlords complained that their incomes were being docked without compensation.

At this stage Rudolph Stadion resigned, and on the following 21 April (1847) the Staatskonferenz (against the votes of many of the Konferenzrat, who regarded him as a dangerous progressive) appointed his brother, Count Francis Stadion, at that time Governor of the Littoral, Statthalter. Soon after arriving in Lemberg. Francis Stadion, who was in fact a very progressive man, and also a highly competent and intelligent one (the brothers were probably the best senior administrators in the Austria of the day), sent in a report urgently recommending a number of reforms: further improvements in the position of the peasants, an amnesty for political prisoners, combined with the expulsion of the chief agitators 'to Algiers, America or somewhere', a drastic purge of the administrative services and the reinforcement of them, and the transference of the judicial work of the Patrimonial Courts to a staff of paid magistrates dependent on the Gubernium.[1]

Effect was given to the two last-named recommendations, and public security was improved by the organization of a special para-military force, but the other reforms were still hanging fire in the early spring of 1848. By that time, order was indeed, prevailing in Galicia, but it was a precarious one. Inside the province, the peasants on the one side, the nobles on the other, were alike seething with discontent, and no one could suggest how to satisfy the one group without alienating the other irretrievably. The Polish emigration, not, apparently, in the least discouraged by the fiasco of its latest enterprise, was gaily laying plans for another.

It was, moreover, relevant to Austria's position that the garrisoning of the province was putting a heavy strain on the Monarchy's meagre military resources, and the administration of it, with the new paid judiciary, a further burden on its groaning finances.

Meanwhile, the peasant unrest had in fact spread to other Lands, many of whose authorities were pressing the Government to take prophylactic measures. Here, again, the Staatskonferenz moved only reluctantly. Its first answer was a Rescript from the Emperor to the Oberster Kanzler, dated 26 May, ordering him to institute a general inquiry into the position in respect of robot and tithe, and expressing the wish that everywhere in the Lands under his authority where the nexus subditelae existed, the redemption of these items 'by agreement' should be facilitated and accelerated. The officials entrusted with this inquiry decided to extend it to all dues and servitudes, but practically the only point on which they agreed was that the

[1] This had been proposed as early as March 1846 and agreed in principle by the Conference but not carried through.

peasants would have to pay for any relief received by them.[1] The Decree issued on 18 December simply informed the Land authorities that a peasant was entitled, if his landlord agreed, to commute his dues against a money rental, or to buy himself out. The one major innovation which the Decree introduced[2] was that, breaking with the old-established rule forbidding any conversion of rustical land to dominical, it made it legal for a peasant to buy himself out by ceding part of his land, but this concession (if it deserves the name, for it rather advantaged the landlords) had, given the peasants' mentality, no practical effect whatever.[3] Otherwise, since the peasant had already enjoyed the rights enumerated for over half a century, it left the legal situation unchanged, so that its sole effect was psychological. This, however, was great. Grünberg describes it as having had 'an enormous immediate effect' and as having been 'immensely important for the future political developments in Austria'[4] – but the effects were the opposite of those desired by the Government. The peasants became convinced that the Government would not help them, whereas if they insisted they would be able to enforce their liberation without paying for it at all. In 1847 they were refusing robot more often than they performed it, and even threatening to burn down the homes of blacklegs. Even in Lower Austria, troops were sent out against them. It is safe to say that only the larger revolution of 1848 forestalled a separate peasant revolution (unless the Government yielded the whole way) in most Austrian Lands.

As it happened, the landlord-peasant crisis coincided with the outbreak of a very severe social crisis in other fields. As we have said, prices had not risen greatly before 1844 (the economy having recovered fairly quickly from the war scare of 1840), and it was only in the latter year that the development of the Zollverein, Kossuth's 'Buy Hungarian' campaign, and a variety of other causes, plunged Austrian industry into renewed difficulties. It was a bad year, with widespread unemployment and machine-wrecking, but still not so disastrous but that, at the end of it, the authorities were expecting that things would be back to normal by the end of it. But the 1845 harvest was bad, and in the autumn came the disastrous floods on the Vistula and others in Hungary and Lombardy, where, too, several successive harvests were ruined. In 1846 there was cattle plague in Hungary, and in Silesia the potato harvest – the only crop to grow at all plentifully on the thin soil of that province – was ruined by blight. While waiting for the next season thousands of people, we are told, 'had nothing to eat except grass and nettles, coltsfoot, or a mess concocted of chaff, clover and blood'. Even in Vienna the bread was mixed

---

[1] On the Commission's inquiries see Grünberg in *L. U. F.*, I. pp. 32 f.
[2] There were a few other minor modifications which need not be enumerated here. They are described in Grünberg, l.c.
[3] I have been unable to trace a single case of advantage's being taken of this concession.
[4] Grünberg, p. 37.

with maize. People 'were spending all their money on food and not paying their debts'. Of 30,000 persons in Vienna liable to the earnings tax, the State in 1845 could get the tax out of half only by sending soldiers to collect it, and out of one-third only by distraining on their effects.[1] In the autumn it became clear that the cereals harvest had failed again, as did the hay harvest, on which the cattle should have been fattened. Prices of food had doubled in two years, firewood had risen 250% in the year. There were shortages in almost every Land, hunger typhus in Styria, Bohemia and Silesia.

In 1847 prices were higher still, being driven up largely by conscienceless speculators who bought the peasants' crops off the field and hoarded them, or sold them on to Bavaria, where there were also shortages, and more money. And now, into the bargain, the worst crisis to date broke out in the Bohemian cotton mills. Several factories went bankrupt and the banks were chary of advancing loans. Unemployment rose to unprecedented heights just at the moment when a full-wage packet was most essential. Then the potato harvest was smitten by blight again and the cereals harvest was bad for the third year running.

The worst foci of distress were in Bohemia and Silesia, but things were bad almost everywhere. In Linz one-third of the population was living below the destitution level. In Salzburg bread was being mixed with clover. Vienna presented a special problem, for great numbers of starving people had flocked into it, especially from Bohemia, in search of work on the railways or other public works. This movement had, indeed, been going on for some years, but it had been chiefly from the German districts, whose inhabitants were unable, at least psychologically, to accept the cut wages for which a Slav had still been willing to work. Now it was joined even by Czechs from the plains.

The railways did provide some employment for heavy manual workers, and for a while, public works were organized on a considerable scale by the Estates of Bohemia, Moravia, and Lower Austria. These, however, were abandoned as the Estates' money ran out, and the relief of distress was left to the parishes, or to private charity. The misery of the starving masses huddled together in the outer suburbs of Vienna was indescribable. There was, naturally, much murmuring against butchers, bakers, millers, peasants, Jews, who were regarded as the profiteers in chief, even against the Imperial family itself. The incidence of common crime, too, rose alarmingly. The police reported that the situation was dangerous.

The general awareness of imminent social danger lent to all the familiar national and constitutional oppositional movements a touch of hectic urgency, and imported new elements of radicalism into most of them. Galicia, as we have said, was simmering. In July 1846 the Estates of Lower Austria submitted to the Government a strongly worded memorandum, insisting on their right to approach the Crown direct with petitions, representations and complaints. The Bohemian Estates were frightened in that

[1] Fischer, op. cit., p. 33.

year into accepting the Government's taxation estimates, but they did so only with a rider re-affirming their constitutional case, as stated in the previous year. Meanwhile, the more radical popular movement had received an extraordinary stimulus for which the Czechs, like the Croats, were indebted mainly to a single individual: in this case, an exceedingly brilliant and intrepid young journalist named Karel Havlíček. Appointed editor of the biggest paper then appearing in Czech, the *Pražké Noviný*, Havlíček had the inspiration of filling its columns with what purported to be reports sent from Ireland of the progress of the 'Repeal' movement there, but were in fact transparent enough descriptions, written by himself, of the sufferings of Bohemia under 'Viennese' rule. Inspired by him, the radicals of both local nationalities (for although an extreme Czech nationalist in the particularist sense,[1] Havlíček contrived to make his agitation acceptable to both) grouped themselves loosely into a movement calling itself by the Irish name of Repeal. Representing as it did the small man, and led by men who were themselves sons of the people, the Bohemian Repeal movement was strongly democratic. It took up the cause of the peasants, artisans and industrial workers, and some of its leaders seem to have found contact with the underground world of extreme social radicalism the centre of which was Paris, and its exponents, some of the Masonic Lodges.

In so far as 'Repeal' meant Home Rule for Bohemia, its programme agreed well enough with that of the aristocrats, and widely as the attitudes of the two movements differed on social issues, certain threads were spun between the two. Dehm's Liberal group, in particular, gave the 'Repeal' movement all the support in its power.

In May 1847 the Estates recovered their courage and again rejected a demand from the Government for an increased land tax, which they declared that they would not pay unless given detailed information on how the money was to be spent. The Government simply sent the demand to the Gubernium, with instructions to collect the money, and relations between Vienna and Prague reached a new record of tension. The situation was rendered a little more uneasy still when, as described below, the Archduke Stephen was called away to succeed his father as Palatine of Hungary. He had not taken a big part in affairs, but the presence of an Archduke in any provincial capital always lent its atmosphere a certain benignity.

The Moravian Estates, too, began to stir, although the movement here was more pacific than in Bohemia and seems to have been purely constitutional, with no admixture of Czech nationalism.

Transylvania – to get its affairs out of the way at this point – was a wheel within a wheel, and its spin was individual, but here, too, the pace of the rotation increased. In 1847 the Magyars won a victory on the linguistic issue,

---

[1] Havlíček had spent a couple of years in Russia, and had come back convinced of the unrealism of Pan-Slavism.

for the Crown issued a ruling which gave them most of their wishes in that field, leaving German only as the language of inner administration in the Saxon districts and that of correspondence between the Saxon Nation and other jurisdictions. The Saxons were infuriated, and Roth got into trouble with the authorities for an inflammatory speech.

The Roumanians had found a new and important leader, Mgr Şaguna, later to become their Orthodox Bishop, who in June 1846 had been appointed Vicar-General to the Orthodox See on the belated death of Bishop Moga. He was a strong Roumanian nationalist, and had also endeared himself to the Austrian authorities by his skill in coping with a threatened peasant rising.[1] Meanwhile, the social grievances of the Roumanian peasants of Transylvania were as bad as ever; indeed, called upon by the Crown to review and revise the status of the peasants, the Diet of 1846–7 had produced proposals which would actually have aggravated still further the miserable conditions of this class. It was perhaps fortunate for all parties, lords included, that the law never came into force, for although the Crown accepted it, with minor amendments, it had not been promulgated when it was superseded by the new laws of 1848.[2]

The scenes in Galicia had a direct and important effect on political developments in Inner Hungary. They convinced Apponyi, who had now got a comparatively free hand, for Majláth had been sent on indefinite leave and the Palatine was falling into his last sickness, that the programme agreed with Metternich in 1844 was no longer adequate to the situation. He therefore added to it a number of items which, if not meeting all the Opposition's demands, went a considerable way towards many of them. They included the extension of taxation to noble land, the abolition of the aviticitas, facilities for peasants to buy in their holdings, the foundation of an agricultural bank, the reform of the penal code, and others.

He also took the important step, new to Hungarian history, of organizing his followers in a political party. The 'Government Party', as the new organization styled itself, was much wider than Apponyi's original group, and contained many men whose conservatism hardly deserved the epithet 'progressive', but the shock given to the Hungarian landlords by the fate of their Galician cousins had been very general, and a large number of them had

---

[1] See above, p. 279, n. 3. According to Helfert, l.c., Şaguna actually kidnapped the agitatrix in chief from the middle of a gathering and bore her away in his carriage to a near-by fortress.

[2] A provisional survey made in 1819 was to be taken as the basis for determining what land was urbarial and what allodial. If land was shown by the survey as being cultivated allodially, the onus was on the peasant to prove that it had been taken from him unlawfully; if shown to be cultivating land registered as allodial, he had to restore it within two years. The size of a sessio was fixed at the minute figure of 4 hold arable and 2 ley for the best land, ranging to 14:6 for the worst; yet the robot was to be the same as in Inner Hungary, where a sessio was four times as large (52 days haulage or 104 hand). The tithe and the landlords' other dues were left unchanged or extended.

come round to the view that a measure of reform was not only inevitable, but desirable, provided that the question of compensation was settled satisfactorily, and in March 1847 they adopted Apponyi's draft as their programme for the Diet when it should next meet, in the following autumn.

The Opposition politicians, for their part, felt the need both to step up their own social programme (partly because opinion in their ranks, too, had been affected by the events in Galicia, partly to avoid being outbidden by the Government), and also to match the Government Party with an organization of the same type.[1] Given the wide differences of opinion on many points which existed between the various factions, the problem of producing a generally acceptable programme was not easy, but the Centralists magnanimously allowed the *Pesti Hirlap* to be used as a common organ for all branches of the Opposition, and after protracted conversations, all the chief men constituted themselves an 'United Opposition', pledged to an agreed programme, which was issued in June 1847 under the title of an 'Oppositional Declaration'. This document, which had been chiefly inspired by Kossuth, but revised by Deák, declared that its authors stood, legally, on Law X of 1790, and objected only to such features in the system, as then practised, as infringed that law; those, however, it condemned as 'foreign and non-national' and unconstitutional, and demanded their repeal. For the rest, the Declaration covered the special wishes of all the groups of the Opposition. To satisfy the Centralists, it asked for a genuinely national Ministry, exercising effective control over the collection and expenditure of revenue; to please the democrats and social reformers, it demanded extension of representation in the Counties and municipalities to non-nobles; general equality before the law; religious freedom and equality; complete and compulsory redemption of all peasant servitudes, against compensation for the landlords; noble taxation, abolition of the aviticitas and the establishment of an adequate credit system; freedom of the Press, and the abolition of the censorship on books. The Partium were to be incorporated unconditionally, Transylvania, if its Diet voted for the union. On the tariff question, Hungary was prepared to negotiate amicably with the Austrian Lands.

Another important passage in the Declaration laid down that while it was essential that Hungary should have these Constitutional institutions, these would not be safe unless similar reforms were introduced in the Austrian Lands.[2]

The Diet would have before it at least two more questions. The old Palatine had died on 13 January, shortly after celebrating the completion of

[1] Some of them had been considering these points as early as 1845.
[2] For the influence exerted on later developments by this declaration, see below, p. 323, etc. Although it was Kossuth who was normally the most persistent advocate of the thesis, others, including Eötvös, also held the view more strongly. It was actually put forward by one speaker in the debates of the 1825 Diet.

half a century's tenure of his office, and his successor would have to be elected. The real choosing in this respect had already been done: Ferdinand had personally insisted that the candidate proposed to the Diet must be Joseph's thirty-year-old son, the Archduke Stephen, then figuring at the head of affairs in Prague. The candidature was agreeable to the Hungarian nationalists, for Stephen, who had been born and brought up in Hungary, and spoke its language, was known to be deeply attached to the country. The Staatskonferenz and the Hungarian Conservatives regarded it with correspondingly misgivings, and in fact, Stephen's enthusiasms were somewhat uncritical, and although genuinely loyal to the head of his family, he lacked his father's understanding of the dynastic interests, and also his extraordinary knack of making Hungarians content with receiving less than they had asked for. They had, however, perforce bowed to Ferdinand's decision.

The Croat question was certain to come up. Haller had resigned in December 1845 and the office of Ban was still vacant (a fact that was to be important a few weeks later). Pending the appointment of a new Ban, Croatia was in charge of Mgr Haulik, the Bishop of Zagreb, a man close to the councils of the Court. Under his benign gaze, the Sabor had cast restraint to the winds. It passed a Resolution 'to work for the unification of Croatia-Slavonia with Dalmatia, the Military Frontier, Fiume and the Littoral'. As interim measures, Vienna was asked to establish a Croat section in the Court Chancellery and a separate Croat Consilium, to elevate the See of Zagreb to an archiepiscopate and to introduce Croat as the sole language of administration and education (as which it was in fact already being used) in Croatia. The Croat Counties returned unread communications addressed to them by Hungarian Counties, and Croat officials addressed their opposite numbers in Croat, refusing even to append a Latin translation.

On their side, nearly all the Hungarian Counties had instructed their delegates to raise the linked questions of the Turopolyans' grievances and the legality of Haller's action in 1845.

When, on 7 November, the Diet met, it was not at all certain how its proceedings would end. The elections had left the two parties very evenly balanced. The Liberals had emerged with a small advantage at the Lower Table, but were in a clear minority among the magnates. Their unity, moreover, was still only very superficial. Deák had declined his mandate on grounds of ill-health, and in his absence, the Opposition was led by Kossuth, now sitting in his own right, as Deputy for Pest County, which had elected him by a large majority; but his authority over his colleagues was far from firm. In fact, when, the election of the new Palatine having been affected, as tradition demanded, by unanimous acclamation, the Government put forward its 'Proposita' (now in the form of draft Bills), these went such a long way towards realizing the Liberals' own programme of social legislation as to fill Kossuth and his fellow-radicals with well-founded fears that their more lukewarm colleagues would be satisfied, and the Diet end with the political side of the Governments's programme endorsed, and a number of three-quarter social reforms enacted on which it would be difficult to go back later.

Kossuth tried to reunite the Opposition and to reassert his own authority, which was really in danger, by proposing a formal complaint to the Crown against the system of administrators, as contrary to Law X. To this he proposed to add the rest of the Opposition's demands, as set out in the Declaration. The question of the administrators was one which the Crown and the Government Party were bound to take as a direct challenge, and the considerable number of men on both sides who were anxious to avoid a head-on collision proposed this and that concession in return for the dropping of the crucial demands. Proposals and counter-proposals flew about like young swallows just out of the nest, and under strong pressure from Széchenyi and other moderates, the Government gave a great deal of ground. Municipal reform, the abolition of the aviticitas, and the re-incorporation of the Partium had already figured among the Proposita. The Government now agreed to extending taxation for the cassa domestica (although not for the contributio) to noble land, and in principle, to the abolition of the nexus subditelae. It agreed that the Consilium Locumtenentiale should be answerable to the Diet, which would have meant that, while foreign affairs, defence and finance remained under central control, Hungary would have been almost completely autonomous in respect of her 'interna'. On 1 February it even suddenly produced a Royal message promising that the system of administrators should be regarded as an emergency measure only, which would not be maintained when conditions became normal.

It seemed possible that this last, very big, concession, would satisfy enough of the Opposition and make it possible for the Crown and the Diet, after all, to resolve their differences peaceably, for on 5 February the Lower Table voted to accept the message, thus inflicting on Kossuth his first Parliamentary defeat. But it had done so only by a majority of a single vote, and that cast by a Croat, so that the prospects of peace were obviously extremely precarious. Meanwhile, Magyars and Croats had been wrangling with great acerbity over the Turopolyan vote, the language of communication between the two countries, and much more serious, the question to which of them the Slavonian Counties and Fiume belonged. The Croats for their part were displaying great irritation, not only against the Hungarians, but also against the Crown for its hesitancy in backing their demands.

The situation in Italy had, quite suddenly, become the most dangerous of all. The elevation of the supposed Liberal, Pio Nono, to the Holy See in June 1846 had opened the sluices to an enormous rush of pent-up national and Liberal feeling throughout the Peninsula. While the inhabitants of the Papal States looked to the new Pope, with almost idolatrous veneration, to lead

Italy in casting off the Austrian yoke, agitation against their rulers grew in all the Principalities which ranked, directly or indirectly, as Austrian dependencies, while the one Italian Prince not tarred with the foreign brush, Charles Albert of Savoy, prepared almost undisguisedly to place himself at the head of a Crusade for national unification.

Metternich was practically helpless in the face of all this. His one intervention outside the frontiers of the Monarchy – the occupation of Ferrara in July 1847 – did Austria more harm than good, for it evoked added resentment against her in Italy, besides drawing down on her the disapproval of Britain.[1]

And now Austria's own subjects caught the infection. Even in Venice, whose passivity had made her a by-word,[2] the authorities had to imprison two agitators, Daniele Manin and Nicolo Tommaseo, in the autumn of 1847. On 31 December there were street riots in Milan, the first for a generation. The nationalists organized a boycott against the Austrian State lottery and tobacco monopoly. Bands of young men strutted through the streets, knocking cigars out of smokers' mouths. Riots followed, in Milan itself, Padua and Pavia. There were signs of irredentism even in the Trentino.

Radetzky, commanding the Austrian army in the Kingdom,[3] had kept his forces excellently trained and organized, but their numbers had been reduced in 1832, on grounds of economy, to 62,000, approximately one-third of them Italians,[4] although this last circumstance seems, strangely enough, to have caused the Austrian authorities, military and civil, no misgivings.[5] With this

[1] The diplomatic crisis was smoothed over by a compromise under which the Austrian troops were withdrawn from the city of Ferrara, but a small garrison left in the fortress.

[2] Two young Venetians who toured Italy in the autumn of 1847 experienced to their shame that toasts were drunk to all the other Italian cities, only not to Venice, which was mentioned only with 'contempt and abuse' for its passivity and lack of sympathy with the Italian cause (Helfert, I. 121).

[3] There is a first-class account of the military position in Lombardo-Venetia on the eve of hostilities in R. Kiszling (ed.), *Die Revolution im Kaisertum Oesterreich, 1848–9* (Vienna, 1948. 2 vols.), I. 86 ff.

[4] So Kiszling, p. 87. Twenty-four of the sixty-two infantry battalions in Radetzky's army were Italian (ten of these ended by deserting, although not all of them immediately) and two Friulian. There were few Italians in the artillery, which was mostly German, or the cavalry, which was mainly Hungarian. Hain in his *Statistik* writes that in 1846 there were then in all 53,000 Italians (plus 4,000 Friulians) in the armed forces of the Monarchy, the total of which he puts at 492,000.

[5] See Hartig, p. 65, n. 'The greatest part of the Austrian forces (sc., in Lombardy-Venetia)', writes Hartig, 'consisted of Italian troops; but almost up to the very commencement of the revolution their loyalty had not only not been doubted, but every allusion to such doubts which are said to have been not wanting in the Cabinet, was looked upon as a violation of military honour. This prejudice was so extensively prevalent that even in the month of February, when martial law against high treason and rebellion was proclaimed in the Lombardy-Venetian Kingdom, and the military were made subject to it, this latter circumstance was even in the highest circles of Vienna looked upon with displeasure, as an attack upon the honour of the soldier, although the Field-Marshal himself had consented to the measure.'

force, the Field-Marshal had to keep order in Lombardy-Venetia, garrison Ferrara, and guard against a possible attack from Piedmont; and he might have had also to garrison Naples, for when trouble broke out there in January 1848, King Ferdinand appealed to Austria for help, invoking a secret treaty of 1819, but the Pope refused to allow the troops passage. Radetzky's men were, moreover, scattered over the length and breadth of Lombardy-Venetia, since the civilian governors of every town reported that they could not do without the garrisons. The troops in Milan numbered only 9,000. There was a small naval force based on Venice, but it consisted only of a few vessels used for coastal patrols,[1] and was even less reliable than the army, since the big majority of the officers and practically all the ratings were Italians.

Radetzky sent repeated appeals for reinforcements, saying that he could not guarantee the safety of Lombardy-Venetia without at least 150,000 men. Between December 1847 and February 1848 the Hofkriegsrat, grudgingly, sent him down (in driblets) another 20,000 men[2] and Metternich promised him that the required figure should be at his disposal if war broke out[3] – a promise which, in the event, could not be honoured, since when the unrest did break out, it was not, as Metternich had complacently anticipated, confined to Italy. Meanwhile, Radetzky had already decided that, failing adequate reinforcements, he would have to withdraw his forces into the Quadrilateral if war broke out with Piedmont.

By this time it was, indeed, clear that the demands of the military could no longer be resisted absolutely, and the allotment for the army had been increased: in 1847 it was 62.96 m.g., an increase of 10 m.g. in two years. But the State finances were even less able than ever before to stand an additional strain. In 1845 there had actually been a small budget surplus, of 7 m.g., but the suppression of the Galician revolt had not been cheap, and the new paid administration there was another big item. In 1847 the Government spent nearly 10 m.g. on constructing new railway lines and 24 m.g. on buying out lines from private holders. On the other side, the bad harvests resulted in a falling-off of revenues. Thanks to this, and to a compassionate reduction in the excise duty, the budget deficit rose in 1847 to 51 m.g. Another loan of 80 m.g., underwritten by four Viennese banking-houses, was raised at the beginning of the year, part of which was meant to go on buying out the railway shareholders, but the Treasury needed the money for current purposes and the operation had to be suspended. Fears were widespread that

---

[1] On acquiring Venetia, Francis, with his typical blend of parsimony and realism, had decided that Austria did not need a big fleet, since England would look after the seas in time of war. The bulk of the Venetian fleet had therefore been sold to Denmark.

[2] For details, see Hartig, l.c.

[3] Kiszling, I. 90.

another 'State bankruptcy' was round the corner – fears and hopes, for the Left believed that this would be the spark to touch off the political revolution for which they were hoping.[1] In the event, they were not far wrong.

[1] Violand, one of the radicals of the 1848 Reichstag, writes in his *Enthüllungen* (p. 6) that he and his friends did not expect revolution to come in 1848, 'but were convinced that it must come when the State bankruptcy, towards which Austria had long been tottering, occurred. For that reason we were overjoyed when Lombardy and Venetia, in the autumn of 1847 ... did everything in their power, even abstaining from the enjoyment of tobacco, to bring this State bankruptcy about, since, as I said, we were convinced that this would bring about a general rising and the end of absolutism.'

It should be noted that the figures on the State finances were never published. This was a precaution which defeated its own end, for rumour usually exceeded even the truth.

6

1848

In the opening weeks of 1848 there was a widespread feeling that a conflagration was imminent, but the quarter in which it was most generally expected to start was Italy. It was towards Italy that Violand and his friends were looking, and when Austrian papers took one of the downward turns which, although small, were frequent during these weeks, this was usually in reply to some disquieting items of news from the Peninsula.

It was, in fact, in Italy that the first armed uprising of the year took place – the Sicilian revolt of January – and in the following weeks the situation in the Peninsula grew steadily more threatening. Ferdinand of Naples' promise of a Constitution was followed by a spate of similar concessions from the rulers of the Principalities. Charles Albert began moving troops up to the Lombard frontier and the Piedmontese Press clamoured for war. On 22 February, Radetzky proclaimed martial law in Lombardy-Venetia.

Nevertheless, it was in Paris that the fuse was lit that touched off revolution in the Habsburg Monarchy. Vague rumours of unrest in the French capital reached Vienna on 26 and 27 February; the definitive news of the abdication of Louis Philippe and the proclamation of the French republic, on the 29th, when the *Augsburger Zeitung* bearing the news arrived.

The reaction of the honest Viennese bourgeoisie was unromantic, but unhesitating. It was convinced that Metternich meant to launch another crusade, involving more heavy expenditure and another inflation. When the rumours first reached Vienna,[1] the big holders of Austrian *Métalliques* began selling them heavily. On 25 February they still only stood just below par, but on 29 February they were down to 92¼. When the rumours were confirmed, there was a run on the banks and savings banks which cleared them out of metallic currency and forced some of them to close their doors. Some shopkeepers were refusing to take paper money. The scenes in Vienna were repeated in every big city of the Monarchy.

Metternich had, in fact, been doing, or trying to do, exactly what the genius of the people suspected. His reaction to the news, which was first brought him by his friend, Rothschild, had been to set on foot a grand

---

[1] The Bourse seems to have got wind of what was happening a day even before Rothschild informed Metternich.

diplomatic campaign. Prussia was to be asked to send an emissary to Vienna to discuss the situation in France, Switzerland and Germany; Russia, to concert ways of preventing France from flooding her neighbours with revolutionary propaganda, and perhaps attacking them; Britain, to hold Piedmont back from attacking Lombardy-Venetia and to thwart the anti-Austrian activities of the 'sects' in Southern Italy. Although he had fainted on the first receipt of the news from Paris, he had quickly recovered a reasonable measure of confidence and did not, apparently, believe the situation in the Monarchy, outside Italy, to be dangerous.

It may, however, be said at once that none of these plans came to anything. Palmerston rejected the idea of intervention flatly, accompanying his refusal with harsh words on the folly of Metternich's past refusal to make timely and necessary concessions and reforms. The Czar had already sent some money – six million roubles in silver; it was all he was prepared to sacrifice for Austria – and was all for repressing revolution, but he thought Austria too weak in 'the moral absence of an Emperor' to take charge of the operation, in which he could not himself take an active part, on account of the slowness of mobilization in Russia. It was therefore the King of Prussia whom he exhorted 'to be the saviour of Germany and the good cause, show himself worthy of the good cause, and shrink not from the task laid upon him by destiny'. Prussia's own emissary, Radowitz, who arrived in Vienna on 4 March, brought proposals for immediate action, even an offer to guarantee Austria's possessions, including those in Italy, against attack by France. But these offers were conditional on 'an open and generous settlement of Germany's national needs' through a reform of the constitution of the Bund in a sense which brought about that German union under Prussian leadership which Metternich had made it his life's work to thwart. And by the time Metternich and Radowitz had agreed on a Conference of Princes, the plan had been swept away by events. Developments in Germany were taking a wholly different course, which drew its inspiration from Heidelberg and Frankfurt.

Meanwhile, one man in the Monarchy had perceived how to transmute financial panic into political capital. That man was Lajos Kossuth. On 3 March he delivered in the Lower House in Pozsony the speech which afterwards was generally hailed as having constituted the inaugural address of the revolution. Putting his finger unerringly on the sore spot, the memory of the financial crisis into which Hungary had been plunged a generation before through operations over which she had had no control, and appreciating, with equal acumen, that the remedy lay in the Centralists' programme, he denounced in ringing tones 'the pestilential air which breathes on us from the charnel-house of Vienna, an air which dulls our nerves and paralyses our spirit'. From this Hungary could not be guarded until she controlled her own finances. He therefore proposed that the Diet present to the Crown an Address, a draft of which he laid before the Lower

House. Broadly, it comprised the Oppositional Declaration *in toto*, but the kernel of it was the demand for 'the transformation of our present system of government by committees[1] into a responsible and independent Hungarian Ministry'.

Hardly less important than this demand for Hungary was another passage in Kossuth's speech, in which he declared that constitutionalism in Hungary could never be safe so long as absolutism prevailed in the rest of the Monarchy, which could only remain united if it were linked by 'general constitutional institutions, with respect for the different nationalities'.

The Hungarian reformers had as we have seen voiced this proposition before, but rather among themselves,[2] and the public enunciation of it by Kossuth at this point was very important, in encouraging the Austrian constitutionalists and in making them feel that their cause was linked with that of the Hungarian Opposition; and we may add here that when the issue was reopened a decade later, the Austrian constitutionalists again owed a great deal – far more than their historians usually admit – to Deák's quiet but invincible insistence on the same principle.

It is certain that not all the Lower House was ravished by these proposals,[3] but in the excited atmosphere, no one liked to oppose them, and the House duly adopted the draft. An odd pause then followed.

An Address to the Crown had to come from both Houses, and the adhesion of the Magnates was far from certain. Further, on 29 February the Hungarian Chancellor, Count Apponyi, who was confident that if allowed to hold new elections, he could produce an amenable Diet, had won the consent of the Staats- und Konferenzrat to the dissolution of the assemblage; only at the last minute had Metternich objected that the Palatine ought to be consulted. The Archduke arrived in Vienna on 1 March, and in his turn insisted that the other great dignitaries of the realm, the Tavernicus and the Judex Curiae, must be heard. They, too, were summoned to Vienna, and their absence was used as an excuse not to convoke the House of Magnates. So for some days an extraordinary impasse prevailed. The House of Magnates did not meet. The Lower House adopted draft Laws in the sense of the Address, the text of which it also had printed. The Rescript dissolving the Diet was drafted but got lost somewhere in the Staatsrat. When it was rediscovered, Apponyi had fallen sick and nobody else much seemed in favour of dissolving the Diet; Apponyi's deputy, Szögyény, advised against it. The Palatine was, however, urged not to allow the Address to reach Vienna, and accordingly, delayed his own return to Pozsony.

---

[1] *Collegiális kormányrendszerünk.*   [2] See above, p. 316.

[3] Széchenyi afterwards wrote to Apponyi that the majority had been against them, but had been terrorized into silence; but his word 'majority' may contain some exaggeration. Széchenyi himself was thrown into great confusion by the developments. He offered his services as plenipotentiary dictator, but they were rejected.

1848

Reports of Kossuth's speech, however, reached Vienna, where they combined with the further news from Paris and from Germany (where by this time half the States were demanding constitutions and demonstrating for German unity) to put heart into the Liberals and constitutionalists, who were further encouraged by the belief that the Archduchess Sophie and her husband were on their side. Rumours to this effect had sprung up, suddenly and mysteriously, round the turn of the year 1847-8; and they had circulated round all the salons of Vienna, and had even reached Hungary, as certain broad hints in Kossuth's speech show. Actually, although the belief acquired such vitality that the legend has survived to this day, there was little or no foundation for it;[1] but its existence was a most important factor in the situation, through the stimulus which it gave to the courage of those who held it. Meanwhile, there was now staying in the Hofburg one man who was a genuine reformer and a real opponent of Metternich's and partisan of Kolowrat, the Archduke John, the most sensible as well as the most popular of the older generation of Archdukes, whom Count Colloredo, President of the Lower Austrian Gewerbeverein, had persuaded to come up from Graz to use his weight in the family councils. The Archduke in fact several times urged his brother to make concessions, but in vain.

In the first days of March several institutions, including the Booksellers' Association and the Juridical-Political Reading Circle, submitted petitions to the Emperor asking for the redress of various grievances. One meeting,

---

[1] It is impossible to trace the origin of the belief. It was doubtless strengthened when the anonymous author (who was, however, known to be Captain Möring, tutor to the Archduke Rainer's children) of the pamphlet *The Sybilline Books out of Austria*, which appeared in January 1848, with its famous apostrophe by Austria to Metternich 'to give her back her lost thirty years', dedicated it to the Archduchess; but Möring himself must have had it from somewhere. The legend is accepted, and some or all of the stories based on it repeated, by such serious later historians as Friedjung (*Oe. 1848-60*, I. 13), Eisenmann, Redlich (*Franz Joseph*, p. 26) and Srbik (*Metternich*, II. 26), although Srbik admits the absence of any direct evidence for the alleged contact between the 'dynastic opposition' and the Lower Austrian Estates, or for the dramatic scene when Sophie allegedly prostrated herself before the feet of the Archduke Ludwig, imploring him to grant a Constitution. But Corti's scrupulous examination of the Archduchess's private papers in his *Von Kind bis Kaiser* gives an entirely different picture. The papers contain no reference to any contacts whatever with the Opposition, or with Kolowrat, still less to any self-prostration. Whereas rumour credited her with speaking the decisive word in favour of the issue of a Constitution on 14 March (see below, p. 332, n. 3), her papers show that, on the contrary, she felt that 'she could not welcome such concessions', since they would have tied her son's hands when he ascended the throne (op. cit., p. 265), and Corti is categoric that she had no hand in the fall of Metternich; she was not one of the little group who tried to persuade him to withdraw his resignation, 'but everything beyond that is untrue' (id., p. 231). Exactly the same conclusion is reached by another writer who examined the Archduchess's papers (F. Reinohl, *Aus dem Tagebuch der Erz.*, *Historische Blätter*, Heft 4, Vienna, 1958, p. 111). Her husband did, as will be seen, take a mildly Liberal line on two or three occasions, but there is no evidence that he was prompted to do so by his wife, who may not have had him so totally under her thumb as is generally believed.

that of the Lower Austrian Gewerbeverein, although it produced nothing more than an assurance of loyalty to the throne, was lent significance by the fact that both the Archduke Franz Karl and Kolowrat attended it, and the former promised to convey its wishes to the Emperor. None of these bodies had any official standing, but the Estates of Lower Austria were due to meet on 13 March, and their preparatory Committee met on the 3rd to draw up the agenda. Thirty-three of its members signed an Address, destined for the plenary session, strongly claiming more powers for the Estates, as against the bureaucracy. Another memorandum was drawn up by the poet Bauernfeld and the later Minister Dr Alexander Bach. It asked for immediate publication of the Budget and State debt, periodical convocation of corporative assemblies, representative of all Lands, classes and interests in the Monarchy, with the right to vote taxation, control the budget and participate in legislation, a modern system of local government and such civic liberties as freedom of the Press and public trial. It was circulated for signature among the most influential bourgeois circles, and after a large number of signatures had been collected, handed to the Committee of the Estates on the 11th. It was to be formally presented on the 13th.

The Archduke Ludwig and Metternich took all this calmly enough, having been reassured by Sedlnitzky that the agitation was unimportant, and that he had the situation in hand. A communiqué issued on the 10th by the Staatskonferenz denied any intention of intervening in France, but declared that the Government would be on its guard against any attempt to overthrow law and order, and would be strong enough to do so. This was taken as an indication that the Government would refuse any reform, and instead of allaying unrest, aggravated it. The radicals warned the Estates that unless they acted vigorously, they, too, would be swept away. Then, on the 12th, which was a Sunday, the students of Vienna met and resolved to present to the Emperor a petition, which some of them had drafted on the previous evening, the main demands of which were for freedom of the Press, instruction and religion, and general popular representation. Two liberal and popular Professors, Hye and Endlicher, persuaded them to let them deliver the petition in their names. They had a prolonged interview with the Archduke, but were obliged to report back that they had 'received no positive answer'.

Actually, the Staatskonferenz did on that day decide to make a concession: the Estates 'of all Lands whose Estates' rights rested on old, hitherto unmodified Constitutional Charters' were to be invited to meet and consult with a Committee to be appointed by the Crown on 'possible measures appropriate to the requirements of the moment'.[1] Instructions to the effect

[1] The actual proposal had come from Kübeck, who argued that if representatives of the Estates were called to Vienna and the financial situation explained to them, 'they might find ways and means of restoring equilibrium between the national revenue and expenditure' (Hartig, p. 103); but Metternich seems to have put Kübeck up to it (Srbik, II. 210 f.).

were issued to the Oberster Kanzler, Inzaghi. But the forlorn attempt by Metternich, who talked the reluctant Archduke into accepting it, to apply his favourite nostrum, was not publicized – by the next morning few members even of the Estates had so much as heard of it; if it had been, it would certainly have been dismissed as derisorily inadequate.

But excitement was now running high. The word had gone down the grapevine that 'the morrow was going to be the day'. All the salons had it, and the students had passed it to the workers. Early on the morning of the 13th the streets of the Innere Stadt began to fill with sightseers, including several hundreds of workers from the suburbs, for whom Monday was the best day of the week,[1] some of them obviously bent on mischief.[2] By the time the members of the Estates reached their assembly hall in the Landhaus, in the Herrengasse, a dense crowd was filling the street outside. While the crowd waited for the Estates to emerge, a great body of students arrived, marching in formation from the Aula. They forced their way into the courtyard of the Landhaus, and a young doctor named Adolf Fischhof addressed the multitude in support of freedom of the Press and of instruction, and of trial by jury. The crowd broke into tumultuous cheers for Fischhof, the Emperor, the Archduke Franz Karl and his wife. Another young man, a certain Goldmark, called on the crowd to enter the Landhaus and force the Diet to carry their demands to the Court. It was decided to send a deputation on this errand, and while the members of this body were being chosen, another student, a certain Maximilian Goldner, arrived waving a bundle of leaflets. They were printed copies of a hurriedly-prepared German translation of Kossuth's speech in Pozsony, which a Tirolean named Patz read aloud to the cheering crowd. The excitement was now indescribable. Feeble attempts by spokesmen of the Diet to suggest half remedies were swept aside, and in the end a deputation of their number willy-nilly carried to the Hofburg the demands of the excited crowd for a Constitution and the fall of Metternich.

These representations, too, looked like achieving 'no positive results'. Metternich, who had been fetched over under an armed escort from the Ballhausplatz, where he had been consulting with Radowitz, informed the deputation of the Konferenzrat's decision of the previous day and told them that when the Committee's report was ready, the Emperor would take the necessary action on it. The Archduke Ludwig said that he was not entitled to make any concessions impairing the Emperor's absolute sovereignty without Ferdinand's own consent.

---

[1] Owing to the curious mutually conflicting institutions of official Sunday work and the unofficial 'blue Monday', when hangovers were slept off, far more workers were unoccupied on Monday than on any other day of the week.

[2] See the vivid description by Violand in the *Soziale Geschichte*, p. 44, of the huge, truculent workman whom he saw striding down the street, his pockets bulging with what were obviously stones.

But all this took time, and meanwhile, the situation in the streets was getting out of hand. Few precautions against disorder had been taken;[1] and although the garrison of Vienna had been alerted and issued with live ammunition, and a fairly strong guard placed outside the Palace and pickets at one or two other strategic points in the Innere Stadt, the bulk of the force, in any case a small one,[2] commanded, unfortunately for all concerned, by the Archduke Albrecht,[3] had been kept in their barracks outside the glacis.

The various civilian authorities had, however, been authorized to call in the military if necessary. About 11 a.m. the crowd in the Herrengasse grew restive; rowdies broke into the Landhaus and began wrecking the furniture, while others gathered in the Ballhausplatz and raised a clamour for Metternich's resignation. The President of the Landesregierung sent a message to the Archduke. A couple of hours later the troops arrived. Some reinforced the guards outside the Palace; some took up positions outside the gates leading into the Innere Stadt, these being closed against further intrusion from the suburbs; others formed a ring round the centre of disturbance, and began clearing the streets round the Landhaus. Repeated adjurations to the crowd to disperse quietly proved less than effective,[4] and eventually one patrol – a detachment of Italian pioneers – opened fire. The first volleys killed four persons, and wounded many more, while an old woman was crushed to death in the panic.

The shots, far from restoring order, precipitated the reverse. The soldiers were hooted and pelted with missiles, and mobbed by bands many of which were headed by those workers who had got into the Innere Stadt before the gates were closed. There were many ugly affrays, and more mortal victims. In the outer suburbs, the rookeries of the wretched proletariat, shops were looted, factories wrecked, better-dressed persons molested. One exciseman was thrown living into a bonfire.

The menacing eruption of the submerged tenth introduced a new element

---

[1] It has even been suggested that Kolowrat, who was ultimately responsible for security, had purposely omitted to take precautions in order that the clamour against Metternich should not be stifled (Bibl, *Tragödie*, p. 127), but this is probably a calumny. As we have seen, Sedlnitzky himself had not thought the situation dangerous, and the Landmarschall had been equally confident.

[2] It consisted of three infantry regiments, one battalion of grenadiers and one of chasseurs, two regiments of cavalry, one of artillery and a few specialist troops, but all the units were under strength. The total strength was fourteen thousand.

[3] Albrecht, then thirty years of age, was the eldest son of the Archduke Charles. He had been destined for a military career, but this was his first independent command.

[4] The picture of a licentious soldateska being wantonly set on an inoffensive crowd is completely false. The Archduke himself went forward on foot to exhort the crowd to disperse, and was hit on the head by a missile. The aged *Platzkommandant* of Vienna, making a similar attempt, was severely injured and barely escaped with his life. The detachment which first opened fire had been met with a hail of stones which knocked out the Commanding Officer. The fatal shots were fired only at 1.30 p.m.

into the political struggle. The bourgeoisie were as hostile as the Court itself to the proletariat. The Burgomaster of Vienna, Czapka, who was titular O.C. the Civic Guard,[1] approached the Archduke asking that the preservation of order should be entrusted to his Corps, which should be expanded into a full-scale National Guard, adequately armed. But this demand, conservative in one sense, was revolutionary in another, for the Guards were not prepared to act simply as auxiliaries to the military, being rightly convinced that in such case the soldiers, after crushing the workers, would simply turn on the burghers themselves. They therefore demanded that the troops be withdrawn and the preservation of order left solely to their own body.

If the burghers mistrusted the Court and the military, the converse was equally true, for a National Guard in control would be simply the arm of the bourgeois revolution. Still less reassuring was a clamour which now arose from the students, that they too should be given arms and allowed to form an Academic Legion. But from another point of view, both demands were difficult to resist. The military were so detested that the mere sight of a soldier's uniform was a red rag to the people, whereas the crowds trusted the students, whom they felt to be on their side, and did not too much mind the Civic Guard.

Up to the late afternoon, the 'party of resistance' at the Court was still in the ascendant. It was felt by all, himself included, that Albrecht must, for the sake of the dynasty's popularity, be taken out of action, but F.M.L. Prince Alfred Windisch-Graetz, Military Commander in Bohemia, a man equally devoid of fear and pity, happened to be in Vienna on private business. On Metternich's suggestion, he was called to the Palace early in the afternoon and asked whether he would be able to restore order. He replied that he could do so provided that the unrest did not spread to the provinces, and was then asked to come back again after dinner. When he did so, about 6.30 p.m. (having dined with Metternich), he was told that he was going to be invested with plenipotentiary powers, civil and military, to carry out the task. He went to his home to change into uniform, but when he got back later in the evening, he found that feeling in the Palace had changed. Another deputation, bringing the 'burghers'' petition, had arrived and declared that while the burghers regarded the satisfaction of all their demands as indispensable, one concession would 'comprise all the others within itself', this being the dismissal of Metternich. The Rector of the University appeared, pleading for the students to be armed, as the only way of pacifying them. A deputation of the Civic Guard said that the Guard would guarantee order on three conditions: that the troops were withdrawn, the students armed, and Metternich

[1] This *Militärisches Bürgerkorps* was a body consisting nominally of two regiments of infantry, with detachments of grenadiers, cavalry and artillery and commanded by the Burgomaster of Vienna, which had been formed during the Napoleonic Wars to replace the garrison of Vienna, which had been sent to the Front. After 1815 its functions had been purely ceremonial.

dismissed. But these conditions must be fulfilled by 9 p.m. These successive representations broke the will even of the Archduke Ludwig. First the arming of the students was conceded, then the demands of the Civic Guard: the organization was to be expanded into a full-scale National Guard, and meanwhile the present members, and the armed students, were to take over the preservation of order from the military. The change-over began immediately, each detachment of troops retiring to the barracks in the Josephstadt as its relief took over, and with the disappearance of the uniforms, the temper of the crowds cooled perceptibly. But the key concession had still to be made. Reluctantly, the Archduke Ludwig himself now told Metternich that he must resign. The old man, in reply, treated his audience to an hour and a half's oration. Then the Archduke John took out his watch and said: 'Prince, we have only another half hour, and we have not yet decided what answer to return to the people.' 'Your Imperial Highness', said Kolowrat, 'I have been sitting in this Conference with Prince Metternich for twenty-five years, and I have always heard him talk like this, without coming to the point.' Ferdinand made one of his rare but pithy utterances: 'After all, I'm the sovereign and the decision lies with me. Tell the people that I agree to everything.'

Metternich still insisted that he would not resign unless released by the Imperial family from his oath to the Emperor Francis. He was released, and tendered his resignation, which, typically, he insisted on announcing (at great length) to the Civic Guards when they arrived for their answer. Windisch-Graetz tried to make him withdraw his resignation, but he refused. The following night, still completely unconvinced that he had ever been wrong and that his going was not a calamity, he left Vienna, first for Prince Alois Liechtenstein's castle in Feldsberg, on the Moravian frontier, later to make his way, by laborious stages, to England. None of the Imperial family had troubled to ask him how he was going to make the journey or how he would fare after it; but Baron Rothschild had more decency and sent him sufficient cash to get him and his family to safety.[1]

The two other personal victims of the evening of 13 March were Sedlnitzky and Apponyi, who voluntarily resigned his office of Hungarian Chancellor.

Scenes of enormous jubilation greeted this popular victory. Streets were illuminated, torch-light processions marched through them, crowds assembled before the Palace to cheer the Emperor, who was reported to have said that the firing had taken place without his consent and that he would not allow it to be repeated.

The Archduke Ludwig was, however, still determined to keep the concessions to the minimum. That night Windisch-Graetz was, after all, invested with his plenipotentiary powers, and he took over his functions next morning, although oddly enough, taking no action in virtue of them that morning.

[1] Another of Rothschild's benefactions (in this Sina participated) was to provide meals for the student patrols.

1848

After much argument it was decided that the two promises of the previous day must be honoured. A proclamation was issued authorizing the establishment of a large-scale National Guard, with the duty of ensuring 'the maintenance of lawful order and the protection of persons and property' and an office opened for the registration of recruits. Another Rescript announced the abolition of the censorship. But there was no word of any other concession, and public unease mounted again when, in the afternoon, Windisch-Graetz's appointment was made public. Rumours ran round that the notorious Field-Marshal was planning some bloody action, and in the evening he, in fact, drafted and sent to the Municipality, for printing and distribution, a proclamation placing Vienna in a state of siege. This extreme measure was, indeed, averted, for a compositor in the printing office leaked the news to a student, who persuaded Professor Hye to make representations in the Palace, and the proclamation was softened down into an austere exhortation to the people to preserve order; but the news sent the popular temperature rocketing up again.

But then another change came. Some time in the evening the Archduke Ludwig must have been induced, by what family representations we do not know, to hand over the Presidency of the Staatskonferenz to his younger nephew,[1] and at 11 p.m. Franz Karl convened a Conference of State to which the Archdukes Albrecht and Francis Joseph, and also Windisch-Graetz, Kolowrat, Kübeck and some others were invited. The Archduke said that in his view it would be wiser to volunteer a Constitution and then stand fast against further political demands. The laconic minutes of the Conference[2] tell us that it agreed.

It was, however, pointed out that Hungary and Transylvania already possessed Constitutions, and that it was impossible to volunteer a 'Constitution' for the Monarchy which did not take those institutions into account. It was therefore decided to make a separate promise for the rest of the Monarchy, and the Conference, for somewhat involved reasons, decided that it would be dangerous to use the word 'Constitution' in this connection.[3] Accordingly,

---

[1] It is a curious fact that no source (to the writer's knowledge) records this important event; but it is a fact that Franz Karl presided, not only over the Conference of the 14th, but over all subsequent meetings of the Staatskonferenz. Ludwig attended these, but as an ordinary member. It cannot have been the Archduke John who arranged the change, for he had already been persuaded to go down to Graz 'to pacify Styria'.

[2] These are reproduced in Friedjung, op. cit., I. p. 847.

[3] The only explanation of this is in Hartig's *Genesis*, p. 151. It should be authentic, for Hartig was one of those present at the meeting, but I admit that I cannot, myself, understand the argument put forward. It was that to divide the Monarchy into a number of constitutional States would endanger its unity, since they would put forward mutually conflicting demands.

The final decision had another important aspect, to which some writers have rightly drawn attention: it was the first step which led towards the ultimate creation of a single legislature for all the Western Lands of the Monarchy – the complex later known as the 'Kingdoms and Lands represented in the Reichsrat'.

the wording was agreed that the Emperor had decided 'to assemble round Our throne representatives of the Estates of Our German-Austrian and Slavonic Realms and of the Central Congregations of Our Lombardo-Venetian Kingdom' – the phrase is interesting for it envisages, for the first time, an Austrian representative body, and may thus be regarded as a precursor of the later Dualism – 'with the purpose of assuring Ourselves of their advice on legislative and administrative questions'. The meeting was to take place on 3 July, if not earlier.

A Rescript to this effect was issued on the morning of the 15th. But this proved too little for any but the smallest appetites. The streets were emptier that day, out of fear of the soldiers, who had been reinforced by detachments hurriedly rushed in from outlying garrisons,[1] but everyone was at some meeting or other, and the vast majority of the bourgeoisie, and the students to a man, condemned the Rescript as totally inadequate. In the early afternoon, the Emperor was persuaded to take a drive (in which he was accompanied by his brother and nephew) through the Innere Stadt, 'to show that he was not afraid of the people'. This, like everything Ferdinand did, evoked outbursts of loyal enthusiasm, but it was still shrugged off as only a gesture. The National Guard refused to go into the workers' quarters to restore order, because they were afraid to leave the Innere Stadt to the soldiers, so that disorder continued to reign in the suburbs, and the Innere Stadt, where a 'Burghers' Committee' of twenty-four members, headed by Bach, had taken charge, forcing Czapka to resign,[2] was itself little better. Menacing crowds gathered again round the Hofsburg.

This time they were rewarded. Another change of councils – again one for the origin of which we have no unimpeachable evidence[3] – had taken place in the Palace. At 5 p.m. a mounted herald appeared at the Palace gate leading out of the Michaelerplatz and read a proclamation to the assembled crowd. This began by confirming the abolition of the censorship and the establishment of the National Guard, and went on to say that the Emperor 'had taken the necessary steps to convoke, as quickly as possible, representatives of all provincial Estates and of the Central Congregations of Lombardy-Venetia, with increased representation for the burghers, for the purpose of the Constitution which We have decided to grant'.

This time it was enough. The jubilation which had greeted the fall of

[1] It had now been brought up to a figure of some 20,000 by reinforcements from Lower and Upper Austria and Styria.

[2] Czapka was threatened with physical violence and fled the capital. He was an intelligent man and far from illiberal, but public opinion chose to associate him with Metternich, with whom he had been on personally friendly terms.

[3] Friedjung (and others) attribute this initiative, like so many, to the Archduchess Sophie, who had allegedly been told by her personal physician that nothing short of a Constitution with specific mention of the magic word would satisfy the people; but see above, p. 325, n. 1.

1848

Metternich broke out again. Houses were illuminated, Ferdinand, when he showed himself, cheered to the echo.

The first Viennese Revolution was over.

After this, it was Hungary's turn again. Kossuth had already lost patience, and had been urging that the Lower Table should present its Address to the Crown, without waiting for the Magnates; but his colleagues had hesitated to make this unconstitutional move. In the early hours of the 14th a messenger sent by the Archduke Ludwig brought the news of Metternich's fall, and now the Palatine, who had arrived in Pozsony the previous evening, decided to side with the national party. He convoked the Magnates for that afternoon. Everybody – the Archduke and Széchenyi not excepted – agreed that the original Address was no longer adequate to the new situation, and it was therefore revised and strengthened; it now demanded the abolition of the entire existing top-level administrative system, and the appointment of a 'responsible and independent Ministry', with its seat in Pest. Other points now specifically mentioned in it were popular representation, popular education, trial by jury and the 'Union' (sc. of Transylvania with Inner Hungary). The validity of the Pragmatic Sanction was not questioned. On Széchenyi's suggestion, it was resolved that a deputation from the two Houses, led by the Palatine himself, who promised the Hungarians to get the demands accepted, should take the Address to Vienna the next day.[1]

The Deputation, a large and tumultuous one, arrived in Vienna on the evening of the 15th, its appearance enhancing the intoxication of joy into which their own successes had plunged the Viennese. They were not able that evening to have audience of poor Ferdinand, who had passed out completely, but the next day they were received by him, and handed him the Address. It appears that Windisch-Graetz and the Archduchess Sophie wanted him to reject it, but the Palatine and the Vice-Chancellor, Szögyény, talked them over by representing to them the danger that if her demands were refused, Hungary might revolt and secede from the Monarchy (the Palatine was suspected, although probably unjustly, of readiness to accept the Crown), and Ferdinand declared himself, in general terms, willing to fulfil the Hungarians' wishes. On the 17th the Palatine was handed a Rescript, the essential passage of which ran:

I am prepared to consent to the wish of the loyal Estates for the formation of a responsible Ministry in the sense of the Laws of the Fatherland, subject to the preservation intact of the unity of the Crown and of the link with the Monarchy.

The Palatine was appointed Plenipotentiary for the King, and empowered to propose to him a suitable Ministry.

[1] According to G. Spira, op. cit., p. 91, the deputation further revised and strengthened the Address *en route*. It was only then that it was decided to ask for plenipotentiary powers for the Palatine.

Meanwhile, on the same day, the Staatskonferenz had met again, again under the Presidency of Franz Karl, and had decided that the Western Lands, too, must have a 'responsible Ministry', to replace the old system of 'collegial' Hofstellen (this concession was announced in the *Wiener Zeitung* of the following morning). On the 20th the Conference met once more, and decided to recommend the appointment of Kolowrat as Minister President – an honour which he accepted only with reluctance, and stipulating that the appointment must be only 'provisional'. The remaining Ministers selected that day were all heads, or near-heads, of existing Hofstellen, and almost all of them, like Kolowrat himself, men of advanced years: Freiherr von Kübeck, ex-President of the Hofkammer, became Minister of Finance; Count Ludwig Taaffe, head of the Oberste Justizstelle, Minister of Justice; Count Ludwig Ficquelmont, President of the Hofkriegsrat, 'Director of the Imperial and Royal House, Court and State Chancellery', i.e. Minister of Foreign Affairs; and Freiherr von Pillersdorf, Chancellor of the Vereinigte Hofkanzlei, Minister of the Interior. Two Ministries were added later: on the 27th, Freiherr von Sommaruga, one of the Archduke Franz Karl's old tutors, was made Minister of Education, and on 2 April, F.M.L. Zanini, of the Hofkriegsrat, Minister of War. It may, however, be mentioned here that Kübeck stuck it out only until 3 April, when he was replaced by Freiherr Philipp von Krausz, of the Gubernium of Galicia. Kolowrat resigned definitively on 17 April; on the 19th, Ficquelmont took over the Minister Presidency, again 'provisionally'. Taaffe resigned on 20 April, Sommaruga taking over his portfolio 'provisionally', and Zanini on the same day; the new Minister of War, appointed on 30 April, was General Count Baillet de Latour. Meanwhile, Pillersdorf, too, had tried to resign, but his resignation had not been accepted.

On 3 April, Windisch-Graetz's special commission was terminated. He departed, disgruntled, to resume his command in Bohemia, although on the way, he treated himself to a generous holiday. The Archduke Albrecht, whom the voice of the people somewhat unfairly made the scapegoat for the bloodshed of the 13th, was replaced in his command[1] by the peaceable and popular F.M.L. Count Karl Auersperg. The Archduke now went down to join Radetzky's army in Italy, where he took command of a division.

With the appointment of a 'responsible Ministry' the old Governmental apparatus disappeared. The Staatskonferenz and the Staats-und-Konferenzrat were, on Kolowrat's earnest advice, abolished on 4 April, when the Archduke Ludwig finally retired into private life; the Emperor's Privy Chancellery on the next day. The Emperor could now constitutionally listen to no other

---

[1] It is fair to say that on the 14th he had himself asked to be replaced temporarily by Windisch-Graetz. He asked for his definitive release on 27 March and it was granted on 30 March.

1848

advice except that of his Ministers, although the Archduke Franz Karl was appointed as a sort of go-between between him and them. All minutes of the Ministerial Conference were to be sent first to him, and submitted by him to the Emperor; it was understood that if he objected to any Ministerial decision, it was to be reconsidered by the Ministry.[1]

The student of the history of the next months should, however, remember that at least until a Parliament or other body had been created to which the Ministers in their turn could be made to answer, the change of the form of regime meant very little. The Government represented a certain concession to revolution, but was in no sense a product of it. Its members were all old and trusted servants of the Crown, the nominees, direct or at one remove, of the Staatskonferenz, and continuing their service under a new name, but in the same spirit as before and with the same object – old wine, even old bottles, only new labels.

They were, moreover, entirely inexperienced in any form of government except the bureaucratic. Poor Pillersdorf remarks ruefully and with justice, that this was probably the first Ministry ever formed none of whose members had ever previously exchanged political ideas with any other.[2]

Few of them were even at all liberal in their personal politics. Kolowrat's liberalism, as we have seen, was simply anti-Metternichism; Kübeck's, as we shall see, had by now given place to a fanatical worship of the purest reaction. Of the new men whose views are worth recording, Pillersdorf was liberalism's best hope. He was a genuine constitutionalist, so much so that in 1852 he was deprived of his Privy Councillorship for his allegedly subversive conduct in 1848.[3] He was experienced, intelligent and honourable, but his career had been that of a quiet civil servant, and neither his training nor his character fitted him to take quick decisions in emergencies, and to stand by them.

Krausz seems to have believed in reform, and although he did not succeed in the impossible task of putting order into Austria's finances, he behaved throughout with integrity and courage. Sommaruga, a very distinguished academic, was a moderate Liberal.[4] Some of the others were pronounced anti-democrats. Ficquelmont was a career officer with some diplomatic experience. This had brought him into contact with Metternich, whose admirer and pupil he was reported to be. His appointment was unpopular, and especially resented by the Poles, for he had been serving in Petersburg during the 1830 revolution, and had shown demonstrative pleasure at its failure (his wife, too, was a Russian). As for Latour, who was to meet so dreadful an end, he was heart and soul a man of the old regime, and presently became an

---

[1] Walter, p. 12.
[2] *Rückblicke*, p. 17.
[3] His dignities were, indeed, restored to him in 1861.
[4] Rumour credits his with being one of the voices which persuaded the Court to its fateful promise of 15 March to grant a Constitution.

active partner with Windisch-Graetz and Jellačič in the moves which carried the counter-revolution into power. It must be said for him, that disliking his dual role, he accepted his portfolio only with reluctance and made many attempts to be relieved of it.

The same words apply to the staffs of the old Chancelleries and Hofstellen, now become Ministries, not to mention the Corps of Officers.

The real transfer of power to the people's representatives had yet to come.

The new Ministry took some hurried steps to ease the social and political pressure. The tax on articles of prime necessity was abolished, as was the turn-over tax on very small transactions, and some other indirect taxes were reduced. A general amnesty for political offenders was enacted. Another measure of wide application was a Rescript dated 28 March, and addressed to Land authorities,[1] establishing the principle of the abolition of the 'Robot obligation', against compensation for the landlords which was to be settled by the local Diets, as far as possible by agreement between the parties. This principle was to be completely realized 'within a year, at the latest by 31 March 1849', and the necessary measures to be worked out 'by legal procedures, with all practicable speed'.

But this was only one of the Ministry's preoccupations. It was no longer responsible for Hungary's 'interna', but the relationship of Hungary to the rest of the Monarchy – what institutions were required 'to preserve the unity of the Crown and the link with the Monarchy' – remained to be defined. In the western half of the Monarchy, the Ministry had to consider the wishes and demands, not of the Viennese alone, but of all its half-dozen peoples; one of these – the Italian – had already had its case taken up by an outside Power, Piedmont, with such verve that actual war was to be expected at any moment. Further, the situation in Germany was completely uncertain, but could well develop into a shape dangerous at least to Austria's hegemony over the other members of the Bund, and conceivably even to her politicial integrity.

All these problems rushed on the Ministers simultaneously, and each, of course, interacted on all the others, a fact which must not be forgotten, although the limitations of his craft compel the historian to describe them one by one. It will be simplest to begin with the question which was the first to achieve a legal settlement: that of the new status of Hungary.

The Palatine had no sooner arrived back in Pozsony on the 17th, than he had appointed Batthyány 'provisional' Minister President, and ordered him to produce the names of a 'provisional' Cabinet. In doing this, the Archduke had exceeded his powers, and had been told so when he reported his action

[1] Strictly, this was issued at first only to the Gubernia of Bohemia, Moravia and Silesia. It was extended in April to Styria, Carinthia, and Carniola. It was never addressed to Galicia, where it was replaced by Stadion's action (see below, p. 368).

1848

to Vienna on the 18th. The appointment had, however, been confirmed, and on the 19th the Palatine convoked the two Houses in joint session, read the Royal Rescript to them, and presented Batthyány to them as Hungary's Minister President. The Diet, without more ado, turned to its law-making business.

So far as Hungary's 'interna' were concerned, things went smoothly and swiftly, their progress being accelerated by the news which had arrived from Pest. Some time before, Kossuth had asked his friends there to arrange for pressure to be put on the Diet through a petition, and his friends had entrusted the preparation of this document to a group of young men calling themselves 'The Youth of Pest', whose *spiritus rector* was the poet, Petőfi. The petition was soon ready. Entitled *What does the Hungarian Nation demand?*, it summed up those demands in twelve Points, which included, besides the social and internal political demands which were already the commonplaces of the Opposition,[1] an independent Ministry in Buda-Pest with a Parliament meeting annually, in Pest, a National Guard, a provision that Hungarian soldiers should take their oath to the Hungarian Constitution, a National Bank, and the Union with Transylvania.

This should have gone to Pozsony with only a few signatures under it, but when the news of Metternich's fall arrived on the 15th, brought with the steam-packet, the Youth organized a vast meeting, which adopted the proclamation by acclamation. Plans were also made for Petőfi to address another meeting on the Rákosmező, an open space outside Pest on which peasants coming in to the big markets were accustomed to camp. One such market was due, and several thousand peasants were in fact congregated on the field; and reports reached Pozsony that Petőfi was marching on the city at the head of a host armed with scythes and flails, like that which had done such dreadful execution in Galicia. The rumours were unfounded, but they completed the intimidation of the Magnates and the conservatives in the Lower House, who now did little more than assent to the programme of the Opposition, as dictated to them by Kossuth.[2] In a few days the Diet was thus ready with a corpus of Bills which transformed the entire administrative and social institutions of the country. There was to be, as before, a bi-Cameral Parliament, and the composition of the Upper House was left unchanged, but the franchise for the Lower House (which was to be elected for a three-years' term) was extended to all males of the age of twenty or over, subject to certain, fairly modest, property qualifications; the lower age limit for the passive franchise was twenty-four, and knowledge of the Magyar language was obligatory. The franchise for the Counties and municipalities was

---

[1] The demand for the liberation of the peasants, however, said nothing about compensation for the landlords.

[2] Some of these Bills had been adopted as early as 14 March; the Lower House had simply passed the appropriate Resolution, and the Magnates had agreed to them without argument.

extended correspondingly; the institutions themselves, and their competences, were left unchanged.

All 'received' religions (among which the Unitarian was now included) enjoyed complete freedom and reciprocity.[1] Taxation was to be borne 'equally and proportionately' by all inhabitants of Hungary, without distinction. The Patrimonial Courts were abolished; the law was to be equal for all. All dues and servitudes attaching to 'peasant' holdings were abolished, the villein peasants thus becoming, at one blow, the freehold owners of their lands. The compensation of private landlords was left to 'the honour of the nation'; the Church renounced the tithe altogether.[2] An agricultural credit bank was to be established to help landlords over their difficulties. The aviticitas was abolished. Other laws authorized the establishment of a National Guard, and guaranteed the freedom of the Press, trial by jury for Press offences and freedom of instruction and learning.

Another Bill enacted the incorporation, with immediate effect, of the Partium, and another, the union with Transylvania, subject to the Transylvanian Diet's voting to that effect when it met. The Ministry was to collaborate with the Transylvanian Diet in preparing legislation of a nature to preserve 'all special rights and liberties of Transylvania which are favourable to national freedom and equality without hindering the complete unification'.

Besides all this, the Diet framed Bills to regulate the relation of Hungary to the Crown, and its position within the Gesammtmonarchie. These had to be agreed with Vienna, and here agreement proved very difficult.

The Diet's main proposals were ready by the 22nd. The Monarchy was, of course, retained, the Palatine representing the King in the latter's absence from the country, and in such case, enjoying plenipotentiary powers; but the Monarchy now became a limited, constitutional one in every respect, for no enactment by the King or the Palatine was valid unless countersigned by the appropriate responsible Minister. The Cabinet was to consist of the Minister President and Ministers *a latere* (for Foreign Affairs), Interior, National Defence, National Finance, Justice, Public Works and Communications, Cults and Education, and Agriculture, Trade and Industry; the previous organs of Government (the Chancellery, Consilium and Camera) disappeared.

By this time Batthyányi had composed his provisional Cabinet, a Ministry of all the talents; the designated holders of the eight portfolios, in the above order, were himself, Prince Pál Esterházy, B. Szemere, Colonel G. Mészáros, Kossuth, Deák, Széchenyi, Eötvös and G. Klauzál.

But the Staatskonferenz, then still in being, had already taken fright.

---

[1] That this provision was confined to 'received religions' was due to a strong wave of anti-Semitism which was then sweeping over Hungary.

[2] In practice this had for a long time past been universally paid to the landlords.

When the Palatine appeared in Vienna with the proposed legislation, and the provisional list of Ministers, the Staatskonferenz objected, with reason, that the proposed laws would reduce the connection of Hungary with the rest of the Monarchy to a simple personal union. On the 29th Staatthaltereirat Zsedényi was sent to Pozsony with a Rescript which agreed to the appointments of Széchenyi, Szemere, Deák, Eötvös and Klauzál, but proposed four important amendments to the Hungarian draft. The Palatine's plenipotentiary powers to act for the Monarch in the latter's absence from Hungary were to be restricted to the existing holder of the office, not enjoyed by every holder of the office. The Court Chancellery was to continue in being as a sort of overlord, standing above the Ministers and responsible only to the Crown, not to the Hungarian Parliament. The Monarch wished to retain his control over tariff and commercial policy, and further, the financial resources thitherto used to meet the expenses of institutions serving the whole Monarchy were not to be handled by the Hungarian Ministry of Finance, but, as thitherto, paid into the 'Common Treasury of the Monarchy'. The Monarch reserved his rights in respect of the organization of the army and of national defence, and these rights were not to be exercised by the Palatine in the Monarch's absence.

A second Rescript ordered that the peasants' servitudes were not to be abolished until the Parliament had made effectual provision for compensation for the landlords.

When these documents were read out to the Diet, a great storm arose. Batthyány himself wanted to resign; Kossuth shouted that 'the fatherland was in danger', and there were rowdy demonstrations in Pest. Batthyány, Deák and Eötvös went back to Vienna to argue the case, and the Court, fearing open revolution, conceded practically all their points, only stipulating that, since Hungary was now to have complete control over her own Camera, the next Diet must make proper provision for the upkeep of the Court and other expenditure previously met from their source, and that adequate provisional arrangements must be made for the intervening period.

The new Royal Rescript, which the Palatine brought back to Pozsony on the 31st, limited the Palatine's powers, when representing the King, only by the stipulation that his exercise of them must not impair 'the unity of the Crown and of the Monarchical association'. The King promised that he (or his representative) would exercise his executive powers only 'through an independent Hungarian Ministry, and that no enactment, appointment, etc., made by him was valid without the counter-signature of the appropriate Minister, each Minister being responsible for his official actions'. The list of Ministers was that proposed by the Hungarians, thus including the Ministries of National Finance and National Defence, and the competence of the Ministers extended to 'all questions which hitherto fell, or ought to have fallen, within the competence of the Court Chancellery, the Consilium, and the Camera, including the Department of Mines', and in general, 'to all civilian, Church, fiscal (aerarial) and military questions'. The Minister *a latere* represented Hungary 'effectively' (*befolyván*) and 'with responsibility to the country' (sc. Hungary)[1] 'in all questions of common interest to the Fatherland and to the Hereditary Provinces' and his counter-signature was required for all Royal enactments in this field, which, however, was not more nearly defined.[2]

The Monarch reserved for himself certain rights which were either the usual prerogative of Royalty or special rights enjoyed by the wearer of the Holy Crown (appointments to higher ecclesiastical offices and to some State dignities, and the conferment of titles of nobility), and also specifically reserved to himself 'the employment of the Hungarian armed forces outside the frontiers of the Kingdom, and appointments to military offices'. Even for these a counter-signature was necessary, but it was that of the Minister *a latere*.

The Diet, having accepted this Rescript, not without considerable grumbling from the Left, duly voted a provisional contribution of 3 million gulden towards the common services, and agreed to consider the regular contribution at the next Diet. It did not, however, meet the Staatskonferenz' wishes on the very important question of Hungary's contribution to the accumulated State debt. The Rescript had passed this question over in silence, but on 7 April a letter reached the Palatine asking for an interim assurance (since it was now too late to settle the matter by legislation) that Hungary was prepared to take over a quarter of the total debt, paying an annual contribution of 10 million gulden. The Hungarians' official reply was that the question would be submitted to the next Diet; the decision of the Ministers, which was unanimous – even Széchenyi and Deák concurred – was that the request was unacceptable.

[1] The German text had only *unter Verantwortlichkeit*.

[2] It remained to the last very obscure. It seems that Batthyány himself had used the title 'Minister *a latere*' when compiling his original list, but in speech had used the term 'Foreign Minister', and the latter title was regularly used thereafter, not only by other Hungarian Ministers, but by Esterházy himself, in his official correspondence, and even by Austrian Ministries addressing him (see Hajnal, op. cit., pp. 20 ff.). It seems, however, certain that the Staatskonferenz regarded Ficquelmont (whose official title, it will be observed, was the same as that which had been borne by Metternich – he, too, was 'Foreign Minister' only in common parlance) as the Foreign Minister proper for the whole Monarchy. As the Hungarians did not at that time question the validity of the Pragmatic Sanction, nor the Monarch's right to control foreign affairs, they do not seem to have been thinking of setting up a Ministry of their own parallel to the Haus- Hof- und- Staatskanzlei, but since the Foreign Minister was to be 'responsible' (undefined as the term was) in Austria, some similar 'responsibility' had to be introduced in Hungary. How far the Hungarian Minister's 'effectiveness' would make him the other man's equal in power, no man could say. The ambiguity of the whole position was heightened by the fact that the Hungarians habitually spoke of Austria as a 'foreign' country, so that their relations with the Hereditary Provinces were to them already 'foreign affairs', while to Vienna foreign affairs meant dealings with countries outside the Monarchy.

1848

Finally the Crown dropped its condition on the prior consideration of the landlords' compensation, contenting itself with the general promise contained in the relevant draft law. No other points of dispute having arisen, the Diet completed the drafting of its laws, and on 11 April Ferdinand himself, accompanied by Franz Karl and Francis Joseph, came to Pozsony and formally sanctioned the corpus of legislation (thereafter formally known as the 'April Laws')[1] enacted by the 1847-8 Diet, which he then declared closed.

We may now turn back to the West. Vienna itself had simmered down quickly enough after the appointment of the Ministry. Most of the bourgeoisie wanted little more than what they had already received, or been promised: assurance that there were going to be no more expensive adventures to keep foreign places in order, a guarantee of some control by the tax-payer over the public purse, freedom to grumble without the risk of going to prison for it, protection against the workers. The workers, for their part, had been driven back into their rookeries, after a considerable number of trouble-makers had been arrested; but they had not been subjected to repression. The Government, as we have said, had taken off or lightened some of the taxes which bore particularly heavily on the poorest classes. Then, when the news arrived that the ten-hour day had been introduced in Paris, many of the Austrian employers, the railway companies taking the lead, agreed between themselves to introduce the same reform. In establishments where this was impracticable, wages were raised in compensation. A tenants' strike forced the landlords to reduce rents all round. Unemployment fell, for the simple reason that employers whose machinery had been wrecked took on hand labour again, and public works were organized for those still unable to find employment.

According to the one contemporary authority who has left a serious account of this side of 1848,[2] the factory workers and journeymen were, at this juncture, content with what they had gained, provided these gains could be consolidated.[3] At any rate, April was a peaceful month on the labour front. Thus only the students and a handful of Left-wing intellectuals remained in their self-cast role of guardians of the new public liberties.

The students were, however, in a powerful position. The arrangement

---

[1] Not, as stated by many English writers (who presumably confuse them with the March Days), the 'March Laws'. The Laws comprised all those enacted at the 1847-8 Diet. Law I of them thus records the death of the Palatine Joseph, and Law II, the election of his successor.

[2] Violand, op. cit., p. 145. See also Zenker, pp. 124 ff. Brügel is entirely uninformative on this subject.

[3] Zenker, op. cit., gives in his sixth chapter a conspectus of the left-wing ideas and literature of the day. The chief requests were for a minimum wage, a maximum proportion of machines to hands, reduction of the excessive number of apprentices, help for the sick and invalids, and humane treatment by foremen. There were few demands for vocational organization, and only one workers' organization came – for a short time – into being: an *Erster Allgemeiner Arbeiterverein* which was founded on the 'self-help' principle. It was afterwards drawn into politics by the agitator Chaizes (see below, p. 401).

hurriedly reached on the 14th had been that all the paramilitary forces should be under the command of one man, F.M.L. Hoyos. The Civic Guard retained its autonomy, but the Academic Legion was to be part of the National Guard, although forming a separate unit of it. In practice, the Civic Guard carried out the duties assigned to it in orderly fashion enough, but the National Guard was from the first something of a shambles. There was a great initial rush to join it, but Hoyos, who was an old man with little real military experience (for many years he had performed only Court duties – he was Master of the Royal Hunt) proved unable to introduce order in the force. The Guard came to comprise a large number of 'companies', under officers elected by themselves, with ill-defined duties[1] and most varying sympathies, some siding with the Court, some with the more sober elements among the bourgeoisie, others with the radicals.

The Academic Legion formed a compact body of 5,000 members, by no means all of them students, but organized as such, by Faculties. Their Commander, Count Colloredo-Mannsfeld, was even more elderly than Hoyos.[2] He was not unpopular with the Legionaries, but he left them largely to their own devices, and the orders which they obeyed were concocted by a 'Students' Committee', a little group chosen by themselves.

The students carried out their self-appointed tasks in the appropriate spirit. When, on 1 April, Pillersdorf issued a provisional Press law, they made such a fuss because they had not been consulted first (although the law itself was by no means illiberal) that Pillersdorf weakly withdrew it for re-drafting. They organized rowdy demonstrations outside the houses of unpopular persons; it was their behaviour that caused Kübeck, Kolowrat and later, Taaffe to resign.[3] Above all, they amused themselves with concocting and publishing a vast flood of inconceivably cheap lampoons, the abundance of which was matched only by their vulgarity, against their pet Guy Fawkeses: the aristocracy, the bureaucracy, the Church, etc. . . .[4] They were, however, already somewhat isolated, even among their own fellow Germans.

The Alpine provinces had quickly got over such social and purely political unrest as they had ever experienced, which had not been much. In the few centres where there was a bourgeoisie of perceptible dimensions, that class had shown pleasure at the fall of Metternich, but more anxiety for the safety of its own persons and property: the demand for a national guard came high on every list of desiderata submitted to Vienna. The only counterpart to the

---

[1] Pillersdorf (*Rückblicke*, p. 41) remarks with acerbity that while elaborate provision was made for the training, organization and equipment of the Guard, its exact duties were never defined.

[2] He had been born in 1777, Hoyos in 1779.

[3] Zanini resigned for a different reason: 'that he was unable to get his way against Generals senior to him in rank, service and experience.'

[4] For specimens of these see in particular Rath, op. cit.

1848

students' agitation in Vienna was among their opposite numbers in Graz, and they were not numerous enough to have much even of a nuisance value. The organized political requests were uniformly modest; none of them asked for more than some democratization of the Estates in the shape of increased representation in the Diets for the burghers and peasants; none of them even touched on the question of new institutions for the Monarchy as a whole, or for parts of it. There was little social unrest. The workers were too few to create it (only in Linz was there some rioting) and the peasants did not need to. They knew that the robot was on the point of disappearance, and simply stopped doing it, and nobody tried to force them.[1] The national conflicts in these Lands were mostly a pale reflection of the more powerful movements elsewhere which will be described later. There was considerable, but not universal, unrest in the Italian South Tirol. The German Lands were mildly German National: both Graz and Innsbruck petitioned to 'join Germany'. The Slovene leaders in Carniola, on the other hand, and the Slovene students' organization, asked for the constitution of all Slovene-speaking areas in one Land, in which Slovene should enjoy the same status 'as German and Italian in their Lands'. It is true that they opened their mouths wide enough: their Slovenia was to include all Southern Carinthia (including Klagenfurt) and the entire Littoral. The leaders of the Carinthian Slovenes, indeed, protested against the demand. The German majorities in the Lands of mixed population – Tirol, Styria, Carinthia – opposed any suggestion directed against their integrity, but did not object to some administrative decentralization and wider use of the local languages in the non-German areas.

But outside the Hereditary Lands, it was a different picture. In Italy, as soon as the news of Metternich's fall crossed the Alps, tumult had broken out in all the main cities under Austrian rule, most clamorously in Milan. On the 18th the Vice-Governor, O'Donnell (the Viceroy and the Governor were both away) published the Imperial manifesto of the 15th, but it made no impression. O'Donnell himself was taken prisoner. Street fighting broke out, and in the next few days, the little garrison lost nearly one-third of its numbers in casualties and desertions. On the night of the 22nd/23rd Radetzky withdrew the survivors and retired on the Quadrilateral. The Milanese formed a provisional Government. Meanwhile Venice had fallen on the 21st, without a shot fired, for the military governor, Count Zichy, simply capitulated to the insurgents, who thereupon proclaimed a Republic with Manin its President.[2] About one-third of the land forces and three-

---

[1] Zenker writes (op. cit., p. 46), 'By the summer not one peasant was doing robot or rendering other services and no lord was asking for them'.

[2] Zichy was afterwards court-martialled and broke. He is supposed to have been blackmailed into surrender by threats to the life of his mistress and children (Benedikt, *Kaiseradler*, pp. 183 ff.).

quarters of the fleet declared for Italy. The land forces which remained loyal set out to join Radetzky and a few naval units escaped to Trieste. On the 23rd Charles Albert issued a proclamation declaring his sympathy with 'the heroic struggle of the people of Lombardy and Venetia' and crossed the frontier. The smaller cities rose in succession. Meanwhile Papal troops were assembling at Bologna, the Duke of Modena had fled, Leopold of Tuscany declared for the Italian cause, and even Ferdinand of Naples was bullied into sending an expeditionary force northwards. Disorder broke out also in the South Tirol, where local insurgents were reinforced by volunteers from across the frontier.

All Radetzky could do was to concentrate the remnants of his army, reduced by the desertion of many of its Italian components to about 50,000,[1] in the Quadrilateral, from which vantage point he was at least able, with the help of local German Tiroleans, to restore order in the Trentino. He appealed urgently to Vienna for reinforcements, but unless and until these arrived, he could at best hope to repel attack on his southern front, but not to take the offensive.

It was not even certain that he would be asked to do so. Liberal opinion in Vienna was at this time, on grounds of principle, in favour of allowing Lombardy-Venetia self-determination; many papers advocated this eloquently.[2] The financial circles to whom Austria owed much of the national debt were for letting the provinces go on the grounds that a campaign to recover them would cost more than the country could afford. Other Viennese business interests feared for their trade or their investments.[3] The Government itself inclined towards cutting its losses in Italy. As early as 20 April Pillersdorf suggested to a Ministerial Council that Austria should recognize the independence of Lombardy.[4] Then Ficquelmont thought the proposal 'premature', but it was, as we shall see, only a month before he was taking diplomatic steps in the same direction.

While no other Land of the Monarchy actually rose against Austrian rule, Galicia seemed for a few days on the verge of doing so. When the news from Vienna reached the province, which was not until 18 March, there were excited demonstrations in Lemberg, and a deputation of Poles appeared before Stadion with a list of demands, which besides the usual ones for constitutional liberties, social reforms (including abolition of the robot) and a national guard, included a political amnesty and a number of highly nationalist postulates: Ferdinand to be proclaimed King of Poland; the introduction of Polish as the language of administration, the Courts and

[1] According to Horsetzky, op. cit., p. 536, about 20,000 officers and men had deserted. Radetzky himself said that four-fifths of his Italian troops deserted.
[2] For sample quotations, see Bibl, *Tragödie*, p. 110: Rath, op. cit., pp. 148 ff.
[3] Hartig, p. 191.
[4] Walter, p. 60.

education; only native Galicians to be employed in the public offices; convocation of a national Diet on a broad basis, and a separate Provincial administration and 'national' military force; the 'foreign' troops were to leave the country. Stadion agreed to release any prisoners held locally;[1] and to let the burghers and students form a guard in Lemberg (but not elsewhere),[2] but said that the other demands must be presented to the Emperor. A large deputation, mainly composed of Polish noblemen, but including some artisans and five Jews, but no Ruthenes (whom the Poles had ignored completely), then set out for Vienna. On the 21st a 'Central National Council' (*Rada Narodna Centralna*), under a seven-man directorate, was constituted in the city.

Very similar scenes took place in Cracow, whose citizens, again, extracted from the local Austrian authorities release of the political prisoners and permission to form a 'Burghers' Committee'. Here, too, a petition (containing substantially the same demands as the other), was drawn up and a deputation appointed to carry it to the Emperor. The two deputations met in Vienna and conflated their demands into one even stronger one, which asked *inter alia* for the establishment of a Polish Provisional National Committee 'to undertake the internal reorganization of Galicia on a purely national basis'.

Now, however, they met with a check, if only because the Government was frightened of incurring Russia's resentment if it showed too much sympathy with Polish nationalism. The Poles were kept hanging about for their answer, which, when it came at last, amounted to no more than a non-committal assurance that Ferdinand 'would consider carefully all measures conducive to the welfare of his loyal subjects'.

Meanwhile, various circumstances had worked together in Galicia to subdue the effervescence of the first days. One was that Stadion was personally a man of great common-sense, energy and courage; the second, that he found local allies to his hand. The peasants assembled in many villages and sent emissaries to Lemberg and Tarnow to ask hopefully whether their help was required, and although they were not called on, their attitude strongly damped the enthusiasm of the Poles. Further, the attitude of the Ruthenes, although not yet defined, was disquieting to them.

With this backing, and that of the local military, Stadion was able to take a strong line. He forbade the Lemberg National Guard to carry arms and vetoed the formation of any guards at all in the local centres, where they would have been purely Polish, so that for the time, authority was re-established. Things did not go so easily in Cracow, where the Burghers' Committee paid little attention to the Austrian authorities. The Committee, however, regarded itself as the local representative of the Polish *émigré*

---

[1] 151 were released in Lemberg.

[2] It will be noted that at that time Lemberg was largely a German town. The burghers at least, could thus be presumed to be on the side of order.

'Government', whose interest was at this time concentrated almost entirely on Poznán, where the local Poles were trying to extract from Prussia an independent territory which could then be made into a base for an attack on Russia. So long as this possibility existed, the Polish leaders themselves did not want a premature move in Galicia, which therefore relapsed, for the time, into a condition of suspended animation.

The Roumanians of the Bukovina (to conclude the list of relatively peripheral movements) had followed the general pattern in establishing a National Guard in Czernowitz and a National Committee, which in due course drew up a twelve-point petition,[1] the main demand of which was for the separation of the Bukovina from Galicia and its constitution, within its existing frontiers, as a separate and autonomous province. It also asked for a 'national' education system, Roumanian-speaking officials, inter-confessional equality, financial autonomy for the Greek Orthodox Church, and certain other local reforms. The petition appears not to have been sent in until June, when it was accompanied (or followed) by another, which some Roumanian leaders had drafted in consultation with colleagues from Transylvania, asking for the unification of all Roumanian-speaking territories (including Moldavia and Wallachia) in a single 'Roumania' under Habsburg sovereignty.

No notice appears to have been taken of either of these documents, and in January 1849, a deputation took the former, or a re-draft of it, to the Court. It was passed to the Kremsier Reichstag, with the results described below.[2]

Meantime the National Guard had been disbanded for disorderly conduct, and Czernowitz put under martial law, but the reverberations of the unrest in the province, such as it was, were not audible outside its boundaries.

The demographical and geographical situation of the Czechs forbade them to think of separation from Austria, or even to threaten force in support of their claims; but they, too, put forward their demands, which, lying as their homes did at the very heart of the Monarchy, raised problems which were even more fundamental for its future than those of Lombardy-Venetia or Galicia, possibly even than those of Hungary.

The Czechs had begun staking out their claim very early, and it was important for the development of this chapter of our history that, in their case, it was the intellectuals and radicals who took the initiative. The Estates were not in session in March, but on the 8th posters appeared in Prague, signed by a certain Dr Kampelik, a Left-wing member of the Repeal Association (which was certainly behind his action, although the fact was concealed), inviting all interested to attend a meeting at the 'Wenzelsbad', a hostelry frequented by local politicians, on the 11th. The meeting, which was

[1] Text in Fischel, *Materialen*, pp. 319–21.　　[2] See below, p. 420.

attended by both Czechs and Germans, chiefly men who at that time were little known, adopted a twelve-point programme dictated to it by a friend of Palacký's, a Czech lawyer named Brauner. This contained the usual Liberal postulates – freedom of the Press, abolition of the robot, etc. – including – in this respect it was unique among all the documents of the period – regulation of the labour market and wages (there had been fairly severe workers' riots in Prague) – and further: 'maintenance and assurance of the constitutional link between the Lands of the Bohemian Crown (Bohemia, Moravia, Silesia)' and representation of them on a reformed Diet to sit annually, alternately in Prague and Brunn; a central administration for these lands, in Prague; complete equality for the Czech and German nationalities in all Czech Lands, schools and offices; all appointments to be restricted to natives, who must have complete command of both languages.

The petition was remitted for drafting to a Committee of Twenty, under the presidency of another lawyer, a certain Adolf Pinkas. The Committee intensified its Czech national tone by inserting a verbose preamble on the inequality under which the Czechs had long been suffering; on the other hand, it watered down the social side of it; thus the demand for the abolition of the robot was changed to one for 'humane improvement of the peasants' conditions'.

This 'revision' was submitted to another meeting, which took place only on the 15th, by which time the news of Metternich's fall had reached Prague, and the Oberstburggraf, Count Rudolph Stadion, had announced that the Monarch had consented to grant a Constitution, freedom of the Press and permission (of which the students were already availing themselves) to form a National Guard. Appetites were increasing, and Pinkas's draft was much criticized, not for its additions but for its omissions. Finally it was decided to take both drafts to Vienna, together with a separate petition from the students, who had objected that the other petitions took too little account of them. A deputation set off, amid scenes of great enthusiasm, on the 19th. They arrived in Vienna on the 20th, and were at once received by Kolowrat, who was benign but fairly ineffectual, except that he arranged for them to be received by Ferdinand on the 22nd. That evening or the next morning they seem to have seen Pillersdorf, or possibly one of his assistants, who went through the petition with them point by point, agreeing with them, or at least informing them of, his answers.[1] These appeared that day in the form of a Rescript from Ferdinand to Pillersdorf.[2] Most of the demands, this document said, had already been fulfilled; satisfaction of others was on its way. The complete equality of the two languages was already laid down by the

[1] Helfert, I. p. 423, writes definitely that Pillersdorf met the deputation, and either he or someone else in his Ministry must have done so. But neither Pillersdorf himself, in his memoirs, nor Walter refers to it, so that someone else may possibly have acted for the Minister.

[2] This appeared in the unusual form of a leaflet issued from the Vienna State printing press.

Vernewerte Landesordnung, and if this was not always observed in practice, the failures should be put right. The reform of the Bohemian Constitution, and any revision of the relationship between Bohemia, Moravia and Silesia could be effected only through the Estates, for the convocation of which the Patent of 15 March had provided.

The petitioners' audience of Ferdinand was, of course, a formality, although the Emperor was his usual kindly self. A second Rescript issued on the 23rd, went a little further than its predecessor, saying that 'modernizations of the Landesordnung would be welcomed', although the channel of the Estates would still have to be followed, as laid down in the Patent of 15 March.[1]

When, on 27 March, the deputation returned to Prague with this answer, there was consternation. Reports had gone round that 'everything had been granted', and a festal illumination of Prague had been planned. Now this was cancelled, and the deputation roundly abused for half-heartedness and reactionary sentiments which had brought the Czechs results so meagre in comparison with those meanwhile achieved by the Hungarians. The 'Wenzelsbad Committee', which had by now swollen into a large and confident body, on which the radical element was strongly represented, while the Germans had disappeared from it almost completely, decided to draft a new petition. In view of the Hungarians' success, it was now thought possible to put the constitutional demands more strongly, and the new draft, which was drawn up by the 29th, demanded *inter alia*, equality in every respect for the Czech and German nationalities, guaranteed by a new Fundamental Law – the Vernewerte Landesordnung was no sufficient guarantee – and the 'indissoluble unification' of all Lands belonging to the Bohemian Crown in respect of their internal autonomy, with a single Diet elected on the broadest basis and representative of all classes, a responsible Ministry for the internal affairs of the three Lands, and the requisite central administrative authorities – these concessions were to be enacted by the King of Bohemia, *jure majestatis*. Further the Citizens' Guard must be armed, and the social reforms introduced without delay.

As it had been argued that the signatures to the previous petitions had not carried enough weight, the leading figures in Prague were now pressed to add their names, and a number did so, including Stadion himself, who then went to Vienna to prepare the Government for the reception of the new document.

The new petition, accompanied by an address in the same sense, signed by thirteen members of the highest Bohemian nobility, was handed in on 1 April, and this time, important results were achieved.[2] The Ministers, at their wits' end to deal with the flood of problems which threatened to overwhelm them,

---

[1] In this document Ferdinand promised also to consider the establishment of a Supreme Court of Appeal in Prague.

[2] For this paragraph, see Walter, op. cit., pp. 25 ff.

were not anxious to commit themselves to any more constitutional concessions, and spent some time in devising other ways by which they hoped the Czechs could be placated, these including the appointment, which was actually announced on the 6th, of the young Archduke Francis Joseph to be Statthalter of Bohemia. Pillersdorf told Hofrat Kletzansky, formerly head of the Bohemian section in the Vereinigte Hofkanzlei, to work something out with the deputation, and after this had (obviously) been scrutinized by Pillersdorf himself, and apparently (although no one afterwards remembered anything about it[1]) shown to the Ministerial Council, the end product was published on the 8th in the form of yet another Rescript from Ferdinand to Pillersdorf.[2]

This repeated that the question of the 'unification of the Lands of Bohemia, Moravia and Silesia under a central administration in Prague and with a common Diet' was one which must be negotiated 'at the next Reichtag'. But it authorized a number of immediate concessions, including the establishment in Prague of 'a responsible central administration for the Kingdom of Bohemia, with extended competence'. Elected representatives from the towns and rural communes were to be added to the Estates, which were to meet shortly, with the right to debate and resolve on all Land questions. The German and Czech languages were to be, in principle, on a footing of complete equality in public life and education, and all persons occupying administrative or judicial posts in Bohemia would have in the future to be conversant with both languages. The Rescript further acknowledged the Vernewerte Landesordnung to be the basis of Bohemia's relationship to the Crown: in other words, the Vereinigte Hofkanzlei was repudiated.

Pillersdorf afterwards maintained that everything in this Rescript 'simply recognized the individual rights which were to be sanctioned in the forthcoming fundamental law, and could, like everything done up to the convocation of the Reichstag, acquire permanent validity only subject to the condition of its confirmation' (by that body).[3] But while the Reichstag would, presumably, be able to repeal any earlier legislation, none of these far-reaching concessions were described as 'provisional', and the 'Bohemian Charter', as the Czechs dubbed the Rescript, naturally awakened enormous jubilation among the Czech nationalists, and corresponding consternation elsewhere. The Diet of Moravia, when it met on 24 April, sent in a caveat that 'the Margravate of Moravia was an independent Land, linked only with the Constitutional Empire of Austria',[4] while the Silesian Diet repudiated the

[1] Walter, p. 30.
[2] The text is in Fischel, *Sprachenrecht*, pp. 73 ff., but by a fatality, the most important line of all has dropped out from the foot of the page. There should be added: Landtage hat einen Gegenstand der Verhandlung auf dem nächsten Reichstage.
[3] *Rückblicke*, pp. 20 ff.
[4] The Diet repeated this declaration in September, when it added that Moravia's link with the Empire was 'organic' and its 'only' link.

idea of unification with Bohemia without a single dissentient voice.[1] The local Germans, too, were getting seriously anxious. They had begun by fraternizing with the Czechs in the joint cause of liberty; many of them had signed all the earlier petitions, and they had accepted the principle of equality between the two nationalities almost universally. But the word 'equality', as applied where there is a majority and a minority, is capable of diverse interpretations and the Germans had soon taken fright at some of the Czech interpretations of it, which amounted to the proposition that either party was equally entitled to impose its will totally if it was in a majority. Various disorderly anti-German demonstrations had also been taking place in the streets of Prague. No Germans had signed the petition of 29 March. The Germans began hurriedly to organize[2] and soon counter-petitions were pouring in on Vienna asking that at least the use of the Czech language should not be extended to schools and administrative offices in German districts and also, to quote one of them, protesting against 'any separation of Bohemia, Moravia and Silesia from the other German Austrian Lands'.

With this the Bohemian question became a part – and a particularly intractable part – of Austria's German problem, now in full spate.

This question was one completely *sui generis*. The new element in it, the epidemic of acute nationalism, impregnated with liberalism and sometimes republicanism, which had been ravaging Germany since late February, had caught the Austrian Government entirely unawares. Metternich, as we have said, saw in it nothing but revolutionary feeling, to be suppressed, and no remedy but concerted repressive action by governments. The Austrian Germans had been practically unrepresented on the Heidelberg Committee which had organized the Frankfurt Vorparlament. Later, however, both government and people had been forced to take cognisance of the new situation by the further spread of the popular movement for German unity and in particular, by the antics with the help of which the King of Prussia was trying to jump a claim and to put himself at the head of united Germany.

The new Austrian Government's reaction to Prussia's move was the

[1] The Silesian Diet contained no Czech representatives. The figures in Moravia were 124 Slavs to 123 Germans, but the Moravian Slavs were at this time, as before (see above, pp. 215, 298), no Czech nationalists; many of them even regarded themselves as belonging to a separate, 'Moravian' nationality.

[2] Living as they did in widely dispersed areas, the Germans of Bohemia had not possessed any central organization of their own, and the lead was taken for them by an 'Association of German Bohemians in Vienna' which was hurriedly formed after 13 March. According to an unsigned article in *Die Bauernbefreiung* 1848 (Leitmaritz, 1923, pp. 32 ff.), this Committee then saw Pillersdorf and gave him some material; they also saw Francis Joseph 'who did not seem to know what it was all about'. On 9 March they sent in to the Ministry a strong protest against the 'Charter'.

obvious one. On 24 March, almost as his first action on taking office, Ficquelmont circularized the appropriate quarters with a statement, which was also published, that while Austria was willing to co-operate in negotiations, carried out in the right place and by competent organs (i.e. the headquarters of the Bund in Frankfurt) for the reform of the Federal Constitution, she could not accept any modification of it made without her consent. In fact, Schmerling, one of the most competent and most German-minded of Austria's public servants, was sent to Frankfurt to sit on the Committee of seventeen sages which the Federal Diet appointed to elaborate a reformed Federal Constitution.[1]

But already by this time popular opinion in Central and Western Germany had almost lost interest in the Diet, in favour of the Vorparlament, which, totally unofficial as it was, had somehow succeeded in becoming the incarnation of the German people's hopes. On this body, too, which held its first formal session on 31 March, Austria was as good as unrepresented: 141 interested persons had come to it from Prussia, 84 from Hesse-Darmstadt, 72 from Baden, while a single Austrian had attended its opening session, and he, a certain Wiesner, was a political *émigré* of the Left; later, another (Count Bissingen) looked in.

This, however, was a little misleading: more would have been there but they had (typically) taken too long preparing for the journey. By now, Austrian opinion had awakened to the German question, but saw it, naturally, through Austrian spectacles.

There were some quarters which had caught the national-liberal infection in its pure, south-west Germanic, form. Chief of these were the students of Vienna and Graz; it was characteristic that the first organization to start wearing the German colours in their button-holes was the Academic Legion.[2] And from the day of the appearance of this phenomenon, it spread very rapidly, until the old black and yellow was almost lost in the new multitude of black, red and gold cockades and button-holes. It was not only the students who were fired by the vision of the progressive and enlightened united Germany which was to emerge from the deliberations of the Vorparlament: all the Austrian German progressives looked forward to seeing Austria take her place in this new Germany, introducing its ideas and its reforms into her own body politic. On 2 April, Ferdinand had to follow the example of his Brother of Prussia in allowing the new colours to be hoisted on the tower of St Stephen's Cathedral, in Vienna, on the University and finally, on the

---

[1] It should be added that Ficquelmont's ideas on German nationalism were not very different from Metternich's. Orders had actually been sent to Austrian troops to reinforce the home garrisons in some of the more turbulent German towns, when the local governments themselves took fright and the moves were called off.

[2] The students' petition of 12 March had already asked that the German Lands of the Monarchy should be represented at Frankfurt.

Palace itself. The crowd gathered outside the Palace sang *Was ist des Deutschen Vaterland*.

But no less typically, the day on which the popular Germanic demonstrations began was that on which the news of the King of Prussia's famous ride through Berlin, draped in the German colours, had reached Vienna. There was in the whole Austrian movement a strong element of rivalry to Prussia. The republican element was very small. When they came to debate the matter, the Austrian Germans divided into the partisans of a confederation, and of a federation. A confederation would have left the sovereignty of its component members intact, while most even of the federalists assumed as a matter of course that the capital of the federation would be in Vienna, and its head, a Habsburg.

All of them, moreover, were acutely conscious of the special problem presented by Austria's largely non-Germanic character. Many of them agreed with the Liberals of central Germany, and of Prussia itself, in wishing to exclude from the future Germany those lands which had not belonged to the old German Bund, or its predecessor, the Reich. They would not have minded seeing Austria renounce her rule over Galicia and Lombardy-Venetia (there were some doubts about Dalmatia) and letting Hungary make what terms she would and could. But for all of them it was axiomatic that the Lands of the Bohemian Crown and the Slovene South would have to remain inside the new formation. Indeed, the federalists were particularly strong precisely among the Germans of the Bohemian Lands, who saw in Austria's adhesion to Germany an additional safeguard of their own position against the Slavs.

It was a move by the Vorparlament that made the question *actuel*. On 2 April it adopted Gagern's proposal to entrust the framing of the future German constitution 'solely and entirely, without any consent from the Governments' to be organized by a Committee of Fifty; and then decided to increase its meagre quota of Austrians in that body by six more, and sent invitations to the Viennese Bach, von Schwarzer and Schuselka,[1] the Tiroleans Baron Adrian Warburg and Schuler and the Czech Palacký. It was to this invitation that on the 11th Palacký made his famous reply, in a letter which was printed in all available newspapers, and also in pamphlet form. 'I am not a German,' he wrote; 'at least, I do not feel myself to be one... I am a Bohemian of Slavonic stock.' Bohemia, he went on, had never been an integral part of the Reich. Moreover, he was convinced that if the labours of the Frankfurt Parliament succeeded, the result of them would be to weaken Austria irremediably, indeed, to make its existence impossible; whereas, in his view, the 'preservation, integrity and reinforcement' of Austria were necessary – in view, he alleged, of the danger from Russia's

[1] Von Schwarzer had been born in Moravia and Schuselka in Bohemia, but both had come to live in Vienna.

'natural' expansive south-western urge. 'Truly, if it were not that Austria had long existed, it would be necessary, in the interest of Europe, in the interest of humanity itself, to create her.'[1] Vienna, not Frankfurt, was the centre 'suited and called by destiny to assure and protect the peace, freedom and rights of my people'. The solution was a united Germany without Austria, a united Austria without Germany, the two linked by a perpetual offensive and defensive alliance and perhaps a customs union.

It was an open bid, which was backed by the Slovenes,[2] to get the Crown to rest its power on its Slavonic subjects. The time was, however, not yet ripe for the Crown to accept 'Austro-Slavism' as the basis of its rule. It could, after all, still hope to do better for itself in Germany than accept an alliance and a customs union with a Germany under Prussian hegemony, nor was it yet prepared to antagonize its German subjects. It did not even wish to do so. When a deputation came to Ficquelmont to ask him what the Government's line was, he told them that: 'The Government of Austria has always been a German one; it is not to divest itself of that character.' Only, the Austrian body politic was something quite peculiar, and therefore 'In the changes imminent in Germany the Government must see to it that the political agreement with Germany does not endanger the Emperor's position in his own dominions. We should remain Germans without ceasing to be Austrians.'

The Government would, in fact, really have preferred to see the whole Frankfurt business dropped, but since it could not stop it and dared not boycott it for fear of being outdistanced by Prussia, it could do no more than let the delegation go, while reserving its rights. In fact, a delegation of relatively sober Liberals went off,[3] whose subsequent attitude their colleagues on the Committee themselves described as 'wondering how they can unite with Germany without uniting with Germany – like trying to kiss a girl with your back turned to her'.

The Committee decided that the elections for the Parliament itself should be conducted 'through constitutional channels'; the Parliament would then 'agree the German Constitution with the Governments'. The Federal Diet abandoned the struggle, gave up its plan of holding its own elections and agreed to recognize those organized by the Committee, which would thus have the recognized character of a Constituent, although still without legal power to enforce its decisions. The Austrian Government made sundry more attempts to get the elections postponed, but finally acquiesced in their being

[1] This famous phrase was not Palacký's original invention. It had been used by Perthaler in an article in the *Wiener Zeitung* on 23 March 1848.

[2] In their petition, which reached the Court only on 1 April, but had been drafted earlier, the Slovenes said that as Slavs, they could not belong to the German Bund, based as it was on German nationality.

[3] These were very different from the rather random lot selected by the Vorparlament, all of whom had refused, except Schuselka. The other five to go then were Kuranda, Endlicher, Hornbostel, Mühlfeld and Schilling.

held at the end of April, making, on the 21st, a last statement to the effect that, while anxious 'to take every opportunity of expressing her attachment to the common German cause', Austria could never agree to 'a complete renunciation of the special interests of those of her territories which belonged to the German Bund, a complete subordination to the Bundesversammlung, a renunciation of the independence of her internal administration'. The primary elections were held on 26–7 April, the secondary on 3 May, and the delegates elected on the latter occasion then set out for Frankfurt. The party was, indeed, composed exclusively of Germans, the Slavs having boycotted the elections. This, however, was no loss to Austria, for the result was that most of the men who went were solid men and good Austrians, some of them men of much distinction.[1] One said that the purpose of this journey was to check the revolutionary tendencies of the West and South Germans, and the instructions agreed between the Viennese delegates contained the sentence: 'The sovereignty and integrity of Austria cannot and must not be sacrificed by adherence to Germany.'

The opening of the Vorparlament also elicited a move from Hungary. Up to that date the Hungarian Government had made no motions to carry out any independent activities abroad, although in April Batthyány had tried (unsuccessfully) to persuade the Foreign Office to recognize the Hungarian Government and to send a diplomatic representative to Buda-Pest. On 14 May, however, two Hungarians, László Szalay and Dénes Pázmándy, were instructed to go to Frankfurt, where they were to 'work towards the maintenance and reinforcement of friendly relations between the German and Hungarian States' and to convince the Germans 'that they could find in Hungary and in a strong Hungarian people their best and most reliable ally'. They were also to warn the Germans of the danger to Germany of allowing those Provinces of Austria which had previously belonged to the Bund 'to become a Slav State'.[2]

Meanwhile, for nearly a month after the issue of the Patent of 15 March, only one person had made any motions at all towards implementing it, and he was not a member of the Government, but Count Montecuccoli, the Landmarschall of Lower Austria, who, apparently on his own initiative, had sent out invitations to all the 'Austrian' Lands to send representatives to Vienna for preliminary discussions on the modernization of the Estates. Galicia and Bohemia ignored the invitation, but all the other Lands invited sent representatives, and the discussions opened on 10 April. Meanwhile, however, the Viennese reformers were clamouring with increasing impatience for a Constitution, and it seemed unlikely that they would be satisfied with a sort

---

[1] Their numbers included such notable figures as Schmerling, 'Anastasius Grün', Andrian, Mühlfeld, Bruck and Perthaler.
[2] Horváth, *Magyarország Függetlenségi Harcza*, I. 120–2.

of Estates General modernized by 'increased representation for the burghers'. The delegates themselves decided that a full-dress Constitution, with a Parliament, would be needed, and said as much to Pillersdorf, who then sat down and compiled his own draft, taking as models the two most liberal Constitutions of the day, those of Belgium and Baden, but adding certain provisions to meet the special conditions of Austria. This was shown to various experts, including the Ministerial Council, the representatives of the Estates, and a number of Archdukes, among them Francis Joseph,[1] and revised in the light of their comments.[2] It was fully expected, and even intended, that the Reichstag, when it met, would make further changes, and some questions were even left open altogether, for the Reichstag to fill in the answers, but it was decided that in view of the urgency, the best course was to begin by publishing this first draft, really as a basis of discussion, as an octroi. It was first hoped to publish it on the Emperor's birthday, 19 April, but as that date fell that year in the last week of Lent, publication was postponed to the day after Easter Monday, 25 April, when the document was issued as an Imperial Patent, but counter-signed by the entire Ministry.

The first paragraph laid down that 'all Lands belonging to the Austrian Imperial State form an indivisible constitutional Monarchy', but the second recognized the separate positions which had already been granted, or were to be granted, to Hungary and Lombardy-Venetia by laying down that the provisions which followed applied only to the Lands belonging to the German Bund, Galicia-Bukovina, and Dalmatia. 'The existing territorial division of the Provinces' (*die bisherige Gebietseintheilung der Provinzen*) was not to be altered, and there were to be provincial Landtage (the Parliament, when it met, was to decide on the composition of these bodies), which would 'take account of provincial interests and meet requirements arising out of those interests', but the key position in the structure was held by a single Parliament, which was to consist of two Houses: a 'Senate' composed of the members of the Imperial House who had completed their twenty-fourth year, an (unspecified) number of life-members nominated by the Emperor, and 150 members elected for the lifetime of the Parliament (five years) from among their own members by the largest landowners[3] of each Land; and a Lower House of 383 members (the franchise law was to be enacted later). The legislative competence was divided between the Parliament and the Emperor, who was given an absolute veto on any legislation, and had the right to dissolve the Parliament or to prorogue it, but not indefinitely. The question of Ministerial responsibility was to be settled by the Parliament.

[1] As the prospective Monarch, who would have to work through it.

[2] Francis Joseph had, apparently, none to make.

[3] The qualification was purely material; birth did not enter into it. The owners of small landtäflich estates thus lost their former privileged position. The Prelates of the larger Houses, however, got into the list in virtue of the property owned by their foundations.

The later paragraphs enumerated the conventional civic liberties which the peoples of Austria were to enjoy. The list, which was a comprehensive enough one, need not be enumerated here; but it may be mentioned that it included the phrase that 'all peoples of the Monarchy are guaranteed the inviolability of their nationality and language'.

Several points in this field, including that of just how much religious equality Austria was prepared to allow, were among those which the Reichstag was asked to settle for itself.[1] It was also to enact the definitive franchise for its successors; a provisional law for the elections to the first Parliament was promised for the near future.

The Pillersdorf Constitution has been dismissed too contemptuously by many writers. It had been compiled hastily, under the pressure of popular impatience, but it was by no means an incompetent piece of work, nor an illiberal one. The catalogue of popular rights and liberties was as full as any known to the Europe of the day. It was centralist in the sense that the competences of the Landtage, although not very exactly defined, were clearly subordinated to those of the central Reichstag, but in this respect it did not differ from the system under which Austria settled down twenty years later. Nevertheless, like all attempts to solve the Austrian problem, it found more critics than admirers. The Polish deputation, which was still in Vienna awaiting the answer to its petition, entered a formal protest against the disregard of their claim for a separate status. The Czechs took exception to the general centralist tone of the document, and entered, in particular, a strong caveat that it could not be taken as over-riding the Rescript of 8 April, which the draft had passed over in silence, as though it had never been issued. The same centralism satisfied most of the Germans, but the extreme chauvinist party which was now beginning to raise its head objected to the exclusion of Hungary and the Italian Lands; and others took offence at the omission of any reference to a possible union with Germany, while the radicals of Vienna, headed by the students, found the document too conservative, especially in respect of the two Houses and the Crown's veto. They also objected to the octroi of a Constitution from above – innocent as Pillersdorf's decision had been, and taken only to avoid delay; in their view it should have been born of the deliberations of a Constituent Assembly.

The publication of the document was therefore followed in Vienna by a renewal of the disorderly scenes of March: the processions, the deputations, the *Katzenmusik* under the windows of individuals who found disfavour in the

---

[1] Pillersdorf's first draft had laid down the principle of complete religious freedom and equality, but the Estates had objected to the complete and immediate emancipation of the Jews, 'not on principle, but on account of popular feeling' (Walter, p. 49). The revised draft provided therefore only for freedom of worship for all recognized Christian confessions. The Reichstag was to deal with 'the question of the abolition of all inter-confessional inequalities'.

1848

eyes of the students, and now events in the capital succeeded one another with dizzy rapidity. On 4th May Ficquelmont resigned, under the threat of actual violence,[1] whereupon fairly extensive changes were made in the Ministry. For his new 'Head of Chancellery and Minister of Foreign Affairs' the Emperor fell back on Freiherr von Wessenberg, a retired diplomat who was then passing the evening of his days in Freiburg in Breisgau, a man of courage, integrity and intelligence, and no ultra-Conservative, but of advanced years (he was then seventy-five years old) and frail health. Pending his arrival (he was not even consulted before his appointment), Pillersdorf acted as President of the Ministerial Council. Freiherr von Doblhoff, a liberal and popular member of the Lower Austrian Estates, was brought into the Ministry in charge of trade and industry (this being the first Ministerial appointment made from outside the ranks of the regular State services), and A. Baumgartner, Director of a State tobacco factory, became Minister for State Enterprises and Public Works,[2] with the special charge of doing something to relieve unemployment. At the same time, several personal changes were made outside the Ministry; a number of persons were replaced or retired, including some figures suspected of exerting an undue influence behind the scenes.

The Radicals were not satisfied with this victory, and on 10 May formed a new 'blanket organization' in the shape of a 'Political Central Committee of the whole National Guard', a body which, in fact danced to the students' piping. Then on 11 May an Imperial Rescript announced the convocation of the Reichstag for 26 June, and published the franchise law for it. The Upper House was to be composed as previously announced, but its total membership was not to exceed 200 – a provision which left the big land-owners, who were still to contribute 150 members, constituting an overwhelming majority in it. The elections to the Lower House were to be indirect, the primary electors choosing a smaller number of secondary electors, who then chose the members of the Reichstag, and the primary franchise excluded workers paid by the day or week, domestic servants, and persons in receipt of public assistance.

The Central Committee promptly protested against this franchise, whereupon Hoyos ordered the members of the National Guard not to participate in

---

[1] According to Strobl von Ravelsberg's entertaining and sometimes well-informed work, *Metternich und seine Zeit* (I. 386), the campaign against Ficquelmont was organized largely by certain Polish ladies who bore him a grudge from earlier days. See also Walter, op. cit., pp. 67–8.

The Church was another special butt of the reformers of these weeks. The Archbishop of Vienna was one of the persons treated to *Katzenmusik*, and the Liguorians and Penitent Sisters were actually terrorized into leaving Vienna.

[2] *Oeffentliche Arbeiten*. The phrase included State enterprises such as the tobacco factories, the nationalized railways, etc., as well as 'public works' as that phrase is usually understood in English.

the Committee's proceedings. When they objected, he suggested that the Committee should dissolve itself. Instead, the students, National Guard and workers held a mass meeting on 15 May. The streets were packed as not since the March days. Crowds besieged the Palace, in which the Ministers happened to be assembled, demanding the cancellation of the dissolution of the Committee and the withdrawal of the draft Constitution and franchise in favour of a single-chamber Constituent Assembly elected on a popular franchise. The unfortunate Government did not dare refuse, and the next day posters appeared, bearing an announcement, which was signed by Ferdinand and counter-signed by the entire Ministry, that these wishes were granted. Another Rescript, issued the following day, promised specifically that the Reichstag should be uni-cameral and that there should be no property qualification for the primary vote. After the 18th the National Guard was even to share with the military sentry duty at the Palace itself.

The concessions of 15 May constituted the biggest victory yet achieved in Austria by the *vox populi*; but they proved also to be the high watermark of its success. They resulted directly in a move which, while looking at the time like another retreat by the Court and its supporters, can be seen today, in its historical context, as powerfully facilitating the course of the reaction, and even as constituting an important, if unintended, move in it. The tumultuous scenes, and perhaps still more, the prospect of having National Guards watching outside their doors, threw the ladies of the Palace into a panic. They decided to take Ferdinand, to whom they communicated their fears, to safety. Hurried preparations were made, in the deepest secrecy; only a handful of trusted men and women in the Palace were initiated. On the afternoon of the 17th the Emperor and Empress set out as though for an ordinary drive, allegedly to call on the Palatine's wife, but instead drove all night and all the next day, arriving late in the evening of the 19th in Innsbruck, where they were joined, a few hours later, by Franz Karl and his wife and two younger children.[1]

From this place of safety the family sent back a defiant proclamation saying that Ferdinand had been forced to leave Vienna because 'an anarchical faction, supported chiefly by the Academic Legion, which had been led astray by foreigners, and by certain detachments of the Citizens' and National

[1] Francis Joseph was now in Italy. The Ministerial Council, although (as said) announcing his appointment as Statthalter of Bohemia on 6 April, had itself decided on the 8th 'that it would be better, in the circumstances, if he did not hurry to take it up', but waited to see how things developed. On 19 April, Windisch-Graetz suggested to the Archduchess that the boy should be sent down to Radetzky, where he would be safe from political pressure. Francis Joseph himself was burning to see active service; the suggestion was accepted, and the young man started from Vienna (incidentally without the Government's having been informed) a week later.

Guards, had, wavering in their accustomed loyalty, wished to deprive him of his freedom of action'.

The ladies' motives in compassing the abduction of the Emperor had been simply those of panic, which they had communicated to Ferdinand himself,[1] but the political effects of the *coup* were enormous. In Vienna the news of it produced an extraordinary succession of moves and counter-moves the immediate outcome of which was another advance, in the capital itself, for the Left. The initial effects of the news, even here, had been to sober spirits. While extremists had raised jubilant voices that this was Austria's flight to Varennes, which would have the same sequel in Austria as it had had in France, and had fêted the coming of the republic, these extravagances only intensified the widespread consternation and fear which the flight had produced among the more sober elements in the capital. There was another heavy run on the banks and savings-banks, and the citizenry rallied to defend itself. The Central Committee transformed itself into a 'Central Association of the National Guard for the preservation of security and order', under Montecuccoli. All the armed formations of the capital, the National Guard, the Civic Guard and the Academic Legion, promised to place themselves under the orders of the commander of the Garrison, F.M.L. Auersperg, in the event of disorders breaking out.

But unhappily for the 'party of order', its defenders went too far. The Government had posters pasted up threatening the proclamation of martial law, should this prove necessary. This threat, coming on the intemperate language of the message from Innsbruck, set rumours buzzing that Windisch-Graetz was *ante portas*. Then, on 24 May, the Ministry of Education declared the University closed, and the next day Colloredo invited the Academic Legion to dissolve itself. The students refused. Next morning a proclamation by Auersperg and an order by Montecuccoli declared the Legion 'in its present form, as an independent component of the National Guard' dissolved; its members were simply to be incorporated in the National Guard. By an unfortunate accident, the proclamation contained some wounding phrases. The students barricaded themselves in the Aula. Once again many workmen flocked to their help, and many other members of the Guard took their side. The Government called out troops, and as on 13 March, this only inflamed spirits. The Government, having no alternative, yielded all along the line. It recalled the troops, retracted the dissolution of the Legion, reaffirmed the concessions of 15 May, and sanctioned the formation of a new 'Committee of Security' (by its full name, 'Committee of the Burghers, National Guard, and Students of Vienna for the maintenance of peace,

---

[1] Sophie wrote in her diary: 'we are like a mouse in a trap here' (Corti, p. 209), and Ferdinand himself wrote, in a little diary which he kept of his journey: 'We were told that the people and the students meant to storm the Palace, set it alight, and murder us; that was the reason that forced us to leave Vienna.' See also Walter, pp. 94 f.

security and order and the preservation of the people's rights') to which it delegated official responsibility for the maintenance of public order and security.

New men took charge of the National Guard and the Academic Legion.[1] The Committee of Security, or rather, the Executive Committee which it in its turn elected, now became the real ruler of Vienna. The Executive Committee numbered among its eleven members several sober and responsible figures, not least its President, Fischof, and in many respects it exercised its powers wisely and well. But the full Committee contained many extremists and the first days after 25 May were another period of turbulence. Warrants were issued for enemies of the people, including Montecuccoli and even Hye and Endlicher, to be called to account for their reactionary activities. Bands of hooligans, besides molesting members of the aristocracy against whom they bore personal grudges, raised a hue and cry against the class as a whole, and many of its members fled the capital.

To the Committee's difficulties were added new ones arising out of an economic situation which, even before this, had been growing steadily more critical. Foreign suppliers of raw materials needed by the Austrian factories had become nervous, and the gulden was now being quoted at a discount of 20–25%. Where shipments from abroad did reach frontiers, their movement across the country, especially from Trieste, was impeded by the claims made by the military on communications. Factories were having to close down for lack of supplies. Revenue was slow in coming in; exchequer receipts for March–May were nearly 14 million gulden below estimate, and the quarter ended with a deficit of nearly 16 million gulden. By June the silver reserves of the National Bank were down to about 20 million gulden, while the note issue was round 160 million gulden. Prices were rising, this in itself causing a fall off in demand, which was aggravated by the flight of the Court and of so many members of the bourgeoisie. This hit, not only the factories, but at least as heavily, the small artisans and shopkeepers. This brought back the threat from the dreaded proletariat. When unemployment grew serious again, a radical student named Willner[2] whom a self-constituted Workers' Committee had made its president, persuaded the Committee to adopt the principle of work or maintenance, that is, that the State was obliged to provide work for any person unable to find private employment. He further got the rate for public works fixed at 25 kreuzer daily for men, 20 for women or 12 for juveniles, this being equal to the top rate paid by private enterprise

---

[1] Hoyos, after being arrested and kept prisoner for some days, had been deposed from the command of the former body; Colloredo resigned from that of the latter. Their successors (a retired Colonel named Pannasch and a retired Captain named Koller) were respectable nonentities.

[2] On him, and the 'navvies' crisis in general, see Violand, op. cit., pp. 125 ff., Zenker, pp. 24 ff.

for unskilled labour. The effect was disastrous. The local unemployed were reinforced by a great influx of masterless men from Bohemia, and many of them simply went each morning to the site of the works in the suburbs,[1] drew their 25 kreuzer (sometimes from several stations) and disappeared, the officials in charge being afraid to protest. Many of the Czechs among these men, incidentally, preached national disaffection. Even some factory workers found it easier to go and draw the dole (which was what the payment amounted to) than to earn the 40 kreuzer or so which they could get for a day's work in a factory. The 'navvies' now numbered some 50,000, a formidable force, especially since it was largely composed of very rough elements, and one which was a constant source of apprehension to the rest of the population. This situation, in its turn, further increased the unpopularity of the Committee of Security and its supporters, and even discredited the whole idea of democracy, for many who had sympathized with the constitutional movement in its early stages, were horrified and disgusted at a regime dominated by 'students who played at politics instead of studying' and 'Lumpenproletariat'. Thus while the Left triumphed for the moment in Vienna, its victory even there cost it a heavy price. Outside the capital, the flight of the Court both created the psychological pre-conditions for a counter-offensive by the Right and put its supporters in a far more favourable position to act. In the Alpine provinces it had the simple and predictable effect of evoking in full measure that chronic antipathy of the Austrian provincial to the capital which is so constant a feature in Austria's history, and one so constantly underestimated by its historians. It produced a great surge of affection for the Emperor and of resentment against his alleged persecutors.

It had also legitimized opposition to the recent trend of events. The first manifesto setting out the Emperor's reasons for his flight – drawn up in Salzburg by Franz Joseph's old tutor, Bombelles – had been so intemperate that the Imperial family itself – presumably Franz Karl – had rejected it. It had been first watered down, then, at the insistence of messengers sent posthaste after the fugitives by the Government, withdrawn,[2] and the Innsbruck manifesto had at least promised to respect popular feeling and had refrained from abusing the Government, But the Empress and the Archduchess Sophie were now making no secret of their hatred of everything that had been done since March, including the April Constitution, nor were they concealing their view that the Ministers themselves were simply the tools of subversion.[3]

[1] It had been proposed at first to use the labour for carrying on the construction of the Südbahn from Gloggnitz to the Semmering, but the plan had to be dropped, and the 'works' consisted almost entirely of shifting earth on various sites on the periphery of Vienna.

[2] On this see Helfert, II. 233; Walter, op. cit., p. 107.

[3] This view was shared by Francis Joseph. 'The Ministers', he wrote to his mother on 23 May, 'are really to blame for everything' (Schnürer, p. 100). He warmly approved both the flight and the Innsbruck Manifesto, which was multiplied and circulated to the troops in Italy (Id., p. 107).

The ill-concealed rift between the Crown and the Ministry raised issues which went far beyond approval and disapproval of 15 May; it was now respectable to question 25 April, and even 15 March. The flight had also suddenly smoothed the path in one important respect for those who wished to do so. In spite of the ladies' fears, the person of Ferdinand had never been in the slightest danger from the honest citizens of Vienna. But there had been, from the point of view of the *Camarilla*, as the Court circle and its close supporters were now beginning to be called, a real danger residing not in the alleged ill-nature of the Viennese, but in Ferdinand's own good nature, which had already led him into sanctioning so many concessions, and might lead him into sanctioning more, so long as he was within reach of petitioners for them. It was on this ground that Windisch-Graetz had told the Archduchess Sophie, as early as 19 April, that he would have liked to see Ferdinand out of Vienna, and viewed from this angle, the importance of the move to Innsbruck was enormous. It was, of course, completely unjust to identify the unfortunate Government with the forces which were in reality its captors.[1] They themselves had sanctioned the concessions of 15 May only with great reluctance, and under *force majeur*, and after it they had resigned *en bloc* and were carrying on only 'provisionally' until a new Minister President could be found. But pending a successful outcome of this search, which was proving difficult,[2] they were perforce remaining in office, and they were also pledged, and determined, to make the April Constitution work. And now the boot was on the other foot, for Ferdinand in Innsbruck was within reach of anyone who cared to make the journey there, but out of reach of his Ministers. Wessenberg, who had been delayed by sickness on his journey from Freiburg, had, when able to resume it, gone straight to Innsbruck, where he arrived on 2 June. But the Ministry as a whole clearly could not leave Vienna. All Pillersdorf could do was to send Doblhoff down to Innsbruck to act as the Government's representative there.

His services were soon in demand, for no sooner had the fugitives arrived in Innsbruck than the attempts to play them off against the Government began. Everybody who objected on any ground to the present position turned to Innsbruck in hope of remedy. The partisans of complete absolutism, with whom the ultimate victory was to lie, were not yet in a position to raise their voices openly; their strength would be with the army, which was then still engaged in Italy. But there were plenty of demands for a different kind of constitutional institution. Even some of the Alpine Provinces sent in far-

[1] As Pillersdorf writes, they asked the National Guard on 15 May whether it had enough troops to restore order; the answer was in the negative. They then tendered their own resignations, these were refused. They had no other choice but to yield (*Rückblicke*, p. 43).

[2] The first man approached was Wessenberg, who declined on the plea of his advanced years and unfamiliarity with domestic problems. Then Stadion, who had come to Vienna for consultations; he, according to Helfert (II. 269), 'felt that his time had not yet come'. Montecuccoli also declined.

reaching demands for provincial rights.¹ These could be, and were, refused, as was an invitation from Hungary that Ferdinand should come there.² But one initiative of the days was more important. This was a move from Bohemia, which ended, indeed, to the profit of the ultimate victors, the absolutists, but only after a bizarre series of happenings which sent the graph of the Czech national movement rising to a peak before the abrupt fall with which it ended.

Rudolph Stadion had resigned the Presidency of the Bohemian Gubernium on 5 April, and to succeed him the Government had appointed Count Leo Thun-Hohenstein, one of those high Czech aristocrats who were prepared to ally themselves with the Czech middle-class intellectuals in the cause of a federal reorganization of the Monarchy based on its Slav elements. Thun had been unable to leave his post (in the Lemberg Gubernium) immediately, and during most of April Prague had in practise been governed by the Wenzelsbad Committee; for when, as one of his last acts, Stadion had called into being a 'Governmental Committee'³ and had ordered the Wenzelsbad Committee to dissolve itself, that body had refused, instead, after some negotiation, combining with the Governmental Committee in a new 'National Committee'⁴ in which the Wenzelsbad element was, in fact, much the stronger.

Thun arrived in Prague on 1 May, where he was soon in touch with the Czech national leaders, then elaborating the plans described below. The events in Vienna seemed to the Czechs to play into their hands. When the news of them reached Prague, Thun announced that he would recognize no concessions extracted from the Emperor by force, and ordered the Bohemian Diet to meet on 7 June, before the Reichstag met in Vienna; the object of realizing the Czech national programme was hardly concealed. On 29 May Thun announced the establishment of a 'Provisional Responsible Council of Government', composed of two members of the high Bohemian aristocracy, four Czech national leaders, and two Germans. This body was to organize the 'responsible central administration' promised in the Rescript of 8 April, and meanwhile, to act in its lieu, 'if necessary, taking measures far exceeding the competence of Land Authorities'. He then sent two emissaries (Count Nostič and Palacký's son-in-law, Rieger) to Innsbruck to obtain authorization for these steps and convey a message of loyalty to Ferdinand, saying that Bohemia would remain true to the Dynasty, but could not 'submit to the rule of the rebellious Viennese people'. They were also to ask that

---
¹ The Estates of Styria, for example, asked that Styrian soldiers should not be sent on active service without their (the Estates') consent.
² See below, p. 388.
³ *Gubernialkommision.*
⁴ *Nationalausschuss, Narodni Zbor.*

Francis Joseph, then still in Italy,[1] should do so without further delay, as representative of the King of Bohemia.

This request was strongly backed by Windisch-Graetz, who, his holiday over, had returned to Prague, where Thun had made him privy to his plans. He now wrote to the Court assuring it in eloquent language of the 'absolute purity' of Thun's motives, and taking the opportunity to ask for himself authority to assemble under his command a force sufficiently strong to enable him 'to fulfil the functions of acting to preserve the safety of the Emperor's Throne and the welfare of the Monarchy as a whole'. He wanted plenipotentiary powers to take such action when he thought fit, without reference to the Ministry.

On this occasion the Government succeeded in asserting itself. Thun had published his intentions, and his arguments, a week before, and Pillersdorf had protested to him vigorously against the falsity of his picture of conditions in Vienna and his allegation that the Government there was not in charge of the situation. He had also written to Innsbruck urgently begging the Emperor not to sanction any illegal action by Thun. Doblhoff pleaded personally with the Emperor in the same sense, and was successful. The convocation of the Diet was sanctioned, although with a caution that it was not to exceed its competences – the Constituent would be deciding on the constitutional question – but not the appointment of the Council of Government, which Thun was ordered to dissolve.[2] And shortly after, other events occurred which brought further disaster to Czechs' national hopes.

Palacký, after rejecting the invitation to Frankfurt, had conceived the idea of countering Frankfurt by a Slav congress, to open in Prague on 1 June. Invitations to send representatives to this meeting had gone out on 1 May to all the Slav peoples of Austria, and also to non-Austrian Slavs.

The Congress was a parallel move to Thun's, with which it was intimately connected (Palacký himself and Rieger were two of the four Czech members of the Council of Government), and to which it should have lent force and persuasiveness – a bid to the Crown to rest its authority on a basis of 'AustroSlavism', which the Congress was meant to organize, as well as demonstrate its existing strength. It did not, however, work out according to plan. To begin with, the membership proved much more radical than had been expected, for the respectable aristocrats who had first agreed to attend it (the names had included two Princes Schwarzenberg, two Counts Czernin, etc.) had taken fright and cancelled their acceptances. In the event, a Prince

[1] He was sent back from the front, where he had displayed considerable dash, soon after, at Radetzky's earnest request. He arrived in Innsbruck on 9 June.

[2] The account given here of the absolute rejection of Thun's principal proposals rests on the incontrovertible documentary evidence quoted by Walter, op. cit., pp. 145 ff. It is thus certain that the version which, according to Denis, op. cit., pp. 280-1, was still being maintained in his day by some Czech historians, that Ferdinand had agreed to the emissaries' proposal, was erroneous.

1848

Lubomirski appeared as leader of the delegation of Poles from Galicia, and a Prince Sapieha of the Ruthenes, but nearly all the participants were intellectuals, such as Palacký himself and Safařik (who played a big part in the proceedings), while several Polish extremists arrived from Poznania and elsewhere, and the anarchist, Bakunin, from Russia.

The Austrian Slavs, after a great deal of often violent debate (for their respective programmes often proved to be mutually competitive, if not mutually incompatible), succeeded in drawing up an Address to the Emperor which asked *inter alia* for a status for Galicia similar to that which the Rescript of 8 April had given to Bohemia, with equality for the Polish and Ruthene languages, but no partition of the Province;[1] the union of Bohemia, Moravia, and Silesia; the union in one body of all the Serb territories of Hungary; the Triune Kingdom for Croatia; and a single administration for all the Slovenes. But the non-Austrian Slavs, of whom, indeed, only the Serbs had sent a delegation worthy of the name (Bakunin was the only Russian to appear) had seemed to consider that the purpose of the Congress was not at all to consolidate Austria, but to realize Slavonic ambitions which might prove highly dangerous to Austria itself. Under the direction of Libelt, a former member of the Polish National Committee and now one of the delegates from Prussian Poland,[2] they persuaded the Congress to adopt a manifesto protesting against the Partitions of Poland and attacking in succession the Governments of Prussia, Saxony, Hungary and Turkey; and, in general, they indulged in much radical language highly alarming to the Court.

Furthermore, as it happened, the week of the Congress coincided with the climax of a long-drawn-out crisis in the Prague cotton mills, which were suffering from very severe unemployment.[3] There were street demonstrations in which the workmen were supported by sympathetic students.

This gave Windisch-Graetz the opportunity for which he had been panting. He, too, had been disappointed in Innsbruck, having been told that he must obey his constitutional superiors, and a suggestion made by him on

---

[1] The conflict between Poles and Ruthenes (who, according to Fischel, *Panslavismus*, p. 268, had arrived in Prague in large numbers, 'firmly determined', as they told the Military Commandant of Cracow, 'to oppose anything suggested by the Poles') had been the most difficult inter-Austrian problem facing the Congress. The Ruthenes had been developing their ideas quickly since March and now asked that Galicia be partitioned into a Polish and a Ruthene Crownland. Thanks largely to the mediation of the Czechs, they dropped this demand; on the other hand, the Poles agreed that the two languages should be on a complete equality in public life and education, the decision which should be used in each District being left to the local majority to take. This agreement was submitted to the Crown, with the Address.

[2] Libelt had been sentenced by a Prussian Court in 1847 to twenty years imprisonment but had been released in March 1848 and then elected to the Frankfurt Vorparlament.

[3] The chronic technological crisis due to the introduction of machinery had been aggravated by the failure to arrive of supplies of American cotton, owing to the difficulty (of itself caused by the military operations in Italy) of getting them up from Trieste (Endres, op. cit., p. 107).

23 May that he should march on Vienna had been rejected; but the rebuff had not lessened his conviction of his own mission to stamp out revolution wherever it raised its head, and he chose to regard the activities of Libelt and his colleagues, and the students' and workers' processions, as symptoms of a deep-laid revolutionary plot.[1] On 6 June he began taking 'precautionary measures'. The demonstrations were in fact largely directed against the Prince himself, as the recognized *spiritus rector* of the reaction, and might not have been so vigorous but for his 'precautions', which were taken as provocations. But they in their turn were seized by him as excuse for further troop movements, and soon the inevitable occurred. On Whit Monday, 12 June, demonstrators came into collision with the military. Street fighting developed;[2] barricades were thrown up. The Government sent two commissions to Prague to mediate; Windisch-Graetz ignored them. On the 15th he threatened to bombard the city unless it surrendered unconditionally, and the next day in fact had a few shots fired. The city surrendered. A state of siege was proclaimed in Bohemia, and tribunals set up to try disturbers of the peace, which they did with great severity. The meeting of the Bohemian Diet was postponed indefinitely (the Council of Government had already been dissolved).

With the fall of Prague, the teeth of another national movement were drawn. The short-lived alliance between blood and brains disappeared for a decade and a half. The aristocrats drew back for the rest of 1848, and indeed, until their re-emergence in 1860,[3] they confined their political activities to leading the reaction in matters of social policy, but left both federalism and Czech nationalism alone. The intellectuals prepared to send their representatives to Vienna, whither, as Havliček admitted, 'they would never have gone but for Windisch-Graetz'. All this was pure gain for the Crown, for any attempt to realize the extremist Czech programme would certainly have produced elemental reactions among the Austrian-Germans, who had watched all that went on in Prague with undisguised hostility.[4] As it was, the question of the future structure of Austria was back in the safe channels of the Constituent. And while it was true that the leadership of the Czech movement

[1] Thun likewise maintained strongly, in a later letter, that the revolt in Prague 'was *not* started by the ultra-Czech party from nationalist motives; it had been organized by French, Polish and Viennese extremist agitators in the interests of their republican ideas'. Other authorities, including Sacher-Masoch, testify to the part played in it by Polish *émigrés*.

[2] Among the dead (who ultimately numbered four hundred) was Windisch-Graetz's own wife, who was killed by a stray bullet as she stood at her window.

[3] See below, p. 497 f.

[4] The *Volksfreund* of 24 June registered the utmost pleasure at the catastrophic fate of what it called 'the Slavic association of lunatics in Prague'. 'The victory over the Czech party in Prague', it wrote, 'is and remains an occasion for rejoicing' (the article is quoted in full in Rath, op. cit., pp. 262–3). 'The Prince', writes Bibl (*Tragödie*, p. 155), 'received enthusiastic addresses of thanks from numerous associations in Germany.'

was now again in the hands of men who stood fairly far to the Left on social and purely internal political issues, they were so much more interested in the national question than the social that there was no danger that they would ally themselves with the Austrian Left. It was rather to be expected that they would adopt the course which in the event they followed, of supporting the Government in the hope of being rewarded by it with national concessions.

And meanwhile things had been taking what were, from the point of view of the Court, pronounced turns for the better alike in Galicia, in Italy and in Germany.

In March, German Liberal opinion, including that of Prussia, had been sympathetic enough to the Poles, and had actually advocated the restoration of Poland. The Poles of the Grand Duchy were claiming full independence, and for a time Prussia had been near granting it. The Polish *émigrés* were being allowed to return from Western Europe across Germany to their homes, where it was hoped that they would prove themselves the advance-guard of the armies of liberty. But very soon the Prussians took fright at the possibility of war with Russia, and also at the exaggerated demands of the Poles, who claimed for their future State many areas which were purely, or largely, German. On 10 April actual fighting broke out between Prussian and Polish troops. Prussia refused to allow any more *émigrés* to enter her territory, and the trains were diverted to Cracow.

Stimulated by these new arrivals, the Poles of Cracow formed a Rada, or National Committee, which turned itself into a sort of government in exile and behaved as though it were the real government of Galicia. The threads with Lemberg were taken up again, and a plan hatched for a new *coup*. The Councils in Cracow and Lemberg were to proclaim simultaneously that they had taken over the government of Galicia from the Austrian authorities; and the proclamation was to be accompanied (as had been planned in 1846) by an announcement to the peasants abolishing the robot and all other servitudes as from 3 May. The proclamation was to be made at the great national Easter festivity of Święcone, which fell that year on 25 April (Easter Monday). Posters appeared announcing that this particular day would be made the occasion for especial celebration.

The Austrian authorities, however, suspecting the real motives of the proclamation, set a cordon round Cracow, refusing entry to any except Austrian subjects. Further, an order was issued prohibiting the manufacture or carrying of unauthorized arms (i.e. the scythes which had achieved such dire prominence in 1846). On the 25th, then, street fighting really broke out, and lasted that day and the next, on a scale so considerable that the garrison had to use artillery before it was quelled. But at 7 p.m. on the 26th the Poles capitulated. They were granted an amnesty, but the National Committee was dissolved, all arms had to be surrendered, and all *émigrés* who were not Austrian citizens had to leave the city.

Meanwhile, the Galician Diet had met in Lemberg (apparently self-convoked) on the 25th, had announced that it no longer represented authority in Galicia, delegated one member from each Kreis to join the Rada, and prorogued itself. But here, too, the Government succeeded in reasserting itself. On 15 April, Stadion had learned of the Poles' intention to emancipate the peasants and had sent an urgent message to Vienna to say that he would be unable to hold Galicia much longer in its existing relationship to Austria.[1] The Ministerial Council received this message on the 17th, and acting with unusual promptitude, sent him back permission (or orders) to forestall the Poles' move, by himself announcing the liberation of the peasants, as from the Government. On the 26th accordingly, Stadion announced in the Emperor's name that all dues and servitudes arising out of the nexus subditelae would cease in Galicia as from 15 May.[2] Compensation for the landlords was to be paid by the State, at a rate determined later through constitutional channels. At the same time he had the Rada's premises closed and forbade it to meet again.

Now, too, the Ruthenes went into action. When one of them had asked the meeting which constituted the National Council to include in its demands equality for his people, he had been physically maltreated. The Ruthenes had therefore been forced to seek their own salvation. After consultations conducted under the auspices of the St Georgites, they sent a message to Stadion assuring him that all they asked was 'to be freed from the yoke of the Polish overlordship, to be recognized as a nation[3] and to be allowed to live as one nation among the others in Austria, as an integral factor in Monarchy, with their own institutions'. They asked to be allowed to form their own Rada.

With great relief, Stadion granted their request. The Rada constituted itself, made an official announcement that it wished to remain loyal to Austria and would never seek adherence to Russia, and drew up a petition which, compiled as it had been in consultation with Stadion, was an extremely modest one: it did not even ask for what was afterwards the Ruthenes' main desideratum, the constitution of East Galicia as a separate Land, but only for adequate instruction in its own language where the population was

---

[1] Helfert, II. 1–2; Walter, op. cit., pp. 62 ff. The usual tradition attributes the suggestion of liberating the peasants to Stadion; Till in his biographical note on Stadion in *Gestalter*, p. 382, even writes that he acted without consulting Vienna at all. The documents quoted by Walter do not bear this out; according to them, Stadion wrote in despair saying that he saw only two possible courses, either to give Galicia up altogether, or to hand it over to 'a national Government under Austrian protection', for the head of which he suggested Goluchowski. The proposal to forestall the Poles with the peasants came from Pillersdorf himself, and was supported by Krausz, whose earlier career had been passed in Galicia. It is of course, possible that the messenger by whom Stadion sent his letter made the suggestion verbally.

[2] The order was extended to the Bukovina on 1 July.

[3] 'Nation' is obviously used in the technical sense of a corporate autonomous body.

1848

wholly or mainly Ruthene; that officials in those areas should understand Ruthene and laws, etc., be published in that language; that the Uniate Church should be treated on an equality with the Roman Catholic, and that Ruthenes should be eligible for the public services.[1]

On 3 May, Stadion wrote to Vienna, enclosing the petition and reporting the formation of the Rada, in which body, he said, 'he at last saw a means of paralysing the Polish influence and getting a backing for Austrian rule in Galicia'. The Ministerial Council, with equal relief, returned the Ruthenes a friendly answer, granting most of their requests. At the same time the Poles were at last given the definitive answer to their petition, and to their complaints against the Constitution: some of the points in the petition had already been fulfilled, others, including the request for the formation of a national army, were incompatible with the Constitution, and must be rejected.

These moves took the sting out of the Polish agitation (Prussia, too, was getting the situation in Poznania under control), and the situation in Galicia went for a while off the boil, but continued to simmer.

The turn of events in Lombardy was even more encouraging. Latour, a stalwart defender of the old order, had been sending all available troops down to Radetzky. At San Lucia, outside Verona, Radetzky on 5-6 May had won a victory over the Piedmontese which, although the forces involved were small[2] was so important strategically that one of his biographers has described it as the turning-point in the whole history of Austria in 1848.[3] It marked an unmistakable turning of the tide, and had an enormous effect in heartening Austria's defenders and intimidating her enemies. It still, indeed, left Radetzky's position extremely hazardous, for the Austrian armies were still confined to the Quadrilateral, where Peschiera itself fell on 30 May. Negotiations for fusion were going on between Turin, Milan and Venice; they were not going easily, but it seemed clear that Turin and Milan, at least, would soon reach agreement. The Austrian Government was still in favour of cutting its losses in the south, and on 24 May sent an emissary, Hofrat Hummerlauer, to London to ask the British Government to mediate

[1] The text of the petition, which is signed by Jachimowicz and two others from 'the Institute of the Lemberg Stauropygia, as representatives of the Ruthene people', is given in Fischel, *Sprachenrecht*, pp. 285 ff. It is dated there 19 April. I cannot account for the date, unless the Ruthenes were using the Old Style calendar. The documents in general show that Stadion did not take the initiative towards the Ruthenes nearly so decidedly as is generally believed; he seems to have been very nervous about their possible Pan-Slav tendencies. The often-quoted quip that he 'invented' the Ruthenes was first launched by the well-known journalist Moritz Gottlieb Saphir.

[2] The total Austrian losses in dead, wounded and missing, were only eighteen officers and 318 O.R., but it was a victory won over what seemed to be great odds, and it meant the failure of the Piedmontese attempt to take Verona, which would have meant the collapse of the entire Austrian positions. See the description in Kiszling, op. cit., I. 116-24.

[3] Frh. von A. Wolf-Schneider, *Der Feldherr Radetzky*, cit. Kiszling, op. cit., p. 123.

peace on the basis that Lombardy should be ceded, while Venetia remained part of the Monarchy with full administrative and national autonomy. But Palmerston refused to mediate except on the basis of total cession by Austria both of Lombardy-Venetia and of the Italian Tirol, and when Wessenberg then repeated the Austrian offer to Count Casati, head of the Provisional Government in Milan, telling Radetzky to offer Charles Albert an armistice during the negotiations, Casati, too, rejected the offer, on 17 June. The prospects of a political compromise had vanished the more completely because in the preceding week first Lombardy, then Venetia, had announced its adherence to Savoy.

But meanwhile larger reinforcements, from Moravia and Galicia, had been reaching Radetzky,[1] and on 11 June he had won another important success, when he re-took Vicenza. He now thought himself able to foresee complete victory if he could have another 20,000–25,000 men. When he received the instructions to offer Charles Albert an armistice, he put them in his pocket,[2] and instead sent an urgent message to the Court asking for the reinforcements (also insisting that the Frontier Regiments must not be recalled)[3] and begging the Court not to conclude an armistice. The messenger bearing this letter, Windisch-Graetz's brother-in-law, Prince Felix Schwarzenberg arrived in Innsbruck on the 19th.[4] He persuaded the Court, in principle, to suspend the armistice negotiations, and then went on to Vienna, where he convinced a Ministerial Council, met under the presidency of the Archduke John,[5] that Lombardy could be saved if Radetzky's army was reinforced. On 1 July the Government issued an official declaration that it had resolved to prosecute the war in Italy and to leave its outcome to be decided in the field.

A few rather hot-headed speeches had been made in Frankfurt when the proceedings opened there on 18 May, and the Vorparlament's decision to create its own central authority, obtaining the consent of the Government's *ex post facto*, was alarming, but the danger that anything might really be done diminished steadily as the talking got into its stride, and almost vanished for Austria when, on 29 June, the assemblage elected the Archduke John 'Imperial Vicar' (Reichsverweser) of the New Germany, and on 18 July chose the Austrian, Schmerling, to be Minister of the Interior in the new

[1] The first of these under Nugent arrived on 29 May, having defeated a force of papal troops en route.

[2] It used afterwards to be said, with a good deal of truth, that the Monarchy owed its survival in 1848 to the disobedience to their orders of three Generals: Radetzky, on this occasion; Windisch-Graetz, who several times overrode orders from Latour; and Jellacic, whose defiances of authority are too numerous to be listed.

[3] For the conflict then in progress between Hungary and Croatia over the Frontier regiments, see below, p. 379 f.

[4] A laudatory account of Schwarzenberg's part in these transactions will be found in Kiszling, op. cit., pp. 34 ff.

[5] The Archduke had just arrived in Vienna to act as the Emperor's *homo regius* there (see below, p. 372).

'Reich Ministry'.[1] Finally, Hungary was more than preoccupied with her own internal problems, which had created a situation in which her Government also thought it worth while to bid for the favour of the Crown; it, too, sent messages to Innsbruck condemning the violence of the Viennese mob and inviting Ferdinand to come to Buda, where he would be safe.

In this situation, the Court consented to a move towards reconciliation with Vienna. The Government had repeatedly begged Ferdinand to return, or if he would not do so, to send the Archduke John to represent him.[2] Hitherto, Ferdinand had withstood all pleas, but after Wessenberg and Doblhoff had repeated their representations most earnestly, on 14 June,[3] he (or his mentors) relented and agreed that the Archduke should go. This, in the event, proved to lead on to another period which brought the Right further advantages, for during it they increased and consolidated their forces while the Left further dissipated theirs; but it is by no means certain that the move was the mere piece of time-saving hypocrisy as which Left-wing historians commonly represent it, for John himself was a sincere friend of constitutional reform and there can be little doubt that he hoped that his presence in Vienna would help the moderate reformers to consolidate their position.[4] At all events, when he arrived in the capital on 24 June, he promised the crowds which welcomed him to respect all popular rights and liberties; and no one doubted his sincerity.

The Committee of Security and its allies, for their part, were far from regarding their battle as lost. They continued to besiege the Government with imperious demands, two of which they pressed with especial vigour: that the franchise for the Reichstag should be to their liking, and that Windisch-Graetz and Thun should be called to account for their doings in Prague. Pillersdorf had given them partial, but incomplete, satisfaction on the former point: the revised franchise issued by him on 30 May gave the vote to independent workers domiciled in their constituencies, but still excluded other categories of workers, and retained the system of indirect voting. But he would not, or dared not, touch Windisch-Graetz, nor, for that matter, Thun.[5]

[1] He was promoted Minister President when the first holder of that office, Prince Leiningen, resigned it.

[2] The Archduke Franz Karl was out of favour with the people, who regarded him as tarred with the Metternich brush. They probably also believed him to be entirely under the thumb of his wife, the legend of whose democratic sympathies had by this time been thoroughly exploded. John had arrived in Innsbruck at the end of May.

[3] Walter, p. 199.

[4] It is interesting that Sophie disapproved of the choice, because, she said, John was 'too thick with other people' (Corti, op. cit., p. 299).

[5] Perhaps out of timidity, Pillersdorf had not even rebuked Thun for his constitutional *extratour*, merely sending him the Emperor's decision. After the Whitsun fighting, the Government had decided that the situation was too explosive to disavow either man publicly. Windisch-Graetz had received an effusive letter of thanks from Ferdinand, and a high decoration from the Czar, for his achievement.

Consequently, the Committee, which only six weeks before had begged Pillersdorff to remain in office, now decided that he was a reactionary, and on 8 July, demanded that he should be replaced by Doblhoff. The Archduke, without resistance, let him make an unreluctant exit from public life.[1] John then had to go to Frankfurt to be invested as Imperial Vicar, but he came back on 17 July, and the new Ministry was announced the next day. It was not altogether what the Liberals had asked for, for they had demanded a clean sweep of the old men, and the Court had insisted on keeping its own men in the three Gesammtmonarchie posts, and Wessenberg now became Minister President, since Doblhoff did not want that post, preferring the Interior for himself,[2] while Latour and Krausz retained their portfolios. But the others were new men, and all with political reputations satisfactory to the Committee: Dr Theodor Hornbostel (Trade, Industry and Agriculture) was a prominent Liberal; Bach (Justice), the 'Minister of the barricades' and himself a member of the Committee of Security; von Schwarzer, a journalist (State enterprises), was one of the five men nominated by the Legion for seats in the Reichstag.

With feeling running as it already was in Vienna against the Slavs, the Committee was probably no less pleased at the Germanic and centralist complexion of the new Government, which was far more pronounced than that of its predecessors. Since Kolowrat's resignation, most of the previous Ministers would, if pressed, probably have called themselves Germans, but nearly all of them had been really of the a-national mentality of the old Austrian civil servant.[3] Most of the new men were quite consciously Germans, and political centralists. Evidence of this was given when, a week after his appointment, Doblhoff dismissed Thun.[4]

In any case, the Left accepted the new Government with reasonable satisfaction, and the next weeks passed in an atmosphere of general cordiality, for which the Archduke's tact and his personal popularity were largely responsible.[5] Meanwhile, the elections for the Reichstag had been held (at various dates over the turn of June/July), with results which history was to prove to have been characteristic for the course of such events in Austria. The astute Czechs, once they had decided to go to Vienna, had picked their best men to go there, these including Palacký, Rieger, Havliček, Breuner, Pinkas and Trojan. The Italians of the Littoral and the Slovenes had also

[1] He allowed himself to be elected to the Reichstag, but took no part in its proceedings, and never held another public office.

[2] He also took over provisionally the Ministry of Education.

[3] When, early in May, Sommaruga had asked to be relieved of his post, his colleagues had thought it important that the post should go to a Slav, and had offered it to Palacký, who, however, had declined it.

[4] His successor was Frh. von Mecséry, an official of the Prague Gubernium.

[5] He was also sagacious enough to parade round with him his agreeable morganatic wife, who had a considerable success.

1848

sent national leaders. The 'elections' in Galicia, which had been held under the pressure of two factors operating in opposite directions – Polish landowners and Austrian officials – had produced an incongruous assemblage of Polish nobles and Polish, Ruthene and Roumanian peasants.[1] The lists of the Germans, many of whose best men were in any case away in Frankfurt, and who had made no attempt to organize their representation (they had also taken conspicuously little interest in the elections)[2] contained representatives of every imaginable social stratification and local interest, from Tirolean ultra-clericals to Viennese pinks. Neither of the social extremes was strongly represented; there were few Deputies with titles, except from Galicia, and no industrial workers. 94 of the 303 Deputies were peasants, but most of them from well-to-do families; middle-class intellectuals provided the next largest occupational group.[3] There were very few real reactionaries, and only a handful of true radicals;[4] most of the Deputies were a little to the right, or a little to the left, of the centre. 160 of them were Germans, 225 Slavs, Italians or Roumanians.

In fact, the Reichstag's activities while it was in Vienna were to prove barren enough, except for one achievement. The Government's Rescript on the peasant question had not had the desired effect of bringing about an agreed and equitable solution of the problem. According to the chief authority on the subject,[5] it had even 'awakened the most lively mistrust' among the peasants, who saw in it an indication that their servitude was going to be prolonged over another harvest, and they boycotted the negotiations on the compensation problem in the hope that if they delayed matters long enough, the State would pay any compensation to which the landlords managed to make good a claim. They simply stopped doing the robot, and the Estates of most Lands, themselves anxious not to negotiate from a position of disadvantage, accepted this, formally renouncing the robot with an expression of hope that they would be given equitable compensation. It was in any case difficult for them to make any binding agreements while their own future was so uncertain.

At the third session of the Constituent, its youngest Deputy, a Silesian

---

[1] Seven of the eight Deputies from the Bukovina were peasants. The Galicians divided about equally into Poles, and Ruthenes or Government nominees.

[2] In no constituency were more than 100 of the possible 2,500 primary votes cast; in one, only 20.

[3] The full occupational list, according to the *Oesterreichischer Kalender* for 1849, was: priests, 20; higher nobles, 19; lesser nobles, 27; industrialists, 18; merchants, 9; advocates, 48; officials (this title probably includes private black-coated workers), 74; doctors, 22; professors, 13; journalists, 9; 'miscellaneous bourgeois occupations', 22; peasants, 94; unknown, 9.

[4] Five of the fifteen Deputies for Vienna had been nominated by the Academic Legion, and passed for Left-wing, but not all of them proved to be so. The other ten Viennese Deputies were sober bourgeois.

[5] Grünberg, *Grundentlastung*, I. 378.

peasant's son named Kudlich, proposed a motion that 'the subject-nexus, with all rights and duties deriving therefrom, be immediately abolished, without prejudice to the question whether and how compensation is to be paid'. Many objections to this vague wording were raised from the landlords' side, while the peasants and their friends opposed any compensation being paid at all. After this point had been decided in the landlords' favour by a small majority,[1] the question 'how' was referred to a Committee, which discussed it for weeks. Finally, on 9 September, the Reichstag accepted a revised motion that the nexus subditelae, whether on rustical or dominical land, with all laws, etc., deriving from it, was abolished in all Lands for which the Reichstag was competent. The landlords' rights were divided into three categories, according to which they were to receive: (a) no compensation at all; (b) 'equitable compensation, to be supplied in part from public funds'; (c) the full value, to be paid by the beneficiary.[2] The details were to be worked out in the form of a law.[3] The Patrimonial Courts were abolished.

With this exception, the Reichstag's history in Vienna was one of frustration. The Deputies began to trickle in early in July, but so slowly that the original opening day had to be postponed, and it was only on 10 July that a quorum could be reached, even for preliminary business. Early on during this, the Deputies came up against the problem which neither they nor their successors ever completely solved, of how to reconcile the principle of national equality with the practical requirement of getting any effective work done at all. While all the Ministers were German-speakers, as were more than half the Deputies, most of the Polish, Ruthene and Roumanian peasant Deputies understood not a word of that language, while the Czechs and Italians, although able to speak it, would not consent to its being adopted as a 'language of State', nor even as the language for the proceedings of the Reichstag. The immediate problem was solved empirically; those who could speak German did so 'without prejudice to the question of principle', while the rest got through as best they could, sometimes simply obeying a leader's signal when it came to voting. Then came the question how the Reichstag should organize itself for its proper task, the preparation of a Constitution, for the results would probably depend largely on the machinery devised to achieve them. Eventually, on 31 July, a 'Constitutional Committee' was formed, composed of three members from each Gubernium (this was a victory for the Germans), and this in turn appointed a Committee of Three[4] to

[1] 174 in favour, 144 against, 36 abstentions. It is alleged by some Left-wing writers (e.g. Fischer, op. cit., pp. 82, 86) that the Galician peasants, who had to have everything explained to them through interpreters, voted for the compensation under a misapprehension.

[2] For details, see below, p. 461 f.

[3] As we say below, the Reichstag wanted its conclusions to be adopted immediately as a law, and had to be told by Bach that it could not adopt a valid law without the Emperor's sanction.

[4] Rieger (Czech), Violand (German Left), Hein (German Centre).

draw up a charter of 'fundamental rights' and a Committee of Five[1] to cope with the structural problem.

For the rest, the Reichstag, after its formal opening on 22 July, spent most of its time,[2] when not engaged on Kudlich's motion, in nationalist squabbles which were often undignified enough. It was symptomatic that when the Deputies came to take their seats in the building allotted to the Reichstag for its meetings,[3] nearly all of them did so in national blocs. The Bohemian Czechs sat in a solid phalanx on the right, the Moravian Czechs and Ruthenes in the centre, the Poles, Southern Slavs and Italians on the left; only the Germans distributed themselves, some in the centre, others on the left.[4] Except in the case of the Germans, whose more radical members chose the left of the House to demonstrate their social views, while the more conservative among them sat in the centre to dissociate themselves from the left, these choices did not reflect any 'left' or 'right' wing feeling in the usual sense of the terms, for the Poles on the left were far more conservative on social issues than most of the Czechs. The grouping by nationalities did, however, express the truth that practically all the Deputies, except the peasants, regarded the national issue as being the prime one at stake. And it soon took that place: it was not long before the Czechs and most of the Germans were abusing one another with a virulence prophetic of the proceedings of later Reichsrats. The Czech Deputies were even assaulted in the street outside the Reitschule. This was, indeed, an outcome of the developments which we shall trace, which brought the Czechs into the position of supporters of the Court and the Government, in contrast to their opponents among the German left. With this, it was not long before a change, imperceptible in its stages but pronounced in their cumulative effect, took place in the relations between the Government and the Reichstag. At first, the latter had been treated with flattering deference. The Speech from the Throne, read by the Archduke, had addressed it by the title of 'Constituent', but this apart, had seemed to regard it as an ordinary legislative Parliament. It had been allowed to express opinions on any subject, and even, as in the case of Kudlich's motion, to draft legislation in the social field. Some of its members had come to take the view, in which they were encouraged by the

---

[1] Mayer (German Centre), Smolka (Pole), Palacký (Czech), Gobbi (Italian), Goldmark (German Left).

[2] It did, however, adopt motions guaranteeing the immunity of the Reichstag as a whole, and of its members individually.

[3] This was the *Reitschule* opposite the Hofburg.

[4] Some of the Germans refused to the last to join any grouping, but the bulk of them ended by dividing into three groups: the *Verband der Deutsch-Oesterreicher*, who were really *schwarzgelb*, opposed to any closer link with Germany and strongly centralist for Austria; the *Zentralclub*, led by Lasser, also 'Austrian', but prepared to allow the Landtage a fair measure of autonomy; and the Democratic Left, left-wing on social issues, and still hankering after co-operation with the left in Frankfurt.

Committee of Security,[1] that they were not only a regular legislature, but a sovereign assemblage.

But as time went by, the old tradition reasserted itself that decisions were the province of 'authority'. Even those Ministers who were elected members of the Reichstag (Bach, Hornbostel, and until his resignation, Schwarzer) appeared in it more and more rarely, and when they did so, it was increasingly often as mouthpieces of a superior authority. Bach had a violent clash with the Reichstag on 2 September, when he denied its sovereign character and its right to publish as a 'law' the result of its labours on the land reform, pointing out that the measure had still to be sanctioned by the Emperor.

But the Reichstag was still a recognized part of the political structure of the new Austria, and the reconciliation between Parliament, Ministry and Crown, and between Vienna and the rest of Austria, seemed to be complete when, yielding at last to the repeated supplications which the Reichstag had added to those of the Ministry, Ferdinand returned to Vienna. He arrived in the capital on 12 August, and in his turn expressed the hope that co-operation between the free peoples and its constitutional Monarch would result in the creation of a new Austria.

The loyal Viennese welcomed their Emperor back with heartfelt rejoicings, which were marred only by a foolish and tactlessly facetious demonstration on the part of the students. And yet, the doom of constitutional life in Austria had by now been sealed, by the very event which had given the Imperial family the courage to venture back from Innsbruck.

On 25 July Radetzky had inflicted a resounding defeat on the Piedmontese armies at Custozza. By a few days later, he had driven them clean out of Lombardy. On 8 August, Charles Albert signed an armistice at Vigevano. Venice still held out, but since none of the Powers showed any disposition to intervene in its favour, its reduction could only be a matter of time, and, meanwhile, a small force was sufficient to contain it.

Radetzky's victory did much more than crush Piedmont; it changed the whole balance of forces inside the Monarchy, for the units which had previously been engaged in Italy, or had had to be kept in reserve for possible use there, were now available for 'restoring order' in the interior of the Monarchy.

This was precisely what Windisch-Graetz was panting to do, and he was now chafing with strong impatience against any form of civilian authority. In July he had again appealed to the Court for plenipotentiary powers – again in vain. In mid-August he challenged the authority of the Government when it released the Czech leader, Breuner, now a Reichstag Deputy, from the

[1] The Committee had sent it an eloquent address (reproduced by Hartig, pp. 324 ff.) which opened with the words 'Sovereign Assembly of our Reich'.

durance in which Windisch-Graetz wanted him held. On this occasion the Government, headed by Bach, stood up to him and defeated him, but he now applied again to the Court and this time received, under a top-secret order of which Latour himself was not informed, the powers for which he had asked in vain six weeks earlier, viz.: authority to assume, in case of emergency, the supreme command of all the Monarchy's armed forces outside Italy, with plenipotentiary powers also in the civilian field.[1] The most elastic imagination could not, indeed, construe the situation in Vienna, at that juncture, as constituting an emergency, so that Windisch-Graetz could only hold his hand here. He did, however, get a friend of his, Prince Lobkowitz, appointed Adjutant-General to the Emperor, and instructed him that 'if he observed that any further concessions were being demanded, or that the person of His Majesty was in any way endangered, he was to take Ferdinand and his family under armed escort to Olmütz'.[2] 'Then,' he told the Empress, 'I shall conquer Vienna, then His Majesty will abdicate in favour of His nephew, Francis Joseph, and then I shall take Buda.'

He again warned the Empress that the time for the abdication had not yet arrived. The time was, however, ripe to move against Hungary.

The achievement of the April Laws in the social and purely internal political fields had proved to be sufficiently solid. They could not be called radical. The franchise still excluded something like 93% of the total population.[3] Nothing was done for industrial labour, nor for that very large fraction of the agrarian population which failed to qualify for the material side of the reform. But the class which did benefit was still a considerable one, over one quarter of the total population,[4] and even the poorest enjoyed the relief of equality before the law. The franchise was broad, judged by the standards of the day, and the general civic liberties were among the most generous in Europe.

The situation during the first few weeks was, of course, characterized by the usual social turbulence. There was considerable unrest among the 'contractual' peasants, and still more, among the *zsellers*. There were a number of local demonstrations by the factory workers, and more by the artisans, these being directed chiefly against the Jews, and the German burghers of some towns joined in the anti-Jewish demonstrations with a zest which necessitated the intervention of the National Guard in some places. In the larger towns,

[1] See Walter, pp. 191 ff. The powers were ante-dated for form's sake for 25 May, so that he appeared to have been in possession of them at the time of the June outbreak in Prague.

[2] The date of this letter was 28 August.

[3] In the elections of 1870, which were held on the 1848 franchise, there were 890,000 persons qualified to vote, this being 6·7% of the total population.

[4] For figures on land distribution, see above, p. 269. 634,134 heads of families, occupying in all 254,629 whole sessions (thirty-seven per cent of the arable land and leys under cultivation), received their land in freehold.

especially Pest, there was the usual disorder, with various more or less self-constituted bodies of students and others putting themselves forward as the representatives of authority. On the whole, however, all this died away comparatively quickly (the national difference which prevented the German burghers and the Magyar students from joining forces may have had something to do with this), and the authorities were always able to 'restore order' without any excessive difficulty.[1] When, in June, the elections for the new Diet took place, the power of habit reasserted itself. The extreme Left – using the word in its modern sense – came out almost empty-handed: almost the only genuine social radical to secure election was the devoted but eccentric 'peasant Tribune', Tancsics. Peasants, workers and tradesmen together secured a bare 2% of the mandates. There were 30–40 representatives of the radical intellectuals, including Perczel and the two Madarász (but not Petőfi, who was defeated at the polls), but no less than 72% of the elected Deputies were landlords, most of them indeed, but by no means all, Liberals and 'Left-wing' in the national sense, i.e., supporters of Kossuth on the national issue.[2]

Another satisfactory phenomenon, for the Magyars, was the virtual disappearance of separatist feeling among the Magyars (including the Szekels) of Transylvania, where the Diet voted the Union on 30 May without a single dissentient voice from that quarter.

But several other quarters were bitterly hostile to the new Hungary.[3] Her own aulic magnates regarded the land reform as sheer spoliation, and from the outset adopted the attitude which soon hardened into the 'Old Conservative' policy of pulling every wire within their reach to have the bulk of the April Laws undone.[4] To the centralist supporters in Vienna of the old regime the Rescript of 17 March, and still more, that of 31 March, had been mere concessions to panic, and they were resolved to re-establish at least control over foreign policy, defence and finance the very moment they were strong enough to do so. In this respect, the gaps and ambiguities in the hastily-drafted laws gave them ample opportunities. Pillersdorf writes frankly[5] that since none of the Austrian Ministers had been officially informed of the transference of any of their powers, they decided to continue acting as

---

[1] When Pulszky went to Vienna in late April, he was struck by the disorderly conditions still prevailing there, whereas in Pest already 'the city had hardly any revolutionary character any more, the flags and cockades had vanished, the noise of the popular assemblies had died away, the intoxication of fraternization was over' (op. cit., II. 117).

[2] Spira, op. cit., p. 208.

[3] Pulszky (II. 159) adds another to the list which I give below: the Bourse. This is probably fair enough, when we consider the later attitude of Viennese financial circles, but these influences operated too far below the surface to be recorded.

[4] Lest these sentences should give a misleading impression, it should be emphasized that the Old Conservative programme accepted the emancipation of the peasants.

[5] *Rückblicke*, pp. 31–2.

though no such transference had taken place. They did, he writes, suggest to the Hungarians that they should consult together on agreed lines of co-operation, and never got any answer. The Hungarian sources do not mention the suggestion.

No trouble arose at first over foreign affairs, for Esterházy, who had not wanted the post and had accepted it only at the urgent request of the Court, was an old career diplomat who knew the ropes. He hardly seems to have regarded himself as concerned with 'foreign affairs', as such, at all, but only with mediating between Hungary and the Court,[1] and in any case, took his duties remarkably lightly.[2] Batthyány, as we have mentioned, made one or two moves in this field on his own initiative, but these seem, perhaps strangely, to have met with no opposition in Vienna.[3]

But innumerable difficulties soon arose in the two other fields. At first, the Viennese Hofkammer went on quietly pocketing the yields of the Cameral enterprises in Hungary and of the Customs. When he took over, Kossuth found only half a million gulden in the Treasury, and nothing coming in (the landlords had not yet begun paying the taxation to which they were now liable). Neither had he any recognized means of obtaining credit, and no Bank of Issue. All the emergency measures which he took to provide for current needs raised objections from the Hofkammer or the National Bank, which complained that its rights were being infringed; and it was obvious that Vienna proposed to maintain this attitude at least until Hungary yielded over the question of the national debt.

There was also much stuff for explosion in the military field. Little friction, indeed, arose at first over the Imperial units quartered in Inner Hungary, of whom there were about eighteen thousand (mostly Germans, Czechs or Italians, but a few Hungarians[4]). Zanini instructed them to swear loyalty to the new Hungarian Ministry, and to take their orders from the Hungarian Minister of Defence, and they did so; in any case, Batthyány, who was in charge of the Portfolio of Defence pending the arrival of Mészáros, left these forces pretty well to their own devices. But early trouble arose over the Military Frontier. During their negotiations with Vienna, the Hungarians had demanded formal re-incorporation of the Frontier, and the Minister President in Vienna had at first been inclined to concede the point. The new Ministry of War, on the other hand, claimed that the control of the Frontier was one of the Monarch's 'reserved rights', and therefore remained with it (the Ministry) as the legal successor in respect of such rights of the Hofkriegsrat.

[1] Pulszky, II. 145.

[2] Id., p. 115.

[3] The instructions for the Hungarian emissaries to Frankfurt (see above, p. 354) were shown to Pillersdorf, who found nothing to object to in them. The emissaries were received in Frankfurt by the Archduke, although boycotted by Schmerling. The instructions had been very carefully worded.

[4] All Hungarians called up during this period were being sent straight down to Italy.

The question was of great practical importance to both sides, especially as almost the entire front-line force of Frontiersmen (twenty-two regiments) was then serving in Italy, where it formed an important part of Radetzky's army. In any case, neither party was willing to see this important military force under the control of the other. The April Laws did not specifically provide for the re-incorporation, but the new franchise law tacitly assumed it by providing for representation of the Frontier districts in the new Parliament.

On 12 April the Hungarian Government agreed to leave the military organization of the Frontier undisturbed pending a future legal settlement: the Austrian Ministry continued thereafter to claim complete control over the Frontier, and its commanding officers, to recognize only the Ministry as entitled to issue orders to them. We shall return to the later developments of this dispute.

The other malcontents were to be found in Croatia, and among the non-Magyars of Inner Hungary and Transylvania.

The spirit in which the Hungarians dealt with the Nationalities and with Croatia in the April Laws was much less that of the conscious national aggression as which it is so often described, than of naïve optimism. The laws in fact did not mention the Nationalities at all, nor the linguistic question, except only in the provisions (which themselves were not new) that the language of Parliament was Magyar, and knowledge of it a requisite for membership of that body. Neither did they modify the legal status of Croatia, as interpreted by Hungary: they recognized the existence of the Zagreb Diet; allowed the partes adnexae to hoist their own colours, side by side with the national ones; and specifically stated that their County Congregations were free to use 'their own mother tongue'.

But it was also true that the new Hungarian constitutional laws allowed no place for devolution, except in purely ecclesiastical respects; that the central Parliament and Ministries were likely to be overwhelmingly Magyar; and that the preponderance of the Magyar element would clearly be increased by any weakening of the links with Austria. The non-Magyars of Transylvania had special reasons to fear the effects of the Union with Hungary, and the laws seemed to leave little space for the exercise of Croat autonomy (the competencies of the Croat Diet were not defined). Moreover, the franchise law recognized as 'Croatia' only the three Counties of 'Zagrab, Várasd and Körös', with the Free Towns and Districts lying within them, and the Croat Frontier districts, thus implicitly denying Croatia's claim to either Fiume or Slavonia. And all this was voted by majority, overriding the objections of the handful of Croat Deputies and thus ignoring the Croats' thesis that *regnum regno non proscribit leges*.

Many of the Hungarians seem genuinely to have believed that they were doing all that man could wish. Kossuth in particular had persuaded himself that the Nationalities wanted nothing more than the civic liberties and social reforms which the laws were now extending to all citizens of Hungary (especially as the Greek Orthodox Church was now being admitted to full equality). 'The magic of liberty', he cried enthusiastically, 'is stronger than nationality, faith, affinity of blood and friendship.' And why should the Nationalities mind Magyar being the official language 'when the State sincerely accepts the principle that it respects the right of every people to have its own language and to use it freely in its internal affairs, or its Church questions'.

And it is fair to point out, and important to realize, that this was not a complete illusion. The first days which followed the fall of Metternich saw innumerable scenes of fraternization between Magyars and Germans, Magyars and Slovaks, even (in Inner Hungary) Magyars and Roumanians. To the very last, practically all the Swabians and Catholic Southern Slavs, the great majority of the Ruthenes and at least a large fraction of the Slovaks took the Hungarian side; so, on the whole, did the Roumanian Uniates of the Partium, and even the Orthodox Roumanians of that area tended to regard the Serbian leaders of their Church as worse enemies than the Hungarian officials.

But this attitude was very far from universal. There were early stirrings even among the Slovaks,[1] a group of whom, as early as 28 March, put forward requests – modest ones enough – for the wider use of the Slovak language in the Courts and in public life. The Hungarians persisted in sniffing 'Pan-Slav agitation' behind any Slovak national movement, and rejected all these requests. Thereupon, on 10 May, a meeting of Slovak nationalists at Liptószentmiklós drew up a resolution which in substance asked for the transformation of Hungary into a 'Nationalities State' on a federative basis, with, for themselves, an autonomous territory in which Slovak should be the sole official language.

A few other Slovaks were coquetting with the idea of Czecho-Slovak union, both national and political, and were finding alarming encouragement in certain Czech quarters.[2]

[1] It has seemed convenient to take these movements in inverse order to their importance, thus getting the minor figures off the stage before the *dénouement*.

[2] The leaders of this group were the pronounced nationalists, Štur and Hurban, but even their attitude was ill-defined. Štur, in a speech at Špere on 2 April, called for Czech help against the Magyars, and again asked for help when he went to Prague for the Slav Congress, but he objected when some Czechs wanted the Slovak areas attached to Bohemia-Moravia, and Hurban, who was with him, said that the Slovaks 'were only seeking protection against the Magyars: they did not want to destroy the historic bonds linking them with Hungary'. the Slovaks' programme at Prague (with which the Hungarian Ruthenes associated themselves) asked for the transformation of Hungary into a multi-national State of equal 'nations', with appropriate facilities for the language of each in administration and education. Incidentally, not all the Czechs at the Conference wanted Czecho-Slovak union, although Havlíček wrote a series of articles in favour of it in *Národny Noviny*.

For the rest, the Slovaks' attitude in general was completely *quot homines*. While, later, some

The Transylvanian Saxons were divided and dubious about the new course. Few of them regarded the prospect of the Union without misgivings, and in mid-May the Saxon 'University' sent a deputation to Vienna to try to get the Union postponed. The deputation missed the Court, which had just moved to Innsbruck, and when the Transylvanian Diet met on 29 May the Saxon Deputies were sharply divided. They eventually decided that it would be imprudent, as the situation stood, to exercise their veto against the Union[1] and the next day voted unanimously for it, while declaring that they reserved their right to submit to the Hungarian Diet proposals for the safeguarding of their rights, their nationality and their language. Another deputation then went to Pest with proposals to this effect; but a petition bearing twenty thousand signatures was also sent to Ferdinand, asking him not to ratify the Union.

The Roumanians were frankly hostile. A first big meeting was held at Balázsfalva on 24 April to protest against the Union, and another, attended by forty thousand participants and presided over by the two Bishops, on 15 May. This congress protested against the Diet's voting on the Union before the Roumanians were properly represented on it, swore loyalty to Ferdinand *qua* Grand Prince of Transylvania and asked for recognition as a 'nation'. The Roumanians present at the Diet's meeting voted for the Union, on which Bishop Leményi actually called down a blessing; but the Roumanians, too, sent a deputation to Innsbruck to try to prevent the ratification of the decision.

But the primitive Roumanian shepherds, the hardly more civilized (and completely disunited) Slovak peasants, the handful of cautious Saxon burghers, were too weak in themselves to threaten the Hungarian State, and because they were weak, the Crown did not at this stage think it worth while antagonizing the Hungarian Government for their sakes. The Croats and the Hungarian Serbs were a different proposition. Both were organized communities, the former politically, the latter, at least ecclesiastically. Both could almost be called nations in arms, for nearly half of each people were domiciled in the Military Frontier, and although the first-line formations were out of the country, even the reservists were trained soldiers, and armed. They were also in any case, through the organization of the Frontier, closely connected with the centralist regime, accustomed to obey the orders of the Hofkriegsrat, and they were the traditional instruments to which the Viennese centralists

---

of them joined the bands raised by Hurban to invade Hungary, others enlisted in the Hungarian Honvédség; one of the Slovak battalions of that force was reported to be one of the two finest units in the Hungarian army. The later so-called Polish Legion was composed largely of Slovaks passing themselves off as Poles (see Leiningen, op. cit., pp. 193–200).

[1] See above, p. 25. This constitutional rule, or usage, would have enabled a negative vote by the Saxons to veto the Union even in the face of a much larger vote in favour of it from the two other Nations.

had become accustomed to look when seeking a counter-poise to excessive Hungarian demands. In the spring of 1848 the Court had especial reason to wish to preserve their good will, because, as has been said, they formed a very important component of Radetzky's army in Italy.

Thus from the very first days of the revolution, the Court and the two Southern Slav peoples of Hungary were potential, and up to a point, actual, although surreptitious, allies. As relations between Hungary and the Court deteriorated, so that alliance became more intimate and more open until September found the Croats invading Hungary in the name of its King, with the Serbs fighting at their side. Conversely, the encouragement given by the Court to the Southern Slavs was a main factor in the breach between Hungary and the Court. The story was not, however, a straightforward one. In the spring Hungary was still technically loyal to the Dynasty, and the great majority of its Government, quite sincerely so; and even if the Court had been quite indifferent to its pledged word, it could not have afforded to throw away this asset and to provoke a hostility not less dangerous than that of Piedmont itself. Moreover, Radetzky's army did not consist only of Frontier units; it contained a number, almost exactly as large, of Hungarian regiments. Finally, the support received by the Serbs from the Principality of Serbia was not altogether without its disquieting features even in the eyes of Hungary's worst enemies at the Court. For many weeks, therefore, the Court wavered between law and interest, or between one legal case or one argument of expediency and another; it was not until July that the die was irrevocably cast.

It should be said that it is a misrepresentation of history to depict even the Croat movement, still less the Serb, as purely the result of Viennese intrigue. There were times, during these weeks, when the Court stood officially on the side of Hungary; but it usually did so half-heartedly, although not without duplicity.

The Croats had raised their voices almost as early as the Magyars, and an alliance between them and Vienna had been adumbrated before the Magyars had fairly extracted from Ferdinand his initial consent to a responsible Hungarian Ministry. It happened that the office of Ban of Croatia was vacant, and as early as 14 March, Baron Josika, then still Transylvanian Chancellor, had advised the Archduke Ludwig to appoint an 'energetic and reliable man' to that office.[1] On 16 March mass assemblages had gathered in Zagreb and other Croat towns with the usual purpose of framing national demands, without, indeed, reaching any very definite result. But among the innumerable voices raised, one was particularly resonant: that of a certain Josip Jellačić, Colonel of one of the Frontier regiments, who a few years

[1] He also advised the dispatch of a Royal Commission to Transylvania to prevent the Union.

previously had been an enthusiastic Magyarone, but had since fallen under the influence of Gaj and turned fanatical Illyrian. No politician and (as it afterwards transpired) a very poor soldier, Jellačić was now completely Croat nationalist and anti-Magyar, and the burthen of his utterances was that Croatia must emancipate herself from Magyar tyranny and cleave in undying loyalty to the Crown.

The Föispán of Zagreb County, Baron Kulmer, who was also an Illyrian in politics, went up to Vienna to report. On 20 March, Kolowrat submitted to the Staatskonferenz a memorandum embodying Josika's advice, and on Kulmer's suggestion, proposed Jellačić for Ban.[1] On the 23rd, before Batthyány had time to protest, a Rescript, signed by Ferdinand and countersigned by an official in the Hungarian Court Chancellery, appeared appointing Jellačić Ban and nominating him Privy Councillor and Major-General and Colonel in Chief of the Croat Regiments.

Kulmer hurried with the news to Zagreb, where, on the 25th, a mass meeting, without waiting for confirmation or for the legal forms to be observed, acclaimed Jellačić Ban. It also resolved to petition the Crown for the unification of Croatia, Slavonia and Dalmatia in a single polity, with its own responsible Ministry and Diet. A deputation bearing these demands arrived in Vienna on the 29th.

The petitioners, it is true, got little satisfaction: even if the Court had been willing at that stage to affront the Hungarians, it was not prepared to part with Dalmatia. The deputation was told only that its legal grievances would be remedied. But Jellačić, who arrived in Vienna in the first week of April, was benignly treated. Although he declared that he would not take the oath as Ban (which he would have had to swear to the King of Hungary), he was, on 8 April, again promoted, this time to Field-Marshal-Lieutenant, and made General Commandant of the Croat Frontier Districts. He returned happily to Zagreb, where he announced that he regarded the Palatine as 'his peer, not his superior', forbade Croat officials to communicate with Buda-Pest, and assumed dictatorial powers, not only over Croatia but also over Slavonia and Fiume.

By now the Hungarians had finished drafting the April Laws, which were obviously incompatible with the Croats' wishes (although, as the dating shows, it was not the Laws that produced Croat counter-demands, but if anything, the reverse). The Hungarian Government was anxious to reach a modus with the Croats; an invitation was sent to Jellačić to come to Buda-Pest for consultations, in the hope of finding a basis of agreement. The Government offered the concession that the Croats might use their own language in communication with the central authorities. Jellačić replied on 19 April by announcing the 'rupture of relations' between Croatia and Hungary. On the

---

[1] Gaj, too, was in Vienna and seems to have given the same advice, which was passed to Kolowrat by Windisch-Graetz.

27th he announced that a number of offences would be punishable by Court Martial: these included the offence of ascribing the liberation of the peasants in Croatia to the Hungarian laws. On this, the Palatine went to Vienna and extracted from Ferdinand three Rescripts. One of these, dated 6 May, was addressed to Jellačić, told him that Ferdinand 'would never allow the legal bond between the Lands of the Hungarian Crown to be loosened by arbitrary orders or unilateral decisions' and ordered him to obey orders received by him from the Palatine or the Hungarian Ministry. The second, of the same date, authorized the Palatine, if he thought it necessary, to send a Royal Commissioner to Croatia to repress any dangerous separatism. The third, dated 7 May, informed all the three officers commanding in the Military Frontier that they would in future be receiving their orders through the Hungarian Ministry of War.

None of these documents had any perceptible effect. The Palatine wrote to Jellačić ordering him to retract his pronouncements of the 19th and the 27th. Jellačić returned the letters unopened. Meanwhile, he had convoked a 'Ban's Conference' for the 9th, and this, on the 11th, produced a long Address to the Crown complaining of the 'inordinate excesses of the Magyars', denying the legality of the Hungarian position and asking for an independent Ministry for the 'Triune Kingdom'. The Palatine now ordered General Hrabowski, commanding the Pétervárad Frontier District and the senior of the three Frontier Commanders, to go to Croatia, annul all illegal measures taken by Jellačić and institute proceedings against him. These orders increased the confusion. Both Hrabowski and his colleague, Piret, had appealed both to the Crown and to both the Austrian and Hungarian Ministries of Defence to postpone placing the Frontier districts under Hungarian command, saying that the Serbs would revolt against it; Hrabowski had even refrained from publishing the order. Correspondence between the two Generals and Latour produced a situation which reached the very limit of obscurity: Latour perforce confirmed the Rescript of 7 May, but told both Generals to inform him immediately of all orders received by them from Buda-Pest. Then, on 3 June, he extracted from Ferdinand a Rescript to the effect that orders from the Hungarian Ministry of Defence must be obeyed, but that this did not mean that the administration of the Frontier was taken out of the hands of 'the Minister of War of the Gesammtmonarchie, nor that the Supreme Command of the Army was to be impeded. As we shall see, even this sibylline instruction was to be over-ruled within a few days. Meanwhile, Hrabowski made no motions to obey the Palatine's order. A crowd burnt the Palatine in effigy in Zagreb. Jellačić called on 'the inhabitants of the Triune Kingdom' to enrol in a National Guard, and convoked the Zagreb Diet for 5 June.

The thread of the Croat question now began to run together with that of the Serb.

Like practically all the nationalities of the Monarchy, the Hungarian Serbs had held innumerable meetings in the first days of freedom, and these had also conformed to rule in speaking with various voices, although most of the programmes produced had been pronouncedly nationalist. Then, on 27 March, the Serbian Church Council at Ujvidék drew up a 16-Point programme which, while 'willingly conceding the supremacy of the Magyar language and nationality in the political and domestic structure of the Hungarian State', asked for legal recognition of their own 'nationality', guarantees for the free use of the Serbian language in all their internal and religious concerns, and the right to hold an annual national congress at which all Serbs, including those of the Military Frontier, should be represented.

A deputation took the programme to Pozsony, where they arrived on 8 April. They came into head-on collision with the Hungarians' insistence on the political unity of the Hungarian State. They were assured that they would receive all the political, social and religious liberties enjoyed by all citizens of Hungary, but that there could be no talk of their getting corporate organization on a 'national' basis. After an auspicious beginning, tempers became frayed, especially in a private interview between the Serbs and Kossuth. One of the Serbs, a young ex-officer of hussars named Stratimirovics, asked for the recognition of the Serbs' 'Leopoldinian Privileges', and said that if the Serbs did not get satisfaction in Pozsony, they would find it elsewhere. 'In that case,' said Kossuth, 'we shall cross swords.' 'A Serb was never frightened of that,' answered Stratimirovics. He could afford to say this, for besides the forces which they could muster themselves, the Serbs were already in touch with the Principality of Serbia, which was not only egging them on but also winking at and itself secretly organizing the dispatch of armed volunteers to them – this with the full knowledge and approval of Colonel Mayerhofer, the Austrian Consul in Belgrade, who assured his Government that it could without danger accept help offered from this quarter.

The next important move was a meeting of the Serbian Church Council at Karlóca, on 14 April. This went much further: it demanded the establishment of a Serbian Voivody under its own Voivode, and comprising Syrmia, the Bánát, Bácka and Baranya. This was to form an autonomous unit within the Triune Kingdom of Croatia, Slavonia and Dalmatia. The Hungarian Government sent down a commissioner to South Hungary, who offered the Serbs a Congress at the end of May to discuss the organization of their religious institutions. But meanwhile the extremists were gaining ground. There were by now several thousand Serb guerillas in Hungary, and small outbreaks of unrest were almost continuous. Even the Frontier troops were obviously unreliable. Now the Serb Archbishop, Rajačić, took charge and convoked a grand 'National Congress', to meet at Karlóca on 13 May. This was attended by several thousand Serbs from Inner Hungary and the

Frontier, and by numerous visitors from Serbia. It registered its decisions on 15 May in the form of ten points. The first recorded the election of Rajačić as Patriarch, and of Stephen Suplyikać, Colonel of a Frontier regiment then serving in Italy, as Voivode. The second announced the constitution of the 'Nation of Hungarian Serbs' as a free and independent 'Nation', under the House of Habsburg and within the framework of the Hungarian Crown. The third proclaimed the establishment of a Voivody, consisting of Syrmia and the Bánát, with the adjacent Frontier Districts. The fourth declared the Voivody to be in political alliance with the Triune Kingdom. The fifth established a Committee to draft a Constitution, with a permanent executive Committee (Glavai Odbor) to act as provisional 'Government'. As Suplyikać, like Mészáros, was on active service in Italy, the Presidency of the Odbor, with the duty of organizing an army, was entrusted (in spite of his youth) to Stratimirovics, the hero of the verbal duel with Kossuth.

A delegation of Serbs took these resolutions to Zagreb, where they arrived on 29 May. This move penetrated Hrabowski's composure, and he met Jellačić, but let himself be reassured when the Croat protested that he was a loyal subject of the Monarch. But it was under these threats that the Hungarians began the series of moves to which the Court in its turn afterwards appealed as evidence of their disloyalty; although the whole story from this point on is really one of hens and eggs, the situation growing steadily worse with each succession.

Many local authorities, especially in South Hungary, had already been recruiting National Guards, which were little more than detachments of special constabulary. But on 16 May Batthyány, who was still provisionally in charge of defence (Mészáros not having yet returned from Italy) appealed for ten thousand volunteers for a new force known as the Hónvédség (Home Defence) for defence against the Serbs. To keep it within the letter of the law, this force was placed under the Minister Presidency and ranked, technically, as a civilian body, but pay and rank in it were equated with those of the army, and officers and other ranks were invited to transfer into it. Vienna regarded it, with reason, as the nucleus of a national army. The response to the appeal was not, indeed, very encouraging in Hungary itself.[1]

Kossuth, who had already been negotiating with the Commercial Bank of Pest for a loan, undertook to finance the arming of this force, and issued, first governmental bonds, then small currency notes, turning the bank, to all intents and purposes, into a bank of issue.

[1] See the letter by Leininger (op. cit., p. 80): 'Nobody wants the National Guard, the rich because they are too indolent, the poor, because they believe that it is intended to make "Grenzer" of them. And the mere thought that they might be wanted for the protection of their country is sufficient to turn these men into rebels.' The letter was, indeed, written on 11 April (in connection with local recruiting in South Hungary), but seems to have summed up general feeling fairly enough. Many contemporary accounts and reminiscenses testify to the widespread indifference to, or ignorance of, the national cause shown by the peasants.

The Government, however, still hoped to keep the law on its side. It had instructed Esterházy to follow the Court to Innsbruck. At the end of May the Palatine, accompanied by Széchenyi and Eötvös, went there, bearing requests to Ferdinand to sanction the convocation of the Diet for 2 July, and himself to come to Buda to open it – he would be safe among his loyal subjects. Ferdinand was asked also to order Jellačić to cancel the convocation of the Zagreb Diet, which he was not entitled to order.

The mission was almost completely successful. Ferdinand's family refused to let him leave Innsbruck, but the Palatine was authorized to open the Diet for him, and a letter was sent to Jellačić ordering him to cancel the Zagreb Diet and to come immediately to Innsbruck to explain his conduct. Then when, a few days later, Batthyány arrived, bearing the Transylvanian Diet's resolution in favour of the Union, for ratification, Ferdinand ratified the Union (this was on 10 June) and the Roumanians and Saxons, who arrived the next day, were told that they were too late.

Batthyány also promised the Court that if Hungary felt secure from attack by the Croats and Serbs, the Diet would vote forty thousand men, and supplies, for the campaign in Italy. In return he got Ferdinand's signature to three documents. One, dated 8 June, told Mészáros (who had now reached Hungary) that in future all orders to all troops in Hungary, including the Frontier, would be issued through him, the Palatine being empowered to sign for the King. The two other documents were dated the 10th. One announced the suspension of Jellačić from all his offices, civil and military; the other instructed the Military Frontier commanders to take their orders from Hrabowski. These two documents were, however, to be used only if Jellačić, when he arrived, failed to justify his conduct, and Esterházy did not put his counter-signature to them.

Meanwhile, Jellačić had been taking his time. He had disregarded altogether the order to cancel the Diet, allowed that body to meet, and had himself ceremonially (although illegally) installed. The Diet then approved the Serbs' programme (with a reservation in respect of Syrmia), accepted their proffered alliance, and proceeded, under Jellačić's benign guidance, to work out its own programme for a great Illyrian Province, comprising all the Southern Slav areas of the Monarchy and enjoying extensive Home Rule; although it wisely placated the Court by allowing the control of defence and finance to remain with the central government. This having been completed, a joint deputation of Croats and Serbs set out for Innsbruck on the 12th. Jellačić went with them. Travelling slowly, they reached Innsbruck only on the 18th, by which time Batthyány, unable to wait the Ban's pleasure any longer, had gone back to Hungary.

Both the Serb and the Croat petitions were rejected, but Jellačić personally had much better fortune. Received in audience on the 19th, he protested his loyalty so eloquently that his audience, according to a witness, was moved to tears. This touching scene might still have left history unaltered (although it was important for the future that Jellačić won the hearts of the ladies of the Court);[1] but this was the very evening when Prince Schwarzenberg arrived from Italy with Radetzky's letter.[2] This put the trumps back into the Croat's hand. The Court decided to leave him, for the time, in the position of *de facto* Ban, and the Archduke John was asked to mediate between him and the Hungarians. Jellačić for his part issued a proclamation to the Frontier troops in Italy, exhorting them to stand fast and do their duty.[3] Then he set out on his return journey.

Meanwhile, fighting had broken out in South Hungary. Stratimirovics had collected a considerable force, which included some ten to twelve thousand partisans from the Balkans. On 10 June he ordered the Serbs of the Voivody to arm and take up battle-stations. By the 12th fairly widespread, although local, fighting was going on. This 'little war', as it was called, went on intermittently throughout the summer.

Under the impact of this news, the Hungarians resorted to the desperate and dubious expedient of publishing the two Rescripts of 10 June, the missing counter-signature being supplied by Szemere. It was not a successful venture. Hrabowski refused to act on the documents, as having no legal validity in the absence of Esterházy's signature. Jellačić, whom the news reached on his return journey, was naturally infuriated, but then said cheerfully: 'Now I will act on my own, and will get better results than I could with my hands tied.'

He could not yet take much positive action, his troops being away in Italy, but he could afford to wait, for whatever the technical constitutional position, he had by now reached a clear understanding with Latour and with the centralists in the Austrian Government, who in the last days of June sent Buda-Pest two extraordinary Notes: one demanding that Hungary reconcile herself at all costs with Jellačić, 'otherwise it would be obliged to renounce its neutrality towards Hungary'; the other, requiring it to pay 150,000 gulden in silver for Jellačić's forces. A third Note protested against Kossuth's issue of paper money, as infringing the monopoly of the Austrian National Bank.

In remarkable contrast with this stood the first proceedings of the Hungarian Diet, which duly opened on 4 July and heard the Palatine read it two Rescripts, both dated 26 June, the one enjoining him to inform the Diet of Ferdinand's fixed determination to preserve the integrity of the

[1] The Archduchess Sophie was thereafter a fervent admirer of his: she used to speak of him as 'the admirable Jellačić' (Corti, p. 307).

[2] See above, p. 370.

[3] This, as it happened, marked a very favourable contrast with something that had occurred in Hungary. A Hungarian squadron in Galicia had left its station to come back to Hungary, where the Ministry of War had admitted its conduct to be an offence but had excused it as an 'excess of patriotism'.

Hungarian Crown and to maintain the April Laws, the second investing the Palatine himself with quite unlimited plenipotentiary powers and enjoining all ecclesiastical, civil and military authorities in Hungary, Transylvania and the Partes Adnexae, including the Military Frontier, to obey him implicitly. There appeared to be one more hope of reconciliation with the Crown, on the basis of Batthyány's offer to reinforce Radetzky's army; but here, too, things went wrong, largely owing to Kossuth, who had become increasingly impatient with 'Vienna'. For weeks past he had been absenting himself from the Ministerial Councils (partly on genuine grounds of ill-health) and on 1 July had begun issuing a paper of his own, 'Kossuth's Journal', the radical nationalist tone of which was extraordinarily embarrassing to his fellow-Ministers. Nevertheless, he was so popular in the Parliament that his colleagues decided to let him be the Government's spokesman when it asked the House for the men and money; and when he did so, on 11 July, he put the request purely in terms of Hungary's own needs. Announcing that 'the Fatherland was in danger' from attacks by Serbs, Croats and Czechs (inspired, he hinted plainly enough, from Vienna) he asked the Diet to vote two hundred thousand men, forty thousand of them immediately, and forty-two million florins, ten million of them immediately, these to be raised either by a loan, or by the issue of paper money. The smaller figures might still have constituted a move to honour Batthyány's promise, but the larger ones could only mean an intention to raise and equip a national army; especially when the Government decided that most of the recruits should be enrolled in Honvéd formations, where they would be safe from 'Imperial' influences.

Worse followed. The Government wanted to include in the reply to the Address from the Throne a passage pledging itself to send the promised troops to Italy, and Kossuth again was entrusted with sponsoring this passage to the House – his colleagues dared not pass him over, and felt that probably no one else could get the promise out of the reluctant House. But Kossuth again let his feelings run away with him. He put the motion, on 20 July, but himself proposed that it should be made conditional on Austria's ceding Lombardy. His horrified fellow-Ministers forced him to go back on this, but he still asked the House to stipulate that Lombardy-Venetia should be given a status so independent as to amount to a personal union.

The day before this, the Government had instructed Szalay, in Frankfurt,[1] to seek to conclude with Germany an alliance of mutual defence against attack from 'a Slav element, or other Powers allied with a Slav element'.[2] On 3 August the House passed with acclamation a Resolution (again sup-

[1] Pázmándy had returned to Hungary to assume the Presidency of the Lower House.

[2] For the fate of this offer, see Horváth, op. cit., pp. 341–7. At first there was considerable enthusiasm for the proposal in Frankfurt, but it gradually petered out as the difficulties became apparent.

ported by Kossuth from the Government benches) that 'should the Viennese Government become involved with the 'German' Central Executive over the question of German unity, it can in no wise count on Hungary's support'.

No one in Vienna now doubted that Hungary was simply preparing to create her own army and her own fiscal system, and to separate herself entirely from the Monarchy.

This was the situation as between Hungary and the rest of the Monarchy when the news of Radetzky's triumph in Italy arrived. As we have said, this completely altered the balance of the military forces, for not only was there now no further need for Hungarian troops in Italy, but Croat and other units could be brought back from Italy and used against Hungary.

But we should be falsifying the picture if we represented what followed simply as a drive against Hungary by the reinforced military arm of the 'Camarilla'. The protagonists on the Austrian side were, indeed, the Court and the three Generals, Windisch-Graetz, Latour and Jellačić, with Radetzky helping where he was needed. But it is important to emphasize the full, and in the case of most of them, willing support which the Generals received from the Austrian Ministry. The Ministry's position *vis-à-vis* Hungary had always been somewhat ambiguous, for, as we have seen, the definition of the 'common' subjects under the April Laws had been unclear, and none of the three Ministers in Vienna holding the Portfolios concerned had ever fully accepted the Hungarian interpretation of them; Latour, in particular, had opposed it with all his resources. The other Ministers, however, had regarded themselves as competent solely for Austrian 'interna'. But a change had come in July, with the appointment of Bach, who was a convinced and even a fanatical centralist for the Gesammtmonarchie, and in the following weeks, by appropriating for himself the role of interpreter of the constitutional position in relation to the Gesammtmonarchie, firmly turned the Austrian Ministry into an instrument of the Camarilla's Hungarian policy, overriding the doubts of his more hesitant colleagues, among whom neither Wessenberg nor Doblhoff seems to have been quite happy about the way things were shaping.[1]

Neither should we be justified in drawing any sharp contrast between the policy of the Ministry and Austrian public opinion in general, inside the Reichstag or outside it. This was divided. The convinced and doctrinaire Left, conveniently forgetting their rejoicings over the Czechs' disaster in

[1] Bach set out his views on the Hungarian question in a memorandum (printed in Friedjung op. cit., I. 489 f.; cf. id., pp. 65 ff.) which he addressed to Doblhoff some time in the summer or early autumn (it is undated, but certainly written before the October revolution). There is little difference between the proposals set out here and the measures actually adopted six months later.

On these developments see also Friedjung, op. cit., pp. 67–8, Redlich, *Staats-und Reichsproblem*, I. 190. Walter, unfortunately, does not regard the subject as relevant to his theme.

Prague, and as conveniently ignoring the national element in Jellačić's case, and regarding him simply as a tool of the reaction, stood for national freedom all round, both on grounds of principle and because they saw that the defeat of one opponent of the gathering reaction would further weaken the position of all the others. For them, the Hungarian Government was leading the battle for national and political freedom in the Monarchy.

But these views were now practically confined to the Viennese Left and the Polish radicals. The Czechs were not going to lift a finger to help the Hungarians, especially in view of the latters' activities in Frankfurt. And many even of those Austrian Germans who a few months before had called themselves Liberals, had rejoiced sincerely in March in the overthrow of the 'system', and perhaps still genuinely believed (as Bach himself did) in constitutionalism for themselves, had since been finding it increasingly hard not to be unregenerate where other peoples were concerned. Every student of Austrian history is familiar with Grillparzer's apostrophe to Radetzky after his victory at Santa Lucia:[1]

> 'Glück auf, mein Feldherr, führe den Streich,
>   Nicht bloss um des Ruhmes Schimmer;
> In deinem Lager ist Oesterreich,
>   Wir andre sind einzelne Trümmer.'

Grillparzer had been a vigorous and sincere critic of the Metternich system. Yet he was able to rejoice in these glowing verses over an event which not only dealt a heavy blow to what everyone regarded as the cause of popular liberty in Italy, but marked a signal success for the forces of reaction in the Inner Monarchy.

Radetzky's second victory, which was celebrated no less memorably by another Muse (in Strauss's famous march), brought an extension and intensification of these feelings. Black and yellow was advancing, red retreating, all along the line. Increasing numbers now wanted only to see Austria consolidated and powerful, no matter whether she was free or not, and consequently sympathized wholeheartedly with the known objectives of the impending action against Hungary.

Incidentally, opposition to the Government based on German national feeling was going the same way as Liberal opposition. It had flared up in May at the time of the Slav Congress, and when there had seemed to be a danger that the Court might go over to Austro-Slavism. Now, however, that this threat had passed over, those who looked to Frankfurt were only the same group who pinned their hopes on Hungary, and both feelings were becoming increasingly identified with social radicalism, and objectionable to the Court on both social and national grounds.

This development was, of course, important for the evolution of events in both halves of the Monarchy, since the anti-Hungarians hesitated ever to

[4] These famous verses were published in the *Donauzeitung* of 8 June.

embarrass the forces which were preparing to move against Hungary. More and more, the Right of the Reichstag developed into a solid force on which the regime could call in all its actions. The hostility of the Czechs, in particular, to Hungary – whether it was justified or not is another question – was undoubtedly one of the factors which facilitated the triumph of the reaction also in Austria.

The first move in the new *parti* was played by Jellačić. The conversations *à trois* under the Archduke John's chairmanship had never taken place, for first Jellačić made excuses not to appear, then the Archduke had to go to Frankfurt, and contented himself with calling Batthyány and Jellačić to him, on 25 July, and exhorting them to agree. They met the next day, with their advisers[1] and then the Croat not only demanded fulfilment of both the Croats' and the Serbs' national programmes, but also, as though he were the very mouthpiece of the Camarilla, demanded that Hungary should give up her separate Ministries of War and Finance and take over a share of the national debt. Oddly, he seems at the end to have been overtaken by a fit of Slavonic sentimentality and to have held out prospects of concessions if Hungary would make further proposals, and Batthyány returned from the interview not altogether despondent. But in the next days, the civilians went into action. Batthyány committed the curious tactical error of asking the Austrian Ministry whether it stood by the Pragmatic Sanction or not, and whether or not it would support Hungary against Croat separatism. The Austrians replied that it was they, and the Croats, who were standing loyally by the Pragmatic Sanction, but before giving a definitive answer, they must study the question.

The Court's next step, which came on 22 August, was to withdraw the Palatine's plenipotentiary powers, which meant that sanction for any law now had to come from Vienna. A week later Batthyány and Deák came to Vienna to ask sanction for the bills for putting the Army vote into effect, and it was refused – the Court no longer wanted a Hungarian army.

Neither did it want Buda and Zagreb reconciled. Latour, having obtained a credit for the purpose, was now sending down arms, supplies and money to the considerable, if motley, force which Jellačić was assembling on the Drave. The second-in-command of this force, General Neustädter, told the troops that they would shortly be marching into Hungary in the name of the Emperor.

This situation determined the fate of the new proposals for a Hungaro-Croat settlement which the two Hungarians had brought with them. These had been worked out by Deák and Szemere, and went to the very limit of concession. The Ban was to be head of both the civilian and the military

---

[1] One of these (on the Hungarian side) was Pulszky, who has left an account of the meeting in his memoirs, II. 134 ff.

apparatus in all Croatia-Slavonia, including the Frontier Districts. A Minister for Croatia was to sit in the Hungarian Ministry, and a Croat Secretary of State to be attached to the Minister *a latere*. Croat was to be the sole official language in Croatia-Slavonia. The Hungarian Ministry, when it approved this draft, had decided that if the Croats did not accept it, they would be satisfied if Croatia simply concluded an alliance with Hungary. Only Fiume and the Hungarian Littoral must remain with Hungary, as essential to her economically.

The Hungarians did not even get as far as the Crown with this offer. They were referred to Latour, who told them that nothing short of cancellation of the April Laws would suffice. On 31 August they were presented with a letter from Ferdinand to the Palatine saying that he had received a memorandum 'from his Viennese Ministers', warning him that the April Laws were themselves illegal, since Austria had not consented to them, and that Hungary's course since the spring had been such as to endanger the unity of the Monarchy. The Palatine was invited to send members of the Hungarian Cabinet to negotiate with the Austrian Ministerial Council on the basis of the memorandum, the conditions for the conversation including:

That Jellačić, reinstated in his offices and dignities, should take part in them.

That the Military Frontier should be placed provisionally under the Viennese Ministry of War.

That all attacks by Hungary on Croatia-Slavonia and the Frontier should cease.

The memorandum was attached to the letter. The fruit of the 'studies' initiated by the Austrian Government, it was an extensive piece of legal argumentation, which, however, ended in the purely political conclusion that 'the existence of a Kingdom of Hungary separate from the Austrian Empire must be described as politically impossible'.[1]

Thus not only was the Court now openly taking Jellačić's side against Hungary, and openly repudiating Ferdinand's signature to the April Laws, but the 'Viennese Ministry' as a whole was identified with the Government of the entire Monarchy, and the proposition (for which there was no shadow of legal or historical justification) laid down that the representatives of the Austrian Lands had, and had even possessed in March 1848, a right to be consulted on the Monarch's transactions with Hungary.

The same day, Croat troops occupied Fiume and proclaimed its incorporation in Croatia.

The Hungarians, naturally, denied absolutely that 'Austria' had any right

---

[1] This document was printed by Helfert in his *Revision des ungarischen Ausgleiches* (Vienna, 1876), pp. 157 ff. It is analysed at length in Springer, II. 496 ff. and Redlich, op. cit., I. 191 ff. It was the work of Hofrath Pipitz, an Austrian *Referent* for Hungarian affairs, and had been approved by the Austrian Ministerial Council on 27 August.

to intervene in their relations with the Crown, and took hurried measures of self-defence. New Honvéd formations were authorized and appeals issued for recruits for these units, to which Hungarian officers and men from the regular forces were invited to transfer. The Diet, however, on Kossuth's proposal, resolved to make one more appeal to the Crown, and to send a deputation with it to Vienna. It is true that the memorandum, reflecting as it did the extreme anger of the nation, was more defiant than suppliant in tone. It asked Ferdinand to come immediately to Hungary, to free his entourage of members of the Camarilla, to remind the troops in Hungary of their duty and to order them to take up arms against the rebels, and to secure the evacuation by the Croats of Fiume and Slavonia.

The deputation, one hundred members of the Diet, led by its President, reached Vienna (where Batthyány had been waiting for them) on the 6th. They were not received at all until the 9th, because their demands were considered 'impertinent',[1] and when at last they were admitted to the Presence, they were given only a completely non-committal answer. Their real answer came in a communication which, to their stupefaction, they read that same morning – in a copy of the *Agramer Zeitung*. This was a Rescript, dated the 4th, from Ferdinand to Jellačić, which revoked the Innsbruck Rescripts, reinstated Jellačić in all his offices and dignities, and expressed the Emperor's confidence in him.

On the 11th, Jellačić led his troops across the Drave.

The constitutional position in Hungary now fluctuated wildly for some days. The Government had already lost several of its members. Széchenyi's reason had given way; on the 5th he threw himself into the Danube, and on being rescued, was taken to an asylum outside Vienna. Esterházy had resigned in protest against the Austrian memorandum, and Eötvös had taken refuge in Germany. When the Archduke Franz Karl confirmed to Batthyány that the report in the *Agramer Zeitung* was authentic, Batthyány himself resigned, his resignation entailing that of the Ministry as a whole. The Court charged the Palatine with the conduct of affairs *ad interim*, but when the Rescript to this effect was read out in the Diet on the 11th, Szemere and Kossuth declared that since the Rescript was not counter-signed, they refused to resign their portfolios.[2] Kossuth asked the House to let him put the Army vote into effect, and when this was agreed, at once set about raising the recruits and printing new money. The Palatine begged Batthyány to form a new Government, and Batthyány got together a list of names which excluded Kossuth, Szemere, and even Deák, but he stipulated that the Court must order Jellačić to leave Hungary. The Court delayed with its answer,

---

[1] Corti, op. cit., p. 308.

[2] Deák himself had objected to the Rescript as illegal. Kossuth had taken his seat on the Opposition benches, but returned to the Government bench after Szemere had given the lead.

and Jellačić continued his advance, which so far had been unopposed.[1] At the same time the Serbs opened a new offensive in the South, and Hurban led a troop of partisans which had been organized in Moravia, into North Hungary, where, on 19 October, they proclaimed an 'independent Slovakia'.

On the 20th the Palatine himself sought a meeting with Jellačić, but the Croat refused to come to the rendezvous. Now the poor young Archduke lost heart; he posted to Vienna, where, on the 24th, he laid down his office.

On the 19th, meanwhile, the Diet, sacrificing legal principle to political expediency, had sent a deputation to Vienna with a request to be allowed to address the Reichstag. The Left wanted them received, but the Conservatives, headed by the Czechs, opposed the request tumultuously. It was opposed also by the Government, for whom Bach read out the Pipitz memorandum to prove the Hungarians' position illegal, and they were refused admission by 186 votes to 108.

The Court tried one more expedient. General Count Lamberg, himself a Hungarian, a friend of Batthyány's and a highly respected man, was to go to Hungary as Commissioner Extraordinary, with supreme authority over all troops in the country, Hungarian and Croat alike, to restore peace. Baron Vay, the Hungarian Government Commissioner in Transylvania, was to be appointed Minister President and the Diet adjourned until 1 December.

Lamberg went to Buda to get Batthyány's counter-signature to these documents. But the news of his commission had leaked out,[2] and the Diet issued a proclamation forbidding the troops to obey him. By a mischance, he missed Batthyány and could not get the papers counter-signed. They were in his pocket, still lacking the essential counter-signature, when a mob recognized him on the bridge between Buda and Pest, and lynched him bestially.

That was on 28 September. Now both sides finally lost patience. A manifesto by Ferdinand, issued on 3 October and counter-signed by a retired General named Retsey, appointed Minister *a latere ad hoc*, declared the Diet dissolved and its most recent decisions null and void, and appointed Jellačić representative of the Crown in Hungary and supreme commander of all troops there. On the other side, Kossuth had on 22 September persuaded the Diet to constitute an 'Extraordinary Governmental Council', under his own chairmanship, nominally to assist the over-worked Batthyány. Now, Batthyány having resigned for the last time, this Council was enlarged, transformed into a 'Committee of National Defence' and invested with emergency governmental powers which, in practice, made Kossuth dictator.

Already for a month past, Kossuth had been throwing all his superb energy

[1] Batthyány and Jellačić had agreed at their meeting to withdraw their respective troops from the Drave. Batthyány had honoured his word, so that West Hungary had been left undefended. Jellačić had broken his.

[2] A Hungarian compositor in Vienna who had set up the proclamation told Pulszky of it, and Pulszky advised the Diet (Pulszky, II. 207).

and eloquence into the task of organizing Hungary's army. Volunteers had been coming in in good numbers, and what was certainly no less important, the confusion of competences and loyalties between the Emperor of Austria and the King of Hungary, the Ministry of War in Vienna and that in Buda, had by now become so inextricable that a perfectly honourable officer could feel completely free to follow the promptings of his sympathies.[1] Accordingly, nearly all the Magyar regiments, and a few others, had taken the Hungarian side, and the Hungarians had also secured possession of many of the fortresses, including the key one of Komárom.

Even so, the Hungarians might well have despaired, but two things came to encourage them. The first was that Jellačić proved a conspicuously incompetent commander. The relative speed of his advance up to the Balaton, near Székesfehérvár, had been due to the fact that it had been practically unopposed. But when, on the 28th, he met, for the first time, a considerable Hungarian force, he broke off the engagement almost before it had been joined, and retreated hurriedly to the Austrian frontier, sacrificing his entire rear-guard, some ten thousand strong, which surrendered to a Hungarian force half its strength. Thus by the time that the proclamation appeared nominating him Commander in Chief of all troops in Hungary, he was on the point of leaving the country ingloriously.

The second factor which gave the Hungarians at least the hope of a respite was a renewed outbreak of Left-wing unrest in Vienna

In spite of the temporary appeasement that had set in with the return of the Court, the situation in Vienna had remained uneasy. Trade and industry were still stagnant, prices of both foodstuffs and industrial articles rising. There were two severe outbreaks of social unrest. One was among the navvies, who had grown more and more unruly, insisting now on their dole on work-free days. When the new Government took office, it took over the control of the public works, the financing of which had previously fallen on the municipality of Vienna. On 2 August Schwarzer issued an appeal to any trained worker to return to his trade, when he would be given all possible help. Hardly anyone responded. Then, on 19 August, Schwarzer cut the rates for women and juveniles; it was understood that the men's turn would follow. The workers invaded the city. They were dispersed, but returned in force on the 23rd. The National and Civic Guards could not cope with the situation. The troops were called out, and opened fire; before the crowds were driven back, they had lost eighteen dead and nearly three hundred wounded. On 11–13 September there were more demonstrations, this time by the artisans, whose situation had deteriorated steadily throughout the summer with the dwindling of demand, especially since the flight from

[1] Latour had circularized the forces in Hungary releasing them from their oath to the Hungarian Constitution.

Vienna of what had been their chief customers, the Court and the aristocracy. The artisans' movement was in a sense a counter-revolutionary one, for one of their chief demands was for repeal of the 'liberal' industrial legislation of the preceding twenty years and restoration of the guild restrictions, but their chief immediate need was for credit, in default of which many of them were being forced out of business, and the actual outbreak was touched off by a curious incident, the collapse of a sort of private bank in which many of them had placed high hopes.[1]

They, too, had to be dispersed by a show of force, although this time, no shots were fired.

Each time the authorities won, and each time they used their victory to tighten the screw another turn. After the August riots they placed the National Guard under their own direct control and forced the Committee of Security to dissolve itself. The Ministry of Public Works was wound up and its agenda taken over by the Ministry of the Interior,[2] which sent thirty thousand of the casual labourers to work on railway construction at a safe distance from Vienna, leaving in the capital only the relatively manageable figure of twenty thousand native Viennese. After the September riots, the University was definitively closed and a vacation proclaimed. Many students went home, and the membership of the Academic Legion fell to some fifteen hundred.

Thus first the proletariat, then the *petite bourgeoisie*, had been reduced to impotence. The peasants had deserted the cause of reform as soon as the law giving them their land and freedom (which in any case they believed themselves to owe to Ferdinand) had passed through the Reichstag. Constitutional issues and fundamental rights interested them not at all. The peasant Deputies in the Reichstag voted solidly with the Government, and in their homes, the peasants formed a solid conservative bloc.[3]

The bourgeoisie outside Vienna had long been conservative to a man, and now its surviving members in the capital who were able to do so moved out

[1] An eccentric watchmaker named Swoboda had founded a sort of credit institute, based on highly idiosyncratic financial principles: a subscriber could get an assignat entitling him to considerable credits, on the sole security of his own future industry. The idea had in it certain beguiling aspects, and Doblhoff himself gave it his official blessing and subscribed to it, although he did not draw on it. In September Swoboda, after collecting a large number of subscriptions, opened his institute and began issuing his assignats. The subscribers rushed to draw their chits, but no one would honour them. The disappointed holders then clamoured that Doblhoff should recognize the assignats as official currency, and the rioting began when he refused to do so.

[2] The take-over took place only on 23 September, but Schwarzer had resigned after the August riots.

[3] A private contest had, indeed, developed inside the agrarian population, for the dwarf-holders and landless men had asked to be given holdings by enclosure of common land. The possessing peasants opposed these claims vigorously, denouncing the unfortunate claimants as 'communists', and joined forces with the authorities, under that banner.

into the country, or to suburban retreats such as Mödling or Baden. Those who had nowhere to go ventured into the streets as little as possible, for fear of molestation at the hands of dubious elements.

The Reichstag acquired further odium (which, rather unfairly, extended to the whole body) when, on 13 September, it refused by a majority to vote an address of thanks to Radetzky's army in Italy.

More and more, the Left was being reduced to a little band of German-Austrian intellectuals, nearly all of them Viennese, in the Reichstag, and to their sympathizers among the students and workers of Vienna; and they were looking more and more to Hungary as their sole remaining hope. Threads were spun between Buda-Pest and the Viennese Left, and the snubs dealt out to Hungary in September by the Government and the majority of the Reichstag were answered by warm demonstrations in Hungary's favour from the Left.

It was over the Hungarian question that the powder-keg exploded. At dawn on 6 October a regiment ordered to Hungary to reinforce Jellačić refused to entrain.[1] Troops sent down to the railway station fired on the crowd, or the crowd on them, causing considerable loss of life on both sides. Soon the whole city was in uproar. The popular rage was directed especially against Latour and Bach, the two men particularly blamed for the Government's policy. Fanaticized mobs started a hunt for them. Bach managed to evade his pursuers, but Latour was hunted down in the Ministry of War and lynched. Afterwards his body was stripped naked, hung from a lamp-post, and bestially mutilated. Another mob attacked the arms depot in the Innere Stadt and eventually got possession of its stock of thirty thousand muskets and some pieces of artillery.

The Students' Committee (unlike the Academic Legion, which had taken a prominent part in the fighting[2]) did its best to restore order. It even persuaded the Reichstag to carry a petition to the Emperor which, while demanding the revocation of the Manifesto of 3 October, the banishment from the Court of 'irresponsible advisers' and the replacement of the Government by one enjoying the popular confidence, yet assured Ferdinand of the loyalty of his subjects and promised him their peaceful co-operation on the new conditions. Ferdinand actually promised to appoint the new Government. But the excesses of the day had been the worst to date, and had decided Lobkowitz to act on his orders. Early next morning Ferdinand and his family left Vienna for Olmütz under a heavy armed escort, leaving behind him a proclamation in which he announced his flight and called on 'all men who loved Austria and freedom' to rally round him.

This was the signal for a great turning of backs on Vienna. Of the Ministers,

---

[1] There is a very detailed and vivid description of the events of this day in Kiszling, op. cit., I, 239 ff. Extracts from the subsequent inquiry into the murder of Latour are given by Hartig, op. cit., pp. 335–461.

[2] The National Guard had been divided, some units taking one side and some the other.

Wessenberg followed the Imperial family straight to Olmütz, where he was presently joined by Bach,[1] and a whole company of public men who had either never possessed, or had lost, confidence in the way things were developing – Schwarzenberg, Kübeck, Stadion, Hübner[2] and many others – took the same road. The Czech members of the Reichstag, except for two radicals, decamped *en bloc*, the Bohemian contingent reassembling in Prague, whence they issued a strongly worded proclamation denouncing the Left and declaring that 'Vienna was not Austria, and was not entitled to impose order on the Assembly'. The Moravians went to Brünn. Practically all members of the bourgeoisie of Vienna who could do so left the city.[3]

On receiving the news, Windisch-Graetz set his long-prepared plans in motion. Leaving one-third of his command in their stations in Bohemia, he gave marching orders to the rest, sent to Moravia and Galicia for reinforcements, and himself made for Olmütz, where he arrived on the 15th. The next day an Imperial Manifesto went out from the city. It had been dictated by Field-Marshal (as Ferdinand now made him) Windisch-Graetz himself, with Hübner's assistance. It condemned in the sharpest terms what had been done in Vienna and announced the despatch against the rebellious city of troops under the command of Windisch-Graetz, 'whom I invest with the appropriate plenipotentiary powers to restore peace in My realm with all speed, by such means as he thinks fit'. Windisch-Graetz now set his troops in motion, having arranged to effect a juncture outside Vienna with Auersperg, when the total force at his disposal would amount to about seventy thousand men.

On his way he was, much to his annoyance, overtaken by a second proclamation, dated the 19th. Stadion had managed to extract this from the Emperor.[4] It was much milder than the first. The Emperor, who expressly described himself as 'constitutional', promised to leave his peoples 'in undisturbed enjoyment of the rights and freedoms conceded to them', and although the Reichstag was prorogued, it was instructed to reassemble on 15 November[5] at Kremsier, near Olmütz.[6] Windisch-Graetz, however, ignored this document and continued his march, himself on the 20th addressing a proclamation to the capital summoning its inhabitants to submit themselves to his authority.

[1] According to Hübner (op. cit., p. 224), he had, after his narrow escape from the mob, first tried to disguise himself as a woman, until someone pointed out the incongruity of this dress with his luxuriant moustache. He then disguised himself as a lackey. He first went to Salzburg, surfacing in Olmütz on 5 November.
[2] Hübner gives a vivid description of his experiences on his own flight, op. cit., pp. 231 ff.
[3] *M.K.P.*, III. 143, puts the number of refugees at a hundred thousand.
[4] Stadion seems to have been first approached by the Czech Deputies of the Reichstag but he was supported also by Schwarzenberg, and, very strongly, by Wessenberg.
[5] The date was changed afterwards to the 22nd.
[6] The choice is said to have been made on Palacký's suggestion.

1848

In Vienna, meanwhile, high confusion prevailed.[1] Auersperg had withdrawn his garrison from the Innere Stadt, a move for which he was much blamed in some quarters, but one which probably saved a lot of bloodshed; for the first week they were camped just outside the city, in the Belvedere and Schwarzenberg gardens. The rump Reichstag elected a new President (the Pole, Smolka) and a Standing Committee of twenty-five, which declared itself in permanence and solely competent to exercise the legislative power in Austria. There were also, at first, three Ministers, two of whom – Hornbostel and Doblhoff – soon resigned. The third, Krausz, remained to the last, to represent the principle of legal continuity, and even persuaded the Reichstag to vote the Budget for 1849.[2] But both Reichstag and Minister were operating in a vacuum. Even inside the city, no one much listened to them, nor to the Municipal Council. Such authority as there was in the city lay with the students, and with a self-constituted 'Central Committee of All Democratic Associations', which, since the conservatives and moderates had withdrawn into passivity, was composed almost entirely of elements of the extreme Left.[3] They, while still maintaining that their cause was the lawful one, which they were defending against mutinous Generals, were under no illusion that what was developing was a death-struggle between Left and Right. They turned their energies to throwing up improvised fortifications round Vienna and organizing a force to man them. The kernel of this should have consisted of the National Guard, but that body, too, had been deserted by its more conservative elements, nor could any such man be found to command it. Eventually, after five successive nominees had either made no motions to take up their post, or had been driven from it, the command of the National Guard, carrying with it that of the Civic Guard and the Academic Legion, was, on 12 October, conferred on an ex-regular subaltern named Wenzel Messenhauser, a curious and innocent enthusiast for democracy who acted throughout in such complete good faith that after the fall of the city he voluntarily submitted himself to Court Martial, declaring, most mistakenly, that he had nothing to fear. Besides these forces, which were voluntary, a 'Mobile Guard' was set up, which, as it was paid, attracted many recruits,

---

[1] The best of the many accounts of these days is that by Ehnl, *ap.* Kiszling, loc. cit.

[2] Krausz's position was a very odd one. He stopped in Vienna, partly because he believed the regime there to be lawful (he acquired much popularity by refusing to countersign Ferdinand's Proclamation of 7 October, on the grounds that it was illegal), partly to save the Treasury from being plundered. In this cause he periodically made small *douceurs* to various more or less illegal bodies of the Left. But he kept in touch with Olmütz, which he visited frequently, for the train ran between Vienna and Olmütz, quite placidly, until the capital was invested, and the purity of his motives and the value of his services were appreciated there. Hübner, who admired him greatly, has some interesting remarks on him (op. cit., pp. 251 ff., 259 ff.). He was on good terms with the students, and probably did a lot to calm them down.

[3] Its President was a certain Awrum Chaizes, calling himself Dr Adolf Chaizé, a Jew of unknown origin.

and became the largest single para-military force in the capital, although also the least disciplined. Appeals were sent out for help, and produced one individual who was a host in himself, the Polish soldier of fortune, Bem, who was afterwards to play so large a part in the fighting in Hungary; he was put in charge of the Mobile Guard. Otherwise, the appeals were almost totally ineffectual. A few volunteers from Graz, Linz and Brünn tried to reach the city, but most of them were stopped by Imperial forces. The peasants were indifferent or worse,[1] the Czechs openly hostile. The Frankfurt Parliament sent two emissaries, the Deputies Blum and Fröbel, to Windisch-Graetz, who told them, in effect, to mind their own business, and that was all they could do: Frankfurt had no arms except words. The two then went on to Vienna, where, however, they could give nothing more than moral support. The only real hope lay in the Hungarians, and it seemed to be at hand, for as Jellačić beat his inglorious retreat, Hungarian forces, after a pause due to their own stupefaction, for they could not at first believe that Jellačić could have drawn such large consequences from so small a reverse, had followed them, and reached the frontier on the 13th. Now, however, the regular officers in the Hungarian army objected to crossing the frontier unless instructed to do so by lawful authority, while the Government was anxious not to present an excuse for further intervention. Messenhauser, on the other hand, refused to call on the Hungarians for help on the grounds that he was no rebel, and would not identify the cause of Vienna with that of the Hungarian rebellion. Meanwhile, Jellačić's retreat had interposed the remnants of his army, with which that of Auersperg now joined up, between the Hungarian frontier and Vienna.

A deputation from the Municipal Council sent to Olmütz returned on the 20th with a simple answer from Wessenberg that all messages must be addressed to the Field-Marshal, who by this time had joined forces with Jellačić and Auersperg and encircled the city. Oddly, neither of the Imperial manifestos reached the capital until the 22nd, when that of the 19th appeared in the morning edition of the *Wiener Zeitung*, sending a sigh of relief through Vienna. But only a few hours later, the Manifesto of the 17th and Windisch-Graetz's own became known in their turn, and deputations to the Field-Marshal came back with the answer that he recognized only the Municipal Council as lawful authority. The Council in its turn received an ultimatum on the 23rd to surrender unconditionally within twenty-four hours.

Fighting began on the 24th, although it was confined at first to the suburbs, and did not become heavy until the 28th. On the 29th the defenders decided

---

[1] Zenker writes bitterly that the peasants, 'far from helping Vienna, everywhere welcomed the *Kaiserliche* enthusiastically' (op. cit., p. 185); and see the Archduchess Sophie's description of the Imperial family's triumphal procession through Moravia (Corti, pp. 314-15). Kudlich went on a crusade to try to stir the peasants up and only got arrested for his pains; he was, indeed, allowed to go unmolested.

1848

that further resistance was useless, and sent a message to Windisch-Graetz agreeing to open the City gates on the following morning.

Most unhappily, that was not the end of the story. The Hungarians had, after replacing the recalcitrant officers by others who did not share their scruples, overcome their hesitations,[1] and precisely on the morning of the 30th a detachment of their cavalry reached the suburbs, and the defenders, expecting relief, repudiated their promise. Windisch-Graetz, who afterwards told Schwarzenberg that this breach of faith 'made mercy impossible', now turned his guns on the city, while the Hungarians provided Jellačić with the single military success of his career by fleeing before him. The resistance in Vienna soon collapsed; it had cost, in all, about two thousand dead. Afterwards, another two thousand were arrested, of whom twenty-five were shot as ringleaders. Most of the minor offenders were drafted into the army and sent down to Italy. All Left-wing associations were dissolved, and the city was put under strict military discipline.

Among those shot were Messenhauser and one of the Frankfurt emissaries, Blum. The execution of Blum, in spite of his parliamentary immunity, appeared as a studied insult to Frankfurt, and seems to have been meant as such by Schwarzenberg, who specifically authorized it when consulted by his brother-in-law. Fröbel, too, was condemned to death, but reprieved because he had not taken any active part in the fighting.[2] Bem escaped, to surface shortly after in Hungary. Chaize also escaped. He was seen in the Dresden Opera, alive and flourishing, a month later,[3] but after this, history loses sight of him. He presumably assumed yet another identity.

The fall of Vienna marked the real end of the revolutionary movement in the Western half of the Monarchy. It was not merely that the counter-revolutionaries were now everywhere in control; their vigilance and their arms were hardly needed. The Viennese bourgeoisie was now ninety-nine per cent on the side of 'order'; 'everyone', wrote a historian from the other camp, 'who was or appeared to be even half tarred with the brush because he belonged to the Reichstag, the Legion or the Press, found any door on which he knocked closed against him, or met embarrassed faces which clearly betrayed the wish to see him gone'.[4] On 29 November a deputation of Aldermen waited on Windisch-Graetz to express to him their thanks and their admiration; the next day, all the trading and industrial corporations of the city presented him with a grovelling address of gratitude for having 'liberated all men of good will out of the night of anarchy, the chains of a terror-rule of a party which had sworn the destruction of all good citizens'.

---

[1] They had made a small advance a few days earlier, but then had retreated again.
[2] For his curious later career, see below, p. 535.
[3] Pulszky, II. 301–2.
[4] Rogge, *Oesterreich von Vilagos bis zur Gegenwart*, I. 92.

In general, it could be said that social revolutionary feeling had ceased to be an active force among the German-Austrians. With it 'Pan-German' feeling breathed its last gasp. The German-Austrians followed the Czechs into the paths of 'Austrianism', anxious only to secure the best terms for themselves in an Austrian State which most of them, indeed (but by no means all), still wanted to be constitutional.

The last, belated outbreak of political revolt[1] came in Galicia, and it was short-lived. Here the situation had developed along rather peculiar lines during the summer. Stadion had not returned to Galicia after his summons to Vienna, but had gone on to Innsbruck, whence he allowed himself to be elected to the Reichstag as member for an East Galician constituency, finally resigning his post as Statthalter on 30 July. He had left the civilian government of Galicia temporarily in the hands of Count Agenor Goluchowski, the senior of the few officials of Polish nationality then in Lemberg; a little later, Hofrat Freiherr von Zaleski, Referent for Polish affairs in the Ministry of the Interior, had been definitively appointed to succeed Stadion, with Goluchowski as his second-in-command. Both these men were unquestionably loyal to the Crown, but they were also Poles. Zaleski had quietly cancelled an order which Stadion had secured just before leaving Galicia, but had taken no steps to put into effect, for the partition of Galicia into two administratively separate halves, had got Polish introduced as the language of instruction in Lemberg University and all but one of the gymnasia of East Galicia,[2] and most important of all, had relaxed Stadion's restrictions on the formation of National Guards. The guard in Lemberg, the core of which was composed of students, had expanded into a considerable force, and other bodies formed in the smaller centres.

This policy had seemed to justify itself during the summer. The elections to the Reichstag had passed off with no more disorder than is customary in Galicia,[3] and both Poles and Ruthenes had taken part in the proceedings of the Reichstag on the assumption that their task was to make the best terms possible for their peoples within the Monarchy.

Meanwhile, however, the Polish hot-heads were using the greater freedom which they now enjoyed to plan a new rising, and thought the occasion for this come when Vienna rose and Windisch-Graetz withdrew part of the garrison of Galicia for his operations against the capital. The revolt, however, was belated: it did not come until 2 November, and then was confined to Lemberg. The Austrian Commanding General, von Hammerstein, put it down easily enough – the bombardment of the city which he carried through was almost superfluous – and proclaimed a state of rigorous siege (*verschärfter*

---

[1] Some outbreaks of unrest in Silesia and the Bukovina were purely social in character.

[2] Fischel, *Sprachenrecht*, No. 1177. The date of the decree was 29 September.

[3] In fact, the peasants, mistrusting the unaccustomed device, had taken little part in them. In one constituency, only five votes were cast.

Belagerungszustand) throughout Galicia which trod out the last embers of active revolt. The compromised extremists fled the country, while a few enthusiasts crossed into Hungary to help the Hungarian armies.[1] The rest of the population settled down.

The centre of Austria's political life now lay partly in Kremsier, where the members of the Reichstag were gathering, but much more in Olmütz, where preparations were going on, in deep secrecy, for the formation of a new Government. Among the promises which Windisch-Graetz had extracted from the Court was one that he should be consulted on all important business of State, and he had insisted that the Wessenberg Ministry must be replaced by a new one, for the Presidency of which he had nominated his brother-in-law, Schwarzenberg. Schwarzenberg accepted the post, more reluctantly than Wessenberg ceded it, and also took for himself the portfolio of Foreign Affairs. The rest of the list, which was completed and approved by Ferdinand on 21 November, ran: Stadion (Interior); Bach (Justice); Krausz (Finance); Freiherr Karl von Bruck (Commerce and Communications); von Thinnfeld (Agriculture and Forests); von Csorich (War).[2]

It was an able team. Schwarzenberg himself had great weaknesses.[3] His conception of the task of foreign policy was simply to exalt his own Monarch above all others, and he had little understanding of what were the real forces at work in the Europe of his day. He was, for example, totally unable to realize that the national feeling of the peoples constituted a force with which Governments need reckon. He himself lamented that he had not worked harder in his youth. But he had qualities which served him well in this field: a gambler's hardihood in taking risks, and an arrogance so limitless as to make him incapable of imagining that his will would ever be opposed, and accordingly, it seldom was. He was quite unfamiliar with domestic problems, but here again his defects helped him. Windisch-Graetz abhorred only the middle and lower classes; he conceded to Counts and Barons a right to exist, and wished to base the new political structure of the Monarchy on an oligarchy of these classes. Schwarzenberg despised even his fellow-nobles; it would indeed be desirable, he wrote to his brother-in-law in January 1849, to see the aristocracy governing the Monarchy, were they capable of doing so, but there were not among them a dozen men of sufficient political insight or experience to justify entrusting them with real authority. It was, moreover, no small asset

---

[1] Not, however, very many (see above, p. 381, n. 2). It was characteristic that the Ruthenes retorted by raising a 'legion' to hold the frontier against them. It was they who afterwards guided the Russians across the passes.

[2] The man to whom the Ministry of Education had been offered, Freiherr von Helfert, had declined Ministerial rank on the score of his youth, so Education was made a department of the Ministry of the Interior, under his charge. Helfert survived many years, to become in his old age one of the best historians of the Monarchy.

[3] For the various estimates which have been made of Felix Schwarzenberg's abilities, see Adolf Schwarzenberg, op. cit., *finis*.

in him that he was not afraid of Windisch-Graetz, who on his side was unable to treat with complete contempt a man who was his fellow-Prince, as well as his own brother-in-law.

Class prejudice had thus not blinded Schwarzenberg in his selection of his assistants, of whom Stadion and Bach were two of the best administrators in the country, Bruck an extremely able business man,[1] von Thinnfeld, a Styrian, experienced in his field, while Krausz had served his country with courage and ability during the previous months.

The cardinal question was what attitude the Government would take up on the question of constitutionalism versus absolutism. There is no mystery about the views of most of its members. Stadion was a convinced and almost fanatical believer in free institutions (he accepted office only on condition that the new State should be based on the principle of the 'free commune').[2] Krausz, Bruck and at that time, Bach seem to have been, in their own ways, sincere constitutionalists; Thinning was a Liberal of the Hornbostel-Doblhoff type. The enigma is Schwarzenberg, of whom all historians until recently, have assumed, in view of his connections, his character and his later conduct, that he was always in favour of absolutism, and that any professions made by him in another sense were pure hypocrisy. Recent researches have thrown doubt on this, for they show him stoutly defending constitutions and popular liberties, in letters not meant for the public, on grounds, not of expediency but of principle.[3] In view of his cynical and self-confessed indifference to truth, the question must remain undecided.

In any case when, on 27th November, he presented his Ministry to those members of the Reichstag, some two hundred and fifty in all, who had by that time reached Kremsier, they were gratified (as well as surprised) to hear him open his address with an almost lyrical profession of faith in those things. 'The Ministry,' he declared, 'does not want to lag behind in the attempt to realize liberal and popular institutions; it rather regards it as its duty to place itself at the head of this movement. We want constitutional Monarchy, sincerely and unreservedly.'[4] He also pledged the Ministry to the equality of

---

[1] Bruck was in some ways the most interesting of the whole team. Born in Elberfeld in 1798, son of a Protestant book-binder in modest circumstances, he had started out for Greece in 1821 to fight for liberty, but got stranded in Trieste. There he married the daughter of a rich merchant, founded the *Oesterreichischer Lloyd*, and soon made a considerable fortune. His abilities had already attracted the attention of Metternich. See R. Charmatz, *Minister Freiherr von Bruck*, Leipzig, 1916.

[2] Till, *Gestalter*, p. 384.

[3] See Walter, op. cit., pp. 260 ff. Even Redlich (*Franz Joseph*, p. 43) takes the other view, but Walter seems to me to prove his point conclusively. It is worth noting that Hübner described Schwarzenberg in his diary *ad* 1–5 October 1848, as 'a man of authority but not at all an absolutist'.

[4] These particular words, it is true, did not spring from Schwarzenberg's heart. They came from Hübner, who drafted the programme, and on his own admission (op. cit., pp. 311 f.) put in the phrase about 'taking the lead' knowing it to be a piece of hypocrisy, but inserting it

all citizens before the law, equality of rights for all peoples, publicity in all branches of the administration, and the principle that the free commune is the basis of the free State.

It was, however, only towards Austria proper that Schwarzenberg used such conciliatory words. In his references to German, Italian and Hungarian affairs, he let the menacing undertones be heard. The Frankfurt Parliament, which just a month before had nerved itself to pass a resolution excluding any non-German land from the new Germany (if such a land had the same Monarch as a German one, the link between the two must be only personal), was told that

> ... the continued existence of Austria as a political unit is a German as well as a European necessity. Permeated by this conviction, we look to the natural development of the still incomplete process of transformation. Not until rejuvenated Austria and rejuvenated Germany have achieved new and definitive forms will it be possible to regulate their mutual relations on State level. Until then, Austria will continue loyally to carry out her duties as member of the Bund.

The Italian provinces were informed that the organic connection between Lombardy and constitutional Austria afforded the Italians the best guarantee for the preservation of their nationality. The reference to Hungary was brief: the war [*sic*] was not against liberty, but against those who would deprive the peoples of their liberty, and the Government would support those peoples in their struggle, the end of which was to be 'the unification of the Lands and races of the Monarchy in one great body politic'.

Before this political programme could be put into effect, one more step had to be taken: Ferdinand had to be got out of the way. This was a step which had actually been delayed, rather than precipitated, by the revolution, for Ferdinand's wife had herself long been anxious that her husband should be relieved of a position for which he was clearly unfitted and which taxed his frail energies so sorely. In November 1847 she had agreed with Metternich that Ferdinand should abdicate, not in favour of his brother, whose capacities Metternich mistrusted, but of his nephew, Francis Joseph, when the latter should have reached his eighteenth birthday, i.e. on 18 August 1848.[1] On 13 March she had wanted her husband to abdicate at once, but Metternich dissuaded her: Franz Karl was not strong enough to cope with the situation,

---

'*ad captivandam benevolentiam* of the Liberal faction of the Cabinet' and Schwarzenberg smiled at Hübner as he read it out. Schwarzenberg had not deleted certain phrases 'the hollowness of which had struck him', because some of his colleagues asked for them.

[1] Srbik, II. 182. Contrary to the usual belief, all these preliminaries to the abdication seem to have been arranged, so far as the Court was concerned, exclusively by the Empress. The Archduchess Sophie was not initiated for many weeks, presumably because the proposals involved passing over her husband; according to her diary, she discussed it with him for the first time in mid-June, this because the Archduke John had then been pressing for the abdication to take place on Francis Joseph's birthday (Corti, p. 296). It was only then that Francis Joseph himself was initiated into the plans (id., p. 297).

and his son was still too young. Afterwards the situation passed into the hands of Windisch-Graetz, who entirely agreed that Ferdinand would have to abdicate. This was not because of the inadequacies of the poor Emperor's intellect. It might be more convenient for Austria to have a sensible Monarch on her throne in this her hour of crisis, but it was not essential: indeed, Windisch-Graetz might himself well have preferred a rubber stamp. But apart from his concessions to revolution in Austria (a point which came up later), Ferdinand had given his sanction to Hungary's April Laws, and showed an inconvenient disposition to regard himself as bound by his word, and Windisch-Graetz wanted a Monarch who was at least not personally so bound.

When, therefore, the Empress approached him again (in July), he replied: 'Impossible; the time is not yet ripe for the Emperor to abdicate.' But he reached an understanding with her that the abdication should take place when he gave the word, and that it should be in favour of Francis Joseph. He put her off again in August. But by the time of the Court's retreat to Olmütz he (and Schwarzenberg, who agreed with him) felt that the time had arrived, and pressure was accordingly put on Ferdinand to renounce his throne, and on Franz Karl to give up his own rights. Neither objective was reached quite easily, for poor Ferdinand clung with unanticipated tenacity to the shadow of power which was his, and Franz Karl, too, showed himself unexpectedly reluctant to stand down in favour of his own son; allegedly, it had been necessary for Francis to appear to him in a vision and to lay his hand in blessing on his grandson's head before the representative of the intervening generation would give way. Eventually, however, the persuasion prevailed, and on 2 December the fateful change was accomplished. At a small gathering, convoked without indication of its purpose, Ferdinand renounced his thrones.[1] Then Franz Karl's renunciation of his claims was read out, then a declaration that Francis Joseph had attained his majority. Then the boy knelt before his uncle, who stroked his hair, raised him, and said: 'God bless you, Franzl. Be good. God will protect you. I don't mind.' The change of dynasty was proclaimed, to a flourish of trumpets, before the City Hall of Olmütz and outside the doors of the Cathedral.

The boy who knelt that day at his uncle's feet was assuming a charge which was destined to rest on his shoulders for the unexampled span of well-nigh seventy years. The personality of the wearer of the Austrian Crown affected the lives of all his peoples so enormously as to make every detail of it a matter of legitimate interest to history, but so much has appeared on Francis Joseph's private life from pens qualified to describe it (as well as others) that it would be otiose to go over this well-gleaned field again; nor, in view of the almost superhuman ability shown by Francis Joseph in keeping

[1] He retired to Prague, where he lived in seclusion until his death in 1875.

his public and his private lives in separate compartments, is it necessary for a history such as ours. Our plan makes it, however, necessary to say some words on his conception of his public duties, and on the qualities which he brought to the performance of them.

His chief mentors, direct or indirect, in respect of politics and *Weltanschauung* had been his mother, his *ajo*, Count Bombelles, his military tutor, Count Coronini, his tutor in philosophy, Mgr. Rauscher, and Metternich. All of these had been much of a mind – Rauscher had been the Empress-mother's choice, while Bombelles had been the selection of Metternich, who afterwards described him as 'one of the few men who thought as I thought, saw as I saw, and wished as I wished'. Coronini was a stiff soldier, 'dynastic to the marrow'. From these instructors the boy had absorbed a political philosophy which did not differ greatly from that of his grandfather, whom, indeed, he resembled in many ways. Kingship was a gift of God, which placed the families born to it apart from the rest of humanity and made them masters of their subjects in the fullest sense. The end of all policy was, in the last resort, the preservation and consolidation of the Monarch's rule, and he was entitled, and even bound in duty, to take any steps conducive to this end, nor had his subjects any right to question either the end or the means. This did not mean that he wanted to be a despot, for his nature was un-despotic, and again like his grandfather, he recognized that kingship carried duties with it. But in those fields in which he saw the essentials of his position, he insisted that his will must be absolute.

It was this feeling of the majesty and omnipotence of kingship that made him insist most rigorously on punctilious observance of the elaborate Court ceremonial,[1] and prevented him from establishing a truly human relationship with any one of his subjects. His punctilio in these respects is the more remarkable because there is no doubt that his nature was unpretentious and even *kleinbürgerlich*; but – to his loss – he was never able to assume the appropriate allures which brought his grandfather so much (undeserved) popularity; he always remained a figure apart.

He was, however, ready enough to delegate authority, and even to allow his subjects to order their own affairs within prescribed limits, for he had none of his great-great-uncle's itch to poke his finger into every pie. In any case, he had, of course, to have his agents, and his choice of them was largely governed by his assessment of their efficiency and reliability as his servants. But it was affected also by certain temperamental predispositions. Among the

---

[1] It is told of him that once, when he had been taken seriously ill in the night and his doctor, roused from sleep, rushed into his room unceremonially dressed, Francis Joseph, struggling as he was for breath, found enough of it to send him back with the gasped work '*Frack!*'. Characteristic of his regard for the attributes of Monarchy was his insistence, when ceding Lombardy in 1859, on retaining for himself, for his own lifetime, the Grand Mastership of the Order of the Iron Crown.

strongest of these was his predilection for military advisers, to whom he listened all his life more readily than to civilians; he also outgrew only slowly a liking for military solutions of problems, and a faith in his own ability as a military leader. The big political role which the army came to assume under him, especially during the first years of his reign, was, as we shall see, a factor of major importance in the earlier social and political development of the Monarchy. He attached extraordinary importance to his position of supreme Head of the armed forces of his Monarchy, and was almost pathologically sensitive to any attempt to question this or to weaken his authority here.[1] A large part was obviously played here by the undoubted fact that it was the army, and the army alone, that had saved his Crown in 1848, but this probably did no more than turn a taste of temperament into a principle of policy, for from early youth he had shown an interest, rare in his family, in military matters, and had shown a preference, which afterwards became a habit seldom broken, except when he went shooting, for wearing military uniform.

By contrast, Francis Joseph seems to have been remarkably uninterested in police methods. Under him, we hear little of the censorship, police espionage, etc., which had been so notorious a feature of his grandfather's reign.

He looked on all his subjects from a pedestal too high above them to reject any of them for being of humble origin. In the first years of his reign he leant heavily on Bach, the peasant's son, and Kübeck, the provincial tailor's; later he perforce worked much with Ministers and civil servants of bourgeois origin. But he never outgrew his family's traditional habit of seeking its immediate servants chiefly in the aulic aristocracy, which, according to a close observer of his character, 'was always nearer to him than his other subjects', held by him to be 'something superior'.[2] We shall see how, when forced to retreat from absolutism, he turned first to the great aristocrats, and when absolutely compelled to appoint a bourgeois cabinet in Austria, still picked a high aristocrat to preside over it.

The Catholic Church was more to him than a servant, for he was a good enough Catholic, especially in his youth, when the teachings of his mother and of Rauscher were fresh in his mind. When in the first years of his reign he took a large personal part in reinstating the Church in a power-position such as it had not enjoyed for many decades, he was probably moved by a sincere wish to increase the glory of God, and religious conviction hardened

[1] As mentioned below (p. 455), Francis Joseph in 1852 even abolished the post of Minister of War, restoring it only when he renounced absolutism. Eisenmann (p. 155) rightly emphasizes the psychological importance of this step, which made the contact between the Monarch and his armed forces direct, without the 'intervention', which had irritated the Army, of a third instance.

[2] Margutti, p. 223. Francis Joseph always shook hands with a noble at the end of an audience, never with a commoner.

his hostility to the undoing of the work fifteen years later. But he was no bigot or fanatic – for that his nature was too pedestrian – and was Josephinian enough in his view of the Church's relationship to the Crown, demanding (and receiving) from it service which made it another of the main props of his rule. How far he was actuated by religious feeling in fighting his duel with Prussia, and how far he made use of it, perhaps no man could say.

As Monarch of a polyglot State which depended for its cohesiveness largely on keeping the national feelings of its inhabitants a-political, Francis Joseph clearly stood himself, in some sense, above nationality. Being human, he could not do so altogether. German was the language which he spoke in his home, and in which he thought; his home was in Vienna, and his favourite summer resort, in the Austrian Alps. He could hardly help feeling himself 'a German' as he could never have felt himself a Czech, a Magyar or a Pole, and feeling a certain human affinity between himself and his German subjects which did not exist between him and those of other nationalities. But the political importance of these feelings was very small. If, in internal politics, he leant more naturally on his German subjects, this was because they were the largest and in most respects the most advanced of his peoples, and the traditional 'cement' of his Monarchy. The partnership seemed to him the natural, as it was the traditional, one; Margutti has recorded of him that he never really succeeded in realizing, psychologically, any other.[1] But he never tried to mould his State internally as a German national one, nor was his foreign policy ever 'national' in the modern sense of the term. If he clung with especial tenacity to his House's leadership in Germany, this was because the title which implied that leadership was more august than any other to which he could aspire, and also more rewarding. He demanded of his German subjects that they, on their side, should serve him in the old a-national spirit. When they thwarted him he unhesitatingly used other peoples in pursuit of his aims, and he probably even resented disaffection from his Germans more bitterly than when it came from any other of his peoples, because it seemed to him unfilial.

He brought to the performance of his duties diligence, conscientiousness, and a fair mental equipment. His intellect was always pedestrian and unimaginative. He was, for example, totally blind towards the arts in any form, lacking even that pleasure in music that watered the aridity of Francis I's personality. Although not obscurantist of policy, like his grandfather, he had little interest in abstract thought, or use for its adepts; we have not included 'intellectuals' among the props of his rule. But he was not stupid, being quick enough to size up a situation or a personality. He was gifted with a fabulous memory, and with the family gift of tongues; besides his native German, he

---

[1] Margutti, op. cit., p. 252; and see below, p. 749.

'I am first of all an Austrian,' he told the Fürstentag in Vienna in 1862, 'but I am decidedly (*entscheiden*) German.'

spoke Hungarian fluently, as well as all the major West European languages, and had a fair understanding of Czech and Serbo-Croat.

His seventy years of rule probably never modified Francis Joseph's innermost convictions, but it made him less quick to assert them. After domestic tragedy had sobered him and repeated defeats in war, diplomacy, and even at the hands of his own subjects had shown him the weaknesses, international and internal, of his position, he, as we shall see, resigned himself to accepting the situation. He renounced foreign adventure, renounced even complete internal authority, and contented himself with preserving what could be preserved, as best it could be done. In this, although always unimaginative and insensitive, he developed, thanks to his diligence, his memory, his gift of tongues and an experience of men and affairs which had become unrivalled, an expertise which served his purpose sufficiently. He was, indeed, incapable by now (if he would ever have been capable) of appreciating those new and spacious ideas which, according to their authors, might have saved the Monarchy by a drastic reshaping of its whole structure and philosophy.

But the worldly wisdom which he acquired in those later years was the fruit of painful experience. He had none of his grandfather's deep internal diffidence, rather resembling his great-great-uncle in his impatience and dogmatism. Now, at his accession, his eagerness to restore the order which alone seemed to him right was equalled by his confidence in his ability to do it. His accession thus ushered in a new period of intense activity, although not, immediately, in every direction.

We must leave it undecided whether Schwarzenberg's influence over him, which is always said to have been very strong at this time, was enough to make him a temporary convert to constitutionalism, or whether – the other possibilities – he did not know what words were being put into his mouth, did not appreciate their significance, or appreciating it, permitted a deliberate deception. In any case, after breaking – this much is certain – a definite promise to the Archduchess Sophie and to Windisch-Graetz that Ferdinand's Act of Abdication should contain a meaty denunciation (which Kübeck had composed) of the sins of the Austrians which had driven Ferdinand from the throne,[1] Schwarzenberg next day read out to the Reichstag, in the new Monarch's name, an address which affirmed if possible even more strongly that faith in popular liberties and in constitutional institutions which Schwarzenberg had professed in his own name a few days earlier, and wished the Reichstag speedy success in its labours.[2] But it also repeated Schwarzen-

[1] See Walter, pp. 262 ff. The breach of faith was a very bad one. A piquant touch is that Windisch-Graetz did not become aware of it during the ceremony, because he did not listen attentively to the declaration; he only noticed that it seemed a little short. He only became aware – to his fury – of the deception which had been practised on him when he read the Declaration in the *Wiener Zeitung*.

[2] This speech also seems to have been drafted by Hübner, but subjected to amendments by some of his colleagues, among whom Bach, in particular, found the first draft 'insufficiently constitutional' (Hübner, p. 310).

berg's words about 'uniting all Lands and peoples of the Monarchy in one great body politic'. This was practically a declaration of war on Hungary, and the point was emphasized by the fact that the only two outsiders among the handful of persons invited to attend the abdication ceremony – all the rest had been members of the Imperial family, Ministers, or Court officials – had been Windisch-Graetz and – Jellačić;[1] and by a second Rescript, read out on 3 December, which appointed Baron Kulmer to the post of Minister without Portfolio in special charge of Croat affairs.

The Hungarians naturally did not miss the significance of the change of dynasty. There was a group in the Diet (the nucleus of the later 'Peace Party') which held resistance to be hopeless and favoured making the best terms which could be got; but Kossuth's bolder view prevailed, and under his influence, the Diet on 7 January adopted a Resolution which declared the change of throne to be 'a purely family affair' of the Habsburgs', by which Hungary, not having been previously consulted, was not bound. Hungary would recognize no King other than Ferdinand until he had been legally crowned and had taken the oath to the Constitution. This was represented by the April Laws, in the defence of which Hungary would continue to fight.

The gauntlet had thus been thrown down and taken up, and both sides nerved themselves for the decisive struggle.

Both had been utilizing as best they could the pause in active operations which had followed Jellačić's retreat. The Hungarians were now securely in command of the centre and north of their country. They had driven back Austrian troops which had entered Hungary from Galicia and had stamped out the rising among the Slovaks which had followed Hurban's enterprise, brutally but effectively; the Slovaks long remembered, under the name of 'Kossuth gallows', the trees from which itinerant Commissioners had hanged the leading insurgents. It was here, in the north-west, that the Hungarians' main military dispositions were being made. The operations had thrown up a young soldier of outstanding military genius, Arthur Görgey, whom (Moga having resigned after the failure of the Schwechat operation), Kossuth had appointed Commander-in-Chief of the main Hungarian force, the 'Army of the Upper Danube', and Görgey had been turning this into a serviceable army, some thirty thousand strong, with great energy and efficiency. In doing so he had, unfortunately, given considerable offence to the local National Guards by simply sending them home, as useless; he had also offended Kossuth himself, although not yet to the point of awakening mistrust in his loyalty or capacities, by his realistic appreciation of the facts of the situation.

In Transylvania and the South the position was different. Many of the

[1] The President of the Reichstag, Smolka, had been left out because, having remained in Vienna after 6 October, he was – most unjustly – regarded as a revolutionary.

Saxons had disagreed with their representatives' decision to vote the Union, and their discontent grew as Hungary drifted into war with the Crown, while practically none of the representations which they had made to the Hungarian Diet were favourably received. While opinion among them was still divided, most of them announced in September that they regarded the Union as annulled, and most of their villages raised defence forces of their own, although primarily as Home Guards. The Roumanians went the same way, but further; a guerilla leader named Avram Jancu raised a force of fifteen 'Legions', each officered by 'tribunes' and 'centurions'; it is true that its numbers were more imposing than its discipline.

On 18 October Field-Marshal Puchner, the officer commanding the Imperial forces in Transylvania, had assumed the 'provisional supreme authority' there and called on the population to obey him. Most of the Saxons and Roumanians had recognized his authority, and Puchner had set up a 'Committee of Pacification', consisting of representatives of these two nations, to function as a local Government under him. Vay had replied protesting against Puchner's action and calling on all officials, and the population in general, to obey him, as Royal Commissioner. The Magyar and Szekel districts did so in the main, so that there were two Governments, each supported by a very small number of regular troops and a much larger one of irregulars. The irregulars on both sides committed grievous atrocities on the populations belonging to the other camp, while the regulars engaged in smaller operations. The result of these was to leave Puchner in possession of most of the fortresses and key positions, but with only a few thousand men available for operations outside these. Each rural district was really caring for itself.

The position in the south was equally obscure. The Austrian military authorities had taken alarm at Stratimirovics's Pan-Slav and Pan-Serb enthusiasms, and had asked Radetzky to give the Voivode-elect, Suplyikać, whose loyalty was above suspicion, leave of absence to come home and take over his duties. Suplyikać reached Karlóca on 7 October, and was acclaimed Voivode by a second National Congress, which Rajačić had convoked to welcome him. The Serb forces were now combined with the regular units in the vicinity in an 'Austro-Serb Army Corps', of which Suplyikać was given the command. It had, indeed, now to do without the help of the Balkan volunteers, many of whom had already returned home, while shortly after, Prince Alexander, on whom some diplomatic pressure was being put, officially recalled the remainder; but even so the Corps constituted the considerable force of twenty-one thousand men with a hundred and eight guns, and it could be trusted to carry out Vienna's orders. It was, however, not of an order to take the offensive, and something of a stalemate had developed on this front. Local skirmishing, particularly atrocious in its details, went on, but neither side was able to gain much advantage.

1848

Meanwhile Suplyikać, a singularly modest man as well as an entirely correct one, had refused to assume the title of Voivode unless and until so appointed by the Crown. He confined himself to military duties, leaving Rajačić, assisted by a new Odbor, to act as the political, as well as ecclesiastical, head of the nation. Rajačić had by now worked himself up into a state of high excitement. He suspected, not without reason, that some at least of the leading Croats, and also some members of the Government itself, were hostile to him (in fact, Stadion had reported to the Emperor that it would be wiser to defer the creation of the Voivodina, or at least the delimitation of its frontiers, to a later date) and besieged Olmütz, Kremsier and Vienna with deputations, petitions and single emissaries. At the end of November the Hungarians offered him peace terms. He rejected these contemptuously, but this did not prevent him from hinting, in his next communication to the Austrian Government, that if the Serbs did not get satisfaction in Vienna, they might change sides and find it in Buda. It was only the Hungarian Diet's announcement of 7 December that finally resolved the Court's hesitations. On the 14th and 15th Francis Joseph, in a series of Rescripts, nominated Suplyikać Voivode and Rajačić Patriarch[1] and promised the Serbs a 'national internal organization', on the basis of the equality of rights of all peoples, when the hostilities should have ended. On the 16th Windisch-Graetz led an army of fifty-two thousand men across the Hungarian frontier, while other detachments advanced from Styria and Galicia. Suplyikać and Puchner undertook diversionary attacks, and another force of Slovak volunteers which had been assembling in Moravia re-entered North-West Hungary.

The Court had hoped to carry through, quickly and almost simultaneously, the military operation of crushing Hungary and the political one of imposing its own system on Austria (following which, it would dictate its own terms to Germany). Both were delayed, the one by Windisch-Graetz' incompetence, the other by his obstinacy. At first his advance went easily enough. Görgey, whose forces were far weaker than the Imperial ones opposite him, withdrew his troops north of the Danube, and Windisch-Graetz reached Buda-Pest almost unopposed on 5 January, the Hungarian Diet – after trying to parley and receiving the usual demand for unconditional surrender – retiring to Debrecen.[2]

Windisch-Graetz believed his military task accomplished, and reported to that effect to Vienna. But he had not confined himself to military operations.

[1] Under the form of words chosen, these appointments derived from Francis Joseph's sovereign authority. The appointment of Rajačić involved him in a dispute with the Czar, who denied his right to appoint a Patriarch of the Orthodox Church.

[2] Matters had been made worse by Kossuth's interference. Perczel, commanding a small independent force south of Görgey's, had also been retreating on Buda, and Kossuth, anxious to raise the spirits of the population, had ordered him to join battle. He did so, at Mór, on 30 December, and was heavily defeated.

The Hungarian aulic magnates, whose leaders had come together in a group calling themselves the 'Old Conservatives', had for weeks past been bombarding the Court with memoranda maintaining that the revolution had been the work only of a handful of Protestants who had seized the power, against the will of the people. They went further than this: they repudiated the April Laws themselves, although admitting the need to confirm the liberation of the peasants and the abolition (against compensation for the landlords) of all dues and payments, including the tithe, arising out of the nexus subditelae. If, they maintained, the *status quo ante* 1848 was restored, with this modification (and they also wanted the internal customs line between Hungary and the West abolished), and no territorial mutilations inflicted on Hungary, it would be possible to re-establish in that country a loyal regime resting on the Catholic Church, the aristocracy, and a contented peasantry.

The Old Conservatives had received short shrift from Schwarzenberg, but Windisch-Graetz, who had many friends among them and was even in a sense one of them (he owned large estates in Hungary and possessed Hungarian Indigenat listened to them willingly enough. He promised them, on his own responsibility, to get the Voivody abolished, to have the Muraköz left with Hungary, and even to have Magyar retained as the official language. He then began establishing a civilian administration in West Hungary, on this basis.

Neither was his optimism entirely unfounded. The population of Buda had welcomed his armies enthusiastically when they entered the city. Much more serious, the Hungarian officers were themselves divided; a considerable number of them had left Görgey's army, saying that their oath to Ferdinand bound them to obey his designated successor.

Nevertheless, Hungary remained unconquered. On 6 January Görgey issued a proclamation to his troops announcing that 'the Army remains loyal to the 1848 Constitution and takes its orders only from the Royal Hungarian Minister of War or his deputy'. Most of his officers accepted this, particularly since the Proclamation added that the Army 'also opposes Republican tendencies'. Görgey's force remained intact, a constant source of apprehension to Windisch-Graetz's troops. That Kossuth gave the supreme command of the armies to a Polish General named Dembinski, who failed to gain the confidence of his Hungarian subordinates, was a retarding factor, but not a fatal one. His countryman, Bem (who had made his way into Hungary after escaping from Vienna) had been given the command in Transylvania, where he won a series of victories over the local Imperial forces. New troops were raised, and Damjanics was equally successful against the new commander of the Austro-Serb Corps, Thodorovics.[1] Windisch-

---

[1] Suplyikać had died suddenly on 22 December. After this, Stratimirovics was appointed acting Vice-Voivode, in charge of civilian affairs, but Thodorovics, an officer from the Frontier, took over the miiltary command.

Graetz ventured out of Pest, lost heart and withdrew again.¹ It was not until 27–28 February that his armies met the Hungarians in force, at Kápolna, and won a technical victory, for after the encounter the Hungarians withdrew behind the Tisza.

Meanwhile, the Deputies in Kremsier, much heartened by Schwarzenberg's comfortable words, had settled down in earnest to the engrossing and psychologically revealing, although, as the event was to prove, politically fruitless[2] task for which they had originally been called together, of framing an Austrian Constitution. The Constitutional Committee's Sub-Committee on fundamental rights (which included the definition of the powers of the Crown) had got through its work fairly quickly (most often, it had simply written out extracts which pleased it from other Constitutions), and its proposals had been circulated to all members of the Reichstag, which was to begin its general debate on them on 4 January 1849. That debate, however, at once brought a head-on collision with the Government. The draft opened with the words: 'All sovereignty proceeds from the people, and is exercised in the manner prescribed in the Constitution.' Before the debate could open, Stadion rose to declare solemnly, in the name of the Ministry, that this dictum was absolutely unacceptable to it: the inalienable source of sovereignty in Austria was not the people, but the hereditary Monarchy. A large number of the Deputies were, for their part, greatly incensed by this intervention, and a prolonged storm followed, which ended, indeed, with the offending words being dropped. The rest of the Committee's proposals were, however, adopted, so far as time allowed. They retained the institution of the Monarchy, and left the Crown almost complete control over foreign policy: the Monarch took the decisions for peace or war and concluded treaties, with the single reservation that any treaty involving the citizen in financial or other obligations had to be approved by Parliament. His domestic powers were less extensive. He appointed and dismissed Ministers, but they were responsible to Parliament, as well as to him, and his powers *vis-à-vis* Parliament were limited by a number of safeguards. He could not prorogue Parliament for more than a month, and although he could dissolve it, he was bound to convoke its successor within three months. His sanction was required for legislation, but if Parliament repeated its decision twice, it was valid even without his consent. For the rest, the Reichstag's proposals were radical enough. All titles of nobility were abolished. The Roman Catholic Church was deposed from its position of 'ruling religion'. Civil

---

[1] To do him justice, he seems to have been misled by reports from his intelligence service which led him to believe that if he waited, the Hungarian resistance would disintegrate spontaneously.

[2] Except in this respect, that it spared later individuals and bodies much work. In general, when peoples and politicians came to discuss constitutional problems again, they took up their arguments exactly where the Reichstag had laid them down.

marriage was introduced. All citizens were equal before the law, and there was a long list of guaranteed civil freedoms: freedom of the Press, of speech, of association, of instruction, etc.

The Reichstag had also decided to treat the questions of 'national' liberty and inter-'national' equality as ones of fundamental rights. The Constitutional Committee and the Reichstag plenum found it relatively easy to agree on the basic principle. The plenum rejected, indeed, a first draft which is interesting in that, while it would have put all the languages of the Monarchy on an equality in respect of education and of the 'outer service' (i.e., the language used by officials in dealing with the public), it left the language of 'inner service' (that used by officials communicating with each other) unmentioned, presumably on the assumption that it would continue to be the German.[1] But it ended by agreeing on a more general wording which added the idea of equality of rights to the Pillersdorf draft, but did not particularize how this was to be realized. The paragraph (No. 21) now ran:

All peoples (*Volkstämme*) of the Empire are equal in rights. Each people has an inviolable right to preserve and cultivate its nationality in general, and its language in particular. The equality of rights in the school, administration and public life of every language in local usage (*landesüblich*) is guaranteed by the State.

But this amounted only to the marking out of the field, within the limits of which there then followed the manoeuverings for position, which in practice turned round two questions: how should the sub-units of the State be delimited, and what should be the relationship between the central power and the local constituents. For it was the answers given to these questions that would determine the real power-positions of the various nationalities within the Monarchy.

A legend has grown up about the proceedings of the Reichstag in this field, that once escaped from the nefarious influences of the Court, the aristocracy, and other reactionary forces, the peoples of the Monarchy found each other in mutual affection and sweet reasonableness, and would have produced a solution on the basis of which Austria would have lived peaceably, had the reaction not prevented it. Nothing could be further from the truth. The work eventually accomplished by the Reichstag was, indeed, very valuable. But the will to produce it had been generated, n t by the absence of the non-democratic forces, but by their too close presence in the background, for everyone in Kremsier was acutely aware that even while they worked, Windisch-Graetz was only awaiting his chance to sweep their work aside.

---

[1] 'The right to preserve nationality, and in particular, national language, is inviolable, and guaranteed by the State. Every person is entitled to present his case to the competent authority in his own language, if it is in local usage (*landesüblich*), and to be judged in it. The detailed rules for the execution of this principle by the organs of the State will be laid down in separate laws. Provincial languages (*Landessprachen*) are to be given equal treatment in the establishment of schools and of higher educational establishments.'

1848

The Sub-Committee of Five to which the Constitutional Committee had originally assigned this problem had proved unable to reach an agreed draft at all, and the Committee had been obliged to ask them for individual proposals. It took two of these – one from Palacký and one from the German Silesian, Cajetan Mayer, as bases of discussion when it opened its own debates on 22 January.

When these discussions began, each people (sometimes each of several factions of a people) fought for its own cause with unqualified egotism, so that the first proposals were completely irreconcilable with one another.

The peoples to whom the existing Land system was unfavourable tried to get it remodelled in their favour. So the Slovenes (or rather, those of Carniola, for those of Styria and Carinthia were lukewarm) wanted historical boundaries swept aside altogether, and all the Slovene areas of Austria united in a great new Kingdom with its capital at Laibach. The Italians of the Trentino wanted their homeland to be attached to Lombardy-Venetia, or failing that, formed into a separate Crownland. The Ruthenes (going back on the concessions made by them at Prague) wanted a new Land of East Galicia,[1] and Palacký, who led the Czechs, began by taking a similar line: he proposed that the Monarchy should be partitioned on national lines, which would have involved the sacrifice by the Czechs of the German districts of Bohemia and Moravia, in exchange for the Slovaks of Hungary (whom he claimed as Czechs).[2]

On the other hand, the majority nationalities in the mixed Lands regularly refused to let the minorities go. A German Deputy from Bohemia[3] suggested giving Galicia and Dalmatia a separate status, and altering the frontiers of the other Lands to make the German areas into a unit, which should then join Germany. But this proposal, although variants of it were, as we shall see,[4] taken up by the German nationalist parties many years later, found no

---

[1] The Ruthenes had petitioned the Crown for the division of Galicia as early as 26 October.

[2] His other proposed 'groups of Lands' were the German (Upper and Lower Austria, North Tirol, North Styria, North Carinthia, Salzburg, Vorarlberg, and the German districts of Bohemia, Moravia and Silesia); the Polish (Galicia, North Bukovina, North-Eastern Hungary – he did not dare offend the Poles for the sake of the Ruthenes); the Illyrian (South Styria, South Carinthia, Carniola, the Littoral); the Italian (Lombardy-Venetia, South Tirol); the Southern Slav (Dalmatia, Croatia-Slavonia, South Hungary); the Magyar; and the Wallachian (Roumanian).

[3] Löhner. He made the proposal very early, on 26 July 1848. It appears, however, that while his was the only voice raised in this sense in the Parliament, the idea was not unpopular among his fellow-countrymen; see the letter from Palacký, quoted by Burian, op. cit., p. 78, n. 152, complaining bitterly enough that the Germans wanted to dismember Bohemia and get rid of Galicia, thus ensuring a majority for the Germans in the rest of Austria. According to the article in *Bauernbefreiung* quoted above (p. 350, n. 2), n. 40, a meeting of German Bohemians on 28–30 August had drawn up a programme which called for the abolition of provincial frontiers and the establishment of Kreise delimited ethnically.

[4] See below, p. 419 seq.

favour with his countrymen at this time, outside Bohemia. The German Tiroleans, Styrians and Carinthians would not hear of their Lands being partitioned, nor would the Poles, and his own countrymen did not support Palacký in his proposals, which in any case went beyond the Reichstag's terms of reference (which did not extend to Hungary); they came down instead on retaining the historic boundaries of Bohemia and Moravia, these two Lands then to be united with Silesia on the alleged authority of the April *Majestätsbrief*.

As the Germans would not hear of this last proposal, which the Moravians and Silesians also opposed, it was dropped, and since the Czechs, once they had decided to go for the inclusion of the Sudeten Lands, backed the Poles, and refused to support the Italians, or even the Slovenes, a large majority emerged in favour of retaining the existing 'historic units', and this was duly decided, with the sole exceptions that the Vorarlberg was to be attached to the Tirol, and Gorizia, Gradiska, Trieste and Istria were to form one Land (the Küstenland, or Littoral). On the other hand, the Committee recommended reinstating the Bukovina as a Crownland, on the interesting argument that if the Roumanians got their own Landtag, their favourable political situation would exercise such an attraction on the Roumanians of the Danubian Provinces that they would wish to join the Monarchy.[1] The Italians' claim for a Crownland of their own in the Trentino was rejected, as was that of the unfortunate Ruthenes. It was, however, recommended on Cajetan Mayer's proposal that the larger Crownlands should be subdivided into Kreise, delimited on an ethnic basis.[2]

The all-important decision taken that the structure of the Monarchy should be based on its historical components, the weight of the struggle shifted to the division of powers between the central authority and the Lands. Here, again, each nationality fought for itself. The Germans (those of them, that is to say, who thought in national terms at all, these being chiefly the Viennese and the Sudetic Germans, for the Tiroleans were purely egocentric, the most extreme federalists of all, and the Styrians little better) based their policy on the fact that the Germans were the strongest single nationality in Austria, and were represented in most Lands, but in many of them, only as a minority. They thus fought for a system which should place the effective authority in the hands of a central Government and a Parlia-

---

[1] Geist-Lanyi, op. cit., pp. 171–2. The Roumanian Deputies in Kremsier, all but one of whom, as has been said, were peasants, do not seem to have been vocal on the point. But when the Court passed the Roumanians' memorandum (see above, p. 346) on to the Parliament, it was argued in detail by others. The Ruthenes, whose very existence in the Bukovina the Roumanians had ignored, counter-petitioned for the province to be divided on ethnic lines, or alternatively, left with Galicia, and they were supported by the Czechs, but the Germans and Poles took the Roumanians' side.

[2] Galicia was to have 10 of these, Bohemia 9, Moravia 4, Lower Austria and Tirol 3 each and Styria 2.

ment elected on an all-Austrian basis, institutions which they could hope to dominate; when forced to concede the principle of some representation for the Lands, they argued that all Lands were equal in status, so that all must be represented equally. The Poles and Czechs contended for a federalist system with the maximum of authority resting with the governments of the Lands, which would have left them free of central control and have left the Ruthenes and the Sudetic Germans respectively at their mercies. The representation of the Lands in any common institutions should be weighted in accordance with their sizes and populations.

In the course of the prolonged discussions, all parties retreated somewhat from their first and most extreme positions. They agreed to recommend a Parliament of two Houses, the 'Federal Chamber' being composed of representatives of the Lands, and deference was paid to the principle of inter-Land equality by the provision that each Land was to be represented in this body by six delegates; but the resultant practical unfairness to the bigger Lands was partially redressed by a proviso that each Kreis should also send one representative. The second Chamber, which was to consist of 360 members, was to be elected on a direct franchise limited to persons paying a minimum of six gulden annually in direct taxation. The respective competences of the Reichstag and the Landtage were not exactly defined, but the Lands were to enjoy a fair, but not inordinate, measure of autonomy, and the Kreise in their turn were to receive enough autonomy to shelter them against the naked tyranny of the Lands. In Lands of mixed nationality arbitral Courts were to be set up to decide disputes on purely national issues.

It was, as we have said, a scheme of considerable merit, which certainly did not mete out general justice (which the Ruthenes most emphatically did not receive), but contained many constructive ideas, and represented a working compromise between the stronger of the innumerable conflicting interests which might have worked out well enough so long as the will to make it work prevailed. It should, however, be emphasized that it was the German Austrians who really (by majority) accepted it with pleasure, and only their historians who praise it warmly, while neither the Czechs nor the Poles, not to mention the Ruthenes and Italians, ever admitted it as anything better than a *pis aller*.

In any case, its merits were not destined ever to be put to the test. Long before the drafts were ready sentence of death had been secretly pronounced on the Reichstag and all its works.

Several of the Ministers – not Schwarzenberg alone – had from the time of their appointment disliked the alleged Left-wing character of the body, and had complained of various sins by it of omission or commission (including dilatoriness in dealing with the question of the landlords' compensation under the land reform). Its worst offence, however, lay in its Constitutional proposals. It is hardly imaginable that the proposals for abolishing titles and demoting the Catholic Church could ever have been accepted by a Court backed by an armed force; but what actually sealed the Reichstag's fate seems to have been its unlucky attempt to declare the people the fount of sovereignty, and to deny that the Emperor bore his crown 'by Grace of God'. Even constitutionalists like Stadion could not accept this dogma, and although the Reichstag had withdrawn it, it had irrevocably forfeited the confidence of the Government and the Court by ever proposing it. 'If', said Windisch-Graetz, 'they will not hear of the Grace of God, they shall learn of the grace of canon.'[1] But even without the offending clause, the Reichstag's work would have been unacceptable to Francis Joseph and his new advisers, for they were determined on principle to accept no Constitution which derived from the popular will.[2] It was a minor point for them that the terms of reference of the Constituent were too narrow for their purposes, since the system planned by them must include Hungary and Lombardy-Venetia.

As early as 20 January the Ministerial Council had taken a formal decision to dissolve the Reichstag and simultaneously to promulgate a Constitution of its own devising, and Stadion, with some assistance from Bach, set about drafting the new document; that another six weeks passed before this was done was due partly to the apparent absurdity of enacting a Constitution to apply to Hungary while Hungary was still unconquered, and partly to the opposition of Windisch-Graetz, who wanted to restore a system resting on the great aristocracy, and had even (as described above) reintroduced such a system as a 'provisional civilian administration' in those parts of Hungary which had come under his *de facto* authority. And Windisch-Graetz had been promised that the new Constitution should not be issued without consulting him. It took painful argument before Schwarzenberg and Stadion could talk the Field-Marshal round, and by the time he yielded it was too late to wait for complete victory in Hungary, for the Constitutional Committee of the Reichstag was nearing the end of its work; in fact, it finished it on 2 March, and a plenary session was to be called immediately which, it had been agreed, was to pass the Committee's work quickly and proclaim the Constitution on 15 March, the anniversary of Ferdinand's promise to grant it.

The battle of Kápolna came just in time. It was not much of a victory, for the Hungarians, although they retreated, had done so unmolested. But it was proclaimed, perhaps in good faith, as heralding the end of Hungarian resistance. On the evening of 6 March, Stadion appeared in Kremsier, had the leaders of the Reichstag called together and told them, to their astonishment, that the Emperor had determined to proclaim a Constitution for the

---

[1] Another offence of theirs was to have re-elected as their President Smolka, who had remained in Vienna.

[2] When told of the Government's plan, the Reichstag offered to accept Stadion's draft in place of their own, but the proposal was rejected, because it would still have left the authorship of the Constitution with the Reichstag.

entire Monarchy; their own labours had therefore become otiose. The protests of even the conservative members of the Reichstag were so vehement that Stadion himself wavered. He promised to see what could be done, and drove back to Olmütz. But Bach, whom he woke from his sleep at three in the morning, simply answered: 'Your Excellency knows very well that it's too late to alter anything now' – and went to sleep again.

In the morning a proclamation, dated the 4th, appeared, announcing the dissolution of the Reichstag on the ground that it had wasted its time on 'dangerous theoretical discussions' instead of completing its work. All Stadion could do for its members was to pull strings with the police to enable the radical ones to escape[1] before the constables sent by Schwarzenberg to arrest them arrived. At the same time, the new Constitution was promulgated.

This document differed from the Reichstag's draft[2] in defining the powers of the Crown unambiguously (and extensively). The Monarch had, indeed, to swear to the Constitution, but his powers in the Crown's traditional fields of foreign relations and defence were almost unlimited. He was supreme commander of the defence forces; he took the decision for war and peace and concluded treaties, with the single reservation that 'treaties imposing new burdens on the Reich' had to be approved by the Reichstag. He was head of the executive, and appointed or dismissed Ministers, as well as other public servants. All enactments by him had to be counter-signed by a 'responsible Minister', but the definition of 'responsibility' was reserved for later legislation. He exercised the legislative power 'together with' (*im Vereine mit*) the Parliament and the Landtage, and Parliament was to be convoked every year; but he had an absolute veto over legislation, and was empowered to dissolve the Reichstag 'at any time'. If he did so he had, indeed, to convoke its successor within three months, but an important paragraph (no. 87) empowered him, if a case of emergency arose when the Reichstag or a Landtag was not in session, to rule by Order in Council, such enactments having 'provisional legal effect', although the 'reasons and consequences' of them had afterwards to be 'submitted' (*dargelegt*) to the Reichstag or Landtag. The wording did not, however, make it clear whether the body to which an emergency measure was submitted could invalidate it retroactively. The Emperor was assisted by an advisory council (Reichsrat[3]), nominated by the Emperor himself.

The proposed Parliament was also a comparatively staid body. It was to

[1] Those who fled were Violand, Goldmark, Füster and Kudlich. All landed up eventually in the USA. Three (including Fischof) who refused to flee were arrested. They were detained in prison for many months awaiting trial, but eventually acquitted.

[2] Although, as will be seen, most of the Stadion Constitution was never translated into practice, and the whole instrument was cancelled less than three years after its issue, it is worth while summarizing these provisions at some length, since they were taken over almost verbatim in the Constitution of 1867 (see below, p. 561).

[3] Its numbers were fixed afterwards at twenty-one.

consist of two Houses, both composed by election, but the franchise for the Upper House was indirect (it was to be composed of delegates from the Landtage) and for the Lower, comparatively restricted; there was to be one Deputy for every ten thousand electors, the voting qualification being payment of direct taxes to amounts ranging from six to twenty gulden. Voting was open.

For the lower levels, Stadion had at first thought of abolishing the Lands, as political entities, altogether, and making the Kreis the effective unit of local administration. He had been persuaded that such a breach with tradition would cause too much ill-feeling, and therefore adopted for the time being (although hoping to carry through his own change later) the Reichstag's proposed hierarchy of Land, Kreis (where the size of the Land called for this) and Gemeinde, intercalating above the last-named an innovation of his own, the Bezirk (Rural District), but in compensation abolishing, except in the single case of the Littoral, the Gubernia in which the smaller Lands had been grouped before 1848.[1] The Ministries gave their orders direct to the Kreisämter, the Statthalters of the Crownlands thus being little more than decorative figureheads unless the Crownland was too small to justify dividing into Kreise. In such a case, it was given a Landesregierung, which performed the same functions as the Kreis of a larger Land. The Statutes for the Landtage were to be promulgated later.

In interesting contrast to the centralization on the higher levels, the Gemeinde, the basis of the whole structure, was completely self-governing in respect of its own affairs, and its elected President was responsible for securing enforcement of the law of the land. Elected representatives from the Gemeinde Councils formed the Bezirk Council, and representatives of these again, the Kreis Council, so that those units also enjoyed some autonomy. The whole judicial system was now a State service (the Patrimonial Courts disappeared). The judiciary and the administration were separate, and mutually independent.

The Constitution proper guaranteed all citizens of the Reich equality before the law and equality of admission, given equal capacity, to public office. The nexus subditelae, in all its forms, was expressly abolished. The principle of inter-national and inter-linguistic equality was repeated in the opening words of the Kremsier draft, although omitting the State guarantee of linguistic equality in public life and education. An accompanying Patent, valid this time only for the Austrian Lands, guaranteed all their inhabitants freedom of conscience and of the private practice of their religions, and laid

---

[1] As suggested by the Reichstag, Vorarlberg remained attached to the Tirol, while the Bukovina became an independent Crownland, in token whereof it was promoted to the status of a 'Duchy'. Galicia was divided into two *Statthaltereiabteilungen*, with their centres in Cracow, which now became a Duchy, and Lemberg respectively. Bohemia was divided into seven Kreise, Tirol-Vorarlberg and Styria into three each, Moravia and the Littoral each into two.

down that the enjoyment of civil and political rights was irrespective of confession. All legally recognized Churches were further entitled to the public and communal practice of their foundations, etc. Knowledge and teaching, expression, the Press, petition, assembly and association were, subject to certain exceptions in the interests of security, free. Other provisions in the generous list related to the inviolability of the person, domicile and the post, etc.

But the real significance of the Constitution, besides its character of an octroi, lay in its pan-Monarchic and strongly centralist character. The Monarch was crowned only once: as Emperor of Austria. There was to be only one citizenship, one legal system and one central Parliament, the *Allgemeiner Oesterreichischer Reichstag*. The whole Monarchy also constituted a single Customs Union; all internal tariffs were abolished.

To this complete centralization and uniformization there was one real exception, and one nominal one. Lombardy-Venetia was to be given a separate status, to be determined later. It was further stated that 'the Constitution of Hungary remains in force, with the reservation that those of its provisions which are contrary to the present Imperial Constitution are abrogated, and that equality of rights is assured to every nationality and every locally current language in all fields of public and civic life; a special statute will regulate these questions.'

As the document further reinstated the Military Frontier, and also divided civilian Hungary into three 'Crownlands' – the Kingdom of Hungary, the Grand Principality of Transylvania (to which the Partium were reattached) and Croatia-Slavonia (which received Fiume and perhaps Dalmatia – this question was left for later decision[1]) while again promising 'the Serbian Voivodina' suitable institutions (the question whether it should be united with 'another Crownland' was again left for later regulation) – it might have been simpler to omit this sentence altogether.

[1] Deputies from Dalmatia were to negotiate with the 'Congregation' of Croatia-Slavonia on the attachment of Dalmatia to that unit, and the result submitted to the Emperor for his sanction.

10

The Decade of Absolutism

It is never easy to say where one chapter of history ends and its successor begins; it is certainly quite impossible to designate any single date or event in the history of the Monarchy in 1848 and 1849 as marking the end of the revolution and the beginning of the years of absolutism, at first unconfessed and afterwards open, which followed it. A case could be made out for any of half a dozen, from the appointment of the Schwarzenberg Ministry in November 1848 or the abdication of Ferdinand in December, to the capitulation of the Hungarian armies at Világos in August 1849, or for that matter, the surrender of Komárom in October. If, in preference to any of these, we take the dissolution of the Kremsier Reichstag and the proclamation of the Stadion Constitution, the choice is certainly too early from some points of view, too late from others, but it is convenient, for these events really signalized the victory of the Counter-revolution in the Western Lands of the Monarchy and provided it with a base – one, indeed, which its architects were soon themselves to demolish – from which to conduct its final operations elsewhere.

In fact, the consolidation of the Counter-revolution in the West was now immediately taken in hand, simultaneously with the establishment of it, and the securing of acceptance of it, elsewhere, but it is easier to deal with the latter operations first, before returning to pick up the threads of the developments nearer at hand.

There were three quarters from which the March *coup* could be expected to evoke reactions which its authors would have to take into account: the Austrian Constitutionalists, Hungary, and Piedmont; and to these three Schwarzenberg immediately added a fourth by announcing to Frankfurt that he was now ready to negotiate on a settlement of the German question, but, of course, on his own terms: there could be no question of splitting up the unitary Austrian State. Unofficially it was intimated that he would consider a Bundesdirectorium under Austrian Presidency, the division of Germany into Kreise, of which Austria (viz., the new centralized Monarchy) should constitute one, Prussia a second, and the smaller States the other four, and a 'Staatenhaus' appointed by the various Governments in numbers proportionate to their populations (which would give Austria thirty-eight seats and the other German States together, thirty-two).

Another message, which arrived on 5 April, stated categorically that Austria would never allow 'a foreign legislature' to extend its influence over Austria.

Reactions came indeed from all four quarters, but in three of the four cases the story is quickly told. The unfortunate Charles Albert had been deeply mortified by the rage and contempt with which the people of Milan had greeted his surrender in the previous August. He burned to prove that he was neither a coward nor a bad Italian, and further believed that his army was in fighting trim again, and that France would help him. He therefore answered Francis Joseph on 13 March by denouncing the armistice, which provided for a truce of eight days before the resumption of hostilities.

But Louis Napoleon was not yet ready to embark on the intricate Italian policy which he was to pursue some years later. The French Cabinet's reply to Charles Albert's request for help was that 'they were not going to offend Austria for the sake of pleasing Piedmont'. They refused even to lend a Field-Marshal to command the Piedmontese troops; the post was given to a Pole, Chrzanowski, who knew neither the people, the language, nor the terrain. The Lombardese themselves showed little enthusiasm for the enterprise. On 23 March the Piedmontese army was defeated by Radetzsky at Novara so crushingly that Charles Albert abdicated in favour of his son, Victor Emmanuel, who signed a fresh armistice on the 26th and opened negotiations for a definitive peace. Pending the conclusion of this, Lombardy remained under Radetzsky's military administration. Venice still held out, but a small force sufficed to contain it. The final peace was concluded at Milan on 6 August; to save international complications, Schwarzenberg demanded nothing more than confirmation of Charles Albert's abdication, and an indemnity.

In Germany, Schwarzenberg's messages forced the Frankfurt Parliament at last to draw the consequences. It now decided, by a majority, to exclude Austria and to form the rest of Germany into an Empire, the hereditary throne of which was to be offered to Prussia. Schwarzenberg withdrew Austria's representatives from Frankfurt, but the sting of the declaration was drawn when, on 3 April, Frederick William refused the offer which a deputation from Frankfurt brought him. His refusal meant, in fact, the end of Frankfurt. The other important German States refused, or retracted their consent to, the Constitution and withdrew their representatives. Germany was its old multifarious self again, and the 'German quesion' reassumed its familiar form of a duel between Austria and Prussia, each trying to enlist so much support among the smaller rulers as would enable it to impose a Constitution which assured its own leadership. Endlessly complex diplomatic moves and counter-moves went on, out of which the fact indeed emerged that Germany was not going to accept Schwarzenberg's terms easily; but neither were the medium and smaller rulers going easily to put Prussia into the dominant position which would be hers if the Austrian counterpoise was eliminated.

Most of the Western Lands, including Vienna itself, Galicia and Prague, were under military regimes of varying degrees of severity which would have made it difficult for their inhabitants to revolt, even if the will to do so had been present; and of such will, it must be said, there were few perceptible signs.

But Hungary was a different matter. As early as 5 March, Damjanics, coming up from the south, had defeated the Imperial troops outside Szolnok. The Austrians were thrown back beyond Pest, whereupon Görgey turned north and, after winning another engagement at Nagysalló, brought his troops round in a great semi-circle to Komárom. Meanwhile Bem had almost recovered Transylvania (although the Czar had sent twelve thousand men to help the Imperial forces there) and the Serbs had been pressed back in the south. A few days later the main Austrian army, now commanded by General Welden (on 12 April Schwarzenberg had found the courage to dismiss his brother-in-law) was back on the Austrian frontier. The Hungarians' success would have been even greater if Kossuth had not insisted that Buda must be retaken, and a considerable force had been detached to invest the city, which fell only on 21 May. Meanwhile on 14 April the Diet, assembled in the great Calvinist Church of Debrecen, had answered the Proclamation of 4 March by declaring Hungary, with all its annexes (Transylvania, Croatia, etc.) a completely independent State, and deposing 'the perjured House of Habsburg-Lorraine' from its throne for ever. Pending the settlement of the future form of State, Kossuth was proclaimed President Regent;[1] he now appointed a Government under Szemere.

But this was the high-water mark of the successes of the Hungarian Left. Probably only a minority of the Diet had agreed with the deposition of the Habsburgs. A considerable number of Deputies had absented themselves from Debrecen altogether, and some of those present had formed themselves into a 'Peace Party'. They were cowed into silence by the extremists, but they remained a powerful potential opposition.

More serious than the qualms of the politicians were those of the army officers, very many of whom were entirely unable to stretch their oath to cover obedience to a regime which had deposed the Habsburgs. Relations between Görgey and Kossuth had already long been strained; Kossuth disapproved of Görgey's Fabian tactics, which involved allowing so much of Hungary to pass into Austrian hands, while Görgey resented Kossuth's

[1] Kormányzó elnök. The statement often made, that Hungary was proclaimed a Republic, is incorrect. The title Kormányzó, which simply means 'Regent', was that worn in the fifteenth century by János Hunyadi, and in the twentieth, by Admiral Horthy. Szemere, however, whom Kossuth appointed Minister President, when expounding his programme, included in it the establishment of a republic.

frequent interferences with his strategic dispositions. The cleavage deepened still further after the Proclamation of 14 April, although Görgey swallowed it, called on the army to fight on against 'the forsworn dynasty' and even entered the new Government as Minister of War. But he was known to have disliked the dethronement, and now some of his officers began asking him to break off relations with Kossuth, proclaim himself military dictator, move his troops to the Western frontier and open negotiations with Vienna. Kossuth's entourage, knowing this, suspected Görgey himself of 'treachery' to the national cause.

Thus Hungary was divided internally at a time when she needed all her strength. The Debrecen Proclamation had broken down the bridges between Vienna and Hungary. Both sides prepared for a fight to the end, and both looked for support from abroad; but only one, with success. Liberal opinion everywhere in Western Europe sympathized with the Hungarians, in whom it saw the standard-bearers of its own ideals of liberty and democracy, but of the Chancelleries, only Piedmont and the U.S.A., if one does not count Venice, then still holding out in a state of siege, would even listen to them, and none of these could help. Kossuth sent Pulszky, who had taken over the Foreign Ministry when Esterházy resigned, to London, but he got nothing out of Palmerston, since the Foreign Office regarded Austria as 'an European necessity'. France took up the same attitude. Much less, of course, could the Hungarians hope for help from the Conservative Powers, which were only too anxious to save Austria. Berlin, indeed, set a price on the help which it offered Francis Joseph – recognition of Prussia's leadership in a Germany from which Austria was to be excluded – which the Austrian Government refused to consider. But ever since Francis Joseph's accession, the Czar had been sending him reassuring messages that Russia would stand by him with 'help and advice' in the spirit of Münchengrätz; he had also stationed a considerable army on the frontiers of Galicia, under the command of Paskiewicz, Duke of Warsaw, as a precaution against any infections invading his own territories, so that the help could come quickly, and as we have seen, some Russian troops had actually been helping the Austrians in Transylvania since February 1849. The only condition which Nicholas laid down was that Austria should ask for the help, and this Schwarzenberg long hesitated to do, on grounds of prestige. By April, however, the Generals in Hungary were agreed that they could not win the campaign without the help, and at last Schwarzenberg, 'subordinating his personal feelings to the needs of State', withdrew his opposition.

The official request went off on 1 May; the Czar sent his orders to his troops within two hours of receiving it. Plans were quickly co-ordinated, and in mid-June Russian armies, led by Paskiewicz, entered Hungary from Galicia. Meanwhile Welden in his turn had been replaced by Haynau, recalled from Italy, with a number of officers, competent like himself

(Radetsky had said that he could not spare men, but could send able officers), and the Austrians began a new advance south of the Danube.

The end could now only be a matter of weeks, which might have been days but for the daemonic energy of Kossuth and the great strategic ability shown by Görgey, Bem and some of their lieutenants, notably Klapka, who held out grimly in the key fortress of Komárom. But Dembinski was less successful, and in any case, the odds in men and metal – 152,000 men with 450 guns against 280,000[1] with 12,000 – were too heavy. The Hungarians were driven relentlessly back into the south-eastern corner of the country. Dembinski's army, the largest in the field, should have joined up with Görgey's at Arad. Instead, without waiting for Görgey, Dembinski retreated on Temesvár, where his army was annihilated by Russian forces arrived from Transylvania. The appeals for further volunteers were now falling on deaf ears. When the Hungarian Parliament reassembled at Szeged on 21 July, for what was to prove its last meeting, only one magnate – the aged Baron Perényi – was there to represent the Upper House and many members of the Lower House absented themselves. Many of those who did appear did not conceal their hostility to Kossuth. A last attempt by Szemere to placate the Nationalities by offering them extended linguistic facilities brought no response from them whatever.[2]

On 12 August Görgey told Kossuth that further resistance was useless, and arranged for the transference of the supreme authority to himself. Kossuth fled to Turkey after burying the Holy Crown under a mulberry tree outside Orsova.[3] More than four thousand of his fellow-countrymen accompanied or followed him. At Világos, the next day, Görgey made both military and civic surrender to Paskievicz,[4] who reported to the Czar: 'Hungary lies at the feet of Your Majesty.'

This was not, in fact, entirely accurate, for there were other Hungarian

[1] 176,000 Austrians and 104,000 Russians.

[2] This law was so obviously a last-minute gesture of despair that many historians of Hungary do not even mention it, but it has its interest as a term in the series of proposals to solve the Hungarian nationalities problem. Broadly, it retained Magyar as the language of top-level official usage (*diplomátikai használat*) but placed no restrictions whatever on the use of non-Magyar languages on lower levels in schools, and in local government up to the County level. It also guaranteed the autonomy of the Greek Orthodox Church.

The Diet also passed a law admitting Jews to complete equality, in recognition of the part played by them in the national movement. This law was not quite without its effects: it had, of course, no immediate results, but was remembered thereafter by the Hungarian Jews with real appreciation.

[3] In 1852 the Austrian police succeeded in bribing an *émigré* Hungarian to betray the cypher record of the hiding-place and recovered the Crown, which was then brought back to Vienna. The police report on the search is reproduced in A. Schlitter, *Aus der Regierungszeit Kaiser Franz Josephs* (Vienna, 1910, pp. 33 ff.).

[4] Strictly, to his subordinate, F. M. L. Rüdiger, who, in spite of his name, was a Russian officer. Paskievicz had previously refused to accept a political surrender, as being outside his competence to receive.

forces still operating in various parts of the country, and several fortresses still holding out, which Görgey's capitulation did not affect. The troops in the field, however, now soon surrendered or dispersed, some of their leaders following Kossuth into exile in Turkey, and the fortresses capitulated one by one. The last of these was Komárom, which actually held out until 4 October, when it surrendered with the honours of war, but as early as 1 September Haynau had felt himself justified in issuing a proclamation which declared the 'rebellion' at an end.

The Emperor's authority was now re-established everywhere in his dominions, for Venice, the last surviving point, outside Hungary, to hold out against him, had capitulated on 22 August. But it will be appropriate to chronicle in this chapter one more episode, which was really an act rather of war than of peace, the vengeance taken on Hungary. In his proclamation, Haynau ordered all soldiers, officials and members of the Hungarian Parliament to appear before the authorities for screening. His pathological brutality was so notorious that Francis Joseph sent him down an order that no death sentence must be executed without sanction from Vienna; but he protested so vehemently that Francis Joseph, on Schwarzenberg's advice, revoked the ban, although Haynau still had to report executions which had taken place. The principle on which he worked was, as he said, 'to hang all chiefs, shoot the Austrian officers who have taken service with the enemy and have Hungarian officers who had formerly been civilians or N.C.O.s in our army conscripted as private soldiers'. His Courts began at the top. Görgey had to be spared, because the Czar intervened personally for him, but on 6 October, thirteen Imperial officers who had served as Generals in the Hungarian army were shot or hanged, and on the same day Batthyány, who had tried to cut his own throat in prison, was shot. Several other personalities shared his fate, including Baron Perényi, who had presided over the Upper House when it pronounced the deposition of the Habsburgs. Haynau's courts-martial pronounced the death sentence further on 231 more officers and on many civilians, including almost everyone – Bishops not excepted – who had taken a prominent part in the 'rebellion', but on 28 October, Haynau was, to his annoyance, told that the executions must stop.[1] In all, according to Hungarian sources, about five hundred death sentences were pronounced, 114 of which were carried out, and nearly two thousand persons sentenced to terms of imprisonment, often very long, in prisons or fortresses. There were seventy-five symbolic executions of persons who had fled the country. Persons who had served in the Honvédség as junior officers or other ranks were conscripted into the Imperial army and sent to serve outside Hungary; it is true that many of them had to be released, since the military authorities were unable to cope with the numbers.

[1] His claim was that he should have been allowed to show the clemency himself: to order it was derogatory to his reputation.

The unhappiest feature of these measures, from the point of view of future relations between Hungary and the Crown, was that they were known to be endorsed by both Schwarzenberg and Francis Joseph himself. There appears to be no documentary evidence for Schwarzenberg's alleged remark when the question arose of withdrawing Haynau's unlimited powers, 'Yes, but first we'll have a little hanging', but it was he who, in fact, persuaded Francis Joseph to give way to Haynau.[1] The 'cold vampire', as Széchenyi called him, notoriously detested all Hungarians ('except for a few pretty women') and repeatedly expressed the opinion that not one of them, not even the most aulic magnate, was any better, under his skin, than any other. His offensive snub to Palmerston when the British Foreign Secretary tried to intervene – that England should begin by sweeping her own doorstep – is, at any rate, well authenticated.

Francis Joseph, too, must bear his share of the responsibility. If he had human scruples, he swallowed them. It is said that his vanity had been deeply wounded by Görgey's choosing to surrender to the Russians instead of the Austrians, and that this was his way of salving the injury by proving himself the master.[2]

It is characteristic of Haynau that he never at all appreciated what hatred he had incurred in Hungary. On his retirement he bought an estate there, and was surprised when his neighbours did not invite him to their parties. He died in 1853. His great-grandson, the last of the line, was found in an attic in Budapest in 1951, dead of cold and starvation.

The end of the fighting in Italy and Hungary left Austria in an international position which was precarious in the sense that it depended ultimately for its maintenance on force, and the Monarchy was perennially short of the sinews of war; but subject to this reservation, in most respects very favourable. The Czar Nicholas looked on the young Emperor with hope, affection and trust: not only had he no designs on his protégé's territory, as he proved by withdrawing his armies from Hungary as soon as their task was accomplished, but he was prepared to protect and support him against others. He had not revealed – perhaps not yet begun to entertain in very clear form – those designs of his on the Balkans which were to trouble Austro-Russian relations so disastrously five years later.

Palmerston was disapproving of Austria's methods but (except in respect of Lombardy-Venetia) positive in his attitude towards the Austrian Power, as Britain's official attitude showed when Kossuth landed on her shores. The danger that France would again become a focus of world revolution seemed over, and the new threat that was presently to emerge from Louis Napoleon's restless ambition was still in the incubation stage. He had, indeed, beaten

---

[1] Corti, *Mensch und Herrscher*, pp. 44 ff.
[2] This is borne out by the fact that of the thirteen 'Martyrs of Arad' those hanged were those who had surrendered to the Russians, while those surrendering to the Austrians got off with shooting.

Austria in the race to occupy Rome, but as the Pope's attitude proved when he did return to the Vatican, this brought Napoleon no political influence in Italy, and the links between him and Piedmont which in 1859 were to bring about Francis Joseph's next great military defeat were still unforged. Piedmont herself was obviously not reconciled to her defeat, and it was to be presumed that she would try again to reverse it as soon as she was in a position to do so, but for the moment she was clearly too weak, and too fully preoccupied with internal troubles, to venture the attempt. In the rest of Italy, Austria's power-position had been re-established firmly enough. The Bourbons were back in Naples. Austrian troops had brought the Grand Duke back to Florence and were stationed in the Duchies and Legations, but they did not need to do much more than walk about and show themselves; Parma and Modena, as well as Tuscany, were little more than Austrian dependencies.

It was only in Germany that Austria had not yet re-established a position satisfactory to herself and it will be convenient, before turning to a description of the Monarchy's internal affairs, to summarize the course taken by the 'struggle for the leadership in Germany' during the next eighteen months, after which this question, also, reached a temporary standstill.

The diplomatic coming and going which had set in after Frederick William's rejection of the German Crown[1] went on during the summer of 1849 without producing any perceptible advantage to either Austria or Prussia. On 30 September the two Powers eliminated one factor in the equation by signing an 'Interim Compact', under which Frankfurt was to disappear (it was formally liquidated in the next months) and Austria and Prussia jointly to conduct 'German' affairs through the old Bund machinery until 1 May 1850, by which time it was hoped that a joint Austro-Prussian Commission, which the Compact established, would have worked out a definitive settlement. But the negotiations which followed brought no advance whatever. Schwarzenberg refused to depart from his terms that the entire Monarchy must be included in the new Reich, which he hoped thus to dominate both politically and economically, for in his and Bruck's plans the next step was to have been the adherence of the Monarchy (entire) to the Zollverein, which was coming up for revision in 1853.[2] Prussia steadily rejected this demand, which was, of course, abhorrent to all German national feeling (a factor to which, as we have said, Schwarzenberg was completely blind, as he was to all popular forces) and busied herself with attempts to establish a 'Small Germany', under her own leadership, from which Austria should be excluded altogether. The diplomatic manoeuvrings and counter-manoeuvrings went on, diversified by episodes in which one or both sides

---

[1] See above, p. 427.

[2] Bruck wanted that the final stage should bring the incorporation of Italy and Switzerland in the economic free trade area. He was not the first author of the idea: it had been mooted at Frankfurt by two Austrians, Deym and Möring.

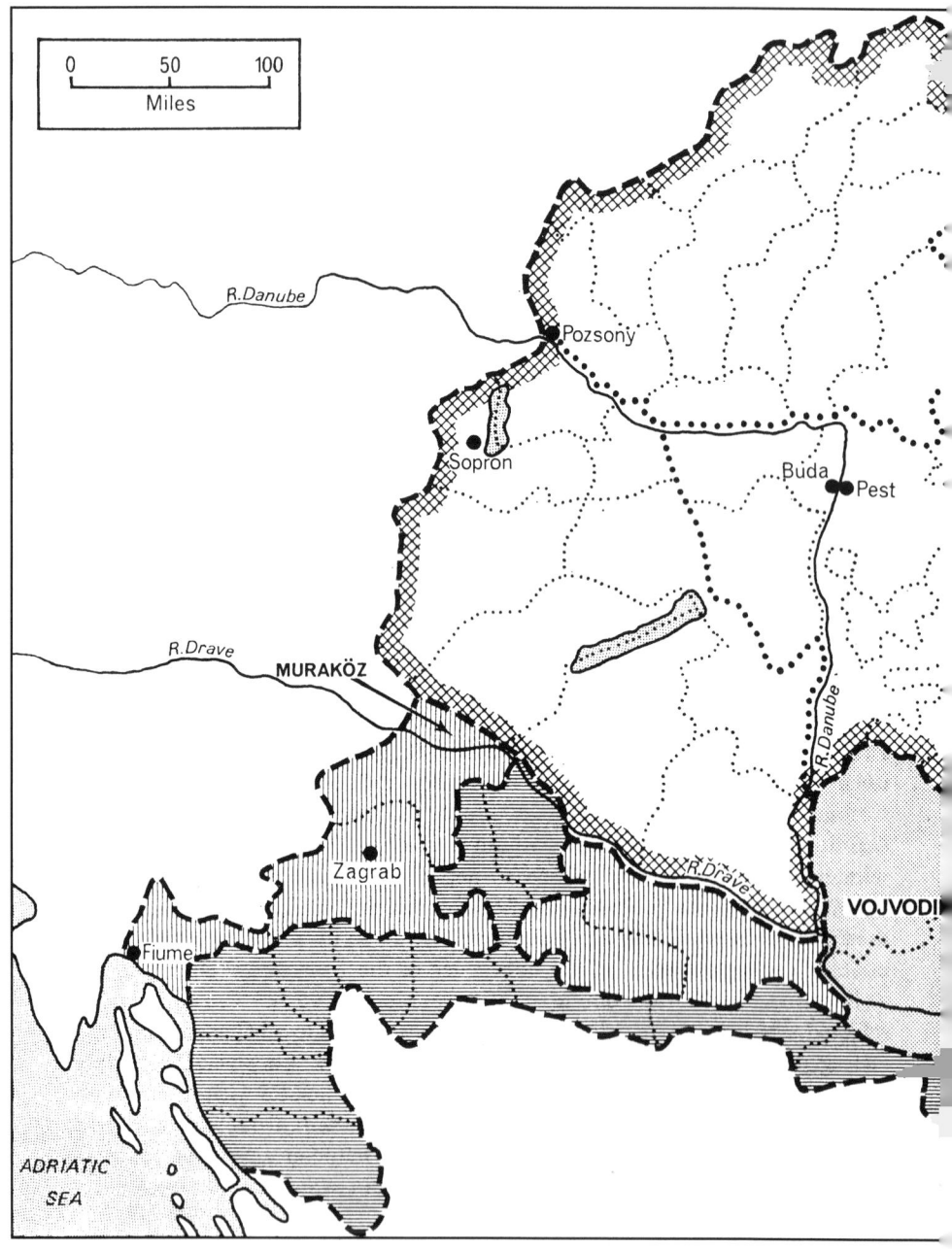

Map 4

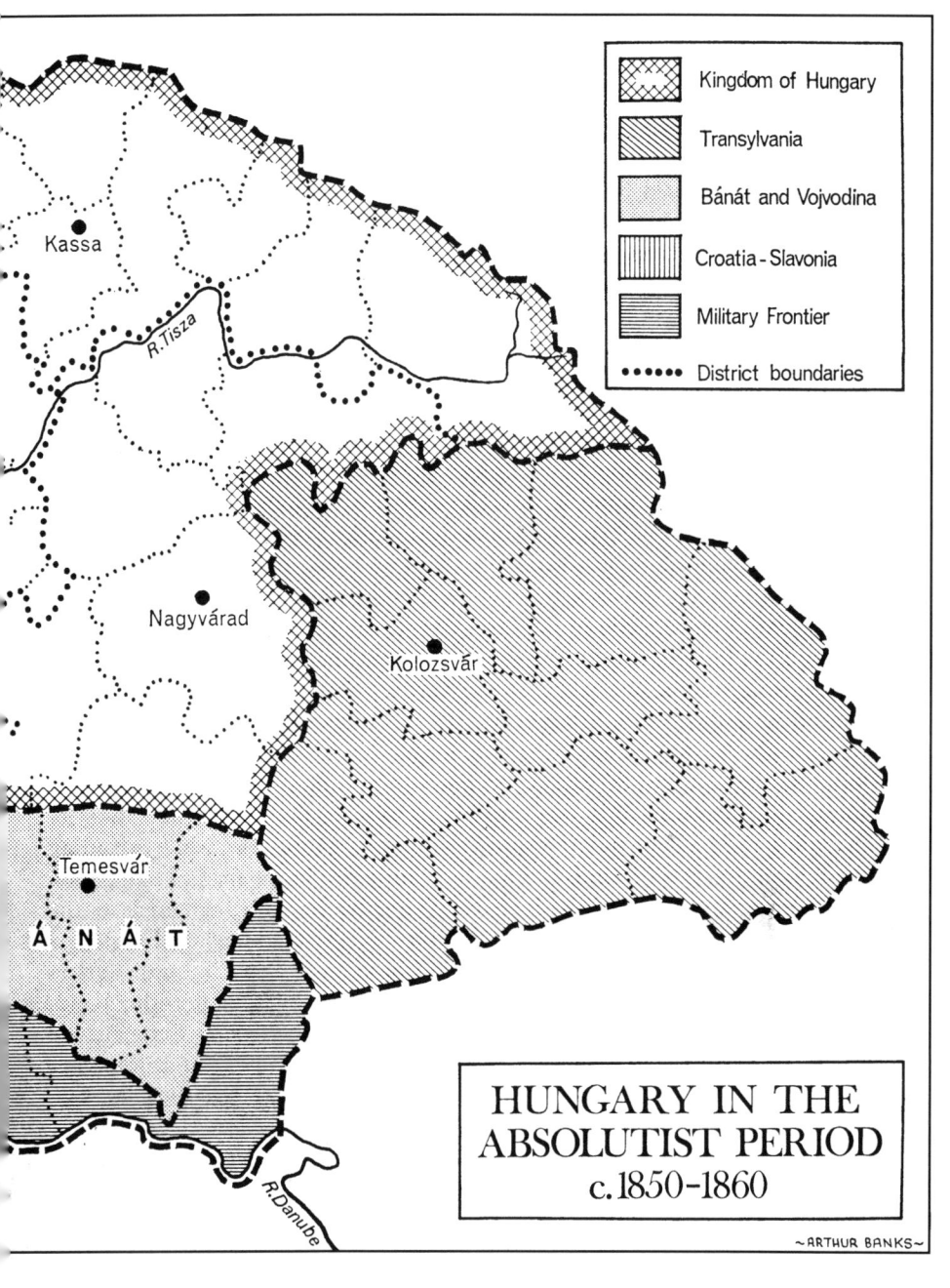

took action appropriate to the position of leader of Germany. One such episode, in the autumn of 1850, which was essentially a question of prestige,[1] brought the two States to the verge of war, which Schwarzenberg was prepared to risk. But Francis Joseph, for once, opposed him and the Czar threatened to march into Prussia unless she yielded. She had no choice but to do so, and on 29 November signed an agreement at Olmütz which marked a humiliating retreat from the position which she had taken up on this particular issue. This agreement, however, did not prejudice the larger question of the future organization of Germany, on which the parties could only agree to hold another meeting to devise a definitive replacement of the Interim. This, which took place at Dresden in April 1851, was the real trial of strength, and Schwarzenberg was within a hair's-breadth of gaining his point, but at the last moment, and by the smallest margin, the fears of the smaller German Princes (and also of the non-German Powers) proved too strong, and the end of the Conference was that Schwarzenberg renounced his demand for including Austria's non-German Lands in the new organization, while Prussia renounced her claim to revise the Bund Constitution in her own favour, and her efforts to create a rival political organization, dominated by herself, and excluding Austria. The old Bund was, after all, resuscitated in its earlier form. At the same time, Austria and Prussia signed a secret Treaty of Mutual Defence, valid in the first instance for three years, but renewable.

From the long-term point of view, and from that of realism, the Dresden Agreements were a heavy defeat for Austria. The Presidency, regained by her, of the futile Bund, brought her no real advantage whatever,[2] and her treaty with Prussia, no enduring one, for all Prussia was smarting under the 'humiliation of Olmütz' and determined to avenge it at the earliest opportunity. Furthermore, if it was possible to tolerate the political anomaly of including one half of a unitary State in another organization, while excluding the remainder, this fiction could not be maintained in the field of economics. Hanover and Schaumberg-Lippe had already, in 1851, adhered to the Zollverein, leaving outside it only Austria and the members of the Steuerverein, Mecklenburg, Holstein, the three Hanse towns and Limburg. Austria now failed to gain admission to the Zollverein, with which, on the other hand, the Steuerverein fused in 1854, leaving Austria the only German State outside it. Prussia's leadership of this great economic bloc was worth far more to her than the Presidency of the artificial protocol-world of the Bund was to Austria.

Her only real profit was that the treaty with Prussia gave her a few years'

[1] The Elector of Hesse had appealed for help against his subjects. The question was, who should intervene. Both Austria and Prussia sent troops into Hesse and there was actually some skirmishing between them.

[2] Only two or three years later, when she tried to get the Bund to promise her military reinforcements against Russia, the young Bismarck succeeded in thwarting the proposal completely.

breathing-space before the struggle should be resumed.[1] Meanwhile, it had been a gain that the tension which had marked much of the diplomatic manoeuvring had never quite reached such a pitch as to interrupt the internal political reorganization which had been proceeding during the same years. By the time of the Dresden meeting this was nearly complete, although the course followed by it had, inevitably, been far from straightforward.

Under normal conditions, the publication of the March Constitution should have been followed by the issue of enactments putting it into force immediately, and throughout the Monarchy, but with the best will in the world, this could not have been done in March 1849. Hungary and Lombardy-Venetia were still theatres of war, and the introduction of constitutional institutions in those areas would clearly have to be postponed until a later date. The situation there also affected the position in the Western Lands, for it would hardly have been practicable to convoke a Rump Parliament consisting of representatives of those Lands; nor were conditions, even there, yet those of peace, for important centres and areas – Vienna, Prague, Galicia – were still subject to military regimes of one type or another. Here, however, the competence of the military extended only to the maintenance of security and jurisdiction over offences dangerous thereto; in other respects, the writ of the civilian government ran. Moreover, the Constitution itself specifically allowed parts of it to be put into force 'provisionally', subject to scrutiny, and perhaps revision, by the Parliament when it should meet. The course which the Ministers were entitled to, and did, follow was therefore to issue a wide range of 'provisional' enactments, with immediate application to the Western Lands, the extension of all or part of them, perhaps in modified form, to Hungary and Lombardy-Venetia being deferred until the establishment there of civilian government. Many of these enactments were, however, in fact applied immediately in Hungary and Transylvania, where the heads of the civilian administration mentioned below were from the first directly responsible to the Ministry in Vienna.

The reader of the following pages will be struck by one odd feature of the record: the far-reaching thoroughness of those measures which could equally well have been carried through by a dictatorship, compared with the extreme paucity of those which provided for any form of popular representation, in which latter field comparatively few measures – none of them above the lowest level – ever became effective. This was not the course which most observers would have predicted, or what the public expected, in the spring of 1849, for Stadion had begun his work with a speed and energy which made it seem probable that constitutional life in Austria would soon be a reality. While drafting the Constitution he had already, simultaneously, been working out the statutes for the 'free commune' which was to replace the previous

[1] The treaty was renewed for a further three years in 1854.

manorial system and to be the foundation of the 'free State', and his proposals had been agreed by a Ministerial Council, presided over by the Emperor, in February, with the result that the Patent embodying them could be issued as early as 17 March. The term by which this measure is usually known, the 'Communal Autonomy Law', gives a misleading impression, for Stadion's 'communes' (*Gemeinden*) consisted not only of communes as ordinarily understood: the local communes (*Ortsgemeinden*) formed only the lowest stratum, and above them were 'District' (*Bezirk*) and Kreis communes, to which the law also applied. The law defined the sphere of the autonomy, which was a wide one, to be enjoyed by the communes of each category, and laid down the procedure for the composition of their Councils. Those of the local communes were to be elected by their inhabitants, on a fairly wide franchise; those of the Bezirk by the local communal Councils, and those of the Kreis, by the Bezirks.

The larger towns were to have their own statutes, the issue of which was promised for the near future.[1]

Stadion also began drafting the Statutes of the Landtage, which would have been genuinely representative bodies, distinctly democratic by the standards of the day.[2]

[1] Many of them in fact received municipal Statutes (Vienna on 6 March 1850) which provided for elected Councils.

[2] These instruments were never destined to be put into force, even in the amended form in which they were promulgated some months later (see below), but they testify to the purity of Stadion's intentions, and are also both of interest as showing the ideas current in the spring of 1849 among the more progressive members of the Government, and of historical importance; for further amended (in a retrogressive sense) they constituted the bases of the statutes actually promulgated by Goluchowski a decade later, and via these (again amended, in a direction which brought them back closer to Stadion's intentions) of those issued by Schmerling, most of which then remained in force, with further amendments, until the last years of the Monarchy.

Stadion's drafts departed from those of the Reichstag, which themselves provided for separate vocational representation, but differentiated only between urban and rural communes, and allowed no separate representation based on birth or wealth. Stadion thought some weighting of the bodies necessary if they were to be uni-cameral, and therefore added to the two categories of urban and rural communes a third, representative (as in Pillersdorf's draft, of which they may themselves be regarded as a re-edition) of the highest taxpayers (the financial qualification varying from Land to Land), whatever the source of their wealth. In most of the statutes the three categories were represented in almost equal numbers; only in that for Galicia were the peasants given more voices. The representation was thus still strongly weighted in favour of property, but far less so than in the old Estates, and the overwhelming predominance enjoyed in those bodies by the landowners was greatly reduced, while the small manorial landlords who had owed their position to a birth qualification alone lost it altogether. It was a change which undoubtedly reflected the Government's wish to favour the middle classes, in recognition both of their growing economic importance and of the fact that politically they, on the whole, represented centralist and pan-Monarchic interests against the more federalist interests of the provincial landowners and, in particular, against the unreliable Hungarian and Polish nobilities.

But in April Stadion's reason, which for some time past had shown signs of tottering, began unmistakeably to give way: Venus was taking her revenge on him, as she did on so many figures of the period. Bach then took over his portfolio provisionally, while retaining his own. On 28 June, when it had become clear that Stadion was not going to recover,[1] Bach became definitive Minister of the Interior, ceding the portfolio of Justice to Schmerling; at the same time, education was promoted to an independent Ministry, and entrusted to Count Leo Thun (who, on his own insistence, also took charge of 'Cults', i.e. questions relating to religion).[2]

It is easy to judge Bach too harshly for what followed. His situation was very difficult. He knew that his own position, despised as he was by the aristocracy and the military for his bourgeois origin and hated for his revolutionary past, was precarious in the extreme; he knew also that the great nobles, headed by Windisch-Graetz, were agitating with all their might to get the emancipation of the peasants revoked, and he may well have felt that unless he showed sufficient pliability to retain his post, the reforms which he thought to be of key importance might never be put through at all. It may also be guessed that he was influenced by the consideration (which could not have escaped Stadion himself) that freedoms granted to Austria could not be withheld indefinitely from Hungary, and, strong centralist as he was, he was convinced that a free Hungarian was a rebellious Hungarian. However all this may have been, it is reasonable to suppose that had Stadion retained his faculties, he would have pressed for some further early steps to be taken to put into force a further substantial part of the self-government for which his Constitution provided, and given his great authority, would most likely have been successful. No such pressure came from Bach, and so far as can be told from the sources, all the other Ministers seem to have felt that it would be time enough to call in the people when they themselves had straightened out the tangles left by their predecessors. The fact thus remained that Stadion's Communal Autonomy Law proved to be the last, as it had been the first, measure taken by the Schwarzenberg Government to introduce any effective self-government into any part of Austria, and even it suffered emasculation. Elections were indeed held in most of the Austrian Lands at the beginning of 1850, but immediately thereafter, on 7 March, Bach issued a new statute which reduced the autonomous powers of the local Councils to a shadow and suspended altogether the elections to the Bezirk and Kreis Councils, of which nothing more was heard thereafter. Similarly, a blueprint for the Landtag Statutes was issued at the turn of the years 1849–50,[3] with an announcement

[1] He died in an asylum in 1853.

[2] On the same day, von Cordon was replaced as Minister of War by General Gyulai, who in his turn left the Ministry in July 1850 to take over command of the Milan Army Corps. He was replaced as Minister by F. M. L. von Csorich.

[3] The form adopted was that the Government submitted its proposals to the Crown in a written exposé dated 29 December 1849, and this was published on 4 January 1850, with an

that the Landtage were to be convoked in the autumn of 1850 and the Reichsrat itself in the spring of 1851. The Statutes for the Hereditary and Bohemian Lands were actually promulgated in the spring of 1850, and that for Galicia in the following September. But elections for them were never held; instead, all persons still holding office by virtue of election[1] were declared to be government servants, and all places falling vacant were filled by appointment. The entire administrative system had thus become purely authoritarian.

Meanwhile, however, there had been other chapters in the Constitution – the reshaping on a unitary basis of the administrative and economic structure of the Monarchy, and the introduction of the principle of 'national' and linguistic equality, which Schwarzenberg and Francis Joseph were positively anxious to see introduced; others, such as the liberation of the peasants, which they were prepared to accept. These reforms could be put into effect without prejudice to the question of popular representation or self-government, and, in fact, the work on them went forward at speed, from the outset, and in a straight line.

The blueprint for the new administrative structure (of the Western Lands) was announced on 14 June 1849. The plan bore Bach's signature, but in fact it simply reproduced Stadion's proposals, with the single exception that Bach gave Galicia three Statthaltereiabteilungen[2] for Stadion's two. It was to come into effect in December, when the additional officials which the extended apparatus required, had been selected and trained – a task into which Bach threw himself with great energy.

The corresponding reorganization of the judicial hierarchy had been announced in another Patent, issued on 26 June, and embodying the separation of the judiciary from the executive which the Constitution had promised. At the top of the new pyramid stood the Ministry and the Supreme Court of Justice; under these came Courts on the Land and Kreis level, and under these again, Bezirks-Gerichte, some fifteen judicial Bezirke going to each Kreis. These constituted the lowest judicial instance, taking over all the work formerly carried out by the Patrimonial Courts, which now disappeared.

---

order from the Emperor approving it. The exposé seems to have taken over Stadion's drafts of the previous spring with few alterations, except in respect of Galicia, where, since Bach had already changed Stadion's proposed bisection of the Province into a sort of trisection, the draft Statute provided for three Landtage, but there was a single Executive Committee (called here the *Wyzdial Krajowy*), composed of five representatives from each Landtag; also a 'Central Committee' (*Wyzdial Centralny*), in which these fifteen were reinforced by six more representatives from each Landtag, whose task was to bring about agreement between the three Landtage if they differed.

[1] In many Lands much of the work had been carried on since 1848 by the Standing Committees of the Landtage elected in the spring of that year.

[2] A Polish (with centre at Cracow), a mixed (Lemberg) and a Ruthene (Stanislavov).

The pattern, here again, was Bach's work; the further tasks, in this field, fell on Schmerling, who had many modern ideas, and took the occasion to introduce a number of important reforms, including trial by jury for all criminal and major civil offences, and the substitution of public and interlocutory examination of witnesses for the old system of written depositions taken in private.

Our statement that Francis Joseph and Schwarzenberg were anxious to introduce the principle of inter-national and inter-linguistic equality will seem surprising to those who have been brought up in the traditional view that the 'Bach era' was one of 'ruthless Germanization', and are able to quote, in support of that view, many measures extending the use of the German language in administration and education. It is nevertheless true in this sense, that according to the fundamental philosophy of the system, the State was a-national. National feeling was to be de-politicized completely, and this ban on any political aspirations based on national feeling applied to German feeling as much as to any other. Conversely, all national cultures were to be allowed equal and complete freedom of non-political development, and this again applied to the German as to any other, no more and no less.

The administration, however, was to be unitary, and the same pragmatic necessity which had governed the decisions of Maria Theresa's advisers dictated that it should be conducted in the German language. The administrative solution adopted drew a sharp distinction between the 'inner' and the 'outer' languages of the administration. The inner language of all public services was German, but the outer language treated all languages currently spoken in the Monarchy equally. Any citizen was entitled to use his own language in addressing the authorities, and they were expected to reply to him in it. Officials were enjoined to familiarize themselves with the local language, and to make this easier, the Kreise of multilingual Lands were, as far as possible, delimited along ethnic lines. The Official Gazette was published in all the ten major languages of the Monarchy, every version being equally authentic, and other official communications, in the 'locally current' language or languages.

The rules governing the use of the different languages in education were analogous. The 'Draft Statute of Education' published on 16 September 1849, laid down the principle that primary education should be given in the pupil's mother tongue; secondary and higher education, in that tongue, subject to 'need and possibility'. The pupil's mother tongue was always to be taught as a subject, as were all languages current in the Crownland concerned; and German was always to be taught as a subject 'because it is a necessity for a great Empire that at least the educated classes of all parts of it should be able to understand each other, and this is most easily achieved by their learning that language which is already most widely current among the educated classes'.[1]

The Government was busy translating these principles into action as early as the summer and autumn of 1849, although it proved not at all easy to introduce even so much instruction as the draft Statute provided, in the more backward languages of the Monarchy. For several of them, there was a grievous shortage of primary teachers, and for some, the primers themselves had to be written, and fundamental questions of orthography and vocabulary decided. On this level, the Ministry had further to contend with a special difficulty, arising out of the land reform: many landlords who in the bad old days had kept up village schools as part of their obligations towards their peasants simply let them go when bought out, and the communes often took their time about replacing them. On the higher levels, it was often necessary to go on teaching a subject in German for the good reason that there existed no books on it in the local language. Nevertheless, the records of the Ministry prove that (contrary to the general belief) a genuine attempt was made during these years to honour the principle of linguistic equality, as thus understood.

In general, it is probably true to say that the 1849 system came as near as was humanly possible to establishing inter-national equality in principle. But it also introduced more linguistic Germanization than ever before by virtue of the simple fact that the German-speaking bureaucracy was larger, and its tentacles reached further. The system was therefore, in spite of its principles, a real instrument of Germanization, because the man who entered the public services and spent his career speaking and writing German usually ended by feeling himself a German. It was inevitably resented by the non-Germans, and while it is true that some nationally-minded Germans also resented it (seeing what they felt to be their preserves invaded by an army of 'new Germans' from the Bohemian gymnasia),[2] it probably confirmed more of them in the tacit and comfortable belief that they were the chosen people of the Monarchy. The resentment of the German Liberals against the absolutist regime sprang from quite other considerations, and the fact that they regarded its political and economic drawbacks as outweighing its national advantages to themselves is due largely to the obdurate under-estimation with which, as before 1848, they viewed the importance of the national feelings of Austria's non-Germans.

There was also another set of transactions of the highest importance the first results of which were promulgated without waiting for the completion of the regime's other moves in Hungary and Lombardy-Venetia. The intellectual

---

[1] The text of this is printed in Frommelt, op. cit., pp. 163 ff.

[2] 'There was', wrote one historian, 'no spectacle more wounding to the dignity of the Germans than to see German civilization served up by Czech officials on a plate of state of siege' (cf. Eisenmann, p. 189).

leaders of the Catholic Church, like those of the nationalities and social classes, had seen in the 1848 revolution the opportunity to press their own claims; but their ideal was, of course, different from those of the national and social leaders. Rauscher, who was the moving spirit in everything which followed, saw in the situation the opportunity to realize what he had long been urging, the establishment of a common front against subversion composed by a Crown unhampered by Constitutions and a Church freed from the fetters of Josephinism.

As early as 19 April 1848, a Committee of priests had petitioned Pillersdorf to include complete liberty for the Church in his Constitution,[1] but Pillersdorf's draft had contained little more than a guarantee of freedom of conscience and of worship (for recognized religions). The Reichstag's draft still left the Churches under the supreme control of the State, and could for many other reasons not be acceptable to Catholics; neither was Stadion's Constitution. Meanwhile, anti-clerical feeling in Vienna had been running so high that the Church had not dared to move publicly, but in January 1849, the Minister President's brother, Cardinal Schwarzenberg, who was an old patron of Rauscher's, had (with Rauscher in attendance) been pressing his brother, and the young Monarch, to conclude a Concordat with the Vatican, a preliminary whereto a Bishops' conference should be held in Vienna, similar to the Würzburg Conference of the German Bishops of the previous November.

The Archbishop of Vienna, Milde, although a convinced Josephinian, left all the arrangements to Schwarzenberg,[2] and the Conference duly opened in Vienna on 30 April. It set up a permanent Committee, which in practice consisted of Schwarzenberg and Rauscher, to frame its demands. The Committee's memorandum re-stated the thesis that the revolution had been due, essentially, to the godlessness of the people, which set them whoring after such false idols as enlightenment and nationalism.[3] To avert repetition of it, and to enable the Church to throw its whole weight into the struggle against the forces of evil, it should be reinstated in the position from which Joseph II had ousted it. All restrictions imposed by Joseph should be removed, and the work crowned by the conclusion of a Concordat.

When this memorandum came before the Ministerial Council, some of its demands were opposed by Schmerling and a few even by Bach, devout Catholic as he was, and the discussion of them lasted over many months. Most of them were, however, strongly supported by Thun, and the young

[1] Weinzierl-Fischer, op. cit., p. 27. The following paragraphs are based on this work.
[2] He was of bourgeois origin, and it seems likely that he was over-awed by his colleague's rank (Weinzierl-Fischer, p. 38).
[3] A Pastoral Letter of 17 June 1849 condemned nationalism as a revolutionary principle. 'The variety of languages' was itself described as 'only a consequence of sin, and of falling away from God'.

Monarch himself insisted that some of them should be met. The concessions which it was agreed to make were eventually published in the form of two Rescripts, dated 18 and 23 April 1850. The Placetum Regium disappeared: thenceforward communication between the Bishops and their congregations and the Holy See was free, and all restrictions on the publication of Papal Bulls and Encyclica were lifted. Bishops recovered their right to impose disciplinary penalties on their clergy, whom they could even have imprisoned, being required only to notify the lay arm, which was bound to carry out the sentence if it was in conformity with Canonical Law. The powers assumed by Joseph to regulate Church services or calendars vanished. The Church became exclusively competent for promotions and appointments within its own ranks, except appointments to Bishoprics, on which the Emperor promised to take the appropriate ecclesiastical advice, and was given exclusive control over the seminaries and the decisive voice in the appointment of teachers of Catholic religion in all educational establishments, and in all questions relating to theological studies. In July 1851 the Society of Jesus was reinstated in 'its former position'. Finally, the Emperor invited further representations on these wishes of the Church which the Patents did not satisfy, and promised to make the necessary preparations 'in so far as an agreement with the Holy See is necessary'.

The Constitution, as we have seen, had envisaged a special regime for Lombardy-Venetia. Pending the elaboration of this, a 'Provisional Administrative System', issued on 17 October 1849, made Radetzky military and civilian Governor of the Kingdom, with practically unlimited powers in almost all fields except those of taxation, which Vienna reserved for itself. Under him, each of the three main centres (Milan, Venice and Verona) was given a military Governor with a civilian co-adjutor. None of the centralizing measures described above were applied in the Kingdom in 1849-51, with the single exception that the Supreme Court in Verona was abolished, final appeals in law going to Vienna. All other enactments either exempted the Kingdom from their application or, at least, gave it special treatment.

The Lands of the Hungarian Crown, on the other hand, were to be made in every respect into an integral part of the new centralized Monarchy – this was, indeed, the principal object of the whole exercise.

There was one important field in which the Government could, and did, begin its work at once: this was the economic and fiscal integration of the Hungarian Lands into the Gesammtmonarchie. The biggest obstacle in the way of this operation had been removed by the Hungarian Diet of 1848 itself, when it renounced the nobles' exemption from taxation. The next steps, which were directed by Bruck, were to extend the Austrian system of direct taxation to the Hungarian Lands and to introduce into them the tobacco monopoly and other excise duties from which they had formerly been exempt. This was done gradually in the course of 1849 and 1850, and in the latter year breaches were made in the customs barrier between the two halves of the Monarchy. By the spring of 1851 the fiscal assimilation had been completed, and on 1 July of that year the last remains of the customs line were abolished.[1]

The political integration was a more complicated business, and several intermediate stages had to be traversed before the final dispositions could be taken.

The first need had been to get round the inconvenient half-promise to the Hungarian Constitution contained in Stadion's production. Guarded as this was, it still constituted a paper shackle on the Government's working; but Bach snapped it for the paper that it was when the Debrecen Parliament pronounced the deposition of the Habsburgs, by announcing that Hungary had by this act herself rendered her Constitution null and void. Then Windisch-Graetz's private experiment, which had proved a total failure (the Hungarian peasants were as hostile to the Old Conservatives as were the Austrian centralists themselves) was quietly liquidated, and when Haynau was given command of the forces in the field, he was also appointed Governor-General, but given a civilian colleague, Baron Gehringer, a respectable Transylvanian Saxon from the Hungarian Court Chancellery, who was the direct subordinate of the Ministry of the Interior. Gehringer was instructed to introduce the new system as quickly as possible. His subordinates took charge of the civilian administration behind the armies (including the Russian) as they advanced, and the reorganization was thus beginning to take shape in some parts of Hungary while the fighting in others was still in progress. This did not, indeed, yet apply to the machinery of government, including its internal language, but the equal treatment of languages in the outer services was introduced, teaching in some schools changed over to local languages, and preparations began for some other measures, including the realization of the land reform.

The 'rebellion' having been officially declared at an end by Haynau on 1 September (and his 'pacification' got under way), the Government, on 17 October (the day of the issue of the corresponding document for Lombardy-Venetia) issued a 'Provisional Administrative System' for Hungary. Haynau remained Governor-General, and Gehringer 'provisionally' head of the civilian administration, but Hungary was divided into six Military Districts, with their headquarters at Sopron, Pozsony, Kassa, Buda-Pest, Nagy-Várad and Temesvár respectively. Each of these was under a Military Governor, to whom, in some cases, a civilian 'adviser' was attached. The Counties and their subdivisions composing each Military District were similarly placed under Military Commissioners, to each of whom a civilian was attached.

[1] Details of this operation can be found in R. Sieghart, *Zolltrennung und Zolleinheit* (Vienna, 1915).

The rule was, of course, dictatorial, the County Congregationes having lost their title to exist with the abolition of the Constitution, but otherwise some attempt was made at this stage to respect the national traditions. The old administrative divisions were retained; the civilian officials were given their old titles (Föispán, Szolgabiró, etc.) and recruited, as far as possible, locally; German was required only for communications with the military authorities, and the Alispáns were allowed to prescribe their own 'inner language', for which most of them chose Magyar. A petition by the Slovaks for an independent territory of their own in North Hungary was rejected.

A similar system was introduced in Transylvania. The senior officer commanding the Imperial forces there, F.M.L. Wohlgemuth, was installed as Military Governor, with a civilian adlatus in the person of Eduard Bach, the Minister's brother. Here there were six Military Districts.

As foreshadowed in the Constitution, the Partium were included in Transylvania, while the Muraköz and Fiume were assigned to Croatia.

The next step was to make the motions of fulfilling the promises made to the Serbs – a task which was not, indeed, accomplished easily, nor without acrimonious wrangling between the Government and Rajačić, and also between the Government and Jellačić, and between Jellačić and Rajačić; for Jellačić had tried to jump control of the area and had even installed a provisional administration of his own in it; while Rajačić wanted all Slavonia under himself. Meanwhile, the non-Serb populations of South Hungary, including its Swabians, had been protesting against being put under Serb rule, and Schwarzenberg's advisers had themselves, after looking more closely into the problem, come to the conclusion that it was impossible to draw ethnic frontiers in that area, and that the best policy was 'to create a unit which should as far as possible assign equal weight to all local interests, as well as those of the Austrian State, which latter demanded that as large an area as possible should be detached from Hungary'.[1]

Their answer was embodied in a Patent of 18 November 1849, which constituted the three Bánátal Counties, the Hungarian County of Bács-Bodrog, and the two easternmost Districts of Srem (Rum and Illok) a separate unit, with the status of a Crownland, under the designation of the 'Bánát and Voivodina'.[2] To mark its dignity, Francis Joseph himself assumed the title of 'Grand Voivode'. This solution did, indeed, answer one of the Government's conditions, for the area thus detached from Hungary was extensive enough; but it was not Serbian in either an inclusive or an exclusive sense, for on the one hand, it included inside its frontiers many more non-Serbs than Serbs, and on the other, it left outside them more than two-thirds of the Serbs of the

---

[1] See on this I. Jánossy in the *Jahrbücher des Institutes für ungarische Geschichtsforschung in Wien*, Vienna, 1933.

[2] This, of course, reduced the number of Hungarian Military Districts to five.

Monarchy.[1] Nor did the Patent give the Serbs any political self-government: it simply appointed an Austrian General[2] Statthalter.

Soon after this (on 2 December, the anniversary of Francis Joseph's accession), a formal announcement was issued that the March Constitution was now to be considered as in force in the Hungarian Lands, but although the Ministries in Vienna were now flooding all the Lands with orders and instructions (often causing acute conflicts of competence between the civilian and military authorities) the pattern was left unchanged until the following spring. Then the Croat 'Banal Council' forced the issue by refusing to promulgate the Constitution, on the grounds that it was invalid in Croatia unless and until it had been ratified by the Sabor, and in any case, violated Croatia's historic rights by excluding from its territory Dalmatia and the Croat Districts of the Military Frontier. To this the goaded Government replied on 7 April with a Patent which, while thanking the Croats effusively for their past services, intimated to them that they must accept the frontiers they had been given and the other provisions of the Constitution, and dissolved the Sabor without providing for the election of a successor. The effect of this was to bring Croatia directly under the jurisdiction of the Viennese Ministries, although the Croats received the concessions that the internal structure of their country was not altered, and that they were expressly assured the continued use of Croat in their inner services.

A Patent for the Military Frontier, issued on 7 June 1850, put the area back where it had belonged before 1848, and restored its internal institutions with little modification. The Government was still hesitant to touch the military regimes in Inner Hungary and Transylvania, but in June Haynau was dismissed, after a quarrel with his superiors of more than usual intensity. No suitable military successor to this thorny post presented himself, and the civilian Ministers were anxious to secure the unimpeded execution of their work. On 8 September, accordingly a new Provisorium[3] was issued for Inner Hungary, which retained, indeed, martial law, thus leaving the military competent for jurisdiction over offences against security, but put the country in other respects under a civilian regime, and directly under the control of the central Ministries. Here, in contrast to Croatia, no concessions whatever were made. Lip-service was paid to the name of Hungary in so far as it was left nominally under a single 'Governor', who was even given his own staff, under the old name of Consilium Locumtenentiale; but the functions of this

[1] The population of the Voivodina, according to the military census of 1851, consisted of 407,000 Serbs, 395,000 Roumanians, 325,000 Germans, 241,000 Magyars and 32,000 others. The total number of Serbs in the Monarchy at that date was 1,438,000.

[2] General Ferdinand von Mayerhofer. Mayerhofer was, indeed, a man of local experience and, according to Friedjung (op. cit., pp. 429 f.), common-sense and humour, who carried out his difficult duties well.

[3] The popular genius distinguished the *Provisorium* from its predecessor by dubbing the latter the *Provisorissimum*.

central office could easily be nullified, for the division of the country was maintained, the five surviving Military Districts becoming as many Provinces.[1] Each of these was placed under a Provisional Governor, who corresponded both with the Governor and also directly with Vienna (his position thus corresponding to that of the head of a Galician Statthaltereiabteilung), and was the head of all administrative services in his Province. These were organized in a pattern corresponding to the Western Kreise and Bezirke.[2] German was made the inner language of all administration.

For the judiciary, too, the Austrian pattern was introduced, with the same separation of the judiciary from the executive and consequent transference of the work of the old Courts to a new network of State Courts of the first instance. The Supreme Court in Buda was abolished, final appeal going to Vienna. The replacement of Hungarian law by Austrian could not be completed overnight, but a beginning was made in several fields.

Among the other institutions to disappear was the old Hungarian police force of *Pandurs*, who were replaced by the Austrian gendarmerie.

The only other change in Inner Hungary up to the end of 1851 was that Gehringer was replaced in August 1851 by the Archduke Albrecht.

In 1850, Wohlgemuth had resisted any change in the regime in Transylvania, but he died suddenly in April 1851, and the Grand Principality then in its turn received its Provisorium. Here the path was slightly cluttered by memories of inconvenient promises, or half-promises, which Francis Joseph had made at an earlier stage, when his position had been less secure, both to the Roumanians and the Saxons. The former had petitioned him in February 1849 for a national territory analogous to that promised to the Serbs, and in June, for the constitution of a Roumanian autonomous territory under Habsburg rule, comprising all the Roumanians in the Monarchy. Francis Joseph had never promised them a territory, but he had promised them 'equal rights and organic institutions, in accordance with their needs and the unity of the Monarchy'. To the Saxons, he had promised the maintenance of their old liberties in words which, on their natural interpretation, would have implied full self-government in a territory which might even constitute a separate Crownland. The Government seems to have had no qualms about breaking its word to the Roumanians, for it made no motions whatever towards giving them any 'organic institutions' of a political nature, but it did, for a brief while, seem to feel itself obligated to the Saxons, for the first Transylvanian 'Provisorium' made the Sachsenboden into separate Kreis, and allowed the Saxon 'University' to meet. A revised edition, however, cancelled this politically scandalous arrangement, which,

---

[1] The official designation was *Regierungsbezirk* (German) or *Kerület* (Hungarian). Both words are usually translated 'District', but that term is used also for much smaller units, and 'province' is a more appropriate word for these formations.

[2] Generally, a County was equated with a Kreis and a *járás* with a Bezirk.

it must be admitted, was also inconvenient, since the Sachsenboden did not constitute a geographical continuum. The Kreise were abolished altogether and the country divided into twenty *Bezirkshauptmannschaften*, directly under the Gubernium, whose powers were thus equated with those of a Landesregierung. The Saxon University was dissolved, and the administration, here too, was made exclusively bureaucratic; and here, too, German was made (or rather, confirmed, following the practice already introduced by Wohlgemuth) the inner language. The centralization was even a little more complete than in Inner Hungary, for the Governor, Prince Carlos Schwarzenberg (the Minister President's cousin) was also commander of the military forces.

The definitive Patent for the Voivodina came last of all, in July 1851. It confirmed the purely autocratic dispositions of its predecessor. The Serbs received no political self-government of any sort. The 'Vice-Voivode' doubled the offices of civilian governor and G.O.C. the military forces, the Government thinking the precaution necessary in view of the presence in and near the Voivodina of so many 'dangerous elements'.

Since the fiscal and economic integration of Hungary into the Monarchy had now been completed, the Patent for the Voivodina made complete (except as regards Lombardy-Venetia) the 'unification of the Lands and races of the Monarchy in one great body politic' which Schwarzenberg had announced to be his programme.

The extension of the new regime to the Hungarian Lands had, of course, been a much larger task than the introduction of it into the Western Lands. There, few, if any, changes had been necessary among the professional civil servants, and to change Standing Committees of locally elected authorities, or magistrates paid by manorial lords, into Government employees, had required a mere stroke of the pen. In most of them, moreover, the designation of German as the inner language of administration had been no innovation, since it had long occupied that position in the Czech and Slovene areas, not to speak of the German.

But in the Hungarian Lands the substitution of autocratic-bureaucratic rule for the old self-governing institutions had meant a genuine change of system, and the linguistic requirements had also been a real innovation. To these difficulties had been added the reluctance of many Hungarians to serve under the new regime, and the suspicion with which the Government regarded those who professed themselves willing. To ask whether the reluctance begat the suspicion, or vice-versa, is to ask whether the hen preceded the egg, for while it is certainly true that Bach's hand was often forced by the difficulty of finding Hungarians both willing and qualified to serve him;[1] it

[1] Of 117 applicants for posts in the Commissioner's office in June 1850, only 9 were Magyars. All the others were from Western Lands (80 of them from Bohemia) (Berzeviczy, op. cit., p. 267).

is equally certain that he and his colleagues jumped at every opportunity to
break the political influence of the old Hungarian ruling class. In any case,
many Hungarians boycotted the new system; others who volunteered to
serve it had their offers rejected out of doubts of their reliability; others,
after the introduction of the Provisorium, were failed on the language test
(which was rigorously applied in Hungary) or for inability to master their
duties. Some of the gaps were filled by Swabians, a few by Slovaks, or, in
Transylvania, by Saxons, but qualified and reliable Hungarian-born men
were thin on the ground, and the regime, unreluctantly, resorted to importation, so that within a few months of the end of the Provisorissimum, a
substantial proportion of the civil servants, high and low, governing Hungary
and Transylvania for the regime, the magistrates judging them and the
tax-collectors garnering (or trying to garner) their resources, were not only
non-Magyars, but non-Hungarians: Czechs (these provided the largest
contingent), German-Bohemians, Slovenes or even Poles.[1]

By this time Galicia had received, in practice although not on paper, a
status of its own. Zaleski had resigned after the *blamage* which his policy had
suffered through the November rising, and the province had remained for a
little while under exclusively military control. The Government, however,
still clung to the hope of conciliating the Poles, and on 9 April 1849, appointed
Goluchowski civilian Governor of the Province. This was an important move,
and one which proved in the event the first step towards the peculiar
relationship which existed during the rest of the Monarchy's existence
between the Monarchy and its Poles, for Goluchowski, first of his nation,
possessed both the will to sponsor a policy of activism and the authority to
enforce it. His task was not easy, for the idea of activism was still unpopular
among the Polish nobles and its corollary, the relaxation of complete
centralist control over Galicia, equally unpopular among the Viennese
centralists. He was, however, a favourite both with the Archduchess Sophie
and the Emperor himself[2] and with their support was able to secure many
concessions. He got the subdivision of Galicia cancelled and the province
re-established as a single unit, centralized on Lemberg.[3] The Ruthenes' protests had obtained the revocation, on 4 December 1848, of Zaleski's first
attempt to effect the near-complete Polonization of secondary and higher

---

[1] In Transylvania the immigrant officials were currently known as 'Galicians'. They were probably recruited largely from among the sons of German officials in Galicia.

[2] *Cambridge History of Poland*, II. 431. Goluchowski had been educated in the Jesuit school at Tarnopol and was a strong Catholic, which may have contributed to the Archduchess's partiality towards him.

[3] There were, however, thereafter, endless administrative manipulations, some of them involving the Bukovina, with which the reader need not be troubled. In the late 1850s Cracow again had its separate Gubernium, which was only finally abolished by Goluchowski in 1860, when he was Minister of State.

education in Galicia,[1] and Bach saw to it that the University of Lemberg should remain German, but Goluchowski resisted the Germanization of the University of Cracow, secured the establishment of a Chair of Polish at Lemberg, and kept secondary education in Eastern Galicia mainly Polish, even during the later period of Germanization.

The completion of the administrative pattern for the Lands of the Hungarian Crown should have made it possible for the Austrian Government to turn its serious attention to the putting into force of the political chapters of the Constitution, and there seems no doubt that up to the middle of 1850, at the latest, most if not all of the Ministers not only expected but hoped that they would soon be so engaged. Schmerling was a constitutionalist in principle, and both he and Bruck believed that a central Parliament was necessary if the Monarchy was to achieve political unity. Krausz thought that the foreign bankers would not give Austria credit without Parliamentary control of the Budget. Bach, willingly as he served autocracy later, was not pressing for its introduction in 1850, and there is no proof that he desired it. Even Thun, although anything but a democrat, held (as did Krausz) that Schwarzenberg's promises, and Francis Joseph's own, constituted obligations of honour which could not in decency be broken. It is never possible to say of Schwarzenberg himself when he was lying, but so far as can be judged, he had not yet turned against constitutional institutions on principle,[2] and if he had done so, he certainly did not want them abolished in Austria so long as the issue with Prussia was undecided, and opinion in the strongly democratic States of South and West Germany wavering.

Yet by now, sentence of death had already been passed on constitutionalism in the Monarchy, and by its Monarch himself. It is not our task to reconcile Francis Joseph's actions at this juncture with the punctilious sense of honour which his biographers ascribe to him, nor do we know just whose voice persuaded him that if his tongue had sworn, his mind had remained oathless. But it is quite certain that by 1850 at the latest he had convinced himself that whatever words Schwarzenberg had put into his mouth on his accession, it was both his right and his duty to ignore them, and to make himself absolute ruler of his dominions.

The carpenter of the ladder up, or down, which Francis Joseph climbed to his objective was Kübeck, whom, as the years advanced, various psychological reasons among which may be reckoned snobbish pleasure at the

[1] The Government had then decreed that Ruthene should be used in the gymnasia in Ruthene areas as far as, and as soon as, possible. Where this was still impracticable, instruction was to be in German, 'since national feeling among the Ruthenes is less hostile to the German language, than to the Polish' (Fischel, *Sprachenrecht*, No. 178).

[2] His contemptuous term of the 'Mis-Constitution' and ugly pun (*Misverfassung* = mis-Constitution, *Mistverfassung* = dung Constitution) seem to have been levelled, not at Stadion's work, but at the Kremsier draft, his dislike of which he never hid.

deference with which he, the provincial tailor's son, was being treated by Metternich, with whom he had struck up a close friendship, Windisch-Graetz, and the Imperial family itself, and an inordinate vanity which had been deeply wounded when Schwarzenberg had preferred Krausz to him[1] when composing his Ministerial team, had turned from the enlightened youth which he had once been into a devotee of the most complete absolutism. Already in Olmütz he had opposed Stadion's plan for a Constitution, recommending instead the proclamation of a state of siege throughout the Monarchy, with Windisch-Graetz as dictator,[2] and he was now pleased to regard Bach as a dangerous revolutionary, and Schwarzenberg as little better, 'since he depended on Bach, while supposing himself to lead him'. He was no kinder to the other Ministers, and wanted to see the whole Ministerial system abolished.

The recorded history of the carpentry begins on 19 October 1850, when Kübeck, who had just returned to Vienna from Frankfurt, where for some months past he had been representing Austria on the Federal Council, was summoned to the Imperial presence, told by Francis Joseph that he had decided to call into being the Reichsrat, or Advisory Council, for which the Stadion Constitution provided, and instructed to produce draft statutes for that body, defining its competences, and proposals for its membership.[3] When, after talking to Schwarzenberg, Kübeck came back on 1 November with his first blueprint, he was told that he was himself to be President of the new body.

We do not know what considerations, nor whose voice, had led the Emperor to these decisions,[4] and it is possible that at this juncture Francis Joseph had still nothing more radical in mind than to bring into being an

[1] Krausz had also offended Metternich, who inspired many of Kübeck's moves, by insisting on an inquiry into some of Metternich's financial transactions, and by haggling over his pension.

[2] Hübner, pp. 248–9.

[3] The Constitution had left these questions to be settled by subsequent legislation.

[4] It is remarkable that we should have to write this, but such is the case. Redlich, who promises us (*Problem*, I. 1. 387) 'a detailed account of the genesis of the Reichsrat', contrives, when he does give the account (id., I. 2. 111 ff.), not even to raise the question of original authorship, much less answer it. Older historians such as Friedjung believed the suggestion to have come from Schwarzenberg, but Walter's account (op. cit., pp. 438 ff.) shows this to be a mistake. When Kübeck first saw Schwarzenberg, after his first audience with the Emperor, the Minister President was 'aware of the situation, but obviously not entranced by it'. He thought that the Reichsrat might relieve the Ministerial Council of some work, but was anxious that it should not become dangerous. Bach hoped that it might 'prove a transitional move towards activating the Constitution'. But Kübeck himself did not produce the idea; he only took advantage of his opportunity. It is not impossible that the idea of using the Reichsrat as a lever to overthrow the rest of the Constitution came from Metternich, who had by now moved to Brussels and was deep in his favourite employment of teaching everyone else their business. At any rate, if he did not originate the plan, he warmly approved it (Srbik, *Metternich*, II. 368).

institution, headed by a figure, which would give the foreign moneylenders that confidence in Austria's credit which Krausz was arguing to be essential, without Krausz's remedy of a Parliament (we shall find the Emperor thinking and acting along very similar lines ten years later). If this was the object, Kübeck, who was in any case the obvious man to draft the blueprint (it was he who had secured the insertion of the provisions for a Reichsrat in the Constitution, and had then written a memorandum on the subject), was also, apart from the fact that he was at the time Austria's principal elder statesman outside the Ministerial ring, a particularly suitable candidate for the Presidency of the new body, for he had the reputation of being a financial wizard, and of being on good terms with the financial world.

If, however, Francis Joseph's thoughts were still halting at this point on 1 November, they soon advanced beyond it. As early as the 19th he told Kübeck, at another audience, that the Reichsrat was to 'supersede, and in a certain sense replace, the Constitution', and Kübeck got the impression that 'they' (*man*) wanted, and wanted strongly, to be rid of the scaffolding of 4 March, and did not know how to do it. He showed them. In memoranda which he now submitted to the Emperor, he attacked the very root of the constitutional principle by arguing that responsibility belonged to the Monarch alone. Ministerial responsibility must therefore be abolished. The Ministers were not even to be the Monarch's direct advisers. There was to be no Ministerial Council; Ministers were to forward all proposed legislation, in any field, to the Reichsrat, which was to be composed of eminent elder statesmen, and only after that body had given its advisory opinion should the file go up to the Monarch for his decision. The Ministers would thus sink to the position of Departmental heads, similar to that occupied half a century earlier by the heads of the Hofstellen and Hofkanzleien *vis-à-vis* the Staatsrat, of which Kübeck's Reichsrat was, in fact, a simple re-hash.

The Reichsrat was duly called into being in April 1851 and some of its members appointed, but prolonged and envenomed argument, with which the reader need not be troubled, went on between Kübeck on the one hand, and the Ministers on the other, over the relationship between the Ministry and the Reichsrat, with which the question of Ministerial responsibility, and thus, that of constitutionalism versus absolutism, was taken as bound up. In the course of this, Schmerling and Bruck resigned (24 January and 23 May), their places being taken by Karl Krausz (Philip Krausz's brother) and Baumgartner respectively. On 17 August, Francis Joseph gave his decision – of the significance of which he was well aware[1] – on the point of principle in favour of Kübeck, whereupon Philip Krausz resigned also, although consenting to remain in office provisionally (his resignation became effective on 31 December, when Baumgartner took over his portfolio also). The other

---

[1] 'Today', he wrote to his mother, 'we have taken a long step forward. We have thrown our constitutional stuff overboard' (Schnürer, p. 160).

Ministers, to Kübeck's malicious enjoyment, bit on the bullet and swallowed their scruples. The Constitution had not yet been formally abolished, but the conclusion of the Dresden Agreements had already removed one of Schwarzenberg's arguments for further delay, and when Louis Napoleon brought off his *coup* in Paris on 2 December, Francis Joseph refused to wait any longer. On 31 December 1851, he issued what was generally known thereafter as the 'Sylvester Patent',[1] although it consisted actually of three documents, all addressed by the Emperor to Schwarzenberg. In the first, Francis Joseph informed his Minister that the March Constitution was cancelled, except that the provisions enacting the equality of all citizens before the law, and the liberation of the peasants from servile dues (subject to equitable compensation for the ex-landlords), remained in force. The Emperor now assumed full and exclusive political responsibility for the conduct of all public affairs. The second cancelled the 'fundamental rights' guaranteed to the peoples of Austria in March 1849, with the saving clause that all 'recognized' Churches and religious communities were still guaranteed freedom of worship and the enjoyment and management of their own property.[2] The third, consisting of thirty-six paragraphs, described what was to be the future political, administrative and judicial organization of the Monarchy, and the principles on which it was to be governed.

This last document represented the purest embodiment of reaction, in the strictest sense of the term, which its authors could devise. A Commission presided over by Kübeck had been painfully going through the entire public law of the Monarchy, marking down for elimination not only anything which allowed for any popular representation or control, but anything (the two measures mentioned in the first Patent excepted) which, even if free from this taint and *prima facie* beneficial, yet owed its origin, directly or indirectly, to the abominable revolution of 1848. Consequently, the administrative and judicial hierarchies promulgated in July 1849 were to survive, above the lowest level; but since the principle of the separation of the judicature from the executive was a product of revolutionary thought, the separate political and judicial Bezirke were to be replaced by 'mixed Districts' (*Gemischte Bezirke*) and the administration and justice alike, on the lowest level, to be entrusted to Bezirksämter acting in both capacities.

The other change in the pattern was that large noble allodial estates could, under conditions to be determined in each land, be taken out of the communal organization and brought directly under the Bezirk. The nobles were, incidentally, promised favourable treatment in the formation of entails.

The Landtag Statutes were cancelled; there were to be no representative bodies on any level – Central, Land, Kreis or Bezirk (only the Communal

---

[1] i.e. New Year's Eve Patent (*Sylvesterabend*=New Year's Eve).

[2] Kübeck, the chief author of the three documents, had wanted to include here equality for the Jews, but Francis Joseph himself had struck this out.

Councils, being a traditional institution, and no product of revolution, remaining in being, but without autonomy). The hereditary landed nobles, the larger and smaller landed proprietors and representatives of 'industry' were, however, to be allowed to furnish advisers to the Land and Kreis authorities.[1]

Another casualty was the principle of 'freedom of national development' and of inter-national and inter-linguistic equality, although the practical effects which would result, in administration and education, were not described.

Practically all Schmerling's reforms, including trial by jury and interlocutory procedure, were abolished. Austrian law, both civil and criminal, was now definitely extended to the Hungarian Lands.

The Patents thus inaugurated a period of true personal absolutism, and an event which occurred soon after made it more personal still. On 5 April 1852, Schwarzenberg died with extreme suddenness. Francis Joseph, who mourned him very deeply, at first thought of making Bach Minister President, but the Minister's aristocratic and military enemies, with whom Kübeck associated himself, raised strong objections, and after hearing them, Francis Joseph, who felt that 'he could not rely on anyone as he had on Schwarzenberg',[2] decided to dispense altogether with a Minister President, and keep the supreme control and co-ordination of policy in his own hands. He did, indeed, appoint a Foreign Minister, in the person of Count Buol-Schauenstein, a career diplomat, but the Emperor insisted, and made it clear, that the direction of foreign policy (which, as he then saw it, was not only the prerogative of Princes, but most efficiently conducted by personal communication between them) lay with himself. The next year, when Csorich resigned, his post, again, was not filled: Francis Joseph was his own Minister of War, the agenda of the Department being conducted chiefly by his Military Adjutant, Grünne.[3]

As Kulmer's post, too, had been abolished in January 1852, this left as Ministers, besides Buol, Bach, Thun, Karl Krausz, Baumgartner and Thinning;[4] with one quasi-Minister, for on 11 April the police was made once again into an independent instance, reporting directly to the Emperor. The blow to Bach was severe, especially as the new Chief of Police, von Kempen, was his old rival and enemy. In another respect, however, he, with

[1] This paragraph was in fact never invoked.
[2] So he wrote to his mother (Schnürer, p. 179).
[3] The 'Military Adjutant' or Head of the Military Chancellery was the supreme instance for all questions relating to 'the personnel, organization and officering of the armed forces'. He represented the armed forces at all Ministerial Conferences and reported to the Emperor on all military aspects. On the psychological significance of the Emperor's step, see above, p. 410.
[4] Thinning was replaced in 1853 by a civil servant, who was not given Ministerial rank.

the other Ministers, came off better than had looked likely when the Patents were issued, for Kübeck's Reichsrat proved as much of a fifth wheel as the old Staatsrat had been. While Kübeck lived, he was often called in to give advice, especially on financial questions, but the Reichsrat as such never had the slightest effect on policy. When Kübeck died suddenly, on 11 September 1855, it was put into cold storage. The name, as will be seen, was revived five years later to preserve the appearance of historic continuity, and even survived until 1918 as the official title of the 'Austrian' Parliament, but the bodies which it designated in its later avatars differed essentially from Kübeck's creation. Meanwhile, the Ministerial Council behaved as though no Reichsrat existed.

In spite of the loss of the police, Bach was still the man in charge of most of the internal services of the Monarchy, even if the principles which he now had to put into execution were not of his devising, but Kübeck's. In this sense the decade of absolutism deserves the name by which it is commonly known, of the 'Bach era'. In another sense, the term flatters him, for his role was in any case confined to internal affairs, and even there it was rather to devise the machinery for carrying out the Emperor's will, than himself to dictate policy (it is true that then as later, Francis Joseph concerned himself little with the details of internal affairs, concentrating on foreign policy and defence as the Monarch's traditional field, and at home, insisting only on the principle of absolutism).

More important, ultimately, than Bach were those persons whose influence over Francis Joseph was strong enough to mould his outlook on affairs, and his will. After Schwarzenberg's death, three persons appear to have exercised such an influence. One was his mother, with whom (and with his unimportant father) he still shared his family life up to his marriage, and even, disastrously, after it; her influence, however, was mainly indirect: she did not intervene on specific issues of policy, unless where the Church was concerned. The second was his old tutor, Rauscher; the third was Grünne, who contrived to make his office much more than a military one, and between whom and the Emperor there soon developed a relationship curiously resembling that between Francis I and his old tutor, Colloredo; it had even begun in a similar way, for Grünne, before his military appointment, had for a couple of years been Francis Joseph's 'Head Chamberlain' (*Kammervorsteher*), an office closely resembling that of tutor.[1] Much the older man of the two (he was born in 1808), Grünne quickly acquired a strong ascendancy over the younger man's mind, and soon not only made himself dictator of the whole military machine of the Monarchy, but much more; for since,

---

[1] He had first been Head Chamberlain to the Archduke Stephen, but had resigned when Stephen identified himself too closely with Hungarian nationalism in March 1848. This had endeared him to the Archduchess Sophie, who in June 1848, when Bombelles retired, had got Grünne given his post.

as one of Francis Joseph's biographers has written,[1] the Emperor himself 'regarded his monarchic office as primarily a kind of military command', and therefore actually preferred that many political questions should be settled through military channels, Grünne became Francis Joseph's real private secretary, and his voice became from month to month more decisive in determining his young master's views, decisions and dispositions in all possible fields.

Like Colloredo, Grünne was an extreme conservative, permeated with pride of birth, for whom the 'common people' meant simply nothing. He also represented in extreme form the military mentality of his own day, which regarded, and depicted, the army as (outside the Catholic Church, of which he was a devout member) the only reliable support of the dynasty; and he strongly encouraged Francis Joseph in this view, already implanted in him by Schwarzenberg. Unhappily, he also shared with Colloredo an extreme mediocrity of brain, with which, it must be said, he coupled great diligence and a genuine devotion to his young master.

Actually, once the 'mixed Districts' had been established, there was little to be done to the internal services, except in two respects. Firstly, German was now the official language of the Monarchy, and although communications to the public in non-German districts were still accompanied by translations into the local language, the German text was the official one. Corresponding changes were made in the language of education. Primary instruction was still given, in principle, in the pupil's mother tongue, but even here, 'mixed' schools multiplied. German became a compulsory subject of instruction in all secondary schools in the Monarchy, including Lombardy-Venetia, and outside those provinces it became the predominant language of instruction in all secondary schools, and almost the exclusive one in High Schools.

Secondly, the last remaining geographical leak in the system, outside Lombardy-Venetia, was plugged. On 19 January 1853 the *Provisoria* in the Hungarian Lands were turned into *Definitiva*. This made no practical difference in Inner Hungary, Transylvania or the Voivodina, but Croatia was now brought into line with other Lands. It was divided into six Regierungsbezirke, each under a head nominated from Vienna. German became the inner language here also. A Commission arrived to screen the officials, and those found not up to standard were sent to learn German or dismissed, the same army of foreign replacements (in this case, chiefly Slovenes from Carniola) arriving as had already flooded other Hungarian Lands. Jellačić was made Count and left as Statthalter of the Crownland, but his position was as empty as that of other holders of the office; he devoted the greater part of his remaining years of sanity[2] to the composition of poetry.

[1] Redlich, *Franz Joseph*, p. 56.
[2] His reason, like that of Stadion and so many others, gave way; he died in 1858, a lunatic.

Meanwhile, the promised negotiations for a Concordat had been taken up, Archbishop, as he now was,[1] Rauscher acting as negotiator in chief for the Emperor. They lasted unexpectedly long, since some of the Holy See's demands were too extensive even for Rauscher, not to speak of the Ministers, and there were other difficulties.[2] Eventually, however, agreement was reached, largely through Austria's giving way to the Holy See,[3] and the instrument was signed on 4 August 1855,[4] and promulgated by Patent on 5 November. It confirmed and extended considerably the concessions previously made to the Episcopate. The Roman Catholic religion, with all its rights and prerogatives, was to be 'maintained for ever' in the whole Monarchy and all its components. The freedom of communication between the Holy See and the Austrian bishops, etc., was confirmed. The freedom of the Church in ordering its own affairs became practically unlimited. All instruction given to Catholic children, in public or private schools, had to be in conformity with the doctrines of the Church and approved by it; only men approved by the Church might teach theology in secondary or higher establishments. All teachers in Catholic schools were subject to supervision by the Church. The Church had the right to designate a book as objectionable on religious or moral grounds, and the lay arm would then prevent its circulation. The jurisdiction of the Church was restored for all questions relating to the faith and its observance, including questions of marriage law, on which the State Courts were competent only for their 'civil consequences', as was the disciplinary jurisdiction of the Bishops over their clergy, although the lay arm was entitled to arrest and punish a priest for an offence against the civil law. The Emperor promised not to tolerate any utterance derogatory to the Church, or its faith or institutions. The property of the Church was declared sacrosanct and inviolable, and the funds derived from Maria Theresa's and Joseph's confiscations were transferred to its keeping. A secret annexe contained further concessions, including the Emperor's promise not to change any confessional or inter-confessional law without the previous consent of the Holy See.

A supplementary Patent on marriage law, dated 6 October 1856, made the ecclesiastical Courts competent in this field also where both parties to a marriage were Catholics, or one a Catholic and the other a Protestant. A Bishop was empowered to prevent a marriage 'if he feared that it would give rise to serious dissension, offence or other scandal'.

[1] He was made Archbishop of Vienna in 1853, and Cardinal in 1855.
[2] Thus the Cardinal-Primate of Hungary objected tenaciously to the inclusion of Hungary in the instrument.
[3] The Austrians retreated from their first positions on eleven points relating to Church-State relations and seven relating to doctrine (*M.K.P.*, III. 173).
[4] A translation of this document will be found in Weinzierl-Fischer, pp. 250 ff.

The other important event of these years was Francis Joseph's marriage. This romantic story has been told too often to need detailed retelling here. Scores of readers know how the young Emperor's mother invited her sister, Ludovica, wife of Duke Maximilian of Bavaria, to bring her daughter Helena to a family party in Ischl, in August 1853, the intention being that Francis Joseph should marry Helena. But Ludovica included her second daughter, Elisabeth, a young girl of only sixteen, wild and tomboyish but exceedingly lovely, in the party, and Francis Joseph lost his heart to her at first sight. Bearing down all opposition, he insisted that she, and only she, should be his bride, and they were duly married on 24 April 1854, the pompous ceremonial inaugurating a tragic human relationship in which the happiness of Francis Joseph's love – deep, enduring and astonishingly romantic, in such a pedestrian nature – was constantly thwarted by his own conscientious pre-occupation with duty, Elisabeth's inexperience and waywardness, and above all, the jealous bossiness of the intolerable Archduchess Sophie.

The Concordat is usually taken as the high-water mark reached by the Austrian 'reaction', and its conclusion forms a convenient point at which to halt and look back on the achievements of the absolutist regime up to that date. They had been very large in many fields. Bach was an excellent organizer, as well as a devoted one. (Eisenmann has written of him, with justice, that while for Schwarzenberg bureaucratic absolutism was a means to an end, for Bach it was an end in itself.[1]) The instructions which he issued to his staff in respect of keeping in touch with the 'public', finding out their real needs and wishes and treating them humanly and sympathetically, are a model of their kind. Where so many new recruits had to be found and trained, it was inevitable that some mistakes should have been made, but nearly all writers testify that in the Austrian Lands the instructions had appreciable results, and that the standards of the new bureaucracy were in almost all respects noticeably higher than those of the old. This was helped by another of Bach's reforms: he secured better pay and conditions for the civil servants themselves, thereby reducing the temptations to which many of the older generation had succumbed, of taking bribes and of engaging in secondary occupations after, or even during, their office hours.

It also seems to be generally agreed that Schmerling's new magistrates were more efficient than their predecessors, and although his more modern reforms in the field of procedure were retracted, he had done good work in clearing away a jungle of antiquated backwoods Courtlets whose proceedings had not always borne much recognizable relationship to the law.[2]

[1] Op. cit., p. 162.
[2] In Carinthia, for example, no less than 497 such Courts had existed before the reform. They were replaced by twenty-nine *Bezirksgerichte* and six higher Courts.

Judgments of Thun's personal merits as a Minister vary greatly,[1] but whatever his opinions (or the view taken of them) he was certainly no fool, and he had at his right hand several very keen and able assistants. Partly owing to the very real difficulties mentioned above, comparatively little was done for the primary schools, but the Ministry carried through reforms, based on Prussian models, of the secondary and higher establishments, on which later Ministers found little to improve during the remaining half-century of the Monarchy's existence. Some of the institutions now founded, including the Austrian Institute of Historical Research, achieved enduring fame. In the wider field, the years of Thun's regime were something of a blossoming-time for several of the more backward national cultures – especially, of course, those which the regime wished to encourage as counterweights to others which were politically more dangerous.[2]

Bruck, besides the considerable feat of making the Monarchy into an economic and fiscal unity, had carried through a great amount of useful work in a number of fields. He created a network of Chambers of Commerce and Industry, whose statutes empowered them to offer the Government advice on economic questions.[3] He reorganized the postal services (concurrently concluding a postal union with Germany), developed shipping, both seaborne and on the Danube, and pushed on with the expansion of the railways, which, under his regime, were nationalized as far as possible: all new lines were constructed at State expense and run as State enterprises, and the owners of the old private lines were bought out as occasion presented itself.

In 1849 and 1850 he had also been busy preparing for the creation of the 'seventy million Reich' (of which the economic assimilation of Hungary would have been the essential preliminary). Schwarzenberg's retreat at Dresden had put paid to these larger hopes, and negotiations which Bruck then initiated with several individual German States brought no immediate result, but in connection with them he had begun preparations for a general simplification and reduction of Austrian tariffs.

After Bruck's resignation, Baumgartner carried forward, almost unaltered,

---

[1] On Thun, see also C. Thiènen-Adlerflycht, *Graf Leo Thun im Vormärz* (Graz, 1967). The Jewish Liberal historians of the later nineteenth century, who hated Thun for his clericalism and his Czech nationalism, are in general very hard on him. On the other hand, Frommelt credits him with 'extreme devotion to duty and conscientiousness' and 'passionate zeal' for his work (op. cit., p. 57).

[2] In 1859 the Czechs presented Thun with an address thanking him for what he had done for their cultural development. While the number of elementary schools remained almost static under his regime in the Austrias and Lower Bohemia, they increased by 118% in the Bukovina and by 142% in Carniola.

[3] It is interesting that these were the only forms of popular representation not abolished in the succeeding period, and that they were also retained as a separate electoral college when constitutional life recommenced (see below, p. 514).

his predecessor's policy, which must have seemed to Francis Joseph (from the encouragement which he gave it) to be conducive to the strengthening of Austria's political and strategic position. The construction of the railways was pushed on: railway mileage had risen by 1854 to 2,240 kilometres, an increase of nearly forty per cent on the 1848 figure of 1,620 kilometres; they included the remarkable railway over the Semmering Pass. All the lines in the Monarchy except two (the Rothschilds' Nordbahn and Sina's Vienna-Raab line) were now nationalized.

The import prohibitions vanished altogether, except for a few maintained on moral or medical grounds; the number of tariff duties was reduced from 614 to 338; the maximum possible duty was lowered by over 66% and the duties on a number of important articles, including pig-iron and cotton, reduced in the same proportion. Then, in 1853, although the hope of Austria's entering the Zollverein and eventually constituting a vast free trade area with Germany was off for good,[1] Buol (or rather Bruck, who conducted the negotiations for him) concluded with Prussia, and thus with the rest of the Zollverein, a commercial treaty providing for another big reduction of tariffs and mutual m.f.n. treatment for the duration of the treaty, which was fixed at twelve years.

The biggest of all the operations carried through by the Government was the implementation of the law emancipating the peasants. The recognition of the principle of equality before the law and the abolition of manorial authority had been dealt with by the reorganization of the administrative and judicial systems; it remained to determine how much the former 'subject' should pay, and how much his ex-lord should receive, in return for the abolition of payments and services formerly rendered by the former to the latter in virtue of the nexus subditelae.

The problem was examined in each Land by a Commission, consisting of two or three officials with assessors representing the landlords and peasants respectively, and local conditions and usages were found to vary so greatly that no two of the Patents eventually issued were quite identical; nor, for that matter, was the work completed (in so far as it was ever completed)[2] simultaneously in all Lands; thus the Patents establishing the funds into and out of which the compensation was to be paid were issued on 11 April 1851 for all the Hereditary and Bohemian Lands, but not until 2 March 1853 for Hungary and Croatia, 29 October 1853 for Galicia and the Bukovina, and 28 June 1854 for Transylvania.[3] But in very brief outline, what was done was this:

[1] For an account of the negotiations, see Charmatz, *Bruck*, pp. 86 ff.
[2] When the main commissions were wound up some questions of detail were left for later regulation, and not all of these had been finally settled in 1918.
[3] The reform did not extend to Lombardy-Venetia, where the nexus subditelae did not exist, nor, for the same reason, to Dalmatia.

All occupants of any piece, however small, of rustical land became freehold owners of it. The dues, payments and services formerly attaching to such holdings were divided into three categories. Those payments or privileges formerly received or enjoyed by the lord in virtue of his legal position and supposed to compensate him for the legal or administrative duties carried out by him in that capacity were simply cancelled; neither did the peasant pay compensation for his release from them, nor the lord receive it for the loss of them. The lord was, however, himself released from the expenses entailed by his former duties.

For the real rents in money, kind and services paid by the peasants for the usufruct of their holdings (this was far the most important of the three groups)[1] the principle of 'equitable compensation' (*billige Entschädigung*) was followed. In the Western Lands, the money value of these rents was assessed, the value of a day's robot being taken at one-third of that of a day's free labour, and that of the dues in kind, proportionately low. Of the resultant sum, one-third was retained by the State in lieu of the taxation formerly paid by the lord out of his rentals; the other two-thirds were paid to the lord in the form of four per cent bonds. In the Hereditary and Bohemian Lands, half of this sum (i.e., one-third of the total) was paid by the peasant, from whom the State collected it in annual instalments, half by the Land exchequer.

In Galicia and the Bukovina, the peasant paid nothing, so that the full two-thirds fell on the Land. As this burden proved too heavy for the Land exchequer, the landlords' compensation here was eventually paid by the State.

In Hungary a different method of assessment, based on the quality of the land, was adopted. In general, the landlord received about one-third of the market value of the land. Here, too, the rustical peasants paid nothing, and the whole compensation came out of the State budget.

In all cases, the landlord was released from his countervailing obligations towards his ex-tenants.

Thirdly, payments made by the peasants for communal services of value to themselves were 'redeemed' (*abgelöst*) at their full assessed value, the payment now going to the State, in the form of mortgages.

As the reform was concerned only with the liquidation of the nexus subditelae, these arrangements did not apply to ordinary lease-holding tenants of former allodial holdings. But peasants holding their land on the Raab system and other 'emphyteutic' tenures on allodial land got their land freehold, but paid both the two-thirds.

It is impossible to say exactly how much land passed into new ownership under this reform, or how many persons were affected by it in one capacity

[1] In this group was included (outside Hungary, where the Church had voluntarily renounced it) the tithe, which in most places had long ceased to be a special payment to the Church.

or the other. In the West (the Hereditary and Bohemian Lands and Galicia-Bukovina) 2,625,512 persons are listed as having 'made payments',[1] but many of these were probably only small redemption payments for communal dues.[2] Here there were 54,267 recipients, about half of whom received their payments under the heading of 'equitable compensation', the other half as 'redemptions'.[3] In Hungary, excluding Transylvania, about 625,000 peasants (i.e., all sessionati urbarial peasants, including holders of eighths of a sessio), received land, an average of 12 hold each; to which must be added a considerable number (although the area affected was small) of small vintners.[4] I have not traced the number of recipients of payments. In Transylvania, 63,940 villein peasants received between them 670,500 Magyar hold. In Galicia, 527,875 peasant holdings were liberated.

The total cost to the State of the reforms is put at 297 million gulden in Austria and 203 million gulden in Hungary-Croatia.

In Hungary, although not elsewhere, the authorities seized the occasion to carry through a much-needed consolidation of the holdings allotted to the peasants. It is true that within a few years the curse of *Streusiedlungen* was back in as virulent form as ever.

The abolition of the nexus subditelae was an act of inestimable importance. It was the first and indispensable preliminary to the modernization of the social and political structure of the Monarchy. It is greatly to Bach's credit that in the early months he insisted on it in the face of all opposition from Windisch-Graetz and his fellow-thinkers; but in the event, that opposition could not be long maintained: it soon transpired that the ex-'subjects' appreciated so widely their promotion to full citizenship as to exclude any serious thought of re-establishing either the nexus subditelae, or the rustical system of land tenure.

The economic effects of the land reform were less uniform. The first accounts of them were enthusiastic.

[1] Grünberg, *L.u.F.*, p. 70 ff.

[2] In the Tirol, where almost all the peasants were free, and only fifty days' robot had been worked in the entire Land, 278,000 persons were recorded in the list of payers. The total sums paid under these headings were, however, small; the communes in Austria only received, in the end, 29 million gulden, while 225·9 million gulden went to private landowners and 34·9 million gulden to the Church.

[3] Other figures are slightly higher: 12,872,000 'payers' and 506,975 recipients.

[4] A large proportion of the vineyards in both Hungary and Transylvania (according to Fényes's statistics, 913,410 out of 1,399,836 Magyar hold in the Kingdom and 82,415 out of 103,615 in the Grand Principality) were allodial land, but cultivated against payment of a so-called 'grape tithe' (*szölödezsma*), usually by zsellers, sometimes by villein peasants, as extensions to their holdings, occasionally even by nobles. There was a strong movement, which was supported by the more progressive nobles themselves, to equate such vineyards with villein peasant holdings, and the Hungarian Diet adopted a Resolution to this effect on 15 September 1848. This was afterwards implemented by the Austrian commissioners.

'The ex-villein,' wrote Czoernig, 'now become freehold owner of his land, is able to devote his whole labour to the cultivation and profitable exploitation of his land, while the woodlands formerly owned by him, which had been deteriorating progressively, are now preserved and rationally exploited. Capital . . . is interesting itself in real estate and fructifying big areas which were formerly insufficiently cultivated, or not at all; industry is entering into close touch with agriculture, and the improved communications provide the increased work and give the capital secure prospects of remunerative return.'[1]

This rosy picture was undoubtedly true for the thrifty and enterprising ex-villeins, especially those whose holdings were favourably situated for marketing. Such men indeed worked for themselves as they had never worked for their masters, and found the new order to offer them opportunities to enrich themselves which the old had denied them.

The change was not, however, an unmixed blessing even to the peasants. The truth soon emerged that the old landlord-peasant relationship had been less one-sided than the peasants had admitted, or perhaps even realized, since like most people, they had been more perceptive of what they gave, than of what they received. The loss of the easements which they had enjoyed on their masters' lands, and of the services which they had received, proved unexpectedly heavy; and even where, as happened in some cases, they received monetary compensation for lost rights, this was usually inadequate. Other intensely complex questions, some of which had not been finally sorted out by 1918, involving disputes not only between peasant and landlord, but also peasant and peasant, were connected with common rights and various forms of shared usufruct. Most of the common lands, which had been very important for the economy of many peasants, were now largely reduced. Some benefits here went to big peasants, more, as a rule, to the ex-landlord. The smaller peasants were the sufferers in either case.[2]

A particular difficulty for almost all the peasants was that almost all their

[1] Czoernig, *Ethnographie*, I. 501.

[2] A vigorous statement of the 'case for the prosecution' in this field can be found in the interesting book by the Austrian Social Democrat leader, Otto Bauer, *Der Kampf um Wald und Weide* (Vienna, 1925), pp. 102 ff. The Patents discussed by Bauer are:

(1) The *Forstpatent* of 1852, which gave the owner of any piece of afforested land free disposition over it, subject to the provision that it must not be de-forested.

(2) The *Jagdpatent* of 1853, which assigned the sporting rights over any land to its owner, but if it was smaller than 200 yokes, he could not exercise them himself; they were in charge of the commune, which could either exercise them itself, or lease them, the owner then receiving a share of the proceeds.

(3) The *Servitutenpatent* of 1853, which abolished the peasants' easements over the lord's forests. For these they were compensated in land, if the lord agreed, or by a cash payment, which, according to Bauer, was always below their real value. Often the change was not wanted by either party, and the old system continued in being.

The common lands were usually divided between the landlord and the commune, the usufruct of the commune's share going to the ex-rustical peasants proportionately to the size of their holdings.

transactions with authority, and in increasing measure, also those of everyday life, had to be transacted in money, to which many of them were unaccustomed, and in which they were almost regularly overreached. Even where used to small sums, they could nearly always be dazzled by large ones, not appreciating what a short way money went off the farm.

This arose particularly over the question of credit, which few of them had required in money before 1848, since it had been the landlord's obligation to see them through crop failures or extensive damage due to catastrophes of nature.[1] Now they needed it for a number of purposes: for working and improving their farms, for paying their taxes (which rose inexorably), and outside Hungary and Galicia, for paying off the purchase of their lands. They were, indeed, partially protected during the absolutist period by a law which limited the rate of interest chargeable to 5% for a mortgage, or 6% for a commercial transaction, but this law was too easily evaded, and where applied, resulted in a financial stringency which restricted the efforts precisely of the more enterprising peasants to expand.

Credit, other than surreptitious, was practically impossible for the peasant to obtain. In 1855 the National Bank was allowed to set up a mortgage department, but it was not allowed to make loans of less than 5,000 gulden. In most Lands the only other sources were the few savings banks and private bankers, and even the charitable foundations now usually preferred – or were pressed – to put their funds into State papers. The *Galizischer Ständischer Creditverein* existed, as the name implies, exclusively for the benefit of the big landowners.

In the more backward parts of the Monarchy the peasants were not money-minded at all, and their reaction to their liberation was, as we have said, to raise what they needed for themselves from their plots, and then go to sleep.[2] Nor should we underestimate the addition in human happiness that thus accrued to them; but the demands of the taxpayer drove them, after all, to earn cash, and since the local markets could not absorb more than a limited amount of their produce, they were presently back again at work on the fields of their old masters.

The picture of the general fate of the class after the reform may well contain more lights than shadows; but honesty cannot deny that it was less uniformly bright than perhaps anyone had expected in 1848, and it owed a good many of its comforting features to two provisions which in fact left their

[1] It has been stated that the only case, not, indeed, a rare one, in which a peasant ever required to borrow a substantial sum before 1848 was when he wanted to set his sons up as technical 'peasants', by buying or leasing for them farms, in order to procure for them exemption from military service.

[2] It is interesting that Leiningen (who did not object to the reform on his own account) prophesied precisely this effect on the peasants. 'Here in Becse' (in South Hungary, where his estates were), he wrote, 'there is no doubt that the peasants will reap no advantage from their liberation, for when there is no one to make them work, their innate idleness and indolence will lead them to fall a prey to speculation' (op. cit., p. 76).

complete 'liberation' imperfect: one the law mentioned above, limiting the legal rate of interest; the other, the maintenance in force, in all Lands, where it had previously existed, of the old Bestiflungszwang, which the Law of 1848 did not affect.

The effects of the reform on the landlords are closely bound up with those of the development of communications and above all, of the abolition of the internal Austro-Hungarian customs barrier. Here, again, the picture is full of contrasts. Those landlords who were already operating a market economy were only too glad to exchange robot for compensation (which in their case was usually paid promptly and often amounted to large sums),[1] which could be usefully employed on modernization. The big Hungarian wheat-growers and cattle-farmers scored doubly, since they were now able to place practically all their produce on the Austrian market, where it did not go abroad. Many of them took advantage of the situation to develop their estates into very efficient and profitable enterprises. Many of the big German-Austrian and Bohemian landlords answered this intensified competition from Hungary by reducing their acreage under cereals, dropping altogether the farming of their marginal lands, and concentrating on cash crops, such as sugar-beet, raised on their best lands, and on the exploitation of their forests; and these, too, proved profitable devices.

For the smaller landlords, especially those of Galicia and Hungary, who had not owned the capital to employ hired labour and had thus really depended on the robot, the land reform often proved a sheer disaster. They were given no advances on their compensation, for which they often had to wait many years. The peasants asked rates for working outside their land which were much higher than the landlords could afford to pay; in many places they could not be induced to work for any consideration whatever – they simply took enough out of their own holdings to satisfy their unexacting needs and then went to sleep. Private credit cost 30–40% a year. This class was largely ruined: in Hungary something like twenty thousand distraints took place in a single generation. Their difficulties were, indeed, the opportunity of the strong; the land which came on the market was bought by their richer neighbours, either directly or at second-hand, after the transaction had enriched a Jewish speculator *en passant*,[2] so that one effect of the land reform was to increase the disproportionate share of the land, especially but by no means exclusively in Hungary, held in mammoth estates.

It is true that this, like the opening up of neglected woodlands to rational exploitation, of which Czoernig writes with appreciation, must indeed be

---

[1] The total amount paid in compensation in Cis-Leithania alone was no less than 230 million gulden. The Schwarzenberg family alone received 1,870,000 m.g. for its seven main estates (607,000 g. for the Krumslov estate alone); the Assems, of Styria, 1,236,000 g.

[2] Jewish speculation in land went on on such a scale that in 1853 the Government forbade the sale of land to Jews. This measure had very important effects described below, p. 484.

counted, on balance, as a profit from the Mancunian point of view, in so far as it tended to place the national resources of the country in the hands of those able to exploit them most efficiently, but in this respect as in others, the conquerors' chariot passed over the bodies of innumerable victims.

The effects on the other branches of the Austrian economy of the various economic measures of the time – the land reform, the fiscal unification of the Monarchy, the liberalization of the tariff policy, the development of communications, etc. – were, again, not uniform. It was a time of rapid modernization, and as always in such periods, the gains of the strong were made in part at the expense of the weak. The weak, it may be said at once, included both the small independent craftsmen and the factory workers. The Church did use its influence to prevent the abolition of the guilds, which thus did not take place until 1859,[1] but otherwise, in spite of its strong position, did nothing to check the Mancunian ruthlessness of the Ministries and the employers. Cardinal Rauscher's ultra-conservative philosophy rejected the principle of Christian brotherhood, and while it admitted that of Christian paternalism, it did little to enforce it.

Thus the small men were continually on the defensive; the complaints of the Viennese artisans against the competition of sweated factory labour were as bitter in the 1850s as they were to be in the 1880s. For the factory workers, the gains which some of them had achieved in 1848, which had never been statutory, disappeared when 'order' was restored, leaving hours and conditions of labour almost completely unregulated and wages dependent purely on the relation between supply and demand. The bright side of the picture for them was that demand was usually good and the acute crises of technological unemployment which had blackened the previous decade did not recur.

The new conditions brought the collapse of many of the smaller Hungarian industries, driven out of the field by Austrian competition, and even of some Austrian firms which had owed their previous survival to import prohibitions or near-prohibitive tariffs. On the other hand, entrepreneurs who possessed the resources, enterprise and intelligence to take advantage of the new freedom and the widened opportunities, profited substantially. The stronger Austrian industries gained more from the opening up of the Hungarian market than they lost from the weak Hungarian competition. Many of them also gained considerably from the freer trade with Prussia, for certain branches of Austrian industry, especially the textile, were at that time stronger than their Prussian counterparts. For several years, moreover, the discount on silver at which the gulden was quoted acted as an export premium. A large number of new industries were founded, especially in Bohemia and Moravia, and production in some fields rose very rapidly.

---

[1] See below, p. 501, n. 1. A draft *Gewerbeordnung* had been prepared in 1854, but laid aside 'since it was soon outdated by the general national economic development' (Czoernig, I. 338).

Both textiles and woollens enjoyed a long boom. Heavy industry received a big stimulus from the expansion of the railways: the production of iron, pig and cast, in the Monarchy rose from 2,985,000 tons in 1849 to 5,269,143 in 1854; that of coal, from 17,352,825 tons to 37,345,827.

It should be added that although the biggest gains were made by the Bohemian Lands and Lower Austria, the balance-sheet even of Hungary was not entirely passive. The absolutist era itself regarded the Monarchy as a unit from the point of view of planning, and, partly out of strategic considerations, did even more to improve Hungarian communications than those of the West, and in connection therewith, Hungary had her share in the expansion of mining and heavy industry. Furthermore, the economic unification of the Monarchy made Austrian capitalists and entrepreneurs, where not held back by considerations of national patriotism (and the wealthier a capitalist, the less, as a rule, did such considerations weigh with him) perfectly willing to invest capital in any Hungarian industry which promised to yield good returns. Thus the same years which witnessed the destruction of some Hungarian industries saw a rapid development of others for which natural conditions were favourable – flour-milling (this above all), brewing, etc.[1]

On balance, therefore, the period was one of prosperity and expansion for the industry of the Monarchy, and as a corollary thereof, also for its trade. The net imports of the Monarchy (Dalmatia excluded) rose from 92,480,787 gulden in 1849 to 219,165,017 in 1854; exports even more largely from 62,428,820 to 228,924,871. There are no figures for internal trade, but it may be assumed to have increased at least as fast.

A feature of this development which was to prove very important for the future of the Monarchy was the active part which mobile capital now, for the first time, began to play in it. The Rothschilds passed through an eclipse after 1848, and were even for a while unrepresented in Vienna,[2] but their Parisian rivals, the Pereires, saw money in the country and, sometimes in association with Baron Sina, financed a number of enterprises there. Besides this, a private Austrian bank, the *Niederoesterreichische Eskomptegesellschaft*, founded in 1853, did creditable business. Then in 1855 Bruck got together with the Rothschilds, who were now desirous of driving the Pereires and Sina out of the field (old Salomon Rothschild had just died and his son, Anselm, had succeeded to the Paris branch of the business). In November 1855 a

[1] The growth of factory industry in these years was actually faster in Hungary than in Cis-Leithania. See the irrefutable figures given by Futó, op. cit., p. I. 301, which show that the number of machines worked by steam in Hungary rose from 79, with 1,175 h.p., in 1852 to 480, with 8,134 h.p., in 1863. The figures for the rest of the Monarchy were: 1852, 551 machines with 6,298 h.p.; 1863, 2,361 machines with 36,276 h.p.

[2] The popular antagonism in 1848 against Salomon Rothschild had been so formidable that he had fled the country, to which he did not return. The Austrian Ambassador in Paris, Hübner, surprisingly, in view of his alleged origin (he is reputed to have been a natural son of Metternich's), preferred the Pereires and Sina to the Rothschilds.

great new private bank, the *Creditanstalt,* was opened in Vienna under Bruck's auspices, and with Rothschild help. It was a grandiose enterprise, which numbered among its directors, besides the Rothschilds, persons bearing such historic names as Schwarzenberg, Fürstenberg, Auersperg and Chotek.[1] Founded largely to enable the State to sell its railways, in the fashion described below, the new bank also did much general business, and the fortunes of many leading citizens of the Monarchy became bound up with it.

There were, however, two Departments of State which showed less satisfactory results. One was the unfortunate Ministry of Finance. Expenditure in 1848 closed with a deficit of 64 million gulden, and 1849 was worse still; in it, military expenditure rose to the unprecedented figure of 145 m.g. – and that although the campaign in Italy was largely financed through levies on the population,[2] while the administrative services were already costing 56.6 m.g. and the judiciary, 4.99, and taxation brought in only 56.6 m.g.; the year closed with a deficit of 154 m.g. Krausz (who rejected Kübeck's idea of applying again to the Rothschilds) helped himself through by various devices, including fresh borrowing from the National Bank, the flotation of more loans, and the issue of various forms of assignats, which, however, were quoted on foreign bourses at a discount of 8%. He also introduced a new income tax and raised existing taxes, and as these now applied to Hungary, revenue in 1850 showed an increase; receipts from taxation rose to 158 m.g. in 1850 and 184 m.g. in 1851, total ordinary revenue from those years being 180.3 and 205.8 m.g. The war indemnity from Piedmont brought in another 75 m.g. in silver, out of which the Government was able to repay about half its debt to the Bank. Ordinary military expenditure was also slightly lower, but still far above the pre-revolution level, and there were substantial items of 'extraordinary' military expenditure, including 15.2 m.g. on armaments, 2.4 on the dispatch of an army corps to Germany and 2.3 on payment to Russia for the cost of her intervention in Hungary. Ordinary civilian expenditure continued to rise: the cost of the administrative services was 72.8 m.g. in 1850 and 92.9 in 1851 and that of the judiciary, 10.99 and 17.53 respectively. In addition, large sums were being spent on the railways – a total of about 255 m.g. between 1849 and 1855. Thus there was still a deficit – met by further borrowing – of 80 m.g. in 1850 and of over 50 in 1851, and the premium on silver rose to 150 in November 1850 (on the eve of Olmütz) and was still 133 at the end of the month, and averaged 126 in 1851.

Baumgartner was, nevertheless, not entirely pessimistic when he took over

[1] The list, it will be observed, does not contain the name of Windisch-Graetz. The Prince refused to soil his fingers with 'business'.

[2] According to Reuchlin, *Geschichte Italiens,* III. 140, 422 million franks were collected in this way in Lombardy between August 1848 and December 1851, and 240 in Venetia. Friedjung, who quotes these figures (*Oe. von 1848–1860,* I. 243), does so with a certain scepticism, but agrees that in any case the deficits of the war years would have been larger 'if the war had not financed the war in Italy'.

the Ministry of Finance at the end of 1851. There would certainly be another deficit in 1852, but he hoped that the curve was flattening out. When political order was restored it would be possible to collect more of the taxes, the arrears of which were heavy in Hungary,[1] and to reach equilibrium by 1858. By that time, however, another 150 m.g. deficit would have accumulated; furthermore, the bank must be put in a position in which it would be able to resume convertibility (for which purpose the State would have to repay it its debt of 75 m.g.) and the State paper money be withdrawn from circulation. For this purpose, another 175 m.g. would be necessary.[2]

Baumgartner had various suggestions for raising the wind, including the flotation of a new loan abroad, which was in fact successful, although the terms were onerous.[3] In February 1854 (the interval seems to have been spent largely in argument between the different financial experts)[4] an agreement was reached with the Bank, which took over all the governmental paper money, to the tune of 155 m.g. It was to exchange this gradually for its own notes, the Government pledging itself, once again, to issue no more paper money, and to pay back the 155 m.g. at the rate of 10 m.g. yearly.

But meanwhile the deficits had, as always, turned out larger than expected: not far short of 150 m.g. in the three years 1851–3 alone, making the State's total deficit since 1848, on ordinary and extraordinary expenditure, something like 920 m.g.[5] And 1854 brought, as we shall see, a further turn for the worse.

The other Department of State which entirely failed to keep pace with the demands of the new age was, curiously enough, that of defence. Both

[1] 67% of the taxes from Inner Hungary were in arrears, 68% from the Voivodina, and 52% from Transylvania (Beer, op. cit., p. 236).
[2] Ibid.
[3] It was issued at 94, to bear 5% interest. The date was May 1852.
[4] See Beer, op. cit., pp. 237 ff.
[5] Czoernig's *Ethnographie* (a remarkable work which contains information on much more than ethnography) gives on Vol. I. p. 325, the ordinary budgets for 1848–53 as follows:

Millions of gulden

	Revenue	Expenditure	Deficit
1848	122	167	45
1849	144	190	46
1850	194	230	36
1851	220	261	41
1852	226	275	49
1853	237	286	49

But besides this, the State had by the end of 1854 incurred extraordinary expenditure as follows:

On the amortization of the funded and floating debt	290 m.g.
On 'extraordinary armaments and costs of intervention'	241 m.g.
On railways and telegraphs	125 m.g.

This had been covered by loans, advances from the Banks and issue of uncovered paper money, together with a few 'extraordinary' receipts, these consisting largely of the proceeds of sales of State property.

Grünne and Gyulai, who was Grünne's favourite and nominee as Minister of War (later, and disastrously, as Commander-in-Chief in Italy), were guilty of many faults. Perhaps the worst of all was their favouritism: in particular, their assumption that high social rank entitled its possessor to high military command. The senior posts in the army, the number of which doubled, were distributed between members of great families, nearly all of whom were equally lacking in military knowledge, and capacity. Neither Grünne nor Gyulai had ever seen active service, and the training which was prescribed to the troops consisted almost exclusively of spit and polish. The equipment of the army was equally neglected, and it was widely and circumstantially alleged that under Grünne's careless eye, gross extravagances were committed in the administration of the defence budgets and that unscrupulous contractors made fortunes at the expense of the troops.

In any case, all these measures, good or bad, had, as we have seen, been imposed by completely authoritarian decisions, and had been enforced by methods which permitted no contradiction. The military, where they were in charge of security – and this was often left in their hands even when the ordinary conduct of affairs had reverted to civilian authority – were entirely high-handed, laying down their own disciplinary rules, making their own arrests and conducting their own trials. They were assisted by a new force of gendarmerie which Bach had called into being as one of his first acts as Minister of the Interior;[1] and while there was undoubtedly room for such a force – for before its creation, public security had, in most parts of the Monarchy, been left to the local authorities, whose efficacy in safeguarding it had left much to be desired,[2] it had not been used only for its nominal purpose of maintaining public safety (in which, when it was extended to

[1] The Order establishing it was issued on 8 June 1849. The force then consisted of thirteen battalions (afterwards raised to nineteen.)

[2] The Liberal historians of the period, such as Rogge, represent Bach's gendarmerie as simply a new instrument of political oppression, called into being for that purpose, but the improvement of public security had long been an item on the programmes of many reformers, for the existing forces maintained for the purpose in most parts of the Monarchy had been notoriously inadequate, where they existed at all. A para-military gendarmerie had been introduced by the French into Lombardy and the Trentino, during their rule there, and had been kept in being under Austrian rule, on the urgent advice of F. M. Bellegarde. There was an analogous civilian body, of similar origin, in Venetia, and as we have seen, a special force had been created in Galicia in 1847. In most parts of the Monarchy, however, security had been left to the Patrimonial Courts or the Estates, most of which maintained only a handful of men, chiefly for the purpose of arresting criminals (in Hungary these were called Pandurs), the military being called in when such phenomena as highway robbery became indecently prevalent. A few of the larger towns kept their own police forces, which appear to have been of the Dogberry type.

It must, however, be said that none of the foreign travellers who toured the Monarchy in the first half of the nineteenth century, and published records of their experiences, appear to have been molested. Many of them have complaints of 'impudent' inn-keepers, postmasters and drivers, but all seem to have come through their adventures unscathed.

Hungary, it proved singularly ineffective, for the population combined against it, and banditry flourished as never before), but as a political instrument. It was particularly unfortunate that a gendarme arresting a person who was then judicially sentenced received a graduated premium rising from four florins for a prison sentence of less than a year to sixty florins for a death sentence. The ordinary police had been largely reinforced, and under Kempen, also worked in the military spirit which took a real delight in showing the strong hand to civilians.

Spies and informers abounded, and a close watch was kept on all suspicious elements. The press was under strict censorship.

The severity of the regime relaxed only very gradually: in the first couple of years it rather increased as the security services got into their stride. The censorship was stricter in 1851 than it had been in 1850. An attempt made on Francis Joseph's life, on 18 February 1853, by a Hungarian tailor named János Libényi, resulted in a new intensification of the police terror, not in Hungary alone.

It is true that martial law was lifted from Vienna and Prague on 1 September 1853, and that Francis Joseph's marriage the next year was made the occasion for many acts of clemency. A large-scale amnesty was enacted, and on 1 May, martial law was lifted from Lombardy-Venetia, Galicia, Inner Hungary, Croatia and the Voivoidina, leaving only Transylvania under it[1] (and this exception was removed on 15 December). But in general, the hand of authority grew little lighter. A new Press Law, enacted in 1854, was even severer than its predecessor, and another law proscribed almost every form of association. The changes enacted in the civilian law after the Sylvester Patent included the reintroduction of corporal punishment for 'workmen and servants', on the ground that this was traditional in Hungary, and indispensable there, and that it was unfair to make a distinction between Hungary and the rest of the Monarchy.

The ultimate question for the Monarchy was, of course, whether its peoples could be brought to accept absolutist rule, and – more fundamental still – the ideology of the a-national State. Up to 1854–5 the prospects had seemed not unfavourable in the Hereditary and Bohemian Lands. The embers of the revolution had smouldered on in Vienna for some weeks or months after the fall of the city. Survivors of the heroic October days met in cafés and wineshops which were regarded as safe, recognizing one another by codes and pass-words, to lament the past over their cups and even sometimes to indulge in pipe-dreams of the future. Since few of the rendezvous were in fact safe from the cocked ears of the innumerable police spies, the list of persons arrested for treasonable activities was a long one, and there were even some executions (although most of the unfortunates sentenced to death were

[1] This seems to have been due to the dangerous situation then prevailing in Russia.

reprieved). Prague, in these early months, was another centre of unrest, and here, too, a large number of victims suffered imprisonment or flogging (a punishment particularly favoured by the military courts, whose hand here was especially heavy). And in Prague, in April 1849, the authorities came on what they described as a serious 'conspiracy', the participants in which were punished barbarously.[1]

This 'conspiracy', however – a queer affair in which some students had struck up an underground alliance with the Left in Saxony – was almost the only seriously meant subversive move in the history of these Lands,[2] and its participants were only a handful. The vast majority of the penalties inflicted were for minor acts of insolence, or more often, for mere expressions of opinion which a more humane regime would have disregarded. And nearly all the culprits were Left-wing social and political extremists. The bourgeoisie of Vienna, large and small, was only too happy to see the spectre of Red rule banished and its city restored to the position of capital of a great Monarchy and residence of its Monarch. Factories were restarted and shops reopened, with all practicable speed. The Court, with a young and *lebensfroh* Monarch as its central figure, in place of the ailing Ferdinand and before him, the thrifty and ageing Francis, was gayer than it had been since the palmy days of Maria Theresa; the carnival of 1851 was celebrated as the most sumptuous and lighthearted that Vienna had ever known.

To the provincial bourgeois, the linked domination of Church and State was as congenial as it was familiar; while the peasants everywhere were concerned exclusively with consolidating their gains.

A few of the old Austrian Liberals produced a small oppositional literature (usually, owing to the restrictions on the Press, in pamphlet form). Most of these productions, however, came during the first months, when it was expected that the Stadion Constitution would really come into force, and were directed against features of that document of which the authors disapproved: most of them thought it too centralist. Some of them also expressed impatience at the delays in putting it into force. But as the prospects of a constitutional regime faded, interest in its nature died away, and so, to judge by the outward signs, did even interest in the institution itself. The issue of the Sylvester Patent evoked hardly a murmur;[3] the middle classes seem to have minded the clerical legislation far more than they did the political dictatorship.

[1] They were detained without trial for eighteen months, after which six of them were sentenced to death (although not, in the event, executed) and several others to long terms of penal servitude.

[2] Libényi's act seems to have been rather personal than political in its motives. Libényi's father had been hanged in 1849. A large number of Hungarians were arrested when it occurred, but no connection between any of them and Libényi was ever proved.

[3] A big police swoop in Styria in the spring of 1852 was quite unconnected with the general political situation: it was directed against the sect known as the German Catholics.

The open reactions to the new regime of disappointed national hopes were were quite astonishingly weak when it is considered that the most important of all the aspects of the regime was its refusal of any political expression to those hopes. We hear of no national unrest at all among the Slovenes. The central political organization of the Czechs protested strongly against the dissolution of the Reichstag, and after it Palacký for a while continued the struggle: at Christmas 1849, he again promulgated in the Press the idea which he had first put forward in the Reichstag, of federalizing the Monarchy on lines of nationality. When, however, the paper containing this article was suppressed, he withdrew from active politics for a decade. Rieger went into voluntary exile. Havliček, the most single-minded of them all, continued, under great difficulties, to issue another small paper, the *Slava*, until August 1851, but when that, too, was closed down,[1] he found no successor. Palacký's own party was defeated in the local elections of 1850 by moderates who favoured collaboration with the regime. Altogether, once the initial unrest in Prague had died down, Bohemia became one of the quietest areas of the Monarchy. For this, indeed, economic factors were largely responsible. Bohemia enjoyed the full benefit of the boom, which brought its business classes prosperity and its workers at least full employment, and outlets in plenty for its aspiring young men, for any of whom, if he could find no place at home, a job was waiting in Hungary, or in the gendarmerie, which was largely composed of Czechs. There is no indication that the youth of Bohemia showed any reluctance, during these years, to learn enough German to qualify for these jobs. When Havliček returned from his exile, his most painful impression was that 'the reaction is in ourselves, and chiefly in ourselves'.

Peace reigned even in Galicia, where Goluchowski was gradually gathering round him a party of adherents of his own policy of activism.[2] Most important of all, he was persuading considerable numbers of his fellow-countrymen to enter the Government service, and finding places for them,[3] by evicting the former German or Czech officials (many of whom then moved to Hungary or Transylvania), so that the administration of Galicia was becoming mainly Polish. It cannot be said that he had yet converted the Galician Poles as a whole to activism, but the atmosphere among them was changing perceptibly from frank hostility to readiness to collaborate on acceptable terms: put

---

[1] Havliček was put on trial before a jury for alleged subversive activities. The jury acquitted him, but he was then arrested under an administrative order and deported to Brixen.

[2] The representatives of this school of thought afterwards (after 1866) called themselves 'Sztanczyks' (from the name of Sigismund III's Court jester) because they could not at first venture to express their unpopular opinions except in satirical form. Their opponents, the Lemberg Democrats, who even after 1866 refused to abandon hope of a resurrected Poland, were known, from the name of a comic paper, as the 'tramtradists'.

[3] Goluchowski's success in this respect was probably due largely to the severe economic crisis into which the land reform and other factors had plunged the middle and small Galician landowners.

otherwise, territorial demands were beginning to give way to political ones. In any case, the extremists were, for the time, out of action.

The bill for this was, as usual, paid chiefly by the Ruthenes. The central authorities still managed to afford them a shadow of protection against Goluchowski's pressure,[1] and in 1849 they had been allowed to open a 'national House' in Lemberg as a cultural centre; it was visited by Francis Joseph when he toured Galicia in 1856. But the Ruthenes had to lay aside all hopes of administrative concessions, and the cultural crumbs which they were allowed to pick up from under the Polish table were desperately meagre. The House was not, incidentally, the only cultural centre of this people. While the St Georgites were still their official leaders, their authority was being increasingly challenged from two sides. On the one hand, there were the younger 'Ukrainophiles', against whom, indeed, everyone in authority combined; yet their movement had in itself the great innate force that the language and popular culture which its leaders were trying to develop was really that of the local peasant masses. Secondly, following Pogodin's earlier tours[2] another Russian emissary had come to Lemberg in 1850 and had founded there a little circle whose tenets were that the Ruthenes were a branch of Great Russians and their language, a dialect of Russian, and their programme, to make it so. Another branch of their activities was the conversion of the Uniates to the Orthodox Church; this, it is true, was propagated less in Galicia than in Cholm, across the Russian frontier. Supplied with funds from Russia, this group founded its own institution (the Matyca) and issued a newspaper of its own. Strangely enough, it was left unmolested both by Vienna and by Goluchowski, who seems to have seen an advantage in any movement which split further unity of the Ruthenes.[3] For the rest, the St Georgites, finding the dice weighted too heavily against them, adopted the favourite Central European device of 'retiring into passivity'.

This acceptance of the ruling order did not, however, extend either to Lombardy-Venetia, or to Hungary. It is true that the police discovered only one serious conspiracy in the former provinces the origin of which was wholly domestic, and that was on a relatively small scale (the 'martyrs of Mantua', i.e. the persons suffering the death penalty on this occasion, numbered only five, although five more death sentences were passed). The rising which led to the storming of the main gate in Milan was more serious (ten Austrian officers and other ranks were killed and fifty-nine wounded), but the initiative here had come from abroad – from the exiled Mazzini.

---

[1] Strangely enough, Goluchowski was regarded by his own fellow-countrymen as a Ruthenophile, a judgment which must appear entirely incomprehensible to anyone who has never tried to fit Polish spectacles on to his nose.

[2] See above, p. 284.

[3] The same policy was (unfortunately for himself) followed by another Governor of Galicia half a century later; see below, p. 802.

Radetzky put this down with a severity (Milan was placed under a 'rigorous state of siege', seventy-nine persons were executed and several hundreds imprisoned, while 209 political exiles suffered the confiscation of all or part of their properties)[1] which was effective, and in general, he was able to maintain 'order' adequately enough; but this was because the country was too full of spies and soldiers for disaffection to organize or manifest itself on a large scale. Here, even more than in Vienna or Prague, imprisonments and floggings were frequent,[2] and the great bulk of the population, at least above the peasant level, undoubtedly regarded the Austrian regime as one of foreign domination, and a hateful one at that. Such relative acceptance of it as was shown was due chiefly to the fact that during these years the stimulus of official encouragement of revolt from abroad was lacking.[3]

If we dwell in greater detail on the development of feeling in Hungary, this is not only because it was more complex (the populations concerned were also far larger), but also because it mattered far more to the Monarchy what course it took. Lombardy was destined in the event to be lost to the Monarchy within a few years after 1855, and Venetia, only a few years later, and in neither case were the feelings of the populations concerned the decisive factor; nor were the losses fatal to the Monarchy. But without Hungary, the Monarchy could hardly continue to exist, and whether it could be retained would depend, not on the ambitions of outside Powers, but on whether the country itself would accept the regime; or if not that regime, then any alternative one which Francis Joseph might offer.

In the years which we are now discussing, there were many variants of opinion, not only among the total population of the Hungarian Lands, but even among the traditional 'Hungarian' ruling class. Even among these, there were some active collaborators – the contingent which every nation throws up, in every situation, of time-servers and place-seekers, and of men only concerned to take advantage of the opportunities for self-enrichment offered by some aspects of the regime; even some who acted out of conviction, either because they approved the regime or because, while disapproving it, they yet thought Hungary's own best hope for the future lay in her accommodating herself as best she could to an inevitable situation;

---

[1] Some of the sufferers were Piedmontese citizens, and the consequent quarrel ended in Cavour's breaking off diplomatic relations with Austria.

[2] It is, however, fair to say that Radetzky abstained from mass physical retaliation against the population, and it is also fair to record that the act which brought Haynau ('the hyaena of Brescia'), and thus Austria, into such particular disrepute, and for which he just escaped a ducking in the Thames at the hands of the workers in Watney's brewery, had not been unprovoked. He had had certain women of Brescia stripped and publicly flogged during the 1848 campaign. These trollops had, however, been escorting Italian cut-throats round the hospitals and pointing out to them which of the wounded were Austrians. Those unfortunates had then been butchered in their beds.

[3] Cavour actually warned the Austrian Government against the 1853 plot.

this last group included one or two distinguished figures whose presence in it surprised their old associates.

At the opposite extreme there had stood, from the first, a party which was committed to nothing short of the separation of Hungary from the Monarchy, and was therefore a *limine* irreconcilable. In the first three or four years after Világos, the views of this party were given much international publicity and attracted much sympathy, especially in Britain and the USA, owing to the activities of the *émigrés*, and especially of Kossuth. The position of the emigration had been the occasion of a stormy international incident at the very outset of its existence, for after Kossuth and those who had crossed the Danube with him had been provisionally interned in Vidin, in North Bulgaria, Austria and Russia had demanded their extradition. Britain and France had, however, put very strong pressure, going to the length of a naval demonstration, on the Porte to refuse the demand, and a compromise had eventually been reached under which Kossuth and a few others had been interned in Kiutahia, in Asia Minor, the rest of his followers either returning to Hungary under promise of an amnesty, or dispersing into various Western countries. Kossuth had stayed in Kiutahia until October 1851, but then the United States had invited him to visit them as their guest, and sent a frigate for him. He had not been allowed to land in Italy or France, but had broken his journey at Southampton and made a tour of England, where he was greeted with an enthusiasm such as the country had, perhaps, never before shown to a foreigner. After a month he had gone on to America, where he had addressed over five hundred meetings, to audiences no less enthusiastic. He had then returned to London, to make his home there, until times changed.

Kossuth had not, indeed, been able to persuade any Western Government to accord him diplomatic recognition, or to take any other official action in that direction, but the sympathy which his beguiling personality and his magnificent eloquence had aroused, and the identification which he had created of the cause of Hungary with that of freedom, had been a significant factor in the international atmosphere of the day and a strong embarrassment to Austria's endeavours to win foreign sympathy for her regime.

Kossuth had his followers in Hungary, although what proportion they constituted of the Hungarian people, no man can say. The police records, were they available, would not help, for hundreds of people were arrested as dangerous opponents of the regime whose only recorded offence had been to sport a buttonhole in forbidden colours, strike up a seditious song over their cups, or use a drastic expression to some officious foreign clerk or gendarme. Equally, many escaped the notice of the police who really deserved it. There were, however, a goodly number – more than would have been found among a people less sanguine and more realistically minded than the Hungarian – who were willing to put their convictions to the test of action. In the autumn of 1851 the police came on the tracks of one really widespread conspiracy, the organizer of which, a certain Colonel Mack, proposed to raise the country in the name of Kossuth, as its lawful Head of State. The centre of the plot was in the Szekel area of Transylvania, but it had its agents, who were organized on a secret system borrowed from Mazzini, all over the country. The ringleaders of this conspiracy, with a number of people probably quite unconnected with it, were arrested in the spring of 1852. Another conspiracy, headed by a certain Oszlopy – this time an entirely hare-brained enterprise – was unmasked (and easily repressed) in the following June.

Had the odds against such enterprises been less obviously overwhelming, many Hungarians would certainly have joined them; had they reached the stage of action, and had that action promised success, they would have found more adherents still. But even if successful, they would not have been universally popular among the Hungarians themselves, for the opposition to the extremists in 1849 had not been based solely on fear. Not only the aulic magnates who had formed themselves into the Old Conservative Group, but many other Hungarians had been genuinely shocked by the dethronement of the Habsburgs. They regarded the Pragmatic Sanction as constituting both the legal basis for Hungary's existence and the best real guarantee of it, and had heaved a sigh of relief when Kossuth and his fellow-extremists had left the country. Far from being irreconcilable, they had been truly anxious for a reconciliation with the Crown, and had even believed, naïvely but none the less sincerely, that events would now follow the course which they had taken after Rákóczi's wars – which had been far more prolonged and whole-hearted than that of 1849 – and would see the conclusion of a new Peace of Szatmár in which the Crown and the nation would join hands again on a basis of mutual respect for one another's historic rights.

Bach's announcement declaring the Hungarian Constitution null and void had done relatively little to diminish these hopes. It had been regarded as an act of war, which would be cancelled in its turn, with the dethronement. Haynau's bloody purge had given the optimists a severer shock, particularly in view of Schwarzenberg's and Francis Joseph's own open endorsement of it. But even that blow had not been mortal, for Generals are expected to be bloody-minded and military regimes are by definition temporary. And in fact, some measure of optimism had not seemed entirely absurd even during the Provisorissimum. The regime had made one or two concessions which had been taken (and probably with justice) as indications that its mind was not yet fully made up as to the future.[1]

Meanwhile, Gehringer, who was genuinely anxious for a reconciliation

---

[1] One of these was the delay in appointing accredited civilians at the head of the five Provinces; the choice of the word 'adviser' for those who were appointed was allegedly made deliberately to suggest the provisional nature of the division. It is said that the rejection of the Slovaks' petition for an autonomous territory was due to the influence of the Old Conservatives.

between Hungary and the Crown, had made things as smooth as possible for the Hungarians. The authorities had not been unduly severe towards those not falling into the prescribed categories. The screening of officials had been carried out mercifully enough, the excuse of duresse being accepted wherever it was at all plausible,[1] and the regime was, as we have said elsewhere, still national in many respects.

The Old Conservatives had been particularly optimistic during these months, and had continued to press their case on the Court, and to expound it in print, with great fluency and cogency.

Then, however, had come the second Provisorium, which was generally, and correctly, recognized as signifying the Crown's intention to make the new regime permanent. Hungary was thus to lose – for ever, unless she could recover them by persuasion or force – the constitutional freedom and territorial boundaries in defence of which she had many times laid down far more lives than had fallen victim to Haynau. These losses were, of course, far deeper than those inflicted by the absolutism on the Monarchy's Western peoples, who had suffered no territorial mutilation at all, and whose self-government had for a century past been purely nominal. And the absolutism itself was far more burdensome to Hungary than it was to the Western Lands, and brought fewer compensations. The benefits most freely acknowledged by Hungarian writers are the reforms introduced in the judicial services. All non-Hungarian writers are loud also in their praises of the efficiency of the new administrators, satirically dubbed by Széchenyi (the name then caught on) the 'Bach Hussars',[2] and we may concede them the virtues of industry and incorruptibility, but we cannot but feel that their efficiency was perceptibly reduced by the inability of most of them to understand a word of the language spoken by the populations whose affairs they were supposed to order, and by their unfamiliarity with the local psychology and habits.[3] And it may be added, parenthetically, that their own life was not particularly happy. They were usually almost without company in the country town or village in which they were stationed, boycotted by the local gentry, at cross-purposes with the rest of the population. They were paid relatively well, but

---

[1] The staffs of two Counties (Sáros and Pozsony) survived the screening entire.

[2] The reference was to an elaborate pseudo-Magyar uniform, complete with flowing cloak, high boots and spurs, which Bach designed for them and made them wear. These uniforms, adorning the persons of honest Czech or Slovene post-masters' or small tradesmen's sons, were a constant subject for mockery by the Hungarians and incidentally, no less antipathetic to their unfortunate wearers, who found them extraordinarily difficult to put on and off, and to wear with dignity, besides eating up a substantial proportion of their salaries.

[3] One of them who spent several years in Hungary left humorous reminiscences of his experiences. On the morning after his arrival he found almost the entire adult male population lined up outside his office. They had been sentenced to prison for their conduct in 1849, but as the jail could not hold them they lived in their own homes and drew a daily dole in lieu of the prison fare with which they should have been provided.

also burdened with heavy expenditure, in which the cost of their uniforms was a large item.

Efficient or not – and for the reasons given, it was certainly less efficient than that of their colleagues in the West – their role was expensive to the country, whose old system of government had at least been cheap. And besides much more for her own administration, Hungary now had to pay her full quota towards the central services of the Monarchy, and also a proportionate share of the national debt. Thus taxation of all kinds had risen enormously; and if the bulk of direct taxation was now falling on the nobles, the poorest peasant had to pay more for his meat, his drinks and his tobacco.[1] Many Hungarians suffered very heavy additional losses when the Government refused to accept the 'Kossuth notes' as legal currency.

Some classes were, it is true, making bigger incomes: the large landlords were doing very well out of the economic unification of the Monarchy, impinging on a situation of high agricultural prices, and fortunes were being made out of some of the new industries. But the country as a whole regarded the big landlords as a foreign class, and many of the industrial profits were actually going to real foreigners. The medium and small landowners who constituted the backbone of the real nation had, as we have said, been largely ruined by the land reform, particularly since many of them were, for political reasons, deliberately kept waiting for their compensation.

There were cultural grievances also: the Protestants groaned under the Catholic reaction imposed by Thun and Rauscher, which was not even agreeable to many Hungarian Catholics, who regarded it as another Viennese move against Hungary, and while the lower clergy resented the increased power now placed in the hands of the bishops, the bishops themselves found their historic importance reduced. The Jews, too, remembered that Hungary's Parliament had given them full freedom and equality.

The appointment of the Archduke proved another change for the worse. When announced, it was represented as a concession to Hungary's status, and at first was welcomed as such by certain circles, especially the magnates, who had despised Gehringer for his bourgeois origin and his personally unpretentious habits. But in respects other than glamour, the light of which reached only a narrow circle, it was the opposite of beneficial to the Hungarian people, for the Archduke was an austere military figure, to whom every Hungarian was a rebel, actual or potential.

One effect of the Definitivum was obviously to fan extremist feeling – the more so as its enactment practically coincided with Kossuth's emergence from internment. The Mack conspiracy, in fact, followed immediately on these two events. There was, however, relatively little increase in active

---

[1] In 1847 the yield of direct taxation in Hungary had been 4,280,000 fl. and of indirect, 5,300,000; the corresponding figures for 1857 were 41,500,000 and 65,600,000. There were a number of riots against the tobacco duty.

resistance to the regime, particularly since after the bloody repression of the conspiracy Kossuth himself warned his adherents to attempt no more such ventures until the international situation grew more favourable.[1] But there was no corresponding growth of willingness to collaborate with the regime: rather the contrary. The Old Conservatives, partly in dudgeon at their repulse by the regime (which had rejected them far rather than they it), partly out of fear of compromising themselves irretrievably with their fellow-countrymen, withdrew into a passivity whence they were hardly to emerge until 1859–60, when they played the transient but important role to be described, as offering the only alternative to absolutist bureaucracy which Francis Joseph was then prepared to consider. The reaction of the bulk of the nation was one of relatively passive, but obstinate, hostility. It was an attitude rather than a movement, and one which at that time lacked leadership, a positive programme, and even much hope,[2] for the man who was later to give it all three, Francis Deák, having been saved rather by happy chance than by his own will from Haynau's and Schwarzenberg's vengeance,[3] was now living in almost hermit-like retirement on his estate in remote Zala and had himself no advice for those who consulted him except that they should on no account countenance the regime by serving it, even with the best intentions. But it was steadfast, and as time passed it hardened rather than crumbled into a solidity which transcended religious, political and even social differences.

Francis Joseph, who did not lack courage, made an extended tour of the country (including Transylvania, the Voivodina and Croatia) in 1852. An amnesty was enacted on this occasion and honours and decorations distributed lavishly. His marriage in 1854 was celebrated, here as elsewhere, with another amnesty, and martial law was, as we have seen, lifted from all the Hungarian Lands in 1854. These gestures possibly chipped the surface of the national hostility; but they did little or nothing to melt it.

The greatest disappointment of all to the regime was that the opposition to it in Hungary was not confined to the country's old traditional ruling class. Bach had always counted with their hostility, but he had reckoned that he would be able to neutralize it with the support which he expected to receive from the peasants, the 'Nationalities', and Croatia. And even this was not forthcoming. The peasants appreciated their liberation, but persisted in

[1] Mack had announced himself to be acting in Kossuth's name, but it is to this day uncertain exactly how far Kossuth had had fore-knowledge of the plans. He denied ever having heard of Oszlopy.

[2] Ferenczy, *Deák Élete*, II. 233, writes that in the early 1850s 'most men believed that the new Austria . . . had finally succeeded; only Deák kept alive confidence and hope in the nation's strength'.

[3] He had been sent with Batthyány on a mission to Windisch-Graetz early in 1849, had been cut off by the advance of the Imperial troops and had thus been unable to rejoin the Diet. He had been court-martialled, but acquitted on the ground that he had taken no part in any treasonable activities.

attributing it, not to Vienna, but to Kossuth, and there is little evidence that they preferred the relatively efficient but alien Bach Hussars to their own traditional masters, whose oppression of them was of a type which they understood and had to some extent learnt how to counter (the Germanic peoples would be less universally unpopular if they could rid themselves of their cherished illusion that anyone except themselves wants or likes efficiency). Having now no more fears that the landlords would try to get the old system restored, they made common cause with them against the representatives of the new authority.

The Slovak nationalists found that they had got, after all, very little more out of Vienna than they had out of Pest, and their Lutherans, an influential body among them, shared the religious grievances of their Magyar coreligionists. The Serbs fretted against the ill-faith which had given them, instead of their own self-governing province, an absolutely ruled Department full of Germans and Roumanians. They were soon wondering whether they would not have done better to make terms with Hungary, after all. In Transylvania, both the Saxons and the Roumanians were solid in opposing reunion with Hungary, but both were bitterly disappointed with the new absolutism. The Saxons, as Lutherans, had their special grievance against its clericalism. The Croats brooded over Dalmatia, and found the yoke of the imported foreign officials as heavy as the Hungarians did; all the books quote the remark made by a Croat to a Hungarian friend, 'we have got as reward what you have been given as punishment'. When Francis Joseph visited Croatia after his Hungarian tour, his reception was so bad that the tour was cut short, on grounds of security, after only six days.

Whether the ideologies of absolutism and depoliticization of national feeling could under any circumstances have finally overcome the demands for self-government and national self-expression which they were challenging, they could most certainly not hope to do so without the continuance of a tranquil and favourable international climate. That climate was still relatively benign in 1852, although even then not cloudless, for in that year Austria ruffled the Czar by intervening in defence of Montenegro, whose Prince had provoked the Porte by certain completely wanton acts of aggression. The Czar decided to swallow this, and to take it as a filial act. Then in the spring of 1853 he began to hint to Francis Joseph, in private correspondence, his intention of himself attacking the Porte; thereby placing Austria – which had itself set the bad example – in a position of extreme difficulty. For several months Francis Joseph did his best to dissuade the Czar from his enterprise; in spite of this, Nicholas, in July, sent his troops into Moldavia and Wallachia. Francis Joseph tried to mediate between him and the Porte, but again without success; on 4 October Turkey declared war on Russia. Britain and France now came to the support of the Porte; in March 1854 they declared war on Russia. Francis Joseph did not join them in this final step, but he mobilized considerable forces (three Army Corps in South Hungary in the autumn of 1853, and in April 1854 four more Corps in Galicia, besides a general call-up in the interior), associated himself with their programme, which amounted to the exclusion of Russia from the Principalities and the Danube, and from any influence over the internal affairs of the Porte, and after Russia had evacuated the Principalities, sent an Austrian occupation force into them. By this time Buol had begun to urge that Austria herself should enter the war and take the Principalities for herself as her reward, and in December he actually concluded an alliance between Austria and the Western Powers (this without informing Prussia, as should have been done); but to the anger especially of Louis Napoleon, who felt himself betrayed, Francis Joseph still refused to take the final step of war. Thus 1855 saw Austria still non-belligerent with even her military preparations relaxed, for she had again demobilized most of her forces, while Turkey, France and Britain, now joined by Piedmont, fought Russia in the Crimea. Then, in March 1856, a Conference in Paris, attended by the belligerent Powers and Austria, concluded a peace which duly excluded Russia from the Danube, but instead of assigning the Principalities to Austria (which Napoleon would have let her have, but only if she renounced Lombardy-Venetia in exchange), left them under Turkish sovereignty with increased autonomy.

Most historians have passed very severe judgments on the policy followed by Francis Joseph and Buol during this crisis. According to some, Austria ought to have done what her Generals wanted: to have associated herself with Russia from the first, taken her share of the booty in the Western Balkans, and preserved in being the Holy Alliance between despots which had saved her in 1849. According to others, she should have cast in her lot wholeheartedly with the Western Powers, when she would have emerged with unimpaired prestige, with allies, and probably also in possession of the Principalities. As it was, she fell between two stools.

The accusations of clumsiness and vacillation are not ill-founded, but it is at least arguable that the most far-sighted determination would have availed Austria little. The breach which ensued between her and Russia was bound to come if the Czar set himself to realize ambitions which he could not but know (he had had a foretaste of it in the little Montenegrin crisis) that Austria regarded as constituting a threat to her vital interests. In his long correspondence with the Czar, Francis Joseph made his position abundantly clear, and if Nicholas disregarded the warnings, it was with his eyes open. The offence to Prussia could have been avoided, but this would not have destroyed Prussia's fundamental determination sooner or later to oust Austria from the leadership of Germany. Louis Napoleon had been offended, and Piedmont had managed to seize the opportunity to steal a march on Austria; but it is hard to think that an alliance between France and Austria would have postponed for long that later understanding between France and Piedmont which was so much rather the natural expression of Napoleon's whole political outlook; still harder to believe that diplomacy could long have dammed the elemental tide of Italian nationalism. Equally elemental, if at the time less turbulent, was the Roumanian national movement. If Buol had really succeeded in annexing the Principalities, the developments of the movement would have taken another form, but it is doubtful indeed whether this would have been a more tractable one. This consideration applies equally strongly to the course advocated by the Generals.

In short, what was undermining Austria's international position was less faults of her own policy than the advance of nationalism in Central Europe. But the fact remained that the end of the war found that position gravely weakened. Bismarck had been given his chance to begin organizing anew resistance to Austrian hegemony in Germany. Piedmont had gained the confidence and prestige which marked her out again as the future nucleus of a united Italy. An alliance between this rising Power and France could be no more than a matter of time. It could also be no more than a question of a few years before the Danubian Principalities had achieved enough national consolidation to exert a strong centrifugal pull on the Roumanian subjects of the Monarchy.

And the new Czar was bitterly disillusioned with and hostile to his father's ex-protégé. Never again could Francis Joseph count on such help as Nicholas had given him in Hungary in 1849 and against Prussia in 1850.

The crisis had also dealt another blow to Austria's hopes of early financial recovery. That she had kept out of war at all in 1854, and had remained mobilized for only a few months, had been due mainly to Baumgartner's insistence that she could not afford a campaign. Even so, the costs of arming and mobilization and of the occupation of the Danubian Principalities, had sent her military expenditure rocketing up, and the premium on silver, which had sunk to 108 in 1853, rose again sharply.

The Government attached extreme importance to wiping out the premium, but it was clear that this would not vanish until the National Bank had recovered at least the bulk of what the Government owed it. A few small international loans had been raised, on onerous terms, but now the foreign financial houses refused to help any further at all, in view of the international situation and still more, out of resentment against the recent enactment forbidding Jews to buy real property in Austria. This measure had, in particular, brought Baumgartner into bad odour with the Rothschilds, who had helped him in 1852, but now refused to do so any longer.[1] In June 1854,

---

[1] Beer, op. cit., p. 256, quotes Baumgartner's statement to this effect to a Ministerial Council; and cf. Hübner's report from Paris (cit. Corti, *The House of Rothschild*, p. 347) that when the veto was reimposed 'a kind of coalition was formed on the bourses of Paris and London, its object being to damage Austrian credit'. The veto was, apart from the Eastern question, 'the sole topic of conversation in Paris', and James Rothschild was 'beside himself'.

accordingly, a great internal loan of five hundred million gulden, the largest in Austrian history, was floated for the express purpose of paying off the State's debt to the Bank. Much propaganda was made for the loan, and more than propaganda,[1] so that the full five hundred million were subscribed; but the proceeds were swallowed up almost entirely by the army, and the State was still left owing the Bank (from which it had meanwhile taken further advances), as much as before. Military expenditure for the year totalled 198 m.g., the service of the debt was now 85 m.g., the deficit 157 m.g. and the premium on silver 140.

Now Baumgartner resigned in despair, and in March 1855 Bruck succeeded him as Minister of Finance. Bruck attacked the situation with all his usual energy. There were still bills for the army to be paid, as the aftermath of 1854, so that military expenditure for 1855 still totalled 257 m.g., but now it was cut down drastically. Taxation was raised. In October, State property valued at 156 m.g., the amount of the State's direct debt to the Bank under the 1854 agreement, was handed over to that institution, which was authorized either to hold and manage the estates, or to sell them.

The biggest retreat of all was over the State railways, the construction and management of which had been a heavy passive item in the Budget. As early as 1854 the Government had begun back-pedalling on railway construction; a Patent of that year, setting out which lines were to be built in the near future, had allowed for most of them to be constructed by private concessionaires, who received in return sundry concessions, including a State guarantee of five per cent on their invested capital at two per cent amortization. The Pereire group in Paris, acting in conjunction with Sina, had begun negotiating for the construction of a number of lines in the north and southeast of the Monarchy, on conditions which included the cession to the group, on very favourable terms, of several big iron and steel works. Next, the State began selling off its own lines outright. The Pereires hoped to acquire these, too, through the Credit Mobilier, and actually bought some of them on 1 January 1855, but meanwhile Bruck had accomplished what was not the least important of his achievements: he had re-established good relations with the Rothschilds. Rothschild had succeeded in organizing the Creditanstalt, and in May 1856 that institution bought the Lombardy-Venetian railways for a hundred million francs. Other lines followed – first, most of the State lines in the north of the Monarchy, then, in 1858, the still unfinished Südbahn, the purchaser of this (another foreign company behind which, again, the Rothschilds stood), undertaking the obligation, on which the Government insisted in view of the possibility of war with Piedmont, of completing the line as far as Trieste.

[1] The Communal Councils were allotted quotas and ordered to raise them. When they failed to do so, the money was raised by forced sales (Charmatz, *Bruck*, p. 124).

The sales although very disadvantageous to the State,[1] yet brought it in some ready money, and one way and another, the deficits, which had still totalled 158 m.g. in 1855, were really brought down: to 81 m.g. in 1856, 53 in 1857 and 52 in 1858. The premium on silver sank to a figure so small that on 28 September 1858 the National Bank resumed convertibility, for the first time for over ten years.

By this time, however, the State had come near to exhausting its realizable assets, and had pledged pretty nearly all its credit; and what was hardly less important, private money in liquid form was also running short. 1855 and 1856 had still been golden years for the speculators. The Creditanstalt, with its glittering names, had attracted a great crowd of eager investors, who had sent its shares soaring in spectacular fashion, and many fortunes had been made. But in 1857 the great Stock Exchange crisis, travelling eastward from New York via London and Paris, reached Vienna. Countless small speculators found themselves ruined, and the Rothschilds themselves had to draw in their horns. Moreover, they were now such heavy creditors of the State, directly as holders of large quantities of State loans, indirectly as owners of railways, that their interest in the solvency of the State was vital. The day was over at last when they could keep old payments going by sponsoring new loans.

Thus, as in the Vormärz, a powerful movement arose which demanded, for economic-financial reasons, constitutional control over Government expenditure. Its chief representatives were, indeed, no longer quite the same as the German bourgeois who had called for the resignation of Metternich. It was no accident that the leaders of the new Opposition were particularly hostile to the Concordat and all its works, nor that the first concessions made by the Crown in 1859 should have included promises to allow autonomy and freedom of worship to the non-Catholic religions and 'to regulate the position of the Israelites along modern lines'. But it was an opposition which found itself in natural alliance with the other forces now fretting against the absolutist system.

The strongholds of these forces were, as before, Hungary and Lombardy-Venetia, and in both of these danger-spots the resistance grew with the change in the international situation. In Hungary, it is true, the extremists had lost some further ground. Kossuth himself had been shocked by the fiasco of the 1851 rising, and had advised his followers to draw in their horns until the international situation changed for the better. His hopes had been raised again by the outbreak of the Crimean War, and he had set about organizing a legion, but had had to abandon the plan when Austria decided on neutrality. Thereafter he had slipped down into the ranks of the *émigré*

[1] The Südbahn was sold for 91 m.g., about one-third of what it had cost the State to construct it.

revolutionaries, consorting intimately with Mazzini, and for the rest, engaging with Polish *émigrés* and sometimes with official personalities in Serbia and the Danubian Provinces in plans for the reorganization of East Central Europe as a federation of independent States which have a considerable historic interest but were, perhaps, fortunate in never being put to the test of practical application.

By this time, too, the emigration was becoming weakened by quarrels among its leaders, many of whom thought Kossuth inclined to take too much on himself. Several important figures among them, including Count Gyula Andrássy, accepted the amnesty, signed declarations of loyalty to the Crown, and returned to Hungary.

On the other hand, Deák had in 1854 sold his estate in Zala and moved to Pest, where he soon became the centre of a circle which, at first consisting of a few friends, widened until it came to comprise most of Hungary's political thinkers and potential leaders outside the Old Conservatives on the one hand and the irreconcilables on the other. Therewith the moderate opposition, then generally described as the '1848-ers',[1] acquired a leader, a programme, and, not the least important things, discipline and courage. Deák's programme was perfectly simple and perfectly logical. For him, the legal situation for Hungary was that created by the April Laws. He did not regard them as immutable; they could be revised, and in some respects obviously required revision. This, however, could only be done in the legal way, by agreement between Hungary's lawfully crowned King and her lawfully elected Parliament. Pending this, any other system was unlawful, and need not be obeyed. His prescription, in a phrase, was passive resistance until the other side should accept his postulates.

Deák admitted unreservedly the validity of the Pragmatic Sanction, so that his attitude, unlike that of Kossuth, offered the possibility of a settlement between Hungary and the Crown which would give the Monarch Hungary's loyalty and her co-operation in maintaining the further existence of the Gesammtmonarchie. But it also required nothing less than the complete retraction by the Crown of everything that it had done in respect of Hungary since Ferdinand had sanctioned the April Laws. And it was no mere statement of a legal case, for Deák's followers now adapted, with enthusiasm, his doctrine of the illegality of the regime as justifying them in refusing to pay their taxes. Arrears of taxation from Hungary continued to be an important item on the debit sheet of the national finances, and to collect what did come in cost the services of large numbers of troops.[2]

The resistance in Lombardy-Venetia was less systematic, for the local

---

[1] At a later date Deák's party became that of '1867' (of the Compromise of that year) while the nationalist opponents of the Compromise appropriated the name of 1848.

[2] It is said that in 1859, 156,000 troops were stationed in Hungary, being largely engaged in collecting arrears of taxation, which then amounted to 32 m.g.

Italians possessed no Deák. It may even have been less widespread. But here, too, there was enough obvious disaffection to compel Austria to keep a considerable garrison in the provinces.

In 1856 and 1857 Francis Joseph made various attempts to popularize his regime, and to make it deserve popularity by relaxing its severity. In the autumn of 1856, taking his wife with him, he made an extended tour of the Italian provinces, visiting all their main cities and spending a considerable time in Milan. He granted another amnesty, under which thousands of political prisoners regained their freedom (the military and the police had advised against this measure, but Elisabeth pleaded for it), and the sequestrated properties of the exiles were restored to them. Radetzky, who had, indeed, reached the ripe age of ninety-one, was retired, and the Emperor's own brother, the mild and affable Maximilian, sent down in his place.[1]

In May of the next year Francis Joseph and Elisabeth began[2] a similar tour of Hungary. Here, too, another amnesty was enacted and many confiscated properties restored.

But these gestures implied no change in the principles of the absolutist regime, in respect of which Francis Joseph was still firmly convinced, not only that it was philosophically right (this was a faith which probably remained with him all his life), but also that it would end by proving itself – was, indeed, already doing so – a success in practice, an illusion which Bach not only encouraged, but seems himself to have shared. In 1855 Francis Joseph had written cheerfully to his mother that 'a State which can mobilize two hundred thousand men without trouble and can raise an internal loan of five hundred million gulden is not sickening for revolution'. Before his journey to Hungary he ordered the authorities 'to make it absolutely clear to the Hungarians that His Majesty is absolutely determined not to depart by a hair's breadth from His principles', and the arrangements for the trip were designed to make this absolutely clear: thus Francis Joseph refused to appear in the uniform of a Hungarian officer, wearing instead the dress of an Austrian Field-Marshal; streamers had to be black and yellow, the national colours being forbidden, and so on.

Francis Joseph seems to have come back from his trip with his confidence unshaken, for he wrote on his return:

'Resolved to uphold unswervingly the fundamental principles which have hitherto guided Me in governing My Empire, I desire that they be generally recognized and more particularly adopted for guidance by all organs of My Government.'

But in fact the trip had done more harm than good. The ostentatious

---

[1] The Archduke took over only the civilian side of Radetzky's functions. The Military Commander (F. M. L. Gyulai) came under the direct orders of Vienna.

[2] The visiting pair's little daughter died in Buda while her parents were in East Hungary. Elisabeth then went back to Vienna, while her husband finished the tour alone.

trampling on national susceptibilities had largely outweighed the effects of the amnesty, and in any case, it was not clemency for which Hungary as a whole was asking, but a change of system. The blow had been especially severe for the Conservatives, who had pinned high hopes on the visit, and had compiled another extensive memorandum, to which they had secured the signatures of 227 prominent members of various walks of Hungarian society, asking, once again (in most loyal terms) for the restoration of the *status ante* 1848. This had been given to the Cardinal Primate to convey to Francis Joseph, but means had been found to thwart his repeated attempts to do so, and the signatories threatened with dire reprisals if they tried to break through the cordon. The Archbishop eventually gave up the attempt in despair. The Conservatives' embitterment over this ran very deep,[1] and their position in Hungary also further weakened by the snub, to the advantage of that of Deák, who had refused to associate himself with the memorandum; for there was no point in compromising on 1848 if the Crown was unwilling to concede anything at all.

Thus disaffection ran higher in Hungary after the visit, than before it, and it was accompanied by a similar growth of disaffection among the Croats.

The Italian tour seems to have been less positively disastrous, although there, too, there were difficulties: for example, the projected balls had to be cancelled because the Italian ladies refused to dance with Austrian officers. And in any case, it was not the feelings of the Emperor's Italian subjects that mattered now. Manin, now in exile in Paris, said frankly: 'We do not want Austria to mend her ways in Italy; we want her to get out of it'; and it is recorded that Cavour actually asked his friends 'if they could, to force Austria to re-impose the state of siege'.

For by 1858 the international dangers which were the heritage of the Crimea were advancing from potentiality to imminence. In July of that year Cavour met Napoleon secretly at Plombières, and plans were laid on the basis that Cavour was to devise a 'respectable' pretext for war against Austria, after which Italy was to be constituted as a federation of four States: North Italy under the house of Savoy; the Papal States; the Kingdom of the Two Sicilies; and a new Kingdom of Central Italy. A calculated indiscretion by Napoleon on New Year's Eve gave what was generally taken as an advance notification of the allies' intentions.

The plan of this work allows for only the briefest registration of the results of foreign political negotiations; for no description at all of the course of either. It therefore allows us to pass over the diplomatic exchanges of the next few months with the bare statements that they left Francis Joseph and his advisers under two convictions: one that France and Piedmont were so bent

---

[1] Rogge, op. cit., II. 461, writes that this was 'the turning-point'. Before it, relatively small concessions would have satisfied Hungary, but this was no longer so after it.

on war that nothing would deter them (whereas Napoleon had begun to hesitate and was putting pressure on Piedmont to back down); the other, that the war would inevitably spread, and involve the opening of another front on the Rhine, where the French would be met by a combined force to which Prussia would send a contingent.[1] Acting on these assumptions, all of which proved to be mistaken, and after a fateful delay which was due partly, indeed, to the financiers' hesitations, but partly to Buol's grotesque misapprehension of the situation, Austria, on 19 April, sent Piedmont an ultimatum to demobilize, and when Cavour rejected this, an Austrian army commanded by General Gyulai and consisting of a force which, when the late arrivals came up, should have consisted of nine Army Corps of twenty thousand each, but in April was much smaller,[2] crossed the Piedmontese frontier.

Now, however, everything went wrong. Neither Britain nor Russia intervened on Austria's side (this, too, had been hoped), and the Prince Regent of Prussia made difficulties, telling the emissaries sent him by Francis Joseph that he was not obliged, under the Bund law, to help Austria unless Bund territory was attacked, and at least hinting that he would require a political price for his services.[3] Gyulai failed to engage the Piedmontese troops seriously while the French reinforcements were still north of the Alps, and when the news of their arrival reached him, retreated back across the Ticino. The armies first met seriously on 4 June, at Magenta, and here, although the Austrians had not even much the worst of the fighting, and were left in superior force to the enemy at the end of it, Gyulai took it as a defeat, thereby turning it into one, and retreated further, while Napoleon entered Milan in triumph.

[1] On 28 May, Francis Joseph told a Ministerial Council that the whole policy of the ultimatum had been based on the assumption that the war would not remain localized (Redlich, *Franz Joseph*, p. 241). He had faced this prospect with equanimity, and when Bruck objected that the country's finances would not stand a general war, had replied that the financial sacrifices would have to be made (Corti, *Mensch und Herrscher*, p. 227). Buol had said earlier that 'it was unimaginable that in a war against France Prussia would fail to stand by Austria' (id., p. 213), and when Bruck pleaded the financial difficulties and both Grünne and Gyulai, to do them justice, warned Francis Joseph that the diplomatic situation was dangerous and the Army weak, Buol thought that there was 'no danger' (id., pp. 208, 216).

[2] Gyulai began his operations with five Army Corps and one Cavalry Division. Two more Corps arrived at the beginning of June and two in July.

[3] The open condition which Prussia had laid down was that the Prince Regent should command the armies on the Rhine. This Francis Joseph refused to consider. But according to Redlich (op. cit., p. 248), the Prince Regent 'was only prepared to fulfil the obligations which, in Austria's view, devolved on him under Bund law, if the leadership of Germany was, on this occasion, left to Prussia and Austria declared herself willing to withdraw from the Bund, as much as possible'. See on this also Friedjung, *Die Kampf um die Herschaft*, II. 28 ff; J. Joll in *The New Cambridge Modern History*, X. 506. Prussia had been annoyed by the relatively trivial incident in 1856 when Austria refused to help her re-assert her rights in Neuenburg when it severed its connection with Prussia.

Meanwhile, Francis Joseph himself had, on 29 May, started for the field, leaving the Archduke Rainer *fils* to deputise for him in Vienna. He took over personal command of the army on 17 June, but on 24 June, at Solferino, the Austrian army was again defeated – again, not having had very much the worst of the fighting, but having suffered casualties which drew tears from the young Emperor's eyes and from his lips the exclamation: 'Rather lose a province than undergo such a horrible experience again!'

Now Napoleon made overtures to him for an armistice, offering relatively favourable peace terms. Austria was to retain Venetia, plus the Quadrilateral, ceding only the rest of Lombardy. Eventually, Italy was to be constituted as a federation. The idea of a federation appealed to Francis Joseph, who at that time thought that Venetia would be able to join it, while remaining part of the Monarchy, and Austria could then even dominate it through Venetia, the secundo-genitures in Tuscany, Parma and Modena, if their rulers (who had been driven out by revolution) were restored, and the alliance of Naples and the support of the Papacy. He therefore accepted the offer in return for a promise from Napoleon not to oppose the restoration of the secundo-genitures, provided it was not effected by force; a face-saving stipulation that Lombardy was not to be ceded direct to Piedmont, but to Napoleon; and a reservation to himself, for his own lifetime, of the right of conferring the Lombard Order of the Iron Crown. On this basis, preliminary peace was signed at Villafranca on 12 July.

We may note that the definitive peace, signed at Zurich on 10 November, was very much less favourable to Austria than the preliminary peace. The territorial provisions were, indeed, not altered; but meanwhile it had proved impossible to secure the restoration of the secundo-genitures, whose territories, with Emilia, were annexed by Piedmont in the following spring. It had also been found constitutionally impossible to give Venetia a dual status, as part of the Monarchy and simultaneously, member of an Italian federation. The whole idea of a federation faded away, leaving Austria with no foothold in Italy except her possession of Venetia.

For our purposes it is not the course of Austria's catastrophe that is chiefly important, but the reasons for it. If we pass over the singular ineptness of Francis Joseph's and Buol's diplomacy, we should presumably put first the extraordinarily poor showing in the field made by the Austrian army. Gyulai proved himself an almost inconceivably incompetent commander, and his senior subordinates, with the single exception of Benedek, failed almost as badly. It should be added that Francis Joseph himself proved quite unequal to the task, entirely new to him, of commanding a large army in battle.

The rank and file did not lack courage, but they lacked everything else. In the past years, only a relatively small proportion of the men called up had been kept with the colours, and they had simply been drilled on the barrack square: they had never been exercised in field operations, nor even hardened for them physically. The reservists had been left untrained, and there had not even been enough of them to make up the force mobilized, although this had not comprised the full nominal war strength of the army. The numbers had been brought up to strength by hurried recruiting reminiscent of the old *Abstellung ex officio*, and with the same results. Their equipment was exceedingly poor, and the commissariat broke down badly, many of the defects being, as it transpired afterwards, due to scandalous corruption. A number of 'volunteer' formations, hurriedly beaten together, were not ready for action when hostilities ceased.

For all this, Grünne was held the scapegoat, and he was certainly primarily to blame for the unfortunate choice of commanders (it must be said for Gyulai that he had protested his unfitness for the command), for the bad training, and for overlooking the corruption. But behind all this had lain the creeping sickness of Austria's financial weakness. The failure to keep the army properly trained and equipped had been due at least in large part to the financiers' insistence on economy, particularly in this field, on which they had concentrated their endeavours. Thus the defence budget had been cut from 139 m.g. in 1856 to 127 in 1857 and 122 in 1858. Then the prospect of war opened up by Napoleon's calculated indiscretion had brought matters to a head. The course of Austrian papers had plunged down again;[1] the National Bank had been forced to suspend convertibility again, and silver had again been at a premium. To finance the war, when it came to regard it as inevitable, the Government had clapped a 20% surcharge on all taxes and cut payments on its own loans, but these devices could not be expected to cover a major war. An attempt to raise money in London brought in only about £1,000,000, and an internal loan for 200 m.g., although pressure amounting to near-compulsion was put on banks and institutions,[2] yielded only 80 m.g. To meet the rest of its most immediate needs, the Government again borrowed from the National Bank, which advanced it 147 m.g. (20 m.g. in silver), but even so, Bruck had insisted that the resources for a big mobilization and a prolonged campaign were simply not there. The ultimatum was sent in the hope of escaping these by crushing Piedmont with relatively small forces before Napoleon had time to intervene, if, indeed, he was not prevented from doing so by the other Powers (as we have said, Austria's diplomatic calculations were at fault); and in this hope, only twelve Corps had been mobilized. That, of these twelve, only nine were sent down to Italy and those only gradually, was due chiefly to the situation in Hungary, where the spring of 1859 had seen, not only a further hardening of the resistance *à la* Deák, but the re-emergence of a threat of actual revolt. Like everyone in history who

---

[1] The quotations for them in Frankfurt fell in four weeks from $81\frac{7}{8}$ to 38. The Rothschilds were extremely hostile to the war (see Corti, *The House of Rothschild*, pp. 370 ff.).

[2] Among the few voluntary subscribers were members of the Imperial family, including the ex-Emperor, Ferdinand.

has ever harboured designs on Austria, Napoleon and Cavour had thought of using Hungary against her, and round the turn of the year both men had talked to Klapka, their first simple idea having apparently been that Hungary should oblige them by staging a rising (to break out in the Szekel area) when hostilities broke out.[1] Klapka, however, consulted Kossuth, who saw Napoleon on 5 May, and agreed to co-operate, but on conditions. The rising, which he assured the Emperor would be general when it came, was to be touched off by the landing of a legion (which he agreed to organize) on the Dalmatian coast, and this must be accompanied by a French detachment; further, Napoleon must officially proclaim the independence of Hungary as a French war aim.

When Napoleon objected that the appearance of France on the Adriatic might lead Britain to intervene against Austria, Kossuth cheerfully announced that he would personally so influence opinion in the British elections which were just impending as to secure the return of a non-interventionist government in Westminster, and Napoleon having accepted this astonishing offer, and agreed to Kossuth's other terms, the dauntless exile, who had already sent 'instructions' to Hungary to rise when he gave the signal (but not before), formed a 'National Executive Committee', consisting of himself, Count László Teleki and Klapka, and set on foot the organization of the legion;[2] whereafter he left for London to talk the British people into so casting their votes as to force Queen Victoria to form a government favourable to Hungarian independence.

The Austrian Government of course knew of these preparations, and when the army was mobilized, a Corps was left behind in Hungary to guard against the anticipated revolt: this Corps, moreover, was composed chiefly of reliable German and Czech troops, while Hungarians were sent down to Italy. Of the remaining eleven Corps, two were at first kept in reserve, but one whole Corps, composed of Hungarian units, showed itself so unreliable that it was sent back to Austria. Other Hungarian and Croat soldiers were taken out of their units and sent to the rear, and of those who were left with the colours, a not inconsiderable number, with some of the Italians, deserted to the enemy.[3] Thus, although not a shot had, in the event, been fired in Hungary, her contribution to the Monarchy's disaster had been substantial.

It had been larger even than the foregoing lines would suggest, for fantastic

[1] Kossuth's own account of these negotiations is given in his *Memoirs of My Exile*, vol. I. His 'instructions' to Hungary are on pp. 97 ff.

[2] An interesting feature of these preparations was an agreement concluded between Klapka and Prince Couza, Prince-Elect of Moldavia and Wallachia, under which Couza undertook to help the Hungarians in Transylvania, while Hungary was to help the Roumanians to recover the Bukovina. Serbia's co-operation was to be secured, the final goal being 'the confederation of the three Danubian States, Hungary, Serbia and Moldo-Wallachia'. See Kossuth, op. cit., pp. 300 ff.

[3] The number of desertions is put at fifteen thousand – six per cent of the troops involved.

as it had sounded, Kossuth had made good his promise to Napoleon, and it had been largely thanks to him that Britain had refrained from intervening against Napoleon on Austria's side.[1]

Then, when the war began to go badly, the political unrest raised its head in another quarter. This time it was the Liberals and financiers,[2] the opponents of the war and the sworn enemies of the whole system which had embarked on it, who unleashed a Press campaign so vehement that the censorship was powerless to silence it, not only against individual scapegoats such as Grünne, Bach and Kempen, but against 'the whole policy of the Concordat and militarism' and the absolutist regime and its pillars, the whole Court and the Emperor himself, in person. The outcry was so formidable that on 9 June the Ministers, meeting in council, decided that it was their 'sacred duty' to warn the Emperor, and composed an alarming report. Count Johann Rechberg, who on 15 May had been appointed Foreign Minister and acting Minister President, *vice* Buol, carried it down to the Emperor and himself endorsed its warnings in the gravest terms. According to most authorities, it was this report, coming on the heels of information from Prussia that made him despair of help from that quarter,[3] that tipped the scales for Francis Joseph and led him to make what terms he could with Napoleon, and hurry home.

[1] This sounds incredible, but a serious British historian (F. A. Simpson, England and the Italian War of 1859: *Historical Journal*, 1962, pp. 111 ff.) agrees that 'it was in fact Kossuth who, far more than any single Englishman, kept England out of the war'. It was, of course, only a question of tilting a nicely balanced structure by applying the right pressure at one or two key points; but even so it is impossible to withhold astonished admiration from the achievement.

[2] Almost all writers describe this agitation in quite general terms as 'domestic unrest', but the description of it given in Redlich (op. cit., pp. 256–7), which I have summarized here, shows quite clearly the particular character of the circles behind it, and its particular direction.

[3] In this respect, again, Francis Joseph had been over-precipitate, for on 14 June Prussia had, after all, ordered the mobilization of six army corps. The Prince Regent certainly had no intention of fighting a serious war for the sake of Austria's *beaux yeux*, but the news had seriously alarmed Napoleon, and if Francis Joseph had been less impatient and less irritated by Prussia's earlier haggling, he might have salvaged more than he did out of the wreckage.

11

Eight Years of Experiment

It was on the morrow of Villafranca that Francis Joseph began the retreat from absolutism which was to end, eight years later, in the constitutional settlement known as the Compromise. The road to this goal was not only long, but tortuous, and littered with the wreckages of unsuccessful experiments, for Francis Joseph did not willingly give way at all: each concession was wrung from him painfully, by overwhelming pressure. Nor were the forces with which he ultimately 'compromised' – those of Viennese business and Hungarian nationalism of the Deák brand – by any means those most congenial to his spirit. If he had had to ally himself with any forces at all, he would have preferred different ones. But this very fact that other solutions to the problem of the Monarchy were tried, and failed, is in itself proof that the final settlement, so reluctantly reached, was not the mere accident or trick as which it is so often represented, but possessed the essential virtue of resting on what were in fact the strongest forces of the day. That the balance of forces inside and outside the Monarchy changed later, making the settlement anachronistic, does not alter the truth that when concluded, it was historically inevitable.

It should be emphasized that Francis Joseph's changes of policies were not due to any spiritual conversion, but simply to forced recognition that the methods which he had employed thitherto were not effective to achieve his ends. Furthermore, his policies in 1859, and at least up to 1866 – more hesitantly, after that still – were characterized by no sort of resignation. Even the consolidation of the Monarchy within the frontiers accepted at Villafranca was in the last instance less an end in itself than a means to foreign political ends; first, the reversal of the decision in Italy itself, and when that had at least to be postponed, then the recapture of the secure hegemony in Germany.

We can date the retreat as beginning after Villafranca, for the replacement of Buol by Rechberg two months earlier had been unconnected with the internal situation.[1]

[1] The dismissal of Buol is generally attributed (as it was by himself) to a desire to placate the Czar, who bore a grudge against him from earlier days. But the documents quoted by Corti (*Mensch und Herrscher*, p. 223) suggest that the cause was more general. Buol had shown

But the Ministers' report, and Rechberg's own representations (which included a warning that the throne itself was in danger) had also convinced Francis Joseph that he must make some concessions to his critics at home. Accordingly, when, on 15 July, having returned from Italy, he issued to his peoples a Manifesto[1] communicating to them the signature of the preliminary peace, he added to it a promise that he would use the 'leisure' which peace would give him to place Austria's welfare on a solid basis 'by appropriate development of its rich spiritual and material resources, and by modernizing and improving its legislature and administration'.[2]

The first steps which he took to translate this vague assurance into concrete terms were, however, short and typically uncomprehensive; they were, incidentally, announced only after six weeks, which had been spent in consultations on which, since they were conducted almost entirely in private,[3] we have little information. It was early decided that some changes of personnel would be necessary, and Bach and Kempen seem to have been given notice of dismissal in July,[4] but it was not so easy to find the new men or the new policies. Rechberg began consultations,[5] at first à deux with Thun, who, however, then brought in his brother-in-law, Heinrich Jaroslav Clam-Martinic, at the time Statthalter in Cracow.[6] Their prescription was a slightly modernized form of feudalism, which would have transferred most

---

himself quite fantastically incompetent during the preceding months, and Francis Joseph had at last awakened to the fact. The deciding voice was probably that of Metternich, who during these last months of his life seems to have recovered a good deal of his old influence over Francis Joseph: the Emperor had been consulting him frequently during this crisis. Rechberg was a pupil and old confidant of Metternich's, incidentally, a Bavarian by birth, although he had passed his whole career in Austrian service. His principal qualification was his expertise, which was considerable, in both German and Italian affairs.

[1] Known from its place of origin as the 'Laxenburg Manifesto'.

[2] The Manifesto also contained an extraordinarily ill-tempered dig at Prussia for having allegedly left Austria in the lurch.

[3] The Ministerial Council was not once convoked between 15 July and 23 August.

[4] Bach's letter of resignation was dated 28 July; Kempen, even before that date, had in practice handed over his duties. Bach was then appointed Minister to the Vatican, an appointment which he held until 1870. He died, almost forgotten, in 1893. Grünne, the third special object of popular resentment, was not retired until 20 October, when he was given a Court position as Master of the Horse, being succeeded by General Count de Crenneville. In practice, however, de Crenneville had taken over Grünne's duties some weeks earlier.

[5] On these, see W. Goldinger, Von Solferino bis zum Oktoberdiplom (*Mitteilungen des oe. Staatsarchivs*, Vienna, 1950, pp. 106–126). Goldinger, unfortunately, does not describe the course of the conversations after Clam's retirement from them.

[6] On Clam see Denis, p. 424, and Höglinger, op. cit., pp. 10 ff. Clam's own family was one of the most illustrious in Bohemia, and linked by marriage to the Schwarzenbergs as well as the Thuns, so that he was a member in virtue of several titles of the arch-Conservative ring of the highest Bohemian aristocracy.

of the effective power from the Crown and its servants to the Provincial landed magnates. Neither Rechberg, nor Francis Joseph, would accept this, and Clam retired in dudgeon, resigned his official post, and set himself to carrying his fellow-Bohemian aristocrats back into political life. Since he possessed energy and ability, as well as family connections, he carried this task through with great speed and success.

A very different course was preconised by Bruck, who, immediately on the Emperor's return, had sent him a detailed memorandum on 'What Austria must do',[1] afterwards arguing his case in a long audience at which the Archduke Rainer was present. In his memorandum Bruck used bold language, denouncing strongly 'the obstacles which hamper the spiritual, confessional, social and political development of the Monarchy', and pleading for a far-reaching liberalization of the Monarchy's social, economic and intellectual life and a re-modelling of its structure to promote the interests and influence of the middle classes. Religious freedom and equality of rights must be granted to the Protestant and Greek Churches, and there should be a Constitution, based on 'sound municipal and communal institutions', but also allowing for Landtage and a central organ in the form of a re-organized and enlarged Reichsrat.

Another set of persistent and vigorous representations came from Hungary – not, of course, from the Kossuthists, nor even from the Deàkists (Deàk seem to have kept silence at this juncture). But as soon as Kossuth's renewed agitation gave them their cue, the Old Conservatives had begun again where they had left off eight or ten years earlier, arguing that Hungary did not want Kossuth, and could be made completely loyal by the appropriate concessions. Rechberg, who had personal connections with them, and believed that the proper policy for the Monarchy was to take them into partnership, had approached the men who were now their leaders, Josika (his confidant in chief) and Szécsen, almost on the morrow of Villafranca, and had elicited from them a memorandum, the work of Emile Dessewffy.[2] This was, indeed, no very modest document: it asked for the restoration of Hungary's 'historic rights' and territorial integrity, cancellation of the absolutist system and re-installation of the old administration, and early convocation of the Diet, as well as concessions over recruits, taxation, etc.

It is probable that Francis Joseph also received advice from many other quarters, of which no record remains.[3] At all events, it was not until 21 August that the composition of the new Ministry was announced. Rechberg Thun (who once again swallowed his scruples) and Bruck retained their

---

[1] Reproduced in Charmatz, *Bruck*, pp. 241 ff. A version of it had been published as early as 1860 in pamphlet form, under the title *Die Aufgaben Oesterreichs* (Austria's Tasks).

[2] The memorandum is summarised by Eisenmann, pp. 212 ff.

[3] For example, it seems likely that Francis Joseph was strongly influenced by the Archduke Rainer's views; but the Archduke's papers, if he left any, have never been published.

Portfolios, Bruck taking over the agenda of the Ministry of Trade and Communications, which was wound up. The new Minister of the Interior was Goluchowski, an appointment which surprised everyone, for he was the first Pole to be given a high appointment outside Galicia, and was not generally reputed a great light, but he was unimpeachably loyal, and had taken Rechberg's side against the Bohemians over the issue of State versus feudal authority. Hübner, back from Paris, who (again for unexplained reasons) had been in on the Rechberg conversations almost from the start, took Kempens's place, and there was a new Minister of Justice, Joseph von Lasser. The interests of the defence forces were to be represented by the Archduke Albrecht, *qua* head of the Supreme Army Command, a post which had been created for him.[1]

Two days later, came the publication of the Government's programme, showing where Francis Joseph was prepared to yield ground, and where not. Drafted by Hübner, it contained a few verbal concessions to Thun, but these were safeguarded by reservations. By and large, it constituted a notable victory for Bruck and his postulated fellow-Liberals (for his cannot have been the only Liberal representations to reach the Emperor) which was, perhaps, partly due to the ingenious way in which Bruck had put his case, representing the purpose of all his suggested reforms as that of strengthening Austria's international position in general, and her hegemony in Germany in particular (his own King Charles's head and one which at that juncture made a special appeal to Francis Joseph), through the direct accretions to her intrinsic strength which they would bring, and the increased influence which they would give her abroad.[2] The word 'Constitution' was studiously avoided, nor was there any reference to the Reichsrat, but many of Bruck's other recommendations, including the creation of a number of what the ordinary mind would regard as constitutional institutions, appeared (in each case, indeed, with certain dilutions and reservations) as promises. There was to be 'effective control' of all expenditure, both civilian and military (although how, or by whom, this was to be carried out was not stated). The legally recognized non-Catholic Churches were to be assured autonomy and the free practice of their religion, and further (a point not mentioned by Bruck, at least on paper) 'the position of the Israelites regulated along modern lines, account being taken of local and provincial conditions'. The Communal Autonomy Law was to be revised to make it appropriate to the particular conditions in each Crownland; a 'substantial part' of the duties hitherto carried out by officials was to be transferred to local bodies, 'if possible autonomous'; and after completion of these 'first and

---

[1] He was succeeded in October by his brother Wilhelm.

[2] The grant of equality for the Protestants and both constitutional and industrial reform are specifically advocated for their effects in Germany; equality for the Greek Churches as a means of preventing Austria's influence being outstripped by that of Russia in the Balkans.

most urgent tasks', bodies representing the Estates (*ständische Vertretungen*) were to be called into being in the various Crownlands.¹

Very different was the fate of the Hungarian representations. Hungary had not in fact risen, for Francis Joseph's acceptance of the peace overtures had been so quick that – it must have been one of the brightest features for him in the whole situation – there had been no time before the armistice for France to make any serious moves in the Adriatic² and after it, Napoleon and Victor Emmanuel had cheerfully thrown their Hungarian protégés overboard.³ But the damage Kossuth had done had been deep enough to fill the Emperor with a strong resentment against the whole 'rebel' nation,

¹ This (to Western eyes) contradiction between Francis Joseph's willingness to grant a fair measure of self-government on certain levels and in certain fields, and his stubborn and repeated insistence on the maintenance of his absolutist power, must beyond doubt seem paradoxical. The insistence is on record: thus in June 1860 he told a Ministerial Council that 'he would allow no curtailment of the Monarchic power through any Constitution; he would face any storm rather than that', and he forbade his Ministers 'even to discuss the possibility'. Yet this was nearly a year after the issue of the Rechberg-Goluchowski programme. In view of this, some historians have dismissed the programme as a piece of hypocrisy, but that view seems to me incompatible with the documents. The key probably lies rather in the tradition which had made it second nature to the Habsburgs to distinguish sharply between those questions over which they claimed absolute control, by virtue of their royal prerogative, and those which they left to their subjects. Communal self-government belonged to the latter category; Bruck himself argued in his memorandum that it was purely administrative. He was more doubtful about the Landtage, which he thought would be bound to stray into politics, which was why he wanted their influences counteracted by an enlarged and strengthened Reichsrat. Why Francis Joseph, while rejecting the enlarged Reichsrat, yet accepted the Landtage one cannot explain; someone must have persuaded him that the *Landtage* would be harmless so long as he retained the *jus legis ferendae*. On the other hand, he regarded foreign policy and defence as fields in which his absolute power was not to be questioned, and so long as they were safe, so was the essential. So when the October Diploma was issued, he wrote to his mother: 'We shall, indeed, have a little Parliamentary government, but the power remains in my hands' (Schürer, p. 302), and in conjunction with the February Patent he enjoined the Ministerial Council 'to confine the activities of the Reichsrat strictly to the field defined, and to reject decisively any attempt by it to interfere in the conduct of foreign affairs, or army affairs, or the business of the Supreme Command' (cit. Redlich, *Problem*, I. 808).

There remained, of course, the ineluctable fact that the Monarch's full control over his armed forces, and consequently, his freedom in the field of foreign policy, was illusory if his subjects could refuse him the sinews of war. This was the real issue, as was to appear even more clearly in the subsequent years, in the course of which Francis Joseph was driven back, step by step. His retreats were, however, always made under compulsion and with the worst of grace, and I find it impossible to believe that the 'control of expenditure' promised in the August programme meant anything more than careful supervision to guard, for example, against the extravagances and abuses for which the defence services and the army contractors, in particular, were then being pilloried.

² A French squadron had anchored outside Fiume on 6 July, and French troops had occupied the adjacent island of Lussin Piccolo for a few days.

³ All they had done had been to secure from Francis Joseph the promise (which was none too scrupulously kept) of an amnesty for the deserters from the Imperial Army who had joined the Hungarian legion, which was then dissolved.

impartially. At that juncture he, like Schwarzenberg before (and Francis Ferdinand after) him, was not prepared to regard one Hungarian as any better than another, and the Emperor refused to listen either to Rechberg, or to any Hungarians. There was no hint in the programme of any modification of the unitary structure of the Monarchy, or, indeed of any concession whatever to Hungary.[1]

A few days later, Hungarian opinion was even provoked further still by a 'Protestant Patent', issued by Thun on 1–2 September, nominally in fulfilment of the Government's pledge to the non-Catholics. This did in fact bring the Hungarian Calvinists and Lutherans some material advantages, but its character of an octroi violated the autonomy which both Churches felt to be essential to their existences. Hübner, to whom Rechberg had entrusted the further conduct of the conversations with the Old Conservatives, and who had sponsored their cause too warmly, paid for his intervention with his post. 'Nothing,' Francis Joseph told him, 'would satisfy the Hungarians. If we announced a Constitution now, we should have a republic within a year.'[2]

In consequence, the autumn passed with the deadlock in Hungary unbroken, and the situation there dangerous in the extreme. The police reported a state of disaffection which could at any moment erupt into revolution. Resistance to the tax-collectors was almost universal among those respectable enough to dare defy the law;[3] the local authorities refused to distrain on defaulters, and the soldiers sent down to do it met with a resistance which they were simply powerless to overcome.

In the West, meanwhile, many weeks passed with little sign that any real concessions were coming. Goluchowski made no perceptible motions to introduce any self-governing institutions, or, indeed, to do anything much except again to rearrange the Crownlands so as to make Galicia once more into an administrative unit.[4] The only noteworthy internal enactment of the period, outside the purely financial field, was the 'industrial regulation' (*Gewerbeordnung*) of 10 December, which satisfied the economic doctrines of

---

[1] Almost all historians write the contrary: that Villafranca was followed by immediate concessions to Hungary. This is not the case: these came only at the next stage, in 1860. It is true that on 8 August a decree had appeared laying down that German 'need not be employed so exclusively as before in the secondary schools and gymnasia of the Monarchy: it was enough if pupils, on leaving them, were able to read, write and speak German.' But this order did not apply to Hungary alone, but to the entire Monarchy: it was issued by Thun, and seems to have been a sort of celebration by him of Bach's retirement.

[2] Corti, op. cit., p. 247. Hübner resigned on 21 October. His successor was Baron Thierry.

[3] When the Hungarian Diet met in 1861, every single Deputy in it was in arrears with his taxes. In January 1862 the Minister of War said in a Ministerial Council that 45 m.g. of taxes in Hungary had to be raised by distraint by the military. He suggested that the Ministry of Finance ought to take over the costs of this operation (Regele, *Benedek*, p. 318).

[4] The details of these measures need not be given, since all of them were cancelled by Goluchowski's successor a couple of years later.

its inspirer, Bruck, by instituting near-complete freedom in the labour market.[1]

There was, however, one problem which admitted of no temporization: that of the national finances. The outbreak of war had sent the course of Austrian papers plunging again, the confusion being accentuated by one of its effects, the bankruptcy of the house of Arnstein and Eskeles. On 2 July Bruck had proposed floating another large loan (500 m.g. inside the Monarchy and 100 abroad), but failed to get the proposal through the Ministerial Council. The Government had perforce borrowed again from the National Bank, which had made a new issue of paper money, promptly quoted at a heavy discount. The war had ended with a note circulation of 600 m.g., the national debt at 2,265 m.g. and the premium on silver at 140. The army was demobilized almost precipitately at the end of hostilities, but the estimated expenditure for 1860 was still 541 m.g. and the estimated revenue only 261.

Finally, at this inauspicious moment, the news leaked out that whereas the amount actually subscribed for the 1854 loan had been 508 m.g., it had overspent by 111 million, the fact having been concealed from the public.

A few steps were taken in this field. A committee to study the reform of taxation was set up in September, and late in October – not, it seems, before – the question of the promised control of expenditure was taken up. Prolonged and very obscure arguments went on in the Ministerial Council,[2] where Bruck fought bitter verbal wars against the Army leaders and against Thun, who

[1] This measure finally abolished the guilds, in the place of which it set 'craft associations', which had, however, no authority over their members, although membership of them was compulsory. A licence of competence was required to practise a small number of trades to which special considerations applied, but these numbered only fourteen in all (among them were building, shipbuilding, chimney-sweeping, the making of firearms and the sale of poisons). Any other trade could be practised by any person legally qualified to administer his own property and with no criminal record. The measure was a revised edition of one drafted by Toggenburg in 1855. It had been re-drafted under Bruck's supervision in 1857-8, but the influence of the Church had then still been strong enough to prevent its enactment. It was now specifically advertised, in accordance with Bruck's recommendation, as proof that Austria was leading Germany in economic liberalism, and was in fact welcomed by the employers: a writer quoted by Charmatz (*Bruck*, p. 135) described it as 'a payment on account which the absolutist State had to offer the bourgeoisie in its obscure thrust for political supremacy'. The weaker categories of workers, on the other hand, now lost all protection (such as the guild restrictions had still afforded some of them) except for the restrictions on the employment of child labour still existing under the general law. To describe it, as a recent English writer has done, as a piece of protective social legislation, is singularly mistaken.

[2] The history of all this is very obscure. Neither Charmatz (on Bruck) nor Beer had access to the archives, and Redlich, who summarizes the relevant minutes of the Ministerial Councils (*Problem*, I. 2. 179) for once does so only in a few lines, leaving it quite unclear how far Bruck was the attacker, and how far, as Uhlirtz suggests, the reform was forced on him. He actually resigned on 22 October, but apparently on a minor issue, and was retained in office (against the opposition of Thun).

was his envenomed enemy, while he himself was being attacked by the public for his part in faking the figures of the 1854 loan. Finally it was agreed that a Committee should be set up to investigate the State debt, and on 11 November the Emperor announced his intention, firstly of getting the 1860–1 Budget balanced,[1] and secondly, of setting up a Committee 'to examine the State credit in all respects and to work for the realization of this objective'. Meanwhile, as Redlich writes,[2] 'the view had gained ground that only a Committee which was independent of the Government and not composed of officials could to some extent restore the confidence of capitalist circles, and of the population in general, in the financial administration', and on 23 December the appointment was announced of a 'State Debt Committee', to report direct to the Emperor, who was its own nominal president, and to consist of seven persons: a Vice-President and two others nominated by the Emperor, two chosen by the National Bank, one by the Lower Austrian Chamber of Commerce and one by the Bourse of Vienna.

This was followed by a series of Orders lifting, in one Crownland or another, one or another restriction to which its Jews had been subjected.[3]

These half measures were, however, received almost with derision, and when the Government issued a new loan of 200 m.g., out of the proceeds of which it hoped to repay its debt to the National Bank, only 76 m.g. were taken up. If, then, the financiers were to be reassured – and the necessity for this seems to have been generally accepted – some further concession to their susceptibilities seemed inescapable. This recognition led to the next step, which was an important one. It had been suggested from various quarters[4] that the desired objective could be achieved by enlarging and giving more

---

[1] This announcement has been the subject of much derisive comment, but it had a reasonable purpose. It was designed as an indirect intimation that military expenditure was going to be cut.

[2] Redlich, l.c.

[3] The most important were two Patents of February 1860 which allowed Jews to own real property in various Lands. The restriction (imposed, as will be remembered, in 1853) was lifted altogether in Lower Austria, the Bohemian and Hungarian Lands, the Littoral and Dalmatia. In Galicia and the Bukovina the full concession was limited to Jews holding a certificate of higher education, although other Jews were still allowed to buy or lease certain categories of land. The Alpine Lands were presumably omitted because their Jewish population was then practically non-existent.

Another measure repealed in Galicia was Joseph II's Edict of 1789 forbidding Jews to manufacture or trade in alcoholic liquors outside the towns. The Statthalterei said this ban might as well be lifted, since it was notorious that in spite of it, the entire traffic in strong liquors had remained in Jewish hands.

[4] The spiritual authorship of it is generally attributed to Hans von Perthaler, a Tirolean awyer occupying the somewhat secondary post of Counsellor in the Supreme Court in Vienna, but a prolific writer on constitutional problems. At the beginning of 1860 he had published anonymously a series of articles (*Neun Briefe über die Verfassungreform in Oesterreich*) in which most of the ideas later embodied in the Patent were advocated. Bruck, however, had already proposed the move in his memorandum.

importance to the Reichsrat, and the friends of the idea in the Ministerial Council (who were headed by Rechberg and Bruck) advised that that body should be given a quasi-representative character by including in it representatives of the Landtage. This meant not only that the Landtage would – unlike those promised by Stadion and Bach – really come into being, but that they would have a genuine voice in public affairs, if only in the one aspect of them which related to finance. It was a step towards Constitutionalism, and opposed on that ground by Thun. This time, however, Francis Joseph agreed with the progressives,[1] and on 5 March a Rescript was issued to the effect that the Reichsrat was to be enlarged by the addition to its existing members of a further ten nominated by the Emperor, and thirty-eight more who were to be elected for six years by the Landtage, pending the constitution whereof they, too, would be nominated by the Crown. It was to meet on 31 May, and its first purpose was to be to consider and advise upon (for it was only an advisory body) 'the determination of the Budget, examination of the closed accounts and of the data of the State Debt Committee'.

Six of the thirty-eight elected members were to come from Inner Hungary, three each from Transylvania, Bohemia and Galicia, two each from Lombardy-Venetia, Lower Austria, Croatia, the Voivody and the Tirol, and one from each of the other Crownlands.

And these proposals, in their turn, raised, in acute form, the problem of Hungary, at that time still divided into five provinces. Several of the Ministers advocated convoking a separate Landtag for each of the five; Nádasdy, the only born Hungarian in the Ministerial Council, warned it most solemnly that to convoke a single Diet for Inner Hungary would at once lead to very strong pressure for further concessions. This, however, would undoubtedly have raised a fearful storm, and Francis Joseph shrank from it, taking instead the fateful decision to experiment – for the first time in twelve years – with conciliation towards Hungary on a point of principle. On 19 April, therefore, a further Rescript abolished the Provinces and centralized the administration of Inner Hungary in the capital. It was explicitly stated that Inner Hungary would have only one Diet, and further, that the lower autonomous units would be the old Counties, with their traditional Congregationes and Committees. In addition, the Archduke Albrecht was replaced as Governor by General L. Benedek, himself a Hungarian, although of modest parentage, and, incidentally, a Protestant.[2]

On 15 May, Thun's Protestant Patent was revoked, and another amnesty

[1] The documents do not explain this strange fact; but Redlich tells us (op. cit., I. 490 n.) that Francis Joseph at this time was actually pressing his Ministers to get on with the statutes of the Landtage, and of the Communal Councils. It may well be that Francis Joseph was influenced by the conversations which he had been having with Metternich, who had also wanted the Lands represented on his Reichsrat.

[2] This change had been decided earlier, the Archduke having repeatedly expressed his wish to be relieved of his post.

enacted. Shortly after, certain analogous concessions to Venice were announced.

On 1 May the proposed membership of the 'Reinforced Reichsrat' was announced. The selection had been made by Francis Joseph himself.[1] It was, as it was meant to be, an assembly of notables. The original core included three Archdukes, one of whom (the Archduke Rainer) was designated President,[2] and various Elder Statesmen (many of these survivors of the original body) such as Krausz and Gehringer; the life-members, Cardinal Rauscher, several Generals and more civilian Privy Councillors. For the nominees, Francis Joseph seems honestly to have tried to pick men who could speak authoritatively for every sectional interest as he understood the term. Thus the list included some bourgeois (by definition, Germans) from Lower Austria and Styria, one (Dr Hain) from Bohemia, and a Transylvanian Saxon, Maager. There were two Roumanians: Şaguna, the Uniate Bishop from Transylvania, and Mocsonyi, a landowner from the Bánát, a Serb (Masirevics, the Orthodox Bishop of Temesvár), two Ruthenes (the Uniate Bishop of Lemberg and a lawyer), and a couple of Italians from Venice and Dalmatia. But most of the nominees, including the two Poles, the two other men from Bohemia and all six Hungarians, belonged to what was in fact the most important class in those Crownlands, the great feudal nobility. All six gentlemen who eventually turned up from Hungary (the wording must be used, because all of them made a point of stating that they were there in their individual capacities, not as representing Hungary) were Old Conservatives; this not altogether of Francis Joseph's fault, since he had tried to throw his net wider, but three of the men first invited by him (Barons Eötvös, Vay and Pál Somssich) had refused the invitation, as had Bánffy from Transylvania. The six who did appear were Counts Apponyi, Barcocsy, Majláth, György Andrássy and Szécsen, and Bishop Korizmics.[3]

With the opening of the sessions of the Reinforced Reichsrat, on 31 May, there began the second stage of the Monarchy's progress towards constitutional life – a stage which proved to be much longer than Francis Joseph had expected, and to end at a different stopping place. The Reichsrat's terms of reference were, as we have seen, modest: it had to advise on certain financial questions, nothing more. In fact, its first action was to appoint a Committee which did go into the financial condition of the Monarchy, and on 19 July elicited from Francis Joseph a concession of quite prime importance in the shape of a promise that no new taxes should be imposed, nor existing ones raised, or loans floated, without its consent. But meanwhile, the Hungarians, who were easily the most skilful and experienced politicians of all those

[1] Redlich, op. cit., I. 489.
[2] The two others were the Archdukes Wilhelm and Leopold.
[3] Josika had just died, a week before Széchenyi.

present, had blandly taken charge of the Reichsrat to turn it into a sort of Constituent. This being so, the fact that all the Hungarians were Old Conservatives was very important for the direction taken by the proceedings; for the Old Conservative philosophy regarded Vienna, whether under its autocratic, its centralist, its bureaucratic, its reformist or its Germanic aspect, as the enemy in chief, whereas it was ready to see Bohemia and Galicia enjoy as wide a federal status as it was asking for Hungary; while at the same time conceding the need for some common institutions for them all.[1] These weeks were the Old Conservatives' hey-day, and during them they achieved an astonishing success story. Clam had now got together a group of adherents and they had already been petitioning the Emperor to restore them their 'historic rights'.[2] The Hungarians welded them, and their remaining opposite numbers from the other Crownlands, into a 'Party of the Federal Nobility', led by themselves, and produced a report, which was actually after it Constitution, of strongly federalist tendencies. It laid down 'the equality in principle, of all Lands of the Monarchy', and while admitting, in principle, in a phrase so obscure as to be practically unintelligible,[3] the need for some institutions, possibly representative, common to the entire Monarchy, it declared the necessity of reconstructing the Monarchy on a basis which took into account 'the historic-political individualities of its various components' and 'linked up with the formerly existing historic institutions'. Hungary's former self-governing institutions should be reactivated, and similar bodies created in the other Lands, and the Diets convoked.

In view of these proposals, a group of the non-Federalist members of the Reichsrat – this party was headed by its German bourgeois members, but some of the smaller nationalities associated themselves with it[4] – plucked up courage also to recommend constitutional institutions, but with a larger Reichsrat which assured 'the complete maintenance of the unity of the Monarchy and of the legislative and executive authority of the Government'.

The two drafts were presented to the Monarch on 27 September in the form of a majority and a minority report, the former signed by thirty-four

---

[1] This was not a mere tactical move, for Eötvös, the brains of the Hungarian higher nobility, had endorsed exactly the same thesis in his *Garantien der Macht und Einheit Oesterechs*, published in 1859. Eötvös is even in favour of allowing the Lands of the Bohemian Crown to form a unit.

[2] A memorandum signed by nine of these gentlemen (four Princes and five Counts) is reproduced in extract by Redlich (and discussed, in Redlich's typical manner, in words more diffuse than its own) in his *Problem*, I. pp. 642 ff. It is undated, but was written after the convocation of the Reinforced Reichsrat and before the issue of the Diploma. Large parts of it appear almost verbatim in the Federal Nobility's report.

[3] *Die definitive Feststellung, Sicherung und Vertretung ihres gemeinsamen staatsrechtliches Verbandes.*

[4] In the voting, the Croat and Italian representatives had voted for the majority report, the Serb and Mocsonyi for the minority. Șaguna and the Ruthene Bishop had voted against both reports, while the other Ruthene had abstained.

members of the Reichsrat, the latter by sixteen. Two Councillors were absent, and six, including the Archdukes Wilhelm and Leopold, and Cardinal Rauscher, had voted against both reports.

Both sets of proposals were undoubtedly highly objectionable to the Emperor, and he hesitated for a fortnight before taking his decision. But the Hungarian Old Conservatives, who were now regular visitors to him, pressed their proposals on him strongly, warning him that revolution would break out in Hungary if they were rejected and assuring him (and this was the decisive argument) that the country would be pacified if they were accepted. Francis Joseph was due to meet the Czar and the King of Prussia in Warsaw on 21 October in the hope (Rechberg's idea) of reconstituting the Holy Alliance, and did not want to arrive at the meeting with half his dominions on the brink of revolution. In the end, he made his decision suddenly (Szécsen is reported to have convinced him finally on a train journey), and when he had done so, acted on it with the precipitancy characteristic of him at this stage of his life. Szécsen was actually told to prepare a draft of the document in which the New Order was to be announced, and was present, with Apponyi, at the discussions on it which were held with Rechberg. The results were thus mainly (although not entirely, for they had to make a few concessions) the Old Conservatives' work. They were embodied in a 'Diploma' (known in history as the 'October Diploma', and announced as a 'permanent and irrevocable instrument') and a number of subsidiary Rescripts, all issued on 20 October. They did indeed represent a big step forward from absolutism, although not such a large one as might have appeared to those unacquainted with Austrian political terminology, for the words 'legislature' and 'legislative' appearing in them were operative, since the Emperor continued to maintain that foreign affairs, and the conduct, command and organization of the armed forces, were prerogatives of the Crown, and not subject to legislative control, and without stating in so many words the exclusion of these questions from the competence of the Reichsrat, the Diploma assumed it *ex silentio*. The Crown accepted, however, considerable restrictions on its authority in the internal field, for it promised that it would thereafter exercise its right to enact, alter or rescind legislation only with the co-operation of the Landtage and of the Reichsrat. The latter was to be competent (in conjunction with the Crown) for legislation on questions affecting the entire Monarchy, these being defined (and here the exclusion *ex silentio* of foreign affairs and defence became operative) as weights and measures, customs and trade, central communications, the modalities and organization of liability for military service (although not the number of recruits to be supplied), taxation and credit operations. Taxation – and herein lay the most important concession in the whole document – required the 'consent' of the Reichsrat; other questions, only its 'co-operation'. Legislation on all other questions fell within the competence of the Diets: in the Kingdoms and

Lands belonging to the Hungarian Crown, 'in the sense' of their previous Constitutions, in the other Lands, constitutionally, in conformity with their Statutes. An important provision, a presage of the later Dualism, enacted that the Reichsrats of the non-Hungarian Lands could be convoked without the Hungarians when questions were under discussion which had long been 'handled and decided' for them as a unit.

In the Rescripts, the membership of the Reichsrat was fixed at one hundred, the numbers being brought up by increasing the representation of the Crownlands, and a large number of special concessions to Hungary were made. The validity of the main Hungarian 'fundamental laws' (i.e. the Leopoldinian corpus) was reaffirmed, the effect being, broadly, to re-establish in Hungary the *status quo ante* 1848, except that the validity of the April Laws enacting noble taxation, general admissibility to public office, and the emancipation of the peasants, was confirmed. The other April Laws, however, being incompatible with the Diploma, were 'reserved for revision and cancellation through the Diet'. The Hungarian Court Chancellery was re-established, Baron Vay, until recently in prison for sedition, being appointed Chancellor. The Chancellor was to be a member of the central Government, into which Szécsen was also taken as Minister without Portfolio. Magyar was restored as the central official language, and that of the 'inner service' and of higher education, but adequate facilities were to be given to non-Magyars to use their language in elementary education and local administration. Immediate elections were to be held for the County and Municipal Diets, after which the old system of autonomous local government would be resumed. The old Hungarian judiciary system was reinstated. The Diet was to be convoked in 1861, to submit further proposals for recasting the relationship between Hungary and the Crown.

The Transylvanian Court Chancellery was restored and the Chancellor instructed to consult with qualified representatives of the different local nationalities, religions and classes, and then to submit proposals for a genuinely representative Diet. The Ban of Croatia was required to convoke the Sabor, and to submit proposals for a new internal Constitution, and for the relationship between Hungary and Croatia. The Voivodina was reincorporated administratively in Hungary, with immediate effect; but a Commissioner was to be sent down to report on the wishes of its peoples as to their future.

In Cis-Leithania the government was to work out statutes for the Landtage, assuring them 'representation adapted alike to their historic development, their present requirements, and the interests of the Empire'.

The central Ministries of the Interior and Cults were abolished, since these questions now fell within the competence of the Land authorities. Goluchowski became Minister of State, Baron Mecséry, Minister of Police, and Degenfeld, Minister of Defence.

Unhappily for its authors, the Diploma was ill-received almost everywhere. In spite of its federalist nature, it failed to satisfy even the Czechs or the Poles: the Czech politicians, suddenly re-emerged, complained that they, alone among the peoples of the Monarchy, had not been represented on the Reinforced Reichsrat (they did not count Clam-Martinic as a Czech), and were aggrieved that the Diploma did not recognize the *Böhmisches Staatsrecht*, while the Poles organized a deputation to Vienna to demand a separate status for Galicia as complete as that given to Hungary.

These were reactions based on national feeling, and the most ominous sign of all for the regime was not that such feelings should find the Diploma unsatisfactory, but that they should exist at all; for this meant that the most fundamental of all the suppositions on which Francis Joseph's and Schwarzenberg's State had rested – that it was possible to de-politize the national consciousnesses of its peoples – had now proved false in the West, as it had from the outset in Hungary. The thesis that Austria was not an a-national State but a multi-national one had been restated, and was to be reasserted, from this date onward, with increasing cogency, until it drove its rival almost – never, indeed, quite – out of the field. It is true that every step in its advance made more clear the difficulties of finding a solution for it compatible with the existence of the Monarchy.

The Germans of the Monarchy themselves did not escape this resurgence of national feeling Nationally-minded. Germans cried out that the Diploma handed over the Germans of the Bohemian Lands to Czech rule. The centenary of Schiller's birth, which was commemorated on 8 November, was made the occasion for fiery speeches of purely Germanic national self-exaltation in which the students' *Burschenschaften* were particularly vocal.[1]

But the German and German-speaking bourgeoisie was hostile to the Diploma also on other grounds. The bureaucrats *à la* Bach saw the control over Hungary slipping out of their hands, while the Liberals saw landlords and clericals installed as the masters of Austria and genuine control by the tax-payer over public expenditure still not guaranteed (if the Diploma did not make things worse than ever in this respect; for it seemed possible that Hungary might use her new freedom to cut down her contributions to the exchequer). The Liberals' discontent was increased when Goluchowski began publishing the Statutes for the Landtage, four of which, for Styria, Tirol, Salzburg and Carinthia, he produced between 30 October and 13 November. Except that the towns gained a little more representation – and even this was counter-balanced by the restoration of a separate Curia for landed property, as such – these were little more than re-hashes of the old Estates, and to emphasize the continuity, the members of the higher Benches were to be allowed to wear their old uniforms. The Landtage were not even given free

---

[1] Students' *Turnverbande*, etc., were now springing up in great numbers. The police thought them undesirable, but were afraid to prohibit them.

choice of their representatives to the Reichsrat: they were to present lists, from which the Emperor would make the final choice. The German Liberals and nationalists formed a loose common front (another precursor of 1867) united by the slogan that 'Austria must be treated as favourably as Hungary', i.e., if Hungary had a central constitutional Parliament, the West must have one also.

The Government was particularly sensitive to these political (and in the last resort, financial) reactions, because public confidence in Austria's financial stability had received another shock in the preceding April when, largely, it would seem, as the result of undeserved calumny, Bruck had committed suicide, his act releasing another cloud of rumours.[1] His successor, Ignaz von Plener, had various ideas for restoring the position, but had not had time to put them into effect when, in the autumn, the international situation erupted again. Garibaldi took Naples in September and Piedmont sent troops into Umbria and the Marches. The Warsaw meeting had ended in nothing more than fairly hollow words, while it had infuriated Napoleon, who saw in it an attempt to isolate him. When the question of sending troops to Italy, or to the Rhine, was discussed, Plener replied, like so many of his predecessors on analogous occasions, that the money simply was not there, and that it could not be raised through increased taxation. Credit would be the only resort, and the outer world was unapproachable.

Thus Francis Joseph, who only a few months before had flattered himself that he would be back in Lombardy in a year or so, had had to watch the unification of Italy almost completed under his nose, because he had not the money to prevent it.

Meanwhile, the biggest disappointment of all had come from Hungary. Szécsen had assured Francis Joseph that the country would accept the Diploma, but even he and his colleagues had admitted that time would be necessary to prepare public opinion, and had been horrified when the documents were published almost before the ink on them was dry. In any case, it quickly transpired that the Old Conservatives had, as usual, totally misjudged opinion in their country. It was quite true that practically the whole of Hungary was now anxious to find a settlement with the Crown:

---

[1] Inquiries had been set on foot in the previous autumn into the irregularities in the commissariat during the Italian campaign. The culprit in chief, Q.M. General Eynatten, hanged himself in prison, leaving a confession. Among the other persons arrested were several Trieste contractors, former associates of Bruck's. Rumour linked Bruck's name with them. Although completely innocent, as was afterwards proved, Bruck submitted his resignation, and the Emperor, after first refusing it in a gracious message which left Bruck completely reassured, wrote to him two days later that he was retiring him 'temporarily' and appointing von Plener 'provisionally' to take his place. No one knows why he took this step, which he seems not to have expected Bruck to resent; but Bruck was shattered by it, and cut his own throat in a fit of mortification.

The real scandals were glossed over with conspicuous lightness.

Villafranca had at last convinced all but the most incorrigible dreamers that anything else was impracticable. But no one except the Old Conservatives themselves were willing to accept any octroied settlement at all, nor even so much control as the Diploma allowed to the Reichsrat, let alone the institution itself, in those dimensions and on those foundations, which gave it, after all, the character of a central Parliament of the Gesammtmonarchie, and one which enjoyed the cardinal right of voting taxation; not to mention the continued separation of Transylvania and the continued treatment of Hungary as one 'Crownland' among many, even if it was to be, in many respects, a privileged one.

Being genuinely anxious to find a settlement which Hungary would accept, Francis Joseph received Deák and Eötvös in audience on 27 December, but Deák[1] told him flatly that Hungary could never accept a common 'Reichsrat' or Parliament, nor any enactment which denied the validity of the April Laws. He agreed, indeed, that the Laws might be amended, and he afterwards persuaded a conference of the Hungarian law officers to admit the possibility, even the desirability, of such amendment; but this could be done only by agreement between the Crown and a legally constituted Hungarian Parliament. Less inhibited spirits demonstrated noisily. The first action of the Congregatio of Pest County (which, in the absence of a Diet, set the tone for the whole country) was to reaffirm truculently the validity of the April Laws, to ask the Chancellery to have the Diet convoked on the basis of those laws, and pending this, to suspend the collection of arrears of taxes. Other Counties elected to membership of their Congregationes such figures as Kossuth, Louis Napoleon and Cavour.

With practically everyone against it, the Diploma would clearly have to be revised to meet one set of objectors or the other, and this time, the Hungarians had overshot the mark. Francis Joseph and his advisers believed that any more concessions to them would lead straight to separation, and their reply to the agitation was therefore simply to reinforce the garrisons in the country. But this was no answer to the financial problems of the Monarchy, which were more pressing than ever. During the international crisis of the autumn, quotations of Austrian bonds sank to a new level, and the premium on silver rose to the record figure of 164. As for the domestic market, when, in January 1861 the Government floated a new loan for the modest sum of 30 m.g., it had to pay the subscribers nearly 9%.

Plener maintained that given time, he could put things straight, but only if the world of finance recovered confidence in Austria's credit-worthiness, and for this, not only abstention from adventures abroad was necessary, but also more constitutionalism at home. And as it happened, this course seemed also to be that required for the realization of those foreign political ambitions

[1] What passed between Francis Joseph and Eötvös has never been published.

which now lay closest to Francis Joseph's heart. If he had not yet finally renounced all hope of recovering his Dynasty's position in Italy, yet he had been forced to realize that this could not be done quickly. But the renunciation, even if only temporary, of the Italian prize made the German all the more desirable, and it was impossible to deny the truth of poor Bruck's thesis that a relatively liberal and German-minded Austria would command more sympathies among the smaller German States than a near-autocratic one with Magyar, Polish and Czech magnates playing all the chief instruments.

So Francis Joseph switched his policy again. On 14 December Goluchowski, who had been the target of particularly vehement and scurrilous attacks by the Liberal Press (who hated him alike as an aristocrat, a federalist, a clerical and a Pole) was abruptly and ungraciously dismissed[1] and replaced next day as Minister of State by Anton von Schmerling, generally regarded as the white hope of the German centralists (although, interestingly enough, the decisive backing for his candidature seems to have come from the Hungarian Old Conservatives).[2]

The arguments which went on behind the scenes on the nature and extent of the move occupied some weeks,[3] for there was still a big gap between what the Liberals thought necessary for political pacification and financial consolidation, and what Francis Joseph was willing to grant. Von Plener, the Liberals' representative in the inner ring, argued that the confidence which he regarded as essential for the success of his financial plans could not be assured by anything short of a genuinely representative system, and wanted the 1849 Constitution restored. Francis Joseph, however, was implacably opposed, not only to many features in that instrument,[4] but on principle to any Constitution of popular origin. All that Schmerling was able to extract from him (and that with great difficulty) was his consent to the halfway house

[1] On entering his Ministry, he found his resignation lying on his table for his signature. This anecdote is told in relation to several Austrian Ministers, sometimes apocryphically, but seems to be authenticated in this case.

[2] Von Plener, the Finance Minister, invariably attributed the appointment to his own influence, but Schmerling himself in his recollections, which are still unpublished but were utilized by F. Fellner in an interesting and informative article, Das Februarpatent von 1861 (*Mitteilungen des Instituts für oe. Geschichtsforschung*, 1955, p. 549, ff.) most specifically attributes the decisive intervention in his favour to Rechberg, who in his turn was passing on the views of the Old Conservatives. This, of course, does not necessarily mean more than that Francis Joseph's decision, already half-conceived, was clinched by the assurance that Schmerling would go down also in Hungary.

[3] On the genesis of the Patent, see Eisenmann, pp. 261 ff., Redlich, *Problem*, I. 672–701, and F. Fellner, op. cit.

[4] These included its chapter on popular rights, of which Francis Joseph would hear nothing. Schmerling bowed to his objections, although he may not have liked them, but he himself 'did not believe that basic rights were of the essential of a Constitution' (Fellner, p. 555). As Fellner remarks, both the Diploma and the Patent admitted the principles of equality before the law and inter-Confessional equality. These, however, had survived the cancellation of the 1849 Constitution and had figured in the Sylvester Patent.

of a relatively conservative document, issued by himself in the form of an octroi and thus bearing no stigma of popular sovereignty. After agreeing with the Emperor on the limits which the new instrument must not exceed, Schmerling rapidly worked out its details with the help of Lasser and Perthaler, whom he had attached to himself as a sort of one-man brains trust (although he seems, strangely enough, then to have been unaware of Perthaler's authorship of the *Neun Briefe*) and having meanwhile avoided the Charybdis of his other colleagues' objections by keeping them in the dark as to his preparations, bullied them into accepting the result.

Meanwhile, the Ministry had been reconstructed, the appointments being announced on 4 February 1861. The Archduke Rainer became Minister President,[1] Rechberg remained Foreign Minister, and Schmerling, Plener and the Hungarians retained their portfolios. Lasser became 'Minister for administration', Frh. A. Pratobevera taking over Justice from him.[2] Then, on 27 February, there appeared the series of enactments known collectively as the 'February Patent'. In form, these were enactments putting into effect the October Diploma, with certain modifications of detail – a device which met Francis Joseph's objection to anything but an octroi, and also avoided the absurdity of revoking what had been described only four months earlier as a 'permanent and irrevocable instrument'. In fact, too, they made no changes to substantial parts of the Diploma (the common description of the Patent as a complete reversal of the Diploma is erroneous). The powers of the Crown were further restricted in one respect only, although that was, indeed, an important one: the consent of the Reichsrat was now required not only for taxation, but for all 'legislation'. Even this concession, however, to which Francis Joseph agreed only with extreme reluctance,[3] was partly counter-balanced by a provision that 'taxation, once voted, remained valid until superseded', and by the resuscitation of the 'emergency paragraph' (now paragraph 13) from the 1849 Constitution, enabling the Government to enact legislation when the Reichsrat was not in session. The Reichsrat, although it now had the right of initiating legislation, remained, technically, an advisory body, and there was no mention of Ministerial responsibility.

---

[1] The appointment seems to have been made in order to spare the Hungarians from sitting under an 'Austrian' Minister.

[2] Replaced in December 1862 by F. Hein. The Ministry of Administration took over the administrative duties of the Ministry of the Interior, leaving the Minister of State to deal with the Reichsrat and the Landtage. He was also in charge of Cults and Education.

[3] How reluctantly, may be seen from the fact that two days after the issue of the Patent, he told his Ministers that 'the extreme limit had been reached of such limitations on his sovereign power as he was prepared to recognize as admissible' and he demanded of them 'a solemn promise that they would use all their energy and the combined application of all their forces to defend the throne against the forcing from it of further concessions, either by pressure from the Reichsrat or the Landtage, or through revolutionary attempts by the masses' (cit. Redlich, *Problem*, I. 808).

The Monarch appointed the Ministers, as his officials, responsible to him alone; he similarly appointed the Presidents and Vice-Presidents of the Reichsrat and the heads of the Landtage, and retained the right of convoking, proroguing and dissolving the Reichsrat and the Landtage. Foreign Affairs and defence were, as in the Diploma proper, assumed *ex silentio* to fall outside the field of 'legislation' and within the exclusive competence of the Crown.

The composition of the Reichsrat was, however, altered radically, and its relationship to the Landtage put on an entirely different footing. The new body was to be bi-cameral, consisting of an Upper House (Herrenhaus) composed of the adult Archdukes, the Princes of the Church, the adult male members of aristocratic families 'distinguished by their extensive landed properties', on whom the Monarch conferred hereditary membership of the House, and life members nominated at his discretion by the Monarch for their distinguished services to the State or Church, learning or the arts; and a House of Deputies (*Abgeordnetenhaus*) composed of delegates, 343 in all, sent to it by the Landtage in proportions reflecting their different populations, taxable capacities and certain other factors; the numbers ranged from eight-five for Inner Hungary and fifty-four for Bohemia to three for Salzburg and two each for the subdivisions of the Littoral and Vorarlberg.[1] All questions relating to 'rights, duties and interests which are common to all Kingdoms and Lands' came, as in the Diploma, before the full Reichsrat: the list of such questions was enumerated in the words of the Diploma, and was not extended. Again as in the Diploma, the representatives of the non-Hungarian Lands could be convoked without the Hungarians when 'objects of legislation which are common to all Kingdoms and Lands with the exception of the Lands of the Hungarian Crown' were under discussion; in that case the Reichsrat sat as a 'Narrower (*engerer*) Reichsrat'. There was, however, an important difference in the Patent's allocation of competences between the Narrower Reichsrat and the Western Landtage, inasmuch as all questions not specifically assigned to the competence of the Landtage fell within that of the Reichsrat, and the former category of questions was defined very narrowly: it comprised only local cultural questions (*Landeskultur*); the local application of central laws relating to the Church, schools, the provisioning of troops, etc.; public works executed at Land expense; welfare institutions maintained at Land expense. For these objects the Landtage were entitled to levy rates up to a 10% surcharge on the direct taxation, but no more, except by special permission.

[1] The full list was: Hungary, 85; Bohemia, 54; Galicia, 38; Transylvania, 26; Moravia, 22; Venice, 20; Lower Austria, 18; Styria, 13; Tirol and Upper Austria, 10 each; Croatia, 9; Carniola and Silesia, 6 each; Dalmatia, Carinthia and the Bukovina, 5 each; Salzburg, 3; Gorizia, Istria, Trieste and Vorarlberg, 2 each. Now (and again in 1867) Dalmatia was assumed to lie in the Western half of the Monarchy, its Italian-controlled Diet having taken no steps to initiate the consultations with Croatia.

An appended document contained new statutes for the Western Landtage. Their membership ranged from 241 in Bohemia and 150 in Galicia (which was once again divided into a Polish and a Ruthene Statthaltereiabteilung) to 20 for the Vorarlberg. For their composition, the system of 'Curias' was kept, but the structure was more progressive than that of Goluchowski's drafts, although more conservative than Stadion's and Bach's. While there were a few variants to allow for special local conditions,[1] the general rule was that each Landtag was composed of four Curias, each elected, by open suffrage, by its own constituents, and each being allotted a fixed number of seats in the Landtag (these proportions were retained in the delegations sent by the Landtage to the Reichsrat). The first was reserved for the 'great landlords', the qualification being, normally, ownership of an estate registered as landtäflich and of an annual taxable value of 250 gulden. This Curia usually included also one or two 'virilists' or *ex officio* members (high-ranking prelates and Rectors of Universities). Wealth other than that based on real property was given a separate Curia, its representatives being elected by the Chambers of Commerce and Industry. The third and fourth Curias went, as usual, to the urban and rural communes, the voters' qualification for these being payment of at least ten gulden in direct taxation,[2] or the possession of certain professional or educational qualifications.

If the Landtag of any Land refused to carry out the elections, the Crown could order direct elections to the Reichsrat to be carried out in it. These were still by Curia, and the proportions were unchanged.

Venice was allowed to retain its traditional 'General Congregation' for Diet, and a Rescript instructed the Hungarian Court Chancellor to submit proposals on how the Hungarian representatives to the Reichsrat were to be selected.

Finally, the original small advisory body which had swollen to such considerable proportions, and had assumed such large new functions, reverted to the name of Staatsrat and to its earlier numbers and duties of examining and reporting on all proposed legislation, central or local.[3]

The Patent was thus a far more centralist instrument than the Diploma, even in respect of the position of Hungary in the Monarchy; for while it did not extend the range of subjects in which Hungary might have to submit to

---

[1] Thus Dalmatia, Trieste and Vorarlberg had no great landlords' Curia, the first Curia here being composed of the biggest tax-payers, and in some of the smaller Crownlands the Chambers of Commerce were included with the towns. There were several local variations in the composition of the first Curias. In Bohemia, this was divided into two Colleges; the owners of *fideicommissa*, with 76 electors, and the remainder, with 541.

[3] In Vienna, exceptionally, the qualification was twenty gulden – the city's penalty for having so sinned in 1848.

[2] It was abolished in 1868 after having proved itself as ineffectual as all its predecessors. Its President, Frh. von Lichtenfels, was, however, one of the important figures behind the scenes of the regime.

the will of an extra-Hungarian majority, it made that subjection more apparent and altered its nature. The Reinforced Reichsrat could still conceivably be regarded as a consultative assemblage of notables meeting to discuss a limited number of subjects of interest to them all; the Patent's Reichsrat was, for all its limitations, a recognizable Parliament expressing the will of its constituents, a majority of whom would always be non-Hungarians.

But the main effect of the Patent, and its principle object,[1] was to increase the influence over the affairs of the Monarchy, directly over those of the West, but indirectly also, through the composition of the Reichsrat, over those of Hungary, of the German bourgeoisie. To describe it, as many writers have done, as 'enshrining the domination of the German *haute bourgeoisie*' is, indeed, something of an exaggeration. The class which, by modern standards, was even now greatly over-represented was that of the big landlords; for even if the Upper House, which was largely composed of men of this class, was left out of account – and it was in fact a powerful and effective body – the Curia system, and the key adapted for it, was still inordinately favourable to them. In Bohemia, for example, they had 70 seats out of the 241, in Galicia, 44 out of 150, in Moravia, 30 out of 100, in Lower Austria, 18 out of 66, in the Narrower Reichsrat, as a whole, 59 out 203.[2]

Incidentally, but importantly, it was precisely the big representation allowed to this class that made it possible for the Government, or the Crown, to influence elections one way or the other by putting pressure on a very small fraction of the electors. For the irremediably Germanic and the irremediably non-Germanic Crownlands balanced out fairly evently, leaving the balance to be tipped by the two great 'mixed' Crownlands of Bohemia and Moravia. And in these again, the German and the Czech constituencies were fairly evenly balanced, so that the majorities in their Landtage, and consequently, in the Reichsrat,[3] depended on the voters in the Great Landlords' Curias, of whom the wealthier were often open to personal persuasion and the poorer (many of whom were heavily indebted to the banks) to arguments of another nature.[4] That influence did not have to be, and in fact

---

[1] Redlich, *Franz Joseph*, p. 270, records that before accepting office, Schmerling had elicited from the Emperor an assurance that his work in the Western Lands, above all, the Landtag Statutes, 'must secure for the bourgeoisie and the German element a power-position appropriate to its importance for the Monarchy'.

[2] These figures include the virilists.

[3] Each Landtag voted as a whole on what representatives to send to the Reichsrat. A Party with a fifty-one per cent majority in the Landtag thus nevertheless provided all its representatives in the Reichsrat.

[4] Another means of influencing the voting in this Curia was provided by the fact that ownership of a landtäflich estate was now no longer tied to a birth or local qualification, so that it was possible to make sure of a vote by simply buying up an estate of sufficient taxable value, if necessary, through a man of straw. As we shall see (below, p. 640, n. 2), not infrequent use

was not always, influenced in favour of the Germans; there were occasions when the Crown exerted it against them.

It was, however, true that the bourgeoisie, with sixty-five seats in the Narrower Reichsrat, had gained a long stride on the Feudals, and if they in their turn had lost much ground to the rural communes (entirely unrepresented before 1848, outside the Tirol), yet they were still over-represented, proportionately to their numbers. In Bohemia, for example, there was one representative for every 11,000 urban constituents and only one to every 49,000 rural. Furthermore, the Germans undoubtedly came off better than most of the other nationalities, and not only through the advantage enjoyed by them in virtue of their higher economic level. The German Lands on the whole sent proportionately larger delegations to the Reichsrat, while the over-representation of the towns automatically favoured the Germans. In some mixed Lands, in addition, the German constituencies, rural as well as urban, were smaller than the non-German.

The Patent thus really opened the door for the entry on to the scene of Austrian political life, as a recognized and effective factor, of a class and creed which was destined to play a leading role in it for a long generation to come: German 'Liberalism' and its representatives. Some words on this force will therefore be in place here, and we may fittingly prefix these by some lines on the changes in the composition of the German-Austrian bourgeoisie which were beginning to come about as the result of the large-scale infiltration now commencing into its most important groups, especially in Vienna, of the Jewish element.

One must write 'large-scale', for individual Jews had, as we have seen, played a most important part in the life of the Monarchy even in the earlier years covered by this history. We have ventured the statement that Salomon Rothschild had been in many respects the most important figure in the Austria of the Vormärz, and although he had towered above the rest, he had not been alone. The salon kept by the brothers-in-law von Arnstein and Eskeles (both had been ennobled) and their consorts, of whom Fanny von Arnstein had been known as the 'Viennese Récamier', had been one of the most brilliant in the glittering Vienna of the Congress. There had been other important business men besides Rothschild; a recent writer has said that 'a large part of Austria's economic life got into Jewish hands during the Vormärz, all restrictions notwithstanding',[1] although those restrictions had

---

was made of this device, which was, indeed, restricted in many Lands by the fact that so many of the large estates belong to *fidei commissa*.

The Crown had another shot in its locker: the Constitution placed no limit on the numbers either of the hereditary magnates, or of the life members, of the *Herrenhaus*, so that the Crown could alter the balance in that body at will. Francis Joseph exercised this power on a number of occasions, often to get through legislation towards which he was personally unsympathetic.

[1] Tietze, op. cit., p. 44.

been really formidable; it had taken Rothschild himself twenty years to get permission to operate a mine. The retail trade of the Monarchy lay already largely in Jewish hands. Nor had the role played by the often impoverished and radical intellectuals who then constituted the other element in Viennese Jewry been unimportant. The often-heard gibe that the Viennese revolution of 1848 was made by Jews is an over-simplification and an exaggeration, but it is not difficult to make out a superficial case for it. Thus the three first speakers to address the masses on that memorable morning of 13th March were all Jews, and Hungarian Jews at that.[1] The fourth, a bull-voiced Tirolean named Patz, was only put up to read out Kossuth's speech because the crowd could not hear, or could not understand, Goldner's German. Afterwards Fischof and Goldmark were members of the Constituent. Fischof was President of the Committee of Security. Most of the men who kept up the vital link with the workers were Jewish students, and three out of the four Presidents of the Aula at the end of October,[2] were Jews. Again, Jewish influence was certainly one of the two main internal factors (Hungarian nationalism being the other) which brought about the abandonment of absolutism in the Monarchy in 1859. In this decade, however, the Jewish influence was chiefly exercised from outside. In the Monarchy itself the Jews, after their total liberation in 1849, were again subjected to various restrictions after 1851.[3] They were still not numerous outside Galicia, Bukovina and the old-fashioned but curiously self-contained and static community of Prague; before 1848 there had never been as many as two hundred 'tolerated' families in Vienna, and even a considerable influx after 1848 had only brought these numbers there up to 6,200 in 1860.[4] They were moreover, still a *corpus separatum*. The operations of the National Bank, even more the hidden influence exercised by Rothschild on Metternich's foreign policy, were conducted on the highest level, and remained a secret from 99·9% of the population of Austria.

But all this then changed, with increasing speed. While after 1859 Francis

[1] Fischof, Goldmark, Goldner. Fischof was a doctor, a profession open to Jews, and one in which they were already numerous, the other two, medical students.

[2] For the names of very many other Jews who played important parts in the Viennese Revolution, see Violand, *Soziale Geschichte*, a work not at all written in an anti-Semitic spirit.

[3] The Kremsier draft had removed all these restrictions and disabilities, and Stadion's Constitution had taken over the paragraph. Bach had specifically affirmed that this entitled Jews to acquire real property. When the Sylvester Patent cancelled the Constitution, no one quite knew whether this meant the re-imposition of the restrictions, and the provision forbidding them to acquire real property was treated as having lapsed until it was specifically re-enacted in 1853. But the Concordat and its attendant legislation undoubtedly denied them equality in other fields.

[4] The true numbers were of course substantially higher than an average of five to a family would give. Tolerated Jews got numbers of protégés entered as members of their families. Others bought Turkish passports, or lived unmolested under various pretexts, or even (by bribing the officials) under none at all.

Joseph's Governments had removed the most important restrictions, they had done so under pressure, reluctantly, and piecemeal; but it was otherwise when the Liberals came into office, for they were committed, on principle and out of conviction, to complete religious and civic equality for all citizens. The constitutional laws of 1867 abolished all civic inequalities, and the inter-confessional legislation 1868 crowned the work. Now practically all doors were open to Jews, just at the moment when the railways were completed which gave them physical access to Vienna (few of them went beyond the capital).[1] The influx began: most of it direct from Galicia, a smaller stream, of the same ultimate origin, from Hungary. By 1870 the Jewish population of the capital had risen to 40,200 (6·6% of the total); in 1880 it was 72,600 (10·1%) and in 1890, 118,500 (8·7%).

Most of the immigrants arrived poor, and some remained so, but their successful members soon acquired a position of extraordinary importance in the economic, intellectual and even the political life of Vienna, and hence of the whole of Austria. They practically dominated the entire central credit system (only the provincial banks were less wholly in their hands), and they owned a big part of the large-scale industry, most of its wholesale and much of its retail trade. The central Press was almost entirely in their hands; of all the big Viennese newspapers of the Francis Joseph era, only the Christian Socialist organ, the *Reichspost*, was not almost entirely owned and staffed by Jews – this giving them an extraordinary power, which was by no means always wisely, or even reputably, used, of influencing public opinion. They were also particularly strongly represented in publishing and in the theatre business. They had long been allowed to practise medicine, and by 1881, 61% of all doctors registered in Vienna were Jews. Up to 1862 they were in practice excluded from the Bar, but by 1888, 394 out of the 681 advocates in Vienna were Jews and 310 out of 360 articled clerks (*Konzipienten*). They were only beginning to enter the teaching profession (the lower levels, which were mostly staffed by clergy, hardly at all), but already constituted a substantial proportion of the University professors. The student of Austrian history who takes his information at second-hand, from the best-known native works, will not do ill to remember that Redlich, Friedjung, Pribram, Kolmer and many others, were Jews. So, for that matter, were many of the leading figures in the artistic and literary world of the day.

In Galicia, the Jews had lived in a spiritual ghetto. When they came to Vienna their religion was all that they wished to keep distinctive: in social and political life they attached themselves to an existing faction. It was natural, even had calculation not enjoined it, that practically all Jews in the Hereditary and Bohemian Lands should line up with the Germans in 'national' respects,[2] and they did so most completely, often sincerely feeling

[1] Railway communication between Vienna and Galicia had been established in 1856.
[2] In Galicia, where they assimilated at all, it was usually to the Poles.

themselves 'Germans' and being accepted as such by others. Fischof, for example, in his correspondence with Rieger, regularly speaks of 'us Germans'. Friedjung and Viktor Adler, both Jews, were among the authors of the 'Linz Programme' for a 'German People's Party'.[1] These examples could be multiplied *ad infinitum*, and non-Germans as well as Germans thought the attitude natural. Rieger, in his replies to Fischof, never accused him of false pretensions. Earlier, in the Vormärz, when a single Jew, one Siegfried Kapper, had gone Czechophile, Havliček himself had told him that 'the Jews should go with the Germans, since German was already their second mother-tongue'.[2]

In politics, accordingly, the Jews associated themselves almost exclusively with two parties, the Liberals and the Social Democrats, both of which they provided with most of their brains, while accentuating certain of the characteristics of each which were most antipathetic to its opponents: in the former, its doctrinaire anti-clericalism and its intimate and often unfortunate association of politics with financial interests; in the latter, its international tenets and its extreme anti-clericalism.

Their influence on the policies of each of these parties was most important, but perhaps more important still was the reaction which set in against it, especially after the 1873 *Krach*. For the last forty years of Austria's existence, the Jewish question was a major issue in the politics of Vienna and of German-Austria as a whole, and anti-Semitism was a chief plank in the platforms of practically all the parties in those areas which were not themselves 'Jew-run'.

The German Liberals were drawn from the German and Jewish upper and middle bourgeoisie of Lower Austria (i.e., Vienna and its environs), the Bohemian Lands, and, to a lesser extent, Styria and Upper Austria. Both components, the German and the Jewish, contributed essential elements towards the final synthesis, although on different planes: the 'Liberal' Ministers and Deputies were, at this stage, all Germans by blood; while the Jews supplied the finance, the Press and most of the brains. Politically, the Liberals were up to a point the heirs of the men who had carried through the bourgeois revolution of 1848 in Vienna, and they were 'constitutionalist' and 'Left' in that they demanded limitation of the Monarch's authority, especially in financial matters: he who paid the piper should call the tune. They also stood for the most complete liberty of the citizen *vis-à-vis* the State: liberty of Press, of association, etc., equality before the law and liberty of religion. They were 'Left-wing' also in their hostility to the 'feudal' landlords, this partly on material grounds, representing as they did industrial and

---

[1] See below, p. 654.
[2] Tietze, op. cit., p. 159. The Austrian census, which listed the population by its 'mother-tongue' (which was then almost invariably taken as the criterion of 'nationality'), counted Yiddish as German.

commercial interests against agrarian, partly as their rivals for political power.

It is important for the history of the Monarchy that their feelings on two points were almost fanatically violent. Their invariable and embittered opposition to the military estimates was not due only to tenderness for their own pockets. The military's own claim to have saved, not only the integrity of the Monarchy, but also the authority of the Crown, in 1848, and Francis Joseph's acceptance of it, had produced their own reaction. The Liberals regarded the army as the pillar of absolutism, and as such, as their deadly enemy, and their hatred of its internal role led them to oppose, year in and year out, even estimates barely sufficient to defend the Monarchy against obviously imminent danger from foreign Powers.

Their second Guy Fawkes was the Church. This feeling was no doubt sharpest in the strong Jewish element in their ranks, but by no means confined to them: it, again, was a reaction to the position which the Church had claimed for itself in the Concordat era. The anti-clericalism of the Liberals, like their anti-militarism, was almost obsessive: as we shall see, a large part of their energies while they were in power were spent on undoing the Concordat and all its works.

In other respects they had, indeed, shed any revolutionary ardours which they had ever possessed. They were at least as hostile as the feudalists to allowing any political power to the classes below them. Their economic philosophy was one of pure Mancunian *laissez-faire* (except on the issue of free trade versus protection, on which they divided according to their particular interests), and allowed and approved the most ruthless exploitation of the economically weak.

There were nuances of difference between them in their attitude towards the structural problem of the Monarchy; their Styrian wing, in particular, which took shape as Kaiserfeld's 'Autonomists', had a strong local tradition. The other two groups, however, were strongly centralist, the Viennese as citizens of the capital of the Monarchy, the Bohemians, for protection against the Czechs (very much of the political struggle of the Monarchy was the struggle between Czechs and Bohemian Germans, fought out in Vienna). The Jews, for economic reasons, wanted the largest and closest unit possible. Taken as a whole, the Liberals represented the most powerful centripetal force in the Monarchy, outside the Monarch himself and his direct servants, and were thus in some respects the natural allies of that latter group, as in others they were often its most vociferous opponents.

Their attitude towards the State was, indeed, curiously ambivalent. While strongly attacking many of its policies, they admitted a sort of self-identification with it which went even beyond their own description of themselves as *staatserhaltend*. At this stage they were even able to make their attitude towards their own Germanic nationality a function of their attitude towards the State. 'The interests of the Monarchy as a whole' was a maxim of their leaders, 'were also the interests of the Germans in it', and, at least on paper, the former were to take the precedence; their purpose, as it has been well said, was not to make the Austrian State German, but 'that *Deutschtum* should adapt itself to the requirements of the State and subordinate its specific national life to them'.[1] Thus not only had they no room for irredentism: they even refused to adopt any specifically German national policy, as degrading them from the position of a Pan-Cis-Leithanian party to that of representatives of a single element in it.

It is true that in practice they often, perhaps unconsciously, reversed the maxim, assuming that what were the interests of the Germans must also be the interests of the Monarchy as a whole; but also true that in this period they were thinking more in terms of liberalism (and of economics) than of nationalism – so much so that the Liberal Party, besides freely admitting Jews, usually contained one or two Italians and even Slovenes.

The practical effect of this ambivalence in 1862 was that in calling the German bourgeoisie, as led by Schmerling, to office Francis Joseph was on the one hand, yielding ground in the economic and financial fields, and even in the constitutional field, meaning by that term the relations between the Crown and the representatives of the subjects, as such. From the structural point of view, on the other hand – from the angle, that is, of centralism versus regionalist aspirations, especially those of Hungary – he was concluding an alliance with a partner who, on this issue, took the same view as himself.

The alliance, on this tacit understanding, was possible in 1862, because it harmonized well enough with the assumptions – perhaps unconscious – on which Francis Joseph was still basing his policy, both foreign and domestic. He still regarded its German element as the natural 'cement' and main prop of his Hausmacht, and Austria itself, primarily as the leading German State, his chief foreign political objective being, at that time, to make that position a reality again. Later developments – the exclusion of Austria from Germany and the advance of the non-Germans of Austria to political, social, economic and cultural maturity – were to make the position untenable, and the Liberals' gradual retreat from it will be a leading motif in the political history of Austria during the next decades. It may perhaps even be argued that the Patent itself, in establishing in Austria for the first time a genuine (if limited) Parliamentary system, marked the first stage in the downward path of its Germans. For once the principle had been established that the destinies of Austria lay in the hands of its peoples, its Germans had to take their place among those peoples, and it would be impossible for them to keep it indefinitely a privileged one. It was the Liberals' tragedy that their decline and ultimate fall were due to the developments which they had themselves done so much to bring about.

[1] Molisch, op. cit., p. 15.

Meanwhile, it must be emphasized that the Liberals represented only one trend of opinion among the Germans themselves (a fact often forgotten by historians, who tend, too frequently, to describe as 'German' feeling or policy what was in fact only the feeling or policy of the Liberals). Many of the voters in the Alpine Lands, especially the Tirol, disagreed profoundly with the Liberals' doctrines (especially their anti-clericalism) and their centralism. They organized, in their turn, parties or groups whose main objective was to counter those tendencies, and were often more antagonistic to the German Liberals than to Slavs whose views on cultural and structural questions agreed with their own. They were, indeed, themselves clearly divided on the question of centralism versus federation.

The elections for which the Patent provided were held in the month after its issue, and in the West, with the results which could have been predicted. Among the non-Germans national feeling had reasserted itself as the political motif *par excellence* with such easy assurance that no one remarked, or perhaps even remembered, that for ten years the regime had refused it the right to any political expression whatever. Almost all of them found the Patent unsatisfactory on national grounds. When, on 1 May, the elected Deputies met in the wooden building (dubbed by the popular wit the 'Schmerling Theatre') which had been run up to accommodate them, the Poles, whose representatives had organized themselves in a disciplined *Polenklub*, took up the attitude that nothing short of complete autonomy for Galicia was acceptable to them.[1] The Czech bourgeois representatives, now led by Rieger,[2] had at first proposed to boycott the Reichsrat altogether. Then, however, they had taken the momentous decision to ally themselves with Clam-Martinic's group of Bohemian magnates on the basis of a joint demand for the restoration of the *Böhmisches Staatsrecht* and to attend the Reichsrat in order to press for revision of the Patent in this sense[3] (a decision which had, indeed, led a rival group of Bohemian magnates, led by Prince 'Carlos' Auersperg,[4] to constitute themselves, with certain fellow-thinkers from the Alpine Lands, as a party of 'Constitutional Great Landlords'). The Slovenes, too, were oppositional, while the Venetians ignored the elections altogether and the Italians of the Trentino elected 'Italianissimo' representatives who then did not attend the Reichsrat. The only non-German supporters of the Patent were the Ruthenes from Galicia, who saw in it a protection against the

[1] The Polish Landtag passed a Resolution to this effect in April, also demanding the exclusive use of Polish in all official transactions in Galicia.

[2] The Emperor had nominated Palacký to membership of the Herrenhaus.

[3] See on this Denis, p. 444, Eisenmann, pp. 339 ff. One factor in bringing about the alliance was undoubtedly a snobbishness from which neither Palacký nor Rieger was free It appears to have been mediated by Thun.

[4] 'Carlos' was actually a nickname: he had been baptized the ordinary Germanic Karl. But he was so commonly called Carlos that the name has passed even into the history books.

Poles, the Italians from Trieste and Dalmatia, who, similarly, regarded it as a shield against the local Slovenes and Croats, and the Roumanians from the Bukovina.[1]

The German-Tiroleans, led by a fiery priest named Greuter, declared that they would never attend the Reichsrat 'unless given firm guarantees against the bureaucratic, absolutist encroachment of Liberalism on our fathers' moral and legal heritage'.

German Clericals and Federalists constituted themselves as another group oppositional to the Patent, with a programme of wide autonomy for the Lands, with protection and equal status for all nationalities in the Monarchy, and maintenance of the Concordat. With this platform they were able to establish a working alliance with the Slavs (the Slovenes ended by actually adhering to this group).

All these oppositional groups together could, however, muster only about 70 Deputies,[2] whereas the 'German Left' alone had returned 118, who did not, indeed, for a single 'party' in the modern sense of the word. They with their allies, divided into three groups: 30 'Great Austrians', led by Mühlfeld, 68 'Unionists' (Herbst) and 20 'German Autonomists' (Kaiserfeld),[3] and the attitude of the three towards the Patent was not identical. It was too centralist for the Autonomists, whose main strength lay in Styria,[4] not centralist enough for the Great Austrians, who were largely Viennese, or for the Unionists, most of whom came from the Bohemian Lands. All three were, however, prepared to take it, subject to later amendment in one direction or another, as an acceptable solution of the structural problem of the Monarchy, and to play the constitutional role of a Government party under it. These 118, with the twelve Ruthenes (who attached themselves to the Unionists) and the four Italians and the Roumanians made up a majority in favour of the Patent large enough to enable it to work as a system for governing the Monarchy if no insuperable difficulties came from Hungary.

[1] The Bukovinian Roumanians adopted in 1860 the principle of always voting with whatever Government was in power. They remained faithful to this principle up to 1918, even though, of the two main parties among them which held the field up to 1892, the 'Federalists or 'Autonomists' and the 'Centralists' (the names explain themselves), one might be in the majority in the Diet in Czernowitz and sending its Deputies to Vienna when the Government there was of the opposite complexion. For example, the Centralists, after gaining the majority in 1871, held it until 1892, but always voted for Taaffe. For the rest, both Parties were merely the followers of rival cliques of landed proprietors, and equally reactionary on social issues.

[2] Excluding the Venetians. All works of reference, in counting numbers, ignore the Venetians altogether and reckon the full nominal membership of the Narrower Reichsrat at 203, but the text of the Patent (para. II) excludes only the Lands of the Hungarian Crown from that body.

[3] At this stage the Constitutional Landowners did not form a separate Club. Most of them associated themselves with the Unionists.

[4] Kaiserfeld himself came, as he never denied, of Slovene stock: his full name was Moritz Blagintscheff, Ritter von Kaiserfeld.

There, however, the Patent was received with almost universal hostility. Further concessions had been made to the country in the intervening weeks. The Commission sent down to the Voivody had recommended its incorporation in the Kingdom, and it had been placed under the Hungarian Court Chancellery (on the understanding, indeed, that a status satisfactory to the Serbs should be agreed between them and the Hungarian authorities). The Muraköz had been transferred back from Croatia to Hungary. But these sops counted for nothing compared with the fact that another Centralist constitution had been imposed by octroi on Hungary, and one which, besides perpetuating her territorial dismemberment, again subjected her (and that in aggravated form) to the control of a pan-Monarchic Parliament. The indignation evoked by the Diploma mounted still higher now. When the Rescript was issued ordering elections to the Diet, as a preliminary to the designation of representatives to the Reichsrat, a party of opinion favoured boycotting the elections altogether. Deák, who had now become a sort of one-man Court of Appeal on constitutional questions, advised that the order was legal, and should be obeyed. But a meeting of the country's law lords convoked to decide on what franchise the elections should be held[1] pronounced unanimously in favour of that of the April Laws,[2] and the result of this decision was disastrous for the Old Conservatives. With the Counties in charge of the electoral apparatus, not one Deputy was returned who supported the Patent, which few even among the magnates found the courage to defend. Practically all the Deputies were agreed that Hungary's programme must be insistence on the validity of the April Laws, amendment of which, by legal methods, might then be considered once the recognition had been given, and almost exactly half the House, led by Count László Teleki and Kálmán Ghyczy, argued that since Francis Joseph had not submitted himself to coronation, and Hungary had consequently no legal king, the proper course for the Diet was simply to express this attitude in the form of a Resolution of the House. Deák, who did not want the breach made irrevocable, invoked an historical precedent,[3] and after nearly a month's debating, a bare and largely fortuitous majority[4] agreed to let the Diet's

[1] This meeting, the so-called '*országbiroi érteklezet*', was an important one in many respects, for it gave a general ruling that the April Laws were legally valid and that Hungary was not legally bound by any enactments of the absolutist regime. Its immediate effect was to strengthen Deák's hand. Later, Hungary invoked it to declare herself not bound by the Concordat (see below, p. 690).

[2] The qualification that a Deputy must command the Magyar language was, however, dropped.

[3] In 1608 a Hungarian Diet had negotiated with the Hungarian King Mátyás II (the Emperor Matthias) before his coronation certain laws which were afterwards recognized as valid.

[4] Count László Teleki committed suicide, owing to a conflict of conscience, just before the voting. The shock caused several Resolutionists to waver and absent themselves from the decisive meeting.

statement take the form of an Address to the Throne. But the Address, which Deák drafted, although courteous in tone, was completely uncompromising in substance. It stated that Hungary had never known, and did not now recognize, any link with any other dominion ruled by the Monarch except the personal one of the common dynasty. She refused to attend the Reichsrat, or any representative body of the Monarchy, and denied such a body any competence to dispose of Hungarian affairs; she was only prepared 'to enter into contact, if the circumstances required it' with the 'constitutional peoples of the Hereditary Lands as one independent, free nation with another'.

The Crown was also reminded of its obligation to restore the political integrity of the country, and in general, to honour the April Laws, the validity of which the Address reaffirmed.

The sequel was inevitable. On 22 July a Rescript[1] was read to the House contesting Hungary's legal case and insisting that the Pragmatic Sanction itself imposed a unity in respect of foreign affairs, defence and finance which went far beyond a personal union. The Union of Transylvania was legally invalid, and unacceptable 'so long as Transylvania's inhabitants of non-Hungarian tongue see their national interests threatened by such a union, and so long as the necessary guarantee of the interests and requirements of the State as a whole is not given'. The Diet was summoned to send its representatives to Vienna forthwith. A second Address, again drafted by Deák, re-stated Hungary's legal case (with arguments which, from the purely legal point of view, wiped the floor with Perthaler), this time in terms of some acerbity; and the Crown's reply to this was to dissolve the Diet (21 August). Vay (who had not signed the Patent) and Szécsen had already resigned, Vay being replaced by Count Antal Forgách,[2] one of the few Hungarian aristocrats who had chosen the Civil Service of the Monarchy as a career, and Szécsen, by Count Moritz Esterházy, an eccentric and enigmatic figure whose political views fell into no known category. On 5 November Field-Marshal Count Moritz Pálffy was nominated Statthalter of Hungary; all surviving representative bodies were dissolved, martial law proclaimed for a number of offences and dictatorial rule, exercised through returning squadrons of Bach Hussars, reintroduced, officially, it is true, only 'provisionally'. The Hungarians fell back again on passive resistance. 'The Government,' wrote Szécsen in 1864, 'has not so far been able to induce one single Hungarian citizen in the smallest village to serve on the provisional municipal Councils.'[3] The quartering of an entire regiment of cavalry on Kálmán Tisza's estate failed to induce him to pay his arrears of taxation.[4]

Meanwhile, the Croats' private logic had led them to conclusions which,

[1] This was composed by Perthaler.
[2] Replaced in his turn in April 1864 by Count Imre Zichy. Incidentally, Forgách was a good enough Hungarian, who often mediated usefully between his countrymen and Vienna.
[3] *Drei Jahre Verfassungsstreit*, p. 146. [4] Eisenmann, p. 351.

mutatis mutandis, were much the same as the Hungarians' When the Sabor met in April 1861 one party, led by the Bishop, Haulik, was for accepting the February Patent another, the so-called 'Magyarones', under Baron Levin Rauch, for coming to terms with Hungary, while the majority (to which Strossmayr belonged) wavered, equally mistrustful of Vienna and Budapest. Outside all these groups stood the 'Party of Right'[1] founded by a young fanatic (afterwards to exercise a great influence over Croat politics) called Starčević, who was equally opposed to Austria, Hungary and the Serbs, and produced a programme which in the last instance desired complete independence for Croatia, with at the most a personal link with any other State, and a slogan that 'to exist, Croatia needs only God and Croats'.[2] After protracted debate, the Sabor resolved by a single vote[3] not to send delegates to Vienna; on the other hand, it declared (in its so-called 'Article 42') that 'the events of 1848 had had as legal consequence the dissolution of all bonds, legislative, administrative and judicial, between the Triune Kingdom and Hungary, except that of their common king, whom the same act of coronation, with the same crown, should instal at once as King of Hungary and of the Triune Kingdom'. The Sabor was, however, willing to negotiate with Hungary provided Hungary accepted Croatia's full territorial claims and its view of the constitutional relationship between the two countries.

Other demands made by the Sabor, or some of its members, were for the incorporation not only of the Military Frontier and Dalmatia, but of Carniola and the Slovene parts of Styria and Carinthia. Strossmayr also tried to preach a crusade for the liberation of Bosnia and Herzegovina.

The Crown 'sanctioned' some of the Sabor's productions, including Article 42 (although exactly what 'sanction' meant in this connection it is difficult to understand);[4] but for the rest, it drew exactly the same consequences from Croatia's refusal to attend the Reichsrat as it had from Hungary's. The Sabor was dissolved, a near-absolutist regime reintroduced and recalcitrant officials dismissed.

Of all the Lands of the Hungarian Crown, it was only in Transylvania that Schmerling achieved a success, and that only a partial one. The Chancellor, Baron Kemény, and the President of the Gubernium, Count Mikó (both of them Hungarian magnates) succeeded in putting off the preparations for a Diet for something like two years. Then Schmerling lost

[1] i.e. of constitutional or historic right, not of 'Right' as opposed to 'Left'.

[2] Totally unpractical as he was, Starčević, like the equally unpractical Radić after him, possessed an extraordinary power over the Croat masses. To them he appealed as no other Croat politician had ever done, and the democratization of Croat political life was largely his work.

[3] According to Czedik (I. 17–18) even this result was achieved only 'through the strong influence of a person who carried great weight at Court'. I have not been able to identify this individual.

[4] It certainly did not mean that the Crown bound itself to accept all Croatia's claims.

patience and replaced Kemény by Count Nádasdy, an extreme centralist, and Mikó by an Imperial officer, F.M.L. Crenneville. A Catholic Bishop who had been a stalwart champion of the Magyar cause was got rid of by the device of appointing him Archbishop of Carthago *in partibus*. A revised franchise was now octroied, and elections held, which returned forty-six Roumanians, forty-three Magyars and thirty-two Saxons, the Crown adding eleven 'Regalists' from each nationality. The Diet was then convoked, and in the absence of the elected Magyars, who refused to attend it, announced its recognition of the Diploma and Patent, and passed laws admitting the Roumanian people and its two national Churches to full equality with the other 'received' nations and churches of Transylvania, and proclaiming the complete equality of all three local languages for all official business. The Roumanians received a further important concession, in that their Orthodox Church was released from its bondage to the Serbian Patriarchate and made autocephalous. Bishop Şaguna was promoted Archbishop, with his see at Nagyszeben, and given two Bishoprics (at Arad and Karansebeş) under him.

The Diet then chose twenty-six of its members to represent it in the Reichsrat, and nine Transylvanians were nominated to the Herrenhaus.[1] The little group presented itself in the Schmerling Theatre on 20 October 1863.

One development which had taken place in Hungary before the breakdown had an important influence on later events. As we saw, the Rescripts with which the Crown accompanied the issue of the October Diploma had contained a provision insisting that the non-Magyar languages must enjoy adequate facilities under the new Hungarian regime. Francis Joseph had also declared that he would set his face against any action of nature to provoke or aggravate inter-national ill-feeling. During the later exchanges he formally demanded legislation safeguarding the rights of the non-Magyars.

The Nationalities themselves had also raised their voices. As the result of the Commissioner's visit, the Serbs of the Voivodina had, in April 1861, held a National Congress which had accepted the reunification of the Voivodina with Inner Hungary (incidentally contrasting Viennese absolutism unfavourably with Hungarian constitutionalism), but asked for the re-constitution of a new Serbian territory (within frontiers excluding the Roumanian Eastern Bánát and the Magyaro-German North Bácska) within which they should enjoy extensive self-government under a Voivode elected by themselves and confirmed by the Monarch, and sitting among the chief dignitaries in both Pest and Zagreb.

A little later (on 6 June) a Slovak Congress at Thurócz Szent Márton

[1] It is often written that only the Saxons went to Vienna. This is not the case: the 26 were composed of 13 Roumanians, 10 Saxons and 3 Magyars. All the 3 Magyars, and 13 of the other 23, were, however, Regalists nominated by the Government.

forwarded to Pest (it was a sign of the times that it was Pest, not Vienna, that they addressed)[1] a petition asking for the following points:
(1) The recognition by law of a Slovak 'nation'.
(2) An autonomous 'North Hungarian Slovak Territory', in which Slovak should be the sole language of administration, the judiciary and education (Magyar was, however, to be the language of communication with the central authorities).
(3) The repeal of all Hungarian laws which infringed the principle of of inter-national equality.
(4) A Slovak Academy of Law and a Chair of Slavonic literature at Pest.

This was followed by a petition containing the same demands, *mutatis mutandis*, from a group of Ruthenes.

The Hungarians were thus under pressure from several quarters; but pressure was not necessary, for many of them, including Deák, were already convinced that both justice and expediency called for the enactment of legislation of nature to satisfy the 'justified demands' of the nationalities; although they also maintained that this was an internal Hungarian question, which must not become entangled with the relations between Hungary and the rest of the Monarchy. Hungary's acknowledged expert in this field was Eötvös, who during the preceding decade had published a number of works on the national problem in the multi-national State, and when the representations from the nationalities reached the Diet, Eötvös arranged that the question should be referred to a Committee, which would then lay a Nationalities Bill before the Diet.

This was a step which had big long-term consequences, for although the Committee was twenty-seven strong and fairly enough composed, to allow all shades of opinion to be represented on it, Eötvös's authority was such that in effect he dictated the principles on which the law should be based, and even, in large part, its specific provisions. And while these were, indeed, never given legislative sanction (although the Diet 'approved' the report) because the dissolution of the Diet came only a few days after the Committee had submitted its report, yet the documentation was, as we shall see, taken as its *point de départ* by the later Committee which resumed work on the subject in 1866, which found nothing to alter in the principles which had guided its predecessor, and made only minor changes in the provisions. Thus the Law of 1868, equally with the draft of 1861, simply expressed, with very slight modifications, Eötvös's personal solution for Hungary's nationalities problem. They even did so so faithfully as to make it unnecessary for us to give any separate description of Eötvös's philosophy, for this, although

---

[1] Shortly before, indeed, Hurban had sent in a petition to Vienna asking for the constitution of an autonomous 'Slovakia' which, he promised, would send its representatives to the Reichsrat. The man behind the Thurócz Szent Márton petition was the Slovak Bishop, Moyses.

intellectually acute and morally lofty, was essentially inductive; the reader can induce it for himself out of the report and Bill.

The report stated that the Committee had considered the memoranda from the Slovaks and Serbs, with a third document, compiled for it by two members of the Committee, on the wishes of the Transylvanian Roumanians,[1] which, like the other two, asked for Hungary to be divided into autonomous 'national' territories. It rejected this solution as incompatible with the political unity of the country, as exposing local minorities to the danger of tyranny (and it was a fact that the Slovak memorandum had been completely ruthless in its references to the large minorities which would have been included in its Slovak national territory) and as calculated to perpetuate friction between the nationalities. It maintained that 'the just demands of individual citizens' and consequently 'the possible corporate development of the individual nationalities, through free association', were better safeguarded under Hungary's traditional system of communal, jurisdictional[2] and denominational autonomy. It then laid down two 'main principles' which between them embodied Eötvös's central philosophy on the place of ethnic or linguistic nationalism in the multi-national State:

(a) That the citizens of Hungary, of every tongue, form politically only a single nation, the unitary and indivisible Hungarian nation, corresponding to the historical conception of the Hungarian State.

(b) That all peoples living in the country, to wit, the Magyar, Slav, Roumanian, German, Serb, Russian, etc., are to be regarded as nationalities equal in rights, whose separate national claims can be made good freely within the limits of the country's political unity, on a basis of freedom of the individual and of association, without any further restriction.

The draft law laid down that the language used by the State authorities and that of Parliament and the University (Hungary at that time possessed only one) was to be Magyar, but every Ministry had to contain officials of non-Magyar nationality able to deal with papers in other languages coming up to it, and the University must contain Chairs of the non-Magyar languages and literatures. The use of any language on lower levels was left to the choice of those concerned, but County and communal officials must always deal with members of the public in the language (if locally current) in which they were addressed. Every citizen was entitled to use his own language in communications to the State or local authorities. Churches were free to conduct their own affairs and to choose their own language of business and the language of instruction in the schools maintained by them, including

---

[1] The Transylvanian Roumanians themselves had not approached the Diet, which they regarded as not competent for Transylvania. The Diet, however, regarded the Union of 1848 as valid, and therefore took steps to ascertain their wishes.

[2] The 'Jurisdictions' (*törvényhatóságok*) were the Counties and autonomous municipal boroughs.

secondary and higher schools, which every denomination and nationality was free to erect, and each was equally entitled to claim assistance if it could not meet its own church or educational expenses. The Ministry of Education prescribed the language of instruction in State schools, but must take into account the language spoken in the district where such a school was founded. Finally, the draft 'emphasised the maintenance in their full substance' of the Laws guaranteeing the rights of the Protestant and Orthodox Churches.

As we have said, the Diet had no time to do more than give general approval to this report, but it may be mentioned that neither the Slovaks nor the Serbs were satisfied with it. The Slovaks sent another deputation to Vienna to ask for an independent Slovak territory (advance proof that their later dissatisfaction was not, as is so often alleged, simply with the failure of the Hungarian authorities to apply the 1868 Law – although failure there was – but with the Law itself). They got no political satisfaction, but were allowed to found a Cultural Association (Matica) and two Protestant and one Catholic gymnasia. The Ministerial Council could not decide what to do about the Serbs, and ended by adjourning consideration of the problem.

Schmerling himself had not thought that Hungary would accept the Patent at once: he had even expected her to answer by a revolt which would have to be put down by force.[1] But he had been confident that she would end by toeing the line – 'We can wait', he had said – and meanwhile, the business of the Monarchy could and should be conducted without her. The Reichsrat in Vienna had, in fact, started with some pieces of useful work. It had elicited from Francis Joseph – only, indeed, with extreme difficulty, and by threatening not to pass the accounts – a declaration that the Ministers were to regard themselves as responsible *also* to the Reichsrat for the maintenance of the Constitution and the exact execution of the laws[2] and secured recognition of

[1] Fournier, op. cit., p. 131.
[2] Strictly, this had taken place in two stages. The Reichsrat had pressed strongly for legal affirmation of the principle, to which Francis Joseph was equally strongly opposed. 'I am in no way prepared', he told his Ministers on 24 June, 'to dismiss a Minister simply because the Reichsrat is displeased with him and he gets outvoted. Ministerial responsibility is an impossibility in Austria and I will never sanction it' (Corti, op. cit., p. 272). He was, indeed, equally uncompromising with his Ministers. When Rechberg disapproved of the idea of the 1863 Fürstentag and wanted to resign over it, Francis Joseph refused his resignation with the remarkable words: 'I cannot accept that a Minister should walk out on me if he disagrees with some measure' (Bibl, *Tragödie*, p. 311). On 2 July 1861, Schmerling had produced a 'Declaration', which, while affirming strongly that the executive power rested exclusively with the Crown, yet conceded that Ministers recognized themselves as 'also responsible to the representatives of the Reich for the maintenance of the Constitution and the exact execution of the laws'. As this still did not satisfy the Reichsrat, Schmerling, on 1 May 1862, read out a message from the Emperor confirming that the previous declaration had been made with his authority and announcing that the enactment of August 1851, relieving Ministers of all responsibility except to the Crown, was now to be considered as no longer valid in so far as it conflicted with the Declaration of 1861.

the principle of the immunity of its own members.[1] It had re-regulated, this time in satisfactory fashion, the position of the Protestants, who now received full equality before the law and acceptance of most of their other wishes,[2] and had enacted another Communal Autonomy Law, almost identical with that of 1849, which left the communes complete autonomy in their own spheres of action, subjecting them to State control only when they were acting as executants of central legislation. It had spoken up in favour of the separation of the executive from the judiciary, and in December 1862 had secured the establishment of a Permanent Committee, drawn from both houses, to control the State debt.

Then, however, it had run into trouble. A premature assault by Mühlfeld on the Concordat had made the German Clericals declared enemies of their Liberal fellow-countrymen. The Poles withdrew in dudgeon when martial law was proclaimed in Galicia, in connection with the 1863 revolution in Russian Poland.[3] The Czech Deputies, up to 1863, adopted the tactics of regularly objecting to the competence of the Reichsrat to legislate on Pan-Monarchic questions, on the ground that, in the absence of any representatives from the Hungarian Lands, those present were in fact only the 'Narrower Reichsrat'. On 17 June 1863, after first Clam-Martinic, then Rieger himself, had been treated with gross discourtesy by the President of the House and the German majority, Rieger withdrew his followers from it altogether.[4] The German Left, which should have been the Government's chief prop, spent their time largely in attacking it, in language often more bitter than that used by the Opposition itself, for its loyalty to the Concordat, its failure to secure civil liberties and its inability to cut budgetary expenditure to the limits of such revenue as they were willing to see raised.

Schmerling himself was perhaps more of a Josephinian than a true Liberal, at least in the anti-clerical implications of the term, and if he had

[1] This Bill was brought in very early, but passed the Herrenhaus only on 30 September 1861.

[2] The date of this important enactment was 8 April 1861. A 'Presbyterial and Synodal Constitution' was issued the next day. Amongst other things, the Protestants received under it extremely wide autonomy in the ordering of their own affairs, complete freedom of conscience and the right of public worship 'for all time', the right to employ foreigners in their Churches and schools and disciplinary powers for their clergy. To this, too, Francis Joseph consented only with very great reluctance. It was not applicable to the Tirol or Dalmatia.

[3] The Poles, except for the inevitable minority of hotheads, had not attempted to extend the revolt of 1863 to Galicia; they had rather hoped that Austria would help them and that in the end the Archduke Maximilian would assume the Crown of Poland. The Committee which they established in Galicia (headed by Smolka, Ziemalkowski and Count Alexander Dzjedniszycki) had therefore told their countrymen to 'wait', and had confined themselves to supplying arms, medical equipment, etc., to their countrymen fighting in Russian Poland. The Austrian Government, however, were not satisfied that the trouble would not spread into Galicia and therefore dissolved the Landtag and put the province under martial law.

[4] The Germans, incidentally, were just as rude to the Slovenes.

felt differently, his hands would have been tied by the Emperor. He was, moreover, sensitive and impatient of opposition (he once told a friend that he was 'by nature a soldier'). He came more and more to govern by the methods of Bach, forcing essential legislation through by the threat of the application of the emergency clause, Para. 13, and over-riding or stifling opposition. A new Press Law, enacted in December 1862, while purporting to eliminate abuses in its predecessor of 1852, was in certain respects still more severe, and was very strictly applied.

Schmerling tried to organize reliable support for himself in the Reichsrat, and in September 1863 persuaded the majority of the Great Austrians and Unionists to fuse in a new 'Club of the Left' to act as a Government Party, but they were none too disciplined, while those Liberals who refused to join the Club (the Autonomists and the Constitutional Landowners, who now formed their own Club, which called itself the 'Left Centre') were more hostile still.

Finance remained the great problem. Plener set himself two objectives: to put the Austrian currency back on parity, and keep it there; and to balance the budget. He made considerable progress towards the former end. After the public had so signally failed to subscribe to the 1860 loan, he persuaded the Rothschilds to under-write part of it,[1] and the National Bank to take over most of the remainder, making for the purpose a new issue of five gulden notes. Then in 1862 the Bank was given a new Statute, running until 1876, which definitively established its independence, while the State's debt to the Bank, now totalling 221·8 m.g., was to be repaid, out of a variety of sources, by the end of 1866. During this time the Bank's note issue was to be reduced to a maximum of 347·4 m.g., while the silver reserve would have risen to 147·4 m.g. The premium on silver sank to 117 in 1862 and 110 in 1863, and the balance of trade became strongly active.[2]

But the budget remained obstinately passive. The deficit was 110 m.g. in 1861, 94 in 1862, 62.5 in 1863, 93 in 1864.[3] It was still necessary to borrow, and the State debt had risen by the end of 1864 to 2,500 m.g., not counting 500 m.g. due to landlords expropriated under the land reform, and the service on it, to 113 m.g., forty per cent of the nett national revenue. The estimates for 1865 foresaw a nominal deficit of only 8 m.g., but Plener asked for a credit of 11 m.g. to help repay the debt to the Bank.

And the approach to balance, such as it had been, had been achieved almost exclusively by cutting expenditure. Voices were sometimes raised,

---

[1] As reward for this, Anselm Rothschild was made a member of the State Debt Committee, and afterwards, of the Herrenhaus.

[2] Expenditure for this year was swollen by the bill for the Danish war and by an advance of 20 m.g. to Hungary, where the harvest had failed disastrously.

[3] Exports rose from 251 m.g. in 1860 to 345 in 1865. Imports also went up, but not nearly so fast (from 224 to 253 m.g.).

Schmerling's among them, that the better policy would be to increase the national wealth by productive investment, improvement of communications, etc. Plener maintained that Austria's credit would stand no more than the minimum of borrowing necessary to square accounts with the Bank. He insisted on a rigidly deflationary policy, which produced an acute monetary shortage, and this caused widespread difficulties in industry and agriculture, these aggravated in the latter field by a series of bad harvests. In Carniola alone there were 26,000 distraints for non-payment of taxes in the one year 1865. The difficulties of the peasants were debated at length in every Landtag, although opinions on the advisability of de-restricting the sale or subdivision of peasant holdings were sharply divided. Industry was hit by the shrinking market, and some branches of it, by special circumstances; the American Civil War drove up the price of imported cotton by five hundred per cent, and at one time, 300,000 of the 350,000 operatives in the industry were unemployed.

A law passed in 1865, in an attempt to attract foreign capital, allowing any foreign enterprise, except an insurance company, to establish branches in the Monarchy, had had little immediate effect, the capitalists being too mistrustful of the Monarchy. An Anglo-Austrian Bank (regarded by Rothschild as 'a personal declaration of war' on himself) had, indeed, been founded in 1863.

The Liberals of the Reichsrat saw in the financial stringency all the more reason to leave what money there was to fructify in the pockets of the taxpayer, and combined with their representatives in the Government, as whom we may count Plener and, up to a point, Schmerling, in insisting on the cutting of Government expenditure, as the only remedy; and faithful to their creed, they concentrated their attacks on the defence estimates. Plener, as Finance Minister, waged a stubborn war against the men responsible for the defence of the Monarchy.[1] As we saw, it had been his veto which prevented Austria from making even the motions of intervening in Italy in 1860: when, in June of that year, the Archduke Wilhelm protested that it was impossible to 'maintain' the essential defences of the Monarchy with the sums allowed in Plener's estimates, Plener replied that 'he could give the army only what he could spare after covering other expenditure'.[2] The estimates to which he did agree then came before a Reichsrat Committee headed by Giskra (the same man who afterwards admitted to having accepted a personal *douceur* of 100,000 fl. in connection with a railway contract), popularly known as the 'Scrape Quartet',[3] which pared them further, and defence expenditure was

[1] That is, up to the issue of the October Diploma, the Army High Command; thereafter, the Minister of War.

[2] See Regele, op. cit., p. 341. Regele's chapters VII and IX are the most convenient source known to me for the history of the struggle between the financiers and the soldiers.

[3] '*Streichquartett*', a play on the word '*streichen*', meaning either to play a stringed instrument, or to cancel a word.

in fact cut from 179 in 1860 and 1861 to 139 in 1862 and 118 in 1863, with its inevitable results for the army. Once again, units were left under strength, men being sent on leave, sometimes indefinitely, and the re-equipment of the army neglected. It was on grounds of forced economy alone that the Austrian army was not equipped with the breech-loading rifles which gave Prussia such an incalculable advantage in 1866, and this was only one instance of many. Francis Joseph had actually watched trials of the new breech-loader in April 1865, had convinced himself of its superiority, and on 20 January 1866 had given orders that the army should be equipped with it. But on 27 February the Minister of War had told him that owing to fresh cuts in the Budget there was money only for 1,840 new rifles.[1]

Meanwhile, Prussia's challenge to Austria's leadership in Germany was growing ever bolder. The *Nationalverein*, founded to provide popular backing for the movement for the unification of a smaller Germany, under Prussian leadership and excluding Austria, was making rapid progress. In the summer of 1862 came the Franco-Prussian commercial treaty, the effect of which, when the consequential instruments had been agreed, was 'to make definitive the economic divorce between Germany and the Monarchy' – a consummation which was actually welcomed by Austria's businessmen, on economic grounds, but most certainly constituted a big political gain for Prussia.[2] On 27 September of the same year Bismarck became Prussian Foreign Minister.

It should be emphasized that at this juncture, Francis Joseph was far from feeling defeatist; and with reason, for many of the smaller German States found the prospect of continued Austrian leadership – in practice, almost imperceptible – far less frightening than that of Prussian domination. His concessions to constitutionalism seemed to be having the desired effects, and to be worth pursuing. Thus a queer little interlude opened, very reminiscent of 1806. Black-red-gold flags were hoisted in Vienna; Press articles appeared on Austria's and the Habsburgs' German mission, the Archduke Charles's statue

---

[1] See the article by O. Regele, Oesterreichs Armee und Flotte im Kriegsjahr 1866, *Donauraum*, 1966, II. 3, p. 127.

[1] The quotation is from Werner, *100 Jahre*, p. 383. For a detailed account of the negotiations, see Benedikt, *Wirtschaftliche Entwicklung*, pp. 57 ff. In 1862 Prussia agreed with France on the draft of a commercial treaty on the m. f. n. basis, which would exclude the special preferences which Prussia, and with her, the other members of the Zollverein, allowed Austria under the Treaty of 1853, which was due to expire in 1865, in which year the Zollverein also was due to come up for revision. Austria made a counter-proposal to institute complete free trade between herself and the Zollverein, except only that the fiscal and excise duties were to be retained. Prussia retorted on 2 August by signing the treaty with France, leaving the other States with the alternative of following suit or letting the Zollverein break up. In the event they accepted Prussia's conditions, while Prussia agreed to negotiate a new treaty with Austria. This was concluded in April 1865, the tariffs being (at Austria's wish) made substantially higher than those of 1853. Austria then negotiated her own treaties, both on the m. f. n. basis, with France and Britain. Both were concluded in December 1865, to enter into force on 1 January 1867.

in the Heldenplatz was inscribed 'to the tenacious fighter for Germany's honour'. Visiting parties from Germany were made welcome at congresses and festivities, and across the frontiers, Austria's cause was popularized by a *Reformverein*, a counter-blast to the Nationalverein, called into being, interestingly, by the same Julius Fröbel who had come to Vienna from Frankfurt in October 1848 as an emissary of the German Left and had barely escaped with his life.

It was Fröbel who was responsible for the idea of inviting the Princes of Germany to a Fürstentag at Frankfurt in August 1863.[1] The avowed object was to revise the Constitution of the Bund (of course, in Austria's favour), but it is probable that Francis Joseph hoped to be offered the Imperial Crown. But the Fürstentag proved the beginning and the end of the enterprise. The ceremony was gorgeous, but Bismarck had (although with great difficulty) persuaded his King to absent himself, and with Prussia absent, the Congress could do nothing but speechify. The same year the complicated diplomatic manoeuverings occasioned by the Polish revolt saw Russia closer to Prussia, and further from Austria, than before, and the autumn saw the beginning of the tedious Schleswig-Holstein imbroglio.

In this, Austria and Prussia managed to act as partners, but all the real advantage, as well as a further access of prestige, went to Prussia, while Austria was left in charge of a province which she did not need and had only cost her money and blood which she did need. And it was the end of the partnership. By now Bismarck was ready to face a direct trial of strength with Austria, and Francis Joseph was beginning to glimpse the red light. Up to that date he had not only been hopeful of success in his German plans, but had genuinely believed that they could be achieved without serious objections from Prussia. As late as the spring of 1864 he had still regarded Napoleon III, whom he never liked,[2] as the true common enemy of Austria and Prussia alike, and in the summer of the same year he could still write to his mother that 'alliance' (*die Alliance*) 'with Prussia is the only right policy'.[3] He complained of his partner's 'lack of principles and juvenile pranks', yet 'the relationship to Prussia is the keystone of our policy'.[4]

But his meeting with the King of Prussia and Bismarck at Schönbrunn on 24 August seems to have convinced him that Prussia could not be checked except by force. Rechberg, who still favoured conciliation, believing as he did that war with Prussia would entail also war with Italy, and that the odds

[1] The plan seems to have originated with Fröbel, who succeeded in interesting Francis Joseph's brother-in-law, Prince Thurn und Taxis, in it, and the Prince fired the Emperor with the idea.

[2] 'The Emperor is and remains a scoundrel', he wrote to his mother on 1 September 1859 from Italy, where he was negotiating the armistice terms.

[3] See his letter to Albert of Saxony, cit. Corti, op. cit., p. 307.

[4] There was no technical 'alliance' with Prussia at that date; the negotiations for one had broken down in April 1861.

would be too heavy for Austria to face, might, perhaps, have bought a few more years of peace, but at a price, and Francis Joseph was not willing to pay what might be a heavy price for uncertain advantage. In October he replaced Rechberg by Count Mensdorff-Pouilly, who, with Hofrat von Biegeleben, the *éminence grise* of the Foreign Ministry, was in sympathy with the forward policy on which Francis Joseph was now decided.[1]

In this situation Francis Joseph found himself again at loggerheads with the Austrian Liberals, for they refused obstinately to admit the need for rearmament. When, at the end of 1862, Degenfeld had drawn attention to the mounting armaments expenditure of Austria's potential enemies, Plener had replied airily that 'he had his own sources of information: the Press, the House of Rothschild, and other bankers; Austria could safely go on disarming'.[2] In 1864 he pronounced that 'the Schleswig-Holstein match seemed unlikely to start an European conflagration';[3] he wanted another reduction of the defence budget, which 'exercised a depressing influence on the world of finance'.[4] The Schleswig-Holstein campaign brought army expenditure up again to 155 m.g. in 1864, but it was cut down again to 101 in 1865, when Schmerling, who said that 'today we are enjoying the certainty of European peace', proposed reducing the Monarchy's forces in Italy,[5] and the estimates for 1866 were cut further still, to 80 m.g. for the army and 7·8 for the navy.[6]

Nevertheless, the international situation brought about the next, and as the event was to prove, the decisive, turn in Francis Joseph's internal policy.

Since their victory, the great majority of the German Liberals had regarded the Hungarian question as settled. Most of them accepted, as a correct statement of the legal situation, the so-called *Verwirkungstheorie*, i.e., the case (restated in 1862 in book form by a Professor named Lustkandl) that Hungary had rendered her own Constitution null and void when the Diet declared the Habsburg Dynasty deposed in 1849,[7] and they did not take the rumours of Hungarian discontent seriously.[8] Like Schmerling himself, they were confident that Hungary would come to heel.

But in this respect also Francis Joseph's horizon was wider than theirs. He knew that if Austria became involved in war with either Prussia, or Italy, or

---

[1] The remarkable negotiations in Schönbrunn, when Rechberg's hope of agreeing with Bismarck on a policy which should direct the Austro-Prussian partnership against France were frustrated by Biegeleben, are excellently described in Friedjung, *Vorherrschaft*, I. 101 ff.
[2] Regele, p. 318.
[3] Id., p. 319.
[4] Id., p. 320.
[5] Id., p. 321.
[6] On this occasion the Liberals were, indeed, guiltless: the cuts were volunteered by the Belcredi Government.
[7] E. von Plener in his *Erinnerungen*, I. 18, testifies that this was his father's view, and that of the great majority of his contemporaries.
[8] Id., p. 16.

both – and he knew that the prospect was not to be laughed off – a disaffected Hungary in her rear would be a serious danger to her. And his agents did not cease to report disaffection. Besides the purely internal passive resistance, Kossuth's Italian backers had resumed touch with him, and their plans again provided for risings in Hungary and Transylvania; several Hungarians were arrested for complicity in these preparations.

The question was whether Hungary could be reconciled. Esterházy, whose influence over the Emperor was very great at this stage,[1] was emphatic that the possibility existed, but he can hardly be credited with the fatherhood of the developments which followed, for he still believed in the possibility of a Hungarian regime based on the Old Conservatives. Strangely enough, it seems to have been the Archduke Albrecht who advised his cousin to get in touch again with Deák, as the really important man.[2] At any rate, Francis Joseph sent down an intermediary[3] to Deák, in deep secrecy, in December 1864.

And Deák proved more approachable than had been expected. Public opinion had, in fact, changed very considerably in Hungary in 1862-3. In December of the earlier year Deák himself, with many others, had been seriously perturbed by the indiscreet revelation in a foreign newspaper of Kossuth's latest proposals for the future of Hungary, this time, a plan for constituting Hungary with Croatia-Slavonia, Serbia, and the Danubian Principalities as a Federal State, with a Parliament meeting in turn in the four capitals. The idea had few charms for a people accustomed to pride itself on its Western traditions, and to regard its Balkan neighours as unlettered barbarians, and the revelation of it had had a very big effect in turning opinion against the emigration.[4] If this was the alternative to an accommodation with the West, then the latter was worth seeking, if it could possibly be achieved. The efficiency which the Austrian police had shown in detecting Kossuth's correspondence, and arresting his correspondents, had made another deep impression, and there were also economic considerations. Hungarian agriculture was in difficulties, which reached a climax in 1863 with a disastrous harvest, so devastating that Schmerling's Government itself, financially embarrassed as it was, had to make Hungary a special grant in aid, whereas the Austrian Government's programme of public works, especially of railway expansion, promised constructive improvement. Quite suddenly, Deák had found his own policy of 'waiting' denounced as unconstructive and over-passive.

[1] It is probable that it was he who was responsible for the replacement of Rechberg by Mensdorff-Pouilly.
[2] Redlich, *Franz Joseph*, p. 280.
[3] Freiherr von Auguss, Vice-President of the Buda Gubernium.
[4] S. Pethö writes that 'at one blow, it altered the psychological dominance of Kossuth's influence, and greatly helped forward the possibility of a reconciliation with the Crown, even if this should cost sacrifices' (*Világostól Trianonig*, p. 74).

Finally, Deák himself appears to have been impressed by the support for Austria shown by the German Princes at the Fürstentag, and also, perhaps, by the backing which Schmerling seemed to be enjoying among most of the Austrian Germans. On the other hand, there was a group among the Austrian Germans which was beginning to favour agreement with the Hungarian Liberals. In 1863 Kaiserfeld had actually concluded an inter-Party agreement between his 'Autonomists' and the Deákists, and was exercising his influence in favour of what proved in the event the basis of the new structure of the Monarchy, Dualism based on an alliance between its German and its Hungarian elements. It is true that Kaiserfeld himself at that time envisaged treatment in a single Parliament of all 'common' subjects.[1]

Nevertheless the development was of the utmost importance, for it meant that those Austrian-Germans who took Kaiserfeld's view were now pulling on the same rope as the Hungarian Liberals, and not, as Schmerling and his followers were still doing, against them. The shift in the balance of forces was not yet big, but from the delicacy of that balance, even a small change might prove decisive.

Deák told the intermediary that Hungary recognized the validity of the Pragmatic Sanction, but could not renounce her constitutional position. Francis Joseph must accept coronation and undertake the appropriate obligations. Transylvania must be re-incorporated and Croatia's relationship with Hungary regulated in a fashion which did not defy history. But he was ready to reach a reasonable compromise with the Croats, and to give the 'nationalities' the treatment outlined in the 1861 report. He was also now prepared to admit that the personal union established under the Pragmatic Sanction entailed 'community' with the Monarch's other dominions, not of the person of the Monarch alone, but also of those questions which had fallen within his royal prerogative in all his dominions, notably foreign policy and defence. There remained the problem of how these questions were to be treated under constitutional regimes, since a common legislature was quite unacceptable; but the ex-Chancellor, Apponyi, had shortly before thrown out a suggestion, which struck Deák as acceptable, that there could be two Parliaments and that these 'common' subjects might be discussed by 'delegations' from them on a footing of complete equality.

On 16 April 1865 the Easter number of Deák's organ, the *Pesti Napló*, carried an article (it was unsigned, but Deák's authorship of it was at once generally known, as it was meant to be), in form a polemic against something written in Schmerling's organ, the *Botschafter*, in which Deák expressed, in general terms, the view that a constitutional Hungary and a constitutional Austria could easily exist together under a common ruler and with a common defence system, provided that Hungary's constitutional rights were in fact

[1] Patzelt, op. cit., p. 15.

respected. A month later a series of articles inspired by him appeared in the *Debatte*, an organ maintained in Vienna by the Old Conservatives,[1] formally admitting the existence of 'matters of common interest' to the two halves of the Monarchy – the Monarch's household,[2] foreign policy and diplomacy, defence, the taxation necessary to cover these items, and commercial and tariff policy, and advocating the system of 'Delegations' from two equal Parliaments as the machinery for dealing with them constitutionally. Francis Joseph in return demonstrated his intention of reconciling the Crown with Hungary by paying Pest a brief and almost unannounced, but very effective, visit. This was on 6–9 June. During his visit, he restored the full competence of the Hungarian Consilium, and suspended the operation of the military courts. On 26 June, Zichy was replaced as Chancellor by György Mailáth.

The Emperor had done all this without consulting, or even informing, his Ministry, and when the change of Chancellors was thus made over their heads, the Archduke and Schmerling tendered their resignations. Schmerling was kept provisionally in charge of affairs until 27 July; then the Reichsrat was dissolved and the names of a new Ministry announced. Of the old Cabinet, only Mensdorff and Esterházy retained their portfolios. The new Minister President was Count Richard Belcredi; the Minister of Finance, Count Larisch-Mönich. The other Ministers were ephemeral figures, whose names are not worth recalling.

The dismissal of Schmerling was an admission that the idea of total centralization of the whole Monarchy, including Hungary, had been dropped; but what was to take its place was still obscure. Francis Joseph was still far from accepting the full programme of Deák and his followers, further yet from envisaging them as his partners in the governance of Hungary. The Hungarians on whom he placed personal confidence were, as his retention of Esterházy and appointment of Mailáth showed, still the Old Conservative aristocrats, who themselves had not yet given up hope of returning to power. And they, as we have seen, were the allies of the federalist feudal nobles in the West, and Belcredi, who was another of Esterházy's nominees, was connected by birth and career with the Bohemian aristocracy, and so far as was known, a federalist in his sympathies.

Belcredi's first moves threw little light on his, or Francis Joseph's, intentions. An Imperial Manifesto and Patent, both issued on 20 September, 'suspended the operation' (*sistierte*) of the February Patent so far as the

---

[1] Although Deák never adopted the Old Conservatives' political theories, he was at this time, as his biographer (Ferenczy, op. cit., III. 4) writes, 'convinced that only they could bring about the overthrow of Schmerling', and was therefore in close touch with them.

[2] Deák afterwards dropped this item from his list.

composition (and, consequently, the operation) of the central Reichsrat was concerned, pending the outcome of negotiations, to be initiated with Hungary and Croatia, on such modifications of the February Patent as would secure their co-operation with the rest of the Monarchy. The Hungarian Diet and the Sabor were both convoked for December, explicitly for such negotiation; the Transylvanian Diet was convoked also, for 14 November, with a single item on its agenda, 'the revision of the Act of Union of 1848'.[1]

While these negotiations were going on, necessary Governmental business relating to the Monarchy as a whole was to be carried on by emergency decree, but the Landtage were convoked for November, and they were promised that the results of the negotiations with Hungary and Croatia, when complete, should be submitted to them 'for the hearing and appreciaton of their views, which would be given equal weight'.[2]

These edicts were naturally received with great indignation by the German centralists, and when the Landtage did meet, those of Upper and Lower Austria, Styria, Carinthia, Salzburg, Silesia and Vorarlberg protested against the suspension of the Patent; of the German Crownlands, only the incorrigibly federalist Tirol went the other way. Galicia, on the other hand, which had once again been administratively reunited, took the opportunity to demand Home Rule again, Moravia rejected, although only by a small majority, a resolution in favour of the Patent, and both Bohemia and Carniola (in both of which Slav majorities had been returned) saluted the change and pressed demands: Bohemia, for coronation of the Monarch in Prague, a Bohemian Court Chancellery, revision of the Landtag Statute to give more weight to the Czech element, and linguistic concessions to the Czech language in administration and education; Carniola, for concessions in favour of the Slovene language and a similar revision of the Landtag Statute. Belcredi in fact promised the coronation and made several concessions in the linguistic field in both Lands.[3]

But the important issue was clearly what was going to happen in Hungary. The elections for the new Diet, which had been held in November 1865, had been fought exclusively on the constitutional issue, and they had returned twenty-one 'Conservatives', a hundred and eighty 'Deákists', prepared to accept their leader's interpretation of the Pragmatic Sanction (most of the

[1] Deák had maintained that since the Union of 1848 had been legally valid, no rediscussion of its terms was constitutional. 'Revision' therefore could really mean no more than 're-enactment' (Ferenczy, op. cit., III. 25).

[2] *Um ihren gleichgewichtigen Ausspruch zu vernehmen und zu würdigen.*

[3] The most important of these in Bohemia was the sanctioning of a by-law (which had been passed by the Bohemian Landtag in 1864 but not then sanctioned) making instruction in both local languages compulsory in all secondary schools. This law, popularly known as the *Sprachenzwanggesetz* (Linguistic Compulsion Law) was repealed as soon as the Germans returned to power; see below, p. 563, n. 2.

representatives of the Nationalities, who did not constitute themselves as a separate group, sat with the Deákists), ninety-four members of Tisza's and Ghyczy's 'Left Centre', who were still reluctant to go beyond the personal union in its purest form, and twenty members of the 'extreme Left'. The country had thus pronounced decisively against the Conservatives, so that the Hungarian problem reduced itself, for Francis Joseph, to the questions whether he could agree with Deák, and whether Deák, for his part, could carry his countrymen with him. His majority was not too safe, for many of his followers were secretly rather sympathetic to the Left Centre, but it was soon strengthened by the result of the decision of the Transylvanian Diet, which had been duly packed by the nomination to it of suitably-minded 'Regalists'.[1] When it met, it decided by majority (the Roumanians and some of the Saxons dissenting) that the 1848 Act of Union had been valid, that all legislation passed since it had been illegal and that its own existence had no legal basis. It therefore begged the Crown to call Transylvania's legal representatives to Pest, where they should resume the negotiations interrupted in 1849. The Crown having granted this request, new elections were held on the 1848 franchise, which resulted in the return of an overwhelming majority of Magyars, a small phalanx of Saxons, and only two Roumanians. The Deputies now appeared in the Pest Diet, where nearly all the Magyars attached themselves to the 'Deák Party'.

The negotiations did not go easily. Francis Joseph himself opened the Diet, on 14 December, with a speech in Hungarian, in which he made the important concession of admitting the legal validity of the April Laws. But he said that they would have to be revised in the sense of the October Diploma, and still asked for 'common Parliamentary treatment' of the common affairs enumerated in that instrument. He had at that time no intention of going much further.[2] The Diet's reply, drafted by Deák, again refused to entertain the idea of a common Parliament, and the whole spring passed in an exchange of notes in which neither side yielded any perceptible ground, although Deák was able to persuade his own fellow-Deputies to elect a Committee of sixty-seven (which in turn elected a sub-Committee of fifteen) to work out the details of the machinery for putting Hungary's wishes into effect, when she had gained her point.[3]

The Croat position reached a similar deadlock, for when the Sabor met at the end of 1865 the Crown had, in effect, told it to agree with the Hungarians, but in the subsequent negotiations the Croats had refused to accept anything short of their full demands, constitutional (for a personal

---

[1] 129 Regalists were nominated, of whom ninety were Magyars.

[2] 'The people in Vienna', he wrote to his mother on 17 February 1866, 'are, as usual, terribly nervous and think that I might make concessions – for instance, appoint a Ministry. I have naturally no intention of doing anything of the sort' (Schnürer, p. 350).

[3] The sub-Committee's report, in fact, figured in the later Law almost textually.

union pure and simple) and geographical (for Fiume and the Muraköz), and the Hungarians had declared these demands unacceptable.

The constitutional question was thus still in the melting-pot when the accumulated powder of Austro-Prussian relations exploded in war. What followed proved again the truth of Francis Joseph's own later admission that he had 'no lucky hand', although the word unlucky is perhaps more appropriate than any adjective expressing strong moral reprobation. Austria was manoeuvred into declaring war, and the domestic responsibility for the declaration undoubtedly falls squarely on the Emperor's shoulders, but he took the final decision only after Bismarck and others had created a situation which left him no other choice, unless he had been willing to acquiesce without a blow in the loss of Austria's leadership in Germany and of her remaining possessions in Italy. If Francis Joseph miscalculated the forces involved, so that his choice proved, in the event, fatal, the blame was not his alone: his General Staff had, indeed, repeatedly called attention to the inadequacies of Austria's armaments, but von Crenneville, whose sympathies were strongly with the war party, seems entirely to have failed to enlighten his master on the true facts,[1] while his civilian advisers, as we have seen, brushed all warnings aside with something more than impatience, and their representations were actually among the factors which made him decide on war.[2]

But the fact remains that the miscalculation was made, and that if Francis Joseph had been better informed, and if at the same time he had been psychologically capable of the voluntary renunciation, Austria would, indeed, have lost the disputed ground in Germany and Italy, but she would have lost it bloodlessly, and would even have recouped her finances in the process. In November 1865 Bismarck offered to buy Austria out of Holstein, and almost at the same time, the Italian Minister President, La Marmora, secretly offered to buy Venetia as far as the Isonzo, for 400 million Austrian gulden. Italy was prepared further to conclude an advantageous commercial treaty with Austria and to adopt a benevolent attitude on the Papal question.[3] Francis Joseph rejected both offers, whereupon Bismarck concluded an offensive and defensive alliance with Italy (8 April 1866). Mensdorff's riposte was to conclude, on 12 June, a treaty with Napoleon III, under which

[1] The miscalculations were not confined to Austria: Richard Metternich, the Austrian Ambassador in Paris, reported that the whole French Army, 'from the Minister of War to the most junior subaltern, was convinced that Austria would be victorious'.

[2] He had persuaded himself that the war would not be expensive, since it would end in a speedy victory, after which Austria would receive an indemnity, and then be able to disarm. 'We must in any case come to a result', he wrote to his mother on 11 May 1866, 'after spending so much money and making so many sacrifices ... Better war than prolongation of the present situation' (Schnürer, p. 355).

[3] It is true that under a secret clause, Italy was also to have been promised the eventual acquisition of the Trentino.

Austria promised after all to cede Venetia, even if she won the war.[1] Her only reward was France's neutrality, and as things turned out, she could hardly have fared worse with France against her.

When war (which broke out immediately after this, Prussia finding a pretext in Holstein to force the issue), Francis Joseph made another grievous false move. The Archduke Albrecht was given the command on the easy Italian front, with a first-class Chief of Staff in the person of Field-Marshal G. John, while the command of the northern armies was forced on the unfortunate Benedek, despite his protests that he was unfitted for so large a command and totally unfamiliar with the terrain. Albrecht and John defeated the Italians at Custozza, on 24 June, and Admiral Tegetthof won a naval victory over the same easy opponents at Lissa on 20 July. But on 3 July, Benedek was crushingly defeated at Königgrätz (Sadowa) by the Prussian armies, which proved far superior to the Austrian in both leadership and armament.

A preliminary peace was signed at Nikolsburg on 6 August and the definitive treaty, at Prague on 23 August (peace with Italy had come on 10 August). Austria had to consent to 'a new formation of Germany, from which the Austrian Empire should be excluded', and to pay Prussia an indemnity. She ceded Venetia to Napoleon, who re-ceded it to Italy.

These were mild terms, and ought to have been even milder, for Bismarck had been willing not to ask even for an indemnity if Austria left the Bund immediately; but Esterházy, who seems to have been Francis Joseph's evil genius in these negotiations, suspected a trap and Francis Joseph's answer accepting the offer reached Bismarck half an hour too late.

The finishing touch to the many foolish and wicked actions which marred this sorry story was provided by the Emperor's unforgivable treatment of Benedek, who was publicly disgraced for his failure to succeed in a task for which he had protested his unfitness. It does not, indeed, appear to be proved that Francis Joseph deliberately allowed Benedek to risk defeat in order to spare the Archduke the danger of it; for one thing, he did not expect defeat, and according to one authority[2] had not even himself wanted to give Benedek the appointment, which was forced on him by the unanimous voice of the army, Austria's South German allies, and public opinion in general. It also seems clear that Benedek really lost his head. Nevertheless, there is something mysterious and unsavoury about the exaction from him of a pledge (which he kept most honourably) to say nothing in his own defence, a few

---

[1] This was to be in compensation for the territorial acquisitions which France proposed, in that event, to make in Germany. Napoleon was further to attempt to persuade Italy to remain neutral. The Treaty also contained numerous provisions governing the cession of Venice and many more limiting Austria's gains after she had defeated Prussia.

[2] Jedlicka, *Gestalter*, p. 355.

days before the appearance (of which he was given no pre-warning) of a most vicious and gratuitous attack on him.

The war, of course, also wrote finis to Austria's immediate hopes of balancing her budget. The Minister of Finance had not expected it to have this effect: he had calculated that it would end in a speedy victory, after which Austria would receive an indemnity and be able to disarm, so that it would actually be a profitable enterprise – a view which seems, as we have seen, to have been shared by Francis Joseph. The operation had, however, to be financed by borrowing, since the Reichsrat would not loosen the pursestrings, and when the inevitability of war became apparent, Larisch sent an emissary, von Becke, to Western Europe in search of a loan. The moneylenders were less optimistic than he, mistrusting as they did political conditions in the Monarchy, especially after the suspension of the February Patent. Lionel Rothschild demanded recognition of the Kingdom of Italy and advised Austria to sell Venice; James Rothschild advised her to sell Holstein. In November 1865, von Becke got a loan of 147 million gulden (nominal) in Paris, but it was floated at 69, so that Austria received only 90 million, and the interest on it came to 9·6%. It was repayable at par in 37 years. On top of this, the underwriters exacted a commission of nearly 10%.[1] For another 60 m.g., lent by the Bodenkreditanstalt, the Treasury had to pledge State forests and estates.

When war broke out, the State took over the 1 and 5 gulden notes of the National Bank, at an obligatory course, to the tune of 150 m.g., the Bank being authorized to issue notes of higher denominations to the same value, and to deposit them with the State. In the next two months the issue of another 150 m.g. was authorized.

In the event it was, of course, Austria that had to pay the indemnity (which again had to be raised with the help of the banks),[2] while military and naval expenditure for the year was 256 m.g. The deficit was 292 m.g., and the debt rose to 3,049 m.g., with a service of 127 m.g.

Meanwhile, the Bourse had taken a different view of the prospects from the Minister's. When the news of Königgrätz came, quotations rose on the Bourse, which preferred quick defeat to a prolonged war, even should it be followed by victory.

The exclusion of Austria from Germany brought with it far-reaching changes in the balance of political forces inside the Monarchy, most of these being indirect, and deriving from its direct effect, that which it had on the position of her Germans. For those of them who were very strongly nationally minded the event came as a grievous spiritual shock: no longer able to feel

[1] For details, see Plener, *Erinnerungen*, pp. 47 ff.
[2] It was, indeed, a modest one: 20 million thaler indemnity plus 5 million for the cost of maintaining the Prussian troops.

sincerely that in serving Austria, they were also serving Germany, they became prey to a painful conflict of loyalties. For such men the natural policy for the Germans of Austria would henceforward be 'to work for the separation of its German districts from Austria and their return to the mother-land'.[1]

Even for those who drew no such conclusions a new situation had in fact been created by the loss by Austria of her membership and nominal leadership of the German Bund. Austria's authority over the other German States had long been a mere shadow, while theirs over her internal affairs had been non-existent. Nevertheless, the connection had, in a way which was perhaps irrational but none the less real, given the Austrian-Germans courage and confidence, and had made them feel that their claim to leadership within the Monarchy was natural and even unquestionable. If the Treaty of Prague was to be final, this backing was lost to them for ever. Austria, no longer even titularly a German State, must adjust itself to becoming a multinational one, and in that its Germans must fight their own battle, as one national group among the many. They were still the largest of those groups, and still socially, economically and culturally the most advanced of them, but their numerical superiority was only relative – the non-Germans outnumbered them by three to one and the Slavs, taken together, by two to one – and their other advantages were bound to dwindle as education spread among the non-Germans and wealth accumulated in their hands. Whatever shape the Monarchy took in the future, it could not, on any reasonable calculation, be that either of Bach's absolutism, or of the February Patent. It would have to allow some further concessions, either to the Slavs, or the Magyars, or both.

Actually, very few of the Germans appreciated all this in 1866–7. As Kleinwächter says bitterly of the change in their policy which, in his view, ought to have come, 'nothing of the sort occurred'. The only immediate reactions of a nature to influence immedate political developments in the Monarchy came from a small group in Graz, connected with Kaiserfeld's Autonomists, which very early after the Peace of Prague[2] began to ventilate ideas some of which were later to become popular. For an immediate policy, they began to advocate going further even than the Dualism which the Autonomists were already supporting, and giving Galicia-Bukovina a similar status. With Dalmatia attached to Hungary, this would leave a unit consisting only of the Hereditary and Bohemian Lands, in which the Germans would be in a safe majority. They also held that history would end by bringing about the break-up of the Monarchy and the adherence of its German parts (including the Bohemian Lands) to the new Germany, and

[1] Kleinwächter, op. cit., p. 196.
[2] The first articles setting out these ideas appeared in the Autonomists' organ, the *Grazer Telegraf*, early in 1867 (Molisch, op. cit., pp. 71–2).

this should be prepared for by economic and cultural assimilation. A German national party should be founded to realize this programme.

The Autonomists' Party Conference at Aussee in 1868 later formulated the new ideas more precisely. Not only 1848 and 1861, but also 1867 had been too ambitious, for the predominance of the Germans in 1867 Reichsrat was founded on an undemocratic franchise, which could not (and ought not to) last long. 'We must give up the untenable Cis-Leithania, and put in its place German-Austria, which once belonged to the German Reich'. The link with Galicia and the Bukovina should be reduced to a personal union, Dalmatia attached to Hungary. Then the Germans could stand up to the Czechs and Slovenes in the Reichsrat, and negotiate with them, 'for the strong can safely grant what the weak must refuse'. 'Today we cannot and may not seek the Anschluss with Germany, but we must form a national body in Austria.'[1]

A 'German-national Association', with this programme, was founded in Graz in 1869, and similar bodies in Vienna and Klagenfurt.

But at this crucial juncture (1866), none of the Germans outside Styria seemed to realize that their position had changed at all. Those who grieved at Austria's catastrophe told themselves comfortably that it would soon be reversed. The Liberal leaders actually believed that the defeat had strengthened their position by the discredit it cast on the war party, whom 'it just served right'.[2] There was no need for any concessions to anybody: rather the contrary.

But others were not so blind. The non-Germans saw clearly that the balance of forces had changed, and were preparing to make their dispositions accordingly. In this situation it was important that the Hungarians were the only nation among them which offered the Government a firm foundation on which it could build.

The Poles had, indeed, just carried through a very important readjustment of their political line. Finally disillusioned by the failure of the 1863 revolt as to the possibility to which they had thitherto clung,[3] of an early restoration of Polish independence through help from the West, they had decided (a group of Conservatives taking the lead) that the best long-term hope for Poland lay in a strong Austria, no longer a threat to their national existence now that Austria was excluded from Germany. The Austrian Government had met them more than half-way, if only because their good will would

[1] *M.K.P.*, III. 219.

[2] I should like to quote here the penetrating comment by Eder (op. cit., p. 151) that the (German) Austrian masses 'still regarded war and its events, politics and political happenings, as something which was not their concern, but that of 'the people above'. It was, at bottom, the attitude of the audience in a theatre, applauding or hissing the play and the actors.'

[3] Even after their Landtag had been restored in 1861, the Poles had put off building premises for it, because they had hoped shortly to be sending their representatives to a Parliament of united Poland in Warsaw (Bienaimée, p. 129).

strengthen Austria's international position. Martial law had already been lifted in April 1865; an amnesty for political prisoners had followed in the same November, and in the following September Belcredi had reappointed Goluchowski Statthalter, accepting his conditions: that the administrative partition of Galicia should be definitively abandoned, Polish made the exclusive language of administration and education above the primary level, and the services purged of their remaining non-local elements. Meanwhile, a meeting of Polish leaders had agreed on a programme of loyalty to the Crown in return for far-reaching autonomy for Galicia, and in December the Galician Diet voted an Address to the Crown which expressed this policy in gratifyingly lyrical terms.

This, however, was a purely self-regarding policy which was not even necessarily hostile to Centralism in the rest of the Monarchy, provided it did not extend to Galicia. The Czechs saw that they could not realize their ambitions except in the framework of a general federalization, and in August, called a 'Federalists' Conference' in Vienna, to which they invited Goluchowski, and also Strossmayer from Croatia, and to which they submitted a plan for reorganizing the Monarchy into a 'Pentarchy' of five federal units, 'Old Austria', 'Inner Austria', the Bohemian Lands, Hungary-Croatia and Galicia. But this failed to satisfy Goluchowski, who thought he could make better terms for Galicia alone, nor Strossmayer, who wanted Croatia released from the link with Hungary. Still less, of course, did it satisfy the Slovenes, who had not even been invited to the Conference which disposed of them so cavalierly,[1] and who now produced their own programme for a Great Slovenia. Belcredi himself asked how he was expected to realize a programme the authors of which were not agreed between themselves. Meanwhile, both Czechs and Slovenes indulged in demonstrations of hostility against the Germans which made the latter determined to maintain the maximum of centralism in the Hereditary and Bohemian Lands, even if it meant letting Galicia and Hungary go their own ways.

To all this, the attitude of the Hungarians presented a refreshing contrast. There had, of course, been voices enough in Hungary, when the war broke out, that Austria's difficulty was Hungary's opportunity, and a Hungarian legion had been enlisted to serve with the Prussian arms. This enterprise, however, had proved a fiasco[2] which had done the extremists more harm than good, while when the peace came to be signed, Bismarck had forgotten his Hungarian tools as completely as Napoleon III had done seven years before. Deák had – not without difficulty – kept the country behind him, and when, after Königgrätz, Francis Joseph asked him, in a personal interview, what his

[1] It had been calculated 'that the Slovenes would have to be sacrificed to the Germans, if Austria was to receive the desired Federal Constitution (*M.K.P.*, III. 209).

[2] A group of volunteers, led by Klapka, had entered North Hungary, but the Slovak population had been hostile to them and they were forced to retreat.

terms were now, he had replied that they were exactly the same as before Austria' defeat.

It was also very important that the man now figuring as Deák's right-hand man and negotiator-in-chief was none other than Count Gyula Andrássy, recently returned home, under an amnesty, from an exile in the course of which his name had been nailed to a gallows-tree for his services to Kossuth. Benevolent fairies had blessed Andrássy with exceptional personal charm, a most persuasive tongue, and a lineage which made him *hoffähig*. Further, although far shallower in mind than Deák, he had more appreciation of non-legal, political considerations. And one element in his political creed strongly influenced the direction in which the further negotiations developed. As a native of North Hungary, Andrássy was by his very environment keenly alive to the Slav danger, and the movements among the Slovaks, coupled with certain indiscreet utterances by Palacký, had bred in him a conviction, which afterwards determined his whole policy, including his foreign policy, when he became Foreign Minister of the Monarchy, not only that Hungary would not be safe unless she formed part of a Great Power – that is to say, her safety lay in a close connection with Austria – but that that Power must not be dominated by Slavs. He therefore disagreed with the Hungarian Feudalists even to the extent of not allowing the realization of the *Böhmisches Staatsrecht*. In a memorandum which he submitted to Francis Joseph in 1866 he argued that 'an artificial reconstruction of the Bohemian Crown and a grouping of the Slav provinces round it would only begin in Austria a work which would necessarily end outside it',[1] and in private audience he is said to have summed up the principle of Dualism (of which he may almost be called the main author) in the words: 'You look after your Slavs and we will look after ours.'

He could not, of course, dictate what the structural arrangement of the Monarchy outside Hungary should be, but he did make it clear to the world that the hopes of a settlement with Hungary would be the brighter if his views were met, with the consequence that not only Kaiserfeld's Autonomists but the German-Austrian politicians in general (except the hard core of Greater Austrian centralists) began to look on the Hungarian Liberals as their natural allies against the Austrian-Slavs.

The Hungarian demands still seemed to Francis Joseph excessive, and his personal sympathies were strongly with Belcredi and his circle in Austria, and with the Old Conservatives in Hungary. But the balance was tipped by two individuals. One was the Empress, who had fallen victim to the insidious Hungarian charm and used all her influence with her husband to persuade him to meet the Hungarians' wishes.[2] The other was a new-comer to Austrian

[1] The text of this is given in Wertheimer, *Andrássy*, I. 224.

[2] Much the best account of the Empress's part in these negotiations is Corti's in his *Elisabeth*, pp. 138 ff. (Wertheimer's references to it are little more than incidental). Elisabeth

politics in the person of Friedrich Ferdinand von Beust, Minister of Foreign Affairs for Saxony, whom, on 30 October, Francis Joseph suddenly appointed his own Foreign Minister, *vice* Mensdorf.

The primary object of the appointment was foreign political. Francis Joseph was still unreconciled to his defeat at the hands of Prussia, and Beust's mission was to organize an anti-Prussian front among the lesser German States (the existence of the secret treaties which Bismarck had concluded with Bavaria, Württemberg and Hesse was not yet known in Vienna and could hardly have been suspected, seeing that *after* their conclusion Bismarck promised to leave those States the possibility of joining a South German League), and beyond that, among other States jealous or frightened of Prussia. He had, as yet, no mandate to intervene in the internal affairs of the Monarchy, of which he had, as his enemies did not tire of pointing out, little knowledge. But it was, after all, obvious that the Monarchy could not hope to stand up against Prussia, much less wage a successful war against her, without internal political appeasement. The appointment of Beust would certainly help appease the German-Austrian Liberals – he was himself a Liberal and a Protestant, as well as something of an anti-Slav,[1] and the very fact that he was a foreigner was an advantage where Hungary was concerned, for it would have been difficult to find an 'Austrian' with whom the Hungarians could agree (poor Elisabeth wanted Andrássy made Foreign Minister, but this would have outraged the Austrians in their turn, besides being unacceptable to Francis Joseph, at that stage, on many other grounds). At all events, Beust wasted little time. On 20 December he made a surprise visit to Buda-Pest, where he established personal contact with the Deákists, and thereafter strongly urged Francis Joseph to come to terms with the Hungarians, himself assuming the role of intermediary.

There were still obstacles to be got over, for although, when the Hungarian Diet met in November, Francis Joseph now declared himself willing to appoint a responsible Hungarian Ministry (for the Presidency of which

---

seems to have taken a liking to the country on her first, personally tragic, visit to it in 1857. In 1860, on her return from Madeira, she 'took it up' seriously, perhaps out of opposition to her horrid mother-in-law, who was strongly on the other side, learnt the language, and got attached to herself a Hungarian lady-in-waiting, Ida Ferenczy, to whom she became warmly attached. The Hungarians soon noticed her feelings, and played on them, but they were also, no doubt, genuinely touched and delighted. Elisabeth accompanied her husband to Buda in February 1866, where she had a *succès fou* and struck up a warm personal friendship with Andrássy, who called her 'our lovely Providence'. She really played an important part in the following months, not in the sense of finding solutions to specific problems, but in that of making her husband well disposed towards the Hungarians. This was perhaps the only case during Francis Joseph's long reign when he let his political judgment be influenced importantly by a woman.

[1] On one occasion he talked of 'a common front of Germans and Hungarians against Pan-Slavism' (Corti, *Mensch und Herrscher*, p. 386).

Andrássy was designated,[1] he still asked for more central control and more 'common' institutions[2] than Deák was willing to concede. Deák, on his side, had to fight against continuous pressure from the Left Centre in the Hungarian Diet, who regarded what Deák was prepared to grant as unnecessarily generous, and even as treachery to the Hungarian cause,[3] while Croatia contributed its mite when the Sabor met by again appealing to Vienna, restating the majority's thesis of Croatia's complete independence and asking for direct negotiations with the Monarch, as King of the Triune Kingdom, on the relations of that Kingdom with the Gesammtmonarchie.

Nor were the difficulties confined to the Lands of the Hungarian Crown. Belcredi, as we saw, had promised the Cis-Leithanian Diets that any agreement reached with Hungary should be laid before them, and Beust, too, was at that juncture of the view that the agreements would have to be laid before the Narrower Reichsrat.[4] It seemed, however, highly unlikely that that body would agree to anything which the Hungarians, for their part, would accept; it certainly would not if Belcredi could help it. On 2 January 1867, he procured the issue of a Patent dissolving the Cis-Leithanian Landtage and ordering preliminary elections for an 'Extraordinary Reichsrat', which was to meet on 17 February for the promised consideration of the outcome of the Hungarian negotiations. The Landtage were to be free to elect their representatives to the Reichstag either by Curia or from their plenums. The result, which was that intended by Belcredi, was that Bohemia, Moravia and Carniola, with the Tirol, returned federalist majorities large enough to dominate the House. These were certain to reject any Dualist settlement, and would presumably try to substitute for it some federalist system agreeable to themselves. The Centralists among the German Liberals were themselves hostile to Dualism, although from a different angle to the Slavs, and they made the deadlock complete by announcing that they would not attend the House manufactured by Belcredi, nor, indeed, any 'Extraordinary' Reichsrat at all.

There were, however, two quarters whose attitude was not entirely negative. Among the Poles, Smolka's 'Federalists' favoured an alliance with the Czechs, but the other Poles intimated their readiness to support Beust in return for an assurance of some measure of autonomy for Galicia. On

---

[1] Deák refused the post for himself, and recommended Andrássy for it.

[2] For example, Francis Joseph's Austrian advisers wanted the whole railway system of the Monarchy made a central service.

[3] This fact needs to be emphasized, in view of the practice of most Austrian and almost all foreign historians of representing the Compromise as a near-total surrender to Hungary's wishes, and complete satisfaction of them. But the whole political history of Hungary from 1867 to 1918 is unintelligible unless it is realized that by no means all of the men representing Hungary in 1867 regarded the Compromise as acceptable at all, and many of those who did so viewed it, not as an ideal settlement, but as a *pis aller* which Hungary's difficult situation forced her to accept. [4] This was, at the time, Deák's and Andrássy's own view.

10 September 1866, Kaiserfeld had convoked his followers to a meeting which was also attended by some sympathizers from the other German groups, and persuaded it to adopt a resolution in favour of Dualism.[1] This gave Beust enough to go on with. He demanded a show-down, and on 7 February the Emperor, with great personal reluctance,[2] decided in his favour. Belcredi resigned, and Beust took over his portfolio. The German Liberals as a whole consented to attend the Reichsrat on condition that it was an 'ordinary' one, although the centralists said that they would not take their decision on the settlement with Hungary until they saw what its terms were. The Poles were not agreed between themselves just how much self-government they wanted, but Beust gave them general sympathetic assurances which they agreed to accept, and they decided by a majority to attend the Reichsrat and support the Government. Since the Czechs and Slovenes were not open to similar transactions, Beust dissolved the Landtage of Bohemia, Moravia and Carniola[3] and ordered new elections in those three Lands. The Reichsrat was to meet in May. Meanwhile, he got together a non-Parliamentary administration to carry on current business.[4]

The negotiations with Hungary were now taken in hand seriously. The Croats were told that their request was incompatible with the Pragmatic Sanction and ordered to send representatives to Pest to negotiate a settlement with Hungary within the framework of that instrument. On 18 February Andrássy was entrusted with the formation of a responsible Hungarian Government, and this body[5] took the oath on 13 March. The report of the sub-Committee

[1] The original resolution provided that 'common' affairs should come before a single Parliament, but a fortnight later modified this phrase to ask for no more than 'constitutional treatment' of these subjects (Patzelt, op. cit., p. 18).
[2] As Belcredi afterwards reported the scene, the Emperor had tears in his eyes when he made the decision.
[3] The Tirol escaped because, as Beust frankly confessed, new elections would not have altered the composition of the Landtag.
[4] The chief members of this were Count Eduard Taaffe, who was made Minister of the Interior and of Cults and Education on 7 March and promoted to be Deputy Minister President on 27 June; Frh. von Becke, Finance (later also Commerce and Economic Affairs); Frh. Hye (Justice, later also Cults and Education); and F. M. L. John (War). Of these, von Becke was a permanent civil servant; Hye, a University professor who had played a Liberal role in 1848 but had since seen the light; John, a serving soldier who had held his post since September 1866, having previously served as Chief of Staff to the Austrian armies in Italy. Taaffe, who was later to play a very large role in the government of Austria, was the descendant of an Irish family settled in Bohemia since the seventeenth century. As a young boy he had been one of Francis Joseph's selected playmates. Later, he had been Landespresident of Salzburg, then Statthalter of Upper Austria.
[5] Its composition was: Andrássy, Minister President and Minister of Defence; Eötvös, Education and Cults; Count Menyhert Lónyay, Finance; Balthasar Horváth, Justice; Baron Béla Wenckheim, Interior; István Gorove, Trade; Count Imre Mikó (a Transylvanian), Communications; Count György Festetics, Minister *a latere* to the Crown.

of Fifteen was taken as a basis for the further negotiations, which were, indeed, carried on under continuous pressure against them from both sides, especially the Hungarian Left. On 26 May, on the very eve of the conclusion of the negotiations, a Hungarian paper published a 'Cassandra Letter' addressed by the exiled Kossuth to Deák, prophesying woe to the Compromise and accusing its author of having sacrificed the honour and vital interests of the country to a short-lived and illusory expediency. 'The existence of the Habsburgs,' Kossuth wrote, 'is incompatible with the independence of Hungary.' Reprinted as a pamphlet, this letter had an enormous circulation in the country, where it reinforced the already widespread belief that Hungary was making a bad bargain.

This, however, actually helped Deák and his supporters to resist the counter-pressure which was coming from the Viennese centralists and the Hungarian Old Conservatives, and if in the final negotiations on details the Hungarians gave way on a few points, the Crown conceded many more; while in the haste many points, some of them of great importance, were (to the great detriment of later relations between the Crown and Hungary) left without any proper definition at all. But to both sides, speed seemed more important than scholarship, and on 29 May the Diet accepted the results of the discussions as 'Law XII of 1867', voting it in the end by the comfortable majority of 257 to 110. On 8 June, Francis Joseph was crowned King of Hungary, with all the traditional pomp. On 28 July he gave his Royal sanction to Law XII.

The Law satisfied Hungary's basic demand in that it explicitly recognized the principle of legal continuity, the changes, as compared with the April Laws, being described as amendments to the earlier instruments. Those amendments were, however, fairly extensive in practice. Foreign Affairs, Defence, and the financing of those two items, were recognized to be 'common subjects' – i.e., common to Hungary and to the rest of the Monarch's dominions, and each of them was to be conducted by a 'common' Minister. These three Ministers were the executants of the Monarch's old *regia potestas*, which, as we know, had formerly been unlimited in these fields, but the Hungarian Law now limited the Monarch's treaty-making powers by the stipulation that the foreign representation of the Monarchy 'as well as the requisite dispositions with regard to international treaties' fell within the sphere of the common Foreign Minister, 'acting in accordance with the Ministries of both parts [of the Monarchy] and with their consent'.

In the field of defence, the law laid down that 'all questions relating to the unitary command, control and internal organization of the whole army, and consequently also of the Hungarian army, *qua* constituent part of the whole army, are recognized as falling within the competence of His Majesty'. But again as in the old days, the Parliament was competent for voting the intake of recruits, and for questions relating to recruiting, quartering and supply.

Any Parliamentary discussion of the business of these portfolios was to be conducted through equal 'Delegations' of the two Parliaments, meeting separately and exchanging views by notes; if exchanges of notes failed to bring about agreement, they met and the point was decided by majority vote; in the event of a deadlock, the Monarch decided. The Delegations had to settle the total budgetary expenditure on the 'common' portfolios, and also what proportion thereof each half of the Monarchy should bear. This figure was to be re-discussed after ten years. When the sums had been agreed, each half of the Monarchy voted and collected the required taxes for itself.

The Law also admitted that there were certain other questions on which the Pragmatic Sanction did not impose unity, but which could nevertheless be usefully treated by common agreement and on identical principles. These included the customs and commercial policy of the Monarchy, credit and currency, weights and measures, indirect taxation and communications of interest to both halves of the Monarchy. Agreements reached on these points were, again, to be reconsidered decennially.

On all other points Hungary was, as the Laws of 1722–3 and 1790 provided, to be ruled exclusively by her own laws, as agreed between the King and the Parliament. The form of the latter was that given to it by the April Laws, and the powers of the Monarch *vis-à-vis* Parliament represented a modernization of those enjoyed by his predecessors before 1848. They were strictly limited in certain important respects. All enactments by the Monarch had to bear the counter-signature of the 'responsible' Minister. He was bound to rule 'in agreement' with Parliament, and did not even possess a legal veto on legislation duly enacted, although this gap was made good soon after by a conventional right conceded him by Andrássy to give or refuse 'preliminary sanction' to a Bill before it was introduced at all. He had the right to appoint the Minister President of his choice: there was no provision limiting his discretion in this respect, and it was his confidence, not that of Parliament, that the Minister President had to possess, so that he was entitled to retain a Minister President in office even in face of an adverse Parliamentary vote. He could also convoke, prorogue or dissolve Parliament at will. He could not, however, leave it *in absentia* indefinitely, for the annual budget had to come before Parliament and be voted by it, and the Hungarian Constitution, unlike the Stadion Constitution, the February Patent or the Austrian Law of 1867, contained no emergency provision enabling him to rule by Order in Council.[1] The office of Palatine was declared to be 'in suspense' until agreement should have been reached on the legal position of its holder.

[1] It will be remembered that the Diet of 1790/1 had extracted from Leopold II a promise not to use this device.

Belcredi's promise to the Landtage of the Narrower Reichsrat had now to be honoured. The new Landtag elections had brought no change in Carniola, but in Bohemia and Moravia influence brought to bear largely by the Emperor himself[1] on the Great Landlords' Curiae had changed the majorities in them and consequently in the Landtage as a whole, producing German majorities in them. When the Reichsrat met, on 20 May, the 'German Left', whose various fractions had managed to re-combine under the common nomenclature of 'Party of the Constitution', or 'Constitutional Left',[2] numbered 118 Deputies, against only seventy-one Federalists and eleven German Clericals,[3] and of the Federalists, not only were the Poles committed to vote for the Government on the Hungarian settlement, but the fourteen Czechs from Bohemia were absent: in April Palacký and Rieger had led a great deputation of Czechs[4] on a 'pilgrimage to Moscow',[5] where they made extravagant speeches, in a tone which was far more Pan-Slav than Austro-Slav, hailing Russia as 'the rising sun of the Slavs' – thereby, of course, giving their enemies a powerful handle against them, and especially incensing the Poles, whose kinsmen in Russian Poland were groaning under the reprisals which had followed the defeat of the 1863 revolution. On their return, the Czech Deputies adopted the policy, which they followed for the next twelve years, of boycotting the Reichsrat.

The German centralists were still unhappy about ceding their control over Hungary, but they were not prepared to risk a federal majority in Cis-Leithania, and more of the Left was now of the Autonomists' view. After all, it was 1849 that had been the novelty, not 1861. Beust had thus a reasonably safe majority for the Compromise, although in the event he hardly called on it. For the Hungarians were now maintaining that Law XII was a bilateral contract between the King of Hungary and the Hungarian nation: no other party had been entitled to be consulted while it was being negotiated, and for validity, once negotiated, it required nothing more than ratification by the King (except, indeed, for those of its provisions which envisaged action by Parliamentary representatives of Austria). Beust had become converted to this view, and accordingly proceeded by one of those quadratures of the circle so common in Austrian history. Francis Joseph informed the Reichsrat in the Speech from the Throne that a 'satisfactory agreement' had been concluded with Hungary, to which 'he hoped that the Reichsrat would not

[1] He sent his brother, the Archduke Karl Ludwig, to Prague and Brünn to tell the Bohemian nobles 'that he wished an electoral result favourable to the Government' (Beust, op. cit., II. 111).

[2] This meant that the Party stood for the existing Constitution against any federalist, etc., amendments: the contrast was not with absolutism.

[3] There should have been 203 Deputies, but three seats were vacant through death.

[4] The party included a few Croats, Slovenes and Ruthenes, but the great majority were Czechs.

[5] Officially, they were visiting the Ethnographic Exhibition there.

refuse its assent'. The agreement was, however, presented to the Reichsrat only after Francis Joseph had ratified Law XII, and as a *fait accompli*.

Reluctant, but not at that stage prepared to face a collision with the Crown, the Reichsrat then appointed representatives to negotiate the various 'common' questions with Hungary. It was agreed in November that the common services should be financed in the first instance out of the yield of the joint Customs duties, the residue being made up by Austria and Hungary in the proportions of 70% to 30%. For the first period, the Monarchy was to constitute a Customs Unit (Zolleinheit) with a single commercial policy; the other questions of common interest were to be regulated on identical principles. The old crux of the national debt was the object of prolonged wranglings; finally, the Hungarians, while not admitting any legal liability, consented as an act of grace to pay a fixed annual contribution of twenty-nine million gulden towards the annual service of the debt, then running at 122 m.g., and 1,150,000 gulden annually towards its amortization.

The 'Delegations' were to consist of 60 representatives of each body (20 from each Upper, and 40 from each Lower, House), meeting in Vienna and Budapest in alternate years.

On 21 December the Reichsrat adopted the laws embodying these arrangements. It did so with an ill enough grace. Skene, the German Centralist leader, described the laws as 'Austria's domestic Königgrätz'. From outside the House, the Czechs did not conceal their passionate dislike of the Dualist system. The aged Palacký wrote a Jeremiad in which he prophesied that Dualism would bring about the end of the Monarchy; he comforted himself with the reflection that 'we Slavs were here before Austria, and we shall be here after it'.

The Monarch now formally appointed the three 'common' Ministers: Beust, Foreign Affairs; von Becke, Finance; John, War.[1]

Even including the Austrian legislation connected with it, the central settlement with Hungary formed only a part of the great mass of legislation of the period. Further laws were needed in Hungary to fill in gaps left in Law XII; the Reichsrat had to have its counterpart to that instrument, and the new constitutional picture necessitated some readjustments of the central machinery of the Monarchy. Some of these pieces of work were not completed until after several years, but it will be convenient to describe at this point all of them which can fairly be taken as forming integral parts of the great general settlement of which Law XII was the first-fruit.

That Law itself contained two points, both connected with the Army, over which difficulties arose which it took some years to settle. The military leaders in Vienna objected to the phrase in the Law which spoke of 'the Hungarian

[1] Von Becke and John had already been acting as 'common' (in the terminology of the year, 'Reichs') Ministers since the previous July. Beust, in his capacity of Foreign Minister, had, of course, always represented the Gesammtmonarchie.

Army, *qua* constituent part of the whole Army'¹ as breaching the unity of the defence forces. The Hungarian Left insisted on them, precisely for that reason, and tried to interpret them as authorizing the establishment of a separate Hungarian Army, controlled, commanded and organized by the Crown, but using Hungarian badges and Magyar as the language of service and command.² This conflict was resolved in 1868 by a compromise: the full central regime, with the German languages of service and command, was to be applied to all the regular armed forces, including the Hungarian units of them; but each half of the Monarchy was to have a second-line force, known in Austria as the Landwehr and in Hungary as the Honvédség, composed of infantry and cavalry only. In these, the indigenous language of command was to be used (in Hungary this was at once made Magyar),³ and these two forces were under Ministers of National Defence, who also represented the Crown in putting the votes for them to the Parliaments.

The higher Viennese military circles, led by the Archduke Albrecht,⁴ also fought a stubborn rearguard action against the 'provincialization' of the Military Frontier, and it took all Andrássy's eloquence to convince Francis

¹ The Austrian counterpart to the Law did not contain these words.

² In view of the terrific controversies which afterwards raged round the language question in the armed forces, an explanation of this term is desirable (this has been kindly supplied to me by the Austrian *Kriegsarchiv*). No official definition of the term 'language of service' (*Dienstsprache*) was, in fact, ever given, but from the days of Maria Theresa onward the rule prevailed that all written communications between the military authorities and 'commands' in the Army (with exceptions which afterwards lapsed, and need not concern us here) must be in German; after 1848 the same rule was extended to the Navy. How far downward and outward this compulsion applied was never defined, but all officers had to know German; this was officially made compulsory in 1876 for all officers and cadets of the k.k. forces and the Austrian Landwehr. The language of instruction in the Military Academies was German, and German 'Rhetoric' was also taught there as a subject. Some other languages of the Monarchy were also taught as subjects.

The 'language of command' (*Kommandosprache*) which in any unit was the same language as that of service, consisted only of a few score words, which every recruit had to learn by heart. Otherwise, a private soldier was not compelled to learn a foreign language, but O.R.s were enjoined to acquire a knowledge of German 'as soon possible'. If they aspired to non-commissioned rank, they were well advised to do so, for a man not knowing the language of service was unlikely to gain promotion. German was taught as a subject in the schools for N.C.O.s.

Every regiment had also its *Regimentssprache*, which was the language of the district in which it was recruited (by custom, when a regiment was recruited from a mixed district, a twenty per cent minority qualified to rank as a subsidiary *Regimentssprache*). This was the language in which instruction was given to the rank and file, and other purely internal regimental business transacted. It was obligatory for every officer to know the regimental language of his regiment, and such knowledge was a condition for his promotion in it. When, later, the Archduke Francis Ferdinand took such mortal offence because the officers and men of the Hungarian regiment talked Magyar in front of him, he was in the wrong; Magyar was their regimental language, and if he had not been an Archduke, he could not have held a commission in the regiment without learning it.

³ Croat in Croatia-Slavonia.   ⁴ For the Archduke's position, see below, p. 578, n. 1.

Joseph that it would be a breach of faith to keep the Frontier under its old dispensation. Even after the Monarch had given way in principle, the provincialization was carried through only in stages, the last of which (the complete introduction of the regular Hungarian tax system) was not completed until 1886. It was, incidentally, very unpopular among the Frontiersmen themselves and in October 1871 two crack-brained adherents of Starčević – Kvaternik and Ljudevit Bach – collected some hundreds of armed Frontiersmen and tried to incite the inhabitants of the Lika – always a storm-centre – into a rebellion which was to culminate in the establishment of a fantastic Southern Slav State. The rising was, indeed, easily and quickly put down, and its chief effect was to discredit the Croat extremists.[1]

Of the subsidiary or consequential arrangements in Hungary necessitated by the Compromise, the main step with regard to Transylvania had already been taken when it had *de facto* incorporated itself in Hungary in December 1866. Its separate status was formally abolished in 1868 (under Law XLIII of that year); the steps taken later to complete its integration are described elsewhere.[2] The Compromise itself should have included a law embodying a new Hungaro-Croat settlement, but it had not proved possible to achieve this in time. After the dissolution of the Sabor, the Croats had still refused to approach Pest, and attempts by the Hungarians, and even by Francis Joseph himself, to move them had failed. In May they sent another petition to Vienna; thereupon the King dissolved the Sabor.

Croatia was not even represented officially at the Coronation.[3] Immediately after this, however, the Ban resigned and Andrássy appointed Baron Levin Rauch, the leader of the 'Magyarone' Party in Croatia, to succeed him. Rauch promulgated a new electoral law, ordered new elections, and exercised such effective administrative pressure at these as to secure a substantial Magyarone majority.[4] The diminished Opposition withdrew from the Sabor, and the majority dropped the idea of trialism and reopened negotiations. Agreement was reached in September 1868. This *Nagodba* (*Hungarice*, Law XXX of 1868) declared Hungary and Croatia-Slavonia-Dalmatia to constitute 'one and the same State complex', whence it followed that they had the same representation, legislature and executive in respect of all affairs common to the Lands of the Hungarian Crown and the other territories of the Dynasty: Croatia was therefore to be proportionately represented on the Delegations, etc. Questions left to Hungary as interna under the Austro-Hungarian Compromise were again divided into 'common' Hungaro-Croat affairs and Croat interna. The former included taxation, credit and currency, commercial policy and communications of interest to both countries (broadly the subjects treated as 'pragmatic' under the Austro-Hungarian

---

[1] See below, p. 735, n.   [2] See below, pp. 690, 696.
[3] Only the Ban and the Bishop of Zengg attended, and three towns sent deputations.
[4] 66 Unionists (including 34 officials) and 14 Opposition.

Compromise). When these matters were under discussion in the Hungarian Parliament, Croat Deputies (to the number of forty)[1] attended that body; they were allowed to speak in Croat. A Croat Minister without Portfolio represented Croatia's interests in these fields in the Hungarian Government. All other questions were Croat interna, and in respect of them Croatia was completely autonomous, although the value of her independence was reduced by the fact that the Ban, who was the head of the Croat 'autonomous provincial Government', was, while responsible to the Croat Diet, yet appointed by the Crown on the proposal of the Hungarian Minister President. The official language in Croatia was solely Croat.

The ratio of contributions towards common expenditure was generous towards Croatia, which was allowed to retain forty-five per cent of the yield of her taxes for her own interna. Territorially, Hungary gave up her hopeless claim to Slavonia, but retained the Muraköz. The Hungarian text declared Fiume (in which the Hungarian administration had already been installed) a *corpus separatum* of the Hungarian Crown, whose future status would have to be regulated by negotiation between Hungary, Croatia and Fiume itself; the Croat text simply stated that agreement on this question could not be reached.[2] In the event, the town remained attached to Hungary.

As regards Dalmatia, Francis Joseph announced that it could be incorporated in the Triune Kingdom only if its Landtag voted to that effect. This, under the conditions of the day, was tantamount to a refusal, for the Italians, tiny minority as they were in Dalmatia, still constituted the majority in its Landtag.[3]

After reassembling at the end of 1865, the Diet had appointed another Committee, again under the presidency of Eötvös, to resume the interrupted preparation of a Nationalities Law. This time there were no Slovak nationalists on the Committee (none had been returned to the Diet in the 1865 elections[4]), but it now contained representatives of the Roumanians and

---

[1] That is, after the provincialization of the Military Frontier: before it, twenty-nine.

[2] When the document (in both Magyar and Croat versions) was presented to Francis Joseph for ratification, a Croat translation of the Magyar version was pasted over the Croat text. R. W. Seton-Watson (*The Southern Slav Question*, p. 81), following Croat authorities, waxes very indignant over this; but if the two texts are examined carefully, there is little difference of substance between them, and I do not know that it has been proved that the Magyar text is a 'falsification'. It is not impossible that the Croat text misrepresented what was agreed in the negotiations.

[3] From about 1860 onward they held back the rising flood of Croat nationalism by allying themselves with the local Serbs. For the later developments, see below, p. 645 f.

[4] They had put up thirty candidates, but not one had been elected. The 'Slovaks' in the Diet, and their representatives on the Committee, were all moderates. The Slovak nationalists' case was represented for them in the Committee by a Ruthene named Dobriansky, not to their advantage, for Dobriansky was currently believed to have been the man who guided the Russian armies across the Carpathians in 1849, and was consequently intensely unpopular among the Magyars.

Saxons from Transylvania, as well as Serbs from the Voivodina, so that the opponents of the politically unitary State were not lacking, and they fought their battles tenaciously, and sometimes bitterly enough. But they were still in a minority compared with the Magyars and the less extreme representatives of the Nationalities who sided with the latter,[1] and were reduced in the end to what amounted to gestures of protest; the two Serbs and a Roumanian laid their own Nationalities Bill before Parliament[2] (which rejected it by an enormous majority), while the Slovak nationalists, unable, owing to their lack of representation in Parliament, to follow this example, announced in their Press that the Thurócz Szent Márton memorandum remained their programme.

The majority of the Committee, however, simply took the 1861 report for its starting-point, and proposed such amendments or additions to that document as it thought advisable.

The Committee was genuinely anxious (as was the Diet as a whole) to reach an acceptable settlement with the Nationalities, and no attempt was made to go back on the cardinal principle of the international nature of the Hungarian 'political nation' and the equality in principle of its components. Nor did the changes in the operative clauses of the Bill place further restrictions on the use of non-Magyar languages. These, outside the addition of some paragraphs regulating linguistic usage in Courts of law[3] which followed the general pattern of linguistically Magyar top-level services with provision for the use of other languages on lower levels, were chiefly in the direction of tidying up and introducing greater precision, and in some cases were even more generous than the 1861 draft: thus the Minister of Education, who prescribed the language to be used in State schools, was bound, not only, as in the 1861 draft, 'to take into account the languages in use in the district of the school in question', but 'to ensure that citizens living together in considerable numbers, of whatever nationality, shall be able to obtain instruction locally in their mother-tongue, up to the point at which higher academic instruction begins'.

There was, however, one point on which the Diet insisted: that the Nationalities, as such, could be allowed no corporate recognition whatever. It

[1] These included the Slovaks on the Committee and the Bunyevac. The Swabians, if they were represented at all, do not seem to have spoken.

[2] This Bill would have reconstructed Hungary as a multinational State in its machinery, as well as its theory. The languages of all six recognized Nationalities were to enjoy equal status in the central Ministries and Parliament. Counties were to be delimited on national lines, and in each the language of official business was to be that of the local majority. Each nationality was to be entitled to create a corporate organization for the regulation of its own cultural and 'national' life, and although this self-government was to apply nominally only to cultural questions, the 'national' organizations were to be empowered to make representations to the Government also on political questions.

[3] The 1861 draft had, probably out of haste, left this field untouched.

rejected a proposal made by Eötvös himself to allow the 'national' districts to form administrative units, and it eliminated from the draft all wording which seemed to confer any corporate rights on the Nationalities: for example, while the 1861 draft had declared 'every denomination and nationality' free to set up secondary and higher schools, its successor conferred that right on 'individual citizens, communes, churches and congregations of whatever nationality'. As the wording of Eötvös's 'principles' had been unsafe in this respect, Deák provided the Law with a preamble which, while reaffirming in lapidary form the rest of the 'principles', avoided this danger. This ran:

Since, according to the basic principles of the Constitution, all citizens of Hungary constitute a single nation, the indivisible, unitary Hungarian nation,[1] of which every citizen, to whatever nationality (*nemzetiség*) he belongs, is equally a member: and since this equality can be qualified by special regulations only in respect of the official use of the different languages current in the country,[2] and only in so far as is necessitated by the unity of the country, the practical possibilities of government and administration and the claims of the administration of exact justice: while the complete equality of rights of all citizens remains intact in every other respect, the following rules will serve as guidance in respect of the official use of the various languages.

The Diet adopted this law on 1 December 1868, under the official designation of 'Law XLIV of 1868 on the equality of rights of the Nationalities' (*a nemzetiségek egyénjoguság tárgyában*).

Even had the Hungarian Law XII not provided for the introduction in Austria of 'complete constitutional institutions', which was more than it could be said to be enjoying under the February Patent, the German Left itself was determined that Austria must receive constitutional liberties not inferior to those which Hungary had secured for herself. The Reichsrat therefore devoted most of the summer and autumn to devising the appropriate legislation, the main results of its efforts being embodied in five laws, which were given the status of 'fundamental laws' which could be altered only by a two-thirds majority. These were adopted *en bloc*, together with the legislation giving effect to the Compromise, on 21 December.

The Government had stood aside from this work (in any case, Beust was sympathetic) and with the Czechs absent and the Poles treating what went on in Vienna as almost irrelevant to themselves, the German Left had had a fairly clear field, their only important opponent being the Emperor himself,

[1] It was unfortunate that historical usage compelled Deák to use for this phrase the words '*Magyar nemzet*'. It is, however, a fact that the correct translation of these words here is not 'Magyar nation' but 'Hungarian nation'. We have seen that Eötvös counted the Magyars as a 'Nationality' (*nemzetiség*).

[2] R. W. Seton-Watson, *Racial Problems in Hungary*, p. 148, unfortunately, in what was for long the only English version of this Law, mistranslates this essential phrase, writing: 'Since, moreover, this equality of right can only exist with reference to the official use', etc., 'only' (not 'and only') 'in so far', etc.

who disliked them for their bourgeois origin and their anti-clericalism, and resisted with determination their attempts to limit his control in the fields of foreign relations and defence. At that juncture, however, he had not felt capable of opposing them on as many points as he would have wished, and the 'December Constitution', as this corpus of laws was thereafter generally known (it remained in force, with only minor modifications, for the rest of the Monarchy's lifetime), was therefore in most respects a faithful and complete enough expression of the German Liberals' wishes, with reservations where the Emperor had dug his heels in.

The Crown in fact emerged with its powers not greatly shorn.

In respect of foreign affairs, the only limitation placed on the Monarch's discretion was that commercial treaties or treaties involving 'the Reich', parts of it, or citizens, in 'burdens' or obligations had to be approved by the Reichsrat. The Monarch was declared 'supreme commander of the armed forces' without further definition of their nature or of his competences. In most other respects, the Austrian laws followed the provisions of the Stadion Constitution so closely that it is unnecessary to do more here than note the few points, beyond simple changes of wording, made in the interest of clarity, on which it modified that instrument. The term 'Ministerial responsibility' received the definition that the Ministry was 'responsible' to the Reichsrat for the legality of all measures enacted in its period of office, even if lacking a counter-signature. The defence budget and the determination of the intake of recruits were added to the list of measures for which the consent of the Reichsrat was required. The emergency paragraph was expanded to make abuse of it more difficult: it must not be used to modify the Constitution or to place a lasting burden on the exchequer or to alienate public property, and the validity of a measure taken under it lapsed if it was not laid before the next Parliament within four weeks of its convocation, or if one of the two Houses then rejected it.

On the other hand, the Monarch retained the right of veto over legislation and his right to prorogue or dissolve Parliament, and as in Hungary, no restriction was placed on his choice of Ministers, who were 'responsible' to Parliament only in the sense that they could be impeached if they violated the Constitution: they were not bound to obey the wishes of a Parliamentary majority.

Few changes were made in the 'structural' field. The Speech from the Throne, when presenting the Reichsrat with the Compromise, had said that this must necessarily be followed 'by the grant, through agreement in the Reichsrat, of all possible extensions of autonomy to the Kingdoms and Lands'. The Liberals did not want to abuse their position, but they were, after all, centralists. Owing to Kaiserfeld's influence, the competence of the Reichsrat compared with that of the Landtage was actually slightly reduced by the change that the questions for which the Reichsrat was competent were enumerated, and all others fell automatically to the Landtage. But the essential pattern of the February Patent, the principle that questions affecting all Cis-Leithania came before the central body and local questions before the Landtage, was left unaltered, as were the composition of and franchise for the latter bodies, and the method of composing the Reichsrat of delegates from them, with the emergency procedure of direct elections if a Landtag refused to send its representatives. The bi-cameral composition of the Reichsrat and the composition of the Upper House were left unaltered. Quorums were fixed of one hundred for the Lower House and forty for the Upper.

This time Parliament was not to be done out of a legal inventory of the fundamental rights of the citizen, of which it produced a very imposing list. The Austrian citizen was guaranteed immunity of his person, his property, his domicile and his mails, and freedom of belief, of religious practice (public in the case of the legally recognized Churches[1]), of speech, of the Press (the censorship was abolished) and of learning and instruction (subject to the general supervision of the State). All citizens were declared equal before the law, and all public offices were open equally to any of them, and the enjoyment of all civil and political rights was expressly declared to be independent of religious confession.

The general law recognized the principles of freedom of association and assembly, but it left the application of the principle to be defined by a special law, and this placed fairly severe limits on both these rights: the authorities had to be notified in advance of public assemblages and could forbid them on grounds of public security, and they could forbid the formation of, or dissolve, an association on the same grounds. Political associations, moreover, were forbidden to found branches, or to combine among themselves.

The principle of national and linguistic equality, recognized in 1848 and reaffirmed in 1849, reappeared in the Kremsier wording, slightly amended and expanded, but still only as an enunciation of principle, the Reichsrat, unlike the Hungarian Parliament, having shrunk from the task of framing interpretative legislation, as beyond its powers, as Paragraph XIX of the Law on the Rights of Citizens, in the following wording:[2]

All peoples (*Volksstämme*) of the State enjoy equal rights and every people has an inalienable right to the maintenance and cultivation of its nationality and language.

---

[1] These, in 1867, were the Catholic (Roman and Greek rites), Evangelical, Greek Oriental, Evangelical Fraternities, Lippovan and Armenian.

[2] As a matter of curiosity, it may be remarked that books which do not reproduce this text, even where they write about it for scores of pages, include Hantsch (both in his *Geschichte* and in his book on the National Question), Hugelmann, Taylor, Kann and Fischel (*Sprachenrecht*). May mistranslates it. Fischel gives it incidentally in his *Materialen*, when reproducing a speech by a Deputy who was criticizing it. It may be found, with the rest of the Law, in Bernatzik's *Verfassungsgesetze*, p. 370.

The equality of rights of all locally current (*landesüblich*) languages in schools, administration and public life is recognised[1] by the State.

In Lands inhabited by several peoples the public educational systems are to be so organised that each of those peoples receives the necessary facilities for education in its own language without being compelled to learn a second language.[2]

Another law reintroduced the separation of the judiciary from the executive, irremovability of judges, interlocutory procedure in the Courts and trial by jury for serious offences. Another provided for the establishment of an Administrative Court of Appeal to deal with conflicts of competence between public bodies and to hear complaints by citizens of violation of their rights.

A point to which the Left attached particular importance was the liberalisation of the confessional system. The Law on the Rights of Citizens touched on this in the important respect that, without mentioning the Jews, it in fact removed all the inequalities to which they had been subject. The Liberals wanted to go much further and to have the Concordat revised radically, and Beust (himself a Protestant) also held that some revision of it would be necessary. Francis Joseph's heart was entirely with the Catholic party, but in view of the strong feelings of the Parliamentary majority, and also of the international situation, he agreed that some concessions were necessary. He sent an emissary to the Holy See with a message to that effect, and publicly rebuked his Bishops for failing to support his endeavours to solve the Confessional problem 'in a spirit of conciliation and concession'. Meanwhile, the Lower House, before adjourning, sent up to its sister body two more Bills which directly contradicted important provisions of the Concordat: one, to restore the Josephinian marriage law, making marriage again a civil contract'[3] the other to place the control of the education in the hands of the lay arm, the Reich, Lands, etc., being responsible for higher and secondary establishments, and the communes for elementary.[4]

The Monarchy's new Defence Law, although it became law only in the Parliamentary period, being adopted by the two Parliaments (by the

[1] As in Stadion's Constitution, 'recognition' was preferred to 'guarantee' because it was objected that a guarantee would be unenforceable.

[2] This paragraph was added at the wish of the German-Bohemian Deputies to celebrate the interment of the *Sprachenzwanggesetz* (see above, p. 540) which was then expressly repealed by the Bohemian Landtag on 5 October 1868. German in fact remained official (outside the Army) as the language of the Delegations of the Supreme Court and of the seal of the National Bank – the German test of laws was the authentic one. German was also the language of the service of the State-owned railways.

[3] The Law also made it possible for a couple, under certain conditions, to contract a marriage without any religious ceremony at all.

[4] The Law provided, however, for compulsory religious instruction in the pupil's religion. It was a very advanced Bill, providing for eight years compulsory primary schooling, and for a largely increased number of schools, not all of which were in the event constructed in the remoter rural areas.

Austrian with much more difficulty than by the Hungarian) in December 1868 and coming into force in 1869, is so truly a part of the general settlement that this is the proper place to describe its provisions.[1] It laid down the principle of universal obligatory service for all able-bodied male subjects of the Monarchy. The term of service was set at twelve years, the first three of them with the colours, and the next seven with the reserves. The Landwehr and Honvédség were composed partly of regular soldiers passing their last two years of service in these formations, partly of members of the annual intake of recruits surplus to the requirements of the regular army. The number of recruits actually required from Austria and Hungary respectively was to be settled decennially in advance, by negotiation between the two Parliaments, the numbers to be proportionate to the populations of the two countries. For the first decennial period, the number was to be that required to give a war strength of 800,000 for the regular army and 100,000 each for the Landwehr and the Honvédség, and the first annual contingents were fixed at 95,474 (54,541 from Austria and 40,933 from Hungary) for the regular army, 10,400 for the Landwehr[2] and 12,500 for the Honvédség.

The conclusion of the Compromise also made it necessary to change the nomenclature of the Monarchy and its central organs and services.

In a letter to Beust, dated 14 November 1868, Francis Joseph informed him that he proposed to entitle himself in the future 'Emperor of Austria, King of Bohemia, etc. and Apostolic King of Hungary; for short, Emperor of Austria and Apostolic King of Hungary', with the descriptions 'H.M. the Emperor and King' or 'His Imperial and Royal' (k. und k.) Apostolic Majesty'. His dominions were to be known as the 'Austro-Hungarian Monarchy' or 'Austro-Hungarian Empire' (Reich), alternatively. The word still displeased the Hungarians, and these names were eventually dropped in favour of the simple 'Austria-Hungary'.

The central services now became *kaiserlich königlich* (Imperial-Royal, the kaiserlich referring to the Gesammtmonarchie, the königlich to Hungary. In 1889 the word *und* was inserted in the nomenclature of the armed forces, which thus became k. und k., and in 1895 the 'and' was inserted in the title of the Foreign Minister, who now became 'Minister of the Imperial and Royal House'. The title of Reichskanzler, bestowed on Beust at his own request to put him on a level with Bismarck, was in any case not renewed, and of the two other 'common' Ministers appointed in 1867, in each case as Reichsminister, the Common Finance Minister lost the 'Reichs' as early as 1868; he and his portfolio were thereafter always known simply as 'common' (gameinsamer, közös). The Minister of War remained Reichskriegsminister until 1911, when he, too, became k. und k.

[1] It had actually been drafted in 1866 and parts of it enacted by decree in the following spring. [2] The Landwehr was to include a contingent of *Schützen* from the Tirol.

This still left the Western half of the Monarchy without a name, for Francis and his successors had never ruled over an 'Austria' composed of these territories, and the champions of Bohemia's State rights, not to mention the Poles, would never admit the existence of such a unit. These Lands therefore continued up to 1917 to bear no other official name than that of 'the Kingdoms and Lands represented in the Reichsrat' (the word 'Reichsrat' was of course itself tendentious, but seems to have got by), or for short, unofficially, as Cis-Leithania,[1] writers and speakers who found themselves forced to use this name revenging themselves by calling the other half of the Monarchy Trans-Leithania. The demand for the introduction of the name 'Austria' as official denomination of these territories figured regularly in the programmes of German National Parties, and in 1917 the Emperor Charles sanctioned the change. This 'Austria' had a life-span of only one year.

As we have seen, these two main 'Constitutions' still left the Crown in a very strong position *de jure*, and *de facto* it was even stronger, especially in the Western half of the Monarchy. In spite of its wording, Law XII does not seem to have been meant to assert any claim to impose a Ministerial or Parliamentary control over the Crown's general conduct of foreign policy, but only, like the Austrian law, to make commercial treaties and such-like subject to Parliamentary consent.[2] The Delegations did regularly discuss such treaties, and difficult enough they used to find it to reach agreement on them. The Monarch's freedom to conduct his own foreign policy in the broader sense was in any case rendered practically complete by the unlimited freedom enjoyed by him in the appointment, retention or dismissal of his Foreign Minister. Francis Joseph always insisted on these rights,[3] and he never felt

[1] The Leitha is the somewhat insignificant stream which then formed the frontier between the two halves of the Monarchy

[2] I cannot find the point discussed in any source which I have consulted, but Ferenczy, III. 225, writes that at a meeting held on 9 January 1867 between Beust, Belcredi and some Hungarians, at which a draft (which was word for word Deák's) of the proposed agreement was discussed, the participants 'included in the sphere of competence of the Foreign Minister international *commercial* (Italics mine) treaties', with the stipulation that both Ministries must communicate them to their Parliaments. This text seems to have been what afterwards emerged as Art. 8 of Law XII, and I cannot attribute any significance of intent from the omission from the final text of the word 'commercial'. Deák at the time was exclusively interested in delimiting the 'common' subjects from the 'interna'; not at all in defining the limits of the *regia potestas*.

[3] Corti, *Der alte Kaiser*, p. 196, records that Bánffy, as Hungarian Minister President, counter-signed the appointment of Goluchowski, *fils*, as Foreign Minister. Francis Joseph objected to this as irregular.

As a matter of convention the Foreign Minister was alternately an Austrian and a Hungarian (although Kálnoky was only very nominally a Hungarian, his estates lying in Moravia, and by no means Hungarian in sympathies) and all three Common Ministers at any given time did not come from the same half of the Monarchy. This practice was not, however, compulsory in law.

himself bound to take any notice whatever if either Parliament disapproved of any action by his Minister.[1] He was not entirely indifferent to the opinion of others, and the idea that the Monarch should have advisers (whose opinion he was not bound to follow) was familiar to him, and did not seem to him incompatible with his own absolute powers. In the earlier years of the period now opening it was his habit to submit questions of the highest importance to Crown Councils attended by the three Common Ministers, the two Ministers President, and sometimes other individuals. It may, however, be doubted whether over these questions he ever entirely shed the mental attitude expressed in his remark to Rechberg, quoted above.[2]

In the first years after 1867, Francis Joseph still conducted many of the top-level negotiations himself. Later, he left more to his Ministers. Aehrenthal once or twice convoked 'Conferences of the Common Ministers', which, again, were attended by the two Ministers President, perhaps also by the Chief of the General Staff. These Conferences became common after July 1914.[3] The Ministers President, if forceful characters, then really exercised an influence on the Monarchy's foreign policy, and Burian, who was Foreign Minister in the First World War, complains how difficult this made his task.[4] Even then, Francis Joseph had the last word: the Foreign Minister took the Council's decision to him, and he did not regard himself as bound to accept it.

Francis Joseph never admitted anyone's right to question his 'reserved rights' (as enumerated in Law XII) in the military field, although he was sometimes driven to accept interpretations of them which would not have been his own. The competence of the Reichsrat or the Hungarian Diet to vote the Budget and the intake of recruits was, on the other hand, a real one, although the latter could, owing to the provisions of the Army Service Law, be exercised only at the end of each decennial period. Cases of conflict between the Crown and the legislatures were thus possible in this field, as in others in which the legislatures enjoyed a voice, and where they did occur, the difference in the real relationship between the executive and the legislatures in the two halves of the Monarchy became operative.

That the Crown had no power to veto legislation in Hungary was of little

---

[1] The Hungarian Parliament did force Kálnoky to resign in 1898, but that was because he had been interfering in Hungary's domestic affairs, and when Francis Joseph accepted his resignation, this was as a matter of policy, not in virtue of a constitutional obligation. He ignored a vote of non-confidence in Andrássy passed by the Reichsrat in 1878. The end of that conflict was that the Government went and Andrássy remained.

[2] See above, p. 530, n. 2.

[3] The minutes of all these Conferences were published, with a long introduction on the prehistory of the 'Common Ministerial Council', by M. Komjáthy, *Protokolle des Gemeinsamen Ministerrates*', etc., Budapest, 1966.

[4] Burian, op. cit., p. 151.

Much depended here on the personal factor. Stürgkh seems seldom to have volunteered an opinion on foreign affairs, but Tisza insisted on seeing, and expressing his opinion on, all papers, including top secret ones (Singer, *Czernin*, p. 26).

practical importance, for the unofficial right of 'preliminary sanction' filled the gap. In either half, the Monarch was equally entitled to appoint the Minister President of his choice and to retain him in office in face of an adverse Parliamentary majority. But the difference in the constitutional legislation of the two countries, and still more, differences of a more pragmatic kind, made it harder for him to govern against the will of Parliament in Hungary, than in Austria.

In Austria, if the Reichsrat was not in session (*nicht versammelt*), the Government was legally entitled to enact necessary measures under the 'emergency Paragraph' (Para. 14), and although such measures were only 'provisional', and required endorsement by the Reichsrat when it did meet, there is no case on record of the Reichrat's refusing its retrospective endorsement. The immense complexity of parties and interests represented in the Reichsrat, and the ingrained tradition of subservience to the Crown, made it certain that the Crown would always get its way, and seldom with much difficulty. On the one occasion on which a Party on which a Government rested refused to vote a military budget, out of hostility to Francis Joseph's foreign policy, the Government fell, the Party was relegated to the Opposition, and the policy was pursued. Usually, if an adverse vote threatened, one or another Landtag was manipulated until the threat vanished.

In Hungary, if a Budget was not voted within the year, a situation called by the lawyers *ex lex* came into being. Any demands by the Government for taxation or recruits then lacked legal sanction, and the Counties and autonomous municipalities were within their legal rights in refusing to comply with them. The Hungarian tradition of resistance to Vienna, especially over these questions, made them actually enjoy doing so. Here, too, the Crown could mobilize enough forces to be sure of coming out top in the end, but the process was a painful and arduous one. In Hungary it was really difficult to govern without a Parliamentary majority; in Austria such a majority was nothing more than a convenience.

The Compromise was not, even in intention, a general settlement of the problem of the Monarchy, still less, of that of Central Europe. It was an *ad hoc* agreement between Francis Joseph and the Hungarian leaders, other parties intervening with more or less effect, under which each 'compromised' by making certain sacrifices of rights and aspirations in the interests of security.

The principals to the transaction did not themselves regard it as ideal. Each thought the price of it excessive. It was, of course, still more unpopular with those who had hoped for a different structural arrangement for the Monarchy: the Hungarian Left, the centralist Germans, the Czech partisans of Austro-Slavism formed round a nucleus of Bohemian State rights, the Croat Trialists, the Hungarian Nationalities opposed to the idea of the unitary Hungarian State.

Any of the alternative plans advocated in these various quarters would have satisfied certain ambitions which the Compromise disappointed; most of them would have avoided some hardships and injustices which the Dualist system inflicted. But before we condemn Dualism on that ground we must be clear that the tangle of claims, ethnic, historical and the rest, in the Monarchy was so unutterably complex, many of them so flatly irreconcilable with each other, that no conceivable settlement could have done justice to all equitable cases, still less, satisfied all wishes. Any possible alternative to that of 1867 would have created other discontents, inflicted other injustices, and the real touchstone by which Dualism must be judged is not whether it was good, but whether it was better (or less bad) than the possible alternatives to it.

When one reads the lucubrations, contemporary and later, pretending that everything in the Monarchy would have been lovely but for the accursed Dualism, one is reminded irresistibly of Saki's story 'Excepting Mrs Penberthy'. We must certainly beware of accepting the facile and frequent assertion that the Compromise 'dealt the death-blow to the Monarchy' because it 'delivered over the other peoples of the Monarchy to the hegemony of the Germans and Magyars', and thus drove them into irredentism. Even apart from the fact that what the Compromise was designed to do, and did, was to reconcile the Germans and Magyars to the Monarchy, there is no particle of evidence that the break-up of the Monarchy in 1918 was due to a dissatisfaction among its 'subject peoples' which would not have been there if the structure of the Monarchy had been different. Irredentism among those peoples was no stronger among those who were really ill-treated than among those, such as the Italians, who had no substantial grievance whatever. As for the Italian, Serb, Roumanian, etc. Governments which in 1918–19 demanded (and received) satisfaction of their 'national aspirations', they did not in the least do so (although some of them sometimes pretended otherwise) because their ethnic kinsmen in the Monarchy were ill-treated – some of them were, some not – but out of pure national determinism.

Dualism was not the product of any sudden, thought-free and care-free inspiration. During the preceding twenty years, effort after effort had been made to find an answer to the problem which history had created, and all of them – Francis Joseph's, Kossuth's, Palacký's, Jellačić's, Széczen's, Schmerling's and the rest – had failed because the forces against them were too strong. Dualism, for all its defects, possessed the overwhelming merit that it satisfied sufficiently the strongest forces in the ring. That was why it could come into being, and why, when established, it did not share the fate of its many ephemeral predecessors. The proof of the pudding is in the eating, and the case for Dualism is that it lasted, and the Monarchy resting on it lasted, for fifty years. This is a long period of life for any Central European settlement. The life-span of its successor was a bare twenty.

12

Intermezzo (1868-71)

The structure of the Monarchy established by the Compromise and its accompanying instruments was destined to stand, substantially unaltered, until the Monarchy's own last days: in the summer of 1918 the constitutional relationships between the Crown and Hungary, and between Hungary and 'Austria', were still those of 1867, and if in 'Austria' the relationships between the central and Land authorities, legislative and executive, had been adjusted, the changes had been slight, the essential dichotomy was still there and the components themselves unaltered. The only structural change in the Monarchy had been the inclusion within it of the formerly Turkish provinces of Bosnia and Herzegovina.

In these respects, the Dualist Era constitutes a distinct and well-defined chapter in the internal history of the Austrian Monarchy, and it was also one during most of which the foreign political relationships of the Monarchy followed a straight course, the dominating feature of which was Austria's friendship, later, her alliance, with the German Reich. But this position, domestic and foreign, was reached only after an intervening period in which Francis Joseph was within an inch of committing himself, in his foreign policy, in a very different direction, and during that period it turned on a hair whether Dualism would survive at all, or whether it would prove to have been simply one more in the long line of unsuccessful experiments. This was because the allocation of power-positions within the Monarchy seemed to depend on its foreign political orientation, and in 1868–70 this was still uncertain. If foreign political considerations, either of offence or of defence, required it, Francis Joseph was prepared to carry through, in their interest, another political reconstruction of the Monarchy which would have modified radically, if it did not entirely destroy, the Dualist system. It was only when he accepted as final the relationship of Austria to the new Germany, and with it, the thought of internal reconstruction – the appointment of an Austrian Minister President committed to the spirit of Dualism and of a Foreign Minister devoted to a policy of reconciliation with Germany occurred within a fortnight of one another – that Dualism could be said to be firmly established, in so far as anything in the Monarchy was ever firm.

The first years after 1867 thus form a distinct sub-chapter of the Dualist Era; and the period which opens in about 1903 forms another. In this, although the Dualist system still stands, it is being subjected to increasing criticism, from both the parties between which the Compromise was concluded: the Hungarians themselves, and the Crown – less, indeed, the man who was then still wearing the Crown, than the man who by all human reckoning must soon succeed to it; and this encourages other enemies of the system, the oppositional forces and nationalities in Hungary, and even some circles in Austria. At the same time, while the Monarchy's own foreign political orientation does not change, other forces appear, so aggressive that her alliances no longer safeguard her existence. Her foreign relations, too, thus enter on a new phase.

In describing these three periods it is, however, not easy to follow the purely chronological method which was appropriate to our earlier chapters. The internal histories of Cis- and Trans-Leithania go such different ways after 1867 that it would be only confusing to treat them together, and during much of the period, the history of the Monarchy's foreign relations, too, is so distinct from that of its internal developments that the two subjects are more appropriately treated in separate chapters. But this is not true of the whole period, and not always equally true of both halves of the Monarchy. From 1868 to 1871 the threads of the Monarchy's foreign relations, and those of internal developments in Cis-Leithania, are so closely interwoven as to make separate treatment of them impossible,[1] whereas there is practically no interconnection between foreign policy and internal events in Hungary. We therefore describe the years 1868–1903 under four headings: the 'intermezzo' of 1868–71, dealing simultaneously with foreign relations and with internal events in Cis-Leithania; foreign policy, 1871–1903; Cis-Leithania, during the same years; and Hungary, 1868–1903. After 1903, on the other hand, it is Cis-Leithania which goes its own way, while the foreign political developments, the internal struggle in Hungary and the relations between Hungary and the Crown form a single story the threads of which can no longer be disentangled. Then 1914 brings all the three stories together again for the final and fatal dénouement.

1868, then opened with Francis Joseph still smarting under his defeat at the hands of Prussia, and Beust, as his Foreign Minister, engaged in tangled negotiations with France, Italy and the South German States. These, however, were of their nature preparatory, and could not be expected to yield

[1] It is true that foreign and internal political considerations clashed severely on one occasion after 1871 (1877/8) but the outcome was simple; Francis Joseph simply dismissed from the conduct of internal policy the party which opposed his foreign political concept.

quick results, even if they were wanted to do so – and they were directed less towards creating a situation than meeting one which might arise through the initiative of others. Immediate developments could come only in internal affairs, where the Ministries in Vienna and Buda-Pest were savouring their first tastes of responsible Government.

In Buda-Pest this was still the same team as had taken office in the previous March, but Beust had given up his internal charges when the December Laws were through, and Francis Joseph, while leaving him Chancellor and Foreign Minister, had, on 30 December, appointed a new Ministry for other business. It was characteristic of him that although the German Liberals were much the strongest Party in the Reichsrat, he could not bear to make one of them Minister President: he conferred that office on Prince 'Carlos' Auersperg, who had, indeed, Liberal leanings and something of a Liberal family tradition (he was a cousin of Anastasius Grün, the mildly progressive poet of the 1830s), and was now, as a Constitutional Landowner, allied with the Liberals, but was, after all, a very great aristocrat, member of one of the highest families of Bohemia, and nicknamed 'the first cavalier of the Reich'.[1] Taaffe remained Deputy Minister President, also taking over the portfolio of Defence (Austrian), and a third high aristocrat, Count Potocki, a Polish landowner of great estates and independent political views, became Minister of Agriculture. The rest of the Ministers, however – Eduard Herbst (Justice), Leopold von Hasner (Education), Karl Giskra (Interior), Brestel (Finance), Ignaz von Plener (Commerce) and Berger (without portfolio) – were all drawn from the German middle classes – largely from German-Bohemia[2] – so that the team deserved its nickname of the *Bürger-Ministerium*. With its appointment the true history of Austria under Dualism begins.

The Burgher Ministry was naturally concerned chiefly[3] to carry on the work of the Parliament from which it had emerged. In 1868 and 1869 it took much of that work a long step further, largely in the form of enacting laws which put into effect general principles enunciated in the Fundamental Laws. The separation of the judiciary from the executive was implemented,

---

[1] Eisenmann, p. 339, finds the explanation for Auersperg's Liberalism and centralism in family rivalry between the Auerspergs and the Schwarzenbergs, but he surely does too little justice to Auersperg's genuine convictions. Incidentally, Schäffle has the same jealousy story (op. cit., II. 7), but according to him, it was the Clams of whom the Auerspergs were jealous.

[2] Herbst, although born in Vienna, came of Bohemian stock; his grandfather's name had been Padzinnek, and his parents regarded themselves as Czechs. Hasner, Giskra and Berger were all from Bohemia, Hasner being another nationally ambiguous case (both Germans and Czechs had offered him a mandate). There were no capitalists in the team: they were lawyers, University teachers, or civil servants. Brestel, who had been a Deputy in Kremsier, had since been earning a painful living as a bank clerk.

[3] 'Chiefly' because they also adopted (with extreme reluctance) the Military Service Law. This received sanction on 5 December 1868.

the Gemischte Bezirke being replaced by a new dual structure of Bezirkshauptmannschaften and Gerichtsbezirke, and other judicial reforms enacted.

The Ministry of Police was abolished. Two important measures reflected the Liberals' faith in the virtue of economic *laissez-faire*: the legal maximum of interest which could be charged on a loan was abolished (although it was still illegal 'to take advantage of the borrower's frivolity, inexperience or imbecility' to charge 'a rate grossly disproportionate to that locally in use'), and all prohibitions on the sub-division of peasant holdings vanished, giving a peasant-holder free disposition, testamentary or otherwise, over his land.

It was their confessional legislation which the Liberals pressed most strongly of all, and it was over this that they met with most resistance, for the representatives of the Church put up an embittered defence of their positions. But Francis Joseph had, however reluctantly, resigned himself to the inevitable: when the Bill on marriage law and the Schools Bill came before the Upper House he instructed his Marshal, Prince Hohenlohe, to vote for them,[1] and they were passed (on 21 and 30 March respectively), amid scenes of immense jubilation. Vienna was illuminated and Auersperg given ovations. They were followed by a third law 'on the regulation of inter-confessional relationships' which laid down the principle of complete inter-confessional equality in questions relating to mixed marriages and their issue, conversions, etc.

Once these laws had been adopted, the abolition of the Concordat could only be a matter of time. Beust asked the Holy See to renounce it, but Pope Pius IX replied only by denouncing the Austrian laws as 'destructive, abominable and damnable' and as 'absolutely null and void'. Several Austrian Bishops refused to recognize the validity of the Austrian legislation. One (Bishop Rudiger of Linz) called on his clergy to resist it publicly, and was actually condemned to fourteen days imprisonment (which he was not, indeed, required to serve) for conduct detrimental to the public order. The Liberals, however (who were supported by a clamorous Viennese mob), set their teeth, and eventually won their main point – only, indeed, under Auersperg's successor, Potocki; but this will be the most convenient point to mention that, when the Oecumenical Council of 1870 adopted the dogma of Papal Infallibility, Beust represented to the Emperor that the pronouncement had invalidated the Concordat by altering the character of one party to it, and on 30 July, Francis Joseph, accepting the argument, cancelled the Austrian legislation implementing the Concordat.[2]

[1] Under the Constitution the Emperor could not sit in Parliament, but could appoint a representative to the Upper House, who voted for him.

[2] The procedure was unusual, especially since Potocki refused, out of religious scruples, to counter-sign the document, which was thus couched in the peculiar form of a letter from the Emperor to the Austrian Minister of Education and Cults, instructing him to prepare new legislation to replace the 1855 Patents. Hungary was regarded as released from the Concordat under the ruling that legislation issued during the absolutist period was invalid. Strangely

Much of this work was valuable, but much of it was also highly controversial. Even in the German Crownlands, the confessional legislation was bitterly opposed by the Clericals and by the bulk of the peasant voters, while the Tirol objected to the centralist structure of the new Cis-Leithania, as did practically all its non-Germans. The Polish Landtag, after a long argument between their different fractions,[1] ended by producing, on 24 September 1868, a joint Resolution which demanded a viceroy for Galicia who was to be responsible to Galicia's own Parliament, which was to be competent for all subjects except the most important ones affecting the whole Monarchy; when those questions were being discussed, Galicia would send her representatives to the Reichsrat, which otherwise they would not attend. A Polish *Landsmannminister* was to be attached to the Crown, and Galicia to have its own Supreme Court of Justice.[2]

The Slovenes demanded linguistic and administrative concessions in the Lands inhabited by them, and a Slovene Congress in Gorizia, in October 1868, demanded the constitution of a Slovenia comprising all the Slovene territories of Austria, with its own Diet and Slovene for the language of administration and education. The Italians of the Littoral clung to Vienna for protection against the local Croat and Slovene majorities, but those of the South Tirol demanded complete administrative separation from the north of the Crownland.

The Bohemian Czechs were infuriated that the Hungarians had succeeded where they, the Czechs, had failed. They boycotted a visit paid by Francis Joseph to Prague in July 1868, and on 22 August of that year eighty-one members of the Bohemian Landtag signed a Declaration which set out their constitutional claim in uncompromising terms. They affirmed, indeed, their wish for an equitable settlement with the Germans of Bohemia on a basis of

---

enough, Francis Joseph seems to have acted willingly on this occasion. Cardinal Rauscher had gone down to ask the Pope to consent to revision of the Concordat and had found him quite implacable. Then nearly all the Austrian Bishops, including Rauscher, had spoken against the dogma and had left the Conference before it was accepted. They promulgated it afterwards, in duty bound, but *à contre cœur*. Francis Joseph wrote to his mother that his action was 'the best, and also the mildest, answer to Rome's unlucky decision' (Schürer, p. 377).

[1] Smolka's group had still wanted a general federalist reconstruction of the Monarchy, to be brought about through alliance with the Czechs. The Conservatives preferred to demand a status for Galicia (such as, they maintained, Beust had promised them) which should differentiate it clearly from any other Land in the Monarchy, but were not agreed what this should be. Goluchowski thought it unsafe to do more than get *de facto* concessions which would leave the framework of the Constitution nominally intact; but he had few followers. A larger group, led by Ziemalkowski, wanted a status for Galicia within Cis-Leithania similar to Croatia's in Hungary; another, headed by Count Borkowski, demanded as much as Hungary itself had got within the Monarchy. Eventually Smolka was shouldered aside and the other groups agreed on the Resolution described.

[2] When this Resolution was adopted, Goluchowski resigned, but his disappearance only consolidated the front of the more extreme parties.

equality; but they declared that the only constitutional basis of Bohemia's position in the Monarchy was formed by the settlement accepted by Ferdinand I at his Coronation (even the Vernewerter Landesordnung was illegal, as having been imposed by force) and the *Majestätsbrief* of Ferdinand V (I) of 8 April 1848. The Bohemian Lands had never stood in a 'real union' with any Austrian State. The October Diploma and the February Patent were illegal, and the Deputies of Bohemia were neither obliged nor entitled to attend the meetings of the Reichsrat, whose decisions were not binding on Bohemia. They demanded the negotiation of a new settlement based on the rights of the Bohemian Crown.

On the same day, the Czech members of the Moravian Diet subscribed to a declaration in similar terms. The Diets of Moravia and Silesia, it is true, immediately announced that they had no use for any closer connection with Bohemia.

It was in these years that the Czechs initiated what afterwards became a permanent feature of their national campaign: its appeal to foreign sympathies. The 'pilgrimage to Moscow' has already been mentioned; now the Czech leaders turned their eyes towards France, initiating the special Czech-French connection which played so big a part in the disintegration of the Monarchy fifty years later. When Prince Jerome Napoleon visited Prague in 1868, he received Palacký and Rieger, and the Czech Press wrote proudly that 'the eyes of Europe are fixed on Prague'. The next year Rieger went to Paris, where, indeed – France being then hopeful of agreeing with Francis Joseph – he failed to get an audience either of Napoleon III or of Jerome Napoleon; but the next year again, on the eve of the outbreak of the Franco-Prussian War, Rieger addressed a memorandum (the text of which leaked out) to the French Ambassador in Vienna, arguing the identity of France's interests with those of the Czechs. 'As soon as Bohemia's independence is assured, it separates Northern from Southern Germany ... A French army could reach Bohemia faster than a Prussian army advancing from Berlin could reach Frankfurt on the Main.'

Characteristically, the only concessions to malcontents made by the Government in 1868 and 1869 were to the Poles. The Government rejected, indeed, the Polish Resolution, partly on principle, partly out of fear that Russia would disapprove. In January 1869, however, all education in Galicia below University level was entrusted to a Land Educational Council, which promptly Polonized all schools above the elementary level (an Imperial Rescript extended this to the Universities), the Ruthenes being told that their language was too primitive to be used in secondary education. In July 1869 Polish was made the 'inner language'[1] of the entire administration and judi-

---

[1] The 'outer language' remained as regulated in 1859 and 1860; Polish and German were treated as *landesübliche Sprachen* in the four westernmost Kreise, and Polish, German and Ruthene in the other twelve.

cature throughout Galicia, and German officials dismissed wholesale – the number is put at between 4,000 and 5,000 – in favour of Polish. It is equally characteristic that the concessions proved totally futile; the Galician Landtag merely reaffirmed its Resolution of the previous year. No similar softness was shown towards the other nationalities. In Bohemia the Germans declared the signatories of the Czech memorandum to have forfeited their mandates, and Prague and its suburbs were under a state of siege from October 1868 to April 1869.[1] Severe measures were taken against the Czech national Press and associations. Auersperg, indeed, resigned over the Czech crisis (his place was taken by Taaffe, on 26 September), but this was not because he sympathized with the Czechs, but on the contrary, because Beust had tried to talk to Palacký and Rieger behind his back.

The discontent was, however, so serious and so widespread that in December the Government itself split: five of its members (Plener, Hasner, Giskra, Herbst and Brestl) were for continuing the existing course, making this possible by amending the electoral law to make elections to the Reichsrat direct, while three (Taaffe, Potocki and Berger) thought some change of course necessary. Francis Joseph took the unusual course of letting both groups express their views in memoranda, having these published, and letting Parliament debate them. As the Houses decided in favour of the majority, the three dissident Ministers resigned and their places were filled by Germans, Hasner taking over the Minister Presidency. Thereupon, however, the Poles put in their Resolution again, and when it was again rejected, resigned their mandates *en bloc*, and when Hasner proposed filling the gaps by the emergency procedure, the Slovenes, Italians and some of the Roumanians walked out in their turn, as did most of the Clericals, thus reducing the active membership of the Reichsrat to the Liberals and the handful of faithful Ruthenes. The Emperor turned, after all, to Potocki, who, when he took office in April, decided to make a fresh start. He dissolved the Reichsrat and the Landtage, ordering the latter to meet again in the summer to elect their representatives to the new Reichsrat, which was to assemble in September.[2] But before it met, the obvious imminence of war between France and Prussia in July 1870[3] faced Austria with the necessity of taking a crucial decision in the field of foreign policy.

[1] Military law had to be proclaimed also in Dalmatia, where a full-scale revolt broke out in the Cattaro region in the spring of 1869. This, however, was due to special causes (an order depriving the inhabitants of certain special traditional privileges and making them subject to compulsory military service).

[2] Potocki exempted the Bohemian Landtag from immediate dissolution, in the hope of reaching an agreement with it. As the negotiations proved fruitless, this body was dissolved on 31 July, and the Bohemian elections held in August. The other Landtage held their elections in June and July.

[3] The French declaration of war was actually delivered on 19 July, but war had been recognized to be inevitable for several days before that.

Historians today seem agreed that the conventional view that Francis Joseph and Beust spent the years 1866–70 in seeking to organize 'a war of *revanche* for Königgrätz' is an over-simplification. There was a powerful party at Court of which the description would be true: it was headed by the Archduke Albrecht, 'Inspector-General of the Armed Forces' since January 1868, and Baron Kuhn, Minister of War since the same date,[1] and the 'aristocratic Court circles' were reputed to be of the same mind, not least because they believed that a victorious war would bring with it the fall of the Liberals in Austria. The Emperor and Beust were more cautious, because they took more account of foreign political realities, especially the danger of intervention by Russia, and much of Beust's endeavours were really devoted to the harmless objective of building a defensive front against Prussia. But it is also an exaggeration to depict the two as wanting nothing more than the *status quo*. Both of them wanted to get Austria in a situation of which she could safely take advantage if Prussia became involved in war with another Power. If that could have been achieved they would have taken their *revanche*, even at the cost of war.

Unfortunately for them, the situation was not easy to create. Beust got nowhere with the South German States (Bismarck had got there before him). Italy, when the question of an alliance with her came up, asked too high a price: the cession of the Trentino and Austria's consent to the annexation of the Papal States, in return for no more than neutrality. Napoleon III, the dynamic factor in the Europe of the day, was anxious to commit Austria to active help against Prussia, and as early as April 1867 offered her an offensive and defensive alliance, out of which Austria was to have got Silesia as reward for her share in the victory; but Beust was frightened to commit himself. The Emperor might have gone further, but just when the *rapprochement* seemed to be in full swing, the news arrived of the tragic death of his brother, Maximilian, in Mexico, court-martialled and shot by his opponents on 19 June 1867. It was Napoleon III who had largely contrived Maximilian's luckless venture, promising him military support which he had, then, not given, and Francis Joseph bore him a personal resentment for this which was certainly a factor in postponing agreement. Then, other difficulties apart, both parties had been largely preoccupied with internal affairs, and by the end of 1869 the only agreement between the two States was an understanding, reached in September of that year in the form of an exchange of notes between the two Monarchs, which pledged Austria to benevolent neutrality in case of war between France and Prussia, and active intervention if a third party (under

---

[1] The Archduke Albrecht, as Head of the Army High Command, had interfered so intolerably with John's work that John, who had also had difficulties with Andrássy, had resigned in January 1868. John's post had then been given to Kuhn, while Albrecht's (which had been created for him) had been abolished, and he had been given instead the position, the duties of which were somewhat undefined, of 'Inspector-General of the Armed Forces'.

which Russia was understood) came to the help of Prussia.[1] France promised to support Austria in the case of an Austro-Prussian war.

Conversations in the spring of 1870 which might have made the understanding binding broke down,[2] and Austria's hands were thus still fairly free when a Crown Council – one of the most crucial in the history of the Monarchy – met on 18 July to decide how she should act. Those present were the Emperor, the Archduke Albrecht, Beust, the two Ministers President (Potocki and Andrássy), and the Ministers of War and Joint Finance (Kuhn and Lónyay[3]). The Archduke and Kuhn wanted Austria to mobilize quickly and to intervene in the decisive battle, which they expected to take place near the frontier of Saxony.[4] Beust wanted her to arm, but not to intervene, but to impose her will on the belligerents when both were exhausted. Andrássy, however, strongly opposed even mobilization, arguing that it was essential for the Monarchy to avoid Russia's intervention (reports had arrived from Berlin that the Czar had promised the King of Prussia to intervene if Austria moved), or at least to conserve its strength against such an eventuality. As both the ex-Minister of War, John, and Col. Beck, Head of the Emperor's Military Chancellery, had, when consulted by Francis Joseph, represented to him most urgently that the Army was in no state to undertake another war, the Emperor decided on a neutrality accompanied by only the most long-term preparatory measures, and the subsequent course of the war excluded any thought of entering it later.

This decision was to lead Austria, in the event, into friendship, and later into alliance, with Germany, but the immediate effect of the outbreak of the war, and of Prussia's swift and sensational successes in it, was rather to strengthen Francis Joseph's conviction of the urgency of coming to terms with his Slav subjects. For the foundation of the later Austro-German friendship was Germany's renunciation of a *grossdeutsch* policy at Austria's expense, and in 1870, although Bismarck had already begun dropping hints of his good intentions, no one in Vienna yet felt assured of their sincerity. Kuhn had supported his case for intervention by the prophecy that if Prussia won in the West, she would then turn eastward;[5] but even if she did not do so

---

[1] It has been rightly pointed out that the first purpose of this treaty, for Austria, was to protect her against Russia.

[2] The Archduke Albrecht went to Paris with plans for military co-operation, but when the French generals made closer inquiries, they decided that Austria's mobilization would be too slow for their purposes.

[3] Lónyay had succeeded to this post in May, on the death of von Becke.

[4] Kuhn had gone further before the Conference: in a memorandum which he circulated in advance of it, he wanted Austria to intervene immediately, 'even at the risk of setting all Europe in flames', to send 200,000 men to Warsaw against Russia, 200,000 to Berlin and 200,000 to the Rhine, to take King Wilhelm prisoner. Austria was to take as her prizes Bavaria, Württemberg, Baden, the Danubian Principalities and Bosnia.

[5] The memorandum contained the words: 'Prussia on the Inn means *finis Austriae*.'

immediately, national feeling of the *grossdeutsch* type among the Germans of Austria, a potential asset to the Crown so long as the possibility existed of using it to help Austria recover the leadership in Germany, could at best be a potential danger, perhaps a real one, if that leadership passed irrevocably to Prussia.

And perversely, the war had sent an unprecedented wave of that feeling sweeping over Austria's Germans. While official policy was still uncertain, important bodies, including the Municipalities of Vienna, Brünn and Linz, had, after debates which throbbed with adulation of Prussia, adopted resolutions calling for strict neutrality. Students organized collections for German wounded; some tried to enlist in the Prussian army. The same circles which four years before had taken the defeat of their own country with such indecent composure celebrated the fall of Sedan with bonfires and illuminated windows.

One very well-known Austrian historian tells us that in the spring of 1871 'almost all members of the Imperial House, except the Empress Elisabeth, were convinced that the existence of Austria and the rule of the Dynasty depended on dividing the Germans of Austria, so joyfully excited by the German victories, into two halves and entrusting their Sudetic branch to the safe keeping of a Bohemian-Czech State'.[1] It may be prudent to take this statement with a grain of salt;[2] but the manifestations cannot have failed to aggravate in Francis Joseph's mind the resentment already inspired in it by the Liberals' attacks on the Church, and for that matter, by their parsimony over the budget, which was, in the last instance, what had forced John to his admission; and however sincerely he loved peace, it cannot have been easy for Francis Joseph to lay aside for ever dreams so long and so dearly cherished; his disappointment when France was defeated had been deep. And meanwhile, the new situation had boosted the value of Czech national feeling *pari passu* with its devaluation of German. The opening lines of Rieger's famous memorandum, with its appeal to France for an 'independent Bohemia', read treasonably enough; but words like 'independence' and 'State' are often, of necessity, used in Austria in senses which lack their full English implications,[3] and the end of the memorandum had been entirely Austro-Slav. The Dynasty, it had run, 'was entering on a false path which

---

[1] Friedjung, *Historische Aufsätze*, p. 469. Friedjung writes in this connection: 'It is all too easily forgotten that after the exclusion of Austria from Germany it took an extraordinary effort to prevent the Court, the aristocracy and the clerical circles from setting up a Bohemian State as a bulwark against the newly founded German Reich, that all efforts had to be exerted to defend the unity of Austria west of the Leitha.'

[2] Friedjung writes that 'he who did not know already' (the state of opinion attributed by him to the Imperial House) 'can read it in Schäffle's memoirs'. I can only say that I have searched Schäffle's *Aus meinem Leben* vainly for this statement, or anything remotely resembling it, nor have I found confirmation of this far-reaching statement in any other work.

[3] This is well illustrated by Friedjung's use of the word 'State' (*Staat*) in the above quotation.

might lead to its destruction by sacrificing the Slavs to the Magyars and Germans, so that the injured national feelings' [of the Slavs], 'if they erupted during a war, might lead to the dismemberment of the Monarchy. If France wishes to preserve the Austrian Imperial State . . . it must turn its sympathies to the Austrian Slavs.'

The appeal to France had lost its value in the new situation, but if Austria's Germans were going to prove unreliable, the argument that the Dynasty had 'entered on a false path' by trusting them was cogent indeed.

The August elections, although Potocki had left them entirely free, had already weakened the Liberals' position. They had split into two mutually hostile fractions of 'Olds' and 'Youngs', while their anti-Clericalism had mobilized Conservatives and Clericals against them. They had lost considerable ground even in the Alpine Lands, while in Bohemia, the Feudalists had won the first Curia from the Constitutional Landlords, leaving the Czechs in a big majority in the Bohemian Landtag. As the Czechs continued to boycott the Reichsrat, the Liberals still just commanded a majority in that body, which they managed to increase by another twenty-four by insisting on emergency elections in Bohemia. But the establishment of a small Parliamentary majority, thus achieved, for a party which was so obviously in a minority in the country was clearly no solution of the problem. As the Czechs and Poles refused to enter the Reichsrat without further concessions, Potocki resigned on November 24, and even before he had done so, the Emperor had begun looking for a successor to him, this time a man who could hope to reach agreement with the Czechs and their allies. The negotiations were conducted in the deepest secrecy between a handful of men which did not include even Beust[1] and the first that the world knew of what was on foot was on 7 February 1871 when the new Ministry took over from Potocki (who until then had remained in charge *ad interim*).

Potocki's Minister of Finance, Holzgethan, had, at Francis Joseph's wish, retained his portfolio. All the other members of the team were new to office. The Minister President, Count Karl Sigmund Hohenwart, who also took over the Interior, had hitherto been known to the public only as the holder of a series of administrative posts (the last of them that of Statthalter of Upper Austria) in which he had conducted himself with moderation and impartiality; but he was at heart an extreme enemy of German centralist Liberalism. He had been offered a post in the Potocki Government, and had declined it 'because he foresaw the uselessness of further patchwork';[2] and later he was to

---

[1] Those in the know were Potocki and Taaffe from the old Ministry; Hohenwart and Schäffle among the Ministers designate (the others only at the last minute); one or two of the Czech feudal nobility (Clam-Martinic and Thun) and a few men connected with the Court: the Emperor's Chamberlain, Prince Hohenlohe, the head of his Civilian Cabinet, Hofrat Braun, his ex-Aide-de-Camp, Count Dürkheim, and possibly one or two more.

[2] Schäffle, op. cit., II. 189.

evolve into the leader of the extreme Conservative-Feudal group. Two of the departmental Ministers were Czechs – the famous historian, Jireček (Education) and Dr Habietenik (Justice), and the list was made up of a professional soldier, General Scholl, for Defence, while the Ministries of Commerce and Agriculture were assigned to the *spiritus rector* and recognized brains of the whole business, Professor Schäffle, a Württemberger by origin, a Protestant by confession and a man of strongly democratic views which were made palatable to the Emperor by his passionate dislike of Austrian Liberalism and its exponents.

The Government announced itself as non-Party, and in its programme, promised no more than conscientious realization of the principle of equality, but by that it clearly meant changes in the existing system, and in fact, Grocholski was brought into the Cabinet in April as Minister without Portfolio representing the interests of Galicia, and a Bill introduced which would have given Galicia a wide measure of home rule, although less than what the Poles were asking. Another Bill would have extended the competences of all Landtage. The Germans opposed both Bills bitterly, getting the latter defeated outright and the former embogged in Committee.

Meanwhile, negotiations had been going on behind the scenes between the Government and the Czechs, and between the Czechs themselves. Rieger, taking as basis certain proposals made by Adolf Fischof[1] (but modifying them substantially), had worked out a draft 'Nationalities Law' for Bohemia. This contained one important and constructive proposal (originally Fischof's[2]): it divided the Landtag into 'National Curias', and laid down that any law containing rules relating to linguistic usage in public life or in educational establishments not serving one nationalitity exclusively was, after its second reading, to be submitted to voting by Curia, and would be taken as rejected if an absolute majority in either Curia voted against it. The budget for cultural purposes was to be divided proportionately to the taxes paid by each Bezirk, and each Curia was to decide the allocation of its own funds. The Landtag was to be bilingual. The official language of each Gemeinde was to be that of its own majority, but in any Bezirk or Gemeinde containing a twenty per cent minority of a second language[3] and in any case, in Prague, that language could also be used as a 'subsidiary language'. Czechs and German were to be used on an equal footing in the central offices. Finally, all members of the provincial Crown (*Landesfürstlich*) services[4] serving in any part of Bohemia were to be able to read and speak both languages.

Meanwhile, Schäffle had been in Prague in May, where he had consulted

---

[1] In his pamphlet *Oesterreich und die Burgschaften seines Bestandes*.
[2] It had, however, already been suggested at Kremsier by the Czech, Pinkas.
[3] This figure had been adopted in the Hungarian Nationalities Law and was afterwards very generally used, as in the inter-war legislation of Czechoslovakia and other countries.
[4] Thus excluding local employees of the Commune, etc.

with the Czech political leaders. They had presented him with their political demands, some of which he had got toned down, while accepting the remainder as a reasonable basis of discussion. These were then put into the form of eighteen 'Fundamental Articles'. They accepted the Compromise, with the institution of Delegations, the Cis-Leithanian members of which were to be nominated by the Landtage; Bohemia allotted itself a quota of fifteen. All questions relating to Bohemia and not 'common' were to fall within the competence of the Bohemian Landtag. The office of Bohemian Count Chancellor was to be revived, and he, with other Land Chancellors or Ministers, was to form a Ministry to deal with those questions described in the Compromise as best settled on agreed common principles. The quota to be paid by Bohemia towards common expenditure was to be decided by negotiation with the representatives of the other Lands.

Finally, an Address from the Crown to the Bohemian Landtag was agreed. That body was, indeed, asked to work out its proposals for the relationship of Bohemia to the other Lands 'in a spirit of moderation and conciliation'; but Francis Joseph also declared that 'he gladly recognized the rights of this Kingdom' (sc. the Kingdom of Bohemia) 'and was prepared to renew that recognition in his Coronation oath'.

When all was ready, including the appointment of suitable Statthalters to the difficult Lands, the Reichsrat and the Landtage of Upper and Lower Austria, Salzburg, Styria, Carinthia, Moravia, Silesia and the Tirol (six of which had previously had centralist majorities) were dissolved, and all Landtage required to assemble on 12 September to elect their representatives for the new Reichsrat. Some franchises were manipulated[1] and strong pressure applied, with the result that when the elections were over, the Government had secured a comfortable majority (137 to 66) in the Reichsrat. When the Bohemian Landtag met, it was presented with the Imperial Rescript promising coronation, and an agenda which included Rieger's language law. On 6 October the Landtag was presented with a draft reply to the Rescript, which set out the 'Fundamental Articles' as the Czechs' proposals.

Such was Hohenwart's famous experiment, and it proved no more successful than any other of Francis Joseph's attempts to solve the structural problem of the Monarchy – except only Dualism. Schäffle's memoirs show that he honestly believed, not only that the presumptive opponents of his plan would have no legitimate grounds for objecting to it, but that the opposition to it would not be widespread. He regarded his programme as

[1] In Vienna, for example, rates were allowed to count as well as direct taxes for a voter's financial qualifications, a change which raised the number of voters from 18,000 to 36,000. New appointments were made to the Upper House, as Schäffle writes (II. 35), 'by giving their proportionate weight to the nationalities, confessions and classes previously left at a disadvantage'. The Emperor exercised his personal influence in Upper Austria (ibid.), where, and in some other Lands, the lists of voters for the First Curia were arbitrarily revised.

one of conciliation and justice, and thought that it would be accepted as such by all except a handful of 'Stock Exchange Kings'. But he overestimated the stocks of reasonableness in Austria. The German members of the Bohemian Landtag had walked out of it when they heard the Rescript. The Liberal members of the Reichsrat announced that they would not attend it. There were riots in German-Bohemia. The Silesian Landtag protested against the idea of union with Bohemia (for prudence' and correctness' sake, the Fundamental Articles had confined themselves to Bohemia and had not raised the question of the *Böhmisches Staatsrecht*, but everyone knew what was behind them). The military feared that the unity of the defence forces would be impaired. Holzgethan himself said that the Fundamental Articles were 'tantamount to State bankruptcy'. The Poles disliked a plan which would have lessened the contrast between the position in Galicia and that outside it. Beust, who was now advocating friendship with Germany as the best prophylactic against German aggression, feared complications if the Germans of Austria felt aggrieved, and in fact, discreetly disapproving voices came from Germany, Bismarck's among them, and even the Emperor's; these, moreover, were coupled with utterances designed to lessen Francis Joseph's fears of German designs on a well-behaved Austria.[1] The most effective opposition of all came from Andrássy, to whose views the Emperor was at the time disposed to pay particular attention, and who was, of course, deeply hostile to any extension of Slav influence in the Monarchy. After first listening to his views privately, Francis Joseph gave him the opportunity to express them constitutionally by inviting him to a Crown Conference on 20 October. There he argued that the Fundamental Articles were, in spite of their careful wording, incompatible with the Compromise as it stood. His opposition seems to have tipped the balance.[2]

Another Conference of 'Ministers of the Reich' drew up a reply to the Bohemian Landtag's address, inviting it to send its members to the Reichsrat, for discussion of its proposals there. This was tantamount to an intimation that the Fundamental Articles were unacceptable, and the Czech leaders made it clear that they would not modify their terms. The Hohenwart Ministry resigned.[3] A search for a new Ministry began, Holzgethan meanwhile holding the fort *ad interim*. Although Francis Joseph had repeatedly declared that he would never again appoint a Liberal Ministry, it soon

---

[1] A first message had come as early as 2 September 1870.

[2] Andrássy is often represented as having forced his way into the Monarch's councils and destroyed the Czechs' hopes single-handed. This is not the case: he behaved entirely correctly, and actually did not at first want to intervene at all; he did so only under strong pressure (which annoyed him very much) from Beust. But when invited to express his views, he did so with eloquence, and his voice was probably in fact the decisive one.

[3] Schäffle tendered his individual resignation on 23 October. Hohenwart sent in his resignation, entailing that of the Ministry as a whole, on 25 October. It was formally accepted on 30 October.

transpired that there was simply no alternative, short of suspending the Constitution altogether. Another aristocratic Minister President was, indeed, dug up in the person of 'Carlos' Auersperg's brother, Adolf,[1] but his team, except for a politically colourless soldier at the Ministry of Defence and a Moravian landowner (but of a *Beamtenadel* family) in charge of agriculture, was composed exclusively of Liberals.[2]

Meanwhile, Beust had resigned (by request) on 6 November. On 14 November Andrássy was appointed to succeed him as Minister of Foreign Affairs.[3]

The intermezzo was over.

[1] Prince 'Carlos' was unwilling to return to active politics.

[2] The full list was: Auersperg, Minister President; Baron Lasser, Interior; Banhans, Commerce; Stremayr, Education; Glaser, Justice; Holzgethan, Finance (after January 1872, de Pretis); General Horst, Defence; Baron Chlumetzky, Agriculture; Unger, without portfolio.

[3] The title of Reich Chancellor died with Beust.

13

The Foreign Relations of the Monarchy, 1871-1903

In placing our account of the foreign relations of the Monarchy after 1871 before that of its internal developments, we are giving them the precedence which they enjoyed in practice, for Francis Joseph himself always put them first, and let no domestic considerations override what he held to be his realm's foreign political interests. And it was Francis Joseph's view that mattered, both in respect of priorities and of the general line of foreign policy itself. This being so, it is hardly possible to over-emphasize the importance for the Monarchy of the increased mellowness – or resignation – which came to colour Francis Joseph's outlook on foreign affairs as he reached middle age. As he had accepted the loss of Venetia even before it was inflicted, and never thereafter entertained serious thoughts of *revanche* against what was now the Kingdom of Italy, so after Prussia's crushing victory over France, he finally accepted the truth that his Monarchy could not recover its old leadership of Germany.[1] That his new Foreign Minister was a Magyar, while the outgoing man had been a Saxon, was itself symbolic of the *renversement* which now took place in his foreign policy. It was the first time in all its history that the Monarchy genuinely and without *arrière pensée* faced East. It had, of course, still to safeguard its rear; the attainment of this security was Andrássy's immediate aim, as the maintenance of it was to be a chief preoccupation of his successors; but what made this so vital was the supreme need to keep eyes and hands free for the East.

Even in this direction, the Monarchy's policy was now almost always essentially defensive in purpose, even where a move was made which looked aggressive. Here, too, Francis Joseph's mentality was a factor, for besides inclining increasingly as the years went on towards peace for peace's sake, he seems to have inherited something of his great-grandmother's indifference towards prizes of backward peoples and undeveloped territories. Andrássy saw his whole problem in terms of Russia, which in his view constituted a permanent and active threat both *qua* Power and *qua* inspirer of the Slavs

[1] The change had, of course, begun, more hesitantly, before 1871, but now it became final. The parallel with Maria Theresa's conversion after the Peace of Dresden is interesting.

outside her own frontiers, to his own Hungary and to the Monarchy on whose survival, as he was now convinced, that of Hungary itself depended. But he thought the Monarchy too weak to challenge Russia, and never seriously entertained any designs against her (he would have liked to see her weakened by the re-establishment of an independent Poland, but that was only an ideal, and he never made any move towards realizing it), so that his policy towards Russia resolved itself into deterring her from moving, both by himself preserving a correct attitude towards her, and by acquiring allies to help him hold the front, or at least neutralizing those who could not be gained as allies. It was very important that he was actually averse from the Monarchy's expanding itself, even if it could do so with Russia's agreement, through a deal such as Catherine had wanted to make with Joseph II. Not only would any such deal almost certainly bring Russia more profit than Austria: the effects of it would have been unwelcome to him on domestic grounds. For the result of any such expansion could only be to add more Slavs or Roumanians to the population of the Monarchy, and if these were incorporated in Hungary, they would increase the proportion of non-Magyars there; if in Cis-Leithania, or if they were given their own political formation, they would tilt the painfully-established Dualist balance against Hungary.

These calculations were no monopoly of Andrássy's. There was, of course, a party which thought differently. Especially in the early years, when the Archduke Albrecht was still active, there existed at the Court a 'party of action', headed by him, from whose influence the Emperor himself was not altogether immune. Certain other influences, which will be mentioned in due course, were also in favour of the Monarchy's expanding, for one or another reason. But considerations of the Monarchy's weakness, or of ethnic balance, or both, weighed as heavily at least with Andrássy's first three successors at the Ballhausplatz as with himself, and those of balance were shared not only by all Hungarian politicians, but also by the German-Austrians, in whose minds they were reinforced by their hostility to the military and their eternal preoccupation with the money-bags.

The policy of territorial abnegation was always faced with one great difficulty in the increasingly precarious hold of the Porte over its own Balkan subjects. If her rule over them should prove quite impossible to maintain, the objections to Austria's herself stepping into the consequent power-vacuum could be met by the reply that any possible alternative would also be unpleasant and even dangerous to her. If the Roumanians and Serbs became fully independent, they would exercise a strong pull on their fellow-countrymen inside the Monarchy. This might in theory be partly counteracted by the establishment of a strong Bulgaria friendly to the Monarchy, but that was hardly a practical possibility. The Czar was unlikely simply to cede the Sultan's place to the Emperor. It was far more likely that he would take it for himself, either directly, or masking the process by allowing a nominal independence to States which in reality would be mere Russian satellites. In such case, a forward policy for Austria might well be argued to be no more than self-defence.

The clouds of a potential conflict with Russia in the Balkans were already visible on the horizon when Andrássy took over the Ballhausplaz. Unrest was growing year by year among the Balkan peoples, and Russia, too, seemed to be preparing to move. In 1870 she had already unilaterally denounced the clauses of the Treaty of Paris which related to navigation on the Danube – thereby conjuring up a major diplomatic crisis the details of which may be omitted from this volume. Her wishes as officially made known did not go beyond the revision of the surviving dispositions of the Treaty, but she had obviously made no spiritual renunciation of her traditional role of patroness and protectress of the Christian peoples of the Balkans. She was in constant touch with Prince Nicolas of Montenegro, and had given strong support to the ambitious plans which Michael of Serbia had pursued until his assassination in 1868. When a Bulgarian revolutionary movement took root after the establishment of the Exarchate in 1870, it received much encouragement and substantial financial support from Pan-Slav circles in Russia. Ignatiev, the Russian Ambassador to the Porte since 1864, was personally an enthusiastic Pan-Slav.

Nor, at that juncture, was Austria entirely defence-minded. A party in Vienna was urging that Austria should find a pretext to annexe Bosnia-Herzegovina. The general argument, which made some appeal to the Emperor (who had not yet quite reconciled himself to the role of eternal loser) was that the annexation would bring Austria some compensation, in the only direction still open – for annexation of the Danubian Provinces, which had looked more tempting twenty-five years earlier, was no longer a practical possibility – for her losses in Italy and Germany, and the military party also argued that now that Venetia was lost, Austria needed a hinterland to Dalmatia, to protect her sea-borne commerce from Trieste and Fiume. More remotely, both military and business interests were beginning to dream of securing for Austria an outlet on the Aegean at Salonica.

Another group wanted the annexation on ethnic-political grounds. These were the *Habsburgtreu* Croat nationalists, who would have liked to see all their countrymen united under Habsburg rule; that the admitted Croats of Bosnia-Herzegovina, designated as such by their Catholic faith, numbered only some 20% of the populations of the two provinces, against twice as many Orthodox Serbs and 34% Moslems of Serbo-Croat stock,[1] weighed little with them against what they called the historic claim to 'Turkish Croatia'. Although these men were few, they were influential, for they included several high-ranking officers from the old Military Frontier. One of these,

[1] See above, p. 82.

THE FOREIGN RELATIONS OF THE MONARCHY (1871–1903)

General Rodić, had been made Statthalter of Dalmatia in 1870 (it was he who had pacified the insurgents there in the previous year), and had already established intimate connections with the Croat nationalists across the border.

Andrássy himself, while he did not belong to the party of action, and would have preferred to see the rule of the Porte maintained, yet thought that it would be a lesser evil that the two provinces should come under Austrian rule, in some form or another, than that they should be partitioned between Serbia and Montenegro, which might then unite and confront the Monarchy with an uncomfortably large Southern Slav State, probably under Russian patronage, on its southern frontier. In any case, the pressure in favour of annexation coming from within the Monarchy itself made it still more unlikely that the *status quo* in the Balkans could last much longer, so that a clash of interests between Austria and Russia seemed inevitable and even imminent, and Austria's need for allies, urgent. The search for these therefore constituted his chief preoccupation when he took office.

Andrássy did not put all his eggs in the German basket – one of his first moves on taking office was to offer Britain an understanding, and although this was rejected, he never quite lost hope of achieving it. But Britain was in any case far away; an alliance with France was out of the question, if only on account of the Emperor's feelings. To meet the immediate situation, and also to preserve the anti-Slav balance within the Monarchy, Germany was the obvious partner. It was Andrássy's good fortune that Bismarck, for his part, was anxious to have Austria friendly to him (to eliminate for good and all the possibility of a Franco-Austrian combination against Germany) and personally well disposed towards Andrássy for his decisive intervention in 1870 (later the two men developed a genuine personal liking), so that he met Andrássy's overtures half way, and it took only a few diplomatic conversations to establish, although not yet in contractual form, that special relationship between Germany and Austria which was to remain until 1918 the most important given fact in all the Monarchy's foreign relationships. Andrássy secured, indeed, one cardinal point almost immediately: even in these early conversations Bismarck assured the Austro-Hungarian Ambassador in Berlin that he would not tolerate an attack by Russia on the Monarchy.[1]

The objectives of the two men were not, indeed, quite the same. Andrássy did not want an offensive alliance against Russia, but he wanted, and for some time hoped to achieve, a full defensive alliance against her between Vienna and Berlin. Both Bismarck and his sovereign, on the other hand, were quite determined to preserve the old friendship between Germany and Russia, if only to prevent Russia from linking up with France. What Bismarck wanted to bring about was solidarity between Germany, Austria and Russia, and it was his will that prevailed as the result of the first exchanges. First it

[1] Cf. Wertheimer, *Andrássy*, II. 24.

was arranged that the new Austro-Russian relationship should be signalized by personal gestures, and accordingly, after Wilhelm had been in Salzburg and Gastein, Francis Joseph was booked to visit Berlin in September 1872. The Czar, however, who was nervous about the developments, invited himself to the party, and the results of this meeting, of a journey by Wilhelm and Bismarck to Petersburg in April 1873 and of the appearance of the Czar and Gorčakov in Vienna a month later, were a complex of understandings and treaties, on the whole along lines desired by Bismarck. In Berlin Andrássy and Gorčakov told one another frankly that either would go to war if the other resorted to force in the Near East, but reassured each other on their respective intentions. In Petersburg Germany and Russia signed a secret convention for mutual support if either were attacked by a third party, but Francis Joseph and Andrássy refused to adhere to this. In Vienna, on 6 June, Austria and Russia signed the so-called 'Convention of Schönbrunn', agreeing to consult on any question on which their interests disagreed, ' in order that these disputes should not overshadow the considerations of a higher order which they had at heart' (a codicil pledged them to joint resistance against revolutionary socialism), and Germany adhered to this agreement on 22 October, thus bringing into being the so-called 'League of the Three Emperors' (*Dreikaiserbund*).

The reconciliation between Austria and Russia was made spectacular: Francis Joseph visited Petersburg and laid a wreath on the grave of Nicholas I, who had saved his Empire in 1849. But the test of the understanding was not far away. Gorčakov, who had for a while been concentrating his activities on Central Asia, suddenly turned his attention back to the Balkans, especially Bulgaria, and the forward party in Austria was equally active. In the spring of 1875 Rodić arranged for Francis Joseph to tour Dalmatia. The visit was made the occasion for irredentist demonstrations from across the frontier, and there was much talk of the possibility, even the imminence, of the annexation. Meanwhile, Austria had stolen a march against Russia in Serbia. Russia had been offended when, after the assassination of Prince Michael, the Serbs had placed his fourteen-year-old cousin on the throne (she would have preferred Nicholas of Montenegro), and when the Regents made her overtures, had rebuffed them. The Regents, and the young Prince, as he grew up, had then turned to Austria, to which Milan had in 1875 pledged himself in extravagant terms. The attachment was, indeed, a personal one: it was not shared, either by the Serbian Liberal Party, which had won the elections in both 1874 and 1875, or by the powerful underground nationalist organization, the *Omladina*.

Then, in the summer of 1875, a revolt broke out in the Herzegovina, initiating a European crisis which lasted almost exactly three years; a crisis of immense complexity, of which only the barest outline can be given here. It would be quite mistaken to suppose that the *Dreikaiserbund* proved

THE FOREIGN RELATIONS OF THE MONARCHY (1871–1903)

altogether ineffectual in face of the situation. When the revolt broke out, Andrássy and Gorčakov agreed on a policy of reforms in the Balkans, the territorial integrity of the Porte remaining intact; and a Note summoning the Sultan to introduce reforms was handed in at Constantinople in December 1875. But the 'reforms' enacted were derisory, and in any case, remained on paper. The unrest among the Balkan peoples grew, and on 30 June 1876 Serbia and Montenegro declared war on Russia (Prince Milan reluctantly, but under irresistible pressure from the Liberals and the *Omladina*) to 'redeem' (for themselves) Bosnia and the Herzegovina respectively.

In this situation Andrássy and Gorčakov met again, at Reichstadt, on 8 July and again reached, or thought themselves to have reached, agreement. If the Turkish armies got the better of the campaign, the territorial *status quo* was to be upheld; but if Serbia and Montenegro won the day, there were to be territorial changes. Unfortunately, Andrássy's and Gorčakov's versions of the precise nature of these changes afterwards proved not to agree. In both, Russia was to recover Southern Bessarabia, besides acquiring certain areas in the Caucasus; but Andrássy's text allowed Austria to annex the greater part of Bosnia-Herzegovina, Serbia and Montenegro getting only relatively small gains; while the Russian version gave Montenegro the whole of the Herzegovina and Serbia a large part of Bosnia, Austria receiving only 'Turkish Croatia and some parts of Bosnia contiguous to her frontiers'.

If Turkey in Europe disintegrated altogether, Bulgaria and Roumelia (in the Austrian text, also Albania) might form autonomous States (the Russian text said, independent principalities) while Greece should receive territorial extensions. Constantinople with the area round it was to become a free city.

In the event, the Turkish armies won big successes against the Serbs, but meanwhile, the revolt had spread to Bulgaria. Russia now began to threaten war on Turkey. The prospect brought the other Powers definitively into action, and after a flurry of diplomatic exchanges, a Conference of the Powers met in Constantinople in December. Their main proposals were for autonomy, under Turkish sovereignty, for Bosnia and for two areas of Bulgaria. Turkey was to suffer no actual territorial losses except to Montenegro, which was to keep the ground held by her armies. Turkey rejected the proposals and the conference broke up. Meanwhile, anticipating this result, Gorčakov had again approached Andrássy, and on 15 January 1877, the secret 'Budapest Conventions' were signed under which Austria undertook to preserve benevolent neutrality in case of a Russo-Turkish war. If Russia were successful, Austria was to receive all Bosnia-Herzegovina, except a slice of the latter province (to go to Montenegro) and its southern extremity, the Sanjak of Novi-Bazar (to remain with Turkey). Serbia and Montenegro were to get further compensation on their southern frontiers. 'The establishment of a great compact Slavic or other State' was to be excluded, but 'Bulgaria',

Roumelia and Albania might be constituted as independent States, and Greece enlarged.

In April, Russia declared war on Turkey, and although held up by the stubborn defence of Plevna, which was broken only with Roumanian help, eventually (on 31 January 1878) forced her opponent to sign an armistice. On 3 March the world was confronted with the Peace of San Stefano. In Europe (she made other acquisitions in Asia) Russia only took for herself Southern Bessarabia, in exchange for which she presented Roumania with the Dobruja; Roumania also became independent. All the heart of the Balkans, as far south as the Aegean coast of West Thrace and as far west as Ochrida, was constituted into a great autonomous Bulgaria. Serbia received independence, with enlargements in the Niš-Mitrovica area and in the Sanjak; Montenegro, independence and territory in the Sanjak and Albania; and the rest of Bosnia-Herzegovina might remain under Ottoman rule.

But Ignatiev, whose work this treaty was, had overshot the mark. Not Andrássy alone was outraged (at these flagrant breaches of the earlier understandings) but other Powers, Britain above all. Bismarck decided to back Andrássy. After a last, elemental crisis, a Congress of the Powers met in Berlin in June 1878. Its members signed a new Treaty in August. The biggest changes made, in comparison with the Treaty of San Stefano, were that the Bulgaria established a few months earlier was broken up into three parts: the northernmost was left as an autonomous Principality; Eastern Roumelia (the Maritsa valley) became a semi-autonomous province, under a Christian governor, while Macedonia was restored to direct Turkish rule. Otherwise, most of the San Stefano frontiers in the Northern Balkans were confirmed, Serbia's being even a little more generous. But now Austria did not come out empty-handed. She made no direct territorial acquisitions, but was authorized to 'occupy' Bosnia-Herzegovina indefinitely, under a European mandate. She further received the right to station garrisons in the Sanjak of Novi-Bazar, which thus continued to separate Serbia from Montenegro and to constitute a gate through which Austria might later expand into the Southern Balkans.

It should be added that when Austria did set about occupying her prize, she met with a disagreeable shock. Andrássy, in his cheerful and superficial way, had said that the occupation would take 'a platoon headed by a military band'. He was grievously disillusioned. The Moslems of Bosnia-Herzegovina were, with the possible exception of the Pomaks of the Rhodopes (like them, Slavonic converts from Christianity), the most fanatical upholders in all the Balkans of the pure doctrine of Moslem supremacy and of its time-honoured and, to them, profitable institutions. It is often forgotten that of the numerous revolts which shook those unhappy provinces in the nineteenth century, those in which Christian peasants rebelled against the tyranny of their masters were less numerous, and less bloody, than those in which the Bosnian Moslems were resisting the efforts (often, indeed, enforced and reluctant ones) of their own Sultans to introduce reform. In these the poor Moslems had regularly made common cause with the rich.

Now, too, when the Porte accepted the dictate of Berlin, the Bosnian Moslems expelled (or occasionally slaughtered) their own officials, formed a local Home Defence Corps, which was reinforced by sympathizers from other parts of the Balkans, including some Turkish regiments who were also in mutiny, and put up a considerable resistance to the Austrian troops when they advanced into the provinces. The modest force originally thought sufficient for the operation had to be reinforced until it reached the considerable figure of 150,000 men, and it suffered over five thousand casualties; the Government was forced also to ask for a retrospective supplementary credit of 25 million gulden on top of the 60 m.g .which it had originally extracted from a sulky Reichsrat.

Neither did Austria's troubles in the provinces end with the completion of the occupation: but the history of her later woes is told in a later chapter.[1]

The crisis had important effects on the development of Austria's international commitments. His experiences during it had deepened Andrássy's awareness of the Russian danger and his consequent eagerness to secure a close contractual relationship with Germany, as defence. Fortunately for him, Bismarck, too, was nervous about Russia's intentions, and also about Austria's, for he was not unaware of the existence of a party in Vienna, headed by the Archduke Albrecht, which still wanted Austria to ally herself with Russia for a war of *revanche* against Prussia. Negotiations began between him and Andrássy. They did not go easily, for the German Emperor, and many of his entourage, were still determined to refuse any obligation inconsistent with friendship with Russia, and if, for Austria's sake, they did undertake any commitment, even purely defensive, against Russia, they wanted Austria to repay it with a similar obligation against France; and this Andrássy, supported by Francis Joseph, absolutely refused to undertake. Eventually, however, agreement was reached on a text which provided that if either party was attacked by Russia, the other would help the party attacked with all the forces at its disposal. If the attacker was a country other than Russia, the party not attacked would preserve benevolent neutrality, but would help the party attacked if Russia assisted the attacker.

The Treaty was to run for five years, but was subject to renewal. It was to be kept secret, but divulged to Russia if she made threatening war preparations. It was signed on 7 October 1879; ratifications were exchanged ten days later.

[1] See below, pp. 740, ff.

This Treaty, which was in fact regularly renewed thereafter, was destined in due course to become not only the fixed pole in all Austria's foreign relationships, but also an influence in them which ended by being something like dominant. At first, however, it made singularly little difference either to her position, or her problems. It gave her final security against Germany; but in practice, she had enjoyed that since 1872, or earlier. For the rest, the only one of her relationships which it affected directly was that with Russia. Here it gave her an ultimate assurance of Germany's support in a conflict not provoked by her, but this, too, she had enjoyed before. Bismarck still remained no more than an honest broker between Austria and Russia, and on 18 June 1881, even elicited from Andrássy's successor, Haymerle,[1] his signature to a new *Dreikaiserbund*. This contained a general clause binding the signatories to benevolent neutrality should any of them become engaged in war with a fourth Power – an undertaking of great value to Germany, whose position in the event of a Franco-German war it strengthened immensely, but one of relatively little importance to Austria. Its remaining provisions were designed to prevent a collision between Austria and Russia in the Balkans, its tacit assumptions being that the maintenance of the integrity of the Porte was desirable in the general interest, but that the western half of the Balkan Peninsula belonged to Austria's sphere of influence and the eastern, to Russia's. Turkey was not to be attacked without previous consultation and agreement on the ensuring peace settlement. Russia agreed that Austria might annex Bosnia-Herzegovina (although not necessarily the Sanjak) when she wished; Austria and Germany agreed not to oppose the eventual union of Bulgaria and Eastern Roumelia. Finally, the three Powers agreed to compel Turkey to maintain the principle of closing the Straits to warlike operations.

The *Dreikaiserbund* was renewed in 1884, but in 1886 extraordinary events occurred in Bulgaria, where the Principality and Eastern Roumelia proclaimed their union under such peculiar circumstances that the reactions of the Powers were the opposite to those envisaged under the *Dreikaiserbund*: Russia opposed it, while Austria raised no objections. The Bulgarians then elected a Prince of the House of Coburg, whom Russia proposed to have ejected, while Austria and Britain supported him. The tension between

---

[1] Andrássy had resigned on 22 September 1879, saying in his frivolous way that statesmen, like opera singers and dancers, ought to retire when their powers and their popularity were still at their height. In fact, however, he had been vexed by the opposition to his policy raised by some Court circles and by attacks made on it in both Austria and Hungary. He had wanted to resign when the Congress of Berlin closed, but had stopped on to see the treaty with Germany through.

Haymerle himself died prematurely on 10 October 1881. His successor, Count Kálnoky, was a Hungarian aristocrat, but unlike Andrássy, no Hungarian nationalist. His contemporaries describe him as personally disagreeable and arrogant, but hard-working and able. The documents do not altogether bear out this last adjective.

Austria and Russia was so great that Bismarck (while also applying pressure to Austria to accept Bulgaria as falling within Russia's sphere of influence) published the text of the Austro-German alliance. The crisis passed over, but had left too much ill-feeling behind to allow the renewal of the *Dreikaiserbund* in 1887. Austria and Russia were never again allies, and their relationship thereafter was never anything much better than one of jealous rivalry.

It was, however, and remained up to the end of the period now under review, nothing worse than that, and for a few years, even Germany's position in the triangle did not alter appreciably, since to compensate for the lapse of the *Dreikaiserbund*, Bismarck, on 18 June 1887, concluded a secret 'Reinsurance Treaty' with Russia, under which Germany promised Russia neutrality unless she attacked Austria, and Russia undertook the same obligation unless Germany attacked France.

What later developments showed to have been a turning-point (also for Austria) did come in 1890, when Bismarck's successor, Caprivi, refused to renew the Reinsurance Treaty, which Russia had wanted renewed and even made permanent; for Russia now turned to France, with which she reached an understanding in 1891, which developed into a military Convention and an alliance. The increased confidence which this gave her prompted her to resume an active policy in the Balkans. In 1894 she achieved a formal reconciliation with Ferdinand of Bulgaria, and the next year she was again planning an advance on the Straits. Berlin seemed inclined to let her have Constantinople, advising Austria to compensate herself in Salonica. Then Lord Salisbury's Foreign Office floated a curious suggestion for the dismemberment of the Turkish Empire. Count Goluchowski,[1] who had succeeded Kálnoky that May, was against partition, if only on the old grounds of not wanting to increase the number of unreliable subjects within the Monarchy, and tried to organize European resistance against Russia, but Europe seemed once again on the verge of war.

Yet even in these years, Austria's relations with Russia had not been implacably hostile. During the most critical of them, in 1894, Kálnoky had reached a loose standstill agreement with Giers, the then Russian Foreign Minister, to the effect that Austria would refrain from meddling in Bulgaria's internal affairs if Russia did the same for Serbia. Something like friendly relations were re-established when Russia, chiefly owing to French hesitations, dropped her plan of seizing Constantinople and was then induced by Japan's victory over China to turn her attention to the Far East. In April 1897, Francis Joseph and Goluchowski visited Petersburg and found the new

[1] This was Agenor Goluchowski, *fils*, son of the former Minister of State. Kálnoky had offended the Hungarian Minister President, Bánffy, by countenancing a visit to Hungary by the Papal Nuncio, Agliardi, who had allowed himself to criticize publicly Hungary's anticlerical legislation.

Czar, Nicholas II, prepared to accept the *status quo* in the Balkans. Now Goluchowski reached another understanding with Giers's successor, Muraviev. Austria and Russia would work together to preserve, if possible, the *status quo* in the Balkans; neither would seek Balkan territory for itself, nor permit another Power to do so. If and when territorial revision became inevitable, a new State of Albania should be established on the Adriatic, and the rest of Turkey in Europe, with Constantinople and the Straits zone, should be distributed equitably among the Christian States of the Balkans, none of which should be allowed to become disproportionately strong.

The agreement was not quite watertight, for once again, the understanding on Bosnia-Herzegovina was imperfect: Goluchowski reserved the right to annex the two provinces, with the Sanjak, while Russia said that the annexation 'would require special scrutiny at the proper time' and that 'the boundaries of the Sanjak would need to be defined'. Nevertheless, the tension was relaxed, and did not recur for a decade. Preoccupied as Russia now was elsewhere, Austria could, indeed, probably have stolen a march on her in the Balkans, had she wished.[1] But Goluchowski, Pole as he was, was a peaceable man by nature and also convinced that Austria was both politically and financially unfit for war, and Francis Joseph had become it with years. They honoured their word, and when unrest broke out in Macedonia in 1903, Austria and Russia again joined hands, at a meeting brought about through Austrian initiative,[2] to work out the 'Mürzsteg Programme' of 3 October, which in effect confirmed the 1897 Agreement; the two Powers undertook to co-operate in the creation of an international gendarmerie to restore order in Macedonia, which was to remain under the sovereignty of the Porte.

Meanwhile, Austria's relations with Germany had stood the test of time, although the emphasis in the relationship had changed, slightly but perceptibly. It does not seem that Bismarck's successors were quite so enamoured of the connection as he had been; on the other hand, Francis Joseph clung to it more closely precisely with the passing of Bismarck, whom he had always disliked in his heart as the true author of 1866; also the young Emperor was more sympathetic to him than his predecessor. Thus although the relationship was clouded after the Badeni Decrees, when the complaints of the Germans of Austria were being vociferously endorsed in the Reich, and there were rumours that Gulochowski's understanding with Muraviev was going to lead to a real reorientation of the Monarchy's foreign policy, the cloud quickly passed over. There had never been any real danger that Austria

[1] Goluchowski is strongly reproached for not having done so by Hantsch, *Graf Berchtold*, I. 10.

[2] The suggestion had come first from Aehrenthal, then Austro-Hungarian Ambassador in Petersburg.

would change sides, and once the Germans realized this, even the temperamental Kaiser, who had joined in the chorus, simmered down.[1]

Gradually the alliance developed, at least in Francis Joseph's eyes, into something much more than a limited defensive agreement: it was a real partnership of peculiar intimacy. The danger was now another one. Austria was, indeed, assured of Germany's protection, which was invaluable to her. But Germany, especially under the Kaiser Wilhelm, was no longer the safe, satiated power which she had been under Bismarck, and although the alliance in no way bound Austria if Germany provoked a conflict with the West (or even with Russia) it might be morally difficult for her to stand aside in such a conflict. With time, too (although this came a little later), Germany herself began meddling in Balkan affairs, not always in strict accordance with Austria's wishes.

By this time Russia was no longer the only quarter from which danger threatened the Monarchy, although if Treaties meant anything, its position at the turn of the century was extraordinarily strong. In 1878 the Minister President of Serbia, Ristić, although personally a strong Russophile, had been obliged to sign an agreement with Austria providing for a railway convention and closer commercial relations, to culminate in a customs union. When Ristić evaded honouring his bargain, Austria retorted with commercial pressure which compelled Milan to dismiss him in favour of a 'Progressive' (i.e., Conservative) Government, and this in April 1881 signed a commercial agreement with Austria, valid for ten years, which came near a Customs Union.[2] Three months later, Milan personally signed a secret agreement undertaking to conclude no treaties with any foreign Power without Austria's permission[3] and to prevent all agitation against Austria in Austrian territory, including Bosnia.[4] In return, Austria promised to recognize Milan as King of Serbia if he assumed the title, and (rather vaguely) to support Serbia's claims to extension in the Kossovo area and in Macedonia.[5]

Austria could have had more than this, for Milan actually offered to let her annexe his country – an offer which Kálnoky refused, saying that Austria

[1] See below, p. 626 f. A convenient short account of this pseudo-crisis is given by Miss Wiskemann in her *Czechs and Germans*, chapter VI. The German documents are in *Grosse Politik*, 13, Kap. LXXXVII. It is obvious that in fact Badeni had never thought of his language ordinances, which sparked the trouble off, as affecting the Monarchy's foreign political orientation at all, nor was Goluchowski in the least trying to change sides. A lot of people lost their heads, not least so the German Emperor.

[2] Between 1884 and 1892, 87% of Serbia's exports went to the Monarchy, and 66% of her imports came from it.

[3] It was afterwards agreed that this veto did not apply to non-political treaties concluded with Powers other than Russia.

[4] For full details of this and the Monarchy's other secret treaties, see Pribram, *Geheimverträge*.

[5] The form of words excluded the Sanjak of Novi-Bazar.

would have more profit from 'a peaceful and flourishing independent Serbia, in friendly relations with us', than from 'a rebellious province'.[1] But the treaties did initiate a couple of decades during which Serbia was really a Austrian satellite, in the modern sense of the term. It was during these years that Austrian business interests entertained their rosiest visions of establishing at least an economic empire in the Balkans, with its outlet at Salonica. Various factors, among them fear of Russia's jealousy and Austria's own shortage of capital, prevented the realization of these plans, and the result of the relationship was, in effect, to leave Serbia an agricultural State, although during these years, a flourishing one enough.

Shortly after, Italy became Austria's ally, and that although during the Eastern Crisis feeling in Italy had run very high against Austria, whose 'yoke' Garibaldi had described as 'no less heavy than Turkey's'. Corti, the Italian Foreign Minister, had been denounced for a traitor for favouring a *rapprochement* with Austria, and enthusiasts had actually planned to make the *rapprochement* impossible by sending irregular bands into Austrian territory. Even official Italy had tried to blackmail Austria into buying Italy's support by ceding her the Italian-speaking areas in the Monarchy, and then at least to obtain compensation if Austria enlarged her frontiers.

Nor, it must be said, had Austria been in a hurry to turn the other cheek. She was still at loggerheads with Italy over the Rome question, and thought little or nothing of her military value as an ally. The alliance came about because Italy's resentment against France (chiefly, although not solely, owing to France's occupation of Tunisia in 1881) was so strong that she approached Germany, and Bismarck, while glad of another ally against France, insisted that Italy must agree with Austria, which obeyed only with great reluctance. The negotiations ended in the three States signing (on 20 May 1882) the Triple Alliance, under which (after a preamble describing the purpose of the Treaty to be the preservation of peace and the maintenance of the Monarchic principle and of social and political order), each party promised to preserve peace and friendship towards the other two, and to enter into no alliances or agreements directed against either of them. Germany and Austria promised to support Italy, and Italy, to support Germany, in the event of an unprovoked attack by France, and the *casus foederis* was extended to all partners if one or two of them was attacked without provocation by two or more Great Powers. If one of the partners made war on a fourth Power which menaced its security, the other two promised it benevolent neutrality.[2]

In 1883 had followed an alliance with Roumania, whose resentment against the Dual Monarchy for containing so many Roumanians within its frontiers was not perhaps outweighed, but balanced by anger against Russia

[1] The refusal was, indeed, largely motivated by fears of Russian objections.
[2] Italy stipulated that the Treaty was in no case to apply against Great Britain.

THE FOREIGN RELATIONS OF THE MONARCHY (1871-1903)

for the treatment accorded by her to Roumania in 1878 after the help which she had received from Roumanian armies. The loss of Southern Bessarabia, for which the Dobruja seemed a totally inadequate compensation, was bitterly resented, and not only Roumania's German King, but her Premier, Bratianu, feared that Russia had designs on Roumania's independence itself.[1] On 30 October 1883, then, Austria and Roumania concluded a treaty (to which Germany adhered the same day[2]) providing that neither party should enter into an alliance directed against the other, that Austria should come to Roumania's help if the latter were attacked without provocation, and Roumania to Austria's if she were attacked without provocation 'in a portion of her territories bordering on Roumania'.[3] This treaty, again, was valid for five years, but renewable.

All these agreements were still in force in 1903. The *Triplice*, although modified in 1889-90, had been renewed in those years, and in 1900; the Roumanian Treaty, to which Italy adhered in 1889, regularly, as it was until 1914; the Serbian economic treaties, in 1889 and again in 1893. But all of them had been concluded with Monarchs, or Governments, not with peoples, and none of them was popular in the country concerned. The Treaty with Roumania had been concluded with the King. Its very existence was unknown except to a handful of men,[4] and it certainly did nothing to prevent popular feeling against the Monarchy, especially Hungary, from continuing to grow, while relations between the two countries were further disturbed by a tariff war which lasted from 1886 to 1891 and did considerable damage to the economies of both.[5] Serbia's treaty relationship with the Monarchy was favourable enough to the Serbian peasant, who was able to get rid of most of his exportable surplus at reasonable prices, but the dependence on the Monarchy which it expressed was unpopular in the nationalist circles represented by the Radical Party, now rapidly becoming the strongest in the

[1] Another motive was probably fear lest the Monarchy should become too intimate with Bulgaria.

[2] This arrangement seems to have been made at Bismarck's wish, partly to spare the susceptibilities of the German Emperor, who was still very hostile to the idea of commitments against Russia.

[3] This phrase was substituted for the word 'Russia', again out of consideration for the German Emperor.

[4] It is even arguable that it was invalid, as incompatible with the Roumanian Constitution, but a case to the contrary can be made out; see R. W. Seton-Watson, *History of the Roumanians*, p. 365.

[5] This broke out because when a new treaty was being negotiated in 1885 to replace its predecessor (which had been distinctly favourable to Roumania), Roumania refused to submit to the veterinary regulations required by the Austro-Hungarian negotiators, and when they refused to relax the regulations, applied her (very high) autonomous tariff to her industrial imports from Austria. It is true that the Hungarian cattle-breeders were desirous of reducing competition from Roumania, but also true that strict inspection of Roumanian cattle was absolutely necessary. The 'war' reduced the Monarchy's exports to Roumania by about 50% and Roumania's exports by some 80%.

country, and the military societies, all of which bore an implacable grudge against the Monarchy for having occupied Bosnia. The dynasty – both Milan and his son, Alexander, who succeeded to the throne when Milan abdicated in 1889 – remained loyal to the Austrian connection[1] but the country was against them. One effect of this, which was to prove fatal to poor young Alexander, was to create a nexus between the unpopularity (already considerable on other grounds) of the dynasty and the Austrophile orientation.

As to Italy, the Austrian alliance had from the first been an offence to romantic spirits, who had carried on a fairly unbridled agitation against it, and against Austria, in their Press. But the first leaders of this agitation were also subversives, even Republicans, in domestic politics, and the Government was chary of encouraging them, if only in the interests of inter-Monarchic solidarity, which was, after all, one of the declared objects of the Triple Alliance and one of those features of it which made King Umberto a loyal and convinced supporter of it, although even in those years, no Italian statesman would have dared (or wished) to make an open and sincere renunciation of all irredentist claims on Austrian territory. And the situation soon got worse, in respect both of public opinion and of official policy. For when Italy, having completed (except as regards the Monarchy) her internal unification, began, as it was *de rigueur* for European States to do in that age, to look round her for directions in which to expand, she cast her eyes, not only on Africa, where Austria had no ambitions of her own, but also on Turkey in Europe. Once she had thus entered her name on the list of claimants for the heritage of the Porte in the Balkans, Austria had only the choice of rejecting her claim, at the risk of seeing her combine with Russia, or of reaching an accommodation with her. In 1887, when the Triplice first came up for renewal, the tension between Germany and France, and between Austria and Russia, put Italy in a strong position, and she extracted from Austria an important concession: the two Powers pledged one another to use all their influence to prevent any territorial change 'in the East' detrimental to either of them. Should, however, the maintenance of the *status quo* in the Balkans, on the Ottoman coast or in the islands of the Adriatic or the Aegean prove impossible, and should either party find 'itself forced to undertake a long-term or permanent occupation' [of any parts of these areas], this was to take place only after previous consultation with the other party, and on the basis of 'mutual compensation for any territorial or other advantage, over and above the present *status quo*, achieved by either party and satisfactory to the just interests and claims of both'.

Concluded in 1887 as a separate bi-lateral agreement between Austria and Italy, this undertaking was incorporated into the main Treaty in 1891, as its seventh article, and subsequently Austria made a further concession,

---

[1] When Alexander succeeded, the Regents (he was a minor) renewed the secret political Convention in 1895.

promising Italy that if and when the Albanian State envisaged in the Austro-Russian understanding of that year came into being, Italy should have a predominant influence in it: this promise, given by Goluchowski verbally in 1897, was put into writing in 1900.

These agreements, however, still left Italy smarting under a feeling that Austria was standing in the way of her realization of what she was now beginning to regard as objectives vital to her security, while Austria, on the contrary, regarded Italy as an interloper into fields traditionally Austria's own. The understanding was, moreover, incomplete, for while Austria believed herself to have stipulated that the annexation by her of Bosnia-Herzegovina was not to be regarded as altering the *status quo*, in a sense entitling Italy to compensation, Italy had not formally accepted the reservation.[1]

Almost simultaneously with this emergence of a fresh source of international rivalry between the Monarchy and Italy, the direct irredentist campaign took a new turn. The romantic and extremist furore, after reaching a peak about 1886–7, ebbed away but it was succeeded by a new agitation which was much more systematic and much more dangerous, for two reasons. Firstly, it appealed to wider circles, and most important, having discarded its one-sided Republican and Oppositional character, it could, and did, enlist adherents from among supporters of the Government and Conservative circles. Secondly, it asked for more. Most of the old national idealists had only clamoured for genuinely Italian territory: the Trentino as far as Solurn, and Friule. The new school raised 'natural', historical and strategic claims: to the Brenner frontier, to Trieste, to Istria, to Dalmatia. After Mazzini had voiced these claims in his *Unità Italiana* in 1866, they became the tacit programme of the great Dante Alighieri Society, founded in 1887, an institution which was nominally unofficial, but was publicly patronized by politicians of the Government party, high-ranking civil servants, and Generals. To support the Italian cause inside the Monarchy, another society was founded, the *Lega Nazionale*, the purpose of which was to support every aspect of Italian life within the Monarchy.

Even now the official encouragement received by this agitation was not constant. Crispi, the Sicilian, when he was Minister President, found it a

[1] Cf. Fellner, *Dreibund*, p. 28. Inexplicably, Kálnoky did not ask Italy directly for this assurance, but told Berlin his Government's point of view and contented himself with Herbert Bismarck's reply that Italy had given satisfactory assurances on this point, and on Austria's other condition, that the Trentino and Trieste could never be traded as compensation for any acquisition in the Balkans. In fact, the assurances had been verbal ones, given by the Italian Ambassador in Berlin, and the Austrian request had never been forwarded to Rome. On Art. VII, Burian's opinion (op. cit., chapter VI) is interesting. He describes it as 'the Archimedean point for giving effect to Italy's national and Balkan policy in the World War ... What was capable of being read into Art. VII was a revelation to us.' To this clause, again, Austria had agreed only with great reluctance and under pressure from Germany.

hindrance to his African plans, discouraged it, dissolving some of the associations and dismissing his own Minister of Finance for an incorrect utterance. But things changed again after Crispi's fall, and after the assassination of King Umberto in 1900. His successor, Victor Emmanuel, was no friend of the Triplice, and when the government came into the hands of Zanardelli, a native of Brescia, and Prinetti, an old and declared enemy of the Triplice, the agitation 'assumed almost threatening forms'.[1]

The Triplice had become a completely artificial conception, which was in no way endorsed by Italian public opinion. Italy was held to her alliance simply by the prospect which it offered her of support for her colonial ambitions, and in the event of a clash with France. But the latter possibility, very real in the early 1890s, diminished swiftly after 1897, when Visconti-Venosta initiated a *rapprochement* with the French Ministers, Delcassé and Barrère, and in 1900 concluded with them agreements which practically eliminated Italy's fears on this point. In the spring of 1902 Britain gave her consent to Italy's African designs. In June of that year Prinetti again renewed the Triplice, this time unchanged, but almost simultaneously exchanged Notes with Barrère pledging Italy to strict neutrality even if France took the initiative in declaring war, provided that she did so in defence of her honour or her security, in consequence of a direct provocation. The declaration was carefully worded to avoid literal conflict with the text of the Triple Alliance, but its practical effect was to make Italy far rather a potential partner, in a European war, of her allies' enemies, than of her allies.

It remains to be added that her support of him in 1886 had brought Austria into friendly relations with the new Prince of Bulgaria. Ferdinand, however, was too *rusé* to put all his money on one horse, and balanced successfully between the two groups of Powers.

[1] Fellner, op. cit., p. 51.

14

Cis-Leithania under Dualism

I FROM AUERSPERG TO TAAFFE
1871–1890

The dismissal of Hohenwart meant that Francis Joseph had renounced the idea of replacing Dualism as the outer bracket of the formula defining the relationship of the Lands and peoples of the Dual Monarchy towards the Crown and with each other. Once having taken the decision, he adhered to it with complete rigidity. In the third and last of the periods into which, as we have suggested, the history of the Monarchy under Dualism falls, plans for substituting something else for Dualism were, as we shall see, again in the air; but it was Francis Joseph's heir presumptive who was considering them, and even he had no thought of putting his intentions into action until he should have succeeded to the throne. So long as Francis Joseph lived, Dualism had to be accepted; and awareness of this was so general that, as one who knew him writes, no one of his entourage even dared whisper in his presence the idea of modifying it 'for this would have brought the man who ventured it into lasting disgrace with the Emperor', and of that, everyone was afraid.[1]

This assumption that, given Francis Joseph's attitude, the Dualist system was a *noli me tangere* seems to have extended from the Emperor's entourage to the politicians of Cis-Leithania, and even to most of its thinkers. They, too, accepted the irrevocable, and up to the dawn of the third period, not only made no attempt to change it (if they had, they would immediately have encountered, not only the Emperor's displeasure, but also his veto) but, while grumbling against it, hardly even discussed what might be put in its place; devoting themselves exclusively to their own mutual relationships within its framework. This being so, one would logically have expected the political history of Cis-Leithania after 1871 to be one of Parliamentary government in accordance with the 'Constitution' of 1867; and also, in accordance with Beust's and Andrássy's premise, to which the Emperor seemed to have

[1] Margutti, op. cit., p. 239.

reverted, of the political hegemony of the Germans in the West, balancing and supporting that of the Magyars in the East.

It did not, in fact, bear out either of these presumptions. The abandonment of the Hohenwart experiment had, indeed, brought with it, perhaps for the same reason of consciousness that the Emperor would not tolerate it,[1] also the dropping of any serious attempt to alter radically the inner structure of Cis-Leithania. Many adjustments, not all of them enjoying a legal basis, were made in the relationship between the central authorities and the Lands, but these never went beyond adjustments, not all of which were given a constitutional basis. The essential dichotomy of the whole and the parts remained unaltered. Nevertheless, although the tendency of the adjustments was, on balance, towards more centralization, and although many of them were actually initiated, in their own interest, by the Germans, yet the Germans lost their political hegemony after less than a decade, and never recovered it completely; when, after that, they were represented in a Government, it was only as one party in a coalition.

Yet this did not mean that the political power had passed to the non-Germans; it has passed away from the people's representatives altogether, back into the hands of the Emperor and of his civil servants, through whom the Government was conducted; the Reichsrat had become in fact little more than it was in name, an advisory body to the Crown.

This, of course, is putting the position with some exaggeration. Francis Joseph still left the representatives of the people considerable elbow-room, so long as they did not touch fundamentals, and, within those limits, the rules of genuine Parliamentary government were applied: votes were taken, and a Minister President regarded himself as bound (under normal conditions) to get for his decisions the affirmative support of a Parliamentary majority. Where, however, fundamentals were at issue, the Monarch's will was enforced, if necessary, over Parliament's head.[2] The system was a purely Austrian one, an adaptation to the facts of Austrian life of the general theories on which the enthusiasts of 1867 had built up the corpus of laws; and one, moreover, which adjusted itself constantly as those facts changed. No analysis can reach the heart of it: all that the historian can do is to record the facts as they occurred.

[1] Among the ideas which, according to Margutti (l.c.), no one dared even whisper in the Emperor's presence were not only the revision of Dualism, but 'the grant of autonomy to the Czechs of Bohemia, Moravia and Silesia' – i.e., precisely what Hohenwart would have carried through. The Czechs talked often enough of the 'Bohemian State Rights', and repeatedly made reservations that whatever they did was without prejudice to their continued affirmation of this principle, but they never brought Parliamentary life to a standstill in pursuit of them as they did over less fundamental linguistic issues.

[2] According to Steed, op. cit., pp. 24–5, the Auersperg Cabinet was formed 'on the basis of an express agreement with the Emperor that he would follow a constitutional policy provided the German majority should grant him the military credits which he might demand'.

In 1871 Auersperg and his team regarded themselves as constituting a genuine Parliamentary government, and as entitled to express and realize the wishes of the element to which most of them belonged – although to secure this they had first to dissolve several of the Federalist Landtage and carry through new elections, which gave them a safe majority in the Reichsrat,[1] and, after this, to carry through two of the structural modifications of which we have spoken. One was openly designed to strengthen the centralist element in the structure of Cis-Leithania. This was a new Franchise Act, which became law on 2 April 1873. The franchise was not extended (the Liberals were strongly against any reform in this direction), so that as before, only 5·9% of the population enjoyed the vote. The system of voting by Curias was retained also, on the insistence of the Constitutional Great Landlords, as was the provision for emergency elections when a Deputy refused to exercise his mandate,[2] but each Curia of each Land now elected its own representatives to the Reichsrat direct. At the same time, the number of Reichsrat Deputies was raised to 353. The proportion of Deputies from the different Lands was left substantially unaltered, but the numbers allotted to the different Curias were changed to the advantage of the towns and the disadvantage of the Great Landlords. These now sent, in all, eighty-five Deputies to the Reichsrat, the Chambers of Commerce, twenty-one, the urban communes, 116, and the rural, 131. Certain further manipulations gave the German element a little further weight still.

The second operation was, in form, a concession to decentralization, although the purpose of it was to strengthen the Germans' position within the narrower field into which they now withdrew. The Hohenwart experiment had shown the Germans that they would not be strong enough to retain the power if all the Slavs combined against them, while the Poles, for their part, awoke to the financial advantages of retaining the constitutional link with the rest of Cis-Leithania. Agreement was reached in 1873. The Poles withdrew their demand for autonomy (the Bill for which had become stuck in Committee); instead, a Minister for Galicia (in this case, Dr Ziemalkowski) was again taken into the Government, as from 21 September 1873, with unwritten powers which, as they developed, gave the Poles almost complete control over Galicia.[3] To mark the reconciliation, Goluchowski became for the third time, Statthalter of Galicia.

[1] The Landtage first dissolved were those of Upper Austria, Carniola, Bukovina and Moravia. Carniola then proved resistant, but the other three changed sides, and that was enough. The Bohemian Landtag was dissolved later. Thanks to strong intimidation and corruption, the Constitutionals won the majority in the First Curia, giving the Germans a majority in the Landtag. The Czechs refused to attend that body, which accordingly sent German representatives only to the Reichsrat.

[2] This proved in the event practically ineffectual, since whenever such a situation arose, the person elected at the second poll invariably belonged to his predecessor's party.

[3] For a convenient description of these powers, see Hugelmann, op. cit., p. 736. The

This was an event of extraordinary importance for the whole subsequent domestic political history of Cis-Leithania. As their side of the bargain, the Poles stopped fighting for more concessions, and thereafter, until 1917, regularly supported whatever Government was in power, and helped, so far as they could, to get the essential legislation through the Reichsrat; the assurance of this was really the single stable factor in Austria's Parliamentary life. The position was exceedingly favourable for the Poles, to whom it gave the best of both worlds, enabling them as it did to intervene at their pleasure in the affairs of the rest of Cis-Leithania without risk of retaliation. It proved ultimately far less advantageous to the Germans, for it was *all* Governments that the Poles supported thereafter, not German ones only. When, a few years later, the Poles joined a coalition Government which relegated the Liberals to the Opposition, the latter then awoke with a shock to this truth, but they were never able to undo their work, although they were trying to do so as late as 1918.

In 1873, however, the agreement served their purpose, and the tolerance of the Poles and continued absence of the Czechs[1] gave the Adolph Auersperg Government a very free hand. It had begun by adding various finishing touches to its constitutional programme: the extension of trial by jury to almost all serious offences and the establishment of the Administrative Court. But it had not got far before the Liberals' prestige was shaken and their own internal unity greatly weakened by an extraordinary turn for the worse in the economic situation.

After the Prussian war, the Monarchy had enjoyed a spell of unexampled prosperity, which had been triggered off, strangely enough, by the very speed and completeness of its defeat. The extra currency issued to finance the war which hardly took place had, as one expert writes, 'come as a real release to the whole economy:[2] it eased the financial stringency to an extraordinary degree, and such was the confidence engendered by the apparent ending of the struggle in Germany, the establishment of constitutional conditions in Austria and the settlement with Hungary, that the currency suffered no depreciation. On the contrary, the word went round that Austria was the

---

Polish *Landsmannminister* saw all proposed measures before they were enacted, and was able to object to any of them which seemed unfavourable to the Poles. 'His influence', writes Hugelmann, 'went so far that no important decision or initiative could be taken by any Departmental Ministry without the Polish Minister's first being given the opportunity to state his views on it.' Every Ministry contained a number of senior officials of Polish nationality, who were regarded *de facto* as the exponents of the *Polenklub*; the Ministry of the Interior, for example, contained a special section under a *polnischer Sektionschef*.

[1] At first there had been more absentees, including most of the Slovenes and many of the Tirolean Germans, but these reappeared in due course, as did the Moravian Czechs. The latter regularly attended their Landtag, which, unlike that of Bohemia, functioned throughout the period.

[2] A. Gratz in *100 Jahre*, p. 254. Gratz is most emphatic on the role played by this factor.

place where fortunes were to be made, and there was a great influx of foreign money, including 'refugee funds' from North America during the Civil War, and later, a considerable proportion of the indemnity paid by France to Germany in 1870. Much of this money was deposited with one or another of the foreign banks which now took advantage of the 1865 Law to open branches in Vienna.

Money came into the country in other ways also. There were two bumper harvests in Hungary, the biggest on record, and by singular good fortune for the Monarchy, the harvests in West Europe were bad. The whole surplus could be exported, and that at high prices, which were paid in silver.[1]

The first effect of all this was a big new expansion of railway construction. This had, indeed, been carried on fairly steadily, even during the years of financial stringency, owing to its obvious importance for the national economy: railway mileage had risen by 1860 to 2,927 km. in Austria, 1,614 in Hungary, and 525 in Lombardy-Venetia.[2] Then, in 1864, the Government had (largely with an eye to the expected conflict with Prussia) worked out an extensive programme, and had promised prospective investors exemption from taxation, subsidies, and/or a guarantee of five per cent on their invested capital. Licences to construct the projected lines had been granted to a number of 'consortiums', almost all of which were composed, on paper, of members of the highest Austrian aristocracy, who figured, as Kolmer, who gives a list of them, writes, 'as stool-pigeons to attract foreign capital'.[3] The new construction had been on a considerable scale even before the onset of the boom; the mileage had reached 3,965 km. in Austria and 2,158 in Hungary. Now it was accelerated to an extraordinary extent, partly in direct connection with the bumper harvests, for in many parts of the Hungarian Plain lines were hurriedly thrown down to carry away the contents of the groaning barns. By 1873 the mileage had risen by 250% in Austria and by 300% in Hungary.[4]

Danubian shipping, too, had record years. The railway companies bought new rolling-stock, thus further stimulating the iron and steel industries and coal-mining,[5] and extending the boom into industry. The banks took over the flotation of joint-stock companies (the fashionable form of the day). A

---

[1] On 9 March 1868, Beust had concluded a treaty with the Norddeutscher Bund, which allowed free export of Austrian (in practice, Hungarian) cereals. The export of cereals (in Doppelzentner) was:

1866	8,436,786
1867	20,869,905
1868	27,817,158

[2] 1859 figures. [3] Kolmer, I. 236–7.

[4] The figures, kindly supplied to me by the Austrian Statistical Office, were 9,354 km. in Austria and 6,219 in Hungary.

[5] The production of pig iron rose from 6·31 million tons in 1861 to 8·63 in 1871 and 10·07 in 1873. The figures for coal are 81·30, 200·96 and 237.

great *Gründungsfieber* swept over the Monarchy. New banks and industrial enterprises sprang up like mushrooms;[1] many of them were bucket-shops, and not a few of the enterprises in which the guileless public was induced to invest existed only on paper. The shares even of solid enterprises were driven up to ridiculous heights.

'When,' wrote a visiting American statesman, 'we look at the vigorous and varied agriculture, and the stupendous works of material improvement, we might fancy ourselves at home in the United States.'[2]

Almost every class of the Monarchy enjoyed, for a few years, great prosperity, in which even the State shared, for the yield of taxation rose, and as military expenditure had been cut back, the budgets for 1869–72 inclusive actually closed with surpluses[3] and the Ministry of Finance was able to consolidate the miscellaneous State debt of which there were then no less than 32 different headings, into a 5% *rente* which, as it was subject to a tax of 16%, cost the State only 4·2%.[4]

Then, however, the harvest was poor again, and the clouds gathered. By the end of 1872 the big banks, including most of the foreigners, were beginning to extricate themselves. But most of the native speculators, large and small, held on, confident that the boom would last at least to the end of the great World Exhibition, which had been billed for May 1873, to advertise Austria's 'economic miracle', and organized on the most lavish scale. In fact, some of the royal guests invited for the occasion, including the German Crown Prince and the Prince of Wales, had arrived, and Francis Joseph had already opened the Exhibition, when, on 7 May 1873, the bubble began to leak. It burst two days later, on that 'Black Friday' which Austria remembered long after, coupling its memory with that of the great 'State bankruptcy' of 1811. The inflated values collapsed in one day (the losses totalled over seven hundred million gulden), ruining many thousands of small speculators. By the end of the year eight banks, two insurance companies, one railway and seven industrial companies had gone bankrupt; and forty banks, six insurance companies, one railway, eighteen building and thirty-four industrial enterprises had gone into liquidation. Several railway companies left their lines unfinished.

It was politically relevant that nearly all the enterprises carried away by the storm were mushroom foundations of the boom years. All six of the Viennese banks founded before 1868 survived the crisis, but only eight of the

---

[1] Between 1868 and 1 January 1874, 1,005 concessions were granted for the foundation of joint-stock companies, 682 of which actually came into existence. These included 443 banks, 63 building companies, 38 industrial and 29 railway.

[2] Cit. May, op. cit., p. 65.

[3] 1869, 22·7 m.g.; 1870, 23·25; 1871, 105.

[4] The debt then amounted to 1,056 m.g. in paper and 275 m.g. in silver. 1,007 m.g. were owned abroad. The State had also been obliged to sell more of its properties, including the Eisenerz works in Styria.

seventy founded in or after that year. Only one of the seven older provincial banks failed, but forty-four of the sixty-five new ones.

We shall return later to the long-term economic effects of Black Friday, which was made more dismal still by natural disasters later in the year: an outbreak of cholera, a bad cereals harvest, phylloxera in the vineyards, while bark-boring beetle and black arches destroyed large tracts of forest. Its immediate political effect was to deal a shattering blow to popular faith in the blessings of economic Liberalism, and also, in the personal integrity of a number of its practitioners in high places. Herbst and Brestl seem to have kept their hands clean, but according to one writer[1] few others among the Liberal leaders did so. Giskra and Banhals were especially badly compromised, and a remarkably high proportion of the Deputies had business interests, in the service of which they used their political influence quite openly.[2] The outcry against the scandals, the call for 'a party with clean hands', was not the least loud among the younger generation of the Germans themselves, whose dissatisfaction was aggravated by their resentment against their Party leader, Herbst, a man of ability and courage, and also of financial probity, but dogmatic and dictatorial, compelling obedience through his choleric temper and bitter tongue, but unable to evoke affection.

When the scandals came, the threads snapped, and a number of malcontents formed themselves into a new fraction of 'Progressives' (these were largely identical with the old Autonomists), and a few, whose revulsions had been still stronger, into a group calling themselves 'Viennese Radicals'.

Elections were due in the autumn, and as these three groups still formed a single 'Club', the Left still emerged as much the strongest single party, with 150 Deputies (eighty-eight 'Old Liberals', fifty-seven 'Progressives' and five 'Viennese Radicals'). Of the other mandates, fifty-four went to the 'Constitutional Great Landlords', led by Carlos Auersperg. Hohenwart had brought together the German Clericals, Slovene Clericals and Moravian Czechs in a 'Party of the Right' which secured forty-three mandates. Forty-nine went to the Poles, thirty-three to the Bohemian Czechs, fourteen to Ruthenes, three to Slovene Liberals and ten to smaller parties and independents. As the Bohemian Czechs still refused to attend the Reichsrat, the Left (to which the Ruthenes attached themselves) still had a clear majority, and the Emperor reappointed Auersperg, who made only a few changes in his Government.

[1] Uhlirz, II. 2,945.

[2] Those interested can find piquant details, both on the *Krach* itself and on the persons involved, in Rogge's work; also in Schäffle, op. cit., *passim*, and in Tschuppik, p. 231. Of the 167 Reichstag Deputies (excluding the absentees), 46 held business positions. The 18 Deputies from Lower Austria included 12 Company Directors, holding between them 38 directorships. The Herrenhaus, which contained many newly elected peers, was no whit better. It is fair to point out, as Plener does in his recollections, that the corruption was not confined to the Liberals and was in full swing under the Hohenwart Government.

The second Auersperg Government concentrated on filling in those gaps in its anti-clerical programme which had had to be left open until the Concordat was out of the way, and succeeded in passing laws providing that the appointment and dismissal of priests lay with the Government, levying the 'Religious Fund' on ecclesiastical property and conferring legal status on the non-Catholic confessions. But all these measures had rough passages, and the Emperor refused his sanction to a Bill for putting monasteries (the membership of which had doubled again since the Concordat) under State control, while another, for facilitating mixed marriages, failed to pass the Herrenhaus.

And the fight against the Church seemed to have exhausted the energies of the Liberals. They had put through the bulk of their demands in this field, although at the cost of making many implacable enemies – among them the Emperor – and they had also realized practically all the rest of their positive political programme, this again at a cost to themselves: for many of their reforms had inevitably gone to strengthen classes and forces fundamentally hostile to them. Now little remained for them to do but to exercise a financial-economic domination which had shown its feet of clay. The virtue had gone out of them, and their last two or three years of office were practically barren. They incurred a good deal of unpopularity for their handling of the negotiations with Hungary on the economic clauses of the Compromise, which came up for revision in 1877 – this rather unfairly, for the results were not unfavourable to Cis-Leithania; its quota towards the common expenses was reduced by 1·4%, leaving the respective figures of 68·6% and 31·4%; the Hungarians accepted a quota of 70:30 for the amortization of the debt to the National Bank, and agreed on a reorganization of the Bank (now called the 'Austro-Hungarian Bank') which gave them a somewhat larger voice in its operations.

But all Austrians always thought that they were being overreached by the Hungarians in any transactions between the two (the Hungarians reciprocated the belief quite as fixedly) and the Liberals were abused for not having done better still. Their end came with the outbreak of the Eastern Crisis described in another section of this chapter. As soon as the possibility of Austria's either annexing or occupying Bosnia began to be canvassed, either course was vigorously opposed by a section of the Liberals, headed by their official leader, Herbst, who disliked either, partly on grounds of economy, and partly because they did not want to see the number of Slavs in the Monarchy increased. Moreover, they claimed, as a point of principle, that Parliament had a right to a voice in foreign policy; at least, that foreign political enterprises involving expenditure (as either annexation or occupation must do) could not constitutionally be undertaken without the consent of the Reichsrat. When Andrássy, who had been something less than candid about his intentions when addressing the Delegations, after all begged for and received a European mandate for the occupation, the resentment of the Liberals ran very high. They protested vehemently against the *fait accompli*, asserting the constitutional claim described above, and threatened to refuse to vote either the occupation, the credits for it, or the army estimates, which had now come up for their decennial renewal, even demanding that the war strength of the defence forces be reduced from 800,000 to 600,000. They were in a strong position because the Minister of Defence wanted a new Army Law, for which a two-thirds majority was needed.

Herbst's constitutional claim was entirely justified by the wording of the Constitution, but it seems clear that Francis Joseph had never understood that document as capable of such an interpretation, and the cup of his resentment against the Liberals was filled. He had never liked them, but he had stuck to them in default of an alternative, and partly, perhaps, on Andrássy's advice. When on 5 July, the defection of his own followers caused Auersperg to offer his resignation again (he had already offered it once, over the negotiations with Hungary), it was not refused.

This was the first great conflict which had occurred between the Crown and the Reichsrat over the fundamental point of their respective competences, and the fact that the Crown got its way was probably the turning-point in the political development, in this respect, of Austria. The defeat, over it, of the German Liberals also marked the real end of their political hegemony. The change to the new era did not, however, come abruptly. Auersperg had to remain in office for a long six months more, during which enough German Liberals more pliable than Herbst were found to enable the Reichsrat to vote acceptance of the Treaty of Berlin, and to vote the army a year's credit and a 'provisional' quota of recruits.[1] In February 1879, a new Government was formed under Dr Stremayr, but this was admittedly only a stop-gap until the Emperor's old henchman, Count Taaffe, should have collected enough followers to form a stable administration.

Even now, Francis Joseph did not want a complete change of course; he had put aside the idea of Austro-Slavism for good and all, and his quarrel with the German Liberals was by no means with their Germandom, nor even with their internal policy; but only over their attitude towards those questions which he regarded as falling within his own sphere of prerogative. He would have let them continue in office if they had met him on this point, and Taaffe even hoped at first to form another administration composed purely of Liberals.[2] But they remained obstinate, and also disunited. They could, or would, give Taaffe none of the assurances which Francis Joseph regarded as essential, and the Emperor felt it impossible to rely on a Party

[1] Later the House consented, with an exceedingly ill grace, and demanding budgetary cuts in return, to prolong the existing arrangements until 1889.
[2] Czedik, I. 304.

which was capable of disavowing its leader at a crucial moment, or one which could not be trusted to support the Emperor in his foreign policy.[1]

On the other hand, Taaffe found it fairly easy to get promises of support from the Poles, and from the Clericals and most of the Feudals.[2] This would still have been too little for a secure majority, but an important change was coming about in Czech politics.

Some years before a malcontent group had come into being in Prague which in 1874[3] had constituted themselves as a 'Young Czech Party', under the leadership of Dr Skladkovsky[4] and the brothers Eduard and Julius Gregr. The Young Czechs were much more radical than the Old on social issues, and strongly anti-clerical. In these respects their tenets were so similar to those of the German Liberals that the latter, in their innocence, actually thought of them as potential allies. This was a disastrous illusion; but it was a fact that the Young Czechs disapproved of their elders' alliance with the Feudal Landowners and the Clericals.

Another illusion of the Germans', fostered by the fact that in 1875 Eduard Gregr had written in a pamphlet that 'the Bohemian State Rights, as then formulated, were not worth a pipe of tobacco', was that the Young Czechs were nationally less chauvinistic than their elders. The reverse was the truth, and even on the point of State Rights the Young Czechs, when they got the chance, opened their mouths even wider than the Old.[5] But they did hold, as a point of tactics, that it was unprofitable for the Czechs to absent themselves from the Reichsrat, on the theoretical ground that it was not legally competent to legislate for Bohemia; in practice, this was simply playing into the Germans' hands. Since their constitution as a Party they had been urging that the Czechs should return to the Reichsrat, and under pressure from

[1] Bruegel, *Gesch.*, II. 257, quotes the Minutes of the Crown Council of 22 May 1879, at which the question of getting the Czechs into a future government was discussed. Francis Joseph said that it was necessary to have a majority 'on which one could count in general questions'. Taaffe described the general attitude of the Left as 'definitely directed against the power-position of the Monarchy'.

[2] The 'Feudals' usually so called were safely on his side, and he now persuaded a section of the Constitutional Landowners to go over to them. Of the remainder, twenty continued in alliance with the Left, while a smaller number, mainly from Moravia, formed a centre Party, often known, after its leader, as the 'Coronini Club'.

[3] The break-away had begun in 1863, when the younger generation had objected to Palacký's and Rieger's endorsement of Russia's repression of the Polish revolt. The group had, however, not split away so long as it seemed possible that the alliance with the Feudals might bear fruit, and had thus constituted itself as a Party only when the Hohenwart experiment had been irretrievably abandoned.

[4] Skladkovsky (popularly known as 'the honest Czech') had been condemned to death for complicity in the 'conspiracy' of May 1849, and although reprieved, had spent several years in prison.

[5] During the negotiations with Badeni in 1896 this same Gregr had wanted to make his Party's consent to the agreement conditional on recognition by the Government of Bohemian State Rights (Suttner, op. cit., I. 138).

them, which was strong (for, although as yet hardly represented in the Landtag, they already had a big following in Bohemia[1]), the Czech leaders now intimated to Taaffe their willingness to come to Vienna, on terms.

The negotiations did not go easily, partly because of Francis Joseph's mistrust of the Czech nationalists, especially the Young Czechs,[2] but eventually the Czechs agreed to return to Vienna if they received adequate administrative and cultural concessions. When their terms had been agreed (although not published), elections were held (July 1879) which gave a majority, although a small one, for the Right[3] and the Emperor appointed Taaffe Minister President.

Even this did not signify an abrupt or immediate change of front, for Taaffe announced his Government as standing 'above the Parties', and as first composed it included three, if not four, men who ranked as German Liberals,[4] and the only immediate concession to the Czechs was the appointment of one of them (Prazak, incidentally, a Moravian) as Minister without Portfolio in charge of Czech interests. But the Germans accepting portfolios had done so as individuals, not as representatives of their Party, which had not even been consulted when the appointments were made and did not regard them as committing it to support of the Government;[5] while Taaffe, for his part, did not regard them as binding him to consult the Party's wishes. Between 1880 and 1882 the Czechs' bill was accordingly honoured in the form of three enactments. The first, dated 19 April 1880, and itself the work of the German, Stremayr, was a new set of language decrees for Bohemia and Moravia, which laid down that all State administrative and judicial officials, in any part of either Land, were bound to use the language employed by the 'party'

[1] The conflict between the two parties is described by Denis, op. cit., II. 562 ff.

[2] At the Crown Council referred to above, Francis Joseph was most insistent that if the Czechs came in, the Great Landowners must be represented 'for without them, the Czechs would be no advantage to the Conservative side in the Reichsrat'. Taaffe agreed. Even Rieger would be dangerous unless yoked to the Feudalists, and it would be exceedingly dangerous if the Young Czechs came in alone.

[3] The figures were complicated, especially by the disintegration of the Constitutional Great Landlords. The main strength of the Right lay in three big groups: the Polish Club (which included five Ruthenes) with 57 Deputies; the Party of the Right, or Hohenwart Club (German Clericals, the Bohemian Feudalists and some Slovenes, Croats and Roumanians) also with 57; and the Czechs, now comprising all the Czechs, including those of Moravia, with 54. The backbone of the Left consisted of the 91 'Liberals' (this figure includes 20 former Constitutional Landowners), 54 Progressives, 8 Styrian 'Progressives', 5 'Viennese Democrats' and 2 German Nationalists. The remainder, the Coronini Club, the Italians and some non-Party Deputies, divided their votes. The Right was generally reckoned to have 179 members and the Left, 174.

[4] Stremayr (Cults and Education, and Justice), Horst (Defence), Korb-Weidenheim (Commerce), Baron von Chertek (Finance). The other members of the Cabinet were Ziemialkowski (for the Poles), Prazak (for the Czechs) and Count Julius Falkenhayn (Agriculture).

[5] See Plener, *Erinnerungen*, II. 167 ff.

with whom they were dealing, either orally or in writing. Officials of these services had to address autonomous bodies in the language of the latter. The second modified the franchise to the Bohemian Landtag in such fashion as to increase the representation of the Czechs in the First Curia, which was now to elect its representatives by constituencies, instead of *en bloc*, and also in the Chambers of Commerce. The third divided the ancient University of Prague into two entirely distinct foundations, one Czech and the other German.

It was difficult to deny the justice of the second and third of these concessions (although the Germans managed to do so). Even the first did not put Czech on a full equality with German, which it left as the language of inner service. But it did create equality for the outer service, and that for the whole of each Land, so that any official in it, even if his district was one inhabited exclusively by one of its nationalities only, was, in theory, required to know both languages. The Germans protested furiously, and when Taaffe refused to give way, Stremayr, Horst, Chertek and Korb-Weidenheim, tired of being abused as traitors, left the Government. The Liberal Party now declared itself to be 'Oppositional', leaving as 'Government Parties' what came to be known as the 'Iron Ring' of Feudalists, Clericals and Slavs. The vacant Ministerial posts were filled accordingly. A Pole (Dunajewski) became Finance Minister, Prazak took over Justice, and two non-Party men (Baron Pino and Count Welter von Welfersheimb) became Ministers of Commerce and Defence respectively.

This was the beginning of the 'Taaffe Era', which was destined to last until 1893, so that Taaffe holds the record of having kept going at the head of Austrian affairs longer than anyone since Metternich and Kolowrat before him, and much longer than anyone after him. But he did so because his government was, at bottom, not Parliamentary. It was supported by the 'Iron Ring', and in internal affairs, paid, within limits, deference to the wishes and interests of the parties which formed the Parliamentary 'majority'. Thus, generally speaking, agrarian interests were favoured rather than industrial, clerical more than free-thinking Liberal, Slav more than German. But it must be emphasized that the parties of the 'Iron Ring' were not the masters of Austria even to the extent that the Liberals had been. Taaffe was not their servant, but the Emperor's: so he described himself, and this was why Francis Joseph, who also saw his regime in that light,[1] gave him his confidence for so long. And his internal policy was far from being one-sided, as the Germans, for whom not ruling with them was equivalent to ruling

---

[1] When, after Taaffe's resignation, the question arose of appointing a Coalition Ministry, and Francis Joseph hesitated, someone said to him that Taaffe's regime, too, had been a coalition, Francis Joseph replied, 'It was not a Parliamentary coalition, but an Emperor's Ministry' (Corti, *Der Alte Kaiser*, p. 180).

against them, always called it.[1] He himself once described it, in an often-quoted phrase, as 'keeping all the nationalities of the Monarchy in a condition of even and well-modulated discontent'. In fact, his concessions to his supporters[2] never went beyond the reasonable; above all, he made no single move to alter the structure of the Monarchy in the direction of more federalism.

He has been accused equally of fomenting national passions, and of repressing them. In fact, he did neither. Except in the case of the international workers' movement, he repressed nothing, and neither did he foster. He let things take their course, balancing and adjusting when they threatened to get out of equilibrium. His opponents described his policy as one of 'muddling through' (*fortwürsteln*),[3] which, in a way, was what it was; but he muddled with very considerable adroitness. His regime was not only the longest experienced by Austria after the Vormärz, but also the least tumultuous.

But it was also the least constructive, for good or ill. Taaffe not only did not produce an answer to the riddle of the Monarchy; he did not even look for one. Thus in the whole decade after the Czechs had re-entered the Reichsrat there is only one single event which is most appropriately recorded in this sketch of Austria's central political life.[4] In 1882 another franchise reform was enacted, which extended the vote in the urban and rural communes. This enfranchised large numbers of peasants and *petits bourgeois*,[5] both classes the sworn enemies of big business and financial interests. In consequence, when the next elections were held (in the summer of 1885) they brought a further swing to the Right. The Poles (fifty-seven), Czechs (fifty-six) and Clericals held their own, although the nineteen German Clericals now formed a separate group under the Princes Alfred and Alois Liechtenstein, leaving the Hohenwart Club with thirty-four members. Various splinter groups (there were in all twelve Parliamentary Clubs) brought the voting strength of the Right up to 190. The 'German Left' was down to 136 in all, including four Radicals; the non-Radicals re-grouped into a 'German-Austrian Club' (eighty-four) and a 'German Club' (forty-eight),[6] who, however, agreed to sit together under a single chairman as the 'United German Left'. With its splinter groups, and counting in the eleven members of the Coronini Club, the Left mustered a total voting strength of 163.

---

[1] See on this Redlich, *Franz Joseph*, p. 371. He was also a favourite of the Archduke Albrecht's (Charmatz, *Lebensbilder*, p. 151). Taaffe presided over no less than twenty-two Ministries.   [2] For the educational legislation of the period, see below, p. 621.

[3] The phrase, often attributed to Taaffe himself, was in fact coined by Herbst.

[4] Unless we count the decennial renewal of the Compromise, which this time (1889) went through without substantial changes.

[5] The reform increased the number of voters in the rural communes by 34% and in the urban, by 26%.

[6] The German Club was itself composed of three fractions: the *Deutscher Klub* (24); the *Deutschnationale Vereinigung* (18); and the *Verband der Deutschnationalen* (6).

The other developments of the period are more conveniently described under subject headings, allowing us to bring up to date the general picture of the state of the various economic, social and national forces in Austria at the point near the end of Taaffe's regime when the pressure of them compelled the end of temporising.

In the half-century up to 1890, the population of Austria had again increased rapidly. The 17½ millions at which it had stood at the end of the Vormärz,[1] had risen to nearly 20½ millions in 1869, over 22 in 1880, and nearly 24 in 1890. This growth had been accompanied by further differentiation and urbanization, although neither of these processes had gone on so fast as in England or Germany. The biggest gainer among the occupational groups had been industry, but its progress had been neither easy nor uniform. The year after the reorganization of 1848 had been very favourable for those Austrian industries whose chief markets lay inside the Monarchy, and even to some of the exporting industries, but the freer trade with the West had proved a two-edged sword, and the balance of advantage had been in Austria's favour only so long as the depreciation of the currency acted as an export premium. After the abrupt check administered to the boom by the Stock Exchange crash of 1857, industry had suffered for a decade under the rigidly deflationary policy adopted by the Government, the shortage of private credit, and the impoverishment caused by the over-numerous wars and mobilizations. As, under these conditions, Austrian industry had developed more slowly than German, the Austrian industrialists welcomed the 'economic divorce' of 1865 between the Austrian and German systems, and this was, in fact, followed almost immediately by the spectacular boom years of 1868–72, which brought with them another very rapid spurt of industrialization. This, however, was followed in its turn by the ultra-sensational *Krach* of 1873, the dimensions of which may be indicated by the single fact that the consumption of iron in the Monarchy fell by almost half in three years (from 18·2 million tons in 1872 to 9·5 million in 1875), the number of workers in the iron and steel industries falling in the same measure. Meanwhile, even the increased protection which Austrian industry had secured against German had been partly counter-balanced by the treaties with the West, to which a similar treaty with Italy had been added in April 1867. Austrian woollens and textiles, in particular, complained of under-cutting from Britain.

The strong agitation for protection which this situation had evoked among the Austrian manufacturers had been opposed by the agricultural interests, especially those of Hungary (with whom the commercial policy of the Monarchy had to be agreed), who not only wanted maximum freedom for the exportation of their own products, but naturally preferred a system which allowed them to import cheaper and better articles from abroad to one which

[1] Excluding that of the Italian Lands lost to the Monarchy in 1859 and 1866.

confined them to the expensive and far inferior products of the Austrian factories; and Hungary made her consent to the introduction of protection conditional on revision of the financial clauses of the Compromise. The competition from other countries continued, and meanwhile, the internal effects of the *Krach* were slow to work themselves out. The foreign capital which had so largely contributed to the boom had retreated out of the Monarchy, and the Austrian public, reverting to its old mentality, preferred to put its savings into savings-banks or Government stocks, rather than invest them in equities or deposit them with the banks, which were themselves short of money for financing industry.[1] Industry found it almost impossible to obtain long-term credit, while short-term credit was exceedingly expensive.

The Government itself, although at that time still a 'Liberal' one, had been frightened by the *Krach*, and to avoid a repetition of it, discouraged the formation of new joint-stock companies, for which it issued licences only sparingly.[2]

The depression had worsened steadily until 1876, and for two or three years after that had been kept on the low level then reached by the threatening international situation. It was not until 1879 that the war clouds in the Balkans passed, and confidence returned, assisted by another series of good harvests. By this time, too, agreement had been reached with Hungary to continue the old customs alliance (in practice, union) and to allow the introduction of some protection against the outer world, provided it was kept on a low level. On 1 January 1879, Austria had then introduced a new autonomous tariff, and whether as an effect of this or in spite of it (both views have been maintained), and whether thanks to or in spite of Government policy, which certainly favoured agricultural interests where they clashed with industrial,[3] but presumably wanted at least some industries developed – a number of industries made important progress in the next few years. The history of the railways has been mentioned elsewhere: the steady but modest progress during the years of financial stringency, followed by the feverish expansion during the great boom. Private activity in this field also had been abruptly halted by Black Friday, but there had been this difference, as compared with industry, that the State had perforce seen to it that the railway construction was carried on, partly to relieve unemployment, partly on

---

[1] This attitude, general before 1848, now became almost a fixation. In 1904, the capita deposited with savings-banks and building societies was 5,922 million kronen, while only 1,818 million kronen was in bills of exchange. 250 million kronen were on deposit with the banks, and 5,000 million kronen in savings-banks, 59·96 of this being invested in mortgages.

[2] The number of joint stock companies in Austria in 1895 (299) was only seven higher than in 1878.

[3] Benedikt, op. cit., p. 125, even attributes the social legislation of the Taaffe period to a wish 'to hinder the development of industry, the detrimental effects of which, in the form of flight from the land and higher agricultural wages, the big landlords were feeling'.

strategic grounds. By 1880 the Cis-Leithanian mileage had risen to 11,429 km.

Trade and finance had followed the same rhythm, and so, on the whole, had urbanization. Throughout the period there had been a steady drift to the towns of the victims of agricultural depression or rural congestion, so that the increase in the urban population, especially that of the larger towns, had always been faster than that of the rural. The movement, however, had been rapid only at the times of industrial prosperity; during the slumps it had slowed down, and there had even been a certain reverse flow of unemployed factory workers returning to the land.

The overall picture in 1890 was thus one of an economy which stood halfway between the rural societies to which Austria herself had belonged a century earlier, such as Russia and the Balkans still were, and the much more advanced ones west of her frontiers. The pattern was still mainly agricultural, and mainly rural. Agriculture still employed 62·4% of the working population,[1] and two out of every three Austrians still lived in a scattered farm or a small village. The great majority even of the towns were small and essentially semi-rural; of the 1,312 'towns' of Cis-Leithania, 1,062, with an aggregate population of 3,011,000, had populations of less than 5,000, and 150 more (967,000) of 5–10,000.

At the same time, industry and mining accounted for 21·2% of the gainfully employed population, and the figures for some industries were quite imposing: 296,000 persons were employed in textiles, excluding home-workers – perhaps half a million in all; 149,000 in food-processing, breweries, etc.; 99,000 in the metal industries, 72,000 in stone and glass; 57,000 in the machine industry; 33,000 in the chemical. The manufacturing industry employed in all 2,880,000 persons. There were a few really large cities; thus Vienna (including its suburbs) had a population of 1,305,000; Prague had 184,000; Trieste (whose municipal boundaries had been enlarged), 150,000; Lemberg, 128,000; and Graz, 114,000. Brünn, Cracow, Czernowitz and Pilsen were all over the 50,000 mark and Linz not far below it. The aggregate population of the twenty-two towns with populations of 20,000 plus, was 2,870,000, and those of the sixty-eight of 10–20,000, 920,000.

The smaller towns now included a number of a type hardly before known to Austria, the factory or mining community pure and simple.

Trade, banking and communications now employed between them 6·2% of the employed population, and the professional and leisured classes, too, had increased.

While the changes so far effected had been relatively modest, the trend was a fairly steady one. Every year saw the percentage of the population em-

[1] This figure, moreover, is almost certainly too low, for the Austrian statistics, like the Hungarian, contained a rubric for 'day labourers in various occupations', and many of these were certainly employed in agriculture.

ployed in agriculture a little smaller, that of most other groups, especially industry, a little larger, and every year the percentage living in towns, especially the largest towns, increased.

Important for the future of Austria was the shift that was taking place in the distribution of the population. Galicia, where the natural increase had been particularly rapid, now had well the largest population of any Land, with over 6.5 millions, Bohemia coming next with 5.8. The growth had been much slower in the German Lands, except Lower Austria, where the figure had been swollen by the rapid growth of Vienna and its suburbs.

The chief centres of industrial expansion were still the traditional areas: Lower Austria and the Bohemian Lands (which had increased their lead owing to the development of the North-Moravian-Silesian area into a great industrial complex).[1] The iron works of Styria, too, had recovered with the foundation in 1881 of the great Alpine Montan concern, and thereafter had expanded greatly. Otherwise, there had been relatively little industrial development in the Alpine Lands, except Upper Austria, where a munitions industry had been founded in Steyr. A textile industry was taking root in Vorarlberg. A newcomer to industry was Galicia, where oil had been discovered (as a commercial proposition) in the 1870s, and the exploitation of it was growing into one of the big industries of the Monarchy (although the profits from it went largely abroad). Galicia remained, indeed, overwhelmingly agricultural: in 1890 seventy-seven per cent of its population was still employed in agriculture, forestry or fisheries, the highest figure of any Land except Dalmatia.

Here we may record the pleasing fact that by the end of the period, Austria's finances had at last reached equilibrium. The hard-earned gains of 1868-73 had, indeed, soon been lost again, for the *Krach* caused a grievous falling-off in State revenue, and the State had also been forced to step in and take over bankrupt railway lines, and carry on with their construction, and with other public works, to relieve unemployment. Thus, although attempts had been made to increase taxation, every budget up to 1885, except only that of 1880, had closed with a deficit, which had been covered by the regular device of borrowing.

The deficits, however, had not been heavy, except in 1878, when the Eastern crisis and the occupation of Bosnia had involved the Monarchy in a deficit of 93 m.g. (18% of its total expenditure). After the introduction of the autonomous tariff the balance of payments became favourable, and with the

[1] In 1890 59% of all industrial enterprises in Cis-Leithania, 65% of their labour force and 59% of industrial production were concentrated in the Bohemian Lands. Since 1848 industrial production in these Lands had risen from 46% to 59% of the total for Cis-Leithania, while the share of the Alpine Lands had sunk from 40% to 33% and that of the other Lands from 14% to 8% (*M.K.P.*, III. 277).

easing of the situation in the Balkans, the national credit improved (although that the bank-notes reached parity in 1879, was due to the fall in the world price of silver, and rather an embarrassment than otherwise). The new loans were raised on comparatively easy terms. There were deficits again in 1887 and 1888, but 1889 closed with a surplus, which now became regular. Another tax reform came in the same year, and at last tapped so much of Austria's own resources as to make her independent of borrowing abroad.

As these economic developments occurred, the pattern of Austria's social and political forces had, up to a point, adapted itself to them, although the effects had inevitably lagged behind the causes which produced them. The most immediate and obvious of them were those deriving from the growth in numbers, wealth, and in the influence which it was able to exert through such channels as the Press, of the upper strata of the German-Austrian bourgeoisie of the German and Bohemian Lands. This class, as we have seen, supplied the Ministries and their supporters from 1861 to 1878, and the legislation enacted by the Reichsrats of those years was, in the main, dictated by their interests and their *Weltanschauung*. Even after the government slipped from their hands as from 1878, their wishes and interests remained something which no government was able to, or tried to, ignore.

The advance of the bourgeoisie was naturally accompanied by retreats on the part of its chief opponents, the aristocracy and the Catholic Church. By 1890 the direct power of the aristocracy was a shadow of what it had been in 1848, not to speak of 1748. Its fight against the bureaucratic neo-absolutism of the 1850s had been doughty and pertinacious – it had been one of the main threads of the political history of the decade – but had, after all, ended in defeat. The new political system, especially during Taaffe's regime, was still weighted in favour of the aristocrats, but it did not depend on them. They were now in the essentially false position of a class which still enjoyed the privileges conferred on it in earlier ages in return for the performance of public functions which were now no longer exacted from it. Where its members took part in political life at all, it was now, even more than in the Vormärz (when the process had already begun), merely as representatives and defenders of their own class interests, which, since the positions defended were those of excessive and anachronistic advantage, brought on them the hostility of all other interests and classes. Many of them turned their backs altogether on the rest of Austria (except the Emperor). They formed a tight little clique in which everyone knew everyone else, and if of the same sex, was on *du* terms with him, and spent their time in gambling, horse-racing, exchanging scandal and seducing other people's wives and daughters. The more respectable and/or impoverished (the terms were nearly, although not quite, interchangeable) shut themselves up on their country estates, which they formed into miniature projections into the nineteenth century of a dream-world which had been reality in the eighteenth. It has been remarked that after the loss of their power, they treated the bourgeoisie with more disdain than in the days when they could afford to do so.

The Church had suffered sharp reverses with the passage of the anti-clerical legislation of 1868–73. It never quite made these good. Efforts by Cardinal Rauscher to found a Pan-Cis-Leithanian Catholic Party broke down on the usual rocks: the different peoples could not be persuaded to sink their national differences, and even the Germans were unable to agree on the issue of federalism versus centralism (it was this difference that killed the 'Casino movement' of the 1870s out of which the party should have emerged).

One must, however, be careful not to exaggerate the extent to which the bourgeoisie had triumphed over its rivals. The losses of those two factors were not mortal, and those of the Church, hardly even crippling. Francis Joseph himself perhaps grew somewhat more Josephinian as the influences of his mother and of Rauscher faded,[1] but he remained a staunch enough Catholic. In spite of repeated efforts, some of which had important political consequences,[2] the Catholic Party failed to obtain either the re-Catholicization of the elementary schools, or the general reduction of the school years to six, but in 1893 it got the 1878 Act amended to provide that the 'responsible head of a school' must be 'a person qualified to give religious instruction in the confession of the majority of its pupils', and Lands were given power to reduce the pupils' hours of schooling in their last two years.[3] In practice, most of the schools outside the big centres were still staffed with products of the seminaries, and the adult peasant still usually took his political cue from his parish priest's Sunday sermon. The very virulence and vulgarity of the Liberals' attacks awoke in Catholic circles a spirit of combativeness which made *croyant* Catholicism a more living force in Austria than it had been, perhaps, since the days of Maria Theresa. This found impressive expression in the 'Catholic Congresses' (*Katholikentage*), the first of which met in Vienna in 1877. The movement itself contained an element of revolt against the extreme hierarchical spirit of the traditional Church, and it was none the weaker for this tinge of democratic appeal. One way and another, in spite of Rauscher's failure, Catholicism came nearer than any other political force in Austria, except perhaps that of Social Democracy, to transcending nationalism, and for many years it remained the chief challenger to Liberalism for the allegiance of the German bourgeoisie; as, when Liberalism withered, it challenged German nationalism longer than any other force.

Its spiritual strength still enjoyed ample material backing, for the Church

---

[1] The Archduchess died on 5 May 1872, Rauscher, on 24 November 1875.

[2] It was the decision taken by the Old Czechs in 1868 to support a proposal by Prince Alois Liechtenstein to reduce the term of school years to six (five days in the week) that was largely responsible for the downfall of their Party in the 1891 elections.

[3] It is fair to point out that the eight-years schooling was almost universally unpopular among the peasants themselves.

and its institutions remained among the biggest landowners of Austria, and their wealth increased rather than diminished.[1]

Nor were the great landowners at all a negligible force, even in 1890. The Curia system still left them an influence out of all proportion to their numbers in the Landtage and the Reichsrat, and it was even greater in the Herrenhaus, and perhaps most important of all, in the innermost circles of the Court. Aristocrats still filled a large proportion of the highest administrative posts: in 1905–7 twenty-one of the thirty-four officials in the Ministry of the Interior of the grade of Ministerialrat and upwards were Counts or Barons, eight out of nineteen in the Ministry of Agriculture, and nine out of twenty-four Heads of Departments in that of Railways. Only aristocrats were heads of *Statthaltereien*: one Prince, seven Counts, five Barons, and one Ritter.[2] And this position, too, was still backed by great wealth. The landed magnates had had their share of the difficulties that had overtaken all Austrian agriculture after 1849, when it had had to face the full competition of Hungarian wheat, live-stock and wine, to which, after the mid-1870s, had been added the competition (which threatened Hungary also) of overseas wheat and cattle. But as we have said elsewhere,[3] most of the big men had survived this. With the compensation which they had received under the land reform, and the credit which they had been able to obtain after it, relatively easily and cheaply (although money had been tight for all classes in the 1850s and 1860s), they had been able to modernize and rationalize their production, cutting their labour costs by mechanization and extensive employment of seasonal labour,[4] and to go over largely to the production of industrial crops, among which an enormous part was played by the production of sugar beet. The cultivation of this crop, after its small beginnings in the 1830s, had made extraordinary progress after 1850: in 1892, 175,800 hectares were under it in Bohemia and 73,500 in Moravia (it was almost confined to these two Lands).[5] Most of this was grown on the big estates, and where it was grown by peasants, they took it to the local magnate's refinery. Thus in 1886, eighty out of the hundred and twenty refineries in Bohemia belonged to magnates, as did five hundred of the nine hundred breweries and three hundred of the four hundred distilleries. Another source of their wealth was timber and its products. Many of the forests had, indeed, been bought by the big new

---

[1] Tiefen, op. cit., quotes on p. 23 figures showing that in 1902 the income of the Church in Bohemia was 15·2 million kronen, of which it spent only 8·96 and re-invested 6·26.

[2] Tiefen, op. cit., p. 63.

[3] See above, p. 466.

[4] At the German-Austrian Conference of 1872, when the Prussian agriculturalists were complaining of labour shortage, it was stated that the Austrian landlords were not suffering from this, because they had mechanized their production in time. Seasonal labour was always available from North Hungary and Galicia (Brügel, *Gesch.*, II. 177).

[5] Outside them, only 9,354 ha. were under sugar-beet in Silesia and 575 ha. in Lower Austria. 212 of the 216 refineries were in Bohemia and Moravia.

industrial companies, but the magnates still had a large share in the ownership of the forests and the exploitation of their products, including paper. In Bohemia, in 1886, they had in their service 72,000 workers, 300,000 day labourers, 15,000 foresters and gamekeepers and 40,000 carters.[1]

It is true that the appearance was often rosier than the reality, for many of the great estates were heavily mortgaged, and when Prince x figured as owner of a sawmill or a refinery, he might well be only a very minor participant in its profits. Nevertheless, the big landowners had been able not only to retain the nominal ownership of most of their estates, but to extend them. The number of legalized *fidei-commissa* had increased steadily. It was stated in the Reichsrat in 1883 that there were over 292 of these institutions in Austria, comprising 880 estates and with a total acreage of 1,140,193 hectares. 579,000 hectares lay in Bohemia; 178,000 in Moravia; 126,000 in Lower Austria; 70,000 in Carinthia, etc.; only Salzburg, Vorarlberg and the Bukovina had no *fidei-commissa*.[2]

The agrarian statistics for 31 December 1896 showed another increase, although a small one, since the Reichsrat, whose consent was now required for new formations, was growing reluctant to give it. Nevertheless, the number of *fidei-commissa* had risen to 297 and their acreage to 1,200,000 ha.[3] At the latter date, 8,700,000 hectares in Austria, or 29% of the whole area of the country, fell into the category of 'large estates', defined as estates of at least 200 ha. and paying at least 200 Kronen in land tax, and of this, perhaps three-quarters consisted of really large estates of 2,000 ha. plus. In Bohemia the figure was 1,436,089 ha., owned by 151 persons, out of 5,194,500 ha.; in Moravia, 558,625 ha. (73 owners) out of an area of 2,222,200 ha.

A few of these very large estates were commercially owned, and another fraction belonged either to the Church, or to the Crown or the Imperial family; a few to business enterprises. But the great majority were still owned by the *Hochadel*. Thus in Bohemia, Prince Johann Schwarzenberg's estates covered 177,000 ha., those of Count J. Colloredo-Mansfeld, 57,000, of Prince Egon Schwarzenberg, 39,000 and of Prince Johann Liechtenstein, 36,000. In all, the few hundred biggest families of Austria probably owned at least twenty per cent of its area.

The feudal landlords had thus salvaged quite a lot, but by no means all that they lost went into the balance of the bourgeoisie. That class, after all, owed its years of office chiefly to the fact that they were Germanic and centralist, and at the time, the Monarch's most useful agents for the

---

[1] Bignon, *La Grande Propriété en Bohème* (1886), cit. Denis, p. 330.
[2] Kolmer, III. p. 323.
[3] I take these and the following figures from Tiefen, op. cit., p. 190. Tiefen is quoting the statistics published in the *Statistisches Monatsschrift*, 1900–1, which is unfortunately not available to me.

domestic, and still more the foreign, policy which he was then pursuing. And its heyday was short. After 1878 Austria never again saw a Government composed solely of their representatives, nor even a Minister President representative of them (Koerber, although untitled, came from exactly the same class of *Beamtenadel* as, for instance, Gautsch).

The men who inherited by far the greater part of the power lost by the aristocrats were the bureaucrats, who were, indeed, now overwhelmingly middle class in origin and circumstances (it was only a few plums, chiefly in the foreign service, that went almost exclusively to bearers of great names), but in their mental attitude classless (subject, of course, to the antagonism towards the poor inevitable in all States founded on property). Momentarily submerged in 1859–60 by the wave of anti-étatism which financial panic had sent washing over the country, they had very soon resurfaced to reoccupy the place in the State in which Bach had set them a decade earlier. Taaffe's regime was already a bureaucratic one in nearly all but name; those of some of his successors even dispensed with the mask.

Modern Austrian writers have a stock adjective for the rule of the Austrian bureaucrats, over their own kinsfolk or others, in the old Monarchy: it was exemplary (*vorbildlich*). Some non-Austrians have outbid even this adjective. *De mortuis nil nisi bonum*, but also μηδὲν ἀγάν. It was not as exemplary that the Austrians who knew them face to face saw their masters. Their favourite personification of the bureaucratic machine was the *Amtschimmel*, an aged and decrepit nag plodding along with infinite slowness under an enormous burden of accumulated files.[1] And the poor creature was in fact slow of foot, cumbersome, unimaginative, and snobbish, and pried into the lives of the citizens in a manner which Westerners experiencing it found quite intolerable.[2] But it is true that the Austrian service stood head and shoulders above those of Russia, or of the Balkan countries. Some of its technical services were quite outstanding, and the worst of them usually produced some result in the end. Most of its members were financially incorruptible, and they were generally prepared to help the public so long as it approached them cap in hand. From the Crown's point of view, they possessed, at this stage, the virtue of absolute loyalty. It was only in the next that they began to be influenced by national feeling, and then indeed, the Monarchy was ripe for dissolution. Until then, they helped hold it together, and in so far as the wheels of its public life went round at all, they did so mainly thanks to the efforts of its devoted, and usually competent, bureaucrats.

The other main prop of the regime was the Corps of regular officers, which was now composed, in overwhelming measure, of the same class as the bureaucrats; for after the introduction of general military service, the high

---

[1] A pun on the two meanings of the word 'Schimmel': mildew, and a white horse.
[2] For the impressions of one Briton who did know what this service was like, see Steed, op. cit., pp. 73–90.

aristocrats had 'withdrawn almost completely from the career of officer . . . Before that, the feudal magnates had been accustomed to serve at least up to the rank of Major or Captain. Now they contented themselves with that of Lieutenant of Reserve'.[1] The bulk of the officers now came out of the two Military Academies, while a few 'one-year reservists' took regular commissions when their year expired.

The change presumably made for greater efficiency, and politically, the Corps of Officers proved a 'cement' of the Monarchy more reliable even than the civil servants. The officers who took sides with their respective nationalities in the final crisis of the Monarchy were almost exclusively non-regulars.

The position of the Cis-Leithanian peasantry, as a whole, declined steadily in the 1870s and 1880s. The general effect of the removal by the Liberal Government in 1868 of these protective (or restrictive) provisions relating to peasant land which the reform of 1849 had retained had been, like those of the reform itself, to create a dichotomy between those to whom freedom came like a fertilizing spring wind and those whom its blast withered. But the earlier change had come at a time when the prices of the peasant's produce were generally high and the trade in them still largely carried on in the local market square. By 1868 the importation from Hungary was organized, and that from overseas standing on the threshold.

The freedom to borrow at will certainly benefited the thrifty farmer who employed his borrowed money productively: it enabled him to re-equip, consolidate and even enlarge his holding. Success stories were by no means unknown, especially in the fertile parts of the Alpine Lands, where the population was economically mature and credit comparatively easy. When the subject was debated in the Reichsrat in 1889 it was stated that the percentage of farms which had become more heavily indebted since 1868 was 'minute', and that indebtedness was heavier in the Tirol, to which the law had not applied, than in the Lands in which it had been applied.[2] But it is difficult to suppose that the speaker was not referring only to the Alpine Lands. Other writers give a very different picture of, for example, Galicia.[3] Here, we read, the peasant borrowed either from his ex-landlord, from a neighbour, or from the local Jewish money-lender. The landlord usually did

[1] Horsetzky, op. cit., p. 716.
[2] See the article by A. Braf in *L. U. F.*, II. I. pp.
[3] The usual rate charged by the Rustical Bank of Gablic, a Jewish enterprise which operated from 1868 to 1884, and to which one Galician peasant in every twenty was indebted, was 40%; and the bank was much less exacting than the village money-lender. At an inquiry into peasant conditions in 1882, the authorities in Galicia and the Bukovina gave as the causes for the peasant distress, 'over-population, religious, moral and intellectual degradation, frivolity, extravagance, lack of diligence and thrift, shortage of industry in the Land, competition, the many holidays and market-days, the high cost of legal procedure, and above all, the high taxes and dues' (Kolmer, III. 322).

not ask for payment in cash, but required the peasant to work his debt out, on terms which might or might not be reasonable. The neighbour usually charged 30–50%, the Jew, 50–150%, and cases of 500% were not unknown.[1] The Galician peasant, moreover, seldom borrowed for productive purposes, but usually to help himself out after a bad harvest, to pay his taxes, or for such purposes as weddings, which it was a point of prestige to celebrate on the most extravagant scale imaginable.[2] An enormous number of peasants were unable to meet these obligations, and were either evicted altogether from their homesteads, or turned into tenants of them, working for rentals more exorbitant than their old obligations when they were unfree men. According to figures given in the Reichsrat in 1880, over 37,500 holdings of real estate, by far the most of them peasant properties, came under the hammer between 1875 and 1879 alone. The creditors, incidentally, recovered only sixty per cent of their claims.

The lifting of the bans on division and alienation of peasant holdings was followed by very rapid parcellation, especially in those Slav areas where national tradition prescribed equal, or near-equal, division of an inheritance among all children. In Bohemia, where, according to Drage,[3] 41,537 new holdings were carved out of peasant properties between 1869 and 1888, 330,489 of the holdings in 1896 (38·0% of the total) were between 0·5–5 ha., and 373,088 (42·9%) under half a hectare. The figures for Moravia were, if anything, worse: 196,403 holdings (36·2%) of 0·5–5 ha. and 268,940 (49·6%) under half a hectare. Silesia showed much the same picture. In the Bukovina 90% of all holdings were of 5 ha. or less, and 59% of 1 ha. or less.

In the Bohemian Lands the rural congestion was partly relieved by the industrialization, which took many surplus hands off the land – into conditions, it is true, of miserable exploitation – and many dwarf-holders remaining on it made good enough livings growing beet for the local factory, and then working for it in the harvest weeks. But even here, and still more in primitive Galicia-Bukovina, the limit was quickly being reached when the land could support no more mouths, and the dwarf-holder's surplus children would have to follow the sold-up man into the towns, or overseas.

Among the Germans, national custom favoured the retention of the undivided *Bauernhof*, and it was stated in the 1889 debate that 'most of the holdings had remained intact'.[4] But this statement, again, is hard to reconcile with the figures. In Styria, in 1896, 62·4% of the total holdings paying land tax (covering 7·9% of the whole area) were of under 5 ha., and only 34·9%

[1] For further details on peasant indebtedness see the article by M. Ertl in *L. U. F.*, I. 512 ff.

[2] This was regular among Slavs, among those of the South even more than those of the North. It was not uncommon for a girl to be left unmarried all her life, although she had a fiancé who wanted her, because her parents could not raise the money to marry her in the style on which they insisted.

[3] Cf. Drage, op. cit., p. 65.

[4] Kolmer, IV. 293.

(covering 44·3%) between 5–50. In Upper Austria, the traditional stronghold of the comfortable yeoman farmer, the figures were 61·6% (6·8% of the area) and 37·3% (62·3%).[1] Drage writes that 'the comfortable homestead . . . still exists, but it is gradually being replaced by allotments, or else it is swallowed up in the ever-widening territory of the capitalist landlord'.[2]

The fight was, in fact, hardest of all for the occupants of the marginal Alpine farms, whose costs were increased by bad local communications and other difficulties, including the irrational siting and shape of many of their holdings.[3] If they did not subdivide so much as the Bohemian peasants, this was partly because they had, as a rule, fewer children, but even more, because their children did not want to stay on the land at all. These holdings were not divided; they simply vanished altogether. After 1869, Drage writes,[4] 'the sale of small farms began on a large scale. In one District (Bezirk) of Styria 700 small farms were put up for sale, and in one commune the peasant proprietors had diminished by 33 within a very few years'. In some mountainous areas, the population was decreasing by the end of the 1870s.

Some of these farms were bought up by valley peasants, who used them as adjuncts to their own farms, but more often, they passed out of peasant hands altogether, the purchasers being either big landlords or *nouveaux riches* industrialists, who sometimes exploited their agricultural or forestal resources (this happened where the process took place, as it did on a smaller scale, in Bohemia), or turned them down to deer forest. Even these purchasers often got the farms only at second-hand: they were first bought up by unscrupulous middle-men, who dazzled the simple peasants by dangling before their eyes sums of ready money which seemed to them enormous, but melted in their hands once they took it into the town.[5]

Some of the peasants, and some Catholic associations which took up their cause, began to agitate against these abuses in the 1870s, but got little satisfaction out of the legislature. A blanket law allowing the re-establishment of

---

[1] Figures from Tiefen, op. cit., pp. 31, 33.

[2] Op. cit., p. 64.

[3] Consolidation had not been carried out in Cis-Leithania in connection with the land reform (see above, p. 463). The shape of the plots sometimes perpetuated extraordinary relics of earlier conditions. Schiff (op. cit., I/II. p. 223) writes that in some places, 'plots 4 km. long and only 7 metres wide were no rarity'. The introduction of the free market for land aggravated the *Streusiedlung*, since a plot coming on the market might be miles away from the purchaser's other holding. In 1916, 83% of the holdings in the Tirol were dispersed, and in Dalmatia, 100%.

[4] Drage, loc. cit.

[5] In my book, *The Social Revolution in Austria*, published as long ago as 1926, I quoted Peter Rosegger's famous novel, *Jakob der Letze*, for a picture of this gradual disappearance of a Styrian mountain parish. I make bold, even at this date, to refer the reader interested in the peasant question in Austria to chapter 7 of my book. It relates, indeed, only to the Alpine Lands which formed the later Austrian Republic. Still more heartily do I recommend Rosegger's classic to any reader.

the indivisible Bauernhof was, after years of debate, adopted by the Reichsrat in 1889, but the Landtage, who were left to apply it with such modifications as seemed desirable in the light of local conditions, simply left it lying on their tables, and the same fate seems to have attended a law of the same year on *Güterschlachterei* (buying up peasant holdings, or parts of them, for profit); I have, at least, failed to find any reference to them in the Parliamentary debates of the 1890s.[1]

The *Knecht*, especially, perhaps, on a peasant farm, existed under conditions of great squalor. He usually slept in the stables, along with the horses and cows, ate miserably and was paid a pittance. He enjoyed no protective legislation at all, and his working day often began at 4 a.m., and lasted till dark. 'It is a subject of wonder,' wrote Tiefen, 'that there are grown people who would give a whole day's work for such pay,'[2] and by the 1880s they were beginning to refuse to do so, and to migrate into the towns, or overseas. Landlords were complaining of the wages which agricultural labour was demanding. It is rather difficult to reconcile these complaints with the figures recorded by observers of the wages actually paid, but it seems a fact that these were often more than the masters could easily afford to pay. Tiefen, writing of the year 1892, put the number of this class at over two millions[3] but it is not clear how they are defined. At harvest time, the bigger landlords relied chiefly on gangs of seasonal labour, who sometimes came from a long distance, or help from local dwarf-holders.[4] For this work the payment was, traditionally, chiefly in kind, in the form of an agreed proportion of the crop harvested.

Up to 1890 the richer peasants voted strictly Conservative, usually Clerical, as did most of the men enfranchised under Taaffe's reform. Almost the only stirrings of oppositional life among these classes, up to this date, were at least

[1] Opinion on the indivisible *Bauernhof* seems always to have been divided. Although the farms were, by custom, always assessed very low for the purpose, the son inheriting the Hof often found the portioning off of his co-heirs a millstone round his neck. When an inquiry into the subject was instituted in 1882, nineteen local authorities favoured re-imposition of the indivisibility, sixteen were against, and ten refused to commit themselves (Kolmer, III. 322). For a detailed account of this question, by a strong partisan of the undivided *Bauernhof*, see the article by Dr Ertl in *L. U. F.*, I. 468 ff. The 1889 Law in any case applied only to medium-sized farms.

[2] Drage, op. cit., p. 168. Both Tiefen, pp. 44, 51–5, and Drage, pp. 66 ff., give some wage figures, but these vary so much and are so complicated by payments in kind and other considerations, that it seems useless to reproduce them.

[3] Id., p. 66.

[4] When J. Howard, a travelling Englishman, made a tour of investigation, he was told in Galicia that the labourers were 'mostly small peasants with their own houses. They often had a little land of their own, or rented plots from the landlord.' (J. Howard, *Continental Farming and Peasantry*, London, 1870, p. 134.) In Bohemia, imported gang labour was used. Howard's is another hair-raising description of the miserable conditions under which Austrian farm labourers worked. It is true that they were not noticeably worse than those observed by him in France and Belgium.

half national – Czech peasants against German landlords, or Ruthene against Polish. The dwarf-holders and landless men, not possessing the vote, were politically inarticulate, although the next years were to see them driven to other ways of venting their grievances.

An important social factor which began to operate towards the end of the period was that of emigration.[1] Before about 1880 emigration from the Monarchy had been almost negligible, and where it occurred, had been chiefly the product of local and special causes,[2] but about that date a stream of emigration to the New World had set in, which had then increased steadily in volume, the annual figure rising from some 20,000 in 1880 to nearly 40,000 in 1890. The nett loss of population to the Monarchy was about 80% of this, for on an average, about 20% of the emigrants returned after a few years, either because they had made abroad what seemed to them a sufficient fortune, or because they had despaired of ever doing so.

Except for the special case that a large number of Jews, some of whom were well-to-do and came from urban centres, including Vienna, left Austria,[3] nearly all the emigrants were from the land, the great majority of them landless men or dwarf-holders. Far the biggest number came from Galicia-Bukovina, with smaller contingents from other Lands, such as Dalmatia, in which the rural population was reaching saturation point.[4] There was also a considerable seasonal migration of harvest workers, chiefly to Germany, although some went as far afield as France and Belgium. Most of these, again, came from Galicia.

The other important phenomenon at the lower end of the social scale had been the emergence of a really big industrial proletariat – a change which had been larger than the mere figures of increased industrialization would indicate, for thanks in part to the deliberate policy of the men who had governed Austria from 1849 to 1880, the growth had been almost entirely in

---

[1] On this see *International Migrations* (National Bureau of Economic Research), vols. 14 (1929), pp. 588–97, and 18 (1931), pp. 390–411. The former volume gives the statistics, the latter, 'interpretations', by Dr Klezel.

[2] The total emigration had only occasionally reached a figure of 10,000 in a single year; more often it was only 2–3,000. The Land with the largest figure was regularly Bohemia, whence a fair number of Czechs went to Russia, where they had been promised land (Drage writes, p. 73, that most of these returned, having found the promises illusory, but there were still some Czech colonies in Volhynia when it passed to Poland after 1918). Another trickle went from Bohemia to the Klondyke in the years of the gold rush. Most of these were presumably German miners.

[3] 300,000 Jews emigrated from the Monarchy to the U.S.A. and England between 1881 and 1908 (Steed, p. 149). Others, of course, went to Germany and other countries. Many of them probably never figured in the emigration statistics.

[4] The statistics given by the National Bureau are not broken down by Lands after 1884, but in 1901 it was stated in the Reichsrat that in the decade 1891–1900, 327,491 emigrants had left Galicia. The total recorded Austrian figure for those years was about 435,000.

the factories, at the expense of the handicraftsmen and artisans. By 1890 some twenty per cent of the entire working population of Austria (including workers in industry proper, miners and home-workers) constituted an industrial proletariat in the true sense of the term. Most of these were now employed by large or medium-sized concerns, for among the factories themselves, the tendency had been towards concentration.

The harsh conditions reimposed under absolutism had not thereafter improved for many years. Only child labour still enjoyed the modest protection enacted for its benefit by Joseph II. Adult labour, male and female (and female labour, excluded by the old guilds, was extensively used in the factories), was quite unprotected. Hours of work were back on their old level; housing and sanitary conditions, miserable; wages, at least for the unskilled worker, as low as the masters could make them – nor is it true (as was frequently alleged) that here was a new tyranny imposed by unscrupulous Jewish blood-suckers and replacing the milder rule of Christian masters, for the latter were no better than the former.[1] The conditions simply reflected the exploitation by the strong of the weaker party which was powerless to defend itself.

Until the advent of Parliamentary Government, the workers had not even been able to make their voices heard in their own defence, since they, like all other classes of Austrian society, had been forbidden to associate even for non-political purposes.[2] In 1867, however, a change did come about in this respect, for the workers profited by the general right of association enacted in that year by the Reichsrat, although that did not include a right to combine for trade purposes. Nevertheless, a large number of associations sprang into being, including the important *Arbeiterbildungverein* (Workers' Educational Association). The movement, however, promptly divided into two camps, one representing the 'self-help' doctrines of Schulze-Delitsch, the other, whose programme linked up with that of the International Labour movement, and was promoted in Austria by Lassalle's pupil, Heinrich Oberwinder, the far more radical tenets of Lassalle. This was strongly political: the programme included State intervention to protect the workers, and to reform society as a

---

[1] In March 1870 the Viennese bakers' assistants wrote to their colleagues in Prague warning parents and guardians not to send their children to Vienna to learn baking. 'These boys are bought on the spot for 50 kreuzer (1/8d.) like cattle. The drudgery and over-work turn them simply into idiot cripples; the Viennese master-bakers have no consciences. So, too, with the apprentices; let them not think that life in Vienna is milk and honey. They are treated like dogs for a weekly wage of one gulden 50 kreuzer (3s.) and a single meal a day, which is worse than a dog's' (Brügel, *Geschichte*, I. 320). There are frequent references in the literature of the time to the 'slave-market' where children from the provinces, especially Prague, were brought by their parents to be sold to Viennese masters.

[2] In 1862 the workers asked for permission to form an educational association, but permission was refused. The official concerned wrote that 'experience in Germany, particularly Prussia, has shown that such movements, however they begin, tend to flow over into subversive politics, and it seems likely that the same thing would happen in Austria'.

whole; complete freedom of association and combination, and of the Press; State help for the workers' co-operative societies; direct and general suffrage; abolition of the standing army and its replacement by a 'people's militia'; and separation of Church and State. That the more extreme current gained the upper hand was largely due to the hostility to any workers' movement shown by the Liberals. Dr Giskra, who is credited with the aphorism that 'the social question stopped at Bodenbach', told a deputation which waited on him in 1868 with a petition for universal suffrage: 'Don't think that we in Austria are going to introduce a mob rule under which the proletariat will storm the House, cap in hand'.[1]

The disheartened self-helpers left the leadership of the workers' movement to their rivals, who, on 13 December 1869, organized a great demonstration: 20,000 workers filed past Parliament to demonstrate in favour of general suffrage, complete freedom of association and assembly, and the right of combination. Actually, the Government had been better than its word: it had already, five months before, referred 'the reform of the *Gewerbeordnung*' to a Committee which, while pronouncing on principle against the legal limitation of hours of work for male adults (on the ground that it would deprive them of the chance to earn more money), recommended protective legislation for women and children and many other reforms (including a large part of those introduced a decade later), with legalization of the right of combination.[2] The Government now sanctioned the last-named right with unexpected speed[3] (again on grounds of principle) thereby legalizing strikes, although revenging itself by arresting fifteen of the workers' leaders for high treason[4] and dissolving all their associations, except those which were specifically non-political, and it was preparing further legislation, but then came its fall. The Hohenwart-Schäffle Government amnestied the imprisoned men, but had no time to deal constructively with the labour question, and the Liberals' second term of office proved as barren in this field as in most others. Austrian and Hungarian delegates met their German opposite numbers at a conference in Berlin, in November 1872,[5] and in the following years the Reichsrat frequently discussed the labour question, but their minds soon became too preoccupied with higher things for them even to carry into effect the good intentions entertained by some of them.

Meanwhile the workers' conditions had become worse than ever. The boom had produced an influx into the factories, causing in particular a great housing shortage in the industrial centres. Workers who had formerly

[1] Another dictum of his was: 'General franchise is never right for Austria, either now or later.'
[2] See L. Brügel, *Gesetzgebung*, pp. 117 ff.
[3] The Bill was introduced the day after the demonstration. It became law on 7 April 1870.
[4] The excuse given was that they had attended the Social Democrat Conference in Eisenach, and had adopted its programme.
[5] Brügel, op. cit., pp. 100 ff.

received free accommodation in the factories (and dismal as this was,[1] it was yet regarded as a benefit) now had to find it elsewhere, and landlords of the Rachman type were driving the rents sky-high. Then the *Krach* caused unemployment on an unprecedented scale. This, however, rather weakened, than strengthened, the workers' movement. The workers were disillusioned with their leaders: moreover, they had no money to pay subscriptions, and dared not complain for fear of dismissal. The membership of the Trade Unions sank to a very low figure. A small Social Democrat Party survived, but was rendered impotent by personal rivalries, and when these had been bridged over (in 1877) it split again on a question of theory into the 'moderates' and the 'extremists', who, embittered by the attitude of the Government, declared even the fight for the vote useless. 'We can hope for no more reforms from the ruling classes', wrote its organ . . . 'we want no milk and water alleviation of conditions; we want total liberation.'

Meanwhile, a parallel movement which had begun in Prague in 1867 had met with a similar fate. Beginning on Schulze-Delitsch lines, it had been driven to the Left in the 1870s, and then to near-disintegration. Although refounded (this time on a Marxist basis) in 1878, it led no more than a shadow existence.

In the 1880s, so-called anarchist tendencies developed. Political crimes were perpetrated, and workers and police came into bloody conflict. The Taaffe Government reacted very strongly against the violence. After 1884 a state of emergency was proclaimed in Vienna and its environs, including Wiener Neustadt, and three hundred workers were expelled from them.[2] In 1886 an 'anarchist law' was enacted which suspended trial by jury anywhere in Austria for offences which had 'anarchist and subversive motives'. This was employed very freely against workers.

Nevertheless, a certain change of heart was coming about in wide circles, although this was perhaps occasioned rather by antipathy towards the Liberals, and especially towards the Jewish element among them, than by sympathy for the workers. The early 1880s saw the birth, in close mutual connection, of two movements, both favourable to the workers. One was the 'socialist' German national movement, the most prominent figure in which was Georg von Schönerer. This is described more fully elsewhere,[3] but it may be emphasized here that all the early agitation developed by Schönerer and his then associates was for social reform, its anti-Semitism being adduced as a social necessity. The second movement represented a revival, in new form,

---

[1] An inquiry held in Vienna in 1872 showed that it was common for apprentices, etc., to be required to sleep two and three in a bed. The beds were, moreover, arranged in tiers of bunks and the rooms grossly filthy and overcrowded. A memorandum from the workers, prepared for the Berlin Conference, said that the average life of a factory worker was only thirty-three years.

[2] The Social Democrat movement, such as it was, now moved its headquarters to Graz.

[3] See below, pp. 653 ff.

of Christian Socialism. Its spiritual rector, Freiherr von Vogelsang, was a recruit both to Austria and to Catholicism, for he came of a family of Prussian Protestants, and settled in Vienna only in the 1860s. There, however, this remarkable man, who absolutely loathed the capitalist system,[1] began to preach a doctrine of social reform on Christian Social lines through a corporative society. His ideas harmonized well enough with those of a group of high Austrian aristocrats, headed by Prince Alois Liechtenstein, who were particularly concerned with the plight of the old craftsmanship and its practitioners under the competition from the sweated labour of the factories. Under their influence, representatives of employers and workers met in Parliament in 1883 for a conference on hours of work. No agreement could be reached, but a valuable precedent had been set. The *Gewerbeordnung* was amended to extend the list of trades which could be practised only by qualified men, and the Government instituted an inquiry into the conditions of factory labour. In 1885-7 a whole series of reforms,[2] most of them modelled on the German legislation, were introduced. Hours of work were limited to eleven daily in factories, ten in mines, with compulsory Sunday rest. The employment of children under twelve was prohibited altogether, and the working day for women and young persons limited to eight hours. Factory inspectors were appointed (at first, indeed, only a handful).[3] Accident insurance was introduced for miners and factory workers, then sickness assurance for many workers, and invalidity, widows' and orphans' insurance discussed, although not enacted, as was a proposal for the establishment of Chambers of Workers, with representation in the Reichsrat. Large as were the gaps which still remained, the Socialist leader, Adler, himself told the Brussels Conference of the International in 1895 that Austria possessed the best social legislation on the Continent, after Germany and Switzerland.

Unfortunately, these laws were very widely evaded, or flatly disregarded,[4] and most of them did not apply at all to home workers, who still constituted a substantial proportion of the labour force. Thus the conditions of the workers were still profoundly unsatisfactory, but at least a considerable improvement upon those of twenty years earlier.

Meanwhile, Social Democracy as a political movement had, after touching a nadir in 1886, begun a recovery which it owed almost entirely to a single man. This was Dr Viktor Adler, scion of a prosperous bourgeois family of Jewish origin, and a medical man by profession. Adler had entered politics as

[1] In a famous passage, Vogelsang compared the system, not to its advantage, with a chariot of Juggernaut, writing that until 'the dark superstition of its worship' had been eradicated and overthrown by 'a serious, purposeful, concentric attack', detailed and individual remedies were useless.

[2] For a full account of these, see Brügel, op. cit., pp. 151 ff.

[3] The first of these were appointed as early as 1883.

[4] See on this point, Drage, op. cit., pp. 102 ff.

a German nationalist and had even been a co-author of the 'Linz Programme' described below, but had been repelled by the violence of German nationalism as it developed under Schönerer's influence, and had been unable to accept its anti-Semitism. He had turned to the workers, prompted, it would appear, by sheer goodness of heart, and had become a convert to Marxism. He soon acquired an extraordinary influence over the workers' movement. He saw that to be strong, this must be united, and began by taking on himself the task of reuniting the various factions – as he insisted, in the moderate sense, for Socialism must be a regulated movement, working in the open and aiming first at achieving universal suffrage, after which it could force through its demands by regular methods and weight of numbers. After three years of labour he succeeded, in a Congress held at Hainfeld in December 1888–January 1889, in uniting the party on a programme drawn up by himself and Karl Kautsky, of orthodox Social Democracy, based on the programme of the German party and in conformity with the doctrine of the Second International, to which the party then adhered. It condemned private ownership of the means of production and stood for the dictatorship of the proletariat; as immediate aims it called for universal suffrage, the separation of Church and State, the abolition of the standing army and an advanced system of social reform.

The emergence of Social Democracy as a real force of which the last years of the Taaffe regime were thus witness practically coincided with the appearance of another party of the 'little men', in this case, of the craftsmen, small shopkeepers,[1] etc., particularly those of Vienna. The 'Viennese Radicals', etc., of the early elections belonged to this group, which, under various titles, all had the same objective, which was that of arresting the economic decline of the very worthy class which they were championing, and all, generally speaking, had the same panacea, a more or less unadulterated anti-Semitism.

The 1882 extension of the franchise gave the vote to a large number of members of this class, many of whom at first showed a disposition to follow the rebel German nationalist, Schönerer. But while Schönerer's anti-Semitism was entirely satisfactory to them, they were repelled by the hostility developed by him towards the Dynasty and the Church, while his national programme passed over their heads. Doctrinally, they were more attracted by the Christian Socialism being preached by Vogelsang and his circle.

Their divisions and their inexperience, however, left them ineffectual until they suddenly found an inspired mouthpiece and leader in Dr Karl Lueger, a young advocate of humble origin (which gave him a natural understanding of the 'little man's' feelings), great ambition, and a charm and an eloquence to match it, who in 1875 had secured election to the Municipal Council of

[1] As well as the factory-owners, most of the pedlars and street traders were Jewish.

Vienna. Originally a Liberal, Lueger transferred his allegiance to the Democrats, and soon made himself a big name by his attacks on corruption and vested interests – attacks which seldom failed to point out the Jewish element in their objects. In 1885 he was elected to the Reichsrat, and soon after came into contact with Prince Alois Liechtenstein, and through him, with a 'Christian Social Union' which two disciples of Vogelsang's, Psenner and Latchka, founded in 1887.

Lueger was at this time still in friendly relations with the German nationals, with whom he succeeded in 1888 in forming an association of 'United Christians'. But this was the year of the great Schönerer scandal,[1] and after it, Schönerer's way and Lueger's parted forever, although Lueger was still able for many years to co-operate from time to time on an *ad hoc* basis with the more moderate German national groups. Now, however, he met Vogelsang himself and accepted his programme, and on this basis, the Christian Social Party was formed, in time to fight the 1891 elections, and to secure in them fourteen mandates, seven of them in Vienna. Its programme, which Prince Liechtenstein then expounded in the Reichsrat, was one of protection for the 'little man', in the town and the country. It emphasized the importance of the Jewish problem, but declared this to be a social one: it rejected racial and religious anti-Semitism. For the rest, it was strongly and even demonstratively dynastic, and 'Great Austrian' in its attitude towards the State, preaching a 'black and yellow' dynastic loyalty which should transcend national feelings; it was thus, in theory, not even a specifically German party, although, as we shall see, it ended up as one, owing to the refusal of non-German sympathizers with its social ideas to dissociate themselves from their national movements.

In spite of their loyalty to the Dynasty and the Church, the Christian Socials were, in these first years, something of political outcasts. Their social radicalism not only alienated their declared enemy, the Jewish capitalists, but made them suspect in the eyes of the Court, the aristocracy and the higher circles of the Church itself: a Pastoral Letter issued by the Austrian Bishops before the 1891 elections was strongly hostile to the movement. But the official Church's own neglect of social issues was now reaping its harvest: denunciations from above could not kill a party which filled a vacuum with a programme that was at once Christian and socially progressive.

This work makes no pretence at being a *Kulturgeschichte*, and nothing is more boring to a reader unfamiliar with a subject than a catalogue of names of which the author simply tells him that they are distinguished without convincing him that they ought to be.[2] It would, nevertheless, be unfair to leave

---

[1] See below, p. 655.
[2] Good brief surveys, with bibliographies, may be found in Zöllner, op. cit., pp. 458 ff., and *M.K.P.*, III. 291 ff.

unmentioned the big progress which Austria had made in the cultural field since 1848. Thanks first to Thun's energy, and later to the Liberals' persistence, the educational system had made up much of its arrears, especially on the middle and higher levels. The medical faculty of Vienna was again one of the leading institutions of its kind in the world, and several of the philosophical faculties not far behind it. The Viennese Institute of Historical Research, founded in 1855, had by the 1870s a list of members which would have done honour to any historical institution in the world – an astonishing achievement when it is recalled that in 1852, when it was desired to make several appointments to Chairs of history, no single native candidate of sufficient stature could be found; all had to be imported. The Viennese Opera and Burgtheater were the finest in Central Europe, if not the world, and there was a busy and productive musical, literary and artistic life. It is true that outside music, which produced Bruckner, Mahler, Wolf and Johann Strauss, jun., few of the figures in any field reached world celebrity status, but the number of Bs and B minuses was large. Typical of these is the painter, Markart, admired in his day in Vienna much as Frith and Landseer were in London. Modern taste finds the architecture of the day more grandiose than pleasing (one of Austria's own historians has called it 'the style of stylelessness'[1]) and probably prefers some of the unpretentious corners of Vienna's Innere Stadt which have survived to the great Ringstrasse round it, which replaced the old fortifications and glacis, with its many spacious and costly buildings, of which no two are in the same style; but it can understand the pride with which Vienna saw it take shape.

Francis Joseph's domestic life during these years had not been happy. As his letters to her prove, he had loved his young wife with a depth and passion which altogether belie the common belief that his nature was one incapable of deep emotion. But their relationship had been made difficult from the first by the pressure of his public duties, and above all, by the interference of the Archduchess Sophie, a regular caricature of a mother-in-law, bossy, jealous, unsympathetic, who lost no opportunity of showing her disapproval of the child-bride, whose talented but Bohemian father had brought her up in a very different atmosphere of unrestraint, which the stiff Archduchess regarded as supremely undignified.

Left much to herself by her husband's necessary preoccupations, Elisabeth had reacted strongly against the draconic discipline which her mother-in-law tried to impose on her. She developed, in particular, a passion for riding, which became an obsession, and spent more and more time on this and similar pursuits, less and less on ceremonial functions. Later, more serious difficulties developed. Although devoted, Francis Joseph was not faithful. Elisabeth's health suffered, and she took to spending long periods abroad, in

[1] H. Benedikt, cit. Hantsch, *Geschichte*, II. 454.

Madeira, in Corfu, where she had built for herself an extraordinary fantasy-palace, and in the hunting-fields of England and Ireland.

Her husband suffered; but the estrangement was not the worst blow which fell on his family life. The couple had, besides their three daughters (of whom the eldest had died in infancy), one son, Rudolph, born on 21 August 1858. Rudolph had in him more of his mother than of his father. He grew up an intelligent, and in many ways a sympathetic youth, gifted with the family talent for languages, a lively interest in the world, particularly natural history, and a marked lack of exclusiveness. Like his mother, he rebelled against the stiff Court ceremonial, and he sought friends in artistic circles, among Liberals and even Jews. The Liberals pinned high hopes on him, but it may be doubted whether, had he ever come to wear the Crown, he would have been a successful reforming Monarch. In politics he was essentially a dilettante, a Prince Hal playing at opposition to his father, with whom he got on only moderately well, and who reacted to his son's velleities by excluding him from any serious role in public affairs.[1]

The direct cause of his tragedy seems to have lain in his love-life. He was married, on 10 May 1881, to the Belgian Princess Stephanie, a singularly plain young woman, who soon failed to satisfy his imagination. He consoled himself with a large number of mistresses, and on the morning of 30 January 1889 his body, disfigured with severe head wounds, was discovered with that of one of them, a young girl named Baroness Marie Vetsera, in his little hunting-lodge of Mayerling. The exact circumstances of the tragedy were, owing to the secrecy imposed on them, never cleared up beyond all possibility of conjecture, although it is practically certain that the simple explanation was the true one: Rudolph, in a fit of nervous depression, had resolved on suicide and had persuaded his unfortunate young lover to die with him.

The effects of this tragedy on the Emperor's spirit are discussed in a later chapter, but one consequence, of vast importance for the future of the Monarchy, must be recorded here. Rudolph and Stephanie's only issue had been a daughter, so that his death left Francis Joseph's brother heir presumptive to the throne; or should Karl Ludwig predecease the Emperor, then his eldest son, the Archduke Francis Ferdinand, born on 18 December 1863.

It is a habit of modern Austrian historians, many of whom seem possessed by a nostalgia for the old Monarchy, to reproach their foreign colleagues with representing the last phase of its history too exclusively as that of a struggle between its component nationalities, devoting too little attention to

---

[1] He also had certain rather mysterious connections with some Hungarian circles, who regarded him as their friend and even dreamed of having him crowned 'junior King' in his father's life-time; but one may strongly doubt whether anything would ever have come of these plans.

the social and economic questions which, after all, formed the main preoccupations of most of its inhabitants, and also under-stressing the centripetal and supra-national forces which still existed, and the amount of friendly co-existence which still went on between individual members of nationalities which, as collectivities, were struggling bitterly against each other.

It is, of course, true that many Austrian men and women cared much more for their bread and butter (and even for their music) than for the 'national' disputes which so excited the politicians; that plenty of friendly intercourse went on between members of different nationalities; and that the real government of the country was still largely being carried on in a supra-national spirit.

But it is also a fact that the attempt of the neo-absolutist era to de-politicize national feeling among the peoples as a whole had failed; that its failure had been apparent from the very hour that that feeling had been allowed to express itself; and that during the following decades nationalism grew steadily more intense and more widespread, not only as the classes to which it had not previously penetrated shrank with the spread of education, but as even educated men to whom their 'nationality' had previously been indifferent now found themselves definitely opting for one national allegiance or another.[1]

Every decade, almost every lustre saw these processes carried a little further. Possibly Taaffe retarded the development by skilful application of his formula; at the beginning of his reign he was really able to keep national discontents 'well-modulated'. But by the end of it, national passions were almost everywhere in full blast. There was no hope any more of using the soft pedal, only of finding some way of harmonizing them. The struggle was still, chiefly, as a distinguished Austrian has written, 'for Austria' (i.e., for position of supremacy in her body politic), not 'against Austria',[2] but it had reached a pitch when some, at least, of the nationalities were beginning to think of turning 'against Austria' unless she found a way of satisfying them within her, and in 1890 she seemed further off than ever from doing so.

The national struggle κατ' ἐξοχήν of the period was that waged between Germans and Czechs in Bohemia; and while it is true that from one point of view, the attention paid to it was excessive – quite ten books appeared on

[1] This increasing definition and unambiguity of national feeling in individuals was an interesting phenomenon of the period. Charmatz, in his *Politisches Denken in Oesterreich*, p.59, quotes striking cases from earlier years of men who described themselves indifferently (or differently at different dates) as Poles or Ruthenes, Germans or Czechs, etc. He rightly points out the importance of this phenomenon of convertibility of national feeling, for while it existed, any nation could hope that if it gained territorial possession of some area, it would be able to convert to membership of itself at least the majority of the local population. This hope still existed in the Taaffe era and beyond it, but the justification for it was vanishing.

[2] Charmatz, op. cit., p. 70 (*um Oesterreich, nicht gegen Oesterreich*).

the subject for every one on the German-Slovene problem, a hundred for every one on the Ruthene, and the proportion of time spent on it by the Reichsrat was as great – yet in other respects it deserves its pre-eminence. More than any other people of the Monarchy, the Czechs sat at its very heart. Unlike any other, they could not dream of complete sovereign independence except in the case of the complete disintegration of the Monarchy, and as, at that stage, this was something which, in their own interests, they did not desire,[1] their efforts had to be concentrated on achieving a status inside the Monarchy satisfactory to their ambitions. Conversely, the aim of Governmental policy must be to place them in that position, provided that this could be done without injury to other peoples. But this was extraordinarily difficult, since the second people in Bohemia, constituting well over a third of its total population, were Germans, whose interests were naturally backed by the other Germans of Cis-Leithania, and at times even by the Germans of the Reich; while the Czechs, although themselves numbering in all a mere five millions or so, were able to link their cause with that of the other Slavs of the Monarchy and at times, more remotely, also of Slavs outside the Monarchy. What made the struggle especially acute was the fact that in Bohemia and Moravia, alone of all Lands in the Monarchy, two developed national bourgeoisies were in rivalry.[2]

In default of the hope of full independence, Czech national ambitions might have been depicted graphically in the form of three concentric circles. The furthest was to gain (with the help of allies) such a position in the Habsburg Monarchy as to swing its whole policy on to a Slav line. The intermediate aim, without which the other could not easily be achieved, but which was also regarded as an object in itself, was to bring about realization of the *Böhmisches Staatsrecht*, i.e., the constitution of the Lands of the Bohemian Crown as a quasi-sovereign unit within the Monarchy; the innermost, which would have been facilitated by achievement of the second, and would in turn pave the way for its achievement, but was again desirable for its own sake, was to remove the last traces of inferiority, *de jure* and *de facto*, under which the Czechs in Bohemia (again we particularize Bohemia, for the heart and nearly the totality of the struggle lay there) were still suffering *vis-à-vis* the local Germans, and ultimately to replace it by domination.

We have seen how in the 1860s the Bohemian Feudalists had aimed straight at the second, perhaps even the first of these targets, and had come within measurable distance of achieving at least the former, and how the Czech nationalists under Palacký and Rieger had allied themselves with the Feudals

---

[1] Jászi, op. cit., p. 387, rightly says that the Czechs' flirtations with Pan-Slavism 'did not signify a possible or serious irredentist movement, but rather a tactical and also a sentimental position'.

[2] In the Tirol, the only other Crownland containing a highly developed bourgeoisie of two nationalities, the Italians and Germans there led such separate lives as hardly to clash.

in that campaign. In doing so, they had shown a sound enough appreciation of what were then the true power-factors in the Monarchy; but for the Feudalists, the Hohenwart experiment would never have been tried. But when it failed, the new generation represented by the Young Czechs operated a change of tactics. They were not in the least indifferent to the *Böhmisches Staatsrecht*, but they concentrated their activities within the innermost circle.

This change was extraordinarily beneficial to the Czechs' cause. They lost the half-hearted support of the Feudalists, few of whom had ever been real enthusiasts for the national cause, but the loss was easily outweighed by the recovery of the democratic quality which was natural to their movement, since the Czechs were still a people of 'little men', socially and economically, and now became its great strength.

The purposeful national solidarity with which the Czechs worked is truly remarkable. No aspect of life was neglected, and the approach to each objective was organized systematically and efficiently. Schools and local culture were promoted through the *Matice Školska*; economic life through a variety of organizations at the head of which stood the very important *Živnostenska Banka*, founded in 1868, originally to finance the Czech cooperatives and the purchase of land by Czechs, but afterwards used also in the interests of Czech industry, and supported by a great network of cooperatives (in these the Czechs led all the peoples of the Monarchy), savings-banks, etc. There was even a great gymnastic organization, the *Sokol* (Falcon), founded in 1863 with objectives which were by no means purely athletic.

The Germans, of course, retorted[1] with their own *Vereine*, *Turnverbände* and local national organizations, such as the *Böhmerwaldbund*, etc.,[2] and the Czech-German national conflict in the 1870s and 1880s was largely fought out in an unremitting *Kleinkrieg* – a cold war in which the adjective became increasingly inoperative as tempers became inflamed and radicalism increased on both sides – between these rival organizations and their supporters.

The official battles turned round the rules for linguistic usage in public life. This question had more or less fallen asleep for many years after 1848, Ferdinand's *Majestätsbrief* of 8 April of that year, although never officially retracted, having long been tacitly regarded by both sides as superseded by

[1] This word is not meant to denote any order of priorities. The *Deutscher Schulverein*, which covered all Austria, was founded in 1880, the same year as the *Matice*, and the *Turnverband* ante-dated the *Sokol*.

[2] One of these organizations deserves special mention: the so-called *Chabrus*, organized before the 1872 elections by the Germanophile Great Landed proprietors, operating through the newly founded Crédit Foncier and other banks, to buy up *landtäfliche* estates which entitled their owners to votes in the Landlords' Curia. The Czechs replied in the same way, through the *Živnostenska Banka*. Sometimes a purchase was real, sometimes a landlord would distribute his estate by sales on paper to his bailiffs, gamekeepers, etc., who then voted as Great Landlords. See Münch, *Böhmische Tragödie*, p. 370.

the numerous later enactments.¹ Even in the 1870s both parties admitted that German must remain as the language of the inner service, while no one denied that Czech must be used as the language of the 'outer service' in the Czech districts. The conflict arose when the Czech claimed that the text of paragraph 2 of the famous Article XIX, enacting equality of rights to all *landesüblich* languages, gave Czech a right to be used in the outer services anywhere in Bohemia, even where there were only one or two Czechs in an entire district. The Germans, pointing out that paragraph 3 of the same Article used the word *Landessprache*, argued that a distinction was to be drawn between *Landessprache* and *landesübliche Sprache*, and that while Czech was indubitably a *Landessprache* of Bohemia, it was *landesüblich* only where it was currently spoken. The argument was possible because, as we have seen, the Article had only enunciated a general principle, and no interpretetive legislation had been enacted.

If the Czech interpretation was adopted, it would clearly give the Czechs a big advantage, because if Bohemia was regarded as an indivisible whole in this respect, any person entering the public services in it would have to know both languages, and in practice, this favoured the Czechs enormously. For the Germans did not know Czech, and did not see why they should. It was, they said arrogantly, a language spoken by only a few million people, mostly peasants and domestic servants, in Bohemia-Moravia and nowhere else in the world, whereas German was a *Weltsprache*, the tongue of some seventy million persons, and also the language of the higher services in Austria itself. They contemptuously refused to learn it, and even reached the point of regarding it as national treason if one of their members did so. The Czechs, on the other hand, made no bones about learning German, so that any post for which knowledge of both languages was necessary automatically went to a Czech.

The Stremayr linguistic ordinances were in accordance with the Czech interpretation, with which Stremayr explicitly agreed when challenged in the Reichsrat. After this, the Germans changed their ground. In 1884 Herbst submitted to the Landtag a formal resolution for the administrative partition of Bohemia into a Czech and a German sector. The central services (which would then be reduced to a minimum) would have to be bi-lingual, but knowledge of the second language would not be required where it was not *landesüblich* as the Germans interpreted the phrase. This, he said, was a demand from which the Germans would 'never retreat'. The Czechs refused, equally flatly, to entertain it, and the parties were still arguing it in 1890.

Another question which involved interpretation of the law – smaller than

---

[1] Even the proposed Czech language law of 1871, while demanding the same equality for the two languages in Bohemia, had not based its claim on the *Majestätsbrief*: the continued validity of that document was asserted only later, and the Germans were astounded as well as scandalized when, on 13 December 1898, the Supreme Court pronounced it to be still valid.

the other, but still argued with great bitterness – was raised by the influx of Czech workers into the growing industrial districts, which lay in German-Bohemia. The Czechs claimed that the law entitled the children of such workers, if their numbers reached the legal minimum,[1] to schooling in their own language. But one ruling of the Courts had been that a commune or District was not obliged to provide a school in a language that was not *landesüblich*, and just when Stremayr had ruled both languages to be *landesüblich* for official use throughout Bohemia, had given an opposite ruling in respect of schools. The Germans claimed that the mere presence in a commune of immigrants who had not acquired *Zuständigkeit* in it and did not pay its local taxes could not make their language *landesüblich* in it; their children must go to German schools. This point, again, was still being disputed in 1890.

By that year, then, the top issues were still unsettled. The validity of the 'Bohemian State Rights' had not been admitted, but neither had the administrative division of Bohemia been sanctioned. The Germans' defence of their positions had been so far successful that the basic ethnic line running through the rural districts had remained practically unchanged, and the ethnic character of the industrial complexes had not altered so much as might have been expected. As the local German populations had been unable, or unwilling, to satisfy the factory-owners' demand for cheap labour, a large number of Czechs had come into these districts,[2] but they were in fact something of a floating element, liable to disappear overnight if a factory ran into difficulties and dismissed all or part of its workers, and many of those who established themselves had Germanized. The Czechs had certainly made some gains: there were Czechs in many districts once purely German, such as Reichenberg and the Komotau-Aussig mining area. Their presence did not, however, affect the preponderantly German character of these districts, and, oddly enough, while the increase of the Czechs had been considerably faster than that of the Germans before 1880, it had slowed down greatly after that date, i.e., just when the German administrative pressure relaxed.[3]

[1] The law of 1869 enacted that an elementary school must be provided where at least forty children of school age (over a five-years average) were to be found within a radius of four km.

[2] The Czech explanation for this is that the Germans were 'decadent', the Czechs, 'more virile'. Another way of putting it is that the Czechs were content to accept standards of living against which the Germans revolted, preferring to emigrate, chiefly to Vienna (where there was a very big German-Bohemian colony), but also to the Alpine Lands. It is true that when the rural congestion in the Czech areas grew intolerable, many Czechs also emigrated to Vienna, where there were 69,000 of them (5·5% of the total population) in 1890. They were chiefly domestic servants, tailors or small shopkeepers.

[3] Denis, p. 570, seems to have got his figures wrong here. See the careful calculations in Waber, pp. 43 ff., 118. In 1846–51, when the Jews were listed separately, the Germans had constituted 38·6% of the population, and the Czechs, 59·8. The figures for 1857 were 37·0 and 61·2. In 1881, when account was taken only of language, they were 37·2 and 62·8: the Germans' increase 1846–80 had been 19·91% and that of the Czechs, 31·71%. But from 1880

But it was only in these respects that the Germans had held their own. They had awakened too late to the danger,[1] and even now their national organizations were less widespread and less purposeful than those of the Czechs, whose leaders, moreover, always remained in Bohemia, while Germans who tired of the struggle migrated to Vienna. Up to 1879 (although not later) the Germans had the forces of officialdom working for them; but working for the Czechs were time and the inevitable effects of economic and cultural development. By 1890 it was no longer possible to recognize in the Czechs the submissive and really half-primitive peasant people of a century before. They had lost most of their aristocratic patrons, and were only just beginning to penetrate into high finance and big business; most of this was still in the hands of Germans or German-minded Jews. But besides a class of industrial workers, they now possessed a substantial small and medium bourgeois class of artisans, shopkeepers and minor officials: they had developed a special aptitude for the career of *rond de cuir*, and supplied easily the largest national contingent, after the Germans, to the administrative services of the Monarchy; it is true that here, too, they were found chiefly in the middle and lower levels. They had long possessed an elementary and secondary educational system adequate for those purposes, and since the opening of the Czech University in Prague in 1882 (a Technical High School had already been given them in 1869) were turning out an annual crop of young men educated nationally up to the highest level to which education went; young men who, moreover, took a pride in spreading what they had learnt among their people.

They possessed a flourishing national culture of their own: a National Theatre, built at the cost of great self-sacrifice out of popular subscription (the sacrifice was two-fold, for the first theatre, opened in 1881, had burned down, and had to be rebuilt), and an ample supply of local reading-rooms, etc. If their literary and artistic products of the time were not, as a rule, particularly distinguished, they were numerous, and in music the Czechs had contributed, in Dvořak and Smetana, two of the Monarchy's, and Europe's, great names. Prague, an almost purely German city two generations earlier, had become an almost completely Czech one. The unemotional Baedeker

---

to 1910 the rates of increase of the two peoples differed little (Germans, 20·13, Czechs, 22·24) and their proportionate shares of the population were:

	Germans	Czechs
1880	37·17	62·79
1890	37·20	62·23
1900	37·23	62·67
1910	36·76	63·19

[1] Kleinwächter, op. cit., p. 131, quotes a story of 'an eminent German political personality' in Prague in the 1870s saying with a laugh: 'the only thing wrong with the Czechs is that no one takes them seriously.'

wrote of it in 1887 that there 'and in the rest of Central and Southern Bohemia, the traveller will hear little but Bohemian (Czechish) spoken, while the names of streets, stations, shops, etc., are generally written in that language'. In fact, the Germans had dwindled to 18·5% of the population in 1880 and they were down to 10% in 1900 and to 8·5% in 1910, a substantial proportion even of these being German-speaking Jews. They lived a strange, unreal existence, almost like that of an army of occupation, meeting only one another, frequenting only their own clubs and restaurants and contriving to ignore the rest of the inhabitants except when (as happened not infrequently) assaulted by them.[1]

It should again be emphasized that, as in earlier years, the national struggle was much less acute in Moravia than in Bohemia. The Moravian Slavs had by now come to regard themselves as Czechs, and after 1881, sat with the Czech Club in the Reichsrat; but they always retained a certain particularist feeling, were not overly keen on the *Böhmisches Staatsrecht*, and were comparatively ready to compromise with the local Germans, as the Germans were with them, on a basis of reasonable give and take.

The Slovene and Croat movements were companion pieces to the Czech, on a smaller scale and in rather less strident colours. The Slovenes, at this stage, were particularist: the old Illyrianism had died away, Yugoslavism was yet to be born. They were thus definitely 'Austro-Slav', a fact which contributed not a little to the relative indulgence with which the Slovene movement was regarded by authority. The goal of their nationalists was, as before, the creation of a Great Slovene Crownland, comprising all Slovene areas of the Monarchy, with its own capital (at Laibach), language of administration and education, and High School.

By 1890 they had got no further than the Czechs with their demand for structural changes in the Monarchy, which were, indeed, in the opposite direction from the Czechs', for while the latter, being in the majority in Bohemia and Moravia, wanted the conservation of existing Land frontiers, the Slovenes wanted Styria and Carinthia partitioned.[2] Neither had they got nearly so far as the Czechs in the development of their national structure. They were still a preponderantly peasant people, with no aristocracy or big landlords, no *haute bourgeoisie* and a relatively small intelligentsia. Their national institutions – Press, co-operatives, patriotic societies and the rest – were all comparatively rudimentary. The older age-groups were still largely illiterate.

[1] On this see Kleinwächter, op. cit., pp. 139 ff.; also (satirically) Gustav Meyrink's novel, *Walpurgisnacht*.

[2] For that reason, when the Slovenes asked the Czechs for support for their programme in 1889, the Czechs refused, lest it should set a precedent.

Nevertheless, they were making progress in all these fields. They had as yet no High School of their own, and their secondary school system was still meagre, partly because the local Germans blocked its development, partly owing to real shortages not yet overcome of teachers and school-books. But they now possessed an adequate network of elementary schools, and the Slovene boys who passed through German secondary schools no longer necessarily, or even generally, emerged from them Germans. The Slovene language had now been admitted to full equality in the public services and the Courts wherever the population figures justified this,[1] so that there were now a substantial number of Slovene officials, as well as the priests and schoolmasters, while Laibach, now an eighty per cent Slovene town, contained a growing Slovene *petite bourgeoisie* of shopkeepers, small professional men, etc. The Slovenes now controlled all the rural districts in Carniola, except the German ethnic islet of Gottschee and one other, and even most of the towns, including Laibach itself, where they gained the majority on the Municipal Council in 1882. In 1883 they acquired the majority in the Landtag itself, and in 1887 the German members of that body were reduced to ten representatives of the Great Landlords' Curia. Outside Carniola, the Slovenes were fully holding their own in South Styria[2] and gaining ground in Gorizia, Istria, and even Trieste. Only in Carinthia was the trend still towards Germanization.

The Slovene areas of Austria were traditionally a stronghold of Catholicism, and for many years the Slovenes' representatives in the Landtag belonged without exception to the Clerical, or Populist Party, a Party which was Conservative in its tenets (although its conservatism was rather of the Christian Social than the feudal brand), and formed part of the Hohenwart Club and of Taaffe's Iron Ring. While the Clericals remained the strongest Slovene party up to 1918, and indeed beyond that date, their political monopoly began to be challenged in the 1880s by the more democratic 'Young Slovenes', or Slovene Liberals. While, however, the two Parties fought one another unsparingly when they had the field to themselves, they habitually combined against any national third party, German or Italian, which was in the field, and there was little to choose between the two in respect of national enthusiasm.

The home of almost all the Croats now represented in the Reichsrat was Dalmatia, where successive censuses showed 'Serbo-Croat' to constitute the

[1] For details, see Hugelmann, op. cit., pp. 459 ff.

[2] The proportion of Slovenes to the total population of Styria showed a small drop, but this was owing to the faster growth (due largely to immigration) of the population in the industrial North of the province. There was no Germanization in South Styria. The Slovenes had made a big gain in 1857, when the Kreis of Marburg (Maribor) was attached to the episcopal See of Lavant, which was already Slovene. The new Bishop, Mgr Slomšek, was a strong Slovene nationalist, and *M.K.P.* tells us (III. 174) that 'after a few decades, there was not one single German parish priest left in Lower Styria, even in the German towns'.

language of the overwhelming majority of the population.[1] Meanwhile, while the Slavs had begun the modern era there as a people of peasants and fisher-folk, with the Italians constituting the bourgeoisie and commanding not only the Landtag but the municipal councils of most of the towns, the former had gained ground steadily, economically, culturally and also politically, until by 1870 they gained the majority in the Landtag, and by a few years later, in all the municipal councils except that of Zara.

One result of this had been partially to reopen the question of the status of Dalmatia within the Monarchy. As we saw,[2] this had been left undecided in 1849, and it had not been reopened by the October Diploma or the February Patent. The Italians were, however, then still in the majority in the Landtag. In 1861 they had refused an invitation from Croatia to resume the negotiations ordained in 1849 and had expressed their gratitude for the Law of 1867, which included Dalmatia among the Lands to be represented in the Cis-Leithanian Reichsrat. On gaining the majority in the Landtag the Croats had, however, announced their wish that Dalmatia should be attached to Croatia-Slavonia, and had continued thereafter (although not unanimously) to press the demand.

The majority of the local Croat politicians were by now vehement nationalists, but the issue was complicated by the existence in Southern Dalmatia of a considerable Serb minority, who during this period protested against the Croats' wish for attachment to Croatia-Slavonia and in 1861 even petitioned for administrative separation 'because they had never been Dalmatians.[3]

The Poles kept faithfully enough to their side of the bargain struck in 1873, completely abjuring irredentism or international conspiracy, and supporting the Government of the day and enabling it to get essential legislation through Parliament.[4] They even abandoned their old boycott of the Austrian State services, which, on the contrary, they now entered on such a scale as to evoke complaints from the Germans of their excessive influence over Austrian affairs. Badeni, Dunajewski and the two Goluchowskis are examples of Poles who in fact in their day largely directed the fortunes of the Monarchy.

This did not mean that they had renounced the re-establishment of an independent and united Poland, as an ultimate ideal, but it is well possible that their impatience to see it realized was growing less acute; certain, that the feeling of national identity between all Poles was becoming qualified by

---

[1] The earliest figures (1846-51) showed 96·2% of the population speaking 'Serbo-Croat' and 3·7%, Italian; the figures for 1890 were 96·2% and 3·1%. There had been an odd shift in 1880, to 93·3% and 5·8%, but this must have been due to some fortuitous cause. It looks as though 20,000 persons had got into the wrong rubric.

[2] Above, p. 425.

[3] Hugelmann, p. 639. Austrian Dalmatia extended further south than the old Venetian province.

[4] A symbol of this was that the premises for the Landtag were now constructed.

an element of particularism, which was developing also among the Poles of Russia and was to produce considerable differences between the two branches, when the question became *actuel* in 1914, as to the form in which the unification should take place.

Another factor reducing their national impatience was probably their growing interest in money-making. According to one writer,[1] the attainment of virtual autonomy by Galicia in 1863 'released the interest of the leading Poles from the political struggle which thitherto had almost absorbed them', diverting it into material channels. This was even more true of the Poles of Russian Poland, which was developing into the leading industrial area of Russia. It should be added that the non-political activities of the Poles were not solely material. During the half-century, Cracow in particular, but also Lemberg, developed into centres of learning and the arts which gave birth to many brilliant products, some the works of native Galicians, others, of Poles from Russian and German Poland who found in Galicia an atmosphere of freedom lacking in their own homes.

The fortunes of the Ruthenes during the absolutist period have been described; it should be added that when Goluchowski became Minister of State in 1859 he set about achieving from that position that complete domination of the Polish element in Galicia which Bach's opposition had prevented him from putting through as Statthalter. The Ruthenes were now forbidden to use the Cyrillic script in communicating with the administrative authorities, and only strong protests from Mgr Joachimowicz prevented the same rule from being laid down for communications to the Courts. Schmerling's appointment recovered them a little ground again: all prohibitions on the use of Cyrillic script were lifted and all officials in East Galicia were required to be conversant with that script, and with the Ruthene language. The Ruthenes secured forty-nine out of the hundred and fifty mandates to the Galician Landtag of April 1861 and eleven in the Reichsrat, all, to whichever school they belonged, solid in their opposition to the Poles' autonomist programme, which they could still hope to see defeated if a centralist government maintained itself in Vienna. When, however, Schmerling fell and federalism was in the air again, the Ruthenes saw themselves being delivered up again to the mercy of the Poles, without any protection whatever. This gave the pro-Russian group its chance, and in 1866 its leader, a priest named Naumovics, announced in the Landtag that the Ruthenes were identical with the Russians, ethnically and linguistically. After Königgrätz the group's organ, the *Slovo*, actually wrote that the future would inevitably bring about the disintegration of the Monarchy and the attachment of Galicia to Russia.[2]

Now the St George Party finally split, or rather, disintegrated. Naumovics's

[1] A. von Guthry, *Galizien, Land und Leute*, Vienna, 1916, p. 111.
[2] Fischel, *Panslawismus*, p. 359.

followers claimed, indeed, to represent the old Party, and consequently took the name of Old Ruthenes; but their thesis of Russo-Ruthene identity differed fundamentally from that of the original St Georgites. The latters' linguistic programme had, however, perished by now of sheer lack of vitality, the fact being that the *Jasicza* was a dead (or still-born) language which it was simply impossible to impose on the masses.[1] The opponents of the Russophiles, who took the name of 'Young Ruthenes', turned instead to the Ukraine, proclaiming the ethnic and linguistic identity of the Galician Ruthenes with the inhabitants of the Great (sc. Russian) Ukraine.

This happened to be just the moment when the full force of Russian chauvinism was being turned on the Ukraine. The Russian Secretary of State for Public Instruction had issued a circular denying the existence of the 'Little Russian' language; what passed under that name was simply 'bad Russian spoilt by Polish influences'. It was forbidden to print anything in 'Little Russian' except verses, stories and plays. The Ukrainian intellectual leaders consequently emigrated, several of them settling in Lemberg, which, under the benevolent eye of the Austrian Government, became the centre of Ukrainian national culture; the Shevchenko Society, founded there in 1873, became a sort of Academy of Sciences for the entire Ukrainian people. Thus fertilized, the Ukrainian cultural movement flourished mightily in Galicia. A national educational society, the *Prosvita*, produced and distributed good and cheap text-books and by this and other methods firmly established the basic Ruthene-Ukrainian identity. In this respect the Young Ruthenes won easily over the Old; the rival propaganda issued by the latter (with Russian funds) had little effect; indeed, the Old Ruthenes were driven to issuing their own propaganda in the local Ruthene-Ukrainian.

The Old Ruthenes suffered another set-back in 1882, when a number of their leaders were arrested on charges of high treason. The jury acquitted them of that charge, but Father Naumovics and three others were sentenced to terms of imprisonment for conduct prejudicial to the public order.[2] After this, the Old Ruthenes were careful to repudiate any suspicion of disloyalty, and in fact the published programmes of the two parties differed little on essentials, each claiming that the Ruthenes constituted a separate nationality, which must find its salvation within the Austrian State. The main difference between them was that the Young Ruthenes claimed that an agreement with the Poles was possible, while the opponents denied that possibility. In this, it must be admitted, the Old Ruthenes had the better of the argument, for

---

[1] There is an interesting similarity between the fate of the Jasicza and that of the 'Ugro-Rusin' language (of which the writer still possesses a grammar) which the Hungarian authorities tried to introduce into Carpatho-Ruthenia after recovering it in 1939. Ugro-Rusin, like the Jasicza, was swept out of the field by Ukrainian.

[2] On his release Naumovics went to Russia, where he adopted the Orthodox faith and became a professional Pan-Slavist agitator.

while in subsequent elections the Poles allowed a handful of Ruthenes to reach the Landtag and a thimbleful, the Reichsrat, on condition that they sat with the Polish Club and accepted the decisions of the majority, the number was always disproportionately small, and their wishes entirely disregarded; so much so that in 1889 the Young Ruthenes left the Club and formed a new pact with their rivals – only, indeed, to split again a year later.

The Polish pressure was, meanwhile, continuing, and was not proving entirely ineffectual. The proportion of Ruthene speakers to the total population of Galicia fell from 50% in 1846 to 45% in 1857, and 42·9% in 1880, recovering to 43·1% in 1890.[1] Emigration accounts for some of this decline, but it must also reflect an assimilation of some members of the nation to the Poles, just as the Slovaks, Ruthenes and Germans in Hungary were losing some members to the Magyars during the same period.

It was, however, only the weaker and, so to say, peripheral elements that were crumbling away. The core was remaining, and hardening. Thanks to the efforts of the Prosvita and kindred societies, and also to a measure of support received from Vienna and the Bukovina, the Ruthenes were, in spite of all their difficulties, making considerable cultural progress and developing a nationally conscious intelligentsia which no pressure would ever wipe out of existence.

The Italians were already, of all the peoples of the Monarchy, that whose attachment to it was the frailest. This was not due to oppression, nor even to any big tangible grievance. It is true that in Gorizia, Istria and Dalmatia they were inexorably losing ground to the local Slavs, with the inevitable disappearance of the old conditions which had given them a weight disproportionate to their numbers. In the Trentino, where they had actually been gaining ground on the local Germans before 1866, their position had become less enviable after that date: the authorities found it necessary to exercise more vigilance in that area now that it had become a frontier one, and its middle classes had lost an appreciable source of income, for while Lombardy-Venetia had belonged to the Monarchy, the Government had staffed their administrative services largely with Italians from the Trentino.

But the Italians controlled the municipality of Trieste, and while their demand for the constitution of the Trentino as a separate Crownland was regularly refused (partly owing to the objections of the Tirolean Germans, partly for fear of creating a precedent), they were fully represented, proportionately to their numbers, in the Innsbruck Landtag, and administration, justice and education, primary and secondary, in the Trentino were purely Italian.

[1] The proportionate increase of the Polish language was larger than this, but this was due to the linguistic assimilation of Jews and 'other' elements, few of whom joined the Ruthenes.

But the heart of the problem of the Monarchy's Italians lay in the geographical location of their homes, just across the frontiers of the new Italy, and in Italy's open ambition to annexe them. These factors made the problem as much an international, as an internal one, and not only strengthened among the Italians of the Monarchy an irredentism to which all questions of their *de facto* conditions were fundamentally irrelevant, but led the Austrians themselves to accept this as a fact of life to which resistance was useless and even moral indignation over it out of place.

There have even been Austrians, of the most various schools of thought, who have written that the Monarchy was unwise in not ceding the Trentino to Italy in 1866, when it could have done so without much further loss of face, their argument being that this minor sacrifice would have made a reality of the Triplice, and saved for the Monarchy, certainly the German South Tirol up to the Brenner, and probably the Italian Littoral as far as Trieste.[1] The present writer doubts strongly whether the sacrifice would have glutted Italy's appetite indefinitely; but that the idea could have been held by serious thinkers indicates the special light in which the Italian national problem was viewed in the Monarchy itself.

Of the Italians within the Monarchy, by no means all were irredentist. Precisely in the Trentino, the Catholic Church long threw its weight into the Austrian scale, and its Party, the Partito Populare, contained many *Austriacante*. The local nobility was divided, most of the peasants still nationally indifferent and often instinctively loyal to the traditional authority. In Trieste the business interests, many of which were, indeed, German or Jewish, were pro-Austrian, and the Social Democrats there (although not in the Trentino) came down on the same side. But the 'intellectuals' nearly everywhere, and especially in Trieste, were Italian nationalist, often very turbulently so. Trieste was the scene of many and rowdy demonstrations, and it was there that a fanatic (whose name, characteristically, was the German one of Oberdank) achieved the distinction of being the only man during this period to attempt the life of the Monarch as a purely national gesture.[2]

The Roumanian educational system in the Bukovina made very large strides after the lifting of the Polish control over it. It is true that when (in 1875) the Duchy received an University of its own, this was a German one, as were many of the secondary schools, and a large number of the primary schools

---

[1] The view is expressed by writers so different in their outlooks as Kleinwächter (pp. 185-6) and Jászi (pp. 394-5).

[2] This was in 1882, when Francis Joseph was visiting Trieste for the celebrations of the quincentenary of the city's inclusion in the Habsburg Monarchy. Oberdank, who was not a Triestiner but a German Austrian who had deserted from his regiment during the occupation of Bosnia, had come from Rome as one of a band of twelve who had sworn to assassinate teh Emperor. He was arrested before he could carry out his design, and executed. As the place of his burial was not revealed, irredentists made his mother's grave a place of pilgrimage.

were mixed. But these, too, were of benefit to the Roumanians, who in time received also a number of elementary and even secondary establishments of their own. Thanks to these, a perceptible intelligentsia emerged, while numerous associations occupied themselves with raising the cultural and economic standards of the peasants.

The local Roumanian nationalism of the time was, however, extraordinarily pacific. The landowners, who, with the higher Orthodox clergy, dominated the Duchy, made loyalty to the Monarchy a fixed principle of their policy, and were even themselves largely denationalized to the point of forgetting their own language. There was practically no irredentism, nor even political disaffection,[1] and the connections of the local Roumanians with their kinsfolk in the Regat, and even in Transylvania, were of the loosest. There was no trace here of such hostility to the Monarchy, or to the local Germans, as prevailed among the Transylvanian Roumanians towards the Hungarian State and the Magyar people.

If the Germans of Austria were slower than any of its other peoples to evolve a specifically 'national' policy, and if a far larger proportion of them denied to the last the necessity, or even the propriety, of any such thing, this was not due to any quality in the German soul which lifted it above national emotion. Where, in any Land or commune, its Germans felt their position threatened or their self-esteem injured, they were as quick as any others to resort to self-defence, and did so with fully as much intolerance and intransigence. But it was one thing for an individual German to react 'nationally' to a personal or local stimulus; quite another for the Germans to organize themselves politically on a national basis. One obstacle lay in their very geographical distribution, scattered over so many Crownlands, each of which had its own special traditions, its own problems, even in respect of nationality – those of the Tirolean Germans were quite different from those of the Bohemian, those of the Styrian and Carinthian other again – even its own type of German, often far more conscious of his local affiliations than of his kinship with a man from another province.

They were also more highly differentiated socially, economically and culturally, than most of the other peoples, and thus more naturally prone to think in terms of class or confessional interests, which in their case could not usually be translated into national terms, as could the grievance of a Czech worker against a German employer, or a Ruthene peasant against a Polish landlord (we shall see shortly how much the German national movement, when it did take root, owed to the case which was the exception to this rule), and had become habituated to thinking in these terms before nationalism emerged as a rival for their political allegiance. They were *beati possidentes* with

[1] There was no single prosecution in the Bukovina for a political offence during the absolutist period; the first case was in 1871.

no national grievances of their own, and consequently inclined to underestimate the strength of others' feelings. Most important of all was the influence on their outlook of the fact that they had so long been accustomed, with reason, to regard themselves, if not as the Monarchy's *Staatsvolk*, at least as its *staatserhaltendes Element par excellence*. Up to the 1860s this view of the relationship between the State and its Germans was not confined to the Liberals: it was held, consciously or subconsciously, by most educated Germans, and it implied in itself a sort of national philosophy which made a specifically national policy not merely undesirable, but superfluous. And it was not purely selfish: those who held it could maintain, with much reason, that any other was detrimental to the State, as weakening the 'cement' which held it together, and further, as encouraging and even justifying reactions against it among other peoples.

As we have suggested, this attitude was basically incompatible with a political philosophy which assumed that the destinies of Austria were in the hands of its peoples, represented in their Parliament – unless, indeed, its non-Germans accepted it, which they had most emphatically refused to do when Parliamentary life opened. That all the Germans in the Narrower Reichsrat had still been able to maintain it (for the Clericals had regarded themselves as above nationality exactly as had the Liberals) is explicable by the safe cushioning with which the Schmerling franchise had provided them. Nearly all of them had still held it through 1866, a fact more difficult to explain, except by the power of acquired habit to blind humanity to present reality.

A bigger change came in 1870, when Prussia's victories over France evoked such an unprecedented wave of enthusiasm among Austria's Germans. Even this, however, still hardly ruffled the political surface. The Graz and Vienna associations drew up political programmes, based on that of Aussee, for the 1870 elections, but neither put up a candidate. The 'Constitutional Left' included in its programme a phrase that Austria was a 'German State' – words to be read in their old connotation – but no more. Then came the Hohenwart experiment, which did, indeed, arouse deep national passions among the Germans, although Beust exaggerated when he told the Emperor that it had turned the Liberals into a German national Party.[1] And when they returned to power, the Liberals put away their fears. With the Poles appeased, the Slovenes hardly yet awake and the Czechs, as they thought, decisively defeated (an illusion which the Czechs' policy of absenteeism did much to foster) they regarded themselves as completely safe at home; while Austria's official friendship with Germany strengthened the illusion, by giving them a comfortable assurance that Bismarck would see to it that no harm would come to them, and enabled them to feel that Austria was, after all, still a 'German State' so far as the world was concerned.

[1] Beust, op. cit., II. 106.

They thought it unnecessary to make any move to conciliate the Czechs, although they also did not think it necessary to repress them: it is fair to say that while the Czechs suffered much during this period from police and bureaucratic tyranny and social arrogance when they did raise their voices, they were not subjected to 'Germanization'. Herbst himself said that to limit the freedom of other peoples would be contrary to the principles of Liberalism.[1] Art. XIX was applied without distortion, nor did the Government try to fill what the German nationalists later regarded as a principal gap in Austria's political structure by making German the official language of Cis-Leithania, or even of the Reichsrat.

This unconcernedness about the national issue was very general in the Liberal Party during its second term of office. When the great split came in 1873, one of the sins with which the young rebels reproached their elders was, indeed, slackness in defending the national interests of their countrymen in Bohemia. But the larger cause of the split was revulsion against the exploitation of the poor which was sanctioned by orthodox Liberalism, and above all, against the corruption in high places uncovered by the *Krach* – a revolt which was 'national' only in the special sense that it contained an element of anti-Semitism generated by the frequency with which Jewish interests had been revealed as lying behind the corruption scandals. The Progressives of the 1870s still sat with the Old Liberals in one Parliamentary Club, and still accepted the doctrine that the Party was concerned with the interests of the State, not those of one national group in it. The only Reichsrat Deputy in this decade to call for a German National Party was Georg von Schönerer, a doughty eccentric[2] who had developed extreme racialist doctrines which were presently to lead him into hostility to the Monarchy and everything for which it stood. But Schönerer himself was at this stage primarily a social revolutionary. When he left the Progressives, as he did in 1876,[3] because they were 'insufficiently nationally-minded', it was the Jewish question, not that of the relationship between the Monarchy and its Germans, that drove him out of the Liberal fold; and at the time, he failed to take a single colleague with him.

Even their defeat in 1879 did not move the Liberals to change their principles: the furthest they went was, in 1882, to adopt new statutes which declared the Party's objects to include 'the protection of the constitutional (*staatlich*) and national interests of its members', who, it emphasized, were not all Germans.[4] It rejected another motion by Schönerer that it should

[1] Molisch, op. cit., p. 93.
[2] He used to call the Feasts of the Church and months of the year by Old Germanic names of his own invention, such as *Julfest* (Christmas), *Heumond* (June), etc. It was he who introduced the greeting 'Heil', afterwards institutionalized by Hitler (who greatly admired him) in place of the pleasant Austrian 'Grüss Gott'.
[3] He had been elected as a Liberal in 1870 and had joined the Progressives in 1873.
[4] See Plener's *Erinnerungen*, II. 167 ff.

transform itself into a German national Party, and although Schönerer then definitively left the Party, all its other members continued to accept the doctrine that the Party was one of 'the State', not of its German element only.[1]

The German clericals, meanwhile, continued cheerfully to combine with Slavs against Viennese Liberalism, and the German feudalists against Viennese centralism, still regarding any other attitude as treason to the true unity of the State.

The rigidity of the Liberals over the national issue did not, however, mean that public opinion was equally immobile. It expressed the ideological beliefs of a group which was rapidly losing ground in the country, largely for that very reason. The 1870s had seen a considerable upsurge of national feeling in the Lands of mixed nationality, especially Bohemia-Moravia, which were then the national bull-rings in chief (the Slovene areas were still relatively quiet), and this had increased when the Germans fell from office. In the 1880s came a series of developments, the best publicized of which is that associated with the name of Schönerer. After finally leaving the Liberals, Schönerer joined a group of intellectuals which included the historian, Friedjung, and the later Socialists, Pernerstorfer and Viktor Adler, to produce a programme (known from its place of origin as the 'Linz Programme') for a 'German People's Party'. This contained a number of advanced social and political postulates, such as extension of the franchise, progressive taxation and protective legislation for the peasants and workers; its national programme was that the Kingdoms and Lands represented in the Reichsrat were to be reduced to the Hereditary and Bohemian Lands, with German as the language of State and sole language of internal administration in them. There was to be the closest possible political, economic and cultural relationship with Germany; this was to be expressed in contractual form.

The Linz Programme does not deserve the place of honour accorded it even by many German historians in the family tree of the German national movement. Its national demands were simply a rehash, slightly coarsened, of the Aussee Programme; nor, for that matter, was there anything new in the social demands. Moreover, its only immediate political progeny was an illegitimate one, for opposition in high quarters prevented the proposed People's Party from ever coming into being. Schönerer, however, took over its social items, added an anti-Semitic spice of his own, and founded his own party, known as the *Deutschnationaler Verein*. This was frankly extremist. 'We gravitate,' Schönerer announced as early as 1882, 'not towards Vienna, but towards wherever there are Germans.' He wanted the Monarchy to disappear, and the Hereditary and Bohemian Lands to be incorporated in the German Reich, and he declared war on everything in the Monarchy which separated or even distinguished it from the Reich: on the Catholic Church

[1] Id., pp. 213 ff.

and on the Dynasty itself, which he believed to be systematically undermining the position of the Germans in Austria.

Henceforward there existed in Austria an avowedly German irredentist movement on the Reichsrat level, but precisely the irredentist plank in Schönerer's platform was that which carried the fewest followers. The High School students used to go through irredentism as regularly as they had gone through mumps and chickenpox a few years before, but nearly all of them got over it within a couple of years of leaving the Aula.[1] Hardly any Austrian of maturer years really wanted to see his country swallowed up in a Germany dominated by upstart, Protestant Prussia, and if his personal inclinations pointed that way strongly, he emigrated (as did Hitler, who admired Schönerer immensely). For the rest, 'Ritter Georg's' picturesque eccentricities and his patent sincerity and sympathy for the victims of oppression always earned him a fairly wide personal popularity, but the very comprehensiveness of his programme made it impossible for more than a handful of fellow-fanatics to accept. Its most popular item was its anti-Semitism, but here it had many rivals, while it also earned him the undying hatred of the Jewish financial and intellectual supporters of the Liberal Party, and the hostility of the Social Democrats, whose leadership was also largely Jewish. His anti-Catholicism drew down on him the wrath of the Catholic Church and cut him off from the pious peasantry among whom he had at first had many followers, while his hostility to the Dynasty offended others, including, not unnaturally, Francis Joseph himself. Finally, he was intolerably autocratic as a leader. In the 1880s he never had more than three followers in the Reichsrat, and in 1888 his enemies (including the Emperor himself) took advantage of one of his numerous indiscretions to have him publicly disgraced.[2]

The comparative failure of the extremist movement did not, however, mean that German nationalism was on the decline. The contrary was the case. Popular feeling had really changed, and most German bourgeois Parties in the mixed Lands were giving the same priority to the national issue as were the Czechs, Slovenes, Croats and Italians. An enormous

---

[1] One writer (Wandruschka, in *Republik*, ed. Benedikt, pp. 374–5) has shrewdly pointed out the influence, in this respect, of the year's military service which students had to do among the professional officers, with their still largely dynastic and supra-national outlook. Naturally, too, they tended to shed their social radicalism as they grew older and acquired settled jobs.

[2] In 1888 a (Jewish-edited) Viennese newspaper published a premature report of the death of the German Emperor, Wilhelm I. Schönerer, with some of his followers, entered the newspaper's offices and assaulted members of its staff. For this and for toasting Wilhelm publicly as 'our glorious Emperor', he was deprived of his mandate and sentenced to six months' imprisonment, and Francis Joseph took away his patent of nobility (Charles I restored this to him in 1917). Francis Joseph is said to have been especially wounded by Schönerer's having voted against the Army estimates on the ground that world power position was a luxury which a rotten edifice like Austria could not afford.

number of self-help organizations had come into being, most of them local, but some, like the *Deutscher Schulverein*, on a wider basis, and some, incidentally, receiving effective help from Germany, where official circles, indeed, held aloof, but the *Alldeutscher Verein*, while refusing to work for the break-up of the Monarchy, took the view that the cause of the Germans in Austria was the cause of all Germans. Among the bourgeois political groups in Austria, the German Clericals sat apart from their Slav colleagues after 1882. The German Constitutional Landowners were already a specifically German Party, and the Liberals more than halfway towards becoming one, or being shouldered aside by others who had done so.

When the Party split before the 1885 elections, even the stalwarts, now led by Ignaz von Plener's son, Ernst,[1] although still maintaining that the interests of the Germans were identical with those of the State, consented to call themselves 'German Austrian'. The dissidents who then formed the 'German Club' laid down as the first point of their programme that 'our supreme principle, which must determine our attitude on all questions, is the welfare of the German people in Austria. The Germans must no longer be put in a minority by a Slav coalition, and the overwhelming Polish influence must be eliminated'. The German language must be made the language of State and the bonds with the German Reich drawn closer. The identity of interests between the Germans and the State was not absolute. When the two groups combined after the elections in the 'United German Left', the joint programme included a demand for 'the protection of *Deutschtum* and the position due to them for the Germans in Austria'.

The more nationalist wing, which was led by Otto Steinwender, was still the smaller one in the Party in 1885, and dwindled further in 1888, when twenty-four of Steinwender's followers returned to Plener's fold in combined defence against the Liechtenstein educational proposals. Those who remained true to Steinwender's leadership formed themselves into a *Deutsch-nationale Vereinigung*, which now produced a programme which, while still containing many social postulates, was also definitely national. It condemned as fruitless all efforts 'to cling to the February Patent and to achieve the power without sacrifice of the most important national interests' until Galicia-Bukovina and Dalmatia had been discarded, and adjured the Germans to obey no other consideration than their national interest. A novelty was a declaration of disbelief in Parliamentary government and a call for 'a neutral Government standing above the nationalities'.

Steinwender's Parliamentary followers numbered only a score or so, but

---

[1] Herbst (who died on 25 June 1892) had lost favour by proposing concessions to the Italians of the Trentino, in order to entice them into the Liberal fold. Plener was elected official leader of the United German Left in 1889. The choice showed the curious capacity of the German Liberals for picking the wrong men to lead them, for Plener, as his memoirs show only too abundantly, was as doctrinaire as Herbst and almost as unpleasant personally.

their programme, including its repudiation of Parliamentary rule, undoubtedly expressed the feelings of a very much larger number of the Germans of Austria than would have been gathered from the Press, standing as that did still almost entirely in the service of the old Liberals and their Jewish backers.

The Germans as a whole were, indeed, still reluctant on principle to step down from the position of a *Staatsvolk* to that of a 'national group', and still very open to economic or cultural considerations. Only a small fraction of the Liberals had yet left them for either Steinwender or Schönerer, and still fewer Clericals. Of the two big Parties which came into being at the end of the 1880s, the Christian Socials and the Social Democrats, one of which was entirely German in membership and the other mainly so, both were in theory a-national in philosophy and at least Pan-Cis-Leithanian in scope. Both gained far more adherents from among the newly-enfranchised classes than did the German Nationalists, and even more of the deserters from the Liberals. But it should be remembered that the strongholds of both these Parties were in Vienna, that untypical city with its special super-national tradition and its abnormally high proportion of inhabitants who were 'German' only by recent linguistic assimilation; and as we shall see, the Christian Socials never succeeded in becoming other than German in composition and ended by becoming it in philosophy, while the Social Democrats found themselves forced a long way along the same road. Similarly, practically all the other Parties, even if the main substantive in their titles was social or cultural, came to prefix it with the adjective 'German', and to include some dose of German nationalism in their nostrums. Their prescriptions were, indeed, astonishingly various.

II FROM TAAFFE TO KOERBER
1890–1903

It was over the Bohemian question that Taaffe's position was first seriously shaken. As we have said, the Germans had not ceased to protest against the language decree of 1880, and this had also brought the Czechs less than their full wishes; but every attempt to reach agreement had broken down on the intransigence of one side or the other. In 1890, the Emperor having expressed serious alarm over the Germans' discontent, Taaffe persuaded leaders of both nationalities to meet in Vienna, and both sides made concessions. The Germans yielded a comparatively small point on schools for 'immigrant' populations,[1] while the Czech negotiator in chief, Rieger, gave way on the much bigger issue of the administrative unity of Bohemia. Kreise and Bezirke were to be re-delimitated, as far as possible, on national lines;

[1] Forty children of school age were to have a school if their parents had resided in a commune for five years, three years sufficing if there were eighty children.

when this had been done the Stremayr Decree was to be reconsidered. Only twenty-six of the forty-one Judges of the Supreme Court needed to be bilingual. Fifteen could get by without Czech.[1] The Bohemian *Landeskulturamt* and *Landesschulrat*, and possibly also the Landed Proprietors' Electoral Curia, were to be divided into national sections. Reasonable compromises were promised on several other points.

This was one of the most sensible and equitable agreements ever reached on the Bohemian question, but the account had been drawn up in the absence of one of the hosts. Whoever was responsible,[2] the Young Czechs had not been invited to join in the negotiations, and they seized this chance to declare the results unsatisfactory and to denounce the aged Rieger as a 'traitor'. There were tempestuous scenes, so violent that even Czechs who privately approved of the agreements were afraid to say so, or to counsel moderation. In the end, only the division of the Cultural and School Councils ever came into effect.[3]

This would have been just another of the innumerable failures to solve the Bohemian problem, but the elections to the Reichsrat were due. These took place in February–March 1891. They brought little change in the numbers of the Conservative parties, the Poles, or the representatives of the smaller nationalities, but the German Liberals lost nearly a quarter of their mandates, being left with only 109 representatives: seventeen seats went to Steinwender's followers, who had taken the name of 'German National Party',[4] and fourteen to the Christian Socials. Much more important still was the change in the composition of the Czech Club, for the agitation of the Young Czechs, which made a special appeal to the newly enfranchised 'little men' (those whose German opposite numbers had voted Christian Social and German National) had been so successful that they emerged with thirty-seven mandates, leaving the Old Czechs with only twelve.[5] The

---

[1] Prazak, as Minister of Justice, had already issued a decree on 23 September 1886, ordering Czech to be treated on an equal footing with German in the *Oberlandesgerichte* of Prague and Brünn.

[2] Some say it was Rieger who failed to issue the invitations; others, Taaffe. In any case, it seems likely that the omission was due to the wish of the Emperor, who held a low opinion both of the intelligence and of the loyalty of the Young Czechs. But it was a grievous error, for the Young Czechs had made a spectacular advance at the expense of their seniors in the Bohemian Landtag Elections of 1889.

[3] The agreement was opposed also by the Germans of the Alpine Lands, who were nervous that it might set a precedent.

[4] For the moment, the Schönerer group (of four Deputies) accepted Steinwender's leadership.

[5] The full figures were: United German Left, 109; German Nationals, 17; Christian Socials, 14; Hohenwart-Liechtenstein Group, 29; Bohemian Feudalists, 18; 'Centre Party' (dissident feudals, mainly from Moravia, otherwise known as the 'Coronini Party'), 8; Polish Club, 58; Ruthenes, 8; Italians, 15 (11 Liberal-National, 4 National Clericals); Slovenes, 16; Croats, 7; Serbs, 1; Roumanians, 4; Old Czechs, 12; Young Czechs, 37.

foundations of Taaffe's majority were shaken, for there was clearly no hope of making the Young Czechs into a Government Party. The only alternative possibility was to reconcile the Germans, and in that hope Taaffe had, even before the elections, dismissed Dunajewski, whom the Liberals, and the Germans in general, regarded as a particular enemy of theirs,[1] replacing him by a permanent civil servant, Emil Steinbach. After the elections he took into the Cabinet a German Liberal, Count Khuenburg, as Minister without Portfolio,[2] and sanctioned the establishment of a German *Landesgericht* in Trautenau (Teplice) in a mixed District of Bohemia. On this, however, Prazak resigned, and the Young Czechs initiated the practice, soon to become general, of frustrating the work of the Reichsrat by organized obstruction. In Bohemia, there were new demonstrations of friendship for France, and anti-dynastic riots in Prague, which led the Government, in September, to proclaim a state of emergency in the city and its environs and to arrest over seventy persons, members of a Left-wing organization known as the *Omladina*, on charges of subversion. A number of organizations were dissolved and papers closed down.[3] In view of this, Plener's Liberals began fishing for office, but this was not the turn events took. The workers were now demonstrating repeatedly, and vociferously, for franchise reform, and this was also being pressed in the Reichsrat by its radical members. Taaffe himself thought that something would have to be done to meet this demand,[4] but the real moving spirit in the developments which now followed was Dunajewski's successor, Steinbach.

Steinbach was a highly intelligent and progressive man, whose sympathies, in spite of his origin (by birth, he was a Hungarian Jew), were strongly with the Christian Socials: he had been the real author of the social legislation enacted in the preceding years. It was his view that the 'national' struggle was essentially a middle-class one, and that democratization of the suffrage would reduce it to reasonable proportions by opening the gates to social and economic forces which were of their nature far less centrifugal than the national ones; the 'lower, politically uncorrupted classes', he argued, 'were sound; they would make social, not national politics; they were dynastically-minded, not irredentist; they were reliable, appreciative and easy to rule.' He did not find it difficult to convince Francis Joseph, to whose emperor's-eye-view the small bourgeois was no more remote than the large, but the Monarch was still unwilling to dispense with the traditional Habsburg bodyguard. The Bill

[1] He had once let fall the remark that 'it was possible to rule Austria without the Germans'.

[2] Khuenberg was, indeed, forced by his colleagues to resign a few months later.

[3] In the course of the emergency, 179 persons were prosecuted and sentences totalling 278 years passed; 7 papers were forced to stop publication and 17 associations dissolved.

[4] In two Ministerial Councils (on 18 June 1893, and again three days later) he said that there was so much agitation, and there were so many proposals for electoral reform, that it was absolutely necessary for the Government to take the lead.

which the Emperor authorized Steinbach to prepare thus kept the curia system intact, and did not alter the proportion of representatives elected by each curia; but it extended the suffrage for the third and fourth curias to practically every male tax-payer who had reached his twenty-fifth year and was able to read and write his locally current language. The electorate was increased from about 1,725,000 to nearly three times that number.[1]

Prepared in deep secrecy[2] and launched without previous announcement in October 1893, the Bill had a disastrous reception. Of all the major parties, only the Young Czechs approved it.[3] That the Left (in the British sense of the term) found that it did not go far enough was no matter, from the Parliamentary point of view, but precisely the parties on which Taaffe was counting were horrified for the opposite reason. The Poles saw their traditional representatives outnumbered by Polish and Ruthene peasants. The Clericals and Feudalists cried out that the farm-hand would be made as good as his master. The German Liberals rightly saw half their former mandates going to Christian Socials and Social Democrats. The three parties united to reject the Bill, and on 10 November, Francis Joseph relieved Taaffe of the Minister Presidency.[4]

Francis Joseph's own inclination seems to have been to appoint as the new Minister President another 'Emperor's Minister', and his mind had already turned towards Count Casimir Badeni, Statthalter of Galicia, a Polish aristocrat who had made a name for himself as a strong and efficient administrator, and had particularly earned the praises of the military authorities for his 'highly patriotic' and able handling of the local situation during the war scare with Russia in 1877–8. But the leaders of the three Parliamentary Clubs which had compassed Taaffe's fall insisted on their claim to his heritage, and the Emperor, reluctantly, consented. He still could not bear to give the Minister Presidency to the German Liberals, and after Hohenwart himself had declined the office on the plea of his advanced years (drawing from the

[1] The literacy provision would, however, have actually reduced the number of voters in Galicia, the Bukovina and Dalmatia.

[2] So much so that Kálnoky, the Minister for Foreign Affairs, only learnt of the whole business when he received a query about it from the King of Greece, who had read of it in the newspapers. Kálnoky complained bitterly, and not unreasonably, to Taaffe, and his objections are generally believed to have been one of the causes which made Francis Joseph dismiss Taaffe. The move had possibly been kept from Kálnoky out of fear that he would try to stop it.

[3] The result of the reform would in fact have favoured the Czechs. According to Denis's calculations, the 400 Deputies would have consisted of 145 Germans, 92 Czechs, 64 Poles, 53 Ruthenes, 22 Slovenes, 13 Serbs and Croats and 11 Italians and Roumanians.

[4] This is the correct wording, for Taaffe did not resign, but was dismissed. The favourite example adduced by those who like to dwell on Francis Joseph's ingratitude towards his servants is that Taaffe thereafter sank into complete obscurity; he never again was consulted on public affairs. But his retirement seems to have been at least in part voluntary, and he died only two years later.

Emperor the bitter comment, 'you are too old to build up, but you weren't too old to pull down') he gave it to a member of his party, Prince Alfred Windischgraetz, grandson of the hero (or evil genius) of 1848, who then formed a Ministry composed of representatives of the three 'Coalition Parties'.[1] The parties agreed between themselves to relegate political and national questions to the background and to introduce no measures 'altering the national *status quo*'.

In the event, however, the Coalition Government, although several of its members were brilliant men, proved one of the worst ever endured by Austria. It did get the essential legislation (the Budget, etc.) through Parliament, but almost all the other measures which it tried to introduce were thwarted by obstruction from the Opposition, the Young Czechs and Christian Socials leading the field in the application of this device. On the Emperor's insistence, a Parliamentary Committee debated extension of the franchise, and here, while the Opposition pressed for reforms, the Government sabotaged them. After only two years of this inglorious existence, the Government fell on a 'national' question of absurd triviality. The Slovenes had been pressing for more secondary education in their own tongue, and had asked for a Slovene *Untergymnasium* in the little South Styrian town of Cilli – a German outpost in a Slovene countryside – or alternatively, parallel classes in Slovene in the German Gymnasium there; as things stood, Slovene children had to attend the German classes there.[2] The Germans, while not denying the justice of the Slovenes' claim to more education in their own language, insisted that the school must not be in Cilli, the *Deutschtum* of which it would endanger. In 1895 Plener, as Minister of Finance, sanctioned the Budgetary appropriation for the parallel classes, whereupon his party disavowed him and withdrew from the coalition on the plea that the inter-Party agreement had been broken, and on 19 June the Government resigned.[3]

The Emperor now reverted to his earlier plan and after a stop-gap Government of permanent officials, under Count Kielmansegg, had bridged the interval for a few weeks,[4] after all, appointed Badeni, who formed a

[1] The list was: Windischgraetz (Hohenwart), Minister President; Marquis Becquehem (Hohenwart), Interior; Ernst von Plener (German Liberal), Finance; Count von Schönborn (Hohenwart), Justice; Count Wurmbrand (German Liberal), Commerce; Count Julius Falkenhayn (Hohenwart), Agriculture; Ritter von Madeyski (Pole), Cults and Education; Count Welfersheimb (Non-Party), Defence; Ritter von Jaworski (Pole), Minister for Galicia.

[2] In fact, there were more Slovene than German pupils in the gymnasium.

[3] Under Kielmansegg, the appropriation was passed without difficulty. The Slovenes were satisfied, and Cilli in fact remained an essentially German town until 1945, when its inhabitants were expelled or massacred. See Suttner, op. cit., I. 112. (Suttner's work contains a very detailed account of the Cilli crisis).

[4] The delay was simply to allow Badeni to carry through the Landtag elections in Galicia.

Ministry which was in effect non-Party, although the Polish element in it was conspicuous.¹

Badeni, who was by no means lacking in ability (German writers are uniformly unjust towards him), made a beginning which was not at all bad. He was civil enough towards the Germans to secure their support in getting the Budget passed, and placated the Czechs by lifting the state of emergency; soon after which, the Emperor amnestied some of the persons sentenced in connection with the Omladina affair, and Count Thun, who had been closely associated with the repressive measures, was relieved of his post of Statthalter.² The Left accused Badeni of reaction, a charge which his attitude towards the Christian Socials, in particular, seemed to justify, for it was largely on his advice that Francis Joseph so long refused to allow Lueger to become Burgomaster of Vienna.³ On the other hand, he attacked the question of franchise reform seriously – and the fact that this now went through without difficulty, although the Parliament of the day was the same which had overthrown Taaffe for introducing it, shows how far the Emperor's will was mandatory. Taaffe's draft was, indeed, modified, the four existing curias being left intact, except that the property qualification for the third and fourth of them was lowered slightly;⁴ but a fifth curia, electing seventy-two members, was added, the voters' qualification for this being simply a lower age limit of twenty-four, literacy, and six months' residence in the constituency. When this had gone through in June 1896, after a debate in which the chief criticisms came from the Left, who objected to it as insufficiently radical,⁵ Badeni dissolved the Reichsrat, and in March 1897 new elections

¹ The list was: Badeni, Minister President and Interior; Ritter von Bilinski (Finance); Frh. von Gautsch (Cults and Education); Count Ledebur (Agriculture); Count Gleisbach (Justice); H. Glanz (Commerce); Welfersheimb (Defence); Dr Rittner (Galicia). Soon after, the Railways were given a separate Ministry, under a soldier, F. M. L. von Guttenberg. Ledebur was a Bohemian Feudalist; Gautsch, Glanz and Gleisbach, permanent Civil Servants; Bilinski and Rittner, Poles. As the Ministry of Foreign Affairs had also just changed hands, and its new holder, Count Agenor von Goluchowski, jun., was a Pole also, five of the portfolios, including four of the key ones, were in Polish hands.

² Eleven persons who had received long sentences benefited from the amnesty; the shorter sentences had already been served.

³ See below, p. 672. Badeni's chief motive seems to have been a wish to placate the Hungarians, whom Lueger detested both for their *bruyant* nationalism and on account of the Jewish influence in their leading circles, and to whom he had been repeatedly and grossly abusive. There is also reason to believe that indirect pressure was applied by the House of Rothschild. But Badeni himself disliked violent anti-Semitism.

⁴ From ten to eight kronen. The currency reform described elsewhere had now been carried through, so that this was equivalent to lowering the qualification from five to four gulden.

⁵ The reform in fact was very far from honouring the principle of one man, one vote. The electors for the 85 Deputies in the Landed Proprietors' Curia numbered 5,431; those for the 21 representatives of the Chambers of Commerce, 556; for the 118 urban communes, 493,804 and for the 129 rural, 1,505,466, while the 72 representatives of the General Curia were chosen by 5,004,222 electors.

were held, on the extended franchise. It goes without saying that these resulted in a more complicated position than ever, from which the only conclusion to emerge clearly was that both social and national radicalism were on the increase. The Great Landowners were sheltered by the retention of the Curia system, so that they came back with their absolute numbers undiminished (although these, of course, now constituted a smaller proportion of the total), but their thirty 'Constitutional' members (all Germans) formed, as before, one group, the nineteen 'Bohemian Federals' another, while the Poles continued to sit with the Polish Club. The Hohenwart Club had dissolved, most of the German members joining either the Constitutional Landowners, or a new (German) Catholic People's Party which got thirty-one mandates, while its eleven Croat and fourteen Slovene members marched under national flags. The Czech Club had retained its unity, but within this, the Young Czechs had swept the board, with sixty mandates out of sixty-two. The Polish Club lost nine members to dissident Poles, and the eleven Ruthenes left it. The German Liberal Party had collapsed completely after the Cilli fiasco and the *Freie Deutsche Vereinigung*, as the little band who remained faithful to Plener called themselves, numbered only fourteen, almost all elected by Chambers of Commerce. Steinwender's followers, figuring now as the 'German People's Party', numbered forty-one, a 'Progressive Party' under a certain Funke, thirty-three; and there were five *Schönerianer*. Finally, the Christian Socials, with twenty-eight Deputies, were now a considerable force, and the Social Democrats, with fifteen, a perceptible one, and there were a few splinter parties and independents.[1]

Up to this point, Badeni, although on presenting himself to Parliament he had announced that his Government 'was preserving a completely free hand *vis-à-vis* the parties', had yet succeeded in getting essential legislation through Parliament without invoking Para. 14, which at that time was still an expedient from which Austrian Ministers shrank. Now, however, a new situation confronted him, for the decennial revision of the Compromise with Hungary was due.[2] Badeni needed a trustworthy Parliamentary majority, and expediency, if not inclination, led him to approach the Young Czechs, who laid down as their price a new 'Bohemian settlement'. Badeni, it is true, consulted also the German leaders, but took little account of their wishes and seems not to have understood the full complexity of the problem. On 5 April 1897 he issued, by Ministerial Enactment (i.e., as orders interpretative of the Law of 1867), two language decrees, for Bohemia and Moravia respectively. These followed the general pattern of the Stremayr ordinances, but extended their scope considerably. As regards the outer language of service, the rule that a member of the public must be answered in the language in which he made his first application, in any District of either Land, was extended from the

[1] I base these figures on Kolmer (VI. 218) but no two lists ever agree exactly.
[2] For the details of this, see below, pp. 701–2.

administrative and judicial services to cover also those operated by the Ministries of Commerce, Finance and Agriculture, and complete equality was introduced also in respect of the inner language by a ruling that all correspondence connected with any case should be in the language in which it had started. As from 1 July 1901, no person was to be employed in the services covered by the first order who was not acquainted with both languages, and even before that date all offices were, as far as possible, to be held only by persons conversant with both languages.

It was now the Germans' turn to revolt, and they did so with a violence such as Austria had not seen since 1848: a violence which went on *crescendo* throughout the entire spring and summer. Extremely tumultuous scenes took place, not only in Prague and German Bohemia, but also in Vienna, where there was severe rioting, and in Graz, where passions had already been whipped up by the Cilli affair, and whose Germans feared that the Slovenes would demand that the Bohemian precedent should be taken as valid for Styria. In the Reichsrat, the Germans took up and improved on the example of obstruction which had been set by the Czechs, utilizing to the full their great tactical advantage of the Government's need to get the negotiations with Hungary through Parliament.[1] The Government, in despair, threatened to use Para. 14, whereupon the Christian Socials and Social Democrats, who had not obstructed on the language issue, did so on that of Parliamentary rights. The Government, by a trick, amended the Standing Orders of the House to provide a remedy against the rowdiest filibustering,[2] but this simply poured oil on the flames. On 28 November, after the rioting in Vienna had reached near-revolutionary dimensions, Francis Joseph accepted Badeni's resignation, making the unfortunate Pole one of the three Austrian Ministers, in the whole 128 years covered by our narrative, to be unseated by public opinion.[3]

Many writers take the fall of Badeni as marking a turning-point in Austrian history: the end of Francis Joseph's attempts to govern Austria 'against the Germans'.[4] But even if we allow for exaggerations in the terminology (for it is unfair to Francis Joseph to represent him as ever deliberately trying to rule

---

[1] This was the occasion on which the Liberal Deputy, Lecher, spoke for thirteen hours. The feat was the more remarkable because all the speech was, allegedly, to the point. When Dr Lueger tried to speak, it was three hours before he could make himself heard.

[2] Count Falkenhayn (after whom the measure was subsequently called) proposed it in a voice heard only by the President of the House and the official stenographers. The President, a Pole named Abrahamowycz (strictly, a Polonized Armenian), declared the measure adopted before the obstructionists had noticed that a vote was being taken. In fact, the measure was mild enough. It empowered the President to exclude a Deputy for three days, or the House to do so for a term up to thirty days. The next day ten Deputies were forcibly ejected by the police.

[3] I count as the other two, Metternich and Ficquelmont.

[4] So, for example, Redlich, *Franz Joseph*, p. 393.

'against' any of his peoples: he tried to mete out justice and to create contentment among them all, and on his insistence, the 'pro-Czech' governments always, if possible, included a German, and vice versa) it was not the end but only, at most, the beginning of the end. The only immediate fruit which the Germans' agitation brought them was the head of the unfortunate Pole. Francis Joseph seems also to have accepted the impossibility of maintaining the Badeni Ordinances. But for the rest, his reactions to the Germans' demonstrations, and to the indiscreetly sympathetic echoes to them coming from the Reich (the nationalist Press raged and there were even street demonstrations in Saxony), was rather to irritate him and harden his heart against them than to incline him to take them into partnership. As a first step he appointed a stop-gap government of permanent civil servants, headed by Gautsch, which carried on for three months without a Reichsrat, enacting legislation (including a six-months' budget and a short-term prolongation of the economic relationship with Hungary) under Para. 14 and then, on 5 March 1898, produced a new, tentative answer to the German-Czech linguistic problem by issuing new decrees (described as 'provisional and pending legislative settlement') for Bohemia and Moravia, making the language in which any case should be handled that of the Bezirk in which it originated, the Bezirk ranking as Czech, German or mixed, according to the census figures. Two days later, Gautsch gave way to Count Franz Anton Thun.

Thun was the man whom Francis Joseph had, it appears, had in mind from the first as Badeni's real successor. He had long been regarded as the coming man among the Conservatives,[1] and to some extent he had a foot in both camps. A member of one of the great Bohemian feudal families (Leo Thun was his uncle), he had, some years before, identified himself with the federalists by calling for Francis Joseph to submit to coronation in Prague. But he described himself as a German, spoke only a few words of Czech, had supported the alliance with Germany in the Delegations, and as Statthalter of Bohemia, had been responsible for the severe repression of the unrest there a few years earlier: his recall from that position had been one of Badeni's concessions to the Czechs. Since then, however, he had partially made up his feud with the Czechs, whose support he hoped to enjoy, and his reason for delaying to enter on his post seems to have been a wish to escape the odium of superseding the Badeni Ordinances.

The administration which he now formed was not unbalanced. Half its members were permanent civil servants, and to these he added, besides the usual Pole (Ritter von Jendrzewicz), a Young Czech (Professor Kaizl) and a German Constitutional Landlord, Dr Joseph Baernreither. Baernreither,

---

[1] Taaffe, before his resignation, had said once that he had only two possible successors: Badeni and Thun. Badeni would last for three years and Thun for two. Both estimates were over-generous.

indeed, resigned after a few months, but Thun succeeded in inducing Freiherr von Dipauli, Chairman of the Catholic People's Party, to take his place, so that all three major nationalities of Cis-Leithania were represented in his Cabinet; and he made sincere efforts to get Czechs and Germans to agree.

His efforts were, however, fruitless. Neither the Germans nor the Czechs were satisfied with Gautsch's enactments. Bohemia was a scene of constant unrest, sometimes bloody. One side or the other was always making work in the Reichsrat impossible; it grew so rowdy that Thun was, or felt himself, forced to govern largely without it. He invoked Para. 14 no less than twenty-eight times, using it even to enact a substantial increase in indirect taxation, as well as a further prolongation of the economic Compromise. This completely illegal action brought the Social Democrats into the field against him. The Hungarians, who disliked him for his federalist past, made difficulties over the Compromise. The German parties (except the Clericals and the All-Germans) formed a hostile coalition.[1]

Strong representations came also from Germany. The Kaiser himself had 'not always very tactful advice' conveyed to Goluchowski that Germany might refuse to renew her alliance.[2] This was in connection with certain aspects of Goluchowski's foreign policy – the *rapprochement* with Russia described elsewhere,[3] which the Germans seem to have taken far more seriously than it deserved, and need not have had any bearing on Austria's internal policy. But the Czechs in the Delegations were indiscreetly advocating a reversal of Austria's international alignments, and the German Ambassador in Vienna, Count Eulenburg, made really strong representations to the Emperor himself on the ill effects on German public opinion – effects which Wilhelm himself 'would be unable to ignore, with the best will in the world' – of 'a Czech majority as Government Party' [in Austria].[4]

In the winter of 1898 and the spring of 1899, when most of these exchanges were taking place,[5] Francis Joseph and Thun, who were extremely angry with the Germans, especially over the support which Schönerer's *Los von Rom* movement was enjoying in Berlin,[6] seem to have given as good as they got. But the Germans' warnings cannot have left the Emperor unaffected, and for that matter, he himself, although more hostile to the 'Schönerianer' than to any non-German national movement, probably never felt it entirely natural to disregard the feelings of his German subjects in favour of those of

[1] See below, p. 681.
[2] Redlich, *Franz Joseph*, p. 394.
[3] See above, pp. 595 ff.
[4] *Grosse Politik*, XIII. 3486 (of 15 December 1898); see also id., 3480.
[5] The last of the despatches recording exchanges in this vein reproduced in the *Grosse Politik* is dated 13 April.
[6] It was being vigorously applauded and supported by the Superintendent General of the Lutheran Church in Berlin.

Czechs or Slovenes.¹ It was the situation of 1871 over again. What may have tipped the scales now in the Emperor's mind was an incident at the end of July when Aehrenthal, then Ambassador in Petersburg, sought him out in Ischl. Kálnoky, who had died in the preceding February, had bequeathed his papers to Aehrenthal, who found among them a memorandum destined for the Emperor, urging him to base his internal policy on the Germans, thus cementing the alliance with Germany and securing the loyalty of Hungary. Aehrenthal took this memorandum to the Emperor, adding to it his own representations in the same sense and expressing the uneasiness of the Constitutional Landowners, to which group he belonged, at Thun's policy.² To whichever of the many considerations we assign the decisive role, it seems certain that in the summer of 1899 Francis Joseph experienced the decisive change of heart and decided, as he expressed it to Eulenburg, 'to turn towards *Deutschtum*.³ After various attempts to form another Parliamentary or pseudo-Parliamentary Cabinet on a coalition basis had failed,⁴ he accepted Thun's resignation on 2 October, and appointed Count Clary-Aldringen, Statthalter of Styria, with the avowed mission of repealing the Badeni-Gautsch Ordinances; which he duly did on 14 October.

Clary's short reign was only another period of confusion, for again, the Czechs were enraged and the Germans, who wanted the Stremayr Ordinances repealed also, unsatisfied. The representatives of the two peoples vied with each other in disorder, thereby creating a situation which was personally impossible for Clary, since in view of the great indignation aroused by his two predecessors' abuse of Para. 14 to put through measures affecting the taxpayers' pocket, he had promised not to invoke the paragraph, but found it impossible to govern without it. Being an honest man, he resigned on 21 December, and after an interim administration headed by Ritter von Wittek had carried on for a few weeks (during which it used Para. 14 extensively), the Emperor, on 18 January 1900, appointed to the Minister Presidency Dr Ernst von Koerber, another permanent civil servant with Ministerial experience.

¹ Another factor which may have been important, and is given by Tschuppik (p. 356) as the actual reason for Thun's fall, was a campaign started by the Czechs that recruits called up for service, and not yet in uniform, should answer their names with *Žde* instead of *hier*. This sounds trivial, but we cannot dismiss it when we recall how enraged Francis Joseph was, a few years later, when the Hungarians tried to tamper with the sacrosanct unitary language of command in the Army.

² See on this Kolmer, VII. 338 ff. Redlich, op. cit., is curiously unreliable on this question. He describes Thun's Cabinet as 'a purely civil servant' one, omits all mention of the Kálnoky-Aehrenthal incident and says that Francis Joseph underwent another of his 'sudden changes of mood' and dismissed Thun 'ungraciously'. None of these statements is correct. As Kolmer shows, the negotiations went on for weeks and Thun remained in high favour.

³ Eulenburg to Hohenlohe, *Grosse Politik*, XIII. 3513 (21 November 1899). 'Die von dem Kaiser eingeschlagene, von höchstdemselbem mir persönlich bestätigte Wendung zum Deutschtum.'   ⁴ On these, see Kolmer, l.c.

This was a real change, if only one of nuances and one which was easier to feel than to define, for, like his predecessors, Koerber composed his Cabinet chiefly of civil servants and called it 'neutral', and although most of its members were Germans, he included in it, besides the usual Pole, a Czech *Landsmannminister* (Dr A. Rezek),[1] and again like his predecessors, he began by trying to mediate a German-Czech settlement in Bohemia, on the basis, to which all his successors adhered, that he would accept any settlement agreed between the parties, but not impose one. Like the rest, he failed: the Czechs, who now felt themselves on the defensive, announced that they would go on obstructing the work of the Reichsrat until they received 'satisfaction for the crime of 17 October 1899' (i.e., the repeal of the Badeni-Gautsch Ordinances), while the Germans retorted by making work in the Prague Landtag equally impossible. Neither side would listen to Koerber's proposals, although they were sensible enough.[2]

In 1900, meanwhile, an economic crisis had broken out; Koerber tried to meet this by economic treatment,[3] and in September dissolved Parliament, which he accused, in a singularly outspoken manifesto, of having wasted its time on barren controversy over the use of the official language in a few Crownlands – an issue which did not even affect much of the Monarchy – and invited the electorate to choose a successor which would pay attention to its real social and economic interests.

This it refused to do. When the elections were held, in January 1901,[4] almost every nationality returned some Deputies representing class interests,[5] but almost all (except the German Social Democrats) voted with the specifically national parties on national issues, whose trumpeters continued to make the Reichsrat's work impossible, and, competent as he was – perhaps the most able Minister President in Austrian history – Koerber could do no more with that body than any of his predecessors. The public works and other measures initiated by him helped Austria to recover from the economic depression, and these and other of his measures, which included salutory reforms to the structure and spirit of the bureaucracy, made his five years of

[1] Succeeded in 1903 by Professor Randa.
[2] Since none of these were realized, the reader is spared a recital of them.
[3] See below, p. 670.
[4] The delay was due partly to preparations for the census; partly to business connected with the Archduke Francis Ferdinand's morganatic marriage and renunciation of the succession for his issue.
[5] The full figures, according to Hugelmann (p. 217), were: German (Constitutional) Great Landed Proprietors, 30; German Clericals (Catholic People's Party), 37; German Progressives, 39; German People's Party, 48; Pan-Germans (Schönerer), 21; German Liberals (*Freie Deutsche Vereinigung*), 12; Styrian Peasant Party, 1; Christian Socials, 22; Social Democrats, 10; Young Czechs, 53; Czech National Party of Work, 5; Czech Agrarians, 6; Czech Catholic People's Party, 2; Czech Great Landed Proprietors, 16; Polish Club, 53; Stojalowski's Group, 5; Polish People's Party, 3; Polish Social Party, 1; Slovenes, 16; Croats and Serbs, 11; Italians, 19; Ruthenes, 10; Roumanians, 5.

office in many respects the most fruitful which Austria had known for many years. But they were fruitful because, although Parliament still met during them, and although Koerber allowed the Press more freedom than it had enjoyed for many years, they were in effect another period of enlightened absolutism. All that the innumerable Party groups did was to howl and obstruct until bought off by some concession – a local railway here, a subsidy to an industry there – thus even distorting and rendering irrational the public works programme. Meanwhile, the continued efforts which Koerber, like his predecessors, made to find a solution to the national controversies, particularly that between Czechs and Germans in Bohemia, were as unavailing as before. When, on 30 December 1904, he resigned, he had proved that Austria could still be governed, but only by non-Parliamentary methods, which could, of course, only be applied so long as she possessed a sufficient number of disciplined servants willing and able to carry them through.

We need not say much on the general demographic, economic and social developments of the period, since they were straightforward enough protractions of those of its predecessor. In spite of the continued emigration, the figure of which reached 93,000 in 1902 and 103,000 in 1903, the population registered another substantial increase, reaching in 1900 a figure of well over 26 millions. Thanks to, or in spite of, a new tariff policy which the Monarchy adopted in 1891, when it abandoned its autonomous tariff and adhered to the Caprivi system, with its high measure of freedom of interchange between Austria, Germany, Belgium, Italy and Switzerland – experts are divided on the effects of this policy, as they were on those of its predecessor – industrialization had gone on at a pace which, if slower than that of Germany, was yet much faster than anything which Austria had known since the boom years before 1873. In 1900 7,004,000 persons, or 25·9% of the population,[1] were deriving their livelihoods from industry or mining. These occupations were taking up the bulk of the increased population; agriculture, fisheries and forestry were barely holding their own in absolute figures, with 13,709,000 persons (52·1% of the total) deriving their livelihoods from them.[2] Parallel with this process, the move into the towns was going on. By 1900 the population of Vienna had risen to 1,675,000. Prague had 201,000, Trieste 178,000, Lemberg 160,000, Graz 138,000, Brünn 109,000. There were 44 towns with populations of 20,000+, with an aggregate population of 3,775,000, 74 of 10–20,000 (1,103,000), 198 of 5–10,000 (1,340,000) and 344 of 2–5,000 (3,874,000). Except in Galicia, the towns were taking up

[1] Inclusive of dependents; this applies also to the other occupational figures quoted.
[2] The other groups were: finance, commerce and communications, 2,604,000 (10·0%); public services, 864,000 (3·4%); free professions, 107,000 (0·4%); rentiers and capitalists, 831,000 (3·2%); active military, 263,000 (1·0%); others and unknown, 760,000 (3·0%).

nearly the entire increase in the population; the rural population in the Alpine Lands and Central and Southern Bohemia was declining.

It was, on the whole, a prosperous period. Industry enjoyed a continuous boom through the 1890s. This was interrupted in 1900 by the crisis mentioned on another page, which, breaking out over labour disputes in the Bohemian coal-fields, spread to industry and for a while, caused widespread unemployment; but its own resilience, aided by Koerber's programme of public works,[1] enabled it to weather the crisis better than had been expected, and the upward trend was resumed. It is true that this was mainly financed by the banks, who controlled an unhealthily large proportion of the Monarchy's more important enterprises. Agriculture was still reeling under the impact of foreign competition, but was beginning to organize its defences. The foundation of agricultural colleges, the importation of improved strains of stock and seeds, and other measures of the kind, some of them the work of the Government of the day, some of their predecessors, had brought about a considerable rise in the yield of most main crops, and the improvement was helped, towards the end of the period, by a recovery in world prices.[2] It was important that knowledge of the improved methods was spreading to the peasant cultivators, who were helped also by the growth of the co-operative movement, a feature of the period. There were, indeed, still black spots. If the curve of distraints and of more or less forced or fraudulent sales of marginal farms in the Alpine areas was flattening out slightly, this was simply a sign that the weakest members had been eliminated altogether; the declining population figures for these areas showed that the process was still going on, as was parcellization of the surviving peasant holdings. In other areas, notably Galicia-Bukovina, where the growth of the population was almost unrelieved by industrialization,[3] rural congestion had reached terrifying proportions. Here social conditions were becoming extremely critical. The large-scale emigration, overseas or seasonal, to which the landless men were now resorting, saved some of them from death by starvation, but now the landlords complained that they were unable to get labour at all, at prices which they could afford to pay.[4] It appears that regular wages had

[1] The programme, which was originally estimated to cost 480,000,000 kr., but although never completed, cost, imperfect as it was, far more than that sum, was mainly concerned with communications. There was to be a second railway line (the Tauernbahn) to Trieste, other railways in Galicia, Bohemia and North Styria, and canals joining the Danube to the Oder, and thence to the Vistula and the Dniester, and between the Danube and the Moldau, to link up with the Upper Elbe; also extensive improvements to the harbour of Trieste.

[2] The price of wheat touched almost rock-bottom in 1891, when it was only 14 kr. After that it rose gradually: the average over the decade was 17·3 kr.

[3] Industry was developing, even in Galicia, especially the oil industry, in which production rose from 32 million tons in 1880 to 1,763 m.t. in 1910. This industry, however, is one which employs relatively little manpower.

[4] In 1896 they had secured the passage of a law making it a penal offence to incite a person to emigrate by holding out false prospects to him.

in fact risen considerably,[1] although still not to an extent to give a decent livelihood to the recipients. On the other hand, the landlords had combined to drive down the share of the harvest paid in kind to the seasonal labourers, which by 1902 they had reduced to a maximum of one-twelfth.[2] From 1897 onward harvest strikes occurred, which the landlords countered by introducing machinery and importing 'foreign' workers. In 1903 there was serious unrest; the houses of Jewish landlords were burnt and their lives endangered.

In 1892 Austria went over to the gold standard, establishing a new currency, the krone (2 kr. = 1 gulden) which was to be interchangeable with the notes of the National Bank.[3] The success of the operation exceeded all expectation. For a couple of years the krone sank against gold, but the public had been so long accustomed to paper that it preferred the familiar notes to gold. Soon only 160 of the 416 million kronen originally minted were in circulation.[4] The rest retired to, or remained in, the vaults of the National Bank, which thus found itself in possession of a very large gold reserve, with which it was able to keep the krone at parity (at which it remained until 1914) and to eliminate the speculation in the national currency which for nearly a century had bled Austria white for the benefit of a few dubious individuals. A 4% loan to acquire gold was taken up easily, and another, issued in 1895, actually reached a quotation of 119. The service of the national debt was now only about 15% of the total expenditure, compared with 32·7% in 1868, and most of it was held at home. With this, Austria's financial connections had widened. Dunajewski is credited with having 'emancipated Austria from the rule of the Rothschilds' by calling in French capital. Afterwards, indeed, French financial interests in Austria were outstripped by German.[5]

As the reader will have gathered from the first section of this chapter, the period brought with it certain new developments in the nature and strength of the political forces in Austria. On the social plane, the emergent political forces were those of the Left. In spite of the terrorism habitually exercised at the polls in Galicia, thanks to which the landlords, who already possessed forty-four Landtag mandates as a Curia, usually managed to secure also most of the seats for the rural communes, a Ruthene 'agrarian socialist' priest named Stojalowski got into the Landtag in 1896 with five followers calling themselves 'Christian Populists', and he and one of his adherents even got as far as the Reichsrat. A Polish counterpart headed a group of three 'Polish

[1] According to Drage, op. cit., p. 67, agricultural wages in Austria rose from 20-250%, according to district, between 1877 and 1902.

[2] Drage, op. cit., p. 69, attributes this move to a ring of Jews, who by now owned 453 of the 2,430 large estates in Galicia, leased 800 of the 1,000 which were leased, and held the whip hand, through mortgages, over many others. Thirty per cent of the estate managers were Jews.   [3] For a brilliant description of this operation see Steed, op. cit., pp. 138 ff.

[4] Drage, op. cit., p. 237.   [5] See on this May, op. cit., pp. 231 ff.

Populists', and a third peasant party, the 'Bojko Party', entered the Landtag in 1901. A fair number of peasant representatives were now getting into other Landtage, and occasionally into the Reichsrat. The structure of the Monarchy, however, made it practically impossible for any peasant movement to develop on anything wider than a Land basis. Important advances were, however, made by both the Christian Social and the Social Democrat Parties.

The Cardinal Secretary of State, Rampolla, was sympathetic to the Christian Social movement, and on his intervention the Pope, early in 1891, received Professor Schindler, one of the leading spirits in the Catholic revival, and on 13 May, in effect, gave his blessing to the Party and Papal authority to its programme in his Encyclical *Rerum Novarum*. In 1893 the Party received another influential supporter in Vienna in the person of the new Nuncio, Mgr Agliardi. The movement, however, still had to fight an uphill battle against powerful opponents. In 1893 the Government actually sent the Vatican a memorandum describing the Party as 'both superfluous and subversive', and Cardinal Schönborn, Archbishop of Prague, went to Rome to make the same points in the name of the Austrian Episcopate. The Hungarians, to whom Lueger was consistently and demonstratively offensive, also used their influence against him, as, allegedly, did the House of Rothschild. In 1895, when the Christian Socialists gained a large majority in the Municipal Council of Vienna and Lueger's name was put forward, for Burgomaster, the Emperor, on Badeni's advice, refused to confirm the appointment.[1] In 1896, the Council having re-elected Lueger, the Emperor intervened personally and persuaded him to accept the post of Vice-Burgomaster under his Party colleague, Josef Strobach.

But the Party was not to be denied, and when the Reichsrat elections of 1897 brought it 27 mandates, Francis Joseph bowed to the popular will. Strobach resigned, and Lueger became Burgomaster. His integrity, his handsome appearance and his homely humour won for him an immense personal popularity; he was also both an administrator of genius and an unscrupulous and ruthless political tactician. With the help of certain changes in the statutes of both bodies which he induced the Wittek Government to put through for him, he consolidated his Party's position in Vienna and won for it a two-thirds majority at the 1902 elections for the Lower Austrian Landtag, when it won practically every seat in Vienna. Under his regime the administration of Vienna and its municipal services – transport, water supply, health services, public libraries, etc., became among the most progressive and imaginative in Europe, and those of Lower Austria came near matching them. The Party's stronghold was still Vienna, but it now had a considerable

---

[1] The voting in that year had been 92 Christian Socialists to 46 others. In the previous year the elections to the Council had given the Christian Socials 64 seats to 66 Liberals and 8 others. Lueger had been elected but had himself declined the appointment and the Council had been dissolved, with the above result.

following in many of the Alpine Lands, among the parish priests, for whose tastes the 'Bishops' Party' (as the Catholic People's Party was generally known) was too conservative, and for the same reason, among the peasants of the more advanced districts.

The Christian Social Party, however, never succeeded in gaining serious support among the industrial workers: attempts in which Leopold Kunschak, then a young journeyman's apprentice, took the lead, to found Christian Trade Unions, met with small success. The Trade Union movement and the political movement among the organized industrial workers remained the domain of the Social Democrat Party, which, once Adler had given it its fresh start, also went ahead very fast. Exact figures of its membership are extraordinarily difficult to discover, but by 1906 it had 90,797 members in Vienna, organized in 47 'political associations'.[1] There were about 17,500 members in Styria, 20,000 in Bohemia-Moravia and a few thousand elsewhere. The Party now possessed its own Press – the daily *Arbeiterzeitung*, the weekly *Kampf* and other organs – and a whole network of women's and youth organizations, etc.

These were not, indeed, large absolute figures, at least outside Vienna, but the sympathizers with the Social Democrats outnumbered many times their organized members. The great strength of the Party lay in its close association with the Trade Unions, which also made great progress. In 1892 there were still only 46,606 organized workers, but the figure for 1902 was 135,178; for 1905, 323,099. This figure, again, was still relatively small compared with the total number of workers: in Vienna, where it was much the highest, it was still only about 25%, and in some of the outlying Lands, 5%, 2%, or 1%. The only trade in which a majority of the workers was organized was the printers (77·75%). Then came the dock labourers (almost entirely in Trieste), with 38·46%. No other trade had an organized membership of 30%, and only ten others, one of 20% or more. These numbers were, however, rising very rapidly.[2]

The Party devoted especial attention to training and indoctrinating the Unions and to eliminating from them all influences except its own. In this it was extraordinarily successful. Naturally, not all members of the Unions were Party members, but in practice, the Party organization and that of the Unions were almost identical. The Party could count on the votes of nearly

[1] Brügel, *Geschichte*, IV. 384. This gives a 'Progress Report' by Lands, but most Lands give only the Trade Union membership.

[2] Tiefen, pp. 186–7, gives figures for the end of 1905, quoted from the *Gewerkschaft*. The chief ones are: Vienna, 97,198; Lower Austria (outside Vienna), 19,893; Bohemia, 94,325; Moravia, 37,599; Styria, 18,693; Silesia, 14,496. Galicia had only 8,017 (out of 113,839 workers in employment), the Alpine Lands a few thousands each and the tail was brought up by Bukovina (508) and Dalmatia (133). But Tiefen's own calculation of the ratio of organized to total workers does not agree with his absolute figures.

all Union members in any election and their support in matters of policy. In particular, it mobilized them regularly, and with great frequency, in strikes and demonstrations, not only for improvements in working conditions but also for political purposes, above all, for extension of the franchise, which Adler had designated to be the chief goal at which the Party must aim.[1] The period saw a very large number of strikes, which brought about considerable further improvements in working conditions,[2] and certainly contributed largely to the extensions of the suffrage which took place in this period and its successor.

Between them, the Social Democratic Party and the Trade Unions made the workers' movement into a powerful factor in the Austrian political life of the day. It is true that their influence was almost confined to central affairs, and locally, to the life of Vienna, Bohemia-Moravia and Styria; elsewhere it was negligible. It is also true that the strength of the movement was greatly diminished by the national conflicts within it described below.[3]

The parties representing the other end of the social and economic gamut were now fighting a rearguard action with dwindling numbers. The Liberals, as we have seen, almost disappeared in 1897; had the franchise not been extraordinarily favourable to them, their downfall would have been more spectacular still. The conservative elements in the Catholic Church put up a better fight against what they regarded as their three enemies in chief, Godless Social Democracy, Protestant extremist German nationalism and subversive Christian Socialism. The Catholic People's Party which entered the lists in the 1897 elections with the objective of rallying the Germans of Austria under this flag had considerable success, especially in its stronghold, the Tirol; and it represented a spirit which enabled the Church to remain a powerful factor, especially in the Alpine Lands, up to the end of the Monarchy.[4]

The most important political phenomenon of the period was still the continued growth and exacerbation of national feeling among the peoples of Austria. From this radicalization of feeling no single one of the peoples, except perhaps the 'satiated nationality' of the Poles, was exempt, and several of them also began to look, much more than before, across the frontiers, if not of the Monarchy, at least of the Leitha.

[1] See Cole, op. cit., p. 535.
[2] The chief benefit of these went to the miners, whose conditions really improved, especially in respect of safety; they also got a reduction in their working day. Outside mines, the biggest advances were in connection with factory inspection and the Sunday rest, which became law in 1895, and the extension of accident insurance to transport workers.
[3] See below, pp. 684 f., 803 f.
[4] See on this Hantsch, *Geschichte*, II. 470–1. After the fusion of the People's Party and the Christian Socials in the next decade, the name and nominal leadership of the two components passed to the Christian Socials, but the Catholic People's Party contributed more of the spirit.

After German rowdyism had enforced the repeal of the Badeni Ordinances, Czech rowdyism failed, as we have seen, to get them restored and the position with respect to the use of the two languages in public life remained that of the 1880s, with German still enjoying a certain advantage. The Czechs had, however, caught up more ground in the economic, social and cultural fields and were now the Germans' equals on all but the very highest levels.[1] Meanwhile, the Czech leaders had begun to interest themselves again in the wider objective of swinging the foreign political alignment of the Monarchy away from Germany, towards the new Franco-Russian axis.

The moving spirit in these endeavours was Dr Karel Kramář, who emerged in the 1890s as one of the most prominent Young Czech leaders. During the politically uncertain latter years of the decade Kramář was strongly urging in the Delegations that Austria should change her foreign political orientation, and his speeches and writings to this effect contributed not a little to the *refroidissement* which prevailed for a little while between Austria and Germany. The passing of the coolness only hardened his determination; in 1902 he sent Delcassé a memorandum warning France of the danger of the *Drang nach Osten*. His heart was, however, less with France than with Russia, for which he had a deep attachment, especially after he had married the daughter of a rich Kiev merchant and taken to spending much time in Russia, where he was in close touch with the Slavophile politicians and writers.

The other prominent Czech politician who refused to hobble himself to the Bohemian parish pump was Thomas Garrigue Masaryk, the later President of the Czechoslovak Republic. Masaryk had, indeed, begun his career by mortally offending the conventional Young Czech politicians by a work in which he exposed the true origin of the 'Königinhof forgeries'[2] (this being not the only occasion on which he braved unpopularity by championing an unpopular cause).[3] In 1890 he and a few friends had founded a 'Realist Party' which gave itself that name because it rejected as 'unrealistic' making the *Böhmisches Staatsrecht* the basis of Czech claims; Masaryk wished to derive these rather from natural right, and said that he would be satisfied with an Austria organized as a democratic federation of equal peoples.

Most of Masaryk's early associates, who included Kramář, soon forsook him for the Young Czechs, and in the years which we are now describing his party in the Reichsrat usually consisted only of himself and one other, and its influence on immediate political developments was negligible. On a wider view, however, Masaryk proved more dangerous to the Monarchy than Kramář himself. Although he did not begin as a declared enemy of the

---

[1] Surveys of the positions of the two nations in these fields are given by Hugelmann, op. cit., pp. 416 ff., and Münch, op. cit., pp. 456 ff. [2] See above, p. 219.

[3] He also wrote a book denouncing the legend of Jewish ritual murder. This, indeed, later brought great advantage to his national cause, for it helped to win it much support from the Jewish communities of Britain and the USA during the First World War (see Sir Tom Bridges, *Alarms and Excursions*, 1938, p. 213).

Monarchy and his conversion to the view that it was *delenda* was only gradual;[1] and although when he reached that view, he still had no clear programme for the Czechs after the Monarchy had disappeared,[2] yet he gradually became convinced that the Monarchy was irreparably lacking in the qualities of justice and democracy which would justify its existence and set himself 'to de-Austrianize (the Czechs) thoroughly while they were still in Austria'.[3]

Masaryk was such an incomparably disruptive force because he expounded ideas of such moral loftiness that they made an irresistible impression on foreign observers; at the same time, they lent themselves to translation by less scrupulous men on to political planes some of which were far less lofty.

Meanwhile, he also became one of the most dangerous enemies of Dualism. His lectures at the Czech University in Prague (to which he had been appointed on its creation in 1882) were attended by many students, including Croats, Slovaks and Serbs from Hungary, who sought its relatively free atmosphere. Himself a Moravian Slovak, Masaryk probably did more than any one other man to revive the then rather drooping plant of Czecho-Slovak nationalism, and he was also a great advocate of Serbo-Croat unity. His affections did not lie with Russia, which he found even less satisfactory than Austria, and he never acknowledged himself to be particularly pro-Slav, even in cultural respects, but his was probably one of the chief influences in the Monarchy in promoting the self-confidence and ambitions of its Slav inhabitants.

If now, as always, less was heard of the Slovenes and Croats than of the Czechs this did not mean that they were, fundamentally, more quiescent. The national consciousness of the Slovenes had been enormously stimulated by the Cilli episode and they were now making progress at a great pace in almost every field and area. Only in Carinthia were they still losing some ground through assimilation: they were holding their own ethnically in Styria, advancing in the rural districts of Gorizia-Gradisca and penetrating Trieste.[4] In Carniola (as in South Styria) only the landlords and the *haute*

---

[1] In the very last speech made by him in the Reichsrat (in 1913) he said specifically that 'he could not indulge in dreams of the collapse of Austria, and knew that this Austria would endure for good or ill'. Cit. Hantsch, *Nationalitätenfrage*, p. 66.

[2] Masaryk, *The Making of a State*, p. 46.

[3] Masaryk, op. cit., p. 47.

[4] The statistics show the Slovenes in Carinthia as declining both percentually (1880, 29·7%; 1900, 25·1%) and absolutely (102,000, 90,000). In Styria their percentage went down, owing to the increase in population brought to North Styria by industrialization, but their absolute figures rose slightly. In Carniola their percentage rose from 93·7 to 94·2. In Gorizia-Gradisca the population figures show little change in the proportions, but the school statistics, which show the language spoken by the majority in each commune, indicate a steady Slovene advance. In Trieste the number of Slovenes remained almost static round 25,000 from 1880 to 1900, but bounded up to 57,000 in 1910, apparently owing to an influx of workers into the new shipyards.

bourgeoisie were still German. Laibach was an almost purely Slovene city,[1] and in it, and other local centres, the Slovenes now possessed a considerable middle and lower bourgeoisie which had definitely discarded the role of a 'servant people' with which the Slovenes had been content a century before. The same could be said, *mutatis mutandis*, of the Croats of Dalmatia, who were also becoming very strongly conscious of their national identity with their kinsfolk in Croatia and the Herzegovina.

The voice of the people had by now definitely answered in favour of Ukrainian the question of what the Ruthenes were, or at least, what their language was,[2] and since Russia, during these years, was devoting little attention to the peoples across her south-western frontiers, the Ukrainophiles, or Young Ruthenes, had matters pretty well their own way against the 'Muscovites' or Old Ruthenes. By now, however, the Young Ruthenes had been forced to see the futility of their hopes of getting anywhere by collaboration with the Poles, who maintained unabated their grip on the political life and educational system (above the elementary level) of Galicia,[3] and the relations between the two peoples were now openly hostile. The statistics continued to show a further slight diminution in the relative numbers of the Ruthenes,[4] and this doubtless reflected some continued assimilation, though the influence of emigration was probably greater. But the hard core was hardening further,[5] and the Ruthenes were now clamouring, in truly bellicose tones, for satisfaction of their national desiderata, especially equality of official usage for the two *Landessprachen*, to which was added a demand for the administrative division of Galicia, and more educational facilities, in particular, an independent Ruthene University in Lemberg (in favour of which seven hundred Ruthene students walked out in 1902).

The deplorable social conditions in East Galicia, and the circumstance that the Ruthenes constituted the social and economic underdogs there,

[1] In 1910 it contained only 5,900 Germans against 33,800 Slovenes.

[2] Another factor was the introduction by the Government (in 1892 in Galicia and 1895 in the Bukovina) of the phonetic orthography in school-books, Old Slavonic being retained only in liturgical works. The identity with Ukrainian of the language spoken by the Ruthenes at once became apparent, and the Ukrainian movement received a big impetus.

[3] For school figures in 1911–12 see Hugelmann, p. 709. The Ruthenes had their full quota of elementary schools, but only 8 out of 79 boys' gymnasia and one out of 21 girls' and no other institution whatever above primary level, except 2 out of the 54 schools for teaching trades. Of the elections to the Reichstag and the Landtag, it is enough to say that the terrorism and corruption practised in them left their Hungarian counterparts in the shade, and that the number of Ruthenes returned in them was always only a small fraction of what their total numbers would have justified.

[4] The figures were: 1900, Polish, 54·8%, Ruthene, 42·2%; 1910, Polish, 58·5%, Ruthene, 40·2%.

[5] Kleinwächter writes (op. cit., p. 177): 'I have myself observed how, especially in circles which had received academic education, Ruthenes who as youths had Polonized completely, reverted to their nationality and now became national Ruthenes.'

suffering under the dual oppression of Polish landlords and Jewish tradesmen and usurers, had the result that their national movement became strongly tinged with extremist Left-wing or even near-anarchist elements; although it might be more accurate to say that the unrest described elsewhere,[1] while primarily social, acquired a national colouring in consequence of the national stratification of the social classes involved.[2]

Even the Roumanians of the Bukovina grew more active. In 1892 their two traditional Parties fused with certain other groups in a 'Roumanian National Party of the Bukovina', under the slogan of 'solidarity of all Roumanians in political, national and ecclesiastical questions' – a more specifically 'national' line than that of either of its predecessors. Almost at the same time, the Bucharest *Liga Culturale* began extending its propaganda to the Duchy.

This was, naturally, not without its effects, and the police reports on unreliable elements, suspicious strangers, etc., grew longer. At the same time, the policy of the official leaders, nearly all of whom belonged to the old cliques, remained as impeccably loyal as before, and there was little trace of anti-German feeling. The Roumanians now saw their chief national antagonists in the local Ruthenes. Whatever had happened a century earlier (when, according to the Roumanians, there had been a big immigration of Ruthenes from Galicia and Russia just when many Roumanians had been emigrating to Moldavia – for it had not been landowners and priests alone who had preferred Moldavian to Austrian rule: there had also been a steady clandestine trickle of peasant emigrants), the respective shares of the two peoples in the total population of the Duchy had since remained almost constant,[3] and the main line between their respective ethnic territories had

---

[1] See above, p. 671.

[2] The harvest strikes were supported and (it was alleged by the Poles) fomented by a 'National Committee' organized in 1901 by the Ruthenes, who had just walked out of the Landtag. It was also alleged that the Ruthenes organized the seasonal migration to Germany, in order to embarrass the Polish landlords. In some cases the more extreme Left-wing Polish parties supported the Ruthenes.

[3] The population figures for the Bukovina are particularly perplexing. The official figures of the *Tafel* for 1846 practically reverse those of Hain, who gives a Ruthene majority even for that year. Hain is almost certainly right: presumably some scribe concerned with the *Tafel* simply put the figures in the wrong columns. The official linguistic figures from 1857 to 1900 are:

	German	%	Ruthene	%	Roumanian	%	Other	%	TOTAL
1857	37,885	8·47	188,288	42·1	175,679	39·3	45,394	10·1	447,095
1880	108,820	19·1	239,690	42·2	190,005	33·4	29,938	5·3	568,453
1890	133,501	20·8	268,367	41·8	208,301	32·4	32,326	5·0	642,495
1900	159,486	22·0	297,798	41·2	229,018	31·7	37,202	5·1	723,504

The 'others' included Poles, Magyars and Armenians. Yiddish was counted as German. It will be seen that while both Ruthenes and Roumanians lost ground percentually, their losses were rather to the German group, than to each other.

hardly changed, but the Ruthenes, who, after all, outnumbered the Roumanians, had become nationally conscious and were demanding the share in the Crownland's affairs to which their numbers entitled them. The Roumanians, whose extremists regarded the Ruthenes as interlopers without any justification at all for their existence, opposed these demands with acerbity, although even in this respect the very complexity of the national conditions and the presence of the big German and Jewish elements, which formed a mediating cushion between the two antagonists in chief, prevented the struggle from becoming as envenomed as it was in the more advanced provinces.

The Italian question had grown perceptibly more acute, as a result, especially, of the developments in Italy. The *Lega Nationale* and its sister body, the *Pro Patria*, were now carrying on an embittered positional warfare of the familiar type with their opposite numbers, the *Deutscher Schulverein* (1880), the *Südmark* (1889), the *Tiroler Volksbund* (1905) and the Slovene *Cyrill and Method* Society. The language of every village school, the appointment of every minor official, the ownership of every border farm, was made into a national question and any grievance, real or imaginary, magnified into a scandal by the chauvinistic Press of the side affected.

It was as true now as in the preceding period that the Italians of the Monarchy had few genuine grievances, unless the continued refusal to constitute the Trentino a separate Crownland be counted as such. This demand of theirs was, indeed, never granted,[1] nor did the Austrian Government ever find a way to satisfy what was at the time their Italian subjects' other chief demand, which was for a University of their own – a refusal which was due less to ill-will than to the extraordinary intractability of the problem.[2] For the rest, the higher Austrian authorities (it must be admitted, the lower authorities and local populations were less indulgent) went out of their way to avoid

---

[1] To the earlier considerations motivating this refusal were now added strategic ones, for many of the new fortifications which Austria was building against her ally lay in the Italian-speaking area. Koerber refused a petition for this, in very decided terms, in October 1900.

[2] While Lombardy-Venetia still belonged to the Monarchy, its Italians had gone to the Universities of Padua and Pavia (where, incidentally, many of them had imbibed strong Italian nationalism). After 1859 and 1866 they could no longer do so with practical profit because the Austrian Government did not recognize degrees from foreign universities as qualifying for admission to the State services or professions. The Italians of Austria therefore asked for their own University, which they wanted to have in Trieste, as the one big Italian town in the Monarchy. The Austrian authorities were reluctant to allow this, fearing, and certainly with reason, that an Italian university in Trieste would be a hot-bed of irrendentism. The idea of putting the University in Rovereto was considered and dropped; the townlet had, indeed, no qualification except that of inaccessibility. An Italian Law Faculty was opened in Innsbruck in 1904, but riots between Italian and German students promptly broke out, on so severe a scale that the Faculty had to be closed. In 1914 the Italians were promised a Faculty in Vienna, as a provisional measure until a solution for the problem had been found; but it was still baffling authority in 1918. Another difficulty was the insistence of the Slovenes that if the

presenting the Italians with legitimate grievances, and even turned a blind eye to much which they might legitimately have resented.[1]

And awareness of this fact was not altogether lacking among the Italians of Austria themselves. The number of *Austriacante* among them was not insignificant and perhaps not even greatly on the decline. But more than ever, Austria's 'Italian question' was not one between her Government and her Italian subjects, but between the Austrian Monarchy and the Kingdom of Italy. As such, it was growing steadily more acute, and also acquiring a scope which made it far more dangerous to the Monarchy as Italy's new ambitions reached out towards objectives the loss of which would cripple the Monarchy's very existence.[2]

Ultimately most dangerous of all to the Monarchy was the growth and radicalization of national feeling among its Germans. We should not, indeed, follow those Austrian-German historians who call either the Cilli episode or the Badeni Ordinances a 'decisive turning-point' in this development, for the trend had been there long before. But the impetus given to it by each was enormous. Cilli was momentous not only for the violence of the passions which it awoke in an area in which they had previously been relatively restrained[3] but also for the realization (previously obscured by differences between their tactical interests) which it brought to the Germans of the Alpine Lands that their national problem was fundamentally identical with that of the Germans of Bohemia. The issue of the Badeni Ordinances was the first event in Austrian history which really shook the Germans' faith that somehow or other Fate, or the Emperor, or someone, would keep Austria essentially a German State.

Historians have tended to depict the developments which followed in terms of the fortunes of Schönerer's extremists. Schönerer did now become increasingly unrestrained. He insisted on his party's taking the name of *Alldeutsch*, and said openly in the Reichsrat that 'he longed for the day when a German army would march into Austria and destroy it'. In his campaign against every prop on which the Monarchy rested he and his lieutenant, Karl Hermann Wolf, launched in 1898 a *Los von Rom* movement for conversion to

---

Italians had a University, they must have one too (in Laibach); and this brought the Germans out against them.

Another enormous outcry arose in 1913, when the Governor of Trieste forbade the Municipal Council to employ Italian subjects. This, however, was only ending an abnormal situation.

[1] See the anecdotes in Sosnowski, *Politik*, I. p. 286, n. 2, and 267, n. 1. On one occasion, when Italians and anti-Italians planned rival demonstrations in Trieste, the authorities authorized the former to carry red, white and green banners and forbade the latter to carry black and yellow ones. The second anecdote describes how a subaltern quartered in the Trentino was officially censured for having sung the *Gott Erhalte*, with friends, at a private party, with windows open, on an evening when a prominent Italian agitator was visiting the town.   [2] See above, p. 601.   [3] See Sutter, op. cit., pp. 127–8.

the Protestant Church, which Schönerer promised to join (Wolf was a Protestant already) when twenty thousand other converts had done so. The Heir Presumptive was entirely right when he said that *Los von Rom* meant *Los von Oesterreich*.[1] We can hardly doubt that this was the spirit that prompted certain circles in Germany[2] to give the movement, as they did, generous support.

As before, Schönerer was unable to make his a mass movement. In spite of widespread resentment among the othr Germans when the Catholic People's Party joined Thun's government, the *Los von Rom* movement gained in the end only between 50,000–100,000 converts.[3] If the *Alldeutsch* Party secured twenty-one mandates in the 1901 elections, this was due chiefly to the efforts of Wolf, who had organized an *Alldeutsch* Party of his own in German Bohemia, where spirits had been excited to near-hysteria by the Badeni Ordinances, and the success even of that movement proved, as we shall see, short-lived.

But the events of 1897–9 also had an impact, which was far more important, on those Germans in the Monarchy who took the view that it must be preserved, but that its shape must be one satisfactory to themselves. The Badeni Ordinances produced a very widespread and extremely strong feeling that the existing Austria did not answer this demand, and a great cry for an agreed German national policy. In November 1897 the German People's Party, Progressives, Constitutional Landowners, Old Liberals and Christian Socials – thus, if we exclude the Social Democrats as being theoretically supra-national, all the German political parties except the Catholic People's Party (who still refused to make their programme specifically national[4]) and the Alldeutsche, who condemned the others as lukewarm – agreed to form a 'German Front' (*Deutsche Gemeinbürgshaft*). At Whitsun, 1899, they issued a joint programme, which was in fact, with small modifications, that of the German People's Party.[5] This began by stating that the signatories had been forced to act by 'the systematic thrusting back of, and increasing threat to, the German national group (*Volksstamm*) in Austria'. The national struggle in

---

[1] Nevertheless, it had a directly national and not necessarily irredentist appeal in the Bohemian Lands owing to the fact that a disproportionate number of the clergy there, even in the German districts, were Slavs: only 15% of the clergy were German, while the figure should have been 38% had it been proportionate to their total numbers. (Figures from Dr Emil Pfersche, *Die Parteien der Deutschen in Oesterreich*, 1915, p. 11).

[2] Notably the Lutheran Church in Berlin and the Gustav Adolf Verein.

[3] Zöllner, p. 432, puts the number at 70,000, including converts to the Old Catholic confession. About 100,000 converts joined the Lutheran Church up to 1918, nearly all from the Roman Catholic Church, but we cannot suppose all of them to have been disciples of Schönerer and Wolf.

[4] The Party was, however, now entirely German in membership, and contained a strong nationalist wing.

[5] The full text of the *Pfingstprogramm*, as it was commonly called, is given by Kolmer, VII. 297 ff. There is also a long summary and commentary in Hugelmann, pp. 204 ff.

Austria could be eliminated only 'by recognition of the position of the Germans won by them many centuries ago, the maintenance of which was a central necessity for the future of the State', and consequently by 'termination of the long-practised system of satisfying the claims of all other nationalities at the expense of the Germans'. For the Monarchy as a whole, the programme demanded the usual fidelity to the German alliance and closer cultural connections, and in speaking of Hungary it asked only for a reorganization of the Dualist system on the basis of 'equality of rights' with that country.[1] For Cis-Leithania it was in some specific respects so modest as to allow Hugelmann to describe it as betraying a 'far-reaching resignation', and in fact, some of its proposals deserve that name. The greater part of it consists of detailed proposals for the regulation of the linguistic question, Land by Land. Nearly all of these proposals are fair, some of them (e.g. those for the Tirol) even generous,[2] and some of the proposals suggest that the signatories were withdrawing on to the inner lines of the Linz Programme. Thus there is a rather obscure reference to the *de facto* autonomy enjoyed by Galicia, which the signatories seem prepared to admit provided that 'the principle of reciprocity is applied and the Germans in Austria safeguarded from unjust influencing of their national life'; and the proposed Land linguistic rules do not make any proposals for Galicia or Dalmatia, and only very brief and vague ones for the Bukovina and the Littoral.

On the other hand, the official name of Cis-Leithania is to be 'Austria'. In it German is to be 'the general language of communication' and the language of the Reichsrat and of all Ministries and central offices dealing with its affairs as a whole. All State officials must have a thorough knowledge of German and 'educational establishments which prepare pupils for the State services' must instruct them adequately in that language.

These demands largely nullified the implicit or explicit concessions made in other parts of the programme; and in any case its sting lay in its head, in the demand for the recognition for the Germans of a special position 'as won by them many centuries ago'. This was a demand to which, it was quite obvious, the non-German peoples of Austria could never submit in 1899, and if those were its Germans' terms for Austria, then Austria was lost indeed.

Given all the circumstances, it is probably no exaggeration to say that the Whitsun Programme was the most definitive death-sentence which had yet been pronounced on the Monarchy, by any nationality or any party.

The period also brought lamentable proof that Steinbach had been mistaken in thinking that the newly enfranchised classes would prove any less nationalistic than their betters. The party styling itself 'Christian Social', without any

[1] A demand for the stricter use of the German word of command in the Army may perhaps be interpreted as a reference to Hungary.

[2] This *cannot* be said of the proposals for Carinthia, Carniola or Styria.

qualifying adjective, turned out to be a purely German one, and although it never produced any 'national' programme, it habitually took a German nationalist attitude on all national questions (we have seen that it was a signatory to the Whitsun Programme). The Czech, Polish, Italian and Slovene Christian Social parties which came into being during the decade habitually stood solid with their respective nationalities: no Austria-wide Christian Social movement or party ever came into being.

An even worse disappointment came from the Social Democrats. At the Hainfeld Conference the Party, in duty bound, adopted the Marxist slogan that the national struggle 'was only one of the means by which the ruling classes ensured their domination and prevented the real interests of the peoples from finding effective expression'. At the Conference held by them in Brünn in 1899 they called for a sensible regulation of the national question in Austria on the basis of national equality, and advocated the reconstruction of Austria as a 'federal State of nationalities', to achieve which the Crownlands were to be replaced by autonomous territories, delimited nationally. All territories of one nationality should then form a single association, which was to be completely autonomous in 'national' and cultural questions. A separate law, enacted by the central Parliament, was to safeguard the rights of national minorities.

These ideas were afterwards elaborated by two important German-Austrian Socialist thinkers[1] into more detailed blueprints for the reconstruction of the Monarchy, or at least, Cis-Leithania,[2] as a supra-national State. Karl Renner, whose ideas had begun to take shape before he was at least an active Socialist,[3] produced the idea of the dual organization of the State on administrative and national-cultural lines. For the former purpose, Austria was to be organized in eight Gubernia, corresponding to natural and geographic units,[4] and these again into four main groups,[5] with a central Government responsible for foreign and military affairs, common finance, economic life and social welfare and justice, and a central Parliament. Side

[1] Karl Renner, in *Der Kampf der oe. Nationen um den Staat* (1902) and *Grundlagen und Entwicklungsziele der oe. u. Monarchie* (1906) (both published under the pseudonym of Rudolf Springer) and many other works; Otto Bauer in *Die Nationalitätenfrage und die Sozialdemocratie* (1907).

[2] Renner made his proposals applicable to Cis-Leithania only, arguing that if they were carried through there, the success of the example would cause it to be followed in Hungary, but he probably adopted this attitude out of tactical considerations; certainly not out of approval for the national position in Hungary – his *Grundlagen* is conspicuous even among Austrian works for the venom of its references to Hungary. Bauer was prepared to see his system enforced in Hungary. Both men were obviously thinking in terms of the *Gesammtmonarchie*.

[3] He began his career as librarian in the National Library in Vienna, and joined the Social Democrat Party only after 1900, when he was already over thirty years of age.

[4] Galicia-Bukovina, Bohemia, Moravia-Silesia, Carniola-Littoral, Lower Austria, Upper Austria-Salzburg, Tirol-Vorarlberg, Styria-Carinthia.

[5] Alpine, Bohemian, Galician, Littoral.

by side with this, each nationality was to be constituted, on the basis of a national register, in a national 'University' completely autonomous in all 'national-cultural' affairs. Otto Bauer's very brilliant study advocated, in substance, much the same ideas, supported by a wealth of historic background.[1]

Both men thus stood for the integrity of the Austrian State, and by no means simply out of considerations of personal prudence. They sincerely believed that a large multi-national State was a more suitable political form for an area like Central-Eastern Europe, with its multifarious and closely intermingled peoples, than a number of so-called national States; and they believed that Austria had a historic role to play, if only as defender of western civilization against Russia. But truth to tell, their ideas, and even those of the Brünn Programme, were never very popular in the Monarchy. The majority of the German-Austrian Social Democrats themselves only accepted the Brünn Programme as a *pis aller*; what they really wanted was a Socialized version of the Liberals' programme – a centralized Austria basically run by its Germans. And most of their non-German colleagues did not want any German leadership at all. Their revolt was headed by the Czech workers, whose independent movement of 1867[2] had already been strongly national. Their initial programme, as expounded in their organ, the *Delnik*, had attributed the misery of the Czech workers to exploitation by German capital, which was, indeed, pitiless – the condition of the Czech workers was far worse even than that of the German – and a banquet held to celebrate the inauguration of the movement had been attended by Palacký, Rieger, the two Gregrs, and several Czech manufacturers.[3] A police report of 1870 said that when approached by the German Bohemians, the Czechs had, on the advice of the Young Czech leaders, refused, saying that 'they preferred to go their own way until the Bohemian question was settled'.[4] They had even for a time considered joining the Young Czechs.[5] The party re-founded in 1878 had agreed to join the 'Austrian' party after Hainfeld, but had made difficulties from the first. To meet them, the Brünn Congress converted the Party into seven national sections,[6] each largely autonomous, although there was to be a federal executive and the Party was to act in the Reichsrat as a united whole. But even this, while going too far for the Germans, did not go far

[1] These plans are interesting not only in themselves but as having formed the basis of the nationalities policy afterwards introduced by the Bolsheviks in Soviet Russia.

[2] See above, p. 554.

[3] Charmatz, *Kampf der Nationen*, p. 31.

[4] Brüghel, *Geschichte*, I. 319.

[5] In 1873 the police even believed that 'the politicians' (i.e. the Young Czechs) had 'called the workers' movement into being in their own interest' (Brügel, II. 258). Another report said that the German employers 'tried to Germanize their workers', to which the Czechs objected.

[6] German, Czech, Croat(!), Slovene, Italian, Polish, Ruthene.

enough for the Czechs, and as we shall see,[1] further trouble soon broke out.

Thus of all the political parties in Cis-Leithania, only the 'Christian People's Party' and the main Social Democrat Party were not yet, in theory, on a national basis. It was, of course, true that very few men – a fraction of the Italians and a very small proportion of the Germans and Ruthenes – were yet actively disloyal to the State, but for the others, their prime political interest now was not to advance the welfare of the State but to strengthen the position of their own nationality in it. And those circles in the innermost councils of the Monarchy which still retained the old spirit were by now small indeed.

The habitual public disorder of the period in Austria had, as the reader will have seen, called for increasingly frequent intervention by the Monarch, and this was perhaps something which he welcomed, not out of lust of power, which had left him, but because otherwise he would simply not have known how to occupy himself. Francis Joseph had not, it appears, felt any very deep devotion to his son. Nevertheless, the young man's death, in such tragic and discreditable circumstances, was a blow from which he found it hard to recover. It was made far worse by the effect which the tragedy had on his wife. It brought her distraction to overflowing, and after it, she was seldom seen in Vienna. Always dressed in black,[2] she wandered over Europe like an unquiet ghost, until on 10 September 1898, she met her equally tragic and senseless end, assassinated by an Italian anarchist on a quay at Geneva.

Now Francis Joseph was really alone. He was fond of his younger daughter, Maria Valerie, and a reasonably affectionate grandfather to his daughter's children. But he had little use for the rest of his family. He did not care for his surviving brother, Ludwig Viktor,[3] and seems to have been deeply mortified over the numerous cases in which members of his august House rejected its rules by entering on morganatic marriages, or even contracting out of it altogether.[4] He had sympathies for some, although by no means all, of his fellow-Monarchs,[5] but his contacts with them were, of necessity, rare. He was too conscious of his rank ever to have a real man friend not of royal blood since he outgrew boyhood. The only truly intimate human contacts

---

[1] See below, p. 803 f.

[2] After the tragedy she put off mourning only for a single day in her life, the wedding of her daughter Valerie.

[3] Margutti, p. 146. On these intimate details, Margutti is far better informed than Redlich, or even Tschuppik.

[4] The sensational case in this respect was that of the Archduke Johann Salvator, who, shortly after Rudolph's death, had renounced his membership of the family, taken the name of Johann Orth, and simply disappeared. There seems to be no doubt (although popular opinion long refused to believe it) that he went down with a sailing-ship which he was commanding in Pacific waters in 1891.

[5] Perhaps his only real friend had been Albert of Saxony, who, however, died in 1902.

which he had with any human being after his wife took definitively to her nomadic life was with a charming actress, Katherina Schratt, whose closer acquaintance with him Elisabeth herself arranged. Frau Schratt, whom for many years he visited almost daily, undoubtedly gave him much comfort and consolation, but even with her, he remained the Monarch. She never exercised, or even tried to exercise, the slightest influence over his political decisions. If she guided him at all – and here her recommendations were not always fortunate – it was on literary and artistic questions.

Uninterested as he was in literature – either serious or light – or the arts, Francis Joseph devoted himself after 1890 almost exclusively to the business of governing his Monarchy. Outside his visits to Frau Schratt, the shooting expeditions, principally after chamois, which still gave him great pleasure, and the ceremonial functions which he still performed punctiliously, but without gusto, he took little time off from his desk, rising at an unconscionable hour (a sore trial to his entourage) and spending long hours over his papers. The Court ceased to be a social centre, although the full ceremonial was maintained for occasions of State.

In these years he probably exercised little less personal control over the destinies of the Monarchy than he had in the years when he was in theory its absolute ruler. He now left, indeed, minutiae to his Ministers, reserving to himself only final decisions, but the impotence of the Austrian Parliament placed on his shoulders the burden of an inordinate number of these, and the cases were innumerable when he had to intervene and decide because everyone else had reached a deadlock.

The rule thus exercised by him was fundamentally conservative. The truth of this statement is not invalidated by the fact that he was, as we have seen, something like the prime mover in what might have been called the near-revolutionary innovation of suffrage reform. For his motive, even here, was basically conservative: it sprang from the belief that the working classes of the Monarchy would save it from the subversive nationalism of its bourgeoisies. Suffrage reform was for him an expedient like any other to keep the Monarchy ticking over. This had become the end of his statecraft, and he followed it with considerable skill, the fruit of an experience which had by now become unique.

15

Hungary under Dualism, 1867–1903

I POLITICAL DEVELOPMENTS

The salient difference between the political working of Austria and Hungary for a generation after 1867 was that while in the former the Dualist system achieved in 1867 was, after some initial hesitation, generally accepted as an unpalatable but unalterable fact of life, this was not the case in Hungary. It has been said that while Francis Joseph looked on the Compromise as the end of a process, the Hungarians regarded it as a beginning. This is not entirely true of the Monarch himself, in the first years, and certainly not true of some of his advisers; it was only when he grew older, and felt himself too tired to reopen the series of experiments, that Francis Joseph himself insisted that the settlement reached in 1867 must be taken as final. But it never occurred to the Hungarians, whose entire political history had consisted of a series of periodical re-statements of their relationship to their Monarch, that this one was to be regarded as sacrosanct and immutable. If satisfactory to them, it should be maintained; if it proved unsatisfactory, they were as a nation neither legally nor morally bound to refrain from trying to get it amended. And the effect of the inveterate traditional national assumption (which had some historical justification) that all Hungary's problems were governed, in greater or less degree, by her relationship with her king, was that this question of the maintenance or revision of the Compromise – the 'issue of public law',[1] as it was called, was from the first the central theme of her entire political life.

The primacy might not have been so absolute if the country had really been making a fresh start in the autumn of 1867. But the Diet of 1865 had been convoked for the specific purpose of reaching (if it could) agreement with the Crown. No other item had been on its agenda – the settlements with Croatia and the Nationalities and the completion of the Union with Transylvania had been parts of the main problem – and the Deputies had been the less tempted to stray into other fields because, elected as they had

[1] *A közjogi kérdés.*

been on a franchise which, relatively broad by the European standards of the day, yet embraced only 6·1% of the population, and elected, moreover, by traditional methods, they practically all held an outlook which was broadly homogeneous on questions of social and general internal politics.[1]

The Parliament of 1867 was simply the Diet of 1865 in continued session. It was entirely natural that the Deputies' minds should still have been filled with the great Issue, and as natural that, almost without exception, they should have taken up the traditional attitude which invested it not only with the primacy over all other problems, but with the governance of them, and that the Party alignment which now took place should have been determined almost exclusively by the Issue. That alignment was fairly simple. Twenty-one Deputies, led from outside by the ex-Chancellor, Apponyi, and inside Parliament, by Baron Pál Sennyey, formed a loose 'Conservative' group. There were 120 Deákists, twenty Deputies of the Extreme Left, who rejected any Compromise whatever, and a 'Left Centre' of ninety-four, led by Ghyczy and Tisza, whose programme, drawn up in March 1868, and known, from its place of origin, as the 'Bihar Points', accepted the Pragmatic Sanction, but asked for the abolition of the Delegations and of the Common Ministry of Finance, an entirely separate Hungarian Army and separate diplomatic representation for Hungary: in brief, very little short of personal union, pure and simple.

If this development was natural, it was none the less profoundly unfortunate for Hungary, particularly as it proved self-perpetuating. It meant that precious energies were wasted in barren wrangling over the Issue which ought to have been devoted to constructive work, and that such work as was accomplished was often distorted because its authors had been all the while keeping one eye on the Issue. At the junctures at which the two sides were closely balanced, any such work was well-nigh impossible.

At the outset, the Government's position was fairly strong. The Conservatives, if they sometimes played for their own hand, at least refused to join forces with the Left, which was thus outnumbered by nearly two to one in Parliament. A number of factors were in the Government's favour. Deák's personal prestige was enormous, and Andrássy's almost as high after he had gained his points over the questions of nomenclature, the Military Frontier and the Honvédség (had he failed on them it would, on the contrary, have sunk to zero, and that of the whole Government with it, and he had been obliged to use that argument to Francis Joseph). The extraordinary harvests of 1868 and 1869 brought an influx of money which started a boom in Hungary even more spectacular than its Austrian counterpart. Enormous

---

[1] As Gratz writes (*A Dualiszmus Kora*, I. 90), 'In the years after the Compromise, practically everyone, except the small group of Conservatives, Deák Party, Left Centre, Extreme Left and Nationalities alike, called themselves Liberals. Even those who were not Liberals in their hearts dared not confess it.'

numbers of banks and similar institutions were founded,[1] and many industries, and above all, a great expansion of the railway system was initiated, usually, as in Austria, on the basis that foreign entrepreneurs undertook and financed the construction, while the State guaranteed the interest on their capital. Some of the new institutions brought real and unmistakable benefit to the country, and many individuals derived much personal profit from them as Directors on their boards. Very many more believed themselves to have made fortunes through investing in the shares of the companies. The budgets for 1868 and 1869 closed with surpluses, although small ones.

The country was happy, and its mood allowed the Government to address itself seriously to the problems before it, which were generally much larger than those confronting its opposite number in Austria. The latter were often able to build on solidly-laid foundations, whereas the Hungarians had sometimes to start from the bottom, and sometimes worse than that; for the sequence of revolution and counter-revolution, followed by a series of regimes each of which had been principally concerned with undoing the work of its predecessor, had produced in many fields a condition of the utmost complexity, not to say chaos.

The matters to be settled included even the basic political structure of the country. Besides the settlements with Croatia and the Nationalities, neither yet completed in 1867, there were the problems connected with the incorporation of Transylvania and the Military Frontier, and another which concerned the whole country: that of the relationship between the central and the local authorities, viz., the Counties. This was a problem which revolved very largely round the Issue, although those who took the side of the Counties were more numerous than the direct opponents of the Compromise. Broadly, however, this party wanted the autonomous Counties preserved, both because, with Kossuth, they saw in them the purest expression of the national genius, and still more, because they felt that Hungary would not be safe against possible future encroachments by Vienna if any breach were made in this traditional national bulwark. The other party thought that the Compromise safeguarded Hungary adequately, and therefore wished, in the cause of efficiency, to introduce the greater measure of Governmental centralization for which Eötvös and his fellow-'Doctrinaires' had been campaigning before 1848. The question was complicated by the circumstance that some of the most extensive autonomous liberties in Hungary were enjoyed by non-Magyar communities such as the Transylvanian Saxons, and, for that matter, the German burghers who still controlled many of the boroughs.

The settlements with Croatia and the Nationalities are described elsewhere. The political assimilations of the Partium and the Military Frontier were

[1] In 1867 there had been only five banks in Hungary; 126 new ones were founded in the next five years.

carried through by simply extending the normal County organization to the areas concerned, a process which, as mentioned elsewhere, it took several years to complete in the Frontier. That of Transylvania was more complex. A Law of 1868, which legalized its incorporation, abolished the political prerogatives of the Three Nations, thereby depriving the Saxon University of its judicial functions, but promised the *Königsboden* a Statute which should do justice to its historic rights, and the office of *Sachsengraf* was to be retained, although its holder was thenceforward to be nominated by the Government (in fact, the last elected *Sachsengraf*, Konrad Schmidt, who had, indeed, been a very vehement opponent of the Union, had been relieved of his office as early as 8 February 1868).

The 'Jurisdictions' suffered only a minor change at this stage: only half the membership of their organs was to be elective, the other half being composed of virilists, usually the highest tax-payers.

Another big complex of problems was that relating to Church-State and inter-Confessional relations. Here the position in Hungary differed from that in Austria inasmuch as Hungary declared herself not to be bound by the Concordat, or any legislation deriving therefrom, but to be bound by her own earlier legislation, including that of 1848, which had not yet been fully implemented. The separation of the Roumanian Orthodox Church from the Serbian having now been sanctioned, the Roumanian Church received, in 1868, a Statute of Autonomy which placed it on a complete level with all other established Churches, with the same extensive self-government in its internal affairs (including its schools) and right to financial assistance, if required.[1] The principle of equality and reciprocity between established Churches brought with it the corollary that the legality of mixed marriages was confirmed, with the rule that the male issue of such marriages should follow the father's religion and the female, the mother's.[2]

Another Law of 1868 placed Jews on a footing of complete civic and legal equality with Christians. This was as far as legal changes in the confessional field went at the time, for the Roman Catholic Church was unable to agree on a statute of autonomy for itself acceptable to the Government, or, indeed, to all its own members, and presently gave up the attempt to do so (with the result that it was still without any such statute when our history ends, and indeed, also so after the Second World War).[3]

Again in 1868, Parliament adopted an Elementary Education Law (the work of Eötvös) which made education compulsory between the ages of six

[1] There is a full description of this law in R. W. Seton-Watson's *History of the Roumanians*, pp. 392–3. Hungary also took over the Statutes already enjoyed by the Unitarians and Transylvanian Lutherans. The latter thus retained their separate organization.

[2] The Holy See had already sanctioned this, for Hungary, although not for the rest of the Monarchy, in 1841 (see above, p. 263).

[3] The Roman Catholic Church of Transylvania, however, retained the autonomous organization (the 'Status Catholicus') which it had acquired in the seventeenth century.

and twelve and obliged every commune in which there were thirty or more children of school age, to establish a school, unless it already contained a confessional or other school. Instruction was to be in the pupil's mother-tongue. The law did not touch existing confessional schools, except to impose on them a minimum of State supervision, which was, however, strictly limited by the Churches' autonomy.

In 1869 justice was separated from administration, on all levels (this, again, only after a hard struggle) and a beginning made with a complete renovation of Hungary's judicial system.

1868 and 1869 were thus genuinely constructive years. Nevertheless, when elections were held in 1869, the Government, although it applied considerable pressure, lost sixty seats to the Left Centre and the Extreme Left, which now had thirty-two Deputies, and took the name of 'Party of 1848'. This still left the Deák Party with a comfortable majority, but clouds were gathering round it. The harvests were no longer good, and the new State apparatus cost a lot of money.[1] The railway programme proved to have been over-ambitious; by 1871 the State had already paid out 20 m.g. in interest, while in one case a foreign entrepreneur's capital gave out and the State was left to meet the loss; in another, a speculator simply decamped with the funds, leaving the investors ruined. The utility of some of the lines was dubious, and it was notorious that some members of the Party and their friends were making fortunes out of rigged contracts.

The Government lost its personal prestige. Andrássy moved to the Ballhausplatz; Eötvös died;[2] Deák retired into private life, himself to die not long after.[3] To succeed Andrássy, Francis Joseph, on Andrássy's advice, appointed Menyhért Lónyay, the Common Finance Minister, who was a competent financier, but unpopular in the Party and with Deák personally (also, as was not unimportant, with Francis Joseph).

The Opposition succeeded in talking out a Bill which the Government had introduced to alter the franchise (to its own advantage). In the elections of July 1872, the Government, by exerting strong pressure, nevertheless increased its majority slightly, securing 245 mandates against 116 of the Left Centre and 38 of the Party of 1848. But the Party was divided internally and unsure of itself, and immediately after, a series of catastrophes overtook it. Lónyay was attacked for having observed insufficiently the distinction between the public financial interest and his own; he resigned the Minister Presidency, but put himself at the head of a group of sympathetic malcontents in the Party. His successor, József Slávy, was admittedly an honest man, but lacking in energy and in ability to hold the Party together. Then came the *Krach* of 1873, which was as damaging to personal reputations of

[1] 1867, 110 m.g.; 1870, 277 m.g.; 1871, 282 m.g.
[2] 2 February 1871.
[3] 29 January 1876.

Hungarian politicians, as of Austrian, brought financial ruin to many thousands of individuals,[1] and also produced an acutely critical situation in the State finances.

To finance her programme of railway construction, etc., Hungary had followed the traditional course of borrowing, and had boasted, and believed, that her 'virgin credit' would fare better than the speckled hide of Vienna. On the contrary, the bankers had shown themselves notably cautious. A first loan, issued in 1868, had been floated at 81 (the underwriters also taking a large commission) and 6%, and a second, in 1870, at 75, so that Hungary had been paying 8–9% for her accommodation. Now the budget closed with a deficit again, and when the unfortunate Finance Minister, Kerkapoly, applied to the Rothschilds for an emergency loan to tide him over, he was, indeed, given a loan to the face value of 153 m.g. (although much less in practice, since the subscription rate was 85), but repayment had to be within five years, and the entire State properties had to be pledged as security. Kerkapoly had to help himself out with an issue of State bonds, issued at 85½. He resigned. Szlávy was literally unable to find anyone to take his place, and had to take over the finances himself.

Meanwhile, the Croats were, as described elsewhere, agitating against the Nagodba, and trouble was threatening with the Nationalities. Most of these had let their national organizations fall into hibernation when the Nationalities Law was passed, but a foolish outburst of Magyar chauvinism in 1872 had revived their fears, and they were girding themselves for defence again.[2]

The Party which had made the maintenance and fulfilment of the Compromise its *raison d'être* looked, and indeed was, on the verge of collapse, but the remarkable sequel was that while the Party indeed collapsed, the Compromise survived. The truth was that all this time, the politicians of the Left Centre had simply been shadow-boxing – for prize-money. They knew perfectly well, although they did not dare tell their electors so, that their programme was quite unrealistic. As things stood, there was no possibility of altering the Compromise to Hungary's advantage; the only conceivable change might be that if goaded too far, Francis Joseph might alter its terms in the other direction – a threat which his recent flirtation with the Czechs had made appear very real. Tisza in particular, who was emerging as the leader of the Left Centre, took very seriously the threat that the Crown might

---

[1] Thirty-one banks went into liquidation in 1874–5.

[2] In November 1872, when Parliament was debating the municipal unification of Buda and Pest, a Deákist Deputy (himself a German) proposed to his Party that the sole language of proceedings in the new Municipal Council should be Magyar, although only a very few inhabitants of Buda, and a minority of those of Pest, understood it. Only Deák and one other, the ex-Minister Gorove, opposed the motion in the Party conclave, and both the Party and Parliament adopted it. The next year Magyar was made the exclusive language of service on the Hungarian railways. For a lively account of this, see Rogge, op. cit., I. 101 ff.

ally itself with the Croats and the Nationalities, and he was convinced that if it did so at that juncture, Hungary would be defeated. On the other hand, he thought the unfavourable balance of forces to be not immutable. He believed that a sufficiently energetic and systematic policy of assimilation would Magyarize a sufficient number of the Nationalities to tilt the national balance in Hungary decisively in favour of the Magyars.[1] The correct tactics for Hungary were therefore to conclude an armistice with the Crown by dropping those points in the Bihar Programme which were totally unacceptable to the Monarch, at least until the national position had been consolidated.

It was also by now quite clear that the Rothschilds (it was they who, in practice, had the say) would not advance money on acceptable terms to any Hungary which threatened the smooth functioning of the financial structure of the Monarchy.

The Party accordingly quietly decided to take over its former opponents' positions on what amounted, in all essential points, to their opponents' programme.

The process took place in stages. As early as 1872 Ghyczy had advised his followers to accept the provisions of the Compromise relating to foreign policy and finance, and to stand out only over the army. In 1873 he and some others founded a Coalition Party with a programme of fusion with the Deák Party. In March 1874, Tisza agreed to the fusion in principle, while still holding out on certain formal points. Next, Szlávy resigned in favour of István Bittó, whose contribution to the problem was to get through a revision of the franchise, which, by raising the property qualifications, reduced the voters to 5·9% of the population. Ghyczy now actually took over the Ministry of Finance, and Tisza consented to say that revision of the Compromise was not, at that juncture, a burning problem; it would be better to concentrate on other questions. The two big Parties agreed to fuse. In March 1875, a caretaker Government was formed under Baron Wenkheim, with Tisza in charge of the Interior. The two Parties fused under the name of 'Liberal Party'. Then elections were held. The Liberals secured 333 seats, the Extreme Left 33,[2] a party of Conservatives who had refused to accept the fusion 18, and various representatives of the Nationalities, 24. On 20 October the King appointed Tisza Minister President.

This appointment marked the opening of thirty years' rule in Hungary of the Liberal Party, the first fifteen of them under Tisza's own guidance. During them the central theme of Parliamentary life continued to be what it had

[1] In coming to this view, Tisza had been strongly influenced by a book of the writings of the well-known publicist, Béla Grünwald, which took a very rosy view of the prospects of such a policy, especially among the Slovaks.

[2] Twenty-six of these took the name of 'Party of Independence', while D. Irányi and six others retained the old name of 'Party of 1848'.

been from 1867 (one might say, since our narrative opened, or indeed, almost since Hungarian history began), the 'issue of public law'; the struggle differed from that of earlier decades only in the respect that between Vienna and the Hungarian nationalists there now stood the link, or buffer, of a responsible Government which was indisputably Hungarian. That Government's position was far from easy, for if the nationalists looked on it as Vienna's front line, its own politicians by no means took that view of themselves. Most of them regarded the Compromise as unduly unfavourable to Hungary in detail; nearly all of them, in any case, looked on the decennial revision of its economic and financial clauses as an opportunity to press for every advantage which they could secure for their country at the expense of Austria (whose representatives took exactly the same view, *mutatis mutandis*), and all of them were alert to repel any infringement by 'Vienna' of Hungarian rights. They were thus under fire from both sides, and this inevitably thinned their ranks until the line could no longer be held.

The deterioration was gradual, for at first Tisza's regime was more broadly based than Deák's had been: most of his adherents had followed him when he changed sides, and when to these were added the remnants of the Deákists, his following constituted a substantial proportion of Hungary's then politically active class. Tisza, who was a superb organizer, and as unscrupulous as he was capable, constructed a complex party machine whose components, popularly known as the *Mameluks*, were dependent on him in every way, and consolidated his position by carrying through, in 1877, a redistribution of constituencies, the effect of which was that the Magyar constituencies of the Alföld, which were difficult to dragoon, elected one Deputy to 7–8,000 voters or more, while in the non-Magyar districts the educational qualification confined the number of voters to what was sometimes a mere handful[1] and one which, the voting being opened, could often be coerced into returning the Government candidate. If the Government put out its whole strength, it could always be sure of obtaining a safe majority.

The Liberal Party had thus little to fear from most sides within Hungary. The limited franchise excluded the poorer classes from representation and kept the Nationalities in check. The Conservatives, although their leader, Sennyey, was one of the most upright and capable of Hungary's politicians, and socially by no means the least progressive, were too heavily tarred with the brush of their predecessors' association with 'Vienna' to be popular in the country, and the Crown did not need their support while it had the Liberals.[2] And so long as the Liberals kept (in his eyes) their side of the bargain, Francis Joseph stood loyally by his. He guarded Tisza against the

---

[1] Two constituencies in Transylvania had only one hundred electors each; one, only sixty-nine.

[2] There was a moment before the fusion when a Conservative Government had seemed a serious possibility, but this passed when the fusion was successfully consummated.

HUNGARY UNDER DUALISM, 1867-1903

intrigues (which were numerous) spun against him at Court and repelled all attempts from oppositional quarters, notably the nationalities, to appeal to him over the Government's head.

The strongest threat to Tisza's regime still came from the 'national opposition'. The Extreme Left (which had reunited under the name of 'Party of Independence and 1848') secured eighty-eight seats in 1881, seventy-five in 1884 and eighty in 1887. This was still manageable; but the Left Centre re-emerged as early as 1877, after Tisza had failed to secure the concessions (which, it may be remarked, were not desired by those Hungarian circles who took a more realistic view of their country's financial strength) demanded by them in respect of the National Bank. Several notable members of the Party, including Dezső Szilágyi, left it, and in 1878 these malcontents joined up with others, the most prominent of whom were E. Simonyi and the ex-Chancellor's son, Count Albert Apponyi, in an 'United Opposition', which before the 1881 elections changed its name to that of 'Moderate Opposition' (*Mérsékelt Ellenzék*). Simonyi's death soon left Apponyi leader of this group.

Their numbers, too, were fairly modest – eighty-four representatives in 1881, sixty in 1884, forty-eight in 1887, and they professed themselves to accept the Compromise in principle, only demanding more satisfaction for 'legitimate Hungarian wishes' within its framework; and so long as those wishes were confined to the financial and economic field, they did little harm beyond aggravating the chronic irritation between the Austrian and Hungarian halves of the Monarchy. With time, however, they strayed into the far more dangerous field of army affairs. This was, indeed, strewn with ample tinder. The military clique in Vienna were themselves entirely unreconciled to the Compromise. They still regarded all Hungarians as undesirable rebels, and the Cis-Leithanian forces quartered in Hungary took their cue from them.[1] There were many provocative incidents, including one committed on the very highest level, which stirred deep passions in Hungary.[2] But Francis Joseph felt instinctively with his Field-Marshals on this point. Any hint of tampering with the army touched him on the raw, and although the 'Moderate Opposition' was not at this time asking for anything even

---

[1] After 1882 these were, indeed, rather less numerous, for in that year the important change was introduced in the organization of the Army that, in order to reduce delays during mobilization, regiments were normally stationed in that area of the Monarchy from which their rank and file were recruited. An officer was, however, often posted to a regiment of another nationality than his own, and many Austrian officers were thereafter still serving in Hungarian regiments.

[2] This was in 1886, when General Jansky, commanding the garrison in Budapest, had a wreath ceremoniously laid on the grave of General Hentzi, the officer who had defended Buda for the Monarchy in 1849 against the Honvéds and had made his name hated by bombarding Pest, which the Hungarians were not defending. Things were made worse by the Archduke Albrecht, who publicly supported Jansky's action.

remotely subversive,[1] nothing, in fact, which the Monarch did not end by granting – their demands engendered in him an acute and mounting irritation.

His own expertise, and the Monarch's support, enabled Tisza to weather these Parliamentary storms without too much difficulty, and his reign, like that of Taaffe in Austria, with which it coincided for so many years, brought few innovations which call for record here. It may be mentioned that during it Hungary, like Austria and in step with her, achieved financial solvency. Kálmán Széll, Tisza's able Minister of Finance from 1875 to 1878, succeeded, like Dunajewski in Austria, in emancipating his country from dependence on foreign bankers, and in floating a series of internal loans on reasonable terms. Under Wekerle, another most competent Minister, the budget achieved balance in the same year (1889) as Austria's, and that although Hungary, like Austria, was spending large sums on her railway system.

The development of Budapest's relations with Croatia, and with the Nationalities, is described elsewhere; here we will say only that although the event proved the undercurrents to have been setting against Budapest, the surface movements were favourable enough for many years.

A series of measures carried further the rather tentative moves towards political centralization made by the Government of 1867–72. In 1876 the *coup de grâce* was given to Saxon autonomy: the functions of the Sachsengraf were abolished altogether, the title becoming merely a decorative appendage to that of the Föispán of Nagyvárad, and those of the Saxon University reduced to the administration of its funds, which were to be used exclusively for cultural purposes. Later in the same year, a grand tidying up of the administrative pattern was carried through. The Sachsenboden, as well as other districts which had previously stood outside the County system – the Cumanian, Jazyge and Haiduk 'Privileged Districts ' – were taken into it. A number of dwarf Counties and rotten boroughs were abolished, and boundaries rationalized – the Sachsenboden had consisted of several widely separated districts, and the County of Fejer, in Transylvania, of no less than fourteen enclaves, scattered clean across Transylvania. There were left a total of seventy-three Counties and twenty-four boroughs of County status, besides Budapest and Fiume, which remained under a separate dispensation. With these two exceptions, the pattern was now uniform throughout Hungary.

The defenders of County autonomy fought for their cause as stubbornly as ever, and a second law on the subject, put through Parliament by Tisza against strong opposition, produced another half-way solution. The autonomy of the 'Jurisdictions' was reaffirmed. They retained the right to administer their own affairs autonomously, within the limits of the law of the land, and

[1] The only specific request which it was making at this time was for a Hungarian military academy. Otherwise it was asking only for more 'Hungarian spirit' in the common Army.

also to protest against, and provisionally to refuse to execute, Governmental enactments which seemed to them illegal, or ill-advised in the light of local conditions. If the Government insisted, they had to submit, but they retained the cardinal right of refusing to execute demands for taxes or recruits which had not been duly sanctioned by Parliament. They further retained their right to discuss any question of general political interest, to adopt Resolutions and petitions, to submit these to the Government and communicate them to other Jurisdictions.

At the same time, the powers of the Föispán, who was now the political representative of the Government – he was appointed on the proposal of the Minister of the Interior – were strengthened. He was the head of the administration, could enact, if necessary, emergency measures, and could in his turn veto, pending report to the Government, any measure taken by the Jurisdiction which he regarded as illegal or as prejudicial to the public security.

This was as far as the law took the position, for although in 1891 the Government introduced another, extremely comprehensive Bill for defining the powers of the Jurisdictions, the opposition to it was so frenetic that the Government had to drop all the specific clauses and content itself with the enunciation of the general principle that 'administration in the Counties was a Government duty'.

In 1896 an Administrative Court was established to settle conflicts of competence between the Government and the Jurisdictions.

It is, of course, obvious, that while the Counties had saved their faces, the last word on essentials was now always with the Government, while the extension of the national law to an ever-widening field of subjects brought with it a proportionate diminution in the Jurisdictions' sphere of autonomous activity.

No attempt was made to alter the relationship between the Crown and Parliament, and the structure of the House of Representatives underwent no significant change, although the franchise for it was, as we have said, made more restrictive. Its term was changed in 1886 from three to five years. The composition of the Upper House, as the old Bench of Magnates was now called, was revised in 1885: it now consisted of the male adult Archdukes and male adult members of Hungarian or Transylvanian families of the rank of Count or Baron, being resident in Hungary (a provision which excluded the class possessing titular Indigenat but residing outside the Kingdom) and paying a minimum of six thousand fl. in taxation – these as life members; as *ex officio* members, the holders of certain high State dignities, fifteen in all; all Roman and Greek Catholic Archbishops and Bishops, and four other dignitaries of that Church, the heads and Bishops of the Greek Oriental Churches, six representatives of the Calvinist Church, six of the Lutheran, and one of the Unitarian; and finally, a maximum of fifty persons appointed for life by the Crown, on the proposal of the Minister President, for distinguished service.

Legislation could originate in either House,[1] but had to pass both before being submitted for Royal promulgation. Government Bills were introduced first in the House of Representatives. In 1881 the police was reorganized, and a new gendarmerie, the *Csendőrség*,[2] created.

It was an army question that eventually brought the end of Tisza's reign. An Army Bill introduced by his Government in January 1889 contained two provisions[3] which both wings of the national opposition chose to regard as objectionable, and their Parliamentary blustering, which was supported by street demonstrations, was so virulent that Tisza sickened of office. In March 1890, when a more popular pretext presented itself,[4] he resigned.

His resignation was a personal one, and did not affect his Party, which continued to supply Hungary with its Governments for another fifteen years, under a succession of six Ministers President: Count Gyula Szapáry (1890–2), S. Wekerle (1892–5), Baron Dezsö Bánffy (1895–9), Kálmán Széll (1899–1903), Count Károly Khuen-Hedérváry (1903) and Count[5] István Tisza (1903–5). During the term of office of the first two of these the Issue of Public Law was, indeed, temporarily shouldered out of the forefront of public interest by another. The Liberals had not thitherto succeeded in putting Church-State and inter-Confessional relations on the footing desired by them. Successive Governments had wanted to put through what they regarded as the key measure, compulsory civil marriage, but all their attempts had foundered on the opposition of the Catholic leaders in the Upper House, and of Francis Joseph himself.[6] Then, in 1900, a Protestant Deputy complained in Parliament that Catholic priests were, by various devices, violating the

[1] The position in this respect was still awaiting legal definition in 1918. In practice, the initiative was exercised almost exclusively by the Lower House.

[2] The name of the ordinary police force was *Rendőrség*. *Őrség* means guardians, *rend*, order and *csend*, quiet. Why quiet should have required a special force to maintain it in the country, and order, in the towns, is a question to which I have never succeeded in obtaining an answer.

[3] One of these, although obscurely worded, was thought to limit Parliament's right to control the number of recruits supplied by Hungary to the Common Army, in that the number was not to be voted decennially, but to remain fixed until further notice. The other imposed on the 'one-year volunteer reserve officers' an obligation to pass an examination in German at the end of their year, under pain of serving a second in the event of failure. The same measure, when brought forward in the Reichsrat, evoked strong protests from the Czechs (Kolmer, V. 470).

[4] The occasion was a Bill for depriving Hungarians living abroad of their citizenship after ten years, unless they registered at an Austro-Hungarian Consulate. Tisza tried to get an exception made in favour of Kossuth, and resigned when he was outvoted in the Ministry.

[5] After Kálmán Tisza's death in 1902, Francis Joseph conferred the title of Count on his sons.

[6] The Bittó Government was actually obliged to withdraw a Bill which it had been going to introduce, as Francis Joseph refused his preliminary sanction to it.

rule in respect of the issue of mixed marriages. Other speakers seized the occasion to raise the whole complex of problems, in particular, the questions of civil marriage and of the status of the Jews. An embittered controversy ensued which before it ended, as it did, in well-nigh complete victory for the party of change – it left Hungarian legislation in this field in line with that favoured by the Liberal political thought of the day, and corresponding fairly closely to that achieved by Austria some thirty years before[1] – had largely absorbed public attention for some five years, had entailed the resignations of two Ministers President, Szápary because he was against the changes and Wekerle because he was for them,[2] and of one Imperial and Royal Foreign Minister[3] and had been won by the victors only by threatening the Upper House with a large change in its composition and carrying through a small one,[4] and Francis Joseph, with the possible collapse of a Parliamentary majority in favour of the Compromise. This question had played havoc with Party alignments: it had split both the Liberals and the Independence Parties from top to bottom, and had even produced the unique phenomenon of a non-Socialist political Party (the Christian People's Party) with a programme which was primarily social. It had also, for a time, brought the Liberals and Francis Joseph into flat conflict. But even now, the Issue had dominated the scene from behind it: Wekerle broke Francis Joseph's resistance to the anti-Clerical Bills by representing to him the danger that if he persisted in opposing them, he might drive a substantial proportion of the Liberal Party into permanent revolt and thereby jeopardize the Parliamentary majority in favour of the Compromise. Once this question had been settled, through the Crown's yielding on it, and after another short interval during which the Parties observed a truce for the duration of the millennary celebrations,[5] the pattern returned to the normal one of a Government

---

[1] Five main Bills eventually reached the Statute Book (in 1894 and 1895). (1) Civil marriage became compulsory. (2) All births, deaths and marriages had to be State-registered. (3) Any person was free to register himself as having ceased to be a member of any Confession, or to have joined another, or to have become a member of no Confession. (4) Parties to a mixed marriage were authorized to agree in advance that all issue of it might be brought up in the Confession of either parent (but not as members of no Confession). (5) The Israelite Confession was made 'established'. The established Confessions were now the Catholic (Roman, Greek and Armenian), Calvinist, Lutheran, Unitarian, Orthodox (Serbian and Roumanian) and Israelite. The Moslem was added after the annexation of Bosnia in 1908.

[2] Wekerle in fact resigned twice. The first time was on 1 June 1894, when the Upper House rejected the Bill on civil marriage. Francis Joseph reappointed him, but he resigned again on 24 December, because he felt that he did not enjoy the Monarch's confidence.

[3] Kálnoky (see above, p. 660, n. 2).

[4] The threat was to lower the financial qualification for a magnate to sit in the House from 6,000 to 2,000 fl., which would have let in over thirty Calvinist magnates from Transylvania. In the event, four new members of the House were created.

[5] I.e., the celebrations (which were held on an extremely grandiose scale) of the thousandth anniversary of the Magyars' occupation of Hungary.

committed to the Compromise, and supported on that understanding by the Crown, and a nationalist Opposition.

The elections of the period always gave these Governments comfortable majorities, and before those of 1901 Széll even persuaded Apponyi to rejoin the Liberal Party (some of his followers, indeed, refused to follow him, and joined instead the Party of Independence[1]). Nevertheless, it is probably true to say that the tumultuous scenes of 1889 ended the period when it was possible to think of the Compromise as constituting a long-term settlement of Hungary's position within the Monarchy. If Francis Joseph accepted defeat at the time on the points over which the trouble had broken out (on Andrássy's advice, he allowed the first of the objectionable clauses to be withdrawn, and the second to be modified), and if he shrank from undertaking another big reconstruction, he never again trusted Hungary, and not often, a Hungarian. On the other side, the extremists perhaps lost some ground, for Kossuth's death in 1894 deprived them of their great rallying-point, and the fact that his son, Ferenc Kossuth, then returned to Hungary and, after his election to Parliament in 1895, was given the leadership of the Party of Independence, proved, if anything, rather a source of weakness to the Independence cause, for Ferenc Kossuth was a conciliatory, rather timid man, probably not even wholly convinced of the rightness of his father's doctrines, and in any case, quite incapable of expounding them with his father's fire. Under his leadership, his Party became lukewarm and disunited. On the other hand, Apponyi, who was gifted with all the eloquence and personal magnetism which Kossuth lacked, began from 1889 onward (he himself in his memoirs describes the Army debate of that year as the turning-point of his views) to expound the doctrine that neither the Pragmatic Sanction nor any other later act had in any way affected Hungary's sovereignty, She was a completely independent State, entitled in principle (although he did not press for their immediate introduction in practice) to all her own State apparatus – her own diplomatic representation, her own army, her own financial system, etc. – and the Monarch could possess in her no 'reserved rights' which he could exercise independently of Parliament. He claimed this to be the true interpretation of all Hungary's Constitutional legislation, including the Compromise, in token whereof he described himself as a supporter of that instrument, and in 1900 allowed Széll to tempt him back (not, indeed, for long) into the Liberal fold; but in the eyes of Francis

[1] As with the Reichsrat, no two sets of figures on Party membership in Parliament ever agree exactly. Those given by Graz, from which others differ slightly, are: 1892, Liberals, 243, National Party (the former 'moderate' Opposition), 60, Party of Independence, 97 (of whom 15 formed a semi-independent 'Ugron Group'), others, 15; 1896, Liberals, 287, National Party, 32, Party of Independence, 60 (Ugron Group, 8), People's Party, 19, others, 15; 1901, Liberals, 276, Party of Independence, 94 (Ugron Group, 24), People's Party, 24, others, 19. The 'others' in each case were composed mainly of representatives of the Nationalities.

Joseph and of such men as the Archduke Albrecht, and after him, Francis Ferdinand, Apponyi's support of the Compromise, as interpreted by him, was indistinguishable from rejection of it, and this was, generally, the light in which it appeared to Hungarian public opinion. In fact, his followers found themselves on a slippery slope. They might maintain that they were supporting the Compromise, but they ganged up increasingly with its opponents, often shouting louder than they.

Apponyi's doctrines were very popular, and if, as we have said, the electoral results continued to show big majorities for the supporters of the Compromise, this was no safe guide to the development of feeling in the country, particularly as they usually reflected a considerable measure of administrative pressure (this was especially true of those of 1896, when Bánffy, a Transylvanian by birth and political experience, employed pressure and corruption on a scale which astonished even the case-hardened politicians of Inner Hungary). The truth was that the Liberal majorities were growing increasingly artificial, and the national opposition in its various forms, which now included the Christian People's Party, increasingly popular with the electorate. The last two years of Liberal 'rule' were, as we shall see, not so much rule as continued and disorderly battle.

The economic relationship with Austria, too, was becoming very strained. The 1887 revision of the economic clauses of the Compromise simply renewed that of 1877, with some minor and relatively non-controversial amendments. In 1897, however, both sides wanted changes made. The Austrians were asking for a big revision of the quota to take account of Hungary's increased wealth and population (at first they actually suggested a figure of 58:42), while the Hungarian national extremists were pressing both for an independent National Bank and an autonomous Hungarian tariff in place of the Customs Union with Austria. In favour of this, they unleashed a 'Buy Hungarian' campaign similar to that of the 1840s.

The conversations between the experts had not been completed when Badeni's Government fell in Austria, whose Parliament then plunged itself into a chaos which forbade any hope of fulfilling the condition laid down in the Compromise legislation, that the decennial revision must be approved by the Parliaments of both countries.

The Hungarian Independence politicians took advantage of this situation to claim that when the 1887 revision lapsed, at the end of 1897, Hungary automatically recovered her tariff autonomy. Bánffy, this time helped by Apponyi, managed to wheedle the House into granting a breathing-space up to May 1898, subject to the stipulation that agreement must be reached by that date, and ratified by both Parliaments by the end of the year. He then succeeded in agreeing with Thun's Government on a new settlement which was, in fact, reasonably equitable: Hungary conceded an upward revision of the quota (to 34.4:65.6), but secured in return recognition of the principle of parity in the National Bank and satisfaction for another demand, that the yield of all indirect taxation derived from consumption should go to the country in which the consumption took place.

This, however, did not satisfy the nationalists, and their tempers were further roused when the news leaked out that Bánffy and his Finance Minister, László Lukács, had secretly agreed that the arrangements should not expire automatically at the end of ten years, but remain in force until the Hungarian Parliament should demand revision of them.[1] A new storm arose, which was the direct cause of Bánffy's downfall. His successor, Széll, produced a new formula which admitted that the Customs Union had really lapsed. Hungary would, however, not exercise her right to introduce an autonomous tariff unless she had failed to reach agreement with Austria by 31 December 1902 to continue the *de facto* union. In default of such agreement, no commercial treaty should be concluded by the Monarchy as a common customs territory beyond the end of 1907.

The new negotiations, which this time were conducted between Széll and Koerber, ended just in time, on the evening of 31 December 1902, in an agreement which retained the customs union *de facto*, while calling it a treaty, and for the rest, confirmed without substantial modification the agreements reached in 1898. The effect of the whole episode, however, had been to strengthen the movement for economic independence in Hungary, and to enhance the ill-will, already copious, with which each half of the Monarchy regarded the other.

II THE FACE OF HUNGARY

The material development of Hungary after 1848 was similar in trend to that of Austria. In one important respect conditions in Hungary changed even faster than in Austria, for the growth of the population was a little more rapid still. The 13 millions or so of 1850[2] rose by 1869 to 15·5. In the next decade the cholera came back, and the 1870 census showed an advance of only about a quarter of a million, but after that, the pace was resumed. The figure for 1890 was 17·5 millions, that for 1900, 19·25, and that although emigration was now going on on a scale exceeding even the Austrian.[3]

---

[1] This was known as the 'Ischl clause' under the impression (in fact, an incorrect one) that it had been signed at Bad Ischl, where Francis Joseph was residing at the time.

[2] These figures include Croatia-Slavonia.

[3] On this, see *International Migrations*, vol. 14, pp. 710–728, and vol. 18 (the 'interpretations', by Dr Thirring), pp. 411–39. No figures were kept before 1885, but overseas emigration on a large scale had begun only shortly before that date. The registered overseas migration was about 25,000 annually between 1886–95, the figure then rising to 43,000 (1889), 55,000 (1900), 51,000 (1901), 92,000 (1902), 120,000 (1903). As in Austria, about 20–25% of the emigrants returned after a few years. In addition to the overseas migration, nearly 300,000 Hungarians emigrated to Austria between 1880–1910 (most of these Hungarian Germans

HUNGARY UNDER DUALISM, 1867–1903

The two major factors determining the economic structure in which these growing masses found their places were the condition of the country before 1848 – that has been sufficiently described elsewhere – and the integration of its economic and financial system into that of the Gesammtmonarchie which was consummated in 1851 and reaffirmed by the nation's own decision in 1867.

The first effects of this were, as we have seen, favourable to Hungary's agriculture, placing as it did the whole Austrian market (above the local level) at the disposal of her producers, and leaving as the only limitations under which her landlords then suffered those imposed by her own conditions: the relatively backward methods of cultivation still prevalent in most of the country, the sparse labour force, the bad communications. The initial advantage thus gained by her agriculturalists was self-perpetuating, for it gave them an interest in opposing any development of a nature to draw off the land the supply of labour, which, until the 1880s, was, in most parts of the country, regularly below the demand for it, or to compete with their requirements of credit.

We have also seen that the first effects of the integration on the other branches of Hungary's national economy were mixed. On the one hand, a great shortage of accumulated mobile capital, a deficiency, much larger than the Austrian, of experienced entrepreneurs and skilled workers, and many other difficulties, including those of communications, placed Hungarian industry, as a whole, at a big disadvantage where it had to compete with its stronger Austrian neighbours, so that the integration proved immediately fatal to a number of Hungarian enterprises, and in the later years many branches of industry found it impossible to strike root. But there was another side of the medal, in the benefits conferred on the country by the Government's public works, and in the fact that the unification had allowed, and tempted, Austrian capital to interest itself in the development of those industries for which the natural conditions were more favourable than in Austria. The flow of this investment dried up in 1857, with the collapse of the Austrian money market in that year, but another spurt came in the boom years after 1867, which again was carried out largely with the help of capital which Hungary could not have provided out of her own resources.

This opening-up process conducted by foreign capital in its own interests was again interrupted by the 1873 *Krach*, which brought with it the withdrawal of a large amount of the capital, and although the process recommenced, it suffered further setbacks, although less serious ones, in 1878 and

---

from West Hungary, moving to Vienna or Graz), 42,000 to Germany and 102,000 to Roumania. About two-thirds of these last were Hungarian Roumanians, but there was also a considerable emigration of Szekels to Bucharest, which was said to have the third largest Hungarian population of any European city. Finally, there was a substantial Jewish emigration to the West; this was, indeed, balanced by continued immigration of Jews from Galicia.

1895. By this time, however, substantial sums of native capital had been accumulated, and its ambition to assert itself had found a helper after 1867 in the politically emancipated country's national pride – the ambition to see Hungary in possession of the material equipment of a progressive modern State, adequate institutions and communications, a worthy capital city, and also a national industry, this if only as a pre-condition of true political independence. The large position held by the State in the national economy made it possible for some of these aspirations to be given practical satisfaction by direct action. Thus the construction of communications was carried on regardless of the difficulties, and in 1881, the essential communications being now complete, Hungary introduced a law which authorized the Government to foster her domestic industries by subsidies, interest-free loans, freight concessions, and similar devices. As this law proved not very effective, it was supplemented by others in the same sense in 1890 and 1899.

Developments were still retarded by shortage of capital, the pressure of vested interests in other camps, and other factors, but they were nevertheless still considerable. The combined result of the various forces operating was that in 1902 Hungary was, like Austria, in a state of transition from the predominantly rural and agricultural conditions of half a century before to one in which industry, trade, etc., played a larger part; but one in which the transition had not yet proceeded so far as in Austria. Both industrialization and urbanization had been making appreciable progress, the pace of which had, moreover, been gathering momentum as the years went on, especially after April 1890. The figures for 1857 had shown 409,616 persons in the Lands of the Hungarian Crown as occupied in industry; those for 1869, 646,964 (an increase of 57·94%, compared with a total population increase of 11·91%), and those for 1880, 788,970 (92·61% more than in 1857, against a population increase of 13·57%). The 1900 census showed 2,400,000 persons (including dependents)[1] in Inner Hungary – 14·2% of its total population – as deriving their livelihood from industry proper and 161,000 (1%) from mining. Some of these industries, especially the rougher branches of heavy industry, food-processing (flour-milling, brewing and distilling) and the industries connected with building, were well-established and large; others, including textiles, chemicals, and sugar-beet refining, were making promising beginnings.

Similarly, the increase in the urban population, which had been 6·4% between 1869 and 1880, had sprung up to 10·7% in 1881–90 and 14·9% in 1890–1900. In the last-named year 20% of the inhabitants of the Kingdom lived in places with populations exceeding 20,000, among which Budapest, which had grown by 45·6% in the single decade 1890–1900, and now possessed over 700,000 inhabitants, was outstanding. Another 7 towns in the

---

[1] This applies to the other occupational figures given hereafter. The 1900 figure was almost exactly double that for 1890.

Kingdom had populations of 50–100,000 each, and over 60 more had reached 5 figures.

In other occupational fields, 524,000 persons (3·1%) were deriving their living from the public services[1] and free professions, 520,000 (3·1%) from commerce and banking, 407,000 (2·4%) from communications, and there were 248,000 (1·5%) rentiers and pensioners, and 404,000 (2·4%) domestic servants.

Nevertheless, the country was still mainly rural, and agriculture was still by far its largest single industry. In 1900, 11,200,000 persons in the Kingdom (66·5%) still derived their living from agriculture, forestry and fisheries,[2] and 80% still lived in scattered farms, villages or small towns. Even the figure of 20% for the larger conglomerations might easily mislead, for several of these were 'village towns', most of whose inhabitants were agriculturalists.[3]

Croatia was even less 'developed'. Here 82% of the population still derived its living from agriculture, and only 8·3% from industry, 2% from the professions, 1·5% from commerce and banking. Only 0·8% were rentiers or pensioners. Zagreb was the only city with a population of over 50,000 and only one other, the garrison town of Eszék, topped 20,000.

Moreover, even if Hungarian agriculture had lost a little ground percentually to other occupational groups, it had in other respects fully maintained its leading position in the national economy. Nowhere had the face of Hungary changed more than on the land.[4] The cultivable area of the country itself had been greatly enlarged through various enterprises, including the regulation of the Tisza, which alone reclaimed 6·5 million *hold* for cultivation.[5] The area of arable land had risen from 10 million ha. in 1870 to 12 millions in 1890, and in 1900 only 5% of the total area of the country was classified as uncultivable, compared with 15% in 1848. In absolute figures, considerably more people were working on the land in the latter year than in the former. There had been much improvement in methods of cultivation. Crop rotation had cut by half the amount of land left fallow each year. The vineyards had been ravaged by the phylloxera, but with that exception, the

[1] Exclusive of the armed forces.

[2] Excluding the 606,157 (3·6%) 'day labourers in various occupations', most of whom were probably employed in agriculture (see above, p. 618 and n.).

[3] Of the larger towns, Szeged itself (second on the list), Szabadka (third), Debrecen (fourth), Hódmezövásárhely (sixth) and Kecskemét (seventh) belonged to this category. They had, of course, genuinely urban nuclei.

[4] In this connection it is fair to record the remarkable work accomplished by the Ministry of Agriculture, especially during the eight years (1895–1903) when it was headed by the exceptionally enlightened and efficient Ignácz Darányi. Important technical work was accomplished also by the landowners' vocational organizations, especially the O.M.G.E. (*Országos Magyar Gazdasági Egylet* – Hungarian National Agricultural Association).

[5] Unfortunately, as it transpired later, the flooding which this operation had been designed to eliminate had been necessary to keep the land sweet, and expensive irrigation works had to be undertaken to counteract the effects of the regulation.

yield of all crops had risen substantially, and the stocks of horses, cattle and swine had been greatly improved. Consequently, the national production of almost all crops had risen substantially: that of wheat, sensationally, from 12 million *q*. in 1851 to 17 in 1865, 21 (average) in 1871–9, 30 in 1880–9 and 50 in 1890–9.

This last development had, indeed, not been altogether healthy. The high wheat prices prevailing in the 1850s and again in the boom years round 1870 had tempted the cultivators to concentrate heavily on this one crop. The big landlords, in particular, had often sold their large herds of cattle and put the former pastures under wheat. Shortage of manure was already beginning to exhaust the new ploughland, and the whole national economy had become dangerously dependent on the price of wheat. Two landowners who visited the U.S.A. in 1878 warned their colleagues of the danger, and an Agricultural Congress in 1879 advised producers to go over to other crops, but with little success: the area under wheat, still only 2 million ha. in 1870, had reached 3 million in 1890 – 30% of the total area under plough.

When it celebrated its millennium in 1896, the Hungarian people indulged in something like an orgy of self-congratulation. The historians of later generations have, on the other hand, seen in the Liberal era little more than a dismal story of wasted opportunities and achievements which profited the individual at the expense of the community. As when the record of any period is reviewed in perspective, a case could be made out for either judgment.

The material development had, after all, been considerable. The industrial shape of the country reflected the truth that it belonged economically within a larger unit. Thus some industries which would have been present in an autarkic system, notably the textile industries, were in their bottle-fed infancy, others almost entirely absent, but others which were based directly on the native raw materials were really important. Agriculture was undermechanized, but technically on a high level. The great obstacle which had so long retarded the entire development of the country – its backward communications – had been largely overcome. Hungary now possessed an extensive network of railways[1] which had, indeed, been planned to radiate outwards from Budapest, so that cross-country journeys were slow and difficult, and direct communication across the frontier from outlying parts even more so (this was a particular grievance of Croatia's, and a justified one), but communications between the capital and the chief points on the periphery were excellent. The whole system had been given a great impetus by the introduction in 1889 of a zone tariff which made cheap long-distance travel possible. The main roads had been improved out of recognition, and many of the chief waterways made fully navigable.

[1] The length of line had been 222 km. in 1850, 947 in 1851, 2,285 in 1967, 7,058 in 1879, 10,870 in 1889, 17,817 in 1904.

The devotion – and the substantial sums of money – which had been lavished on making Budapest the capital of a proud and independent country and the peer of Vienna had yielded impressive results. Besides the original Suspension Bridge which had been the child of Széchenyi's inspiration, four more bridges for road traffic and one for railway now connected the twin cities. Both of these contained large numbers of grandiose new buildings: the Royal Palace, reconstructed as an enormous building containing 860 rooms,[1] the great neo-Gothic Parliament, built in a style reminiscent of Westminster, a Court opera and Court theatre, and a host more. The art galleries, museums and libraries of Budapest could vie with those of any European State of comparable size.

Budapest had been pampered at the expense of the provincial towns, but many of these had modernized at least their centres in styles which aroused the admiration of the age, if not always that of its successors.

It may be worth emphasizing that of the latter, some which had made the biggest progress lay in the non-Magyar periphery of the country, for the initiative in establishing new industries had been left almost entirely to private entrepreneurs, who had sited their factories where labour was cheap and natural conditions favourable. Only the great munition works at Csepel had been deliberately sited, for national reasons, in the heart of the country.

We have mentioned Széll's and Wekerle's work in bringing order into the national finances and in breaking the vicious circle of deficits met by borrowing which only left them larger. This had been consolidated by taxation reforms which had raised the revenue. In 1892, when Hungary accompanied Austria on to the gold standard, the total national debt was consolidated into gold *rentes*. It is true that the public debt was still heavy, totalling about 5,000 million kronen, with an annual service of nearly 300 m.k., and that more than two-thirds of it was held outside the country; also that to achieve the result, a large amount of State property had been sold, usually (as is the rule in such transactions) on terms advantageous to the buyer.[2]

The reorganization of the administration had been a big achievement, and the general level of the administrative services had been greatly improved in connection with it. The Hungarian Courts, after their reorganization, enjoyed a deservedly high reputation, except, indeed, where political issues were at stake. Public security was good.

The execution of Eötvös's elementary education act had been hampered by material difficulties, and by conflicts of competence between Church and State, and became involved with the Nationalities issue in the fashion described below. Nevertheless, the number of elementary schools had

---

[1] This was not completed until after the period covered by this chapter. The foundation stone was laid by Francis Joseph at the millenary celebrations.

[2] According to Mód, op. cit., p. 120, an average of 14,000 *hold* of State lands had been sold every year, at an average price of 170 fl.

increased largely, and illiteracy, while still remaining high for many years, was diminishing in a measure which could not be denied.

The number of secondary and higher educational establishments was substantial. It included a number of technical and specialist colleges, a second University (in Kolozsvár)[1] and a technical High School of University rank in Budapest.[2]

The period had been one of great intellectual, artistic and literary activity, the products of which, if lacking something of the freshness of those of the preceding generation, and of the distilled but often bitter refinement of the next, were yet imposing in quantity and in some cases – the novels of Jókai and Mikszáth and the paintings of Munkácsy and Szinnyey-Merse may be given as examples – indisputably high in quality. A number of valuable historical works came from the Academy, and in Loránd Eötvös and Ignác Semmelweiss Hungary produced two of the outstanding scientists of the Europe of the day.

All this added up to a very considerable sum of achievement, but it had been accompanied by a social development which in some respects had been remarkably slow, and in others, unhealthy, and this in its turn found expression in a political system which was singularly unmodern, if not in its institutions, at least in its operation of them.

One conspicuous feature of Hungarian society even as late as 1903 was the absence of a middle class possessing its own outlook and interests, and yet constituting an integral part of the national structure.

It contained, of course, its administrative class, which towards the end of the period had come to play a very important role in the national life. But it was not an independent role. A certain contingent of these services (in some of the Ministries an important one) came, indeed, from old German burgher families, or families of prosperous Swabian peasants.[3] The great majority of the Grade A civil servants, however, were members of the old landlord class, or their sons, whose acres could no longer afford them a living. And the change of habitat and occupation, and even of direct economic interest, left the social outlook of these men unchanged to an extent which would appear almost uncanny to an observer unfamiliar with the national psychology. To them, the only real difference between their old positions and their new was the unimportant one that the salaries received by them for administering Hungary were no longer paid to them direct by their peasants, but collected and handed to them by the State, of which they remained at once the servants

---

[1] Founded in 1872.

[2] There was also, as mentioned below, a University in Zagreb.

[3] The Swabians, like the Germans of the Alpine Lands, by custom retained the tradition of the undivided Bauernhof, the sons, other than the heir (who was usually the youngest), being given portions and then going into the towns to seek their living outside agriculture. The Magyars divided a holding among all the children.

and the beneficiaries, and most truly the incorporation. It was no less remarkable how completely this outlook was adopted by the minority among them whose origin was different.

The result was the curious phenomenon of a system which seen from one angle, had changed completely, from one of decentralized self-government to one of centralized bureaucracy, but had remained practically unaltered in the spirit in which it was administered.

The other section of what are usually known as the middle classes – the traders, industrialists, etc., would in any case have played a less important role than their counterparts in Austria because, owing to the slower economic development of their country, their numbers were smaller. But the social and political weakness to which the paucity of their numbers in any case condemned them and to some extent, also the professional men, was accentuated by other factors of a different order. That the German-Austrian bourgeoisie had, during the same period, been able to play a political role which was even disproportionate to its numerical strength had, as we have seen, been due to the reinforcement which it drew from various adventitious circumstances. It represented the centralism which was one of the two great rival principles which were contending for the mastery in Austria. It was ethnically or at least linguistically identical with the largest single nationality in Cis-Leithania. It was of the same stock from which the bulk of the Austrian administrators were drawn.

While the stock of the older industrial and commercial classes in Hungary had been the same Germanic one as the Austrian, this, in the different national context, had had precisely the opposite effects on their position, the national difference accentuating the conflict of social and economic interests which divided them from the Magyar landlords. The development of the bourgeoisie after 1848 did little to efface these differences. It was true that the Germans who formed its nucleus now Magyarized, and as a rule, quite whole-heartedly; but they themselves were now ousted from the leading positions in Hungary's industry and commerce, and to a large extent, in her professional classes, by the Jews, whose invasion of these fields was even far more complete in Hungary than in Austria.

The arrival of the Jews in Hungary, as in the Western Lands, had been mainly a nineteenth-century phenomenon. In 1787, when they were first counted (soon after Austria's acquisition of Galicia) they had numbered only 87,000 (1% of the population), but immigration, chiefly from Galicia,[1] coupled with a high rate of natural increase, had raised their figures, in spite of considerable emigration westward,[2] to 249,000 (1·89%) in 1840,

[1] There had also been a small immigration, chiefly on to the Esterházy estates, from Bohemia and Moravia.

[2] About 110,000 Jews left Hungary between 1870 and 1910 alone. This movement was not usually overseas: the first stage of it was generally Vienna.

343,000 (2·65%) in 1850, 542,000 (4·0%) in 1869, 625,000 (4·6%) in 1880 and 830,000 (8·49%) in 1900. They were then still thickest on the ground in the Carpathian and sub-Carpathian regions which formed the first stage of their journey, but there was now no town, and hardly a village (except an occasional German settlement in the south) from which they were entirely absent, and Budapest itself contained over 167,000 of them – 23·4% of its total population.

All that has been said elsewhere of the commanding position acquired by the Jews in Austria applies even more fully to Hungary, where their opportunities were much greater and the competition which they had to face much weaker. The capitalist development of modern Hungary, in so far as it had been carried out by 'domestic' forces at all, had been almost entirely of their making, and the results of it were concentrated chiefly in their hands. The occupational statistics for 1910[1] showed that 12·5% of the 'self-employed' industrialists and 21·8% of the salaried employees in industry, 54% of the self-employed traders and 62·1% of their employees, 85% of the self-employed persons in finance and banking and 42% of their employees, were Jewish, and even these figures, failing as they do to distinguish between enterprises by size, do not reveal the whole position, which was that practically all banking and finance, far the greater part of all trade, and most industry above the artisan level, were owned and staffed in their higher branches by Jews, and most of the money earned in these occupations, outside the wages – direct profits, dividends, and higher salaries – went into Jewish pockets. The only source of privately-earned wealth which seemed not yet to be chiefly in Jewish hands was the land; but even here, Jews now owned 19·9% of the properties of 1,000 hold+ and 19·0% of those between 1,000 and 200 hold and constituted 73% of the lessees in the former bracket and 62% of those in the latter. And what proportion of the rent-rolls from the larger estates went straight into the pockets of their owners' Jewish creditors, statistics do not record; but it was undoubtedly a very large one.

Tradition kept them out of the Civil Service, and out of the regular armed forces,[2] and they were naturally confined to their own proportions in the Churches and Church schools, but in the free professions generally, they had reached almost as strong a position in the intellectual life of the country: 11·5% of the teachers in the burgher schools were Jewish, and a substantial and growing number of the University teachers; 26·2% of the persons entered under the rubric 'literature and the arts', including 42·4% of the journalists; 45·2% of the advocates and 48·9% of the doctors, were Jews.

[1] The 1900 census does not give the corresponding figures.
[2] They were, however, numerous among the reserve officers – the University graduates who were allowed to do only a single year with the colours, after which they received commissions as officers of the reserve. The Army reserve of doctors was largely composed of Jewish reservists.

HUNGARY UNDER DUALISM, 1867–1903

The contribution made by the Jews to the development of the new Hungary was, beyond doubt, enormous. Given the incurably conservative mentality of the Magyars, it is hard to see how, without the Jews, Hungary could ever have accomplished the transition from a 'feudal' to a modern capitalist economy. Their contribution to Hungary's intellectual and artistic life was hardly smaller: a very great number of the nation's most boasted achievements in learning, science, literature and the arts were the work of Jews. It is, however, undeniable that their infiltration of the national life, on such a scale, raised a problem quite different from that presented by the German or Slovak newcomers to the national middle class. The habits, religion, even the family trees of the latter, if traced back far enough, differed little from those of the old-established 'Magyars', and old and new fused easily, and, as it then seemed, completely enough. If they took from the original product a little of its happy-go-lucky charm, they enriched it in return with their own qualities of sober worth, and the Magyar psychological strain nearly always proved the dominant one.

The Jews entering Hungary, on the other hand, nearly all came to it as the products of many centuries of segregation, partly enforced, partly self-imposed, and distinguished from their neighbours, not only by their religion, but also by their jargon and their dress. Naturally, the longer they stayed in the country, the more they tended to discard the outward distinctions, but precisely those who did so most readily were those who then passed on to the West, while their places were filled, and more than filled, by new arrivals from Galicia. Moreover, few of the Jews themselves were prepared to go the whole way towards assimilation. Many were passionately anxious to appear Magyars in all externals, and even to be Magyars in all except their religion,[1] and when in 1906 the Jewish community in Hungary split into two great bodies, the Neologs and the Orthodox,[2] the latter, which wanted the old ways preserved intact, was much smaller than the former, which favoured complete social assimilation, but even the Neologs discouraged changes of religion, which were, in fact, extremely rare.[3]

In the Vormärz and 1848–9 the great majority of Hungary's Jews had taken her side against Vienna, and in 1867 the Hungarians remembered this in their favour with gratitude. The new Governments saw in them useful allies for the future, both economically, and no less, owing to the Jews' willingness to assimilate linguistically, in the national struggle. At that time there was, moreover, practically no element of rivalry, such as already existed in

---

[1] L. Hatvany's novel, *Bondy and Son*, gives an interesting psychological picture of a young Jewish boy possessed by this longing.

[2] The extreme north-east of Hungary also harboured a few adherents of the peculiar sect of *Chassidim*, or *Gute Yidden*, and there were a few Karaite Jews in Transylvania.

[3] Only 5,000 conversions took place between 1895 and 1907. The number before that was minimal; it was confined to a few families who had been exceptionally successful in business.

Vienna and Bohemia. The middle-class Hungarian did not want to go into money-making himself; he was only too glad to leave that side of the nation's business to the Jews (who, as he was well aware, were much better at it than he was), and to draw his salary out of the profits made by them. To these considerations of expediency were added entirely sincere ones of principle, for the Hungarian Liberals (here understanding under that term not only the political party which bore the name, but the whole generation, including such men as Deák and Eötvös), were as genuinely convinced as their Austrian opposite numbers that it was morally wrong to draw a distinction between man and man on grounds of religion or ethnic origin. All the Governments of the time were therefore, as we have seen, at pains to admit the Jews to full civic and political equality, and to give them their share of social reward.[1] Anti-Semitism was strongly discouraged, and was in fact much less of an open political issue than in Austria. In 1880 a Deputy named Istóczy founded no less than 78 specifically anti-Semitic organizations, and in 1884 got 17 Deputies into Parliament, a year after a notorious 'ritual murder' trial had taken place in Tisza-Eszlár. The Government, however, turned its batteries on the movement, and it soon disintegrated. After it the only major Party to include a touch (not a very big one) of anti-Semitism in its programme was the Christian People's Party.

It is true that when the magnitude of the Jewish influx became perceptible, and in particular, when the Jews began to move in large numbers into the professions, official disapproval could not make all non-Jews in Hungary wholly convinced that the difference of religion between Jew and non-Jew was a mere incidental, not affecting a fundamental identity, nor prevent some Hungarians from wondering whether the nation could really digest such a large and powerful new element without its own character undergoing a change. The question was, however, asked more often than it was answered, at least with a decided negative.

But this apart, a certain feeling was always present (perhaps on both sides) that the bourgeois professions, and also the practitioners of them, whatever their ethnic origin, were not quite an integral part of Hungarian life. Largely as a consequence of this, the bourgeoisie as a class never even attempted to play an independent political role. Its members rather attached themselves, sometimes invisibly, to other parties. In the Tisza era, they nearly always supported the Liberals. Only round the turn of the century did the urban middle classes produce something of their own in the shape of a number of circles and associations of young intellectuals, largely but by no means exclusively Jewish, who initiated a movement for political and social reform on democratic lines. The most important of these groups, which numbered among its members several men destined later to play considerable political

---

[1] Twenty-six Jewish families were promoted during the period to Baronial rank, and 280 given patents of lower nobility.

roles, was best known from the periodical issued by it, the *Huszadik Század* (Twentieth Century).

The Parliamentary and social life of Hungary continued therefore to be dominated by its traditional landlord class, which continued to divide, in its members' own eyes and those of others, and to some extent institutionally, into the traditional classes of the magnates and the lesser men, for whom the name 'gentry' came in these years to supersede the older one of 'nobiles bene possessionati'. As between these, the magnates had maintained their institutional and social lead, and had also come off better economically. The land reform had hit many of them only very lightly, owing to the high proportion of allodial land in their estates, and their punctually paid compensation, coming to them at a time when the price of wheat was very high, had often enabled them, not only to modernize their existing estates, but to buy from distressed smaller neighbours more acres than they had had to cede to their rustical peasants. Later, they had been able to obtain credit with relative facility. The proportion of the soil of Hungary held in very large estates, huge as it had been before 1848, consequently actually increased in the following decades. An agrarian census taken in 1895 showed that just under 4,000 proprietors, mainly, although not entirely, private individuals,[1] then held between them, in estates of 1,000 hold or more, twelve of the 41·7 million hold at which the cultivable area of Hungary-Croatia was then reckoned, this excluding properties consisting solely of forest or rough grazing; had these been counted in, the share of the mammoth estates would have been larger still.[2] Some of the individual estates were enormous: Prince Esterházy's alone covered 516,000 hold, those of Prince Schönborn, 241,000, of the Counts Károlyi, 174,000, of Prince Festetics, 161,000, of the Archduke Friedrich, 145,000, of the Prince of Coburg-Gotha, 141,000.

A fair proportion of these estates were entailed, for between 1867 and 1912 Francis Joseph sanctioned the formation of sixty new *fidei-commissa*, making ninety-two in all. Thirty-five per cent of the area of the country was now entailed.

As individuals, the gentry had not survived the political and economic storms nearly so well. Many families had been ruined by the land reform and even more by the agricultural depression. Ancestrally regarded, the gentry of 1900 were largely a class of new men. In this sense, the Hungarian writers who describe the decay of the old gentry class as one of the major social features of this period, are justified. The newcomers to it had, however, adopted their predecessors' traditional outlook on life and way of living with

---

[1] The proportion of privately owned estates was slightly lower than in Austria, since besides the Roman Catholic Church, many municipalities, especially some of the village towns, were very large landowners.

[2] The total area of the Lands of the Hungarian Crown was then about 325,000 sq. km., or 56·5 million hold (1 sq. km. = 173·7796 hold).

such remarkable facility and completeness, that it would have taken a genealogist's eye to distinguish between the two elements; all its members were, in all essentials, the true successors of the old bene possessionati who had so long disputed, and shared, with the magnates the internal running of Hungary.

There were, as there had always been, a considerable number of points of difference between these two classes, or sub-classes. The natural and traditional rivalry between the smaller man and the larger was generally accentuated by a political difference, again traditional, on the Issue of Public Law; for while there were many exceptions, some of them very conspicuous, it was usual, as it had been before 1848, for the smaller men to be more national, while the magnates stood nearer to the Court and included more of the Gesammemonarchie within their mental horizons.[1] Some members of the very greatest families almost dissociated themselves from any special relationship with Hungary, except as a source of income, and those who did not go quite so far as this usually regarded themselves as the exponents of the Crown in Hungary.

These differences sometimes took demonstrative form. Excluded by the insufficient blueness of their blood from Széchenyi's Casino, the gentry founded a Casino of their own,[2] and there even existed something rather vague called the 'gentry movement'. None of these things, indeed, kept the two classes from presenting a front of perfect solidarity towards the outer world.

It should be added that while the years before 1867 brought the magnates political advantage also at the expense of the gentry, the trend thereafter was in the opposite direction. The Compromise was itself the fruit and expression of a political reconciliation between the Crown and the gentry, and after it Francis Joseph had no need to continue to seek an alliance which in any case had proved ineffectual, and was now superfluous. The truth of this statement is not affected by the fact that 50% of his Ministers President after 1867, and 34% of all Ministers, were of magnate families: such was his personal idiosyncrasy, and the figure was in any case far lower than in Austria. Ministerial figures apart, the weight of Parliamentary importance was inevitably shifting to the Lower House,[3] and outside Parliament, the gentry continued to command the Counties. The Counties themselves were, indeed, losing ground to the bureaucracy; but the bureaucracy was itself now largely stocked with members of gentry families, and if the sons of magnates entered

---

[1] This distinction partly overlapped with that of religion, the Catholics tending to be more aulic and the Protestants, more nationalist. One result of this was that the Transylvanian magnates, many of whom were Protestants, were usually nationalist in sympathies, while in Catholic West Hungary aulic sympathies extended to the middle nobility.

[2] The *Országos Kaszino*, as opposed to Széchenyi's *Nemzeti Kaszino*. Unfortunately, the most obvious English translation for either is 'national'.

[3] It was presumably this fact that led many ambitious young sprigs of the higher nobility to seek their political fortunes in the Lower House. It had not been uncommon before 1848 for a magnate to represent a County on the Lower Bench, and a Law of 1885 made it legal for one to sit in the Lower House without forfeiting his birth-right to the other body.

it, they had to fight their way up its ladder on equal terms with other people. The Permanent Head of a Ministry was no longer automatically a son of a great house – nor, for that matter, was an Archbishop.

It is true that Parliamentary influence was not always the same as effective political power, for behind the scenes, other influences were often stronger than those of the greatest landlord. Not the least reason for the Liberal Party's prolonged tenure of office was the tacit (but notorious) alliance which existed between it and the Jewish capitalist interests. Nationalist writers often complained that Hungary was really ruled by an unholy partnership of 'feudal magnates and Jewish bankers', while Lueger, from Vienna, described the Liberal Party as controlled by Jews. These words, spiteful as they were, contained much truth. It is interesting that the financial unity of the Monarchy, which was the financiers' chief concern, suffered fewer impairments than Francis Joseph's special interest, the formal unity of the organization of the armed forces.

The magnates were, of course, very few, and even the gentry, only a relatively small élite. While no definition of that class existed, it can be taken as roughly equivalent to that of the owners of estates of 200–1,000 hold, of whom there were, in 1895, about 10,000 (3,200 estates of 500–1,000 and 6,700 of 200–500). Below them the pyramid broadened out: there were 10,800 estates of 100–200 hold, 39,000 of 50–100, 235,000 of 20–50 and 460,000 of 10–20.

These medium and small independent farmers formed an important factor in the country's economic life, but not an independent political one. The national tradition, which was reinforced by administrative pressure, that the governance of Hungary was a matter for its substantial landlords, was strong enough to defy the numerical paucity of that class. The smaller men, whether ranking socially as gentle-folk or peasants, dutifully obeyed this unwritten law and unless they were non-Magyars, when if they possessed a vote (but more often they did not) they might cast it for a national party, voted '67 or '48, according to the opinion entertained by or prescribed to them on the Issue of Public Law.

The broad base of the pyramid, meanwhile, was composed of a great mass of dwarf-holders and landless men, who were existing in a condition of complete political impotence and great social degradation, and of extreme material misery.

The land reform had, as we have seen, been generous to its beneficiaries, the rustical peasants, in requiring no compensation from them. But the beneficiaries had constituted little more than one-third of the total rural population, and even to them it had come as no more of an unmixed blessing, in economic results, than it had to the Austrian peasants. In Hungary, too, there were real gainers, commonest among the thrifty German peasants of the South, who had also early adopted the habit of family limitation. But very many ex-rusticalists, even in the earliest years after the reform, had found the difficulties of equipping themselves (credit was even shorter and more expensive in Hungary than in Austria) and of meeting the tax-collector's demands, insuperable, and had simply reverted to a modernized form of their old servitude,[1] in which they were even joined by many sandalled nobles now deprived of their only asset, the robot. Even the small-holders had, however, profited by the high agricultural prices prevailing for some twenty years after the reform, and seem to have maintained themselves fairly well during these years; but the advent of the great agricultural depression of the 1880s, coinciding with a growth of population which far outstripped the development of outlets for it off the land, brought a very abrupt deterioration. A large number of peasant proprietors were ruined altogether,[2] and sub-division of holdings set in on a large scale. The agricultural census of 1895 showed over 400,000 holdings of 5–10 hold in the Kingdom and 110,000 in Croatia, 717,000 and 126,000 respectively of 1–5, 563,000 and 54,000 of less than one, and nearly 1,700,000 persons (wage-earners) totally landless.

The figures for the dwarf-holdings of course include vineyards and market gardens which could provide their owner or lessee with a comfortable existence enough even where only a few acres in extent; many of them, especially of the vineyards, were, moreover, owned by persons who derived only part of their livelihoods from them. A large part were, however, purely agricultural holdings whose owners had no other means of subsistence, and the greater part of these fell below the subsistence level.[3]

The condition of the landless men had undergone a similar deterioration. In the first years after the land reform, when labour was very short, especially in districts where robot had been widely used, the ex-zsellers or members of peasant families willing to supply it had been able to command good wages. These years were followed by the era of the great public works – the construction of the railways, the regulation of the Tisza, and other enterprises – so that labour on the estates was still in short supply, so much so that some landlords were importing harvest labour from Italy and Dalmatia.[4] Wages were still good, as were those earned by the navvies. Then came the 1880s. The public works slackened off, and the landlords, themselves in difficulties, mechanized (although less than in Austria) to save labour, and where they still had to pay wages, cut them. The biggest cuts, as in Galicia, were those made in the

---

[1] According to Mailáth, *La Hongrie Rurale, Sociale et Politique* (Paris, 1909), p. 22, it was now that share-cropping became a common institution.

[2] 118,000 peasant proprietors were sold up in the last three decades of the century (Mód, op. cit., p. 154).

[3] Eight hold was usually taken as the minimum on which a family could exist.

[4] Mailáth, l.c.

harvest labourers' share in kind, and the worst sufferers that class, now a very large one (it included many dwarf-holders, as well as men entirely landless) who depended almost entirely on this work, living from harvest to harvest on the share which they took home of the crop harvested by them. But the farm-hands suffered too, since now the supply of labour exceeded the demand.

The destitution which had now come to prevail among the dwarf-holders and landless men was terrifying. An inquiry undertaken in 1896[1] showed that the seasonal workers when away from their homes often lived exclusively on bread, only very rarely getting warm food. In one Carpathian district, the inhabitants 'lived exclusively on potatoes in vinegar, without fat or meat'; in another, 'exclusively on beans, dry or mixed with maize flour, boiled or roast potatoes in cabbage soup or on raw cabbage, or on a wretched maize bread', etc.

The poverty of the labourer was due not only to the lowness of the wage paid to him for a working day, but also to the fact that his working days did not, as a rule, exceed 70–90 in a year. The long winters of enforced idleness also reduced the earnings of the small peasants and dwarf-holders, while the development of the factories had cut off the subsidiary earnings with which their womenfolk had formerly helped out the family budget.

There had been a similar decline in conditions off the land. When the period opened, Hungary possessed a fairly extensive artisan class, which lived modestly but sufficiently. When the factories began to expand on a large scale, skilled labour was still very scarce. Its exponents were often imported from Austria or Germany,[2] and were able to command relatively high wages and good conditions. But things got worse when the use of machinery became more general and when the surplus population from the country began flocking into the towns. The Liberal philosophy of the day favoured the free operation of the law of supply and demand, and the landlords opposed high wages in industry as tending to draw labour off the land. It was also generally (and not unreasonably) argued by the Government and the employers that Hungary could not afford to let either wages or conditions advance ahead of those in Austria. In fact, wages moved on much the same level: an inquiry in 1900 showed that 28% of the men for whom data were available were earning 14–20 kr. a week, 48% 6–14 and 15% less than 6. Women earned proportionately less. Hours of work for child and juvenile labour were limited by a law passed in 1884, but those of adults (as in Austria) left unlimited. In 1900 an inquiry showed that the commonest working day in factories was 12 hours, inclusive of breaks; 9 or 10 for women. Housing conditions in

[1] See J. Bunzel, *Studien zur Sozial und Wirtschaftspolitik Ungarns* (Leipzig, 1902), pp. 11 ff. A very interesting picture of the lives of this class may be found in G. Illes's autobiographical work, *Puszták Népe*.

[2] A survey made in Budapest in 1875, covering 10,020 workers, showed that 24·9% of them had been born outside Hungary.

Budapest were even worse than in Vienna; in 1910 nearly 10% of the population lived 10 or more to a room, only 6·3% one or two to a room. Some people lived in caves or holes dug in fields; in 1905 a police search revealed 35 individuals roosting in trees, having tied themselves on with ropes.

Meanwhile, the fortunes of the artisan class had been similar to those of its Austrian counterpart. The relative weakness of the competition from the factories had made its decline slower, but its position at the end of the century was perceptibly worse than half a century before.

In recording these facts we must, indeed, beware of adopting without reservation the fashionable picture which contrasts the destitution which undoubtedly prevailed at one end of the social scale with a supposed limitless abundance at the other. The truth was that in 1902 Hungary was still a poor country. It had been backward when the period opened, and the fields towards which its development had then been chiefly directed had, largely owing to circumstances beyond the nation's control, proved to be particularly unlucrative. The development had thus produced only a moderate accession of national wealth: economists have calculated that on the eve of the First World War, Hungary's total national wealth was only just over half of Austria's, whose population was only about 20% larger;[1] and Austria itself was poor by West European standards, not to speak of American. There were, of course, wealthy men in Hungary, but especially on the land, the supposed darlings of fortune were usually not nearly so rich as they looked. The Esterházys of the day no longer built themselves palaces like Esterháza or Kismarton (in general, few of the great country houses of Hungary date from the Liberal era), nor stood themselves luxuries like Prince Miklos's famous uniform of pearls. If the great estates survived, it was even more true of Hungary than of Austria that most of the rent-rolls from them went into other pockets than those of their nominal owners. The lord of less than 1,000 hold usually lived modestly indeed, except in so far as his estates provided him with abundance of food and wine, and domestic service was cheap and plentiful. More big fortunes were probably made out of industry, than off the land, but as Hungarian writers often emphasize, by no means all the plus values created by the Hungarian workers remained in the country.[2] This was even more true of the financial system, where the profits were probably biggest of all; the Hungarian finance houses (which owned

[1] See the calculations made shortly before the war by the Hungarian economist, Fellner, cit. F. Herz, *The Economic Problem of the Danubian States* (London, 1947), pp. 20 ff.

[2] Some calculations on this point will be found in W. Offergeld, *Grundlagen und Ursachen der Industriellen Entwicklung Ungarns* (Jena, 1914), pp. 249 ff. They are complicated and cautious, but seem to justify the conclusion that at the beginning of the twentieth century about 35% of the profits from Hungarian industry were going out of the country. According to an article by W. Federn in the *Oe. Rundschau*, 1908, cit. Hantsch, *Gesch.*, II. 594, 80% of the mortgages then held by the Austro-Hungarian Bank were on Hungarian properties and 65% of its bills of exchange were drawn on Hungary.

much of the industry) were largely subsidiaries of concerns having their headquarters in Vienna, or even further afield.

The fact that part of the picture was not so brilliantly white as is often supposed does not, however, make the other part of it less dark, and the fact remained that nearly one-half of the population of Hungary was living on sub-human material standards, and that for long years the regime spent far more effort on preventing them from revolting against their condition, than on trying to improve it.

The industrial workers had never been entirely denied a right to organize. The compositors had founded their own Trade Union (disguised as a mutual benefit association) as early as 1861, and on their initiative, a 'General Workers' Association' had been brought into being in 1869, the Government raising no objections. In 1870, however, indiscreet demonstrations in favour of the Paris Commune had thrown the authorities into a panic which had led to exaggerated measures of repression. A law enacted in 1872, and re-enacted with amendments in 1884, declared association and strikes lawful, but made incitement to strike a punishable offence, and every form of association, including the Trade Unions, had to be non-political.

The development of a workers' political movement was held up, as in Austria, by rivalries between different schools of thought, and between personalities, but in December 1890 a Social Democrat Party was founded, which adopted bodily the Hainfeld Programme just evolved by the Austrian sister party. The Hungarians also adopted the Austrian tactics of close association with the Trade Unions – in their case, so close that behind every official union was set up an unofficial 'shadow' or 'free' union, which performed the political functions of the union, including the collection, administration and distribution of strike funds. Every member of an official union was at the same time, and automatically, member of its 'free' union, and in most cases also of the Social Democrat Party.

By the end of the century both the Party and the Unions were firmly established, and constituted nuclei which might one day expand into important movements. Their actual membership was, however, almost insignificant, and it was impossible for the Socialists even to think of Parliamentary representation until the advent – of which there was as yet no sign – of suffrage reform. Moreover, while there were now some signs that the social conscience of Hungary's rulers was beginning to awaken to the deplorable condition of the industrial workers, and certain modest reforms were being put through in the field of social legislation, the Social Democrat Party was regarded by the regime with extreme hostility and repugnance, not only as threatening profits, but partly also owing to the international character of its programme and the non-Magyar composition of its leadership, which, after the incubation period, when it had been mainly Swabian, had become almost entirely Jewish.

The element of psychological hostility was absent from the regime's attitude towards agricultural labour; a certain feeling existed in the countryside, among both parties, of membership of the same stock and attachment to the same traditions. On the other hand, the demands of the agricultural proletariat were a direct challenge to the landlords' own pockets, so that the regime was even more strongly opposed to attempts by this class to organize, than to those made by the industrial workers. For nearly twenty-five years after the Compromise it was completely successful. Then, round 1890, trouble broke out, similar to that in Galicia and occasioned by the same cause, that the landlords were progressively reducing the harvesters' share in kind. Now the agricultural labourers on many estates revolted, and in 1891 and again in 1894 there were demonstrations which the military dispersed with bloodshed. The political opposition to the landlords was complicated by the appearance of a strange figure named István Várkonyi, a horse-dealer from Csegled, who first joined the Social Democrat Party, then seceded from it and founded his own party of 'Independent Socialists', the doctrines of which (which he took over largely from Dr Eugen Heinrich Schmitt) were an individual mixture of mystical Christianity, anarchism and revolutionary socialism. Both Várkonyi and the orthodox Social Democrats developed a lively agitation, and in 1897 the labourers carried out a large-scale strike. That year and the next the unrest was very widespread, and there were clashes with the authorities in many parts of Hungary.

The strike was not unsuccessful. Harvest wages were forced up by 40–50%, and in many places a particularly resented institution, the 'robot labour', was abolished.[1] The next year the Government introduced a law commonly known as the 'Slavery Law' which made the contracts of agricultural and day labourers[2] an official obligation, which was undertaken before the authorities, and once made, could not be broken by the labourer except in case of sickness, military service or danger to life. A worker not appearing voluntarily at his work, failing to begin work or failing to bring the implements, etc., stipulated in the contract, became liable to two months' imprisonment. He might be escorted back to his work by gendarmes. Further, all combinations among agricultural workers were declared null and void, and incitement either to combination or to strike became punishable offences. In return, the employer was bound to keep his contract, the truck system was abolished, and certain welfare measures made obligatory.

[1] This was an institution under which the labourer was obliged to undertake a certain number of days, up to forty in a year, of unpaid labour in addition to that for which he contracted. Only if he agreed to this could he be certain of being hired. The term 'new robot' was used also in another sense, when the lessee of a small plot took out his rent, wholly or partly, in service (sometimes including domestic service performed by his women-folk in the big house). This arrangement was sometimes convenient to both parties.

[2] The law was extended subsequently to workers in forestry, tobacco plantations, market gardens, etc.

It is fair to say that the Government now enacted several measures designed to eliminate the worst abuses under which the agricultural labourers were suffering,[1] and even attempted, here and there, to relieve the rural congestion by founding agrarian colonies. The congestion was also being relieved, more effectively, by emigration, which had now set in on a large scale, and to a lesser extent, by the increased pace of industrialization. The 1890s probably constituted a nadir, both in respect of land distribution, and of wages and conditions of labour. If, however, conditions did not worsen after that date, such improvement as they showed was little more than minimal, and there was no relaxation of the political pressure. Várkonyi's movement had been dissolved in 1898. The authorities discouraged any social democratic agitation by all means in their power, and partly for this reason, partly, it must be admitted, for others – the country-folk did not take well to it – it made little impression. In 1900 another dissident Socialist movement, calling itself the 'Reorganized Social Democrat Party', tried to woo the agricultural labourers and dwarf-holders, but it, too, attracted little support, except in the Serb and Roumanian districts, where it contrived to combine national with social agitation.

So far, then, the regime had held its own, at least to the extent of making no political concessions, against the dispossessed classes, but the accumulated explosive stuff was now so formidable as to make it highly doubtful whether it would be able to hold its position indefinitely. Meanwhile, the national question had reached a stage which, as in Austria, was much more dangerous still.

III THE NATIONALITIES PROBLEM

The development of the 'nationalities problem', i.e., that of the relationship between the peoples inhabiting the Kingdom of Hungary,[2] was quite different from that of the national problem in Cis-Leithania. The difference did not lie so much in the law, for the Hungarian Law of 1868 laid down the principle of inter-national equality just as the Austrian Paragraph XIX did, and Austrian usage made concessions to 'the practical requirements of administration and justice' like those for which the Hungarian instrument specifically allowed.[3] Nor, *pace* all German-Austrians who ever wrote, did it lie in national psychology, for the German Austrians, and for that matter, the other peoples of Cis-Leithania, were no more naturally tolerant than the Magyars. But the sheer forces of history and demography had driven all these

---

[1] Here again, Darányi deserves a credit mention, as does Count Sándor Károlyi, the leader of the more progressive landlords and *spiritus rector* of the co-operative movement, which developed rapidly during these years.

[2] This section is concerned only with the Kingdom of Hungary, i.e., Hungary proper, excluding Croatia-Slavonia, and all remarks, statistics, etc., refer only to that area.

[3] It is true that the Hungarian Law went further than Paragraph XIX in defining these requirements, e.g. in laying down that the language of Parliament was Magyar.

peoples to a certain measure of mutual concession, whereas the Magyar and Magyar-minded ruling class in Hungary had never in history regarded their State as either a-national or multi-national, and they did not do so now. They could not feel that the primacy allowed by the Law to their language was simply a pragmatic concession to administrative efficiency, and that the State was no more 'theirs' than it was the Slovaks' or the Roumanians'. They were even convinced – and the conduct of the nationalities in and after 1848 had deepened that conviction – that the very existence of Hungary depended on the maintenance of its Magyar character.

While Deák and Eötvös were alive and politically active, their influence was still strong enough to compel a certain moderation, and at least the main provisions of the Law were observed. But the pot was simmering even then,[1] and a big change for the worse set in when the Ministry of the Interior was taken over by Tisza, with his belief in the practicability (and if practicable, it was certainly desirable) of Magyarizing at least a large part of the Slovaks. Thereafter no Hungarian regime ever thought of Hungary except in terms of Magyar supremacy; they differed only in their views of how far down it was necessary to go with the process of Magyarization, and in the degree of vigour and purpose with which they pursued the aim. And the general trend was always in the same direction, although its graph was not that of a uniform slant; periods when the slope was gradual alternated with others when it was more abrupt, the most marked among the latter, in our period, being when Tisza first took office; the time of the Bosnian crisis, when the Government felt the need to placate public opinion for its unpopular acquiescence in the occupation; the millenary celebrations, with their evocation of a fever of national self-confidence; and the years when Hungarian policy was dictated by the violent and brutal Bánffy, who defended his support of the Compromise as the only way to enable Hungary to develop into 'an unitary Magyar national State, the centre of gravity of the future Magyar-Austrian Monarchy'.

It is, of course, unsafe to generalize superlatives in describing any situation, and this one is no exception. During the worst of these periods, and to the end, there were some officials (more than is generally admitted) who continued to treat the non-Magyar public with whom they had to deal sensibly and paternally, but even they did so as the representatives of a Magyar State. Others made it a patriotic virtue to behave worse even than the recognized practice laid down. The conduct of administration and justice were Magyarized, down to the lowest level, not only in all internal transactions, but, largely, in the outer services: notices to the public, even in purely non-Magyar districts, were in Magyar only, as were all proceedings in the Courts; a defendant could employ an interpreter, but had to pay for his services. The Magyar national culture was treated as the only one deserving respect, or even legitimate, in Hungary; the others were, at best, tolerated

[1] See above, p. 692.

contemptuously, but attempts to cultivate them, above the humblest level, even where specifically authorized by the Nationalities Law, were regarded as potentially or actually treasonable; always discouraged, and whenever a quarter-plausible excuse could be thought up, forbidden. The smear of treason attached even more to any attempt to give political expression to the philosophical assumption of the Law itself: the possibility of a Hungarian patriotism not identified with Magyarism. Every administrative device, including manipulations of the franchise itself (which was more restricted in Transylvania, the chief danger area, than in Inner Hungary), was employed to stifle any such movement. For the extremists, the only ultimately satisfactory solution was, as it had been in the 1840s, that the country should become entirely Magyar. Some measures adopted were pure eye-wash, designed to produce an appearance of achieved reality, not to achieve it. Such was the Magyarization of all place-names, even of villages founded, and inhabited since their foundation, exclusively by non-Magyars, and the official ostracization even of ancient and familiar alternatives to them, such as Pressburg, Oedenburg or Steinamanger. Such, too, was the encouragement (to which, in the case of State employees, pressure was sometimes added) officially given to the adoption of Magyar family names, for which the fee charged was at first five florins (10s.), and later, only thirty krajcar (1s.). This was not useless from the point of view of the national prestige; we have had it dinned into us *ad nauseam* that the great poet Petöfi began life as Petrovicz,[1] but many people today credit the Magyar genius with the achievements of László, Fraknói, Munkácsy, Vambéry, Toldy, Molnár, Marczali and a hundred others whose ancestors, or themselves in their youths, bore very different-sounding names. But determined efforts were made also actually to transform non-Magyars into Magyars, not only by the negative method of denying a man advancement in the official or even the social world unless he Magyarized, but through the educational system. The Nationalities Law itself laid down that the language of Pest University should be Magyar, which meant that knowledge of the language was a precondition for the degree which admitted its holder to the senior branches of the Civil Service, or to many professions. On the lower levels, the hands of the authorities were somewhat fettered by the fact that the educational system was so largely in the hands of the Churches, whose autonomy the Nationalities Law affirmed, and some tradition-bred quirk of national psychology forbade open violation of this provision of the Law. In fact, the non-Magyar confessional secondary schools were subjected only to the reasonable requirement, enacted in 1883, that Magyar language and literature should be compulsory subjects of instruction in their two top forms. But the Orthodox Churches possessed only a handful of such schools, and permission to add to their number was

[1] The change was, incidentally, made by the poet himself, out of sheer, unprompted enthusiasm for Magyarism.

repeatedly refused. The authorities of the Roman Catholic Church, and of the Lutheran (outside Transylvania), not to mention the Calvinists, were themselves Magyars, and saw to it that all instruction in their secondary schools should be in Magyar. Further, from the 1870s onward the State itself began founding schools, and these were largely used as instruments of Magyarization, being deliberately sited in non-Magyar or mixed districts, but with Magyar as the exclusive language of instruction. The Hungarian Statistical Annual for 1906–7 listed 205 gymnasia and Realschulen; in 189 of these the language of instruction was Magyar; in eight, German; in six, Roumanian, and in one, Italian, while one was mixed Magyar and Roumanian. There were 89 training colleges, one of which was Roumanian, two mixed Hungarian-Roumanian, two German, and one Serb, the rest Magyar; and 400 burgher schools, of which 386 were Magyar, five German, four Roumanian, three Serb and two Italian. The Slovaks and Ruthenes had no establishments of their own at all above the primary level, the three Slovak gymnasia founded in the 1860s having been closed a decade later (together with the Slovak Cultural Institute, the *Slovenská Matica*) on the pretext that they had been teaching Pan-Slavism. About 4,400 of the 6,750 Germans attending secondary schools in 1906 were going to Magyar schools, as were all the Slovaks and Ruthenes, 1,400 of the 3,900 Roumanians and 750 of the 1,100 Serbs and Croats. In elementary education, where the law prescribed instruction in the mother tongue, little had been required of non-Magyar autonomous churches except that a Law of 1879 had made the teaching of the Magyar language compulsory in their schools and ordered teachers to qualify themselves to give this instruction; but as teachers were appointed for life and the State could not insist on their dismissal, the law largely remained on paper. But here, again, the Catholics and Lutherans outside Transylvania pressed the teaching of Magyar, not so exclusively as in the secondary schools, but still far beyond its due, and the State again stepped in with its own schools, which in fact were often very popular where they were founded, since, as the State paid for them, the commune got its children's schooling free. In 1906, according to the same source, there were in Hungary proper 16,618 primary schools, of which 2,153 were State, 1,460 communal, 12,705 confessional and 300 private. The language of instruction in 12,223 of them, including all the State schools, was Magyar; in 492, German; in 737, Slovak; in 2,760, Roumanian; in 107, Ruthene; in 270, Serb or Croat; in 10, Italian, and in 19, another. About 475,000 pupils of mother tongue other than Magyar were attending Magyar primary schools, including 180,000 Slovak and 185,000 German children; only 70,000 Slovak and 52,000 German children were attending primary schools in their own language.

Finally, an Act, passed in 1891, for the compulsory establishment throughout the country of Kindergartens and homes for children whose parents were unable to give them proper care was largely utilized for purposes of Magyarization; the Magyar language was used in them almost exclusively and children were often taken from Nationality districts and put in Magyar homes. According to figures given by one reliable authority, in 1914 93.4% of the University teachers, 91·5% of the secondary, and 81·9% of the elementary, were linguistic Magyars.[1]

It should not be supposed that all these efforts were wasted. By the end of the century the State apparatus of the Kingdom – a much larger one than thirty years before – was almost exclusively Magyar in feeling, and by far the greater part of it, also Magyar in speech: according to the same authority, 95·6% of the State officials, 92·9% of the County officials, and 9·68% of the judges and public prosecutors were linguistic Magyars. Social, business and professional life showed the same picture: 89·1% of the lawyers, 89·1% of the physicians, 63·7% of the clergy. Business was overwhelmingly in the hands ot Magyar-speaking persons: figures for joint-stock companies in 1915, based on the language used by the boards or 'the names of the leading men', showed that 97·4% of these companies, with 99·3% of the share capital and 99·5% of the total assets, were in the hands of linguistic Magyars. Only 1·1% of the companies belonged to Roumanians, 0·9% to Slovaks, 0·5% to Transylvanian Saxons and 0·1% to Serbs. Magyar-speaking were 2,228 out of 2,884 owners of plants employing more than twenty persons. Most of the factory-owners and leading figures of the joint-stock companies (and their shareholders) were Magyar-speaking Jews, but the linguistic predominance of Magyar extended down well beyond the leading figures: 83% of the senior black-coated employees, 63% of the skilled workers and 71% of the artisans employing apprentices. Only 237 out of the 1,657 owners of 1,000 *hold* or more gave a language other than Magyar as their usual one.

Magyarization had made astonishing progress in most of the towns. Between 1880 and 1890 alone, the Magyar-speaking population of Hungary's twenty-five largest towns had grown by 29% and that of the 101 smaller towns by 16%; the progress in the following decade had been even greater. Budapest, which had been three-quarters German in 1848, was 79·8% Magyar-speaking in 1900, by which date its population had trebled. Pécs, Sopron, Pozsony, Kassa, Arad, Temesvár had undergone similar transformations.

The figures for the country as a whole, including the rural communes, were not so sensational, but the proportion of the total population giving Magyar as its mother tongue had risen from the 40–42% at which the estimates of the 1840s and 1850s had placed it to 46·65% in 1880, 48.61% in 1890, 51·4% in 1900: in 1910 it was to be 54·9%. In 1900 there were 8·6

---

[1] Jászi, *Dissolution of the Habsburg Monarchy*, p. 280. All the following figures are from this source, except those relating to the joint-stock companies, which come from a Hungarian memorandum submitted to the 1920 Peace Conference.

million linguistic Magyars (over 10 millions in 1910) against under 5 millions shown by the earlier censuses, 6·4 in 1880, 7·35 in 1890. The percentages of all the linguistic groups (except that of 'others') had sunk, and their increases in absolute figures had usually been small. It should further be emphasized that, contrary to so much that has been written, practically all this increase in the Magyar element was real in almost every sense of the term. The censuses (which did not attempt to define the individual's 'national feeling' or 'nationality' but only his 'maternal language'[1]) were usually honestly compiled (if there were occasional abuses, they were very few) and in the overwhelming majority of cases, the man who put himself down as 'Magyar by mother tongue' regarded himself, or at least wished others to regard him, as a Magyar.

But there was another side to the statistics. Nearly all the increases, both absolute and relative, in the Magyar-speaking element in the country had taken place in the central areas, especially Budapest and its surroundings, and it had been due, partly, to the Magyarization both of the formerly German populations of the towns and of some of the smaller non-Magyar (German and Slovak) rural islets; in large measure also to the immigration, which came from two main sources: the Jews, who as they moved southwestward exchanged Yiddish for Magyar, and the overspill from congested peripheral districts, chiefly in the north, come down to find employment in the State services or, on a humbler level, the factories of the prosperous centre. The children of these Slovak and other arrivals Magyarized automatically, almost imperceptibly.

But Central Hungary was by large majority Magyar already. The effects of the attempts to extend the Magyar area outward were practically nil. The non-Magyar pupils in the State schools in the peripheral areas who spent their school years learning a few scraps of Magyar – and very little else – promptly forgot them on leaving school. Where a commune changed its ethnic character, this was due to quite other causes, and the changes were by no means always favourable to the Magyar element. A Magyar writer who investigated the question in 1902,[2] reported that during the Liberal period the Magyars had gained only 261 communes from the non-Magyars, while losing 465 to them. Their chief gains (89) had been at the expense of the Slovaks; their chief losses, to the Roumanians and Germans. Of all the nationalities in Hungary, the Ruthenes had lost most communes (217) but most of these losses had been to the Slovaks, not the Magyars. The Magyars had lost next most, then the Serbs (87 losses, 4 gains); this largely owing to a declining birthrate.[3] The Roumanians had gained most communes – 362

---

[1] Defined as the language which the person speaks habitually and most easily.

[2] D. Balogh, *A Népfajok Magyarországon*, Budapest, 1902.

[3] Partly also to Roumanization when the Roumanians got their own Orthodox Church, and to emigration to Serbia.

gains, 64 losses – then the Slovaks (253 gains, 106 losses), then the Germans (188 gains, 116 losses).

Emigration had some effect on the national totals and proportions, for in Hungary, as in Austria, it began in the districts in which rural congestion was most acute. Thus when it began on a large scale, it came chiefly from the Slovak districts, and the Slovak contingent was percentually the largest up to 1913, and the Magyar, percentually the smallest. In absolute figures, however, the Magyars had passed the Slovaks in 1905, after which they accounted for about one-third of the annual totals.[1] Emigration, however, hardly affected the ethnic map, provided that density was disregarded, for it left no spaces to be filled, or not, at any rate, by non-local elements.[2] Broadly, therefore, the ethnic frontiers in the West, North and East had remained stationary, on almost the exact lines on which they had been stabilized at the end of the *impopulatio*: only in a few, exceptional cases did the growth of a Magyar-speaking town on the linguistic frontier alter the local balance. Behind the main lines, the losses suffered by the Magyar element at least balanced its gains; here, exactly as in Central Hungary, small local minorities were being swallowed up by the local majorities.

Thus the potential danger to Hungary's territorial integrity presented by the non-Magyar ethnic character of its periphery had not even diminished, much less disappeared. It would do so only if Magyarization conquered the periphery of the country, as it had the centre; or if Hungarian policy succeeded in winning over those non-Magyars whom it failed to assimilate linguistically to an activist attitude towards the State; and this would have to be activist indeed if it were to defeat the demands made by Hungary's neighbours, on the basis of national determinism, if the integrity of the State were threatened by outside forces.

For a considerable period it looked as though Hungary might accomplish even this, at least with most of the Nationalities. The Transylvanian Saxons had, as was their wont, conducted such an austerely self-regarding policy and had ended by achieving for themselves a position so special, that a long footnote is the only appropriate way of describing it.[3]

---

[1] According to the USA statistics for 1898/9–1912/13, the number of emigrants from Inner Hungary (we reach this figure, roughly, by omitting the Croats and a small proportion of the Serbs, and note that the American statistics ignore the Ruthenes) was, in thousands: Slovaks, 432; Magyars, 402; Germans, 219; Roumanians, 47; Serbs, 30. The Hungarian estimates for 1905–13 give: Magyars, 287; Slovaks, 193; Germans, 150; Roumanians, 95; Serbs, 50; Ruthenes, 36; others, 8. We must also take into account the emigration into Austria, which, as said elsewhere, was mainly German, and into 'other European countries', mainly Roumanian, with Germans second and Magyars third.

[2] The German areas were not heavily congested, but the persons emigrating were, here too, landless, owing to the Germans' system of inheritance (see above, p. 708, n. 3).

[3] When the Dualist era opened, memories of their attitude in 1848–9, and also of their attendance at the Schmerling Theatre, had made the Saxons deeply unpopular among all

But Hungary's other middle-class Germans, without exception, had taken a different line. They were only too glad to pay the entrance fee which admitted them to business or professional careers in which industry, method and sobriety (in all of which they excelled) were sure to earn enviable rewards: the sons or grandsons of any German burgher or Swabian peasant who had left his village were usually completely Magyarized. If any member of them felt irresistibly German, he emigrated; among those who stayed in Hungary there was, up to 1918, no trace of a German national movement, and when the *Deutscher Schulverein*, after its foundation in 1881, began to occupy itself with Hungarian conditions, the Swabians repudiated it unanimously and vigorously.¹ The same could be said of the smaller and weaker nationalities, the Sokci and Bunyevci, the Armenians, the West Hungarian Croats and Slovenes, even the Ruthenes, and almost up to the close of the century, i had been true also of a large part of the Slovak intellectuals.

At the time of the Compromise the Slovaks still possessed a handful of combative national leaders. As we have said, none of these had got into the

---

Magyars, especially, of course, those of Transylvania, and among themselves, while a small party, calling themselves the Young Saxons, wanted full recognition of the new era and even themselves advocated the abolition of their old separate status, the big majority was stubbornly determined to safeguard every jot of the ancient privileges. The Government's dismissal of the Sachsengraf and the failure to reconstitute the Sachsenboden (see above, p. 698) disillusioned even the Young Saxons, and a mass meeting at Mediasch in 1872 adopted a programme of full defence, by all legal means, of the communities' rights. In 1876 the Government replied, as mentioned above (ibid.), by further gross violations of those rights, and of its own pledged word, and for some years put extreme pressure on the Saxons, who defended themselves by rolling themselves into an even more compact hedgehog than before. Their great strength lay in the autonomy, which even the Liberal Governments respected, of their Lutheran Church. Under its protection they built up a network of schools and cultural institutions, founded banks and co-operatives, and after all, endured the storm. Before long it became apparent to both sides that the only gainer from the quarrel between them was the cause of the Roumanians, and both put out feelers: the Government replaced the more aggressive Főispáns, and the Saxons as early as 1881 stopped asking for the restoration of their old status. Then in June 1890 they drew up a new programme in which they finally accepted the Union and the Laws of 1876, demanding only honest administration and genuine application of the existing Law. The Saxon Deputies, who hitherto had called themselves independent and had confined themselves in Parliament to voicing their own grievances, were authorized to ally themselves with any party which accepted the Compromise. The Government made further concessions which in practice restored to the Saxons much of their old self-Government and they thus became a '*staaterhaltendes Element*', regularly allying themselves with the Government in Parliament and locally, with the Magyars against the Roumanians; although how little they counted the interests of the Hungarian State compared with those of their own community was shown by their action in 1918, when they voted for the attachment of Transylvania to Roumania (having ascertained in Paris that the transference had been decided there).

¹ It may, of course, be suspected that this was due to administrative pressure, but pressure did not prevent the Saxons from welcoming the *Schulverein*.

1865 Diet, but three got elected to the 1869 Parliament as representatives of the Slovak National Party, with a programme of realizing the 1861 memorandum. There was also a rival movement, the 'New Slovak School' (*Nová Skola Slovenska*) which aimed at reaching some compromise with the Magyars. But the Magyars, whose painful experience had convinced them that the Serb and Roumanian national movements, however nefarious, were realities with which policy must reckon, could never be persuaded that Slovak nationalism was anything more than an aberration, which they also believed to be curable. Government pressure was applied against both parties, whose rivalry also split the Slovak vote, and neither got any candidate into Parliament in 1872. Thereafter the *Nová Skola* disintegrated altogether, and the National Party decided to adopt 'a policy of abstention' which had much the same effect. Meanwhile, the full weight of Magyarization was being turned on the Slovaks, in accordance with Grünwald's advice, more completely than on any other nationality. Their three Gymnasia were, as we have said, dissolved in 1874, their cultural association, the *Slovenska Matica*, in 1875,[1] and the number of elementary schools with Slovak as language of instruction sank from a peak of 1,971 (in 1874) to half or a third of that figure.

Other factors, too, were weakening the Slovaks' resistance. The Czech politicians under the Feudalist politicians then leading them, had lost interest in them. Emigration overseas, which was very high in the 1880s, and 1890s,[2] carried away many of their more enterprising members. Sväty Marton (Szent Mártón) survived as a sort of national centre, but one little frequented, and the famous description by a chauvinist Hungarian writer of the secondary school as a sausage machine into which Slovak boys were fed at one end, to emerge Magyars at the other, had much truth in it. A high proportion of the Slovak intelligentsia did Magyarize, and those who achieved eminence in their chosen vocations, among which the Church was a favourite, usually became as devoted to their adopted nation as any Magyar of the blood.

The Serb national movement, too, became less active with time. It had started with a swing in the first years of Dualism, when memories of the lost Voivody – gilded by a somewhat deceptive afterglow of memory – were still vivid, and relations with the Serbian Principality close. Unlike the other Nationalities, the Serb politicians did not boycott the Hungarian Parliament,

[1] On this occasion the Hungarian Government achieved a master stroke. Its statutes declared the assets of the *Matica*, which had come to it chiefly through donations (including one from Francis Joseph), to be 'the property of the Slovak nation'. The Hungarian Government confiscated the lot on the grounds that no such personality in law as the 'Slovak nation' existed.

[2] Exact data on this are not available, but it is known that when inter-continental emigration began on the large scale (after 1880) it was much the highest from the Slovak and Ruthene Counties, and although other nationalities caught up a little later, these two continued to provide the highest rates. Between 1899 and 1914, 300,000 out of the 1,400,000 registered emigrants were Slovaks, against 401,000 Magyars.

and the speeches of the vigorous and outspoken leaders whom they sent to it, Svetozar Miletić and Michael Polit, caused frequent uproars.

Passions became further inflamed when the Eastern crisis broke out in 1876. Miletić and the old fire-brand, Stratimirovićs, began collecting money and recruiting volunteers to help Serbia against the Turks, and a nationalist society, the Omladina, carried on a vigorous agitation which had in it an irredentist element.

Now, however, the Government intervened. The leaders were arrested, and Miletić sentenced to five years' imprisonment, whence he emerged a broken man. The Omladina was dissolved. The Government had already won an important success in 1875, when the Patriarch Masirević having died, it had succeeded in imposing the election of its own candidate, Ivacskovics, to the vacancy, and securing the support of the other Serb Bishops for a policy of *rapprochement*. Now the waves subsided. The Government allowed the Serbian Matica to continue in being (and it became in fact the cultural centre of all Serbian life) and the unchallenged autonomy of the Serbian Orthodox Church provided a regular inflow of young educated men. Thanks to these advantages, there was practically no real assimilation.[1] But the external feelings of the day were unfavourable to the Serbs, as they were to the Slovaks. The Serbian intelligentsia, other than the priests, emigrated largely to Serbia, where they filled many of the higher places in the young State; and Serbia was then almost an Austrian satellite, and irredentism was not encouraged there. The Serbs of Croatia had reconciled themselves with Hungary[2] and of the two Parliamentary parties which divided their franchises, the Liberals, who favoured a *modus vivendi* with Hungary, were the stronger.[3]

This left only the Roumanians as almost entirely resistant, and even among them, opinion was not always uniformly uncompromising. The Roumanians from the Partium, whose leaders Vincentiu Babes and Alexandru Mocsonyi, were among the most important figures among all their politicians, never quite lost hope of reaching a reasonable accommodation with the Hungarian Government, and even in Transylvania the great Archbishop Şaguna preached 'activism' while he lived.

But a larger party among the Transylvanian Roumanians had decided, as early as 1868 (after another mass meeting at Balászfalva, held on 15 May of that year) to demand cancellation of the Union and restoration of Transylvanian autonomy. When they saw that they were unlikely to get the

[1] The 1910 statistics for certain mixed areas, which the writer had to study in 1942, showed exactly the same figure (30,784) for persons of Serbian mother-tongue and for members of the Orthodox Church.

[2] See below, p. 737.

[3] A further curious factor in the situation was that the practice of voluntary limitation of families, which afterwards became so widespread in Hungary, began among the Serbs, whose birthrate was the lowest of any nationality in Hungary.

support, or the allies, to realize this, they decided to follow the fashionable policy of 'passivity', i.e. of boycotting Parliament. When Şaguna died in 1873, 'activism' collapsed, and its opponents were left in undisturbed possession of the field in Transylvania. In 1876 they established a National Committee to direct their policy, and in 1881, constituted a National Party, with a programme the main item of which was the demand for Transylvanian autonomy, although it asked also for remedy against the many administrative and cultural grievances under which, as it justly complained, the Roumanians were suffering. It remained, however, in passivity, an attitude which led most Hungarians – to whom Transylvania was still a remote and semi-foreign land – to believe that Roumanian national feeling was declining, like Slovak; but the contrary was the case. The consciousness of their basic ethnic oneness has, as we have said elsewhere, always been peculiarly deep among Roumanians, and it was only natural that when, in 1866, the Regat achieved the status of an independent Kingdom, the picture of Transylvania united to that kingdom, and its Roumanians elevated from the position of a despised and often ill-treated minority to that of the local master-race, should have dazzled many. Even those who were not yet consciously irredentist felt their pride and confidence in their people enormously stimulated by the achievements of their brothers across the Carpathians.

National feeling in the Regat was, moreover, now being cultivated, as never before, by a young generation, recently emerged from the High Schools, and calling themselves *Junimists*.[1] The Junimist movement did not preach active irredentism, for as it happened, its leaders were largely men trained at German Universities and Austrophile in politics. But its nationalism was of the type which transcends frontiers and class barriers, and it sowed a seed which the Francophile Liberals were to reap; and in Transylvania it found devotees, of whom one was outstanding, a brilliant and fanatical young journalist named Slavici, who was a radical in every respect.

In 1884 Slavici began publishing a new journal, the *Tribuna*, and under his influence the Roumanian national movement took on a renewed activity. The tactical point at issue was whether the Party should or should not openly announce that it had lost hope and faith in any Hungarian Government, and appeal directly to the Monarch for redress, which, in the view of many of them, could be achieved only through abolition of the Dualist system. Owing largely to Mocsonyi's opposition, the proposal was rejected in 1886 and again in 1891, and in both years the Party's programme was reissued unaltered. Meanwhile, however, the relations between the Roumanian nationalists and the authorities were growing more embittered. Proceedings were instituted against Slavici and his sympathizers, and when the Court in Nagy-Szeben refused to convict the defendants, Tisza had the cases transferred to Kolozsvár, where the juries were ultra-chauvinistic. At that point the case

[1] Roum. junimea: youth.

of the Hungarian Roumanians was suddenly spotlighted in two *causes célèbres*. In 1891, the students of Bucharest University published, in Roumanian, German, French, English and Italian, a 'memorandum' on the grievances of their kinsmen in Hungary. The Magyar students of Budapest issued an 'Answer' to this, and to that again Roumanian students (this time Hungarian subjects) answered with a 'Réplique'. The Court of Kolozsvár sentenced the principal author of this, a certain Aureliu Popoviciu, to four years' prison (which he avoided by escaping to Roumania), and the printer to a year.

The appearance of the Memorandum at last tipped the scales in Transylvania, and in 1892 the National Committee drew up its own Memorandum, which a deputation of three hundred carried to Vienna. Francis Joseph refused to receive them, and the Hungarian Government prosecuted fifteen members of the Committee, sentencing them to terms of imprisonment up to five years. The next month, the Party itself was dissolved. The chief effect of the crisis was, however, simply to eliminate the moderates, who dropped right out of politics. The Party carried on under various transparent aliases, and the entire national movement came under the unchallenged control of the extremists; to all of which the Government found no reply except more repression and more Magyarizing legislation.

Battle was, as it were, joined, and the Roumanians had the better of it. In spite of all the efforts of the Hungarian Government, and of a voluntary society, the 'E.M.K.E.',[1] Magyarization was negligible. Şaguna's organization worked admirably, and even the number of Roumanian schools remained almost constant; after dropping a little between 1876 and 1890, it was clearly recovering by 1900. A Roumanian middle class grew up, and if its members attended Magyar gymnasia, they remained Roumanians. A network of Roumanian banks was founded, on the model of the Czech Živnostenská Banka, to help the establishment of Roumanian businesses, and to transfer land from Magyar to Roumanian ownership. The Albina Bank, founded in 1872, opened 152 branches in Transylvania over the next forty years. As Balogh's statistics, if nothing else, prove (362 communes gained by the Roumanians against 64 lost),[2] Transylvania was more Roumanian in 1900 than it had been in 1848.[3]

The Hungarian Roumanians were now receiving effective support from the Regat. The publication of the Memorandum had encouraged the Roumanians in 1891 to found a 'League for the Cultural Unity of all Roumanians'[4] which helped to subsidize Roumanian individuals and

---

[1] Erdelyi Magyarság Kulturális Egyesülete.   [2] See above, pp. 726-7.
[3] Factors in this were the low birthrate of the Saxons, and the decadence of the Szekels. The birthrate of the latter people remained high, but they were now emigrating in large numbers both to Inner Hungary and to Roumania.
[4] Liga Pentru Unitatea Culturala Tutoror Românilor.

institutions, nominally only for cultural purposes, but of course, in a spirit of nationalism which saw every cultural advance as a stepping-stone towards future political unification. The League, it is true, collapsed after two or three years,[1] but its work was carried on surreptitiously by the Roumanian Government, and politicians, especially those of the Liberal Party, openly urged, in the Press and even in Parliament, that the acquisition of Transylvania should be the first object of Roumanian foreign policy. As early as 1893 Sturdza told the King that 'the broadest circles of the nation were beginning to see in the Magyars far worse enemies than the Russians and that the feeling was undermining Roumania's attitude to the Triple Alliance'. The King himself, and his Government, remained loyal to the Alliance, but the ideal of irredentism was by now overwhelmingly strong in the Roumanian public opinion, and only a child could suppose that it was much weaker among the Roumanians of Transylvania.

Towards the end of the century signs appeared that Slovak and Serb nationalism, too, had not been dead, but only dormant. In August 1895 a 'Congress of Nationalities' met in Budapest (Bánffy, oddly enough, raising no objections), and a Roumanian, a Slovak and a Serb delegate (this last, the aged Polit) agreed on a joint programme which repeated the old thesis that Hungary's ethnic composition required that she should be politically, not a national but a multi-national State. They dropped the demand for 'National' territories and organizations, but asked that counties, etc., should be delimited on national lines, the language of administration and justice in each to be that of the nationality inhabiting it; also for general, equal and secret suffrage, and various democratic reforms.

This programme elicited outbursts of unbridled rage from the Magyar chauvinists, and an intensification of Magyarization: four hundred new Magyar State schools were founded the following year. The programme had no further immediate effects, since the politicians even of those nationalities concerned decided not to abandon their 'passivity', while the Germans and Ruthenes continued to stand aside. The meeting may, however, be taken as the first sign of that turn of the tide which, ten years later, was flowing forward visibly and purposefully, particularly among the Slovaks.

Very important, in this connection, was the revival of interest in Slovak affairs which was now setting in in Prague under the influence of Professor Masaryk, himself a man of Slovak stock, although his forebears came from the extreme western outposts of his people, where it had spilled over into Moravia. Under Masaryk's inspiration some of the young Slovaks who had taken to attending Prague University (in default of adequate facilities in

[1] In any case, its funds had not been large, and its chief interest had been the Balkan Vlachs. Of its budget of 483,000 kr., 300,000 had been earmarked for the Balkans, 100,000 for Transylvania and 21,000 for the Bukovina.

their own country) founded in 1896 a 'Czechoslovak Society' (*Ceskoslovenská Jednota*) to work for the national unification of Czechs and Slovaks, to assist Slovak students in Bohemia and Moravia and 'to emancipate the life of Upper Hungary from Magyar influence'; also a periodical *Hlas* (Voice) to propagate their views.

Characteristically, the stimulus produced not only action but also counter-action among the Slovaks themselves, whose particularists and ultra-Catholics objected to the Czecho-Slovak programme on both ethnic and religious grounds (since every Slovak sniffs a crypto-Hussite in every Czech). The old quarrel broke out again and could not be resolved, although one effect of the argument was that the Pan-Slav and pro-Russian movements died away, leaving in the field only the Czecho-Slovaks and the Slovak particularists. The latter found a way out by allying themselves with the recently founded Hungarian Catholic People's Party, which agreed to support moderate Slovak demands in return for Slovak support against the laicizing policy of the Government. In 1901 a Slovak People's Party constituted itself, and, supported by the larger People's Party, got four representatives into Parliament, on a programme which was, indeed, moderate, asking for little more than honest application of the Nationalities Law. Meanwhile, with the two fractions engaged in noble rivalry, a real national revival had set in. Slovak literature, both periodical and other, multiplied, some of the Slovaks entering the professions and business retained their national consciousness, and a systematic 'self-help' movement was inaugurated with the customary apparatus of co-operatives, savings-banks, etc. This received valuable help from the Slovaks in the USA, whose remittances helped to finance the new institutions.

IV CROATIA

The history of Hungaro-Croat relations was somewhat similar to that of the nationalities question, or indeed, the Austro-Hungarian; initial storms were followed by a long period of comparative calm, at the end of which clouds were again gathering.

As we saw, the Sabor had had to be packed before the Nagodba could be got through at all, and the majority of Croat political opinion, whether adhering to Starčević's extremist doctrines or to Strossmayer's more moderate ones, was against it. Rausch simply ignored the opposition for a couple of years, but when, after he had been compelled to resign in January 1871 in consequence of accusations (which were probably, but not quite certainly, justified) against his personal financial integrity, his successor, Bedekovics, held elections in which he applied somewhat less pressure, the National Party (the former 'Illyrians') secured fifty-one out of sixty-five elected mandates and the Unionists (the former 'Magyarones') only thirteen.[1] The Govern-

[1] The other mandate went to Starčević.

ment adjourned the Sabor as soon as it met, whereupon the National Party issued a very bellicose memorandum denying the legality of the Nagodba and demanding the constitution of Croatia as a quasi-independent State, linked to Austria and Hungary alike only through the person of the common Monarch.

Fresh elections, in 1872, still gave the National Party forty-seven seats, with twenty going to the Unionists and eight to a group of 'Independent Unionists', who disapproved of Rausch's methods. The new acting Ban, Vakanović, packed the Sabor with Virilists, thus securing a majority in favour of the Nagodba. This, of course, did not appease the National Party, but they were now discouraged by the failure of the Hohenwart experiment in Austria, while the extremists had been discredited by a lunatic attempt by Starčević's Lieutenant, Kvaternik, to raise a rebellion in the Lika.[1] Lónyay, in Hungary, professed himself anxious to meet the Croats' genuine grievances. The Archbishop of Zagreb, Mihailović, succeeded in gathering the moderates of both sides into a centre party which kept the name of 'national' but dropped the old National Party's clearly unrealizable demands. The Hungarians, on the other hand, agreed to a revision of the Nagodba which satisfied some of the Croats' more reasonable wishes,[2] and after the Sabor had voted the revision, in September 1871, a widely respected Croat, Ivan Mažuranić, was appointed Ban.[3]

Mažuranić, the first non-noble ever to hold this office, and generally known, in consequence, although with some exaggeration (he was actually a professional civil servant of some standing), as 'the peasant Ban', was popular with his countrymen, for whom he did a good deal, especially in cultural respects; himself a poet and author of a famous epic, he did much to foster education – it was under his aegis that the University of Zagreb was founded. Apart from this, his years of office saw the introduction of many administrative and judicial reforms, the counterparts of those being introduced during the same years in Austria and Hungary. The Hungarians kept their side of the new compact, and peace reigned for some years.

The respite, however, was short-lived. The dark side of Mažuranić's regime was his intolerance towards the local Serbs,[4] and the considerable ill-

[1] Kvaternik was an exalté, a super-fanatical Catholic who believed that he had a Divine mission to liberate Croatia and to punish godless Austria. His 'rising', as has been said elsewhere (p. 557), was put down in three days. An attempt had also been made with the help of forged documents to discredit Strossmayer and others as Pan-Slav agents and revolutionaries (see R. W. Seton-Watson, *Southern Slav Question*, pp. 88 ff.). This was so transparent as to damage only its authors.

[2] The three points granted were: the powers of the Ban were slightly restricted; Croatia's contribution to the joint treasury was fixed at fifty-five per cent of her total revenues; and it was made obligatory to convoke the Sabor within three months of its dissolution.

[3] According to Südland (op. cit., p. 153) the appointment was made on Francis Joseph's personal insistence, against the wishes of the Hungarian Ministry.

[4] He actually introduced a Croat Catechism and prayers into the Orthodox schools.

will already existing between the two peoples was enhanced by the outbreak of the Bosnian insurrection of 1875 and the tumultuous developments which followed it, for both nations had their eye on Bosnia. Serbia's ambition to annexe the province for herself was enthusiastically supported by the Serbs of Hungary,[1] while the Croats wanted it annexed to the Monarchy and then combined with Croatia (and Dalmatia) into the Great Croatia of their dreams; each party maintained a one hundred per cent claim to the nationality of the Bosnians with superb disregard of the other's case.[2] The Croats' ambitions brought them into conflict, not only with the Turcophile public opinion in Hungary, but also with official Austro-Hungarian policy, and when, in February 1879, Mažuranić, irritated by delays over the incorporation of the Military Frontier, offered his resignation in a moment of pique, the Hungarian Government hastened to accept it.

The new Ban, Baron Pejačević, although much less of a Croat backwoodsman than his predecessor, was a correct enough man, but under his regime there occurred one of those absurd incidents which, trivial in themselves, raise points of fundamental principle and end by rocking empires. The new Director of the Financial Department in Zagreb, a Magyar named David, introduced courses in Magyar for his staff. Then he made their promotion dependent on their proficiency in the language. Finally, on one August night in 1883, he had the escutcheons with inscriptions in Croat over his office (and some others) taken down and replaced with others bearing inscriptions in Croat and Magyar; his argument was that some of the services performed in these buildings were 'common' ones. The moves were legally defensible, but the Croats took them, probably with reason,[3] as part of a planned campaign from Budapest to Magyarize the common institutions. Riotous mobs tore down the new escutcheons, and troops had to be called in.

The Hungarian Government made reparation of a sort, but it was tardy and ungracious, and feeling ran high on both sides. Twenty-three Deputies resigned from the National Party, to form a new 'Independent National Party'; even more recruits went over to Starčević. Pejačević, whom David had not consulted, resigned, thereby earning for himself the nickname of 'the Cavalier Ban'. Eventually Tisza decided to use the strong hand. The Croat Constitution was suspended and the country administered by a Royal Commissioner until order had been restored. Then Tisza appointed as Ban a cousin of his own, Count Károlyi Khuen-Hedérváry, a man who was Croat (or rather, Slavonian) only technically, and in spirit, a true Tisza man.

Khuen-Hedérváry was only thirty-three at the time of his appointment, and his rule was destined to last for twenty years. During these he proved

[1] See above, p. 730.
[2] Most Croats of the day, including Mažuranić, maintained that the local Orthodox population were 'Orthodox Croats'. The Serbs called the local Croats 'Catholicized Serbs'.
[3] There is reason to believe that David was acting under direct instructions from Szapáry.

himself his cousin's equal as a political tactician. He combined the Unionists with the remnants of the National Party in a new National Party which had nothing in common with its predecessor except the name; it now consisted of a clique of men dependent on the Ban, who were rightly given by the people the same name of 'Mameluks' as had been bestowed on Tisza's followers in Hungary. Strong administrative pressure and corruption regularly secured the return of a big quota of Mameluks to the Sabor, and a revision of its Standing Orders in 1884 (in which Zagreb preceded both Vienna and Pest) enabled them to put through the business entrusted to them. As, however, he could not even so count on an absolutely safe majority, Khuen provided his bow with a second string in the shape of the Serbs, who since the total reincorporation of the Military Frontier, had come to constitute nearly a quarter of the population of Croatia-Slavonia. If his predecessors had given the Serbs much less than justice, Khuen made up for this in full measure. Their culture was strongly encouraged: they were allowed to maintain as many schools as they wished, and these received their full share of subsidies. The Cyrillic alphabet was admitted to full equality with the Latin, and taught obligatorily in all schools. Serbs were admitted in generous numbers into the civil services and professions, while a Serbian Bank, founded in Zagreb in 1895, helped them to develop their own economic life. They were allowed a newspaper in Zagreb, and although it was an open secret that the organ was subsidized from Belgrade, it was allowed more freedom than the Croat Press. The Serbs were allowed to fly the red, white and blue colours which were, indeed, the colours of their own Church, but also those used by the Prince of Serbia.

This was the side of Khuen's policy which has been most bitterly attacked by all Croat writers (and many others) who have invariably refused to see in it anything except a Macchiavellian device for ruling the population by dividing it. It is fair to point out that justice alone would have required any man in authority to protect this important minority against what would otherwise have been the unbridled tyranny of an ultra-chauvinistic majority. But the political motive was, of course, present also, and the political harvest was reaped, for the Serbs regularly supported Khuen in the Sabor[1] and thus ensured its smooth functioning.

For the rest, Khuen was a competent administrator. A peripheral area, and not rich in natural resources,[2] Croatia did not enjoy the more rapid economic development which came during these years to some other, more fortunately situated, parts of the Monarchy. As we have seen, it lagged

[1] An Independent Radical Party, founded in 1877, was oppositional, but it was very small.
[2] One of its great resources, the enormous oak-forests which once covered much of Slavonia was, indeed, ruthlessly torn from it in these years by foreign capitalists. Croat historians complain that Croatia received less than its fair share of Hungarian Governmental subsidies, etc. In default of exact information, the present writer refrains from expressing an opinion on this point.

behind the Kingdom of Hungary in respect of industrialization and urbanization. There was the same problem of rural over-population which was cursing Hungary, with the same effects of agrarian rioting[1] and of emigration, which seems to have been even higher from Croatia than from the Kingdom.[2] But Khuen did much to improve communications (it is true that the new railways were directed towards Budapest, and communications between Zagreb and Cis-Leithania deliberately neglected), raise technical standards of agriculture and in general, to modernize the country as far as could be done with limited resources.

It may be added that Khuen – most properly – made no attempt to interfere in Croatia's cultural affairs. The University and Academy of Zagreb flourished and Croat literature enjoyed something of a *floraison* during the period.

Khuen's tactics met with considerable success, even among the Croats. His enemies complained that he 'corrupted the soul of a whole generation'; what they meant was that he induced a considerable proportion of the Croats to accept the relationship with Hungary in principle, if not in every detail. The national opposition was further weakened by Starčević's habit of pouring intemperate abuse on everyone (Strossmayer not excepted) who refused to follow him blindly. In 1895, however, the Party of Right succeeded in fusing with the Independent National Party in a 'United Opposition', and two years later, under the influence of Dr Josef Frank, a highly intelligent Jew who was becoming the *spiritus rector* of the Right, it revised its programme, dropping the idea of complete independence in favour of a new Compromise, under which the Nagodba was to be replaced by a Treaty between Hungary and a Great Croatia, as two equally 'immediate' parties. In 1896, Starčević died and another split followed. The moderates, who kept the title of Party of Right, asked for little more than a relationship of strict equality between Hungary and Croatia, while Frank and his followers, who now called themselves the 'Party of Pure Right', produced a programme asking for the 'erection of the Unified Kingdom of Croatia by the incorporation of Slavonia, Dalmatia, the town and territory of Fiume, the Littoral, Bosnia, Herzegovina, Istria, Carniola, Carinthia and Styria, within the bounds of the Habsburg Monarchy'. All questions deriving from the Pragmatic Sanction

---

[1] The worst year for this in Croatia was 1897.

[2] It is extraordinarily difficult to be certain of the exact figures. There is an article on the subject by G. J. Prpic (Kroatische Auswanderung nach Amerika vor 1914) in *Der Donauraum*, 9 Jhr., Heft (1964), pp. 167 ff., but his sources often do not distinguish Croats from Slovenes, Croatia from Bosnia and Dalmatia, etc. The official figures, which take account only of persons with passports, show 166,579 persons as leaving Croatia for the USA between 1899–1913, while private calculations, which include persons without passports, give almost exactly double that figure. Südland (op. cit., pp. 464–5) goes higher still; he says that 527,355 persons emigrated between 1900 and 1913. The Croats being partly a maritime people, the proportion emigrating for short periods, and returning, was probably exceptionally high.

and the unity of the Monarchy were to be handled by the Kingdom of Croatia 'on equal terms with the Kingdom of Hungary and the other Lands of the Monarchy'. This demand, with its fantastic geographical extensiveness, was justified as 'the realization of Croat constitutional law and of the natural rights of the Croat nation'.[1]

It is not surprising that this programme elicited vigorous protests from the Serbs. The Slovenes were able to comfort themselves with the thought that their homes were in Cis-Leithania.

[1] A translation of this programme is given by R. W. Seton-Watson, *The Southern Slav Question*, p. 392.

16

Bosnia-Herzegovina, 1875–1903

The European mandate to administer Bosnia-Herzegovina with which Austria was entrusted in 1878 could be no sinecure. At that time the provinces held the repute of being wilder and more backward than any other part of Turkey in Europe (except perhaps the inner fastnesses of Albania) – some said, even of Anatolia. The 'towns', except Sarajevo, the seat of the Pashalik, and perhaps Mostar, were mere hamlets. 'Industry' consisted of peasant handicrafts, trade was done largely by barter: 'if anyone had money', we are told, 'he hid it away'.[1] There were few schools and practically no medical services; plague, cholera and syphilis were rife. There were only three hundred and fifty miles of carriage-roads in the two provinces; work on a single railway was just beginning. For the rest, most movement was by mule-track, and the mule or ass was the usual vehicle of transport, whether passenger or goods.

The agriculture from which the vast majority of the population (except that fraction of it, which was, indeed, not inconsiderable, which practised the calling of banditry) was of the most primitive kind. Some tobacco was grown in the Herzegovina and plum brandy distilled in Bosnia. Otherwise, the peasant scratched the ground with a wooden plough to raise a meagre crop of maize, or pastured his lean cattle, sheep and swine on the hill-tops and in the forests. The latter, which covered a large part of Bosnia, were in theory State property; in practice, a no-man's-land plundered at will by any comer.

There was little law or order, especially for the Christian population. The reforms enacted by the Porte during the preceding generation had, on paper, removed most of the disabilities under which Christians had previously suffered under Ottoman rule, but in practice, the reforms were largely ignored; the governors sent to Sarajevo by the Porte either proved unable to enforce the new order against the opposition of the local Moslems or, more often, collaborated with them in sabotaging it. Most of the Christians were also the bondsmen of Moslem landlords, for the local landlords who had

[1] Stöller, op. cit. We do, however, hear of quite wealthy Christian merchants in some of the towns.

adopted Islam when the Turks conquered the provinces had been allowed to retain their estates. When the central authority of the Porte ceased to be effective in these remote provinces – as it did in the seventeenth century – the descendants of this class were able to extend their estates by usurpation at the expense of the Christian communities; other properties were acquired by ex-officials, tax-farmers or other immigrants. The process was more difficult where the peasant was a Moslem, for a Moslem, even where he was a peasant, was a free man, and in 1878 there were still some 77,000 free peasant holdings, almost exclusively in Moslem hands, but the vast majority of the Christian peasants, put at 80,000 families of Orthodox and 23,000 Catholics, were now 'kmets' on the estates of the Moslem agas, or begs, as they were commonly, although inaccurately, called,[1] of whom there were then some 6–7,000. Thus although there were still a few free Christian families (and many who had lost their freedom only recently, for the process of usurpation had been going on steadily, even in the nineteenth century) and a very few Moslem kmets,[2] the proposition was generally true that a Moslem was a free man and the Christian (outside the towns) a kmet.

The landowners had not only extended their estates, but had altered the form of them from the timar to the much more burdensome *chiflik*, which meant that the kmet's obligations were, in practice, ruled by local custom, but hardly at all by law. As in Austria, these obligations had grown steadily heavier with the increasing demands of the begs, and had been the cause of many revolts. Laws regulating them had, however, been enacted in 1848 and (under pressure from the Powers) in 1859. Under these the robot was abolished (it was still occasionally practised thereafter, but on a small scale, demesne farming being rare). The kmet usually paid his landlord one-third (the so-called *tretjina*) of his produce of cereals, fruit and vegetables, and one half his hay; the payment was usually made in kind, sometimes in cash. The landlord was responsible for the upkeep of the tenant's domicile, farm buildings, etc. In addition, the State took tithe of all produce, and a house-tax. The *haratch*, or poll-tax, had been abolished in 1854, when Christians were made liable to military service, but those not called up (and these constituted the great majority) paid a tax in lieu (the *bedel-i-askeri*) which amounted in practice to the same thing.

When the Monarchy's forces entered the Provinces they met, as we have said elsewhere, with strong resistance from the local Moslems, which it took some time to overcome; and this was not even counter-balanced by friendliness from the bulk of the Christian population, for the Serbs, who constituted

---

[1] The title 'beg' was really a much higher one.

[2] Two thousand families. It is interesting that the figures are almost exactly the same, proportionately, as those given by Südland (p. 211) as correct for 'his day' (he wrote in 1916); he said there were then about 80,000 kmet holdings, of which 58,845 were held by Serbs, 17,116 by Croats and 3,653 by Moslems.

the majority of the Christians, although hostile to the rule of the Porte, had not wanted it replaced by that of Austria; their wish had been for unification with Serbia or Montenegro. Only the local Croats sincerely welcomed the Austrians. For some months the Provinces had remained under military occupation, and this had been succeeded by a period of experimentation which had been frankly unhappy, especially since it was complicated by a dispute between Austria and Hungary over how the authority over the Provinces was to be exercised, neither Cis- nor Trans-Leithania being willing to leave the privilege to the other. On the other hand, neither wanted the Provinces for itself, and they could not be made into a 'Reichsland', as Germany had made Alsace-Lorraine, because Hungary did not admit the existence of an Austrian 'Reich'. The problem was eventually solved by putting the Provinces in charge of the Joint Ministry of Finance – a device which was less absurd than it sounds, for that Minister's other duties were hardly more than nominal. Even when this had been decided, it took some time before the administrative machinery took its definitive shape, of the Minister in supreme charge,[1] three central sections (concerned respectively with internal affairs, justice and finance) and a network of subordinate instances in the smaller towns and districts; and for a time conditions were fairly chaotic. Austria had pledged herself to retain the former Turkish officials, but those gentlemen, who in any case would have been ill-qualified to administer the new order, had, with hardly an exception, fled (where they had not been slaughtered), leaving the country without any administrative services whatever. The Austrian Government appealed to the Austrian and Hungarian Ministries for replacements, and the Ministries naturally unloaded on to the Bosnian service all the corrupt or incompetent officials of whom they wished to disembarrass themselves.

Nor was the Monarchy's general policy fortunate: the only definitive measure enacted in these years in the Provinces was the extension to them of the Austrian military service law. This was greatly resented by the Christian population, which had in general been exempt from such service under the Turks; it produced a revolt, and although this was put down, remained a standing source of grievance among the Bosnians.

A new chapter opened in July 1882, when Benjamin Kállay was appointed Joint Finance Minister, a post which he held until his death, in harness, just twenty-one years later (this was an extraordinary tenure of office for an Austro-Hungarian Minister, but the appointment, like that of the other two 'common' Ministers, was made by the Monarch, and was not dependent on Parliament).[2] Kállay was perhaps a shade superficial and self-satisfied, but

[1] There was also a military garrison, whose commander possessed a civilian *ad latus*. I have been unable to make clear to myself the exact relationship between this official and the Joint Ministry.

[2] Count Welfersheimb, the Austrian Minister of Defence appointed in 1880, held his portfolio for twenty-five years.

he was an honest and just-minded man, and an excellent administrator. Being a Hungarian, he could not help knowing a good deal about Croats, and he also knew the Serbs, for he had spent some years as Austro-Hungarian Consul-General in Belgrade. He also liked them: he had even written a strongly sympathetic history of the Serbian people (which he himself put on the index of books prohibited in Bosnia).

Kállay's regime was one of enlightened autocracy, and its autocratic nature must be emphasized. It was only in 1897 that the towns were allowed a small measure of autonomy, and then the concession was confined to the towns. It was only gradually that native Bosnians were even admitted to the administrative services, and then only on a small scale: as late as 1907 only 2,493 out of the 9,106 officials or State employees[1] were native Bosnians, and hardly any of them were holding positions of responsibility.[2] A considerable force of police, open and secret, was kept in the provinces, and such devices as the subsidizing of a Press favourable to the Government and severe control over Oppositional organs were used freely.

But the regime also deserves the adjective. Kállay began by cleaning up the administration. The service, as it developed under his hand, still did not constitute the cream of the Austro-Hungarian bureaucracy, for the best men did not enter a service which took them into remote, lonely and unhealthy spots and was, moreover, badly paid. Furthermore, while the central serviesc contained some Germans and Magyars, and the financial branch a large number of Jews, the local services, which brought their holders into contact with the population, were necessarily staffed almost entirely with Slavs, and among these there were not even many Czechs, the only Slav people in the Monarchy who were natural bureaucrats.[3] These posts were staffed chiefly with Croats (who constituted about half the total), Slovenes and Poles, peoples on the whole little accustomed to governing others. Consequently, cases of corruption and inefficiency still occurred. But on the whole, the service was incomparably cleaner and more efficient than anything which Bosnia could have produced out of its own resources, or which any of the contemporary Balkan States could show.

Through this instrument, Kállay exercised a benevolent dictatorship, which in certain fields achieved a complete transformation of conditions before the occupation. Security became absolute: brigandage was stamped out and the incidence of crimes of violence became the lowest in the Monarchy. Justice became completely even-handed and accessible to all. The three local religions were placed on a footing of complete and scrupulously maintained equality and the freedom of all of them *in puris spiritualibus* (we

[1] Including messengers and porters, subordinate employees on the railways, etc.
[2] Haumont, op. cit., p. 427.
[3] According to Haumont, l.c., they were not readily admitted because they were suspected of Pan-Slavism.

shall have to return to the qualification implicit in these words) was entirely respected. In matters where expenditure was involved, Kállay's hands were tied by a decision taken by the Austro-Hungarian Government at the outset of the occupation, that the Provinces were to be self-supporting: the central exchequer's only contribution towards them was a 'military credit' of some £300,000 annually, towards the upkeep of the local garrisons, and everything else had to be met out of local resources. The State facilitated the issue of the loans out of which the railways were constructed, but all other expenditure was met out of local revenue. This gravely limited what could be done, especially in respect of public works, and it must be admitted that what was done included a few bad and expensive planning errors.[1] and a certain amount of eyewash.[2] On the whole, however, the available moneys seem to have been allocated between the different departments in just enough proportion to real needs[3] and to have been well and wisely spent. Medical and veterinary services were improved out of recognition. A considerable number of State primary schools and gymnasia were constructed, and some exceedingly valuable technical schools of agriculture, etc., and a great deal done to improve local standards of cultivation. Over 1,000 miles of railways were built – narrow-gauge, indeed, owing to the difficulties of the terrain[4] (these, as has been said, were financed by borrowing) and the figure would have been much larger had not the Hungarian Government persistently obstructed the establishment of direct railway communication between the Provinces and Cis-Leithania. The road system was brought, according to a sensible observer,[5] up to the level of that of the Tirol and other mountainous provinces of Austria. Some valuable afforestation and irrigation was carried through. The State forests were managed on modern lines and made to yield a useful profit. The production of the salt-mines, another Government monopoly, was increased ten-fold. The Government devoted special pains to encouraging cottage industries, and some of these, including carpet-weaving, managed to compete on the Austrian market.

A good deal of development was carried out also by private enterprise, which played a considerable part in modernizing the entire aspect of the Provinces.

[1] The most notorious of these was the expenditure of some £400,000 on a 'river fleet' to compete with Serbian shipping on the Drina. The boats proved too large for the river and had to be sold off at a heavy loss.

[2] This included unnecessarily sumptuous public buildings in Sarajevo, a race-course which no Bosnian ever went near, and the well-meant construction of a watering-place, with modern amenities and diversions, which failed to attract the tourists for whom it was meant.

[3] One of the great complaints made against the regime by its opponents was that the budget for the public safety services was larger than that for education, but in view of the long-ingrained local habits, this was perhaps necessary.

[4] This figure does not include private lines built purely for the carriage of timber.

[5] Drage, op. cit., p. 630.

There was, of course, a reverse side to even the more striking-looking parts of the medal. Where the private enterprise was concerned, it could be argued that in many cases it took much more money out of the country than it put in, especially in the case of some concessions for the exploitation of forests, some of which were granted on incautiously generous terms. The Provinces themselves did not always benefit even by the wage-bills, not always through the concessionaires' ill-will; but the Bosnian mentality was still very pre-economic: workers were apt to disappear once they felt their pockets full enough, or if they stayed, to keep an unconscionable number of holidays. Some enterprises in the Herzegovina were forced, against their will, to work entirely with imported labour from Dalmatia.[1] To the taxpayer, the reverse side of the Government's enterprises was the cost of them. Taxation rose some five-fold between the beginning and the end of Kállay's regime. It is true that it was more justly allocated, more fairly collected and better spent than in Turkish days; also that taxable capacity had risen substantially; but this large increase nevertheless weighed very heavily on some elements in the population, and was one of the main grievances felt by them. It was felt the more bitterly because the Bosnians, on the whole, had little appreciation for such benefits as education, or even sanitation or security; they much preferred *periculosam libertatem* and actually resented much which, had they been modern-minded and correctly-thinking men, they would have appreciated. As that wise man, 'Odysseus', wrote:

> The Porte does not like being reformed, but at least it does not try to reform other people.... However irksome the regulations of the Porte may be, it is the only Government which gives its Christian subjects liberty to fight their quarrels out, and that is the only form of liberty which they really appreciate.[2]

One problem which Kállay preferred not to touch at all was that of the landlord-tenant relationship. Some said that he wanted to placate the Moslems; others, to preserve the social structure as such (himself a member of a very ancient Hungarian 'gentry' family, he is recorded as having said that the Provinces needed a 'gentry' class through which they could be governed); he himself maintained that the kmets were not yet sufficiently worldly-wise to profit by emancipation; and it is a fact that the number both of peasants and of begs who went under when the winds of capitalism struck them was alarmingly large. But the perpetuation of the pre-Occupation system of land-tenure (the Austrians simply kept the law of 1857 in force, with the single modification that rents and taxes were now paid in cash) gave rise to widespread ill-feeling, particularly since a proportion of the chifliks had been recent usurpations which the peasants had fully expected the occupying

---

[1] There was also some feeling in the Provinces against the considerable influx into them of Jews, who, it was alleged, exploited the natives.
[2] *Turkey in Europe*, pp. 381, 382.

authorities to rectify. The authorities, however, had found the task of disentangling usurpations from established title-deeds so difficult that they had simply recognized the entire *status quo* in respect of land tenure, and the only facility granted under Kállay's regime to a tenant wishing to buy his holding was that the Government lent him half the purchase price, at 7%; the other half he had to meet out of savings (which he rarely possessed), or borrow privately, when he was asked an exorbitant charge.

In the cultural field, the Government from the first laid down the principles of inter-confessional equality and of freedom of worship, and its supporters could make a good case for maintaining that it observed strictly both these principles. The religious susceptibilities of the Moslems were respected with a care which impressed observers. The Sultan was prayed for in the mosques;[1] the green banner of the Djihad was hung out on the ritual occasions; the appointment of the clergy was left in the hands of the Sheik-ul-Islam. Moslem recruits in barracks were made to keep the observances of their faith with a strictness unknown in those areas in which the writ of the Sultan really ran, and often unwelcome to themselves. Cases between Moslems affecting such questions as family law were tried by their own judges, in special Courts. Only the administration of the Wakoufs was put under supervision, but this precaution was of great profit to those for whose benefit the institutions were designed to serve.

The Catholics came under the general rules governing the relationship between the Catholic Church and the Austrian Crown, and prospered greatly under them. On the occupation, the Pope created a new Province of Bosnia-Herzegovina, with an archepiscopal see in Sarajevo and suffragans in Mostar and Banjaluka. As the Bishop of Ragusa already held jurisdiction over parts of Herzegovina, this gave the Catholics a large organization which they expanded so successfully that whereas in 1878 they had possessed only thirty-five churches in the two provinces, there were a hundred and thirty-five of them in 1900,[2] some of them in villages in which there was hardly a Catholic to be found.

The Orthodox Church enjoyed full freedom of worship, and received its full quota of Government subsidies. Here, however, the Government did introduce a measure of indirect political control. The practice before the occupation had been for the Patriarch of Constantinople to appoint the Bishops, who were then paid out of a fund, known as the Vladicharina, which was raised by subscription from among the congregations of their sees. The parish priests were elected by their own parishioners, and similarly maintained by them. The Government bought the episcopal advowson off the Patriarch, abolished the Vladicharina, and paid the Bishops regular stipends

---

[1] Not *qua* temporal head of the Ottoman Empire, but *qua* Khalif.

[2] This was the figure given by Kállay to the Delegations. Haumont puts it higher (240 churches and twenty-four monasteries, risen from two).

out of general taxation. The parish priests were still elected by their parishioners, but no priest could be given a cure of souls unless he possessed a certificate of good morals, issued by the seminary.

It cannot be denied that this was a salutary precaution, and as the instruction in the seminary was greatly improved, the effect of the Government's measures was to raise substantially both intellectual and moral levels among the Orthodox priests. But it was equally obvious that an aspirant priest's political views, as well as his personal morals, were taken into account when his certificate was issued, as were those of a candidate for a bishopric.

Although, moreover, the expansion of the Catholics was due to their own efforts – the Government gave them no more than their due quota of subsidies – the fact remained that it was much faster than that of the Orthodox. Catholic children also entered the secondary educational establishments in far higher numbers than those of the Moslems or Orthodox (although not the Jews, whose proportionate quota was easily the highest of all) and were admitted in larger numbers into the State services. This was because they applied more readily, and were better qualified; but it gave colour, if not substance, to the accusation that the Catholics, or Croats, were being favoured at the expense of the Serbs.

What Kállay really wanted was not to favour or 'rule through' any one of the local nationalities, but to call into being among them all a specific local 'Bosnian' nationalism which should transcend their particularist loyalties. Here, indeed, he failed. The Moslems came nearest to feeling themselves simply 'Bosnians', for until the Young Turk revolution of 1908 they had no alternative (those with a strong national feeling emigrated[1]), but even they did not feel themselves one with the local Orthodox or Catholics; simply a special local community. The Catholics from the first adopted a strongly particularist – and militant – attitude. Towards the end of the century, under the influence of their very combative Archbishop, Mgr Stadler, they were immersing themselves completely in the Great Croatia movement, clamouring for the unification of Bosnia with Croatia and Dalmatia and propagating the other Croat extremists' thesis that the Orthodox population of the Provinces were Croats converted to Orthodoxy (unless, indeed, they were immigrant Vlachs[2]). A speech made by Stadler in September 1900 expounding these views drew down on him an official rebuke. Nevertheless, the Party founded by him to express them was the most influential Croat Party in the Provinces.

---

[1] A large number of them did emigrate after 1878, but most of them came back, saying that conditions were worse on the other side of the frontier. After this some emigration took place, but less than was going on from Serbia, Bulgaria or Greece.

[2] There is something more to this theory than is generally admitted. The sceptical reader should note the frequent references to 'Morlachs' (Mavrovlachs) in travel-books of the seventeenth to nineteenth centuries relating to the Western Balkans.

Serbian nationalism seems not to have been very widespread among the Orthodox population in 1879, but, being an emotional and irrational feeling rather than a materialist or logical one, it grew steadily as the years passed. Towards the end of the century the chief complaint, at least as voiced, of the intellectuals was the denial of self-government, and this created a vicious circle, for it was precisely because of his mistrust of the Serb element that Kállay thought it impossible to introduce institutions which would give it any influence over the Provinces. Thus his regime developed more and more into one of opposition to the Serbs, with the inevitable result that the other grievances, just or unjust, of the population – the conscription, the high taxation, the perpetuation of the kmet system, and the rest – came to be represented, and felt, as national injustices.

It should be added that Kállay's regime seems to have deteriorated in its latter years. The reins were slipping out of his hands. A competent observer, visiting the country in 1908, wrote:

> When I was here for the first time, in 1892, the atmosphere was one of energetic progress, well-considered and full of eager hopefulness in the future; today, inactivity, doubt, apprehensiveness are the note. Gone is the organised and conscious activity I admired so much.[1]

---

[1] Baernreither, *Fragments of a Political Diary*, p. 21.

17

The Last Years of Peace

When an organism consists of so many components, each with so much separate life, as the Austro-Hungarian Monarchy at the beginning of the twentieth century, no single event is likely to mark a caesura in the history of all of them. In fact, nothing occurred in 1903 in the inner developments of Cis-Leithania to give them any pronounced new twist.

In that year, however, the long-accustomed cavillings of the Hungarian 'national opposition' against the Compromise developed into a storm so intense and so widespread as to call in question the very existence of the Compromise itself, and thus of the whole internal structure of the Monarchy. Almost simultaneously with this came changes in Serbia which proved the prelude to the emergence of a new international situation fraught with danger to the Monarchy's very existence. The combined effect of these two major events, and of certain others of less obvious significance which, again, occurred almost simultaneously with them – a change of regime in Bosnia, an alteration in the commercial policy of the Monarchy – were weighty enough to justify the treatment of the decade which began with them as a chapter of its own in the history of the Monarchy.

There is another, very important, difference between this period and its predecessor. So long as the reins were in Francis Joseph's hand, it was certain that there would be no radical change in either the foreign or the domestic policy of the Monarchy. He had long since given up all thought of conquest, content to keep what he had, and looking to the German alliance to enable him to do so, and in respect of the central internal problem of the Monarchy, that of its structure, he had also decided to take as final the settlements reached in and immediately after 1867. We have seen that by this time no one was daring so much as to suggest to him any modification of the structure of Cis-Leithania, and he was equally rigid on the still more fundamental issue of Hungary.

It is often said that his unswerving insistence on honouring to the letter his side of the Compromise sprang from grounds of conscience: that he felt himself bound by his Coronation oath. This may well have been one of his reasons, but it is unlikely that it was the deepest of them. In his youth he had often enough found pretexts to break what to most men would have appeared as a pledged word, and he might well have done so again now, if he had seen advantage in it. The deeper explanation probably lies rather in the mental outlook which he had acquired in earlier years, and could no longer alter. He simply did not appreciate the nature and strength of the new forces which had grown large since he was a younger man. Margutti has written that Francis Joseph 'never really understood the political aspirations of the Slavs'. 'He seemed still to regard them for what they had been at the beginning of his reign, a *quantité négligeable*. It often seemed to me that he thought of the Czechs simply as a pendant to the Germans of Bohemia, the Slovenes, to the Germans of Styria and Carinthia, the Slovaks and Serbs as standing in the same relation to the Magyars.'[1] This does not mean that he wanted human injustice done to any of these peoples; but it is probably true that, psychologically, he regarded the political problem of Hungary in the terms of 1866–7. The threat to his rule in Hungary came then from the Magyar 'Independence' Parties, and the effective counter-weight to them lay in the Magyar loyalists of the Deák and Andrássy type. The Compromise was the price which he had paid for the support of these men, and they had in fact, to use a colloquial term, delivered the goods. The results having thus proved at least more satisfactory than those of any other combination tried by him, he proposed for his part to keep his side of the bargain exactly. He demanded, indeed, an equally punctilious observance of it from the other side, but so long as he could compel this, the Compromise was safe.

But in 1903 Francis Joseph had passed the Psalmist's statutory limit of years, and his Crown, with all the immense power wielded by the wearer of it, must by all human reckoning soon pass to another. By now the Archduke Karl Ludwig was dead,[2] and the Heir Presumptive in law, as he had been in the general expectation since Rudolph's death, was Karl Ludwig's elder son, Francis Ferdinand.

By this time Francis Ferdinand had left behind him a youth and early manhood which had not been in all respects happy, especially as he had been troubled by ill-health. The year before his father's death he had shown such alarming symptoms of incipient tuberculosis that he had had to spend a long time abroad. He recovered physically, but the natural morosity of his nature was accentuated by the fact that certain circles had assumed his coming death prematurely, and had transferred their flattery to his younger brother, Otto.

But it had not needed illness to make him a very nasty man. One of his passions was to collect *objets d'art*, but he was exceedingly stingy, and there are many tales of how he practically terrorized dealers into giving him articles cheap. His second great passion was 'sport', and his idea of sport was to have stags driven in front of him or pheasants put up which had been

[1] Op. cit., p. 252.
[2] He died on 19 May 1896, of a fever caught by drinking the waters of Jordan.

fattened until they could hardly fly, while he slaughtered the wretched creatures, beaters handing him a fresh gun when that which he was using became too hot to hold. He was an ill-tempered bully in dealing with men, and in his social outlook, a black reactionary. The one redeeming feature in his personal character was, paradoxically, that which involved him in his most serious conflict with his uncle. He fell deeply in love with a lady, a Countess Sophie Chotek, who, although a member of the highest Bohemian aristocracy, was not *ebenbürtig* by Habsburg family law, so that if he married her, the union would be morganatic. Enormous pressure was put on him, from the most various quarters, to renounce his love. This he obstinately refused to do, and at last Francis Joseph gave way. The marriage was celebrated, on 1 July 1900, but first Francis Ferdinand had had to sign a solemn declaration renouncing the right to the succession of any issue of the marriage. The Emperor conferred the title of 'Princess' on the bride, but this still left her inferior in rank to any Archduchess. Francis Ferdinand's enemies at Court, who were many, saw to it that the ceremonial in this respect was exactly observed. This was another iron that entered into his soul, and not a few of his sympathies or antipathies towards foreign rulers derived from their attitude towards his bride. Two men who treated her with full deference were the German Emperor and the King of Roumania, and Francis Ferdinand repaid both with attachment.

For the rest, he remained a devoted husband and was an affectionate father to the three children of his marriage.

Francis Ferdinand's foreign political conception was already formed. His object here was the obvious one, to maintain the integrity of the Monarchy, and it must be said for him that he was no imperialistic land-grabber; even a man of peace. Thus although disliking and despising the Italian people, and sharing to the full the general (and entirely justified) mistrust of Italy's intentions, in consequence of which he was a strong advocate of the development of the fleet, and also paid much attention to the strengthening of the Monarchy's fortifications on its southern frontier, he was opposed to the idea of preventive war, against either Italy or Serbia. He regarded the Monarchy's alliance with Germany as the king-pin of its foreign relationships: it is entirely untrue that he wanted to alter its orientation. He did, however, attach great value to friendship with Russia; what would have pleased him best would have been a restoration of the *Dreikaiserbund*. 'Russia-ourselves-Germany', he said once to a Russian visitor in 1907: 'What a power! The whole globe would be at our feet!'[1]

By 1903 he had not, apparently, evolved any specific domestic programme, but the prejudices and predispositions which would govern any such programme when it appeared were already there, and they were no secret. He was profoundly undemocratic: he had not for the common people even the

[1] Corti, *Der alte Kaiser*, p. 314.

kindness which years had brought to Francis Joseph, still less any sympathy for their wish to have a say in their own concerns.[1] If he never, apparently, played with ideas of bureaucratic autocracy, this was out of no respect for popular institutions, or for those who represented them; he was immeasurably impatient of any opposition to his own will.

Like his wife, he was an extreme Catholic; his only public intervention in internal affairs before 1903 had been a condemnation of the *Los von Rom* movement, made in his capacity of Patron of the Catholic Schools Association (a position granted him on his own request) so intemperate as to raise a storm in the Liberal Press, and even to draw on him a rebuke from his uncle.

His views on the national question (this was the most important part of his political creed, because of its relationship to the fundamental question of the structure of the Monarchy) were the product, partly of calculation of the usefulness or otherwise to the Monarchy of each nationality, partly of personal prejudice. It is completely untrue that he ever thought of 'remodelling the Monarchy so as to rest it on its Slav elements', internally any more than in respect of foreign policy. Although no emotional German nationalist, he regarded the Germans of the Monarchy as its 'natural cement', to which the leadership in it (under himself) must naturally fall, if only for the sake of efficiency. He had not even any sympathy for any of the Slav peoples, except perhaps the Croats, whom he appreciated for their military qualities, their Catholicism, and, above all, their antagonism to the Magyars. He looked with some favour on the Slovaks, as possessed of the two last-named qualities, the latter of which tended to endear the Roumanians to him. These feelings were, however, essentially political.

Deeply as he loved his wife, he found the Czech people, as such, unsympathetic. He had, indeed, a certain fellow-feeling for the Bohemian feudalists, with whose economic interests his own coincided in his capacity of landowner, for his own biggest estates lay in Bohemia. But this feeling, which his marriage perhaps rather weakened than the reverse (for the ultra-snobbish Bohemian super-magnates were jealous of the Archduke's wife and vented their spite by sneering at her origin – her family was not quite in the innermost ring of all, although very near it – and she retaliated with a natural resentment), did not in any case breed in him any sympathy for the doctrine of Bohemian State Rights, for which he had as little use as for the claims of Hungary.[2]

[1] Of all the ridiculous things that have been written about Francis Ferdinand, few are more absurd than that 'he wanted to create a democratic State'. It is true that he supported the attempt to introduce suffrage reform into Hungary, but this was simply part of his campaign against the Magyar oligarchy. He was against suffrage reform in Austria, precisely because it would have given power to the people.

[2] According to Sieghart, p. 239, and Kiszling, op. cit., p. 226, he was largely responsible for frustrating the Czech-German settlement which nearly came into being in 1912, partly because he feared that if the Czechs and Germans combined, the authority of the Crown

He disliked the Poles strongly, as a subversive and arrogant people, as well as an obstacle to an understanding with Russia. But easily the dominant feeling in his gamut of national sentiments was a real loathing of the Magyars, or at least, of their politicians.[1] How this feeling originated, it is difficult to say. It may have begun with his somewhat humiliating defeat at the hands of the Magyar language, for unlike most of his family, he was a poor linguist, and found that language beyond him,[2] and it seems to have taken firm root during a tour of duty which he did at Sopron as Colonel of a regiment whose officers talked Magyar in front of him and otherwise treated him with insufficient deference, while even the N.C.O.s reported to him in syllables which he did not understand.[3] Later, this resentment was to grow into a real obsession which coloured all his thoughts.

Francis Joseph had been slow to admit his nephew to any share in the business of the State, or even to take him into his confidence. In 1898 the Archduke had been given a sort of roving commission, which he had carried out with great zeal and considerable efficiency, to interest himself in all aspects of the defence of the Monarchy, and he had represented his uncle on some ceremonial visits, including one to Petersburg in 1902, but he had held no post, if we except his unfortunate patronship of the Catholic Schools Association, which gave him any *locus standi* for intervening in the internal politics of the Monarchy.[4] The only influence he had so far been able to exert in these fields had thus been indirect; he could press his views on the Emperor or on his servants, individually. But even by 1903 that influence was perceptible, for there were few public men in Austria quite indifferent to the wishes and intentions of the man who would presumably soon be able to put behind them the whole immense authority of the Crown, and many who actively sought his favour; he already had 'his' party, to which a considerable, and

---

would be weakened, but partly also because the draft agreement spoke of 'Kingdom' and 'Monarch' instead of 'Crownland' and 'Emperor'. See also his remarkable outburst against 'trialism', meaning federalism for the Bohemian Lands (Sieghart, p. 236; Kiszling, p. 140). It is true that Höglinger, *Clam-Martinic*, pp. 72 ff., while confirming the Archduke's objections to the draft agreement, and his reasons for it (another was that he thought it too favourable to the Czechs) says that earlier he had been strongly in favour of reconciliation between the two peoples and had for that purpose wanted the two fractions of the Great Landlords to unite.' Here, however, he was probably thinking in social rather than national terms.

[1] M. Hodža, in his *Federation in Central Europe*, pp. 46 ff., seems to deny that Francis Ferdinand disliked the Magyar people as such, but it would be easy enough to adduce quotations to the contrary.

[2] Oddly, this inability to learn Magyar was shared by the Habsburg who in all history has been most popular in Hungary, the Archduke-Palatine Joseph (see above, pp. 174 ff.)

[3] On this point he was not entirely in the right (see above, pp. 556).

[4] At one time Francis Joseph had entrusted him with the Royal Prerogative, but Koerber had had to ask the Emperor to take it back, as the Archduke did not trouble to deal with the papers (Redlich, *Franz Joseph*, p. 428).

increasing, number of holders of key posts belonged. It is true that Francis Joseph was not of the party, and when the two men's views differed, as was not infrequent, insisted on his own. His influence grew steadily during the years with which this chapter is concerned, especially after 1906, when a new man, Captain (later Lieut.-Colonel) von Brosch took charge of the little 'military Chancellery' which Francis Ferdinand had established in the Belvedere Palace to help him carry out his official duties.[1] Von Brosch was an extremely able and energetic man, and under him and Col. Bardolf, who succeeded him in 1911, the Chancellery expanded into a regular shadow government. Through it, the Archduke was supplied by correspondents in all parts of the Monarchy with information which was certainly far superior (since less tactfully discreet) to what was reaching the Emperor. By now he also possessed his wider political contacts. In Cis-Leithania these were closest with the Christian Social Party; in Hungary, with leaders of the 'Nationalities', notably the Slovak, Milan Hodža and the Roumanian, Vaida Voevode, but he was close also with the Hungarian Minister President of the Féjérváry Cabinet, Kristóffy.

By this time he had stepped well into the fore-ground of the political stage. In 1913 the Emperor made him Inspector General of the Armed Forces of the Monarchy. He still held no office entitling him to intervene in non-military affairs, but nothing could stop him from preparing for the future. That he was doing so was one of the certainties in the political picture; what were the changes that he would try to introduce, one of its major uncertainties.

With these new factors, international and domestic, in the picture, the whole atmosphere of the decade which opened in 1903 was, inevitably, quite different from that of its predecessors. The old feeling which had prevailed for so long that the essential 'problems' of the Monarchy, at home and abroad, had been 'settled' – that was gone. Change was in the air, and very likely, it would be violent change.

The historian must, however, beware of misrepresenting the mood of the day. The event was to prove that the struggles which the decade ushered in were the beginning of the Monarchy's death-agony, and it is not difficult to find Cassandra cries enough in the diaries and correspondence of men in a position to see below the surface of things. But it would be quite erroneous to suppose the general life of the Monarchy during these years as overshadowed by a sense of impending and ineluctable doom. There were very many who believed that what the future held was, on the contrary, rejuvenation, consolidation on a new and firmer basis, perhaps even territorial expansion (and in fact, the period, like the Vormärz which it resembles so curiously in many ways, brought the Monarchy an extension of its frontiers).

[1] Strictly, the office, under that name, was sanctioned only in November 1908. Before that Brosch and his predecessors were only the Archduke's aides-de-camp (Flügeladjutante).

And there was, indeed, much in the picture to justify optimism. Materially, these were the most prosperous years that the Monarchy had ever known, at least since our history opened. While the population had increased again substantially, reaching in 1910 a figure of 28½ millions for Cis-Leithania and nearly 21 for the Hungarian Lands (to which had now to be added, 1.8 for Bosnia-Herzegovina), this increase was no longer bringing with it the old unrelenting pressure of expanding demand on resources unable to keep up with it. Industrialization was now really gathering way in both halves of the Monarchy. In Austria, the percentage of the population employed in industry and mining had risen by 1910 to 26, while in Hungary, where a 'third wave' of economic development set in in 1906, helped by a new set of protective measures, the rapidity of the advance was astonishing. Here, the number of industrial plants increased by 84% between 1898 and 1913, and that of workers, by 76%,[1] bringing the percentage of the population gaining its livelihood from industry and mining up to 17. The new factories, with the expanding communications and growing trading and professional circles, were now able to offer employment to a large proportion of those seeking it. There were still black areas of congestion, notably in Galicia and parts of Hungary, but for these the safety-valve of emigration was operating even more freely than before.[2] If the combined processes of industrialization and emigration were not interrupted, it was reasonable to hope that the scourge of rural over-population from which the economy of the Monarchy had so long been sick would soon have vanished from all parts of it, as it had already from many.[3]

Industrial productivity was also rising rapidly. According to one Austrian expert, the increase per head of the production of ten categories of raw or half-finished materials in Austria ranged from 67·5% (pig-iron) and 43%

---

[1] Hanak, op. cit., p. 277.

[2] In eight of the eleven years 1903–11 over 100,000 persons were officially registered as leaving Austria for overseas, with a grand total for the period of over 1,350,000 (in the peak year, 1913, the figure was 194,402). For continental emigration in the last years before the war, Dr Klezl, in *International Migrations*, II. 402–3, gives the astonishing figure of 450,000 annually. Most of this was presumably seasonal, but Dr Klezl writes that in 1907, 196,000 out of 316,000 Austrian workers in Germany were employed in industry (most of them, presumably, in German Silesia) and many of these probably settled in their places of employment. According to this source, in 1911–12, when the total was 262,944, 80,000 were Poles, 80,000 Ruthenes and 80,000 Germans. The official figures for Hungary were 97,000 for 1904, 170,000 for 1905, 178,000 for 1906, 209,000 for 1907 (the peak year) and about 100,000 a year 1908–13. These figures may well be considerably too low, for after 1881 intending emigrants were required to equip themselves with passports, and as these were often refused, much of the emigration was clandestine. This would hardly affect the figures before 1904, which were based on data collected at the Dutch and German ports of embarkation, but may well have made a difference after 1904, when Fiume began to be used largely.

[3] When the Social Democrat Government of the Austrian Republic tried to introduce a land reform after 1918, very few applicants for land came forward.

(wool), downward, with an average of 31%. Taking into account the increased number of workers, the output of industries and building must, this writer calculates, 'have increased by a percentage of between 90 and 100'.[1] In Hungary, Hanak tells us that 'the H.P. output of machines' rose by 188% and the value of goods produced by 126%.[2] On another page he puts the nett product of industry and mining at 860 million kronen in 1900 and 1,840 m.k. in 1911–13.[3] In agriculture, the average yield per hectare of wheat in Austria rose by 16% between 1901 and 1913, of rye by 24%, of barley by 21·2% and of oats by 33·96%. As the amount of land left fallow each year also fell, the increase in total production was larger. For Hungary, Hanak tells us that the nett product of agriculture rose from 2,209 million kronen in 1900 to 4,549 in 1911–13. According to Gratz, the area under cultivation rose from 12 million ha. in 1890 to 14 m.h. in 1910; the percentage of fallow sank from 15 to 8.8. Total production (metric of tons of wheat) rose from 34·9 in 1898 to 41·2 in 1913; of maize, from 32·3 to 46·2; of potatoes, from 37·8 to 47·7; of sugar-beet, from 14·9 to 47·0; of fodder crops, from 35·8 to 56·2.[4] Both quantity and quality of live-stock improved in both halves of the Monarchy.

The nett output of agriculture, forestry and fisheries rose from 2.236 million kr. in 1901–3 to 4,143 in 1911–13 (85%) and the output per head of the working population from 358 to 633 kr. (77%).

The total national incomes derived from production rose by about 86% in Austria and 92% in Hungary. As prices rose by about 20–25%, the growth of real income was somewhat smaller, and that of real income *per capita* smaller still, when we take account of the growth of the population, but still very substantial. All classes, moreover, had some share in it. The average increase in industrial wages (34%) exceeded that of the cost of living, and the higher prices for agricultural produce resulting from the increased agricultural protection introduced after 1904 seem, contrary to the general belief, to have benefited the small farmers and agricultural labourers almost equally with the larger producers.[5]

This prosperity extended to the State finances. In 1907 the Austrian budget closed with the biggest surplus in the national history (116 million kronen), eliciting from the Minister of Finance words which (so far as the records tell us) had never before fallen from the lips of any holder of his office: 'We are doing well.' The rise in prices (amongst other factors) also reduced the burden of the national debt, the service of which in 1914 called for only 14% of the national expenditure, and nearly all of it was held at home. Budgetary conditions in Hungary were similar. The currency was still stable, as it remained up to 1914.

[1] Hertz, op. cit., p. 43.
[2] Hanak, l.c.
[3] Id., p. 270.
[4] *A Dualiszmus Kora*, II. 213 ff.
[5] Hertz, p. 30.

It is true that the picture was far from being uniformly brilliant.[1] Considerable as had been the increase in agricultural production, the figures pro hectare for almost every crop were still substantially below those being achieved in Germany. Peasant cultivation was still relatively primitive, and the big landlords more concerned to keep up prices than to increase production – a policy which their political weight enabled them to realize with results which often entailed considerable hardship for the consumers.[2] In spite of the increases, the Monarchy had to import foodstuffs in bad years, of which 1907 was one: it could in fact easily have absorbed the Serbian swine excluded from its market during the 'pig war' of that year. The handworkers were still being pressed hard, as they had been for a century, by the competition of the factories, while the unhealthy concentration of so many of the latter in the hands of a few, often inter-linked, holding banks[3] allowed prices in this field also to be kept high by cartels and rings.

Nevertheless, the general material condition of most of the Monarchy could be regarded as at least one of dawning well-being.

In the arts, the robust but sometimes crude productivity of Austria's Victorian age had given way to new fashions, in which the eternally indispensable task of leavening the Teutonic lump, performed in the age of Baroque by Italians, had been taken over by the sons and grandsons of the Jews who had established themselves in the capitals of the Monarchy half a century before. There was a good deal of self-pitying *Weltschmerz* in some of the products of this new cross-fertilization, but at their best they achieved an almost heart-breaking loveliness which was not the less beautiful for the touch of over-ripeness sometimes perceptible in them. German poetry can show little more lovely than the lyrics of Hoffmannsthal and Rilke, nor German prose anything more limpidly graceful than that of Schnitzler.

The opening of the period found Mahler still directing the Court Opera, and if his experiences there were unhappy, Richard Strauss was entering on his years of glory (1911 saw the première of the Rosenkavalier), not to speak of Schönberg or of such lesser but still delightfully scintillating luminaries as Lehár. Klimt was still painting, and a vigorous school of art, not, indeed, admired by all, centred round the 'Sezession'. Sigmund Freud was bringing Vienna renewed fame in other fields.

In Hungary some of the old lights were still burning brightly – Kálmán Mikszáth died only in 1910 – and here, too, there was plenty of frivolous brilliance and plenty of tasteless excess. But the decade saw also a truly

---

[1] The shadow-side of it is well, although briefly, put by A. Brusatti in *Vorabend*, pp. 63 ff.
[2] Prices of cereals rose by 47% in 1899–1909; of meat and fats by 34·3%; of all foodstuffs by 36·3%.
[3] The Creditanstalt, for example, which in 1890 had been associated with one bank and one industrial enterprise, controlled in 1914 forty-three industrial enterprises and five commercial, five banks, two insurance companies and two transport undertakings.

remarkable reaction against the opulent materialism and sentimental romanticism of its predecessor, a revolt which was strongly tinged by political and social radicalism and by populist sympathies. The greatest figure here was Ady, perhaps the most brilliant lyric poet ever produced by Hungary, but the journal *Nyugat* which was his mouthpiece was also the forum for a number of other striking figures: Babits, Zsigmond Móricz, Deszö Szabó, and more. The 'Thalia' society adapted the plays of Ibsen and Hauptman for the Hungarian stage, Béla Bartok and Zoltán Kodály collected folk music, analysed its origin and structure and used its themes in their own work. There were several lively schools of painting, strongly influenced by French Impressionism, but like the writers and musicians, drawing much of their inspiration from Hungary's native soil.

All these achievements, material and artistic, bathe the picture of these years in what seems to us today a beautiful but tragic sunset glow, but can more fairly be taken as proof of the substantial measure of vitality still present in the Monarchy. It is fair to record them before turning to less happy subjects.

In the previous sections in which we divided the narrative of a subject by periods, we began with foreign relations, as in general the dominant influence, then taking the internal developments in Cis-Leithania, as the larger half of the Monarchy; those of Hungary third, and of Bosnia last. For the period with which we are now concerned, another arrangement is more appropriate. The crisis in which Hungary wallowed during practically the whole period was magnificently self-regarding; its Hungarian authors initiated it on a purely national issue, and pursued their point with such complete disregard of any life *extra Hungariam* that as late as 1911 they were justifying their resistance to the increased Army estimates by the serenity of the international picture. In so far as there was any mutual interaction between the developments in Hungary and those of the international situation, the former influenced the latter more than the reverse, and may therefore conveniently be described first of the two. They form, also, a complete story, most comprehensible if it is taken through to its close without interruption. Next comes the foreign political narrative. Austria falls back to the third place, as almost purely recessive, affected by developments in Hungary and abroad, but exercising little influence on either. Finally, Bosnia as a separate heading disappears altogether for some years, swallowed up by the slough of the Southern Slav question, which had become primarily one of foreign politics. Its fortunes, when it reappears, call for little more than an extended footnote.

The eve of the war finds the threads again disastrously running together.

The crisis between the Crown and Hungary broke out over the old question of the Army. Owing to chaotic Parliamentary condition in Austria, it had been impossible in 1899 to fix the new ten-year figure for the annual intake of recruits, and in that year, in 1900 and in 1901 the Government had simply called up contingents of the size fixed in 1889[1] by the use of Para. 14 in Austria, and in Hungary, by annual Bills. But in 1902 the Reichsrat was functioning again, and meanwhile, the results of the 1900 census had been published, showing a large increase of the population on 1890, and a larger one on 1880. The Imperial and Royal Ministry of War therefore decided to raise the contingent, which in any case was far below that of most European Great Powers.[2]

At first the Ministry proposed leaving the nominal annual figure unaltered, but giving the authorities power to call up for actual service certain conscripts who, although registered, had for various reasons not been required to do their actual service. When these proposals, introduced into both Parliaments in October 1902, were resisted in both, the Minister withdrew them and introduced new Bills raising the contingent for the regular forces to 125,000 (71,562 from Austria, 53,438 from Hungary), for the Landwehr to 14,500 (plus the special contingents from the Tirol and Vorarlberg) and for the Honvédség to 15,000.

In Austria, Koerber eventually got the Reichsrat to vote its law, although only after a struggle which lasted nearly a year, and only conditionally on Hungary's doing the same; but the Hungarian Parliament was more stubborn still. The 'Independence' politicians took the occasion to demand, as price for letting the Bill go through, or even voting the annual contingent of recruits, a whole series of 'national' concessions: the term of service to be reduced to two years,[3] the language of command in all Hungarian units to be Magyar,[4] Hungarian regiments to be quartered in Hungary and to be officered exclusively by Hungarians, their oath of loyalty to be taken to the Hungarian Constitution, and the Hungarian national coat of arms to be given a place in the insignia of the common army.

And the 'Parties of '48' were not the only recalcitrants. The fusion which Széll had brought about between the Liberals and Apponyi's party had never been more than skin-deep. Apponyi and his followers had always kept one foot in the opposition camp, and now Apponyi, although a member of the Government Party and President of the Lower House, openly encouraged the Opposition, and himself recommended making Parliament's consent to the Bill conditional on a number of concessions which were less far-reaching

[1] This had been raised in 1889 to 103,100 (60,339 for Austria, 42,761 for Hungary, adjusted in 1892 to 59,211 and 43,229), exclusive of the two reserves. Service in the Navy had been increased in 1884 from three to four years. Even now the effective strength of the army had increased since 1868 by only 12%; far less than the total population.

[2] At that date Germany was calling up 280,000 men annually, France 250,000, Russia 335,000 (including the Cossacks) and Italy 100,000.

[3] This demand was being made also by many speakers in the Reichsrat, and the Government was itself planning to introduce the change as soon as it could do so without reducing the peace strength of the Army. [4] Croat in Croatia.

than those required by the Party of Independence, but in the same direction of emphasizing the distinctive quality of the Hungarian Army. Obstruction now set in on such a scale that the Budget could not be passed, and in May 1903 the country entered on the state of constitutional vacuum known as *ex lex*.[1] Széll resigned in despair, and after Kálmán Tisza's son, István, had failed to form a Government, Francis Joseph appointed to the Minister Presidency Count Khuen Héderváry, who had kept Croatia in order for so long.

Khuen persuaded Francis Joseph to let him withdraw the Army Bill for further consideration, and Kossuth agreed to let the Budget go through, but the extremists of the Left redoubled their filibustering, which they combined with attacks on Khuen's personal integrity. He resigned on 10 August, although perforce remaining in office pending the appointment of a successor to him. The military circles in Vienna judged the situation so serious that Field-Marshal Baron Beck, the Chief of the General Staff, drew up plans for 'Case U' – the occupation of Budapest by Austrian regiments from Vienna and Graz, while other forces were to be supplied by the Army Corps with headquarters in Zagreb, Premysl and Lemberg.[2] The Emperor was unwilling to resort at once to such extreme measures, but on 17 September he issued an Army Order from the Galician village of Chlopy, where he was attending the autumn manoeuvres, declaring that he would tolerate no infringement of his rights as Supreme War Lord, nor any tampering with the unitary character of the army. The Order spoke of the 'Volksstämme' of the Monarchy, including the Hungarians among them – a phraseology evocative of the period of absolutism, and this increased the resentment with which it was received in Hungary.

A compromise was, after all, patched up. Francis Joseph sent a letter to Khuen which filed off the sharpest edges of the Army Order, while a Committee of nine members of the Liberal Party worked out a compromise formula for the Army question. It asked for the immediate grant of certain concessions: the alteration of the Army insignia, the use of Magyar in Courts Martial in Hungarian regiments, the transference of Hungarian officers to Hungarian regiments, more instruction in Magyar in the cadet schools of the Common Army, a ruling that correspondence between Hungarian offices and non-Hungarian units stationed in Hungary, and civilian authorities in Hungary should be conducted in Magyar, and one or two others. The questions of the two years' service and of the intake of recruits were to be considered in connection with the revision of the Defence Law. The Committee's report recognized the Crown's right to decide the languages of service and command, although it maintained that 'the political responsibility of the Cabinet and the lawful influence of Parliament applied on this question, as on any other'. It agreed, however, not to raise the question at that juncture.

[1] See above, p. 567.   [2] Kiszling, op. cit., p. 81. Plan U was in readiness also in 1905.

Francis Joseph agreed to these demands, subject to several amendments to which the Committee of Nine agreed in its turn, and now he let Khuen go; Tisza took over on 31 October, and formed an administration of his own closest and most reliable associates. When the first concessions began to arrive from the Ministry of War,[1] the Hungarian Parliament, in a sudden excess of mingled sentimentality and nervousness, sanctioned the regular intake of recruits (up to the 1889 figure[2]). But Tisza was the Independence politicians' bugbear. He gratified them, indeed, over one notable incident: on 17 November, Koerber, in the course of the debate on the Army Bill in the Reichsrat, had put forward the idea that no reinterpretation by the Hungarian Parliament of the Monarch's reserved rights (the Committee of Nine's caveat was meant) was valid without the consent of the Reichsrat. Amid the cheers of the whole Hungarian Parliament, Tisza declared that Hungary had no need to take into account 'dilettante remarks by a distinguished foreigner' [sic] on her internal affairs. But for the rest, his appointment ushered in a condition of near-anarchy. Outside Parliament, the administration carried on from hand to mouth; inside it, the Opposition, now reinforced, for the incurably unadult Apponyi had refounded the 'National Party' and Bánffy had started a 'New Party' of his own, both joining the Opposition, did its successful best to paralyse the affairs of the country. This lasted nearly a year; then, in November 1904, having repeatedly, and always in vain, tried to persuade Parliament to reform itself, Tisza, like Badeni and Falkenhayn before him, put through a reform of its standing orders by dubious methods. A group of Liberals, headed by Count Gyula Andrássy, seceded from the Party in protest against these dictatorial methods, and Tisza now decided to see how the electorate really felt. He dissolved Parliament on 3 January 1905 and held new elections, which the officials were told not to influence. From these the Liberals emerged with only 159 mandates, while the Party of Independence, into which Apponyi had now taken his followers, secured 166, Andrássy's 'dissidents', who had formed themselves into a 'Constitutional Party', 27, the People's Party, 24, and Bánffy's 'New Party', 17, the remainder being made up out of 11 representatives of the 'Nationalities' (8 Roumanians, 2 Slovaks and 1 Serb),[3] 2 'Democrats', 2 'Agrarian Socialists'[4] and 8 Independents. Subsequent defections from the Liberals reduced their numbers to 102, most of the deserters joining the Party of Independence or the

[1] It must be said that these were very slow in coming; some were not made until 1911 and one or two not at all.

[2] A senior member of the Independence Party, Kálmán Thály, suddenly appealed to his colleagues, in full session, not to oppose this, out of pity for the men who were being kept with the colours past their time. The House was moved by the humanitarian force of this appeal, but it was also afraid of the consequences if it resisted it, for rumours were already current that Tisza was preparing to take some drastic steps if he did not get his way.

[3] The Transylvanian Saxons took their seats with the Liberals.

[4] Three were elected, but one of them was promptly assassinated by scandalized patriots.

Constitutional Party. The Party of Independence, Constitutionalists, People's Party and New Party founded a 'Coalition of National Parties'.

Not all of these professed to reject the Compromise, but the elections were a clear defeat for those who supported it unreservedly. Francis Joseph, however, refused to be intimidated. When Andrássy, in the name of the Coalition, refused to form a Government unless further 'national' concessions were made over the Army, the Monarch for the first time exercised in Hungary the right which had become habitual to him in Austria. He made General Fejérváry, the Minister of Defence in the previous Governments, an old soldier on whose loyalty he could depend,[1] Minister President, at the head of a Cabinet of permanent officials, with instructions to negotiate with the Coalition leaders for a basis on which he could entrust the Government to them. The first conversations having proved fruitless, he relieved Fejérváry of his commission, and on 23 September summoned the Coalition leaders to him and curtly informed them of his conditions, which were: (1) the question of the languages of service and command, on which any concessions were and remained excluded, to be dropped from the programme; (2) no tampering with the common institutions in respect either of the Army or the foreign service; (3) any revision of the economic clauses of the Compromise to be duly negotiated with the representatives of Austria, through the regular channels; (4) and (5) guarantees that the Budget and the new Army Act, which was now ready in draft, would be voted. They were to discuss details with Goluchowski.

The whole audience had lasted only five minutes.

The conversations began and, of course, immediately ended in deadlock, and Francis Joseph then reappointed Fejérváry. The Coalition tried to organize resistance through the Counties, but Francis Joseph again stood firm. He sent a Royal Commissioner to close Parliament, and 'administrators' were sent to take charge of the Counties. Then Fejérváry's Minister of the Interior, Kristóffy, played a trump card: he published the text of a Bill for franchise reform, which he said that he proposed to introduce into the next Parliament. This would have increased the number of voters in Hungary from 1·0 millions to 2·6, a substantial number of the new voters being non-Magyars.

Before this threat, what courage the Coalition leaders had left collapsed. Ferenc Kossuth, at heart a conciliatory man, had already come round to the view that it would be necessary to accept the Crown's terms. He told Fejérváry so, and when informed that the Coalition would be required, in addition, to enact a suffrage reform on at least as broad a basis as that envisaged by Kristóffy, he still did not object, having been persuaded, in curious fashion, that a reform of the sort was inevitable.[2] Andrássy and Apponyi objected very strongly, but sniffing the possibility that Kossuth

[1] He had been Commander of the Royal Hungarian Bodyguard.

[2] These obscure transactions are described in detail by Gratz who was a party to them op. cit., II. 115 ff.

might come to terms with the Crown without them, they joined him in accepting the Crown's conditions, to which was added yet another, that the Minister President was not to be a member of the Coalition, but the old Liberal utility man, Wekerle. The bargain having been struck, in deep secrecy, Francis Joseph, on 7 April 1906, appointed Wekerle Minister President, and he then formed a Cabinet in which Andrássy received the Ministry of the Interior, Kossuth that of Commerce and Communications, Apponyi that of Cults and Education, and Zichy, that of Minister *a latere* to the Crown. Wekerle kept finance in his own hands. Parliament was now dissolved, and new elections held in May. As Tisza had dissolved the Liberal Party, which did not contest the elections, the Coalition Parties, whose candidates did not oppose one another, won an overwhelming victory, the Party of Independence returning 253 Deputies, the Constitutional Party, 89,[1] the People's Party 23 and the New Party 3. The only real opposition was composed of 25 representatives of the Nationalities other than the Saxons,[2] 4 Democrats, 3 Agrarian Socialists or Democrats and 5 Independents.

It is hardly surprising that the years which followed this transaction proved to be among the most ignominious in Hungarian political history. Their promise to the Crown, which was kept a close secret between the Coalition leaders, precluded them from fulfilling practically any of the promises in faith whereof their constituents had elected them to office. In the new decennial economic negotiations with Austria, which took place in 1907,[3] they extracted the barren change in nomenclature that the relationship between the two countries was to be called a 'Customs Treaty', the terms of which were to come up for revision in 1917; but they paid for this with a number of material concessions, including another change of two per cent in the quota, to Hungary's disadvantage. It is true that in the course of the negotiations Andrássy extracted from the Crown (in the face of very strong opposition from the Heir to the Throne) certain 'constitutional guarantees' against further arbitrary action by the Crown;[4] but the practical effect of these was not great. At home, the Minister of Agriculture, Ignácz Darányi, did a little (against much opposition) to improve the conditions of the agricultural labourers, and the Secretary of State for Commerce, József Szterényi, who was in fact the real holder of the Portfolio (ill-health kept Kossuth away from his duties for long periods) introduced another law for the protection of domestic industry. But the Coalition's biggest 'national' achievement was a law devised by Apponyi, and enacted in 1907, which surpassed all records in national chauvinism. *Inter alia*, it made teachers in

[1] Including the Saxon representatives.
[2] Sixteen Roumanians, seven Slovaks and two Serbs.
[3] I.e. ten years after the previous agreement should have been concluded.
[4] The chief of these was to give Counties and Boroughs a right to appeal against demands for recruits. Andrássy's original demands went much further.

Church schools State employees, requiring of them ability to read, write and teach Magyar adequately, and of non-Magyar pupils, that they should, by the end of their fourth school year, be able to express themselves in Magyar, orally and in writing. Something like eighteen of the twenty-two hours of instruction in non-Magyar primary schools was devoted to the language.

Meanwhile, there were two questions on which the Coalition itself was deeply divided. One was that of suffrage reform. One fraction of the Independence Party, led by Gyula Justh, genuinely wanted the reform, as a postulate of democracy; it believed that a democratized Hungary would be able to come to terms with the Nationalities.[1] On the other hand, the '67 members of the Coalition entirely agreed on this point with Tisza, that true franchise reform would mean the end of that Magyar Hungary which, as they and he saw it, was the only kind of Hungary which could exist at all. Kossuth seems to have been undecided on the point. As the Crown insisted, Andrássy, after over two years of rearguard action, produced a Bill set about with the most elaborate devices for safeguarding the supremacy of the Magyar element. Justh's group refused to accept this, and it was withdrawn.

The second bone of contention was the National Bank. Here, again, it was Justh's followers who insisted absolutely that Hungary must have her own Bank by the end of 1911. The '67 Parties in the Coalition opposed this, partly on principle and partly because they thought the retention of the common Bank to be advantageous to Hungary, as the economically weaker half of the Monarchy. It was on this rock that the Coalition finally split, the Party of Independence having divided into two wings, one led by Kossuth and Apponyi, the other by Justh. The Coalition had become unworkable, and on 27 April 1909, Wekerle resigned.

Interminable conversations followed, one suggested combination after another breaking down on Francis Joseph's insistence that he would make no 'national' concession to any Hungarian Government which did not first introduce the suffrage reform. At last Khuen Héderváry said that he would be able to form an administration on these terms with the old Liberals. He was appointed Minister President on 17 January 1910, dissolved Parliament, and held new elections in May. In preparation for these, Tisza had reconstituted the Liberals under the name of 'Party of Work', and this time no holds were barred. The Party of Work secured 258 mandates; Kossuth's wing of the Party of Independence, 55; Justh's fraction, although heavily supported by Kristóffy (acting for Francis Ferdinand), only 41;[2] Andrássy's

---

[1] Oddly enough, this view was now supported by Bánffy, who during his Minister Presidency had broken all previous records for chauvinism.

[2] On this, see Kiszling, pp. 151 ff., and Redlich, *Schicksalsjahre*, II. 179. According to Kiszling, Kristóffy asked Francis Ferdinand's Military Cabinet for money, and secured through it, from the Christian Social Party, the rather inadequate sum of 50,000 kr. (typically, the Archduke himself gave nothing). But according to Redlich (who dates the event wrongly),

followers, 21, and the People's Party, 13. The Saxons had voted with the Party of Work, which had also allowed 8 Serbs to get in on its list; 8 other representatives of the nationalities (5 Roumanians and 3 Slovaks) got in under their own colours and there were also 3 Smallholders, 2 Democrats, one Christian Social and a handful of independents.

The situation was back in the main to the *turbulentia qua ante* 1903, with a Government pledged to the Compromise and the 'Independence' Parties in the Opposition; seasoned, however, with an element more reminiscent of the Coalition period in that the Government was pledged to introduce suffrage reform, whereas Tisza was fixedly determined not to do so. In fact, Khuen, who remained Minister President, did not hurry himself to introduce the reform, and for a while, history repeated itself with uncanny accuracy, for as as soon the House opened, it was presented with another Bill for raising the strength of the armed forces[1] and again the Opposition resorted to wild filibustering and to extravagant counter-demands which they pressed with such vigour that Khuen, caught between the hammer of them and the anvil of Francis Joseph's resistance, resigned in April 1912. He was succeeded as Minister President by László Lukácz, while Tisza took over the Presidency of the House, in which capacity he forced through not only – at last – the long-disputed Army Bill, but also a reform of the Standing Orders which really made Parliament workable – an achievement which came near costing him his life.[2] In return for this, Francis Joseph seems to have been prepared to disinterest himself in the question of electoral reform. Lukács did pass a Bill through Parliament, but it was so excessively cautious that after its enactment the agitation for or against reform went on as though it had never existed. Francis Joseph, however, did not ask for anything more.

Then, in June 1913, Lukács resigned in consequence of attacks on his financial probity.[3] Now Tisza himself took over the Minister Presidency, making the apparent reversion complete.

The reversion, however, was only apparent. The leaders of the 'national opposition' had discredited themselves deeply, but this did not mean that the ideas for which they professed to stand had lost their popularity among their traditional adherents. On the contrary, it was now plainer than ever that

---

Kristóffy secured from a Hungarian source, through the Minister of Finance, Lukács, no less than 318,000 kr. with which to support the Justh candidates. The remarkable thing about this story is that this was the same Lukács who afterwards got into trouble for financing the other side (see below, n. 3).

[1] For particulars, see below, pp. 790-91.

[2] An enraged Deputy fired three revolver-shots at Tisza and a fourth at himself. He missed Tisza completely and the wound which he inflicted on himself proved not mortal. Tisza carried on with the session unmoved.

[3] He was accused of having borrowed 4 million crowns from the National Bank, not, indeed, for his personal enrichment, but for Party purposes – the purposes, be it noted, of the Party of Work. The money which he got for the other side does not seem to have come up.

"48' was far more popular than "67' in the circles within which the political struggle in Hungary was traditionally waged. But far more important than this was the increased growth and determination of the forces which had previously been excluded from that struggle altogether. In 1903 the Social Democrat Party had reorganized, adopting new statutes, but still keeping its intimate association with the Trade Unions, whose numbers had increased rapidly, reaching 70,000 in 1905 and over 130,000 in 1907, the peak year. Meanwhile, the developments in Russia and Austria, and the possibility that franchise reform might come also to Hungary, had given the movement a fresh impetus. In 1905 the workers had organized great demonstrations in favour of the reform, and the dashing of the cup from their lips had not lessened their desire to drink of it. The demonstrations were repeated in subsequent years. In 1912 the Party proclaimed a General Strike. There were mass demonstrations in front of Parliament which cost the participants six dead and 182 wounded after the gendarmerie had opened fire on them.

Still unrepresented in Parliament and still looked on with distrust by most of the country, largely on account of their international tenets and their Jewish leadership, the Socialists now constituted a very real force in the country, and one which might prove a dangerous enemy to the 'system'.

There had been continued unrest on the land. In 1905, when the Counties had proclaimed resistance to the tax-collector and the recruiting officer, Socialist agitators, mostly from among the 'Reorganized Socialists', appeared, claiming the merit for themselves.[1] That year, and again in 1906, there were more harvest strikes, some of them in protest against the new 'labour reserve'[2] and widespread demands among both the agricultural labourers and the dwarf-holders, not only for better wages and conditions, but also for land-reform.

The middle-class 'radical' movement, too, had grown more extreme. By 1906 the more conservative members of the *Huszadik Század* had withdrawn from it,[3] leaving the movement in the hands of a group of radicals, almost exclusively Jewish (a fact of importance, since it widened the gulf between the group and the more traditionally-minded Hungarians). The editor of the periodical, to whom his disciples looked up with almost idolatrous veneration, was Oszkar Jászi (Jakubovics), an acute and fluent sociologist whose mind was, however, essentially destructive.

Further, both the international and the domestic developments of the period had stirred the nationalities into renewed activity. In 1904 the learned and ultra-patriotic Professor Jorga of Bucharest revived the *Liga Culturale*, and when the 1905 elections were announced, the Roumanians of Transylvania decided to abandon passivity and reopen the Parliamentary

---

[1] Mailáth, op. cit., p. 27.

[2] In 1903 the Government had organized a 'labour reserve' several thousands strong, which could be moved to any place where it seemed unlikely that the harvest could be got in by ordinary means.   [3] Gratz, op. cit., II. 140.

struggle on their old programme. At the same time the Slovaks decided to break with the People's Party, with whose attitude on the 'issue of public law' they disagreed, and formed their own 'Slovak National Party'.[1] Neither decision had been unanimous and not many candidates stood, with the meagre result recorded above.[2] But for the 1906 elections the Nationalities stood in force, and the twenty-five successful candidates included several men destined to play an important role in the next years – the Roumanians Maniu and Vajda-Voevod, the Slovaks Juriga and Hodža, not to mention the veteran Serb, Polit.

The Coalition showed itself even more intolerant than the Liberals towards the Nationalities. Broadly speaking, its answer towards their demands was more Magyarization, more abuse, more administrative pressure. Apponyi's egregious Education Act has been mentioned. Besides this, precisely the Coalition's years of office witnessed an unparalleled number of proceedings against the Nationalities. Seventeen Roumanians were sentenced for agitation against the State in 1906 and thirteen in 1907; eleven Slovaks in 1906, thirty-three in 1907 and twenty in 1908, both the Roumanian and the Slovak victims including Deputies, whose Parliamentary immunity was suspended so that they could be sentenced, besides such figures as the Slovak leader, Mgr Hlinka. 1907, moreover, saw the notorious 'massacre of Csernova', when gendarmes fired into a crowd of Slovak peasants, killing fifteen and wounding many more[3] – a deplorable incident which, moreover, did Hungary much harm, for the Slovaks' case, publicised by Seton-Watson, was taken up by a number of well-known figures in several countries, including Björnsen and Leo Tolstoy.

The 1910 elections made things no better, for although the representation of the Nationalities was down again, their spirit, and their hostility to the Hungarian State, were even greater than before.

By 1912 relations between the Kingdom of Hungary and Croatia, too, were back to the pessimum, after a curious series of fluctuations. They had reached a first nadir in 1903, when a refusal by the Hungarian Government to revise in Croatia's favour the financial clauses of the Nagodba had led to violent rioting in Croatia. This had spread to Istria and Dalmatia, and had generated what one of its warmest sympathizers has himself described as 'one of those strange furies which at rare intervals seize upon a whole nation'.[4] Wild rumours spread that some of the demonstrators in Croatia were to be hanged, and a deputation from the Istrian and Dalmatian Landtags went

---

[1] The programme of this Party is given by R. W. Seton-Watson, *Racial Problems in Hungary*, p. 483.   [2] See above, p. 760.

[3] For a full account of this, see R. W. Seton-Watson, op. cit., pp. 339 ff. It is true that the crowd was not demonstrating directly for Slovak liberties, but indirectly so: to prevent a new church from being consecrated by anyone except Mgr Hlinka, who was then in prison for political agitation.

[4] R. W. Seton-Watson, *The Southern Slav Question*, p. 114.

to Budapest to beg the Monarch to intercede for their persecuted fellow-countrymen. He refused to receive them.

The incident was very important, for it gave rise to a feeling among many Croats that they had nothing to hope from Vienna, a feeling which was ultimately to develop into a 'Yugoslav' movement looking outside the Monarchy.[1] But the immediate effects seemed to point in a different direction, for the next important political development was that, on the initiative of one of Masaryk's pupils, a Dalmatian journalist named František Supilo, and of a colleague of his, Anton Trumbić, forty Deputies from Croatia, Dalmatia and Istria met in Fiume on 4 October 1905, and adopted a Resolution offering the support of the signatories to the Hungarian Coalition in return for loyal observance of the Nagodba, democratic reform inside Croatia, and Hungarian support for the re-attachment of Dalmatia to the Triune Kingdom. On 16 October twenty-six Serb Deputies adhered to this Resolution, declaring themselves in favour of joint political action with the Croats, and a little later representatives of both peoples signed a declaration that they were parts of one people.[2]

The Independence Party in Hungary received the Croato-Serb overtures with *empressement*, as strengthening its own hand against Vienna. Ferenc Kossuth sent an open telegram to the signatories of the Fiume Resolution, ending with the words 'May God lead Dalmatia back, via Croatia, to the Crown of St Stephen. We await you with love and hope'. The new Ban who had replaced Khuen Hédervary, Count Todor Pejačević, did not attempt to influence the elections which took place in the autumn of 1906, and these accordingly brought the National Party heavy losses; it secured only thirty-seven mandates, while twenty-eight went to a 'coalition' of Croats and Serbs who accepted the Fiume Resolutions[3] and the Serbo-Croat identity, and twenty-three to the 'Party of Pure Right'.

But Francis Joseph would not hear of any tampering with the position of Dalmatia, and after the Hungarian Coalition came into power it soon got across its friends in Croatia. In May 1907 Kossuth introduced a Bill[4] making

---

[1] In a Court Martial for desertion in 1916 the accused, a Croat sergeant, said that 'the Croats were always loyal to the Emperor, but he did not love them, and delivered them over to the Magyars, so that they were forced to turn to the Serbs, who at least spoke their language'.

[2] Kiszling, *Franz Ferdinand*, p. 231, quotes a document (a report to Francis Ferdinand from Kristóffy) that the Croat signatories to the declaration, in return for the Serbs' promise in respect of Dalmatia, recognized Bosnia as the Serbs' 'sphere of influence'.

[3] Subsequently, twelve more Deputies went over from the National Party to the Coalition.

[4] According, however, to Redlich (*Schicksalsjahre*, I. 12, ad 3 May 1909), this move – always quoted against the Coalition as one of their major blunders – was really the result of a trick played on them by their opponents. The Bill was drafted for Kossuth (who was often away sick) by his Secretary of State, Szterényi, who was put up to it by Wekerle 'in order to put all the responsibility for the settlement' (the impending revision of the Nagodba) 'on the Kossuthists alone, and at the same time, to divert explosive national feelings against Croatia'.

knowledge of Magyar compulsory for all employees on the Hungarian State railway system, including the lines in Croatia, where, however, those employees who had to deal with the public, or with the local authorities, should also know Croat. The Croat Deputies declared this rule to constitute a violation of the Nagodba, and resorted to obstruction in the Pest Parliament, taking advantage (for the first time) of the provision of the Nagodba which allowed them to use their own language there. Meetings were held up and down Croatia, calling for complete separation from Hungary.

The Ban resigned, his successor (appointed on 6 January 1908) being Baron Pál Rausch, son of the midwife of the Nagodba. Rausch, whose suitability for the appointment Wekerle himself (who proposed it officially to the King) seems to have doubted,[1] promptly dissolved the Sabor and held new elections, but feeling was so inflamed that he could not get the Unionist Party together at all. 57 of the 88 seats went to the Serbo-Croat Coalition, 22 to the Party of Pure Right, and the remaining 9 to splinter Parties. Rausch opened the Sabor on 12 March, but, after its members had spent two days abusing Hungary, and one another, in unprintable terms, he prorogued it indefinitely.

After this there came another small improvement. When Khuen Héderváry again became Minister President of Hungary, the leaders of the Serbo-Croat Coalition asked a certain Professor Tomasics to mediate a *modus vivendi* between Croatia and Hungary. Eventually, Khuen had Rausch replaced by Tomasics himself, who re-convoked the Sabor, got it to accept a franchise reform which increased the number of electors from 45,000 to 222,000, then, having meanwhile organized a new Unionist Party called the 'Party of Progress', dissolved the Sabor and held new elections in October. Those, however, gave only 18 mandates to the Party of Progress, 36 to the Serbo-Croat Coalition, 9 to the Party of Right, 14 to a new Christian Social Party, 9 to a Peasant Party founded by the brothers Anton and Stjepan Radics, and one to a Serb Radical, and when the new Sabor met after the elections, all the Opposition Parties insisted with such violence that the Railway Law must be repealed before anything else could be discussed, that Tomasics was obliged, after all, to adjourn the Sabor. He held new elections in November, but again failed to secure a majority, and resigned. His successor, Cuvaj, again suspended the Constitution (31 March 1912), whereupon someone threw a bomb at him, injuring him severely.

It must be said that when Tisza got the reins again firmly in his hands, the curve of trouble in the Hungarian Lands flattened out a little. In particular, Tisza achieved an important *modus vivendi*, the effects of which were perceptible in the Croats' attitude in 1914, with the Croats. In November 1913 he replaced Cuvaj as Ban by a personal friend of his own, Baron Skerlecz, who elicited from all the Croat Deputies, except those of the Pure

[1] R. W. Seton-Watson, *Southern Slav Question*, p. 156.

Right, a declaration that they accepted the Nagodba in principle, although condemning the violations of it which had been committed by Hungary. Tisza in return remedied the Croats' most loudly voiced grievances, the use of Magyar place-names and the linguistic regulations on the railways.

On the other hand, negotiations which he initiated with the Roumanians proved unsuccessful. He offered to lift the ban on the National Party, to extend public facilities to their business enterprises and to make certain concessions to the use of their language in education, administration and justice; but their counter-claims went so far beyond these that he handed the list of them back to Maniu with the comment: 'A Magyar stomach can't digest that'.

The deadlock remained unbroken in essentials, and Tisza was not the man to break it. He could only hold the fort, and with so many hostile forces gathered against it, it is difficult to believe that the synthesis of national and social domination of a minority which he was defending could have survived indefinitely, even given the continued support from outside which had thitherto been at once its strength and its *raison e'être*. And it could not count on enjoying this for much longer. In a sense, it had been taken away already, when Francis Joseph had ordered the franchise to be extended, for Tisza was certainly right in his view of the inevitable effects of any real democratization of the Hungarian franchise.

Francis Joseph may not even have meant this threat seriously, except as a means of putting pressure on the Independence politicians;[1] at any rate, he had contented himself with the travesty of a compliance with it to which Lukács' Act had amounted. In any case, it was to be assumed that so long as he lived, he would do no more than insist on exact compliance with the Compromise. But in the nature of things, the Crown must soon pass to Francis Ferdinand, whose dislike of the Magyars had been fanned into a sort of permanent, pathological rage by what he regarded as their attempts to destroy the efficiency of the army – a fury which he used to vent to his confidants in terms which an English printer would hesitate to reproduce even after 1951, and one which drew no distinction between one Hungarian and another: Tisza, he used to maintain, was no better than the rest of them.

There had been only one small group among the enfranchised classes in Hungary which had envisaged the possibility of following any policy towards the factors outside the ring other than one of simple repression. This was that wing – or a part of it – of the Party of Independence which had followed Justh when the Party split. Justh, as we have said, had been sincerely attached to the idea of suffrage reform, and in its interest, had initiated a certain co-operation in the 1910 elections with the Social Democrats and, in some places, with the Nationalities. Soon after this Justh fell ill (he died in 1913), but meanwhile, his Party had received an unexpected recruit in the

---

[1] See Redlich, *Franz Joseph*, p. 407.

person of Count Mihály Károlyi, a young scion of one of Hungary's most historic and wealthiest families, who, after beginning his public career as an extreme reactionary, had undergone a change of heart. As the new leader of the Party when it reunited after Justh's death, Károlyi had renewed the contact with the Social Democrats, established relations with Jászi and his group, and evolved a theory that if Hungary introduced political and social justice and initiated a new policy (described by himself as 'federalization')[1] towards the Nationalities, she would not merely be righting what was wrong with herself, but also be establishing her own internal solidarity.

While, however, Károlyi's ideas agreed with Francis Ferdinand's on the desirability of suffrage reform, it was a case of extremes meeting at one point which on all others remained poles apart. Károlyi advocated the reform as (he thought) a way of solidifying Hungary; the Archduke meant it as a step towards breaking the country up. Looked at from the point of view of the Gesammtmonarchie, the picture was reversed. The Archduke meant to consolidate the Monarchy, while Károlyi was an extreme 'Independence' man. At this date he does not, indeed, seem to have envisaged complete separation of Hungary from Austria; instead, he adopted the thesis that for his ideas to be realized, the Monarchy would have to break entirely with the Triple Alliance and 'join the alliance of anti-German States', and in the autumn of 1913 he went to Paris on a journey to popularize this idea in France and the U.S.A.

Here, again, he was taking a diametrically opposite view from that of Francis Ferdinand, of whom he writes in his memoirs with extreme hatred.[2]

For the rest, Károlyi's ideas were regarded by all the conventional politicians of Hungary with as much horror as Francis Ferdinand's own. They became popular only in 1917, when the international situation had changed, and the German alliance had really become a debit for Hungary, instead of an asset.

On 29 May 1903, the young King of Serbia, Milan Obrenović, and his wife, were murdered in the Konak by conspirators belonging to a secret nationalist association of officers, who then promptly called to the throne the senior representative of the rival dynasty, Peter Karageorgević.

Austria at first smelt no danger and extended prompt recognition to the new King.[3] It is also possible that Peter himself was not at the time anxious

[1] Károlyi, *Gegen eine ganze Welt*, p. 73.

[2] Id., p. 52. I cannot trace any reference at all to Károlyi in such works as I have consulted on Francis Ferdinand.

[3] According to Bogitschewitsch (*Kriegsursachen*, Zurich, 1919, p. 15), Austria had even helped to prepare the way for Peter's eventual succession to the throne. Bogitschewitsch is not, indeed, a witness who inspires undiluted confidence. But see Steed, op. cit., p. 241, for Austria's foreknowledge of the conspiracy and for her absence of alarm when the change of dynasties took place.

for trouble. But he was the prisoner of the officers who had put him in power, and of the Radical Party, now become the strongest in Serbia and transformed from a Left-wing peasant party into an almost purely nationalist one, the patron and inspirer of a nation-wide campaign for the unification of all Serbs in one State under the new dynasty. The effects of the change thus quickly made themselves felt. Nationalist societies, open or secret, sprang into being in the service of the national aim, and were very soon extending their activities, on the one hand, into Macedonia, and on the other, into both Croatia-Slavonia and Bosnia. The most prominent of these societies operating in the territory of the Monarchy was the *Slovenska Jug* (Slavonic South) founded in 1905.

Almost at the same time an economic issue arose, the origin of which did not lie in Austro-Serbian relations and its effects were not confined to them, but happened to be very important for them, in an unfavourable sense. The Caprivi treaties were due to expire in February 1904. The protectionist opposition to them had won much ground in the slump of 1900, which, as has been said, had been badly aggravated by German dumping, and it was important that the movement for protection was now being supported by the Hungarian agrarians, whose position and interests had changed during the preceding decades: the non-agrarian population of the Monarchy was now large enough to consume most of what Hungarian agriculture could produce, while on the other hand, Hungary's products were being challenged by overseas competition, especially on the German market – thitherto their chief outlet – and even at home. Hungarian industry, too, was reaching a stage at which it could, and did, ask for protection.

Strong pressure for agrarian protection was coming also from the Polish landlords in Galicia.

In 1902 Germany introduced a new tariff which included high duties on agricultural imports, Pending the negotiation of a new agreement, Austria also introduced a provisional regime with relatively high duties, both industrial and agricultural; although these could be reduced by negotiation with trading partners.

The Austro-Serb Commercial Treaty was also due to expire shortly, and the negotiations for its renewal, which opened in 1903, promised to be difficult. Under the existing treaty, Austria was taking 80–90% of Serbia's exports, and supplying her with 50–60% of her imports. Serbia wanted, on political grounds, to reduce her dependence on imports from Austria, but would have liked to keep up her exports. On the other hand, the Hungarian agriculturalists[1] had long been complaining of the cheap Serbian competition. This had been growing increasingly burdensome for some time past, as

---

[1] It is always the 'Hungarian feudal magnates' who are accussed of oppressive behaviour towards the Serbs, but in fact the producers chiefly hit by the Serb competition were the Swabian (and Serb) pig-breeders of South Hungary.

Germany reduced her purchases from the Monarchy, and it had become, as a Hungarian expert has written,[1] 'a dogma in Hungary that she could allow exports from the East only in the measure to which Germany opened her doors to Hungary's exports'.

The Austrian negotiators insisted that Serbia must at least pledge herself not to reduce her industrial imports from Austria.[2] Far from doing this, Serbia, in January 1904, placed a large order for munitions, not with the Austrian Skoda, but with its French rival, Schneider-Creuzot – a move the implications of which were obviously not purely economic. Summoned by Austria to cancel the contract, she refused, and concluded, in the same year, a Secret Treaty of Alliance with Bulgaria, which envisaged the later conclusion of a Customs Union. The existence of the Treaty leaked out through an indiscretion in the Bulgarian Sobranje, and Austria vetoed the Customs Union as incompatible with the treaty of either State with the Monarchy, both of which were based on the most favoured nation clause.[3] As Serbia still refused to accept the Monarchy's terms for the renewal of her commercial treaty with it, a 'treatyless condition' came into existence on 1 March 1906, which lasted, with minor interruptions, until June 1909, when a 'provisional' treaty relationship was restored.

In the event, Serbia emerged almost unscathed from the 'pig war', as it was generally nicknamed. She got more credits from France, with which she built her own slaughter-houses and canning plants, and found outlets for her produce in this form. She supplied herself with imports chiefly from Germany.[4] But her antagonism to the Monarchy had deepened, and she had now an economic as well as a national ground for coveting Bosnia, possession of which would bring her nearer to her greatly desired outlet to the sea. Her agitation in that province redoubled, and found its path smoothed for it by good intentions on the part of the Austrians themselves.

Kállay had died in harness on 13 July 1903, and Francis Joseph had given his succession to Baron Burian (later to become Austro-Hungarian Foreign Minister). Burian took the view[5] that it was not possible to go on governing the Provinces, in effect, against the Serb population, which constituted not

---

[1] Gratz, *A Dualiszmus Kora*, II. 237.

[2] The share of the Austrian industrial interests in the negotiations is also regularly passed over by historians. The Austrian industrialists were also threatened with competition from Germany, which had concluded a new trade agreement with Serbia.

[3] Bulgaria's treaty with the Monarchy had expired in 1903, but had been succeeded by a 'provisorium' on the same terms.

[4] Benedikt, op. cit., pp. 164–5. The value of Germany's exports to Serbia rose from 12·5 million RM. in 1902, to 17·9 in 1910, and of her imports from Serbia, from 5·1 to 19·1 RM. By then the Monarchy's share in Serbia's exports had sunk to 31%, and in her imports to 24%.

[5] The fullest account of these events known to me is in Südland, op. cit., pp. 498 ff. Burian's own account in chapter XVI of his *Austria in Dissolution* is much less illuminating.

only numerically the largest but also the most active and vital element in them. He believed that their demands for cultural liberty and for some measure of self-government could not, at this stage, be resisted, and took the optimistic view that if their legitimate wishes were satisfied, they would not 'gravitate outwards'. In 1905 he agreed with the leaders of the Orthodox community on a Statute[1] which gave the Orthodox Eparchies complete autonomy (subject to the ultimate control of the Crown) in the conduct and administration of their own Churches and schools, and of the properties and funds appertaining thereto. Preparations were also set on foot for the introduction of a measure of local, and eventually District and Provincial, self-government, the first statutes for which were published in 1907. The censorship was eased, and in general, the grip of authority relaxed.[2]

The result of this was, however, not at all to make the Serbs of Bosnia gravitate inward. Liberty under Austrian rule was not what they wanted, still less, what Serbia wanted for them. Her agitation now became exceedingly vigorous. Bands of Serb agents roamed the provinces unrestricted. The printing presses of Belgrade (and also of Cettinje) poured out denunciations of the bloody tyranny of Austrian rule, and these were echoed in the Serbian Press of the Provinces. The *Srbska Riječ* of Sarajevo (which was certainly in the pay of Belgrade) was confiscated some seventy times, and if what was not allowed to appear was worse than what did pass the censor, it must have been subversive indeed, for many articles and poems saw the light which openly called upon the people to rise against the tyrannous foreign rule.

The agitation took a peculiar shape, for while its real object was to bring about the unification of Bosnia with Serbia, yet whether as a tactical move to gain the support of the local Moslems, or because the device was thought less dangerous, the procedure most usually followed was to exploit the fact that the legal sovereignty over the Provinces was still the Sultan's. In 1907 the Serbs actually carried through elections of their own to a kind of mock Parliament. Seventy-one delegates met in Sarajevo, assumed the role of a sort of Constituent, and adopted a resolution which, invoking the principle of self-determination, announced the establishment of an independent Bosnia-Herzegovina as part of the Ottoman Empire. A little later (in May 1908) a labour movement constituted itself in Sarajevo which promptly identified itself with the Serb national cause and for some days 'practically eliminated the authority of the State'[3] in that city.

Some of the Moslems showed a certain sympathy with this agitation, although more of them, not being blind to its true purpose, retreated into an

---

[1] It was promulgated on 1 September 1905.

[2] Burian also introduced a new scheme to enable the kmets to buy their land. They were to get the whole price advanced by a Hungarian bank, the Government guaranteeing the repayments.

[3] Südland, p. 499.

uneasy and non-committal silence. Most of the loyal Catholics, under the leadership of their bellicose Archbishop, Mgr Stadler, felt the need to defend themselves, and in the spring of 1908 obtained permission to found a nominally non-political organization, the Hrvatska Narodna Zajednica (Croat National Union) which, needless to say, promptly adopted an essentially political programme for the annexation of the Provinces by the Monarchy and their unification with the 'Croat Lands' of Croatia-Slavonia and Dalmatia in a new sub-State on an equal footing with Cis- and Trans-Leithania. Even the Croats, however, were not quite unanimous, for some of the younger men wanted a Yugoslav solution, rather than a purely Croat one, and one group, led by some Franciscan Friars, sought contact with the Slovene Catholic Populists.

Serbia's activities in Croatia-Slavonia were necessarily carried on more discreetly, and also less wholeheartedly, for most Serb nationalists were at that time still uninterested in the Croats. But it is highly improbable that the Fiume Resolutions owed nothing to the inspiration of Belgrade, and in retrospect it is completely clear that the important declaration here was not that of 4 October, offering the Coalition's support to Hungary,[1] but its sequel which proclaimed the ethnic unity of Serbs and Croats.

It is easy to over-estimate the number of those who really believed this to be true in the deepest sense: probably very few indeed of the Serbs, and not a very much higher proportion of the Croats, the majority of whom, to the last, would have preferred in their hearts an 'Austro-Croat' solution for their people. But it was fairly certain that most of the politically conscious Serbs of Croatia-Slavonia were now Serbian irredentists, and a growing proportion of the Croats prepared at least to toy with the idea of joining a federal Southern Slav State.[2]

Since the Serbian agitation was always slaveringly anti-Austrian, and the reports of the Austrian and Hungarian Press fully as vicious, the relations between the two countries, at least as expressed unofficially, were by now envenomed to a degree.

Meanwhile, the international situation was changing to Austria's disadvantage in other important respects. In 1903 Russia had still been

---

[1] According to Redlich, l.c., Supilo told him that the offer was only a manoeuvre to frighten Austria into doing something for the Croats.

[2] Voting is no safe guide to opinion in South-Eastern Europe, but the figures for successive elections in Croatia show the Croat Deputies elected as divided fairly evenly between those who accepted the idea of Serb-Croat fraternity, and those who rejected it (it must not be forgotten that a quarter of the electors were Serbs, almost all of whom voted regularly for the Coalition). Besides the Party of Pure Right, the Christian Social Party which emerged in 1910 was strongly Catholic and Austro-Slav. Stjepan Radić's first literary product, a pamphlet written in Czech in 1902, had advocated a reconstruction of the Monarchy on ethnic lines. Radić refused to join the Coalition, and in 1909 produced a programme of his own of Croat-Slovene union.

absorbed in the Far East, and in so far as she was interesting herself at all in Balkan affairs, her favourite client was Bulgaria, with which she had concluded a military Convention, directed against Roumania, only the previous year. Indeed, when Austria recognized King Peter, it had been against the advice of the Russian Foreign Minister, Count Lamsdorff, who had told the Austro-Hungarian Ambassador in Petersburg, Count Aehrenthal, that Austria ought to occupy Belgrade and restore order there. The Mürzsteg Agreements[1] were concluded four months after the murders, and a year later, Austro-Russian relations were still cordial enough to allow Lamsdorff and Aehrenthal to exchange Notes pledging the two countries to loyal and complete neutrality if either became involved in a war, not provoked by it, with a third Power, other than a Balkan State.[2]

What changed the situation was Russia's defeat at the hands of Japan in 1904. This gave birth to two developments, curiously different in their nature.

The first in time was the direct product of the revolution in Russia which followed her defeat and brought into the Duma a number of more or less idealistic men who rejected the policy of Great Russian chauvinism which Russia's Government had been following. They, and the representatives of the non-Russian peoples themselves, really forced through the Duma several considerable cultural and administrative concessions to the Poles, Ukrainians and White Russians of the Czarist Empire.

At the same time, some of them became the adepts of a purified version of the old Pan-Slavism, which they called 'Neo-Slavism', to distinguish it from the older movement. It repudiated imperialism, specifically recognizing the right of every Slav people to its own national individuality, speech, religion and political independence. It aimed only at a close and friendly association between all the Slav States, but was nevertheless fundamentally political in the highest degree, since it counted the Monarchy as a Slav State, which would have, indeed, to be transformed politically so as to give its Slav peoples the weight in it to which their numbers entitled them, the Germans and Magyars stepping down into their proper places of minorities.

These doctrines, while they never bit on the Ukrainians, met with a considerable response from the Russian Poles, among whom, as we have said elsewhere, a school of thought, of which the National Democrats were the chief exponents, had for some time past been growing up which held that the future of Poland lay in a friendly understanding with Russia which would eventually make it possible for the three branches of the Poles to combine against the real enemy, Prussia. The next step must be to convert the Austrian Poles, and to this end the Russian patrons of the movement called in Kramář, who had long held, or professed to hold, views similar to theirs, and

[1] See above, p. 596.
[2] The instrument was dated 14 October 1904 and was to be valid for five years.

indeed claimed to be the true spiritual father of neo-Slavism. Kramař duly organized a 'Preparatory Conference', which was held in Prague in July 1908 and attended by delegates of all the Polish parties of Russia and Austria, except the Social Democrats, all the Czech parties, with the same exception, and a number of Serbs, Croats, Slovenes and Bulgarians, as well as a strong delegation of Russians. The Congress drew up an imposing programme of 'All-Slav' solidarity, which was carefully framed to include no directly political postulates, but was of course admittedly designed to promote conditions in which the long-term political ideal of the movement could be realized.

Neo-Slavism as such was killed by the Russian Government itself, for in 1907 – thus even before the Congress had met – Stolypin had withdrawn almost all the concessions which had been made to the non-Russian peoples of the Czarist Monarchy and reintroduced the old policy of Russification. Nevertheless, the idea of Slav solidarity had become fashionable again in Russia, and was now proclaimed by a multitude of organizations and publications which fiercely denounced all the non-Russian oppressors of other Slavs, Germans, Magyars and Turks. These effusions were not entirely without their effects on the Slav peoples of the Monarchy[1] and the feeling of Slavonic solidarity, in a form which, indeed, had more in it of the old Pan-Slavism than of its variant, thereafter constituted a strong element in Russia's official policy, which, as the second consequence of her defeat in the Far East, was now facing West again.

While Izvolski, who was a convinced adherent of the 'Western' orientation, had become Russian Foreign Minister as early as the summer of 1906, his hands had been closely tied in that year by the revolutionary conditions in Russia, and by the extreme liability of the international situation. Even a revival of the old Russo-German Alliance had seemed a possibility. But by the end of 1907 the tangles had been straightened out. The Franco-Russian alliance had been cemented by the great French loan to Russia. Britain had consummated her entente with France and had reached agreement with Russia on the chief issues which had divided the two Powers in Asia, and *pari passu* with this, the long period of search for friendship between Britain and Germany was drawing to its close. The partition of Europe into the two great power-blocks of Triple Entente and Triple Alliance was broadly complete, subject, of course, to the looseness of Britain's attachment to the one and the ambiguous position of Italy in the other. Russia was still very weak, and desperately conscious of her weakness, but yet not willing to let the Central Powers steal any marches on her in the Balkans without compensation to herself, and Izvolski had even reached the stage of regarding the problem from the other angle: that Russia might herself achieve a positive advance in the area, in the shape of a revision of the regime of the Straits,

[1] See below, p. 801 f.

which would have, indeed, to be brought about in agreement with Austria and paid for by concessions to her.

By this time important changes had taken place in certain key positions in the Monarchy. In October 1906, Goluchowski had been forced out of office, directly, on account of a quarrel between him and the Hungarian Coalition,[1] but also, in large part, because of the hatred with which he was pursued by Francis Ferdinand, who chose to regard him as standing in the way of Austro-Russian friendship.[2] He was replaced, on Francis Ferdinand's recommendation, by Baron Lexa von Aehrenthal, at that time Austro-Hungarian Ambassador in Petersburg. A month later, Conrad von Hötzendorff, another protégé of the Archduke's, replaced Baron von Beck as Chief of the General Staff – *de facto* the most important post in the armed services of the Monarchy[3] – while Baron von Schönaich took over the Ministry of War from von Pitreich, whose head, also, the Archduke had demanded. Changes were made at the same time in the High Command of the Navy and in the Emperor's Military Chancellery.

Some changes at the head of the defence forces were certainly overdue. Von Beck, a highly competent man in his day, had held his post since 1881 and was now nearer eighty than seventy. Many of his coadjutors were of the same generation, and things had got into a rut. Conrad, who belonged to a younger generation, was full of ideas for reorganizing the army, remodelling its tactics and making it an instrument capable of fighting a modern war. He did not, however, regard his functions as confined to such technical tasks, but was constantly pressing on the Government his prescription for the Monarchy's foreign political situation, which was that she should make preventive wars on Italy and Serbia while she could still do so with hope of success.

As this panacea was never adopted – even Francis Ferdinand always set his face against it – Conrad's actual influence over the foreign policy of the

---

[1] He had got across the Coalition leaders in his conversations with them after the 'five minutes audience' so badly that he himself had asked for permission to resign.

[2] See Kiszling, *Franz Ferdinand*, pp. 33–4, 93. The Archduke accused Goluchowski, amongst other sins, of a 'Big Poland policy'. The truth was simply that Francis Ferdinand detested all Poles and could not be fair to one. Goluchowski's reluctance to undertake a forward policy in the Balkans (precisely out of fear of offending Russia) probably also contributed to his fall.

[3] Prolonged controversies had gone on in the 1860s and 1870s on the respective competencies of the Chief of the Army Command (then the Archduke Albrecht), the Minister of War and the Chief of the General Staff. When, in 1881, Beck, who before that had been head of the Emperor's Military Chancellery, and therefore, behind the scenes, perhaps more influential than any of the three, became Chief of the General Staff, he asked Francis Joseph point-blank: 'whose Chief of General Staff he was? The Emperor's, the Archduke's or the Minister's?' He was told that he was 'personally, under the direct orders of the Emperor, but also assistant to the Minister'. As time went on, the Archduke faded out of the picture (he died in 1895), the Emperor became less active, and Beck in practice simply dictated his wishes to the Ministers of War and Defence, who became mere post-boxes.

Monarchy was, until the decisive moment in 1914 when he may have tipped the scales in favour of war, not great, but he did succeed in generating and maintaining an atmosphere of unrest which enhanced the difficulties of the Monarchy's last years.

Aehrenthal was, historically, by far the more important man, for with Francis Joseph now loosening his grip on the reins of policy and his nephew not allowed to take them from him, the foreign policy of the Monarchy was, from the day of Aehrenthal's appointment to that of his death in harness on 17 February 1912, what he made it. He has been most variously judged, and many of the judgments have been very hostile. Some of them are probably unfair, but the documents prove that he was repeatedly, almost habitually, disingenuous even towards his own allies, not to speak of the rest of the world, and his actions also bear out the accusations that he was misled into unwise moves by a desire to score a quick personal success which may well have been due to a certain inferiority complex: rumour credited him with a Jewish strain in his ancestry. The rumour appears to have been unfounded, but he seems to have felt that a prejudice existed against him on the strength of it. And as it happened, these personal weaknesses played a big part in bringing about the unfortunate results in chief of his years of office, which were not only to leave the Southern Slav question more of a festering sore than ever, but also to make Russia, at last, Austria's conscious enemy, with Serbia her preferred client.

Yet Aehrenthal had gone to the Ballhausplatz after a diplomatic career spent largely in Petersburg, with the reputation of a pronounced Russophile, a strong partisan of a revival of the *Dreikaiserbund*, and the actual inspirer of the Austro-Russian agreement of October 1903 (his initiative it had been that had brought about the Mürzsteg meeting which had resulted in the Agreements of that name); and he was fully prepared to let Russia have her share of the prize from the operation which he appears to have been planning long before he reached Ministerial rank.[1] The trouble was that he left other factors out of his calculations, and further alienated his own proposed partner by his dishonesty.

What he proposed to do was to abandon Goluchowski's policy of *quieta non movere* and to revert to the old alternative course of a political partition of the Balkans. Russia was not to be treated ungenerously – he told a confidant that 'he was not afraid of the result of handing over Constantinople and the Dardanelles to her',[2] with, of course, firm control over Bulgaria. Austria, however, was to have the Western Balkans down to Salonica inclusive, under 'some form of protectorate, i.e., the establishment of overlordship by means of alliances, trade and military conventions, etc.',[3] and as he usually expressed his intentions, Serbia was to be left nominally independent and

---
[1] The conversation with Baernreither quoted here took place in the summer of 1899.
[2] Baernreither, *Fragments of a Political Diary*, p. 34.   [3] Ibid.

territorially intact, but put back into the condition of political and economic subservience in which she had stood under the Obrenović. Even this, however, is not certain,[1] and in any case, the method by which he chose to open his operation was such as to arouse Russia's immediate suspicions.

On 27 January 1908, without having done more than hint to Russia of his intentions,[2] he announced in the Delegations, with considerable flourishes, that he had negotiated an agreement with the Porte under which Austria was to build a railway through the Sanjak to link up with the Macedonian system, thus giving the Monarchy direct communication with Salonica.

Aehrenthal afterwards tried to argue that the purpose of the railway was purely economic. Economics were one thing, politics another, and as politics did not come into the question, no one need object. But if the railway had been constructed (and the engineering difficulties were such that the enterprise would have been enormously expensive, and in fact, it was, for that reason, never carried through[3]) it would obviously have strengthened Austria's strategic position in the Balkans, thus contravening at least the spirit of all Austria's international undertakings respecting the Balkans. Moreover, strong suspicions soon became current that Austria had paid the Sultan for the concession by promising to sabotage the reforms which the Powers were pressing on the Porte.

The announcement evoked a tempest of popular wrath in both Serbia and Russia, where the nationalist Press called for the cancellation of the Austro-Russian agreement. In April, Izvolski retorted with a counter-suggestion that a second railway should be constructed from Roumania across Serbia and Montenegro to the Adriatic, and Aehrenthal, the prisoner of his own contention that railways did not involve politics, replied perforce on 1 May, that Austria would not object to this. But Izvolski's heart was really set, not on railways across the Balkans, but on getting the Straits opened to Russia, and on 2 July he sent Vienna a memorandum which, in effect, offered Aehrenthal a bargain: Russia's support for Austria if she annexed Bosnia-Herzegovina and the Sandjak in return for Austria's support for Russia in a revision of the regime of the Straits. Both questions, the memorandum said, were European problems and would have to be discussed on that level, but Russia was prepared first to enter into friendly discussions on them with Austria. This offer must have come to Aehrenthal as a gift from Heaven, for the situation in Bosnia itself (and, in connection therewith, the Monarchy's relations with Serbia) had become genuinely intolerable.

[1] Hantsch, *Berchtold*, p. 438, quotes a reported utterance by him indicating that he really meant Austria to expand territorially as far as Salonica. 'Talk about the saturated condition of the Monarchy was only for the public.'

[2] Carlgren, p. 223; Hantsch, *Berchtold*, p. 85.

[3] Its solitary and murine, although delightful, product was the now almost disused Aspangbahn, which carries, or used to carry, travellers from Vienna to the *'bucklige Welt'* fifty miles away.

Things could not go on as they were, and Austria had in effect only two courses open to her (if one excludes as humanly impossible that of handing the Provinces back to Turkey). One would have been, while leaving the constitutional position intact, to restore order with an iron hand – this was what Conrad, in his bluff way, was advising; the other, which was advocated precisely by those who, like Burian, wanted to create model conditions in the Provinces which would then make them a magnet to draw in the other Serbia, was to annexe them; for without this, as Burian argued, the necessary reforms could not be carried through.[1]

Burian had made representations to this effect in April 1908 and Aehrenthal had probably then become convinced that the annexation would presently be a necessity, although he had thought the international situation inappropriate for immediate action.[2] But then came Izvolski's letter, which arrived almost simultaneously with a piece of news which really forced Austria's hand: on 6 July the Young Turks seized the power in Constantinople and forced the Sultan on the 25th to issue an order convening a Parliament to which Bosnia-Herzegovina, with the other territories of the Ottoman Empire which were in a similar 'occupied' position (Eastern Roumelia and Crete), were to send elected representatives.

It seems to have been this news which decided Aehrenthal that the annexation was inevitable, and on 19 August he submitted to a Ministerial Council proposals (which the Council duly accepted) that Austria should annexe Bosnia-Herzegovina, while withdrawing her garrisons from the Sanjak. She should enter into negotiations with Russia to secure her consent in return for a discussion of the problem of the Straits. On 29 August, as the first step in this connection, he sent Izvolski (who was then in Karlsbad) a memorandum which gave no indication that Austria had already made up her mind – on the contrary, it laid down the principle 'that the two Cabinets will remain true to their resolve to uphold the existing *status quo* in Turkey so long as circumstances make this possible', but said that 'if compulsive circumstances forced Austria to annexe Bosnia-Herzegovina' she would immediately withdraw her garrisons from the Sanjak and definitively renounce any occupation of that territory', and that she was prepared to enter into a confidential and friendly exchange of ideas with Russia on the question of Constantinople, the Straits and the adjacent territory, as soon as the question became *actuel*. Berchtold now placed his castle at Buchlow at the Ministers' disposal, and Aehrenthal and Izvolski met there on 15 September. Aehrenthal believed or at least afterwards maintained, that Izvolski had definitely agreed

---

[1] Hantsch, op. cit., pp. 585–6, quotes a letter to Berchtold from Count Forgách, a high official in the Foreign Ministry, saying specifically that it was Burian who 'instigated and talked Aehrenthal into the ... annexation'.

[2] On this, see Hantsch, op. cit., I. 106–7. The whole complex of Austro-Hungarian relations at the time is admirably treated by Carlgren.

to the annexation, in return, indeed, for a promise of support for her wishes in the Straits and in respect of certain other Balkan questions, all these questions, however, constituting music of the future, to be settled at a future international conference. He did not consult the Russians again, nor go beyond hints to any other Power, even Austria's own ally in chief, Germany. Only on 4 and 5 October was formal notice given to Germany, as to the other signatories of the Berlin Treaty, and the annexation was announced, as a unilateral decision, by Francis Joseph on 7 October, a day after Ferdinand of Bulgaria, probably on the basis of an inspired guess,[1] had proclaimed Bulgaria's own independence.

We shall not attempt to retell the details of the ensuing crisis which kept Europe hovering for months on the brink of war. The Turks naturally resented the violation of their sovereignty. Serbia, although technically without a *locus standi* in the dispute, strengthened her armed forces, demanded territorial compensation and appealed to Russia. Montenegro was equally aggrieved. Izvolski was deeply offended, for he had, or maintained himself to have, understood differently what had been agreed in Buchlow (as at Reichstadt, thirty years earlier, no agreed statement of the results of the conversations had been put in writing): according to him, the whole programme – annexation, revision of the Straits regime and the rest – was to come as a whole before a Conference of the Powers, and Aehrenthal had not revealed that he was going to jump a claim by effecting the annexation so soon, and without further notice. He felt himself duped, and his grievance was accentuated when, chiefly owing to British objections, no Conference was held, so that Russia came out of the transaction empty-handed. Britain and France, which Aehrenthal had treated cavalierly, if not dishonestly, resented the unilateral denunciation of the multilateral Treaty of Berlin, and even Germany was not best pleased, while Italy felt that she had, into the bargain, been cheated out of the compensation which she could legitimately have expected.[2] Angry crowds demonstrated in front of the Austro-Hungarian Embassy in Rome.

In the end, the crisis passed over. The German Emperor decided to back

---

[1] Ferdinand and Aehrenthal had met in Budapest on 23–24 September. It seems probable that Aehrenthal let Ferdinand guess his intentions but did not expect him to act until later.

[2] Italy had not, on the main point, a legal case. Goluchowski had told Tittoni on 1 April 1904 that the annexation, if and when it took place, would not entitle Italy to compensation, unless Austria annexed the Sanjak. There seems no doubt that Tittoni accepted this, although for one reason or another, Goluchowski had failed to get the acceptance into writing. Goluchowski had further warned Tittoni that Austria would not allow Italy to set foot in Albania. Aehrenthal had repeated Goluchowski's statement to Tittoni on 4 September 1908, in Salzburg, and again Tittoni had accepted it. But this time Aehrenthal had undoubtedly lied to the Italian, whom he had promised 'not to surprise with any kind of decision', and Italy could justifiably resent the way in which she had been kept in the dark, only a year after again renewing the Triple Alliance.

Austria to the limit, and Russia was not ready (nor anxious), for war; still less did Britain or France desire it. Confronted by Germany with a very blunt demand to state her position, Russia abandoned her support of Serbia in return for an assurance from Austria that she would not attack that country, as at one stage she had threatened to do. Left to herself, Serbia had no option but to submit, and in a Note of 31 March 1909, recognized the annexation and promised to reduce her armed forces to the level of the preceding autumn, and to maintain good-neighbourly relations with Austria. Montenegro was induced, with even more difficulty, to follow suit, in return for the removal of certain restrictions placed on her by the Treaty of Berlin. Turkey was persuaded to recognize the annexation in return for a cash payment (disguised as the purchase price of the State forests) of £T. 2,400,000. The *coup* had come off. Austria had acquired two more provinces, while no other Power had made any gains at all.

It was an achievement which was hailed in many circles in the Monarchy with great satisfaction as proof of the Monarchy's continued vitality. Yet the end of the crisis probably left the Monarchy's situation, on balance, less comfortable than ever. On the credit side, if it was a credit, was to be set an increased intimacy of her relations with Germany, where leading circles had been seriously wondering whether the dangers of alliance with her did not outweigh its possible advantages, particularly if Austria, on her side, continued to be so lukewarm in her support of Germany on issues where she was not herself directly involved, as she had been at Algeciras. Even before the annexation, however, Bülow had decided that 'Germany and Austria must stand together as a solid bloc . . . loyal co-operation with Austria would be and must remain the fundamental basis of German foreign policy'.[1] Germany had acted in this sense during the crisis, and after it military consultations between the General Staffs of the two countries were resumed.[2] This, it is true, increased the danger that Austria might be dragged in Germany's wake into war with the Western Powers, but Aehrenthal thought the danger not too serious. 'We stand aside,' he wrote in a self-briefing for a conversation with Sir Charles Hardinge in August 1908, 'from the rivalries between Germany and England, especially the competition in naval armaments,

---

[1] See his despatch to Schlözer, 25 June 1908, *Grosse Politik*, XXV, pp. 474 ff.

[2] Such conversations had taken place on previous occasions, notably during the years after 1882, which was a period during which the German General Staff still attached importance to Austrian co-operation. Even then, however, Bismarck had objected to the conclusion of a military Convention, as contrary to the spirit of his Russian policy, and when Von Schlieffen replaced Waldersee at the head of the German General Staff, he thought preparations for joint offensive operations in the East unnecessary, and the contact between the two General Staffs was 'almost completely broken off' after 1896. It was now renewed, on Conrad's insistence, on 1 January 1909, although even now no firm or detailed agreements were reached, and none were in force in the summer of 1914. See the article by A. Wagner in *Vorabend*, pp. 73 ff.

which we regard as not without danger. We are justified in expecting that these frictions between Berlin and London will not be allowed to affect the relationship between Austria-Hungary and England.'[1]

This, however, showed a serious misconception of feeling in the West. The faith of the Western Powers in Austria's value as a counterweight to or barrier against Germany had already been shaken by the Kaiser's tactless description of her at Algeciras as Germany's 'brilliant second'; now it was further diminished. They accept a situation which had been achieved largely through their mediation, but they seem never again really to have trusted the Ballhausplatz.

Another, very important effect of the Annexation, and of the whole international *revirement*, was to bring about a change in the attitude of British public opinion towards national problems in the Monarchy. France had long been cultivating friendly unofficial relations with the Slavs of the Monarchy. Now British opinion began to follow French in seeing Austria, especially as guided by Aehrenthal, in a new light. The two publicists of the day who occupied themselves seriously with the problem, Wickham Steed, then correspondent of *The Times* in Vienna (later to become its Foreign Editor, then its Editor) and R. W. Seton-Watson, both wished and at the time believed in the survival of the Monarchy, but both took up the cause of its 'subject peoples' and wrote arguing that the survival would be possible only if the domination of its Germans and Magyars were broken.

Steed and Seton-Watson were only individuals; there was at the time nothing like any general consensus of British opinion on the Monarchy, and other writings continued to appear which were friendly enough to it. But the judgments of these two men carried exceptional weight, even at the time, and later events were destined, as we shall see, to put them in a position in which their views counted for more than those of all other observers put together.

Italy hotted up her agitation in the Trentino and Trieste still further, and Tittoni revenged himself by concluding yet another agreement with the other side. On 4 October 1909, Italy and Russia agreed, under the Raccognino Agreement, to endeavour to maintain the *status quo* in the Balkans, and if violent trouble broke out there, to uphold the principle of nationality, i.e., not to impede the development of the Balkan States and to exclude foreign domination there, combining to resist any undertaking which ran contrary

[1] Cit. Crankshaw, op. cit., p. 330. It is true that if Aehrenthal's own record, as given in *Oe. U. Aussenpolitik*, I. p. 37, is to be trusted, he omitted the devastating last sentence at the actual meeting, at which, incidentally, he appears to have been unusually dishonest, even for him: while he gave Hardinge the impression that, while he would make no promises, he would try to restrain Germany, he let the Germans believe that 'he had defended their point of view almost passionately'. But he was in general fatuously ignorant of Britain's importance. When visitors during the crisis warned him not to ignore Britain's influence, 'he asked repeatedly of them: "what can England do to us?" ' (Steed, op. cit., p. 233).

to these principles. Further, Italy promised to support Russia over the Straits, while Russia promised not to oppose Italy's designs on Tripoli. Immediately after this, it is true, Italy made another Pact with Austria under which the two Powers agreed to communicate to one another 'any proposal by a third Power which might conflict with the principle of non-intervention or of the *status quo*'. But these diplomatic engagements were coming to look extraordinarily unreal in the light of the open hostility with which the two countries regarded each other. The offence was by no means all on one side. Conrad, when the question of the annexation was first discussed in the summer of 1908, described war with Italy as 'almost inevitable'. The official organ of the Austrian Army, *Danzers Armeezeitung*, actually advocated a preventive war against Italy in 1909, when she was weakened by the Messina earthquake. It is true that Aehrenthal never lent himself to these suggestions, but the relationship between the two States was not improved by the fact that everyone knew that Conrad had received his post through the Archduke Francis Ferdinand's patronage. Francis Ferdinand, himself never, indeed, endorsed either of Conrad's schemes for a preventive war (against Italy or Serbia), but he was convinced that war against Italy, which he regarded as the Monarchy's enemy in chief, was bound to come, and in his military capacity was devoting much attention (which did not escape notice) to preparing for the eventuality.

In the Balkans, Turkey soon got over her resentment, and Bulgaria showed signs of wanting a closer relationship with her fellow-beneficiary of the crisis, although these were not followed up, partly, perhaps, owing to Francis Ferdinand's strong dislike and distrust of Ferdinand of Bulgaria. But Serbia's promise to become Austria's 'good neighbour' proved not worth a pie-crust. Her agitators were as active as ever in Bosnia and Croatia, and they were, as it happened, singularly fortunate in that two attempts by the Austrian authorities to discredit them were extraordinarily badly handled. In March 1909, 53 Serbs of Croatia were put on trial in Zagreb for high treason, viz. conspiracy against the Monarchy with irredentist circles in Serbia, directed by the Slovenski Jug. The indictment adduced many absurd indications of treason, but for 'proof' of the main charge the prosecution relied almost entirely on most unconvincing 'revelations' by a notorious character called Nostić. The moving spirits here were, incidentally, the Croats of the Pure Right, whose hatred of the Serbs had driven them into a curious *Interessengemeinschaft* with Hungary. Not only were the charges flimsy, but the trial was most scandalously conducted, and after the first Court in Zagreb had sentenced 31 defendents to terms of imprisonment totalling 184 years, the sentences were quashed by the Court of Appeal, which ordered a retrial.[1] The second case, which opened immediately after (in December 1909) had an equally ignominious ending. When the annexation crisis was at its height,

[1] This never took place.

and with the purpose of justifying a declaration of war, which then seemed imminent, by Austria on Serbia, the Ballhausplatz supplied the Viennese *Reichspost* and the distinguished historian, Dr Friedjung, with a number of documents purporting to reveal Serbian intrigues in Bosnia.[1] Some of them implicated Supilo and the Serbo-Croat Coalition. The editor of the *Reichspost*, Funder, published a pamphlet and Friedjung wrote an article in the *Neue Freie Presse*, and a libel case followed.[2] It transpired that some, or most, of the documents were forged, and many of the particular allegations contained in them demonstrably unfounded. Professor Friedjung had to eat his words, and the defence collapsed.

The two cases received enormous publicity, particularly since they were unlucky enough to attract the especial attention of R. W. Seton-Watson, then a young man whose genius was at its spate, who wrote them up in very great detail.[3] They undoubtedly did much deserved harm to Rauch's regime in Croatia, and to Aehrenthal's credit in the Chancelleries of Europe; an incidental effect of them was to raise still higher the reputation of Professor Masaryk, who took a prominent part for the defence in both of them.

Yet it would be a gross error to suppose that the collapse of the trials proved either that pro-Serb irredentism did not exist in Bosnia or Croatia, or that it was not being fostered from Serbia. The Slovenska Jug itself had, all official whitewash notwithstanding, been so heavily compromised at the trials that the Serbian Government had to dissolve it, but in its place came a new society, the *Narodna Obrana* (National Defence), dedicated to the same purpose of furthering Serbia's ambition for national expansion. This society, too, was nominally 'cultural', but the propaganda, open and secret, issued by it was so violent as to make the adjective a mockery; and after 1911[4] there stood behind it, and in close connection with it, another society, the *Ujedinjenje Ili Smrt* (Union or death), more commonly known as the *Cerna Ruka* (Black Hand), whose objects, and the methods advocated by it, were militant in the extreme. They included the assassination of opponents, especially in the Monarchy; the execution of these was usually left to young Bosnian Serbs, Austro-Hungarian subjects, who were organized in a subsidiary secret society, the *Mlada Bosna* (Young Bosnia).

---

[1] According to Redlich, *Schicksalsjahre*, p. 44, Aehrenthal told him (on 9 January 1910) that he had asked Friedjung to 'collaborate' in a Press campaign against Serbia, with the object suggested above. Friedjung had then 'done the rest with Sektionschef Jettel'. This version, if true, saddles Friedjung with more conscious complicity and less naïveté than was generally supposed at the time.

[2] Actually, there were three cases: one by fifty-two Deputies of the Coalition against Friedjung; one by Supilo alone against Friedjung and a third by Supilo and two others against the *Reichspost*. Being based on the same material, they were taken together.

[3] His *Southern Slav Question* contains very full accounts of both trials.

[4] The date of foundation was 9–22 May 1911. For the history of the organization see Uebersberger, op. cit., pp. 279 ff., and Dedijer, op. cit., passim.

The Black Hand was only nominally unofficial. Its head was Lieut.-Colonel Dragutin Dimitriević, Chief of the Intelligence Department of the Serbian General Staff, and most of its leaders were serving officers. The Serbian Government, while not necessarily initiated into all its plans, was well aware of its objectives and its preferred methods, and the Crown Prince Alexander contributed to its funds. It is true that before long differences over policy in Macedonia caused a coolness between Dimitriević on the one hand, and the Court and the Radical Party on the other. Alexander founded a second officers' league, the White Hand, which in 1917 liquidated its rival after the famous 'Salonica Trial'. The key to the 'riddle of Serajevo' may well lie in the ambivalent relationship between the two leagues.[1]

The almost limitless resentment which the Serbian agitation evoked in Austria was a very important factor in the history of the Monarchy's last crisis. Conrad advised preventive war here also, and during the annexation crisis Austria came very near following his advice. Aehrenthal himself had by now come round to the view that the only ultimate solution of Austro-Serb relations was for the Monarchy to incorporate 'the non-Bulgarian parts of Serbia' (letting the 'Bulgarian parts' go to Bulgaria). International pressure and other causes, which included the old one of financial stringency, made him draw back now, but again and again during the Monarchy's last years of 'peace' one finds the view expressed that Serbia's provocations were so intolerable as to exclude any peaceful solution whatever. The phrase 'better an end with terror than terror without end' became almost a commonplace expression of a widely held view that the Monarchy must either crush Serbia, or itself go under. It is this argument which is adduced by Austrian historians to justify her declaration of war on Serbia in 1914. It is not perhaps altogether easy to reconcile with the same historians' contention that the Monarchy was nefariously pulled to pieces by outside forces, in spite of its inner solidarity. But logic does not always govern political emotion, and the legitimacy of Austria's irritation was unquestionable, as was its intensity.

Serbia could afford these tones towards Austria because she was now under very open Russian protection. Izvolski had, indeed, soon paid for his *blamage* with his post: he went to Paris as Ambassador, and was succeeded as Foreign Minister by Sazonov, who had not his predecessor's personal grudge against the Austrians, and was certainly not anxious for war. But Russia was now seriously alarmed at the prospect that Austria, backed by Russia, might become over-powerful in the Balkans, and convinced of the need of countering this by an active policy of her own. The policy favoured by Sazonov, towards which, indeed, Izvolski had already been feeling his way – the Raccognigi Agreements, which were concluded while Izvolski was still Foreign Minister reflected it – was not to attempt territorial

---

[1] Dedijer, op. cit., provides the reader rather with a glimpse of the complexity of the problems than a key to them.

expansion for Russia herself, which would be opposed too strongly by the Powers, but to strengthen the Balkan States, individually and collectively, and to bring them under Russian patronage. With this end in view, he set himself to organize the Balkan States in a 'Balkan League'.

The further development of the 'Eastern Question' was dominated by Russia's pursuit of this policy, the only secondary motif in it being that of Italy's attack on Turkey in 1911, which was almost episodic for Austria. The incorrigible Conrad wanted the occasion seized to 'settle accounts' with Italy, but Aehrenthal again rejected the idea, on grounds both of honour and policy (he still did not regard Italy as lost irretrievably) and made only the one condition, that the fighting should not extend to the Continental Balkans. As this was fulfilled, Austria and Italy remained allies (the Triple Alliance was even renewed again, unaltered, on 5 December 1912), although if possible, less cordial ones than ever.

The Italo-Turkish war did not interrupt Sazonov's efforts, but gave the results of them a turn which he had not intended. Thinking that it would be impossible for Russia to take Constantinople herself, and not wishing to see Bulgaria or Greece there in her place, he had wanted to include Turkey in his Balkan League, but the weakness of the Turks, as revealed in Tripolis, was too much of a temptation to the young Balkan States, and Serbia, Montenegro, Bulgaria and Greece concluded a network of alliances between themselves with the object of taking advantage of it.

In all this activity, Russia played a curiously ambiguous role, the complexity of which was due in part to the divided councils prevailing between the more conservative Foreign Ministry in Petersburg and the enthusiastically Slavophile Russian Ministers, Hartwig in Belgrade and Neklyudov in Sofia. Russia was kept informed of the negotiations and resultant Treaties, and even accepted the role of arbiter between Serbia and Bulgaria over the allocation of part of Macedonia. Yet Sazonov continued to insist that there must be no aggression against Turkey. When the intentions of the Balkan States became apparent, Russia even collaborated once more with Austria in a joint Note warning them that no change in the Balkan *status quo* would be permitted. But on the very day on which this was presented (8 October 1912), Montenegro, first of the four, declared war, and the League won such rapid successes that it was soon obvious that the *status quo* was past saving. Berchtold, who had succeeded Aehrenthal as Austrian Foreign Minister on the latter's death in the previous February, refused to take the step, repeatedly pressed on him by the 'forward party', of letting Austria join in the competition for territorial acquisitions ('settling accounts' with Serbia during the process) and confined himself to efforts to keep the readjustments of the map as innocuous as possible, and here he found himself, for once, in agreement with Italy, but at odds, not only with Serbia and Montenegro, but with Russia. In the complex negotiations which occupied the winter of 1912–13,

Berchtold obtained the creation of an independent Albania, and Serbian and Montenegrin forces which had occupied territory earmarked for Albania were forced to withdraw, although to achieve this, an ultimatum had to be sent to Serbia and at one stage it looked as though Austria would after all be involved in war. But the settlement still left Serbia and Montenegro substantially enlarged, now territorially contiguous, brimming with self-confidence and intensely inflamed against the Monarchy. 'The first round is over,' said Pašić, the Serbian Prime Minister, 'now we must prepare for the second, against Austria.'

The situation changed once again after this. One of Russia's great difficulties in negotiating the Balkan League had been the rivalry between Serbia and Bulgaria over Macedonia, and in this had lain Austria's great hope of preventing the formation of the League: but she could offer Bulgaria no price comparable to what membership of the League could give her. Now, in July 1913, the Balkan allies quarrelled over the division of the spoils, and fighting broke out between Bulgaria on the one side and her former allies, reinforced by Roumania and later by Turkey, on the other. Bulgaria had now a natural community of interests with Austria, especially as she had quarrelled with Russia),[1] and Berchtold would have liked to take advantage of this. But she could not support Bulgaria without offending Roumania, who was claiming territory from her. Both the German Kaiser and Francis Ferdinand, amongst others, were very hostile to the King of Bulgaria, and strongly predisposed in favour of Roumania, so that all that Berchtold was able to do was to give Bulgaria a little hesitant diplomatic support, which availed her nothing, and offended Roumania *pro rata*. From now on – if it had not been the case before – the Monarchy's alliance with Roumania was as hollow as that with Italy. The Roumanian and Russian Royal families themselves fraternized. Roumanian publicists attacked the Monarchy – in this case the Hungarian half of it – almost as venomously as the Serbian and Italian.[2] Count Ottakar Czernin, who was sent to Bucharest in November 1913, reported that the Austro-Roumanian Treaty was not worth the paper it was written on.[3] Sazonov's view was that Roumania 'would work with the side which turned out to be the stronger, and offered her more'.[4]

In any case, the Monarchy could certainly not rely on Roumania to help her against Serbia, and probably not against Russia unless the war had already been three-quarters won without her. If the Monarchy got into

---

[1] In May 1913, Sazonov, misunderstanding a phrase in a Bulgarian note, had jumped to the conclusion that Bulgaria was in league with Austria, and denounced all Russia's agreements with her from 1902 onward.

[2] Several Austrian writers date the beginning of Roumanian irredentism as beginning now. In fact, as we have seen, it was nothing like so new a plant.

[3] Czernin to Berchtold, 7 December 1913, *Aussenpolitik*, VII. 901-2.

[4] Sazonov to Nicholas II, 29 June 1914, *M. O. III*, III. 339.

difficulties, she would very likely find Roumania among those seeking to profit from them.

There was another field in which Russia was working directly against the Monarchy. Neo-Slavism had gone under, but Russia had rediscovered the Ruthenes. In 1906 or 1907 a 'Galician-Russian Society' was founded under the Presidency of Count Vladimir Bobrinskij, a leader of the Russian Right, who had repeatedly voiced his belief that the security of the Russian Empire demanded that its flag should be planted on the Carpathians.[1] The agitation which he developed was undoubtedly irredentist in purpose, although it chiefly took the form of propaganda for conversion from the Uniate to the Orthodox Church. His collaborator in chief in Galicia was the Old Ruthene leader, Dr Markow.

Bobrinskij attended the Prague Conference of 1908. After it he toured Galicia and the Bukovina, making propaganda and enlisting agents so openly that the Austrian authorities issued a warrant for his arrest. But the agitation went on apace, financed by subsidies given (with astounding openness)[2] to individuals, or sometimes in other ways: thus when the Galician harvest failed in 1913, large sums were sent from Russia to relieve the distress. Students' hostels were founded, in which students were put up free and taught Pan-Slavism; pilgrimages to Kiev organized, and subversive leaflets circulated.[3]

The Monarchy's material defences against these dangers were still far less than adequate. Conrad's agitation for 'active policies' against Italy and Serbia had grown so embarrassing to Aehrenthal that the Foreign Minister had appealed to Francis Joseph, who had supported him, and Conrad had resigned.[4] Auffenberg-Komarow, another protégé of the Archduke's, who succeeded Schönaich as part of the same transaction,[5] carried through the reorganization of the periods of service in the armed forces,[6] and succeeded in

---

[1] Fischel, *Panslawismus*, p. 505.

[2] See the anecdote in Kleinwächter, op. cit., p. 180, of a Ruthene Deputy in the Bukovina who was accused of subverting some of these funds. He did not attempt to deny having received money from Russia, but claimed that he had devoted it all to the cause, deducting only his expenses for going to Vienna to draw it.

[3] One of these, quoted by Hofrat Barwinsky, *Oe. Ungarn und das ukrainische Problem* (Vienna, 1916), said that Russia was first going to liberate the Balkan States (the date was 1913), then the Ruthenes in Galicia 'who are now groaning under the Austrian yoke'.

[4] The audience took place on 15 November 1911. Conrad handed in his resignation on 30 November and was relieved of his post on 2 December. Aerenthal's argument was that Conrad's agitation would drive Italy into changing sides altogether.

[5] Schönaich had offended the Archduke by his over-leniency towards the Hungarian 'national demands' for the Army.

[6] Service in the infantry was reduced from three years to two. It remained at three years in the cavalry and the artillery, and at four in the Navy. An additional 56,400 men were required for the first year to fill the gap.

getting the regular annual intake of recruits raised to 159,500 (91,313 from Austria, 68,187 from Hungary[1]), which would raise the peace strength of the regular army from 295,000 to 350,000 and its war strength from 900,000 to 1,500,000, with corresponding increases in the strengths of the Landwehr (30,000) and the Honvédség (25,000). Considerable sums were spent on new artillery, fortifications, and the Navy, for which a big new programme was adopted at the end of 1911,[2] while other provisions legalized the conscription of men and resources in case of war.

Even this, however, left the strength of the Monarchy's armed forces very low by comparison with other Powers,[3] and its leadership, too, remained unsatisfactory, at least in the Archduke's eyes, although, at his urgent request, Conrad was reinstated in December 1912, when (as part of the same transaction) Auffenberg-Komarow was replaced by F.M.L. Krobatin.

One unfortunate effect of these developments was to re-import the old uncertainty into the Monarchy's financial situation. The cost of two mobilizations, plus that of two partial mobilizations and expenditure on the railways (which also was largely strategic), was heavy.[4] One consideration which undoubtedly weighed with the Monarchy in the fateful days of 1914 was unwillingness to spend both material and emotional capital on a third mobilization not followed by action.

The history of Bosnia-Herzegovina after the annexation is quickly told. The problem of where the provinces belonged in the structure of the Monarchy was never finally settled; in the end, the Common Finance Minister went on representing them in the Delegations.

The proclamation annexing the provinces had promised them 'provincial representation in a form corresponding to the religious traditions and the traditional social structure of their inhabitants'. A Landtag was to be set up on the traditional Austrian pattern, with four Curias, representing respectively 'the principal dignitaries, the persons of education and substance, the urban communes and the rural communes'. A Committee (from which the Serbs absented themselves) was set up to work out the details, and on 17 February

---

[1] Plus 7,100 from Bosnia. For a good short account of these developments see the article by R. Kiszling, Die Entwicklung der Oe U. Wehrmacht, *Berliner Monatshefte* (1934), XII. pp. 735-49.

[2] It provided for the construction of four battle cruisers, three light cruisers and a number of smaller vessels.

[3] The defence budget of the Monarchy in 1911 was still only 420 million kronen. That of Germany, expressed in the same currency, was 1,786 million kronen; of Russia, 1,650; of Great Britain, 1,514; of France, 1,185; and of Italy, 528.

[4] Both halves of the Monarchy were spending large sums in these years (amounting in 1914 to twenty-four per cent of the total expenditure) on the railways. By 1913 the length of these had reached 22,981 km. in Austria and 22,369 km. in Hungary.

1910 there was introduced a statute defining the competence of the Landtag, a franchise law for the elections to it which assigned to each of the three local confessions a fixed quota of mandates, Standing Orders for its procedure, laws on association and assembly, and a law on District Courts.

Elections were held in May 1910 and the Landtag met in June. The Croats formed a coalition with the Moslems, so that the Serbs were left in the minority. As the outbreak of the Balkan Wars brought renewed tension between the Monarchy and Serbia, Burian, whose policy of trusting the Serbs had produced such disappointing results, was replaced on 20 February 1912 by a Pole, Bilinski, who had not unravelled any of the tangles by the time war broke out in July 1914. Almost the Government's only achievement had been a new agrarian law which proved little more effective than its predecessors.[1] For the rest, Bilinski's rule seems to have been gentle enough; as late as the spring of 1914 he was confident that the Serbs of Bosnia were completely loyal.[2]

During these years the political life of Cis-Leithania underwent a surface transformation which could not easily have been anticipated when the period opened. In 1903 the picture was completely stylized, for the Czechs, dissatisfied with the concessions which were all that Koerber could offer them without driving the Germans into hysteria, had reverted to their old tactics of paralysing the work of the Reichsrat by obstruction, and although a number of causes contributed to bring about Koerber's resignation and the appointment of Gautsch to succeed him on 31 December 1904 – he had lost favour with the Monarch for consenting to the 'Széll formula' in the negotiations with Hungary, was having trouble with Parliamentary Parties over Land finances, and was suffering from nervous strain brought about by over-work[3] – the decisive one was probably an offer by Kramař to Goluchowski to call the obstruction off if Gautsch, with whom he was personally friendly, was appointed. But Gautsch (who made few changes in his Ministerial team) was not expected to strike out on any sensationally new line, and in fact made no motions to do so during his first six months of office. Then, however, came Kristóffy's inspiration to break the resistance of the Hungarian 'Independence' politicians by extending the franchise in Hungary. This inevitably stimulated further the already strong demand among the Austrian workers for a similar concession – the Austrian Emperor, people said, could not refuse what the King of Hungary was granting. Gautsch, who was personally against

[1] A kmet tenant could now, if his landlord agreed, buy his holding by paying instalments to the Government, which compensated the landlord. By 1915, when the operation of the law was suspended, only 45,000 peasants out of 145,000 had taken advantage of it, and eighty-nine per cent of them were in arrears with their instalments.
[2] Sieghart, p. 29.
[3] On this, see Charmatz, *Oe. aüssere und innere Politik 1895–1914*, p. 68, Sieghart, op. cit., pp. 61 ff.

any such move,[1] made reservations and objections, but into the middle of the excitement fell the news that the Czar had promised his peoples a Constitution and the convocation of a Duma. Now the workers' demonstrations in Vienna, Prague and many other industrial centres reached formidable proportions, and on 3 November 1905, Francis Joseph – once again ahead of his Ministers on this question – informed Gautsch 'that he had decided to introduce the institution of general suffrage in both halves of the Monarchy'.[2] Gautsch obeyed.

The reform did not, however, go smoothly, for Gautsch decided to adapt it to Austrian conditions in two ways. Firstly, the priority given by most electors to national questions was to be recognized, and those problems removed from the list of contested electoral issues, by re-delimiting constituencies to make them as far as possible uni-national. Secondly, the old advantage formerly possessed by the wealthier and more advanced nationalities was to be perpetuated by weighting the constituencies in their favour. In the key which Gautsch worked out, the total number of presumed German constituencies was left unchanged at 205 and the Czechs got an increase of 12 (from 87 to 99), but the Poles' figure was reduced from 72 to 64, while that of the Ruthenes went up from 10 to 31. As the total number of mandates was to bre aised to 455, the Germans suffered a relative loss, and the Slavs of all types would have outnumbered slightly the non-Slavs (Germans, Italians and Roumanians). The Germans protested strongly, and the Poles, who demanded no less than 118 seats for themselves, so fanatically, that in April Gautsch resigned. His successor, Prince Konrad Hohenlohe, resigned after only a month;[3] then Francis Joseph appointed another permanent official, Freiherr von Beck (another favourite of Francis Ferdinand's),[4] who revised his predecessor's quotas in favour of the Poles and Germans, the new presumptive figures (in a Parliament of 516) being 241 Germans, 97 Czechs, 80 Poles, 34 Ruthenes, 23 Slovenes, 19 Italians[5], 13 Croats, 5 Roumanians and 3 Serbs. For the rest, the franchise was now extended to all males aged twenty-four and upward who had resided for a year in their commune. After passing

[1] Gautsch was an old protégé of Francis Ferdinand's, who was strongly against extending the franchise in Austria.

[2] Sieghart, op. cit., p. 83. It is important that the reform applied only to the two Parliaments; not to the Austrian *Landtage* or the Hungarian Counties.

[3] He had not wanted the appointment, and took the occasion to resign when the Emperor allowed the Hungarians to call their tariff autonomous.

[4] Beck had been the Archduke's tutor. According to Sieghart (p. 93), the chief qualification which the new Minister President had to possess was 'command of the Compromise question'. But Francis Joseph was also glad to find 'a middle-man between himself and his difficult nephew'.

[5] Interestingly, it was now the Italians who, of all peoples of the Monarchy, were getting the highest number of Deputies, relatively to their numbers (1:38,000). Then came the Germans (1:40,000), then, oddly, the Roumanians (1:46,000). The Ruthenes were, as usual, last, with 1:102,000.

through the Herrenhaus with great difficulty, which was overcome only by strong pressure from the Crown,[1] the Bill received the Emperor's sanction on 26 January 1907. Parliament was now dissolved, and new elections held in May.

The resultant Parliament of course presented an entirely new picture.[2] The accustomed vertical stratification by nationalities (which, incidentally, had not worked out quite according to plan, for fewer Germans and Poles had been elected than had been expected, and more Czechs, and there were also four Zionists[3] and one Jewish Democrat, on whom no one had reckoned) was now crossed by horizontal lines. Many of the national parties wore labels committing them to some social or economic ideology, and some of these refused to sit with their national Clubs, while the Social Democrats dispensed with the national epithet altogether. There was, naturally, a swing to the Left. The Christian Socials, although they had concluded an electoral pact with the Catholic People's Party, in the interests of which they had toned down their programme, still retained some of their original inspiration. The Social Democrats had made a big advance, while a number of the Czech, Polish and Ruthene Deputies, and even some of the non-Socialist Germans, were pronouncedly Left-wing in their various fashions.

Austria thus now possessed a Parliament in which almost all classes of the population were represented – a big change indeed from the situation of only a few years, not to speak of decades, before. Yet if we regard 'democracy' as connoting general and equal opportunity to influence policy on the top level, through constitutional channels, we are bound to reject the description given by a distinguished Austrian historian[4] of the effects of the franchise reform as bringing about 'the democratization of Austria', for the good reason that the Reichsrat did not govern Austria. For perhaps eighteen months after the

---

[1] A clause was also added to the Bill limiting the number of life appointments which could be made by the Crown to this House.

[2] The best figures I have been able to find are in Sieghart, op. cit., p. 102, and in the *Encyclopaedia Britannica*, which agree almost exactly; Hugelmann's, op. cit., p. 240, add up to two short and differ in other small ways. The following is probably about right: Christian-Social-Catholic People's Party alliance, 97 (67+30); German Agrarians, 21; German Progressives, 15; German People's Party, 31; German Radicals, 12; Alldeutsche, 3; Czech Agrarians, 28; Young Czechs, 18; Czech People's Party (Clericals), 17; Old Czechs, 7; Czech National Socialists, 9; Czech Realists, 2; Independent Czech, 1; Polish National Democrats, 25; Polish Conservatives, 16; Polish Populists, 17; Polish Centre, 12; Polish Independent Socialist, 1; Young Ruthenes, 25; Old Ruthenes, 4; Slovene Clericals, 18; Slovene Liberals, 5; Italian People's Party, 10; Italian Liberals, 4; Croats, 12; Serbs, 2; Roumanians, 5; Zionists, 4; Jewish Democrat, 1; Social Democrats, 87 (50 Germans, 23 Czechs, 7 Poles, 2 Ruthenes, 5 Italians); independent, 5; seats unfilled, 2.

[3] There is no place here to go into the Zionist movement, but we may recall that the birthplace of the modern movement was Vienna and its spiritual father the Viennese (by birth, Budapest) Jew, Theodor Herzl.

[4] Charmatz, op. cit., p. 8.

reform Beck did preside over something like a genuine Parliamentary government. Half his assistants were permanent civil servants like himself, but the other half were Parliamentarians, drawn from German, Czech and Polish Conservative Parties who had sunk their differences in the face of the emergent forces of the Left, and in return for various political douceurs.[1] But this phase did not last for long. Although, as we have seen,[2] Austria probably gained more in substance than she conceded in the long and exhausting economic negotiations with Hungary, the Archduke blamed Beck for making any concessions whatever, and for that reason, and because he had presided over the electoral reform, turned against his former favourite with extraordinary bitterness.[3] The annexation of Bosnia was in the wind and the military party demanded a 'Government of the strong hand' in view of the international situation. Beck offended Aehrenthal by opposing the annexation. The Czech Great Landlords started a campaign against him when he tried to introduce a reform of the Bohemian Landtag which would have weakened their influence there. On 15 November 1908 he was intrigued out of office by a combined manoeuvre in which these forces were joined by the Christian Socials, who were playing for the Heir Presumptive's favour, and also hoped to bring about a new coalition government with themselves playing the leading part in it. As, however, the parties whom the Christian Socials had hoped to make their partners proved as greedy as themselves, the idea of a genuine Parliamentary coalition had to be given up, and Francis Joseph appointed as the new Minister President another permanent civil servant, Freiherr von Bienerth, whose position differed from Beck's only in the respect that the Archduke and Aehrenthal were, at least for a time, on his side. Bienerth, whose first instructions had been to govern by Parliamentary methods, formed another Cabinet composed mainly of permanent civil servants, with three 'Landsmannminister' representing the Germans, Czechs and Poles respectively, and the Christian Socials, German nationals (whose leading parties formed themselves in February 1910 into a new association, the *Deutscher Nationalverband*[4]) and Conservative Poles gave him enough

---

[1] Thus a Ministry of Public Works was created and given to the Christian Socials, the Czechs received a linguistic concession in the postal services, etc.

[2] See above, p. 763.

[3] The story is told in detail by Sieghart, op. cit., pp. 138 ff. See also Charmatz, op. cit., pp. 82 ff. Kiszling, pp. 112 ff. Another cause of offence was his handling of the case of Wahrmund, a Liberal-thinking Professor in Innsbruck whose lectures had given offence to Catholic circles. Their complaints in turn evoked protests from the other side. Beck let Wahrmund down too lightly for the Archduke's taste.

[4] This was first concluded between the German People's Party and the Progressives, and later joined by the Agrarians, Radicals and the little German Workers' Party. As before, the Social Democrats refused to join it because it was too national and the Alldeutsche because it was not national enough, and this time the Christian Socials also stood out because they thought they could do better for themselves alone.

formal, although unenthusiastic, support to enable him to keep a nominally Parliamentary regime alive for a couple of years. It was, however, a barren period (described by the historian, Friedjung, as one of 'Parliamentary chaos and administrative absolutism'), for whenever Bienerth tried to get the Reichsrat to carry through any constructive measure whatever, one or another of its thirty parties or five independent members contrived to make this impossible; the scenes in the Reichsrat in February 1909 went down to history as the most scandalous on record. Hoping to get a more secure majority, Bienerth dissolved the Reichsrat in May 1911 and held new elections, but in these, although the parties of the *Nationalverband* increased their vote, the Christian Socials, much of whose virtue had gone out of them with their fusion with the Clericals, and more when Lueger died on 10 March 1910, lost heavily,[1] and the Poles were now hopelessly divided.[2] Bienerth resigned, and the Emperor once more fell back on Gautsch, who again tried to get the Czechs to support him, but as usual, the Czechs asked a price which the Germans refused to pay, and Gautsch gave up in despair on 31 October. The Emperor now appointed Count Karl Stürgkh, a Styrian landowner who had left the administrative service in 1891 to enter Parliament as a member of the United German Left, and had held the portfolio of Education (not unsuccessfully) under Bienerth. Stürgkh got together another cabinet of civil servants, with only one professed 'Landsmannminister', the Pole, although Stürgkh paid tribute to German and Czech national susceptibilities by choosing Departmental Ministers from men of those two nationalities. He avoided raising national issues at all in the Reichsrat, and got through necessary business chiefly by extensive use of Paragraph 14. In March 1914 obstruction, chiefly by the Czech Radicals, forced him to adjourn the Reichsrat altogether, and it had not been re-convoked when Austria declared war on Serbia four months later.

So far, then, all that the extension of the franchise had done had been to prove the complete impossibility of governing Cis-Leithania, with its immense complex of sometimes interlocking, sometimes mutually frustrating national, social and economic interests through the medium of a single Parliament on the conventional basis. If, as an Austrian historian has pointed out,[3] the Landtage were sometimes able to carry out more fruitful

---

[1] The Clerical, or rural, wing of the new party held its own well enough, but the Old Guard of the Christian Socials in Vienna was almost wiped out. They got only 7 urban seats (3 in Vienna, out of a possible 33), but 69 in the country.

[2] The main figures were: German National Association, 104 mandates; Schöneriander, 4; Christian Socials, 76; Social Democrats, 82 (49 German, 24 Czech, 9 others, chiefly Poles); Czech Agrarians, 34; Young Czechs, 19; Czech National Socials, 11; other Czech parties, 20; Polish national Democrats, 25; Polish Conservatives, 22; other Polish parties, 33; Ruthenes, 28; Croats and Slovenes, 34; Italians, 16; Roumanians, 5; miscellaneous and non-Party, 16.

[3] Hantsch, *Geschichte*, II. 475.

work, the answer is that the franchise reform had not been extended to them,[1] and further, that many of them had not to cope with the national problem. Where they had to face the same problems as the Reichsrat, they proved equally unable to deal with them.[2]

It was true that Austria had become more democratic in the broader sense that the political weight of the different social classes had shifted considerably. The Christian Socials had, indeed, sacrificed almost all their original inspiration for the sake of office. After the 1907 elections they and the Catholic People's Party had fused, and if the name of the Party which emerged from the process was theirs, the spirit was that of the other component. They were now essentially a Catholic Conservative Party, resting on the rural electorate of the Alpine Lands.[3] But they still had to make most of their appeal to the peasants, who now constituted much the largest class of rural electors, and were emancipating themselves from the spiritual leadership of the big landowners. Even outside the Christian Socials, the peasants were now strongly represented.

The Social Democrat-Trade Union combination had made big advances.[4] Its strength still lay overwhelmingly in Vienna and its environs, and in Bohemia-Moravia; outside these areas, and to a lesser extent, Styria, it was still insignificant. Moreover, as we shall see, even this party had now fallen a prey to national differences. Yet its strength in the key centres of Vienna, Wiener Neustadt, etc., was now sufficient to make it a force with which every Government had to reckon, to the extent of having to find answers to its demands other than that of organized repression, and was to enable it to play a decisive part in the years of the Monarchy's death-agony. The 'Feudals'

[1] It is true that several of the Landtage were reformed during these years to allow more representation to the poorer classes. This proved, however, impossible in the key case of Bohemia.

[2] The reason why Austria had to enter the World War without a Reichsrat was that the Germans had made the Bohemian Landtag unworkable by their obstruction and the Czechs had retorted that if the Landtag could not work, neither should the Reichsrat. The Landtage in several other provinces, especially where Southern Slavs and Italians clashed, were little more orderly than that of Prague. One may quote a heartfelt remark by the Landeshauptmann of Silesia: 'God forbid that the general franchise should ever be introduced into the Landtage, for if that ever happened, it would have to be extended to the communes, and that would mean reddest anarchy and the ruin of the State' (cit. Kiszling, op. cit., p. 116).

[3] They continued to hold the municipality of Vienna, because the new municipal elections were not yet due there.

[4] Brügel, *Geschichte*, V. 140 ff., gives some more figures for 1913, which, however, are again incomplete. He gives the German national section of the Party as having 142,027 'organized members', and the political Vereine, which were the basis of it, 108,075, 42,705 of them in Vienna. The 'Centralists' in Bohemia had 14,200 members, the Czech 'Separatist Party' 17,000. The total Trade Union membership was 428,363 (322,000 German, 70,000 Czech, 20,000 Polish, 9,000 Italian, 6,000 Slovene, 1,000 Ruthene). The membership of the Czech Separatist Trade Unions numbered 107,263. Only 16,579 members were organized in Galicia, 6,464 in the Tirol and 5,200 in the Littoral and Dalmatia.

were now almost confined to the Herrenhaus, and the old Party of capital was represented only by Plener's handful of followers.

So far as social questions were concerned, Austria might have evolved with time into something like a Parliamentary democracy. The national question, however, was proving as intractable as ever.

Against this statement, when it is made, is often adduced the fact that during these years several Crownlands succeeded in evolving satisfactory *modus vivendi* between their local nationalities. The earliest and most famous of these was the 'Moravian Settlement',[1] reached in November 1905. Under this, the first Curia of the Landtag and its Standing Committees, composed of the two virilist members[2] and the representatives of the Great Landowners, was left bi-national, while the other Curias were divided in agreed proportions between Czechs and Germans, each nationality electing its own representatives, for which purpose electors were registered in national 'catasters', compiled on the basis of free declaration.[3] Either local language could be used equally in any business. The same proportional system was applied to the various vocational, etc., bodies. In local units the language was decided by the local majority, but a 20% minority could claim to be dealt with officially in its own language. In all matters of interest to one nationality alone (schools, etc.) appointments were made only by that nationality, which paid for such appointments out of its own budget. In 1910 the Bukovina introduced a similar system of national catasters (in this case, four: German, Ruthene, Roumanian, Polish).[4] There were six curias, all but the first uni-national. Here German was by general consent used as the language of the Landtag.[5] Negotiations also took place in Galicia, through the mediation of the Ruthene Metropolitan, Count Szeptycki, between Poles and Ruthenes, and a *Landesgesetz* was actually passed and sanctioned by the Crown in July 1914, although never applied, owing to the outbreak of war. This again provided for separate voting to the Landtag, in which the Ruthenes would have received 61 mandates out of the total of 227 – a figure far below that to which their numbers entitled them but still much bigger than

---

[1] For a full description of this law see Hugelmann, op. cit., pp. 226 ff. The author of the compromise was Baron von Chlumecky, Minister of Agriculture (later, of Commerce) in the Auersperg-Lasser Government, a Deputy for nearly thirty years and a man well known to and highly respected by both nationalities.

[2] The Prince-Archbishop of Olmütz and the Bishop of Brünn.

[3] The figures were: urban communes, 20 Germans, 20 Czechs; Chambers of Commerce, 9 Germans, 9 Czechs; rural communes, 14 Germans, 30 Czechs; general Curia, 6 Germans, 14 Czechs. The Standing Committee was composed of 2 Great Landowners, 2 Germans and 4 Czechs.

[4] The local Jews were counted in with the Germans, the Magyars with the Roumanians, the Armenians with the Poles and the Lipovans with the Ruthenes.

[5] Hugelmann, pp. 728 ff.

they had ever previously achieved. At the same time, they were promised also their own University, and certain other cultural concessions.[1] Even in Bohemia talks for a settlement between representatives of the two nationalities got so far that when they broke down, in 1912, one of the negotiators said that 'only the thickness of a sheet of paper' had separated the two parties.

It would, however, be a grave mistake to draw from these words, as certain Austrian historians have tried to do, the deduction that the Czech and the German peoples in Bohemia, or in the Monarchy, had come within a hair's-breadth of composing their differences. The hope of a *rapprochement*, such as it was, had come only after years in which Czechs had made work in the Reichsrat impossible by their obstruction, and Germans had done the same in the Prague Landtag, where business had broken down completely, since the procedure of the Landtag contained no Para. 14 to enable the authorities to carry on in spite of the politicians. Other negotiators, in earlier days (so under Taaffe, in 1892) had actually reached agreement, with no result whatever, and as then, so now, those representatives of each nation who had sincerely tried to reach a *modus vivendi* with the other were virulently attacked by their kinsmen for traitors, German and Czech extremists vieing with one another for the credit of having wrecked the treacherous attempt. In fact, the Bohemian problem remained as intractable as ever up to the end of the Monarchy (and beyond it); in 1914 the Bohemian Landtag was out of action, like the Reichsrat, and for similar reasons.

And it was generally true that during these years the national problem of Cis-Leithania lost nothing either of its venom, or of its priority in the minds of most of the peoples. The one quarter in which national emotions looked to be going off the boil was that of the non-Socialist Germans. In 1903 Schönerer quarrelled with Wolf, who took his followers, and many of Schönerer's, out of the Party, with the result that the number of 'Schönerianer' Deputies fell to three in 1907 (when Schönerer himself failed to secure re-election), and only went up by one more in 1911. The *Nationalverband*, unlike the *Gemeinbürgschaft*, did not adopt an agreed programme on national issues, and the Christian Socials often voted against the other German Parties. Generally speaking, the German Parties supported the Minister President in Parliament, and refrained from making intolerable nuisances of themselves.

And the drop in temperature was not only apparent. It is true that the differences between Schönerer and Wolf were primarily personal, but the latter, with his followers, refused to stand for the dissolution of the Monarchy, while the lack of unity between the other Parties reflected a real

[1] Hugelmann, pp. 715 ff. According to Steed, op. cit., p. 128, Francis Joseph had exercised pressure on the Poles to make them consent to this agreement. The promise of a university was, indeed, whittled down to one of a Faculty of Law, and the outbreak of war made an excuse to postpone granting even that.

reversion, if only a partial one, to the feeling that other issues could be more important than purely national ones.

But this was simply because the Germans had stopped being frightened. One of their historians has described Thun's Ministry as 'the last attempt to rule against the Germans through the forms of Parliamentary rule by majority'. What followed was 'a change of system'; Koerber's Ministry 'answered the demand of the first positive German national programme (sc., the Deutsche Vereinigung's programme of 1897) 'for a neutral Ministry'.[1] The Germans regarded all Ministries after Koerber's, except perhaps that of Gautsch, in the same light.

But the Ministries were, of course, not really neutral. By refusing to let the Reichsrat raise national questions, and insisting on the maintenance of the *status quo* unless the parties concerned agreed to alter it, they were in reality overriding the principles of pure Parliamentary democracy; for the administrative *status quo* was still clearly, on balance, favourable to the Germans, whereas the introduction of general suffrage had already placed them in a minority in the Reichsrat. The Germans' satisfaction was thus achieved by a tacit alliance with the bureaucracy, at the expense of the other peoples, and at the expense of the fair application of that very Parliamentary system for which the German Liberals had once fought so hard.

The more logical among the nationally-minded Germans were already actively supporting the course – to which necessity increasingly drove the Ministers President of the time – of dispensing with the Reichsrat altogether and governing 'administratively', i.e., through the bureaucracy, for good and all. In other words, they were jettisoning the last remnants of Liberalism and reverting to a sort of neo-Josephinianism, based, like its prototype, on the German element in Austria. It was, indeed, possible to maintain that as conditions had developed, this was the only way of keeping the wheels of public life turning at all, but it was simply childish to suppose that a system which had begun to break down as soon as national feeling awoke in the Monarchy could be reimposed as a permanent solution for the Austrian problem at a stage when that feeling had become intense among all its peoples, including – not least important – the Germans themselves.

Among the non-Germans, there was no abatement of national passions and aspirations, and it was also less generally true than it had been that the national struggle was one 'for' Austria, not 'against' her. Irredentism made further advances in the Italian areas, in small part as a reaction against genuine grievances, such as the unsolved problem of the Italian University, but much more, as before, in reaction to the international situation as relations between Austria and Italy deteriorated and the Government-encouraged irredentist agitation grew ever more unbridled.

There were dangerous developments among the Czechs. The results of the

[1] Patzelt, op. cit., p. 63.

1907 elections, giving as they did, in spite of the electoral geometry, a majority in the Reichsrat (however minute) to the Slavs against the combined Germans, Italians and Roumanians, encouraged the Kramař school of politicians who thought in such spacious terms in their belief that the Monarchy could be turned into a State dominated politically by its Slavs, and to them Neoslavism came like manna from heaven.

In theory Neoslavism was, of course, by definition not directed against the existence of the Monarchy, but the distinction between a strongly Russophile movement which was non-irredentist and one which was secretly irredentist was one which it would not be easy to preserve in a conflict between the Monarchy and Russia.[1] Austro-Neoslavism was very different from the Austro-Slavism of the previous century, nor did the difference escape the Russians.

Although Kramař was the leading representative among the Czechs of this new movement, many other Czech politicians shared many of his views. The annexation, in particular, evoked extremely tumultuous scenes. Czechs called up for military service appeared in mourning bands. The Czechs, alone among the peoples of the Monarchy, boycotted the celebrations of Francis Joseph's sixty-year jubilee. The black and yellow flags were torn down in Prague, and Klofač, the 'National Socialist' leader, announced that 'besides the flag of the old Dynasty, I know only one flag, that of the Kingdom of Bohemia, because we are primarily and exclusively Bohemian patriots'. Precisely in these days which ought to have demonstrated the loyalty of the Czech people, a state of emergency had to be proclaimed in Prague, and the Landtag dissolved. After further fruitless attempts to make it workable, the Landtag was replaced in 1913 by an 'Imperial-Royal Administrative Commission'. And while the Czechs, as always, led the Monarchy's army of Russophiles, they were not its sole component. The Polish National Democrats of Galicia, whom the extension of the franchise made into a considerable force (they emerged from both the 1907 and the 1911 elections as the strongest single Polish Party, and their leader, Glombinski, consequently presided over the Polish Club in the Reichsrat and sat in the Government),[2] took the same view as their sister party in Russia of the possibility, and desirability, of a Polish-Russian reconciliation, and they found allies in the so-called 'Podolian Conservatives', i.e., the great East Galician landlords some of whose estates lay across the Russian frontier, who felt their position threatened by the Ukrainian national movement, and combined with the Russians against it. Among these was the Statthalter of Galicia, Potocki,

---

[1] Zeman, op. cit., pp. 16–17, quotes a secret memorandum sent by Kramař to a Russian friend in May 1914, outlining his plans for 'a Slav confederation ruled from St Petersburg', to be brought into being after a war between Russia and the Monarchy, which Kramař assumed would result in the disintegration of the Monarchy.

[2] He was Minister of Railways in 1911.

who paid for his policy with his life, for in April 1908, he was assassinated by a Ukrainophile Ruthene student.[1]

It is true that much of the Galician Poles' enthusiasm for Russia vanished when the renewed Russification set in in the autumn of 1908; among the nobles, the pro-Austrian 'Cracow group' was much stronger than the Podolians, and the Galician socialists, under the influence of Pilsudski and other *émigrés* from Russian Poland, also took the Austrian side. Yet after 1905 the Austrian Government was no longer able to trust its Poles nearly so implicitly as it had between 1870 and that date.[2]

On the figures, the tangible results of the Russian agitation among the Ruthenes do not look very impressive. In the 1907 elections only 5 Russophiles were returned to the Reichsrat, against 22 Young Ruthenes, and in 1911 the number was down to 2; one of their leaders then polled only 581 votes against 25,788 in a straight fight against a Young Ruthene opponent.[3] The 1910 census recorded only three Orthodox villages in Galicia, with 2,770 inhabitants (0·04% of the population of the province).[4] The figure had certainly increased by 1914, but the current phrase of 'mass conversions' seems to be an exaggeration.

The Austrian authorities long attached little importance to the movement. Only in 1914 did they suddenly become alive to it, and suddenly put four persons on trial for treasonable activities, the prosecution maintaining that propaganda to persuade a person to change his religion to the Orthodox faith was treasonable. At the same time, the Hungarian Courts tried a number of persons on similar charges. High treason trials had become rather unpopular since the Friedjung fiasco, and the Lemberg jury (composed entirely of Poles) acquitted all four defendants; the Hungarian Courts were more severe, but still not sensationally so.[5] But the Austrian Government was now really alarmed; Berchtold, in particular, took the movement very seriously. 'I am not exaggerating,' he wrote to Stürgkh, 'when I say that our relations with Russia ... will depend in the future on our success in frustrating the Russification of the Ruthenes.'[6] And he was probably right. The conversions were not artificial: it is highly unlikely that the rolling roubles

---

[1] The assassin, a certain Siczynski, was sentenced to life imprisonment, but escaped after three years and made his way to the USA, where he became a leader of the Ukrainian colony. I met him in London in 1931.

[2] When the Prussian Government initiated the expropriation of Polish estates in Prussian Poland, the Austrian Poles even started a boycott against imports from German Austria. And cf. Redlich, *Schicksalsjahre*, II. 119 (ad. 3 June 1916): 'Since 1905 the Poles, including their Ministers, have for the most part adopted a Russophile attitude and openly described their existence in Austria as now constituting only a disagreeable "provisorium".'

[3] Zeman, p. 4.

[4] The figure for the Bukovina is uninformative, since the Roumanian population there was Orthodox already.

[5] Thirty-two persons were sentenced to a total of 391½ years imprisonment.

[6] Zeman, op. cit., p. 12.

got as far as any of the unfortunate converts themselves.[1] But they reflected a widepsread, if not perhaps always conscious feeling. The Orthodix Church, besides the direct material advantages of membership of it,[2] seems to possess a *mystique* which has a peculiar appeal to the Slavonic soul. It used certainly to identify itself with Moscow, and while it is probable that few of the peasant converts were consciously disloyal, many of them found it impossible to distinguish between the Ruski Czar in Petersburg and the other Czar in Vienna.[3] Moreover, their total ignorance of the facts made it easy to persuade them that their condition would be easier under another Little Father.

Berchtold, indeed, found it hard to suggest a remedy, for he went on: 'We must absolutely avoid, when supporting the Ukrainians, putting the Poles in such a position that they might one day become receptive to Russian influences.'

The position in the Bukovina was complicated almost beyond comprehension by the extension of the franchise, which led to the emergence of a number of new parties and groups – a Social Democrat, a Christian Social, and others, some of which adopted, on principle, a non-national basis, while in others, social and economic conditions having grown very critical in this province (in the same way, and for the same reasons, as in Galicia), the representatives of the poorer classes were prepared to sink their national differences in a common struggle against the landowners and/or the Jewish middle-men. A 'Democratic Party' founded in 1900 by Dr Aurel Ritter von Onciul and a 'Freethinking Association' (*Freisinniger Verband*) with which it allied itself, both included representatives of the non-Roumanian nationalities. Further, as we have said, the various nationalities evolved a model machinery for conducting the public affairs of the Duchy. But the extreme, irredentist Roumanians, although still constituting only a small minority of the people, were probably rather on the increase than the reverse.

Unhappy but convincing evidence of the continued, and increasing, predominance of the national factor in the life of the Monarchy was furnished by the fortunes of the Social Democrat Party, within which another national conflict broke out soon after the Brünn settlement had been reached.[4] This

---

[1] When an Englishman visited some villages of converts, their inhabitants protested to him with tears in their eyes that they had never received a rouble. See R. K. Birkbeck, *Life and Letters of W. J. Birkbeck*, p. 282, cit. May, op. cit., p. 431.

[2] The Orthodox Church levied no tithe; the village Pope was remunerated (very modestly) out of subscriptions levied off his parishioners.

[3] Kleinwächter, pp. 123-4, has another story, dating, indeed, from the war period, of a Ruthene peasant in the Bukovina who was asked how the Russian troops had behaved in 1915-16 when they were occupying his village. His reply was that it had not been too bad; 'only when the Czar got angry and sent the Honvéds, it was terrible.'

[4] A convenient account of this controversy will be found in G. D. H. Cole, *The Second International*, vol. III, part II, pp. 532 ff. See also Brügel, *Geschichte*, V. 77 ff. In 1911 the German and Czech Socialist Deputies in the Reichsrat sat in separate Parliamentary Clubs.

time the Trade Unions were the bone of contention. The Czechs wanted a separate Trade Union organization in Bohemia, and a recognized right of the Trade Unions controlled by Prague to enrol Czech workers in other parts of the Monarchy. The German-Austrians insisted that the Unions had to remain unitary: it was impossible to have workers in the same area, even the same enterprise, belonging to different national unions. The Czechs then complained that their German colleagues were 'denationalizing' Czech workers. After complaining to the Trade Union Congress in 1905, they appealed in 1907 to the International Socialist Congress, and when the decision went against them, refused to accept it and formed what amounted to a separate Party, with its own political organization and Trade Unions. They did not, indeed, altogether abandon the principles of Hainfeld; they rejected the 'Böhmisches Staatsrecht' and continued to stand for an Austria organized as a federation of free and equal peoples, and were hated accordingly by the bourgeois Czech national parties.

The other national sections of the Party remained affiliated to it, but were little less independent. Both the Poles and the Italian sections followed policies dictated by national considerations.

The non-Socialist political parties with social bases (which included a fair number of workers' parties which refused to join the Social Democrats precisely because of their international character[1]) regularly sided with the specifically national parties on any national issue. If the regular commissioned ranks of the Army (and up to a point, the long-service N.C.O.s), most of the higher grades of the central civil service, the bulk of the aulic aristocracy, the episcopate and most of the German members of the lower grades of the clergy, still thought in the old terms, these were now about all who did so. The civil services of the Lands divided almost entirely on national lines, and here even senior posts had often to be given to nationalists, as price for their party's vote in the Landtag or the Reichsrat. The national parties of Slavs and Italians were as often as not led by their clergy, and the reserve officers seldom adopted the outlook of their professional brothers.

It was still true that only a relatively small fraction of the peoples of the Monarchy wanted to leave it. In the great majority of cases they were still manoeuvring for position within the existing Monarchy. A feature distinguishing these years from those preceding them was the increased frequency of the assumption that such plans need not consider the Dualist system, nor even the territorial integrity of Hungary, as immutable data. The ideas of

---

[1] These included several German groups and the Czech 'National Socialists' or 'National Workers' Party', founded in 1898 under Wenzel Choc, Georg Stribny and Wenzel Klofac. Of them it was said that 'they outbid the Young Czechs on constitutional (staatsrechtlich) questions, the Social Democrats on social ones, and everything that had gone before in their readiness to obstruct in the Reichsrat' (Sieghart, op. cit., p. 329).

many of the Czechs, Southern Slavs and Roumanians envisaged a complete reconstruction of the Monarchy, as, confessedly or not, did those of many of the Social Democrat thinkers. The Christian Socials' Party Conference of 1905 adopted a resolution condemning 'the deprivation of the non-Magyar Nationalities of their rights', and demanding that the 'Empire' (Reich) 'be set on an united, consolidated basis in place of the present rotten form of State'.

These ideas were, of course, encouraged by the Heir Presumptive's notorious hostility to the ruling regime in Hungary, for it was almost universally assumed that when he came to the throne, he would enforce radical changes in the structure of the Monarchy at the expense of that element which he so openly detested. This supposed intention of his made him the object of many high hopes while he lived, and has even caused some later writers to write him down as a great statesman. It is difficult to see the justification for these praises. It was easy enough to see the defects in the Dualist system: the test of statesmanship would be the ability to provide something better to put in its place, and if there is one lesson which the history of the Monarchy should teach, it is that there was never, at any time, any ideal answer to its problems. It is, as a matter of fact, quite uncertain what Francis Ferdinand would have done, or tried to do, if he had ever really come to the throne, for he changed his mind on the point many times.[1] The plan first favoured by him seems to have been a sort of re-edition of the system of 1850, a reorganization of the Monarchy into a system of federated provinces, Hungary being broken up into four or five of these, and Bohemia and Galicia into two each. Then he took up the idea, with which his name is most often associated, of replacing the Dualist system by a 'Trialist' one, the third component of which was to be constituted out of the Serb and Croat areas of the Monarchy.[2] This, however, did not last long: he was put off it by the Fiume Resolutions and the Serbo-Croat fraternization.[3] Later he showed some interest in a plan put forward in 1906 by Aurel Popovici, the Transylvanian Roumanian of 'Memorandum'[4] fame, in his book *Die Vereinigten Staaten Gross-Oesterreichs*,[5] but there is no evidence that he proposed

[1] On this subject see Kiszling, pp. 250 ff., far the fullest account of Francis Ferdinand's various plans. The earlier biographies are scrappy on the subject.

[2] Nearly all descriptions of this plan use the phrase 'Southern Slav areas', but I cannot find that Francis Ferdinand ever thought of including the Slovenes of Austria in it.

[3] Oddly enough, Francis Ferdinand was a 'Yugoslav' in the sense that he held Serbs, Croats and Slovenes to be one people (Margutti, p. 125), but before 1906 he does not seem to have drawn the obvious conclusion.

[4] See above, p. 732.

[5] This was a plan for reorganizing the Monarchy into sixteen 'States' (German Austria, German Bohemia, German Moravia with Silesia, Czech Bohemia and Moravia, Magyar Hungary, Roumanian Transylvania, Croatia-Slavonia, Polish West Galicia, Ruthene East Galicia, Slovakia, Carniola, the Voivodina, Szekel-Land, Trentino-Trieste, Dalmatia, Bosnia-Herzegovina), each with its own Government, Parliament and judiciary, but all subject to a strong central authority. For the rest, there is nothing original or particularly

seriously to adopt it. In the spring of 1914 he had committed another plan to paper: this was to postpone his coronation in Hungary, appoint a Ministry with a General at its head and non-Magyar Ministers of the Interior and Justice, enact general franchise by *octroi* and then have a 'people's Parliament' reform the Constitution.[1] He might quite possibly have changed his mind yet again, even towards his avowed enemies, for his bullying manner concealed a deep inner irresolution. Baron Schönaich – not, indeed, a friendly witness – once prophesied of him that 'he would make more concessions in twenty-four hours than Francis Joseph had made in twenty-four years',[2] and there are other witnesses to his essential instability.

Whether any of the Archduke's plans would really have set the Monarchy on a more solid basis, or whether whichever he chose would simply have initiated another period of frustrating experiment, like that of 1859–67, must remain for ever doubtful, for the question was never put to the test. The Army manoeuvres for 1914 were arranged to take place in Bosnia, beginning on 25 June. The close of them brought the Archduke, in his capacity of Inspector General, to Sarajevo precisely on 28 June – Vidov Dan, the anniversary of the Battle of Kossovo, where independent Serbia had been crushed by the Turks in 1389, and ever since charged for all Serbs with a peculiar national emotion. It was obviously a provocative day on which to parade Habsburg rule over Bosnia, and several warnings had been received that the Archduke would be unwise to expose himself, but he did not lack courage, and preferred to ignore them. His wife accompanied him. On the fatal morning a bomb was thrown at the cortège as it drove into Sarajevo from the small summer resort of Ilidže where Francis Ferdinand had spent the previous night. It bounced off the hood of the Archduke's car and exploded under one of those following, severely wounding one of its occupants, but leaving the Archduke and his wife untouched; but three-quarters of an hour later, when the couple were driving to the hospital to visit the wounded officer, a singular series of mischances brought their car to a halt immediately opposite another of the band of assassins, who fired on them with a revolver, mortally wounding both. She died almost immediately, he, ten minutes after her.

Both the unsuccessful and the successful assassins, and all the other persons arrested on the spot, or immediately after, in connection with the crime, were Bosnian Serbs, and Austrian subjects, but the Austrian Government at once suspected Serbian complicity. An investigator sent down to Sarajevo,

---

profound in Popovici's work, which is simply one of the innumerable blue-prints for re-organizing the Monarchy which crowd the shelves of libraries. It appealed to the Archduke because, in spite of the author's past, it saw the future of Transylvania as lying inside the Monarchy.

[1] Redlich, *Schicksalsjahre*, I. 230, II. 66.
[2] See Kiszling, op. cit., p. 315.

Sektionsrat Wiesner, reported that there was 'no proof, nor even grounds for supposing that the Serbian Government was privy to the murder, or the preparations for it', and to this day it has not been possible to prove the contrary quite conclusively. But the investigators had no difficulty in establishing the facts that the assassins had been supplied with arms from the Serbian army arsenal in Kragujevac, trained in their use and smuggled across the frontier by a Serbian organization – that they put the blame on the wrong society, designating the Narodna Obrana as the culprits and missing the very existence of the Black Hand, did not affect the real point; and this discovery, coming on top of so many experiences of acts of similar nature, if less sensational, committed during previous years, was enough for the Austrian Government. The hornets' nest must be smoked out, once and for all, and nothing less than war would suffice.[1]

When the consultations began, the only man among all the Emperor's responsible advisers, civilian or military, to take a different view was Tisza, who not only was (it appears) far less satisfied than the others that a war against Serbia could be localized, but also feared the result of even a victorious war, since he did not want the number of Southern Slavs inside the Monarchy to be increased. From the outset, he wanted 'Serbia to be given time to show her loyalty'. The Emperor himself thought 'the time for military action not yet ripe'. The military, on the other hand, pressed Berchtold to take swift and determined action, and when he consulted Berlin, both the German Emperor and the Chancellor assured him that Germany would stand by Austria even if her action should involve war with Russia – a contingency which, however, they thought remote. Austria was even strongly pressed to act (after the first day, when he had taken the opposite line) by von Tschirschky, the German Ambassador in Vienna.

With these assurances in his pocket, Berchtold convoked the Joint Ministerial Council on 7 July. Tisza was now less confident as to Serbia's behaviour, but nevertheless insisted that the first step must be no ultimatum – the demands must be hard, but not impossible – and if war did come, consequently on Serbia's rejecting the Note, the Monarchy must make it clear that she was not aiming at the complete annihilation of Serbia, and would not itself annexe any part of it. All the other participants[2] were unanimously in favour 'of such far-reaching demands being made of Serbia as justified the presumption of their rejection, in order to open the path for a radical solution through military intervention'.

[1] The story which follows is given fully in Hantsch's *Berchtold*, pp. 557 ff. A short, convenient account by Goldinger in *Vorabend*, pp. 48 ff. The minutes of the Joint Ministerial Council from 1914 to 1918 have been published with annotations by M. Komjáthy, *Protokolle des Gemeinsamen Ministerrates*, etc., Budapest, 1966.

[2] Berchtold, Stürkgh, Bilinsky, Krobatin, Conrad. Admiral von Kailer also attended, representing the Navy, but the record does not show him as speaking.

When Berchtold saw Francis Joseph on 9 July he got no final decision from him. Tisza had sent the Emperor a dissenting memorandum, prophesying that war with Serbia 'would in all human probability bring about the intervention of Russia, and therewith, world war'. Berchtold got no more out of the Emperor than his agreement that 'it was impossible to go back now', and that the Note must demand guarantees that if it accepted it, Serbia would keep its word. He was, however, fully determined on his own course (in which Berlin continued to encourage him), and when, on receipt of Wiesner's report, the Foreign Ministry set itself to draft the Note, it was, after all, deliberately framed to be unacceptable.[1] And now even Tisza agreed to this, subject only to the stipulation that the Ministerial Council should make an unanimous declaration that the Monarchy had no plans of conquest against Serbia and would annexe no Serbian territory beyond frontier rectifications necessary on military grounds.

The Note went off on 20 July, with instructions to the Austrian Minister in Belgrade to present it at 6 p.m. on the 23rd. Serbia was given forty-eight hours in which to reply. Foreign Governments were to be given the Note on the 24th. The Serbian reply in fact accepted almost all the conditions, but Austria made the small reservations excuse to describe the reply as insufficient and declared war on the 28th.

Even the Germans were disapproving now: they had got cold feet when they found that Britain was unlikely to stand aside. But they should have seen earlier that the system of European alliances was so constructed as to make a localized war impossible. Inevitably, Russia stood by Serbia, France by Russia, Britain by France, as Germany stood by Austria. By mid-August Austria and Germany were at war with Russia, France, Britain, Belgium, Serbia and Montenegro. The Monarchy's allies, other than Germany – Italy and Roumania – took the view that the *casus foederis* under the Triple Alliance had not arisen for them, and stood aside.

We do not propose to inflict on the reader a pontifical assessment of Austria's degree of 'guilt' for the 1914 war. It is easy indeed to understand the feelings of the men who took the decision for war. Austria had, in truth, been subjected to intolerable provocation, and the milder remedies which she had often tried to apply had proved unvaryingly ineffectual. It was reasonable for her military advisers to argue that if war was bound to come now or later – and that, too, was a reasonable expectation – then better make it now, before the reorganization of the Russian army was complete; reasonable also that they should be influenced by the fear, for which cause could be shown, that if

[1] According to M. Károlyi, *Faith without Illusion*, p. 56, Berchtold's wife, who was a Károlyi, told him in October 1914 that 'poor Leopold could not sleep on the day when he wrote his ultimatum to the Serbs, as he was so worried that they might accept it. Several times during the night he got up and altered or added some clause, to reduce this risk.'

Austria did not show resolution now, Germany would regard her alliance with her as no longer worth keeping up. It was humanly natural for Berchtold to be influenced by the strong criticism which had been levied at him during the Balkan Wars for not intervening at least to annexe the Sanjak, and thus to decide more easily, as Professor Hantsch writes, 'to break with the inglorious, misinterpreted and, into the bargain, unsuccessful policy of yielding'.[1] If it was really legitimate to use war as an instrument of national policy (and in 1914 this had not yet been formally denied), Austria had a very good case for using it. But her apologists should not over-state the case. The decision between war and peace in July 1914 was hers, and hers the choice for war; a choice made in knowledge that the war might prove general. Professor Hantsch tells us that Berchtold 'would have preferred to localize the war', and we can easily believe him. But he himself admits that Berchtold knew that there was a risk that localization would prove not to be possible, and took it with his eyes open. No pleading can alter that fact.

[1] *Gestalter*, p. 500.

18

The End of the Monarchy

The Austro-Hungarian Monarchy did not survive the conflict which it unleashed when it declared war on Serbia. The end of the war was also the end of the Monarchy. Many is the book which has been written on the question whether this consummation was forced on it, unnaturally, by foreign enemies, some of which had become so only by accident, or whether it was the natural and inevitable result of the forces of decay within its own organism. In fact, the mutual interaction of the internal and external factors was so intimate as to make any distinction between them highly artificial, and if in some cases the former gave the lead to the latter, in others the position was the reverse.

The death-sentence was certainly pronounced by foreign Powers, and the dismemberment carried through partly in the name of general principles sponsored by those Powers, partly in fulfilment of war-time agreements made by them, largely out of military expediency, with neighbours of the Monarchy which coveted parts of its territory, or with elements inside it whose help seemed desirable. Without war, these agreements would not have been made, and it is more than probable that they often went further than the peoples themselves wanted, at the time. Yet the preceding chapters have surely shown that in 1914 the future of the Monarchy was at best problematical. Francis Joseph's attempt to make his peoples forget their national loyalties in an a-national one had never enjoyed even a semblance of success in Hungary or Galicia, and its failure in the West had become obvious by 1859. After that, the a-national spirit had lived on at the Court and, to an extent which at first was very considerable, among the Emperor's chosen servants – the professional civil servants, the Army officers, some of the Catholic clergy, some of the high aristocrats. But the number of those whose loyalty was genuinely 'Habsburg' rather than to their own people had been dwindling year by year. If the Monarchy was to survive, it must be as a multi-national state, not an a-national one, and in 1914 the peoples of the Monarchy were further than they ever had been from finding the basis of an accommodation between themselves.

At the outset of the war, as at that of most wars in most countries, *Kriegsstimmung* in the population was fairly general, particularly since no one envisaged even the possibility of a long war (every European war since 1848 had been virtually over in a few weeks). The Germans of the Monarchy naturally stood behind their Government: the German nationalists, because they saw the war as a struggle between Teuton and Slav, waged at the side of Germany, and the Christian Socials and their sympathizers, because loyalty to the Dynasty was part of their creed. The Social Democrats, whom the crisis caught in the middle of preparations for a great international conference, had, while the storm was gathering and again on the day when war was declared, protested against it and washed their hands of responsibility; but when they failed to arrest the march of events, they, like their colleagues in Germany, found theoretical excuses – in this case, the threat of Czarist tyranny – for human feelings, and became quite astonishingly bellicose. The Hungarian Party of Work naturally backed Tisza (who did not reveal his own initial resistance to the ultimatum) and the Coalition leaders, headed for the time by Apponyi,[1] hailed the news with cries of 'At last!' Afterwards they suggested joining a Cabinet of National Concentration – which proved impossible because they made the condition that Tisza himself should stand down, which he refused to do. Nevertheless, they accepted the necessity of prosecuting the war loyally. The one leading Magyar politician who might have taken a different line, Count Mihály Károlyi, was abroad, trying to convert the United States to his ideas, and got back to Hungary only in October.

The Croats were equally whole-hearted. The news of the assassination had already been greeted with anti-Serb riots, both in Croatia and Bosnia. When war broke out, only a handful of deeply compromised politicians – Trumbić, Supilo and a few more – slipped across the frontier to set on foot abroad the activities to which we shall return. When the Sabor met, the members of the Serbo-Croat coalition sat silent, while the Party of Right poured out objurgations on Serbia and Radić endorsed the war in terms of exuberant loyalty; it is true that in June 1915 the Sabor took the occasion to press for the unification of all the Croats 'in one State organization' under the Habsburgs.

The Austrian Poles were more divided than they would have been twenty years before, and the attitude of the 'Lemberg Democrats' gave the Austrian authorities considerable anxiety. The Parliamentary leaders of the nation, however, decided that Russia was the enemy in chief, and Pilsudski actually raised a legion to fight her. When the Grand Duke Nicholas, leading his armies into Galicia in August, offered them 'a re-born Poland under the sceptre of Russia', there was little response. The Roumanians obeyed their calling-up notices without question and fought bravely, as they did throughout the war; in 1914 their politicians made loyal declarations (Roumania, of course, had not yet decided to break with her former allies). The Italians

[1] Kossuth had died on 5 May.

in 1914 took much the same line as the Roumanians, and the Slovenes, as the Croats.

Jarring notes came from only three of the nationalities in the Monarchy. Very many of the Serbs associated themselves with their nation, rather than their state; the authorities executed a frightening number of them for helping the enemy, and interned or deported even more. Although the Ruthene national parties had declared the war against Russia to be a war for the liberation of the Ukraine, many of the Ruthenes welcomed the Russian armies which occupied their homes in the first weeks of the war. It seems possible, indeed, that not all of them well understood what was happening around them.[1] The disaffection was, however, very widespread. Finally, the Czechs followed that policy of keeping an iron in every fire which many small nations, most sensibly, try to pursue, but in which the Czechs had developed an unique expertise. Many of their political leaders, from Clericals to Social Democrats, volunteered declarations of loyalty, some of which were unquestionably sincere. Others, as there is equally little doubt, worked from the first to bring about the destruction of the Monarchy with Russian help. It was Czech *émigrés* in Russia who obtained an audience of the Czar and expressed to him the hope 'to see one day the free and independent Crown of St Wenceslas shine in the radiance of the Crown of the Romanovs'; a number of leading nationalist politicians at home formed an underground organization, the Mafia, to organize sabotage and passive resistance; emissaries from Bohemia went to Russia to seek Russian support; and forged leaflets were circulated in Bohemia bearing alleged promises by the Grand Duke Nicholas that one of the Czar's family would accept the Crown of Bohemia.

And these efforts, combined with the effects of a hostility to everything German which had by now become second nature to the Czech people, and of a more nebulous and less universal, but still fairly general sentimental attachment to Russia, really resulted in fairly widespread disaffection. Some regiments, in particular two from Prague (the 28th and the 8th Landwehr), demonstrated noisily when sent to the front; in April 1915 the 28th went across to the Russians, or at any rate surrendered without resistance, almost *en masse*; there were many other cases of desertion of individuals or formations to the Russians and the Serbs. Just what proportion of the Czech soldiers behaved 'treacherously' was a matter of dispute, even at the time, but it was not inconsiderable,[2] and in the spring of 1915 the authorities took severe

[1] See above, p. 803.
[2] Some idea may be gathered from the statistics of soldiers fallen in battle. These were not kept by nationality, but the regional statistics give the following picture:

Recorded dead (military)

Purely German areas	(A)	29·7%	Moravian-Slovak areas	(A)	26·7%
Purely Magyar areas	(H)	28·0%	Croatia		25·7%
Purely Slovene areas	(A)	27·5%	Purely Slovak areas	(H)	23·7%

repressive measures. Klofač had been arrested as early as September 1914; now the same fate overtook Kramař (on 21 May 1915) and many others.[1] Kramař was later tried and condemned to death for high treason, although Francis Joseph commuted the sentence to life imprisonment. The Mafia was driven underground, and the few leaders who had escaped abroad to convert the world to the idea of Czech independence – easily the most important of these was Masaryk, who had left for the West as early as December 1914 – were, for the time, almost without contact with their fellow-countrymen at home.

The disciplining of Bohemia did not, of course, mean that those who felt disaffected had undergone a change of heart, but only that they were silenced, but the silencing was, for the time, effectual (incidentally, widely applauded by other Czech politicians), and by the summer of 1915 it really looked as though the centripetal forces in the Monarchy had triumphed fairly decisively over the centrifugal. Neither had the States which were then Austria's chief enemies yet come round to the belief that the assimilation of political to national frontiers was an overriding postulate of international morality:[2] and if France and Britain had held such a view they would have been debarred from acting on it by the fact that Russia – more multinational than Austria herself – was their ally. In any case, they were still impressed by the value of the Monarchy's role as a factor in the European Balance of Power and as a barrier alike to German and Russian expansion.

These considerations explain why Britain and France, at this stage, made no attempt to appeal to national separatism in the Monarchy, and paid very little attention to the *émigrés*: Supilo's success, described below,[3] seems to have been almost fortuitous, and Masaryk and Beneš (who had joined him in September 1915) had no tangible successes at all for a long year after they had begun their work. As for the Russians, they soon lost interest in the Czechs – more, it appears, out of slackness and ignorance than of policy. On the other hand, the big Allies had existing allies, and were seeking new ones, among the Monarchy's neighbours. These had to be bought, or rewarded, and the primacy enjoyed at the time by the 'national' idea made it inevitable

Purely Roumanian areas	(H)	23·0%	Bosnia		19·1%
Purely Czech	(A)	22·5%	Italo-Ladin	(A)	18·3%
Mixed Serb-Croat	(H)	22·2%	Purely Serbo-Croat	(A)	17·0%
Purely Ruthene	(A)	21·5%			
Mainly Roumanian	(A)	19·2%	Purely Polish		16·2%

These figures also give 'mixed Ruthene' (H) 11·9%, but I suspect a misprint. In another passage Gratz gives the Croat figure as 'under the average for the Monarchy'.

[1] According to R. W. Seton-Watson, *History of the Czechs and Slovaks*, p. 287, 'many thousands of Czech civilians were interned as political suspects' and death-sentences by Court Martial numbered close on 5,000.

[2] For the following, see Macartney and Palmer, *Independent Eastern Europe* (London, 1962), pp. 39 ff.   [3] See below, p. 814.

that prices should be stated mainly in 'national' terms. Consequently, this principle was invoked as excuse for a number of bargains the effect of which would be to mutilate the Monarchy drastically. Sazanov himself began by proposing to turn the national principle to Russia's own advantage by annexing East Galicia and rearranging the rest of the Monarchy on 'national' lines. Nothing came of this plan, which did not become an inter-Allied, nor even an official Russian war aim, nor of Sazonov's early efforts to detach Roumania from the Triple Alliance.[1] But on 26 April 1915, Italy signed with the Allies the Treaty of London, which promised her, in return for her entry into and continuance in the war, rewards which included substantial slices of Austrian territory: the South Tirol up to the Brenner, Gorizia-Gradica, Trieste, Istria as far as the Quarnero, then, after skipping the Hungarian and Croat Littoral, Northern Dalmatia as far as Cape Planka. On the strength of this, Italy declared war on the Monarchy on 23 May.

Meanwhile, the Serbian Government had been in continuous touch with the Allied Governments, especially that of Russia, while Supilo, Trumbić and a few others had founded a Yugoslav Committee which in May had established itself in London and developed a lively propaganda in favour of Yugoslav independence. Half-promises had been given to the Serbs in the spring (this was why Italy was denied the Hungaro-Croat Littoral and Southern Dalmatia), and on 17 August the Allies offered Serbia Bosnia-Herzegovina, Southern Dalmatia and, apparently, other parts of the Monarchy, Grey also promising 'to facilitate Serbia's union with Croatia, if the latter so desired'. He appears already to have given Supilo certain assurances, and now, in September, told him that 'provided Serbia agreed, Bosnia-Herzegovina, South Dalmatia, Slavonia and Croatia should be permitted to decide their own fate'. It is true that the records of what was promised are singularly ambiguous, and the Allies appear later to have been themselves ignorant of the extent to which they were bound,[2] but on any natural interpretation of the texts they were now pledged to amputate from the Monarchy all its Serb and Croat territories.

The Czechs, too, had founded a Czecho-Slovak National Council in Paris, under Masaryk's Presidency,[3] and on 3 February 1916, Masaryk got from Briand a promise, which again was at the time personal to the author of it and afterwards not treated as binding in the fullest sense, but yet left its mark on later negotiations, to 'carry out' Masaryk's policy, which appears to have been the creation of a fully independent Czecho-Slovak State, with

[1] Germany, indeed, who at the outset of the war was inclined to make free with her allies' territory, wanted the Roumanians to be allowed to 'occupy' Transylvania 'to defend it against Russia'. Tisza, naturally, would hear nothing of this.

[2] See Macartney and Palmer, op. cit., pp. 52–6.

[3] Other Czech émigré organizations had been established in Russia and elsewhere. For a convenient recent account of these, see Zeman, op. cit., pp. 72–94.

frontiers even larger than those of the later Republic, except that they did not include Carpatho-Ruthenia.[1] And on 17 August 1916, the Allies concluded with Roumania a Treaty[2] (on the strength of which she declared war on the Monarchy on 28 August), promising her, in return for her entry into and continuance in the war, all Transylvania, the Bánát, and a frontier 'running past Szeged and Debrecen to the Carpathians, then East to the line of the Pruth, including the Bukovina'.

The Western Allies had been prevented by consideration for Russia from holding out any prospects to the Poles, but Russia herself had stated her intention of creating an united, autonomous Poland under the Russian sceptre. Thus it was already sure that if the Allies won the war, and fulfilled all their promises, what would be left of the Monarchy would be something for which the word 'torso' would be a strong meiosis. And meanwhile, opinion was hardening perceptibly against allowing even a torso to survive. In particular, the appearance in 1915 of Friedrich Naumann's 'Mitteleuropa', with its vision of an enormous Central European unit which, although Naumann put its capital in Prague, would obviously be dominated by Germany, immensely strengthened the hands of the party which was insisting that the idea that the Monarchy could form a counterweight to, or barrier against, Germany, was mere illusion. The enemies of the Monarchy gave their cause a great impetus when, in the autumn of 1916, a group of them, which included most of Britain's acknowledged experts on the Danube Basin and the Balkans, besides non-British sympathizers, began issuing a journal, *The New Europe*, which pleaded with learning and brilliance that the Monarchy was *delenda*. The view even penetrated the Foreign Office. In the summer of 1916, Mr Asquith asked the Foreign Office to prepare a memorandum suggesting the basis for a peace settlement. The authors of the resultant memorandum boldly advocated reorganizing Central Europe in national States, arguing that the 'conglomeration of States' which would replace the Monarchy would 'prove an efficient barrier against Russian preponderance in Europe and German extension towards the Near East, because those States would be happy and contented in the realization of their national aspirations, and strong as regards their economic future'.

The Central Powers had, indeed, succeeded in making Russia's promises to the Poles look fairly toothless, for in 1915 their armies had not only recovered Galicia, but had driven the Russian armies out of Russian Poland itself, but they, too, had seen that it was necessary to do something about the Poles. Having failed to agree between themselves on a policy, they had ended by shelving the question and keeping in being the two Military Governments, in Warsaw and Lublin respectively, which they had established on occupying

[1] The memorandum for which Masaryk was then seeking Allied approval did, however, ask for a Corridor through West Hungary to link Czecho-Slovakia with the projected Southern Slav State.   [2] One of the numerous Treaties of Bucharest.

Russian Poland, but on 5 November 1916 they issued a Proclamation in the names of the two Emperors, that they intended to constitute Russian Poland a fully independent Kingdom, linked with the Central Powers especially as regards defence. The promises did not apply to either Austrian or Prussian Poland, but Austria promised Galicia extended autonomy. In any case, with both sides offering near-independence at least to most Poles, it was hard to anticipate that Galicia would very long remain part of the Monarchy. That both the Germans and the Austrians continued to believe it up to the late summer of 1918 is one of the curiosities of history.[1]

All of these agreements which had any binding force had, as we have seen, been purely business transactions which took into account the wishes of the Monarchy's neighbours, but not of its peoples; it is true that when Italy and Roumania went over from alliance with the Monarchy to warring against it, the attachment to the Monarchy of its Italian and Roumanian subjects naturally diminished sharply. On the other hand, when the terms of the Treaty of London became known (as they quickly did), the Croats became more bellicosely loyal than ever; Grey's vague assurance to Supilo counted for nothing compared with the prospect of seeing Croat territory given to Italy if the Monarchy were defeated. And right up to the end of 1916 the relations between the little 'Czecho-Slovak National Council' in Paris, still more those between the Czech *émigrés* in Russia and the Czech politicians in Bohemia and Moravia, were still ambiguous to a degree. To talk of the 'loyalty' or otherwise of most of those politicians is to use a misleading term, for their emotional loyalties were exclusively towards their own people.[2] But most of the actively disaffected were under lock and key, and very many of the rest genuinely thought that Masaryk was only doing harm to his people: his ideas could never be realized, and only gave the authorities, and the Austrian Germans, an excuse to trample on the Czechs. The interest of the Czechs was still to work for the maintenance of the Monarchy, and for the optimum terms for themselves inside it. Their not infrequent repudiations of Masaryk's activities, and protestations of their own loyalty to the Monarchy, were insincere only if an emotional connotation was read into them; they were perfectly sincere expressions of what their authors then believed to be the correct tactics for the Czech people to follow.

The continued vitality of centripetal feelings in the Monarchy owed much to the successes achieved by its arms in the first two years of the war. Things

---

[1] The struggle which went on between Germany and Austria for the possession of Poland after the war, both parties assuming that they were going to have a voice in the matter, is well described by Fischer, op. cit. cc. 8, 12, 17, 19 and 23.

[2] This sentence does not mean that no Czechs were genuinely attached to the Monarchy. There were certainly some, in all social strata, who were sincerely loyal.

had not, indeed, gone easily at the outset. Conrad's plan[1] had been to crush Serbia in a swift offensive and then to turn against Russia; a relatively large number of Austrian troops had been employed for the Serbian operation instead of being sent to the Russian front. But the Serbs put up an extraordinarily gallant resistance, twice throwing back the Austrians with heavy losses, and meanwhile the Russians proved more efficient than had been expected; although their right flank was nearly defeated by the Germans, they nevertheless overran East Galicia and the Bukovina in September 1914 and threatened, although, except for small raiding parties, they failed to force, the Carpathian passes. In March 1915 the great fortress of Premysl surrendered, and two months later, Italy's entry into the war opened a third front. Nevertheless, 1915 on the whole passed off well for Austria and her allies. A great Austro-German offensive, which opened on 2 May, drove the Russians far back to a line east of Vilna, Pinsk and Luck, leaving, of Austrian territory, only a corner of East Galicia and the Bukovina in the hands of the enemy. The Italians were held on the Isonzo, and after difficult negotiations had brought Bulgaria into the war in September (Turkey had entered it already in November 1914), Serbia and Montenegro were overrun, and Albania occupied. In 1916 there were again dark months; the Italians won a little ground, Brusilov launched a new big offensive in Volhynia, and when Roumania entered the war, forces of hers penetrated Transylvania, which at the time was almost bare of troops. But the Italian line was stabilized after only a small retreat; that against Russia, after a retirement which was larger, but still stopped east of Lemberg; and the Roumanian armies were quickly thrown back, not only out of Transylvania but even out of Wallachia, and left holding only a precarious line in Moldavia.

But all this cost the Monarchy a heavy toll. Particularly its best officers and men suffered appalling losses in the first fighting (250,000 dead and wounded and 100,000 prisoners in the first four weeks), so that the 21–32 classes had to be called up as early as November 1914, and the 32–42 not long after. There were also very heavy losses in prisoners: 120,000 men were taken on the single day when Premysl fell and over 300,000 in Volhynia in 1916. Those who survived were in grievous state: the supply and hospital services were badly organized, and unscrupulous contractors, who flourished inordinately, especially after Galicia had been overrun, furnished boots soled with paper and uniforms of the most inadequate shoddy. There were also growing difficulties at home, where food soon began to run short. The Russian occupation of Galicia cut off one of the Monarchy's granaries. Italy's entry into the war and the British blockade pressed on other sensitive spots, and the domestic producers began to suffer under shortages of manpower and animal labour, lack of fodder and fertilizers, and deterioration of machinery. There

---

[1] A convenient short account of Austria's military plans may be found in an article by Kiszling, *Vorabend*, pp. 83 ff.

were also severe shortages of industrial raw materials, especially those needed by the textile industry.

With these problems, too, the administrative services dealt inadequately, partly out of inexperience, and partly under the handicap of the Monarchy's non-unitary Constitution, which allowed every component of it a large measure of control over its own internal affairs. Hungary set the example – in 1915 she had undertaken the entire provisioning of the armies, but beyond that she allowed only so much of provisions to go into Austria as her population could comfortably spare, and that at stiff prices. And while Hungary gave the lead, she was by no means the unique offender. Every Austrian Land followed suit, to the best of its powers, so that even by 1915 the food situation was difficult in Vienna and the big Austrian industrial centres. By 1916 it was a big degree worse still. The German Ambassador reported: 'The people in the suburbs of Vienna are starving; they are being driven to despair by long waits, often in vain, in queues.'

Prices, too, were beginning to rise.

The political regime was highly oppressive. Areas designated as operational zones were, of course, under military administration, and the military saw to it that these zones should be as extensive as possible. In addition, jurisdiction over certain offences had, at the very outbreak of the war, been withdrawn from the civilian authorities and transferred to the military, and a 'War Supervisory Office' (*Kriegsüberwachungsamt*: K.U.A.) was established, as a sort of military security organization. As a military body, it was officially competent for the whole Monarchy, but Tisza's vigorous defence of all Hungarian citizens, Magyar or non-Magyar, confined its operations to within very narrow limits in the Lands of the Hungarian Crown; it was thanks to Tisza that the Croat Sabor was able to meet, equally with Hungary's own Parliament, and the regular Croat administration to function, throughout the war. He himself, indeed, set up a very efficient machinery of his own for harnessing Hungary's resources to the service of the war effort. But the Austrian *Landespräsidenten* found it harder to resist the military. The Czechophile Governor of Bohemia, Prince Thun, was replaced in March 1915 and thereafter the military there, in Moravia and in Carniola, did much as they pleased. In all the Monarchy, the factories working for the armed forces – a very wide range of enterprises – were under the military: officers controlled them, the workers were subject to military discipline, and recalcitrants were clapped into uniform and sent to the front. The severity of this regime was one reason – the scandalous prevalence of *embusqués* from the upper classes was another – why the Monarchy never developed such a solidarity of feeling between officer and man, and such a cleavage between serving soldiers of all ranks on the one hand, and munition makers and workers both on the other, as was perceptible in Britain.

The civilian regime was a degree milder than the military, but it was harsh enough. Expression, in particular, was most closely controlled. A clerk was sentenced to death[1] (on moral, not aesthetic grounds) for distributing translations of the then popular American pacifist doggerel 'I didn't raise my boy to be a soldier.' Nor was any protest constitutionally possible in the West, for while the Budapest Parliament and the Croat Sabor met, so that popular feeling could (within the limits of the franchise) express itself, no such outlet existed in Cis-Leithania, owing to the widespread apprehensions that if the Reichsrat were convoked, its non-German members, and the Social Democrats, would give voice to disloyal and defeatist sentiments, and thus hearten the Monarchy's enemies. The German *Nationalverband*, which was the only group to which Stürgkh could reasonably look for Parliamentary support, had informed him that they would oppose the convocation of the Reichsrat unless he had previously met certain demands which they had worked out: these, besides such requirements as a closer political and economic connection with Germany, included a new status for Galicia, under which its Deputies should be excluded from the Reichsrat (although receiving representation in the Delegations); the recognition of German as the 'language of State'; a new Bohemian settlement safeguarding their positions there; and revised Standing Orders. These reforms would have to be enacted by octroi.[2]

As Stürgkh shrank from trying this desperate remedy (to which he might not have got the Emperor's consent), he had simply left the Reichsrat unconvoked and continued to enact all necessary measures through Para. 14. The Reichsrat building was actually turned into a hospital.

It was the impossibility of protesting in any other effectual way against war and its attendant tyrannies that eventually decided Viktor Adler's son, Friedrich – in himself as gentle a spirit as stepped – to resort to desperate remedies. On 21 October 1916 he emptied a revolver into Stürgkh in a Viennese restaurant, then crying 'Down with absolutism! We want peace!' and surrendering himself to his captors. He had not kept a bullet for himself, because he proposed to utilize his trial for the exposition of his views; but before that could take place, several other events of the first magnitude had occurred.

First, in order of time, came the re-election of Woodrow Wilson to the Presidency of the United States, presaging as it did not only the military defeat of the Monarchy when the United States entered the War (as it was now almost certain to do) but also, in the general belief, political calamity for it on account of the President's known devotion to the principles of democracy and 'self-determination'. That he was not going to interpret these doctrines as necessarily fatal to the Monarchy was (most naturally, in view of the language used by him) not appreciated, and his re-election brought

---

[1] Commuted to five years' imprisonment.
[2] On this see Redlich, op. cit., II. 133, 163; Höglinger, pp. 132 ff.; Uhlirz, op. cit., pp. 241 ff.

strong encouragement to those who liked to think of themselves as representatives and leaders of the 'subject races' of the Monarchy.

Then, on 21 November, Francis Joseph passed peacefully away, in the eighty-seventh year of his life and the sixty-eighth of his reign. It has been said that 'the old Emperor's person had, while he lived, come by sheer force of habit to constitute so strong a cohesive force among the peoples of his dominions as genuinely to diminish separatism and subversion among them'; while his end had so long seemed imminent that even the convinced advocates of revolutionary change had to a large extent put their plans into cold storage against the day of his death, after which they could be taken out in what would assuredly be a more favourable atmosphere. Thus the mere fact of his death released a whole multitude of pent-up forces, national and social, throughout the Monarchy, and it was humanly certain that the structure of the Monarchy would yield before their impact, in one direction or another; for the new ruler, Francis Joseph's great-nephew, Charles, was known to be a man of pacific character and great good will, who would not wish, even if he were able, to rule with an iron hand.[1]

Charles was still only twenty-nine years of age, and little was known of his political ideas, but most of his advisers, including the man whom, as one of his first acts,[2] he made his Foreign Minister, Count Czernin, had belonged to Francis Ferdinand's circle and shared his views on the Magyars,[3] and he was generally credited with ideas not dissimilar from his uncle's: that is, of wishing to placate the Slavs and Roumanians of the Monarchy at the expense of its Germans and Magyars. He was in fact in favour of concessions to the Czechs in Austria, and to the Southern Slavs and Roumanians in Hungary, but he had none of Francis Ferdinand's pathological detestation of the Magyars and in any case, he could not, at that juncture, venture to challenge Hungary, which by simply cutting off food supplies could have reduced Cis-Leithania to literal starvation. And Tisza, aware of his strong position, consolidated it by arranging for Charles's early coronation. The ceremony took place in Buda on 30 December 1916 and by the oath which he then swore Charles bound himself to respect Hungary's laws and to maintain her integrity. As reward for this, Tisza consented to a reasonable renewal of the economic Compromise, and a settlement, which was scheduled to last for twenty years, was eventually reached, although the Monarchy broke up before it came into effect.

Meanwhile, one of Charles's promises to his peoples, made on his accession, had been to work for peace, and in fact, negotiations for a peace offer,

[1] Macartney and Palmer, p. 65.

[2] The appointment was made on 22 December. Czernin's predecessor had been Baron Burian, who had succeeded Berchtold on 1 January 1915.

[3] He had brought himself to the Archduke's notice in 1910 by sending him a memorandum urging him to break the supremacy of the Magyars in the Monarchy (see Singer, *Czernin*, pp. 14 f.).

initiated by Burian, had been on foot even before; the Note signifying the Central Powers' readiness to negotiate went out on 12 December 1916. The effect, however, was disconcerting. Wilson offered himself as mediator and invited the two sides to state their terms. The Germans took charge of the Central Powers' reply, which read arrogantly enough: *inter alia* it demanded cessions of territory to the Monarchy from Russia, Roumania and Serbia. The Allies' terms included 'the liberation of the Italians, as also of the Slavs, Roumanians and Czecho-Slovaks from foreign domination'.[1] This did not in fact mean that the Allies had decided to dismember the Monarchy, but it sounded as though they had done so, and Charles and his advisers lost most of their hopes, for the time, of an early peace. This rather increased the urgency of getting wide support for what looked like being a long war yet; in which connection Charles placed considerable hopes in the influences of constitutional government and a measure of democracy.

In Hungary, Tisza was summoned to introduce suffrage reform at last. In Austria, Koerber, whom Francis Joseph had brought back to fill Stürgkh's place, but whose ideas could not be brought into harmony with those of the young Emperor, resigned on 14 December, and after a financial expert, Dr von Spitzmüller, had failed to form an administration, the Minister-Presidency was, on 20 December, given to Count Heinrich von Clam-Martinic, who, unlike Koerber, was prepared to accept the *Nationalverband*'s *conditions préalables*.[2] Clam formed a Government which included, besides the customary Pole (Dr Michael Bobrzynski), two German Nationalists (Dr Josef Baernreither and Dr Karl Urban) and a clerical minded German civil servant (von Hussarek), and opened negotiations with the Germans and Poles on the measures to be enacted by octroi preparatory to the convocation of the Reichsrat. The proclamation announcing the measures was actually drafted.

But hard on these preliminary moves came the news of the March revolution in Russia. The new Russian Government's promises to the Poles in fact went little further than the Czar's, but the Poles of Russia now no longer feared their old masters; more important still, the Western Powers now felt their hands free to go further in their own Polish policies. In fact, declarations encouraging to the Poles came from both countries, and also from the USA, and in August a Polish National Committee was established in Paris. This was then recognized successively by Britain, France, Russia, Italy and the USA. It was now Germany and Austria which appeared as the chief

[1] On the history of this remarkable phrase, see Macartney and Palmer, p. 67. The Central Powers' reply was made on 26 December 1916; that of the Allies on 12 January 1917. In respect of Poland, the Allied Note confined itself to a reference to the Czar's recent proclamation.

[2] A nephew of the other Heinrich von Clam-Martinic who had played such a large role in public affairs half a century earlier, Heinrich *cadet* had begun his public career as a federalist and something of a Czech nationalist, but had changed his ideas (apparently as a result of his war experiences: see Höglinger, op. cit., *passim*) and was now of the view that the only possible Government for Austria was one resting on its Germans and Poles.

obstacles to the fulfilment of Poland's national ambitions. The Russians' more general pronouncements in favour of national self-determination (to which Milyukov added a gloss advocating the disintegration of the Monarchy into national units) whetted national appetites, aad radical ones were encouraged by the amazing ease with which the mighty Czarist regime had been overthrown. Gone, too (although, as events a generation later were to prove, mistakenly), was the fear that the destruction of the Monarchy might result in its components being swallowed up by Russia.

Under the circumstances the Poles refused to accept the measure of autonomy which Clam and the *Nationalverband* were offering them, and on 15 April, Charles withdrew his consent to the *octroi*. Baernreither, Urban and Bobrzynski offered their resignations, but were persuaded, as was the *Nationalverband* as a whole, to bow to the inevitable, and the opening of the Reichsrat – unreformed – was announced for 30 May.

In preparation for this event, the Polish, Ruthene, Czech and Slovene Deputies organized their Parliamentary Clubs more tightly, so that in each, one man should speak for all his colleagues. In every case, the bolder and more radical spirits prevailed over the moderates. The Polish Club had met on 15–16 May and had adopted Resolutions to the effect that the situation afforded no basis for discussions on a separate status for Galicia, and that they would be unable to support the Government. Bobrzynski had thereupon resigned. On 30 May the Poles announced their objective to be 'an independent and unified Poland, with access to the sea'; how this was to be brought about should be a matter for international consideration. The Ruthenes sent a greeting to the Ukrainians of Russia and declared that 'they would not give up the struggle until the great Ukrainian nation was in enjoyment of its full rights on its entire national territory', 'which was to include the Ukrainian areas of Galicia-Lodomeria, as well as Cholm, Podlachia and Volhynia'. They repudiated 'any organic connection between the Kingdom of Galicia and Poland'. Both the Czechs and the Southern Slavs now came a long way into the open. Both had protested their loyalty when the Allied peace terms were published, and both still made the motions, not altogether insincere, of seeing their future inside the Monarchy; but not as then constructed. The Czechs denounced the Dualist system as 'injurious to the interests of both the ruling and the subject nations' and demanded the transformation of the Monarchy into 'a federation of free and equal States', one of which was to include 'all branches of the Czecho-Slovak nation'. The two 'Progressive' Czech Deputies went still further, calling for 'a new Czecho-Slovak State'. The Southern Slav spokesman, the Slovene, Mgr Korosec, demanded 'the unification of all districts of the Monarchy inhabited by Slovenes, Croats and Serbs in an autonomous State, free from any national domination, resting on a democratic basis, under the sceptre of the House of Habsburg-Lorraine'.

Clam in his reply glided over these demands, announcing his programme to be 'Austria. An Austria which has grown up through a splendid historical development.' This satisfied no one, and he was also vehemently attacked for his extreme Conservative past (like his uncle and father, he had been a leader of the Bohemian Feudalists). As the Poles now definitely informed him that they would not support him, although they would consider voting essential legislation under another Government, Clam resigned on 23 June. To replace him, Charles made what was originally meant as the stop-gap appointment of Ignaz von Seidler, a permanent official in the Ministry of Agriculture, the only man anyone could think of who was not tarred with the brush of Para. 14. Seidler, although a German, was no extreme German nationalist. The Slav political leaders in the Reichsrat refused to co-operate with him, but he took into his Cabinet members of all the chief nationalities, and on 2 July, Charles amnestied a number of political prisoners, including Kramař. and made further concessions including restoration of trial by jury. But he was to learn, as others had found before him, that no formula existed for making a square out of the Austrian polygon. The Czechs swallowed the concession and asked for a second helping, while both the loyal 'schwarzgelb' elements and the German nationalists were correspondingly embittered. For the first time in Austria's history, a proportion of German nationalist feeling began seriously to turn against the existence of the Monarchy.

The Germans and Poles nevertheless gave Seidler enough support to enable him to keep Parliamentary government in being for another year, but the Reichsrat led only a shadow-existence, of which few but its own members took any cognisance. The weight of political life in Cis-Leithania now lay almost entirely with the various 'national' committees and associations.

Meanwhile, Tisza had resigned the Minister Presidency on 23 May, rather than introduce what he believed to be the fatal measure of suffrage reform. Charles gave the position to the young Count Maurice Esterházy, who in September, owing to ill-health, handed it on to the old war-horse, Wekerle. The Cabinet was composed of members of the old Coalition, with a few new men, including a professing Jew, Vázsonyi, as Minister of Justice. They declared themselves ready to introduce suffrage reform, and Vázsonyi actually agreed a fairly radical measure with the Social Democrats, but Tisza, who still commanded the Party of Work, refused to agree to it; it was only a year later that Parliament accepted a watered-down version of the Bill, and that in return for acceptance of further 'national' demands, including those concessions over the army which Francis Joseph had refused so brusquely ten years before.[1] Thus those Hungarians who still professed themselves "67ers' had made the link with Austria more tenuous than ever, while more and more ground was being gained by those who went further still.

[1] The excuse for pressing these was the allegation that Hungarian units were being deliberately chosen for dangerous or desperate operations.

Chief among these was Count Mihály Károlyi, who was now propagating the thesis that if the Monarchy broke with Germany and asked for peace, and Hungary broke, or as near as might be, with Austria, and at the same time introduced democratic reforms and made concessions to the nationalities, all her troubles would be solved at once: her neighbours would drop their designs on her when they saw their kinsmen well treated, and the Entente would have no reason to treat her harshly. He soon gained a considerable following, composed partly of naïve nationalists who accepted his thesis, partly of radicals who wanted social reform for its own sake.

Meanwhile, the military situation of Austria and her allies was still far from being altogether unfavourable. The United States had declared war on Germany (although not on the Monarchy), but it would be some time before it could put an army into the field, and the unrestricted submarine warfare which Germany had initiated (against the Austrians' protests) was taking a heavy toll of Allied shipping. Russia's war effort had become almost ineffectual, and on 15 December the Bolsheviks were obliged to sign an armistice, Roumania following suit two days later. In the West, both France and Italy were near-exhausted – in October Italy suffered, at Caporetto, one of the heaviest defeats of the war – and Britain weary. Victory for Austria seemed not impossible, if she could hold on a little longer.

But at home, the autumn of 1917 and the following winter were grim indeed. The harvest was bad everywhere, yielding only half the anticipated quantities in the German and Hungarian districts and one-third in the Slav. Less than this was delivered to the authorities, for the farmers were hoarding everywhere. In a well-meant endeavour to tempt supplies on to the market, Esterházy had abolished the requisitioning machinery in Hungary. The foodstuffs appeared, but were bought up by speculators. Wekerle restored controls and even created an independent Ministry of Public Supply, but the damage was done. The Minister, Hadik, scraped together just enough to feed the army after a fashion, but there was little over for Austria. Then came an early and hard winter.

The prices of basic necessaries were controlled, but these were in such short supply that everyone had to supplement them, if he could, on the free market. Here prices were soaring and inflation setting in.

It was thus a time of great anxiety for the workers and middle classes, especially of Vienna and the big industrial centres, and a great war-weariness set in. Revolutionary feeling was stimulated by Friedrich Adler's defence,[1] which it took him two whole days to deliver – at his trial, in reality an eloquent attack on the 'system' and plea for peace – and by the example of the Russian revolution, of which sanguine stories were brought home by returning prisoners of war, many of them imbued with extremist doctrines.

[1] It was reprinted in a booklet, *Friedrich Adler vor dem Ausnahmegericht*, which is an indispensable source for the social history of the period.

In these circumstances, the Social Democrat Party became a force, the weight of which was on the side of ending the war. At its Congress in October 1917, the Party adopted a programme which in essentials was that of the Independent Socialists of Germany, calling for a peace without annexations or reparations. In January 1918, when the flour ration was reduced from 200 to 165 grammes per day, a strike broke out among the munition workers of Wiener Neustadt, whence it spread to Vienna and even Hungary. It was almost of revolutionary dimensions, and the Social Democrat leaders agreed to pacify the workers only on condition that certain internal alleviations be introduced, and that the peace negotiations with Russia then proceeding at Brest-Litovsk should not be allowed to break down on territorial issues. The Government had to promise formally to fulfil these terms.

At this time an important change came in the Party's policy. Among the repatriates from Russia was Dr Otto Bauer, a very brilliant Socialist thinker who already before the war had made his name by his great study *Die Nationalitätenfrage und die Sozialdemokratie*. Bauer foresaw the break-up of the Monarchy and decided to make friends with the Nationalist leaders. In opposition to Renner's Great Austrian programme, he proposed at the October Congress a resolution which practically endorsed separation on national lines. The Party found this too much, but a Left wing now formed, under Bauer's leadership, and in January 1918, this group produced its own 'nationalities programme', recognizing the right of the non-Germans to self-determination and claiming the same right for the Germans.

The great strikes of January were followed by others in other parts of the Monarchy, and even, on 1 February, by a mutiny of the fleet in Cattaro harbour.

On 9 February the Central Powers concluded a separate peace with the Ukraine which, it was hoped, would relieve the supply situation. In the event, it brought only meagre help, for the task of getting more than a fraction of their hoards out of the Ukrainian peasants proved beyond the powers of the military. It also involved further political trouble with the Poles, since the Central Powers had in return to recognize as Ukrainian the district of Cholm, which was disputed between Poles and Ukrainians, and Austria had further to promise to constitute East Galicia and the Bukovina as a separate Crownland. Until then, a party among the Austrian Poles had still favoured an 'Austrian' solution for the Polish question: Charles was to have been proclaimed King of Poland. Now the Poles denounced him for betraying their cause, and Galicia became demonstratively disloyal – only a few Conservatives remained true to the Monarchy. As by this time the United States, Britain and France had all come out in favour of Polish independence, it was clear that failing a miracle, Polish Galicia, at least, was lost to the Monarchy. On the other hand, its prospects of retaining its Czech, Croat and Slovene districts had brightened, for although the United

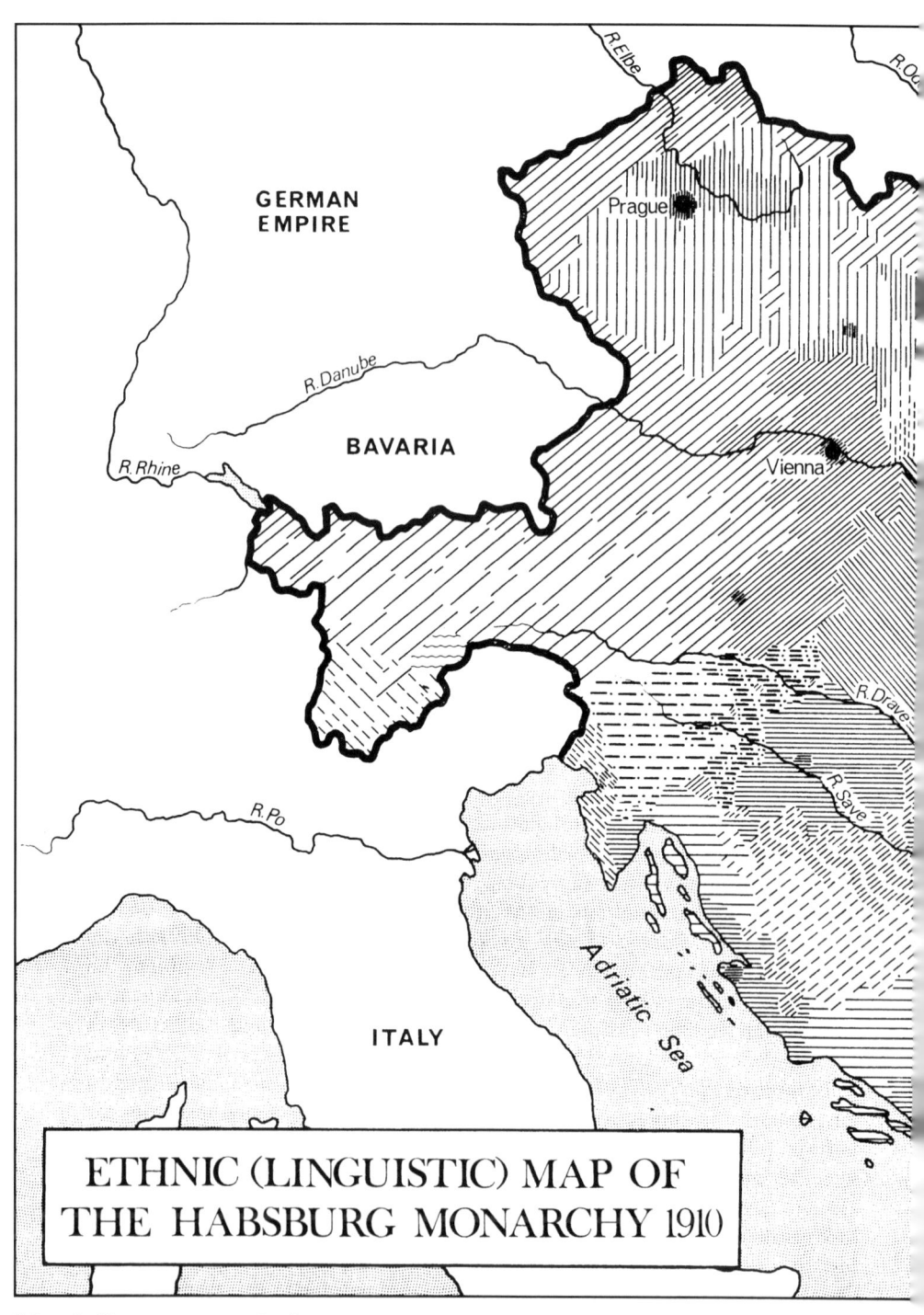

Map 6 (See note on p. 837)

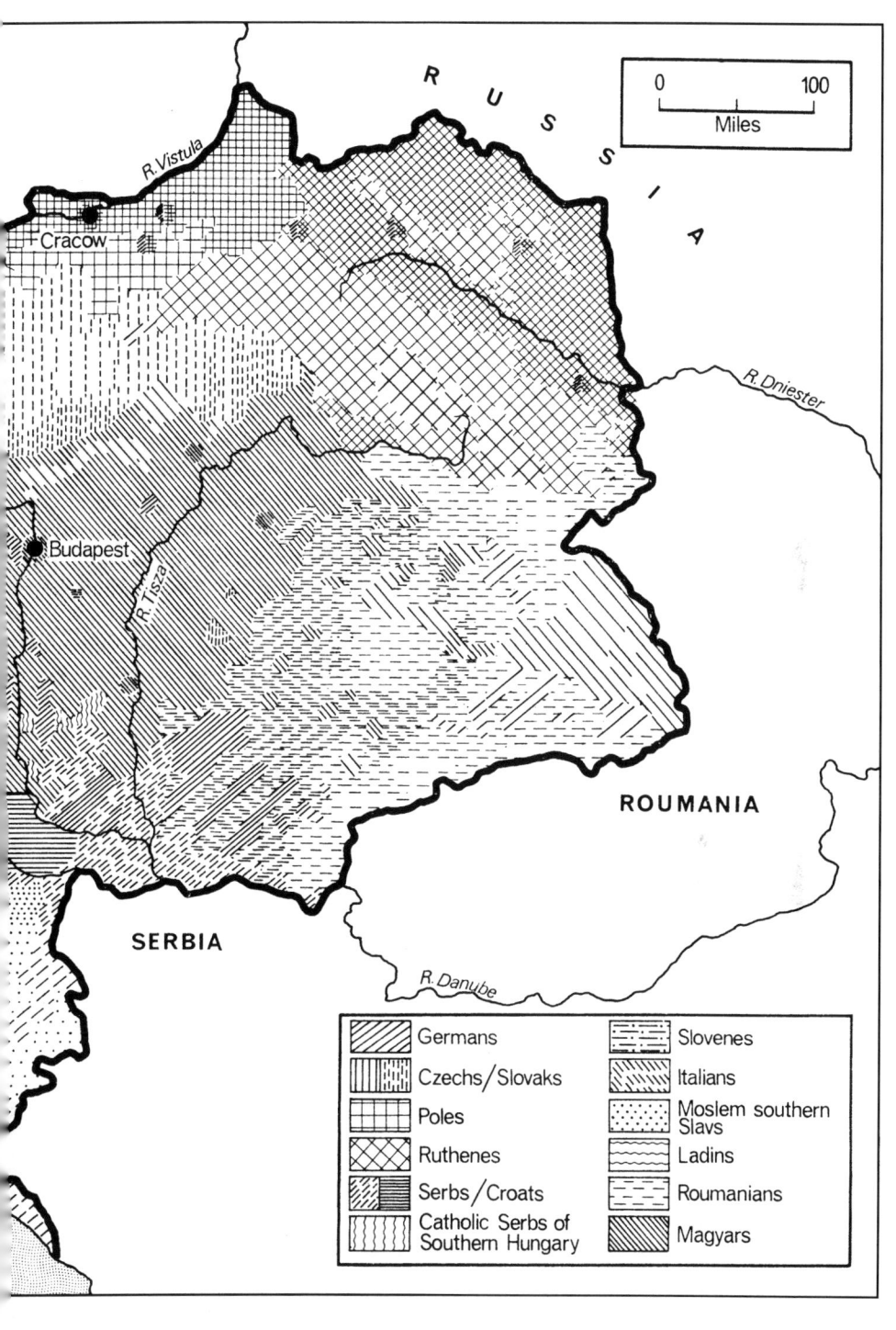

States had now declared war on the Monarchy also, and Wilson was making magniloquent speeches on self-determination as 'not a mere phrase but an imperative principle of action which statesmen would thereafter disregard at their peril', yet in fact, secret endeavours, in which precisely Wilson was a moving force, were being made to entice Austria into a separate peace. If this were to be achieved, her territory would have to be left intact in so far as engagements which could not be repudiated did not absolutely forbid, and the Allies appear not to have regarded their promises to Supilo and Masaryk, or even the Serbs, as falling under this heading. At any rate, they went back on them a long way.[1]

But the spirits that were abroad now could no longer be layed. The Poles were practically ignoring Vienna. The Czechs were by now secretly taking their orders from the National Committee in Paris: these were, to make no move which might hinder or retard the disintegration of the Monarchy. On 6 January 150 Czech political leaders adopted a Resolution[2] which declared that the 'Czecho-Slovak nation' now regarded itself as 'quit of any obligation towards the Dualist Monarchy and the Dynasty' and 'master of its own combatant forces'. It demanded independence in a sovereign State 'erected within the historic frontiers of the Lands of the Bohemian Crown and the Slovak people'.

On 20 July 1917, the Yugoslav Committee and the Serb Government had signed a Pact in Corfu for the union of 'the Serbs, Croats and Slovenes, also known as Southern Slavs, or Yugoslavs' in a single State under the Karageorgević Dynasty. When the news of this reached Croatia, the Serbo-Croat Coalition recovered its position there. Radić went over to the Yugoslav idea, while the Party of Right, in any case weakened by the death of Starčević, ceased to oppose it.[3] Now the Sabor passed Resolution after Resolution in favour of Yugoslav unity, not always troubling to insert the saving clause that this should be achieved within the framework of the Monarchy.

And in the event, their confidence proved well-founded. When the German offensive broke on the French front in March, and an Austrian attack threatened on the Italian, the British propagandists[4] urged, and the Italians (whose hostility to the Yugoslav movement had thitherto been stubborn) agreed, that if defeat was to be avoided, it was necessary to proclaim Czecho-Slovak, Polish, Southern Slav and Roumanian independence as an Allied war aim. The decision does not seem to have been formally ratified on the highest

---

[1] See on this Macartney and Palmer, pp. 68 ff., 78 ff.
[2] Known from its date as the Epiphany Resolution.
[3] Starčević's successor, Pavelić, was a 'Yugoslav'.
[4] Britain had recently established a Ministry of Propaganda under Lord Northcliffe, who had taken the natural but fateful step of putting Steed and Seton-Watson in charge of propaganda to the Monarchy.

level,[1] and in any case, the U.S.A. was not a party to it, but propaganda in the sense of it began, and soon after, there occurred a contretemps which was disastrous for Austria. Charles, through his brother-in-law, Prince Sixtus of Parma, had written to Clemenceau promising to support France's 'just claims to Alsace-Lorraine'. This leaked out through an indiscretion, and the enraged Germans, among whom a party had for some time past been advising tightening the controls over Austria, compelled Charles to journey to Spa, protest his complete loyalty, and on 12 May promise to conclude agreements which, at least in the eyes of the Allies, would have left the Monarchy little more than a political, military and economic satellite of Germany's.

The Allied Powers now dropped their hesitations, and after some hesitation, Wilson followed them. In the course of the next weeks, all Austria's chief opponents pledged themselves, more or less definitively, to independence for Polish and Czecho-Slovak States. Objections by Italy and obstruction by the Serb Government prevented agreement from being reached so quickly on the Southern Slav question – the final answer here was not given until the end of the year – but in June the U.S.A. Government promised the Southern Slavs also 'complete freedom'. Roumania had been forced to conclude a separate peace with the Central Powers on 7 May, thus rendering the Treaty of Bucharest invalid, but the Allied propaganda had not dropped the Roumanians from the list of 'oppressed races' to whom it was promising freedom.

All this became immediately known to the leaders of the nationalities in question inside the Monarchy, and naturally increased their confidence, and meanwhile, the Sixtus Letter and the Spa undertakings had also had disastrous effects elsewhere. The German national politicians saw themselves betrayed by the Monarch himself, and their loyalties moved yet further to the Reich. The Christian Socials and Clericals, on the contrary, being loyal to the Dynasty, found the prospective relationship with Germany intolerable, and saw their only hope of salvation in breaking away quickly. The Social Democrats, who wanted nothing but peace, concluded that only the break-up of the Monarchy could bring it.

Both the latter arguments applied, *mutatis mutandis*, to Hungary, and Károlyi's following increased daily.

A few weeks after this, Austria, under German pressure, launched another offensive against Italy. The Italians, stiffened by British and French reinforcements, resisted it with unexpected stubbornness, and the attack had to be called off on 24 June, after fighting which had lasted only ten days, but had cost the Austrian armies 140,000 casualties in dead, wounded or missing.

[1] Mr Balfour made on it the extraordinarily disingenuous comment that his policies, of promising independence to the nationalities and preserving the Habsburg Monarchy, were not mutually exclusive, since the former could be utilized to blackmail the Monarchy into saving itself by making a separate peace. The whole policy of the Allies on this question is riddled with dishonesty.

By this time, conditions for the civilian populations of large parts of the Monarchy were reaching the limit of human endurance. In the big towns and industrial centres, queues waited all day for the miserable pittances to which their ration cards entitled them, and even those were often not available. Everyone who could went out into the country and brought back rucksacks or pockets full of food, bought from the peasants at enormous and constantly rising prices, or exchanged for commodities. But the peasants themselves, short of labour, of livestock and of implements, had little enough to spare.

The forces at the front were themselves short of rations, of uniforms, even of munitions,[1] and after the failure of the offensive against Italy, a rot set in here also. Desertions to the enemy and mutinies multiplied. Men slipped away from the depots and went into hiding; 'green cadres' composed of such fugitives defied the authorities in parts of Bosnia and Croatia. So many units had to be kept in the hinterland 'maintaining order' as gravely to weaken the combatant strength of the army.

Czernin had resigned after the Sixtus affair, in connection with which he had, in good faith, told what had proved to be an untruth. Burian, recalled to take his place, exhausted himself throughout the summer in telling the Germans that Austria could not face another winter of war. Still confident, even after their armies' 'black day' of 8 August, the Germans refused to listen to him, and on 14 September he himself sent a Note to the Allies proposing informal peace talks. This brought an unhelpful reply from Wilson and a telegram of rebuke from the German Emperor to Charles.

But on 19 September the Bulgarian front cracked, and on the 26th Bulgaria sued for an armistice. Now even the Germans gave up hope, and on 3 October Germany, Austria-Hungary and Turkey sent simultaneous Notes to Wilson asking for an armistice. Wilson took his time over his reply, and on 16 October, while the Monarchy waited for it, Charles, who had replaced Seidler by Hussarek as Austrian Minister President on 23 July[2] made the peoples of Cis-Leithania a new offer, which he hoped would meet Wilson's requirements: the Poles were to go their own way, and the rest to form a federal State, in which each nation was to form its own constitution on its own ethnic territory.[3] But Wekerle, shown an advance draft of the

[1] In one unit there were uniforms only for the men in the front line. The men in reserve wore underclothing only.

[2] Seidler had resigned on 25 June, after the Poles had demanded his head for failing to defend the indivisibility of Galicia at Brest-Litovsk. Hussarek was governing with a makeshift majority composed of the non-Socialist Germans, the Polish Conservatives, the Roumanians of the Bukovina and the Italians of Istria.

[3] Hussarek, although he counter-signed the Manifesto, was not the author. It had been composed in Charles' secretariat and afterwards revised by various hands, including German nationalists, who had insisted on the phrase 'Ethnic territory' in order to save German Bohemia from the Czechs.

Manifesto, had stipulated that no proposals for Cis-Leithania could affect the Lands of the Hungarian Crown, and the Manifesto included a reservation to that effect. The Czechs and Slovenes declared that they rejected out of hand any proposal which did not allow for their union with their brothers and cousins in Trans-Leithania. But they would not in any case have accepted the offer, without claiming the whole Province: a Czech National Committee had already practically taken charge in Bohemia, and on 6 October a 'National Council of Serbs, Croats and Slovenes' had established itself in Zagreb with the declared purpose of 'uniting the whole people of the Serbs, Croats and Slovenes . . . in a single entirely sovereign national State'. Local Councils in smaller provincial centres accepted the authority of this body. The Polish Council of Regency had proclaimed the establishment of a 'free and independent Poland' on the 7th, and thundered against the Manifesto because it did not give them East Galicia. Of the non-Germans, only the Ruthenes accepted the Manifesto, precisely because they hoped it would give them East Galicia, and the National Council which they, in their turn, set up, still looked to Vienna – across a great gulf. And on the 8th and 9th the German-Austrian Deputies of the Reichsrat, on the initiative of the Social Democrats, began discussing their own future, on the assumption that Polish, Czecho-Slovak and Yugoslav States were coming into being.

In Hungary, the Croats were openly going their own way, the Roumanians had set up a National Council on the 12th, and the Slovak nationalists were preparing to do likewise. Nevertheless, Károlyi was clamouring louder than ever to be put in power to negotiate a separate peace, while Wekerle himself announced that the Manifesto reduced Hungary's link with Cis-Leithania to a personal union.

Thus Wilson's reply, which became known on the 20th and said that the President could no longer be bound by the tenth of his Fourteen Points, which had simply demanded 'autonomy' for the peoples of the Monarchy; the Czecho-Slovaks and Yugoslavs must be their own judges of what would satisfy them – did little more than recognize an existing situation. In fact, Charles on the 23rd appointed a Committee (transformed on the 27th into a Cabinet) under the distinguished pacifist, Professor Lammasch, to carry through the peaceful liquidation of Austria, and on the 24th he entrusted the Portfolio of Foreign Affairs to Count Gyula Andrássy, jun., who sent off a Note accepting Wilson's conditions and again asking for an armistice. Again the answer was slow to arrive, and pending its coming, the disintegration went on. On the 28th a Czecho-Slovak Republic was proclaimed in Prague, and the Poles set up a 'liquidation Committee' to wind up relations between Vienna and the already existent Polish State. On the 29th the Sabor in Zagreb proclaimed Croatia-Slavonia, with Dalmatia and Fiume, an independent State, part of the 'national and sovereign State of the Serbs, Croats and Slovenes'. The Landtag in Laibach issued a similar proclamation on the 31st, Serajevo on 1 November. The German-Austrian Deputies of the Reichsrat had already, on 21 October, voted the establishment of an independent German-Austrian State, to include all districts '(of Austria)' inhabited by Germans. A Constituent Assembly was to determine the Constitution of the new State. On the 30th the Deputies met again and declared themselves authorized to speak for the German-Austrian people in matters of foreign policy. A Council of State, to be elected immediately by the Reichsrat, was to take over the executive authority. A Coalition Government took office the next day.

On 1 November the Ruthenes proclaimed their independence. Last of the peoples of Cis-Leithania to be out of one war, they were first to be in the next, for they were promptly engaged in hostilities with the Poles.

In Hungary, Wekerle had resigned on the 23rd. A Governmental interregnum followed while the Archduke Joseph, whom Charles had appointed his *homo regius*, hesitated whom to propose for the succession. Meanwhile, Károlyi's followers from the Party of Independence, the Bourgeois Radicals[1] and the Social Democrats, formed a 'National Council' who mobilized the streets in their favour. On the evening of the 30th the Archduke yielded to the clamour and advised Charles to appoint Károlyi Minister President. The next day (which was also the day on which assassins broke into Tisza's house and murdered him), Charles actually administered the oath of loyalty to Károlyi, but released him from it on 1 November. The new Government announced themselves to be representing an independent State, unconnected with the Habsburgs' other dominions. Their belief that the change of regime would placate the Nationalities had, however, already been negated by the voices of the Nationalities themselves. On 27 October the Roumanians had claimed self-determination. Croatia-Slavonia, as we saw, had gone on the 29th, and on the 30th and 31st a meeting of Slovaks had decided to 'join Czecho-Slovakia'.

Meanwhile, on 24 October, the Allies had launched an offensive at Vittorio Veneto. For some days the Austrian armies resisted valiantly enough, but then the Czechs began to desert to the enemy, and the Hungarians to clamour to be sent back to defend their own endangered country. On the 31st Károlyi's Minister of War, Colonel Lindner, ordered them to return, and some began the journey. The fleet in Pola mutinied, and on Charles's orders its Commander-in-Chief, Admiral Horthy, handed it over to the representatives of the Serb-Croat-Slovene State.

On 1 November the Italian Command communicated to emissaries from the Austrian army the armistice terms on which the Supreme War Council had agreed. These obligated Austria to evacuate, roughly, the areas promised to Italy under the Treaty of London. The Allies were entitled also to occupy such other 'strategic points' within the Monarchy as they thought fit.

[1] A midget group, led by Jérzi, who had constituted themselves a 'party' in July, 1914.

Charles authorized acceptance, and the Austrian armies ceased fire at 3 a.m. on 3 November. The Italians, indeed, suspended hostilities only at 3 p.m. on the 4th. In the intervening thirty-six hours they had advanced, capturing large quantities of stores and 300,000 unresisting prisoners. Those Austrian soldiers who escaped captivity made their ways home, some in orderly formations, others as best they could, jettisoning their arms on the way.

Meanwhile, a mixed French and Serbian force had reached Belgrade. Its commander, General Franchet d'Espérey, maintained that the Armistice of Padua applied to the Italian front only. Károlyi led a delegation to Belgrade to receive terms from him, and the General presented him with a line which authorized the French and Serbian troops to occupy large parts of South and South-Eastern Hungary. To add to Hungary's troubles, Roumania redeclared war on 9 November and marched into Transylvania, while Czech detachments entered North Hungary under the pretext of occupying 'strategic points' under the Padua Armistice.

By this time only one top-level question had still to be decided. Neither German-Austria nor Hungary had yet officially pronounced on its future form of State. It was, however, clear that the majorities of both Governments favoured the republican form, for which rowdy mobs in both capitals were clamouring. After the German Kaiser had abdicated, on 9 November, his advisers warned Charles that even his own person was no longer secure.

On 11 November a proclamation from Charles was posted up in Vienna. 'Filled', it read, 'now as ever with unshakeable love for My peoples, I will no longer set My person as a barrier to their free development. I recognize in advance the decision which German-Austria will take on its future form of State. The people has now taken over the Government through its representatives. I renounce any participation in the business of the State. Simultaneously I relieve My Austrian Government of office.'

The next day, the German-Austrian Provisional Parliament proclaimed the constitution of the German-Austrian Republic. On the 13th Charles, who had retired to his near-by estate of Eckartsau, handed a declaration in similar terms to three emissaries from the Hungarian Parliament, which in its turn proclaimed Hungary a republic on the 16th. The old Monarchy had ceased to exist.

Appendix 1

TITLES

The Habsburgs used 'Great', 'Middle' and 'Small' titles. The 'Great Title' assumed by Francis under his Patent of 4 August 1806 ran:

Wir, Franz der Erste, von Gottes Gnaden Kaiser von Oesterreich, König von Jerusalem, Hungarn, Boheim, Dalmatien, Croatien, Slavonien, Galizien und Lodomerien, Erzherzog zu Oesterreich, Herzog zu Lothringen, zu Salzburg, zu Würzburg und in Franken, zu Steyer, Kärnthen und Krain, Grossherzog zu Krakow; Grossfürst zu Siebenbürgen, Markgraf in Mähren, Herzog zu Sandomir, Massovien, Lublin, Ober und Niederschlesien, zu Ausschwitz und Zator, zu Teschen und zu Friaul, Fürst von Berchtesgaden und Mergentheim, gefürsteter Graf zu Habsburg. Görz und Gradisca; Markgraf zu Ober und Niederlausitz und in Istrien, Herr des Landes Wolhynien, Podlachien und Brzesz, zu Trieste, zu Freudenthal und Eulenburg und auf der Windischen Mark, usw., usw.

Ferdinand's accession diploma added the Kingdoms of Rama, Servia, Cumania and Bulgaria, and in 1840 the following were added: the Kingdoms of Lombardy, Venetia and Illyria, the Grand Duchy of Tuscany, the Duchies of Modena, Parma, Piacenza and Guastalla, Ragusa and Zara; the Principalities of Trient and Brixen and the Countships of Hohenembs, Feldkirchen, Bregenz, Sonnenberg, etc. This list remembered to call the Kingship of Hungary Apostolic.

By 1867 Francis Joseph had added the Bukovina and Cattaro, but dropped Lombardy, Venetia, Würzburg, Franconia, Freudenthal and Eulenburg, and some of the Polish titles.

Appendix 2

CURRENCY, WEIGHTS AND MEASURES

Currency. The basic Austrian coin, during nearly the whole period covered by this history, was the Gulden (H., fórint), stabilized in 1773 at a rate of 20 Gulden to one fine Cologne Mark with a content of 23·39 gr. silver. It was known as a 'Conventionsmünze', the standard having been agreed in a Convention between Austria and certain other German States. Two Gulden were equal to one Thaler, while the Gulden was divided into 60 (after 1856, 100) Kreuzer (H. krájcár) and the Kreuzer into 4 Groschen (H. garas). 20-Kreuzer pieces (Zwanziger, H. huszás) were also minted. The Thaler soon went out of common use, except in Abyssinia, where it remained legal currency up to modern times; in the inter-war period the Austrian mint was still striking Maria Theresa Thaler for that country. The other coins remained in common use, although during the Napoleonic Wars all the silver and most of the copper was called in, and replaced by paper currency, which depreciated very largely in value. The reforms of 1818 re-established the old values, and the new paper again bore the inscription C.M. (Conventionsmünze), although for a time there existed side by side with it another paper currency, the Wiener Währung (W.W.), worth only forty per cent of the C.M. of the same nominal value. In 1892 Austria went over to the gold standard, and the Gulden was replaced by the Krone (H. korona) at the rate of 1 Gulden = 2 Kronen. A Krone now consisted of 100 Heller (H. fillér).

Linear Measures. 1 Klafter = 2·07 feet. 1 Austrian Meile = 4·9782 English miles.

Square Measures. 1 Joch (yoke) = 1,600 square Klafter = 0·576 hectares = 1·43 English acres. The Hungarian 'cadastral hold' was the same as the Austrian Joch, but there existed also an older 'Magyar hold', the size of which varied slightly from place to place, but was usually in the region of 0·43 ha. or 1·07 acres. 1 Austrian square Meile = 22·239 English square miles.

Weights and Dry Measures. The usual Metzen (H. merö) equalled 1·74 English bushels, but there were many variants. 1 Pfund (H. font) = 1·235 English pounds avoirdupois. 1 Zentner (H. mázsa) contained 100 Pfund, or 123·48 lb. Weights were often calculated in Doppelzentner, ten to a ton.

Liquid Measure. 40 Mass = 1 Eimer = 14·95 gallons.

Appendix 3

PLACE NAMES

G German; H Hungarian; I Italian; Cz Czech; R Roumanian; P Polish; Slk Slovak; Slo Slovene; S Serb Ru Ruthene; Cr Croat.

Bácska H. Bačka S.
Balázsfalva H. Blasendorf G. Blaj R.
Besztercze H. Besztercze-Bánya H. Bistritz G. Bistriţe R. Banska Bistriţa Slk.
Bjelovar Cr. Bélovár-Körös H. Kreuz G.
Brassó H. Kronstadt G. Braşov R.
Brixen G. Bressanone I.
Brünn G. Brno Cz.
Buccari I. Bokor S.
Buda H. Ofen G.
Budweiss G. Budowice Cz.

Cattaro I & G. Kotor S.
Cilli I. Cilje Slov.
Czernowitz G. Cernauţi Ro.

Fiume I & H. Rijeka Cr.

Göttschee G. Gočej Slo.
Györ H. Raab G.
Gyulafehérvár H. Weissenburg G. Alba Julia R.

Karlóca H. Karlowitz G. Karlovci (Sremski) S.
Karlovac Cr. Karlstadt G. Károlyváros H.
Kassa H. Kaschau G. Košice Slk.
Kolozsvár H. Klausenburg G. Cluj R.
Komárom H. Komorn G. Komarnó Slk.
Komotau-Aussig G. Ušti Chamutov Cz.

Königgrätz G. Sadova Cz.
Kremsier G. Kromeřiž Cz.

Laibach G. Ljubljana Slo.
Lemberg G. Lwow P. Lvov Ru. Lviv modern Ukrainian (so I am informed). Léopol French.

Máramaros H. Maramureş R.
Marburg G. Maribor Sl.
Munkács H. Mukačevo Cz. Slk.
Muraköz H. Medjumurje Cr.

Nagyszeben H. Hermannstad G. Sibiu R.
Nagyszombat H. Tyrnau G. Trnava Slk.
Nagyvárad H. Grosswardein G. Oradea Mare R.

Olmütz G. Olomouc Cz.

Passarowitz G. Passarovic H, S.
Pécs H. Fünfkirchen G.
Pilsen G. Plžen Cz.
Pošega S. Pozsega H.
Pozsony H. Pressburg G. Bratislava Slk.

Reichenberg G. Liberec Cz.

Sopron H. Oedenburg G.
Szabadka H. Mariatheresiopol G. Subotica Serb.
Szatmár H. Satu Mare R.

APPENDIX

Szeged H. Szegedin G.
Székesfehérvár H. Stuhlweissenburg G.
Szombathely H. Steinamanger G.
Szrem H. Srem S. Syrmien G.

Temesvár H. Timişoara R.
Tisza (R). H. Theiss G.
Trient G. Trento I.
Turopolje Cr. Turmezö H.

Turóczszentmartón H. Turčjanský Sväty Marton Slk.

Ujvidék H. Neusatz G. Novi-Sad S.

Varašdin Cr. Várasd H. Warasdin G.
Virovica Cr. Veröcze H.

Zagreb Cr. Zágráb H. Agram G.
Zengg G. Senj Cr.

Note to Map 6

As bases for this map the Austrian and Hungarian censuses of 1910 have been used, and (for Bosnia-Herzegovina) the Yugoslav census of 1921. Generally, therefore, the map takes the linguistic criterion of ethnic appurtenance, but since the Austrian and Hungarian censuses counted 'Serbo-Croat' as one language, and thus did not distinguish between the two peoples, we have divided this linguistic group by religions. In general, Catholic speakers of 'Serbo-Croat' are equated with Croats, and Orthodox with Serbs; but we have given separate symbols to the Serb-speaking Moslems of Bosnia, and to the Catholic Serbs (Sokci and Bunyevci) of South Hungary.

The Ladins, lumped together in the Austrian census with the Italian-speakers, are also shown separately here. It has not proved possible to show the distribution of the population of Israelite faith.

Such allowance as space permits has been made for density of population by the device of spacing the lines more closely in densely-populated areas, and further apart where the population was sparse. The result is only to be taken as approximate, but it is hoped thereby to correct in some measure the enormously distorted impression of the relative numbers of the different ethnic groups resulting from a map which gives equal weight to the populations of a densely-populated conurbation and a mountain range containing only a few hamlets and scattered farms.

Bibliography

What follows is only a highly selective short list of works in which the reader may find more details on the subjects with which my book has dealt, or a different treatment of them. As in my text, I have cut references to diplomatic and military history, and to *Kulturgeschichte*, to the minimum. I have not listed older works where they have been superseded by later, nor, unless forced to do so by their importance or by the absence of anything more solid, articles in periodicals; for these the reader must consult the bibliographies listed below. I have, with reluctance, included a few books in Hungarian (Mr Péter has helped me in the selection of these), and Roumanian, but only where I have been unable to give anything of comparable value in a more accessible language. That I have not done the same for the Slav languages is due to my deficiencies as a linguist, and I am aware that the Poles, Ruthenes, Slovaks and Southern Slavs consequently come off very badly. The Czechs are better off, for there is a large literature on them in non-Czech, by their friends as well as their enemies.

In the list which follows I have curtailed some of the names where they are very extensive (as is often the case with books by Central European writers) and where I am satisfied that the operation could not cause confusion or difficulty to anyone looking up the book in a library or bookseller's catalogue. I have also allowed myself a few abbreviations: besides the familiar ed., vol, etc. (I also shorten bibliography to bib.), I have regularly used the following abbreviations: in English titles, A for Austria or Austrian, H. for Hungary or Hungarian; in German, Oe.(s) for Oesterreich(s), oe. for oesterreichisch and its declinations, Gesch. for Geschichte, Jht. for Jahrhundert, k. u. k. for kaiserlich und königliche, u.u. for ungarn ungarisch; in Hungarian, M-g, for Magyarország (Hungary) (if a suffix follows, this is postpositional), m. for magyar. When a section or sentence is specifically described as relating to some individual, I have not thought it necessary to exhaust the reader's patience and insult his intelligence by writing out the name in full every time: thus I credit him with the ability to interpret the abbreviation F.J. in the section headed Francis Joseph, and S. in the sentence beginning: 'biographies of Schwarzenberg'.

[N.Y., indicating a place of publication, stands, of course, for New York; Bp., for Budapest.]

General

A. For a very full bib. of the whole subject, see Uhlirz, A. and M., *Handbuch der Gesch. Oe.s und seiner Nebenländer Böhmen und Ungarn*, Graz, 1927, 3 vols, with supplement 1941; new ed. now (1968) in course of preparation. This admirable work, which supersedes all its predecessors, is near-exhaustive for literature in German, especially on the Monarchy as a whole and its German Lands; less so for works in other languages, or for the 'Nebenländer', but the first vol of the new ed. includes bibs. in Hungarian, Czech, etc. and most of the chief works in those languages. It also lists the learned periodicals for all parts of the ex-Monarchy, besides referring in the appropriate places to articles in them. Bridge, F. R., *The Habsburg Monarchy, 1804–1918*, London, 1968, is a valuable list, with short critical notes, of books and pamphlets published in the U.K. between 1818 and 1967. There is a bib. of works in English on Hungary in Teleki, P., *The Evolution of H.*, N.Y., 1923. Since 1965 Rice University, Texas, has issued a useful *Austrian History Yearbook* on work recently appeared or in preparation (I cite this as *A.H. Yearbook*). Many of the works listed below contain bibs. Where these are useful, I mark the work with a *.

B. Works covering all or a substantial part of my period, and all or most of the Monarchy:

Of these, Uhlirz' own 'Handbook', viz. the sections of narrative which link the bibliographical chapters, is far from being the least helpful, until after 1870, when the author's Germanic feelings rather run away with him. Another older work which needs very little revision even today, and is very convenient, is Charmatz, R.'s five-volume series, *Gesch. der Auswärtigen Politik Oe.s im XIX Jht.*, I, *bis 1848*, II, *1848–1895*; *Oe.s Innere Gesch. 1848–1895*, I, *1848–1871*, II, *1871–1895*; and *Oe.s Äussere und Innere Politik, 1895–1915*, all last issued, Leipzig, 1918. Later histories include Hantsch, H., *Gesch. Oe.*, Vienna, 3rd ed., 1964, 2 vols, of which the second covers our period, masterly writing and vision, Catholic-Conservative sympathies; Zöllner, E., *Gesch. Oe.*, Vienna, 3rd ed., 1964, summary for some aspects of the nineteenth century, but text and bibs. good, especially for economic and cultural developments in the German-Austrian Lands; Mayr-Kaindl-Pirchegger (quoted as *M.K.P.*), *Gesch. und Kulturleben Oe.s*, an old work revised and brought up to date by later hands, 3 vols, of which vol 3 interests us, straightforward and informative, 2nd. ed. of last revision, Vienna, 1965. Further, Bibl, V. *Der Zerfall Oe.s*, Vienna, 1922, 2 vols, and id., *Die Tragödie Oe.s* (the *Zerfall* shortened and re-written); 'Liberal' ideology which finds everything in the old regime wrong, irritating, badly arranged and unindexed into the bargain, but stimulating. Benedikt, H., *Monarchie der Gegensätze*, Vienna, 1947, impressionistic. To all these, however, the remarks in my preface about tribal historians apply, least so to Hantsch, but he cannot be excepted.

For institutions, etc. Luschin-Ebengreuth, A., *Grundriss der oe. Reichsgesch.*, Bamberg, 2nd. ed., 1918, extraordinarily useful work, not tribal.

In English, Taylor, A. J. P., *The Habsburg Monarchy*, London, 3rd ed., 1964, individual; Kann, A., *The Habsburg Empire*, London, 1957, short sketch.

I place here, in deference to their scope, Eisenmann, L., *Le Compromis Austro-Hongrois de 1867*, Paris, 1904, primarily a history and appreciation of the 'Compromise' of 1867, but extending far beyond this in every respect, often very brilliant; and Redlich, J., *Der oe. Staats-und Reichsproblem* (quoted as Redlich, *Problem*), Leipzig, 1924–6, 2 vols, primarily a history of the constitutional experiments of 1848–67, on which it is very profuse and heavily documented, but also with long introductory reflections. For 1867–1914, May, A. J., *The Hapsburg Monarchy, 1867–1914*, Cambridge, Mass., 2nd. ed., 1965, incomparably the best work in English in its field, and indeed, the only one to cover all aspects of its subject.

This is also the place to list Jászi, O., *The Dissolution of the Habsburg Monarchy*, Chicago, 2nd. ed., 1929, an essay rather than a history, but including much history in its enormous field; a very brilliant work, which anyone interested in the Monarchy will ignore at his peril. He will, however, also be unwise to make it his sole reading-matter on the subject.

Of the great series, *Die oe. Zentralverwaltung*, begun by Fellner and Kretschmayer, then continued by F. Walter, the volumes quoted below belong to this period.

Several biographical collections are concerned in whole or part with this period. Chief among them, the *Neue Oe. Biographie (quoted as *N. Oe. B.*), 17 vols to date, 1st vol, Vienna, 1923. Several good sketches also in Hantsch, H. (ed.), *Gestalter der Geschicke Oe.s (quoted as *Gestalter*), Innsbruck, 1962. Several good portraits in Charmatz, *Lebensbilder aus der Gesch. Oe.* (quoted as Charmatz, *Lebensbilder*), Vienna, 1947, and in Friedjung, A., *Historische Aufsätze*, Stuttgart, 1919.
Military. v. Wrede, A., *Gesch. der k. u. k. Wehrmacht*, Vienna, 5 vols, 1896–1907. Horsetzky, General A., *Kriegsgesch. Ueberblick über die Feldzüge seit 1790*, Vienna, 7th ed., 1917.
Finance. State finances: de Beer, A., *Die Finanzen Oe.s*, Prague, 1877, still the stand-by of all later writers. Private finance: Scheffer, E., *Das Bankwesen in Oe.*, Vienna, 1924. Believe it or not, when seeking literature on the subject in 1964, I was referred to this book, which is quite a short one.

The inter-Land variety of cultural and economic developments was such that no works have, to my knowledge, appeared on either subject which can fittingly be named in this section; but Tomek E., *Kirchengesch. Oe.s*, Innsbruck, 1949, 3 vols, (running up to 1848) is monumental, and Wodka, J., *Kirche in Oe.*, Vienna, 1959, handy. Education, general: Strakosch-Grossman, G., *Gesch. des oe. Unterrichtswesens*, Vienna, 1905.

C. General Histories of Lands and Peoples:

General. Nearly all the ethnographical works come more properly under later headings, but I may place here: Auerbach, B., *Les Races et les nationalités en Autriche-Hongrie*, 2nd ed., Paris, 1917, much anthropology and pre-history, but also some later history, etc., with many curious details; and Kann, A., *The Multinational Empire*, 1848–1918, N.Y., 1950, 2 vols, a study of the nationalities, their ambitions and suggested solutions of their problems, which goes back before its professed starting-point; learned. A conference at Indiana in 1966 held a discussion on 'The National Problem in the Habsburg Monarchy in the Nineteenth Century', the record of which was published by the *A.H. Yearbook*, Vol. II, pt. 2, 1967. I received this too late to utilize it fully, but draw attention to the more valuable papers in the appropriate places.

The Slavs in general. Fischel, A., *Der Panslawismus*, Stuttgart, 1919, a mine of information.

Zöllner, *M.K.P.*, etc. are already in reality essentially histories of German-Austria and its rulers: professedly so, Srbik, H., *Oe. in deutscher Gesch.*, Munich, 4th ed., 1936, and many others. Most histories of the German-Austrian Lands are either antiquated, or sketchy, or both, but there are some notable exceptions, e.g. Pirchegger, H., *Gesch. der Steiermark*, Graz, 1920–42, 3 vols, and Gutke, H., *Gesch. des Landes Nieder-Oe.*, St Pölten, 1957–65, 3 vols. For a full list, see Uhlirz. The sentimental literature about Vienna is enormous.

BIBLIOGRAPHY

Bohemia and the Czechs. Denis, E., *La Bohème depuis la Montagne Blanche*, Paris, 1930, 2 vols, grandiose work, strongly pro-Czech. Shorter, Seton-Watson, R. W., *A History of the Czechs and Slovaks*, London, 1943. From the German-Bohemian side, Bretholz, B., *Gesch. Böhmens und Mährens* Reichenberg, 1922-4, 4 vols. Münch, H., *Böhmische Tragödie*, Stuttgart, 1919, is badly arranged but fair and very informative.

The Slovenes are badly served. Least unsatisfactory general account. Loncar, D., *The Slovenes: A social history*, Cleveland, 1949. Zwitter, F., in *A.H. Yearbook*, 1967, is vague. References in Fischel, *Panslawismus* and in the following more general works on the Southern Slavs: Seton-Watson, R. W., *The Southern Slav Question*, London, 1911, Wendel, H., *Der Kampf der Südslawen um Freiheit und Einheit*, Frankfurt, 1925, Haumant, L. X., *La Formation de la Yougoslavie*. Paris, 1930, all three strongly 'Yugoslav'. See also the provincial histories ap. Uhlirz.

Galicia. Both papers on the Poles (by Wandycz, P. and Wereczycki, N.) and that on the 'Ukrainians' (by Rudnytsky, I. L.) in *A.H. Yearbook*, 1967, contain valuable material. Otherwise all I can find to put here is two chapters in the *Cambridge History of Poland*, vol. II, Cambridge, 1940, of which the second by R. Estreicher (1848-1918), is some use, although very short and chauvinistically Polish; the first (1815-48), by R. Fellman, is no use at all. There is no satisfactory full history of the Ruthenes. For the Bukovina, especially its Roumanians, Prokopowitsch, E., *Die rumänische nationale Bewegung in der Bukowina*, Graz, 1965, useful.

Hungary. The classic history is vol 5 (by Szekfü) of Hóman, B. and Szekfü, G., *Magyar Történet* (Hungarian History), Bp., 2nd. ed., 5 vols, 1936, by a brilliant historian. Recent, Spira, G., *A m. Nép Története* (History of the H. People), Bp., 2nd. ed., 1953, Communist interpretation. Very useful is Miskolczy, J. (G), *U. in der Habsburger-Monarchie*, Vienna, 1959, less a history than an essay showing how far Hungary fitted into the Monarchy, and where not, why not; very fair to both sides, and perceptive. Short general histories in English: Sinor, D., *A Short History of H.*, London, 1959, and Macartney, C. A., *H., A Short History*, Edinburgh, 2nd. ed., 1966.

There are about twenty short histories of the Slovaks, none perceptibly better or worse than the others. Of the two papers in *A.H. Yearbook*, 1967, that by Holotik, L., is the better. For the Hungarian Serbs, Schwicker, J. B., *Politische Gesch. der Serben in U.*, Bp., 1860, is still useful. General surveys by Vucinich, W. S. and Djordjevic, D., in *A.H. Yearbook*, 1967. Croatia and the Croats, the works of R. W. Seton-Watson, Wendel and Haumant quoted above, and Kiszling, R., *Die Kroaten*, Graz, 1956, too short; also 'Südland' (I. von Pilar), *Die Südslawische Frage*, informative but intemperately pro-Croat, and Jelavich, C. and Krizman, B. in *A.H. Yearbook*, 1967. Transylvania and its Roumanians: Seton-Watson, R. W., *A History of the Roumanians* (also covers Moldavia and Wallachia), London, 1940, scholarly; Gáldi, L. and Makkai, L., *Gesch der Rumänen* (again includes the Danubian Provinces), Bp., 1942, Hungarian standpoint, but tries to be fair; Jorga, N., *Istoria Românilor din Ardeal şi Ungaria* (History of the Roumanians of Transylvania and H.), Bucharest, 1916, 2 vols, Roumanian standpoint, makes no such attempt; Makkai, L., *Histoire de la Transylvanie*, Paris, 1946, rather sketchy; Jancsó, B., *A Roman Nemzetiségi Törekvések*, etc. (The Roumanian National Aspirations), Bp., 1898-9, 2 vols, by a Hungarian specialist on Roumanian wickedness, well-documented. The papers by Fischer-Galaţi, S. and Oţetea, A., in *A.H. Yearbook*, 1957, are controversial. The Transylvanian Saxons have a monumental history of their own, *Gesch. der Siebenbürger Sachsen*, first published by Teutsch, G., in 1870, later brought up to date, 4th ed., Hermannstadt, 1910, 3 vols, and a shorter *Die Siebenbürger Sachsen*, by Teutsch, Fr., Leipzig, 1916.

CHAPTER I

The Monarchy in 1780

It would obviously be impossible for me to give anything like a full bib. for this section; what follows is the merest sketch. There are, of course, innumerable biographies of Maria Theresa, and all the standard histories describe her reign at length, but the only general picture of the Monarchy in (or slightly after) 1780 which I know is a very old work, Demian, C., *Darstellung der Oe. Monarchie*, Vienna, 1804, 3 vols, a sort of proto-Baedeker, almost forgotten today but containing an astonishing amount of assorted information. Another description of many aspects is contained in vol I of Beidtel, I., *Gesch. der Oe. Staatsverwaltung*, Innsbruck, 2 vols, published 1896 but written fifty years earlier, a remarkable work which describes not only the political institutions of the Monarchy before and after Maria Theresa's reforms, but also its legal, educational, etc. systems, written with a refreshing independence of judgment; much of it superseded today by special studies, but its general picture still unsurpassed. There is a brilliant 'picture' of Hungary in Marczali, H., *Hungary in the eighteenth century*, Cambridge, 1910; good also is Grünwald, B., *A Régi M-g.* (The Old Hungary), Bp., 1889. For Bohemia, Kerner, J., *Bohemia in the XVIIIth Century*, N.Y., 1932, purports to do for Bohemia what Marczali did for Hungary, but is less exhaustive. For Galicia, Brawer, A. J., *Galizien wie es an Oe. kam*, Vienna, 1910, short study, essentially an interpretation of the statistics, valuable. For the Bukovina, Zieglauer, F., *Geschichtliche Bilder aus der Bukowina*, etc., Czernowitz, 3 vols, 1893–8.

Some, but disappointingly few, of the top-level enactments are in F. Walter's three volumes in the *Zentralverwaltung* series, II. I., Halbband I. and II (narrative), and II. 3 (texts), the results conveniently in Luschin-Ebengreuth, op cit. There is an excellent recent sketch of the first reform period in Walter, F., *Der Theresianische Staatsreform von 1749*, Vienna, 1948. For the *Staatsrat*, Hock, C. and Biedermann, J. H., *Der Oe. Staatsrat 1790–1848*, Vienna, 1879.

Demographic statistics: for Western Lands, Gürtler, R., *Die Volkszählungen Maria Theresiens und Joseph IIs*, Innsbruck, 1909; for Hungary, Thirring, G., *M-g. Népessége József II Korában* (the Population of H. in the time of Joseph II), Bp., 1938, first-class study, with commentary; for Galicia, Brawer, op. cit. All these statistics were broken down occupationally (although, as remarked elsewhere, not on the lines which the modern reader would expect), and thus throw light on the economic and social structures of the Lands concerned. Almost all studies of economic problems are local, and most of them to be found only in periodicals, for which see the bibs. (excellent in Zöllner), but Marczali and Kerner describe their respective Lands, and there is a first-class recent study by Otruba, G. **Die Wirtschaftspolitik Maria Theresias*, Vienna, 1963. For Viennese policy towards Hungarian industry, Eckhardt, F., *A bécsi udvár gazdasági politikája M-gon* (The Economic Policy of the Vienna Court in Hungary), Bp., 1922, excellent. For Transylvania, Müller, K., *Siebenbürgische Wirtschaftspolitik unter Maria Theresia*, Vienna, 1959, unfinished, published posthumously (the author was murdered in his hospital bed in 1945 by Czech freedom fighters). All the standard histories, including Luschin-Ebengreuth, have something on the peasants, and travellers' descriptions such as those of Damian and of Riesbeck, *Briefe eines reisenden Franzosen*, English tr., *Travels through Germany*, London, 1787, 3 vols, throw light on how the peasants really lived. The classic work on the reforms is Grünberg, K., *Die Bauernbefreiung in Böhmen und Mähren*, Leipzig, 1894, 2 vols (quoted as Grünberg, *Bauernbefreiung*), much used by writers who do not always notice that it refers only to the Bohemian Lands. For these, see also Kerner and the c. (IX. 12) in Arneth's *Maria Theresia*, valuable for its detailed record of the discussions in high places, but no general picture. Otruba, op. cit., is short but clear. For Hungary, besides Marczali, op. cit., Acsády, I., *A M. Jobbágyság Története* (History of villeinage in H.), Bp., 2nd. ed., 1944, excellent general sketch, and Szabó, D., *A M.-g.i Urbérrendezés* (The 'Urbarial' settlement in H.), Bp., 1933, 2 vols, account, with documentation (chiefly in Latin or German), of the reform imposed by Maria Theresa in 1764. A later (Marxist) work is Spira, G. (ed.), *Tanulmányok a parasztság Történetéhez M-g.on 1711–1790* (Studies on the History of the peasantry in H., 1711–1790), Bp., 1952. Blum, J., *Noble Landowners*, etc. (below) begins with the reforms and gives a valuable picture for the whole Monarchy.

Nationalities

For my population figures I have, as I have said elsewhere, had to work backwards. For early history and distribution, Auerbach, op. cit., the monumental unfinished *Ethnographie der Oe. Monarchie* by Baron K. Czoernig, Vienna, 1855, 3 vols, and the mass of later literature, often polemical, listed in the bibs. It is only recently that the idea of national hierarchies and differentiations has surfaced from the state of unthinking acceptance; for the Monarchy it was, if not invented, then certainly popularized by Bauer, O., in his *Nationalitäten* etc. (below), and is now being taken up with enthusiasm by the Marxist historians, with many illuminating results, although carts, it seems to me, often lead horses. Kann, op. cit., is steeped in it. A valuable article (by a German chauvinist, but an intelligent one) is H. Steinacker's long introduction to Hugelmann's *Nationalitätenrecht* (below). Literature of developments of national movements is given in the next section. For the actual development of linguistic usage in the western half of the Monarchy, Fischel, *Das oe. Sprachenrecht*, Brünn, 1906, good collection, and Gumplowicz, L., *Das Recht der Nationalitäten*, etc., Innsbruck, 1879.

CHAPTER II

Joseph II

Nearly all J.'s correspondence has been published in various collections by the Viennese *Akademie der Wissenschaften*; see the bibs. There is a severely eclectic selection of his decrees, which does not include any relating to Hungary, etc. in vols II. I. 2/2 (narrative) and II. 4 (texts) of the *Zentralverwaltung* series, ed. Walter. There is a complete *Sammlung* of all enactments, ed. Kropatschek, W., Vienna, 1785–90, 18 vols. All earlier biographies of J. and accounts of his reign were superseded by the magnificent and all-embracing work of P. von Mitranov, German trans. by V. von Demelic, *Joseph II*, Vienna, 1910, 2 vols. Of the later biographies the best (although short) is Bibl's *Kaiser J. II*, Vienna, 1944. Padover, S. K., *The Revolutionary Emperor*, London, 1934, Benedikt, E., *Kaiser J. II*, Vienna, 1936, and Fejtö, F., *J. II, Un Empéreur revolutionnaire*, Paris, 1953, are far inferior. Bright, J. F., *J. II*, London, 1907, is almost purely diplomatic.

CHAPTER III
Leopold II

For L.'s published correspondence, see the bibs. Walter's vol on Joseph in the *Zentralverwaltung* series cover L.'s reign also. Kropatschek produced a collection of his *Gesetze* in 5 vols, Vienna, 1792. In spite of its importance for the history of the Monarchy, L.'s reign was for long singularly neglected by historians. The neglect has been largely made good by Wandruschka, A., in a big and important work, *Leopold II*, Vienna, 1965, 2 vols, but this still does not entirely fill the gap, for it is a biography, rather than a history, devotes most of its space to L. in Italy, and often spend more time on explaining what made L. act as he did, than on saying what he did do. The gap is, however, partially filled by Mitranov, who, after describing Joseph's actions, often gives the reactions to them, and L.'s treatment thereof. Kerner covers L.'s reign for Bohemia and Szekfü for Hungary, but a good monograph in a major language on L. and Hungary, including Transylvania and the Serbs, is badly needed. Interesting recent works on L.'s plans, etc., especially as regards Hungary, include Wangermann, E., *From J. II to the Jacobin Trials*, Oxford, 1959, Silagi, D., *Ungarn und der Geheime Mitarbeiterkreis Kaiser L. IIs*, Munich, 1961, and id., *Jakobiner in der Habsburger Monarchie*, ibid., 1962.

CHAPTERS IV–VIII
Francis I (II) and Ferdinand I

A. General and Statistical. There are 'Statistische Tabellen' for several years, still unpublished, in the Austrian archives in Vienna. Censuses were taken every three years, and there is one printed digest of them, covering twenty-five years: Becker, S., *Die Bevölkerung Oe. 1818–1843*, Vienna, 1846, purely demographic. Works which use many statistics, but also go wider afield, like Demian (above) include Bisinger, J. C. *Generalstatistik des oe. Kaiserstaates*, Vienna and Trieste, 1808–9, 2 vols; Springer, S., *Statistik des oe. Kaiserstaates*, Vienna, 1840, 2 vols; and Hain, J., *Handbuch der Statistik des oe. Kaiserstaates*, Vienna, 1852 (but the figures which he uses are those of the Vormärz). All three are mines of information. For the similar works dealing only with Hungary, see below, Section V, E.

B. Francis I, political. For the central documents, Walter's vols in the *Zentralverwaltung* series, II./I/2.2 (narrative) and II. 5 (texts), also covering the reign of Ferdinand; Hock and Biedermann, op. cit.; and another *Sammlung der Gesetze*, etc. in 60 vols, Vienna, 1792–1836, vols 1–25 ed. by Kropatschek, 25–57 by Goutta, W. G., and 58–60 by Pichl, F. X. Another excellent summary of all the main enactments in all fields is given by Beidtel, op. cit., vol II.

Personalities. Biographies of Francis, Meynert, H., *Kaiser F. I*, Vienna, 1872, a curious collection of disconnected studies on various aspects of F.'s personality and activities, sometimes unexpectedly informative; Wolfsgruber, C., *Franz I, Kaiser von Oe.*, Vienna, 1899, 2 vols, only goes up to F.'s coronation; Langsam, W. C., *Francis the Good*, N.Y., 1949, also deals only with F.'s early years. Bibl's *Kaiser Franz*, Vienna, 1938, is a re-write of vol I of his *Zerfall* (above), unfairly hostile to F., of whom a very different picture is given by Hartig in his *Genesis* (below) and by Corti in his *Von Kind bis Kaiser* (below).

There are three main lives of the Archduke Charles: Zeissberg, H., *Erzherzog Carl*,

Vienna, 1895; von Angeli, M., *Erzherzog Carl von Oe.*, etc., Vienna, 1896-7, 5 vols, this rather a history of the Austrian army, and valuable as such; and Christe, O., *Erzherzog Karl*, Vienna, 1912, 3 vols; also a sketch in *Gestalter*. The latest on the Archduke John is Theiss, V., *Erzherzog Johann*, Graz, 1950, popular.

For Metternich, see his own *Nachgelassene Papiere*, ed. Prince R. von M., Vienna, 1880-4, 8 vols, and the monumental biography of him by Srbik, H., *Metternich*, Munich, 1925, 2 vols, extremely full, a storehouse of information. The favourable view taken by Srbik of Metternich was challenged by Bibl in *M., der Dämon Oe.s*, Leipzig, 1937, who accuses Srbik above all, of taking Metternich's own word about himself too uncritically. The lesser scholar, Bibl makes some good points, and proves the advisability of taking some of Srbik's judgments cautiously. What is original in the rest of the enormous literature on M. (e.g. A. Cecil's biography) is exclusively diplomatic, and may be passed over here.

Gentz' diaries (*Tagebücher*), a valuable source for the history of the time, were edited in 4 vols, Leipzig, 1873-4. The latest work on him is Mann, G., *Frh. von Gentz*, Zürich, 1947. Kübeck's *Tagebücher* were edited by his son, Frh. v. Kübeck, in 4 vols, Vienna, 1909-10; further, Walter, *Aus dem Nachlass des Frh. Karl v. K.*, Graz, 1960. About 20 pp. of these are entirely invaluable; the rest could safely be scrapped. There are studies of K. in *Gestalter* and the *N. Oe. B.* Otherwise, the biographical literature for the period is weak; Stadion, Kolowrat and Sedlnitzky have entries in the *N. Oe. B.*

There is a recent life of Andreas Hofer by Paulin, K., *Leben Andreas Hofers*, Innsbruck, 1952.

Narrative accounts. Of the general historians listed in Section I, B, Hantsch gives the most illuminating interpretive account, while *M.K.P.* gives an excellent factual account of the wars, etc. I pass over the enormous special literature on A.'s wars and foreign relations up to 1815; see the bibs. in Uhlirz and Zöllner. Charmatz' is still a very convenient compendium of A.'s foreign relations. For general internal history, Wertheimer, G., *Gesch. Oe.s und U.s im ersten Jahrzehnte des XIX Jhr.*, Leipzig, 2 vols, 1884, 1890, is still the fullest account of its period. Where Wertheimer leaves off, the torch is taken over by Springer, A., *Gesch, Oe. seit dem Wiener Frieden, 1809*, Leipzig, 1883, 2 vols, of which vol I goes up to the 1840s, perhaps the best work on any period of Austrian history ever written, covers the entire Monarchy. Srbik's *Metternich* now also becomes a valuable source. Between them these works, with the standard histories, cover the meagre political history of Francis' later years adequately enough.

Walter provides an acute analysis of the philosophical basis of Franciscean absolutism in his *Zentralverwaltung* volume and in his essay on Francis in *Gestalter*, pp. 299ff. Other pictures are those given by Redlich in the opening pages of his *Problem*, by Eisenmann, op. cit., and to my mind the best of all, by Beidtel, op. cit. On the question of ultimate responsibility, see also Srbik's *Metternich* and the rejoinders by Bibl, who in his various works spreads himself with relish on the oppressive aspects of the regime. The best-known 'foreign observer' of the period is 'A. Sealsfield' (really a German Bohemian émigré named Karl Postl) whose *Austria as it is*, London, 1828, is much quoted, but probably unduly spiteful. Other travellers' accounts include Russell, J., *Tour in Germany*, etc., 2nd ed., Edinburgh, 1825, 2 vols.

C. Ferdinand, political. Walter's volumes cover Ferdinand's reign, to which Beidtel devotes a separate book. On Ferdinand, Ségur-Cabanac, Count V., *Kaiser Ferdinand als Regent und Mensch*. For the intrigues following Francis' death, Srbik and Bibl, Novotny's biography of Kolowrat in *N. Oe. B.* and several periodical articles quoted in Zöllner's bib. Kübeck now becomes important, and the critics and observers of the regime are reinforced by Hartig, F., *Genesis der Revolution in Oe.*, English tr. printed as appendix to vol 4 of Coxe's *House of A.*, London, 1872. An undeservedly forgotten book, *Oe. in 1840*, by 'ein oe. Staatsmann' (Count F. L. Schirnding), Leipzig, 1840, 2 vols, not only gives a clear account, such as I have vainly sought elsewhere, of the actual machinery of government in the *Vormärz*, but also acute criticisms of political and social conditions. The best-known 'anti' pamphlets are Andrian-Warburg, *Oe. und dessen Zukunft*, Hamburg, 2 vols, 1843, 1847; Möring, K., *Sybillinische Bücher aus Oe.*, Hamburg, 1848, 2 vols, and various works by Schuselka, the best-known of which are *Ist Oe. deutsch?*, Leipzig, 1843, and *Deutsche Worte eines Oe.s*, Hamburg, 1843. More favourable impressions by some foreign travellers: so Turnbull, P. E., *Austria*, Edinburgh, 1840, 2 vols, very informative, and Wilde, A. A., *A. and its Institutions*, Dublin, 1842, worth reading.

The movements of the Estates from the mid-1840s on are given most fully by Springer, Hartig and Beidtel, and in Schlitter, A., *Aus Oe.s Vormärz*, four parts: (1) *Galizien und Krakow*, (2) *Böhmen*, (3) *Ungarn*, (4) *Nieder Oe.*, all Zurich, 1920; also Bibl, V., *Die Nieder Oe. Stände im Vormärz*, Vienna, 1911; but see also the sections on Lands and nationalities below.

Excellent account of the annexation of Cracow in Srbik, op. cit., II. 149ff. In general, Srbik covers A.'s foreign relations for the period exhaustively.

D. General questions, 1792–1847.

i. Cultural and religious: exhaustive documentary collection, Maass, F., *Der Josephinismus*, Vienna, 1951, etc., 5 vols. For general developments, no one is better than Beidtel. For Hofbauer, Till, A., *Hofbauer und sein Kreis*, Vienna, 1951.

The police and censorship: Fournier, A., *Die Geheimpolizei auf dem Wiener Kongress*, Vienna, 1913, and Marx, J., *Die Zensur im Vormärz*, Vienna, 1959, also covers Francis's reign.

ii. Finance. Beer, op. cit., is still the stand-by. For Austria's loans, Helleiner, K., *The Imperial Loans*, Oxford, 1965. The State bankruptcies, Kraft, J., *Das Finanzreform des Grafen Wallis*, Graz, 1927; Stiassny, P., *Das Oe. Staatsbankrott von 1811*, Vienna, 1912. Stadion's reforms, a good essay by A. Brusatti in *Oe. und Europa*, Graz, 1965, pp. 281ff. All the more important historians, notably Springer and Beidtel, have much to say on the subject. Certain passages in Kübeck's *Tagebücher* are indispensible. Interesting figures in 'Tebeldi' (pseudonym of C. Beidtel, jun.), *Die Geldangelegenheiten Oes.*, Leipzig, 1847, interesting work, much wider than its title would suggest.

For the bankers, Corti, A., *Der Aufstieg des Hauses Rothschild 1770–1830*, Leipzig, and id., *Das Haus R. in seiner Blüthe, 1830–1871*, ibid.; English trs., *The Rise* and *The Reign of the House of R.*, London, 1928; but the really intimate glimpses are only occasional. Something in Scheffer, op. cit., and in Franz' *Liberalismus* (below).

iii. Agriculture and the peasant question. Blum, J., *Noble Landowners and Agriculture in A., 1815–1848*, Baltimore, 1947, is a first-class work, covering all parts of the Monarchy and dealing with agricultural production, as well as the social question. Its bib. lists the sources, such as they are, on the former subject. For the latter, besides Blum, Grünberg's *Bauernbefreiung* and id., *Die Grundentlastung*, in vol I of the *Gesch. der oe. Land – und Forstwirtschaft* (quoted as *L. u. F.*), Vienna, 1889, 5 vols, an exhaustive survey which, except for Grünberg's contribution, does not go back before 1848. G.'s article is particularly valuable for the developments of 1846–8. Some material in 'Tebeldi', op. cit. (extraordinary as it may seem, no one in Vienna has been able to suggest to me where Tebeldi got his statistics from) and in the works quoted below, ad 1848, of Bach, Violand, Zenker, Fischer and Endres, and Kudlich, H., *Erinnerungen*, Vienna, 1873, 3 vols. All these writers are left-wing, and the impressions of travellers such as Turnbull do not altogether bear out their picture.

iv. Industrial development; the question of industrial labour. Needless to say, nothing for the Monarchy as a whole, and not even anything truly satisfactory for the Western half of it as a whole. Slokar, J.'s often quoted *Gesch. der oe. Industrie*, etc., Vienna, 1914, is little more than a thoroughly uninformative list of foundations of enterprises. There are, however, numerous periodical articles on developments of individual industries, and in individual localities, and it may be hoped that some useful general works will shortly be emerging. The economic fluctuations of the 1840s in the Lands administered by the *Vereinigte Hofkanzlei* are described in some detail in Marx, J., *Die wirtschaftlichen Ursachen der Revolution in Oe.*, Graz, 1965, which combines and revises several earlier studies by the author; much valuable material, but the wood is hard to see for the trees. This work is also good for the social problem of industrial labour, on which see also the chapters in the Left-wing historians of 1848: but here again, compare the travellers, especially Turnbull. For detailed figures of prices and wages, Pribram, K. and others, *Materialien zur Gesch. der Preise und Löhne in Oe.*, Vienna, 1938.

E. Lands and Nationalities. The German-Austrian and Bohemian Lands have no private political histories until the mid-1840s, whereafter see above. For the Czech national revival, Denis, op. cit., very full, Seton-Watson, *Czechs and Slovaks*, and Raupach, N. D., *Der tschechische Frühnationalismus*, Essen, 1938. The French in Illyria, Marmont, *Mémoirs*, vol III, Paris, 1857, and other works listed by Haumant, op. cit., p. 239. Galicia and the Poles: a valuable work from the Austrian side is Anon., *Polnische Revolutionen*, Prague, 1863. The author, L. Sacher-Masoch, was for many years Director of Police, Lemberg. For the 1846 revolution in Galicia, Sacher-Masoch, Schlitter, *Galizien und Krakow*, an unexpected chapter on 'Die nationale Bewegung in Galizien' in vol I, pp. 335 ff., of F. Strobl von Ravensberg, *Metternich und seine Zeit*, Vienna, 1906, 2 vols.

There is no full-length account from the Austrian side of the Austrian rule in Lombardy-Galicia (and, I am informed, nothing first-class either from the Italian side). Glimpses in Beidtel, II. 244 ff., Srbik, I. 465–91, Benedikt, H., *Kaiseradler über dem Apennin*, Vienna, 1964, and vol I of C. F. H. Berkley, *Italy in the Making*, Cambridge, 3 vols, 2nd ed., 1968. Sandona, A., *Il Regno Lombardo-veneto, 1814–1859*, Milan 1912, is a collection of texts. For Venice, Trevelyan, G. M., *Manin and the Venetian Revolution of 1848*, London, 1927.

German bourgeois liberalism in the *Vormärz*, Franz, G., *Liberalismus: die deutschliberale Bewegung in der Habsburgermonarchie*, Munich, 1953; Eder, K., *Der Liberalismus in Alt.-Oe.*, Vienna, 1965; both good. Valjavec, F., *Der Josefinismus*, Munich, 2nd ed., 1945, is slight. Some penetrating remarks in Burian, P. *Die Nationalitäten in Cis-Leithanien*, Vienna, 1962, a good little work.

THE HABSBURG EMPIRE

The much livelier political existence led at this time by Hungary has, on the other hand, evoked a number of works. Besides Szekfü and Spira, Wertheimer (himself a Hungarian) and Springer take adequate cognisance of Hungarian affairs. For the early years, see also Benda, K., *A. M. Jakobinosok Iratai* (The Writings of the H. Jacobins), Bp., 1932, 3 vols, the documentation largely in German or Latin, the sequel to which is Malyusz, E., *Sándor Lipot Föherceg Iratai* (The Writings of the Archduke Alexander Leopold), Bp., 1932, the documentation again mainly in German or Latin; but Malyusz's conclusions were effectively challenged by B. Iványi-Grünwald in his introduction to Széchenyi's *Hitel* in the latter's collected works (below). For Alexander's successor, Domanovszky, S., *József Nádor*, etc. (The Palatine Joseph), Bp. 1945, 4 vols. Vol VIII of Horváth, E.'s great *M. Történet* (H. History), which runs up to 1823, has never been translated, but his next vols have appeared in German as *25 Jahre U. Gesch.*, Geneva, 1866, 2 vols. They are very chauvinistic, but detailed and informative. For the great figures, there have been various eds. of Széchenyi's *Oesszes Müvei* (Collected Works), the most recent a 12 vol one, Bp. 1930 ff. There is no really satisfactory biography of him in any language, Silagi, D., *Der grosste Ungarn*, Vienna, 1967, is short, and patchy at that but profound meditations by Szekfü in his *Három Nemzedék* (Three Generations), 2nd ed., Bp., 1935. See also Grünwald, B., *Az Uj M.-g.* (The New H.), Bp., 1890, and an interesting special number on Sz. in the *Journal of Central European Affairs*, Denver, Colorado, XI. 3, Oct. 1961. Kossuth's *Oesszes Müvei* have also been collected, most recently, Bp., 1948 ff., 15 vols, and an *Emlékkönyv* (memorial vol) on him appeared in Bp. in 1952, in 2 vols. Of him, too, there is no satisfactory biograpqy in any language: Zarek, O., *K. Die Liebe eines Volkes*, Zurich, 1935, is journalistic. There is a classic life of Deák by Ferenczy, Z., *Deák Ferenc Élete*, Bp., 1904, 3 vols. No worthy full-length biography of Eötvös (Söter, E.'s *Eötvös József*, Bp., 1953, does not fill the gap). The excellent study of him in Mervyn Jones, *Five Hungarian Writers*, Oxford, 1966, is literary rather than political. For Eötvös and the Nationalities question, see below, Section IX. General surveys, economic and social conditions. There is a good 'statistical' (in the wider sense) description of H. in the opening years of the century in Schwartner, M. von, *Statistik des Königreiches U.*, Ofen (Buda), 3 vols, 1809–11, and another, very valuable one for the end of the period: Fényes, E., *M-g. Sztatisztikája* (Statistics of H.), Pest, 1842, 3 vols, revised 2 vols ed., ibid., 1847, German tr. *U. im Vormärz*, Leipzig, 1851. J. Springer's and Hain's works (above) cover H. Travellers' impressions include Bright, A., *Travels through Lower H.*, Edinburgh, 1800, Bendant, F. S., *Travels in H.*, London, 1837 (from the French), Paget, J., *H. and Transylvania*, London, 1837, 2 vols, deservedly famous work with excellent pen-portrait of Széchenyi, whom Paget admired greatly; Kohl, J. G., *Reisen in U.*, etc., Leipzig, 1840, 2 vols. For a picture of H. in the 1840s the reader could not do better than look at Eötvös's famous novel, *A Falusi Jegyzö* (The Village Notary), many eds.; has also appeared in German, English, etc. Agriculture and the peasant question, see Blum, op. cit., and for an excellent modern work, Merei, G., *Mezögazdaság és Agrártársadalom M-gon 1790–1848* (Agriculture and Agrarian Society in H., 1790–1848), Bp., 1948. The chapter by Ember, Gy. in various, *Forradalom és Szabadságharc* (Revolution and Fight for Liberty; quoted as *F. és Sz.*) is intemperate. Some good pages in Szabó, E.'s *Harcok* (below). See also Le Play's investigations quoted in the text. Industry: vol I of Futo, M., *A. M. Gyáripár Története* (The History of H. Factory Industry), Bp., 1944,

2 vols; good, many facts and figures; Merei, G., *M. Iparfejlödés* (H. Industrial Development), Bp., 1952, also good. A chapter by Nemes, D., on industrial labour in *F. és Sz.*

The standard work in the cultural field is that of Kornis, G., available in German as *U. Kulturideale, 1777–1848*, Leipzig, 1930. For the linguistic revival, Tolna, A., *A Nyelvujitás* (The Linguistic Revival), Bp., 1929, and an essay on Vörösmarty in Mervyn Jones, op. cit. The spirit of Magyar nationalism, Spohr, A., *Die Geistigen Grundlagen des Nationalismus in U.*, Berlin, 1936, good; analyses the thought of Kossuth, Széchenyi, Eötvös, etc. very fairly. The article by Steinacker, H., 'Das Wesen des Madjarischen Nationalismus', in Walter and Steinacker, *Die Nationalitätenfrage im alten Ungarn*, Munich, 1959, contains some acute observations, but is over-hostile and often unjust; when you find a German writer spelling the national name 'Madjar' you can, for some reason, bet that this will be the case. Thoughtful works in Hungarian, Joó, T., *A M. Nemzeti Szellem* (The H. National Spirit), Bp., 1938, id. *M Nationalismus*, ibid., 1940, Szekfü, G., ed. *Mi a Magyar?* (What is the Magyar?), ibid., 1939, Recent, Barany, G., The Awakening of M. Nationalism before 1848, *A.H. Yearbook*, II, 1966. The 'Nationalities' legislation before 1848, Szekfü, *État et Nation*, Bp. 1945.

The Nationalities: the latest, and far the best work on the Slovaks in this period is Gogolák, L., *Die Nationswerdung der Slowakei*, etc., Vienna, 1963. Denis and other writers on the Czechs include many Slovaks in their surveys; Fischel, *Panslawismus*, is also useful. For the Roumanians and Serbs of Inner Hungary, I have found little beyond the works listed in previous sections; for the Swabians, Annabring, N., *Volksgesch. der Deutschen in U.*, Stuttgart, 1954. Croatia, the Croat question: for the legal position, Miskolczy, G., *A Horvátkérdés Története* (History of the Croat question), Bp., 1927–8, 2 vols, fundamental. For Illyrianism, besides the general Croat histories and Fischel, *Panslawismus*, there is an essay on Gaj in Wendel's *Aus dem Südslawischen Risorgimento*, Gotha, 1921. Transylvania: both Horváth and Szekfü cover the history from the H. side; see also the works on the Roumanians and Saxons in Section I, C. A descriptive work: de Gerando, A., *La Transylvanie et ses Habitants*, Paris, 1845, 2 vols. Paget's work includes a description of Transylvania, where he ended by settling.

CHAPTER IX

1848

A. General. Here, exceptionally, it is possible to recommend a book covering the subject comprehensively and accurately: Kiszling, R. (and others), *Die Revolution im Kaisertum Oe. 1848–9*, Vienna, 1949, 2 vols. This work, the editor and chief contributor to which is a retired military man, covers the whole Monarchy, and gives all that any but the most advanced specialist needs to know on all the military operations. The political sections are less uniformly good, but some are excellent. It is fortunate that this should have appeared, for the other modern works are not satisfactory for the inquirer who wants more than a surface view. The best is *M.K.P.*; but Hantsch gives the whole revolution only 10 pages, mostly interpretation, and Zöllner, only 5. Novotny, A., *1848*, Graz, 1948, is short and popular; Endres, D., *Revolution in Oe., 1848*, Vienna, 1947, purports to re-write Bach (below), but is far inferior to him. Fischer, E., *Oe., 1848*, Vienna, 1949, by a Communist, brings nothing new. The only modern works which add anything to Kiszling's are Corti's *Von Kind bis Kaiser* (below) for the Court, including especially the alleged role of the Archduchess Sophie, and Walter's latest vols in the *Zentralverwaltung* series, III. 1 (narrative) and III. 2 (texts). These, which are far the most informative volumes in the entire *Zentralverwaltung* series, cover the Ministries up to Schwarzenberg's inclusive, and constitute the last word on affairs at the top level. Most of the older narrative accounts are superseded by Kiszling, but the following still have their value: Springer, A., op. cit., vol II; Reschauer, H. and Smets, M., *Gesch. der Wiener Revolution in Jahre 1848*, Vienna, 1898, 2 vols; Bach, M., same title and year, an excellent work, Left-wing sympathies, full social background; Helfert, A. von, *Gesch. der oe. Revolution*, etc., Freiburg, 1907–9, 2 vols, not confined to the Monarchy, covers only the first months. Friedjung, *Oe. von 1848–1860*, Stuttgart, etc., 1908, 2 vols, unfinished work, is short on the revolution itself, but rescues a few documents. Hartig's narrative (the continuation of his *Genesis*, above) is over-personal and ill-tempered, but in places a primary source. Eisenmann is not always accurate. Redlich, *Problem*, discourses learnedly on the 'forces and ideas on the solution of the problem', but gets down to narrative only with Kremsier. A good recent book, less exhaustive, is Rath, A. J., * *The Viennese Revolution of 1848*, Austin, Texas, 1957. Robertson, P., **Revolutions of 1848*, N.Y., 1952, not confined to the Monarchy, is lively but very often inaccurate, as is the chapter (XV) in the *New Cambridge Modern History*, vol X, Cambridge, 1960.

B. The March Days and their sequel in Vienna. Besides the above, Srbik, *Metternich*, II, 245ff. Personal reminiscences, Pillersdorf, *Rückblicke*, etc., Vienna, 1849; Ficquelmont, *Aufklärungen*, etc., Leipzig, 1850; (Montecuccoli), *Die Nieder-Oe. Stände*, etc., Vienna, 1850; 'Ein Mitglied des Aufgelösten Reichstages' (Violand), *Enthüllungen aus Oe.s jüngster Vergangenheit*, Hamburg, 1849; Füster, A., *Memoiren*, etc., Frankfurt, 1850 (on the students). The biography of Windisch-Graetz by Müller, D., *Fürst W.*, Vienna, 1934, is useful; that of the Archduke Albrecht by von Dunker, C., Vienna, 1892, is valueless.

Text of the Pillersdorf Constitution in Bernatzik, *Die oe. Verfassungsgesetze*, Leipzig, 1906, pp. 73–82, and of the revised franchise of May 1848, id., pp. 82–3

For the social question, Bach, op. cit., is valuable, as are Violand, *Soziale Gesch. der Wiener Revolution*, Hamburg, 1852, first-hand, and Zenker, A., *Die Wiener Revolution in 1848*, Vienna, 1897. Less useful, Endres and Fischer (above).

C. The revolutionary months in the West. General, Burian, op. cit., is often useful whether other accounts fail, e.g., for the Slovenes, and his bib. is excellent. There are only small, local works on the Alpine Lands. On the Czechs, all the general works previously quoted are fairly good (Burian best of all), as are Denis and Mach, but all older versions need checking against Walter. See also "Dr Boemus", 'Die Entwicklung des tschechischen staatsrechtlichen Programmes', etc. in *Oe. Jahrbucher*, I. 6 (1918); also the opening pages of Sutter, B., *Die Badenischen Sprachverordnungen*, 2 vols, Graz, 1960.

Galicia. Of the general histories, only Helfert pays much attention to Galicia, and he must be checked with Walter. The *Cambridge History of Poland* is useless here. Papers in the *A.H. Yearbook*, 1967, are slight on 1848. Besides Sacher-Masoch, op. cit., I have used an unpublished dissertation by Sommergruber, J., *Die Nationalpolitischen Verhältnisse in Galizien, 1848–1867*, Vienna, 1941. Burian helps. For the Bukovina, Prokopowitsch, op. cit. German Austria and the German question:

here Friedjung and Bibl are the best of the Austrians, but better is Veit, V., *Gesch. der deutschen Revolution, 1848–9*, Berlin, 1930, 2 vols. There is also a special study by Telle, G. H., *Das oe. Problem*, etc., Kiel, 1933.

On the Slav Congress, besides the historians of Bohemia, Springer and Fischel.

D. Hungary, the first phase. The latest accounts of the revolution in H. are *F. és. Sz* (above), emotional, and Spira, G., *A. M. Forradalom 1848–9ben* (The H. Revolution in 1848–9), ditto, but thorough, and good bib. Old, but still valuable for its detail, Horváth, M., *Gesch. der Unabhängigkeit*, etc., Bp. 1872, 3 vols. The indispensable primary source for the first days is the *Emlékiratai* (Reminiscences) of Szögyéni-Marisch, L., Bp., 1861, 3 vols. The Austrian historians are usually inaccurate on the 'March Days'; Friedjung is the best of them. Steinitz ap. Kiszling overestimates Hungarian extremism at this stage, but his general picture is good. Text of the April Laws in Bernatzik, op. cit., pp. 49–73.

Hungary's 'foreign policy', Hajnal, K., *A Batthyány kormány külpolitikája* (The Foreign Policy of the Batthyány Government), Bp., 1957; some glimpses in Pulszky, F., *Mein Zeit, mein Leben*, Pressburg, etc., 1880–3, 4 vols. Social problems: besides *F. és Sz.*, Szabo, E., *Tarsadalmi és Partharcok*, etc. (Social and Party struggles), Bp., 2nd. ed., 1949, very brilliant pioneer work. Also Szabó, I., *A Jobbágybirtokok Problémája 1848–1849* (The problem of the peasant holdings, 1848–9), Bp., 1948. Some interesting side-lines on general internal developments in Pulszky, op. cit.

The Nationalities: the picture usually drawn is far too generalized. For the Slovaks, besides the histories of Slovakia, Steier, L., *A Tót nemzetiségi Kérdés 1848–1849ben* (The Slovak national question in 1848–9), Bp. 1937, 2 vols. The Serbs: Thim, J., *A M-g, 1848–1849iki szerb fölkelés*, etc. (The rising of the Hungarian Serbs in 1848–9), Bp., 1930, 3 vols, very fully documented but confused reading. For the Croats and Jellačić, it is safer to read accounts from more than one side, e.g., Springer, Horváth and Hubka ap. Kiszling; also Kiszling's own *Kroatien* (above). For Transylvania, the works quoted in Section I above, and the H. histories. There is a biography of Avram Jancu in the *N. Oe. B.*

E. The Reichstag, etc. Springer, Ehnl *ap.* Kiszling and Rath are good on the deteriorating situation in Vienna; Ehnl's account of October in Vienna is first-class. Hübner, A., *Ein Jahr meines Lebens*, Leipzig, 1891, is a valuable and much-used first-hand source for this period. The investigation into the murder of Latour is given as an appendix to vol 4 of Coxe's *House of A* (above). Springer published the records of the Constitutional Committee of the Reichstag – *Protokolle des Verfassungsausschusses*, etc., Leipzig, 1885. His general account of the work of the Reichstag is still among the best. Lengthy analysis of the Kremsier Constitution in Redlich, *Problem*, I.II. I.2 (vol I, pp. 221–323); shorter, in Wierer, R., *Der Föderalismus im Donauraum*, Graz, 1960, pp. 36 ff. Text of the Constitution in Bernatzik, pp. 85–102.

For the debates on the national question, Geist-Lányi, P., *Das Nationalitätenproblem auf dem Reichstag zu Kremsier*, Munich, 1920, very useful.

For Olmütz and the pre-history of the abdication, Walter and Corti op. cit. are indispensable, as is Hübner. Biographies of Schwarzenberg, Schwarzenberg, A., *Prinz Felix zu S*, N.Y., 1948, and Kiszling, *Fürst Felix zu S.*, Graz, 1956. Bruck: Charmatz, R., *Minister Frh. von Bruck*, Leipzig, 1918. Wessenberg, Arneth, A., *Johann von W.*, Vienna, 1898, 2 vols. Fischof, Charmatz, *Adolf Fischof*, Stuttgart, 1910. There are no full-length biographies of the other new men, but sketches of Bach and Stadion in *Gestalter* and the *N. Oe. B.*, and of Krausz in the latter work; of Bach, also in Charmatz, *Lebensbilder*, and Friedjung, *Historische Aufsätze*.

Text of the Stadion Constitution in Bernatzik, pp. 102—48; commentary, Redlich, *Problem*, I.IV.I.

F. The fighting in Hungary in 1848–9 is dealt with sufficiently in Kiszling; further works listed in his bib. The Russian intervention, Andics, E., *Der Bündniss Habsburg-Romanov*, Bp., 1964, shortened version from the Hungarian original: extremely biased, but documented. There is a flood of memoirs on these months; the most important, Görgei, *Mein Leben und Wirken in U. 1848 und 1849*, Leipzig, 1852, 2 vols; on the 'Görgei question', Kosáry, D., *A Görgey-kérdés története* (History of the Görgey question), Bp., 1956. British policy, Sproxton, A. C., *Palmerston and the H. Rev.*, Cambridge, 1919, short.

Francis Joseph and his Family

Far the best psychological study of F.J. is Margutti, A. Frh. von, *Kaiser F.J.*, Vienna, 1924, a work based on intimate knowledge of the Emperor in his old age (M. was employed in the 'Adjutancy-General') and very sensitive and perceptive. Of the shorter studies that by Novotny, A., in *Gestalter*, pp. 433 ff., is perhaps the most understanding. Some brilliant lines in Wickham Steed, *The Habsburg Monarchy*, London, 1911, pp. 55–8. The most exhaustive personal biography is Corti's trilogy, *Von Kind bis Kaiser*, Graz, 1950, *Mensch und Herrscher*, id., 1952, and *Der Alte Kaiser*, id., 1955, which are supplemented by his *Elisabeth, die seltsame Frau*, Salzburg, 1934, easily the best life of the Empress, although there are quantities more of novelettish products. Corti's books go into every detail of their subjects' personal lives, often in excessive detail, and occasionally quote some document which throws light not found elsewhere on some public event, but such flashes are incidental. F.J.'s correspondence with his mother ed. by Schnürer, F., *Briefe Kaiser F.J.s an seine Mutter*, Salzburg, 1930, sometimes important; with Elisabeth, *Briefe Kaiser F.J. an Kaiserin Elisabeth*, ed. Corti, Graz, 1966, 2 vols; with Frau Schratt, Bourgoing, J. de, *Briefe Kaiser F.J.s und Frau K.S.*, Vienna, 1949, totally uninteresting, as are his letters collected by Ernst, O., *F.J. in seinen Briefen*, English tr., *F.J. as revealed by his letters*, London, 1927. The best political biography is Redlich, J., *Kaiser F.J.*, etc., Berlin, 1929, English tr. *The Emperor F.J.*., London, 1930. Works straddling biography and history are Steinitz, E. von, *Erinnerungen an F.J.*, sometimes important, Berlin, 1931; Tschuppik, K., *F.J., der Untergang eines Reiches*, Hellerau, 1928, English tr., *The Reign of the Emperor F.J.*, London, 1930, underrated work: T. was a well-informed journalist who sometimes knew more than the professional historians; *Crankshaw, E., *The Fall of the House of Habsburg*, London, 1963, readable but very inaccurate. Bagger, E., *F.J.*, N.Y., 1927, is inferior.

Far the best life of the Crown Prince is Mitis, O., *Das Leben des Kronprinzen Rudolf*, Leipzig, 1928. Most of the vast literature on the 'tragedy of Mayerling' is romance rather than history.

CHAPTER X

The Decade of Absolutism

Useful short general accounts, the relevant vols of Charmatz (see Section I); also *M.K.P.*, III, 161–88. Springer gives out now, but in his place we get Rogge, W.,

BIBLIOGRAPHY

Oe. von Világos bis zur Gegenwart, Leipzig, 1872, 3 vols; vol I covers this decade, spiteful and irritating, by a rabid Liberal, but well-informed; R. was a journalist attached to the Press Bureau. Friedjung, *Oe. von 1848-1860* covers the beginning.

Austria and Germany, the general histories and Friedjung, op. cit., II.I., Books 1-3; also Charmatz, *Bruck*. The 'Provisoria' conveniently in Friedjung, vol I; comment in Rogge. For Hungary, from now to 1865, Berzeviczy, A., *Az Absolutismus Kora Mg.-on* (The Age of Absolutism in H.), Bp., 1922-32, 4 vols, comprehensive, and Walter, F., 'Von Windisch-Graetz über Welden zu Haynau' in *Die Nationalitätenfrage im alten Ungarn* (above). The economic union with H., Charmatz, *Bruck*, and Sieghart, A., *Zolltrennung und Zolleinheit*, Vienna, 1915.

The transition to pure absolutism, Walter's vols in *Zentralverwaltung*, Redlich. *Problem*, I. IV, 2-3, with the biographies of Schwarzenberg (above), and Walter's ed. of Kübeck's *Nachlass*. Text of the 'Sylvesterpatent' in Bernatzik, pp. 172-85.

The achievements of the regime, Czoernig, K. Frh. von, *Oes. Neugestaltung 1848-58*, Stuttgart, 1858, a magnificent comprehensive work by an official statistician, with detailed data on almost every aspect of the regime, especially in the fields of finance, economics, communications, etc., but recording also administrative innovations, educational reforms, even Army organization. The system at work, general, Rogge, op. cit., and Mayr, J. I., ed., *Das Tagebuch des Polizeiministers Kempen*, Vienna, 1931. Eisenmann overrates the importance of Bach and underrates the role of Kübeck.

The Concordat, etc.: Weinzierl-Fischer, E., *Die Oe. Konkordate von 1855 und 1933*, Vienna, 1960; Wolfsgruber, C., *Joseph Othmar, Kardinal Rauscher*, Freiburg, 1888. Good short sketch of Rauscher by Till in *Gestalter*, pp. 347 ff. The linguistic question in education, Frommelt, K., *Die Sprachenfrage in oe. Unterrichtswesen 1848-1859*, Graz, 1963, useful work, well-documented. Education in general, Ficker, A., *Bericht über das oe. Unterrichtswesen*, Vienna, 1873.

The land reform: texts of Patents in Czoernig; results for Western Lands, Grünberg, *Grundentlastung* (above). Servitudes, consolidation, etc., article by Schiff, W., in *L.u.F.* I, pp. 81-201. For Hungary, Bernáth, G., *Az Absolutizmus Földtehérmentesitése Mg.-on* (The Agrarian Reform of Absolutism in H.), Bp., 1936.

Finance, general, Beer, op. cit., and Czoernig. For the role of mobile capital, the books of Scheffer and Franz (above) and Corti's *Rothschilds*.

The provinces: for Bohemia, Rogge and Bretholz (above). For Galicia, Sommergruber, op. cit. For Lombardy-Venetia, Benedikt and Sandona (above), the various biographies of Radetzky, and the Italian historians. Many details also in Rogge. For Hungary, besides Berzeviczy, op. cit., there is a glowing account of the achievements of the regime, ordered by Bach, Anon., *Rückblick auf die jüngste Entwicklungsperiode U.s*, Vienna, 1857, reprinted 1903, answered by Szechenyi, *Blick auf den Anonymen Rückblick*, 1857, reprinted, ed. Tolnai, V., Bp., 1925. Rogge is full on Hungary. For Deák, Ferenczy, op. cit. The Old Conservatives, Wertheimer, E., *Zur Gesch. der u. Altkonservativen*, Ungarische Rundschau, 1913, pp. 37 ff., and 1914, pp. 52 ff.

The emigration, Kossuth's own *Memories of my Exile*, London, 1880, 2 vols; his speeches in London were also printed. See also Denes, J., *Great Britain and Kossuth*, Bp., 1937, and id., *Die u. Emigration und der Krieg im Orient*, ibid., 1939. Kosáry, D., *A History of H.*, Cleveland, 1941, is good on the emigration; also useful, vol I of Wertheimer's *Andrássy* (below).

For the Crimean War, Friedjung, *Der Krimkrieg*, Vienna, 1907, also some interesting details by Heller, E., in von Steinitz, op. cit. But see the latest general diplomatic histories. The Austrian side of the preliminaries to the 1859 war is best given in the various biogs. of Franz Joseph; there is no large-scale diplomatic study. The official military history of the campaign, is that of the General Staff, K. u. K. Generalstab, ed., *Der Krieg in Italien*, Vienna, 1872-6, 3 vols. Shortly, Friedjung, *Kampf um den Vorherrschaft* (below), with references to other literature.

CHAPTER XI

Eight Years of Experiment

A. The German question. Friedjung, *Kampf um die Vorherrschaft in Deutschland*, 10th ed., Berlin, 2 vols, 1927, classic work, but the diplomatic history, which is relatively short, has now been largely superseded by vols 3 and 4 of Srbik's *Deutsche Einheit*, Munich, 1935, and his *Quellen zur d. Politik Oe. 1859–66*, Berlin, 1934-8, 6 vols. See also the German and general historians, and Engel-Jánosy, J., *Graf Rechberg*, Munich, 1927. The war of 1866, Friedjung, op. cit., and many other works, including the official history by the A.H. General Staff, *Oe.s Kämpfe im Jahre 1866*, Vienna, 1867-9, 5 vols. The Benedek controversy: Friedjung edited Benedek's *Nachgelassene Papiere*, and much literature is based on this work and on his *Kampf*, which is very detailed on the military side. Later, Priestland, J., *Vae Victis*, London, 1934, sympathetic to B., shows careful research into specialist works, but wildly inaccurate background. Far better on technical side, and also more judicious, Regele, O., *Feldzeugmeister B.*, Vienna, 1960, most valuable for Austria's military preparations, or lack thereof, and for the responsibility for the deficiencies. *Donauraum*, XI.I (1966) has interesting articles by Regele on the military side of 1866, and by Engel-Jánosi on the diplomatic. See also Jedlicska's essay on the Archduke Albrecht in *Gestalter*.

B. Internal affairs. Besides the standard histories and vol II of Rogge, op. cit., there is a good short general sketch by Fournier, *Oe.U.s Neubau*, Vienna, 1917. The top-level story in great detail in Redlich, *Problem*, I/II and vol II, and Eisenmann, op. cit. For the negotiations with Hungary, further, Beust, *Aus drei Vierteljahrhunderten*, Stuttgart, 3 vols, 1887-9, very uninformative, vol III of Ferenczy, op. cit., vol I of Wertheimer, E., *Graf Julius Andrássy*, Berlin, 1910, 3 vols, a major work, and Corti's *Elisabeth* (above). Also Fellner, F., *Das Februarpatent von 1861*, Vienna, 1959. Texts of the Diploma and Patent, and of the Patents of 1865, in Bernatzik, op. cit., pp. 185-330. Exhaustive comments in Redlich and Eisenmann.

For Cis-Leithania, G. Kolmer's *Parlament und Verfassung in Oe.*, Vienna, 1902, 8 vols, begins to function seriously from 1861 on. This is a very full summary of the proceedings of the Austrian Reichsrat and Landtage, invaluable for those who need detail; also Czedik, E., *Zur Gesch. der k.u.k. oe. Ministerien 1861–1916*, Vienna, 1917, 4 vols, with pen-portraits of Ministers. These two works, and Rogge, give between them every detail man could want of party and Parliamentary manoeuverings in Cis-Leithania. For the nature of German bourgeois Liberalism in the 1860s, Franz and Eder (above); Charmatz, *Deutsch-oe. Politik*, Vienna, 1910, an acute and thoughtful work; vol I of E. von Plener's *Erinnerungen*, Stuttgart, 1911—13, 3 vols, and biographies of Schmerling, Giskra, Fischof, Plener, Herbst, and others in the collections. For the Viennese Jewry, Tietze, H., *Die Juden Wiens*, Vienna, 1933. For national movements in Cis-Leithania, see the next section.

Hungary, internal. Berzeviczy, op. cit., up to 1865; but the Hungarian historians concentrate inordinately on the 'issue of public law'. On internal conditions, Rogge is as informative as any of them. The negotiations with the nationalities: Nagy, I., *A Nemzetiségi Törvény a m. Parlament elött* (The Nationalities Law before the H. Parliament), Bp., 1930. Translation of the 1861 Report in Seton-Watson, R. W., *Racial Problems in H.*; see also Macartney, C. A., *H. and Her Successors*, Oxford, 2nd. ed., 1965. Eötvös's own main work on the nationalities question is his *Nationalitätenfrage*, Pest, 1865, but he touched on the problem in others of his main books, notably his *Einfluss der Herrschenden Ideen*, etc., Leipzig, 1851-4, 2 vols. For recent discussions of his views on the subject, which changed frequently, see Weber, J., *Eötvös und die u. Nationalitätenfrage*, Munich, 1966, giving a general view (influenced by Steinacker) of the problem; also Macartney, C. A., The H. Nationalities Law, in *Donauraum*, Oct. 1967. For Croatia, Seton-Watson, R. W., *Southern Slav Question* (above), with tr. of the *Nagodba*. For Transylvania, besides works already listed, Mester, M., *Az Autonom Erdély* (Autonomous Transylvania), Bp., 1936.

Texts of the Hungarian Law XII and of the Austrian 'December Constitution' in Bernatzik; of the former, also in Drage, *Austria-Hungary* (below). Judgments on the Compromise, Eisenmann, op. cit., Žölger, L. V., *Der staatsrechtliche Ausgleich*, etc., Leipzig, 1910, Andrássy, G., *Ungarns Ausgleich*, etc. (tr. from the Hungarian), Leipzig, 1897, Andrássy's case for his own work, and innumerable others.

CHAPTER XII
Intermezzo

Besides the general diplomatic histories, see Erichsen, E., *Die deutsche Politik des Grafen Beust*, etc., Kiel, 1927. Beust himself is little help. The best short account of Austrian policy in the crisis is that of Srbik in his essay on John in *Aus. Oe.s Vergangenheit*, Salzburg, 1949, pp. 67–98. See also Wertheimer's *Andrássy*, I, pp. 443–531. For the domestic history of the Hohenwart crisis, Schäffle, *Aus meinem Leben*, Berlin, 1903, 2 vols; but see Friedjung, *Historische Aufsätze*, p. 469. From the Czech angle, especially Denis, II, pp. 499–533 and Münch, pp. 312–63; from the German-Austrian centralist angle, Rogge, op. cit., vol III, *passim*. Two contemporary works are still of great interest: Palacký, *Die oe. Staatsidee* Prague, 1866, and Fischof, A., *Oe. und die Burgschaften seines Bestandes*, Vienna, 1869.

CHAPTER XIII
The Foreign Relations of the Monarchy (1871–1903)

I leave most of this field to the professional diplomatic historians. Charmatz is handy, but written without knowledge of the most secret documents. Vol I of Albertini, L.'s great *Origins of the War of 1914*, London, 1952-4, 3 vols, covers this period, as does Langer, W. L., *European Alliances and Alignments, 1871–1890*, N.Y., 1931. For the early years, Wertheimer's *Andrássy* and Leidner, L., *Die Aussenpolitik Oe.U.s 1870-9*, Kiel, 1934. Bosnia: Herkolović, J., *Vorgesch. der Okkupation Bosniens*, etc., Agram (Zagreb), 1906; Fournier, *Wie wir zu Bosnien kamen*, Vienna, 1909, and the standard works, especially Rupp, G. H., *A Wavering Friendship*, Cambridge, Mass., 1941, and Medlicott, W., *The Congress of Berlin*, etc., London, 1938.

Later period: Pribram, A. F., *Die Geheimverträge Oe. Us*, etc., English tr. *The Secret*

Treaties of A. H., 1879–1914, Cambridge, Mass., 1920–2, 2 vols; Fellner, F., *Der Dreibund*, Munich, 1960, short but excellent; Engel-Jánosi, F., *Oe. und der Vatikan*, Graz, 1960, 2 vols.
There are essays on Kálnoky in the *N.Oe. B.* and by Friedjung in his *Historische Aufsätze*; nothing at all substantial on either Haymerle or Goluchowski.

CHAPTER XIV

Cis-Leithania under Dualism

Political History, 1871–1903. Hantsch, *Gesch.*, pp. 393–492, gives a brilliant picture. Charmatz, as usual, is adequate. May comes in at this point. For more detail, Kolmer, vols II–VII, Czedik, vols II–III and Hickmann, A. L., *Der oe. Reichsrat*, etc., 1877–1901, Vienna, 1901. Redlich's, Corti's and Tschuppik's lives of Francis Joseph are often valuable. Few full-length biographies, but sketches of Taaffe, Koerber and some others in the collections listed in Section I. For the Auersperg Ministry, also Rogge, *Oe. seit der Katastrophe Hohenwart – Beust*, Leipzig, 1879, 2 vols. For the Taaffe era, Skedl, E., *Der politische Nachlass des Grafen T.*, Vienna, 1922, and Jenks, W. A., **A. under the Iron Ring*, Charlottesville, 1963. For the Badeni era, Sutter, op. cit. The best-known memoirs are those of Plener (above) and Sieghart, R., *Die letzten Jahre einer Grossmacht*, Berlin, 1932, important for the intrigues behind the scenes, in which S. took a great part, but subjective and spiteful; see the no less malicious description of him by Steed, op. cit., pp. 143–4.

Economic and Social History, 1848–1903. Both Zöllner and *M.K.P.* have excellent short accounts and admirable bibs, but both concentrate heavily on Vienna and German-Austria. General accounts in Benedikt, H., *die Wirtschaftliche Entwicklung in der F.J. Zeit* (quoted as Benedikt, *W.E.*), Vienna, 1958, anecdotal; Drage, G., *Austria-Hungary*, London, 1909, very thorough and informative work, inexplicably forgotten; Mayer, H., ed., **100 Jahre oe. Wirtschaftsentwicklung* (quoted as *100 Jahre*), Vienna, 1949, valuable chapters on financial, monetary and commercial policy. Agriculture, *L.u.F.*, above; Strakosch, S. von, *Die Grundlagen der Agrarwirtschaft in Oe.*, Vienna, 1916, and see the bibs., Industry, *Die Grossindustre Oe.s*, collective work, 1898, 6 vols.

The peasants: for the post-1848 operation, see above, Section VIII. *L.u.F.* also contains contributions (some of them reprinted separately) on the effects of the Liberal legislation of 1868 (by H. von Schullern), attempts at agrarian reform (by M. Erth), and the history of agr. administration (by Dr. von Herz). Sommeregger, F., *Wege und Ziele der oe. Agrarpolitik*, Vienna, 1912. Drage goes deeply into the decline of the peasantry; see also Tiefen, G. W., *Die Besitzenden und Besitzlosen in Oe.*, Vienna, 1907, Bauer, O., *Der Kampf um Wald und Weide*, Vienna, 1925, by the Socialist leader, and Macartney, C. A., *The Social Revolution in Austria*, Cambridge, 1926.

Industrial labour: conditions, Drage's is one of the best single accounts known to me in any language. Material also in the Social Democrat histories (below), and in Brügel, L., *Soziale Gesetzgebung in Oe. 1848–1918*, Leipzig, 1919.

Emigration: *Nat. Bureau of Econ. Research*, 'International Migration', vol XIV, 1929, figures, and XVIII, 1931, 'interpretations'.

Education, general, Strakosch-Grossman, G., op. cit.

May, op. cit., has some interesting pages on social forces in the old Austria; my account is parallel to his, not derived from it. The picture given by W. Steed, op. cit., is brilliant. Of the standard histories, that of Hantsch (II, 426 ff.) is the most perceptive in this respect. The disintegration of Liberalism well described by Eder, op. cit., and Charmatz, *D.Oe. Politik* (below), and Plener's memoirs are an unconscious confession of it.

For the new forces in general, besides Hantsch, a good chapter by Wandruschka, *'Oe.s Politische Struktur', in Benedikt, ed., *Gesch. der Republik Oe.*, Vienna, 1954, pp. 289ff. Interesting also Fuchs, A., *Geistige Strömungen in Oe., 1867–1918*, Vienna, 1949; Schneefuss, W., *Demokratie im alten Oe.*, Klagenfurt, 1949. Conservative and clerical forces and movements, Allmayer-Beck, C., *Conservatismus in Oe.*, Munich, 1959, short and rather general; also Vodka, op. cit. Christian Socialism, the latest works are: Skalnik, L., *Dr Karl Lueger*, Vienna, 1952, popular; Allmayer-Beck, *Vogelsang*, Vienna, 1952 (also sketch of V. by the same hand in *N.Oe. B.*); Funder, A., *Von Gestern bis Heute*, Vienna, 1952; id., *Aufbruch zur Christlichen Sozialreform*, ibid., 1953 (biography of Schindler). Social Democracy: Brügel, L., *Gesch. der S.D.*, Vienna, 1922 ff., 5 vols, much information, badly put together; Deutsch, J., *Gesch. der oe. Arbeiterbewegung*, Vienna, 3rd ed., 1947; Hannak, J., *Im Sturm eines Jahrhundertes*, Vienna, 1948, popular. Biography of V. Adler by Ermers, M., Vienna, 1932; also sketches in Charmatz, *Lebensbilder*, and *N.Oe. B.* Good sketch of the beginnings of the movement in Charmatz, *Innere Gesch. Oes. II*, 28ff. The Trade Unions, Klenner, F., *Die oe. Gewerkschaften*, Vienna, 2 vols, 1951–3.

Nationality and its Problems

Statistics: Waber, L., *Die Zahlenmässige Entwicklung der Völker Oe. 1846–1910*, Brünn, 1916, a careful analysis; appendix on Hungary.

Legislation: Hugelmann, K., ed., *Das Nationalitätenrecht des alten Oe.*, Vienna, 1934, exhaustive and most valuable work, primarily a compendium of legislation, but contains also much information on political movements. Valuable material also in Fischel, *Sprachenrecht* (above), and id., *Materialien zur oe. Sprachenfrage*, Vienna, 1902, valuable collection of petitions, Parliamentary debates, etc.

General Surveys: Kann, *The Multinational Empire* (above); Auerbach, *Races et nationalités* (above), Samassa, P., *Der Völkerstreit im Habsburger Staat*, Leipzig, 1910; Hertz, F., *Nationalgeist und Politik*, Zürich, 1936; Macartney, C. A., *National States and National Minorities*, Oxford, 1934, Hantsch, H., *Die Nationalitätenfrage im alten Oe.*, Vienna, 1953.

For other general works, see Section XVII, F, below.

Social Democracy and the Nationalities, Mommsen, H., *Die Sozial-demokratie und die nationale Frage*, etc., Vienna, 1963, very full.

The Germans: Charmatz, R., *Deutsch – Oe. Politik*, Leipzig, 1907, much material. Patzelt, J., *Deutsche Politik in Oe.*, Vienna, 1912, very useful. Molisch, A., *Gesch. der deutsch-nationalen Bewegung in Oe.*, Jena, 1926, unclear, and id., *Briefe zur deutschen Politik in Oe. 1848–1918*, Vienna, 1934, very occasionally important. Perceptive but very short, Wandruschka *ap.* Benedikt (above).

The Czechs and Bohemia, besides Denis and Münch, the latter, especially, excellent, Wiskemann, E., *Czechs and Germans*, Oxford, 1938; Plaschka, L. G., *Von Palacký bis Pekar*, Vienna, 1955. The paper on the Czechs by Havranek, J., in *A.H. Yearbook*, 1967, throws interesting light on the economic and social factors. Much information in Suttner, op. cit., and in Fischel, *Panslawismus*.

The Poles: Galicia. Bienaimée, I., *La Diète de Galicie*, etc., Paris, 1910, political; Estreicher, S., Galicia in the Period of Autonomy, in *Cambridge Hist. of Poland*, vol II (above) and the papers in *A.H. Yearbook*, 1967. The Ruthenes, Fischel; also Romantschuk, D., *Die Ruthenen und ihre Gegner in Galizien*, Vienna, 1902, and *A.H. Yearbook*, 1967. The University Library in Vienna contains about twenty theses on the Ruthenes, but none of them seems ever to have been printed. The Slovenes: still nothing comprehensive, but much can be fished out of the works of Hugelmann and Suttner. The Italians: Kramer, H., *Die Italiener unter der Oe.U. Monarchie*, strongly sympathetic to Austria. Older works, Veiter, T., *die Italiener in der oe.u. Monarchie*, Vienna, 1905, and Mayr, M., *Der Irredentismus*, Innsbruck, 2nd. ed., 1907. Very recent, Huter, F., ed., *Südtirol*, Innsbruck, 1965, a large *Sammelwerk* with valuable contributions on Italian nationalism and on the legal position of the Italians in the Monarchy. The bib. gives also works from the Italian side. The Roumanians, Prokopowitsch, op. cit.

CHAPTER XV
Hungary under Dualism

A. General political history. Rogge still regards Hungary as part of the Monarchy, and covers its internal history up to 1879 in vol II of his *Oe. seit der Katastrophe* (above). The later 'standard' Austrian historians simply ignore the place, and in general, practically everything written on Dualist Hungary by German-Austrians or by foreigners dependent on them is valueless, less on account of its prejudice (although this is almost invariable) than of its incomprehension. Foreign works which have taken their material from Hungarian informants fall into the opposite pit. Miskolczy, *U. in der Habsburger-Monarchie* (above) contrives to be fair to both sides, but is rather unfactual. For details it is necessary to go after all to Hungarian writers, especially Szekfü's *M. Történet* (above) and Gratz, G., *A Dualizmus Kora* (The Age of Dualism), Bp., 1934, 2 vols, excellent on Parliamentary history and on personalities, although not always accurate on dates, etc. Pethö, A., *Világostól Trianonig* (From Világos to Trianon), Bp., 3rd ed., 1925, is strongly 'Independence'. Merei, G., *M. politikai Pártprogrammok* (H. political Party Programmes) is a useful handbook. Szekfü's *Három Nemzedék* (above) is a gloomy but brilliant piece of meditation. The speeches of Deák, Szilágy, Apponyi and others have been edited in the original Hungarian, and there are some political memoirs in the same language, but the shortened English ed. of Apponyi's memoirs is valueless. In English, two chs. (10 and 11) in May, op. cit., and shorter in Macartney, *Hungary, a Short History* (above), and id. *October 15th*, Edinburgh, 2nd. ed., 1961.

B. Economic and social developments: Gratz, op. cit., is excellent on economics. A grandiose survey was produced in connection with the millenary celebrations, Matlekovits, S., *A M. Államháztártásának Története* (The History of the H. State Economy), Bp., 1894, 2 vols, followed by id., *Das Königreich U. wirtschaftlich dargestellt*, Leipzig, 1900, 2 vols. Also: Szterényi, J., *La Grande Industrie du Royaume de H.*, Bp., 1901; Mandello, K., *Rückblicke auf die Entwicklung der u. Volkswirtschaft, 1877–1902*, Bp., 1902; Offergeld, W., *Grundlagen und Ursachen der Industriellen Entwicklung H.*, Jena, 1914; and vol II of Futó, op. cit. The *Évkönyvek* (Yearbooks) of the Royal Hungarian Statistical Service are often mines of information.

Szekfü's writings are good on the changing social pattern, but otherwise, this

BIBLIOGRAPHY

seemed, until recently, to interest foreign writers more than Hungarian. I venture to draw attention to my own two books (above) and to my *Hungary* (Modern World Series, 1934). Lately, there has been much retrospective sociological writing on nineteenth-century Hungary, some of it valuable, some merely shrill, but so difficult of access that it seems useless to list it here. It is, moreover, still afflicted with a certain indigestion. Among older works, Bunzel, J., *Studien zur Sozial- und Wirtschaftspolitik U.s*, Leipzig, 1902; Mailáth, J., *Studien über die Landarbeiterfrage in U.*, Vienna, 1905; id., *La Hongrie rurale, sociale et politique*, Paris, 1909; Jaray, G., *La Question Sociale*, etc., Paris, 1909. Some judicious remarks in the works of Drage and May (above).
C. The Nationalities. Statistics in the official publications, summarized in Waber, op. cit. Collection of documents, Keményi, G., ed., *Iratok a nemzetiségi Kérdés*, etc. (Documents on the Nationalities question), Bp., 1955, 2 vols. On Hungarian policy, Seton-Watson, R. W., **Racial Problems in H.*, London, 1908, primarily but not exclusively concerned with the Slovaks, denunciatory, documented; Jászi, *Dissolution of the Habsburg Monarchy* (above); Macartney, C. A., *H. and her Successors* (above); Kemény, G. A., *A m. nemzetisegi kérdés története* (History of the H. nat. q.), Bp., 1946; Farkas, G., *Az Assimilacio Kora* (The Age of Assimilation), Bp., n.d. (1935?), is an interesting study of the large-scale voluntary assimilation, especially of middle-class Germans and Jews, which actually took place. Balogh, A., *A Népfajok Mg.-on* (The Races in H.), Bp., 1901, shows, on the basis of the censuses, which communes actually changed the nationality of their majorities 1870–1900; unexpected results emerge. For the general political history of the problem, the works of Graz, Szekfü and myself. The Slovaks: Seton-Watson, *Racial Problems* (above) and numerous works by Czech and Czechophile historians; from the other side, Steier, L., *A Tót-kérdés Mg.-on* (The Slovak Question in H.), Liptószentmiklós, 1912; Szána, A., *Gesch. der Slowakei*, Bratislava, 1930. The H.-Germans, no special study for this period, which is covered in innumerable more general writings; see the full bib. in Paikert, G. C., **The Danubian Swabians*, The Hague, 1967. The Roumanians: see Section I; also Jancsó, B., *A Román irredentista Mozgalmok Története* (History of the Roumanian Irredentist Movements), Bp., 1920; Popovici, A., *La Question Roumaine en Transylvanie*, etc., Bucharest, 1915; Moroianu, G., *La Lutte des Roumains Transylvains*, Paris, 1933. The Hungarian Serbs have little accessible literature of their own, but are usually given some pages in the works on the Southern Slavs generally, or the Croats. There are essays on the Omladina and on Svetozar Marković in Wendel's *Südslawisches Risorgimento* (above). See also the *A.H. Yearbook*, 1967. For the Croat question, the works listed in Sections I and IX, above; also some facts in Graz. Literature on the Jews is mostly scurrilous, but there are sober statistics in Kovács, A., *A Zsidóság Térfoglalása Mg.-on* (The Spread of Jewry in H.), Bp., 1922.

CHAPTER XVI

Bosnia, 1878–1903

The occupation: Weltze, A., *Unsere Truppen in B.*, etc., Vienna, 1907–8, 6 vols. The administration: Schmid, F., *B. und H. unter der Verwaltung O.U.s*, Leipzig, 1914, very full, based on the official documents; shorter, Stöller, F., *Die Kulturelle Entwicklung B. und H.*, Vienna, 1961. Sugar, F., *The Industrialisation of B.H.*, Seattle, 1963. There is a separate study of the agrarian problem by Grünberg, K., *Die Agrarverfassung und die Grundentlastungsprobleme in B. und H.*, Leipzig, 1911. While Schmidt and Stöller paint very rosy pictures, a flood of Serbian pamphlets, mostly dating from in or about 1907, depict Austrian rule as the blackest tyranny and exploitation. Of the more accessible works, easily the most balanced is that of Drage, op. cit., pp. 596–650, full of facts, but the author does not commit himself much to imponderables. Südland is full of intimate political details, but intemperately pro-Croat; Haumant, strongly pro-Serb. It is a sad pity that 'Odysseus', who understood the Balkan peoples better than any other European of his age, seems to have spent only a couple of days in Bosnia.

CHAPTER XVII

The Last Years of Peace

A. General pictures: an interesting little 'Sammelwerk', Hantsch, H., ed., *Oe. am Vorabend des Weltkrieges, Graz*, 1964 (quoted as *Vorabend*). Economics, general, Hertz, F., *The Economic Problem of the Danubian States*, London, 1947, very rosy, hard to reconcile with Burgatti's essay in *Vorabend*. I have not read two volumes ed. by Barter, R., *Die Agrarfrage in der Oe.U. Monarchie, 1908–1914*, and *Die Frage des Finanzkapitals* ditto, both Bp., 1965, records of a conference of contemporary-minded historians held in Budapest in 1964.

B. Central figures and top-level policies: the best of the many biographies of Francis Ferdinand is Kiszling, *F.F.*, Vienna, 1953; others still worth reading, Chlumetzky, L., *Erzherzog F.F.*, Berlin, 1929, and Nikitsch-Boulles, P. V., *Vor dem Sturm*, Berlin, 1925; the writer was private secretary to the Archduke, and actually liked him. No satisfactory biography of Aehrenthal; Molden, A., *Graf A.*, Stuttgart, 1917, is a wartime product; a sketch of him by Hantsch in *Gestalter*. Many glimpses of him in Fellner, F., ed., *Schicksalsjahre Oe.s 1908–1919, das politische Tagebuch Josef Redlichs*, also of great general interest. For Berchtold, Hantsch, H., *Leopold, Graf B.*, Graz, 1963, 2 vols. Conrad: his own memoirs, *Aus meiner Dienstzeit*, Vienna, 1902–5, 5 vols; the latest of the big literature on him is Regele, O., *F.M. Conrad von H.*, Vienna, 1965. Beck, Allmayer-Beck, J. C., *Baron Beck*, Munich, 1956. Tisza: Erényi, G., *Graf Tisza*, Vienna, 1935; his letters (*Briefe*), ed. by O. von Wertheimer, Berlin, 1928; his speeches (*Beszédei*) and collected works (*összes munkái*) have also appeared in Hungarian. For Koerber, see above.

Foreign policies and relations: exhaustively treated in many works not Austrian in authorship or specifically Austrian in angle, e.g. for the whole period, Albertini, op. cit.; for the diplomatic history of the annexation, Schmitt, Bernadotte, *The Annexation of Bosnia*, Cambridge, Mass., 1937; the diplomacy of the Balkan wars, Helmreich, E. (that title), Oxford, 1938; the outbreak of war, besides Albertini, Fay, S. B., *The Origins of the World War*, N.Y., 1928; Schmitt, B., *The Coming of the War*, N.Y., 1930, 2 vols. I add only a few titles: Musulin, A., *Das Haus am Ballplatz*, Vienna, 1924; for the Austro-Serb-Russian complex, Uebersberger, H., *Oe. zwischen Russland und Serbien*, Cologne, etc., 1958; Carlgren, H. M., *Iswolski und Aehrenthal vor der bos, Annexionskrise*, Uppsala, 1953; Seton-Watson, H., *The Decline of Imperial Russia*, pp. 347ff., brilliant. The Balkan background to the Annexation, best in Südland, op. cit. Some new diplomatic details in Hantsch's *Berchtold* (above). For the last years, the A. Govt. published a series of documents, ed. Bittner, L., *Oe.U.s Aussenpolitik, 1908–1914*, Vienna, 1930, 9 vols. Short account, Pribram, A. F., *A's Foreign Policy, 1908–*

1918, London, 1923, only a sketch, but P. had access to the documents; id., *Austria and Great Britain*, Cambridge, 1931. Wedel, O., *Austro-German Diplomatic Relations, 1908–14*, Stanford, 1932. For Austro-German military relations, a most useful article by Wagner in *Vorabend. Oe. u. in der Weltpolitik 1900–18*, Berlin, 1965, is a product of the Budapest conference. Many novel interpretations, not all of them convincing. For the military side: Conrad's *Dienstzeit* and (shortly) an article by Kiszling, 'Die Entwicklung der oe.u. Wehrmacht', etc., in *Berliner Monatshefte*, XII, 1934, pp. 735ff. The assassination. Most of the enormous earlier literature on this subject is more safely disregarded; Uebersberger, too, should be used with caution. Albertini seems to be sound. The latest special studies are Remag, J., *Sarajevo*, London, 1959, somewhat superficial, and Dedijer, V., *The Road to Sarajevo*, London, 1967. Dedijer goes into every minutest detail of the background and personal lives of the young conspirators themselves, and probes deeply into the history of the Ujedinjenje and its relations with the Serb dynasty and politicians, but he too fails to reach, or at any rate, to convey, any firm conclusion on the ultimate questions. Background often unsound.

On the Monarchy's final decision for peace or war, an interesting, if indulgen article by Goldinger, W., in *Vorabend*.

C. Austria, internal: The course of events can be followed in the last vol of Charmatz series and in Kolmer, with some details of what went on behind the scenes in Sieghart, op. cit., Redlich's *Tagebuch*, Baernreither, J. M., *Fragments of a Political Diary*, ed. J. Redlich, London, 1930, Allmayer-Beck's life of his father, the biographies of Francis Ferdinand, etc.; seen from a socialist angle in Bauer, O., *Die oe. Revolution*, Vienna, 1923. The real interest has, however, passed by now to the development of the national and social movements, for which see previous sections. The Moravian and Bukovinian 'Compromises' are analysed in detail in Hugelmann, op. cit. For Neo-Slavism, Section XI of Fischel, *Panslawismus*, H. Seton-Watson, op. cit.; also Zeman's *Break-up of the Habsburg Monarchy* (below), pp. 15ff. National movements in general, Hanak, P., ed., *Die Nationale Frage in der Oe.U. Monarchie, 1900–1918*, Bp., 1966, another product of the conference mentioned above (see Barter, ed.).

D. Hungary, internal. The crisis of 1905 is told in detail by Graz, Steed, op. cit., Kiszling, *Franz Ferdinand*, and others. For general internal history, see also Erényi's *Tisza* (above). M. Károlyi's own story in *Gegen eine ganze Welt*, Munich, 1924, English tr. *Fighting the World*, London, 1925. His later *Faith without Illusion*, London, 1956, is less informative.

E. I list here a few of the books which appeared during the period setting out proposals for the reconstruction of the Monarchy, or after it, suggesting the reasons of its dissolution:

Steed, *The Habsburg Monarchy* (above); Sosnowski, Th. von H., *Die Politik im Habsburgerreich*, Berlin, 1912, 2 vols, lively and anecdotal; Popovici, A., *Die Vereinigten Staaten Gross-Oe.*, Leipzig, 1906 (for its place in history, see text); Bauer, O., *Die Nationalitätenfrage und die Sozialdemokratie*, Vienna, 1906, Social Democrat solution, to be found also in two works by K. Renner: *Grundlagen und Entwicklungsziele der oe.u. Monarchie*, Vienna, 1906, written under the pseudonym of 'R. Springer', and *Oes. Erneuerung*, Vienna, 1916 (under his own name). Christian Social angle, Seipl, I., *Nation und Staat*, Vienna, 1916. Early works by Jászi, *A nemzeti államok kifejlödése*, etc. (The Development of the National States), Bp., 1912; *Der Zusammenbruch des*

THE HABSBURG EMPIRE

Dualismus, etc., Vienna, 1918; *Magyariens Schuld, Ungarns Sühne*, Vienna, 1923; of these, the *Zusammenbruch* had the misfortune to be published just after events had taken place which proved many of its main premises to have been mistaken; *Magyariens Schuld* explains this away. Other 'plans' in the literature on Francis Ferdinand, including Hodža, M., *Federation in Central Europe*, London, 1942. Analyses of these and other proposals in Kann, *Multinational Empire* (above) and Wierer, op. cit. Jászi's *Dissolution of the Habsburg Monarchy* (see Section I, B) is the most read today of the retrospects, but the best of them (although somewhat Germanic in outlook) is, to my mind, Kleinwächter, F., *Der Untergang der Oe.U. Monarchie*, Leipzig, 1920.

CHAPTER XVIII

The End of the Monarchy

Latest, May, A. J., *The Passing of the Hapsburg Monarchy*, Philadelphia, 1966, 2 vols, comprehensive, covers all aspects. Penultimate, Zeman, A. B., *The Break-up of the Habsburg Empire*, Oxford, 1961, good on some points, especially the Czech movement, but enormous gaps. Macartney, C. A. and Palmer, A. W., *Independent Eastern Europe*, London, 2nd ed., 1967, gives, we believe, all the essential facts briefly. Still useful, although written before the appearance of many documents, Glaise-Horstenau, E., *Die Catastrophe*, Zurich, 1929; English tr., with some cuts, *The Collapse of the A.H. Monarchy*, London, 1930. The narrative in Uhlirz is remarkable and the bib. enormous. Namier, Sir L., *The Downfall of the Habsburg Empire*, London, 1959, is a reprint of an earlier chapter in the *History of the Peace Conference*, London, 1921–3. A brilliant achievement in its day, it is now long out-dated and it was a pity to reprint it.

As most of these works have full bibs., I add only a few other titles. The military history, Oe. Bundesministerium, etc., *Oe.U.s letzter Krieg*, 1914–18, Vienna, 1931, 15 vols; short sketch, Kiszling, *Oe.U.s Anteil am ersten Weltkrieg*, admirable. The Emperor Charles: latest, and far best, Lorenz, R., *Kaiser Karl*, Graz, 1959, exhaustive; Polzer-Hoditz, A., *Kaiser Karl*, Zurich, 1929, is subjective. The diplomats: Burian, S., *Drei Jahre meiner Amtführung*, Berlin, 1923; English tr., *A. in Dissolution*, London, 1925. Czernin, O., *Im Weltkriege*, Berlin, 1919; English tr., *In the World War*, N.Y., 1920. On Czernin, Singer, L., *Ottakar, Graf Czernin*, Graz, 1965, admiring but useful. Andrássy, G., *Diplomatie und Weltkrieg*, Vienna, 1920; English tr., *Diplomacy and the War*, London, 1921.

These works give, or their bibs. indicate, all important literature on A.'s foreign relations, including the Emperor Charles's peace offers (the Sixtus Letter, etc.), and on the attitudes of the Powers towards the Monarchy, and on these points I will add only a second mention of Pribram's *Austrian Foreign Policy* (above), and a couple more titles on A.'s Polish policy: Hausner, A., *Die Polenpolitik der Weltmächte*, etc., Vienna, 1935, and Fischer, F., *Griff nach der Weltmacht*, Düsseldorf, 3rd ed., 1963, by a German hostile to the then regime.

Internal, general. The Carnegie Trust planned an ambitious series of books relating to the Monarchy in its *Economic and Social History of the World War*. All those completed and published are listed in May's bib. The most important (given under their English titles, where available) are Redlich, J., *A. War Govt.*, New Haven, 1929, Gratz, G. and Schüller, A., *The Economic Policy of A.H. during the War* (ibid.) and id., *Der Wirtschaftliche Zusammenbruch Oe.U.s*, Vienna, 1930. Also Löwenfeld, H., *Die Regelung*

BIBLIOGRAPHY

der Volksernährung, etc., Vienna, 1926. Winkler, W., *Die Totenverluste*, etc., is instructive. Internal, Cis-Leithania. Redlich, *Tagebuch*; Adler, F., *Vor dem Ausnahmgericht*, Jena, 1923; Bauer, O., *Die Oe. Revolution*, Vienna, 1923 (these two Socialist works); Macartney, C. A., *The Social Revolution in A.* (above); Höglinger, F., *Minister Präsident Graf Clam-Martinitz*, Graz, 1964; Rumpler, H., *Max Hussarek*, Vienne, 1965. For the national movements, see the general works above.

Internal, Hungary. There is little that it would serve any purpose to record, even in Hungarian, for both Gratz and Pethö are short, and Szekfü stops with the outbreak of war. May, however, has a couple of chapters, and see also Windischgrätz, *Prince L., Vom Roten zum Schwarzen Prinz*, Vienna, 1920, tr. and abbreviated in his *My Adventures and Misadventures*, London, 1967.

For the decisions of the Powers to break up the Monarchy, the recognition of the Governments, etc. of the 'Nationalities', the general works above; Macartney and Palmer is convenient. Also *History of the Peace Conference*, vol IV and bibs., including that in Macartney, *Hungary and her Successors*. For the end in Hungary, Károlyi, op. cit., Jászi, *Magyariens Schuld, Ungarns Sühne* (above); Batthyány, T., *Für Ungarn gegen Hohenzollern*, Vienna, 1930. For Austria, the chapter by Goldinger in Benedikt's *Gesch. der Rep. Oe.* (above) and I end this wearisome task by recording that one of the very few Austrian historians (so far as I know, indeed, the only one) who ever read my *Social Revolution* told me that 'it was to this day the only book in any language to treat the subject from the sociological angle'.

Index

Abrahamowycz, David, Ritter von, 664
Abstellung ex officio, 18
Academic Legion, 329, 342, 351, 358 ff., 398 f., 401
Academy of Sciences (Vienna), 268; (Budapest), 223, 290; (Zagreb), 738
Acsády, I., 72
Aczél, István, 186
Adamovitch, Bishop, 139, 229
Adler, Friedrich, 819, 824
Adler, Viktor, 305, 519, 633 f., 654, 673, 819
Administrators (in Hungary), 197, 293 f., 318, 762
Adrianople, Peace of, 232
Ady, E., 758
Aehrenthal, Baron Lexa von, 566, 596, 667, 776, 778 ff., 784 ff., 790, 795
Agliardi, Mgr, 595, 672
Ágoston, A., 54
Agrarian credit, 265, 465, 466
Agrarian indebtedness, 466, 625 f., 716
Agrarian Socialist Party, 761 ff.
Agricultural labour, 71, 73–4, 273–4, 377, 398, 620, 628–9, 670–1; (Hungary), 716–7
Agriculture, 36, 37, 45, 47, 74, 201–2, 267, 464 ff., 533, 607, 618, 622 ff., 625 ff., 670 f., 703 ff., 756, 757
Albania, 596, 601, 789, 817
Albert v of Hungary and Bohemia, 6 f.
Albert of Saxony-Teschen, 26, 535, 685
Albrecht I, von Habsburg, Duke, 3
Albrecht, Archduke, 261, 328 ff., 334, 448, 497, 503, 537, 543, 556, 578 f., 587, 593, 615, 695, 701, 778
Alexander I, Emperor of Russia, 199, 232
Alexander, Crown Prince (King) of Serbia, *see* Obrenović
Alexander, Archduke, 140, 173, 178, 218
Alföld, 97
Alispán, 21, 122
Alldeutscher Verein, 656, 681, 796
Allgemeine Schulordnung, 112, 113
Allgemeines Krankenhaus (Vienna), 126
Alpine Lands, 41 ff., 71, 83, 97, 110, 271, 342 ff., 361, 522, 625, 627, 658, 797
Alpine Montan, 619
Alsace-Lorraine, 742
Ambrózy, Baron L., 293
American Civil War, 607
Amtschimmel, 624

Andics, E., 285
Andrássy, Count Gyula, 487, 548 ff., 556 f., 566, 578 f., 584 f., 586 ff., 591 ff., 603, 610 f., 688, 691, 700, 750, 761 ff.
Andrássy, Count Gyula, jun., 831
Andrian Warburg, Viktor Frh. von, 263, 277, 301, 305
Angelovitch, Mgr, 217
Anne, daughter of Wladislaw Jagiellon, 6
Anticipationsscheine, 197, 201
Anti-Semitism, 276, 313, 317, 519, 635, 655, 712
Anton, Archduke, 208
Apponyi, Count Albert, 688, 695, 700 f., 759, 761 ff., 767, 811
Apponyi, Count György, 293 f., 297, 315 f., 324, 330, 504, 538
April Laws, 341, 377 f., 380, 384, 390 f., 394, 408, 413, 416, 487, 507, 510, 524 f., 541, 552
Arad, martyrs of, 431 f.
Aristocracy, 52 ff., 152, 206 f., 263 f., 620, 622 f.; (Hungary), 715 f.
Armenian Catholics, *see* Churches
Armenians, 81 ff., 108
Army, 15 ff., 130 f., 158 f., 172 f., 176, 182, 184, 203 f., 259 f., 319 f., 470–1, 491–2, 533–4, 536, 624–5, 695, 778, 790 f.; *see* Defence Law
Arneth, A., Ritter von, 48
Arnstein, banking house of, 501, 516; Fanny von, 516
Árpád dynasty, 7, 224
Aspern, battle of, 188
Asquith, Mr H. H., 815
Auersperg, Prince Adolf, 585, 604 ff., 609, 611
Auersperg, Count Anton von, 241
Auersperg, Prince 'Carlos', 522, 571, 574, 576, 585, 609
Auersperg, Count Karl, 334, 359, 401 f.
Auffenberg-Komarow, F.M.L. M. von, 790 f.
Auguss, Frh. A. von, 537
August, Prince Karl, of Weimar, 133
Aussee Programme, 652, 654
Austerlitz, battle of, 156, 181
Austria Above the Enns, *see* Upper Austria
Austria Below the Enns, *see* Lower Austria
Austrian Netherlands, 2, 10, 18, 33, 131 f.

INDEX

Austrian Succession, War of, 20, 27, 48
Austro-Slavism, 298, 352 f., 364 f., 547, 850 ff.
Autonomists, German-Austrian, 520, 523, 532, 538, 545 f., 548, 554, 609
Avars, 219
Aviticitas, 44, 245, 316, 338
d'Azeglio, Massimo, 229, 282

Babenberg, dynasty of, 3, 110
Babeş, Vincentiu, 730
Babits, M., 758
Bach, Alexander, 270, 275, 302, 326, 332, 352, 372 ff., 391 f., 396, 399 f., 405 f., 410, 412, 422 f., 439 ff., 445, 449 ff., 459, 463, 471, 479 ff., 488, 494, 496, 500, 503, 508, 514, 517, 532, 545, 624, 647
Bach, Eduard, 446
Bach, Ljudevit, 557
'Bach Hussars', 479, 482, 525
Bácka, 386; see Voivodina
Bács-Bodrog, County, 446
Badeni, Count Casimir, 596 f., 612, 646, 660 ff., 672, 675, 680 f., 701, 761
Badeni Ordinances, 663-4
Baedeker, K., 643 f.
Baernreither, Dr Joseph, 665 f., 748, 779, 821 f.
Baillet-Latour, Count, 168, 334 f., 369 f., 372, 377, 385, 391, 397 ff.
Bajza, Josef Ignatius, 226
Bakunin, 365
Balázsfalva, 91, 382
Baldacci, Frh. A. von, 167 f., 175, 182, 187
Balfour, Mr Arthur, 829
Balkan League, 788 f.
Balkan Wars, 792, 809
Balkans, 34, 37, 93, 117, 131, 200, 232, 295, 432, 537, 588, 592, 596, 617 ff., 624, 776 ff., 784 ff.
Balogh, D., 726
Ban (of Croatia), 8, 558, 735
Bánát of Temesvár, 9, 46, 65 f., 81, 93, 139, 141, 386 f., 445; see also Voivodina
Bánffy, Baron Dezsö, 565, 595, 698, 701 f., 722, 733, 761, 764
Banhans, Dr A., 585, 609
Bankozettel, 49, 179 f., 183, 194 ff.
Bárándy, A., 225
Baranya, County, 36, 386
Barbarossa, Emperor Frederick, 7
Bardolff, Col. K., 754
Barrère, 602
Bartok, Béla, 758
Barwinski, Hofrat S. von, 790
Basilians, 284
Batthyány, family, 53
Batthyány, Count Kázmer, 53, 284, 336 ff., 354, 379, 387 ff., 393, 395 f., 431

Batthyány, Count Lajos, 284
Bauer, Otto, 464, 683 f., 825
'Bauer', defined, 71; see Peasants
Bauernfeld, E., 268, 326
Baumgartner, A., 302, 357, 453, 560, 469 f., 484 f.
Bavaria, 109, 117, 131, 156, 188 f.
Bavarian Succession, War of, 49
Baylen, Capitulation of, 186
Beamtenadel, 70
Beatrix, of Modena d'Este, 11
Beauharnais, Marshal, 188 f.
Becher, Johann, 38
Beck, Col. (later F.M.L.) F. F., Baron von, 579, 760, 778
Beck, Max Wladimir, Frh. von, 793, 795, 860
Beck, Baron, 579, 760, 778, 793, 795
Becke, Carl Ritter von, 544, 551, 555, 579
Becquehem, Marquis, 661
Bedekovics, K., 734
Beer, A., 179 f., 183, 195, 198, 203, 236, 257, 265, 470, 501
Beethoven, L. von, 213
Beidtel, F., 32, 70, 152, 158, 202, 206, 263 f., 299, 301
Belcredi, Count Richard, 536, 539 f., 547 f., 550 f., 554, 565
Belgium, 132, 136, 154, 823
Belgrade, 132, 136, 225, 833
Belgrade, Treaty of, 9
Bellegarde, F. M., 208, 471
Bem, Joseph, General, 402 f., 416, 428, 430
Bendant, F., 95, 97, 271
Benedek, General L., 308, 491, 503, 543
Benedictines, 111
Benedikt, H., 209, 229, 343, 534, 617, 636, 773
'Bene Possessionati', 55-6
Beneš, Dr E., 813
Berchtold, Count Leopold, 781, 788 f., 802 f., 807 ff., 820
Bereg, County, 200
Berger, J. N., 303, 571, 577
Bergrecht, 68
Bernatzik, Dr E., 562
Bernolák, A., 225 f.
Berzeviczy, G., 44, 449
Bessarabia, 591 f., 598
Bessenyei, George, 104, 178, 223
Bestiftungszwang, 128-9, 223; abolished, 574
Beust, Friedrich Ferdinand Baron von, 549 ff., 554 f., 560, 563 ff., 570 ff., 574 ff., 584 f., 603, 607, 652
Bezirk: instituted, 424, 438; Judicial, 440; Mixed, 454, 574; Bezirksgerichte, 446
Bibl, V., 206, 212, 255, 302, 328, 344, 366, 530
Biegeleben, Hofrat von, 536

865

INDEX

Bienaimée, I., 546
Bienerth, A., Frh. von, 795 f.
Bignon, A., 623
Bihar, County, 200
'Bihar Points', 688
Bilinski, Leo Ritter von, 662, 792, 807
Birkbeck, R. K., 803
'Bishops' Party', 673
Bisinger, J. C., 29, 271
Bismarck, Count Otto von, 436, 484, 534 ff., 541 ff., 547, 564, 578 f., 584, 589 f., 592 ff., 596, 599, 601, 652, 783
Bissingen, Count, 351
Bisztritz, 81
Bittó, István, 693, 698
Björnsen, 768
'Black Friday' bankruptcy (*Krach*), 608 f., 616 ff., 632, 653
Black George, *see* Karageorge
Black Hand Society, 786 f., 807
Bleiweiss, Dr Johann, 299
Blue Monday, 275, 327
Blum, J., 143, 269, 402 f.
Bobb, Bishop, 139, 229, 297
Bobrinskij, Count Vladimir, 790
Bobrzynski, Dr Michael, 821 f.
Bogitschewitsch, M., 771
Bogomils, 83
Bohemia, 2 f., 6, 11, 14, 18, 21 ff., 36 ff., 41 ff., 49, 55, 58, 60, 64 ff., 69 ff., 77, 85, 87 ff., 97, 99, 102, 105, 113 f., 121 f., 127, 142, 144, 159, 176, 185, 194, 207, 215, 218 ff., 241 ff., 276, 298, 303, 313 ff., 336, 349 ff., 363 ff., 419 ff., 424, 474, 503, 513 ff., 540, 555 f., 582 ff., 613, 619, 622, 626, 639 ff., 657 ff., 744 ff., 779 ff., 812 f.
'Bohemian Charter', 349, 420, 476
Bohemian Federals, 663
Bohemian Feudalists, 612, 658, 660
Bohemian State Rights (Böhmisches Staatsrecht), 347 ff., 420, 565, 575–6, 584, 604, 612, 639, 866
Bojko Party, 672
Bolsheviks, 684, 824
Bolzano, Bernhard, 211
Bombelles, Count H. T., 361, 409, 456
Borkowski, Count K., 575
Bosnia, 10, 83, 94, 106, 224, 287, 610, 736, 780, 806 ff.
Bosnia-Herzegovina, 82, 569, 588 ff., 596, 740, 781, 791 f.
Botschafter, 538
Bourbons, 433
Bourgeois Radicals (Hungary), 832
Braf., A., 625
Brassó, 81
Bratianu, I., 599
Braun, Hofrat, 581
Brauner, F. A., 347, 372, 376

Brawer, A. J., 72 f., 96
Breinl, J. Frh. von, 308
Breisgau, 10
Brestl, Dr R., 571, 577, 609
Brest-Litovsk, 825
Briand, Aristide, 814
Bridges, Sir Tom, 675
Bright, R., 272
Brion, Marcel, 277
Brixen (Bressanone), 2 f., 41, 76, 82, 84, 110, 155
Brosch, Captain A. von, 754
Bruck, Frh. Karl von, 97, 405 f., 433, 444, 451, 453, 460 f., 468 f., 485, 490, 492, 496 ff., 501 f., 509, 511
Bruckner, 636
Brügel, L., 75, 275, 341, 612, 622, 630 f., 633, 673, 684, 797, 803
Brünn, 202, 400
Brünn Programme (1899), 683 f., 803
Brusatti, A., 757
Bucharest, Treaty of, 829
Buda, 44 f., 93, 136 ff., 371, 388, 393, 396 f., 415 f., 428, 448
Budapest, 124, 337, 385, 389, 415, 445, 571, 696, 725
Budapest Conventions, 591
Budweis, 259
Bukovina, 2, 11, 13 f., 18, 25, 28, 47, 61, 66, 82, 97 f., 102, 108 f., 115, 122 f., 217 f., 346, 368, 404, 424, 462, 523, 625, 650 f., 803
Bulgaria, 587, 590 ff., 773, 776, 782, 788 ff., 817
Bulgars (in Monarchy), 81, 82
Bülow, Prince, 783
Bunyevci, 80 f., 559
Bunzel, J., 717
Buol-Schauenstein, Count Karl Friedrich, 455, 461, 483 f., 490 f., 495 f.
Bureaucracy, Austrian, 59, 112 f., 122 f., 124, 165 ff., 259, 263 f., 459, 624; in Hungary, 708 f.
Bürger-Ministerium, 571
Bürgerliches Gesetzbuch, 126
Burghers, 58 f.
Burgundy, 6, 11
Burian, P., 300 f., 419, 820 f., 830
Burian, Count Stephan, 566, 601, 773 f., 781, 792, 820 f.

Caldiero, battle of, 156
Calvinists, *see* Churches
Camera, *see* Hofkammer
Campo Formio, Peace of, 155 f., 172, 180
Caporetto, battle of, 824
Caprivi, Count L., 595
Caprivi Treaties, 699, 772
Carbonari, 230

866

Carinthia, 2 f., 11, 13, 28, 34, 37, 42, 47, 58, 65, 67, 70, 76, 101, 105, 108, 122, 143, 160, 203, 336, 459, 526, 540, 644 f.
Carlgren, H. M., 780 f.
Carniola, 2 f., 13, 34, 37, 60, 65, 67, 70, 76, 97 f., 101, 105, 108, 122, 203, 207, 216, 220, 336, 343, 526, 540, 550 f., 645
Carolina Augusta of Bavaria, 213
Carolina Resolutio (1731), 107
Carthusians, 106
Casati, Count, 370
'Case U', 760
Casino movement, 621, 714
Casidim, 711
Casopis Musée, 214
'Cassandra Letter', 552
Catalans, 81
Catherine II, Empress of Russia, 118, 131, 587
Catholic Church, *see* Churches
Catholic Congresses, 621
Catholic People's Party (Austrian), 663, 666, 673 f., 681; (Hungarian), 699, 700, 701, 734, 761, 763, 765
Cattaro mutiny, 577, 825
Cavour, Count C., 476, 489 f., 493, 510
Censorship, 113, 144, 162 f., 173, 210, 305, 316, 331, 472, 562
'Centralists' (Hungarian), 286 f.; (Roumania and Bukovina), 523
Cettinje, 774
Chabrus, 640
Chaizes, Awrum, 341, 401, 403
Charles I (as Emperor of Austria; IV as King of Hungary), 565, 820 ff., 829 ff., 832 f.
Charles IV (Emperor), 6 f.
Charles V (Emperor), 6, 87
Charles VI (Emperor; III as King of Hungary and Spain), 9, 13, 27, 38 f., 41, 47, 49, 52, 75, 115 ff., 264
Charles VII (Emperor), 11
Charles Albert of Piedmont, 260, 319, 322, 344, 370, 376, 427
Charles the Bold of Burgundy, 6
Charles of Durazzo, 8
Charles, Archduke, 1, 158, 167 ff., 172, 175, 181 ff., 187 ff., 233, 238, 534
Charmatz, R., 210, 242, 301, 406, 461, 485, 497, 501, 615, 638, 684, 792, 794 f.
Chasteler, F.M.L. J. G. Marquis, 187, 189
Chertek, Baron E. von, 613 f.
Chlopy, Army Order of, 760
Chlumecky, Baron von, 585, 798
Choc, Wenzel, 804
Cholera, 243, 702
Cholm, 155, 475, 825
Chotek, Count Karl, 182 f., 234 f., 298; Count Rudolf, 48; Countess Sophie (Duchess of Hohenberg), 751, 752, 806

Christian People's Party, *see* Catholic People's Party (Hungarian)
Christian Populists, 671, 685
Christian Social Party, 635, 657 ff., 663 f., 672 ff., 681 ff., 754, 764, 769, 775, 794 ff., 805, 811
Christian Social Union, 635
Chrzanowski, General Adalbert, 427
Churches:
  Calvinist, *see* Protestant
  Catholic, Armenian, 108, 562
    Greek (Ruthene), 108, 203, 369, 475, 790
    Greek (Roumanian), 91, 108, 229, 381
    Roman, 14, 18, 51, 54, 59 ff., 68, 80, 82 ff., 91 ff., 104 ff., 108 ff., 112 ff., 120, 129 f., 141, 162 f., 184, 212, 217 ff., 225–6, 262 ff., 277, 368, 410 f., 416 f., 422, 443 f., 458, 462, 467, 480, 520, 562, 574, 620 ff., 650, 654 f., 672 ff., 681, 690, 698 f., 713, 724, 744 f., 752
  Evangelical, *see* Lutheran
  Greek Orthodox: general and Serb, 92 f., 108, 117, 121, 141, 142, 225, 226, 381, 415, 436, 530, 699, 723; (in Bosnia), 82, 746–7, 774
    Roumanian, 86 f., 91, 107, 108, 142, 229, 315, 346, 527, 651, 690, 699
    Russian, 475, 790, 802
  Lippovan, 562
  Lutheran, *see* Protestant
  Moslem, 699, 740 ff., 746
  Protestant (general), 104 ff., 141, 211, 225 f., 262 ff., 285, 291, 295, 480, 497–8, 530, 681
    Calvinist, 104, 106 f., 111, 114, 121, 295 f., 500, 699, 724
    Lutheran, 104, 106 f., 111, 114, 121, 229, 295 f., 482, 500, 666, 681, 699, 724, 728
    Unitarian, 106, 338, 699
  'Received' (established) Churches, 107, 454, 562, 699
  Reformed Church, *see* Calvinist
Uniate Church: its doctrines, 108
'Cilli affair', 661, 663 f., 680
Circles (Kreise), 23 f., 29; in Kremsier draft, 421; in Stadion Cpnst., 424
Cis-Alpine Republic, 155
'Cis-Leithania', 565, 570
Civic Guard (Militärische Bürgerkorps), 329 f., 342, 397, 401
Civil Service, *see* Bureaucracy
Clam-Martinic, Count Heinrich Jaroslav, 259, 496, 498, 505, 508, 522, 531, 581, 821
Clam-Martinic, Count Heinrich von, 821 ff.
Clary-Aldringen, Count Manfred, 667
Clemenceau, M., 829

Cloşka, 142
'Club of the Left', 532
'Coalition' (Hungarian), 761-4, 768; (Serbo-Croat), 768, 769, 811, 828
Coalition of National Parties, 761 ff.
Coalition War, First, 179
Coalition War, Third, 177
Cobenzl, Count Ludwig, 153
Cobenzl, Count Philipp, 149, 153, 155 f., 168, 181
Coburg-Gotha, Prince of, 713
Cojz, Baron A., 216
Cole, G. D. H., 674, 803
Collin, J. von, publicist, 186
Collin, F.M.L. Ludwig von, 308
Colloredo, Count Ferdinand, 325, 342, 359 f.
Colloredo, Count Franz, 151 ff., 156 f., 164, 167 f., 181 f., 190, 206, 325, 359 f., 456 f.
Colloredo-Mansfield, Count J., 342, 623
Comes, 24
Commercial Policy, *see* Tariffs
Committee of Nine, 485
Common Ministerial Council, 566
Common Ministries, 552, 555, 564
Communal Autonomy Law, 438 f., 498, 531
Commutation, 68-9, 129, 144, 159, 160, 234, 280, 312
Compromise (1867): Hungarian Law XII, 552 ff.; Austrian implementing legislation, 554 ff.; assessment of, 565 f.: decennial revisions, 1877, 610; 1887, 710; 1897, 663, 701 f.; 1907, 763; 1917, 820
Concordat, 263, 443 f., 458; abolition of, 574 f.
'Concordia', 302
Confalonieri, Count, 230
Confederation of the Rhine, 157
Congregationes (Hungarian), 24, 57, 286, 446, 696 f., 763
Congregations General (Lombardo-Venetian), 208 f., 230, 332, 514
Conscription, 129 f., 172, 175 f., 184, 230, 564, 571, 759, 791
Conservative Party (Hungary), 688, 693
Consilium locumtenentiale, 26, 31, 318, 447
Constantinople, 131, 595 f., 788
Constitutional Great Landlords, 522, 532, 605, 609, 613, 663
Constitutional Left, Party of, 554, 652
Constitutions: Austrian, 'Pillersdorf' (April, 1848), 355 f.; Kremsier (draft), 417 ff.; 'Stadion' (March, 1849), 423-5; 'December' (1867), 560 ff.; Hungarian, 30-1, 140, 338 ff. (and *see* April Laws), 553 (and *see* Compromise). *See also* Sylvester Patent, October Diploma, February Patent
Consumption tax, 236, 336
Continental Blockade, 189, 195, 201 f.

'Contractualists', 70; and land reform, 462
Contributio, 20, 28, 32, 48
Conventionsmünzen, 201
Cordon, F.M.L. Frh. F. von, 439
Corfu Pact, 828
Coronini, Count J. A., 409
Coronini Club, 612, 613, 619
Corti, A., 240 f., 244, 256, 325, 371, 389, 395, 432, 484, 492, 495, 500, 530, 535, 548 f., 565, 598, 614, 751
Corvinus, Matthias, 7
Cossacks, 81, 759
Counter-Reformation, 34, 36, 87, 104, 109
Counties, Hungarian, 24, 32 f., 122, 132, 197, 222, 286, 293, 445 f., 503, 507, 696; *see* Congregationes, Jurisdictions
Court Chancelleries (Hofkanzleien), 26 f.
Couza, Prince, 493
Cracow, 82, 109, 155, 172, 199, 307 ff., 345, 367, 424, 450
Cracow Group, 802
Crankshaw, E., 784
Creditanstalt, 469
Credit Mobilier, 485
Crenneville, F.M.L. Count de, 244, 296, 527, 542
Crimean War, 483, 486, 489
Crişan, 142
Crispi, Francesco, 601 f.
Croat National Union, 775
Croatia, 2, 7 ff., 13 f., 24 ff., 37, 46, 65 f., 73 f., 81 ff., 96 ff., 102, 107, 115, 122, 139, 141, 251 ff., 287 ff., 365, 380, 386, 446 ff., 458, 472, 482, 503, 538, 547, 550, 557 ff., 705, 734 ff.
Croats, 76 ff., 90, 97 ff., 114, 138 f., 154, 216, 225 ff., 238, 250 ff., 313 ff., 317 ff., 382 ff., 393 ff., 482, 489, 492 ff., 526 ff., 541, 551, 557 ff., 588, 644 ff., 692, 736 ff., 767 ff., 811, 831
Csendörség, 698
Csernova, 'massacre of', 767
Csorich, F.M.L. A. Frh. von, 405, 439, 455
Cumanian Districts, 25, 61, 696
Cumans, 78
Customs Union (Treaty), Austro-Hungarian, *see* Compromise
Custozza, battle of, 376, 543
Cuvaj, E., 769
Cyril and Method Society, 679
Cyrillic script, 647, 737
Czapka, Ignaz von, 329, 332
Czartoryski, Prince Adam, 295
Czecho-Slovak National Council, 814 ff., 826
'Czechoslovak Society', 734
Czecho-Slovak Republic, 831 ff.
Czechs, 12, 35, 59, 77 f., 81 ff., 85 ff., 97, 101 ff., 144, 173, 212 ff., 218 ff., 225 f., 252, 301, 313 ff., 346 ff., 356, 361 ff.,

INDEX

Czechs—contd.
375 ff., 381 ff., 391 ff., 419 ff., 449 ff., 474, 508, 547, 554 ff., 575 ff., 581 ff., 604 ff., 638 ff., 652 ff., 734, 750 ff., 792, 798 ff., 812 ff., 821 ff.
Czedik, E., 526, 611
Czernin, Count Ottakar, 789, 820, 830
Czernin family, 88, 364
Czernowitz, 218, 346, 618
Czoernig, Baron K., 464, 466 f., 470

Dacia, 131
Dalmatia, 7, 37, 82, 94, 96, 101, 115, 160, 172, 175, 202, 207, 252, 288, 352, 355, 384, 386, 419, 425, 447, 461, 513, 526, 558, 577, 601, 645 f., 831
Damian, P., 46 f., 60, 72, 95 f., 228, 271
Damjanić, General J., 416, 428
Dante Alighieri Society, 601
Danubian Principalities, 229, 297, 482 ff.; see Moldavia, Wallachia, Roumania
Danzers Armeezeitung, 785
Danzig, 39, 220
Darányi, Ignacz, 705, 721, 763
David, A., 736
Davoust, Marshal, 177
Deák, Ferencz, 246, 272, 285 f., 288, 291, 294, 316 ff., 324, 338 ff., 393, 395, 481, 487 ff., 495 f., 510, 524 f., 528, 537 ff., 547 ff., 552, 560, 565, 688, 691 ff., 712, 722, 750
Debatte, 539
Debrecen, 36, 44, 58, 705; Proclamation of, 428 f.
'December Constitution', see Constitutions
Dedijer, V., 786 f.
Defence Law (1868–9), 562–4; renewals, 698, 752 f., 765
Definitiva (Hungary 1853), 457
Degenfeld, Count A., 507, 536
Dehm, Count Albert, 298, 314
Delcassé, 602, 675
Delegations, 538, 555, 565
Della Torre, Hofrat, 161
Dembinski, General Count Henrik, 416, 430
Denis, E., 214 f., 219, 364, 498, 522, 613, 623, 642, 660
Deperdita, 20
Dessewffy, Count Aurel, 284, 293
Dessewffy, Count Emil, 497
Deutschnationale Partei, see German National Party
Deutsch-nationale Vereinigung, 656, 800
Deutsche Gemeinbürgschaft, 681
Deutsche Volkspartei, 663
Deutscher Schulverein, 656, 679, 731
Deym, K., 433
Dienstreglement, 165–6

Diets, 23 ff.
Diets, Hungarian: 1790–1 (Leopoldinian), 138 ff.; 1792, 154; 1796, 174; 1802, 176; 1805, 157; 1807, 187; 1808, 186; 1811, 196; 1825, 223 f.; 1830, 242; 1832, 246 f.; 1839, 284 f.; 1843, 290 ff.; 1847–8, 317 (and see April Laws); 1848, 389 f.; 1849, 428 f., 430; 1862, 524 f.; 1865, 540 ff.
Dimitrievic̀, Lt-Col Dragutin, 787
Dipauli, Frh. von, 666
Directorium in publicis et cameralibus, 28
'Dissidents' (Hungarian), 760, 761, 763–4; see Constitutional Party
Doblhoff, Anton Frh. von, 302 f., 357, 362, 364, 371 ff., 391, 398, 401
Dobriansky, A., 558
Dobrowsky, Josef, 214, 218, 225
Draft Statute of Education (1849), 441 f.
Drage, G., 626 ff., 633, 744
Drašković, Count Janko, 253
Dresden, Peace of, 586
Dresden Agreements, 436, 454
Dube, H. von, 210
Dugonic, A., 138
Dunajewski, J. Ritter von, 614, 646, 659, 670, 696
Dürkheim, Count Ferdinand, 581
Dvořak, 643
Dwarfholders, see Land Distribution
Dzjedniszycki, Count Alexander, 531

Ebenbürtigkeit, 52
Eder, H., 546
Education, 110 ff., 122, 125 f., 161 f., 183, 212, 216, 405, 441 f., 457 f., 460, 529 f., 559, 563, 576, 621, 642 f., 645, 650 f., 657, 679 f., 690 f., 707 f., 723 ff.
Eger, 106
Ehnl, M., 401
Eichhoff, Peter, 258
Eingekauft peasants, see land tenure
Einstandsrecht, 126
Eisenmann, L., 148, 325, 410, 442, 459, 497, 511, 522, 525, 571
Electoral Capitulations, 154
Elizabeth, Empress, 458, 488, 548 f., 580, 636 f., 685 f.
Elizabeth Wilhelmina Louisa of Württemberg, 152
Ember, G., 269
'Emergency paragraph' in Stadion constitution, 423; in December Constitution (para. 14, q.v.), 561, 567; not in Hungarian constitution, 553
Emigration, Austria, 629, 660, 755; Hungary, 702, 727; Croatia, 738
Emphyteutical tenancies, 70, 129, 462
Endlicher, Professor S., 302, 326, 353, 360
Endres, D., 60, 365

869

INDEX

Eötvös, Baron J., 57, 272, 284, 286, 316, 338 f., 388, 395, 505, 510, 528 f., 551, 558, 560, 689 ff., 707, 712, 722
Eötvös, Baron Lórand, 707
Epiphany Resolution, 828
Erastianism, 120, 230
'Erbländer', 2 f., 6, 13 f., 18, 22 f., 26 f., 33 f., 36, 41, 50, 69, 75, 84, 87, 99, 105, 126 f., 142, 185, 220, 284 ff., 343, 525
Ercole of Modena d'Este, 11
Ertl, M., 626, 628
Eskeles, banking house, 501, 516
d'Espérey, General Franchet, 833
Estates (Stände), 23, 26, 28, 105, 122
Esterháza, 45
Esterházy, family, 40, 713, 718
Esterházy, Count Maurice, 823
Esterházy, Count Móritz, 525, 537, 539
Esterházy, Prince Pál, 45, 53, 338, 340, 379, 388 f., 395, 429, 713
Esztergom, Prince Primate of, 106
Eugene of Savoy, Prince, 40, 117
Eulenburg, Prince, 666 f.
Evangelical Church, see Churches (Lutheran)
Eynatten, Q.M. General, 509

Falkenhayn, Count Julius, 613, 661, 664, 761
Fallmeyerer, Jakob, 268
Febronius, 110
February Patent, 512 ff., 522 ff., 539 f., 545, 553, 560, 562, 576, 646
Federal Nobility, Party of, 505
Federalists' Conference (1866), 547
Federn, W., 718
Feigl, F., 37, 57
Fejérváry, F.M.L. Baron, 762
Fellner, F., 511, 601 f.
Fényes, E., 90, 269 f., 463
Ferdinand I, Emperor, 6, 8, 19, 26, 49, 52, 87, 116, 576
Ferdinand II, Emperor, 8, 23, 27; Ferdinand I (Austrian Emperor), 152, 233, 239 ff., 255 ff., 263, 284, 299, 317, 327, 330, 333, 341, 345, 347 f., 351, 358 f., 362 ff., 370, 376 f., 382 ff., 388, 395 f., 407 f., 412, 426, 473, 492, 640
Ferdinand IV of Naples-Sicily, 239, 322, 344
Ferdinand of Bulgaria, 595, 602, 782, 785, 789
Ferdinand d'Este, Archduke, 234 f., 251
Ferdinand, Archduke, 11, 26
Ferenczy, Ida, 549
Ferenczy, Z., 481, 539 f., 565
Ferrara, 319 f.
Festetics, family, 712
Festetics, Count György, 551
Feudalists (Czech), 497 f., 613 f., 639 f.
Fichte, 300
Ficker, F., 114 f.

Ficquelmont, Count Ludwig, 291, 309, 334 f., 340, 344, 350, 353, 357, 664
Fidei commissa, 53, 623, 713
Finance, National, 20, 47–9, 175–6, 178 ff., 183, 194 ff., 201, 203 f., 205–6, 235 ff., 257 ff., 320–1, 360, 536, 544, 608, 619 f., 671, 790; Hungarian (Dualist period), 691 ff., 696, 707; see also contributio, consumption tax, inflation, loans, National Bank, etc.
Finance Patent (1811), 195 ff.
Fischel, A., 215, 346, 349, 365, 369, 404, 451, 562, 647, 790
Fischer, E., 313, 374, 423, 816
Fischof, Adolf, 274, 327, 360, 517, 519, 582
Fiume, 2, 10, 39, 176, 288, 292, 318, 384, 394 f., 425, 446, 499, 541, 558, 831
Flemings, 12, 82
Föispán, 24, 122, 696 f.
Folberth, Otto, 297
Forgách, Count Antal, 524, 781
Forst Patent (1852), 464
Fournier, A., 530
Fraknói, V., 723
France, 117, 134, 148 ff., 154 ff., 179, 185, 188, 192 f., 197, 232 f., 258, 309, 322 ff., 427, 432, 482 ff., 498 ff., 542 f., 576 ff., 595, 598, 602, 782, 808, 813, 824 ff.
Franche Comté, 6
Franchise: Austria (1848), 357 f.; (February Patent), 514 f.; (1873), 605; (1882), 615; (1893, proposed), 660; (1896), 662; (1905–6), 792: Hungary (1849), 337 f., 377; (1877), 694; (1918), 822; see also Suffrage Reform (Hungary)
Francis I (II), 3, 112 f., 115, 125, 147 ff., 199 ff., 205 ff., 210 ff., 220 ff., 225 ff., 230, 232 ff., 255 ff., 284, 306, 320, 456, 473
Francis Ferdinand, Archduke, 287, 500, 556, 637, 668, 701, 750 ff., 764, 770 ff., 778, 785, 789, 793, 805 f., 820
Francis Joseph, 129, 240 f., 262, 331, 341, 349 f., 355, 358, 361 ff., 407, 415, 427 ff., 436, 439 ff., 446, 448, 451 ff., 456, 461, 472, 475 f., 478, 480, 482 ff., 488 ff., 495 ff., 503 ff., 509 ff., 516 ff., 527, 530, 534 ff., 541 ff., 547 ff., 552 ff., 564 ff., 569 ff., 574 ff., 580 ff., 586, 593, 595 ff., 603 ff., 611 ff., 621, 636 f., 650, 655, 659 ff., 672, 685 ff., 691 ff., 698 ff., 713 ff., 729, 732, 749 ff., 760 ff., 768 ff., 778 f., 782, 790, 793, 799, 806 ff., 810, 813, 820 ff.
Francis Stephen of Lorraine, 11, 37
Frank, Dr Josef, 738
Franz, Georg, 302
Franz Karl, Archduke, 1, 152, 240 f., 256, 326 f., 331, 334 f., 341, 358, 361, 371, 395, 407 f.

INDEX

Frederick II, King of Prussia, 8, 105, 117
Frederick III, Emperor, 3
Frederick William III, King of Prussia, 135, 149, 199, 260
Frederick William IV, King of Prussia, 260, 427, 433
Free Peasants, 61
Freie Deutsche Vereinigung, 663, 668
Freistadt, 34
French Revolution, 134, 138, 149 f., 157, 162, 211
Freud, Sigmund, 757
Friedjung, Professor A., 518, 519, 654, 786; quoted, 129, 325, 331, 332, 391, 447, 452, 469, 490, 536, 580, 796
Friedrich, Archduke, 713
Frint, Mgr J., 211
Frith, 636
Friule, 3, 200
Fröbel, Julius, 402 f., 535
Frommelt, K., 442, 460
'Fundamental Articles', 583 f.
Funder, E., 786
Funke, G., 663
Füster, A., 304, 423
Futó, M., 45, 468

Gagern, Heinrich von, 352
Gaj, Ljudevit, 251 ff., 287, 299, 384
Gáldi, L., 226
Galicia, 2, 15, 18, 21, 26 ff., 33, 35, 37, 39, 46 ff., 55 ff., 61 ff., 65 ff., 72 ff., 82, 93 ff., 100 ff., 108 ff., 115, 118, 122 f., 127 ff., 158, 168 f., 175, 186, 202, 208 f., 217, 220, 234, 243, 263, 281 ff., 300, 307 ff., 344 ff., 365, 367, 404 ff., 419 ff., 424, 428, 439 ff., 450 ff., 462, 472, 474, 503, 513 f., 518, 540, 547, 550, 575 ff., 583 f., 619, 625, 647, 817 ff.
Galicia-Lodomeria, 10 f.
Galician-Russian Society, 790
Garašanin, Ilja, 295
Garibaldi, G., 509
Gautsch, Karl Frh. von, 624, 662, 665 f., 792 f., 796, 800
Gehringer, Baron Karl, 445, 448, 478 ff.
Geist-Lanyi, P., 420
Gendarmerie, 471 f.
'General Civil Code' (1811), 206
'Gentry', 713 f.
Gentz, F. von, 186, 205, 210
George III, King of England, 199
German Catholics, 475
German Clericals, 523, 531, 554, 577, 581, 609, 612, 614, 652, 656, 666, 668, 796
German-Austrian Club, 615
German Club, 615, 656
German (Holy Roman) Empire, 3, 10, 87, 98 f., 116 f., 147, 156 f., 199; German Bund, 199, 211, 323, 350 ff., 407, 426 ff., 433 ff., 490, 534 ff., 542 ff.; German Empire, 578 ff., 589 ff., 666–7, 772, 773, 782 ff., 807, 809, 821, 829, 830; *see also* Prussia
German Federalists, 523, 550, 554
'German Left', 523, 531 ff., 554, 571, 615
German National Party, 658 ff.
German People's Party, 519, 654, 663, 681
'Germanisation', 88 f., 99, 113–14, 123, 144, 216, 220 441 f., 448, 457, 563, 819
Germans, 80 ff., 93, 97 ff., 114, 116, 123, 173, 218 ff., 293, 346 ff., 356, 373 ff., 381 ff., 411, 419 ff., 441 ff., 508 ff., 515 ff., 568, 576 ff., 604 ff., 626 f., 638 ff., 651 ff., 798 ff., 807 ff., 811 ff., 828 ff.
Germans (in Monarchy), 35, 42, 46, 76 f., 78, 80 ff., 98 f., 101–2, 103, 118, 213, 300 ff., 350, 351 f., 356, 366, 372, 374, 381, 392, 411, 419 ff., 508, 515 ff., 544, 604, 638 ff., 651–7, 680–2, 757, 798, 799 ff.; *see also* Swabians, Saxons, Transylvanian
Germany, 3, 10, 14, 34 f., 42, 46, 116, 118, 154 ff., 187, 199, 211, 300, 323 ff., 343, 352 ff., 367, 406, 426 ff., 433, 436 f., 499, 534 ff., 544 ff., 597, 771 ff., 781 ff., 821 ff.
Gewerbeordnung (1859), 500–1, 633
Ghika, Prince, 67
Ghyczy, Kálmán, 247, 524, 541, 688, 693
Giers, 595 f.
Giskra, Karl, 533, 571, 577, 609, 630
Glaise-Horstenau, E. von, 173
Glanz, H., 662
Glaser, Dr Julius, 585
Gleisbach, Count J. N., 662
Glombinski, Dr S., 801
Glück, 116
Gobbi, G., 375
Gogolák, L., 225
Golden Bull (of Andrew II, 1272), 30
Golden Bull (of Charles IV, 1356), 7
Goldinger, W., 807
Goldmark, A., 327, 375, 423, 517
Goldner, Maximilian, 327, 517
Goluchowski, Count Agenor, 404, 438, 450 f., 474 f., 496, 500, 507, 511, 514, 547, 575, 582, 646 f.
Goluchowski, Count Agenor, jun., 563, 595 ff., 601, 605, 646, 662, 666, 778, 782, 792
Gorčakov, 590 f.
Görgey, Arthur, 413, 415 f., 428 ff.
Gorizia, 11, 84, 122, 420, 645
Gorizia-Gradisca, 2 f., 11, 76, 122, 143, 207
Gorove, István, 551, 692
Gotthardy, Franz, 157
Göttschee, 645
'Government Party' (Hungary), 315 ff.
Gratz, A., 250, 606

871

INDEX

Gratz, G., 688, 700, 756, 766, 773, 813
Graz, 41, 211, 240, 303, 342 f., 351 f., 545;
  see also Styna
Great Austrians, 523, 532
Great Britain, 132, 150, 155 f., 161, 185, 195,
  197, 199, 202, 205, 232 f., 319, 369 f., 429,
  432, 477, 482 ff., 493 f., 589, 592, 598, 602,
  782, 813 ff., 821 ff.
Greece, 592
Greek Oriental Church, see Churches
Greek Orthodox Church, see Churches
'Greek Project' (1783), 131
Greeks, 115
Green Cadres, 830
Gregr, Eduard, 612, 684
Gregr, Julius, 612, 684
Greuter, Mgr Josef, 523
Grey, Sir Edward, 814, 816
Grillparzer, F., 212 f., 268, 301 ff., 392
'Grün, Anastasius', 241, 571
Grünberg, K., 69, 159, 269, 311, 373, 463
Grünberg Ms., 219
Grünne, F.M.L. K. L., 455 ff., 471, 492, 494,
  496
Grünwald, Béla, 31, 693, 729
Gubernia, 26 ff., 29, 122, 207
Guilds, 40, 126, 203, 407, 501
Guizot, 309
Güterschlachterei, 628
Guthry, A. von, 647
Guttenberg, F.M.L. von, 662
Györ, battle of, 188
Gypsies, 81 ff., 95, 102
Gyulafehérvár, 107 f.
Gyulai, General Count F., 439, 471, 488 ff.

Habietenik, Dr C., 582
Hadik, Count J., 824
Hagen, Baron von, 210
Hain, J., 97, 319, 678
Hainfeld Conference, 683, 719, 804
Hajdu District (Hungary), 61
Hajnal, K., 340
Halics-Vladimir, 13
Haller, Count József, 154, 294, 317
Hammer-Purgstall, Josef Frh. von, 268
Hammerstein, F.M.L. W. von, 404
Hanak, P., 755 f.
Hanka, V., 219, 298
Hanover, 436
Hantsch, Professor H., 83, 182, 562, 596,
  636, 676, 718, 780 f., 796, 807, 809
Hardinge, Sir Charles, 783 f.
Hartig, F., 166, 319 f., 326, 331, 344, 376,
  399
Hartwig, Baron J., 788
Hasner. Leopold von, 571, 577
Hatvany-Deutsch, Baron L., 711
Haugwitz, Count F. W., 20, 28, 48, 100, 115

Haulik, Bishop, 317, 526
Haumant, L., 743, 746
Haüsler, Innmänner, etc., see Land Tenure
Havliček, Karel, 314, 366, 372, 381, 474, 519
Haydn, 116
Haymerle, 594
Haynau, F.M.L. W., 429, 431 f., 445, 447,
  476, 478 f., 481
Hebenstreit, Franz von, 157
Hein, F., 374, 512
Helena, Bavarian Princess, 459
Helfert, A. von, 405; cit. 279, 300, 315, 347,
  361 f., 368, 394, 405
Helleiner, K. F., 179, 205
Hentzi, General H., 695
Herbst, Eduard, 523, 571, 577, 609 ff., 615,
  641, 653, 656
Herder, 300, 301
'Hereditary Lands', see Erbländer
Herz, F., 718, 756
Herzberg, Count E. F., 132, 149
Herzegovina crisis, 590 ff.
Herzl, Theodor, 794
Hesse, Elector of, 436
Hitler, Adolf, 653, 655
Hlinka, Mgr A., 767
Hoch, C., 285
Hódmezövásárhely, 36
Hodža, Michael, 296, 753
Hodža, Milan, 754, 767
Hofbauer, Klemenz Maria, 213, 277
Hofdeputatio in Banaticis, 93
Hofer, Andreas, 187, 189
Hoffähigkeit, 52, 151
Hoffmann, Professor E., 34, 41
Hoffmannsthal, H. von, 757
Hofkammer, 19, 21, 28, 122, 166, 201, 258,
  334, 379
Hofkriegsrat, 19, 168, 334, 379
Hofrechnungskammer, 19
Höglinger, F., 753, 819
Hohenlinden, battle of, 155
Hohenlohe, Prince Konrad, 574, 581, 667,
  793
Hohenwart, Count Karl Sigmund, 157, 581,
  583 f., 603 ff., 609, 640, 660 f.
Hohenwart Club, 609, 613, 615, 645, 663
Hold, defined, 835
Holstein, 436
Holy Alliance, 232
Holzgethan, Andreas F. H. M., 581, 584 f.
Honoratior, defined, 50
Honvéd, Honvédség (1848), 387, 390, 395,
  431; (1868), 556, 564, 791
Hora, 142, 279
Hormayr, Joseph Frh. von, 181, 186, 189
Hornbostel, Dr Theodor, 302, 353, 372, 376,
  401
Hörnigk, Johann, 38

Horsetzky, General A., 344, 625
Horst, General J., 585, 613 f.
Horthy, Admiral M. (N.), 428, 832
Horváth, Balthasar, 551
Horváth, E., 390
Hötzendorff, Conrad von, F.M.L. (later F.M.), 778, 781, 785, 787 ff., 807, 817
Howard, J., 628
Hoyos, Count E., 342, 357 f., 360
Hrabowski, F.M.L. A. Frh. von, 385, 387 f.
Hradcin (Moravia), 105
Hubertsberg, Peace of, 41, 117
Hübner, A., Frh. von, 406 f., 468, 496, 500; cit, 401, 412, 452, 484
Hugelmann, K., 562, 605, 645 f., 675, 681 f., 794, 798 f.
Hugo, Victor, 247
Hummerlauer, Hofrat K. von, 369
Hungarian National Agricultural Association, 705
Hungary, 1, 2, 6, 7 ff., 14, 24–5, 26, 30–2, 35 f., 37, 43–6, 53, 54, 57, 66, 71, 72, 73, 77–81, 85–7, 89–93, 97, 102, 103–4, 106–7, 114, 121, 122, 127, 131 f., 135, 137–42, 153–4, 172–7, 183–5, 196 f., 221–5, 242–250, 269, 271 ff., 284 f., 288–96, 315–18, 324 f., 333–41, 377–97, 402, 413–17, 425, 428–32, 444–50, 461, 462, 466 f., 476–82, 486–9, 493, 497, 499, 503 ff., 509 f., 524–530, 536–9, 540, 547–53, 557 ff., 567 ff., 687–739, 758–71, 811, 818, 820, 821, 823–824, 829, 831, 833; *see also* Magyars, Croatia, Transylvania, etc.
Huns, 78
Hunyadi, János, 428
Hurban, Josef, 296, 381, 396, 528
Hussarek, Max Frh. von, 821, 830
Hussites, 35, 105, 107, 225, 734
Huszadik Század, 713
Huzuls, 46
Hye, Professor A., 526, 551

Ibsen, H., 758
Ignatiev, 588, 592
Illes, G., 717
Illok, 446
Illyria, Kingdom of, 189, 191, 193, 199, 216
Illyrian Court Chancellery, 141, 154
'Illyrian' language, 113, 114, 123
'Illyrian Movement', 139, 252 ff., 287 f., 292, 294 f., 384, 388
Impopulatio, 80
Independent National Party (Croatia), 736, 738
Independent Radical Party (Serb), 737
Indigenat, 21
Industrial workers and conditions, 75, 274 ff., 312–13, 341, 360 ff., 377, 397 f., 629 ff.; in Hungary, 717 f.

Industrialization, 38 ff., 42 f., 126 f., 265 ff., 275 ff., 291 f., 467 f., 607 f., 616 f., 619 629 ff., 670, 717 f., 755 f.
Inflation, 178 ff., 183, 194 ff., 197–8, 201
Inner Language of service, 418, 441
Innsbruck, 41, 188, 211, 343, 370 f.
Innsbruck Manifesto, 361
Institute of Historical Research (Vienna), 460, 636
Insurrectio, 15, 177, 185, 188
Interim Compact, 43
Interim Relatio, 66
Inzaghi, Count K., 299, 327
Ipek, Patriarch of, 108
Irányi, D., 693
'Iron Ring', 614, 645
Isabella of Portugal, 6
'Ischl clause', 702
Isonzo, battle of, 817
Istóczy, G., 712
Istria, 2 f., 76, 84, 155, 207, 216, 420, 601, 645
Italians (in Monarchy), 76, 81, 82, 84 f., 97, 98, 100, 101, 102, 116, 649 f., 679 ff., 811–12
Italy, Kingdom of, 230, 260, 318 ff., 322, 343–4, 369 f., 376, 427, 433, 489 ff., 542 f., 578, 598, 600–2, 784 f., 814, 817, 828, 829, 832 f.; *see also* Lombardy, Venetia, Piedmont, etc.
Izdenczy, Hofrat J., 175
Izvolski, A. P., 777, 780 f., 787

Jacobi, Baron C. P. W., 133
Jacobins, 165, 169, 211
Jagd Patent (1853), 464
Jagiellon, Louis, 6, 8
Jagiellon, Wladislaw, 6 f., 14
Jagiellon dynasty, 6 f., 14, 85
Jancu, Avram, 414
Jánossy, I., 446
Jansenists, 111
Jansky, General L., 695
Járas, 24
Jarcke, K. E., 262, 293
Jasicza language, 283, 648
Jassy, Treaty of, 136
Jászi, Oszkar, 639, 650, 725, 766, 771
Jaworski, A., Ritter von, 661
Jazyge Districts, 25, 61, 696; Jazyges, 25, 78
Jedlicka, L., 543
Jellačić, Josip, 336, 370, 383 ff., 387 ff., 391 ff., 399, 402 f., 413, 446, 457, 568
Jena, battle of, 185
Jendrzewicz, A. Ritter von, 665
Jesuits, 111, 113, 212 f., 262, 449
Jews, 19, 25, 47, 58 f., 63, 77, 81 ff., 94 ff., 102, 105, 108 f., 121, 128, 180, 184, 205, 225, 243, 276, 285, 302, 304, 308, 338, 356,

INDEX

Jews—*contd.*
377, 430, 454, 466, 480, 484, 502, 516 ff., 563, 629, 653 ff., 662, 670, 675, 690, 699, 703, 709 ff., 745, 747, 766, 794
Jireček, J., 582
Joachimowycz, Mgr, 283, 369, 647
Joanna, Queen of Spain, 6
Jobbágy, defined, 71
Johann Parricida, 3
Johann Salvator, Archduke, 685
'Johanneum', 216
John, Archduke, 181 f., 185 ff., 200, 216, 236, 238, 256, 325, 330, 370 ff., 393, 407
John, F.M.L. F. von, 543, 551, 555, 578 f.
Jókai, M., 708
Joll, J., 490
Jorga, N., 766
Joseph I, Emperor, 14
Joseph II, Emperor, 1 f., 8 ff., 14, 33, 37, 60 ff., 66, 71, 75, 79, 90, 95, 98, 103, 105, 112 f., 115, 119 ff., 141 ff., 148 ff., 158 ff., 162, 164, 172 ff., 178 f., 205, 214, 217, 220, 275, 277, 443, 458, 502, 587, 630
Joseph, Archduke Palatine, 174 f., 183, 190, 316 f., 753
'Josephinism', 120, 148, 151 f., 163, 169, 174, 207, 213, 238, 255, 262 f., 293, 302, 411, 443, 531, 563, 800
Josika, Baron Samuel, 297, 383, 497, 504
Joyeuse Entrée, 123
Judensteuer, 109
Judicial system, 126, 160, 166, 169, 207 f., 507, 571, 574, 691, 696 ff., 707
Jungmann, Josef, 214
Junimists, 731
Juriga, A., 767
Jurati, 247 f.
Juridisch-politischer Leseverein, 302 f., 325
'Jurisdictions' (Hungary), 529, 690, 696 f., 763
Justh, Gyula, 764 f., 770 f.

Kailer, Admiral V. von, 807
Kaiserfeld, Moritz von, 520, 523, 538, 545, 551, 561
Kaizl, Prof. Dr J., 665
Kállay, Benjamin, 742 ff., 773
Kálnoky, Count G., 565 f., 594 f., 597, 601, 660, 667, 699
Kammerknechte, 19, 21
Kampelik, Dr F. C., 346
Kann, A., 112, 562
Kápolna, battle of, 417, 422
Kapper, Siegfried, 519
Karadžić, Vuk, 225, 252
Kara George, 224
Karageorgević, Prince Alexander of Serbia, 295, 414
Karageorgević, King Peter, 771, 776, 828

Karl Ludwig, Archduke, 240, 554, 637, 750
Karlóca, Metropolitan, 93, 108, 142; Congress of (1840), 386 f.
Karlovac, 251
Karlowitz, Peace of, 8
Károlyi family, 713
Károlyi, Count György, 252, 713
Károlyi, Count Mihály, 771, 808, 811, 823, 829 ff.
Károlyi, Count Sándor, 722
Kassa, 445
Katholica Udloga, 747
Kaunitz, Count W. A., 9, 15, 20, 28, 88, 93, 117, 136, 149, 153, 211
Kautsky, Karl, 635
Kay dialect, 252
Kazinczy, F., 103, 137, 157, 178, 221, 224
Kemény, Baron, 526 f.
Kempen, F.M.L. J., Baron von, 455, 472, 494, 496
Kerkapoly, K., 692
Kerner, J., 64, 74, 127
Khevenhüller, Prince, 48
Khuenburg, Count G., 659
Khuen-Héderváry, Count Károlyi, 698, 736 ff., 760, 764 f., 768 f.
Kielmansegg, Count E., 661
Kiev, 217
Kinsky family, 88
Kirschbaum, J. M., 296
Kiszling, R., 319 f., 369 f., 399, 752 f., 760, 764, 768, 778, 791, 795, 797, 805 f., 817
Kiutahia, 477
Klagenfurt, 41, 343
Klapka, G., 430, 493, 547
Klauzál, G., 338 f.
Klebelsberg, Count J., 258
Klein-Micu, Innocentius, 91
Klein-Micu, Samuel, 91
Kleinwächter, F., 545, 643 f., 650, 677, 790, 803
Kletzansky, Hofrat J. von, 349
Klezl, Dr, 629, 755
Klimt, G., 757
Klofáč, V., 801, 804, 813
Kodály, Zoltán, 758
Koerber, Ernst von, 624, 667 ff., 679, 702, 753, 759, 761, 792, 800, 821
Kogalniceanu, M., 297
Kölcsey, Ferencz, 246
Kollar, Jan, 214, 225, 251 f., 290, 295
Kolmer, Dr G., 518; *cit*, 607, 623, 625 f., 628, 663, 667, 681, 698
Kolowrat (Kollowrat) family, 88
Kolowrat-Krakowski, Count L. J., 167, 175
Kolowrat-Liebsteinski, Count Anton, 160, 210, 219, 234 ff., 241, 253, 256 ff., 263, 284 ff., 303 f., 309 f., 325 ff., 330 f., 334 f., 342, 347, 384

INDEX

Kolozsvár, 81, 731
Komárom, 397, 428, 430 f.
Komjáthy, M., 566, 807
Kommerzdirektorium, 202 f.
Kommerzialgewerbe, 39, 194, 205
Konferenzrat, 210 f.
Königgrätz, battle of, 543 f., 578, 647
Königinhof Ms., 219, 675
Kopitar, B., 216 f.
Korb-Weidenheim, Baron K. von, 613 f.
Körös, 227 f., 292, 380
Koroseč, Mgr A., 822
Kossovo, battle of, 806
Kossuth, Ferencz, 700, 760, 762 ff., 768, 811
Kossuth, Lajos, 248 ff., 272, 276, 284 ff., 290 ff., 312, 316 ff., 323 ff., 333, 337 f., 378 ff., 386 f., 389 ff., 395 ff., 413, 415 f., 428 ff., 477 ff., 486 f., 493 f., 497, 499, 510, 517, 537, 548, 552, 568, 689, 698 ff.
Kövár, 9
Közep-Szolnok, 9
Kramař, Dr Karel, 675, 776 f., 792, 801, 813, 823
Krassó, County, 200
Kraszna, 9
Krausz, Karl von, 453
Krausz, Philipp von, 334 f., 368, 372, 401, 405 f., 451 ff., 469
Kreditdeputatio, 19
Kreisämter, 23, 29
Kreise, *see* Circles
Kremsier, Reichstag and draft Constitution of, 405, 415, 417, 420, 422 ff., 426, 517, 562, 582
Krieg, Baron F., 234
Kristóffy, J., 754, 762, 764 f., 768, 792
Krobatin, F.M.L. Baron von, 791, 807
Kübeck, Karl F. Frh. von, 214, 236, 255, 258, 261, 264, 291, 310, 326, 331, 334 f., 342, 400, 412, 451 ff., 469; *cit*, 160, 162, 234, 235
Kudlich, H., 279, 374 f., 402, 423
Kuhn, Baron F., 578 f.
Kulmer, Baron F., 384, 413, 455
Kunschak, Leopold, 673
Kuranda, I., 353
Kutchuk Kainardji, Treaty of, 118
Kutna Hora, Treaty of, 104
Kvaternik, J., 557, 735

La Marmora, 542
Latchka, A., 635
Ladins, 76, 82
Ladislas Postumos, 6
Ladislas of Naples, 8
Laibach, 41, 216, 419, 645, 677
Lamberg, General Count F., 396
Lammasch, Prof. Dr N., 830

Lamsdorf, Count, 776
Land Distribution (1780), 71 ff.; (in Vormärz), 269 f., 273 f.; (under land reform), 462–3; (in Cis-Leithania, Dualist Era), 626 ff., 670; (Hungary, Dualist Era), 713, 716
Land Reform (1848–9), 338, 373 f., 377; implementation of results, 461 ff.; (Bosnia-Herzegovina), 746, 792
Land Tax (pre-1848), 20, 51, 63; Josephinian (proposed), 129 f., 143; Franciscan, 203
Land Tenure (pre-1848), 62 ff., 65, 69; under land reform, 462–3; Bosnia-Herzegovina, 746
Landeshauptmann, 28, 286
Landessprache, Landesübliche Sprache, 418, 562, 563, 641
Landseer, 636
Landstände, *see* Estates
Landtafel, 21
Landtage, composition and statutes, pre-1848, 23 ff.; Stadion Const., 438, 439; Goluchowski's drafts, 508; February Patent, 514 ff.; December Const., 562; Bosnia-Herzegovina, 791–2
Landwehr (1808), 185, 187, 188; (1868), 556, 564, 791, 812
Language of service and command, 556
Lanner, J., 268
Larisch-Mönich, Count Johann, 539, 544
Lassalle, 630
Lasser, Joseph von, 496, 512, 585
Latifundia, 53–4, 623, 712
Latin (language), 90, 123, 137 f., 142, 177, 220 f., 227, 252, 283, 292, 297
Laudemium, 68
Law XII of 1867, *see* Compromise
Laxenburg Manifesto, 496
Le Play, F., 270 ff.
League for the Cultural Unity of all Roumanians, 732 f.
League of the Three Emperors (*Dreikaiserbund*), 590, 594 f., 751, 779
Lecher, Dr O., 664
Ledebur, Count Johann, 662
'Left Centre', Austrian, 532; Hungarian, 541, 550, 688, 691; *see* Moderate Opposition, etc.
Lega Nazionale, 601
Lehár, Franz, 757
Leibgeding towns, 21, 70
Leiningen, Count K., 382, 387, 465
Leiningen, Prince, 371
Leipzig, battle of, 197
Lemberg, 47, 115, 217 f., 220, 307, 344 ff., 367, 404, 424, 450, 475, 647 f.
Leményi, Bishop, 251, 297, 382
Lenau, 302

875

Leoben, Preliminary Peace of, 155
Leopold I, Emperor, 8 f., 31, 38, 48, 59, 66, 92, 106
Leopold II, Emperor, 2, 119 f., 134 ff., 149 ff., 153, 157, 159, 162, 164, 172, 179, 553
Leopold, Archduke, 506
Leopold II, Grand Duke of Tuscany, 344
Leopoldine, Archduchess, 152
Libelt, K., 365 f.
Libényi, János, 472 f.
Liberal Party, Cis-Leithanian, 519 ff., 571, 574 ff., 581, 605 f., 614, 633 ff., 693 f., 733, 760; and see Autonomists, Young Liberals, etc.
Liberal Party, Hungarian, 693 ff., 698 f., 759 ff., 763, 764
Liberalism, German-Austrian, 301 ff., 516–522
Lichtenfels, Th., Frh. von, 514
Liechtenstein, family, 53, 203; Prince Alfred, 615; Prince Alois (sen.), 330; Prince Alois (jun.), 615, 633, 635; Prince Johann, 623
Liége, University of, 125
Lieven, Countess of, 192
Liga Culturale, 766
Lika, 557
Limburg, 436
Lindner, Col. Béla, 832
Linguistic legislation, etc.: under Maria Theresa, 89, 99 f.; under Joseph II, 123. General and Austria, Pillersdorf Const., 336; Kremsier draft, 418; Stadion Const., 424; Bach enactments, 441 f., 446, 448; Sylvester Patent, 455; December Const. (Art. XIX), 562 ff.; *see also* Badeni Ordinances, Stremayr Ordinances, Bohemia, Bukovina, Galicia, Moravia. Hungary (1791–1848), 142, 144, 223, 226 ff., 242, 247, 288; see Magyarisation (1848), 337; (1849), 430; (1861 draft), 527 ff.; Law XCIV of 1868, 558 ff.
Linz, 34, 41, 259, 313, 343
Linz, Treaty of (1645), 107
Linz Programme, 519, 634, 654, 682
Lippovan Church, 562
Liptószentmiklós, 381
Lissa, battle of, 543
'Little Russian' language, 648
Littoral, 23, 37, 57, 65, 73, 84, 102, 160, 189, 203, 343, 420, 424, 513, 575, 650
Livings Patent, 133
Ljubljana, *see* Laibach
Lobkowitz, family, 53, 88; Prince August, 221, 233 f.; Prince Joseph, 377
Löhner, L. von, 419
Lombardy, 24, 41, 48, 97, 122, 155, 208 f., 230, 369 ff., 409, 476
Lombardy-Venetia, 199, 202 f., 208 f., 229, 233 f., 267, 282, 300, 319 f., 322, 344, 352, 355, 370, 390, 419, 422, 425, 437, 444, 461, 472, 475, 486 f., 503
London, Treaty of (1915), 814, 816, 832
Long Haulage, 64
Lónyay, Menyhért, 247, 551, 579, 691, 735
Los von Rom movement, 666, 680 f., 752
Louis XVI, King of France, 149 f., 157
Louis Napoleon, Emperor of France, 427, 432 f., 454, 483 f., 489 ff., 499, 509 f.
Louis Philippe, King of France, 322
Louis the Great, 35, 56
Lower Austria, 36 f., 40 f., 58, 67, 69, 101, 105, 114, 122, 160 f., 169, 202 f., 279 ff., 303, 313, 326, 503, 515
Lower Lusatia, 7, 87
Lower Slavonia, 10
Lublin, 155
Lubomirski, Prince A., 365
Ludovica of Bavaria, 459
Ludwig, Archduke, 239, 241, 255 f., 304, 325 ff., 330 ff., 383
Ludwig, Viktor, 685
Lueger, Dr Karl, 622, 634, 664, 672, 796
Lukács, László, 702, 765, 770
Lunéville, Peace of, 153, 155 f., 175
Lusatia, 7 f., 87
Lussin Piccolo, 499
Lustkandl, Professor W., 536
Lutheran Church, *see* Churches

Macartney, C. A., 80, 627, 813, 820, 821, 828
Macedonia, 596
Mack, Joseph, Hungarian Colonel, 478, 480 f.
Mack, Karl Frh. von, Austrian General, 156, 168, 177
Madarász, J. and L., 247, 378
Madeyski, Ritter von, 661
Mafia, 812 f.
Magenta, battle of, 490
Magyar (language), 114, 123, 137, 142, 175, 178, 185, 221, 242, 285, 288, 292 f., 297, 380 f., 416, 430, 446, 507, 524, 528 f., 556, 692, 721, 736, 753
Magyarisation, 288 ff., 722 ff.
'Magyarones', 288, 294, 297, 526, 557, 734
Magyars, 3, 12, 30, 34 f., 46, 77 ff., 96 f., 107, 226 ff., 287 ff., 414, 527, 558 ff., 568
Mahler, Gustav, 636, 757
Maior, Petru, 92
Majestätsbrief, *see* Bohemian Charter
Majláth (Mailáth), Count Antal, 285, 315; Count György, 239, 539; Count J., 716, 760
Makkai, L., 226
Mályusz, E., 173

INDEX

'Mameluks', 694, 737
Manin, Daniel, 319, 343, 489
Maniu, 767
Manorial system, 21 f., 160
Mantua, 2, 10, 15, 65, 136
Máramaros, 90
Marburg, 41
Marczali, H., 723
Margutti, A. Frh. von, 410 f., 603 f., 685, 750, 805
Maria, daughter of Charles the Bold, 6
Maria, sister of Ferdinand I, 6, 8
Maria Christina, Archduchess, 26, 135
Maria Ludovica of Este, 185, 190, 234
Maria Theresa, Empress, 2, 9 ff., 18, 20 ff., 26 ff., 30 ff., 38 ff., 42 ff., 47 ff., 55, 64 ff., 70, 72, 74 f., 80, 89, 103 ff., 107 ff., 122, 124, 137, 140, 143, 159, 162, 173, 225, 229, 458, 473, 556, 586, 621
Maria Theresa of Bourbon-Naples, 152, 185
Maria Valerie, Archduchess, 685
Marie Caroline, Archduchess, 239
Marie, Louise, Archduchess, 152, 193, 199
Markart, J., 636
Markow, Dr, 790
Martinovics conspiracy, 157, 173 f., 178
Marx, G., 275, 306
Masaryk, Thomas Garrigue, 102, 675 f., 733, 769, 813 ff., 828
Masirević, Patriarch, 730
Matica (Ruthene), 475
Matica Srbska, 224, 530, 730
Matice Školska, 640
Matthias, Emperor, 14, 87, 524
May, A. J., 562, 608, 803
Mayer, Cajetan, 375, 419 f.
Mayerhofer, Ferdinand von, 386, 447
Maximilian I, Emperor, 6, 13, 20, 110
Maximilian II, Emperor, 104
Maximilian, Archduke, 188, 488, 531, 578
Mayr, P., 189
Mazils, 26
Mažuranić, Ivan, 735 ff.
Mazzini, Guiseppe, 475, 478, 487, 601
Mecklenburg, 436
Mecséry, Frh. von, 372, 507
'Memorandum Trial', 732
Mensdorff-Pouilly, Count Alexander, 536 f., 539, 542, 549
Meran, 11
Mercantilism, 38 ff., 126
Merei, G., 269
Messenhauser, Wenzel, 401 ff.
Mészáros, Col. G., 338, 379, 387 f.
Metternich, Prince Clemens, 15, 113, 187, 189 ff., 196, 199 ff., 210 ff., 222 f., 230, 232 ff., 246, 255 ff., 284 ff., 292 ff., 303 ff., 307, 309 ff., 315, 319 ff., 326 ff., 330 ff., 335, 337, 340, 342, 347, 350, 381, 392, 406 ff., 452, 486, 496, 503, 517, 614, 664
Metternich, Prince Richard, 542
Meynert, H., 66, 94, 153, 161, 173
Meyrink, Gustav, 644
Michael, Prince of Serbia, see Obrenović
Migazzi, Cardinal, 112
Mihailović, Archbishop, 735
Mikó, Count Imre, 526 f., 551
Mikszáth, Kalman, 708, 757
Milan, 2, 10, 15, 19, 26 f., 33, 65, 208 f., 229, 282, 301, 319, 343, 369, 444, 475 f., 490
Milan, Prince (King) of Serbia, 590 f., 597, 600
Milde, Archbishop, 443
Miletić, Svetozar, 730
Military Frontier, 2, 18, 25, 61, 81, 93, 102, 107, 114, 122, 141, 379 f., 385, 388 ff., 394, 425, 447 f., 526, 556 f., 689 f.
Milyukov, P. N., 822
Mitranov, P. von, 106
Mittrowsky, Count A. F., 299
Mobile Guard, 401 f.
Mocsonyi, Alexandru, 505, 730 f.
Mód, A., 200, 716
Modena, 11, 199, 233, 344, 433
Moderate Opposition, Party of, Hungarian, 695
Moga, Vasile, Bishop, 229, 251, 315, 413
Mohács, battle of, 6
Moldavia, 11, 108, 346
Molisch, P., 300, 521, 545, 653
Molnar, F., 723
Monasteries, Monastic Orders, 105 f., 111, 121, 144 610; (Bosnia), 746
Montecuccoli, Count, 354, 359 f., 362
Montenegro, 482 f., 589, 591, 788 ff., 808
Mór, battle of, 415
Moravia, 2, 7 f., 14, 23, 26 f., 35, 37, 42 f., 65, 67, 70 ff., 76, 85, 87, 102, 105, 176, 195, 202, 215, 243, 281, 303, 336, 349 f., 365, 424, 515, 540, 550 f., 576, 622, 626, 639 ff., 643
'Moravian Settlement' (1905), 798
Morgarten, battle of, 10
Möring, K., 305, 325, 433
Morlaks, 82, 84, 97, 747
Mortuarium, 68
Moslems, 82 f., 94, 588, 592 f., 699, 740 f., 745 ff., 774
Moyses, Bishop, 528
Mozart, 116
Mühlfeld, Dr E., 353, 523, 531
Münch, H., 640, 675
Münchengrätz, Agreement of, 233, 429
Munkács, Uniate Bishopric of, 217
Munkácsy, M., 708
Muraköz, 81, 416, 446, 524, 541, 558

Muraviev, 596
Mürzsteg Agreements, 596, 776, 779

Nádasdy, Count M., 235 f., 503, 527
Nádor, see Palatine
Nagodba, 557, 692, 735, 768 f.
Nagysalló, battle of, 428
Nagy-Szombat, 45
Nagyvárad, 106, 445
Namier, L., 308
Naples, 10, 155, 204, 222, 230, 320, 509
Napoleon, Prince Jerome, 576
Napoleon Bonaparte, 152, 155 ff., 170 f., 177, 180 ff., 185 ff., 192 f., 196 ff.
Napoleon III, 535, 542, 547, 576, 578
Narodna Obrana, 786, 807
'Nation', 288 f.
National Association for the Protection of Industry (Védegylet), 292
National (later, Austro-Hungarian) Bank, 201, 203 f., 257, 258, 265, 379, 389, 465, 469 f., 474 f., 532, 544, 610, 702, 764
National (State) debt, 48, 49, 179, 205–6, 236, 237, 258, 470, 501, 502, 532, 608, 671 f., 756; Hungary and, 532, 544, 610, 702, 764
National Guard (Vienna, 1848), 329, 331 f., 342, 346 f., 357 ff., 362, 377, 387, 397 ff., 401, 413
Nationalities in Monarchy: numbers and distribution (1780), 75 ff.; national hierarchies, 81 ff.; social and cultural differentiations, 94 ff.; nature of national problem in the Monarchy, 100 ff.; national feeling in 1780, 102 ff.; development of the problem, see Vormärz, passim; 441 ff., 508, 613, 637 ff., 674 ff.; in Hungary, 721 ff.; and see Germans, Magyars, Czechs, etc.
'National Parties', Croat, 734 ff.; Hungarian, 700, 761; Roumanian, 731 ff.; Slovak, 729
National Socialist Party (Czech), 804
Nationalverband, 795, 796, 799, 819, 821–2, 830
Naumann, Friedrich, 815
Naumovics, Father, 647 f.
Navy, 320, 790 f.
Neklyudov, A., Russian diplomat, 788
Nemes, H. D., 267
Neoacquistica Commissio, 10
Neo-Josephinianism, 800
Neolog Jews (Hungary), 711
Neo-Slavism, 776 ff.
Nestroy, 268, 302
Netherlands, 6, 15, 19, 24, 26 f., 38, 48, 65, 81 f., 103, 122 f., 136
Neustädter, J. Frh. von, General, 393
New Party (Hungary), 761, 763

New Slovak School, 729
Nexus Subditelae, 21, 62; see Peasants; abolished, see Land Reform
Nicholas I, Emperor of Russia, 233, 260, 429, 432, 482 f., 590
Nicholas II, Emperor of Russia, 596, 789
Nicholas, Grand Duke, 811 f.
Nicholas, Prince (King) of Montenegro, 588, 590
Niederoesterreichische Eskomptegesellschaft, 468
Niederoesterreichischer Gewerbeverein, 302, 325, 326
Nikolsburg, Treaty of, 107, 543
Nobility, 49 ff., 227 ff., 263 f.; see aristocracy, 'Gentry', bene possessionati, sandalled nobles
Nomenclature of Monarchy (after Compromise), 564 ff.
Northcliffe, Lord, 828
Nostić, Count A., 363
Noszlopy, G., 478, 481
Novara, battle of, 427
Novi-Bazar, Sanjak of, 591 f., 596 f., 780 f.

Oberdank, W., 650
Oberste Justizstelle, 28, 29, 168
Oberwinder, Heinrich, 630
Obrenović, Alexander, Crown Prince (later King) of Serbia, 600, 790
Obrenović, Michael, Prince of Serbia, 295, 598, 590
Obrenović, Milan (d. 1839), 295
Obrenović, Milan, Prince (King) of Serbia, 596, 597, 600
Obrenović, Miloš, Prince of Serbia, 224, 295
October Diploma, 506 ff., 512, 527, 541, 576, 646
O'Donnell, Count Heinrich, 243
O'Donnell, Joseph, Count, 185, 194 f.
'Odysseus', 745
Offergeld, W., 718
Old Conservatives (Hungarian), 478 f., 481, 487, 489, 497, 505 f., 509 f., 524, 537, 539, 541, 548, 552
Old Czechs, 658
Old Liberals, 609
Old Ruthenes, 648, 677
Olga, Grand Duchess, 261 f.
Olmütz (Court in), 399 ff., 405, 408, 423
Olmütz, Archbishop of, 105
Omladina (Czech), 659, 662
Omladina (Serb), 590, 591, 730
Onciul, Dr Aurel Ritter von, 803
'Oppositional Declaration' (1847), 316
Örményi, József, 154
Orsova, 430
Országos Kaszino, 714
Orthodox Church, see Churches

INDEX

Orthodox Jews (Hungary), 711
Oswiecim (Auschwitz), 11
Otruba, G., 38, 42, 48, 75, 179, 266
Ottakar, King of Bohemia, 3
Otto, Archduke, 750
Ottoman Empire, 6, 8 f., 34, 36, 79, 106 f., 131 f., 135 f., 193, 225, 232 f., 365, 482, 508 f., 600, 730, 741, 746, 754, 781 ff., 817
Outer language of service, 418, 441

Padua, 209, 319
Padua, Armistice of, 833
Paget, J., 271 f.
Palacký, Františeck, 214 ff., 219, 226, 298, 347, 352 f., 363 f., 372, 374 f., 419, 474, 522, 548, 554 f., 568, 576 f., 612, 639, 684
Palatine (*Nádor*), 26 106, 137, 140, 338, 339, 393
Pálffy, Count Fidél, 284 f.
Pálffy, Count József, 177
Pálffy, Count Károly, 154
Pálffy, Count Móritz, 525
Palkovic, Georg, 226
Palmer, A. W., 813, 820, 821, 828
Palmerston, Lord, 309, 323, 370, 429, 432
Pandurs, 448
Pannasch, Col. A., 360
Panslavism, 215, 218, 290, 296, 298
'Para. 14', *see* Emergency Paragraph; applications of, 664, 665, 666, 796, 823
Paris, Treaty of (1815), 199
Paris, Treaty of (1856), 483, 588
Parliaments, Hungarian: 1867, 687 ff.; 1872, 691; 1875, 693 ff.; 1881, 695 f.; 1884, ibid.; 1887, ibid.; 1901, 761 ff.; 1906, 763 ff.; 1907, 764 ff.; 1910, 764 ff.
Parma, 10, 199, 233, 433
Partito Populare, 650
Partium, 9, 316, 338, 425, 446, 689
Party of 1848, 691, 693
Party of the Federal Nobility, 505
Party of Independence, 693, 695, 700, 761 ff., 768 ff., 832
Party of Progress, 769
Party of Pure Right, 738, 768 f., 775
Party of Right, 526, 738, 811
Party of Work, 764 f., 811, 823
Pašić, N., 789
Paskiewicz, Duke of Warsaw, 429 f.
Passarowitz, Peace of, 9
Passau, 66
Patrimonial Courts, 22, 74, 160, 279; abolished, 338, 374, 450
Patzelt, N., 538, 551, 800
Paul, Emperor of Russia, 155
Pavelić, M. A., 828
Pavia, 209, 319
Pázmándy, Dénes, 354, 390
Peace Party (Hungary, 1849), 428

Peasant Party (Croat), 768; *see* Radić, S., 769
Peasants, 61 ff., 127 ff., 141 ff., 173 ff., 245, 269 ff., 277 ff., 308 ff., 315, 337 ff., 398 ff., 461 ff., 481 ff., 533, 625 ff., 716 f., 745 f., 729
Pécs, 36, 74, 81
Pejačević, Count Ladislas, 736
Pejačević, Count Todor, 768
Penal Patent, 128
Penitent Sisters, 357
Perczel, Mór, 378, 415
Pereire, Banking House of, 468, 485
Perényi, Count Z., 284, 430 f.
Pergen, Count, J. A., 126, 153
Pernerstorfer, Engelbert, 654
Perthaler, Hans von, 353 f., 502, 512, 525
Peschiera, battle of, 369
Pest, 44 f., 74, 126, 175, 245, 271, 301, 333, 378, 528
Pesti Napló, 538
Pethö, S., 537
Petöfi, S., 337, 378, 723
Pfersche, Emil, 681
Pfingstprogramm, 681 ff.
Pfleger, E. von, 210
Philip, King of Spain, 6
Piacenza, 10, 199
Piarists, 111, 121
Piasts, dynasty of, 23
Pichler, Caroline, 268
Piedmont, 204, 222, 230, 260 ff., 320, 336 376, 426 ff., 433, 483 f., 490, 509 ff.
'Pig war' (1904), 773
Pilgrimage to Moscow, 554
Pillersdorf, Franz Frh. von, 234, 299, 309, 334 f., 342, 344, 347 ff., 355 ff., 362 ff., 368, 371, 378 f., 418, 443
Pilsudski, J., 802, 811
Pinkas, Adolf, 347, 372, 582
Pino, Baron F., 614
'Pious Party', 212 f., 238, 262
Pipitz, Hofrat J. von, 394, 396
Pirchegger, H., 111
Pitreich, General N. Frh. von, 778
Pius VII, Pope, 212
Pius IX, Pope, 38, 574
Placetum Regium, 110, 130, 144, 444
Plener, Ernst von, 536, 544, 609, 613, 656, 661, 798
Plener, Ignaz von, 509 ff., 532 f., 536, 571, 577, 653, 656, 659, 661, 663
Plevna, battle of, 592
Podiebrad, Georg, 85
Podolian Conservatives, 801
Pogodin, M., 284, 475
Poland, 2, 11 ff., 30, 35, 56, 61, 70, 109, 132, 149, 187, 193, 243, 365, 587, 646 f.
Poland, First Partition of, 11, 117

879

Poland, Second Partition of, 153, 155
Poland, Third Partition of, 199
Poles, 12, 30, 82, 92 ff., 100 ff., 132, 169, 187, 208, 217 ff., 234, 242 ff., 282 ff., 307 ff., 344 ff., 356, 367 ff., 373 f., 419 ff., 450, 474 f., 508, 522, 531, 546 f., 550 ff., 576 f., 583, 605 ff., 646 f., 801 ff., 811 f., 815 f., 821 ff., 830
Police, 125, 144–5, 162, 163 ff., 212, 410
Polish Club, 522, 606, 613, 649, 658, 663, 801, 822
Polish Legion, 382
Polish Populists, 671 f.
Polit, Michael, 730
Polizeibetriebe, 39, 194, 205
Pomaks, 592
Poniatowski, Prince J., 217
Popoviciu, Aureliu, 732, 805 f.
Population statistics, 76 ff., 264 ff., 518, 618 f., 642 ff., 669, 676 ff., 702 ff., 709 ff., 715 f., 724 ff., 738 ff., 755 f.
Populist Party, 645
Porte, *see* Ottoman Empire
Portugal, 11, 155
Posen (Poznán), 307, 346
Potocki, Count Alfred, 571, 574, 577, 579, 581, 801
Potsdam, Declaration of, 150
Pozsega, 1
Pozsony, 44 f., 186, 226 f., 292, 296, 333, 337, 386, 445, 479
Pragmatic Sanction, 13 f., 19, 31, 117, 333, 340, 393, 478, 487, 525, 538, 540, 551, 688, 700, 738
Prague, 27, 36, 42, 102, 109, 154, 157, 211, 214 f., 242, 301 ff., 347 ff., 363 ff., 377, 428, 473, 643
Prague, Treaty of, 543, 545
Prandstätter, Josef, 157
Pratobevera, Frh. A., 512
Prazak, Alois, 613 f., 658 f.
Premyslides, dynasty of, 7
Pressburg, Peace of, 156, 189
Pribram, A. F., 518; *cit.*, 597
Prinetti, 602
Privilege of Kassa, 56
Privilegium Maius, 3, 6
Privilegium Minus, 3
'Progressive Conservatives' (Hungarian), 293
'Progressives' (German-Austrian), 609, 653, 663, 681
Prokesch-Osten, 268
Prokopowitsch, E., 94, 218
Propinatio, 63, 168
Prosvita, 648 f.
Protestant Patent (1859), 500, 503
Protestants, *see* Churches
Provisoria (Hungary, 1849), 445 ff., 457
'Provisorissimum', 447

Prpic, G. J., 738
Prussia, 39, 105, 109, 117, 131 f., 135 ff., 149 f., 153, 185, 197 ff., 220, 233, 260 ff., 309, 323, 346, 352, 367, 426 ff., 433, 436, 490 ff., 534 ff., 543, 549 f., 577 ff.
Psenner, Dr L., 635
Puchner, F.M.L. A. Frh. von, 414 f.
Pulszky, F., 378 f., 393, 396, 403, 429
Putz, 327, 517

Quadrilateral, 344, 369

Raab, Frh. von, 70
Raab system, 70, 128, 143
Raccognino Agreement, 784 ff.
Radetzky, Count J., F.M., 266, 319 ff., 334, 343 f., 358, 364, 369 f., 376, 382 f., 389 ff., 399, 414, 427, 430, 444, 476, 488
Radić, Anton, 769
Radić, Stjepan, 526, 769, 775, 811, 828
Radical Party (Serbia), 599 f., 771, 787, 832
Radowitz, J. M. von, 323, 327
Railways, 259, 266, 313, 460 f., 469, 485 f., 550, 607 f., 617 f., 662, 670, 689, 691 f., 696, 706, 716, 744, 780, 791
Raimund, Ferdinand, 213, 268
Rainer, Archduke, sen., 181, 185, 190, 208 f.
Rainer, Archduke, jun., 491, 497, 512, 539
Rajačić, Bishop, 295, 386 f., 414 f., 446
Rákóczi, Prince F., 53, 90 f., 478
Rampolla, Cardinal, 672
Randa, Prof. A., 668
Rastatt, Treaty of, 10
Rath, A. J., 342, 344, 366
Ratio Educationis (Austrian), 113 f., 161 f.; (Hungarian), 114, 183
Ratschky, Hofrat A. von, 161
Rauch, Baron Levin, 526, 557, 734
Rausch, Baron Pál, 769, 786
Rauscher, Joseph Othmar von, 262, 409 f., 443, 456, 458, 467, 480, 506, 575, 621
Ravelsberg, F. Strobl von, 357
Realist Party, 675
Rechberg, Count Johann, 244, 494 ff., 500, 503, 506, 512, 530, 535 ff.
Redlich, Prof. Josef, 518; *cit.*, 54 f., 325, 391, 394, 406, 452, 457, 490, 494, 499, 501 ff., 511 f., 515, 537, 615, 664, 666 f., 685, 753, 764, 768, 770, 775, 786, 802, 806, 819
Reformation, 106, 219
Reformed Church, *see* Churches (Calvinist)
Regele, O., 500, 533 f., 536
Regimental language, 558
Règlement Organique, 297
Reichenberg Convention, 135, 139, 197
Reichshofrat, 33
Reichskammergericht, 33
Reichsrat (1849), 423, 453, 456; Narrower (1860), 513; Reinforced (1860), 503 ff.;

INDEX

Reichsrat—*contd.*
(1867), 554 ff.; (1870), 581 ff.; (1873), 609 ff.; (1879), 613 ff.; (1885), 615 ff.; (1891), 658 ff.; (1897), 662 ff.; (1901), 668 ff.; (1907), 794 ff.; (1911), 796 ff.
Reichstag (1848–9), 373 ff., 398 f., 400, 406, 417 ff.
Reinohl, F., 325
Reinsurance Treaty, 595
Religious Fund, 610
Renner, Karl, 683
Reorganized Socialists, 766
Repeal Movement, 314
Rerum Novarum, Encyclical, 672
'Reserved Rights', Monarch's (defence), 340, 379, 552
Responsibility, Ministerial, Austria, 355, 453–4, 530, 561; Hungary, 339, 353
Retsey, General A., 396
Reuchlin, A., 319, 344, 469
Reviczky, Count A., 236, 242, 284
Rezek, Dr A., 668
Ribay, Juray, 225
Riedel, Frh. von, 157
Rieger, F. L., 363 f., 372, 374, 474, 519, 522, 531, 554, 576 f., 582 f., 612 f., 639, 657 f., 684
Riepl, R., 259
Riesbeck, A., 41, 96
Rilke, R. M., 757
Ristić, 597
Rittner, Dr E., 662
Robot, 63 ff., 159 f., 178, 229, 279 f., 303, 310 ff., 336, 343, 373, 462, 716, 720
Robot Patents, 65
Rodić, General, 589 f.
Rogge, W., 403, 471, 489, 609, 692
Rokitansky, Karl, 268
Roman Catholics, *see* Church
Rosseger, Peter, 627
Roth, Stefan Ludwig, 297, 315
Rothschild, Anselm, 468 f., 492, 532
Rothschild, James, 484 ff., 544, 672, 693
Rothschild, Lionel, 544
Rothschild, Salamon, 205, 238, 259, 322, 330, 461, 468 f., 516 f.
Rottenhahn, Count, 162, 182
Roumania, Kingdom of, 592, 598 f., 731–2, 789, 808, 817, 829; *see* Danubian Principalities, Moldavia, Wallachia
Roumanian National Party of the Bukovina, 678
Roumanians of Monarchy: in Bukovina, 82, 94, 108, 115, 217 f., 221, 229, 346, 373 f., 420, 523, 650 f., 678, 803: in Hungary and Transylvania, 12, 78, 80, 81, 86–7, 90, 91 f., 97, 100, 102, 107 f., 115, 139, 142, 297 f., 315, 381, 382, 414, 482, 527, 529, 730 ff., 766 f., 811, 831; *see also* Vlachs

Roumelia, Eastern, 592, 781
Royal Bohemian Society of Sciences, 214
Royal Free Boroughs, 21 ff., 44 f., 58, 291
Rüdiger, F. J., Bishop, 430, 574
Rudnay, Cardinal, 225 f.
Rudolph I, German King, 3, 10
Rudolph II, Emperor, 87
Rudolph II, Duke, 3
Rudolph IV, Duke, 6, 87
Rudolph, Crown Prince, 637, 750
Rukavina, Baron A., 253
Rum, 446
Ruptași, 94
Russell, J., 97, 109, 301, 306
Russia, 117, 130 ff., 135 ff., 153, 155 f., 185, 193, 197, 199, 204, 221, 225, 232 f., 260 ff., 287, 309, 323, 378, 429 ff., 482 ff., 535, 578 f., 586 ff., 592 ff., 596 ff., 624, 647 ff., 677, 751, 776 ff., 781 ff., 788 ff., 801 ff., 810 ff., 821 ff.
Russian Revolution (1917), 821, 824
Rustical Bank of Gablic, 625
Rustical land, 62 f., 71 ff.
Ruthenes, 12, 45 f., 79 f., 82, 90 ff., 97, 100 ff., 107 ff., 114 ff., 217 ff., 225, 283 f., 289 ff., 345, 365, 368 f., 373 ff., 404 f., 419 ff., 450 ff., 475, 522, 528, 576 ff., 647 ff., 677 f., 812, 822, 830 ff.

Sacher-Masoch, L., 282, 307, 308 f., 366
Safařik, Paul Josef, 214, 225, 365
Șaguna, Mgr, 315, 505, 527, 730 ff.
St Georgites, 283, 368, 475, 647 f.
St Stephen, 24, 106
Saki, 568
Salisbury, Lord, 595
Salm, Robert Altgraf in, 299
Salonica Trial, 787
Salzburg, 2 f., 61, 66, 76, 82, 101, 105, 156, 207, 313, 513
Sandalled nobles, 57 f., 222, 228, 288, 294, 466
San Lucia, battle of, 369, 392
San Stefano, Peace of, 592
Sandomir, 155
Saphir, Moritz Gottlieb, 369
Sapieha, Prince S., 365
Sarajevo, 740, 774, 787, 806
Sáros, County, 479
Saurau, Count, 158, 164
Saxons, Transylvanian, 25, 30, 46, 61, 78 ff., 86, 92, 107, 111, 123, 229, 289, 296, 314, 382, 388, 413, 448 ff., 482, 559, 696, 727 f.
Saxony, 8, 365
Sazonov, Serge, 787 ff., 814
Schäffle, Dr A., 571, 580 ff., 609
Schiff, 627
Schiller, 212, 300, 508

881

INDEX

Schilling, Dr R., 353
Schindler, Dr F. M., 672
Schlegel, August Wilhelm, 186
Schlegel, Dorothea, 212
Schlegel, Friedrich, 186 f.
Schleswig-Holstein, 535 f., 542 f.
Schlick family, 88
Schlieffen, von, 783
Schlitter, A., 310, 430
Schlözer, German diplomat, 783
Schmerling, Anton, Ritter von, 302 f., 351, 370, 438 ff., 443, 451, 453, 455, 459, 511 f., 515, 521 f., 526 f., 530 ff., 536 f., 539, 568, 647, 652
Schmidt, Konrad, 690
Schmitt, Dr Eugen Heinrich, 720
Schnürer, F., 361, 453, 541 f.
Schoischnigg, Kabinettsrat, F., 152, 167
Scholl, General, Frh. von, 582
Schönaich, Baron von, 778, 790, 806
Schönberg, 757
Schönborn, family, 713
Schönborn, Cardinal, 672
Schönborn, Count von, 661, 713
Schönbrunn, Convention of, 590
Schönbrunn, Treaty of, 170 f., 193
Schönerer, Georg von, 632, 634 f., 653 ff., 666, 680 f., 799
Schratt, Katherina, 686
Schreyvogel, Joseph, 213
Schubert, Franz, 213, 268
Schuler, O., 352
Schulze-Delitsch, 630, 632
Schuselka, F., 305 f., 352 f.
Schwartner, F., 73 f.
Schwarzenberg, Cardinal, 443
Schwarzenberg, Prince Carlos, 449
Schwarzenberg, Prince Egon, 623
Schwarzenberg, Prince Felix, 54, 214, 260, 364, 370, 389, 400, 403, 405 ff., 412, 416 f., 421 ff., 426 ff., 431 ff., 436, 439 ff., 446, 451 ff., 459 f., 478, 481, 500, 508, 571
Schwarzenberg, Prince Johann, 623
Schwarzer, Ernst von, 352, 372, 376, 397 f.
Schwind, M., 268
'Scrape Quartet', 533
Sealsfield, A., 160, 206, 271
Secret police, 124 f., 144 f., 163 ff., 472
Sedan, 580
Sedlnitzky, Count Joseph, 206, 210 f., 219, 242, 296, 303, 321, 328, 330
Seidler, Ignaz von, 823, 830
Semmelweiss, Ignác, 708
Semmering Pass, 461
Sempach, battle of, 10
Sennyey, Baron Pál, 688
Serbia, 224 f., 386 f., 589 ff., 597 ff., 736, 749, 773 ff., 784 ff., 788 ff., 806 ff.
Serbs (in Monarchy), 12, 46, 56, 78 ff., 86, 92 f., 97 ff., 107 f., 115, 139, 141, 216, 224 ff., 252, 288 ff., 295, 382 ff., 396, 415, 446 ff., 482, 527 ff., 558 f., 729 f., 733 f., 748, 768, 772 ff., 806 ff., 828 ff.
Serfdom Patent, 127
Serujac, General, 139
Servitutenpatent (1853), 464
Seton-Watson, R. W., 784, 786, 828; cit., 83, 214, 219, 253, 295, 558, 560, 599, 690, 735, 739, 767, 769, 813
Seven Years War, 117
Sezession, 757
Shevchenko Society, 648
Siczynski, R., 802
Sieghart, R., 445, 752 f., 792 ff., 804
Sigray, Count, 157
Silagi, D., 135, 138, 144, 146
Silesia, 2, 7 f., 14, 23, 26, 35 ff., 42 ff., 65, 67, 70, 72 f., 87, 97, 100 ff., 105, 115, 117, 193, 200, 215, 312 f., 336, 349, 365, 404, 576, 626
Simonyi, E., 695
Simpson, F. A., 494
Sina, Baron, 258 f., 330, 461, 468
Singer, L., 566, 820
Sinkay, George, 91 f., 139
Sistova, 136
Sixtus of Parma, Prince, 829 f.
Skene, Alfred, 555
Skerlecz, Baron, N., 139, 226, 769
Skladkovsky, Dr Karl, 612
Skoda, Joseph, 268, 773
Skoda Works, 773
Slava, 474
'Slavery Law', 720 f.
Slavici, I., 731
Slavonia, 7, 10, 66, 74, 97, 141, 226, 384, 386, 395
Slav Congress (1848), 364 f., 381; Stremayr Ordinances, 613 f., 641
Slávy, József, 691 ff.
Slomšek, Mgr A. M., 645
Slovak Cultural Institute, 725, 732
Slovak National Party, 767
Slovaks, 78 ff., 86, 90, 96 f., 101 ff., 107, 114, 225 ff., 253, 289 ff., 295 ff., 381 ff., 413, 419, 446, 450 ff., 478, 482, 527 ff., 548 ff., 558 f., 649, 655, 733 f., 766 f., 767 f.
Slovenes, 76, 81, 84, 86, 97, 101 ff., 111, 113, 215 ff., 252, 288, 299 ff., 343, 352 ff., 372, 419, 449 ff., 457, 522 f., 547, 575, 644 ff., 661, 676, 828
Slovenska Jug, 772, 785 f.
Slovo, 647
Smetana, F., 643
Smolka, 375, 401, 413, 422, 531, 550, 575
Social Democrat Parties: Austria, 630, 632, 633, 664, 666, 668, 673, 683 f., 797, 803 f., 811, 824 f., 832: Hungary, 719 ff., 766, 770, 771

882

INDEX

Social legislation (industry), before 1848, 75, 254, 285; in 1848, 341; later, in Austria, 631, 633; in Hungary, 719; (agriculture), in Hungary, 718–9
Sokci, 80, 81
Sokol, 640
Solferino, battle of, 491
Sommaruga, F. Frh. von, 334 f., 372
Somogy, County, 36
Sonderbund, 309 f.
Sonnenfels, Josef, 111 f.
Sophie, Archduchess (later, Empress Mother), 240 f., 256, 263, 325, 332 f., 358 f., 361 f., 371, 389, 402, 407, 412, 456, 459, 636
Sopron, 45, 58, 445
Sosnowski, M. von, 681
Spanish Succession, War of, 10
Spielmann, Baron Anton von, 153
Spira, G., 333, 378
Spitzmüller, Dr A. von, 821
Sprachenzwanggesetz, 540, 563
Springer, J., 61, 195 f., 263, 394
Srbik, H., 292 f., 309, 325 f., 407, 452
Srbska Riječ, 774
Staatsrat, 20, 140, 165 ff., 185, 209
Staats-und Konferenzministerium, 168, 185; rat, 256, 334
Staatskanzlei, 15
Staatskonferenz, 256, 334
Stadion, Count Franciz, 311
Stadion, Count Philipp, 181 f., 185 ff., 189 f., 201, 203 f., 235, 336, 344 ff., 362, 368 f., 400, 404 ff., 415, 417, 422 ff., 437 ff., 439
Stadion, Count Rudolph, 310, 311, 336, 363
Stadion Constitution, *see* Constitutions (1849)
Stadler, Mgr, 747, 775
Stahl, Frh. von, 202
Stanislavov, 47
Starčević, A., 526, 557, 734, 736, 738, 828
Starhemberg, Count Georg, 117
Status Catolicus, 690
Steed, H. Wickham, 629, 784, 828; quoted, 604, 624, 671, 771, 799
Stein, Karl Frh. von, 271
Steinbach, Emil, 659 f., 682
Steinwender, Otto, 656 ff., 663
Stephanie of Belgium, Princess, 637
Stephen, Archduke, 299, 314, 317 ff., 456
Sternberg, Count Kaspar, 214, 216
Steuerverein, 436
Steyr, 34, 41
Stift, A. von, 213, 268
Što dialect, 252
Stojalowski, J., 668, 671
Stöller, F., 740
Stolypin, P., 777

Stratimirovics, Georg, 386 f., 389, 414, 416, 730
Stratimirovics, Stepan, Patriarch, 139, 224 f., 290, 386 f., 389, 414, 416, 730
Strauss, Johann, 268, 392
Strauss, Johann, jun., 636
Strauss, Richard, 757
Streymayr, Dr Carl, 585, 611, 613 f., 641 f., 658, 663, 667
Stribny, Georg, 804
Strobach, Josef, 672
Strossmayer, J. C., Bishop, 526, 547, 734, 738
Students, in Vormärz, 211, 303 f.; in 1848, 326 ff., 351, 365–6, 376; *see* Academic Legion
Stur, Ljudevit, 296, 381
Sturdza, Demeter, 733
Stürgkh, Count Karl, 566, 796, 802, 807, 819, 821
Styria, 2 f., 12 f., 28 f., 33 f., 37, 40 ff., 58, 65 ff., 76, 84, 97, 101, 105, 108, 111, 122, 143, 146, 203, 281, 303, 313, 336, 363, 424, 644 ff.
Subjects' Patent, 128
'Südland', 83, 735, 738, 741, 773 f.
Suffrage Reform (Hungary), 762, 764, 770, 823
Supilo, František, 768, 775, 786, 811, 813 f., 816, 828
Suplyikać, Col. Stephen, 387, 414 ff.
Supplex Libellus Valachorum, 139, 142, 251
Sutter, B., 612, 661, 680
Swabians, 80, 90, 381, 446, 450, 559, 708, 719, 728, 772
Swoboda, L. E., 398
'Sylvester Patent', 454, 472 f., 511, 517
Szabadka, 44
Szabó, Deszö, 758
Szabó, E., 54
Szalay, László, 247, 354, 390
Szapáry, Gyula, 698 f., 736
Szatmár, County, 200
Szatmár, Peace of, 89
Széchenyi, Count Ferencz, 244
Széchenyi, Count István, 44, 223, 243 ff., 272, 286, 290, 294, 318, 324, 333, 338 ff., 388, 395, 432, 479, 504, 707, 714
Szécsen, Count A., 497, 506 f., 509, 525, 568
Szeged, 44, 430
Szekels, 9, 25, 61, 78 ff., 86, 123, 274, 289, 378, 414, 478
Széll, Kálmán, 696, 698, 700, 702, 707, 759 f., 792
Szemere, Berthalan, 247, 338 f., 389, 393, 395, 428, 430
Szent Endre, 93
Szeptycki, Archbishop Count, 798
Szilágyi, Dezsö, 695
Szinnyey-Merse, P., 708

Szögyény, L., 324, 333
Szrem, 10
'Sztanczyks', 474
Szterényi, József, 763

Taaffe, Count Eduard, 551, 571, 576, 581, 611 ff., 624, 628, 634, 638, 657 ff., 696, 799
Taaffe, Count Ludwig, 334, 342, 523
Tancsics, M., 378
Târgoviste, 107
Tariffs, 39, 126, 253, 261, 461, 534, 617, 660, 772; internal Austro-Hungarian, 44, 176, 261, 291 f.; abolished, 425, 444; 1867– , *see* Compromise
Tarnow, 307 f., 345
Tatars, 46
Tauernbahn, 670
Taxation, *see* Finance, national
'Tebeldi', 269 ff., 301
Tegetthof, Admiral, 543
Teleki, Count L., 284, 493, 524
Thalia Society, 758
Thály, Kálmán, 761
Theresianum, 104, 124 f.
Thierry, Baron, 500
Thiers, 247
Thinnfield, Ferdinand von, 405 f., 756
Thirring, G., 702
Thirty Years War, 8, 34 ff.
Thodorovics, C., 416
Thököly, Imre, 53
Thugut, Baron J. A. F., 153, 155 f., 172
Thun, Count Franz Anton, 665 ff., 680, 701, 800, 818
Thun-Hohenstein, Count Leo, 302, 363 ff., 371 f., 439, 443, 455, 460, 480, 496, 500 f., 503, 522, 581, 636, 662, 665
Thurn und Taxis, Prince, 535
Thurócz Szent Martón memorandum, 527 f., 559
Tiefen, G. W., 622 f., 627 f., 673
Tietze, H., 516, 519
Till, A., 406
Tilsit, Peace of, 185
Tirol, 2 f., 18, 23, 28, 34, 37, 39 ff., 61, 65, 67, 73, 76, 84, 101, 108, 122, 130, 143, 156, 186 ff., 207 ff., 420, 424, 463, 522, 625, 639
Tisza, Count István, 566, 698, 760 ff., 769 f., 808, 811, 814, 818 ff., 832
Tisza, Kálmán, 525, 541, 688, 692 ff., 705, 722, 731, 736 f., 760
Tisza, R., regulations of, 294, 705, 716
Tithe (Church), 63, 68, 338; (Seigneural), 67–8
Tittoni, 782, 784
Toggenburg, A., 501
Toldy, F., 723

Toleration Patent (1781), 121, 127, 133, 141, 144, 225
Tolna, County, 36
Tolstoy, Leo, 767
Tomasics, Prof. M., 769
Tommaseo, Nicolo, 319
Trade Unions: Austria, 630, 632, 673 f., 797, 804; Christian Unions, 673; Hungary, 720, 766
Trans-Leithania, 565, 570
Transylvania, 2, 8 f., 14, 19, 25 f., 30, 36 f., 46, 60, 65 ff., 73 f., 78 ff., 91 ff., 105 f., 108, 122, 140, 142, 168, 208, 217 f., 229, 250, 291, 314 ff., 331, 337 f., 378, 382, 425, 428, 446 ff., 472, 503, 525, 557, 651, 730 ff., 814 f., 831
Trautenau (Teplice), 659
Trautmannsdorf, Count F., 167
Trent, 2 f., 41, 76, 82, 84, 110, 155
Trentino, 84, 160, 319, 344, 542, 601, 649 f.
Tribuna, 731
Trieste, 2 f., 39, 41, 76, 109, 420, 601, 644, 650
Triple Alliance, 598 ff., 733, 771, 777, 788, 808, 814
Triple Entente, 777
Tripoli, 785
Trojan, A. D., 372
Troppau, Protocol of, 232
Trumbić, Anton, 768, 811, 814
Tschirschky, von, 807
Tschuppik, K., 609, 667, 685
Tunisia, 598
Turin, 369
Turkey, *see* Ottoman Empire
Turnbull, P. E., 160, 218, 264, 268, 271, 274 f., 305 f.
Turopolje, 228, 288, 292, 317 ff.
Turopolje, Count of, 220, 292
Tuscany, 11, 134, 136, 145, 199, 433

Uebersberger, N., 786
Ugarte, Count Alois, 198
'Ugron Group', 700
Ugro-Rusin language, 648
Uhlfeld, Count A., 48
Uhlirz, A., 501, 609, 819
Ujvidék, 224 f., 386
Ukrainians, 79, 82, 100, 217, 283, 648, 801 f.; Ukraine, 822, 825
Umberto, King of Italy, 600, 602
Unger, Dr J., 585
Uniate Church, *see* Churches
Union of Brest Litovsk, 108
Unionists (German-Austrian), 523, 532, 557, 734, 769
Unitarians, *see* Churches
'United Christians', 635

INDEX

United German Left, 615, 656, 658, 796
United Netherlands, 2, 14
'United Opposition' (Hungary), 695; (Croatia), 178
United States of America, 811, 819, 821, 824, 829
Universalkommerzdirektorium, 39
Upper Austria, 3, 14, 28, 34, 37, 41 f., 61, 66 f., 74, 76, 101, 105, 108, 114, 122, 160, 203, 627
Upper Lusatia, 7, 87
Urban, Dr Karl, 821 f.
Urbaria, 65
Utrecht, Treaty of, 10

Vajda-Voevode, Dr A., 754, 767
Vakanović, A., 253, 735
Valkó, County, 10
Vambéry, R., 723
Van Sweiten, Gerhardt, 111
Várasd, 46, 292, 380
Várkonyi, Istvan, 720 f.
Vatican, 110, 213, 263, 433, 443, 672
Vay, Baron M., 396, 414, 507, 525
Vázsonyi, V., 823
Venetia, 208 f., 282, 476, 491, 542 f., 586
Venice, 3, 13, 82, 94, 155, 160, 169, 209, 230, 319, 343, 376, 427, 444, 504, 514
Vereinigte Hofkanzlei, 28, 33, 122, 168, 334
Vernewerte Landesordnungen, 6, 8, 23, 27, 88, 298 f., 348, 576
Veröcze, 10
Verona, 209, 369, 444
Verwirkungstheorie, 534
Vetsera, Baroness Marie, 637
Vicenza, battle of, 370
Victor Emmanuel of Piedmont, 427, 499, 602
Vidov Dan, 806
Vienna, 24 ff., 33 ff., 40 ff., 55 ff., 101 f., 108, 114, 116, 124 ff., 132 ff., 139, 147 f., 153, 157, 161, 187 ff., 194 ff., 205 ff., 215 f., 224, 241 ff., 248 ff., 266 ff., 274 ff., 289 ff., 301, 312 ff., 325 ff., 351 ff., 370 ff., 378 ff., 397 ff., 428, 437 ff., 472, 517 ff., 583, 657, 797
Vienna, Congress of, 164, 200 206 f., 211
Vienna, Treaty of (1606), 107
Vienna, Treaty of (1809), 189
Viennese Radicals, 609, 634
Viennese Revolution (1848), 322 ff., 517 ff.
Viertel unter dem Wienerwald, 72
Vigevano, Armistice of, 376
Világos, battle of, 426, 430, 477
Villafranca, Peace of, 491, 495, 500, 510
Village towns, 36, 44, 705
Violand, E., 274, 301, 321 f., 327, 341, 360, 374, 423, 517
'Virilists', 23, 514, 735, 798
Visconti-Venosta, 602

Vittorio Veneto, battle of, 832
Vlachs, 46, 78 f., 81, 91, 95 f., 107, 229, 733; see also Roumanians
Vladicharina, 746
Vlastenci, 298
Vodnik, Mgr, 216
Voivodina, Voivody, 387, 425, 446 f., 449, 457, 482, 507, 524, 527
Vogelsang, Frh. von, 633 ff.
Volhynia, 629
Vorarlberg, 2 f., 37, 42, 76, 101, 122, 156, 207, 420, 424, 513
Vorlande, 2, 10 f., 57, 68, 72, 74, 82, 108, 122, 199 f.
Vörösmarty, Mihály, 221
Vorparlament (Frankfurt), 350 ff., 370, 390, 402, 407, 427

Wagner, A., 783
Wagner, Bishop, 212, 255
Wagram, battle of, 188
Wahrmund, Dr L., 795
Waldmüller, 268
Waldstein (Wallenstein), family, 88
Wallachia, 107, 114, 346, 482
Wallis, Count Joseph, 195 f., 198, 209 f.
Walloons, 12, 82
Walter, F., 309, 335, 344, 347 ff., 356 f., 359, 361, 364, 368, 371, 377, 391, 406, 412, 452
Wandruschka, A., 135, 139, 145, 655
Warburg, Baron Adrian, 352
Weimar, 211
Weinzierl-Fischer, E., 443, 458
Wekerle, S., 696, 698 f., 707, 763 f., 768 f., 823 f., 830 ff.
Welden, General, 428 f.
Welfersheimb, Count Walter von, 614, 661 f., 742
Wels, 34
Wendel, H., 216, 253
Wenkheim, Baron Béla, 551, 693
Wenzelsbad Committee, 348, 363
Werner, K. H., 534
Wertheimer, G., 162, 548, 589
Wesselényi, Baron Miklós, 52, 89, 250 f., 284 f., 296
Wessenberg, J. F., Frh. von, 357, 362, 370 ff., 391, 400, 405
Westphalia, Peace of, 105, 117
Wetzlau, 33
White Hand Society, 787
White Mountain, battle of, 52
Wiener Neustadt, 632, 797, 825
Wiener Scala, 195 f.
Wiener Stadtbank, 49
Wiener, Währung, 198, 201
Wiesner, Sektionsrat F. von, 351, 807 f.
Wilde, A. A., 271, 278

INDEX

Wilhelm I, German Emperor, 506, 533, 579, 590, 597, 655, 666
Willner, 360
Wilson, Woodrow, 819, 821, 828 ff.
Windisch-Graetz, Prince Alfred, 53, 129, 329 ff., 334, 336, 358 f., 362 ff., 370 f., 376 f., 384, 391, 400 ff., 408, 412 f., 415 ff., 422, 439, 445, 452, 463, 469
Windisch-Graetz, Prince Alfred (grandson of above), 661
Wirkner, L. von, 293
Wiskemann, Professor E., 597
Wittek, Ritter von, 667, 672
Wlassics, General, 250
Wohlgemuth, F.M.L. L. von, 446, 448 f.
Wolf, Karl Herman, 636, 680 f., 799
Wolf-Schneider, A., 369
Wolfsgruber, C., 153
Workers' Educational Association, 630 f.
Wscherd, Victorin Cornelius, 85
Wurmbrand, Count Gundaker, 661
Württemberg, 157, 188, 579
Würzburg, 156, 443

Young Bosnia Society, 786
Young Czech Party, 612 ff., 640, 658 f., 663, 668, 675, 684, 804
Young Ruthenes, 648 f., 677
Young Slovenes, 645
Young Turks, 781
Yugoslavs, 101, 828, 831

Zagreb, 227, 251 f., 292, 294, 317, 380 f., 393
Zalán Futása, 224
Zaleski, Frh. Wenzel von, 283, 404, 450
Zanardelli, G., 602
Zanini, F.M.L. P., 334, 342, 379
Zápolya, John, 8, 87
Zara, 646
Zarand, 9
Zator, 11
Zay, Count Károly, 295 f.
Zeman, Z., 801 f., 814
Zenker, A., 266, 270, 275, 341, 343, 360, 402
Zichy, Countess Julie, 212
Zichy, Count Imre, 525, 539
Zichy, Count Károly, 154, 168, 182 f., 185, 210, 235, 343, 763
Zichy-Ferraris, Countess Melanie, 238
Ziemalkowski, Dr F., 531, 575, 605, 613
Zillertal Protestants, 263
Zinzendorf, Count, 185
Zionist movement, 794
Zipser Saxons, 80
Zirc, 60
Živnostenska Banka, 640, 732
Zöllner, E., 34 f., 636, 681
Zollverein, 233, 260, 291, 433, 436, 534
Zsedényi, E., 339
Zseller, defined, 71; *see* Land distribution, labour, agrarian
Zsigmond, Móricz, 758
Zurich, Peace of (1858), 491